The Last Best Place

A Montana Anthology

The Last Best Place

A Montana Anthology

Edited by
WILLIAM KITTREDGE and
ANNICK SMITH

University of Washington Press
Seattle and London

The planning, compilation, and production of *The Last Best Place* was generously funded in part by the Montana Committee for the Humanities, the Montana State Legislature's Coal Tax Aesthetic and Cultural Grants fund, the Montana Arts Council, U S WEST, and the State of Montana's Centennial Commission.

Grateful acknowledgement is made to all those who granted permission to reprint the selections in *The Last Best Place*. A complete list of permissions and bibliographic references can be found on pages 1145-1156.

A Montana Centennial Book

University of Washington Press edition first published 1991
Fourth printing, 1995
Reprinted by arrangement with The Montana Historical Society,
225 North Roberts Street, Helena, Montana 59620

Cover art by Tom Sailor and Kathleen Bogan
Cover and book design by Kathleen Bogan
Typeset in Berkeley Old Style by Arrow Graphics & Typography,
Missoula, Montana
Printed in the United States of America

Library of Congress Cataloging-in-Publication Data
The last best place : a Montana anthology / edited by William Kittredge and Annick Smith
p. cm.
Originally published: Helena : Montana Historical Society Press, © 1988.
Includes bibliographical references.
ISBN 0–295–96974–1
1. American literature—Montana. 2. Montana—Literary collections.
I. Kittredge, William. II. Smith, Annick, 1936–
PS571.M9L38 1991 91–25288
810.8'032786—dc20 CIP

The paper used in this publication meets the minimum requirements of the American National Standard for Information Sciences—Permanence of Paper for Printed Library Materials, ANSI Z39.48–1984. ∞

Contents

6
Literature of Modern Montana

7
Contemporary Fiction

Preface

In May of 1984 the Montana Committee for the Humanities brought scholars, writers, and interested citizens from all over the state to a cultural gathering in Helena to plan for the state's Centennial anniversary in 1989. Irreverently titled "Montana Myths: Sacred Stories, Sacred Cows," this two-day meeting was packed with lectures, panel discussions, and media presentations. It was an event rich with intellectual chemistry, which generated great excitement about our cultural heritage.

Driving back to Missoula we talked about Montana literature and how it could all be gathered into one big book. We knew our contemporary writing was exceptional, but we had not realized how much good writing there had been from Lewis and Clark onwards and had little idea of the great Native American storytelling traditions. The gathering would be an adventure and a pleasure. But we knew such a project was too large for two people, and too expensive to do on goodwill and speculation.

We had made new friends in Helena, and we asked them to join some old friends from Missoula to form an editorial board: Bill Lang, editor of the Montana Historical Society Press; historian Richard Roeder; fiction writer and college administrator Mary Blew; Blackfeet novelist and poet James Welch; and critic and teacher of American literature Bill Bevis. We needed time and money for planning and research. Margaret Kingsland and the Montana Committee for the Humanities provided both with generous grants, and by autumn the book was launched.

The task proved greater than anyone had dreamed. Each editor was responsible for researching at least one of eight chronologically organized chapters, from prehistory to the present. In addition, Chere Juisto was hired to search out unpublished manuscripts and out-of-print books from eastern Montana, where we knew there must be hidden treasures. And researcher Glenda Bradshaw traveled to each Indian reservation, talking to cultural committees and combing libraries to find stories of the Native American pre-white past as well as more recent writings. The resulting manuscript came to almost three thousand pages – far too much for one book.

The cutting began. A year of editing was supported by the Montana state legislature through a grant to Northern Montana College from the Cultural and Aesthetics Fund administered by the Montana Arts Council. At the same time, we were planning for design, illustrations, and publication. Graphic artist Kathleen Bogan, under a grant from the Montana Arts Council, began working on a design concept and selection of individual artists to illustrate the book. Through all this process we were assisted by our secretary, Chris Ransick. Thanks go also to Verna G. Brown, who typed mountains of manuscript pages, and to our editors, Marianne Keddington and Bill Lang.

By the summer of 1987, three years after we started, we had a publishable manuscript. Many selections (sometimes an editor's personal favorites) had been rejected. Other books can and should be compiled from writings we were not able to include. We hope the next generation of anthologists will take up where we have left off.

One job remained. The sale price of the book would have to be subsidized. Otherwise it would be too expensive for most of the Montana audience we wanted to reach. Once more, the Montana Committee for the Humanities stepped into the breach. Their contribution was matched by the Montana Historical Society, under the direction of Robert Archibald. Additional grants and in-kind help were given to the project by the U S WEST Foundation and D. A. Davidson. We gratefully acknowledge the help and support of all these groups.

We also offer thanks to the Montana Centennial Office under the leadership of Lieutenant Governor George Turman and Governor Ted Schwinden, who enthusiastically supported the idea of this anthology from its first days and later helped to subsidize publication costs.

And we give special thanks to the Montana Committee for the Humanities and its director, Margaret Kingsland, whose continuous encouragement and funding made this book possible.

The Last Best Place is not the first anthology of Montana writing, and it will not be the last. But if we have done our work well, it will be definitive for a while. In its pages readers may see the evolution of a literary tradition. In Latin, *familia* means house, and we hope this book will help define the family which is our house here in Montana.

William Kittredge
and Annick Smith, editors
Missoula, Montana, 1988

1

Native American Stories and Myths

■ *Long Time Ago*

JAMES WELCH

 long time ago, the Assiniboine people were in a country almost always covered with snow." Thus begins the first story—or myth—of this remarkable collection of myths—or stories. It is difficult to categorize these pieces. The myths are grounded in the commonplace—a man going hunting with his wife, a wife preparing food for an old woman—and the stories take on mythic proportions—a woman gathering firewood makes love with a snake (who turns out to be a white man). We shall call them stories, for the strength lies in the telling and listening.

"A long time ago. . . ." How far back do these stories go? All the way to creation—of the heavens, earth, the birds and animals, the mountains and streams, the humans. The creation stories vary from tribe to tribe, but not much. They are not much different from the creation story in Christian mythology. Always there is the creator (or creators): Old Man, Napi, Coyote, Man and Woman. Always his crowning achievement (or folly) is the creation of man and woman. Always there is a fall from grace, and life becomes tough for man and woman and their offspring. Sometimes the creator makes a mistake. After Napi (Old Man) creates the first humans, he picks up a buffalo chip and throws it into the water, saying, "If it floats, the people will die for four days and live again; but, if it sinks, they will die forever." Of course it floats. But Old Woman, a gambler herself, picks up a rock and says, "I will throw this rock. If it floats, the people will die for four days. If it sinks, they will die forever." Needless to say . . .

Not long ago (in the history of humankind) the Plains Indians started looking to the sun as their principal ceremonial deity. The people had always known that the sun rose in the east and watched over them all day until he returned to his home in the west. They observed that when he was in his full glory, the grasses grew long, the berries ripened, the buffalo returned, and the winter sicknesses vanished. During these summer months, men went on raiding parties and gained glory, horses, wealth. Sun himself gave them a special ceremony which, if they performed it correctly and fervently, would ensure continued abundance, good health, courage, strength. Perhaps in the first decade of the nineteenth century, the Sun Dance became the principal ceremony of all the Northern Plains tribes. About the same time, and not incidentally, the horse came into their culture and the Indians entered modern times.

With the coming of Sun Chief, the legendary creator figures became long-ago deities. Napi was sent into retirement to his favorite gambling spot in the Backbone of the World (Rocky Mountains). But the old creation stories continued, along with the origin stories ("How the Morning and Evening Stars Came to Be," "The Origin of the Seasons," "How the Sweathouse Came to Be"). It is remarkable how logical and natural these origin stories are. In the Assiniboine story, "How the Summer Season Came to Be," the people send five swift animals to the south to steal summer (spring water is in a bag made from a buffalo's stomach). In the relay race that ensues, each of the animals is killed just as he passes on the bag to the next animal. Finally the long-winded wolf delivers summer to the people, leaving in his wake luxuriant grasses, plants, and flowers. A deal is struck with the southern people that the two groups will share summer, each keeping it for six moons. Then the people decide that they will give it to the cranes to deliver, since they migrate anyhow. But the cranes are very leisurely birds, and if they find good feed along the way they stop there for a while; thus, winter and summer arrive more gradually. In this way, spring and fall came to be. Who among us could doubt that this is the true origin of the seasons? Who are the narrow-minded humans who would wish to kill off the wolf after he had delivered such a good thing to us?

Although the stories are highly entertaining, they were not told merely to entertain. Almost always there was an instruction, a lesson to be learned, which helped shape the moral values of the people. A Chippewa/Cree story, "Why the Crane Is Timid," is an obvious example of an instructive story. At one time the crane was the most handsome of the water birds–he could swim, he had a loud clear voice, and he was not afraid of any bird or animal–but he was vain and mean. He thought he owned all of the waters, and he chased animals away who came to drink in his waters. One day a man came to drink, and the crane tried to chase him away. But the man had been sent by the creator. After explaining that all animals were put on

Mother Earth to get along with each other, the man changed the handsome bird into a long-legged, long-necked, squawking coward. This is the crane we know today. It is not good to be mean to our fellow creatures.

The consequences of being bad could be harsh. In "The Bad Wife," a Gros Ventre woman is captured by the Crows. When the husband with six companions goes to retrieve her, she causes the companions to be killed and the husband to be left to die in a gruesome manner. With the help of a sympathetic old Crow woman, the husband recovers and recaptures his wife. He brings her to the old woman. "I know what to do to her," said the old woman. She went to her, seized her nose, cut it off, and threw it on the fire. Then she cut off her breasts, *ejus vaginae labia*, and her ears, and threw them in the fire. Then they threw the woman herself in the fire. A great crowd stood about, and whenever she crawled out on one side they threw her in again. Finally, she was burned. They all went home rejoicing.

While this is not simply a story of adultery (the wife was bad in other ways as well), adultresses met much the same fate in real life. Men were seldom dealt with such harshness by the group. An adulterous man might be banished for awhile or even killed by an avenging husband, but the social group did not look upon his transgression as seriously as they did in the story. This story served to remind girls and young women of the virtue of faithfulness (or at least the evils incumbent upon unfaithfulness).

Not all of the stories taught such a grim lesson. Some were meant to comfort, to provide hope to those who needed it. In the Blackfeet story, "Mia-wa, the Hard Luck Warrior," Mountain Chief has just returned from an unsuccessful raid and is complaining. Mia-wa tells him, "Your bad luck doesn't compare with the continuous failures of my undertakings." He then enumerates many misadventures, including the humiliating loss of his gun while escaping enemies. Dejectedly, he tells a medicine man of his hard luck. Together they discover that once Mia-wa had not sacrificed properly to the Above Ones and so his power animal had deserted him. After a vision quest on top of Chief Mountain, Mia-wa obtains a new powerful animal helper and his luck changes dramatically. He becomes a successful hunter and warrior, a well-respected man among his people. It is not difficult to see the effect of such a story on Mountain Chief. If misery loves company, then Mountain Chief could identify with Mia-wa's hard luck. If Mia-wa could change his luck, then so could Mountain Chief. He must have gone away feeling pretty good about the future.

Coyote stories. All tribal groups had a coyote figure, a trickster who is by turns benevolent and malevolent, who does good, who does bad, often with the coyote's twinkle in his eye. Often he is a sympathetic figure, a creature whose flaws (like our flaws) get him into trouble. He can be greedy and selfish, unprincipled and disgusting, and he can also be capable of tragic emotion. But Coyote is a trickster; and if good occurs to people as a result of his actions, it often seems secondary to his main purpose: to trick. The Flathead stories, "Coyote Kills the Giant" and "Coyote Kills Another Giant," illustrate how he saves the people and animals by tricking these giants. He even saves Wood Tick, which proves not only his off-handed benevolence but also how wonderfully detailed Indians' stories are.

The Plains Indians were basically nomadic. Even before the coming of the horse, they followed the buffalo herds, their primary source of sustenance. The early Indians traveled lighter, using dogs to pull travois. They traveled less often than did Indians in the later horse culture, but they did not need to move frequently. The buffalo were plentiful, and the pishkun (buffalo jump) was a very effective means of securing meat and hides, utensils, and clothing. By the time the Indians went into their winter camps on river bottoms to escape the harsh winds out of the north, they usually had plenty of meat and berries and roots put by to last them through the hard times. The people who dwelled in the mountains, although less nomadic than those on the plains, had summer and winter camps and traveled often during the warmer moons. It should come as no surprise that almost all of the stories created by these people involved travel and distance–distance in time and space.

There are so many examples of this aspect of storytelling that I will choose only one. In the Northern Cheyenne story, "Yellowtop-to-Head Woman," the people are starving. They have only fish, geese, and ducks to eat, and not many of them. They send two boys, the sons of chiefs, out to search for something to eat. The boys travel eight days and cover a great distance, finally coming to a large mountain far to the north. This is the home of the coyote man, his wife, and his daughter. After a misadventure in which one of the boys is captured by a serpent in a large stream, the boy is healed, marries the coyote man's daughter, and is instructed to look to the various directions from the mountains (the coyote man's lodge). He and his friend see a field of corn, herds of buffalo, elk, deer, and other game, horses, and birds. The boys are further instructed to return to their people, taking the daughter with them, for she is a powerful being and all the animals will follow her. They must rest four times on their journey, and they will reach the village that night. (This journey takes place in a single day, demonstrating that people-time and coyote-power time are not the same.) The next morning the animals will appear (as they do). The woman, furthermore, is instructed never to say "My poor animal" if a little buffalo calf is brought into camp. Coyote man's wife elaborates: "If they ever bring in any kind of fowl, never, never say to it, my poor animal. Do not express pity for any suffering creature."

Some eight years after the woman brings all the animals, she sees some boys dragging a buffalo calf into camp, abusing it, and she exclaims, "My poor calf." That day all the buffalo disappear, and they do not come back for a long time. This story not only demonstrates the importance of time and distance in Indian stories, but it also emphasizes the need to follow the strictures set down by the spirit people. That simple utterance of pity eight years later caused the people great suffering.

Much has been written recently about the notion of "Magical Realism" as practiced by Latin American writers, notably Gabriel Garcia Marquez. Magical Realism, it should be noted, is a term that North American critics have devised to describe the kind of stories common among Latin American writers, especially since the 1960s. These stories are not subject to the usual cause-and-effect relationships as we conceive of them nor to our conventional notions of time and space. Yet, the material is treated matter-of-factly. For example, in *One Hundred Years of Solitude*, ice is considered miraculous, whereas the ascension of Remedios the Beauty (while hanging out laundry) is not. All of these writers, including Marquez, rely not only on their own observations of reality but also on the influences on their observations by stories given to them by their elders. Marquez has acknowledged the degree to which his style and content were shaped by stories told to him as a child by his grandmother, just as Indian storytellers learned from their elders.

Our world views are shaped by the explanations contained in our stories, our histories, our religions. "Yellowtop-to-Head Woman" thus contains many aspects of reality that would be completely accepted by its Indian listeners. Not only would they believe that they had acquired the horse and buffalo and game through the journey to the coyote man's lodge, but they would also believe that the utterance of "my poor calf" would take away the buffalo. In this paradise on earth, that simple phrase might be equivalent to tasting the apple.

Even today, while reading these stories, we will be able to see the value of them as they were told to people. Stories "eased the way" through life by instructing, entertaining, shaping one's view of the world and its creation, by *placing* one within the great scheme of things. The stories are generous in their wisdom, important in their telling. So we might imagine ourselves sitting in a lodge on a cold winter night listening to the storyteller. It is through the stories that we live. "A long time ago, the Assiniboine people were in country almost always covered with snow." Listen.

Dedicated to the memory of Percy Bullchild

Editors' Note: The editors of this anthology have selected only stories for which the tribes have given permission to reprint or stories published by anthropologists who had received permission from their original sources. Most of these stories are secular oral tradition tales. Songs and sacred stories also figure importantly in the oral culture of Montana Indians, and many sacred stories have been omitted from this collection because they are sacred. Thus, we regret that the Chippewa/Cree and Kootenai tribes are not adequately represented in this edition.

Songs have been excluded from the collection because they are less similar to what the dominant culture considers "literature" than the oral tales. Songs would have required more specialized introductory material for the first-time reader.

We regret that no stories of the Montana Sioux on the Fort Peck Indian Reservation in northeastern Montana were available at the time of publication of the first edition of this anthology. Several members of the tribe have been working on transcriptions of oral stories and myths as told by the tribe's elders. We hope they will be available for future editions.

JAMES L. LONG

James L. Long, or First Boy, was a member of the Assiniboine tribe who collected and transcribed traditional stories as told to him by the Old Ones, elders of the tribe. While on the staff of the WPA Montana Writers' Project during the early 1940s, Long collected these stories in an effort to preserve an authentic picture of Assiniboine life in the days before the encroachment of the white man's "civilization." These stories, illustrated by William Standing, were first published in Land of Nakoda, The Story of the Assiniboine Indians *(1942) and have been reprinted in Michael Kennedy's* The Assiniboine *(1961).*

How the Summer Season Came

A long time ago, the Assiniboine people were in country almost always covered with snow. There were no horses and only dogs were used to carry things.

A small war party, that had been gone a long time, returned and went at once to the chief's lodge. They told him to call his counsellors together for they had an important message. The chief set food before them and sent his camp crier to call the council members to his lodge.

The spokesman said, "We have been away from our people for many moons. We have set foot on land that belongs to others; we have set foot on land without snow. It is in the direction of where the sun rests at midday.

"In the middle of a large encampment there is a lodge painted yellow. In this the summer is kept in a bag hung on a tripod. Four old men guard it day and night. One sits in the back, directly under the tripod; another lies across the entrance and two others sit on each side of the fireplace."

The chief and his headmen sat in council until one of them said, "Let us call in a representative of each kind of the fast running animals and ask them to help us bring this wonderful thing to our country." So the camp crier went forth and called to those medicine men, who had fast running animals for their helpers, to invite them to the lodge.

When all were in council the chief said, "My people and my brothers (the animals), far in the direction of midday there is the summer and I call you here to make plans to bring it to our people. The ones who go will never come back alive but they will do a great good to our people and their kind; for their children will enjoy the breath of the summer forever."

It was decided to send the Lynx, the Red Fox, the Antelope, the Coyote and the Wolf. The young warriors, who knew the way, were to guide the runners to the encampment.

After many days' march they arrived near the camp and took council. The spokesman said, "The Lynx will go into the lodge and bring out the bag containing the summer, because nobody can hear him walk. He will give it to the Red Fox, who will be waiting for him along the way. From there, the Antelope will carry it to the Coyote, who will take it to the Wolf who is long-winded, and he will bring it to us by the big river, where we will be waiting on the opposite bank. From there we will take it to our people."

So, the Lynx was left there and the rest went back in the direction from which they had come.

The Red Fox first was told to take his position, and so on until all the animals were stationed a certain distance apart according to the ability of the runner. If an animal was short-winded, it was not required to make a long run, for the bag was to be carried at the fastest speed.

Towards morning, before the light showed and when the slumber was in every lodge, the Lynx softly walked to the yellow lodge and looked in. The four old men were all asleep. The bag, containing the summer, was hanging on the tripod in the back part of the lodge.

The summer was in the form of spring water. It moved about in a bag made from the stomach of a buffalo. Now and then it overflowed and trickled along the ground, under the tripod, and in its wake green grass and many different kinds of plants and flowers grew luxuriantly.

Cautiously, on stealthy feet, the Lynx entered, stepping over the entrance and, with a quick jerk, snapped the cord that held the bag. Seizing it tightly in his teeth, he plunged through the door and sped away.

Almost the same instant the old men awakened and gave the alarm: "The summer has been stolen!" The cry went from lodge to lodge and in a short time a group on fast horses were after the Lynx.

They were fast gaining on the Lynx when he gave the bag to the Red Fox who was waiting. The horsemen then killed the Lynx and started after the Fox who, after a time, gave the bag to the Antelope. The Antelope took it to the Coyote, who brought it to the Wolf, the long-winded one, who was to deliver it to the waiting party. Each time the bag was passed to the next runner, the winded animal was killed by the pursuers.

The fast horses were tired but gained steadily on the Wolf. As he sped across the country, the snow melted away directly behind him; the grass sprang up green; trees and bushes unfolded their leaves as the summer passed by. Fowls seemed to join the pursuit, as flock after flock flew northward.

As the Wolf crossed the river the ice moved and broke up. By the time the horsemen reached it, the river was flowing bank-full of ice. This halted the Southern people. In sign language they said to the Assiniboine, "Let us bargain with each other for the possession of the summer." After a time it was decided that each would keep the summer for six moons. Then it was to be taken back to the river and delivered to the waiting party.

That agreement was kept, so there was summer half of the year in each country. In that way there were the two seasons, the winter and the summer.

After many two-season years had passed, the headmen of the Assiniboines decided to have the cranes carry the summer back and forth. They were always the first of the migratory fowl to go south. They moved by easy stages, stopping for long periods at good feeding grounds. By that method of carrying the summer, the winter gradually followed the cranes, so that, instead of the sudden winter as when the summer was taken south by the men, the fall season, *Pdanyedu*, made its appearance. Long before the cranes returned, there were signs among the plants and animals that the summer was on its way north. That time was called the spring, *Wedu*.

A late fall or spring was a sign that the cranes had found good feeding grounds and tarried there too long. An early winter or summer was a sign that the carriers had winged their way south or north in haste.

As the cranes flew over an encampment they always circled several times and, with their loud calls, seemed to proclaim their arrival or departure.

So, finally, the Assiniboine had four seasons: the winter, *Waniyedu*; the summer, *Mnogedu*; the fall, *Pdanyedu*; and the spring, *Wedu*.

Power of the Peace Pipe

Long ago the *Waziyamwincasta*, People of the North, one of the many bands that formed the great Assiniboine tribe, were camped in the northern part of their territory, in the land claimed by the Red Coats (British).

It was in the Joins Both Sides moon and the weather during that moon was always much loved by the people, because the days were still summer but the nights whispered the coming of winter.

The buffaloes were moving in the direction where the sun reaches halfway on its daily journey. The people had already put much cured meat away for the cold season and soon they would leisurely follow the buffaloes as far as the Cypress Hills, their winter camp grounds.

The people were all in camp, as the big hunting season was about over; no war parties were out so there was rest and peace. Only the laughter of children was heard while at play. It was the time when women were in their lodges making clothing for the cold that was sure to come. The men, too, were busy on new bows, arrows and other things to be made from different kinds of wood now matured. Those men sat outside their lodges or took their work to another's place to work and visit as well. Some old men and women made extra travois to pack the cured meats and berries when moving time came.

There was no need for hurried tasks as the striped-back gopher still frolicked about, a sign that summer would linger yet awhile.

Since this long ago time the snow has fallen many, many winters, so many that only the very old remembered the story as it was told to them by the ones who were there. They say:

It seemed like a skilled hunter was ready to make the kill, so quietly did it happen and so unsuspecting was the victim.

A man, who sat near his lodge, busy at a task, spoke to his wife, who was within. "There is a medicine man going into the lodge of the chief. Have you heard if anyone there is ill?" "I am sure no one is ill. It may be that he is asked to eat with the chief," was the answer. But soon camp talk reached around that Comes Out Chief, only child of the chief, was taken suddenly ill. "He was just playing with the other children this morning," the old grandfather had said of the six-year-old boy.

Soon noted medicine men gathered in the lodge of the chief; not of their own accord, but each one was given gifts and entreated to come. Before the next morning the spirit of little Comes Out Chief had departed to join his only and older sister, who died some years before. There was much sorrow in the camp and the heart of Takes The Weapon, the chief, was heavy. He cut deep gashes on his arms, legs and body as an act of mourning. He refused to be taken to the guest lodge; he wanted to be near the body of the boy, which reposed in the arms of the mother in their own lodge. He cried, "No, my son is still here, for the spirits do not leave the encampment until four days have passed. They always wait for the feast that is prepared for them and then take their departure. It is well that I remain here."

The headmen went in a body to the chief's lodge and sat with him. One of the servers first told of a war deed, then he took the chief's sacred bundle from its place on a tripod. On live embers from the fire he placed pieces of dried sweet grass which he broke off from a long braided coil. He took the bundle and passed it back and forth, four times, over the smoke offering. He filled it with tobacco and lit it with a piece of live ember. After a few puffs he extended the mouthpiece toward the chief and bade him smoke.

"Once," he said, "this pipe has made you happy. That was when you became chief. It now can soothe you and bring your mind back to your people. Talk to us that we may know your wishes."

The chief took the pipe and with his right hand felt of the bowl and other parts in a caressing manner. He closed his eyes and drew deeply on the pipe. Many thoughts passed through his mind, thoughts that brought memories of when he was presented with that very pipe to hold sacred. He had been a good servant of the pipe; he was always kind and generous to his people. Yes, that was what the server had said, "It will bring your mind back to your people." It was one of the times when the power of the pipe became the leader. It was well that its leadership be followed by its keeper.

After a time the silence was broken by the chief, who said, "Everyone knows that not all can reach gray hairs. But being that the pipe has come to me from my father and through three generations before him, it has always been my wish that when my son reached the age of deep thinking then my people might look toward him and honor him with the pipe. His grandfather on his mother's side has always told him many things and much of that remains with him, as you all know. Every day I have offered food and the pipe to the spirits of his grandfathers that they may see and watch over him. You, my people and my relations, as you see me now I am alone with my wife; our family has come to an end; the pipe can no longer go to a keeper in our family; allow that it be presented to my boy as if he had reached the age of leadership. Leave me now and talk it over among yourselves while I mourn." The group voiced approval and went back to the guest lodge.

They talked and planned the best way to console their chief. Their minds were as one. "Send for Wounded Arm," they said, "the pipeman, the giver of pipes to headmen. He is the man who makes chiefs. He has been given that power on account of his many brave deeds in battles. His sacrifices to the Beings are many and his gifts to the poor are known even to other bands."

So a messenger was sent and the pipeman accompanied him back to the guest lodge. He was a noble man, this giver of pipes, tall and kindly, who always wore a smile. Wounded Arm was an example to prospective chiefs and headmen that kindness made leaders.

A lodge was pitched near the guest lodge. Then the group went for the body of little Comes Out Chief. They brought it back and laid it in the honored place. A ceremony was performed the same as if the prospective one was living, only not a new pipe but the one handed down through the boy's family was used. At the end of the ceremony the pipe was laid on the body, with the bowl toward the foot. Then the body and the pipe were wrapped together to make the sacred bundle.

Never before had a bundle been made like that one, but the pipeman gave the instructions so the people were not afraid.

The headman took charge of the burial, which was high up in a tall tree. An untanned hide was wrapped over the body and made secure to the limbs. Then the people moved a short distance away in the direction of Cypress Hills, their winter home.

When darkness spread over the encampment, a white light, which extended upward over the burial tree, was noticed by the people. They gathered in groups and were amazed at the strange sign; they wondered at its meaning. Not knowing what else to do, they burned sweet grass on live embers as an offering and many medicine pipes were raised towards it.

The pipeman with several from the guest lodge went toward it and found the light remained over the burial. To be sure, they circled around to the north of it and back to camp. They told the people that the light came from the sacred bundle.

The people continued to move slowly away from the burial place. At night the strange light appeared and each time it extended a little higher. The feast for the dead was held and that night the light rose higher than ever before until its tip remained directly over the camp. After that no more was seen of it for many moons and, then, only at times.

"The ways of the Beings are wise," the people said, "they have placed little Comes Out Chief in the far north where he can look after us and be chief forever. With the peace pipe, he makes signs to us and we must offer many sacrifices; also erect sweat lodges so our medicine men can fast and purify themselves that they may be shown the meaning of the signs."

When the headmen were in council, the old chief, the father, never sat in the honored place. The decorated backrest was placed there and the spirit bundle, containing the lock of hair of the boy, was hung on it. The council relied a great deal on the spirit bundle, because it spoke to them by signs in the north that always were good for them. The people never failed to look northward at night because without warning the light might appear. Sometimes there were many lights on each side and when that happened Comes Out Chief had much to tell his people. Once he warned them to flee far northward toward him, away from the smallpox that came up the Missouri River. In its wake, many other bands perished, but not this one.

The People of the North invented the buffalo trap. They prospered. Their traps were always successful and the herds were large and came in quietly, because the spirit of Comes Out Chief joined them in the buffalo lodge from where the buffaloes were called. They became a large band and many more headmen were added to the council, but the backrest in the guest lodge was always reserved for the little spirit chief, who guided his people with the light that shone from the peace pipe.

■ ROBERT H. LOWIE
translator

During the summer of 1907, Robert H. Lowie, a highly respected ethnologist, traveled to the Canadian and American West to document the cultures and customs of various Native American peoples. Lowie spent about seven weeks with the Stoney Assiniboine of Morley, Alberta, before traveling south to visit their kinsmen, the Assiniboine of Fort Belknap, Montana. His main objective was "to secure notes on social and ceremonial organization," and "The Gambling Contests" describes one of the ceremonial games Lowie witnessed. His account was published in 1909 as "The Assiniboine," as part of the Anthropological Papers of the American Museum of Natural History *(1909).*

The Gambling Contests

The people were living together in a camp circle. The chief had two sons, the older of whom cared very much for the fox dance. One day the fox dance was to be performed, and all the members prepared for it in their dance lodge. They went around the circumference of the camp. The younger brother thought he would take his older brother's horse and watch. He did so, and followed the dancers. When his brother saw him, he pushed him off the horse, saying that he did not wish anyone but himself to ride it. The young man walked home, picked up some moccasins made for his older brother, and sneaked away, being ashamed of what had happened. His father asked the people to search for him, but he could not be found.

The first night the young man slept out on the prairie. The next day he traveled on. Towards evening, he reached a small herd of buffalo. He said, "I am going around to see whether I can hit one of these buffalo with an arrow." He got ahead of them, and when close to the buffalo he shot one, hitting him in the side so that the arrow stuck in it. The buffalo staggered and fell. The man picked up his robe and approached the dead animal. It had been hit by another marksman on the other side. Each man butchered half of the animal, then they built a fire of buffalo-chips. The other man's name was Crow. They cooked their food. Crow brought his share to the young man, saying, "Friend, eat what I have cooked." The young man reciprocated. They ate. Crow went west, without waiting for the young man, who followed after him. In the evening, they found the same herd ahead of them. The boy sneaked up and killed one buffalo; as he was going up to butcher it, he found that it had also been shot by Crow from the other side. Again they built a fire and cooked. Crow waited on the boy, then the latter reciprocated, as before. When they had eaten, Crow departed. The next day the boy traveled on. Late in the evening he reached a small herd. Sneaking up, he shot an arrow at one of the buffalo. Going to butcher it, he again found Crow's arrow sticking in the other side. They cooked and exchanged their shares again, then they ate without speaking to each other. Crow departed. The next day the boy continued his journey. In the evening he got to a small herd of buffalo. He killed one, which had also been shot by Crow. They cooked, exchanged their shares, and ate, then Crow left. The next morning the boy continued traveling. About noon he saw a man approaching, so he sat down. Crow sat down in front of him. "To-morrow noon," said Crow, "we will play a game, but before that we will smoke." He filled a black pipe and offered it to the boy. The boy took out his red pipe, filled it, and handed it to Crow. Both smoked, exchanging pipes from time to time. Crow said, "Do you understand what I told you? To-morrow we are going to play a game." The boy agreed. Crow went off. The boy slept.

Early the next day Crow came and said, "To-day we will play a game." They were near a rock. Crow untied a bundle, containing a netted wheel and two darts. He gave one stick to the boy, and said, "When I roll the wheel, it will be your turn to throw." Each wagered some of his clothes. The boy hit the net, Crow missed. They walked back. Crow rolled the hoop again. The boy hit it, Crow missed again. Crow rolled it again. The boy hit it, Crow missed. Crow said, "If you hit it again, you win the first game." They threw the darts again; Crow missed, while the boy hit the net and won the first game. Crow bet again. "It will now be my turn to throw first." The boy rolled the hoop, Crow hit the net, and the boy missed. Four times Crow hit the net, and the boy missed. Thus Crow retrieved what he had lost. The boy now staked all his belongings except his clout on the next game. Crow said, "This will be the last of our games. If you win, you get all my clothes. We will do more, we will wager our scalps." The boy took the hoop and rolled it. Crow hit it, and the boy missed. Crow won four times in succession. "I have beaten you," said Crow, and scalped the boy. Then he said, "I don't want to see you go bare-headed, I will cover you with a buffalo robe." And he covered him with a robe. "What will you do now?" he asked. "Eight days from now I shall bring more stakes to wager against you. My father is a big chief, and I have many relatives." Crow said, "The first one to get here shall plant a stick in the ground." They separated.

The boy quickly traveled homewards. It had taken him five days and four nights to reach the gambling site, but he made the return trip so as to get home on the fourth evening. Instead of going to his father, he went to another chief, who was sitting with bowed head before the fire. The chief said, "Old woman, rise, a visitor has come." She stirred the fire. "Who are you, stranger?" "I am So-and-so's lost son." The chief raised him and kissed him. He told the boy that everyone had sought him in vain and that he himself had vowed to adopt him as a son if he were found, not having any children of his own. They arranged his bed, and gave him fine clothes to wear. The boy said, "Father, I have come to get people to accompany me to a place where I was beaten in a game. I should like your band to go there." The crier was summoned to herald the news. All traveled to the gambling-site. On the fourth morning, the boy said, "I'll go ahead to yonder big rock." He dressed up, took a stick that was painted red, and with his tobacco pouch and pipe he rode up to the rock. At a short distance, he saw Crow approaching from the other side with the boy's scalp suspended from a pole. The boy arrived first and planted his stick. When Crow got there, he put his stick next to the boy's. The boy filled his pipe, and they smoked each other's pipes. Both Crow's and the boy's followers camped near-by. The two opponents went to their respective bands. The boy said to his father, "I should like to have a couple of women." The chief appointed an old man to get two of the prettiest girls. The boy was satisfied with them. "I want ten women that have never been married." The women were called. "I want eight young men." The eight young men came. "Now I want some one to ride a race-horse for me." A herd of horses was around the chief's camp. The boy said, "If anyone wishes to ride for me, I will fill my pipe for him and give him a pocketful of food. After the race is over, he may marry the ten women and I will give him ten horses from this herd." He passed the pipe to the young men present, but none accepted it. He then asked his father to send for more young men. Again he filled and passed the pipe, but the young men went out without smoking. Then he had the young boys summoned. He passed the pipe, making the same offer as before, but no one accepted it.

At last, a poor boy living with his grandmother rode up on his crippled horse and inquired why the pipe was being passed. When he heard the reason, he accepted the pipe and smoked it. All those within the lodge raised their hands (as a token of their gratitude). The poor boy ate the berries set before him. He had a wooden whistle suspended from his neck by a buckskin string painted red. His hair was unkempt and lousy. The chief's son had the boy combed, then every one went to the race-ground. From the other side, Crow and his people were approaching. The chief's son said, "I will choose my game, we shall have a horse-race." Crow selected a rider. The boy said, "We will just run once. I bet everything belonging to me; if you win, you can strip me naked and drive me away." Crow accepted these terms. The riders started. There was a long ridge there leading to a cut-bank; ropes were stretched at the bank to prevent the horsemen from tumbling down. They started. The orphan was in the rear. Suddenly he got ahead. He took his whistle, blew it, turned into a hawk, and, clinging to his horse's mane, leapt over the rope and descended with ease. Crow's rider turned back when he reached the bank. The boy won. All Crow's people cried. The boy approached Crow and spread a blanket. "Give me my scalp first." Taking out his knife, he scalped Crow. Then he had all the property belonging to Crow's people taken away and put in his camp. Crow's people were put into an enclosure and ordered to strip. They were told to walk away naked. All of them were crying. All the clothes were laid in a pile. The boy bade Crow wait a while. He called his people together; to his horseman he gave ten horses and two of the largest lodges. He asked him what else he wanted, and granted all his wishes. He gave the orphan sixty horses. He divided the stallions among his relatives and gave the mares and colts to the old women and children. He divided all his property among the people. He had forty horses brought and also some game. Taking pity on Crow, he told him he could take these things along. "You won the first contest; I have won the second contest. If you wish to wager your people, I am willing to play you again." Crow declined, and moved away with his people. The victor's older brother, hearing of his success, came with the horse from which he had pushed the boy and offered it to him. "No, I don't want it, you have thrown me down. You loved your horse better than me."

The camp was broken. The next day they set out to chase buffalo. All started. The chief's son saddled up, and went towards the buffalo. He saw his older brother chasing buffalo and knocked him down. "Never mind," he said to his people, "he threw me away, now I will throw him away. Let none help him." Everyone went home with the meat. The boy was the last to go home. For several days they dried meat and enjoyed themselves dancing. They went home and pitched their camp. The boy's real and his adopted father were the head-chiefs. One day a young man came in and told the boy he was going to make a new kind of dance, but before starting it he wanted to tell how he had obtained it. "Yesterday I was out on the hills and lay down. Beyond the hill I heard a man and a woman singing. It sounded as if they were coming towards me. I walked towards them slowly, thinking it might be enemies. A male and a female prairie-dog were coming along. I greeted them, 'Hau!' He answered, 'Hau!' I asked where they were going. The male answered that he was coming to show people a new kind of dance. 'I'll show you, follow me.' I followed them into a big hole. There was a lodge inside with a smoke-hole. I saw ropes stretched across, and feathered dance-ornaments were hanging from them. The prairie-dog went to the next lodge, and lots of young men came in. The prairie-dog told them he was going to give a dance to the people. He had the young men singing several songs for him. He asked me whether I had learned them, then he bade me look at the buckskin strings and feather ornaments, and I looked at everything. The men put on the ornaments and danced. When they were through, he asked whether I could make a dance like it. One rule is always to camp in the same place (?). The prairie dog then told me to go home and get up the dance. Accordingly, I came out and told you about it." Many young men were invited and were taught the new dance. They learned their songs, then they were told to bring their guns and arrows. Each man was delegated to kill such and such a bird or other animal. They separated and brought back hawks, crows, owls, gophers, prairie-dogs, badgers, and buffalo-hoofs. The skins were dried and tanned, cut in strips, and hung on ropes. The next day they began the dance. All the young men came to watch or to join in the performance. When they were through dancing, the performers took off their apparel and gave it away. The master of ceremonies told them this was the Big Dog dance. Many people joined the society.

After a long time a messenger came to the chief's son, asking him to visit Crow. Crow said, "I have been prosperous and as well off as ever. We must not gamble any more, but we must scalp as long as people live. That is what I wanted to tell you." Thus warfare originated.

JEROME FOURSTAR

Jerome Fourstar is an Assiniboine elder from the Fork Peck Indian Reservation. He was born in Frazer, Montana, in 1918 and was raised by his grandparents. In 1938, he married Mabel Redstone, and together they had six children, thirty-one grandchildren, and six great-grandchildren. Fourstar taught Assiniboine language and Indian culture at the elementary and high schools in Wolf Point and at Northern Montana College in Havre, and in 1978 he compiled an Assiniboine dictionary. "How the Morning and Evening Stars Came to Be in the Sky" is Fourstar's previously unpublished version of a traditional Assiniboine story.

How the Morning and Evening Stars Came to Be in the Sky

Once upon a time, long ago, there was a man and his wife and their two sons who lived in their teepee in the woods. The man would go hunting while the woman stayed in their teepee and did her work, such as tanning hides, and making clothes for her boys, who were twins.

One day when the boys were about 17 years old, their father told them that they had to go on a long journey. So their mother prepared some lunch for them. She made pemmican, rosebuds and grease, and dried meat. Each one of the boys had a dog and a horse, which also looked alike. After the mother got the lunches ready, the two young men were ready to go on their journey. They left early one morning at daylight. They went south-east, traveling while the sun was high and straight over their heads. This is what the white men today call high noon. They came to a fork of a trail and one of the young men said to the other, "You take one of the trails and I will take the other, and every so often we will look at our knives. If the blade of our knife is rusty, you will know that one of us is dead."

So they both went off on different trails. The boy that took the left trail came to a teepee at sundown, where a woman had a camp. She asked him where he was going, and he replied that he was going on a journey to explore the country. She told him he could stay there and sleep there that night, so he tied his horse to a tree with his rawhide rope, fed his dog, then went to bed. Early the next morning he had his breakfast, packed his bedroll on his horse and resumed his journey.

About three o'clock that afternoon he saw a cow elk and chased it, but the elk ran into the woods, where he followed it until dark, when he lost it.

He tied his horse to a tree and started to gather dry wood. After he had enough he made a big bonfire and started to eat his lunch. All of a sudden he heard something coming through the brush. Out came an old woman. She said, "grandson, I am cold, can I sit by the fire and keep warm?" He told her she could sit by the fire and keep warm. He offered her some of his lunch, but she said she wasn't hungry, just cold. She said, "grandson, if you get sleepy, you could go to sleep, as I will sit here and keep up the fire all night." So he lay down on one buffalo robe and covered himself with another one.

After a long while the old lady wanted to know if the young man was sleeping, so she said, "Look out grandson the sparks are jumping toward you," but he did not move. Again she said, "Look out grandson, the sparks are jumping toward you," but again he did not move. She wanted to make sure that he was sleeping, so she took some of the fire and threw it toward him. Again she said, "Look out grandson the sparks are jumping toward you," but he did not move, so she knew that he was sleeping now. So she took out her medicine pouch and put one end of a stick in her medicine pouch. Then she took the stick and touched the young man that was sleeping with it. He turned into a tree and then she went out and touched the dog and horse and they also turned into trees.

About this time the other boy looked at his knife and seeing the rusty blade, he knew that his brother was dead. So he turned his horse around and started back to the fork of the trail where he and his brother separated. When he got back to the fork of the trail, he started on the trail that his brother took. He followed this until sundown where he came upon the teepee where his brother had stayed.

The old woman, still there, said, "Oh, you came back again," he said, "No, this is the first time that I am coming through here," but she said, "No, you were here before and you stayed overnight." Well anyway, she told him to tie his horse up and come in and have supper with her. He tied his horse up, fed his dog, and then took in his bedroll. After they got through eating he said he was going to bed as he had a long way to go the next day, he said he would like to get an early start in the morning. So early next morning when he got up, it was still dark, after he had breakfast and packed his bedroll, it was daylight. He took the trail that his brother took and since dogs have a good sense of smell, the dog led the way, following the trail the other brother took. At about three o'clock that afternoon, he saw the same cow elk that his brother had seen. He also chased the cow elk, but before he could get close enough to shoot it with his bow and arrow, the cow elk ran into the woods. He followed it into the woods and as soon as he went into the woods it got dark. The young man tied his horse up and started a big bonfire after he had gathered enough dry wood, and he started to eat his lunch. As he started to eat, he heard something coming through the brush, but he knew what it was so he was prepared. Soon an old lady came to the bonfire and said, "Grandson, I am cold and I would like to sit by the fire and warm up." He told her she could sit by the fire and warm up if she liked. The old lady said, "Grandson, if you get sleepy you could go to sleep as I can sit by the fire and keep putting on more wood and keep the fire burning all night."

The young man put his buffalo robe down and took his other robe and covered himself, but he cut a hole in the buffalo robe and he was watching the old lady. Pretty soon she said, "Look out grandson the sparks are jumping toward you," but he just lay there watching her. Again she said, "Look out grandson the sparks are jumping toward you," but again he just lay still, so again she said, "Look out grandson the sparks are jumping toward you." This time she threw some burning sticks toward him, but he still lay still and did not move. She waited for a while and then she took out her medicine pouch and took a long stick and took one end of the stick and put it in her medicine pouch. Then she started to sneak toward him. When she was just about to poke him with the stick, he jumped up and out of the way. He grabbed the stick away from her and touched her with the stick. She turned into an old crooked tree. Then he told his dog to look for his brother, so his dog went from tree to tree sniffing, all of a sudden the dog stopped and started to wag his tail. So the young man took the stick and touched the tree with the stick and it turned out to be his brother, then the dog began sniffing around again and stopped by another tree, this time it was the horse. The dog began sniffing around again and stopped by still another tree, so again the young man touched the tree with the stick, this time the tree turned out to be the dog.

So, after that he took the stick and touched a lot of trees and they all turned out to be men. The two young men told all of the men to go back to where ever they came from. The two young twins were getting ready to go, but before they left they told the other men just what had happened. They all said that they too had chased a cow elk and just when they were about to catch it, it would go into the woods and when they went in after it, it would get dark. Then they too would make a fire and an old lady would come to warm up and she would tell them to sleep and that she would keep up the fire and that is all they remembered. The young men that saved the other men told them that she was a witch. They all went back to where they came from. The two young twins stopped at the teepee where the lady told each of them to stay. When she saw both of them together, she knew then that they were twins. They stayed there that night and the next day they started back home.

By sundown they got home and they told their parents what had happened. Their father told them from this day on the two of them were going to be useful to the people as time goes on. He told one of them, "You are going in the direction where the sun comes up, and there you will stay. You will be the morning star. The people will know it is time to get up when they see you coming up." He told the other boy, "You will go towards where the sun sets, and that is where you will stay and you will be the evening star. The people will watch you after dusk, and when you disappear in the horizon the people will know it is time to go to bed."

So that is how the morning star and the evening star came to be in the sky. From that day on nobody turned the people into trees.

JAMES WHITE CALF *as told to* Richard Lancaster

Chief James White Calf of the Piegan told this version of the Blackfeet's creation story to Richard Lancaster during the summer of 1958. White Calf, who was 101 years old at the time, had been Chief since 1897. He lived with his son, Jimmy Eagle Plume, on a small ranch twenty miles outside of Browning on the Blackfeet Indian Reservation. This telling is remarkable because it interprets Christian beliefs and incorporates them into the tribe's traditional sacred story. The story was published by the Texas Folklore Society in and horns on the toads *(1959).*

Why the White Man Will Never Reach the Sun

I am Running Wolf, the same who is Chief White Calf, Chief of the Piegan Blackfeet, given to be chief in the year 1897 by my father, Last Gun, who was Chief White Calf of the Blackfoot Nation before me, and who gave me to be chief because he was getting pretty old. I tell you who I am so you will know that what is spoken here is spoken by me, and you know that I am Chief White Calf of the Piegans and I speak with one tongue. What I say here is the truth, and if anybody says to you that it is not the truth then you ask them how they know, for they were not there at the beginning.

Hear me, I am Chief White Calf of the Blackfeet, and you are my son, Last Gun, for I have given to you the name of my father who was Chief White Calf before me and who was called among the Piegans as Last Gun. I have given you the beaded gloves to show that I am glad to have you for my son and I love you as my son, and your brother, Jimmy Eagle Plume, has given you the beaded moccasins to show he is glad to have you for a brother and he loves you for his brother, and now I give you this story, for this is the way it was in the beginning.

I am Chief White Calf of the Blackfeet, and I am one hundred and one years old, and I give you this story that I got from my father, Last Gun, who got it from the old men of the tribe. I am one hundred and one years but I am not old, for when I was a young man and hunted the buffalo and made war on the Crees and Assiniboines and Crows and counted coup on them and stole their horses I was never afraid because Nah-tóh-seh came to me in a dream and told me that I would live a long time but I would never be old. But he gave me just so long to live and I don't know when I will die, so I give you this story so it will not be lost. No other of the Blackfeet know this story because I have not told them, because it is the true story of how things were in the beginning and it is given by the Chief to his son so it will not be forgotten. You are my son, and I am White Calf, Chief of the Piegan Blackfeet and I give it to you.

Only once before I tried to give this story. There was a missionary and I called him son and gave him a name and tried to give him this story but he would not take it because he said that this is not the way things were in the beginning. But I was not proud to have him for my son because he says there is only one path through the forest and he knows the right path, but I say there are many paths and how can you know the best path unless you have walked them all. He walked too long on one path and he does not know there are other paths. And I am one hundred and one, and I know that sometimes many paths go to the same place.

Hear me, you are my son, Last Gun, and I know you will tell this story the way I tell it to you and not change it the way white men do, and so I give this story to be yours, for this is the way it was in the beginning.

O.K. In the beginning there were just two of them, a Man and a Woman, and they made the whole world. There were no oceans at the beginning of the world, and there were no mountains and no trees and no rivers that flow into the oceans.

So before they began to build the world, the Woman said to the Man, "We have a lot of work to do to build the world, so let us have two children right away so they can help us with the work."

And the Man answered her: "No, we are not ready for children yet. We will have them later on."

But the Woman said that they should have children right away and the Man said no, they were not ready yet. Three times the Woman asked to have children to help build the world, and three times the

Man said no, they were not ready for children yet. But the fourth time the Woman said they should have children, the Man finally said all right and he asked her if she wanted boys.

And the Woman said, "I want two boy children, so they can help us build the world, for girls could not help us as well as boys could."

So two boys were born, and they grew to be eight years old. One of the boys was very wise and clever and he has no Indian name but is known as Mu-ká-kí, which means *very smart* in the Blackfoot tongue. But the other boy, whose name is Náh-pi, was pretty stupid and the Blackfeet call him Mut-tsáhp-tsi, which means *crazy* or *old man*.

Then one day Mu-ká-kí, who was the wise boy, found that his mother was running around with another man. So he told his brother, Náh-pi, who was not so smart, and Náh-pi asked him what they should do about it. And Mu-ká-kí said, "We will tell our father that our mother is running around with another man." And so they told him.

"When our mother goes out to build the world," they said, "she works for only a little while and then she goes down by the big tree and plays with another man."

But the Father said, "This cannot be, for there are only the four of us in the world. We are not yet ready for other people until we finish building the world."

So Mu-ká-kí, who was the smart boy, said to his brother that they would go down and hide by the big tree and spy on their mother. So they hid down there, and pretty soon the Mother came down and began to hit all around the tree. The tree was really just a big stump, and after the Mother had beat all around the big stump for a while, a big snake with a horn on his head came out of the top of the stump and started to crawl down. And when he was halfway down the stump, he jumped, and when he landed on the ground he was a handsome white man. And the white man and the woman began playing together by the big stump. And the boys ran back and told their father that the Mother was playing with the white man down by the big stump, but the Father would not believe them. "There are only the four of us," he said. "We are not ready for other people yet until we finish building the world."

So two more times the boys hid down by the stump and watched the Mother playing with the white man, and each time they ran back and told the Father that when the Mother went out to make the world she would work for just a little while and then go down by the big stump and play with the white man. But the Father would not believe them.

So for the fourth time the boys went down to watch their mother, and this time when they came back to tell their father he believed them. So the Father sent his wife out to work again but pretty soon she came back, and he said to her, "You should keep working. We have a lot of work to do to build this world."

So the Woman went back to work, and while she was busy working, the Man put on a woman's dress and combed his hair like a woman and went down to the big stump and beat on it like a woman. And pretty soon a big snake with a horn on his head came out of the stump and started to crawl down, and when he was halfway down he jumped and when he landed on the ground he turned into a white man. So then they fought, and pretty soon Man killed the big snake.

And then Mu-ká-kí, who was the smart boy, said to his father, "Our mother will be after us now for sure, because we have killed the white man she was playing around with. She will try to kill you, Father, but you should try to kill her first. We are your sons, and we will help you fight."

And sure enough, the Woman chased after her husband and caught him and then they fought for a long time. Finally the Woman got her husband down and was going to kill him, but the boys helped their father fight and together they killed the Mother and cut off her head.

But pretty soon the Mother's head began to chase after them and the Father said, "Boys, we are going to leave here and go some other place."

So they started to travel, and the Mother's head chased after them, so the Father started to build up the timber behind him and the boys so the head could not get through. But the head got through anyway.

So after he built the timber, the Father built up the mountains so the Mother's head could not follow. But the Mother's head followed anyway.

So then Mu-ká-kí, who was a pretty smart boy, said to his father, "Father, Mother's head must be back together again with the body, otherwise she couldn't follow us so fast. Now that the timber and the mountains are finished, we have no place to go. How are we going to get away from our Mother?"

But the Father said, "Boys, we have one more thing to do to get away from your mother." So then he made the oceans all around the place where he was so the Mother couldn't follow, and he stayed on the islands where he was and that was the Indian country. Nowadays they call it United States.

So then the Father started to make the rivers and the streams, and his son Mu-ká-kí, who was pretty smart, said, "Father, you keep this up and pretty soon you'll have this land all covered with water."

But the Father, who was pretty smart too, said, "No, this land will never be covered with water, because I make the streams to run into the rivers and the rivers to run into the oceans."

You can see this is the true story, because even today the rivers all run into the ocean and the land is not covered with water.

O.K. But then when the streams and rivers were finished, Mu-ká-kí, the wise son, went to his father and said, "Father, Mother is here. She came across the ocean."

So the Father said, "Now I don't have any more place on this world to go, so now I'm going to another world. But first I'm going to send your mother to another place so she won't see me go. She will disappear for thirty days, and four days after the thirty days she will be back, but I will be gone. When your mother leaves it will be dark, so she can't see, but when I leave it will be bright daylight so you will all be able to see. No matter how hard they try, nobody will ever be able to get to the world where I am going."

So Woman went up to the moon in the dark of night, and Man went up to the sun in bright daylight, and even today there is a woman in the moon and a man in the sun.

But before he left for his new world, Man spoke to his two sons: "Boys, I've got to leave for my new world, but my work here is not finished because I haven't made the people yet. So you two boys will have to finish my work for me. Mu-ká-kí, who is the cleverest one, will go back across the ocean and make the people there, and Náh-pi, who is not so clever and who will be called Mut-tsáhp-tsi, will stay here and make the people here. Mu-ká-kí, who is clever, will go back across the ocean and make people, and for them he will make machines and big weapons. He will do this because he is clever. But Náh-pi is pretty stupid, so he will stay here and just make the people.

"The people of Mu-ká-kí will have white skins, and in the beginning they will all speak the same tongue. The people of Náh-pi will have red skins and in the beginning they will have their own language that they will all speak. The people of Mu-ká-kí will be clever and have many tools, and one day they will try to build a big tower and reach the new world of Man, but one day when the tower is only just so high, one of the men will say to another, "Hand me that tool there," and at that time the man will not understand him because the language will change and everybody will speak a different tongue. And from then they will be enemies and fight amongst themselves because they cannot understand one another, and they will be so busy fighting that they will forget all about the tower.

"And at the same time that the languages change amongst the whites, they will change among the red men, and each tribe will speak a different tongue and they will fight amongst themselves because they do not understand one another."

And all that Man said came to pass. Even then there were dogs and they spoke like men, so when the Woman in the Moon played around with other men, the dogs could spy on her and tell Man in the sun. But at the same time as the language changed, Woman in the Moon put filth in the mouth of Dog and said, "From this time on, no dog can talk to any man; dogs will understand what men say, but when Dog tries to tell Man about Woman, Man will not understand." And so now when it is four days past the thirtieth day, Dog howls at Woman in the Moon to come and give him his voice back. So when you hear the dog howl at the moon, you know that this is the true story of how it was long ago in the beginning.

I do not know how Mut-tsáhp-tsi worked when he made the people over the ocean, for I do not understand the ways of the white men. But the Indian people were made by Náh-pi, and he made them like little dolls from clay. When he had finished he put them into little groups, so that each one knew what group he belonged in, and then after four days they began to walk around.

Pretty soon Náh-pi married one of his people and then pretty soon they had a boy child. Then Náh-pi said to his wife, "When we die we will die for four days, and then we will come back."

But his wife said, "No, that way there will soon be too many people. Why don't we die for good!" And pretty soon Náh-pi said O.K.

But then their little boy who was their only child died, and Náh-pi's wife said to him, "Why don't you say it again – to die for four days and come back!" But Náh-pi said, "No! It's too late now. We die for good!"

And then Jesus was born across the ocean. When he was born, the Jews tried to find him and kill him as a baby because they were afraid he would become chief of all the tribes. But then he grew up, and finally they found him and crucified him on a cross. He stayed on the cross four days and then came back to the village and said, "Goodbye, I'm going to the other world."

So the Catholics knew there would be a big flood at that time, and they built a big boat and almost everybody got on it. And while they were on the boat a pigeon brought a leaf to them, and then the Priest made magic and all the water turned to land again. So that is why you find the bones of the buffalo in the banks alongside the streams.

So over there they call him Jesus whom they saw going up. So over there they believe in him as God. But here they believe in the Sun and the Moon, and they pray to Sun, the Man, and Moon, the Woman. For Náh-pi said to his people to pray in the nighttime to Mother Moon, and in the daytime to pray to Father Sun. And that is the true story of how things were in the beginning, and you know that it is I who tell you this and that what I tell you is true, for I am Running Wolf, Warrior of the Crazy Dog Clan of the Piegans, known as Chief White Calf, Chief of the Blackfoot Nation.

And now I hear that white men are trying once again to reach the New World, Sun, home of Man. But they will never get there. Their towers will get just so high and no higher, but they will never reach the New World, Sun, where Man and Jesus went up, because their tongues are different and they do not understand one another, and they fight amongst themselves and do not work together.

And the same is true for the Indians. Their tongues are different and they do not understand one another and they fight amongst themselves. So they can never reach the New World.

Only when all men are of one tongue and one heart and work together and stop fighting amongst themselves will Man and Jesus return. In the meantime the only way to get to the New World where Man and Jesus live is to be dead for good.

Hear me, I am Chief White Calf, Chief of the Piegans and all the Blackfeet, and I have spoken.

■ DARNELL DAVIS RIDES AT THE DOOR

Darnell Davis Rides At The Door, who lives on the Blackfeet Indian Reservation with her husband and three children, is the hostess for a local television program produced by and for Montana Native Americans. This story is one of several stories that Rides At The Door wrote and compiled about Napi, a traditional Blackfeet figure who is often a trickster. "All Blackfeet knew of Napi," she writes in her introduction, "from the serious side of his creations to the foolish and spiteful deeds. . . ." The stories that Rides At The Door collected for Napi Stories *(1979) were told by Henry Little Dog, Francis Guardipee, Richard Little Dog, Mae Williamson, Tom Many Guns, Joe Cadotte, and Mary Ground.*

The Story of Marriage

In the old times, men and women lived separately. Old Napi was responsible for bringing them together. The women were skilled in running buffalo over a cliff to get food. They were also skilled in tanning and sewing, so they knew how to make good clothes and fine teepees.

The men killed their game with bows and arrows. They did not know how to tan or sew very well. All their clothes were made of animal skins and fixed crudely. Their lodges were made of green hides.

So Napi went to the Women's Camp and told them of the way the men lived. The Chief Woman took pity on the men. She asked Napi to bring them to their camp so the women could choose mates. Old Napi brought the men to a hill near the Women's Camp. The women had been busy preparing buffalo. The Chief Woman came forward first to choose a mate. She was dressed poorly and looked shabby from cutting buffalo meat. She chose Napi, but he refused her because she did not look appealing to him. This made the Chief Woman very angry.

She returned to her Camp and told the other women not to pick Napi as a mate. She then dressed in her finest clothes and went back to the men. This time Old Napi liked her and tried everything to get her to choose him, but she picked another mate.

All the men had been chosen, except Napi. Then the Chief Woman turned Napi into a pine tree. There he remains as a lone pine tree.

If you ever happen to see a lone pine tree on a side hill, it will remind you of Old Napi and how he never got married.

■ GEORGE COMES AT NIGHT

George Comes At Night was born in 1909 in a log cabin near Big Badger Creek on the Blackfeet Indian Reservation. He remembers with pride the life of his father, Comes At Night, who was born in 1855, the year that the Stevens Treaty was signed, the first treaty the whites made with the Blackfeet. "In his young days the prairie country was still wild," George Comes At Night tells of his father, "he knew all the great warriors of his day." This story about Mia-Wa is included in Roaming Days *(1978), a collection edited by Jane Bailey.*

Mia-Wa, the Hard Luck Warrior

Around 1900, Comes At Night and Yellow Fish, his good friend, were hunting in the St. Mary's area for big horn sheep. One day they went north of the lower St. Mary's Lake to where Chief Mountain stood, and climbed it. There were two skulls up on Chief Mountain. They knew that one of those skulls was brought up there by Eagle Head, a renowned warrior of the early days, but the other one, they didn't know who had brought that one up, so they sought to find some old timers. Warriors went up to Chief Mountain to fast, to pray for visions as they slept, and brought skulls up there for pillows. That much they knew. So they got Lone Charger to tell them the story of Mia-Wa, the hard luck warrior, the one who had brought the unknown skull.

Mia-Wa was one man who had endured much bad luck for many winters. Then because of the vision he obtained upon Chief Mountain with a buffalo skull he carried up there for a pillow, he had great success in all his undertakings thereafter. Mia-Wa, in his old age, loved to tell of his many terrible experiences, how he had failed in everything that he attempted to do and how at last he obtained the power to overcome his bad luck. A number of us were gathered at Mountain Chief's lodge. He had just returned from an unsuccessful raid and was telling of their bad luck. Mia-Wa told Mountain Chief, "Your bad luck doesn't compare with the continuous failures of my undertakings."

This is the story he told Mountain Chief.

At last, one day in the summer, Mia-Wa said to his wives, "Make two pairs of moccasins for me, plain ones. Put an awl in with them, sinew thread, sacred paint, some pemmican meat and put them in my war bag. I am going to try my luck to take Sioux scalps and horses."

His sits-beside-him-wife told him, "Do you know you are leaving us with barely enough meat for two days? Before you take off for war, you bring in some fat buffalo meat so we can cut up some to dry for later use."

Mia-Wa told her, "Your brothers will keep you in supply while I'm gone. Do not worry." And he started out. The Pikuni (Blackfeet) were camped where the Marias River joins the Missouri, so he started out on the plains and traveled eastward, on top, along the Missouri. Old Night Light (the moon) came up big and round. The Seven Stars (the dipper) were up, turning in the clear Northern sky, showing the coming of morning and passing of night. One did not pray to them, as they were different from the Sun and other Above Ones, but they were helpful when not cloud hidden. By the position they were in, a person could tell whether morning was near at hand.

Going on raids to other tribes' areas is one long walk. Mia-Wa thought, "I have been on some raids against the Crows, the Sioux and other enemies but I have never even taken a horse or scalp or enemy gun. Our warriors have no trust in me; they shun me. On this, my one lone journey, I will make a successful raid on the enemy or die trying." Going on raids is night travel. During the coming day, you hid in the brush or jack pines, then come dark, you start out again.

Toward daylight, Mia-Wa dropped down into the bottom brush along the Missouri River to hide. He drank thirstily of its muddy water, went into the brush and ate some of his pemmican. Just then some deer came to the shore to drink. Should he shoot one? He was afraid, but he took a risk. The enemy might not be far off, but he killed a yearling doe and built a little fire. He cooked some meat, ate some, and broiled some to last several days. He looked around, crawled back into the brush and slept till night came on. Then he got up and started his long hike on the plain, traveling eastward. Seven Stars (the dipper) gave him to know it was midnight. From where the Missouri River turns south, he traveled due northeast to the Bear Paws, not far off. He arrived there about daybreak and climbed the steep slope up into a grove of pine for his day's rest. Out on the plain he could see buffalo and antelope grazing. He ate some of his broiled meat, lay down and went to sleep.

Just then he woke up, hearing loud singing. He sat up. There was a spring in a little coulee going down from where he sat, about two hundred yards below him. He was hidden from it in the pines. A war party of many men was at the spring, with many horses. Some had eagle tail feathers tied behind their heads, indicating they were Sioux.

Maybe they stole the horses from the Pikuni, his own tribe. They rode northeastwards along the Bear Paws that night and the following night Mia-Wa traveled south and east to Middle Creek (Cow Creek on the map). The second night he went up into the Little Rockies. Three mornings later he had traveled around the Little Rockies and was on top of Hairy Cap, on the east end.

On its north side Mia-Wa found rocks piled up waist high for shelter. Within that circle he filled his pipe to smoke. After the smoke he lay down to sleep, but a loud noise of ravens flying around above him woke him up. He got his gun and sat up, just as three white tail deer came leaping up over the east end of the butte. They ran close and went on over the north end of the butte. He wanted to shoot one but he thought, "Something scared those deer and they are really moving." So he grabbed his gun and crawled to the east rim of the butte, where the deer had popped up. He peeked down. Saw some men plainly. They were coming up the slope, one tall guy in the lead looking down to the plains. A feather tied on behind his head indicated Sioux. Mia-Wa crawled back a little ways, got up and sped to the west slope as fast as he could run. Then he made for the south end of the butte, the heavily timbered end, and hid in it.

Looking down on the plain south of Hairy Cap, Mia-Wa could see the Missouri breaks about twelve miles off. He could see buffalo bunch up and run toward the breaks. Not far from the buffalo run he saw thirty or more riders going east and at dusk he started for the Missouri breaks.

He went along the north side of the river and three mornings later he was looking down into their camp in a big open bottom with cherry bushes on the ridge going down to the river. On the west side of camp he could see band after band of horses. The best horses were tied at night in front of the owners' lodges. Most of them were stolen.

About midnight is when all fires are out in any big camp, but Mia-Wa waited for a while longer. He'd gotten to the west side of the camp, down along the cherry bushes, when, of all the luck, he stepped down on two lovers. The woman screamed. The man jumped up. So Mia-Wa took a shot at him and beat it to the creek. He didn't know if he'd hit the man but the two ran shouting and really aroused the camp. Men were coming from the lodges, going for the timber, so Mia-Wa made a beeline for the river, made it, and waded in along the shore. Going down it he just about got to Little River (the Milk River), flowing from the north into the Big Water (the Missouri). Darn if he did not step into a water hole, a deep spot, and went in and under. The swift water coming in from Little River pushed him out. Gun in one hand, he tried to swim, but no luck. He needed both hands. As he was sinking, he had to let go of his gun or else drown. He swam to shore below the mouth of Little River. Indians were swarming in the timber, yelling to one another, west of him, and he really had failed again. Going against the enemy, losing his gun in deep water at night and now having only his knife, with many night's travel to get home to his people.

After he wrung out his clothes and moccasins and put them back on, Mia-Wa started up Little River. Not far from the Sioux camp, when light was coming on, he climbed half way up the north slope of the Little River valley and made his way into some cherry bushes. He opened his war sack for pemmican and there was enough to last for three or four days. Bad luck had been his and would, for how long, he didn't know. He slept a little.

When the sun came up, with a clear sky and warm air, Mia-Wa heard people talking and sat up. Looking down into the valley below him, he saw that many riders were coming up along it, a hunting party with women and travois horse behind them. But he was well-hidden in brush, looking down at them. They passed up around the bend and out of sight. He was lying on his side thinking and wondering when he heard shots around the bend, west of him. "Must be plenty of buffalo dead, I hear many shots." So he thought to himself, "I should go now. If I wait till dusk, it will be hard to find their kills. If I go down and travel along the brush by the creek, I'll see them butchering!" He ran down the valley. In a big opening around the bend in the river, where buffalo bedded down for the night, he saw men and women loading meat on horses and travois. Hides too. They finished, got together and went down the valley out of sight. So Mia-Wa slept, under cover, until late evening.

At dusk he went out to the remains of the enemy's kill, and many buffalo they had killed. He got a lot of meat off the heads that the enemy did not take, really nice meat. The home journey was a long walk. Not far from the hills, Mia-Wa built a little fire and cooked meat. He cut thin pieces, dried them near the fire and put them in his war sack. It took him about ten nights to get home to the big camp lodges.

On a warm morning he walked into camp and went to his lodge. "Huh!" his two wives told him. "You've returned from a war raid and you have no gun, no horses, no scalps."

"I have cut meat the Sioux provided me," he said.

His wife told him, "So you've become friends with our enemy."

He never answered or said a word to her. Not long after, his brothers-in-law came in to hear news of his long journey and why he had no luck. So Mia-Wa told all that happened after he located the enemy's big camp where Little River flows into the Missouri, told of hitting a water hole and trying to swim with one hand, holding his gun with the other. Starting to sink and having to drop the gun in deep water or drown. They had great pity for him, for his bad luck.

A few days later he got himself a horse, borrowed a gun from the great medicine man, Talks With The Buffalo, rode out alone and killed himself an antelope. He brought home meat.

His wives said to each other, "Poor you and me, never will he be a good warrior." But they cooked him meat. After he got through eating, he took a nap and late in the afternoon he took the gun to Talks With The Buffalo.

Mia-Wa told him of the bad luck, of his long journey and failure to come home with horses or scalps.

Talks With The Buffalo said to him, "Tell me where you did wrong to your sacred helper. That I must know in order to help you."

So Mia-Wa told him of the animal that came to him in his vision, to help him in whatever he did. Just once he had failed to fulfill his promise. He had forgotten a certain sacrifice to the Above Ones and a dog had eaten it. From there on, his good luck had turned to bad, in all his goings and comings.

Talks With The Buffalo said to him, "You should have told me of your misgivings long ago. As I see it, now you will have to try and obtain a new sacred, powerful helper. I, in my youthful days, had to go for a sacred fast to obtain a sacred helper, a water animal. It was on Feather Woman Mountain. In my sleep, the vision of a sacred helper came to me and I have never failed to make the sacrifices."

Talks With The Buffalo was a very powerful sacred man, a sacred pipe man, and he told Mia-Wa, "I know of a place on top of Chief Mountain, Almost Sacred Mountain, and I know that Eagle Head, a most powerful warrior, obtained his vision there."

Mia-Wa told him, "I do not like to go far from my people to fast."

Talks With The Buffalo told him, "I will talk with the chiefs, Big Lake and others, about moving to Inside Lakes" (St. Mary's Lakes). The chiefs granted his request to move, so in a few days they made camp at St. Mary's Lakes, not far from Chief Mountain. Mia-Wa made a sweat lodge and he and Talks With The Buffalo had a steam sweat. Talks With The Buffalo prayed for him to the Above Ones, and even to his own sacred helper, to pity Mia-Wa and let him obtain a vision during his sacred fast. He loaned his gun to Mia-Wa as a safeguard while he slept on top of Chief Mountain.

The next morning when the horses were brought in, they caught four and Mia-Wa, his two women, and Talks With The Buffalo started out for Chief Mountain. Mia-Wa took one buffalo head about three winters old up with him to use for a pillow. They arrived about noon and rode up the west side of the mountain, dismounted and climbed the short, steep slope of it to the top. The women brought two blankets and a buffalo robe for bedding. They went down to get some pine branches to make a good bed for him and placed the buffalo head at the west end. Talks With The Buffalo knelt down and prayed for him to the Above Ones and to Earth Maker. Again he asked help from his sacred helper for Mia-Wa. Then they left him, got on the horses and went back to camp.

Chief Mountain is high. A person can look a long ways down on the great plain and see the Sweet Grass Hills and our Bear Paw Mountains. Mia-Wa started praying to the Above Ones, the Sun and the Night Light (moon) for a success vision and a secret helper. In these fasts a person could not drink water or eat for four days and nights. On the fourth night, if he did not obtain a vision, it was all off for him. No more fasting then, because that's the limit, four days and nights. If you have no luck, go home and try again, some other place. Hah!

On the fourth night he obtained a vision and a sacred helper, a water animal, an Otter. This animal said he would help in all Mia-Wa's undertakings. In return Mia-Wa should do certain things in the way of prayer and sacrifice. He told this animal whose wake he was in (the Otter was out in front of him) that he would do all he could by prayer and sacrifice. Waking up near morning, he was really weak from thirst and hunger, but how happy he was to get a sacred helper again after all!

That morning, after the fourth night, Talks With The Buffalo and Mia-Wa's women came after him. He told them of his powerful vision and that a certain water animal was to be his helper. They had to half carry him down to the horses. At camp, water and food made him feel like an altogether different person.

Three Bears, a great leader and warrior, was to go on a war raid to the Crows and got Mia-Wa to go with him, along with a party of twenty-five. Many nights they traveled, rafted across the Missouri, crossed Wolf Creek and Arrow Creek, waded Yellow River (the Judith), crossed the Musselshell and Elk River (the Yellowstone) and went up the Big Horn River. They were now in Crow territory. The second night, up at the end of the Big Horn, they ran into a war party of twenty; they killed most right there. One tall heavy Crow make a beeline for the river. Mia-Wa went after him. The Crow dropped his gun and jumped in the river. Mia-Wa caught him and stabbed him, cut his scalp and took his gun. Thereafter, Mia-Wa killed fifteen enemies and took more than a hundred horses. The last six raids, he was a leader of war parties. His people, the Pikuni, were happy because he was a great warrior, a sacred man, and also a camp crier in his old days, so thank you for listening.

■ PERCY BULLCHILD

A full-blood Blackfeet, Percy Bullchild was born and raised on the reservation, where he was known as an artist and a musician. Bullchild published The Sun Came Down, *a book of Blackfeet stories, in 1985 when he was seventy years old. He died one year later. Bullchild spent the last eleven years of his life writing this important book, which has been critically acclaimed as one of the finest collections ever published of traditional Native American literature. These selections from that book include "The Twelve Moons," which is from a much longer story entitled "The Earth's Beginnings."*

The Twelve Moons

The Native American knew all about the effect of the stars, the moon, the sun too. Weather could be known in advance by observing these, the color of the morning or the color of the evening twilight could tell you if it's going to be a slight breeze or a very windy day.

All of the months of the year had names. Rightfully, it was each moon that had a name. Beginning with the month of January, the Natives call it the Moon of Big Smoke, the Moon That Helps Eat. That's because in January, when the air is very still, the smoke from the tipis goes straight upward, and for some reason it comes very big in size from the tipi. "Helps eat" is because the weather is so cold, no one could get out to do anything outside, everyone just about has to stay inside of the tipi. When one is always near the food, it's always tempting to eat, and naturally the food goes faster. So January is the Help Eat Moon.

February is the Moon of the Eagle, when the eagle returns from the winter migration. Also it is known as the Hatching Time of the Owl. The owl takes time to grow, he is awful slow. So to be ready for the spring months and able to fly, the owl hatches in February. This is true for other predatory animals or birds. The owl must be able to fly when all of the summer birds and hibernating animals come out for the warmer months. February is also the moon of the dreaded northern blizzard. The natives call it Taking Orderly Position for the Attack.

March is the Geese Arrive Moon. It is also known as the time Napi Comes Running Down Off of the Mountains, the Moon of the Warm Chinook Winds. It is the moon for gophers, too.

April is the Moon of the Frogs. April is the moon when the frogs come and begin their noisemaking, croaking. It is also the Moon of the Returning Bluebirds. April is also the moon when the thunder returns and all the holy bundles that pertain to the thunder are taken out to honor the return of the thunder.

May is the Moon of the Green Grass. It begins to grow, comes out of the ground, it also is the moon of leaves, when the leaf begins to appear on the growth. It is also the moon that changes the color on some certain animals, the summer color comes on. It is known too for the pretty flowers blooming.

June is the Moon of Hatching, most birds' eggs hatch. It is also the Moon of High Waters, the moon when the sarvis berry begins to ripen.

July is the Moon of Ripe Berries, the gathering of the holy encampment that comes annually, midsummer time.

August is the moon that ends the summer holy encampment, the crows begin to gather or bunch up, the moon to move back to their hunting areas to stock up on meat for their winter use.

September is the moon when the long time rain comes, the departing of the thunder for that year, the yellowing of the leaves, the gathering of the white fish or sharpface fish, the moon that dries the berries up. The moon to move to their wintering areas. To bless all holy bundles and put away for winter.

October is the Geese Go South Moon. Certain animals such as the plains rabbit and the weasel begin to turn white for their winter coat.

November is the moon to knock bullberries off of their thornie bushes, cold and frost really turns them on for the sweetness. All animal hair is prime in November, trapping begins for those early ancestors of ours. The eagle goes on its southern migration. Ice covers most waters.

December is the Moon of Winter Cold. It's also the Moon That Parts Her Hair Right Square in the Middle. This is because of the days, the shortest day and the beginning of the longer days.

Napi and the Sun's Leggings

Napi was the exact image of Creator Sun. He was always so jolly and kind to everyone, all life alike, no matter what kind of life, humans, birds, animals, plant life, water life, and all life of Mother Earth, still life, and active life, he loved them as he was put on Mother Earth to do. He loved and adored life unless he was hungry. He was always hungry. So he uses the power of Creator Sun that was entrusted to him for his mischief, to gain food for himself.

This wasn't too many years ago, a few thousand years ago. Creator Sun came down to earth once in a great while, but it had to be a very, very important happening here on Mother Earth to make him come down to his children. He came down disguised so he could freely roam about among the life he planted here to find out what could be wrong without anyone knowing he was down here and about. He worked like a present-day detective. When he found out what the wrong was about, he didn't punish physically, but through his power and unseen force he meted out punishment to those that were to be punished.

It was one of these times that Creator Sun was down here with his wife, Mother Earth, to see what his disciple Napi was doing. He knew Napi was doing some funny things to the life he was supposed to be taking care of. This wasn't any different from any other time Creator Sun came down to find out the root of the wrong he was investigating. Camping alone or camping among his children of life, Creator Sun was there to get firsthand knowledge of the trouble.

Creator Sun was camping alone at this particular time, along a small creek where willows and quaking aspen were quite thick. People of those days had to camp always near a watering place, and where firewood was plentiful, with a lot of shelter from wind and weather. It was this way where Creator Sun put up his tipi.

Napi, always roaming about for adventure or mostly for food, always ended up doing something foolish. This day wasn't any different. It was getting quite late in the day as Napi walked briskly along by this creek. Again he was tired and hungry, he must find a bite to eat soon, his stomach was a-growling like always when he was hungry. He was going along at a fast pace, with nothing in sight to go to. As he came around the quaking aspens and the willow trees, up ahead he seen this lone tipi. There was smoke coming out from it, so Napi knew someone was home there. What luck, just when he was getting mighty hungry. He didn't waste any time to go there.

As he got to the doorway, before he could get ahold of the doorpiece, a voice within the tipi called out to him and told him to come right on in. This didn't surprise Napi, because he didn't even notice it. Probably he was too hungry to notice anything unusual about this place, or he was just plainly scheming for some mischief. It should've surprised Napi that the man inside of this tipi called him by name and told him to come right in without even seeing him first to recognize him.

Napi went on in and was greeted warmly by this man that was all adorned in red earth paint. "Come on and have smoke with me and we will have something to eat pretty quick." Napi thought to himself this man was extra friendly, for the way he was greeted and welcomed. Even before Napi sat down, his eyes were flitting here and there, taking in everything that was in view. Before Napi knew it, he was eating away, while the owner of this tipi sat talking to him. He offered Napi a place to sleep for the night, as it was late already.

After the meal the two smoked the pipe for awhile, talking as they visited over the pipe. All of this time, Napi's eyes were roving about, flitting here and there until they were attracted by a pair of buckskin leggings. These leggings were somewhat unusual in the way they were made. Instead of the regular buckskin fringes and the usual plain buckskin leggings, these leggings were doused with the red earth paint and the fringes were of red-winged woodpecker feathers, they were mostly outstanding in appearance. Very, very neat in the way they were made. It was these leggings that Napi's eyes were glued onto. He would look away from them, but those eyes rolled right back to those nice-looking leggings.

When it was finally time to go to bed, the man of this tipi pushed all the live ashes of the fireplace to the center and laid a few very large pieces of wood over the ashes. Then the man got into bed, while across the room, Napi was laying there wide awake. It wasn't very long after they went to bed that the man of the tipi went to sleep, breathing heavily and snoring once in awhile.

The night was young yet. Napi stole out of his bed when he heard the man snoring and breathing loudly, and went right to the place where the leggings were hanging. Going about as easy as he could,

Napi took the leggings off of the pole they were hanging from and under his arms they went. Quiet as a mouse he went towards the door of the tipi and out he went. He had stolen the red-winged woodpecker feather fringed leggings.

Napi went along as fast as he could tiptoe until he was out of hearing distance from the tipi. From there he went into a run, on and on he ran as fast as his legs could go. He wanted to get as far as possible as he could before daylight came about. After he had gone over many hills and coulees, creeks, too, then did he slow down. It was getting pretty well towards daylight when he laid down to sleep. He was very tired from all of that running and he knew he was far, far away from that tipi. He used the pair of leggings for his pillow as he laid down near a tree.

Napi slept a long time. It was late in the day when he sat up awake, but to his utmost surprise, he was still in the tipi that he stole those red-winged woodpecker feather fringed leggings from. It was quite astonishing.

Sitting up on the bed he slept in, Napi didn't have anything to say. He thought that it was just all a bad dream. And to make it worse, the pair of leggings were under his head as a pillow. Somehow he tried to lie out of this, telling the man, "I needed a pillow for my aching head, so I got up and got what was in easy reach for me in the dark, and they happened to be your leggings."

It was all right with the man as long as Napi would hang them back up on the pole where he got them from after he got out of bed. All that day it was a puzzle to Napi–how did he get back into the tipi after running away almost all night before he laid down to sleep? This didn't deter Napi's mind one bit, though, he was more determined to steal those red-winged woodpecker feather fringed leggings.

Napi came up with several excuses to sleep there again, and got his permission from the owner of the tipi. Napi had made some foolproof plans for this night.

Night once more came to this tipi. Napi waited until the snoring got very loud this time. Napi did some very foolish things, but this was more foolish than ever. Before getting out of the bed he was in, Napi pinched himself as hard as he could to truly know that he wasn't dreaming again like the night before. He pinched himself so hard that he made tears come to his eyes. He even pulled on his hair as hard as he could to make very sure he wasn't asleep and dreaming.

After being very sure about being wide awake, Napi got up so easy and to those leggings again he went, taking them down, and under his arms he put them. Out of the door he went once again, running as he got out of hearing distance. On and on Napi ran, not stopping for a breather. Through the night Napi ran on. It was getting light enough to see, and Napi was just so very tired he couldn't go on, he must get rest and sleep. Down in the thick part of the willows he laid, and just almost as he laid down, Napi fell asleep.

Napi was so tired from all that running, he slept most of the day. It was very late in the day when he woke up. Without opening his eyes he sat up, and was stretching from the stiffness from that running he did the night before. As he stretched his arms this way and that way, he touched something with his fist or fingers, and it felt like a soft tanned hide. He knew he was sleeping in the thick patch of willows. His eyes still closed, he was wondering about the soft thing that he had just touched. Slowly he opened his eyes and again, to his astonishment, he was back in that strange tipi where those red-winged woodpecker feather fringed leggings belonged.

The man of the tipi acted like he didn't even know what was going on. Like nothing happened, he got a meal ready for Napi and told him to eat hearty, that he may be very hungry. Eating as he sat there in the strange man's tipi, Napi was almost going crazy trying to figure out what was happening to him, why he would wake up back in this strange tipi. He knew he wasn't dreaming like he thought he was. It was a very deep puzzle to him. But for some reason he was determined to steal those red-winged woodpecker feather fringed leggings.

In those early days, even to the time before electricity came into the countryside, on the many Native reservations, those Native people went to bed with the sunset and got up with the sunrise, they were so devoted to Creator Sun. Their last act of the day was devotion to the setting sun, with sweet grass they made incense. As it smoldered on hot charcoal and the smoke went upwards, curling in the air, their prayers of faith could be faintly heard in their tipis, the smell of the sweet grass was all over in the room, that sweet aroma as the prayers were being said. About the time the sweet grass burnt out, the sun had set, and so on to bed they all went. Sometimes there was storytelling from the bed while all waited to go to sleep. As it quieted down, everyone went to sleep.

The older people would get up long before sunrise and the woman cooked by the light of the open fire inside the tipi. Just before sunrise, everyone would be awakened to get up and give their devotion as the sun rose up into view on the eastern horizon. All Natives grew up this way, all Natives know their rightful Creator. The sun that feeds them and gives them the breath of life. And Creator Sun gave to them

Mother Earth's part of this devotion, the greatly honored sweet grass. Not only the sweet grass, but the cedar, the sweet pine, the juniper, the sage, and the pine tree moss—all of these for the people devoted to the sun as they burned them on hot charcoals as they prayed.

This camp wasn't any different from the other camps. This strange man, too, burns sweet grass as the sun begins to rise or as it begins to set and pays his respects and devotion too.

It was so late in the day that it was almost time to go to bed as Napi finished his meal. It wasn't too long after that meal he ate that it was time for bed again. Napi was more determined then ever to get away with those red-winged woodpecker feather fringed leggings. In his mind he knew he was going to try again to steal those leggings. To bed they went and again, as all things quieted down and it was fairly late in the night, Napi stole up again and got at those leggings. Taking them down once more and tucking them under his arms, he went out of this strange tipi once again and off into the night he ran. Away and ever farther away he ran through that night. This time it was morning when he finally stopped running, daylight. He had come to where large quaking aspens grew. Stopping by one very large one, Napi laid down to get some sleep. As he laid down, he tied himself securely to this large tree. Napi felt contented as he went to sleep, again he was just so very tired from all the running in those past few nights. No matter what powers there were to contend with, Napi felt absolutely safe now. Because with the way the rawhide rope tied him to a very large tree, there wasn't any way anyone could take him from this place. And so to sleep he went, this time no worries.

Upon waking up, Napi didn't wait to open his eyes. Yes, he was right back to where he got started, in that strange tipi again, and it was almost dark. Whatever it was that was urging Napi to steal the red-winged woodpecker feather fringed leggings, no one knew, just himself. For sure this time he was going to get away with stealing those leggings, this was the fourth time and the fourth night he tried to get those leggings from this strange tipi.

Once more they went to bed after the sun went down in the west and after evening devotion. Napi acted like he was fast asleep. But as soon as the strange man began to snore again, Napi got up and right back to those red-winged woodpecker feather fringed leggings he went. Down once more they came, right under his arms once again, and off into the night he took off. It was broad daylight when finally he stopped again, once more he found a very large tree to tie himself to, and as always he used the leggings as a pillow. The leggings were always a telltale sign, they were always still under his head when he woke up in that strange tipi. He just didn't have a guilty conscience about trying to steal those leggings from this good-hearted man that wouldn't even mention what was going on. Instead, Napi was treated with kindness.

Napi was sleeping heavily from the running again. When he finally woke up, he didn't open his eyes. He had felt the rawhide rope still tied securely to the big tree and around him too. That's what came into his mind as his eyes were still closed and laying there. This time he had won, he got away with those red-winged woodpecker feather fringed leggings and he was still tied securely to the tree, that's what he knew without opening his eyes yet. He could hardly move with the rawhide rope around him, but he was feeling so great that he finally got away from that strange tipi, and with those wonderful leggings too, that he didn't want to move or open his eyes, but just lay there and rest a while.

Maybe he slept a while again, it was such a relief to get away with something you liked so much. It was late in the day when Napi woke up again. He must go on now that he got free from that tipi. Finally, he slowly opened his eyes. I suppose he would've used all the profane words when he finally opened his eyes, when he seen where he was at. And to make it worse, he was still tied to something.

Fully opening his eyes, Napi seen that he was tied to the tipi poles. Turning his head slowly around towards the opposite side of the room, he was greatly embarrassed, he seen that strange man sitting there on his bed. Napi couldn't face the strange man, he felt so awful guilty of these past few nights, trying to steal those beautiful red-winged woodpecker feather fringed leggings. He just didn't know how to act as he slowly untied himself from those tipi poles he was tied to.

The strange man spoke up like nothing happened, *"Oo-ki Napi, nee-bo-wod, ka-ki-chooi.* All right Napi, get up and eat." Napi was very ill at ease over his behavior these past few nights, he just couldn't look into this strange man's eyes.

This strange man put him at ease with the kind words that came from him. He wasn't mad at Napi for trying to steal his leggings from him. Napi was still treated with respect and kindness.

As Napi ate slowly, this strange man was explaining to Napi about himself, letting Napi know that he too might've tried stealing the leggings from someone else if he got stuck on them. But as he spoke, he told Napi that the best thing one should do was to ask for something he wanted. Like now, Napi should've come right out and asked him for those leggings. "It wouldn't've been a problem to give you them, as you are a visitor here. They were yours for the asking. You can have them red-winged woodpecker feather fringed leggings of mine, take them with you when you leave here." And Napi ate with haste as this man told him he could have those leggings.

Already through with that meal, Napi folded the leggings up neatly and was soon ready to leave. Before he went out of the tipi, this strange man motioned to Napi to wait and he spoke on. "I am the Sun, Creator of all things. Creator of this Earth you are on and the many forms of life here. Any place here on this Mother Earth is my tipi, which you were trying to run away from. You were only running inside of my tipi all the time you were running, that's why you always woke up in that bed you slept on.

"There is a restriction on those red-winged woodpecker feather fringed leggings of mine and if that restriction isn't complied with, you shall find out the consequences. Do not wear them just any time. They are made especially for certain times when one is very happy and devout for the coming day. Only wear them when you are to pray with all your feeling for your coming to this Mother Earth. Remember and take my advice to you, don't wear them just any time, unless your heart is all given to your Creator."

Napi was listening, but the words of this strange man were going right through Napi's ears. He didn't hardly hear a word of the words that were spoken by this strange man. All Napi had in his mind was to get a-going so he could try those red-winged woodpecker feather fringed leggings on, they looked so neat the way they were made.

As the strange man got through with the talk, Napi went on his way, hurrying as fast as he could walk. On and on he went, trying to get out of sight of the tipi. Far from this tipi and way out of sight, far out in the prairies quite a ways from the closest creek, Napi sat down and out came those red-winged woodpecker feather fringed leggings. Off came his own leggings, and on went the red-winged woodpecker feather fringed leggings. Slowly standing up and looking at himself, admiring the leggings on him, how good they looked on him. But then he took a step and as his foot touched the ground, the dry grass burst into flames. He immediately stepped the other way, only to see that foot touch the ground and the grass burst into flames. Away from these flames he walked, first in a fast walk, and then he broke into a fast run. But each time his feet got in contact with the grass, they burst into flame. Faster and faster he ran as the flames followed him right at his heels. His senses coming to him, Napi made a wild dash for the closest creek, where he didn't even stop, but jumped right in, leggings and all. Napi took off those red-winged woodpecker feather fringed leggings as fast as he could and left them in the creek. To this day, those leggings might still be floating down or hanging back in that strange man's tipi.

After all of this, Napi never learned his lesson: to be honest.

■ GEORGE BIRD GRINNELL *compiler*

George Bird Grinnell (1849-1938) was a zoologist, anthropologist, and historian of the American West. Trained at Yale, he first traveled to the western frontier on a zoological expedition in 1870. He returned with Custer's expedition to the Black Hills in 1874 and explored the Yellowstone in 1875. Much of Grinnell's most important work was included in his two-volume study, The Cheyenne Indians *(1923). The story of Yellowtop-to-Head Woman (Ē-hyōph'-sta), as told by Two Crows of the Southern Cheyennes, was brought to Grinnell by John J. White, Jr. "It is a sacred story," Grinnell writes, "and must not be told except at night, and a prayer was made for forgiveness for having told it." Grinnell published the story in "Some Early Cheyenne Tales" for the July-September 1907* Journal of American Folk-Lore. *We reprint it here with respect for its sacred nature.*

Ē-hyōph'-sta (Yellowtop-to-Head-Woman)

This is the story of the beginning of the people, way up on the other side of the Missouri River. It is very level and sandy there.

There was a big camp, and they had nothing to eat; every one was hungry. All they had to depend on was the fish, geese, and ducks in the little lakes. Early one morning an old man went through the village calling out for two chiefs who must be fast runners. They were told to go around to all the small lakes, and see if they could find anything to eat. They were told not to come back until they found something, for the camp was in great need of food; the children were starving.

These two men were to be trusted. They travelled far in different directions, and in four days came back without having found anything. The cry went round for every one to pack the dog travois, for they must move anyhow.

That night when they made camp, all the chiefs gathered in the centre of the village, and sent for two young men, the sons of chiefs, and the chiefs told them to go on ahead of the camp, and not to return until they had found something. They said, "You must try hard. You can hear the old people and children crying for something to eat, so be sure and find something. Do not come back until you do so."

After these boys set out, the elder said to the younger, "Now we must find something before we come back or the people will starve." So they started, going straight north.

After they had been gone eight days, they saw in front of them a high peak, and, just this side of it, something that looked blue. One of them said, "I am nearly dead. I am afraid I cannot travel much farther." The other said, "Do you see that peak over there? We will both go over there and die, and it will be a mark over us; it will be our burying-place." The peak was high and steep. The other said, "We will go there and die together." They walked toward it, and, when they got near, they saw that between it and them ran a large stream. They sat down on the bank and looked across, and saw that the peak came right down to the other bank, and off to one side of the peak ran a high bluff. The elder said, "Take off your leggings and let us cross over to the peak." He took the lead and they waded in. The water came up to mid-thigh; then higher. Finally the one behind called out and said, "My friend, I cannot move. Something has hold of me. I cannot move. Tell my people what has happened to me. Tell them not to cry for me. Some mysterious power holds me." As this man stood fast, he called out, "My friend, come back and shake hands with me for the last time." The older boy turned back and approached his friend weeping, and shook hands with him. Then he left him and the younger gave his war-cry, and the elder went on weeping, toward the peak. He came out of the water and walked up and down the bank weeping.

Just then he saw a man come out of the peak, and come towards him. This man had a large coyote skin around him, the head coming up over his head. He carried a large knife in his hand. The boy ran to him and said, "Something is holding my friend." The coyote man said, "Stand where you are!" and went on toward the boy in the water. Just before he reached him he dived down under the water and cut the big serpent which was holding the boy. He cut its head off with the knife he was carrying. The other saw the serpent rise up, after its head had been cut off, and splash water in every direction. The coyote man then came to the top of the water and called to the boy on the shore, "Go to the peak; there is a big rock there; that is the door. You will find an old woman there. Tell her that grandfather has killed the serpent he has been trying so long to get, and that she must bring some hide ropes."

When the boy reached the place, the rock flew open like a door, and an old, old woman came out. He said, "Grandfather has killed the serpent he has been so long trying to get." The old woman said, "That is true, he has been trying to kill it for a long time." Then the boy went back to where the coyote man was standing. The coyote man said, "Go get your friend and bring him out of the water." When he reached him, the younger said, "I can walk no farther; I cannot move." So the elder turned his back to him and got him on his shoulders, and carried him to the bank and laid him there. Then the coyote man said, "Let him lie there a while; help me to drag out this serpent." They both waded in again and cut the serpent to pieces and dragged them out with a rope. When they had brought it all to the bank, the coyote man said to the elder boy, "Lift your friend on your shoulders, and I will carry his feet, and we will take him up to the peak." Meanwhile the old woman was carrying up all the meat. The elder boy took his friend on his back, and the coyote man held up his feet, and they carried him up to the peak.

When he got close to the rock, the coyote man threw the door open and they went inside, and the boy saw that the peak was a lodge, a very fine lodge, and on one side they had a sweat house. The coyote man told the elder boy to start a fire and to carry his friend into the sweat house. He started a fire, and, after the stones were heated, they put the younger boy in the sweat house. When they got the stones inside, the coyote man sprinkled water on them four times. Meanwhile, the younger boy was beginning to become discolored where the serpent had caught hold of him. Four times they sprinkled water on the stones, and after they had done it the fourth time, they told him that he was cured, and he arose and walked out of the sweat house. The old woman called to them to come and eat, for she knew they were nearly starved. Standing by the fire were two jars, in which she was cooking. She said, "I know you are very hungry." She had two white bowls made of stone; they were as white as snow. She put meat in each dish. She handed each of them a white flint knife to cut with, and told them to eat all they wanted. After they had finished eating, the coyote man, who was sitting on one side of the lodge with the old woman, said, "Look over there!" They looked and saw a very handsome young woman sitting on the other side of the lodge. They looked at her, and the coyote man said, "Now, my grandsons, I want to ask you two things: Do you want to take that woman for your sister, or do either of you wish to marry her?" The elder said, "My friend here is poorer than I; let him take her for his wife." The coyote man said, "Hā-hō′ (Thank you); that is good. I am glad to hear that." (Here Two Crows stopped, saying that he must ask a blessing from above before he continued; so that he might be allowed to finish the story.)

After the younger had chosen the woman for his wife, the coyote man told them to look to the north. They did so, and they saw a big field of corn. He told them to look to the east, and there they saw the country covered with buffalo. He told them to look to the south, and there were elk, deer, and all kinds of game. A little to one side of where the elk were (southwest), as they looked again, they saw herds of horses; and to the west, they saw all kinds of birds. The coyote man said to them, "Now you shall go to your home. Take that woman back with you to your camp; it is very fortunate one of you selected her for his wife; she is to be a great helping power to your people; she will take everything I have shown you to your people; everything will follow her." They went out of the lodge and stood looking toward the south – the direction the two young men had come from. They stood in this order. The old woman on the east side; then the coyote man; then the young woman; then her husband, and then his friend.

Now for the first time the two young men knew that this woman was the daughter of these two old people, for the coyote man said, "My daughter, rest four times on your way." He meant make four stops, not four nights, for he had given her the power to travel fast. The coyote man said they would arrive at their village that night, and that the next morning they would see all these animals around their camp. He also told his daughter that if there was ever a little buffalo calf brought in, not to say to it, "My poor animal." The old woman said, "If they ever bring in any kind of fowl, never, never say to it, 'My poor animal.' Do not express pity for any suffering creature." The coyote man said to her, "I send you there for a special purpose. These poor people only have fish and a few birds to eat, but now that you are there, there will be plenty of game of all kinds; the skins of all these animals will also be useful for wearing."

The three young people started for home and rested four times, and, as they started the fifth time, they passed the crest of a hill and saw the village below. When the people saw that there were three persons coming back instead of two, the whole village came running toward them. They came close and looked at the handsome woman. They spread down a robe and carried her in it to her father-in-law's lodge; he was one of the head chiefs. They all three sat together, and the elder boy was the spokesman. All crowded close about them to hear the news they had brought. He said, "Old men, women, and chiefs, societies of soldiers, and children, we have brought this woman down here from far up north; she has brought great power with her. You people are saved from hunger. Now when the sun goes down and comes up again, you will see many things around you." That night, as they went to sleep, they heard noises all around them.

Early next morning an old man called out, "Get ready, get ready," and they saw the buffalo close to the village; the wind was blowing toward the east and there was just a little open space in front of the village; the buffalo were all around. The Indians ran out with their bows and flint-headed arrows and killed many buffalo. The buffalo were so near that they shot them from the lodge doors. The elder boy told the people that they must kill only what they needed, and that then they must leave the buffalo alone. The buffalo came right up to the lodge, in which lived the woman they had brought down, and rubbed against it, and she sat and laughed.

One of the chiefs went into the lodge where this woman lived, and said to her father-in-law, "All the chiefs will come here in the morning to hold a council and arrange some plan, deciding what to do." This chief said, "We want to talk about returning favors to the girl and her people, because they have been kind to us and brought us these animals." The woman said nothing, but her father-in-law answered, "Come together here in the morning, and we will smoke and talk."

When the morning came, all the chiefs gathered together and came to the lodge to talk with the woman. She was not like the other women; she would hardly ever speak. She did not even go out and look around as other women do, but always sat in the lodge. When the chiefs came in, each in turn thanked her for what she had done and what she had brought, and asked if they could do any favor for her or her father for all that she had done for them. She said her father had not told her to accept favors, and she must do only what her father told her.

Four years after that, this woman's husband said to her, "Let us go back and visit your father and tell him what the chiefs told you, for they asked if they might do you some favor." She said again, "No, my father did not say I was to accept any favors." But after a while she also said, "You are anxious to go there with me, let us go." So her husband went to his friend, and said they were planning to go to the peak again. The woman told her husband to tell his friend not to come to the lodge until late at night; and he came after all the village had gone to sleep. The woman said, "Everything is arranged. We will start now." It was then late in the night. They walked outside the circle of lodges. There they stood and the woman said, "Shut your eyes." They did so, and when she spoke again and said to them, "Open your eyes," they were standing in front of the door of the peak.

The woman said, "Father, we have come back; open the door." The stone moved back and they went in. The coyote man and his wife got up and hugged all three.

After they had eaten, the coyote man said to his daughter, "I did not expect you back, as I did not tell you to return, and I do not ask for any favors. After you have rested, return to your village." The coyote man also said, "None of you must return here again. The only favor I ask is that no one ever says 'Poor animal' in speaking of a bird or a beast; do not disobey me in that." They all stepped out, and as before stood in front of the lodge. The three shut their eyes, and when they opened them they were standing in their own village. Before they started, the coyote man asked if they used the skins of the animals to wear and to make their lodges of. And when they said, "Yes," he said it was good and that he was glad.

Four years after they returned, some boys were dragging a little buffalo calf into camp; they were abusing it by throwing dirt into its eyes. The woman went out and said, "My poor calf"–then she said, "I forgot," and went and lay down in her lodge. When her husband came in, he saw that she was sorrowful and said, "What is it, my wife?" She answered, "I have done what I was told not to do; I said, 'My poor calf,' and my father told me not to."

That day the buffalo all disappeared and there were no signs of them.

Next morning the woman said to her husband, "Go and call your friend." So he came. She said to both of them, "I am going back; if you wish to come back with me I am glad; but if I must leave you here, you will have a hard time." They both spoke and said, "We love you and will go with you; let us go to the centre of the camp and have it announced that we are going to where your father and mother live, so that all the village may know what becomes of us." So it was announced, and all the people came running to where they were. She said that she had disobeyed her father in spite of his many cautions, and that they must go away. When she said that the whole village began to cry. Her friend then stood up and said that he and her husband were going also; he told his father and mother and all his people not to sorrow over him. Her husband also stood up and said the same, and that they now must work for his wife's father and mother. After that, they announced that they would start that evening for the peak. All their relations wept because they were going to leave them forever. That night all three disappeared, and no one ever knew what became of them.

The name of the woman was Ē-hyōph′-sta or Yellowtop-to-head, for she had light-colored hair.

The buffalo never came back till they were brought from the spring by the two young men. This happened long before that.

ALICE MARRIOTT CAROL K. RACHLIN *compilers*

Alice Marriott and Carol K. Rachlin did the research, writing, and photography for Plains Indian Mythology *when they were teachers at Central State University in Edmond, Oklahoma. These stories from that collection were told to them by Mary Little Bear Inkanish, a Southern Cheyenne, and Jessie American Horse, a Northern Cheyenne. One of the stories, "Bear Butte," tells of a sacred Cheyenne place north of Lame Deer, Montana. "If you go to the Bear Butte," the authors warn, "you must take an offering of tobacco with you. . . . Stand on the east side of the butte and pray for mercy and protection, while you scatter the tobacco to the four world corners. Then look on the ground at your feet. If your prayers are to be answered you will find a token, perhaps a white bead, or a quartz arrow point. Then you know that your life will always be blessed by Maheo, the Above Spirit."*

The Bear Butte

as told by Jessie American Horse

Once there was a very beautiful young woman. Her father was a chief, who was a wise guardian for his people. He had no son, but he had many horses, and lots of young men came to ask him for his daughter. He always said no.

A Crow man came, walking proud and handsome, his long hair trailing on the ground behind him, as if he owned the earth.

"Give me your daughter," he said to the chief.

"No," the father answered, "she must stay with her own people."

The Crow man went away, shaking his head, and very angry.

"I don't want a Crow to cut your hair off and paste it to his own to make himself look more handsome," said the chief to his daughter. "You are too beautiful to be treated like that."

Next came a Sioux man, with his great crested war bonnet standing up straight on his head, and his nose hooked and pointed down, as if he smelled something bad.

"Give me your daughter," he said. "I have three wives all ready, and I promise you she will not have to work."

"No," said the father, "she is a good worker, and while I prize her, I want her to work. Otherwise she will become fat and lazy."

"Have it your own way," said the Sioux, and he got on his horse and rode off, never looking back.

"That is no life for a young healthy woman," said the chief. "You shall stay here with me until the right man comes along."

Next came a white man, loaded with traps and furs, and with a little keg on his back. "I hear you have a daughter for sale," he said to the chief.

"She is not for sale," the father answered. "I certainly would not give her to you."

"I will give you all my skins."

"No. I can catch better ones myself."

"I will throw in all these traps, with the skins."

"No. She is not for sale."

"I will throw this in, too," said the trapper, juggling the keg on his back so that it gurgled.

"Go away," the chief shouted, "do you think I would trade my daughter for that stuff that makes men crazy? She is too good and proud for that!"

So the trapper went off into the mountains, and nobody ever saw him again.

At last a very tall, handsome young man, dressed like a Cheyenne, came.

"I am looking for a wife," he said.

"That's better," the chief snorted. "All the others just said, 'Give her to me.' Who are you? You look like one of our own people. Are you Cheyenne?"

"I am Cheyenne," the young man proudly said. "I have been a Cheyenne as long as there have been Cheyennes."

"You are too young," the chief protested. "You could not have lived that long."

"I am as young as I am old," said the suitor, "but I will make your daughter a good husband."

"We will ask her," the chief said, and sent for the girl.

When she saw the handsome, well-dressed young man, with two fine bay horses, the girl hung her head shyly, and thought he would make a very good husband. So she agreed and they were married.

After a while, the husband said, "There is one thing that you must never do. Never turn your back on me."

"Why not?" asked the young wife, who was curious, like most women.

"Because I tell you not to. Something bad will happen if you do," her husband told her.

When they had been married about a year, a son was born. The father was very pleased and happy, and as soon as the little boy could sit up straight, the man began putting his son on the saddle behind him and teaching him to ride.

"Don't do that," the mother protested. "He's too little to start riding yet."

"I know more about this than you do," her husband growled.

"Maybe you know more about riding, but not about babies," she exclaimed, and snatched the boy down and began to run away with him.

"I told you never to turn your back on me!" her husband howled. He got down off his horse and started chasing her.

The woman ran and ran, and she heard him pounding behind her. Once she turned her head and looked back. There was a great grizzly bear chasing her, not a man at all.

"I'll catch you and eat both of you," he threatened.

The woman was running to the east, and all of the sudden she saw a little mound of earth ahead of her. It was not much, but it was better than nothing. She ran to its top.

"Oh, Maheo, Above Person," she wept, "help me. Help me."

Maheo looked down and saw her and took pity on her. The mound of earth began to grow up into the air, carrying the woman and the little boy with it. When the bear got there, and saw what was happening, he was very angry.

"I'll get you yet!" he roared, and began clawing at the side of the mound, trying to get a foothold so he could climb it. But the mound kept on growing until it turned into a great sandstone butte, and the bear was left raging at the bottom. That night Maheo sent the girl's father to get her and take her home where she and her child would be safe.

Today, if you go to Bear Butte, you can still see the claw marks the bear made when he tried to climb it, and if the light is right, you can see the moccasin tracks of the woman and the little boy at the bottom. It is one place in the old Cheyenne country where women can go to look for power.

The Ghost Owl

as told by Mary Little Bear Inkanish

A little girl sat crying in her mother's lodge. She was angry because her mother wouldn't let her do what she wanted to do. It was night time, and her mother told her she couldn't go out of the lodge. Finally, the mother got so exasperated that she picked the little girl up and put her outside.

"Go on," the mother ordered. "The owls can have you if they want you."

It happened that there was an owl just outside the lodge, sitting in a tree, waiting for a mouse or a rabbit to come along. When he saw the little girl, he swooped down and picked her up in his claws and flew away with her. He carried her off to his lodge where his old grandfather lived.

"Here," the owl said, "This is something nice for you to have."

"Good," said the owl grandfather, and he clapped his wings together for pleasure. "You can sleep in that corner," he told the little girl, pointing with his lips to the women's place on the south side of the lodge, "and in the morning you can get busy and make yourself useful."

When the little girl woke up the next morning, the owl grandfather sent her out to get wood for a fire. "If you don't work, you can't eat," he said. "I can't stand daylight, so you'll have to do the outside work, except at night."

As the little girl went through the woods, picking up sticks and dry branches, a sparrow flew up to her. "You're gathering that for yourself," said the sparrow. "They're going to cook you and eat you." The child was frightened, and ran back to the owl's lodge, because it was the only place she knew to go.

"That isn't enough firewood," the grandfather said. "Go on. Go out and get a big pile. Nobody can cook with those little old sticks."

So the girl went out again, and this time a flycatcher flew up to her and warned her that she was going to be eaten. She ran back to the lodge and piled the wood on top of what she had already brought.

"That still isn't enough," scolded the old owl. "How am I going to get any dinner from that little heap?"

A third time the girl went out, and this time a red-winged blackbird warned her, "Don't do that. You're gathering it for yourself." And again she was frightened and ran back to the lodge.

"You'll never make a man a good wife," said the old owl, glaring at her. "Why, you can't even gather enough firewood to cook a meal."

Once again the girl set out to gather wood, and this time a red-tailed hawk flew up to her. "This is the last time," he said. "We have all tried to warn you. Now you must not go back."

"What shall I do?" the girl asked. "Where can I go to be safe?"

"Get on my back," the hawk said. "I will take you to a safe place on a high mountain, and I will tell you what to do when you get there."

So the girl put her hands on the hawk's shoulders, and he carried her away and away, up to the top of a high mountain, and on the way he told her what to do when they got there. The hawk landed right in front of a big rock on the mountain top.

"Now do just what I told you," he ordered.

The girl said to the rock, "My hawk grandfather, I have come to you for protection. My hawk father, I have come to you for protection. My hawk brother, I have come to you for protection. My hawk husband, I have come to you for protection."

Then she heard a voice say, "You will be safe here." The rock rolled aside, and there was a big cave. At first the girl was afraid to go in because she saw only the old hawk grandfather sitting there. "Come on, I won't hurt you," he reassured her, and she went in. Behind her the rock rolled back in its place.

When the old owl realized that the girl had escaped, he was very angry. "Those hawks must have played this trick on me," he said, "but I'll get her back. They can't keep her forever."

He started out for the mountain. Four times on the way he stopped; each time he hooted four times, and when he hooted the earth shook. The girl heard him coming and was terrified. The fourth time the owl hooted he was right outside the door.

"Bring out my meat," he howled. "If you don't, I'll come in and get it."

"Open the door just enough for him to get his head in," the hawk grandfather directed the girl.

She opened the door, and the owl thrust his head in. Then she slammed the rock back in place, and cut his head off so it rolled around on the floor.

"Roll the head out of the lodge with a stick," said the hawk grandfather. "Don't touch it, or any part of the body. Make a pile of dry wood and I will come out and help you."

They did so, and when the pile was big enough, the hawk grandfather set it on fire, and threw the head and the body on top of the flames. The body split open and all kinds of beads and pretty things came rolling out. The girl wanted to pick them up, but the hawk grandfather made her throw everything back in the fire with sticks for tongs.

Then they went back in the lodge, and the girl stayed with the hawks until she was grown up. She did a woman's work, and she became very beautiful. But she still missed her own people, and finally she told the hawks so.

"Well, you are old enough to take care of yourself now," the hawk grandfather said. "But you must do just exactly what I tell you if you are to get back safely."

"I will," the girl promised.

Then the grandfather made her a red-painted robe, and had her make a boy's moccasins and leggings. The grandfather made her a thunder bow with lightning designs on it, and he fastened buffalo bulls' tails to the heels of her moccasins to wipe out her tracks. Last he painted her face red, and tied the skin of a prairie owl on her forehead. She was dressed like one of the Backward-Talking Warriors, who were the greatest warriors of the Cheyennes, not like a girl.

When she was ready to leave, the grandfather gave her a live mink. "Keep this inside your robe," he instructed her. "Never let go of it. Then when you start out, pass by the first four villages you come to. On the evening of the fourth day you will come to your last great danger. An old woman will come out of her lodge and call to you and offer you food. Don't eat any of the first bowl; feed it to the mink. The second time she will give you buffalo meat and you will be safe to eat that. Be sure you keep the mink with you, but let it go when the old lady threatens you."

It all happened just that way. On the fourth evening the girl came to the old lady's lodge, and the woman came out and called to her. "Come in, my grandson. You must be tired and hungry."

So the girl went into the lodge, and the woman fixed her a bowl of brains cooked with mush, and gave her a horn spoon to eat it with. The girl pretended to eat, but instead she fed the mush to the mink.

"My, you are hungry, grandson," said the old woman. This time she gave her dried buffalo meat, and the girl ate it.

"Lie down and rest," said the old woman, and she took the bow with lightning designs on it and hung it on the west side of the lodge. Then she spread out some hides in the man's place on the west side of the lodge and the girl lay down on them and pretended she went to sleep. She even snored a little. "I'll stay up a while and keep the fire going to warm you," said the old lady.

As soon as she thought the girl was asleep, the old woman sat down by the fire and began to scratch her leg. She scratched until the leg swelled up into a great club. Then the woman started for the girl to beat her to death, but the girl let the mink out of her robe. The mink ran across the floor and bit a big chunk out of the woman's leg.

"You've killed me!" she screamed, and fell down dead, while the mink ran away.

The next day the girl went on again, and that night she came to her own village. Everyone came running out to see who the handsome young man was. They all asked her questions, but she was ashamed to say she had been so naughty when she was little that her mother had given her to the owls. She hung her head and would not speak.

"Who are you? What tribe are you? Where have you come from?" all the people asked her.

At last she said, "I am the naughty girl whose mother threw her away. I have had a hard time and come through many dangers, but now I am back with my own people."

Then her mother came to her, weeping and crying to be forgiven. And some young men came to her, and asked if they could wear the same kind of clothes she had on. The girl thought a while and then she said, "Yes. But because I am a woman dressed like a man, you must always do some things backwards. If you are in battle, and someone tells you, 'Go forward,' then you can go back." And that is how the great soldier societies of the Cheyennes got started.

Why the Turtle's Shell Is Checked

as told by Mary Little Bear Inkanish

One time the animals were planning to go to war. There were Turtle, Skunk, Porcupine, Grasshopper, Snake, Cricket, and Willow who were going. They took Willow along to help them find water. Seven of them went on the war party.

So they started out, and in the evening they camped. Next morning, when the others were ready to start on again, Grasshopper had lost one of his legs, and had to stay behind. The others went on without him.

They were on the way all the second day, and that evening they camped again. Next morning when they got up, Cricket was singing, singing under a bush. He wouldn't come out when they called. So the others went on without him.

Now there were only five of them left. They were on their way all the third day, and that evening they camped again. In the morning, Snake went down to the lake and went swimming, and when the others were ready to go on, he wouldn't come out. So they left him, and went on without him.

Now there were only four of them left. They were on their way all the fourth day, and that evening they camped again. They stayed all night close to a creek, and in the morning they got ready to start on again. Then they found that Willow had got stuck in the mud and couldn't pull loose. So the others left him there and went on.

Now there were only three of them left—Turtle, Skunk, and Porcupine. And that night, just at twilight, they came to the enemy village. They decided that they would raid it later on, after everybody was asleep. So, very carefully, when it was very dark, they sneaked into the chief's tipi, and before he could wake they scalped him to death. They cut his head off and took it away with them.

In the morning, when the people in the camp woke up, they found the chief lying there, with his head gone. They all cried and mourned, and hunted around, but they couldn't even find the tracks of the raiders.

Finally, one woman noticed a big wooden meat-pounding bowl turned over and upside down, and a little fine smoke coming out from under it. So she kicked the bowl and turned it over right side up, and there underneath it were the three enemy warriors with the chief's head. They'd already taken his scalp off, and were just getting ready to hold their victory dance.

Everyone came running out to see who had scalped the chief.

"Here they are!" all the people shouted. Porcupine grabbed up the scalp and ran away with it, and Skunk turned around and raised his tail and sprayed at the people, so everyone ran back and he got away with Porcupine. The only one left to be captured was poor little Turtle.

Then the enemy people began to wonder what they ought to do with their prisoner. And all the chiefs sat around and tried to decide, and Turtle shut himself up in his box. Sometimes he popped his head out and snapped at them.

That made the enemy people mad, and they decided to burn him. Some of the young men went off to get the wood to make up a great big fire. When they had brought in stacks of branches they built the fire up, while poor Turtle just sat on the ground and blinked at them.

After the fire was burning up high, the people picked Turtle up and threw him on it. He stretched out his legs and kicked around, and kicked all the wood away, so he was out of danger, but his shell was all cracked and checked from the heat.

So the people wondered again what to do with Turtle, and finally they decided to drown him. Then he pretended to get all nervous and shaky, and begged them not to do it. But still they wanted to drown him, and to have a big dance to celebrate their victory.

The enemy chief said, "Turtle, have you got anything to say before you die?"

Turtle was crying and sobbing. "Yes," he wept. "I want to die like a man."

"That's the way to do it," the chief said. "Die like a man whenever you can. Now, what do you want to say to us?"

"Well," sobbed Turtle, "this is my last request. Let all my sisters know I died like a man. I want two of your biggest chiefs to take me down to the river and put me in the water."

"Oh, that's fine," said the head chief. "Two chiefs are the very ones that will do it."

So two young war chiefs took Turtle, one on each side of him, and hauled and shoved him down to the river, and he hung back and cried and begged every step of the way. But they took him down to the water and put him in, and dragged him out to the middle of the river before they turned him loose. When the two young men were in the water up to their waists, Turtle suddenly grabbed them and pulled them under, and drowned them both.

The people on the bank saw what had happened, but they were afraid to go in the water and bring Turtle out. But one old lady had a good idea. She told the people to go back to camp and get their bowls and buckets, so they could bail all the water out of the river.

The people worked all day, but they couldn't seem to get the river dry. After dark they gave up and went back to camp for a rest. Then Turtle dragged the two young chiefs out of the water and up on the bank, and scalped them both. He cut their heads off, too, although they were dead already. Then he started home with his two scalps.

Just before Turtle got home to his village, Porcupine and Skunk came in with their one scalp. Everybody was excited about their success, and the announcer went around hollering, so you could hear him way out on the prairie, "That's the way to be a man! Look at Porcupine and Skunk! Porcupine and Skunk!"

Then Turtle came quietly home to his tipi, where his sister was sitting weeping because he hadn't come back. Oh, she was so glad to see him, when he came in carrying his two scalps. And while they were talking to each other, the crier came around again, naming Porcupine and Skunk. Then Turtle's sister, Miss Turtle, ran out with her two scalps and sang,

> My brother Turtle,
> He's a man, too,
> Right along with these others,
> He's got scalps.

"Shut up, Old Wrinkle Legs, and come back in here. I'm mad!" Turtle yelled out at her.

So Miss Turtle came back in the tipi and asked her brother what was the matter.

"I did the hard work of getting that scalp they're carrying around, and now I've brought in two more, but their bands haven't named me once. Go and tell our Turtle band I want war with those bands."

So the word got around the camp, and Skunk and Porcupine got scared. They came outside the tipi and called, "Turtle! Turtle! That's the way to be a man! We heard you brought in two more scalps. We're going to have a big victory dance for you!"

Then Turtle cheered up, and went out where his sister was crying about the names he called her. Like all lady turtles, Maheo, the Creator, had given her beautiful leggings with yellow stripes, while to the man turtles he had given red ones, and she didn't like being called Old Wrinkle Legs.

"Sister," Turtle called, "who told you to cry? I went to war to bring you happiness. I fought hard. See – my shell is all cracked and checked from the heat of the fire the people threw me into. But it was worth it to make you happy. Dry your eyes and go and get ready to dance with these two scalps."

So his sister jumped up, happy once more. "Oh, Brother Turtle! Brother Turtle!" she cried. So she ran back to the camp and danced, and they were all peaceful and happy.

That's why we always say Turtle was so smart, and we give him to children to wear, so they will grow up the same way.

ROBERT H. LOWIE

Robert H. Lowie was a pioneering anthropologist and linguist at the University of California whose life's work was to record the language and stories of the Crow tribe. He began making field research trips to the Crow Indian Reservation as early as 1906, returning many times through the summer of 1931.

"Lodge Boy and Thrown-Away" is a traditional Crow myth from the Old-Man-Coyote cycle that Lowie heard from Plentyhawk. "Stories were told on winter nights," writes Lowie. "Old people with a reputation as raconteurs *were invited for a feast and then expected to narrate their tales. The audience were required to answer 'e' (yes) after every sentence or two. People were formerly afraid to tell stories in the summer because, one informant said, the morning-star comes only in the winter time. The reason for restricting the entertainment to the night is that all the stars with names used to live in this world and only come out at night." This selection is from "Myths and Traditions of the Crow Indians," part of the* Anthropological Papers of the American Museum of Natural History *(1918).*

"The structure of the language fascinated him," writes Luella Cole Lowie in her introduction to Lowie's collected translations, which she published after his death. "He was never happier than when sitting under a tree, talking fluent Crow with a group of old men. . . ." "Divorced Women" is excerpted from "The Creation," which appeared in Crow Texts *(1960), collected, translated, and edited by Robert H. Lowie and compiled by Luella Cole Lowie.*

Lodge-Boy and Thrown-Away

A man once went out hunting with his wife. They camped all by themselves. When the man had gone out hunting, a woman came to visit his wife but she always left before he returned. The wife wanted to tell her husband about her visitor, but she forgot. After the second visit she took a little blade of grass and stuck it in her hair as a reminder but when her husband came she forgot again. She did not recollect until she heard the visitor come again; then she wondered that she had forgotten so easily and felt sorry over it. When the woman came in, she cooked for her. Whenever she watched her visitor, she ate like other women, but when the hostess looked away her guest swallowed all the food in a gulp. After a while she went away again. Then the wife took some grass and stuck it into her hair about her temples so as to make her husband ask what it meant. Whenever it was time for her husband to return, this woman dressed up and waited for him. When she saw him, she would joke with him and kiss him. In spite of her reminder, she forgot to tell her husband and did not recollect until after he was gone on the following day. She felt sorry about it. She heard the woman come again. When she entered, the wife got her something to eat. When she had cooked some meat and put it on a plate for the woman, the visitor said, "That is not my plate." She took it away and brought her another. Still she refused. At last the wife asked: "Comrade, what kind of a plate do you use?" She answered: "A pregnant woman,—that is my plate." So the wife lay on her back, pulled up her dress, put the food on herself, and called her guest to come up. She came, sat by her, and ate. While eating, she bit open her hostess's abdomen and saw that there were two babies within. She took one of them and threw him behind the lodge-curtain, and threw the second one into a spring. Then she packed all her hostess's meat to take it away, burnt the wife's upper lip with a firestick to give her the appearance of smiling, then took a pole and made her stand up facing her husband. When the man returned in the evening, he saw his wife standing at the door watching him. She did not come up to kiss him as usual, so he said, "I am tired, why don't you come over to me?" He approached her and gave her a push, then she fell over and he saw her stomach was open. He cried and jumped on her, then he took her to a hill, and buried her in a pine tree. Then he came back crying all the way.

Whenever he returned now, the boy thrown behind the curtain asked him for food. The hunter heard him, but never knew whence the sound came. Curtain-boy was raised by mice. One day when Curtain-boy again asked for food, his father answered, "Whatever you are, come out and eat with me, I have been suffering." But the boy was afraid to come out. One day his father returned late at night, built a fire, and lay down tired out. Again he heard the voice say, "Cook something and I'll eat with you." The man answered, "Come out and I'll cook something and eat with you." The boy now came out from behind the curtain, put his arm around his father's neck and kissed him. The man cried, then he got up and cooked something to eat. He ate with his own son. That morning and the next day he did not go out but stayed with the boy. The following morning he roasted a buffalo shoulder for the boy and told him he might be back late.

When he had gone, his son went to the spring and met Spring-boy; he saw that he had big teeth. He asked him to come out and play with him. Spring-boy said: "I am afraid of your father." "My father is gone. He is very poor; you have no reason to be afraid of him." The boy then came out of the spring and they played together and ate up the piece of meat left by their father. Towards night, Spring-boy said, "It smells after your father." Then he ran back to his spring and went into it. When the man returned, he saw that the meat he had cooked was all eaten up and knew that something was wrong. The next day he cooked two pieces of meat. When he had gone, his son went to the spring and called his brother. Spring-boy answered, "I'll ask my 'father.' " This was a being inside the spring that had adopted him. After asking his "father," Spring-boy came up and they played, then they went to the lodge and ate up all the meat again. That night their father returned and cooked something to eat. Curtain-boy had had his fill but said, "I'll eat with you because you are alone." The next morning he asked his father to make two bows and four arrows for him. His father asked, "Why do you want two?" "When one is spoiled, I'll take the other." He told his father not to go away that day, so he stayed and made the bows and arrows. The boy went to the spring. Spring-boy came out and told his brother to ask his father to cook meat and go away. "Then we shall eat." Curtain-boy told Spring-boy he should do so tomorrow, but that today his father was making bows and arrows.

The next morning the man gave his son one bow and two arrows, tying up the other set on the curtain. He went away after leaving twice as much cooked meat as before. As soon as he had gone, Curtain-boy called his brother. Spring-boy asked whether his father had finished the bows and arrows. "Yes, he has made them." He gave him his own set and got the other from the curtain, then both played and began gambling. Each staked one of the two pieces of meat left by their father, and Spring-boy won both. Then he said, "Come over and let us eat." He felt sorry for his brother and asked him to eat too. He said, "Tomorrow have your father roast three big pieces; the one who wins shall eat two of the three." They played until Spring-boy scented the hunter, when he said, "It smells like your father coming" and went back into the spring again. The next day the father cooked three big pieces of meat and told the boy to keep the fire going. As soon as he was gone, Spring-boy came out, calling Curtain-boy. "Can I come in?" "Yes." He entered the lodge and they cooked the three big pieces. When the meat was done, Spring-boy was eager to gamble, for he thought he could beat his brother. They began to play with their bows and arrows, and this time Curtain-boy beat Spring-boy. Spring-boy wanted to play another game but Curtain-boy would not do it. About sunset the hunter came home and asked the boy what he had done with the three pieces of meat and whether there had been any one with him. "In the spring there is a boy that comes out and plays with me. We gamble over the meat. He always beats me and always eats up the meat." Then he told his father how their mother had been killed. "For three days a woman visited my mother, who always wanted to tell you about it but forgot. She killed my mother and threw one of us into the spring and me behind the curtain. The other boy is in the spring." "Can you get him?" "He has sharp teeth and always talks about his father in the spring and how powerful he is. Spring-boy is afraid of you. Make rawhide cuffs and gloves for me." When the boys wrestled, Spring-boy always bit Curtain-boy, who had to let him go. "Can you get him?" "I have tried several times but he always bit me and I let him go." Whenever the boy caught his brother, he bit him and the spring burst, with fog issuing from it. This had happened three times. The boy told his father to stay close by and watch; he should also bring buffalo guts and pemmican. As soon as Spring-boy was caught and the spring burst and flew towards him, the father was to throw these two pieces into the spring. The next morning the man went out but stayed near by. Spring-boy came out and called Curtain-boy to play. Curtain-boy came with the bows and arrows and lent his brother one set. They began shooting. Curtain-boy wore his rawhide suit. Spring-boy asked him, "Where did you get your clothes?" "My father made them for me." "I want your father to make one for me." They shot their arrows and got to disputing as to which fell nearest the mark. Spring-boy lay down on the ground to measure it, then his brother jumped on him. He had tricked Spring-boy, who had really shot closest. Spring-boy bit him, tearing holes in the rawhide. Curtain-boy called his father, who took the guts and threw them into the spring so that the water went back into the spring again. A fog came forth and covered everything and did not go away. The hunter helped the boy to overpower Spring-boy, and they took him to their lodge. They filed off his sharp teeth, then he was weak. Curtain-boy told his father to sleep with Spring-boy and keep watch over him. Spring-boy said, "We'll have our father sleep between us." The fog did not disappear at all for ten days.

One day the hunter left. The boys stayed home playing. They wondered where their mother was buried and were going to ask their father. When he came back, Spring-boy ran up and said, "I'll ask you something and I want you to tell me." His father told him and then Spring-boy wanted to see the place. His father took him there. When they got back, Spring-boy felt badly over it. One day the father told the boys to stay home, but when he returned they were not there. At last they returned and told their father they had killed something great; it was a buffalo.

The next day the hunter said to his sons: "There is an old woman with a jug; she is dangerous. Whenever she points it at anything it is drawn into the jug, where it is boiled, and then she eats it." He warned the two boys to keep away from her. He left early, then his sons talked to each other about how they might catch that old woman. One of them said, "Let us catch her asleep." The other said, "Let us take a big rock with us and if she points the jug at us we'll throw the rock in and stop up the jug. That's the way we can overcome her." Spring-boy got a stone. When they got near to the old woman, she pointed the jug at him and he was drawn towards the jug but dropped his rock in and jumped aside, falling down. His brother laughed at him. They asked the old woman where she got the jug and how she used it. She said, "Whenever anyone passes by, I use the jug to call him with." They joked with her, then Curtain-boy said he wanted to look at it and she gave it to him. He looked at it and at last pointed it at her. She went in and was boiled inside. They poured her out then and brought the jug home, waiting for their father to return. They told him how they had got it.

That night the hunter told them about another dangerous being they should avoid. "There is a woman over there with a digging-stick; don't go there." "What does she do with it?" "She always kills animals with it. If she sits down and a deer comes she merely swings it and kills the deer. Thus she gets her food." The boys went towards this woman, wondering how they might overcome her. Finally one turned himself into a butterfly and the other into a fly. They flew up to her as she was sleeping on the ground with the stick in front of her. Curtain-boy, as the butterfly, alighted on the stick, while Spring-boy sat down on the old woman's head. Then they turned into boys again and Curtain-boy took the stick. When the old woman arose, he had it and asked her, "What is this stick for?' She wanted it back, but he said, "I am just looking at it." He knocked her in the head with it and killed her. He took the stick home and showed it to his father, telling him how they had killed the old woman.

Curtain-boy said to Spring-boy: "We'll make our mother get up some way." They were going to start right away but Spring-boy said, "Wait till father comes back, we'll ask him for a stone maul (*bū'ptsa*) and also for a stone anvil (*bī'witce*)." They asked him for these, and the next morning after he had left to hunt, they also took the jug and a flesher to the burial site. Under the pine tree, they discussed which of them was to begin. At last Curtain-boy began. Taking the flesher and tossing it up into the air, he said to his mother, "This flesher is going to fall upon you." Then she moved. Next he threw the jug up and said, "This jug is going to fall on you." Again she moved. Then Spring-boy took the maul and threw it into the air, crying, "This maul will fall on you." Then she got up and sat down. She said to the boys: "I have slept for a long time." They took her home, letting her walk between them, and hid her. Their father came home bringing some meat. After he had eaten and when he was lying down for a while, Spring-boy asked his father to say something. The man wanted to know what he wanted him to say. Spring-boy said: "Call for your wife to go to bed." The hunter replied: "Your mother died a long time ago, do not say that any more." Spring-boy kept on saying that he should tell his wife to go to bed. Curtain-boy also asked him to say it. At last he said it. Then the woman came out of her hiding-place. They went to bed together. He watched her at night and did not sleep at all. For four days he did not go away but continued watching her.

The father told his boys that there was a tree leaning over that was very dangerous; whenever anything passed, the tree would drop on it and kill it. One day they went to the tree. When they got there, each shot an arrow over the tree, then they raced towards it. When almost there, they stopped and the tree dropped. Then they jumped on it, played on it for a while, and took some of the limbs home, where they showed them to their mother and told her how they had overcome the tree.

Their mother told them there was a little coulée running through a good flat country. "Whenever any one jumps over it, it spreads out, and if he can't reach the other side he is drowned. It is very dangerous. Keep away from it." One day they said to each other, "Let us look for that coulée." They went to look for it. They saw a coulée coming through the flat and were wondering whether that was it. Both shot arrows across, then Spring-boy went back and took a run. As he got near the coulée, he stopped as if to jump across. Then it spread out, but he did not jump at all. Curtain-boy began to laugh, then both laughed. They both started back and ran quickly, then suddenly stopped. The coulée spread quickly and they ran back, then they jumped over it. Then they played with it and drank from its water and jumped about till the coulée no longer spread apart. They came home and told their mother they had overcome the coulée so that it had no more power.

Their mother told them of a man one of whose moccasins was of fire and who was very dangerous; she bade them keep away from him. One day they said they would look for this man. They found him outside his tipi sleeping with his moccasins off. They wondered what they could do to catch his moccasins. They talked it over and at last Spring-boy turned into a whirlwind and got the moccasins. He used them and went round the tipi, burning up both the tipi and the man. They went homeward saying to each other, "In the morning our mother has a hard time building a fire. We'll take the fire-moccasins home for her."

Their mother told them of a buffalo called Bull-dead-wolf (*tsī'ruptse'tce*), which had killed many people and was very dangerous. Nothing could be done against it, all were afraid of it. She warned them not to go there, showing them where it lived. One day they looked for it. From a high hill they saw it. Down the hill there were very deep roads. They said to each other: "We'll hide in a deep road, and if the buffalo gets one of us, the other shall kill him." They separated. One ran toward the buffalo, hit its tail, and fled. The buffalo pursued him into a hollow, tearing out a big piece of earth each time it struck the ground. The boys said to each other, "We have met something powerful, we may die." The one running, called for help, then the other shot the buffalo twice right in the collarbone, then struck his tail, and now the buffalo chased *him*. Now the other boy shot it twice in the anus. The buffalo stopped suddenly and after a little while fell dead. They were still afraid of it, thinking it was only feigning death. When they found it was really dead, they skinned it, and took the flesh home. They tried to cook it, but the meat was too tough.

One day their mother said, "Keep away from Red-woman. You can do nothing to her, she is too clever. Her medicines go as fast as a wind and she can foretell the future from the clouds." The boys set out and went away from the lodge for a few days. They stayed in the wood and built a little shelter. Spring-boy stayed there and Curtain-boy went out hunting, bringing home meat. They wanted to find out about Red-woman. One day she came to Spring-boy. His brother had told him not to forget to tell him if she came. Before Curtain-boy returned she left and Spring-boy forgot to tell his brother. Three times she came to Spring-boy and every time he forgot to tell Curtain-boy, not recollecting until after his brother had left. At last he stuck one of his arrows at the door, so that Curtain-boy should ask him what the arrow was for when he returned. Thus he remembered and told his brother about the woman. Curtain-boy wished to go home. Spring-boy did not want to. He said, "First we'll try to kill that woman, then we'll go home." It was she that had killed their mother. One day Spring-boy turned into a little boy and watched what Red-woman was doing. He sat on a tree in front of where she was living. She was lying asleep outside with a digging-stick beside her. That was the medicine she used to kill with. He flew back and told his brother they should go and kill her and then go home. They went there. Curtain-boy jumped on the digging-stick and as soon as she got up they hit her on the head with it, knocking her inside. She was dead. Her lodge was an *acta'tsé* (shelter). They tore it down and burnt it on top of her. The firewood popped out and they heard the woman laughing. Then they threw the wood back again. She continued saying, "No matter what you do, boys, you'll be killed." They watched her closely and each time threw the bark into the fire again. When everything was burnt up thoroughly, they went home with the digging-stick and gave it to their mother, telling her to dig with it. They were glad to have killed Red-woman because she had killed their mother.

Their mother told them there was a white tipi that was very dangerous and that they should not go there. After a few days the boys talked it over and decided to look for the tipi. Curtain-boy believed what their mother said, but Spring-boy said, "We can overcome that and can kill anything." He wanted his brother to come also. They set out together, but after a while Curtain-boy said, "Our mother was alone, that is why she got killed. I will stay with her this time." Spring-boy went on and saw representations of snakes on the tipi; near the door there was a picture of a snake facing him and in the back were two more snake pictures. Before leaving, Curtain-boy had told his brother that he was going to watch him. Before Spring-boy got to the lodge he met a jack-rabbit and exchanged eyes with him. The rabbit wanted to go away at once but Spring-boy bade him stay till he was able to see well with his eyes. Then he asked for the rabbit's name and it answered, "Running-jack-rabbit." Below there was a big clump of sagebrush and there Spring-boy told the rabbit to wait for him. Next Spring-boy met Old-Man-Coyote, who said "That tent is dangerous, I can do nothing for you. Get a flat stone and as soon as you get inside, put it under you to sit down on." He got a flat stone and arrived at the door. He asked, "Is there anyone inside?" Some one answered from within, "Whom do you want to see?" Spring-boy said, "Is Snake-face there?" "Yes." Then Snake-face asked him to enter and when he got in they bade him sit down in the rear. He laid down the stone and sat down on it. Hardly had he done this when one of the snakes went into the ground and tried to crawl into his anus but struck the stone. After a while a second one tried to do the same. They were all snakes.

They said they always told stories. Spring-boy said: "That is what I like to hear." They began telling stories and he always answered "Yes." After a while, however, he told them they should go on without waiting for him to say, "Yes." So he fell asleep but his eyes remained open because he had borrowed the rabbit's eyes; accordingly, they thought he was awake. The snakes had sticks to rest their heads on. Several of them tried to enter his anus but they struck the stone. After a while he awoke and asked whether he should tell stories. They said he should, and he told them to reply, "Yes." Spring-boy began as follows: "When a big crowd of people move and reach a river, they are always eager to get there. When they arrive, there will be a big shade and the river will be high. We'll smell the river and see the trees and the leaves floating down and the blackbirds singing over the river. After all have camped, everybody will go in for a swim, and sitting down afterwards in the nice shade they will fall asleep." When he had said this, half of the snakes were already asleep, and no longer answered, "Yes." Then he began again: "In the fall when the leaves have all turned yellow and are falling off, there are sometimes rainy days. They will be out somewhere far along in the evening and get wet, and when they get home they will take a blanket and cover themselves. When they have lain thus for a while, they can't help falling asleep." Again half of the remainder were asleep. He began again: "Late in the fall when the days are windy, they will be out and come back home and lie inside. They will hear the wind blowing, then they can't help falling asleep." Again only half of the rest answered, "Yes," now. The fourth time he spoke as follows: "When they move to the mountains and camp near the pines and the wind strikes the trees, they can bear the rustling in the pines and can't help falling asleep." Now they were all asleep and he jumped up, took his knife and cut off their heads. Only one snake awoke in time to escape. This one said, "Don't do it four times," and ran underground. Spring-boy could not catch him. Then he called out, "Running-jack-rabbit, I have brought your eyes back." Then the jack-rabbit came out and took his eyes back. Spring-boy returned home. He told his mother, "I went into that tipi and told stories and put them to sleep and cut off the heads of all but one. That one said, 'Spring-boy, don't do it four times,' and went underground." His mother said, "Watch yourself closely."

After a while he went out and slept under a sagebrush. Then the snake came out and entered his anus. As soon as he woke up, he broke himself apart at the waist, but the snake had already gone higher. He broke himself apart at the throat, but the snake was already in his brains. He could not do anything now. One day he made it rain. Where his head was lying there was a coulée and a deep hole. He made it rain till the hole was filled with water. Then he caused a strong wind to come, that blew his skull into the deep hole with water. The snake stuck its head out saying, "It is a long time that he has been dead." Spring-boy wanted to catch him but every time the snake went in again. Spring-boy made the sun shine so that it was very hot and the water began to boil. The snake was boiling in the hole. It said, "He has been dead a long while." It stuck its head out but was afraid to come out and stuck it in again. It did this again. Then Spring-boy got up and caught it. He was wondering what he should do with the snake. He took it to the hills where there were big stones and began filing its face off. The snake began to scream. "I'll do nothing wrong any more, I'll never enter any one's anus, I'll be good." Its face was bleeding: the face of snakes used to be sharp and long before he ground it off. When the snake made these promises he let it go. Before it entered the ground, it said, "I'll just bite once in a while." Spring-boy ran towards it but could not catch it. He went back home and told Curtain-boy he had no brains. "I melted my brains," he said. Curtain-boy said, "I'll take little stones and put them in your head." He did this, then Spring-boy said, "I have a rattle now." Then they named him Rattling-head. The boys went about and Spring-boy would rattle his head. There used to be many dangerous beings on earth, but these boys killed them all.

The two boys always went out to hunt. One night when they slept away from camp Long-arm (*bā-ā'ritsg·e*), reaching down from above, took Curtain-boy up into the sky. His brother looked for him everywhere, making medicine to find him, but all in vain. One day he met Old-Man-Coyote and told him about his troubles and asked for his help: "I will kill buffalo and give you a big feast." Old-Man-Coyote called all the birds of the world to come. All came and Spring-boy killed buffalo and gave the meat to Old-Man-Coyote. When all had come, Old-Man-Coyote asked whether they knew anything about Curtain-boy. He told them that he had been gone several days, that his brother had tried every means to find him, but without avail.

He questioned the birds one by one: none had seen him. They were about to go home when one of them said, "Running-crow has not come yet, he is a clever bird, let us wait for him." Old-Man-Coyote waited for this bird, but when it arrived it knew nothing about Curtain-boy.

Spring-boy went home. He lay down one day and looked straight up thinking about his brother. Then he saw in the sky a little hole through which his brother had been taken. He called out, "Mother!" "Yes." "I see where my brother was taken." He showed her and told her he was going up. He made four arrows, painting one yellow, one black, one blue, one green. He went where no one could see him and shot his first arrow into the air. This arrow was himself. He shot the second arrow still farther, then the third farther still, and with the fourth he landed where his brother had been taken. He stood there. No one was around there. He was wondering where the camp was and where his brother might be. Some one came along and the boy asked where the camp was. It was near a river. Little birds lived there. Spring-boy transformed himself into a poor boy and got to the first tipi. An old woman was inside. He waited without, and she called him in and gave him to eat. After he had eaten he addressed her as grandmother and asked whether she knew anything about the boy who had been brought in and what they were going to do with him. "They will eat him, for they have killed many medicine beings on earth. Long-arm brought him here. He made medicine and took him to a second camp and from there, after making medicine, to a third camp and there they made medicine again and then took him to the fourth camp, and there they are going to eat him." The boy asked whether he might get a little piece to eat. She said only prominent people might eat him, poor people would not get anything, so she did not think he would get any piece. He asked her next, whether he might look on. "Yes, some people are going there, you may follow them."

The next morning he followed this party and they got to the second camp, where he again found an old woman. "Grandmother, what are you doing?" She was making parfleches. She told him to go in and find something to eat. He went in. The people in this second camp were storks. He asked her whether he might go to the place where the boy was to be eaten. She told him he might, and he left with a party going that way.

In the third camp he found an old woman working on a hide outside. He came up to her and asked, "Grandmother, what are you doing?" "I am dressing a skin." She told him to go in and have something to eat. Before eating, he asked her, "Where are these people going?" "They are going where they will eat the person brought from the earth. They took him through here yesterday." He asked whether he might see it, and she said, "You'll have a hard time to see it because there are so many people who will look on." He ate and went on with some people toward the fourth camp. The people in the third camp were eagles.

He got toward the fourth camp. He asked a man in his party whether he might get a small piece of the boy to eat. The man turned about and scolded him: "We ourselves shall not get a chance to eat." The boy looked so poor they did not like him and told him to go back. At last he got to the fourth camp, where the people were black eagles. Long-arm was their chief. He got to an old woman and asked, "May I see the boy?" She said, "I don't think so. Go in and have something to eat." He ate and left her lodge, then shot his arrows to the place where Curtain-boy was. Before he got there he played about and stood behind the big crowd of onlookers. There he heard Curtain-boy breathing hard as if in pain. A young man stood near by. The boy asked him, "What are they doing?" "There are two boys who killed many great things on earth whom the black eagles had adopted, that is why they brought him up here to eat him." "Will you hold me up and show me the boy." The young man picked him up in his arms and took him into the crowd. Then the boy saw his brother. Curtain-boy opened his eyes, and seeing Rattling-head he said, "Rattling-head, why have you waited so long? I have been suffering for a long time." Rattling-head heard him and asked the young man to let him down. Then he walked through the crowd in front of Long-arm, who had his arms wound about the boy so that only his head peeped out. He walked up to him, rubbing his bow and arrows, which turned into good ones. He said to Long-arm, "Let the boy go." Long-arm answered, "I would not let him go, no matter what you did, I'll eat you up too." Near them they were drumming and singing over the boy. Long-arm had a stone and he shot it with the bow and arrows so that everybody could see blood coming from the stone. Again he bade Long-arm release the boy, and again he refused. He took an arrow and shot it through Long-arm, and with a second arrow he again shot him through the heart. He fell dead. Then everyone fled. Spring-boy called them back and told them to bring wood to burn up Long-arm. When they had burnt him up, he told all the birds to come down on the earth. "It is a good place and there is nothing harmful there." He bade all the four camps come down. That is why the birds are on earth instead of in the sky. He took his brother homeward. When he got to the sky-hole, he lent Curtain-boy two arrows, and he himself went down on two arrows. When he got back home, he told his father and mother that they had a hard time up above.

One day he told his parents they would arrange it so that they should live forever. They told their mother to be the moon and their father the morning star; Curtain-boy was to be the last star in the Dipper, and Spring-boy the eveningstar.

Divorced Women

If some people were different, if their speech and language were different, it would be well. Our language is one, therefore we cannot feel angry (with each other). For that reason we cannot feel content, we cannot dislike anyone, we cannot get furious, we cannot be happy. If you made our speech different, if we could not understand each other, we could get furious, we could be angry, we could be happy, that's how it is. If one day we're happy, one day we're unhappy, if good and bad are mixed together, we'll have something to do and thus we'll like each other. We shall thence have chiefs. Why, only recently I told you you did not know many good things; flirting with women is a good thing you don't know of. Old Man Coyote it was. For the first time he spoke; while Cirape talked *he* was silent. "Well, these are some very fine things. I like this, I was going to talk about it, I put it off; you were cunning, you knew and were the first to talk about it." Cirape said: "Now how did you know?" Old Man Coyote said: "Why I have known all along." Cirape asked: "If so, how did you know?" Old Man Coyote: "Why, when we go to war, from somewhere we bring horses, we reach a camp, we flirt, we sing tsura songs, at women we make eyes, women look at us. We go to war, kill somebody, strike a coup, take their bows, sing tsuras, make the women dance. That's it, it's good. One thing I'll tell you. Newly-married women are wont to satisfy us; when we've been long married we get dissatisfied. If we marry others, at first it's the same, we have a lively interest. Cirape, I thought you were cunning, but one thing you did not know." Old Man Coyote continued. "Married women when we secretly have them as our sweethearts and under difficulties, they generally give great pleasure." Cirape said: "Why, if there is anyone in this state it is I." "If so, I'll ask something." Old Man Coyote spoke. "All right." "This mutual wife-stealing of ours, have you ever experienced it? Has your wife ever been kidnapped?" he asked. "Why, several times they have been taken away. A hostile charge is less disagreeable, of all different things it stands out." "All right, have you ever taken back a divorced woman?" Old Man Coyote asked. "What! I am honorable. I have self-respect. How could I take back a divorced wife?" Old Man Coyote said: "If so, you truly know nothing. Cirape, the truth is my wife–she must have given pleasure–had been kidnapped, and thrice I have taken back a divorced woman. If they abduct our wives and we take them back, when we do like this (gesture), she recalls the time she was taken; we don't have to remind them, they will do anything at all we desire. Our having wives like this is incomparable, it is grand. You think I've been married, you have never been really married. If some day you will do as I say, then you'll really be married." Cirape answered: "You might think it was grand. But though you do, other people will look at you and mock you. That's why I don't take back a divorced woman, that's it. Anyone knowing would mock you. That's why I have self-respect, (literally, hold myself sacred) that's it." So much for that. Old Man Coyote kept divorced women, hence from then to the present the Crow have kept divorced women.

■ PETE BEAVERHEAD

Pete Beaverhead, an elder of the Salish (Flathead) tribe of western Montana, tells this traditional myth, "The Origin of the Seasons," about the early days of the earth's creation. In this story, a force of nature, the Stolemtk, appears to be a family of humans. Because such stories are told only during the winter months and only at night, the Flathead Culture Committee asks that readers observe and honor their culture by following this ancient custom. "The Origin of the Seasons" is one of several traditional stories that the Flathead Culture Committee has collected and transcribed so they can be passed on to the children of the tribe. This story was published in Stories from Our Elders *(1979), edited by Clarence Woodcock.*

Origin of the Seasons

Many years ago there lived two families. One family lived on the east end of the river and the other family lived on the west side of the river.

The family on the east end, were the chiefs of the cold weather, the Q^{w}ox^{w}míneʔ. They were birds of the Dipper family. They were three brothers and one sister. Since they liked cold weather, their end of the river was frozen over the year round.

On the west end of the river were the chiefs of the warm weather, the Sʼtólemtek^{w}. They were not beings but were part of the weather. In this family were three brothers and one girl. The girl was the wife of the oldest brother. Also living here was their grandmother. This family preferred warm weather, so their end of the river always had clear running water.

The two families were always arguing who should rule the weather.

"All of you come. We are going to gamble in the river," the warm weather beings said to the Dippers one day. The water was frozen over. The Dippers had made the weather cold.

"We are going to race. We will start from here. We are going to run and skate on the frozen water. Whoever reaches the other side first will win," challenged the Dippers.

There was an area that didn't have any ice because the water was strong and swift.

"We will place bets and we will race. Your life will also go along as a bet."

They ran and when they reached where the water was too swift to freeze, the Dippers pushed the Sʼtólemtek^{w} and he fell in the water under the ice.

The Dippers killed them all. So then they became the chiefs of all the twelve months.

"We have control of all the months. We have something to do with everything that happens during these 12 months. We will fix it so there will be no spring and summer months. It will always be winter!"

There was only one Sʼtólemtek^{w} left. It was the old grandmother.

"Leave the old woman. Don't kill her. She will die by herself. She will die from the cold," they said.

Sometime later the Dippers seen smoke. The old woman had already gathered dry wood and made a fire. The Dippers seeing this would take her dry wood and throw them in to the water. Then they'd go back and give her wet wood.

"Here is some wood for you. Don't use this dry wood anymore. It's no good."

The poor old woman couldn't make fire with the wet wood. She took all her blankets and piled it on her. She sat there all covered up.

The sister of the S̓tólemtek^{W} was the last one the Dippers had killed. The brothers were drowned first. The dead S̓tólemtek^{W} floated down stream.

The Bullhead lived at the head of the water. He is a rare person, a rare fish. He lived alone in his home. He is a fish trapper.

One day Bullhead went to see his traps. He seen a woman laying there in the water.

"Ha Yo! There is a person dead, drowned!"

She was ready to give birth when she drowned. Bullhead picked her up and brought her back to his home and warmed her up. She was dead. Frozen!! But there was something moving around inside her stomach! It seemed as if the child was alive.

Bullhead took his knife and sharpened it on a rock until it was very sharp. He cut the woman open and took the child out. He found the child still alive!

"Ha Yo! I have a companion now. Even if there is just the two of us, today little child, I'm very glad to have you. You don't speak, you don't know it now but you're moving your arms and hands and everything." Bullhead was laughing and very pleased and said, "It is good."

Finally the child grew up and started to talk.

"Today you spoke. Is it good to know and see everything? Do you hear well and see well enough?"

"Today I am going to tell you your name. It is Sck̓^{W}eľtelénč, which means cut out of the stomach. Over there, at the end of the lake was where your parents lived. This is where the Dippers killed them all. Their home is still there. They had four children. Today the Dippers are chiefs of all the weather. They are the ones who don't want the summer. They want it to be winter always."

Sck̓^{W}eľtelénč told Bullhead to go pour some water in a wooden bucket for him. Bullhead did. He took a bath, splashed around playing in the water. The next morning again he told Bullhead to pour him some water.

"The water is too warm. Get me some cold water."

The next morning Bullhead asked him if he wanted him to get some more water.

"No. I will go to the water myself and take a bath." There was a hole in the ice where Bullhead got his water.

Sck̓^{W}eľtelénč jumped in this hole. The ice started to melt quite aways and break up. The next morning he went to take a bath again. He ran and jumped in. The ice broke up all the way across to a little island. He did this four times until there wasn't anymore ice all the way to the end of the lake.

"Ha Yo!" The Dippers came out and said. "The S̓tólemtekʷ is showing up. Their power has showed up. Maybe it is the old woman," they thought out loud.

The clouds were turning dark. It was a chinook!!

"I am going over to gamble and challenge the Dippers," Sck̓ʷel̓telénč told Bullhead the next day.

"Okay go ahead," Bullhead told him. He warned him too that the Dippers were very smart. "Because of their smartness, although your mother and elders were smart, they were all killed," he warned.

"Wait, I will help you. I will give you a hand." He picked up his pillow and underneath it lay his white bag.

Bullhead gave this to Sck̓ʷel̓telénč.

"This is going to be your way of getting there. It is fast. It will get you there swiftly. When you get there, you fix this. No one will see what it is." Bullhead took one white bag and untied it and gave it to him. It was a bag of red Indian war paint. A piece of buckskin string was laying in the paint sticking out.

"When you are going to race and skate on the ice, and when you get real close to where there is no ice, you pull this buckskin string out with the red paint on it. You sprinkle this paint on the ice. You won't pass this. You will stop right there and not fall in the water. Then you hit the Dippers on the behind and they will fall in the water. You will get rid of them. They will all die."

Sck̓ʷel̓telénč got ready. He sprinkled the paint on the ice. The Dippers came and got on the ice. He barely touched the Dipper. He hit him and knocked him clear over to the other end of some little island. Sck̓ʷel̓telénč didn't have any trouble getting across the other side. He was quick.

He went to a place near Kalispel. He saw the old woman's home. He went in and seen her wood. They were like icicles. She didn't have a fire going, she was sitting there wrapped up in her blankets.

"Who are you? Who are you?" she asked.

Sck̓ʷel̓telénč told her that one of the S̓tólemtekʷ was his mother and that she had been killed.

"Ah! So you are from that kind."

"Is your wood any good?"

"No," said the old woman. "I am almost frozen to death."

Sck̓ʷel̓telénč took the wet wood outside and cut some dry pitch and built a big fire.

A while later the Dippers seen the smoke. They said the old one has smoke coming out of her house again. One of them went over. A man was sitting there.

"Come in. We are going to talk about something."

"Who are you?"

"I am Dipper."

"And who are you?"

"I am Sck̓ʷel̓telénč."

"My brothers and sister are asking you to come over to race," Dipper said.

"Okay, go on. I will go."

This is when the Dippers were all killed. When they reached the water, they would run real fast racing and skating and Sck̓ʷel̓telénč would sprinkle the paint and he'd stop right there. He'd hit the Dipper on the behind and push them in the water and they'd drown.

"How about another one of you. Come and race. Your other brother tricked me by falling in the water and drowning," he would say.

"You Dippers aren't going to be chiefs forever. When time goes on and mankind begins over there at the head of the water and in the cool places is where you will live."

This is when the S̓tólemtekʷ got back the six months of warm weather–the spring and the summer months.

■ LOUISA McDERMOTT
compiler

Louisa McDermott of Fort Lewis, Colorado, published these Coyote stories in 1901 in the Journal of American Folk-Lore. *Although she titled her article "Folk-Lore of the Flathead Indians of Idaho," most of the stories she records take place in Montana's Bitterroot Valley, the home country of the Flathead tribe. There are many versions of these Coyote stories, but these are of interest because they take place in specific Montana settings, and they seem to have happened after the long-ago times, but before the present.*

Coyote Kills the Giant

From Spokane Falls Coyote came up on to Ravalli. There he met an Old Woman, who was camped close to where Ravalli Station is now. The Old Woman said to Coyote, "Where are you going?"

"Oh," said Coyote, "I am going to travel all over the world."

"Well," said the Old Woman, "you had better go back from here."

"Why should I go back from here?" asked Coyote.

"Because there is a Giant in this valley who kills every one that goes through," replied the Old Woman.

"Well," said Coyote, "I will fight with him and kill him."

Then Coyote started on the trail again. He saw a great big tamarack-tree growing on the hillside, and he pulled it up and threw it over his shoulder and went on his way. He said to himself, "I'll choke that giant with this tamarack-tree. That's what I'll do."

Pretty soon he saw a woman that was nearly dead. "What is the matter with you?" asked Coyote. "Are you sick?"

The woman said, "No, I am not sick."

Coyote said, "I am going to choke the Giant with this tamarack-tree."

The woman said, "You might as well throw that stick away. Don't you know that you are already in the Giant's belly?"

Then Coyote threw the tamarack against the hillside, and it can be seen close to Arlee, a little station on the Northern Pacific Railroad. It stuck against the hillside and grew. All of what is now Jacko Valley was filled by the Giant's belly.

Coyote went on from there and he saw lots of people lying around. Some of them were dead, and some were pretty nearly dead. "What is the matter with you people?" asked Coyote.

They all said, "We are starving to death."

Coyote said, "What makes you starve? There is plenty to eat in here, lots of meat and fat."

Then Coyote cut chunks of grease from the sides of the Giant and fed them to the people, who got better. And then Coyote said, "Now, all of you people get ready to run out. I am going to cut the Giant's heart. When I start to cut you must all run out at O'Keef's Canyon or over at Ravalli."

The Giant's heart was the rounded cluster of mountains north of Flathead Agency, and there are marks on the side which show the place that Coyote cut with his stone knife.

Coyote began to cut the Giant's heart with his stone knife. Pretty soon the Giant said, "Please, Coyote, let me alone. You go out. I don't want you to stay in here. You can go out."

Coyote said, "No, I won't go out. I am going to stay right here. I am going to kill you."

Then he started to cut the Giant's heart. He cut the Giant's heart off and then ran out. The Giant was dying, and his jaws began to close. Woodtick was the last to come out. The Giant's jaws were just closing down on him when Coyote caught him and pulled him out.

"Well," said Coyote, "you will always be flat. I can't help it now. You must be flat." That is the reason Woodtick is so flat.

Coyote Kills Another Giant

Coyote started from there to go up to Stevensville. Between Corvallis and Stevensville there is a very sharp Butte. The Giant lay on top of that Butte. Coyote had a little black squirrel for a dog. He called him One Ear. The Giant had Grizzly Bear for his dog. Grizzly Bear killed all the people that passed through the valley. He never missed one.

At the foot of the hill Coyote saw a little camp of Mice. He said to them, "What will you take to dig a little hole for me from the bottom of this hill up to where the Giant is? I want to go up under the ground. It is the only way I can get up."

The Mice said, "Give us some camas and blackberries and we will dig the hole." Then Coyote gave them some camas and blackberries, and they began to dig. They dug and dug until the hole reached from the foot of the hill to the top. It came right up to where the Giant lay.

Coyote went in about noon. He crawled through the little hole, and pretty soon he came out right under the Giant's belly, where the hole ended.

The Giant was very much surprised. "Where did you come from?" he said.

Coyote said, "Are you blind that you didn't see me come?"

"Which way did you come?" asked the Giant.

"I came right across the prairie," answered Coyote.

"I didn't see you," said the Giant. "I've been watching everywhere all day, and I didn't see any one come."

Coyote said again, "Are you blind that you didn't see me? You must have been asleep. That is the reason you didn't see me."

Just then the dogs began to growl at each other. Coyote said to the Giant, "You had better stop your dog. My dog will kill him if you don't."

The Giant said, "You had better stop your dog. My dog will swallow him."

Then the two dogs began to fight. One Ear ran under Grizzly Bear and cut his belly open with his sharp pointed ear. Grizzly Bear fell down dead.

Coyote said, "I told you to stop your dog. Now he is killed."

Then they sat down and began to talk. Coyote made a wish, and whatever he wished always came true. He wished there were lots of horses and women and men down at the foot of the hill. Pretty soon he could see the people and horses moving down there. The Giant didn't see them yet.

Coyote said, "I thought you had good eyes?"

The Giant said, "Of course I have good eyes. I can see everything."

Coyote answered, "You say you have good eyes. Can you see the Indians moving over there? You didn't see them yet?"

The Giant looked very carefully and he saw the Indians moving. He was ashamed that he didn't see them before.

"Now," said Coyote, "let us be partners. We will kill all these people."

"All right," answered the Giant.

"Now we will go after them," said Coyote. "We will go down to the foot of the hill."

They started down the hill, and when they were half way down the Giant was very tired.

"Give me your knife," said Coyote. "I will carry it for you. It is too heavy for you, and you are already very tired." So the Giant gave Coyote his knife. Then they started on.

When they got to the bottom of the hill the Giant said, "I am not going any farther than this. I am played out."

Coyote said, "Give me your bow and arrows. I will carry them for you." The Giant gave his bow and arrows to Coyote. Then he had nothing at all to fight with.

As soon as Coyote got the bow and arrows he began to jump and yell. "Now we'll start war right here," he said.

"Let me go free, Coyote," begged the Giant. "I won't kill any more people. I'll be good friends with everybody if you'll let me go."

"No," said Coyote. "I am going to kill you now. To-day is your last day."

Then he commenced to shoot, and soon he killed the Giant.

BLIND MOSE CHOUTEH

Blind Mose Chouteh was an elder of the Flathead Tribe. In this unpublished manuscript, transcribed by the Flathead Culture Committee in 1983, Chouteh tells the story of the origins of the sweat ceremony. The ceremony is an important traditional cleansing and healing ritual that is still practiced by many members of the Flathead Tribe and, in their own ways, by other Native American tribes around the country.

How the Sweathouse Came to Be

Long ago, before mankind was created, there was two families camped to the far west across the ocean.

There was a small mountain with Coyote and his mother camped on one side while Fox and his mother had their tipi on the other side.

Coyote and Fox were cousins since their mothers were sisters. They frequently met in the woods to visit.

One day Coyote got restless, he didn't feel like doing anything. He just laid around. "Are you sick?" his mother asked. "No," Coyote answered.

After a few days of his mother watching him lay around she said to him: "Get ready, you are going to leave me. You are to go overseas and help the people. Take pity on them, defend them from the monsters that rule the land. When the human race is created they will be a pitiful sight if you don't go now and kill the monsters."

Coyote sat there quietly listening as his mother continued to instruct him: "When morning is upon you, you must go. Walk to the ocean shore, go in the direction of the sunrise. When you get to the shore you will see some reeds. Cut the reeds and weave them into a boat. You will cross the ocean on this boat. When you get across, you will see a small mountain, you must climb to the top and hide your boat. From there you will walk and start killing the monsters that you encounter. You will die many times because the monsters will kill you time and time again. Coyote's mother had a big bundle which she layed out on a blanket and described each individual little bundle that was inside.

There was four things used: flint, human hair, buckskin, and a bone. Four little dolls were made using these four thing. They were mialtkʷó, kʷeltalálqs, ʼcaʼcel?qʷé, and ʼcacl̓nšen, who would be the strongest and would help Coyote the most. "Your brother, the Fox will follow you and he will always bring you back to life," Coyote's mother told him. With that his mother wrapped these four little bundles up in the blanket and gave it to Coyote to keep and use for his strength.

Early the next morning, Coyote began his journey. He came to the ocean shore, cut some reeds and weaved a boat.

Anxious to get across the ocean, Coyote climbed aboard the boat and headed for the eastern land.

After several days on the water, Coyote reached the shore. Remembering his mother's instructions he began climbing the small mountain carrying his boat. Upon reaching the mountain top he put his boat away then began the journey on foot.

Meanwhile Coyote's brother Fox also became restless. He went to visit Coyote but he was not home. His mother informed Fox that his cousin went overseas. "He went to slay the monsters," she told Fox; "For when mankind is created, the people will suffer and be pitiful if the monsters are not destroyed."

Fox felt very sad, he missed seeing his cousin. He went home and just layed around not wanting to do anything. "Are you sick?" his mother asked. Fox told her: "No, I am just lonesome for my cousin Coyote."

Fox's mother said to her son: "Okay, tomorrow you will follow your cousin and help him." She handed him a bundle and said: "This is what you will use to bring your brother back to life when he is killed, as he will be killed many times before he conquers the monsters. When you use this, you must step over Coyote to revive him."

Fox's mother continued to instruct him: "When you get to the shore where your cousin sailed from, you must cut some cattails and weave them into a boat. You will use the boat to sail across the ocean. When you land, you will see a small mountain. That is where Coyote put his boat away and this also is where you will put yours away. From here you will go on foot and follow your cousin. As you walk on your journey, you will be told that Coyote has been killed over there by a monster. You must go and look for him. If you find just a single strand of his fur or if you see just a small piece of his bones, put them together and sing this song. You sing this song through once. Lay these pieces of your cousin on your blanket and step over them and he will come to life again. He will yawn and say, 'Hi yo, I was just going to lie down and I must have fallen asleep.' You will say to him:

'Yes you were sleeping, you were killed by the monster.' Then you show him which monster killed him," she said.

Fox's mother continued: "Then Coyote will tell you that he is going to kill that monster. You will try to stop him and if he doesn't heed your warning then let him go. He will find a way to kill that monster, any monster."

With all the instructions memorized, Fox began his journey. He did everything he was told. He weaved a boat out of the cattails, sailed across the ocean, climbed the small mountain, put his boat away where Coyote had, then he continued walking.

Fox had walked a long way before he was told: "Way over there is where your brother has been killed."

Fox went looking for Coyote. He found a small piece of a bone and a single strand of Coyote's fur. Fox spread his blanket out, put the piece of bone and fur on it. As he sang his song, he stepped over them and Coyote came back to life.

Coyote opened his eyes, looked at Fox and said: "Oh wow, I was just going to lay down for a little while and I must have fallen asleep."

Fox looked at his brother and said: "Yes, you were sleeping. You were killed by a monster."

Coyote jumped up. "Oh that's right," he said, "that monster is going to get it now, I am going to kill him."

Fox tried to stop Coyote but he wouldn't listen so Fox told him, "Okay, go ahead."

Coyote began walking. He went and killed the monster. He killed the monsters with the help of Fox and the other three little dolls who had power.

Coyote kept on going farther east. He came to a lake. A monster called Ntuk lived at the bottom of the lake. Ntuk was surrounded by many guards, who were everywhere, in the lake, on the lake, by the lake, in the deserts, in the air and even underground. Coyote was killed. He was revived then killed again. He tried again and again then finally after being killed five times he killed Ntuk the monster.

One day as Coyote was traveling around the country, he saw some smoke off in the distance. He said to himself, "Hi yo there must be a sweathouse over there where that smoke is. Well I think I will go over and take a sweatbath. I am tired and my feet are really sore." He went.

As he approached, Coyote was greeted: "So, you are here Coyote."

"Yes, I have come to sweat," Coyote answered.

He was told: "No, you must fix it all yourself. When you are all done, then you can sweat. You will then get well and be in good health."

So Coyote went to work, he got everything ready then made the fire.

Awhile later he was told to go on in the sweathouse and that the rocks would be brought in.

The voice said:

I AM THE SWEATHOUSE,
WHOEVER YOU MAY BE,
WHEN MANKIND IS CREATED,
IF YOU ARE REALLY SINCERE IN THE PRAYERS YOU SAY TO ME,
I WILL HELP YOU.
BUT YOU WHO USE ME
JUST FOR THE SAKE OF GETTING CLEAN,
OR IF YOU ARE JUST PASSING TIME,
OR PLAYING AROUND,
I WILL NOT HELP YOU.

Coyote went into the sweathouse. The rocks were brought in as well as the bucket of water. Then he was told: "That is all. From now on when you get to where there are people, you must make a sweathouse and teach the people how to make one. You, the Indians, must always and forever, build the sweathouse upstream from your home. Eventually, whoever you may be, you will have your own home away from your family and you must always build your sweathouse upstream and the door must always face the sunrise. Also when you pick your rocks, you must always have one rock, two rocks, three rocks, four rocks. That is the very first thing you put in your sweathouse. No matter how small the rocks, when they enter your sweathouse, they will make your sweathouse strong. Your sweathouse will be powerful. You must always build your sweathouse upstream from your home with the door facing the sunrise."

Sweathouse continues to tell how it must be:

ALL OF YOU, WHOEVER YOU MAY BE,
IF YOU LIKE ME, RESPECT ME,
TREAT ME WITH COMPASSION,
I WILL HELP YOU.
I TOO GET HUNGRY AND LONELY,
WHEN YOU BUILD ME AND USE ME,
AFTER AWHILE YOU MAY NO LONGER USE ME,
YOU WILL FORGET ABOUT ME,
YOU WILL LEAVE ME
THEN I TOO WILL BE PITIFUL.
THAT IS THE WAY IT WILL BE,
IF YOU HELP ME, THEN I WILL ALWAYS HELP YOU.

WHEN YOU ENTER ME,
PRAY THAT YOU MAY TRAVEL IN GOOD HEALTH,
THAT YOU EAT GOOD, THAT YOU HAVE PLENTY OF
WHAT YOU NEED.
WHEN YOU ARE ILL, COME SEE ME AND I WILL CURE YOU.
YOU MUST ENTER ME ONE, TWO, THREE, FOUR TIMES
AND I WILL HELP YOU.
FOR A CHRONIC ILLNESS YOU MUST ENTER EIGHT TIMES
AND YOU WILL BE HEALED.
I WILL HELP YOU IF YOU ARE AILING FROM AN ACCIDENT,
OR IF YOU ARE SUFFERING FROM DEPRESSION, HATE OR
RESENTMENT.
IT WILL BE THE SAME, I WILL HELP YOU.
OR, IF SOMEONE HAS DONE YOU WRONG IN SOME WAY,
WHOEVER YOU ARE, IF YOU ARE HONEST AND STRAIGHT
FORWARD
AND REALLY BELIEVE, WHEN YOU ENTER WITH YOUR PLEA TO ME
I WILL HELP YOU.
YOU WHO ARE TO BE THE HUMAN RACE, WHEN MANKIND IS
CREATED,
YOU WILL BE HEALED.
ALWAYS WHEN YOU BUILD ME, YOU MUST USE ME OFTEN
AND YOU
WILL ALWAYS TRAVEL IN GOOD HEALTH.

To Coyote he said: "Eventually you and your brother the Fox will have your camps to the east, on the coast, on an island."

That is where they are camped today. Coyote and Fox both have daughters. When the end of the world comes, we will see them again.

■ FRED GONE, SR.

Fred Gone, Sr., a member of the Gros Ventre, or White Clay People, was employed by the Works Projects Administration during the early 1940s to interview Gros Ventre elders about life as it was before the buffalo were slaughtered. These stories—which appeared with others in War Stories of the White Clay People *(1982)—are written in the same words and syntax that the original storytellers used. Some of the stories tell of the personal exploits of the informants, and some are tribal myths. They relate unusual and memorable events in Gros Ventre history and explain unnatural phenomenon that occurred in the daily lives of the people.*

The Boy Who Was Raised by Seven Buffalo Bulls

There was an Indian encampment, and in this encampment, a young man and a maiden were lovers. They used to meet secretly, but never were engaged to be married, therefore their secret meeting continued until the Indian maiden was not able to keep it up anymore. And when she began to show signs on her person, resulting from those secret meetings she became sad and downcast. Finally her mother noticed her appearance and asked her the reason, but the maiden would not tell, but said she was sick.

Finally when she was about to deliver, she told her mother, "I have had a lover, and now I am ashamed and when the child is born, let us throw it away." The tribe moved camp, and she and her mother fell behind, because she was now in great pain, and when the tribe had moved out of sight, the mother looked for a place where she made a temporary shelter for them, and that night the daughter gave birth to a boy.

Next morning her mother looked around for a likely place to leave the baby, and finally she dug a shallow hole in the bank of a buffalo wallow, and laid the baby in it and covered it up with dirt, and left it there and followed up where the tribe had moved to.

And as the child had cried and struggled it had partly uncovered itself. Now there was a herd of seven old buffalo bulls near by and had started to follow the trail left by the moving tribe.

One of these old bulls left the others and went to the wallows to wallow in them and happened to approach the wallow the baby was buried in.

He heard the sound of the baby crying and did not know what it was, so he stood there listening when the other old bulls reached him. And when they had all arrived there, they finally found the cause of the noise and uncovered the baby. When they knew what it was that they had found, they pitied the child.

One of the old bulls said, "Let us raise it and we will have it for our son." The first one that had found the child began to wallow and when it was done it began to lick the child with its tongue, then another one did likewise, and so on until they all had licked the child with their tongue, and as each one licked the child, the child would advance in age and size, and by the time the seventh and last bull got done licking the child, it was no longer a baby but he was a boy. The bulls told the boy to get on the back of the bull who had found him first, and to hang on by its mane.

The bulls then started off with the boy, and when they finally thought the boy was hungry, they wondered what to feed the boy, because they did not know what to feed him.

Then they asked the boy, "Will you eat grass with us?" "No, I cannot eat it," the boy said. The bulls said, "What do you eat?" "I do not know," the boy said. So one of the bulls said, "They eat buffalo." So they didn't know just how they were to get a cow and kill it for the boy.

They planned, so they went and looked for a herd of buffalo and when they found one they got a cow among themselves, and after coaxing the cow away from the main herd, they killed the cow with their horns. The bulls knowing that the boy did not know how to go about dressing the cow, told the boy, "Break a stone, and use the sharp edges for a knife, and cut up the meat." So the boy did as he was told to do, using the points and sharp edges of the broken stone for a knife.

Thus, the boy was happy for now he had much to eat. He would play by himself and sometimes he would play with his foster fathers, and when the boy would find feathers, he would tie knots in the long hair of mane, and fasten the feathers there, and the boy would sometimes tie feathers to the bulls' tails. When the boy was growed up, the bulls told him to make a bow, but the boy knew nothing of the life of his tribe, therefore the bulls had to instruct him in the making of the bow and arrows.

So, the bulls told the boy, "Go into the brush and cut a piece of cherry wood, cut it so long, and also cut seven sticks of the cherry wood for arrows, and to peel them all then season them, and after the wood is all seasoned, then shape the wood into bow and arrows, then take some sinew, and twist it into a bow string."

The boy did all this as he was told. Then the bulls told him how to break flint rock and shape it into an arrow point. When the boy had finished making his bow and arrows, the bulls then told him to kill his own game himself for food. So when the boy ran out of food, they would carry him into a herd on their backs, and when in the middle of the herd the boy would jump off when he saw the one he wanted and killed it. Thus the boy continued to russel himself. The bulls loved their foster son very much and at no time did they even get angry with him for anything that he done. Sometimes the boy would cut thongs of raw hide and tie their feet together with it, but they never got angry.

Each in turn, they would carry him over the country wherever they went, and he continued to live with them until he grew to be a young man.

Now in their wanderings from place to place they got into a certain territory that was occupied by a very large herd of buffalo well known to the seven bulls, so they cautioned the boy, because this herd was held by a powerful bull, who had nothing but all young cows in the herd and was very jealous of them. Whenever any bull would approach the herd this powerful bull would run it off, so one of the seven bulls told the young man, "You must be very careful when we come to this herd, because the bull of that herd is very jealous and he is powerful, do not go near the cows because you may lose your life." When they reached the place where this herd was, they saw the dangerous bull, then the seven bulls began to watch the young man very closely, but he managed to escape them one day and went toward the herd, and one of the cows saw him and came running to him, and said, "I heard that the seven bulls had a good looking young man, are you he?" "Yes," the man said. Then the cow said, "You are indeed very handsome." Then she began to try and attract the young man's desire, and at last she succeeded, the young man went up to her and put his arms around the cow's neck.

Then the young bull who was a servant to the powerful bull saw them together, therefore went to his master and said, "A young man who is the son of the seven bulls, is with one of your wives." The powerful bull became very angry, and looking, saw them and came very swiftly to where the young man and cow were standing.

When the young man saw the powerful bull coming, he fled, and the bull said, "It is useless for you to try to escape from me, I will overcome you and your fathers, the seven bulls." When the young man reached where his fathers were they said, "We must try and save our son, even though we die for it." So they all got around their son and stood with their tails raised, and when the powerful bull came near, one of the seven went out to meet him. They fought, and the powerful bull broke all four legs of the boy's father so that he was unable to move, then another one went out to meet the powerful bull, and he too was disabled by him, then a third one went, and he too was disabled and so until all the seven bulls were crippled by the powerful bull, and when the seven bulls were all down, the powerful bull said to the young man, "Now it is time for you to be killed." The young man said, "I don't think you will kill me, perhaps you will kill me, but I don't think so." The young man took his bow and placing an arrow preparing to shoot. The young man had a white plume tied on his head. The bull then charged on him and tossed him up in the air, but only the white plume flew up, and when it came down, there stood the young man the bull tossed him up again but the same thing happened each time. But he could not injure the young man.

Then the young man shot the powerful bull with one of his arrows, and the arrow nearly went clear through the bull, and getting on the other side of the bull he shot it the second time and the arrow like the first one almost went clear through the bull, so the young man killed the powerful bull. After killing the bull the young man then said to his seven fathers, "I will try to heal you all."

Placing an arrow to the bow he went to the bull who first found him and drew his bow and motioned four times as if to shoot at bull and at the same time he said, "Get up or I'll shoot you," and when he drew the bow the fourth time, the bull got up well and sound. Thus he repeated this performance to each one of the other six bulls using the seven arrows, one to each bull, he cured them, and when this was done, each one of the seven bulls thanked him, saying, "You have shown that you think well of what we have done for you." Then one of the seven bulls said, "It is time now that you go to your people, we have raised you, and you are a man now, so it is time now for you to go home, we cannot change you into a buffalo, so go to your Father and Mother." So they started out to hunt the camp of the tribe where the young man's parents were, and as they walked they went in single file, one behind the other, and the young man rode one and then the other, he'd changed from one bull to another as they traveled and he'd play with them. When they finally sighted the encampment, they went as near as they dared to before they stopped. The bulls said, "Now your people are there, and had better go on to them, and we thank you for restoring us to life." The young man then thanked the bulls for raising him to manhood and as he was about to leave them, he stopped and said, "I do not like to leave you, my fathers, because I love you, if I go to the camps, I shall not know my people, I shall not understand them when they talk to me, and I won't know my father and mother."

And the bulls said to him, "You will know your father and mother when you get to the camps, and you will understand them when they speak to you and when you talk they will understand you, you are a human being, we are animals, we can not turn you into an animal, that is why we tell you to leave us and go to your own kind, now go, and when you are near the camps, stop, and you will see many young women playing ball, and as you stand there the ball will roll straight to you, and stop right in front of you, then you must pick the ball up, there will be one of the women who will follow up the ball, and will come to you, this woman will be your mother. When she gets to you, you must give her the ball and say, 'Here is the ball, My mother.' "

The young man did all he was told to do. So when he approached the camp, sure enough he saw the women playing ball, so he stopped and waited there the ball rolled to him and as he watched he saw one of the young women come to retrieve the ball and when she got near him he picked the ball up and handing it to her he said, "Here is the ball, My mother." Upon hearing the young man calling her his mother, she got ashamed, and instead of acknowledging him as her son, she turned and ran home crying. All of the other women who were there playing ball were surprised to see this young man following her to the camps, she entered her lodge and he followed her in, and when he entered he saw her father and mother sitting there in the lodge. Then the young man spoke, he said, "My parents, I am here now, and I am your grandson."

When the old people heard this, then the grandmother spoke, she said, "How is it that we are your grandparents?" "Do you not know?" The man said, "That when the people were moving camp, my mother your daughter, gave birth to a child. And after I was born you buried me in the buffalo wallow, then leaving me, then seven old buffalo bulls found me and raised me to now, a young man."

Upon hearing the young man say this, the grandfather was surprised, because he had known nothing of what his wife and their daughter had done in the past of what the young man spoke. So when the young man had finished telling this about himself, his mother stopped her crying, and his grandmother embraced him and kissed him as her grandson. That night the young man said, "Now I will go out and look for my father, and I want my mother to go with me." So he and his mother went out of the lodge.

Now it so happened that there were many young men who were gambling in a certain lodge, a game called hiding buttons, and when they went to the lodge where the young men were gambling, the young man looked in and saw a young man who was doing the guessing in which hand the player had the button. The players then guessed in which hand they held the button, all laid the buttons down and the young man who picked the buttons up was the father of this young man who was raised by the seven old buffalo bulls. When this young man saw this, he entered the lodge and said, "My Father, let us go home." The man was surprised but nevertheless he got up, and they all three left the gambling game and went to the lodge of the mother's parents. Thus, the boy who was raised by the seven bulls had finally found his father and mother in the end, and they all lived together ever after.

Moon Child

Once upon a time, the sun and the moon had an argument and disagreed about women.

The moon said to the sun, "I think those women who live down there on the earth, out away from the water and brush are the prettiest women." (The moon meant human females.) And the sun answered, "No, they are not. When they look at me they always make faces at me. They are not pretty, they are the worst looking women on the earth. The women who live in the water are the most beautiful. When they look at me, they look just as if they were looking at their own, I think they are the most beautiful women on earth." (The sun meant the frog.) The moon then said, "You think the Frog is pretty? You surely have poor judgment of women, the frog has long legs, she is green on the skin and have spots on her back, and large bulging eyes, I do not think anyone who looks like that is pretty." The sun said, "Well, we will compete in this, as soon as I have set to night, I will go to the earth and get a Frog, and I will bring her up here to be my wife." "Very well," said the moon. So that night the sun went to the earth after it set, and got him a Frog without any trouble, and brought her up with him during the night to his mother's lodge up in the sky. The Frog would hop around and each time she leaped she would urinate, and leave a wet spot. Then the mother asked, "What ridiculous thing is that?" And the sun answered, "My mother, be still, that is your daughter-in-law." So his mother was silent. So that night the moon shined in all its glory and he selected a woman on the earth. When the moon set early in the morning he went to the earth.

The woman the moon had chosen was troubled all night and she could not sleep, and she did not know what troubled her, she could not satisfy herself. Early that morning she took a rawhide rope and asked her sister-in-law to go with her after wood, so they both went to the woods, and when they got among the trees they spied a porcupine, so this woman that was chosen by the moon said, "I will kill this porcupine because I want to use its quills for embroidery work." Then she pursued it and the porcupine ran up the first tree it came to, and the woman climbed up after it. And the porcupine kept climbing up further and further up the tree, and several times she could almost touch it and when she would rest in her climbing, the porcupine would rest also, and just a little distance above her.

Thus it continued to do until they reached the sky, this tree that they were climbing on reached a hole in the sky and the porcupine went up the hole. When the woman had climbed up to this hole, she saw a young man standing at the side of the hole. The man said to her, "Let us go to my mother's lodge." So she went through and they started off together, when they arrived at the lodge, the man went inside and the woman remained outside, and when he was inside he said, "My mother, ask your daughter-in-law to come in." Then the mother went outside, and as soon as she was out she saw the woman standing there and then the mother called out gladly, "Oh, what a fine looking daughter-in-law I have, come on inside." Then they both went inside. The Frog was sitting by the sun, and the woman went and sat down by the moon. So the sun and moon's mother had two daughters-in-law to do her work for her. The woman who was the moon's wife did much for her, but the Frog did very little. Whenever the Frog was sent somewhere she'd hop along and was very slow. When the mother-in-law forgot she had a Frog for a daughter-in-law, the Frog would sometimes startle her by her hopping. So one day the mother-in-law took and boiled up the thickest part of a buffalo paunch, and when it was cooked, she cut it in two pieces and gave each one of her daughters-in-law a piece, and said, "Now, my daughters-in-law, I want you to eat this paunch, and I will have the one that makes the most noise in chewing it for my best and favorite daughter-in-law." Of course the woman who had good teeth made the most noise in chewing the paunch therefore was chosen the favorite. The Frog, instead of chewing on the paunch, took a piece of charcoal and chewed on it, and while the Frog chewed on it the blackened saliva ran down from each side of its mouth, and when the moon saw that it made him dislike the Frog, his sister-in-law, so the moon said, "Whenever the Frog is sent anywhere, she only hops and urinates, you should not move at all, Frog, because whenever you move, you urinate, dirty one!" Thus the moon spoke to the Frog whenever she was sent on an errand.

At last the sun could hold his patience no longer, so he picked up the Frog and threw her against the moon's face, and said, "Because you do not like the Frog, she shall always stick to your face, and now I will have your wife." That is why there is a dark spot on the moon when it's in full moon.

■ ALFRED L. KROEBER *compiler*

During the winter and spring of 1901, anthropologist Alfred L. Kroeber collected many Gros Ventre myths and tales on the Fort Belknap Indian Reservation in northern Montana. He did this important work as a member of the Mrs. Morris K. Jesup expedition. Although some of these stories exist in modern forms, Kroeber's transcriptions have a precise and vivid language that preserves the flavor of a tradition in its prime. His informants for these selections were "Assiniboine," a middle-aged man, and Watches-All, an old woman. They appeared in Kroeber's "Gros Ventre Myths and Tales," part of the Anthropological Papers of the American Museum of Natural History *(1907).*

The Woman and the Horse

as told by "Assiniboine"

The people sent out two young men to look for buffalo. They killed one and were butchering it. Then one of them said, "I will go to that hill and look around; do you continue to butcher." He went on the hill, and his companion went on with the butchering. The one on the hill looked about him with field-glasses. At Many-Lakes he saw a large herd of wild horses. He continued to look at them. Then he saw

a person among them. Then he saw something streaming behind the person. He thought it was a loose breech-cloth. He called his companion, and said to him, "Look!" Then they went nearer. They saw that it was indeed a person. They thought that it was something unnatural (*kaxtawuu*). Therefore they did not try to disturb the person, but went back. They asked the people, "Did you ever miss a person?" An old man said, "Yes. A man once lost his wife as the camp moved. She was not found." Thereupon the young men told what they had seen. The people thought it must be this woman. The whole camp went there. All the people mounted their best horses in order to catch her. When they approached the place, they surrounded the whole country. All of them had mirrors. When they had gone all around, they turned the mirrors and reflected with them, signalling that the circle was complete. Then they drew together. The four that were mounted on the fastest horses started toward the herd. The wild horses ran, but, wherever they went, they saw people. The person in the herd was always in the lead. The people continued to close up on the horses. When they got them into a small space, they began to rope them. Six of the horses and the woman escaped. She was exceedingly swift. The people headed them off, and at last drove them into an enclosure. With much trouble they at last succeeded in fastening one rope on her leg and one on her arm. Then they picketed her at the camp like a horse. *Pubis suæ crines equi caudæ similes facti erant.* At night a young man went out. He lay down on the ground near her, looking at her. Then the woman spoke: "Listen, young man. I will tell you something. You must do what I tell you. It is the truth. Long ago the camp was moving. I was far behind. I saw a large black stallion come. He had a rope on him. I jumped off my horse and caught him, thinking he belonged to some one in camp. When I had hold of the rope, he spoke to me. He said, 'Jump on my back.' Then I climbed on him. He is the one that took me away. He is my husband. I have seven children by him, seven young horses. There is one, that gray one; there another one, that spotted one; there a black painted one; there a black one." She showed him all her children. "That is my husband," she said of a black horse that was tied near by. "I cannot go back to the tribe now. I have become a horse. Let me go. Let us all go. Tie a bell on a horse of such a color; then you will be lucky in getting horses. If you will let me loose, I will give you forty persons (you will kill forty enemies). If you do not loose me, many of the tribe will die." Then the young man went to his father and told what the woman had said. The old man went outside and cried it out to the people. Then they freed her and the horses. They ran amid flying dust, the woman far in the lead.

The Bad Wife

as told by Watches-All

There was a camp-circle. A man went out with a war-party. While he was away, the Crows attacked the camp and captured his wife. When he came back and asked for her, the people told him, "The Crows have taken her." Then he took his three brothers and three brothers-in-law with him and started out. They came to the Crow camp. The man said to his six companions, "Wait here in hiding. I will go into the brush, and where the women go to get water I will watch for my wife." He waited all the morning. Many women came, but not his wife. At last she came. The man jumped out, caught her, and said, "I have come to take you back." She asked him, "How many are there of you? Where are they?" He said, "There are your three brothers and my three, and they are in that place." The woman said, "Wait for me there, and I will steal something and bring meat for you to take with you." The man went back to his six companions, and told them, "She will soon come here." The woman went back to the Crow camp, took a coal, chewed it, rubbed it over her face, and, where a number of men sat smoking, said, "This sun has given me seven persons. They are there in the brush." Some of the men said, "That woman is crazy"; but some believed her. She continued to say, "The sun has given me seven persons. They are there in the brush," and she painted her face, and rejoiced. At last the people believed her. They went and surrounded the place where the seven men were hiding, shot at them, and killed six. But the man himself they could not kill. He went straight to the Crow camp-circle. He entered the largest tent, which stood in the middle. There was his wife. A crowd followed him in. He told his wife, "I want to smoke and to drink." The Crows asked her, "What does he say?" The woman said, "He says you are to dig two holes and set two trees into them, and connect them at the top by a pole. Then you are to hang him there by the neck. Stretch his arms and tie them, and leave him, moving camp. Thus he says." Some of the Crows did not believe her. But the woman continued to say the same until they all believed her. Then they dug the holes and stuck up the poles, and hung the man and left him. An old Crow woman pitied the man, and waited until the whole camp, including even the dogs, had gone. Then she unloaded her travois in the brush, went to the man, cut him down, and washed his face. She cooked dried sliced meat and gave him to eat, and then took him along with her hidden on her travois. When she came to the Crow camp, she put up her tent outside of the circle, brought water, and started a fire. Then she called her sons to smoke with the man. She called him her son. The men said, "If you pitied him, you should have told us." They gave him clothes, for he had been hung up naked. Then the man said, "I will go back. I will return soon with all my people in order to get my wife. Always camp together at the rear of the camp-circle, at the end which is in the direction from which you have just come. If the tribe divides, put rocks in a row along the trail which that part of the people have taken with whom my wife is." Then he asked his new brothers, "What kind of a horse does this woman ride?" They told him, "She always rides a black-painted short-tailed horse which is very fast." Then the man went back to his people, running ceaselessly. After he had returned, he cut tobacco into little pieces. Young men took these to the Piegans, the Blackfeet, the Bloods and the North Piegans (Sarcees). Soon all the tribes gathered, and joined the Gros Ventre. They started against the Crows. Whenever they stopped, they raced their horses to discover who had the fastest. They came near the Crows. The man made them all stop behind the hill, and went alone to his Crow mother. Then she called her sons, and the man told them, "Take all your property inside your tent. Hobble your horses close by, and stay indoors." The Crows were just breaking camp. They asked the old woman and her sons, "Why do you remain encamped there?" They answered, "We are going off somewhere." When the Crows had begun to move, the war-party attacked them. While they were fighting and killing the Crows, the man's younger brother, mounted on the swiftest horse, was only looking for the woman. He was far ahead of the fight. Then he saw the black-painted horse with the short tail, and the woman on it. He rode after her and caught up with her. He took her bridle and turned her, and went back with her to the camp of the old Crow woman. On the way the woman said, "Let me kiss you, my brother-in-law; I have been longing for you." He answered, "There will be time for that when we arrive where we are going." As soon as the woman was captured, the people stopped fighting the Crows. The old Crow woman began to sharpen her knife, and had them build a large fire. They took the woman off her horse, and made her stand up. "I know what to do to her," said the old woman. She went to her, seized her nose, cut it off and threw it on the fire. Then she tore in two her bell-covered dress, and threw it on the fire. Then she cut off her breasts, *ejus vaginae labia*, and her ears, and threw them in the fire. Then they threw the woman herself into the fire. A great crowd stood about, and whenever she crawled out on one side they threw her in again. Finally she was burned. They all went home rejoicing.

The Man Who Acquired Invulnerability

as told by Watches-All

There was a poor man. He wandered about. Then he found snakes in a hole. He cut his flesh and fed it to the snakes. He cut himself all over. He gave the snakes even his ears, and cut off his little finger and threw it to them. Then, before he should bleed to death, he jumped into the hole. All the snakes retreated from him as he lay there. Then one young snake said, "Why do you draw back? I pity this man. I will give him power and make him strong." Then its father and mother said, "It is well that you pity him. We will help you to do something for him. You shall go into him and stay in his body. Then he will be unkillable." Then the young snake entered the man's mouth and went into his body, and the two old snakes gave him each a rattle from their tails. The man got up and went off. But now he no longer had scars on him. He came to where the people were shooting bears in a hole. Again he cut flesh from his body and fed it to them. Then he lay down in the den in order to bleed to death there. A young bear said to the others, "You do not pity this man, but I will help him." Then his father and mother said, "We will give him the strength of our bodies, and he will be invulnerable." The young bear entered the man's mouth, and the two old ones gave him each one of their claws. They gave him the longest one on their feet. Then the man went away. A certain young man saw a *bax'aa*^{n}. He told the man who had been to the snakes and the bears. Then the man went to the river, cried, cut off his flesh and threw it in. He also cut his little finger and threw it in the river. Then the *bax'aa*^{n} rose up out of the water halfway. He hooked the water with one of his horns, and where the man had been lying on the bank, bleeding to death, he was now riding a white horse and carrying a shield and spear, and was beautifully dressed. Then the *bax'aa*^{n} hooked the water with his other horn, and a painted horse stood on the bank. "You will not be poor," said the *bax'aa*^{n}, and he hooked innumerable horses of different colors, and much property of different kinds, out of the water, until horses were standing all about the bank of the river. The *bax'aa*^{n} said to him, "You will be the only man on this earth rich in horses (the richest in horses)." After this, the man fed his flesh to many kinds of animals. He gave himself to eagles, to jack-rabbits, to the buffalo, and to horned toads. Then the snakes told him to take six poor people with him. He did so and they started out, seven in the party. They reached a lake. They saw many people travelling toward the lake. Then they went into the water and lay down. The camp arrived, and every one watered his horses at the lake. An old woman came and drove her horse into the water. She saw a mouth in the water, and riding out, told the people, "I have seen persons in the water." Then these people killed the man's six companions; but the man himself they could not kill. Spears, stones, and arrows could not hit him or hurt him. He continued to sing his song. Then they cut him to pieces, and scattered the pieces about. When they moved camp, the man rose up alive. He went to where they were camped, and hid in the brush. A woman came to get wood. He seized her, and with a large knife cut her to pieces. All the people took him and tried to cut and stab him. They cut him to pieces and moved camp. He rose up alive, and again went to where they had camped. Again he killed a woman who was gathering wood. Thus the people would kill him and move camp; but he would return to life, follow them, and kill one of them. Then he killed many, because he felt bad that this tribe had killed his six companions. He continued to do this until his feet became too sore to walk. Then he stole horses and a shield and robes, and returned home, driving the horses before him. When he came back to his own people, he had a bundle of scalps hanging at his side. Thereafter he would go to war, kill a man or a woman, and bring back a herd of horses. He continued to do this until he became very rich. But he would not marry. Then he went off again and returned with horses. While he was away and the people were hunting buffalo, the Cheyenne attacked them, and captured and took away a small boy. When the man returned, he heard about this. The little boy had a sister who was pretty. She was old enough to be married. Then the man said, "I will go to bring back the little boy, and when I bring him, I will marry this girl." When her father heard this, he said, "It is well: if he brings back the boy, he can have my daughter." Then the man started out, accompanied by a party. They killed two persons, and captured horses. The man sent all the rest of the party back with the horses. He himself went to the Cheyenne camp, looking for the boy. The Cheyenne were having a sun-dance. The man looked on. Then he heard a sound, and saw the boy tied to the centre pole of the lodge. His arms were drawn back around the tree, and he was hanging at the fork. He was painted black. The man looked for a suitable pole among those extending over the lodge. He climbed up, went along it to the tree in the middle, and cut the boy loose. As the boy was very stiff, he took the cloth that had been hung at the top of the lodge as an offering, wrapped him in it, and, carrying him as a woman carries her child, began to climb down again. Before he reached the ground, a Cheyenne saw him, and they all stopped dancing. The man said to the Cheyenne, "Do not kill me until to-morrow. Who is the chief? Where is the largest tent?" Then he went to the largest tent and staid there that night. Next day he told the Cheyenne, "Get seven buffalo-skulls and place them in a row. I will jump from one to another, and, if I miss or stumble, you can kill me." Then they put the seven skulls in a row, and he started. He jumped from one to another like a rabbit, and when he came to the last one he continued to leap along, carrying the boy with him. As he went, he turned into a rabbit. He wished for a hole, put the boy into it and covered it with a buffalo-chip. Then he ran on and wished for another hole, went into it and covered it with grass. The Cheyenne were running all about, looking for him in vain. At last the man came out of his hole. He looked for a buffalo-horn. When he found one, he washed it in the river, and brought a drink to his little brother-in-law. He told the boy, "Wait for me, and I will bring horses and meat." He went again to the Cheyenne camp and took two spotted horses, some meat, robes, and a shield. He went back to the boy, and said to him, "Now come out." He tied the boy on a horse, and they started off. At a stream in the mountains they rested. There he cooked for the boy. Then they went on, resting whenever the boy was in need of it. At last they returned to the camp. A tent had been set up for him, and about it stood many horses of different colors; and he married the girl. She wore a dress covered with elk-teeth, and rings and bracelets. The people took the man for their chief. His name was Hat'uxu (Star).

The people were camped. Young men found a herd of buffalo, and an old man cried out that they would hunt. Hat'uxu took many horses with him. He wanted to kill much. He told his wife, "Tie all the horses abreast, and follow me. Give away none of what I kill." Then he went ahead, hunted, killed buffalo, and began to cut them up. Meanwhile the enemy came, and captured his wife and her horses. When Hat'uxu had at last finished cutting up his buffalo, he stuck his knife in his scabbard, and went back to where he had left his wife. She was gone, but he saw her tracks and those of the people who had captured her. He followed her at once. He had no weapons with him except his knife. He reached the mountains where he thought he would be able to intercept the enemy. He tied his horses, and climbed a tree. Soon he saw the enemy coming, riding in file. His wife was among them, carrying on her back their quiver of large arrows. It was nearly dark. Hat'uxu came down from his tree, and went to where the enemy had camped for the night. He threw aside the blanket which they had hung up as a door for their brush hut, and went inside. He saw his wife sitting next to one of the men, who had taken her for his wife. He killed the man. Then he used the arrows, which his wife had been carrying, against the rest. They all ran off into the brush. Then he cut off the dead man's head and took it with him. He told his wife to carry the captured arrows and to collect all the enemy's horses. By next morning he was back at the camp. Then the people celebrated over the head he had brought back with him. Thus he recaptured his wife.

CLAUDE SCHAEFFER *as told by* Simon Francis

Claude Schaeffer, the curator of the Museum of the Plains Indian in Browning, Montana, during the late 1940s, collected this story while doing ethnological fieldwork among Idaho's Bonners Ferry Kutenai in 1947. His informants were Simon Francis, who was fifty-seven years old at the time, and Simon's mother, Lucy. When Francis was young, his father committed suicide by eating the root of the "wild parsnip." To escape harsh treatment from his stepfather, Francis ran away to St. Eugene's Mission in Cranbrook, B.C. "The brief education thus gained," writes Schaeffer, "enabled Simon in later life to fill, successively, the posts of interpreter, police officer and councilman at Bonners Ferry." This selection is from Schaeffer's article, "Wolf and Two-Pointed Buck: A Lower Kutenai Tale of the Supernatural Period," which appeared in the January and April 1949 issues of Primitive Man, *the quarterly bulletin of the Catholic Anthropological Conference.*

Wolf and the Two-Pointed Buck

There was a time long ago when the Whitetail Deer people had their home on a hill some distance west of Yaak River. Their neighbors were the three Wolf brothers, who lived farther south along the Kootenai River. The Deer people wore attractive, well made moccasins, which had been designed and made for them by Young Doe (*nīloquatna'na*). One day the second oldest Wolf (*ka'ke·n*), who had long admired the Deer's footwear, decided that he must have a pair. So he went to live with Young Doe.

The season arrived for making new footwear. Doe prepared to make moccasins for her relatives. She asked her husband, Wolf, if he would not like a pair. Wolf feigned indifference and replied merely that he would accept them. Secretly, he hoped to receive a pair like those of the Deer people. Doe, who was a skilled worker, realized that the one piece type of moccasin (*kokīnalā'ktcu*) would not fit Wolf. His foot was shaped differently and hence difficult to fit. She studied the matter for a long time. Finally, she cut the material round to fit his paw, and thus devised a new type, the *kwī'lqäne* or two piece moccasin, with u-shaped seam.

Doe gave the new moccasins to her husband. Wolf disliked their appearance immediately and refused to try them on. He told Doe bluntly that he had married her because of her skill in sewing, and demanded why she had made his moccasins so clumsy looking. Doe, realizing his disappointment, determined to tell the truth. She explained that the new moccasins were designed for the "pawed group" of animals. That each one of that group, as well as mankind later, would alter the toe of the moccasin to fit a long or short foot. That these new things had to be made properly, so that the humans could make use of them. Wolf retorted angrily that he was not interested in preparing the way for mankind. He again insisted that the moccasins were too large and clumsy. Doe was sure that they would fit properly and urged Wolf to try them on. Upon his refusal, she explained that he could not wear the moccasins of the Deer people, as his paws were blunt. At this remark, Wolf exploded, "So my paw is ugly. We'll see about that." Throwing the moccasins aside, Wolf seized his bow and arrows and left the lodge.

Arriving home, Wolf told his brothers that the Deer people had ridiculed them. Doe, he explained, had told him that his foot was ugly and had made his moccasins large and clumsy. Now the Wolves must remove the Deer people from the face of the earth, so that none of their gifts would be left for mankind. Preparations, Wolf said, would start that night.

When evening came, Wolf started to sing. His brothers joined him. Soon it began to snow. Wolf explained the purpose of the song. "We'll allow them no time. We'll work hard and have everything ready by daybreak. The Deer people think that they are smart, but someone else is smarter. We'll pull them down and even eat their flesh. To do this, we must sing for three different kinds of weather. We'll continue the present song until there is plenty of snow. Then we'll change the songs to bring other kinds of weather." Turning to one of his brothers, he said, "You're the oldest Wolf (*akīnu'küi*). You must watch. We'll make the snow so deep that it will bury the Deer. Go outside and run about. When you think it is deep enough, come back and tell me." The eldest Wolf went out several times to measure the depth of the snow. When it came up to his neck, he returned, saying enough had fallen. Since he was heavier and slower than his brothers, he selfishly allowed more snow to fall than was needed. In this way he was assured of getting his share of the kill.

Wolf now began to sing another song. This time he announced, "This song will bring rain. Go out at intervals and tell me when it has softened the surface of the snow." His elder brother did so. As before, he allowed a greater quantity of rain to fall than was actually needed.

Long before this, Two-pointed Buck (*kiankalīna'na*), the leader of the Deer people, had discovered through his supernatural power what the Wolves were doing. As soon as Wolf began his songs, Buck realized that the Deer were in mortal danger. He warned his people, "The one we have to destroy is Wolf. We must not miss him. This is a struggle to the death." He then explained what Wolf was trying to do. "When I send you out, watch the weather closely. If it begins to snow, move about so as to make runways. You know the hills and the valleys, and the best places to make your trails. You will have to work throughout the night in order to save your lives." The Deer went outdoors. Suddenly the sky, which had been clear, began to cloud up. It started to snow. The Deer ran about to make runways, as Buck had directed. After a time, however, they became tired and went inside. Buck, realizing that they would be of no further help, sent them to bed.

Buck had a wife and small child. To find some way of saving them, he lay down upon his bed and began to use his power. Now he could hear the Wolves talking and singing. He said to his wife, Doe, "We are in desperate trouble. Don't awaken the others as they can do nothing. Wolf is furious and plans to attack us. He knows that he must kill me and won't stop until he succeeds. He has great supernatural power, against which I can do little. We must try to find some way to escape. I'll arrange a place for you and the boy to hide. I'll leave some of my power with you, so that you can raise the child. If you don't hear from me, it means that I am dead. If I succeed in killing Wolf, I'll send for you. Wait for a time, however, before you come." His wife promised to follow his instructions.

Two-pointed Buck now began his preparations. A rock lay close to his bed by the fireplace. He moved it aside to reveal a shallow depression. He thrust his power token (*tcokolta'līs*) into the depression and withdrew it. A room shaped like the inside of a lodge appeared below. Buck next told his wife to take the child, all her robes and clothing, some coals from the fire and go down into the room. Filling a mussel shell with coals and ashes, she took her possessions and the boy into the room below. Buck replaced the rock, lay down upon his bed and through his power removed all traces of his family's hiding place. Then he made one leap through the smoke hole of the lodge to land upon the top of a distant mountain near Kootenai Falls. He stood there a moment, turned so as to face his home, and lay down beside a tree. There he awaited developments.

Wolf, meanwhile, had changed his song for the third time. Now he sang for cold weather. Again he sent his eldest brother out to observe the ice forming on top of the snow. The latter ran over the snow several times until he found that the surface would support his weight. As before, he delayed returning until the crust had frozen quite hard. Wolf now told his younger brother to stop singing. The three then set out for the Deer's home, encircled it and lay down to await daylight.

With the first light of morning, the Wolves attacked the lodge of the Deer. The latter scattered out, each taking to the cleared trail that he had made the previous night. The runways, however, were not nearly long enough and flight was difficult through the crusted snow. The Deer now realized their mistake in not following Buck's advice. The Wolves quickly sized up the situation and took advantage of it. While one pursued his quarry along the runway, the others cut across to intercept it. In this way, the Deer were pulled down, one by one, and slain by the Wolves. From his mountain top Buck watched everything that took place. He was deeply grieved over the merciless slaughter of his relatives. By the time the sun came up, all the Deer had been killed.

Wolf and his younger brother had kept close watch for Two-pointed Buck, but failed to find his body among the slain Deer. The oldest Wolf, who had succeeded in killing several Deer, was little concerned about anything now that he had something for himself. When asked if he had killed Buck, he hesitated and then said that he had. The three brothers went over to the first Deer that he had killed, and found it to be an old buck. The same thing happened, in turn, with each animal slain and finally the old Wolf admitted that he was wrong. The Wolves then examined the balance of the kill and discovered that Buck and his family had escaped. After circling around outside the area and failing to find any tracks, they knew that their chief enemy was still alive. Buck was observing all this from the distant mountain, but his chief concern now was for the safety of his family.

The Wolves proceeded to tear down the lodge of the Deer, leaving only the poles standing. They looked about the lodge interior but could find no trace of Buck. Wolf, however, refused to give up the search. He decided to make use of his power. Stepping over to the spot where Buck's bed had been located, he lay down and stretched out in the position customarily assumed by Buck. He examined the lodge poles, the adjacent trees and the ground but could still find no sign of his enemy. Finally, he glanced up at the junction of the lodge poles and saw there one of Buck's tracks. Through his power, Wolf now traced the course of buck's flight to his resting place on the mountain top. At that spot their "glances locked." Buck, after witnessing the cruel slaughter of his people, had determined never to rest until he had killed Wolf. The latter could see in Buck's eyes that it was a struggle to the death, and his own glance dropped. "Brother-in-law or not, I'm going to kill you," Wolf thought. Buck read his thoughts.

After telling his brothers where Buck had gone, Wolf started running towards the mountain. Buck, seeing this, got up, stretched and relieved himself, and made a leap backwards towards the northeast and landed near the top of another peak. He faced directly about so as to watch towards his rear. At the same time, Wolf was running swiftly towards the first mountain. When near the top, he circled cautiously and silently so as to take Buck from behind. After picking out the spot where Buck should be, he approached it, dodging from tree to tree. When close, he rested for a few minutes before peering out. There was no one there.

Wolf walked over and saw where Buck had lain. There were no tracks there. After circling about, he was still unable to find any trace of Buck's presence. He realized now that Buck was using his supernatural power. Wolf again lay down in the usual position of Buck, worked his power and followed the latter's flight until he came up with him. Their eyes engaged briefly. Once more Wolf set out in pursuit of Buck. It was now about noon. Buck made another leap far to one side, landing this time on a mountain top near his home. In the meantime, Wolf had run to the second peak and found Buck gone. Employing his power as before, he quickly discovered his enemy's whereabouts. This time Buck had not reversed his position, but merely turned his head to the rear. He saw Wolf and their glances held momentarily. Wolf, already on his feet to take up the pursuit, was becoming more and more angry. Again he started out after Buck.

This time Buck arose and ran quickly down the mountain side towards the Yaak River. Now he was in the vicinity of Bullhead's home, located on the east side of the river. He hastened directly to Bullhead's lodge and entered. Wolf, meanwhile, had come up to Buck's last resting place, observed him in flight, and set out in pursuit. Bullhead, aware of everything that had taken place, was prepared to aid Buck defend his life. He was seated on his bed smoking his pipe. Buck said hurriedly, "I need your help. Wolf is after me. He will soon be here." Bullhead remained silent. Buck spoke more urgently, "He wants to kill me." Bullhead smoked his pipe, t-s-ā-k! tsāk! tsāk! tsāk! tsāk! Buck cried out, "He killed all my relatives." Bullhead still continued to smoke. Finally, he asked Buck, "Whose brother-in-law are you talking about?" Buck retorted, "Wolf was my brother-in-law. But would you call him that after he slaughtered my people? You must help me." Bullhead laid aside his pipe and said, "I'll help you." His bed occupied one side of the lodge and directly across the fire was another. He motioned Buck to lie down there and Buck hurriedly did so. Bullhead then placed over him the hide of a young fawn. It was scarcely large enough to cover his middle. Bullhead sat down and resumed smoking.

By this time Wolf could be heard approaching. He had followed Buck's tracks to Bullhead's lodge. Now he bolted in, expecting to find his victim there. Surprised at not seeing him, he demanded of Bullhead, "Has anyone come in here?" Bullhead kept silent. Wolf then inquired about Buck. Bullhead continued to smoke his pipe. Wolf asked the third time but received no reply. Finally, Bullhead spoke, "I think you're speaking of your brother-in-law. He didn't come in here." Wolf retorted, "Yes, he did." Bullhead answered, "Perhaps your eyes have deceived you. You're seeking vengeance." (This last remark was intended as a warning, and if Wolf had heeded it, he might have saved his life. Wolf, however, was too angry to notice.) He insisted that Buck must have entered the lodge. Bullhead told him that Buck may have gone elsewhere. Wolf went out to look around. By this time Bullhead had abandoned his efforts to prevent further bloodshed. Quickly he fashioned the small figure (*tsa'tsa*) of a deer from grass, and hurled it through the wall of his lodge to a place some distance up the river. Since Wolf was being so deceitful, Bullhead knew that his plan would work.

Wolf reentered the lodge and demanded again to know where Buck was. All this time he had been unable to see him lying there on the bed. Bullhead came to the point, saying, "Have you looked along the river for his tracks?" Wolf went out again, glanced upstream and now saw what he thought was Buck standing far up the river. He returned to ask Bullhead if the latter would take him across the river in his canoe. Bullhead refused, and told Wolf to cross as best he could. Wolf ran out, leaped far into the river and started to swim across. Buck now jumped to his feet and looked out to see Wolf in the water. He asked Bullhead to ferry him across in his canoe. The latter temporized and continued smoking his pipe. Buck cried, "Only my wife and child are left of all my people. Take me to him in your canoe, so that I can kill him!" Without asking permission, he seized Bullhead's quiver from the lodge pole. Bullhead tried his best to dissuade him, but without success. Not wanting his weapons to be used in taking life, he forbade Buck to use any but the plain, unfeathered arrow. Then he put on his mittens, went outside and launched his canoe.

By this time Wolf had nearly reached the opposite bank. Bullhead, with one long and one short stroke of the paddle, brought the canoe alongside Wolf. Aware of something at his side, Wolf looked around to see Buck raise his bow and arrow. He cried, "My brother-in-law. Really, I love you. You know I love you very much." Buck retorted, "Brother-in-law, eh! Well, you are pitying yourself. You know that all my relatives have been slain. Therefore, I shall kill you." He released his arrow at close range. It penetrated Wolf's body so as to project equally on both sides, and killed him at once. Buck reached out to withdraw the arrow, but Bullhead stopped him, saying, "Leave it. It's spoiled. I don't want it after being used in this way." All this time Bullhead had been trying to restore Buck to his senses. He knew that Wolf still had two brothers living and he wanted to bring the blood feud to an end. Buck then asked, "Perhaps you will take Wolf's body. The skin may be useful. I'll give it to you." This remark indicated to Bullhead that Buck's anger continued unabated. Bullhead accepted the offer but said, "I'll not use it. It has a bad odor. That is what made Wolf mean." He thrust his paddle under Wolf's body and lifted it into the back of the canoe. He then turned the canoe around, and with one long stroke and a short one, they reached the other side and both got out. Bullhead lifted his canoe from the water and placed it upon the wooden supports. They then entered Bullhead's lodge, where Buck restored the quiver to its place. Bullhead seated himself and resumed smoking his pipe. Now he hoped to induce Buck to live with him for a while, as it was unsafe to go about in his present state of mind. After a few puffs, he said, "It's not proper for young people to travel around when they're angry. Lie down on that bed. It belongs to another person, but you may make use of it." Buck seated himself and considered what he should do. He could find no good reason to refuse Bullhead's offer. He still had certain things to do but didn't feel like leaving immediately. After a time he relaxed and stretched out on the bed.

The bed was used by two young girls, who spent most of their time dipping in the water. They were Water Ousel (*tci'tskom*) and her companion, *wī'tswits*. After sundown, Water Ousel and her friend returned to find a handsome stranger occupying their place. They hesitated to sit down until Bullhead said, "You have someone to sleep with now. He belongs here but you have never met. I told him to sit there. So take your regular places." The girls sat down, one on each side of Buck. This indicated that they accepted him as a husband, according to Bullhead's wish. It was now fall, and Buck remained there throughout the winter. Towards the close of winter, a little girl was born to Water Ousel and Buck. Soon she was running about the lodge. The snow melted and spring came. When the grass grew tall, Buck began to long for his other wife and child.

All this time Doe and her son, Fawn, had remained where Buck had hidden them. She kept the fire going, covering it at night with ashes. The child began to wonder why the two of them were alone. One day he asked, "Are there only the two of us?" Doe had busied herself making moccasins and clothing and had now accumulated quite a store. Some of the apparel was of large size, which prompted the child to ask this question. He inquired, "Is this the only room we have?" Doe replied, "No, there is an entrance above. I can't tell you more now, as there are enemies who might hear me." Several days passed and the boy asked, "May I go outside and play?" Doe had made him a small bow and arrow and the grass figure of a deer as a target (*tsa'tsa*). She told him to practice with his bow and arrow. The boy tried many times but could not hit the target. Finally, an arrow struck it and the game was over. Then he would throw the figure in another direction and shoot again. In this way he soon acquired considerable skill. The room became too small for his sport and he wanted to go outside. He became bored and sat around all day. It seemed to him that there must be other people somewhere, but his mother would not answer his questions.

Doe finally decided to let the child go outdoors, but warned him to keep a sharp watch for strangers and allow no one to see him. At the sound of any noise, he must quickly come inside. She explained that to leave the room, he must push the door to one side but leave a small opening, so that he could come in swiftly. Although there was no ladder, Doe told him to walk up to the opening. He went through the motions of climbing and found himself rising in the air. Next, he pressed the white spot, as instructed, and the door opened. Fawn hesitated to go out, but his mother reassured him. Peering out, he saw that no one was in sight. He pushed the rock aside and went out. The country looked green and beautiful. He rolled the rock back, leaving a small opening. One of the first things he noticed was the lodge poles still standing. He now realized that there were other people in the world. He knew that it was the remains of a lodge and felt that there must be a good reason why his mother could not answer his questions. He decided to remain watchful while playing. In throwing out his target, he found that now there was sufficient space for his game. In a short time he returned to the room below. "It's a beautiful world up there," he said. "Yes," answered his mother. "You must go out again. Soon you will become used to it." He went outdoors regularly, but came inside as soon as he heard a noise. His mother approved his watchfulness and cautioned against staying out too long.

The time arrived for Doe to tell her son more. "Someone will come for us one of these days. We are here only temporarily. The one who comes for us will explain everything. However, don't run to the first person you see, as it might not be the right one." From then on, the little fellow looked forward to seeing the person who would release them.

Meanwhile, Buck's little daughter grew rapidly, and now played outdoors. One day, her father gave her several small deer hooves strung together on a cord to play with. They made a pleasant sound when shaken. "Tie these to your belt," he said, "you will soon use them." Because she obeyed his instructions in running errands, he felt that she could be trusted to deliver a message to his family. Buck realized that he would have to tell Doe of his second wife, and felt that he could best inform her through his daughter. By this time he had forgotten completely his desire for revenge upon the Wolf brothers. Bullhead had been aware of Buck's first wife and child, but arranged the second union in order to take his mind off his enemies. Now he was willing that Buck should return to Doe. By summer Buck could no longer endure the thought of Doe's confinement. He wanted greatly to free her and the child.

One day, Buck called his small daughter and told her the time had come for her to use the deer hoof rattles. She was instructed to cross the Yaak River and take the trail west until she came to a long hill. She was to climb this hill and continue a short distance until she reached the end of the trail. Upon arriving there, she was to look carefully about. "You may meet someone there," Buck said. "Don't let them see you. If no one appears, continue until you come to an abandoned lodge. Hide in the brush nearby and if you still see no one, come back. If you see a person who disappears quickly, return and tell me." The little girl started out carrying the string of deer hoof rattles. She followed her father's directions and found everything as he had described it. Seeing the deserted lodge structure, she approached it carefully. No one was about, however, and she returned home. Every day she was sent out to observe the old lodge. Through his power, Buck had learned that his son came out to play, and he hoped that his daughter would meet him. He instructed her to watch closely for a boy or a grown person. Hearing this, the little girl, who longed for a playmate, tried all the more to find him.

One day, coming around a turn in the trail, she saw something move. It was a good-sized boy, carrying his bow and arrow. As she quickly stepped behind a tree, he threw his target towards her. While he released his arrow, she had a good chance to observe him. The arrow lodged in the target and the boy walked over to remove it. As he approached, the girl stepped into view. Seeing her, he quickly picked up his arrow and ran towards the lodge. She called out, "Young brother, stop!" But he disappeared somewhere about the lodge. She walked over but could find no trace of his hiding place. It seemed very mysterious. The girl lay down and started to cry. She could not understand why her brother ran from her. After a time she returned home. Her father saw that she had been crying and asked her the reason. She told about seeing the boy and how he had run away. She began to cry again, saying she felt as if he were related to her. Buck explained that it was her brother, and that he ran away because he was not accustomed to strangers. But he assured her that they would play together sometime.

As he entered the hidden room, Fawn breathed so heavily that his mother knew that something had happened. He told her that someone had seen him for the first time, a pretty little girl, who had called him brother. He reproached his mother for never telling about a sister, adding that the latter had cried because he ran away. Doe believed that someone would come for them, but hadn't expected it to be a little girl. Now she knew that her husband still lived, had married again, and had a daughter. Further, that having sent a messenger in this way, he wanted to rejoin them. She told Fawn that it must have been his sister, but refused to answer any more questions. She instructed him to go out the next morning at the same time to talk with the little girl. Although he would have preferred a boy as a playmate, Fawn promised to do so.

The next day when he went out, Buck's daughter was already there. Before she left home, her father had said, "This is what you must do. Your brother will run and hide. Go up to the lodge poles and look for a rock beside the fireplace. Roll it aside, look down and you will see him and his mother. Untie the hooves and shake them. The sound will bring him outside. Then shake the rattle and sing, 'Come forward, *kikīsna'na* (Blacktail Fawn)! Come forward, *kikīsna'na*!' " Once the boy began to dance, she could hold his attention. She was to continue singing to make the boy dance towards her, and thus draw him away from the lodge. Then she was to try to catch him before he could escape inside.

The little girl followed her father's instructions. Fawn again ran from her and disappeared around the lodge poles. She found the rock, pushed it aside, and saw the room below. There the mother was sewing and had bags, moccasins and clothing arranged about her. At her side stood the boy. The girl untied the rattles and as she shook them at the opening, he looked up. Doe was certain now that the messenger came from her husband, for the rattles represented his power. The girl started to sing. It was the same song that Buck used to sing to his son. The boy listened to the song and began to dance in time to the rattles. He wanted to reach out for them but was afraid. As the girl retreated from the opening, the boy danced towards her. He turned back several times, but the girl drew him forth again. When he was some distance from the door, she tried to catch him but he escaped to the room. Then she cried and told him that she only wanted to play with him. She returned home as her father had directed. The boy's mother refused to answer any of his questions, except to say that the girl was his sister. She urged him to play with her, as she would explain everything.

The following day, Buck sent his daughter to make a final attempt. This time he foresaw that she would be successful. He advised her to draw the boy far from his place of concealment before she tried to restrain him. He again pointed out that his son, not being used to strangers, suffered from shyness. She set out for the old lodge site. Buck then explained to Water Ousel that their daughter was being sent to get his former family, and that he must leave her to go with them. Henceforth, she would have to manage alone. He told her of his struggle with the Wolves. Water Ousel accepted his decision without question. She realized that the Deer people differed from her own, and that it was better for Buck to return to his first family. Since he had agreed to help her, things would not be too difficult in the future.

Buck's daughter went up to the old lodge, removed the rock and started to sing. The boy came out and she led him some distance away. Previously, his mother had cautioned him not to run away, so that his sister might explain things to him. "You and she have the same father, and he has sent a message by her." So this time the boy did not run fast, in order that his sister might catch him. Now she was very happy. Buck had told her to give the rattles to the boy as a present, as they were intended more for boys than girls. He promised her a gift later from her mother. She handed the deer hooves to her brother, telling him that they belonged to Buck. She then offered to conduct both him and his mother to Buck. Fawn was very glad. He ran quickly to his mother and related what his sister had said. Doe prepared to leave, as she understood everything now. She was happy to be outside again, and to know that Buck had sent for her and their son. They set out and soon reached Bullhead's lodge, where they were joyfully greeted by Buck. Soon after, Buck, together with Doe and Fawn, left to resume their accustomed way of life. Water Ousel and her daughter remained with Bullhead. Before leaving them, Buck told his daughter not to grieve over their departure. He promised that each year, in the summer, Fawn, her brother, would come down to the stream to play with her.

LESLIE B. DAVIS
as told by Pete and Josephine Beaverhead

Pete and Josephine Beaverhead told these four myths to Leslie B. Davis, a professor of anthropology at Montana State University in Bozeman. Davis acknowledges the Beaverheads' foresight and patience in sharing their knowledge of traditional Pend d'Oreille oral narratives and also the assistance of Patrick Adams, whose own interest and recorded tales were useful in providing comparative perspective. Davis published these stories in 1965 as part of the University of Montana's Anthropology and Sociology Papers.

The Flying Head

There was a big camp. One morning Coyote went to the Chief's tipi. Chief told him, "When we woke this morning our young daughter was not here. We don't know where she has gone. Tell all the young men to come to my tipi." After Coyote had brought them, Chief asked if any of them had taken his daughter. None of them had. Chief said, "I want all of you to go out and hunt for her. She will be his wife whoever finds her." They began coming back that evening, the runners first and later the flyers. No one had found her. The next morning Chief told Coyote to bring all the men to his tipi again. He told them to go out again and they said they had already looked everywhere. Coyote said, "There is one who didn't go looking for her. That is Magpie." Chief sent for him and said, "Yesterday you did not go hunting. Today you will go." Magpie answered, "The boys can all stay home. I will hunt alone. I don't want to marry her. If I find her I will only bring her back." He flew east over three mountain ranges and saw smoke. He landed on the third mountain and walked down. He found a tipi, sneaked close and peered inside. The girl was sitting there with Skaɗīokn (Note: a bodiless being, an evil witch) on her lap. Magpie walked back up the mountain, flew back to camp and said, "I found her. Skaɗīokn took her." Chief called the camp together and told the men again that whoever outsmarted Skaɗīokn could marry his daughter. Most of the boys thought they weren't smart enough. Four brothers said they would go. They were White Owl, the youngest, Owl, Eagle, and Osprey, the oldest. Coyote built a stone wall that ran from coast to coast between the last two mountain ranges. He made holes near the top of each wall that stretched far into the sky. When he got back to camp he built a sweat lodge of red stone. Coyote said, "There will be two doors in it. Go in the front one and out the back. The front door will close when Skaɗīokn is inside. Get him back here if you can, White Owl. Go way up high on each wall so you will know how to get back. When you come to the third mountain range walk down, and sneak to the tipi." White Owl did that and whistled softly at the girl. She saw him and said, "Oh, what a beautiful boy." She told Skaɗīokn, "I will lay you down for awhile. I must go outside." White Owl took her, walked a ways and flew away. Skaɗīokn waited, went out and saw them far above. He flew up very, very fast, hit White Owl and killed him. Coyote knew that White Owl had been killed so he sent Owl. (Both Owl and Eagle are killed, each coming progressively closer to escaping. Exactly the same sequence is repeated in each instance.) Coyote sent Osprey, saying, "Do your best. There will be red-hot rocks in the sweathouse and everything will be ready." This time the girl wrapped Skaɗīokn in a buffalo robe as tightly as she could. Osprey didn't sneak away but went straight up. Skaɗīokn tore up the robe to free himself. Osprey waited up high instead of going through the hole in the wall. Skaɗīokn went through the hole expecting to see Osprey ahead of him. Then Osprey dived down and barely got ahead of Skaɗīokn. Osprey flew through the second wall and into the sweathouse, Skaɗīokn right behind him. The front door closed and Coyote slammed the back door. Skaɗīokn rolled around and knocked the water over on the hot rocks. He exploded. Coyote gathered his dead people together and revived them. Osprey married the girl. After several days blisters appeared on the tips of her smallest fingers. Osprey cut them open and two little Skaɗīokns rolled out onto the bed. In a few days they were much bigger. The other children played with them and kicked them around. They banged the children too hard in return and killed them. They would fall into people's cooking pots and eat all the food. The people became hungry and Chief told Coyote, "Maybe you could kill them." "No, but I know who could. Rattlesnake is camped across the river. I'll tell him." He asked Rattlesnake who agreed, but said, "I won't begin until you leave." Then he began singing. He scraped some of his scales off into a pot. Singing still, he put the pot on the fire. The Skaɗīokns knew he was cooking so they jumped into the pot and ate it all up. They went back across the river and laid down. The children wondered why they wouldn't play. The smaller one bounced about and burst. Soon the big one burst and they both turned to ashes. If it wasn't for Coyote the world would be full of Skaɗīokns. That is all.

The Wolves' Sister Marries

Five wolves were camped. There were four brothers and their sister. Šctao was the leader and he and Ntsīitsn and Ikušinou were hunters. Greedy was only the wood chopper. Sister was the cook and she tended to drying the meat. One evening when all the men were home their sister wasn't speaking. Šctao said, "You are lonesome for a husband. It is a long way to where there are other people. You will have to go in the direction of the rising sun. Tomorrow morning get ready and you can go." So that morning came and she packed some food and clothing. Šctao told her, "I don't know how many days you will have to walk but you will finally see some people running up and down beside their camp. They will be gambling. When they stop toward evening a boy will come to meet you, but don't go with that one. When a boy all dressed in red comes you go with him. He is a smart man. That is all the advice I can give you." She walked for several days until she came to a camp where people were gambling. When the game was over boys came over and asked her to go with them. She told them, "No, I didn't come here to be with you." The boy dressed in red was living with his grandmother. His grandmother went out that evening and saw the girl. She told her grandson, "Skudlétm (Red), you go get that girl. She's not from here, but she will be your wife." It was just getting dark when he reached the girl. He asked her to go home with him and live with his grandmother. She agreed and told him that she had been looking for him. He took her back to Grandmother's tipi and told her, "There is my bed. You sit there." Red only went out very early in the mornings and stayed in the tipi all day long when he wasn't hunting. He told his wife, "I don't go out in the daytime. I stay inside all day until they quit that gambling. When they quit that I will go outside again." But his wife tired of staying in the tipi day after day doing nothing. One day she asked him, "Let's go outside and watch the game. We can watch it right from our doorway." She kept begging him. Finally he agreed, "All right, you put on your best clothes. I'll do the same and we will go." Then he took two sticks and a buckskin ball. He gave her one of the sticks saying, "There are two women at the game. Our camp is gambling with them. They are very fast runners and want to take me away. That's why I am afraid of them and stay in the tipi all day." When they left the tipi he said, "You hold onto my belt and don't let loose whatever you do." The Women's goal was to the west and the camp's goal was to the east. The ball ground was a half mile long. Red and his wife stopped in the middle of the grounds and waited. The Women knew him. When they had the ball they ran with it, one on each side of it. One would hit it and then the other. No one could catch them. When they were even with Red he tried to hit the ball but they beat him to it. After the Women had won the game, one of them broke Red's wife's hold on his belt. They grabbed Red and ran away, leaving all their winnings behind. All Red's wife could do was stand there and watch them until they were gone from view. She went back to the tipi and cried. Grandmother told her, "See, you made him go. He didn't want to go. Now they have taken him away from you. You might as well pack up and go back to your brothers. The Women won't let him come back." So she walked back to her brothers. She told them what had happened and they said, "We knew it. We knew you were coming back." She stayed with them and soon she had a baby. When the child was a year old, Šctao told her, "Your husband is back in his camp, but the Women are there, too. Maybe when he sees his son he will keep you and make them go away." The next morning she packed up and started for her husband's camp. When she came in sight they were playing the ball game. She stood there and waited until the game was over. The old grandmother saw her and said, "Red, Red, go get your wife and son. They are waiting for you out there." He went out and got her and his son. Grandmother went back into the tipi and told the Women, who each had a child, to go home to their family. She scolded them for wearing their hair so short and for wearing such short dresses and said, "You don't belong on that bed. It belongs to her." So Red brought his first wife and son into the tipi. The Women took their babies and started home to their family. Grandmother waited for awhile and went outside. She saw the Women just disappearing over a hill and she called, "Red, Red, go after your wives. They just went over that last hill." So he left and followed them. When he was out of sight the Women ran so they could get him away from his camp faster. He hadn't caught up to them by dark but he knew the way. He got there in the morning. The Women's father was Chief of that camp. When Red went into the Chief's tipi no one greeted him or paid him any attention. His father-in-law went out and called all the men and boys to his tipi. He said, "My son-in-law is here. Take him and tie him up tightly." They did as they were told and took everything out of the tipi. "Now make a big fire of pitch and plug all the holes in the tipi." They made a big fire of pitch and it smoked. They left Red in there for a long while. Chief called, "Bring him out."

They took him out and untied him. His red clothes were all smoked up and dark. They saw he was Woodpecker. His wives were Antelope. When they turned him loose, Chief said, "You go home and stay with your people. We are not the same as you are. Don't come around here again." When Red got back to his camp he was pitiful. He told his wife, "Now, you had better return to your brothers. You must leave our son here with me. If you try staying with me all the people will laugh at us because I ruined myself by chasing after those Women. I will always be a Woodpecker. You will always be a Wolf. You go back to your brothers." When she got back, her brothers asked her, "What did you do with your son?" She told them what had happened. Šctao said, "It is good to have you back. From now on we will stay at home with our own kind." That is all.

Frog Takes a Mate

There was a big camp with many tipis. There was another camp close by where Frog lived alone in a brush house. There was a celebration going on in the big camp, and married couples were walking around. Frog was watching and he thought it must be nice to have a wife and be able to walk around like that, arm in arm. He thought he should get himself a wife so he could join the other couples. So he went to the Chief and told him he wanted a wife. Chief told Coyote, the camp announcer, to tell everybody that Frog wanted a wife. Soon the young girls and women went over to see what Frog looked like. They all said they didn't want him for a husband because his eyes were too high in his head. Chief asked him, "Now, what are you going to do? They all say your eyes are too high." Frog said, "Well, I will change things around. Tell the boys that I am looking for a husband." Then the boys and men came around to look him over. Bat was the only one who wanted him. Then the people all prayed to Sun and the Chief married Frog and Bat. Chief told Frog that he must then go to live with his husband. Frog went back with Bat. There was nothing in Bat's tipi – no blankets, no bed, nothing to eat. Bat climbed up a tipi pole to the roof and hung there upside down by his feet. He called Frog to come up there and go to bed with him. Frog got up there with Bat's help and hung there upside down. But he fell asleep and fell out of bed. Frog landed very hard on his head. He sat up and thought, "It is no good having a husband. I will go back and ask the

Chief for his advice." He went back and told the Chief, "My husband's bed is no good. I just fell from there and was hurt. It is no good having a husband or a wife. What can I do? Can I have a grandmother or a grandchild?" The Chief said, "What are you, a man or a woman?" Frog answered, "I don't know," and the Chief told him, "Go back to your own camp and just stay that way." That is all.

Mountain Sheep Boy

Long ago, a man and his family lived high in mountain sheep country. Every day the man hunted mountain sheep and his wife gathered wild roots. Their son played around in the rocks. After several weeks there the man had to hunt and hunt to find any game. The sheep weren't coming down the nearby trail they had always followed from place to place. His wife was finding fewer and fewer roots. They were eating less and less and they were becoming very hungry. One evening their son stopped playing earlier than usual. He came back to the tipi, sat before his parents, and asked, "Why is it that you can kill no sheep and can get no roots? I'm getting very hungry." His father told him that the sheep were still there. He saw fresh sign each morning, but he was never waiting for them at the right time. His mother told the same thing about the roots. The boy said, "I know the time when the sheep pass and I know the time when the roots come up. The sheep pass at exactly midnight, but not before or after. That's when the roots grow, but toward morning they work themselves back underground. Only the sick ones stay above the ground." He went on, "My father, tonight you will be waiting just before midnight along the sheep trail. You will soon see a large herd of sheep coming. You will kill only one. Bring it back without letting it touch the ground. Bring it through the rear of the tipi. If I'm asleep wake me." Then he turned to his mother and said, "Mother, tonight at exactly midnight you will go to where you dig roots. Build a fire and you will see many roots there. Now I am going to bed." So then the parents waited as they had been told. At midnight they went out. The boy's mother built a fire and was surprised to see the ground covered with roots. She began digging them up. The boy's father waited until he heard the sound of horns hitting stone. He saw many sheep coming up the trail out of their hiding place. He picked a fat one, killed it, and carried it on his back, not letting it touch the ground anywhere. When he got home his wife had already raised the back side of the tipi for him. He woke his son. The boy got up and directed his father to cut the sheep open down the middle. Then he was to remove all the tripe and was told to cut out all the fat along the backbone. He was to separate out the meat there from the backbone fat and give it to his son to eat. Then he told his parents to go ahead and eat their fill. The next evening he told his father, "Tonight you will kill the baby sheep for me. When you skin it leave the ears, hooves, tail and everything on the hide. After that you may kill any sheep you want. Just give me the fat next to the backbone." The boy had met a stranger who had told him when to find the sheep and roots, and to bring to him a young sheep's hide with everything on it. The boy's father killed a baby sheep. After carefully skinning it he gave the hide to his son. Time went on. Soon they had much dried meat and roots. One day Father asked his son, "Why don't you let your mother eat some of that backfat you've been eating. Don't you think she might like to eat some, too?" The boy listened quietly. Then he reached behind him and covered himself with the sheepskin. He made sure that his head, arms, and legs were covered and then he began to cry. His father tried to comfort him, but he tired and his wife tried to comfort her son. The parents went to sleep and left their son there crying. Later the man got up and looked at his son. His son looked very much like a young sheep. Father called to his wife, "Look. Look at our son. I think he has become a sheep. Jump up. Let's try to catch him. Watch the door and I'll go behind him." Then the boy jumped up and ran around inside the tipi, his parents trying to hold him. But he escaped out the back of the tipi. They lost him in the woods. They waited week after week for him to return and his father hunted for him each day. Soon they had no more dried meat or roots and they became very hungry. They decided to go down the mountain to the village of their people. There they told what had happened in the mountains. The next spring they returned to their mountain camp. The father looked for his son without success. One night as he sat waiting for the sheep to pass he saw a big, fat sheep leading the herd. The sheep walked up to him in his hiding place and said, "Now look at me, look at me closely. I'm your son. I'm full-grown now. I have my own father and mother in the herd behind me. The one that is following me is my brother, the next is my other brother, and the one after him is my uncle." Then the sheep-boy told his father of his other relations on down through the herd. He told his father to shoot the last sheep because he wasn't any relation. The boy's father and mother intended to stay on the mountain until they starved to death. Each night Father was to shoot the last sheep. Then they had plenty of dried meat and roots again. One night his son came to him on the trail and said, "My father, I would like to see my mother just as I am once more. Bring her with you tomorrow night so I may speak with her." They waited the next night. The lead sheep stopped and said, "Hello, Mother. I am your son although I don't look like him. This will be the last time I speak with you. But I and my herd will pass through here each year when you camp here. You, my father, always shoot the last sheep. From now on I will not speak with you. I have my own home now and I am happy. You should never worry about me. I will be fine. When you see the herd coming you will always know I am the leader. Goodbye, my father, and you, my mother." Then his father shot the last sheep. Soon they had enough meat to last them all winter and they returned to their people. The next year they went back to their hunting place. After a time they had plenty of meat and roots. But one night Father decided to shoot a big, fat sheep that wasn't last in line. He shot one in the middle of the herd, and another one, and another one. He began gathering those he had killed but he couldn't find any of them. In his excitement he hadn't seen them coming to life and running away. So he went back to his wife and told her that he hadn't seen any sheep. But as they already had plenty of meat they started home. Toward the middle of the next summer they packed and headed for their hunting place. They set up their tipi and he went out to look at the game trail, expecting to see it covered with sign. But the trail was overgrown with brush and there were no tracks anywhere. He sat there all night but no game went by. His wife told him she hadn't found any roots either. Father knew then that his son controlled the game and the roots. He knew, too, that he had broken the law when he shot the wrong sheep the year before. They talked it over and decided to stay there anyway until they died. So they lived on until they died without ever seeing their son again. That is all.

2

Journals of Exploration

■ *Montana Is a Foreign Country*

WILLIAM L. LANG

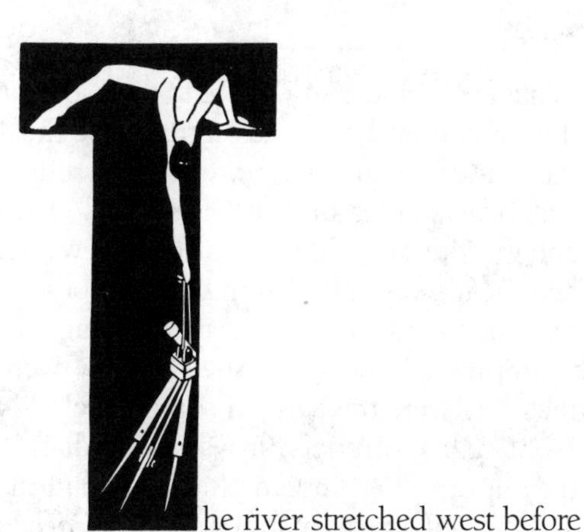

he river stretched west before the Corps, leading them into wilderness. It was 1805 and they were members of the first American expedition to explore the great western territory the young nation had purchased from Spain only two years earlier. Led by two Virginians, Meriwether Lewis and William Clark, the expedition had originated in the enlightened mind of Thomas Jefferson, whose curiosity about the secrets of this new territory and its people matched the expanse of the region. The explorers carried instructions from Jefferson to feel out the new land with their senses and to record the details, grand scenes, and minutiae; to note the terrain; and to determine if there was a continental Northwest Passage. Over two thousand miles up the Missouri River from St. Louis, what opened on the western horizon each morning was the space that map makers label *terra incognita.*

These explorers were from the humid and timbered East, and the expansiveness and strangeness of the Upper Missouri landscape overwhelmed them. The arid, glacier-scraped plains, cut through by silt-laden rivers, seemed to Lewis "truly a dessert [*sic*] barren country," inhospitable but intriguing. On the river, deep in one of its cuts, Lewis marveled at limestone cliffs, "vast ranges of walls of tolerable workmanship so perfect . . . that I should have thought that nature had attempted here to rival the human art of masonry had I not recollected that she had first began her work." At the Great Falls of the Missouri, with its power and beauty at hand, from his displeasure that he lacked a painter's descriptive powers, Lewis wrote:

> I hope still to give to the world some faint idea of an object which at this moment fills me with such pleasure and astonishment; and which of its kind I will venture to ascert is second to but one in the known world.

What Lewis and Clark wrote in their journals, field notes, and diaries during and after their adventure gave the world much more than a "faint idea" of the new western territory. Their maps laid down American names on the terrain and charted the expansive plains, and the journals told readers about new species of plants and animals and the lifeways of western Indian tribes. They portrayed the West as an exotic land, coloring in the unimaginable frontier wilderness.

Impressed and astonished as they were, Lewis and Clark knew that they were traveling in someone else's world. They had come to Montana as intruders; it was the Indians' domain. Like diplomats, they approached Indian chiefs as political and commercial leaders. True to Jefferson's instructions they described the Indians' habits, commerce, politics, and strengths as if scouting an opponent. "We met a party of the Tushepau [Salish] nation," Clark recorded on September 4, 1805:

> . . . those people receved us friendly, three white robes over our Sholders & Smoked in the pipes of peace, we Encamped with them & found them friendly, The Chief harrangued untill late at night, Smoked in our pipe and appeared Satisfied. I was the first white man who ever wer on the waters of this river.

They were unlike any tribes the woodland settlers had encountered east of the Mississippi.

Lewis and Clark's journals were the beginning of a descriptive literature about Montana that informed as it defined wilderness for Americans. But a veil of time and distance separated Americans from their new West. The reports of fur traders and the journals of explorers and adventuresome travelers described but could not quite explain the Montana wilderness. Written when popular literature included James Fenimore Cooper's novels about the trans-Appalachian frontier, Timothy Flint's narratives about the Old Northwest, and Washington Irving's accounts of Astor's and Bonneville's western expeditions, the descriptions of the Missouri River landscape and especially the lives of the Indians read like James Cook's descriptions of Tahiti a century earlier–it was an exotic land.

"Through the whole of this strange land," artist and western traveler George Catlin wrote from the Upper Missouri in the 1830s, "the dogs are all wolves–women slaves–men all lords. The *sun* and *rats* alone (of all the list of old acquaintance), could be recognised in this country of strange metamorphose." Catlin wrote in the language of documentary realism strained through a sieve of romanticism. At the same time that the fur trade and its powerful influences were changing the lives of

Indians forever, Catlin characterized Indians as "noble fellows" who were "yet uncorrupted by the vices of civilized acquaintance."

Certain that they would be the last of their kind, Catlin had come west in 1832 to document these exotic people before they vanished. "From the first settlements of our Atlantic coast to the present day," Catlin reminded his readers, "the bane of this *blasting frontier* has regularly crowded upon them," and time was running out. The Montana Indian was "Nature's man . . . with a soul unalloyed by mercenary lusts, too great to yield to laws or power except from God." Catlin's message from the "strange land" warned civilization to step no further west, no further into this domain.

This "strange land" and its pristine wilderness also pulled Catlin to its breast, and he embraced it. "If you think me *enthusiast*, be it so; . . . I am an enthusiast for God's works as He left them."

> Such of Nature's works are always worthy of our preservation and protection; and the further we become separated (and the face of the country) from that pristine wildness and beauty, the more pleasure does the mind of enlightened man feel in recurring to those scenes, when he can have them preserved for his eyes and his mind to dwell upon.

In the prose of fur traders, adventurers, and travelers, scenes on the Montana landscape underscored the unimagined and defined again and again a new world with new men. In a memoir of trapping and trading in the Upper Missouri country, Warren Ferris asked his readers to imagine a thousand Salish Indians with their "long black locks gently waving in the wind, their faces painted with vermillion, and yellow ochre. . . . the rattle of numberless lodgepoles trailed by packhorses, to the various noises of children screaming, women scolding, and dogs howling." The snow-capped Rockies served as backdrop for Ferris' word pictures, scenes so common, he wrote, "that they scarcely elicit a passing remark, except from some comparative stranger."

For Catlin, Ferris, Osborne Russell, and the others who first wrote about what they saw and experienced in the Montana wilderness, it was a unique landscape of primitive beauty. What happened there, they told their readers, happened nowhere else. But the fur trade dramatically altered that Eden. Smallpox ravaged whole tribes, liquor bewitched unwary Indians as it did whites, and Indians' lives turned more and more on satisfying the trade and all that such commerce brought. "Ah! Mr. Catlin," John James Audubon wrote a decade after Catlin had visited the Upper Missouri, "I am now sorry to see and to read your accounts of the Indians *you* saw—how very different they must have been from any that I have seen!" Audubon's comment reflected his critical appraisal of Catlin's romantic descriptions, but it also documents the lightning, irreversible changes that had taken place. The exotic world of Lewis and Clark had been lost.

From the American Fur Company's outposts on the Upper Missouri during the 1840s, Alexander Culbertson and other company traders looked out on a landscape and culture in transition. For over a decade, they maneuvered among the Indians like ambassadors of commerce, finding ways to co-exist on a frontier of extractive capitalism strung along the river deep into the Indians' territory. Like the English traders in China during the same years, these men built palisaded trading zones on the Indians' land, while the Indians killed bison by the thousands for barter and tried to keep their lives free of the intruders' influences. Beaver had become scarce in the creeks and streams, hide-hunting had begun to erode the great bison herds, steamboat boilers had consumed thousands of cords of riverside cottonwoods, but more importantly the trade had clouded values.

Traders disrupted the Indians' world, and the traders' memoirs tell us how it happened in frightful detail. High up the Missouri, at Fort Piegan, trader James Kipp later told James Bradley that he used a "grand stroke of generosity" to induce Blackfeet to trade:

> For three days the whiskey was given out with lavish hands and for three days the Indian's camp was the scene of carousal and maudlin joy until some 200 gallon had been consumed. . . . a camp of thousands of souls given all the whiskey they could drink and kept drunk for three whole days! It was without parallel.

As the Indians brought their hides to trade for rifles, calico, and steel, their world developed cracks that soon widened.

Montana's Indians had lived for centuries in coexistent spiritual and material worlds; they drew few distinctions between them. It was a place beyond the whites' comprehension, a foreign landscape that was demarcated by natural boundaries and governed by the spirits and natural rhythms. In the winter, Iron Teeth of the Northern Cheyenne told in her memoir, "we considered to sleep much and eat only a little food during the cold weather, the same as the animals and the trees and grass." In a world of danger, challenge, and death, where life's meaning and the importance of honorable behavior were never obscured, Indians worshipped homeland. "The Crow country is good country," Crow chief Arapooish told trader Robert Campbell. "The Great Spirit has put it exactly in the right place; while you are in it you fare well; whenever you go out of it, whichever way you travel, you fare worse."

Indians understood their land and lived their lives differently than the white intruders. Whites could describe Montana, but what they saw they wanted to change. Fur traders in their outposts wrote about what remained of the once exotic land, their lives a busy routine of commerce with Indian and white customers. They clearly understood that future prosperity demanded white settlement. For Nicholas Point, S.J., and other missionaries during the 1850s, what the Indians and their domain needed was civilization through Christianity. Knowing "what fruits grace can produce in willing hearts," Point and his colleagues wrote about the Indians as "children" who needed "only a few minutes of conversation to bring them around to the point to which, for the good of humanity, it would be desirable for all warring nations to be brought."

It all argued against the Indian. In quick succession, the treaty men came to wrangle from the tribes and mark travel corridors through Montana; steamboats powered their way to Fort Benton carrying settlers and goods; John Mullan built a road for white emigrants from the west; and prospectors found the yellow metal in Montana. Henry Edgar and his friends, prospecting as they traveled in May 1863, panned a creek in southwest Montana and made their strike. Edgar scribbled in his journal:

> Staked the ground this morning; claims one hundred feet. Sweeney wanted a water-notice written for a water right. . . . I wrote it for him; then "What name shall we give the creek?" The boys said "You name it." So I wrote "Alder." There was a large fringe of Alder growing along the creek, looking nice and green and the name was given. We staked twelve claims for our friends and named the bars, Cover, Fairweather and Rodgers where the discovers were made.

Edgar and other miners claimed the Indians' universe, putting their names on the land and tethering it to a surely advancing civilization. Their words ring with confidence of a known commodity in an unknown world, and this constituted the change. The landscape that Lewis and Clark, Catlin, Audubon, and Point had described slipped from exotic and foreign to explored and possessed. Montana became claimed country.

■ MERIWETHER LEWIS WILLIAM CLARK

Meriwether Lewis (1774-1809) and William Clark (1770-1838) were commissioned by President Thomas Jefferson to explore the territory of the Louisiana Purchase from the Mississippi to the Pacific. Lewis, who had been Jefferson's secretary, was the best educated of the two in literature and science; Clark was mapmaker, principal waterman, and skilled Indian negotiator. They recorded their discoveries in the famous Journals of the Lewis and Clark Expedition *(1804-1806), which are excerpted here from the Reuben Gold Thwaites edition (1904-1905).*

From Original Journals of the Lewis and Clark Expedition, 1804-1806

edited by Reuben Gold Thwaites

From Fort Mandan to the Yellowstone

[Lewis:] Saturday April 27th 1805

This morning I walked through the point formed by the junction of the rivers; the woodland extends about a mile, when the rivers approach each other within less than half a mile; here a beatifull level low plain commences and extends up both rivers for many miles, widening as the rivers recede from each other, and extending back half a mile to a plain about 12 feet higher than itself; the low plain appears to be a few inches higher than high water mark and of course will not be liable to be overflown; tho' where it joins the high plain a part of the Missouri when at it's greatest hight, passes through a channel of 60 or 70 yards wide and falls into the yellowstone river. on the Missouri about 2½ miles from the entrance of the yellowstone river, and between this high and low plain, a small lake is situated about 200 yards wide extending along the edge of the high plain parallel with the Missouri about one mile. on the point of the high plain at the lower extremity of this lake I think would be the most eligible site for an establishment between this low plain and the Yellow stone river their is an extensive body of timbered land extending up the river for many miles. this site recommended is about 400 yards distant from the Missouri and about double that distance from the river yellow stone; from it the high plain, rising very gradually, extends back about three miles to the hills, and continues with the same width between these hills and the timbered land on the yellowstone river, up that stream, for seven or eight miles; and is one of the ha[n]dsomest plains I ever beheld. . . .

From the Yellowstone to the Musselshell

[Lewis:] Tuesday May 14th 1805

. . . In the evening the men in two of the rear canoes discovered a large brown bear lying in the open grounds about 300 paces from the river, and six of them went out to attack him, all good hunters; they took the advantage of a small eminence which concealed them and got within 40 paces of him unperceived, two of them reserved their fires as had been previously conscerted, the four others fired nearly at the same time and put each his bullet through him, two of the balls passed through the bulk of both lobes of his lungs, in an instant this monster ran at them with open mouth, the two who had reserved their fir[e]s discharged their pieces at him as he came towards them, boath of them struck him, one only slightly and the other fortunately broke his shoulder, this however only retarded his motion for a moment only, the men unable to reload their guns took to flight, the bear pursued and had very nearly overtaken them before they reached the river; two of the party betook themselves to a canoe and the others seperated an[d] concealed themselves among the willows, reloaded their pieces, each discharged his piece at him as they had an opportunity they struck him several times again but the guns served only to direct the bear to them, in this manner he pursued two of them seperately so close that they were obliged to throw aside their guns and pouches and throw themselves into the river altho' the bank was nearly twenty feet perpendicular; so enraged was this anamal that he plunged into the river only a few feet behind the second man he had compelled [to] take refuge in the water, when one of those who still remained on shore shot him through the head and finally killed him; they then took him on shore and butch[er]ed him when they found eight balls had passed through him in different directions; the bear being old the flesh was indifferent, they therefore only took the skin and fleece, the latter made us several gallons of oil; it was after the sun had set before these men come up with us, where we had been halted by an occurrence, which I have now to recappitulate, and which altho' happily passed without ruinous injury, I cannot recollect but

with the utmost trepidation and horror; this is the upseting and narrow escape of the white perogue. It happened unfortunately for us this evening that Charbono was at the helm of this Perogue, in stead of Drewyer, who had previously steered her; Charbono cannot swim and is perhaps the most timid waterman in the world; perhaps it was equally unluckey that Cap[t] C. and myself were both on shore at that moment, a circumstance which rarely happened; and tho' we were on the shore opposite to the perogue, were too far distant to be heard or to do more than remain spectators of her fate; in this perogue were embarked, our papers, Instruments, books medicine, a great part of our merchandize and in short almost every article indispensibly necessary to further the views, or insure the success of the enterprize in which we are now launched to the distance of 2200 miles. surfice it to say, that the Perogue was under sail when a sudon squawl of wind struck her obliquely, and turned her considerably, the steersman allarmed, in stead of puting, her before the wind, lufted her up into it, the wind was so violent that it drew the brace of the squarsail out of the hand of the man who was attending it, and instantly upset the perogue and would have turned her completely topsaturva, had it not have been from the resistance mad[e] by the oarning [awning] against the water; in this situation Cap[t] C. and

myself both fired our guns to attract the attention if possible of the crew and ordered the halyards to be cut and the sail hawled in, but they did not hear us; such was their confusion and consternation at this moment, that they suffered the perogue to lye on her side for half a minute before they took the sail in, the perogue then wrighted but had filled within an inch of the gunwals; Charbono still crying to his god for mercy, had not yet recollected the rudder, nor could the repeated orders of the Bowsman, Cruzat, bring him to his recollection untill he threatend to shoot him instantly if he did not take hold of the rudder and do his duty, the waves by this time were runing very high, but the fortitude resolution and good conduct of Cruzat saved her; he ordered 2 of the men to throw out the water with some kettles that fortunately were convenient, while himself and two others rowed her as[h]ore, where she arrived scarcely above the water; we now took every article out of her and lay them to drane as well as we could for the evening, baled out the canoe and secured her. . . .

From the Musselshell to Maria's River

[Lewis:] Sunday May 26th 1805

Set out at an early hour and proceeded principally by the toe line, using the oars mearly to pass the river in order to take advantage of the shores. scarcely any bottoms to the river; the hills high and juting in on both sides, to the river in many places. the stone tumbleing from these clifts and brought down by the rivulets as mentioned yesterday became more troublesome today. the black rock has given place to a very soft sandstone which appears to be washed away fast by the river, above this and towards the summits of the hills a hard freestone of a brownish yellow colour shews itself in several stratas of unequal thicknesses frequently overlain or incrusted by a very thin strata of limestone which appears to be formed of concreted shells. Cap[t] Clark walked on shore this morning and ascended to the summit of the river hills he informed me on his return that he had seen mountains on both sides of the river runing nearly parrallel with it and at no great distance; also an irregular range of mountains on lar[d] about 50 M[ls] distant; the extremities of which boar W. and N.W. from his station. he also saw in the course of his walk, some Elk several herds of the Big horn, and the large hare; the latter is common to every part of this open country. scarcely any timber to be seen except the few scattering pine and spruce which crown the high hills, or in some instances grow along their sides. In the after part of the day I also walked out and ascended the river hills which I found sufficiently fortiegueing. on arriving to the summit [of] one of the highest points in the neighbourhood I thought myself well repaid for my labour; as from this point I beheld the Rocky Mountains for the first time, I could only discover a few of the most elivated points above the horizon, the most remarkable of which by my pocket compass I found bore N. 65° W. being a little to the N. of the N.W. extremity of the range of broken mountains seen this morning by Cap[t] C. these points of the Rocky Mountains were covered with snow and the sun shone on it in such manner as to give me the most plain and satisfactory view. while I viewed these mountains I felt a secret pleasure in finding myself so near the head of the heretofore conceived boundless Missouri; but when I reflected on the difficulties which this snowey barrier would most probably throw in my way to the Pacific, and the sufferings and hardships of myself and party in thim, it in some measure counterballanced the joy I had felt in the first moments in which I gazed on them; but as I have always held it a crime to anticipate evils I will believe it a good comfortable road untill I am compelled to believe differently.

[Lewis:] Wednesday May 29th 1805

Last night we were all allarmed by a large buffaloe Bull, which swam over from the opposite shore and coming along side of the white perogue, climbed over it to land, he then allarmed ran up the bank in full speed directly towards the fires, and was within 18 inches of the heads of some of the men who lay sleeping before the centinel could allarm him or make him change his course, still more alarmed, he now took his direction immediately towards our lodge, passing between 4 fires and within a few inches of the heads of one range of the men as they yet lay sleeping, when he came near the tent, my dog saved us by causing him to change his course a second time, which he did by turning a little to the right, and was quickly out of sight, leaving us by this time all in an uproar with our guns in o[u]r hands, enquiring of each other the ca[u]se of the alarm, which after a few moments was explained by the centinel: we were happy to find no one hirt. The next morning we found that the buffaloe in passing the perogue had trodden on a rifle, which belonged to Capt Clark's black man, who had negligently left her in the perogue, the rifle was much bent, he had also broken the spindle; pivit, and shattered the stock of one of the blunderbushes on board, with this damage I felt well content, happey indeed, that we had sustaned no further injury, it appears that the white perogue, which contains our most valuable stores is attended by some evil gennii. This morning we set out at an early hour and proceded as usual by the Chord. at the distance of 2½ Miles passed a handsome river which discharged itself on the Lard side, I walked on shore and acended this river about a mile and a half in order to examine it. I found this river about 100 yds wide from bank to bank, the water occupying about 75 yards the bed was formed of gravel and mud with some sand; it appeared to contain much more water as (*than*) the Muscle-Shell river, was more rappid but equally navigable; there were no large stone or rocks in it's bed to obstruct the navigation; the banks were low yet appeared seldom to overflow; the water of this River is clearer much than any we have met with great abundance of the Argalia or Bighorned animals in the high country through which this river passes. Cap. C. who assended this R. much higher than I did has thought proper to call (*called*) it *Judieths* River. the bottoms of this stream as far as I could see were wider and contained more timber than the Missouri; here I saw some box alder intermixed with the Cottonwood willow; rose bushes and honeysuckle with some red willow constitute the undergrowth. on the Missouri just above the entrance of the *Big Horn* (*Judith*) *River* I counted the remains of the fires of 126 Indian lodges which appeared to be of very recent date perhaps 12 or 15 days. Cap[t] Clark also saw a large encamp[m]ent just above the entrance of this river on the Star[d] side of reather older date, probably they were the same Indians. The Indian woman with us ex[a]mined the mockersons which we found at these encampments and informed us that they were not of her nation the Snake Indians, but she beleived they were some of the Indians who inhabit the country on this side of [the] Rocky Mountains and North of the Missoury and I think it most probable that they were the Minetaries of Fort de Prarie. At the distance of six ½ M[s] from our encampment of last night we passed a very bad rappid to which we gave the name of the Ash rappid from a few trees of that wood growing near them; this is the first ash I have seen for a great distance. at this place the hills again approach the river closely on both sides, and the same seen which we had on the 27th and 28th in the morning again presents itself, and the rocky points and riffles reather more numerous and worse; there was but little timber; salts coal &c still appear. today we passed on the Star[d] side the remains of a vast many mangled carcases of Buffalow which had been driven over a precipice of 120 feet by the Indians and perished; the water appeared to have washed away a part of this immence pile of slaughter and still their remained the fragments of at least a hundred carcases they created a most horrid stench. in this manner the Indians of the Missouri distroy vast herds of buffaloe at a stroke; for this purpose one of the most active and fleet young men is scelected and disguised in a robe of buffaloe skin, having also the skin of the buffaloe's head with the years and horns fastened on his head in form of a cap, thus caparisoned he places himself at a convenient distance between a herd of buffaloe and a precipice proper for the purpose, which happens in many places on this river for miles together; the other indians now surround the herd on the back and flanks and at a signal agreed on all shew themselves at the same time moving forward towards the buffaloe; the disguised indian or decoy has taken care to place himself sufficiently nigh the buffaloe to be noticed by them when they take to flight and runing before them they follow him in full speede to the precipice, the cattle behind driving those in front over and seeing them go do not look or hesitate about following untill the whole are precipitated down the precepice forming one common mass of dead an[d] mangled carcases: the decoy in the mean time has taken care to secure himself in some cranney or crivice of the clift which he had previously prepared for that purpose. the part of the decoy I am informed is extreamly dangerous, if they are not very fleet runers the buffaloe tread them under foot and crush them to death, and sometimes drive them over the precipice also, where they perish in common with the buffaloe. . . .

[Lewis:] Friday May 31st 1805

The hills and river Clifts which we passed today exhibit a most romantic appearance. The bluffs of the river rise to the hight of from 2 to 300 feet and in most places nearly perpendicular; they are formed of remarkable white sandstone which is sufficiently soft to give way readily to the impression of water; two or thre thin horizontal stratas of white freestone, on which the rains or water make no impression, lie imbeded in these clifts of soft stone near the upper part of them; the earth on the top of these Clifts is a dark rich loam, which forming a graduly ascending plain extends back from ½ a mile to a mile where the hills commence and rise abruptly to a hight of about 300 feet more. The water in the course of time in decending from those hills and plains on either side of the river has trickled down the soft sand clifts and woarn it into a thousand grotesque figures, which with the help of a little immagination and an oblique view, at a distance are made to represent eligant ranges of lofty freestone buildings, having their parapets well stocked with statuary; collumns of various sculpture both grooved and plain, are also seen supporting long galleries in front of those buildings; in other places on a much nearer approach and with the help of less immagination we see the remains or ruins of eligant buildings; some collumns standing and almost entire with their pedestals and capitals; others retaining their pedestals but deprived by time or accident of their capitals, some lying prostrate an broken othe[r]s in the form of vast pyramids of connic structure bearing a serees of other pyramids on their tops becoming less as they ascend and finally terminating in a sharp point. nitches and alcoves of various forms and sizes are seen at different hights as we pass. a number of the small martin which build their nests with clay in a globular form attatched to the wall within those nitches, and which were seen hovering about the tops of the collumns did not the less remind us of some of those large stone buildings in the U. States. the thin stratas of hard freestone intermixed with the soft sandstone seems to have aided the water in forming this curious scenery. As we passed on it seemed as if those seens of visionary inchantment would never have and [an] end; for here it is too that nature presents to the view of the traveler vast ranges of walls of tolerable workmanship, so perfect indeed are those walls that I should have thought that nature had attempted here to rival the human art of masonry had I not recollected that she had first began her work. These walls rise to the hight in many places of 100 feet, are perpendicular, with two regular faces and are from one to 12 feet thick, each wall retains the same thickness at top which it possesses at bottom. The stone of which these walls are formed is black, dence and dureable, and appears to be composed of a large portion of earth intermixed or cemented with a small quantity of sand and a considerable portion of talk or quarts. these stones are almost invariably regular parallelepipeds, of unequal sizes in the walls, but equal in their horizontal ranges, at least as to debth. these are laid regularly in ranges on each other like bricks, each breaking or covering the interstice of the two on which it rests. thus the purpendicular interstices are broken, and the horizontal ones extend entire throughout the whole extent of the walls. These stones seem to bear some proportion to the thickness of the walls in which they are employed, being larger in the thicker walls; the greatest length of the parallelepiped appears to form the thickness of the thinner walls, while two or more are employed to form that of the thicker walls. These walls pass the river in several places, rising from the water's edge much above the sandstone bluffs, which they seem to penetrate; thence continuing their course on a streight line on either side of the river through the gradually ascending plains, over which they tower to the hight of from ten to seventy feet untill they reach the hills, which they finally enter and conceal themselves. these walls sometimes run parallel to each other, with several ranges near each other, and at other times interscecting each other at right angles, having the appearance of the walls of ancient houses or gardens. I walked on shore this evening and examined these walls minutely and preserved a specimine of the stone.

[Lewis:] Monday June 3rd 1805

This morning early we passed over and formed a camp on the point formed by the junction of the two large rivers. here in the course of the day I continued my observations as are above stated. An interesting question was now to be determined; which of these rivers was the Missouri, or that river which the Minnetares call *Amahte Arz-zha* or Missouri, and which they had discribed to us as approaching very near to the Columbia river. to mistake the stream at this period of the season, two months of the traveling season having now elapsed, and to ascend such stream to the rocky Mountain or perhaps much further before we could inform ourselves whether it did approach the Columbia or not, and then be obliged to return and take the other stream would not only loose us the whole of this season but would probably so dishearten the party that it might defeat the expedition altogether. convinced we were that the utmost circumspection and caution was necessary in deciding on the stream to be taken. to this end an investigation of both streams was the first thing to be done; to learn their widths, debths, comparitive rappidity of their courants and thence the comparitive bodies of water furnished by each; accordingly we dispatched two light canoes with three men in each up those streams; we also sent out several small parties by land with instructions to penetrate the country as far as they conveniently can permitting themselves time to return this evening and indeavour if possible to discover the distant bearing of those rivers by ascending the rising grounds. between the time of my A.M. and meridian Capt C. & myself stroled out to the top of the hights in the fork of these rivers from whence we had an extensive and most inchanting view; the country in every derection around us was one vast plain in which innumerable herds of Buffalow were seen attended by their shepperds the wolves; the solatary antelope which now had their young were distributed over it's face; some herds of Elk were also seen; the verdure perfectly cloathed the ground, the weather was pleasent and fair; to the South we saw a range of lofty mountains which we supposed to be a continuation of the S. Mountains, streching themselves from S. E. to N. W. terminating abbruptly about S. West from us; these were partially covered with snow; behind these Mountains and at a great distance, a second and more lofty range of mountains appeared to strech across the country in the same direction with the others, reaching from West, to the N of N. W., where their snowey tops lost themselves beneath the horizon. this last range was perfectly covered with snow. the direction of the rivers could be seen but little way, soon loosing the break of their channels, to our view, in the common plain. on our return to camp we boar a little to the left and discovered a handsome little river falling into the N. fork on Lar^d side about 1½ M^ls above our camp. this little river has as much timber in it's bottoms as either of the larger streams. there are a great number of prickley pears in these plains; the Choke cherry grows here in abundance both in the river bottoms and in the steep ravenes along the river bluffs. saw the yellow and red courants, not yet ripe; also the goosberry which begins to ripen; the wild rose which grows here in great abundance in the bottoms of all these rivers is now in full bloom, and adds not a little to the bea[u]ty of the cenery. we took the width of the two rivers, found the left hand or S. fork 372 yards and the N. fork 200. The no[r]th fork is deeper than the other but it's courant not so swift; it's waters run in the same boiling and roling manner which has uniformly characterized the Missouri throughout it's whole course so far; it's waters are of a whitish brown colour very thick and terbid, also characteristic of the Missouri; while the South fork is perfectly transparent runds very rappid but with a smoth unriffled surface it's bottom composed of round and flat smooth stones like most rivers issuing from a mountainous country. the bed of the N. fork composed of some gravel but principally mud; in short the air & character of this river is so precisely that of the missouri below that the party with very few exceptions have already pronounced the N. fork to be the Missouri; myself and Cap[t] C. not quite so precipitate have not yet decided but if we were to give our opinions I believe we should be in the minority, certain it is that the North fork gives the colouring matter and character which is retained from hence to the gulph of Mexico. I am confident that this river rises in and passes a great distance through an open plain country I expect that it has some of it's sou[r]ces on the Eastern side of the rocky mountain South of the Saskashawan, but that it dose not penetrate the first range of these Mountains. and that much the greater part of it's sources are in a northwardly direction towards the lower and middle parts of the Saskashawan in the open plains. convinced I am that if it penetrated the Rocky Mountains to any great distance it's waters would be clearer unless it should run an immence distance indeed after leaving those mountains through these level plains in order to acquire it's turbid hue. what astonishes us a little is that the Indians who appeared to be so well acquainted with the geography of this country should not have mentioned this river on wright hand if it be not the Missouri; *the river that scolds at all others*, as they call it if there is in reallity such an one, ought agreeably to their acount, to have fallen in a considerable distance below, and on the other hand if this right hand or N. fork be the Missouri I am equally astonished at their not mentioning the S. fork which they must have passed in order to get to those large falls which they mention on the Missouri. thus have our cogitating faculties been busily employed all day.

Those who have remained at camp today have been busily engaged in dressing skins for cloathing, notwithstanding that many of them have their feet so mangled and bruised with the stones and rough ground over which they passed barefoot, that they can scarcely walk or stand; at least it is with great pain they do either. for some days past they were unable to wear their mockersons; they have fallen off considerably, but notwithstanding the difficulties past, or those which seem now to mennace us, they still remain perfectly cheerfull. In the evening the parties whom we had sent out returned agreeably to instructions. The parties who had been sent up the rivers in canoes informed that they ascended some distance and had then left their canoes and walked up the rivers a considerable distance further barely leaving themselves time to return; the North fork was not so rappid as the other and afforded the easiest navigation of course; six (7) feet appeared to be the shallowest water of the S. Branch and 5 feet that of the N. Their accounts were by no means satisfactory nor did the information we acquired bring us nigher to the decision of our question or determine us which stream to take. . . .

From Maria's River to the Great Falls of the Missouri

[Lewis:] Saturday June 8th 1805

It continue to rain moderately all last night this morning was cloudy untill about ten OClock when it cleared off and became a fine day. we breakfasted and set out about sunrise and continued our rout down the river bottoms through the mud and water as yesterday, tho' the road was somewhat better than yesterday and we were not so often compelled to wade in the river. we passed some dangerous and difficult bluffs. The river bottoms affording all the timber which is to be seen in the country they are filled with innumerable little birds that resort thither either for shelter or to build their nests. when sun began to shine today these birds appeared to be very gay and sung most inchantingly; I observed among them the brown thrush, Robbin, turtle dove linnit goaldfinch, the large and small blackbird, wren and several other birds of less note. some of the inhabitants of the praries also take reffuge in these woods at night or from a storm. The whole of my party to a man except myself were fully pe[r]suaided that this river was the Missouri, but being fully of opinion that it was neither the main stream, nor that which it would be advisable for us to take, I determined to give it a name and in honour of Miss Maria W——d. called it Maria's River. it is true that the hue of the waters of this turbulent and troubled stream but illy comport with the pure celestial virtues and amiable qualifications of that lovely fair one; but on the other hand it is a noble river; one destined to become in my opinion an object of contention between the two great powers of America and Great Britin with rispect to the adjustment of the North-westwardly boundary of the former; and that it will become one of the most interesting branc[h]es of the Missouri in a commercial point of view, I have but little doubt, as it abounds with anamals of the fur kind, and most probably furnishes a safe and direct communication to that productive country of valuable furs exclusively enjoyed at present by the subjects of his Britanic Majesty; in adition to which it passes through a rich fertile and one of the most beatifully picteresque countries that I ever beheld, through the wide expance of which, innumerable herds of living anamals are seen, it's borders garnished with one continued garden of roses, while it's lofty and open forrests are the habitation of miriads of the feathered tribes who salute the ear of the passing traveler with their wild and simple, yet s[w]eet and cheerfull melody. I arrived at camp about 5 OClock in the evening much fatiegued, where I found Cap[t] Clark and the ballance of the party waiting our return with some anxiety for our safety having been absent near two days longer than we had engaged to return. on our way to camp we had killed 4 deer and two Antelopes; the skins of which as well as those we killed while on the rout we brought with us. Maria's river may be stated generally from sixty to a hundred yards wide, with a strong and steady current and possessing 5 feet [of] water in the most sholly parts.

As the incidents which occurred Cap[t] C. during his rout will be more fully and satisfactoryley expressed by himself I here insert a copy of his journal during the days we wer[e] seperated.

I now gave myself this evening to rest from my labours, took a drink of grog and gave the men who had accompanyed me each a dram. Cap[t] Clark ploted the courses of the two rivers as far as we had ascended them. I now began more than ever to suspect the varacity of M[r] Fidler or the correctness of his instruments. for I see that Arrasmith in his late map of N. America has laid down a remarkable mountain in the chain of the Rocky mountains called the tooth nearly as far South as Latitude 45°, and this is said to be from the discoveries of Mr Fidler. we are now within a hundred miles of the Rocky Mountains, and I find from my observation of the 3rd Inst that the latitude of this place is 47° 24′ 12″.8. the river must therefore turn much to the South between this and the rocky Mountain to have permitted M[r] Fidler to have passed along the Eastern border of these mountains as far S. as nearly 45° without even seeing it. but from hence as far as Cap[t] C. had ascended the S. fork or Missouri being the distance of 55 (*45 miles in straight line*) Miles it's course is S. 29° W. and it still appeared to bear considerably to the W. of South as far as he could see it. I think therefore that we shall find that the Missouri enters the rocky mountains to the North of 45°. . . .

[Lewis:] Thursday June 13th 1805.

This morning we set out about sunrise after taking breakfast off our venison and fish. we again ascended the hills of the river and gained the level country. the country through which we passed for the first six miles tho' more roling than that we had passed yesterday might still with propryety be deemed a level country; our course as yesterday was generally S.W. the river from the place we left it appeared to make a considerable bend to the South. from the extremity of this roling country I overlooked a most beatifull and level plain of great extent or at least 50 or sixty miles; in this there were infinitely more buffaloe than I had ever before witnessed at a view. nearly in the direction I had been travling or S.W. two curious mountains presented themselves of square figures, the sides rising perpendicularly to the hight of 250 feet and appeared to be formed of yellow clay; their tops appeared to be level plains; these inaccessible hights appeared like the ramparts of immence fortifications; I have no doubt but with very little assistance from art they might be rendered impregnable. fearing that the river boar to the South and that I might pass the falls if they existed between this an[d] the snowey mountains I altered my course nea[r]ly to the South leaving those insulated hills to my wright and proceeded through the plain; I sent Feels on my right and Drewyer and Gibson on my left with orders to kill some meat and join me at the river where I should halt for dinner. I had proceded on this course about two miles with Goodrich at some distance behind me whin my ears were saluted with the agreeable sound of a fall of water and advancing a little further I saw the spray arrise above the plain like a collumn of smoke which would frequently dispear again in an instant caused I presume by the wind which blew pretty hard from the S.W. I did not however loose my direction to this point which soon began to make a roaring too tremendious to be mistaken for any cause short of the great falls of the Missouri. here I arrived about 12 OClock having traveled by estimate about 15. Miles. I hurryed down the hill which was about 200 feet high and difficult of access, to gaze on this sublimely grand specticle. I took my position on the top of some rocks about 20 feet high opposite the center of the falls. this chain of rocks appear once to have formed a part of those over which the waters tumbled, but in the course of time has been seperated from it to the distance of 150 yards lying prarrallel to it and a butment against which the water after falling over the precipice beats with great fury; this barrier extends on the right to the perpendicular clift which forms that board [border] of the river, but to the distance of 120 yards next to the clift it is but a few feet above the level of the water, and here the water in very high tides appears to pass in a channel of 40 y^ds^ next to the higher part of the ledg of rocks; on the left it extends within 80 or ninty yards of the lar^d^ Clift which is also perpendicular; between this abrupt extremity of the ledge of rocks and the perpendicular bluff the whole body of water passes with incredible swiftness. immediately at the cascade the river is about 300 y^ds^ wide; about ninty or a hundred yards of this next the Lar^d^ bluff is a smoth even sheet of water falling over a precipice of at least eighty feet, the remaining part of about 200 yards on my right formes the grandest sight I ever beheld, the hight of the fall is the same of the other but the irregular and somewhat projecting rocks below receives the water in it's passage down and brakes it into a perfect white foam which assumes a thousand forms in a moment sometimes flying up in jets of sparkling foam to the hight of fifteen or twenty feet and are scarcely formed before large roling bodies of the same beaten and foaming water is thrown over and conceals them. in short the rocks seem to be most happily fixed to present a sheet of the whitest beaten froath for 200 yards in length and about 80 feet perpendicular. the water after decending strikes against the butment before mentioned or that on which I stand and seems to reverberate and being met by the more impetuous courant they roll and swell into half formed billows of great hight which rise and again disappear in an instant. this butment of rock defends a handsome little bottom of about three acres which is deversified and agreeably shaded with some cottonwood trees; in the lower extremity of the bottom there is a very thick grove of the same kind of trees which are small, in this wood there are several Indian lodges formed of sticks. a few small cedar grow near the ledge of rocks where I rest. below the point of these rocks at a small distance the river is divided by a large rock which rises several feet above the water, and extends downwards with the stream for about 20 yards. about a mile before the water arrives at the pitch it decends very rappidly, and is confined on the Lar^d^ side by a perpendicular clift of about 100 feet, on Star^d^ side it is also perpendicular for about three hundred yards above the pitch where it is then broken by the discharge of a small ravine, down which the buffaloe have a large beaten road to the water, (*Qu.*) for it is but in very few places that these anamals can obtain water near this place owing to the steep and inaccessible banks. I see several skelletons of the buffaloe lying in the edge of the water near the Star[d] bluff which I presume have been swept down by the current and precipitated over this tremendious fall. about 300 yards below me there is another butment of solid rock with a perpendicular face and abo[u]t 60 feet high which projects from the Star[d] side at right angles to the distance of 134 y[ds] and terminates the lower part nearly of the bottom before mentioned; there being a passage arround the end of this butment between it and the river of about 20 yards; here the river again assumes it's usual width soon spreading to near 300 yards but still continues it's rappidity. from the reflection of the sun on the sprey or mist which arrises from these falls there is a beatifull rainbow produced which adds not a little to the beauty of this majestically grand senery. after wrighting this imperfect discription I again viewed the falls and was so much disgusted with the imperfect idea which it conveyed of the scene that I determined to draw my pen across it and begin agin, but then reflected that I could not perhaps succeed better than pening the first impressions of the mind; I wished for the pencil of Salvator Rosa [*a Titian*] or the pen of Thompson, that I might be enabled to give to the enlightened world some just idea of this truly magnifficent and sublimely grand object, which has from the commencement of time been concealed from the view of civilized man; but this was fruitless and vain. I most sincerely regreted that I had not brought a crimee [camera] obscura with me by the assistance of which even I could have hoped to have done better but alas this was also out of my reach; I therefore with the assistance of my pen only indeavoured to trace some of the stronger features of this seen by the assistance of which and my recollection aided by some able pencil I hope still to give to the world some faint idea of an object which at this moment fills me with such pleasure and astonishment; and which of it's kind I will venture to ascert is second to but one in the known world. I retired to the shade of a tree where I determined to fix my camp for the present and dispatch a man in the morning to inform Cap[t] C. and the party of my success in finding the falls and settle in their minds all further doubts as to the Missouri. . . .

From the Great Falls to the Three Forks

[Clark:] July 25th Thursday 1805

a fine morning we proceeded on a fiew miles to the three forks of the Missouri those three forks are nearly of a Size, the North fork appears to have the most water and must be Considered as the one best calculated for us to assend Middle fork is quit[e] as large about 90 yds wide. The South fork is about 70 yds wide & falls in about 400 yards below the midle fork those forks appear to be verry rapid & contain some timber in their bottoms which is verry extencive. on the North Side the Indians have latterly Set the Praries on fire, the Cause I can't account for. I saw one horse track going up the river, about four or 5 days past. after Brackfast (which we made on the ribs of a Buck killed yesterday), I wrote a note informing Capt Lewis the rout I intended to take, and proceeded on up the main North fork thro' a Vallie, the day verry hot, about 6 or 8 miles up the North fork a Small rapid river falls in on the Lard Side which affords a great Deel of water and appears to head in the Snow mountains to the SW. this little river falls into the Missouri by three mouthes, haveing Seperated after it arrives in the river Bottoms, and Contains as also all the water courses in this quarter emence number of Beaver & orter maney thousand enhabit the river & Creeks near the 3 forks (Pholosipher's River) We Campd on the Same Side we assended Starboard 20 miles on a direct line up the N. fork. *Shabono* our Intrepreter nearly tired [out] one of his ankles falling him. The bottoms are extencive and tolerable land covered with tall grass & prickley pears. The hills & mountains are high Steep & rockey. The river very much divided by Islands, Some Elk Bear & Deer and Some small timber on the Islands. Great quantities of Currents red, black, yellow, Purple, also Mountain Currents which grow on the Sides of Clifts, inferior in taste to the others haveing Sweet pineish flaver and are red & yellow, Choke Cheries, Boin roche, and the red buries also abound. Musquetors verry troublesom untill the Mountain breeze sprung up, which was a little after night.

[Lewis:] Saturday July 27th 1805–

We set out at an early hour and proceeded on but slowly the current still so rapid that the men are in a continual state of their utmost exertion to get on, and they begin to weaken fast from this continual state of violent exertion. at the distance of 1¾ miles the river was again closely hemned in by high Clifts of a solid limestone rock which appear to have tumbled or sunk in the same manner of those I discribed yesterday. the limestone appears to be of an excellent quality of deep blue colour when fractured and of a light led colour where exposed to the weather. it appears to be of a very fine gr[a]in the fracture like that of marble. we saw a great number of the bighorn on those Clifts. at the distance of 3¾ Ms. further we arrived at 9. A.M. at the junction of the S.E. fork of the Missouri and the country opens suddonly to extensive and bea[u]tifull plains and meadows which appear to be surrounded in every direction with distant and lofty mountains; supposing this to be the three forks of the Missouri I halted the party on the Lar[d] shore for breakfast. and walked up the S.E. fork about ½ a mile and ascended the point of a high limestone clift from whence I commanded a most perfect view of the neighbouring country. From this point I could see the S.E. fork at about 7 miles. it is rapid and about 70 Yards wide. throughout the distance I saw it, it passes through a smoth extensive green meadow of fine grass in it's course meandering in several streams, the largest of which passes near the Lar[d] hills, of which, the one I stand on is the extremity in this direction. a high wide and extensive plain succeeds the meadow and extends back several miles from the river on the Star[d] side and with the range of mountains up the Lar[d] side of the middle fork. a large spring arrises in this meadow about ¼ of a mile from the S.E. fork into which it discharges itself on the Star[d] side about 400 paces above me. from E. to S. between the S.E. and middle forks a distant range of lofty mountains ran their snow-clad tops above the irregular and broken mountains which lie adjacent to this beautifull spot. the extreme point to which I could see the S.E. fork boar S. 65° E. distant 7 M. as before observed. between the middle and S.E. forks near their junction with the S.W. fork there is a handsom site for a fortification. it consists of a limestone rock of an oblong form; it's sides perpendicular and about 25 feet high except at the extremity towards the middle fork where it ascends gradually and like the top is covered with a fine terf of greensweard. the top is level and contains about 2 Acres. the rock [r]ises from the level plain as if it had been designed for some such purpose. the extreem point to which I can see the bottom and meandering of the Middle fork bears S. 15.E. distant about 14 Miles. here it turns to the right around a point of a high plain and disappears to my view. it's bottoms are several miles in width and like that of the S.E. fork form one smoth and beautifull green meadow. it is also divided into several streams. between this and the S.W. fork there is an extensive plain which appears to extend up both those rivers many miles and back to the mountains. the extreme point to which I can see the S.W. fork bears S.30.W. distant about 12 Miles. this stream passes through a similar country with the other two and is more divided and serpentine in it's course than either of the others; it a[l]so possesses abundan[t]ly more timber in it's bottoms. the timber here consists of the narrowleafed cottonwood almost entirely. but little box alder or sweet willow the underbrush thick and as heretofore discribed in the quarter of the missouri. a range of high mountains at a considerable distance appear to reach from South to West and are partially covered with snow the country to the right of the S.W. fork like that to the left of the S.E. fork is high broken and mountainous, as is that also down the missouri behind us, through which, these three rivers after assembling their united force at this point seem to have forced a passage. these bottom lands tho' not more than 8 or 9 feet above the water seem never to overflow. after making a draught of the connection and meanders of these streams I decended the hill and returned to the party, took breakfast and ascended the S.W. fork 1¾ miles and encamped at a Lar^d^ bend in a handsome level smooth plain just below a bayou, having passed the entrance of the middle fork at ½ a mile. here I encamped to wait the return of Capt Clark and to give the men a little rest which seemed absolutely necessary to them. at the junction of the S.W. and Middle forks I found a note which had been left by Capt Clark informing me of his intended rout, and that he would rejoin me at this place provided he did not fall in with any fresh sighn of Indians, in which case he intended to pursue untill he overtook them calculating on my taking the S.W. fork, which I most certainly prefer as it's direction is much more promising than any other. beleiving this to be an essential point in the geography of this western part of the Continent I determined to remain at all events untill I obtained the necessary data for fixing it's latitude Longitude &c. after fixing my camp I had the canoes all unloaded and the baggage stoed away and securely covered on shore, and then permitted several men to hunt.

From the Three Forks of the Missouri to Beaver's Head

[Lewis:] Sunday July 28th 1805.

My friend Capt Clark was very sick all last night but feels himself somewhat better this morning since his medicine has opperated. I dispatched two men early this morning up the S.E. fork to examine the river; and permitted sundry others to hunt in the neighbourhood of this place. Both Capt C. and myself corrisponded in opinion with rispect to the impropriety of calling either of these streams the Missouri and accordingly agreed to name them after the President of the United States and the Secretaries of the Treasury and state having previously named one river in honour of the Secretaries of War and Navy. In pursuance of this resolution we called the S.W. fork, that which we meant to ascend, Jefferson's River in honor of that illustrious personage Thomas Jefferson. [*the author of our enterprize.*] the Middle fork we called Madison's River in honor of James Madison, and the S.E. Fork we called Gallitin's River in honor of Albert Gallitin. the two first are 90 yards wide and the last is 70 yards. all of them run with great volocity and th[r]ow out large bodies of water. Gallitin's River is reather more rapid than either of the others, is not quite as deep but from all appearances may be navigated to a considerable distance. Capt C. who came down Madison's river yesterday and has also seen Jefferson's some distance thinks Madison's reather the most rapid, but it is not as much so by any means as Gallitin's. the beds of all these streams are formed of smooth pebble and gravel, and their waters perfectly transparent; in short they are three noble streams. there is timber enough here to support an establishment, provided it be erected with brick or stone either of which would be much cheaper than wood as all the materials for such a work are immediately at the spot. there are several small sand-bars along the shores at no great distance of very pure sand and the earth appears as if it would make good brick. I had all our baggage spread out to dry this morning; and the day proving warm, I had a small bower or booth erected for the comfort of Capt C. our leather lodge when exposed to the sun is excessively hot. I observe large quantities of the sand rush in these bottoms which grow in many places as high as a man's breast and stand as thick as the stalks of wheat usually do. this affords one of the best winter pastures on earth for horses or cows, and of course will be much in favour of an establishment should it ever be thought necessary to fix one at this place. the grass is also luxouriant and would afford a fine swarth of hay at this time in parsels of ma[n]y acres together. all those who are not hunting altho' much fatiegued are busily engaged in dressing their skins, making mockersons lexing [leggings] &c to make themselves comfortable. the Musquetoes are more than usually troublesome, the knats are not as much so. in the evening about 4 O'Ck the wind blew hard from South West and after some little time brought on a Cloud attended with thunder and Lightning from which we had a fine refreshing shower which cooled the air considerably; the showers continued with short intervals untill after dark. in the evening the hunters all returned they had killed 8 deer and 2 Elk, some of the deer wer[e] in excellent order. those whome I had sent up Gallitin's river reported that after it passed the point to which I had seen it yesterday that it turned more to the East to a considerable distance or as far as they could discover the opening of the Mountains formed by it's valley which was many miles. the bottoms were tolerably wide but not as much so as at or near it's mouth. it's current is rappid and the stream much divided with islands but is sufficiently deep for canoe nagivation. Our present camp is precisely on the spot that the Snake Indians were encamped at the time the Minnetares of the Knife R. first came in sight of them five years since. from hence they retreated about three miles up Jeffersons river and concealed themselves in the woods, the Minnetares pursued, attacked them, killed 4 men 4 women a number of boys, and mad[e] prisoners of all the females and four boys. *Sah-cah-gar-we-ah* o[u]r Indian woman was one of the female prisoners taken at that time; tho' I cannot discover that she shews any immotion of sorrow in recollecting this event, or of joy in being again restored to her native country; if she has enough to eat and a few trinkets to wear I beleive she would be perfectly content anywhere.

Down the Lolo Trail

[Clark:] September 4th Wednesday 1805–

a verry cold morning every thing wet and frosed, we [were] detained untill 8 oClock to thaw the covering for the baggage &c. &c. Groun[d] covered with Snow, we assended a mountain & took a Divideing ridge which we kept for Several Miles & fell on the head of a Creek which appeared to run the Course we wished to go, I was in front, & saw Several of the Argalia or Ibex decended the mountain by verry Steep decent takeing the advantage of the points and best places to the Creek, where our hunters killed a Deer which we made use of, and prosued our Course down the Creek to the forks about 5 miles where we met a part[y] of the Tushepau nation, of 33 Lodges about 80 men 400 Total and at least 500 horses, those people rec[e]ved us friendly, threw white robes over our Sholders & Smoked in the pipes of peace, we Encamped with them & found them friendly but nothing but berries to eate a part of which they gave us, those Indians are well dressed with Skin shirts & robes, they [are] Stout & light complected more So than Common for Indians, The Chief harangued untill late at night, Smoked in our pipe and appeared Satisfied. I was the first white man who ever wer on the waters of this river.

[Clark:] September 5th Thursday 1805

a cloudy morning we assembled the Chiefs & warriers and Spoke to them (with much dificuel[t]y as what we Said had to pass through Several languages before it got into theirs, which is a gugling kind of language Spoken much thro the throught [throat]) we informed them who we were, where we came from, where bound and for what purpose &c. &c. and requested to purchase & exchange a fiew horses with them, in the Course of the day I purchased 11 horses & exchanged 7 for which we gave a fiew articles of merchendize, those people possess ellegant horses. we made 4 Chiefs [to] whome we gave meadels & a few Small articles with Tobacco, the women brought us a few berries & roots to eate and the Principal Chief a Dressed Brarow, Otter & two Goat & antilope Skins

Those people wore their hair as follows the men Cewed [queued] with otter Skin on each Side falling over the Sholders forward, the women loose promisquisly over ther Sholders & face long shirts which come to their anckles & tied with a belt about their waste with a roabe over, the[y] have but fiew ornaments and what they do were [wear] are Similar to the Snake Indians, They Call themselves Eootelash-Schute (*Oat la shoot*) and consist of 450 Lodges in all and divided into Several bands on the heads of Columbia river & Missouri, Some low down the Columbia River

Lewis's Short-Cut to the Missouri, and Exploration of the Maria's River

[Lewis:] Saturday July 26th 1806.

. . . I had scarcely ascended the hills before I discovered to my left at the distance of a mile an assembleage of about 30 horses, I halted and used my spye glass by the help of which I discovered several indians on the top of an eminence just above them who appeared to be looking down towards the river I presumed at Drewyer. about half the horses were saddled. this was a very unpleasant sight, however I resolved to make the best of our situation and to approach them in a friendly manner. I directed J. Fields to display the flag which I had brought for that purpose and advanced slowly toward them, about this time they discovered us and appeared to run about in a very confused manner as if much allarmed, their attention had been previously so fixed on Drewyer that they did not discover us untill we had began to advance upon them, some of them decended the hill on which they were and drove their horses within shot of it's summit and again returned to the hight as if to wate our arrival or to defend themselves. I calculated on their number being nearly or quite equal to that of their horses, that our runing would invite pursuit as it would convince them that we were their enimies and our horses were so indifferent that we could not hope to make our escape by flight; added to this Drewyer was seperated from us and I feared that his not being apprized of the indians in the event of our attempting to escape he would most probably fall a sacrefice. under these considerations I still advanced towards them; when we had arrived within a quarter of a mile of them, one of them mounted his horse and rode full speed towards us, which when I discovered I halted and alighted from my horse; he came within a hundred paces halted looked at us and turned his horse about and returned as briskly to his party as he had advanced; while he halted near us I held out my hand and becconed to him to approach but he paid no attention to my overtures. on his return to his party they all decended the hill and mounted their horses and advanced towards us leaving their horses behind them, we also advanced to meet them. I counted eight of them but still supposed that there were others concealed as there were several other horses saddled. I told the two men with me that I apprehended that these were the Minnetares of Fort de Prarie and from their known character I expected that we were to have some difficulty with them; that if they thought themselves sufficiently strong I was convinced they would attempt to rob us in which case be their numbers what they would I should resist to the last extremity prefering death to that of being deprived of my papers instruments and gun and desired that they would form the same resolution and be allert and on their guard. when we arrived within a hundred yards of each other the indians except one halted I directed the two men with me to do the same and advanced singly to meet the indian with whom I shook hands and passed on to those in his rear, as he did also to the two men in my rear; we now all assembled and alighted from our horses; the Indians soon asked to smoke with us, but I told them that the man whom they had seen pass down the river had my pipe and we could not smoke untill he joined us. I requested as they had seen which way he went that they would one of them go with one of my men in surch of him, this they readily concented to and a young man set out with R. Fields in surch of Drewyer. I now asked them by sighns if they were the Minnetares of the North which they answered in the affermative; I asked if there was any cheif among them and they pointed out 3 I did not believe them however I thought it best to please them and gave to one a medal to a second a flag and to the third a handkerchief, with which they appeared well satisfyed. they appeared much agitated with our first interview from which they had scarcely yet recovered, in fact I beleive they were more allarmed at this accedental interview than we were. from no more of them appearing I now concluded they were only eight in number and became much better satisfyed with our situation as I was convinced that we could mannage that number should they attempt any hostile mesures. as it was growing late in the evening I proposed that we should remove to the nearest part of the river and encamp together, I told them that I was glad to see them and had a great deel to say to them. we mounted our horses and rode towards the river which was at but a short distance, on our way we were joined by Drewyer Fields and the indian. we decended a very steep bluff about 250 feet high to the river where there was a small bottom of nearly ½ a mile in length and about 250 yards wide in the widest part, the river washed the bluffs both above and below us and through it's course in this part is very deep; the bluffs are so steep that there are but few places where they could be ascended, and are broken in several places by deep nitches which extend back from the river several hundred yards, their bluffs being so steep that it is impossible to ascend them; in this bottom there stand t[h]ree solitary trees near one of which the indians formed a large simicircular camp of dressed buffaloe skins and invited us to partake of their shelter which Drewyer and myself accepted and the Fieldses lay near the fire in front of the she[l]ter. with the assistance of Drewyer I had much conversation with these people in the course of the evening. I learned from them that they were a part of a large band which lay encamped at present near the foot of the rocky mountains on the main branch of Maria's river one ½ days march from our present encampment; that there was a whiteman with their band; that there was another large band of their nation hunting buffaloe near the broken mountains and were on there way to the mouth of Maria's river where they would probably be in the course of a few days. they also informed us that from hence to the establishment where they trade on the Suskasawan river is only 6 days easy march or such as they usually travel with their women and childred[n] which may be estimated at about 150 ms that from these traders they obtain arm[s] amunition sperituous liquor blankets &c. in exchange for wolves and some beaver skins. I told these people that I had come a great way from the East up the large river which runs towards the rising sun, that I had been to the great waters where the sun sets and had seen a great many nations all of whom I had invited to come and trade with me on the rivers on this side of the mountains, that I had found most of them at war with their neighbours and had succeeded in restoring peace among them, that I was now on my way home and had left my party at the falls of the missouri with orders to decend that river to the entrance of Maria's river and there wait my arrival and that I had come in surch of them in order to prevail on them to be at peace with their neighbours particularly those on the West side of the mountains and to engage them to come and trade with me when the establishment is made at the entrance of this river to all which they readily gave their assent and declared it to be their wish to be at peace with the Tushepahs whom they said had killed a number of their relations lately and pointed to several of those present who had cut their hair as an evidince of the truth of what they had asserted. I found them extreemly fond of smoking and plyed them with the pipe untill late at night. I told them that if they intended to do as I wished them they would send some of their young men to their band with an invitation to their chiefs and warriors to bring the whiteman with them and come down and council with me at the entrance of Maria's river and that the ballance of them would accompany me to that place, where I was anxious now to meet my men as I had been absent from them some time and knew that they would be uneasy untill they saw me. that if they would go with me I would give them 10 horses and some tobacco to this proposition they made no reply, I took the first watch tonight and set up untill half after eleven; the indians by this time were all asleep, I roused up R. Fields and laid down myself; I directed Fields to watch the movements of the indians and if any of them left the camp to awake us all as I apprehended they would attampt to s[t]eal our horses. this being done I feel into a profound sleep and did not wake untill the noise of the men and indians awoke me a little after light in the morning.

[Lewis:] July 27th 1806. Sunday.

This morning at daylight the indians got up and crouded around the fire, J. Fields who was on post had carelessly laid his gun down behi[n]d him near where his brother was sleeping, one of the indians the fellow to whom I had given the medal last evening sliped behind him and took his gun and that of his brother unperceived by him, at the same instant two others advanced and seized the guns of Drewyer and myself, J. Fields seeing this turned about to look for his gun and saw the fellow just runing off with her and his brother's he called to his brother who instantly jumped up and pursued the indian with him whom they overtook at the distance of 50 or 60 paces from the camp s[e]ized their guns and rested them from him and R. Fields as he seized his gun stabed the indian to the heart with his knife the fellow ran about 15 steps and fell dead; of this I did not know untill afterwards, having recovered their guns they ran back instantly to the camp; Drewyer who was awake saw the indian take hold of his gun and instantly jumped up and s[e]ized her and rested her from him but the indian still retained his pouch, his jumping up and crying damn you let go my gun awakened me I jumped up and asked what was the matter which I quickly learned when I saw drewyer in a scuffle with the indian for his gun. I reached to seize my gun but found her gone, I then drew a pistol from my holster and terning myself about saw the indian making off with my gun I ran at him with my pistol and bid him lay down my gun which he was in the act of doing when the Fieldses returned and drew up their guns to shoot him which I forbid as he did not appear to be about to make any resistance or commit any offensive act, he droped the gun and walked slowly off, I picked her up instantly, Drewyer having about this time recovered his gun and pouch asked me if he might not kill the fellow which I also forbid as the indian did not appear to wish to kill us, as soon as they found us all in possession of our arms they ran and indeavored to drive off all the horses I now hollowed to the men and told them to fire on them if they attempted to drive off our horses, they accordingly pursued the main party who were dr[i]ving the horses up the river and I pursued the man who had taken my gun who with another was driving off a part of the horses which were to the left of the camp. I pursued them so closely that they could not take twelve of their own horses but continued to drive one of mine with some others; at the distance of three hundred paces they entered one of those steep nitches in the bluff with the horses before them being nearly out of breath I could pursue no further, I called to them as I had done several times before that I would shoot them if they did not give me my horse and raised my gun, one of them jumped behind a rock and spoke to the other who turned arround and stoped at the distance of 30 steps from me and I shot him through the belly, he fell to his knees and on his wright elbow from which position he partly raised himself up and fired at me, and turning himself about crawled in behind a rock which was a few feet from him. he overshot me, being bearheaded I felt the wind of his bullet very distinctly. not having my shotpouch I could not reload my peice and as there were two of them behind good shelters from me I did not think it prudent to rush on them with my pistol which had I discharged I had not the means of reloading untill I reached camp; I therefore returned leasurely towards camp, on my way I met with Drewyer who having heared the report of the guns had returned in surch of me and left the Fieldes to pursue the indians, I desired him to haisten to the camp with me and assist in catching as many of the indian horses as were necessary and to call to the Fieldes if he could make them hear to come back that we still had a sufficient number of horses, this he did but they were too far to hear him. we reached the camp and began to catch the horses and saddle them and put on the packs. the reason I had not my pouch with me was that I had not time to return about 50 yards to camp after geting my gun before I was obliged to pursue the indians or suffer them to collect and drive off all the horses. we had caught and saddled the horses and began to arrange the packs when the Fieldses returned with four of our horses; we left one of our horses and took four of the best of those of the indian's; while the men were preparing the horses I put four sheilds and two bows and quivers of arrows which had been left on the fire, with sundry other articles; they left all their baggage at our mercy. they had but 2 guns and one of them they left the others were armed with bows and arrows and eyedaggs. the gun we took with us. I also retook the flagg but left the medal about the neck of the dead man that they might be informed who we were. we took some of their buffaloe meat and set out ascending the bluffs by the same rout we had decended last evening leaving the ballance of nine of their horses which we did not want. the Fieldses told me that three of the indians whom they pursued swam the river one of them on my horse. and that two others ascended the hill and escaped from them with a part of their horses, two I had pursued into the nitch one lay dead near the camp and the eighth we could not account for but suppose that he ran off early in the contest. having ascended the hill we took our course through a beatifull level plain a little to the S. of East. my design was to hasten to the entrance of Maria's river as quick as possible in the hope of meeting with the canoes and party at that place having no doubt but that they [the Indians] would pursue us with a large party and as there was a band near the broken mountains or probably between them and the mouth of that river we might expect them to receive inteligence from us and arrive at that place nearly as soon as we could, no time was therefore to be lost and we pushed our horses as hard as they would bear. at 8 miles we passed a large branch 40 y^{ds} wide which I called battle river. at 3 P. M. we arrived at rose river about 5 miles above where we had passed it as we went out, having traveled by my estimate compared with our former distances and cou[r]ses about 63 m^{s}. here we halted an hour and a half took some refreshment and suffered our horses to graize; the day proved warm but the late rains had supplyed the little reservors in the plains with water and had put them in fine order for traveling, our whole rout so far was as level as a bowling green with but little stone and few prickly pears. after dinner we pursued the bottoms of rose river but finding [it] inconvenient to pass the river so often we again ascended the hills on the S. W. side and took the open plains; by dark we had traveled about 17 miles further, we now halted to rest ourselves and horses about 2 hours, we killed a buffaloe cow and took a small quantity of the meat. after refreshing ourselves we again set out by moonlight and traveled leasurely, heavy thunderclouds lowered arround us on every quarter but that from which the moon gave us light. we continued to pass immence herds of buffaloe all night as we had done in the latter part of the day. we traveled untill 2 OCk in the morning having come by my estimate after dark about 20 m^{s} we now turned out our horses and laid ourselves down to rest in the plain very much fatiegued as may be readily conceived. my indian horse carried me very well in short much better than my own would have done and leaves me with but little reason to complain of the robery.

■ C. C. UHLENBECK
compiler

C. C. Uhlenbeck was a Dutch ethnologist who collected and transcribed a number of first-hand accounts of traditional Blackfeet life during the summer of 1911. Assisted by a young Blackfeet interpreter, Joseph Tatsey, Uhlenbeck heard "How the Ancient Peigans Lived" from Blood (Kainaikoan). The account, which was published in both a Blackfeet language transcription and in English translation, is found in A New Series of Blackfoot Texts *(1912).*

How the Ancient Peigans Lived
as told by Blood (Kainaikoan)

How the ancient Peigans moved about, how they ate, the things they cooked with, the things they had happy times with, how they fought in war, how they played, and how they dressed, the way I heard about them.

Far down on Maria's river [literally: Bear creek], there they stayed till late in the spring. Their horses were really fat, they had done shedding their hair. They [the Peigans] waited for one another. They waited for the bulls, that they had shed their hair. The chiefs talked, they went crying about the camp, they would say: Go about to get lodge-pins. We shall move up [away from the river]. Then they moved up. It was in the Battle-coulee that they camped. In the morning they went round saying: Come on, we shall move. When the buffaloes were far, we overtook them in the Cypress hills; when they were not far, we overtook them in the Small Sweetgrass hills. We would chase the bulls between the Small Sweetgrass hills. The bulls were chased first. And their bodies were oily. They were put straight up [after having been killed]. Their eyes [the bulls' eyes] were dusty. They would rub the knives a little, with them they cut their backs open. They were all skinned from the back down. Then they would throw out their kidneys. And the oil and grease would gather about their navels. They would throw down the yellow back-fat and spread it out. The man would tell his wife: Take and wash the manifold. When she came back, he would say to her: That leg-bone, the oily leg-bone, just break that. It would be broken for him. And the manifold and the marrow of the leg would burst by chewing. He would roll the marrow in the manifold. He would burst it by chewing it.

He had done skinning. Then he began to pack his meat [on a horse]. Then he came home with the meat. Then the woman [his wife] brought it [the horse with the meat] home [to her own parents]. He [her husband] stretched his hand out [that means: gave the meat to his parents-in-law]. And the man [the husband] just sat [inside of his lodge]. His wife came in with the son-in-law's [that means: her husband's] food. The broken boss-rib, the short rib, the gut with the blood in it, the tripe where it is good, with those [four] things he [the son-in-law] was fed [by his parents-in-law]. He was told by his wife: Give an invitation. The old men, those were the ones he invited. The women jerked the skin-meat from the skins which they would make their marks on [the skins that would be used as parfleches]. They made marks on the parfleches, and the long sacks, the real sacks, and the berry-sack. In that way we made use of the hide. The chief then again cried about the camp: When the slices of meat are dry, then we shall move. We shall move down over on Milk river [literally: Little creek]. Close by [that river] are the better buffalo. We shall skin [for lodges]. Again he cried around the camp: We shall move. We shall make a circle [to chase the buffalo]. We shall camp on Bad-water [a lake]. They camped. The lodges were all put up. Everything was quiet in the camp [literally: they – the lodges – were all quiet]. And the chief said: Now begin to catch your horses. Then they went on a hunt. Then they got to the buffalo. They began to get on their horses. Then they chased the buffalo. The carcasses were scattered all over. And they began to skin. They would take the teats of the cows with sucklings. There was foam on the back-fat from rubbing. They would go home with the carcasses.

The horses that had meat on them would be taken all over [the camp]. They were what the married men presented [to their fathers-in-law]. The cooked ribs, that were all carried about, were the food given to the sons-in-law. Inviters would go about. When a man was still at home, [some people on the outside] then would say: A big herd of buffalo is coming towards the camp. The women would say: Over there is [a buffalo], that the people try to kill, that we may go to get the entrails. No one went ahead of them [the women] for the blood, when they went themselves to the carcasses about. They camped a long time, where they got food. All their choice pieces of the meat got dry [during the time they were camping]. Then they dried their skinnings [the hides]. The strong women would quickly get the hair off their hides. The chief said: Come on, we shall move to the Manyberries [a local name]. We shall camp there. There is a young man who went far, he found out [that] the berries are ripe. Come on, you women, you may go for berries. And they had many berry-bags [literally: And many were their berry-bags]. In the evening they all came back from picking berries. The pickings of that one [bunch of women] were sarvis-berries, goose-berries, white-berries [red-willow-berries]. That were the pickings of that one bunch of women. Their children would be delighted in eating the berries. The women prepared [an oil out of] the brains and the liver, mixed up [to oil the hides with]. There began to be many [hides] for their future lodges. They had done the oiling of the skins.

When they moved again, the chief said: We shall move. We shall camp at Buffalo-head [a local name]. There are many berries [of all kinds], [especially] cherries. They took them. When they had brought them home, they mashed them with the whole seed in them. They were picked for future use [for winter-time]. Then they moved again. The chief said: The buffalo is near the Seven-persons [a local name], we shall camp there, and there we shall chase elk. And there they camped. They gathered in a circle [to chase the elk]. Then they chased [the elk]. And there was much hot pemmican, tripe, guts. The choice parts were back-fat, flanks, belly-fat. They all had plenty of food. The chiefs would come together to decide, which way to move the camp. They did not move about [far], they only ate food. And there they moved about [just a little]. When the hides were all good, then [the chiefs] said: We shall move to the mountains [the Cypress hills]. We shall cut the lodge-poles. Then they started to move. Then they separated [by bands]. Then they would move this way. They camped over there at Long-lakes [a local name]. Then they moved again. The chief said: We shall move to Where-the-Women-society-left-their-lodgepole [a local name]. And there are some [buffalo], we have still to chase. We moved back [towards the prairie].

The chief said: Come on, we shall move. We shall move to Green lake. And there they camped. Then stray-bulls were chased. They were taken to use their hides for Indian trunks. The women would use their hides to tie their travois with. The hair on the heads [of the buffalo] was taken also. It was made into ropes. The same [hides] were also made into hard ropes. And the women made a string from the sinews [this string was used in tanning]. They began to tan the skins for the lodges. [The chief] would say: We shall move. We shall move to Writing-stone [a local name]. There are many berries, [especially] cherries. They camped there. The women did not go far for picking berries. And the mashed cherries were dry. They put them away. They put them in calf-sacks. They were the berries for future use. In winter they would skim the grease with them, they would mix them with their pemmican, and they would make soup with them. [The chief] would say: We shall move up [alongside Milk river] to Woman's-point [a local name]. We shall camp about along the river. The meat about [the camp] is getting scarce. Then we had moved away [from the river]. Buffalo and antelopes commenced again to be shot. The prairie-antelopes were fat like dog-ribs. They had sweet livers. There was nothing, we would just look at [without killing it]. Wolves, badgers, skunks, prairie-antelopes were those, that we bought tobacco with.

[The chief] said: We shall cut our lodge-poles from Cut-bank river. When we were near to [the place], where we would cut our lodge-poles, the women would have completed their lodges. They would have done sewing them. Then they [the Peigans] moved fast. Then they camped. It is Cut-bank river, where they always cut lodge-poles from. They would watch the lodge-poles. When they were all dry, then they would stretch their lodges with them. And they would look like leaf-lodges. And it was late in the fall, the leaves would all be white. They began to eat guts [and] tripe. They began to make soup with them. One never turned his head away from the soup. They would begin to eat even hard-seed-berries. They were careful [literally: hard] women, [that] never would be hungry. Over there [near the mountains] it was, they camped about. Black-tails, deer, elk, moose, those were [the animals], they hunted for. These [people] were camped about [near the mountains], those were [the animals] they killed. When it snowed [first] in the fall, then they began to hurry, that they moved down [to the lower country]. There [down] on the river, there they would be camped about. There they waited, where the buffalo would come the nearest. To that place they would move. They would carefully look, where they [themselves] would be during the winter. Then they camped in different places all along the river. They would make the corral [for their horses]. In the beginning of the winter they were all happy.

[The chief] would say: The buffalo would not set warm their [unborn] calves [that means: the buffalo would not have another place than their own bodies to hide their calves]. Then they [the people] were happy. When it cleared up, one person would see the buffalo. In the night he came back, and said: The buffalo are close by, they are many. In the morning you will hunt. They were all gone on a hunt. Then they would chase the buffalo. The buffalo's fur was good already. They [the people] liked the big heifers [four years old], [and] the heifers [two years old] very much. With those they wintered [that means: they ate them during the winter]. They would be like as if their hair were brushed. Oh, happy times there would be in the beginning of the winter, from the food that they got. They all came back home. [After] two, three, four, five [days] the buffalo would go away [from the neighbourhood of the Indians]. They [the buffalo] moved back [they would drift away north]. And here, where they were camped, they would just stay. They would be in a hurry for their robes [to tan them]. They jerked the skin-meat from them. Then they scraped them. Then they oiled them with the brains and the liver. Then they greased them. When they were soaked with grease, they had already warm water. Then they would pull the water [from the fire]. They poured the water on them. When they were soaked with water, they would twist them. [When] the water was all out of them [by twisting], then they would untie them. Then they tied them stretched. Then they began to scrape the moisture out of them. They scraped them with a broken stone. They would brush their fur with sticks. It [the hide] was a little dry, then they pulled it on a string. Then they put it down. Then they stretched it by stepping on it [by holding their feet on the ends]. Then they pulled it again on the string. There were some buffalo-bones, they were called shoulder-bones. With those they also scraped the hide. Then they [the hides] were completed. Then there was nothing to think about [to worry about]. They had done making robes for themselves. The woman, and her husband, and her children, they all had robes for themselves. When they slept, they would sleep as if they were sleeping with fire [the robes were so warm!].

[When] the buffalo was far, the girls would cut a big tree over there. It would fall. She [a girl] would go up to it. Here, where she liked it, she would knock off the bark of it. She would hit it [the tree] lightly. Then she would peel from the same place [where she had been hitting]. The same size [as she had peeled] she would tear in two. She would eat it. It was very sweet. Then the girls and boys – many of them – would go. Over there on the hill-side they dug for false roots [a kind of eatable roots], rattle-sound-roots, [and] make-bleed-roots. Those they ate also. The children never became sick [because those roots were so healthy]. They would find the other [trees] to eat, they took all those trees. They peeled the bark from them. They ate also roseberries, [and] hard-seed-berries. And then there was earth-medicine [black alcali], it was earth. They licked it.

All the mouths would be just white from it. That [the earth-medicine] prevented them from being sick [literally: they would not get sick from]. The women kept bullberries through winter [literally: laid bullberries over night]. They had them also for berries to use them afterwards. When they had real winter, they would provide for wood. The women would go on foot for wood. They would pack the wood on their back. When the wood was far to get, they would put the travois on a horse. They had covered their saddles from one end to the other [with raw-hide]. They carried wood on them [on the travois and the saddles]. They had profit from the travois. They valued it very much. When they had done carrying wood with it, then they began to coil up the ropes, attached to the travois, [for fear] that they might be eaten [by the dogs]. And the old woman had [also] profit from her dog. She would say: Just put it [the dog] short [that means: just put the travois on its neck]. That way she got her wood.

When she had done getting her wood, then she began to put her leg-bones together. She pulled out her stone to hammer the bones on, [and] her stone-hammer. She put her leg-bones down on her half of a hide. She would say: I shall make grease [from the bones]. Then she began to hammer them. She had already put her real pot on the fire. She would make the soup with one of the leg-bones. She had done hammering them. Then she would put the mashed bones in [the pot]. When it had boiled a long time, then she would pull it from the fire. She had already put the cherries [near her]. She took a horn-spoon. With that she skimmed. She put her skimmed grease in a big real [wooden] bowl. Then she had done skimming [the grease]. She put the cherries in [the bowl]. There was much [literally: far] of the cherries with skimmed grease. She told the women: You must get hot this soup of the leg-bones. Her daughter was already hammering the sirloin-dried-meat. [When] she had done hammering, she gave it to [her mother]. And she [the mother] mixed it [the dried meat] up with the skimmed grease [and cherries]. Then she made it all into one roll. She gave that to her son-in-law. He invited the old men.

■ W. A. FERRIS

Born in Glen Falls, New York, in 1810, Warren Angus Ferris was trained as a civil engineer, but he came West in 1829 as a fur trapper and mountain man with the American Fur Company. Ferris, who published his journals in 1842 as Life in the Rocky Mountains, *has given us one of the best early accounts of life in the Yellowstone region. Ferris later participated in the Texas Revolution, became a surveyor, and lived out his life near Dallas, Texas, where he died in 1873.*

From Life in the Rocky Mountains

Expedition to the Fur Country

Westward! Ho! It is the sixteenth of the second month, A.D. 1830, and I have joined a trapping, trading, hunting expedition to the Rocky Mountains. *Why* I scarcely know, for the motives that induced me to this step were of a mixed complexion,—something like the pepper and salt population of this city of St. Louis. Curiosity, a love of wild adventure, and perhaps also a hope of profit,—for times *are* hard, and my best coat has a sort of sheepish hang-dog hesitation to encounter fashionable folk—combined to make me look upon the project with an eye of favour. The party consists of some thirty men, mostly Canadians; but a few there are, like myself, from various parts of the Union. Each has some plausible excuse for joining, and the aggregate of disinterestedness would delight the most ghostly saint in the Roman calendar. Engage for money! no, not they;—health, and the strong desire of seeing strange lands, of beholding nature in the savage grandeur of her primeval state,—these are the only arguments that *could* have persuaded such independent and high-minded young fellows to adventure with the American Fur Company in a trip to the mountain wilds of the great west. But they are active, vigorous, resolute, daring, and such are the kind of men the service requires.

White Traders and the Indians

We departed southwestward for the Jefferson River on the morning of the fifteenth, accompanied by all the Indians; and picturesque enough was the order and appearance of our march. Fancy to yourself, reader, three thousand horses of every variety of size and colour, with trappings almost as varied as their appearance, either packed or ridden by a thousand souls from squalling infancy to decrepid age, their persons fantastically ornamented with scarlet coats, blankets of all colours, buffalo robes painted with hideous little figures, resembling grass-hoppers quite as much as men for which they were intended, and sheepskin dresses garnished with porcupine quills, beads, hawk bells, and human hair. Imagine this motley collection of human figures, crowned with long black locks gently waving in the wind, their faces painted with vermillion, and yellow ochre. Listen to the rattle of numberless lodgepoles trained [trailed] by packhorses, to the various noises of children screaming, women scolding, and dogs howling. Observe occasional frightened horses running away and scattering their lading over the prairie. See here and there groups of Indian boys dashing about at full speed, sporting over the plain, or quietly listening to traditionary tales of battles and surprises, recounted by their elder companions. Yonder see a hundred horsemen pursuing a herd of antelopes, which sport and wind before them conscious of superior fleetness,—there as many others racing towards a distant mound, wild with emulation and excitement, and in every direction crowds of hungry dogs chasing and worrying timid rabbits, and other small animals. Imagine these scenes, with all their bustle, vociferation and confusion, lighted by the flashes of hundreds of gleaming gunbarrels, upon which the rays of a fervent sun are playing, a beautiful level prairie, with dark blue snow-capped mountains in the distance for the *locale*, and you will have a faint idea of the character and aspect of our march, as we followed old Guignon (French for bad-luck) the Flathead or rather the Pen-d'oreille chief slowly over the plains, on the sources of Clark's River. Exhibitions of this description are so common to the country that they scarcely elicit a passing remark, except from some comparative stranger.

Next day we separated into two parties, one of which entered a cut in the mountains southward, while the other (of which was I,) continued on southeastward, and on the 17th crossed a mountain to a small stream tributary to the Jefferson. In the evening a Pen-d'oreille from the other division, joined us and reported that he had seen traces of a party of footmen, apparently following our trail. We ourselves saw during our march, the recent encampment of a band of horsemen, and other indications of the vicinity of probable foes. Pursuing our route, on the following day we reached and descended into the valley of the Jefferson twenty-five miles below the forks. This valley extended below us fifteen or twenty miles to the northward, where the river bending to the East, enters a narrow passage in the mountain between walls of cut rock. The plains are from two to five miles in breadth, and are covered with prickly pear,—immediately bordering the river are broad fertile bottoms, studded with cotton-wood trees. The River is about one hundred yards wide, is clear, and has a gentle current,—its course is northward till it leaves the valley. We found the plains alive with buffalo, of which we killed great numbers, and our camp was consequently once more graced with piles of meat, which gave it something the appearance of a well stored market place. From starvation to such abundance the change was great, and the effect was speedily apparent. Indians, children, and dogs lay sprawling about, scarcely able to move, so gorged were they with the rich repast, the first full meal which they had, perhaps, enjoyed for weeks. The squaws alone were busy, and they having all the labour of domestic duty to perform, are seldom idle. Some were seen seated before their lodges with buffalo skins spread out before them, to receive the fat flakes of meat they sliced for drying. Others were engaged in procuring fuel, preparing scaffolds, and making other preparations for curing and preserving the fortunate supply of provisions thus obtained. Even the children were unusually quiet and peaceable, and all would have been exempt from care or uneasiness, had not the unslumbering cautiousness of the veteran braves discovered traces of lurking enemies.

On the morning of the 19th several of our men returned from their traps, bearing the dead body of Frasier, one of our best hunters, who went out the day previous to set his trap, and by his not returning at night, excited some alarm for his safety. His body was found in the Jefferson, about five miles below camp, near a trap, which it is supposed he was in the act of setting when fired upon. He was shot in the thigh and through the neck, and twice stabbed in the breast. His body was stripped, and left in the water, but unscalped.—In the afternoon we dug his grave with an axe and frying pan, the only implements we had that could be employed to advantage in this melancholy task, and prepared for the sad ceremony of committing to the earth the remains of a comrade, who but yestermorn was among us in high health, gay, cheerful, thoughtless, and dreaming of nothing but pleasure and content in the midst of relations and friends. Having no coffin, nor the means to make one, we covered his body in a piece of new scarlet cloth, around which a blanket and several buffalo robes were then wrapped and lashed firmly. The body thus enveloped was carefully laid in the open grave, and a wooden cross in token of his catholic faith placed upon his breast. Then there was a pause. The friends and comrades of the departed trapper gathered around to shed the silent tear of pity and affection over a companion so untimely cut off; and the breeze as if in sympathy with their sorrow, sighed through the leaves and branches of an aged cottonwood, which spread its hoary and umbrageous arms above his last resting place, as though to protect it from intrusion; while in contrast with this solemnity merry warblers skipped lightly from limb to limb, tuning their little pipes to lively strains, unmindful of the touching and impressive scene beneath. At length the simple rite was finished, the grave closed, and with saddened countenances and heavy hearts the little herd of mourners retired to their respective lodges, where more than one of our ordinarily daring and thoughtless hunters, thus admonished of the uncertainty of life, held serious self-communion, and perhaps resolved to make better preparations for an event that might come at almost any moment, after which there can be no repentance. But it may be doubted if these resolutions were long remembered. They soon recovered their light heartedness, and were as indifferent, reckless, and mercurial as ever.—Frasier was an Iroquois from St. Regis, in Upper Canada. He left that country seventeen years before, having with many others engaged in the service of the Norwest Company, and came to the Rocky Mountains. Subsequently he joined the American hunters, married a squaw by whom he had several children, purchased horses and traps, and finally as one of the Freemen led an independent and roving life. He could read and write in his own language, was upright and fair in all his dealings, and very generally esteemed and respected by his companions.

It commenced raining in the afternoon of the following day, and continued without intermission during the night. Taking advantage of the storm and darkness, a party of Blackfeet boldly entered our lines, and cut loose several horses from the very centre of the camp. An alarm having been given the Flathead chief arose and harrangued his followers, calling upon them to get up and prepare to oppose their enemies, not doubting but that an attack would be made at day break. When he had concluded, a Blackfoot chief, who last summer deserted from his people and joined the Flatheads, in a loud voice and in his native tongue, invited all who were lurking about camp, to come in and help themselves to whatever horses they had a mind to, asserting that as the whites and Flatheads were all asleep, there could be no hazard in the undertaking. Scarcely had he done speaking, when the Blackfeet, to testify their gratitude and appreciation of this disinterested advice fired a volley upon him. Fortunately, however, no one was injured by the firing, though several lodges were perforated by their balls. In the morning we were early on the alert, but the Blackfeet had all departed, taking with them seven or eight of our best horses. As there was no help for it, we had to put up with the loss, and the next day having finished drying meat, we struck our tents, and departed southward up the Jefferson.

■ JAMES KIPP
as told to Lieutenant James Bradley

James Kipp, an American Fur Company trader, opened the first trading post in Blackfeet country in the spring of 1831. He located Fort Piegan on the north bank of the Missouri River near its confluence with the Marias River in northeastern Montana. To win the good will of the hostile Blackfeet, Kipp threw a three-day party featuring all-you-can-drink free whiskey. He also offered the Indians much higher prices for their furs than the British traders of Hudson's Bay Company did. "Establishment of Fort Piegan As Told Me by James Kipp" was reported by Lieutenant James Bradley in Volume 8 of the Contributions to the Historical Society of Montana *(1917).*

Establishment of Fort Piegan As Told Me by James Kipp

For three days the whiskey was given out with lavish hands and for three days the Indians camp was the scene of carousal and maudlin joy until some 200 gallon had been consumed, when Mr. Kipp announced to them that his supply was exhausted. Such liberality astonished the savages and elevated the American traders in their esteem to a higher place than the representatives of the Hudson Bay Co. had ever enjoyed. When they asked themselves was such a thing ever known before, a camp of thousands of souls given all the whiskey they could drink and kept drunk for three whole days! It was without a parallel. The British traders had not approached it in generosity, they could not have believed it possible. Whiskey, as they knew to their cost, was a very dear commodity and for these new comers to have presented them outright with such an enormous quantity was proof enough that they loved the Indians and meant to deal fairly with them. They no longer believed the misrepresentations of their British rivals, saw no snares, in the pretended higher prices offered them and gathered their peltries together besieged the fort in anxious throngs to barter them away for the white mans goods. In a very few days Mr. Kipp had secured 6,450 pounds of beaver skins upon which he realized the next year $46,000. It was a transaction rarely equalled in the annals of the fur trade and amply compensated him for the gift of the single barrel of alcohol, which had sufficed to make the 200 gallons of Indian whiskey consumed in the three days of carousal.

Having completed their trading the Piegans departed for the north. Great was the chagrin of the British traders when they learned the success of their American rivals and as the Piegans had failed them, they now sought to persuade the Blood Indians to undertake the reduction of the fort. They represented the Americans as scoundrels of the deepest dye, whose sole object was to plunder and destroy the Indians and secure their land for themselves. They assured them that the trading posts were not for the benefit of the Indians as they professed but simply a devise to gain a foothold in the country, learning the strength of the Indians and the plan for their destruction. They further represented to the Bloods the advantages that would accrue to them from possessing themselves of such a large stock of goods as they would find in the post as well as the furs which the Piegans had given them in trade. The distrust and animosity of the Bloods having been thus aroused, they readily consented to destroy the fort and prepared to do so as soon as the weather permitted them to advance against it.

Meantime the garrison at Ft. Piegan as the place had been named whiled away the winter of 1821-'22 as best they could and were yearning for the approach of spring, when early in February a Piegan Indian arrived at the fort and disclosed to Mr. Kipp, the startling intelligence of the intended attack. About 100 cords of wood had been cut which he hastily secured at the fort and he then turned his attention to the accumulation of a quantity of ice to supply them with water in case of a siege. This done he was ready and in a few days the Indians appeared to the number of 500 lodges. Finding the gates closed they quickly gave token of the hostile design by surrounding the fort and opened fire at long range, gradually growing bolder until they were near enough for the garrison to have replied with fatal effect. But Mr. Kipp had determined to fire upon them only at the last extremity, as he wished rather to conciliate them and secure their trade than excite their hostility to the point of utter implacability. He therefore gave orders to his men not to fire but let the Indians see that he was constantly ready to repel any attack to carry the place by storm.

For 11 days this state of affairs continued when the garrison had exhausted its supply of ice and were threatened with a famine of water. The besiegers had maintained a desultory fire to which not a single shot had been returned by the garrison, so that the one party protected by their walls, and the other by the forbearance of the besieged they were equally unscathed.

But Mr. Kipp now resolved to disclose to them the resources for defense, and by impressing them with an idea of its helplessness induce them to raise the siege. An immense cottonwood tree, some 9 feet in diameter near the base, with a heavy top of gnarled limbs and shaggy branches grew near the fort and charging a brass four pounder cannon heavily with grape, he fired it into the tree. A tremendous shower of shivered splinters and broken limbs rained down around the tree, which together with the thunder of the discharge, gave the savages such an exaggerated idea of the awful destructive powers of the gun, that seized with a panic, they fled in every direction, the last one of them disappearing in a few moments behind the neighboring hills.

"Now boys, in with your ice," shouted Mr. Kipp, well pleased with the result of his shot, and in a few moments the entire garrison except a small watch was busy with the crystal blocks and rapidly replenished their exhausted store of solidified water. It was at first supposed that the Indians had gone quite off, but presently two appeared in view and cautiously approached the fort. Mr. Kipp went out to meet them and when within speaking distance invited them to come into the fort, promising them protection. They declined to do so fearing their lives would be sacrificed but Mr. Kipp continued to advance toward them in a friendly strain, till by a sudden movement he placed himself in their rear and cut off their retreat. He then ordered them into the fort, still assuring them that they should not meet with harm, and unable to escape, they reluctantly obeyed. They proved to be two of the principal chiefs, and once in the fort talked quite freely of the attack and confessed the part played in the matter by the agents of the Hudson's Bay Company. Mr. Kipp explained to them his friendly designs, showed them the advantages offered to them by his establishment over those of the rival company and proved his indisposition to harm them, by sighting his having refrained for 11 days to fire upon them, when he might have done so and killed many of their tribe. He then proposed that they cease hostilities and make one trade with him, when they would speedily see how much more he would give for the peltries than they had ever received before.

■ GEORGE CATLIN

George Catlin was born in Pennsylvania in 1796. Although largely self-taught, he became one of the great painters of the American West, specializing in images of Indians. In 1832, Catlin joined an American Fur Company expedition and traveled to the Upper Missouri River. These selections are taken from Volume 1 of his Letters and Notes on the Manners, Customs, and Condition of the North American Indians *(1841), two volumes illustrated with more than three hundred engravings.*

From Letters and Notes on the Manners, Customs, and Condition of the North American Indians

Letter—No. 8.
Mouth of Yellow Stone, Upper Missouri

Since my last Letter, nothing of great moment has transpired at this place; but I have been continually employed in painting my portraits and making notes on the character and customs of the wild folks who are about me. I have just been painting a number of the Crows, fine looking and noble gentlemen. They are really a handsome and well-formed set of men as can be seen in any part of the world. There is a sort of ease and grace added to their dignity of manners, which gives them the air of gentlemen at once. I observed the other day, that most of them were over six feet high, and very many of these have cultivated their natural hair to such an almost incredible length, that it sweeps the ground as they walk; there are frequent instances of this kind amongst them, and in some cases, a foot or more of it will drag on the grass as they walk, giving exceeding grace and beauty to their movements. They usually oil their hair with a profusion of bear's grease every morning, which is no doubt one cause of the unusual length to which their hair extends; though it cannot be the sole cause of it, for the other tribes throughout this country use the bear's grease in equal profusion without producing the same results. The Mandans, however, and the Sioux, of whom I shall speak in future epistles, have cultivated a very great growth of the hair, as many of them are seen whose hair reaches near to the ground.

This extraordinary length of hair amongst the Crows is confined to the men alone; for the women, though all of them with glossy and beautiful hair, and a great profusion of it, are unable to cultivate it to so great a length; or else they are not allowed to compete with their lords in a fashion so ornamental (and on which the men so highly pride themselves), and are obliged in many cases to cut it short off.

The fashion of long hair amongst the men, prevails throughout all the Western and North Western tribes, after passing the Sacs and Foxes; and the Pawnees of the Platte, who, with two or three other tribes only, are in the habit of shaving nearly the whole head.

The present chief of the Crows, who is called "Long-hair," and has received his name as well as his office from the circumstance of having the longest hair of any man in the nation, I have not yet seen: but I hope I yet may, ere I leave this part of the country. This extraordinary man is known to several gentlemen with whom I am acquainted, and particularly to Messrs. Sublette and Campbell, of whom I have before spoken, who told me they had lived in his hospitable lodge for months together; and assured me that they had measured his hair by a correct means, and found it to be ten feet and seven inches in length; closely inspecting every part of it at the same time, and satisfying themselves that it was the natural growth.

On ordinary occasions it is wound with a broad leather strap, from his head to its extreme end, and then folded up into a budget or block, of some ten or twelve inches in length, and of some pounds weight; which when he walks is carried under his arm, or placed in his bosom, within the folds of his robe; but on any great parade or similar occasion, his pride is to unfold it, oil it with bear's grease and let it drag behind him, some three or four feet of it spread out upon the grass, and black and shining like a raven's wing.

It is a common custom amongst most of these upper tribes, to splice or add on several lengths of hair, by fastening them with glue; probably for the purpose of imitating the Crows, upon whom alone Nature has bestowed this conspicuous and signal ornament.

Letter—No. 31
Mouth of Teton River, Upper Missouri

Many are the rudenesses and wilds in Nature's works, which are destined to fall before the deadly axe and desolating hands of cultivating man; and so amongst her ranks of *living*, of beast and human, we often find noble stamps, or beautiful colours, to which our admiration clings; and even in the overwhelming march of civilized improvements and refinements do we love to cherish their existence, and lend our efforts to preserve them in their primitive rudeness. Such of Nature's works are always worthy of our preservation and protection; and the further we become separated (and the face of the country) from that pristine wildness and beauty, the more pleasure does the mind of enlightened man feel in recurring to those scenes, when he can have them preserved for his eyes and his mind to dwell upon.

Of such "rudenesses and wilds," Nature has no where presented more beautiful and lovely scenes, than those of the vast prairies of the West; and of *man* and *beast*, no nobler specimens than those who inhabit them—the *Indian* and the *buffalo*—joint and original tenants of the soil, and fugitives together from the approach of civilized man; they have fled to the great plains of the West, and there, under an equal doom, they have taken up their *last abode*, where their race will expire, and their bones will bleach together.

It may be that *power* is *right*, and *voracity* a *virtue*; and that these people, and these noble animals, are *righteously* doomed to an issue that *will* not be averted. It can be easily proved—and we have a civilized science that can easily do it, or anything else that may be required to cover the iniquities of civilized man in catering for his unholy appetites. It can be proved that the weak and ignorant have no *rights*—that there can be no virtue in darkness—that God's gifts have no meaning or merit until they are appropriated by civilized man—by him brought into the light, and converted to his use and luxury. We have a mode of reasoning (I forget what it is called) by which all this can be proved, and even more. The *word* and the *system* are entirely of *civilized* origin; and latitude is admirably given to them in proportion to the increase of civilized wants, which often require a *judge* to overrule the laws of nature. I say that *we* can prove such things; but an *Indian* cannot. It is a mode of reasoning unknown to him in his nature's simplicity, but admirably adapted to subserve the interests of the enlightened world, who are always their own judges, when dealing with the savage; and who, in the present refined age, have many appetites that can only be lawfully indulged, by proving God's laws defective.

It is not enough in this polished and extravagant age, that we get from the Indian his lands, and the very clothes from his back, but the food from their mouths must be stopped, to add a new and useless article to the fashionable world's luxuries. The ranks must be thinned, and the race exterminated, of this noble animal, and the Indians of the great plains left without the means of supporting life, that white men may figure a few years longer, enveloped in buffalo robes—that they may spread them, for their pleasure and elegance, over the backs of their sleighs, and trail them ostentatiously amidst the busy throng, as things of beauty and elegance that had been made for them!

Reader! listen to the following calculations, and forget them not. The buffaloes (the quadrupeds from whose backs your beautiful robes were taken, and whose myriads were once spread over the whole country, from the Rocky Mountains to the Atlantic Ocean) have recently fled before the appalling appearance of civilized man, and taken up their abode and pasturage amid the almost boundless prairies of the West. An instinctive dread of their deadly foes, who made an easy prey of them whilst grazing in the forest, has led them to seek the midst of the vast and treeless plains of grass, as the spot where they would be least exposed to the assaults of their enemies; and it is exclusively in those desolate fields of silence (yet of beauty) that they are to be found—and over these vast steppes, or prairies, have they fled, like the Indian, towards the "setting sun"; until their bands have been crowded together, and their limits confined to a narrow strip of country on this side of the Rocky Mountains.

This strip of country, which extends from the province of Mexico to lake Winnepeg on the North, is almost one entire plain of grass, which is, and ever must be, useless to cultivating man. It is here, and here chiefly, that the buffaloes dwell; and with, and hovering about them, live and flourish the tribes of Indians, whom God made for the enjoyment of that fair land and its luxuries.

It is a melancholy contemplation for one who has travelled as I have, through these realms, and seen this noble animal in all its pride and glory, to contemplate it so rapidly wasting from the world, drawing the irresistible conclusion too, which one must do, that its species is soon to be extinguished, and with it the peace and happiness (if not the actual existence) of the tribes of Indians who are joint tenants with them, in the occupancy of these vast and idle plains.

And what a splendid contemplation too, when one (who has travelled these realms, and can duly appreciate them) imagines them as they *might* in future be seen, (by some great protecting policy of government) preserved in their pristine beauty and wildness, in a *magnificent park*, where the world could see for ages to come, the native Indian in his classic attire, galloping his wild horse, with sinewy bow, and shield and lance, amid the fleeting herds of elks and buffaloes. What a beautiful and thrilling specimen for America to preserve and hold up to the view of her refined citizens and the world, in future ages! A *nation's Park*, containing man and beast, in all the wild and freshness of their nature's beauty!

I would ask no other monument to my memory, nor any other enrolment of my name amongst the famous dead, than the reputation of having been the founder of such an institution.

Such scenes might easily have been preserved, and still could be cherished on the great plains of the West, without detriment to the country or its borders; for the tracts of country on which the buffaloes have assembled, are uniformly sterile, and of no available use to cultivating man.

It is on these plains, which are stocked with buffaloes, that the finest specimens of the Indian race are to be seen. It is here, that the savage is decorated in the richest costume. It is here, and here only, that his wants are all satisfied, and even the *luxuries* of life are afforded him in abundance. And here also is he the proud and honourable man (before he has had teachers or laws), above the imported wants, which beget meanness and vice; stimulated by ideas of honour and virtue, in which the God of Nature has certainly not curtailed him.

There are, by a fair calculation, more than 300,000 Indians, who are now subsisted on the flesh of the buffaloes, and by those animals supplied with all the luxuries of life which they desire, as they know of none others. The great variety of uses to which they convert the body and other parts of that animal, are almost incredible to the person who has not actually dwelt amongst these people, and closely studied their modes and customs. Every part of their flesh is converted into food, in one shape or another, and on it they entirely subsist. The robes of the animals are worn by the Indians instead of blankets—their skins when tanned, are used as coverings for their lodges, and for their beds; undressed, they are used for constructing canoes—for saddles, for bridles—l'arrêts, lasos, and thongs. The horns are shaped into ladles and spoons—the brains are used for dressing the skins—their bones are used for saddle trees—for war clubs, and scrapers for graining the robes—and others are broken up for the marrow-fat which is contained in them. Their sinews are used for strings and backs to their bows—for thread to string their beads and sew their dresses. The feet of the animals are boiled, with their hoofs, for the glue they contain, for fastening their arrow points, and many other uses. The hair from the head and shoulders, which is long, is twisted and braided into halters, and the tail is used for a fly brush. In this wise do these people convert and use the various parts of this useful animal, and with all these luxuries of life about them, and their numerous games, they are happy (God bless them) in the ignorance of the disastrous fate that awaits them.

Yet this interesting community, with its sports, its wildnesses, its languages, and all its manners and customs, could be perpetuated, and also the buffaloes, whose numbers would increase and supply them with food for ages and centuries to come, if a system of non-intercourse could be established and preserved. But such is not to be the case—the buffalo's doom is sealed, and with their extinction must assuredly sink into real despair and starvation, the inhabitants of these vast plains, which afford for the Indians, no other possible means of subsistence; and they must at last fall a prey to wolves and buzzards, who will have no other bones to pick.

It seems hard and cruel, (does it not?) that we civilized people with all the luxuries and comforts of the world about us, should be drawing from the backs of these useful animals the skins for our luxury, leaving their carcasses to be devoured by the wolves—that we should draw from that country, some 150 or 200,000 of their robes annually, the greater part of which are taken from animals that are killed expressly for the robe, at a season when the meat is not cured and preserved, and for each of which skins the Indian has received but a pint of whiskey!

Such is the fact, and that number or near it, are annually destroyed, in addition to the number that is necessarily killed for the subsistence of 300,000 Indians, who live entirely upon them. It may be said, perhaps, that the Fur Trade of these great western realms, which is now limited chiefly to the purchase of buffalo robes, is of great and national importance, and should and must be encouraged. To such a suggestion I would reply, by merely enquiring, (independently of the poor Indians' disasters,) how much more advantageously would such a capital be employed, both for the weal of the country and for the owners, if it were invested in machines for the manufacture of *woollen robes*, of equal and superior value and beauty; thereby encouraging the growers of wool, and the industrious manufacturer, rather than cultivating a taste for the use of buffalo skins; which is just to be acquired, and then, from necessity, to be dispensed with, when a few years shall have destroyed the last of the animals producing them.

It may be answered, perhaps, that the necessaries of life are given in exchange for these robes; but what, I would ask, are the necessities in Indian life, where they have buffaloes in abundance to live on? The Indian's necessities are entirely artificial—are all created; and when the buffaloes shall have disappeared in his country, which will be within *eight* or *ten* years, I would ask, who is to supply him with the necessaries of life then? and I would ask, further, (and leave the question to be answered ten years hence), when the skin shall have been stripped from the back of the last animal, who is to resist the ravages of 300,000 starving savages; and in their trains, 1,500,000 wolves, whom direst necessity will have driven from their desolate and gameless plains, to seek for the means of subsistence along our exposed frontier? God has everywhere supplied man in a state of Nature, with the necessaries of life, and before we destroy the game of his country, or teach him new desires, he has no wants that are not satisfied.

Amongst the tribes who have been impoverished and repeatedly removed, the necessaries of life are extended with a better grace from the hands of civilized man; 90,000 of such have already been removed, and they draw from Government some 5 or 600,000 dollars annually in cash; *which money passes immediately into the hands of white men*, and for it the necessaries of life *may be* abundantly furnished. But who, I would ask, are to furnish the Indians who have been instructed in this unnatural mode—living upon *such* necessaries, and even luxuries of life, extended to them by the hands of white men, when those annuities are at an end, and the skin is stripped from the last of the animals which God gave them for their subsistence?

Reader, I will stop here, lest you might forget to answer these important queries—these are questions which I know will puzzle the world—and, perhaps it is not right that I should ask them.

Thus much I wrote and painted at this place, whilst on my way up the river: after which I embarked on the steamer for the Yellow Stone, and the sources of the Missouri, through which interesting regions I have made a successful Tour; and have returned, as will have been seen by the foregoing narrations, in my canoe, to this place, from whence I am to descend the river still further in a few days. If I ever get time, I may give further Notes on this place, and of people and their doings, which I met with here; but at present, I throw my note-book, and canvass, and brushes into my canoe, which will be launched to-morrow morning, and on its way towards St. Louis, with myself at the steering-oar, as usual; and with Ba'tiste and Bogard to paddle, of whom, I beg the readers' pardon for having said nothing of late, though they have been my constant companions. Our way is now over the foaming and muddy waters of the Missouri, and amid snags and drift logs (for there is a sweeping freshet on her waters), and many a day will pass before other Letters will come from me; and possibly, the reader may have to look to my biographer for the rest. Adieu.

■ OSBORNE RUSSELL

Born in Maine in 1814, Osborne Russell ran off to sea at the age of sixteen. Growing disgusted with the life of a sailor, he determined to try a new frontier and became a trapper for several trading companies in the Rocky Mountains and the Northwest. Moving on to Oregon and California, he became a judge, cattleman, and merchant before he died in 1892. Russell's memoirs, which were published as Journal of a Trapper *(1921), remain one of the finest accounts of a mountain man's life and of the wilderness he loved. This selection from the journal describes Russell's encounter with the Blackfeet at Yellowstone Lake in 1838.*

From Journal of a Trapper

. . . We were encamped about a half a mile from the Lake on a stream running into it in a S.W. direction thro. a prarie bottom about a quarter of a mile wide On each side of this valley arose a bench of land about 20 ft high running paralell with the stheam and covered with pines On this bench we were encamped on the SE side of the stream The pines immediately behind us was thickly intermingled with logs and fallen trees–After eating a few [minutes] I arose and kindled a fire filled my tobacco pipe and sat down to smoke My comrade whose name was White was still sleeping. Presently I cast my eyes towards the horses which were feeding in the Valley and discovered the heads of some Indians who were gliding round under the bench within 30 steps of me I jumped to my rifle and aroused White and looking towards my powder horn and bullet pouch it was already in the hands of an Indian and we were completely surrounded We cocked our rifles and started thro. their ranks into the woods which seemed to be completely filled with Blackfeet who rent the air with their horrid yells. on presenting our rifles they opened a space about 20 ft. wide thro. which we plunged about the fourth jump an arrow struck White on the right hip joint I hastily told him to pull it out and I spoke another arrow struck me in the same place but they did not retard our progress At length another arrow striking thro. my right leg above the knee benumbed the flesh so that I fell with my breast accross a log. The Indian who shot me was within 8 ft and made a Spring towards me with his uplifted battle axe: I made a leap and avoided the blow and kept hopping from log to log thro. a shower of arrows which flew around us like hail, lodging in the pines and logs. After we had passed them about 10 paces we wheeled about and took [aim] at them They then began to dodge behind the trees and shoot their guns we then ran and hopped about 50 yards further in the logs and bushes and made a stand—I was very faint from the loss of blood and we set down among the logs determined to kill the two foremost when they came up and then die like men we rested our rifles accross a log White aiming at the foremost and Myself at the second I whispered to him that when they turned their eyes toward us to pull trigger. About 20 of them passed by us within 15 feet without casting a glance towards us another file came round on the [opposite] side within 20 or 30 paces closing with the first a few rods beyond us and all turning to the right the next minute were out of our sight among the bushes They were all well armed with fusees, bows & battle axes We sat still until the rustling among the bushes had died away then arose and after looking carefully around us White asked in a whisper how far it was to the lake I replied pointing to the SE about a quarter of a mile. I was nearly fainting from the loss of blood and the want of water We hobbled along 40 or 50 rods and I was obliged to sit down a few minutes then go a little further and rest again. we managed in this way until we reached the bank of the lake Our next object was to obtain some of the water as the bank was very steep and high. White had been perfectly calm and deliberate until now his conversation became wild hurried and despairing he observed "I cannot go down to that water for I am wounded all over I shall die" I told him to sit down while I crawled down and brought some in my hat This I effected with a great deal of difficulty. We then hobbled along the border of the Lake for a mile and a half when it grew dark and we stopped. We could still hear the shouting of the Savages over their booty. We stopped under a large pine near the lake and I told White I could go no further "Oh said he let us go up into the pines and find a spring" I replied there was no spring within a Mile of us which I knew to be a fact. Well said he "if you stop here I shall make a fire" Make as much as you please I replied angrily This is a poor time now to undertake to frighten me into measurs. I then started to the water crawling on my hands and one knee and returned in about an hour with some in my hat. While I was at this he had kindled a small fire and taking a draught of water from the hat he exclaimed Oh dear we shall die here, we shall never get out of these mountains, Well said I if you presist in thinking so you will die but I can crawl from this place upon my hands and one knee and Kill 2 or 3 Elk and make a shelter of the skins dry the meat until we get able to travel. In this manner I persuaded him that we were not in half so bad a Situation as we might be altho. he was not in half so bad a situation as I expected for on examining I found only a slight wound from an arrow on his hip bone but he was not so much to blame as he was a young man who had been brot up in Missouri the pet of the family and had never done or learned much of anything but horseracing and gambling whilst under the care of his parents (if care it can be called). I pulled off an old piece of a coat made of Blanket (as he was entirely without clothing except his hat and shirt) Set myself in a leaning position against a tree ever and anon gathering such leaves and rubbish as I could reach without altering the position of My body to keep up a little fire in this manner miserably spent the night. The next morning Aug 29th I could not arise without assistance When White procured me a couple of sticks for crutches by the help of which I hobbled to a small grove of pines about 60 yds distant. We had scarcely entered the grove when we heard a dog barking and Indians singing and talking. The sound seemed to be approaching us. They at length came near to where we were to the number of 60 Then commenced shooting at a large bank of elk that was swimming in the lake killed 4 of them dragged them to shore and butchered them which occupied about 3 hours. They then packed the meat in small bundles on their backs and travelled up along the rocky shore about a mile and encamped. We then left our hiding place crept into the thick pines about 50 yds distant and started in the direction of our encampment in the hope of finding our comrades My leg was very much swelled and painful but I managed to get along slowly on my crutches by Whites carrying my rifle when we were within about 60 rods of the encampment we discovered the Canadian hunting round among the trees as tho he was looking for a trail we approached him within 30 ft before he saw us and he was so much agitated by fear that he knew not whether to run or stand still. On being asked where Elbridge was he said they came to the Camp the night before at sunset the Indians pursued them into the woods where they seperated and he saw him no more. At the encampment I found a sack of salt–everything else the Indians had carried away or cut to pieces They had built 7 large Conical forts near the spot from which we supposed their number to have been 70 or 80 part of whom had returned to their Village with the horses and plunder. We left the place heaping curses on the head of the Blackfoot nation which neither injured them or alleviated our distress We followed down the shores of the lake and stopped for the night My companions threw some logs and rubbish to gether forming a kind of shelter from the night breeze but in the night it took fire (the logs being pitch pine) the blaze ran to the tops of the trees we removed a short distance built another fire and laid by it until Morning We then made a raft of dry poles and crossed the outlet upon it. We then went to a small grove of pines nearby and made a fire where we stopped the remainder of the day in hopes that Elbridge would see our signals and come to us for we left directions on a tree at the encampment which route we would take. In the meantime the Cannadian went to hunt something to eat but without success. I had bathed my wounds in Salt water and made a salve of Beavers Oil and Castoreum which I applied to them This had eased the pain and drawn out the swelling in a great measure. The next morning I felt very stiff and sore but we were obliged to travel or starve as we had eaten nothing since our defeat and game was very scarce on the West side of the Lake and morover the Cannadian had got such a fright we could not prevail on him to go out of our sight to hunt So on we truged slowly and after getting warm I could bear half my weight on my lame leg but it was bent considerably and swelled so much that my Knee joint was stiff. About 10 oclk the Cannadian killed a couple of small Ducks which served us for breakfast. after eating them we pursued our journey. At 12 oclk it began to rain but we still kept on until the Sun was 2 hours high in the evening when the weather clearing away we encamped at some hot springs and killed a couple of geese. Whilst we were eating them a Deer came swimming along in the lake within about 100 yards of the shore we fired several shots at him but the water glancing the balls he remained unhurt and apparently unalarmed but still Kept swimming to and fro in the Lake in front of us for an hour and then started along up close to the shore. The hunter went to watch it in order to kill it when it should come ashore but as he was lying in wait for the Deer a Doe Elk came to the water to Drink and he killed her but the Deer was still out in the lake swimming to and fro till dark. Now we had plenty of meat and drink but [were] almost destitute of clothing I had on a par of trowsers and a cotton shirt which were completely drenched with the rain. We made a sort of shelter from the wind of pine branches and built a large fire of pitch Knots in front of it, so that we were burning on one side and freezing on the other alternately all night. The next morning we cut some of the Elk meat in thin slices and cooked it slowly over a fire then packed it in bundles strung them on our backs and started by this time I could carry my own rifle and limp along half as fast as a man could walk but when my foot touched against the logs or brush the pain in my leg was very severe We left the lake at the hot springs and travelled thro. the thick pines over a low ridge of land thro. the snow and rain together but we travelled by the wind about 8 Mls in a SW direction when we came to a Lake about 12 Mls in circumference which is the head spring of the right branch of Lewis fork. Here we found a dry spot near a number of hot springs under some thick pines our hunter had Killed a Deer on the way and I took the skin wrapped it around me and felt prouder of my Mantle than a Monarch with his imperial robes. This night I slept more than 4 hours which was more than I had slept at any one time since I was wounded and arose the next morning much refreshed These Springs are similar to those on the Madison and among these as well as those Sulphur is found in its purity in large quantities on the surface of the ground. We travelled along the Shore on the south side about 5 Mls in an East direction fell in with a large band of Elk killed two fat Does and took some of the meat. We then left the lake and travelled due South over a rough broken country covered with thick pines for about 12 Mls when we came to the fork again which ran thro. a narrow prarie bottom followed drown it about six miles and encamped at the forks We had passed up the left hand fork on the 9th of July on horse back in good health and spirits and came down on the right on the 31st of Aug. on foot with weary limbs and sorrowful countenances. We built a fire and laid down to rest, but I could not sleep more than 15 or 20 minutes at a time the night was so very cold. We had plenty of Meat however and made

Mocasins of raw Elk hide The next day we crossed the stream and travelled down near to Jacksons Lake on the West side then took up a small branch in a West direction to the head. We then had the Teton mountain to cross which looked like a laborious undertaking as it was steep and the top covered with snow. We arrived at the summit however with a great deal of difficulty before sunset and after resting a few moments travelled down about a mile on the other side and stopped for the night. After spending another cold and tedious night we were descending the Mountain thro. the pines at day light and the next night reached the forks of Henrys fork of Snake river. This day was very warm but the wind blew cold at night we made a fire and gathered some dry grass to sleep on and then sat down and eat the remainder of our provisions. It was now 90 Mls to Fort Hall.

ARAPOOISH, CHIEF OF THE CROWS

Arapooish was a Crow chief whose love for his homeland in the Yellowstone, Powder River, and Wind River country of Montana and Wyoming is expressed in this vivid statement made to fur-trader Robert Campbell. The interview was reported by Lieutenant James Bradley in Volume 9 of the Contributions to the Historical Society of Montana *(1923) and is reprinted in Joseph Kinsey Howard's* Montana Margins *(1946).*

My Country

as told to Robert Campbell

The Crow country is a good country. The Great Spirit has put it exactly in the right place; while you are in it you fare well; whenever you go out of it, whichever way you travel, you fare worse. If you go to the south, you have to wander over great barren plains; the water is warm and bad and you meet with fever and ague. To the north it is cold; the winters are long and bitter and there is no grass; you can not keep horses there but must travel with dogs. What is a country without horses?

On the Columbia they are poor and dirty, paddle about in canoes and eat fish. Their teeth are worn out; they are always taking fish bones out of their mouths; fish is poor food.

To the east they dwell in villages; they live well, but they drink the muddy waters of the Missouri—that is bad. A Crow's dog would not drink such water.

About the forks of the Missouri is a fine country; good water, good grass, plenty of buffalo. In summer it is almost as good as Crow country, but in winter it is cold; the grass is gone and there is no salt weed for the horses.

The Crow country is exactly in the right place. It has snowy mountains and sunny plains, all kinds of climates and good things for every season. When the summer heats scorch the prairies, you can draw up under the mountains, where the air is sweet and cool, the grass fresh, and the bright streams come tumbling out of the snowbanks. There you can hunt the elk, the deer and the antelope when their skins are fit for dressing; there you will find plenty of white bears [grizzlies] and mountain sheep.

In the autumn when your horses are fat and strong from the mountain pastures you can go down into the plains and hunt the buffalo, or trap beaver on the streams. And when winter comes on, you can take shelter in the woody bottoms along the rivers; there you will find buffalo meat for yourselves and cottonwood bark for your horses, or you may winter in the Wind River valley, where there is salt weed in abundance.

The Crow country is exactly in the right place. Everything good is to be found there.

There is no country like the Crow country.

■ JOHN JAMES AUDUBON

John James Audubon was born in Haiti in 1785. His sea-captain father sent him to France to be raised and educated, and in 1803 he was sent to America to avoid Napoleon's draft. Young Audubon studied and painted birds along the Mississippi frontier from Cincinnati to New Orleans, but he could not find backing to explore the Far West until his last expedition in 1843, up the Missouri from St. Louis to Fort Union. Audubon's visual record of wildlife on the Upper Missouri may be found in The Viviparous Quadrupeds of North America, *which his son, John Woodhouse Audubon, completed in 1848. Audubon died at his New York estate in 1851. His "Missouri River Journals" were printed in* Audubon and His Journals *(1877), edited by his daughter, Maria R. Audubon.*

From The Missouri River Journals, 1843

May 17, Wednesday . . . We have seen floating eight Buffaloes, one Antelope, and one Deer; how great the destruction of these animals must be during high freshets! The cause of their being drowned in such extraordinary numbers might not astonish one acquainted with the habits of these animals, but to one who is not, it may be well enough for me to describe it. Some few hundred miles above us, the river becomes confined between high bluffs or cliffs, many of which are nearly perpendicular, and therefore extremely difficult to ascend. When the Buffaloes have leaped or tumbled down from either side of the stream, they swim with ease across, but on reaching these walls, as it were, the poor animals try in vain to climb them, and becoming exhausted by falling back some dozens of times, give up the ghost, and float down the turbid stream; their bodies have been known to pass, swollen and putrid, the city of St. Louis. The most extraordinary part of the history of these drowned Buffaloes is, that the different tribes of Indians on the shores, are ever on the lookout for them, and no matter how putrid their flesh may be, provided the hump proves at all fat, they swim to them, drag them on shore, and cut them to pieces; after which they cook and eat this loathsome and abominable flesh, even to the marrow found in the bones. In some instances this has been done when the whole of the hair had fallen off, from the rottenness of the Buffalo. Ah! Mr. Catlin, I am now sorry to see and to read your accounts of the Indians *you* saw—how very different they must have been from any that I have seen! Whilst we were on the top of the high hills which we climbed this morning, and looked towards the valley beneath us, including the river, we were undetermined as to whether we saw as much land dry as land overflowed; the immense flat prairie on the east side of the river looked not unlike a lake of great expanse, and immediately beneath us the last freshet had left upwards of perhaps two or three hundred acres covered by water, with numbers of water fowl on it, but so difficult of access as to render our wishes to kill Ducks quite out of the question. From the tops of the hills we saw only a continual succession of other lakes, of the same form and nature; and although the soil was of a fair, or even good, quality, the grass grew in tufts, separated from each other, and as it grows green in one spot, it dies and turns brown in another. We saw here no "carpeted prairies," no "velvety distant landscape"; and if these things are to be seen, why, the sooner we reach them the better. . . .

May 23, Tuesday The wind blew from the south this morning and rather stiffly. We rose early, and walked about this famous Cedar Island, where we stopped to cut large red cedars [*Juniperus virginianus*] for one and a half hours; we started at half-past five, breakfasted rather before six, and were on the lookout for our hunters.

Hunters! Only two of them had ever been on a Buffalo hunt before. One was lost almost in sight of the river. They only walked two or three miles, and camped. Poor Squires' first experience was a very rough one; for, although they made a good fire at first, it never was tended afterwards, and his pillow was formed of a buck's horn accidentally picked up near the place. Our Sioux Indian helped himself to another, and they all felt chilly and damp. They had forgotten to take any spirits with them, and their condition was miserable. As the orb of day rose as red as blood, the party started, each taking a different direction. But the wind was unfavorable; it blew up, not down the river, and the Buffaloes, Wolves, Antelopes, and indeed every animal possessed of the sense of smell, had scent of them in time to avoid them. There happened however to be attached to this party two good and true men, that may be called hunters. One was Michaux; the other a friend of his, whose name I do not know. It happened, by hook or by crook, that these two managed to kill four Buffaloes; but one of them was drowned, as it took to the river after being shot. Only a few pieces from a young bull, and its tongue, were brought on board, most of the men being too lazy, or too far off, to cut out even the tongues of the others; and thus it is that thousands multiplied by thousands of Buffaloes are murdered in senseless play, and their enormous carcasses are suffered to be the prey of the Wolf, the Raven and the Buzzard. . . .

June 7, Wednesday . . . We reached Fort Clark and the Mandan Villages at half-past seven this morning. Great guns were fired from the fort and from the "Omega," as our captain took the guns from the "Trapper" at Fort Pierre. The site of this fort appears a good one, though it is placed considerably below the Mandan Village. We saw some small spots cultivated, where corn, pumpkins, and beans are grown. The fort and village are situated on the high bank, rising somewhat to the elevation of a hill. The Mandan mud huts are very far from looking poetical, although Mr. Catlin has tried to render them so by placing them in regular rows, and all of the same size and form, which is by no means the case. But different travellers have different eyes! We saw more Indians than at any previous time since leaving St. Louis; and it is possible that there are a hundred huts, made of mud, all looking like so many potato winter-houses in the Eastern States. As soon as we were near the shore, every article that could conveniently be carried off was placed under lock and key, and our division door was made fast, as well as those of our own rooms.

Even the axes and poles were put by. Our captain told us that last year they stole his cap and his shot-pouch and horn, and that it was through the interference of the first chief that he recovered his cap and horn; but that a squaw had his leather belt, and would not give it up. The appearance of these poor, miserable devils, as we approached the shore, was wretched enough. There they stood in the pelting rain and keen wind, covered with Buffalo robes, red blankets, and the like, some partially and most curiously besmeared with mud; and as they came on board, and we shook hands with each of them, I felt a clamminess that rendered the ceremony most repulsive. Their legs and naked feet were covered with mud. They looked at me with apparent curiosity, perhaps on account of my beard, which produced the same effect at Fort Pierre. They all looked very poor; and our captain says they are the *ne plus ultra* of thieves. It is said there are nearly three thousand men, women, and children that, during winter, cram themselves into these miserable hovels. . . .

After this, Mr. Chardon asked one of the Indians to take us into the village, and particularly to show us the "Medicine Lodge." We followed our guide through mud and mire, even into the Lodge. We found this to be, in general terms, like all the other lodges, only larger, measuring twenty-three yards in diameter, with a large squarish aperture in the centre of the roof, some six or seven feet long by about four wide. We had entered this curiosity shop by pushing aside a wet Elk skin stretched on four sticks. Looking around, I saw a number of calabashes, eight or ten Otter skulls, two very large Buffalo skulls with the horns on, evidently of great age, and some sticks and other magical implements with which none but a "Great Medicine Man" is acquainted. During my survey there sat, crouched down on his haunches, an Indian wrapped in a dirty blanket, with only his filthy head peeping out. Our guide spoke to him; but he stirred not. Again, at the foot of one of the posts that support the central portion of this great room, lay a parcel that I took for a bundle of Buffalo robes; but it moved presently, and from beneath it half arose the emaciated body of a poor blind Indian, whose skin was quite shrivelled; and our guide made us signs that he was about to die. We all shook both hands with him; and he pressed our hands closely and with evident satisfaction. He had his pipe and tobacco pouch by him, and soon lay down again. We left this abode of mysteries, as I was anxious to see the interior of one of the common huts around; and again our guide led us through mud and mire to his own lodge, which we entered in the same way as we had done the other. All these lodges have a sort of portico that leads to the door, and on the tops of most of them I observed Buffalo skulls. This lodge contained the whole family of our guide—several women and children, and another man, perhaps a son-in-law or a brother. All these, except the man, were on the outer edge of the lodge, crouching on the ground, some suckling children; and at nearly equal distances apart were placed berths, raised about two feet above the ground, made of leather, and with square apertures for the sleepers or occupants to enter. The man of whom I have spoken was lying down in one of these, which was all open in front. I walked up to him, and, after disturbing his happy slumbers, shook hands with him; he made signs for me to sit down; and after Harris and I had done so, he rose, squatted himself near us, and, getting out a large spoon made of boiled Buffalo horn, handed it to a young girl, who brought a great rounded wooden bowl filled with pemmican, mixed with corn and some other stuff. I ate a mouthful or so of it, and found it quite palatable; and Harris and the rest then ate of it also. Bell was absent; we had seen nothing of him since we left the boat. This lodge, as well as the other, was dirty with water and mud; but I am told that in dry weather they are kept cleaner, and much cleaning do they need, most truly. A round, shallow hole was dug in the centre for the fire; and from the roof descended over this a chain, by the aid of which they do their cooking, the utensil being attached to the chain when wanted. . . .

After dinner we went up the muddy bank again to look at the corn-fields, as the small patches that are meanly cultivated are called. We found poor, sickly looking corn about two inches high, that had been represented to us this morning as full six inches high. We followed the prairie, a very extensive one, to the hills, and there found a deep ravine, sufficiently impregnated with saline matter to answer the purpose of salt water for the Indians to boil their corn and pemmican, clear and clean; but they, as well as the whites at the fort, resort to the muddy Missouri for their drinking water, the only fresh water at hand. Not a drop of spirituous liquor has been brought to this place for the last two years; and there can be no doubt that on this account the Indians have become more peaceable than heretofore, though now and then a white man is murdered, and many horses are stolen. As we walked over the plain, we saw heaps of earth thrown up to cover the poor Mandans who died of the small-pox. These mounds in many instances appear to contain the remains of several bodies and, perched on the top, lies, pretty generally, the rotting skull of a Buffalo. Indeed, the skulls of the Buffaloes seem as if a kind of relation to these most absurdly superstitious and ignorant beings. . . .

June 11, Sunday. This day has been tolerably fine, though windy. We have seen an abundance of game, a great number of Elks, common Virginian Deer, Mountain Rams in two places, and a fine flock of Sharp-tailed Grouse, that, when they flew off from the ground near us, looked very much like large Meadow Larks. They were on a prairie bordering a large patch of Artemisia, which in the distance presents the appearance of acres of cabbages. We have seen many Wolves and some Buffaloes. One young bull stood on the brink of a bluff, looking at the boat steadfastly for full five minutes; and as we neared the spot, he waved his tail, and moved off briskly. On another occasion, a young bull that had just landed at the foot of a very steep bluff was slaughtered without difficulty; two shots were fired at it, and the poor thing was killed by a rifle bullet. I was sorry, for we did not stop for it, and its happy life was needlessly ended. I saw near that spot a large Hawk, and also a very small Tamias, or Ground Squirrel. Harris saw a Spermophile, of what species none of us could tell. We have seen many Elks swimming the river, and they look almost the size of a well-grown mule. They stared at us, were fired at, at an enormous distance, it is true, and yet stood still. These animals are abundant beyond belief hereabouts. We have seen much remarkably handsome scenery, but nothing at all comparing with Catlin's descriptions; his book must, after all, be altogether a humbug. Poor devil! I pity him from the bottom of my soul; had he studied, and kept up to the old French proverb that says, "Bon renommé vaut mieux que ceinture doré," he might have become an "honest man"—the quintessence of God's works. . . .

July 21, Friday. We were up at sunrise, and had our coffee, after which Lafleur a mulatto, Harris, and Bell went off after Antelopes, for we cared no more about bulls; where the cows are, we cannot tell. Cows run faster than bulls, yearlings faster than cows, and calves faster than any of these. Squires felt sore, and his side was very black, so we took our guns and went after Black-breasted Lark Buntings, of which we saw many, but could not near them. I found a nest of them, however, with five eggs. The nest is planted in the ground, deep enough to sink the edges of it. It is formed of dried fine grasses and roots, without any lining of hair or wool. By and by we saw Harris sitting on a high hill about one mile off, and joined him; he said the bulls they had killed last evening were close by, and I offered to go and see the bones, for I expected that the Wolves had devoured it during the night. We travelled on, and Squires returned to the camp. After about two miles of walking against a delightful strong breeze, we reached the animals; Ravens or Buzzards had worked at the eyes, but only one Wolf, apparently, had been there. They were bloated, and smelt quite unpleasant. We returned to the camp and saw a Wolf cross our path, and an Antelope looking at us. We determined to stop and try to bring him to us; I lay on my back and threw my legs up, kicking first one and then the other foot, and sure enough the Antelope walked towards us, slowly and carefully, however. In about twenty minutes he had come two or three hundred yards; he was a superb male, and I looked at him for some minutes; when about sixty yards off I could see his eyes, and being loaded with buck-shot pulled the trigger without rising from my awkward position. Off he went; Harris fired, but he only ran the faster for some hundred yards, when he turned, looked at us again, and was off. When we reached camp we found Bell there; he had shot three times at Antelopes without killing; Lafleur had also returned, and had broken the foreleg of one, but an Antelope can run fast enough with three legs, and he saw no more of it. We now broke camp, arranged the horses and turned our heads towards the Missouri, and in four and three-quarter hours reached the landing. On entering the wood we again broke branches of service-berries, and carried a great quantity over the river. I much enjoyed the trip; we had our supper, and soon to bed in our hot room, where Sprague says the thermometer has been at 99° most of the day. I noticed it was warm when walking. I must not forget to notice some things which happened on our return. First, as we came near Fox River, we thought of the horns of our bulls, and Mr. Culbertson, who knows the country like a book, drove us first to Bell's, who knocked the horns off, then to Harris's, which was served in the same manner; this bull had been eaten entirely except the head, and a good portion of mine had been devoured also; it lay immediately under "Audubon's Bluff" (the name Mr. Culbertson gave the ridge on which I stood to see the chase), and we could see it when nearly a mile distant. Bell's horns were the handsomest and largest, mine next best, and Harris's the smallest, but we are all contented. Mr. Culbertson tells me that Harris and Bell have done wonders, for persons who have never shot at Buffaloes from on horseback. Harris had a fall too, during his second chase, and was bruised in the manner of Squires, but not so badly. I have but little doubt that Squires killed his bull, as he says he shot it three times, and Mr. Culbertson's must have died also. What a terrible destruction of life, as it were for nothing, or next to it, as the tongues only were brought in, and the flesh of these fine animals was left to beasts and birds of prey, or to rot on the spots where they fell. The prairies are literally *covered* with the skulls of the victims, and the roads the Buffalo make in crossing the prairies have all the appearance of heavy wagon tracks. . . .

August 4, Friday. . . . We saw, after we had travelled ten miles, some Buffalo bulls; some alone, others in groups of four or five, a few Antelopes, but more shy than ever before. I was surprised to see how careless the bulls were of us, as some actually gave us chances to approach them within a hundred yards, looking steadfastly, as if not caring a bit for us. At last we saw one lying down immediately in our road, and determined to give him a chance for his life. Mr. C. had a white horse, a runaway, in which he placed a good deal of confidence; he mounted it, and we looked after him. The bull did not start till Mr C. was within a hundred yards, and then at a gentle and slow gallop. The horse galloped too, but only at the same rate. Mr. C. thrashed him until his hands were sore, for he had no whip, the bull went off without even a shot being fired, and the horse is now looked upon as forever disgraced. . . .

August 5, Saturday. . . . The white horse, which had gone out as a *hunter*, returned as a *pack-horse*, loaded with the entire flesh of a Buffalo cow; and our two mules drew three more and the heads of all four. This morning at daylight, when we were called to drink our coffee, there was a Buffalo feeding within twenty steps of our tent, and it moved slowly towards the hills as we busied ourselves making preparations for our departure. We reached the fort at noon; Squires, Provost, and LaFleur had returned; they had wounded a Bighorn, but had lost it. Owen and Bell returned this afternoon; they had seen no Cocks of the plains, but brought the skin of a female Elk, a Porcupine, and a young White-headed Eagle. Provost tells me that Buffaloes become so very poor during hard winters, when the snows cover the ground to the depth of two or three feet, that they lose their hair, become covered with scabs, on which the Magpies feed, and the poor beasts die by hundreds. One can hardly conceive how it happens, notwithstanding these many deaths and the immense numbers that are murdered almost daily on these boundless wastes called prairies, besides the hosts that are drowned in the freshets, and the hundreds of young calves who die in early spring, so many are yet to be found. Daily we see so many that we hardly notice them more than the cattle in our pastures about our homes. But this cannot last; even now there is a perceptible difference in the size of the herds, and before many years the Buffalo, like the Great Auk, will have disappeared; surely this should not be permitted. Bell has been relating his adventures, our boat is going on, and I wish I had a couple of Bighorns. God bless you all.

■ EDWARD HARRIS

Edward Harris was a wealthy farmer, horse breeder, and amateur naturalist from New Jersey. As John James Audubon's good friend and patron, he accompanied the naturalist on his trip up the Missouri to Fort Union in 1843. These selections are from the journal that Harris kept of that trip, which was published as Up the Missouri with Audubon *(1938).*

From Up the Missouri with Audubon

Excerpts from The Journal: June 1843

Wednesday, June 14th . . . In the afternoon it was proposed that Mr. Culbertson and some of his most expert hunters should show us how wolves were run down on horseback. There was no difficulty in finding the game as they were always to be seen prowling about within a mile of the Fort. It was not long before Mr. Wolf made his appearance—the horses were sent for (to the Prarie) and were soon ready for the chase. Mr. Culbertson got the start and started his beautiful Blackfoot Pied mare at full speed, when within a half mile of the wolf, who turned and galloped off leisurely until Mr. C. was within two or three hundred yards of him when he started off at the top of his speed, at this moment Mr. C. fired his gun to show us his dexterity in reloading while his horse was at full speed. The interest in the chase now became highly exciting but unfortunately the beast took for the rising ground and both wolf and pursuer were lost sight of over a small hill. In a very short time we saw Mr. C. returning at full speed and we soon perceived he was holding the wolf on the horse in front of the saddle. As he came nearer the Fort he practiced a maneuvre which is common among the Indians and hunters which we had not seen before, that of guiding the horse while at full speed by the inclination of the body, the reins being thrown upon the neck, as they necessarily were during the chase for the convenience of loading and firing–it was well done and had a fine effect as he leaned over to one side the mare performed a gentle curve in that direction when he would suddenly shift his body to the other side and the well-trained animal swayed over in the required direction, thus making for the last half mile in a serpentine track. This beautiful exhibition was performed in almost as short a time as I have taken to relate it, the distance rode was about 3 miles and we all regretted that we had not thought of taking the time. The wolf was shot through the lungs and shoulders (both of which were broken) from the horse while both were at full speed, he had two bullets in the gun and both passed through him. The performance of the mare must not be forgotten, and has given us a more favourable impression of the Indian horses than we had before entertained, instead of exhibiting signs of distress we had looked for, the noble little animal did not draw a long breath, and the motion of her nostrils was scarcely quicker than when she started–in a few minutes she was turned out on the prarie to graze with the rest of the horses. I look upon the performance of the horse as excellent when it is considered that she had never eaten a mouthful of grain in her life, but it is said that this is nothing to what she performs in a day's hunt. In the course of the afternoon chase was given to another wolf, but as he took across the hills at a very unfavourable place covered with rocks and stones the hunters did not think it worth while to continue the chase. In returning to the Fort, they gave us an exhibition of loading and firing as they do in Buffalo hunting, frequently killing five and six Buffaloes with a common single barreled flint gun without drawing a rein on their horse. They generally put five or six bullets in their mouth, and when they fire they pour a charge of powder into the left hand from the powder horn which hangs over the right shoulder, throw it into the barrel, which is hastily struck on the saddle to shake down the powder so as to pass into the pan to prime it, then throw in a bullet wet with saliva of the mouth which causes it to adhere to the powder and prevents it falling out when the muzzle is depressed to fire. In this manner these gentlemen fired from 12 to 14 times each in riding about a mile, but without ball. It will be readily seen that a percussion gun cannot be fired with the same facility on account of the inconvenience of putting on the caps. We retired early but had not been long in bed before we were called to attend a ball, we would willingly have been excused but as our host was one of the musicians and took a lively interest in the fun, and moreover it was in the apartment adjoining our room precluding the possibility of sleeping, we all got up to see the fun and admire the Indian ladies of the Fort as they stepped it off to Mr. Culbertson's violin, Mr. Denny's clarionet, and Chardon's drum. It was kept up until one o'clock of the morning when we most willingly returned to our beds. . . .

Wednesday June 21st. . . . Mr. Chardon gave us yesterday a highly interesting but appalling description of the ravages of the Small-pox in 1837 among the Mandans and Ricarees, he was at that time in command of Fort Clark. He says it was brought up by the steamboat Assineboin belonging to the Company, and that the Indians were informed of it and warned not to have any intercourse with the boat, but that a chief came on board and sat a long time along side of one of the men who had just recovered from the disease, and when he went away stole the man's blanket. When Mr. C. ascertained the fact he sent around the village to try to recover the blanket, offering a new one in its place, but the thief being a chief he considered it too great a stigma on his character to be exposed in such an act and as might be expected he was the first victim and in a very short time it began to spread in the village. The men of the nation at this time were principally away in the praries on a hunting or war party. Mr. C. sent a runner urging them to remain where they were if they valued their lives, but they insisted in spite of all remonstrances in coming home to their crop of corn. The disorder now began to spread at a frightful rate and a suspicion arose among the Mandans that it had been introduced by the traders with the intention of killing them off, particularly as the Ricarees who were living with them, mixed up in the same lodges were not yet attacked. Some of the young men attempted to take Mr. C.'s life and the whites were obliged to shut themselves up in the fort. One day Mr. C. and several others ventured to sit out at the entrance of the Fort when a young Mandan advanced and shot the man who was sitting next to Mr. Chardon, dead on the spot. The Indian ran towards the graves of his people and was pursued and overtaken by the whites, he begged them not to kill him until he reached the grave where all his relatives had gone before him, he was spared until he walked to a mound which he mounted and was immediately dispatched. Mr. C. related a singular story of a Dove pursued by a Hawk which flew in at his windows one day when he was seated with several chiefs of the Mandans and Ricarees, the whole party in a melancholy mood brooding over the calamitous situation, the Dove sat still on the table for a minute or more and flew away. One of the Chiefs asked Mr. C. what the bird had said to him. Knowing the superstition of the Indians he instantly conceived the idea of making capital out of the circumstance. He told them it informed him that he had been sent by his great Father down the river who saw his situation and knew that there was some bad young men among the Mandans who sought his life and were using all their art to persuade the people that he was acting treacherously with the Mandans and was in league with the Ricarees to kill off the Mandans, and to assure the latter it was all a lie, and offering his protection against all his enemies. The chiefs all got up and shook hands with him, and expressed themselves satisfied with his good intentions towards them all. He related several instances of self destruction by the Indians after they were attacked by the loathsome disorder, and of some who killed themselves without being attacked particularly one poor fellow who had lost his only child a beautiful boy on whom he doted, as soon as the child was buried he told his squaw that he had always been a good husband to her, that he had not like most of his people took a wife for a short time and then when tired of her cast her off, that he had always been faithful to her and never took another wife, that now they had lost the joy of their life, the bad medicine of the whites was destroying all their people, they had no longer anything worth living for, and begged her to let him shoot her and then he would destroy himself. She consented at once, he took up his gun and shot her and then drawing a knife he gashed himself across the vitals and was soon dead by her side–Another story of two young men who were sitting in the Fort entirely untouched by the disorder, talking of the horrors of their situation and the dreadful death they were certain of meeting. At length they came to the conclusion to destroy themselves and commenced a violent dispute as to the best mode of accomplishing the end, one recommended a mode sometimes practiced among them of placing an arrow at the bottom of the throat and forcing it down with both hands into the lungs, the other insisted that the knife was the best weapon for the purpose, the dispute ran quite high between them at last the one that had recommended the knife told the other to try his method and he would see how he liked it, the words were hardly spoken before the arrow was forced into his head and he was a corpse, the other instantly drew his knife and gashed himself to death. It was some weeks before the Ricarees were attacked and the Mandans were nearly all dead before the men in the Fort caught the disorder, not one escaped an attack, though most of them had been vaccinated, but only 3 or 4 died. His account of the horrors were truly thrilling and such as only could have been given by a witness.

Thurs July 20th . . . About 12 o'clock we reached the valley of Fox River which runs into the Yellowstone, it is a small stream in wet weather, but has no running water at this time. We were just about crossing it when Mr. Culbertson looked back and saw 4 Buffalo Bulls, quietly grazing at the distance of about a mile and which had previously been hid from our view by a rise in the Prarie. We quickly saddled our hunters and arranged our dress and accoutrements for the chace and started with the whole of our equipage in a direct line for the herd covered by a small eminence behind which we left the carriages with Mr. Audubon so that he could ascend the mound and have a fine view of the chace while we filed off to the right, keeping out of sight behind the hill so as to come upon them in such a way as to force them to run in the fine level valley of Fox River, thereby ensuring a fine run and at the same time give Mr. Audubon a good view of the chace. Our approach was a good one and as there was a bull apiece for us we agreed to stick to the bull of our choice without interfering with that of our neighbor. As soon as they commenced to run Mr. C. gave the word for us to start which we all did at full run, the bulls soon separated, two were followed by Mr. C. & Bell and Squires and I took those which went to the right. Knowing that Squires had the fastest horse I waited for him to choose, he fired into his bull and I crossed his track after the other, just as I was passing him his horse had come up with the Bull who turned him, and instead of turning off gradually to the right as he (the horse) should have done (the hunters always ride to the right of the Buffalo) he stopped suddenly and wheeled to the left behind the Bull, this movement being unexpected to Squires he lost his seat and fell to the ground, the bull proceeding without attacking either horse or rider, I checked my horse long enough to ascertain that Squires was not disabled (for he was on his feet in a moment and in pursuit of his horse) and pushed on after my game, which I soon overtook and fired striking him in the middle of the thigh, a few strides more brought me directly opposite him and I shot him in the lungs just behind the shoulder. I rode along side of him reloading my gun, which I had just accomplished when I saw blood gushing in a stream from his mouth and nostrils in such a way that I knew he must soon fall, I therefore turned away and galloped after Squire's horse which I caught and brought back to him. On looking around I saw that my Bull was down. Squires soon mounted and as his Bull had stopped a short distance to look after his companions, he and I started in pursuit, determined if possible to avenge the mishap of poor Squires. We had not proceeded far before Squires discovered that the muzzle of his gun had become stopped with earth in his fall. I exchanged with him, one of my barrels being loaded and on we pushed, on approaching him Squires fired and struck him behind so as not sensibly to arrest his progress, we pushed on again at a rapid pace, but through some difficulty in loading he did not get another shot and from the effects of his fall he felt so much overcome as to be unable to proceed any further and turned back and I took the gun to make another effort to secure the long winded monster who had now led us a long chace. The Bull soon came to a steep clay bank which he stumbled down for about 15 feet, I was fortunately far enough off to check the speed of my horse and walk him down it. This prolonged my chace but at last I came up with him. As I raised myself in my stirrups, leaning a little towards the Bull, and was on the point of pulling the trigger the Bull made a rush at my horse, I was so eager in the pursuit as to have forgotten all the cautions which had been given me on this head and as my horse wheeled off to the right I lost my balance and came to the ground between him and the Bull, I was on my feet in an instant, and as the Bull paused to consider whether he should put his threat into execution I levelled and snapped both barrels at him, broadside to me, at the distance of about 20 feet and the Bull pursued his way. On examining my Gun I found that in falling, the heads of the cocks which cover the caps had become filled with earth, which prevented the caps from exploding. I caught my horse but found myself so completely out of breath with my long chace and my fall that I gave up the chace and slowly wended my way back to the spot where I left my Bull and which I found to be between three and four miles, happy to find that I was not much bruised and had escaped the horns of a vicious old Buffalo Bull, and purchased besides another good lesson in running Buffalo. When I got back I found that Mr. Culbertson & Bell had each killed their Bulls and I was happy to find that Mr. Audubon had had a splendid view of the whole chase. . . .

■ NICOLAS POINT, S. J.

Father Nicolas Point, S.J., was born in France in 1799. In 1841, he accompanied Father Pierre-Jean DeSmet to the Upper Missouri River country and then westward to the land of the Flatheads in the Bitterroot Valley, where they founded the St. Mary's Mission. In 1845, Point went to visit the Blackfeet in northern Montana, but the church soon called him back to Quebec, Canada, where he went against his wishes. Point died in Quebec in 1868. This selection is from his illustrated journal of the return voyage, "A Journey on a Barge Down the Missouri from the Fort of the Blackfeet to That of the Assiniboines: Particulars Edifying or Curious," reprinted in Joseph P. Donnelly's Wilderness Kingdom *(1967).*

A Journey on a Barge Down the Missouri

On the twenty-first, about eight o'clock in the morning, we bid adieu to Fort Clay and in a very short time were floating by the auxiliary fort, called Fort Campbell. Those acting in the place of the absent captain saluted our passing with a few rifle shots which we acknowledged by waving our hats. Then we plunged into a solitude so profound that soon we saw only wild animals. But they were in such variety and abundance that our descent had for us perhaps more attraction than the most beautiful promenade civilization could have offered. Within a few hours we saw wolves, antelopes, deer, bighorns, buffalo, bear, eagles, gulls, bustards. As for the denizens of the water, we saw no samples of them until in the evening. Then we saw a catfish, that is, a fish whose three feelers of different lengths on each side of its head give it the appearance of a person with a mustache. By reason of its fine meat it is called a "Missouri salmon." The delicacy of the meat is proportionate to its size and bulk (which sometimes is such that the eyes are eighteen inches apart), and to the depth of the waters it inhabits. . . .

The situation of man gliding over a beautiful river in a boat always has something magical about it, in that the country traversed seems to be moving by on either side. But on certain parts of the Missouri the charm is increased by reason of the real or fictitious beauty displayed on its shores. By fictitious beauty I mean the great landslides created by the depth of its bed, the adjacent land, and the subsiding of its high water. When seen close by they are, it is true, only hideous ravines, obscure holes, hanging ruins or trunks of uprooted trees–in a word, the picture of desolation. But from ever so short a distance these huge masses seem to assume gracious shapes. Colors are blended, the disparate objects melt together, and sometimes effects are produced which it would be impossible to see without shuddering, or being pleased, or lost in admiration, according to the nature of the beings that [seem to] appear, are transformed, and soon vanish. This is a sensible image of the illusions of this world.

On May 22, these scenes were anything but uniform. But it is perhaps to this variety that the traveler owes his best impressions. Yesterday their yellowish tint bordering on [black] and the too great proximity of their forms gave them an atmosphere [depressing] to the heart. Today the widening banks of the river permit our gaze to embrace a vast horizon, a more gentle verdure, fresher groves, waters nearer to their source, white mountains shaded in rose, and a great open space which lends some of its blue to the over-somber or over-vivid colors of this vast tableau. All this produces in the soul a joyful effect.

The contrast is the more striking because the dreary aspects, of which I have already spoken, were augmented by a still sadder sight–that of civilization fallen into ruin. I am referring to Fort Mackenzie built by order of Mr. Mackenzie under the direction of Mr. [Kipp], and called Fort Piegan in honor of the Indians of this nation who were the first to form an alliance with them. This was a mark of deference, doing honor no less to the Piegans than to the modesty of the founder. This fort was burned by men who apparently did not know that his intentions were benevolent. Mr. Mackenzie had another one constructed a little higher up [the river]. This one, which received the name the first one should have borne [*i.e.*, Mackenzie], prospered until 1844, when reasons of prudence dictated its transference. Apparently the vicinity of the Judith River, together with the beauty of its environs, overly tempted the persons charged with providing for it. For experience showed that these advantages, and others thought to be available there, did not compensate for the grave inconvenience of being an easy prey to their enemies. The fort, leveled only a year after its construction, was transplanted farther up the river. This was the beginning of Fort Lewis, about which I spoke earlier. But this fort, after having a long career, was soon joined to Fort Clay, then under construction. To omit nothing that ought be included in the present article, I should place between Fort Piegan and Fort Clay the additional fort of 1844 (of the Fox and Livingston Company), which lasted only one spring.

What is to be said of the thousand and one army forts scattered along the banks of the Missouri? They are almost as plentiful as the grass in the fields, but do not last as long, for more often than not rebels destroy what has been built. Thus, in this region, more than anywhere else, in spite of prudence, skill, and long experience, of which qualities there was no lack, there was no permanent dwelling. Fort Mackenzie, which lasted for only twelve years, is cited as a rare example of longevity. But let us honor its ashes, for it was to commerce what Fort Lewis has been to religion.

To give continuity to this journal, I have had to omit the events of the day, ancient history, and some of the monuments which merit attention. I wish to speak of what is called here the Citadel, Pierced Rock, and the Steamboat, which are to the Missouri what the *Maison* and the *Cheminée* are to the Platte, with the difference that the Citadel, instead of being a composition of pure sandstone, is composed of fragments of rock which appear to be the product of some volcanic disturbance. As for the Steamboat, which a missionary would rather call *la Cathedrale*, and Pierced Rock, remarkable only for the hole which pierces it through and through, they, like the odd formations along the Platte, owe their formation to erosion by wind and rain. But there is this difference: sandstone is more durable and, by adding antique tint to picturesque form and the impression of greater durability, presents a more venerable aspect.

Here are the events of the day. Almost under the walls of the fort, a bear was killed by Mr. Culbertson just as it was rearing to attack. There was Louis' hat to be had by anyone caring to go for a swim at the foot of Pierced Rock and its owner wailing, "My poor hat; there it goes up the river!" These are perhaps somewhat inappropriate subjects for the sketching pencil of a missionary. Finally, there was a passably comic Indian story, here given in the style of the day and the country!

"One day when it was raining rather hard a Piegan sought shelter in a cave that went deep into the earth. Hardly had he entered when a Snake entered, too. It was not an animal, this snake, but a human just like us; it was a member of a tribe that goes by that name. But the tribe was not on friendly terms with the Piegans. In a moment the Piegan saw him coming, and you may well imagine how little he was enjoying himself. What was he to do? 'Ah! Comrade!' he said to the Snake. The Snake did not see him. He stopped short and strained his eyes. He had to see! 'Ah, yes! Comrade!' said the Snake. 'You see very well that it is not good for you here,' said the Piegan. 'Go away.' 'I will not go away,' said the Snake. 'I am not so stupid; if I turn around you will kill me.' 'I kill you?' said the Piegan. 'Nothing is further from my thought. But if you are afraid to turn your back on me . . . I didn't tell you to turn around. I told you to go away. You can back up.' 'Ah! That's different,' said the Snake, only too happy to get out of this devil of a hole. Then he went back, back, back, just like a crab, until–oops!–he came to the end, and there he was outside. And the Piegan came out, too, for he was not so stupid, either, as to remain in there. When they were both out, the Piegan again said to the Snake, 'My comrade.' Now there was nothing to keep the Snake from going. 'Go away,' said the Piegan. 'No, you go away,' said the Snake. 'No, you go. . . .' 'No, you go. . . .' They stood there for a long time telling each other to go away. Neither one wished to follow the command of the other. 'Well,' said the Piegan at length, 'I can think of only one thing to tell you, but it is good. If we do not wish to take leave of each other in the ordinary manner, we can do it in another way.' 'How?' asked the Snake. 'Just like we did a short time ago, only better. You backed up, but I didn't because there was no way for me to do so. This time both of us can back up. And then, when we are so far apart–now listen carefully–when we are so far apart that we can't see each other, then we can bid each other good day.' 'Good,' said the other. 'You have brains, you have.' And there they went, backing up and backing up until they were out of sight of each other."

So ends the story.

To end the vigil of so great a day in a more appropriate manner, let us say, in praise of our worthy paddlers, that in the midst of the fatiguing occupation of the trip I heard no one murmur. In spite of the many curious things which the rapidity of our progress opened up before us at each step there was more than one of them who regretted leaving *terra firma*, thinking of what he would have done with the missionary the next day, as on Easter. But the barges did not halt.

On the twenty-third, Pentecost, the crew at least had the satisfaction of hearing Holy Mass. Half of my cabin was occupied by the altar, so some of our men were on the bank.

On the twenty-fourth, the feast of Our Lady Help of Christians, ice on the river told us that in two nights the temperature had dropped 43 degrees. This change was due to a new air current and the leveling off of the river banks. When the bank advances out into the river, the resulting formation is called a "point." These points are separated more or less by dry strips. From the *Grande Ile* to the Mussel Shell River, that is, within a space of a few miles, they are so close together that as many as twenty-four of them can be counted. On them the animals of the more inoffensive varieties congregate because of the thick shade and the good pasturage. Thus scarcely an hour would pass without our seeing some herd at close range.

To our right we saw the ruins of a house which had been built, during the rigorous winter of 1845, by A. Hamel, present interpreter at Fort Clay. That winter made him decide not to spend another one there. Near there, through the cotton trees on the left bank, could be seen in the distance the blue hues of the Rocky Mountains, otherwise called Wolf Mountains by the Indians, because of the great number of wolves to be found there. Their presence in large numbers indicated an abundance of deer and buffalo, for the wolves usually follow only big game of good quality. The attention of the passengers was fixed with lively interest on the slope of the neighboring shore. A buffalo cow, with her calf, was under attack by a pack of wolves. The barge stopped to give a better view. The hunter jumped ashore and the captain followed him. Wishing to watch the action, I followed the captain. We rounded the hill where the battle was taking place and soon, without being seen ourselves, we saw an interesting demonstration of the courage of a mother in defending her young.

On these banks there were the most beautiful flowers I had seen since our departure. A blue, star-shaped one tinged with rose had clusters delicately arranged around a pyramidal stem which is graced at intervals with two round leaves of diminishing size. Another, similar to the lupine, but more simple, was of a serene yellow with pale green leaves in groups of three like those of the clover. In honor of the feast of the day I called the first one *auxiliame* and the second one *mariane des Pieds-noire*, for I had found it near Fort Lewis right after the passing of winter.

A little farther below was Dry Point, so called because of the whitened tree trunks covering the ground. Some were still erect; some had fallen or were being supported by others. This melancholy sight, coming right after the flowers, recalled the paintings of Poussin in which playing shepherds are represented. Near them is a gravestone on which are inscribed the words: "And I was a shepherd, too."

Another sign of human poverty was the remains of a sacrifice offered not long before. The rich furs which had served as the holocaust were still on the platform of branches which had served as an altar. The sacrifice had been made to the sun, by Bloods on their way to war against the Assiniboines.

On the twenty-sixth, we saw before us the round butte which is the halfway mark between the fort of the Blackfeet and that of the

Assiniboines. This butte is distinguished from the others by its height and shape. Its flat top gives it the appearance of an overturned vessel. A large tree standing out like a plume to the left shades the summit.

Near the barge we perceived felled trees, trunks stripped of their bark, pieces of wood arranged in mounds, and animals with four large foreteeth, a very flat tail and paws like hands. All this told us we were in beaver country. Everyone knows the industry, the neatness, and the gentle habits of this animal. Thanks to new substitutes for their skins they are beginning to multiply again, and if this continues they will soon be what they once were. This is very probable, for the female produces many young and their lodges protect them from whatever might be a hindrance to breeding.

A fawn was seen on the shore, and the children chased it, caught it and embraced it, wishing to adopt it. But since its mother's milk was failing, it was decided to put it out of its misery.

There was soon a sadder and more grandiose spectacle. This time, not the young, but the lofty and powerful lords of the wilderness that had to undergo fire from all the barges. What would become of them? They were caught between the fire and the inaccessible ramparts of the river. One, struck in the heart, drifted down the river. Some, seeking refuge in a heap of branches, became entangled as in a snare. Some saw safety only in braving the threat of death. The less brave, but nimbler, ones struggle up the high bank. Finally, all that were not dead or mortally wounded disappeared, leaving civilization as mistress of the field of battle.

On the twenty-seventh, there was fog and rain, a kind of mourning of nature, interrupted only by a dismal concert. For there are always some beings who rejoice only at the unhappiness of others, and in this case it was the wolves. The children on the barge, too, had great sport when one of their number got a spanking, which happened often enough.

On the twenty-eighth, we saluted Milk River, which owes its name to the whiteness of its waters, though this color is evident only when the water is low. From the point at which the Milk River joins the Missouri, the latter stream broadens, the mountains fall off into the distance, and the view begins to have something majestic about it. In the evening a nun, that is, a white-headed eagle, killed by our hunter and presented by Mr. Culbertson, had the honor of being painted. The king of the skies is depicted in the spot where he received his fatal wound, that is, under the wall of his stronghold.

On the twenty-ninth, we sighted the nest of an eagle to which attaches a touching memory. At the foot of the tree in which its nest was built, little Josette, oldest daughter of our pilot, had been born eight years before. Several rows of trees, so symmetrically aligned that they might have been planted by a royal gardener, surrounded this nursery. But better by far than their beauty were the piety, the candor, and the happy expression of the child who had been born there. She and her little sister, Marie, did not let a day of the month pass without placing at the feet of the Blessed Virgin the tribute of their piety and their virtuous efforts. They had been the first to crown with flowers the cross now rising on the land of the Blackfeet.

We found more ruins, the remains of a fort built by a dozen men. When the company withdrew, these men wished to enjoy something of Indian life. But either because they could not manage it or because, desiring no other guide but their individual fancy, they had not been able to co-operate, they separated. One of them was killed by the Assiniboines.

On the twenty-ninth, our flotilla almost suffered a serious accident. The wind being stronger than usual, one of our barges was blown against a tree and pierced through both sides. But by dint of rapid work the 360 packs of furs which it contained were unloaded before the water reached them. Out of a hundred barges meeting this kind of fate, so said the pilot, not a single one might be expected to be saved. This accident occurred almost in the same spot where fifteen years before the provision barge had sunk. The loss was estimated at ten thousand dollars, but that was not the worst of it. Since the accident occurred at night, it was possible to see the shore only by flashes of lightning. The barge was borne away by the hurricane winds and several persons who wanted to jump ashore, or who did actually jump, were more or less severely wounded. A Canadian named Benedict was found crushed between the side of the barge and shore; a child of eight years was drowned in its bed, and an Indian woman saved her own life only by jumping into the water. Michel Champagne, then as now pilot of the barge, was hurled ashore by a blow from the rudder. But Heaven protected a man who was to set such good example, and this jump caused him no injury other than that of bringing vividly to his consciousness the wretchedness of the others. The news of the disaster was carried to Mr. Mackenzie, then the captain of the fort. His reply was that his men should not be set ashore, for he had other equipment for them.

On the thirtieth, there was dialogue between a young passenger and an old pilot:

"Skipper, I think I see to our left, over there above the willows, a white thing in the shape of a sugar loaf. Do you know what it is?"

"It is an Indian pyramid."

"An Indian pyramid! But I have been told that these fellows do not concern themselves with architecture. Well, then, this pyramid must be an exception. Which Indians thought of building it?"

"The Crow."

"The Crow! What an odd name."

"No name could be better chosen."

"But why?"

"Because for their neighbors they are almost always birds of ill omen. They are at war with almost all of them and their wars are almost always wars of extermination."

"And they have erected this monument in memory of some great victory?"

"No. It is said that it was intended to dispose their divinities well toward them."

"In what period of their history do you place its erection?"

"The oldest recollections are only of one thing, and that is of always having seen it there."

"Strange! The nearer we approach to this curious structure the more mysterious it appears to me. The side toward the sun shines like silver."

"But it is not of silver at all. It is, however, made of something almost as durable as silver."

"It is made of marble, then?"

"Not at all. It is neither metal nor even mineral."

"What is it, then?"

"It is made of a kind of branch, which grows like a plant, but which is not a plant. It has roots but does not spring from the earth. It is of animal origin but is never animated. Now, can you guess?"

"There are buffalo around here. Is it perhaps made of their horns?"

"You are almost right. It is made of horns, true, but of horns with many prongs, which is as much as saying that they are not really horns."

"Now I follow you. They are antlers. Am I right?" [Some word play on "*bois*" as signifying both wood and antlers is necessarily omitted here.]

"Precisely."

"Why did the builders of this monument choose such strange materials?"

"Among them the stag is a medicine animal."

"Then this great heap of stag antlers is a religious monument?"

"So it is said."

"And the Indian goes there just as we go on a pilgrimage, and each time deposits his offering there?"

"At least whenever he finds a stag with such a set of antlers. When he does, he does not fail to add it to the others. In this manner the monument has become what we now see. Evidently the first builders laid only the foundation."

"Has no one ever thought of destroying it?"

"It was destroyed in eighteen forty-three."

"By whom?"

"By some whites out on a pleasure party."

"And the Crows have not avenged this deed?"

"Others have avenged it in their place."

On the Feast of the Holy Trinity, thanks be to God and the good dispositions of the crew, I was able to say Holy Mass. The time given to God is never wasted. In spite of threats of a contrary wind the day was almost as good as one might have wished, and the evening was delightful. At least no other evening ever seemed so beautiful to me. As the sun set in a light haze, it exchanged the gold of its fire for the color of rubies. Above it, and outlined sharply against a blue background, a formation of clouds tinged with purple, blue, and violet hung like drapery. A row of beautiful trees cast their shadows to the middle of the river. What was the crew doing in the presence of this rich coloring? While the men drove our barges forward like so many chariots racing for a prize, their wives and children sang hymns in honor of the Queen of Angels. Never had the wilderness heard the like. What person devoted to Mary would not have been moved by this refrain:

Qu'on est heureux sous son empire!
Qu'on coeur pur y trouve d'attraits!
Tout y sessent, tout y respire!
L'amour, l'innocence, et la paix.

On the thirty-first, the month of Mary ended and the end of our barge journey was also at hand. At least we thought so, for we would dock in a few miles. But the wind arose, forcing us to call a halt. This offered me another opportunity to observe how a good pilot manages to struggle victoriously against adversity even with an exhausted crew. Our pilot had done this many times.

Here are some of the expressions the pilot used: "Now, men, let's make that point. Keep up your courage. . . . See that snag, don't get stuck on it. . . . Look out for those branches. . . . Make for the shore. . . . Well done; here we are on land. It's all over. . . . Good appetite now."

And the oarsmen certainly did not lack a good appetite. They supped gaily, then lit up their pipes and began to talk about the rest they would enjoy the next day, the cannon shots that they would hear, of the reception to be given, and so on.

On the morrow a magnificent sun rose. To our right were two snow-white peaks. There was a slight wind against us, but it served to cleanse the air rather than to impede our progress. The first cannon shot resounded. A few minutes later the great flag was raised. Artillery pieces answered each other. The bastions came into view. All the occupants of the fort came down to the shore. The barges stopped, greetings and *bon jours* were exchanged. Finally began the handshakes, the gestures of friendship and the manifestations of joy, and so on. All this terminated in a celebration.

I have been among the Indians only seven years, but they have been seven years of missionary work in the closest relationship with them. These give me the right to be interested in everything that concerns them. Having seen in their wilderness, perhaps more than anywhere else, what fruits grace can produce in willing hearts, I have always been happy to recount what I know about them. And today, when they are under attack, I am duty bound to tell what I know about them. This duty is all the more pleasant because its fulfillment is a means of paying honor to my country. I can affirm that if the harvest already reaped cost us efforts, even though consoling, it is, after God, to the French that we are indebted. And, if not to the French of France, then at least to their descendants or to Indians converted by French missionaries. These *voyageurs*, whom Providence scattered throughout these regions, did not, it is true, always conduct themselves in conformity with their faith, but none of them took it upon himself to speak disrespectfully either of his religion, of the priests, or of his country. And since there were those among them who spoke of these things only with the most respectful affection, it was impossible for their sentiments not to be communicated in some measure to their hosts. Hence the surprising confidence the

Flatheads and the surrounding tribes manifested in us when we first appeared in their country; the marvelous facility with which they learned to practice their duties and, finally, the admirable fruits spread from the Rocky Mountains to the shore of the Pacific.

The Blackfeet appeared to many to be too far separated from the Kingdom of Heaven to be able to offer such consolation to our ministry. Still we visited them and among them, as elsewhere, we met with a sympathetic attitude. Upon learning what religion had meant for the prosperity of the Flatheads, the women brought their children to be baptized, and many times warriors would not set out on a campaign without first recommending themselves to the prayers of the missionary. Out of the twenty-five or thirty camp leaders who visited us or were visited by us, not one failed to describe his people in terms that served to encourage our zeal. And twelve Indian women at Fort Lewis, whose religion in a short time made them model wives and mothers, gave us proof that with time and patience a minister of the Gospel could accomplish there what we did elsewhere. This very hope was shared by the two Blackfoot forts to such an extent that there was not a man in these establishments who did not encourage it by alms which would have done honor to a prince. And each professed his faith in a manner which would have done honor to the most religious of apologists. Another thing which redounded both to the credit of American impartiality and to the work of which we were the ministers was the fact that Americans of other faiths were the first to suggest a subscription in our favor. What has been said of the Blackfeet can also be remarked about the Crow. I visited only one part of their tribe, the least attractive part, so it is said.

Though the Crows were mortal enemies of the Blackfeet, whose friend I had declared myself to be, it required only a few minutes of conversation to bring them around to the point to which, for the good of humanity, it would be desirable for all warring nations to be brought. Would it not be the same in the case of the Assiniboines if we could speak with them, or if others would do so in our place? We have every reason to believe that it would be, for they, more than the others, are well aware of their needs.

All of this presents more than enough evidence to prove to a reasonable mind that he who would seek, in one way or another, to vilify religion would instigate a horrible war against humanity. Fort Lewis was so well aware of this truth that one of its men, not without reproach in this respect, repented his sins.

■ FORT BENTON JOURNALS

The "Fort Benton Journals" includes entries from a fur trader's journal at Fort Benton during the fall and winter of 1854-1855. The excerpted reprinted here are from Volume 10 of Contributions to the Historical Society of Montana *(1940).*

"Pretty Busy"

November 1854

Fri. 24–Raining and snowing and altogether very disagreeable. Sent after 2 loads fire wood and another Wagn. to haul wood for fireburner.–

Sat. 25–Clear but cold. Got on well with all the work of the Fort–Hauled balance of our logs, etc. etc. A trader–the white Calf arrived with some five Robes.–

Sun. 26–Late last night Baptiste arrived with a letter from M Champaigne in want of more goods, and states his Wagn. is on the way in with 200 Robes. Put up an assortment in consequence to fill this order in the morning. Windy and cold. The Crows Flag arrived with some 9 Robes for trade.–

Mon. 27–Again late last night Perry arrived from G Vs express, but having lost his way was behind two days He came for three Wagns. to move Revais his Inds having all left him. Started Panton with a Wagn. to Michell containing the goods put up yesterday. Also started 1 Ox Wagn. and 2 horse do. to the Gros Ventres in conformity with express recd. yesterday but scarcely were they started when Mr. Culbertson arrived.

Tues. 28–Put up a small equipment to send to Blackfoot Camp per Baptiste–Arrived three Wagns, and two Carts from Gros Ventres with 619 Robes 2300 lbs. Meat etc. etc. also one Wagn. from M Champaigne with 200 Robes and a few other things–Pretty Busy–. . .

December 1854

Fri. 1–Early Mr. Culbertson started with family on a visit to Blood Inds. Started also Mr. Burd with 2 Carts and equipment put up yesterday, but shortly afterwards he returned having met some Inds. who informed him the Camp he was going to had moved up to Mr. Rose. A few traders arrived and three War parties. Fort crowded.—Late our long looked for Express arrived from St. Louis.

Sat. 2—Indians all cleared out—No new arrivals, quite quiet and able to do a little writing—Yesterday was very windy having blown down our pickets—and today is also a little too windy for us and very cold

Sun. 3—Early Ox Wagns. arrived from M Champ (Champaigne) having 366 Robes etc. etc. and shortly afterwards a few Inds. arrived with some 40 Robes to trade, but they will await Mr. Culbertsons comming—

Mon. 4—Two War parties arrived and these with what came yesterday crowd us a little—No Word of Mr. Culbertson—Ice begins to run pretty briskly—

Tues. 5—Warriors all started—Our Ox Wagn. arrived from Gros Ventres with 52 Robes Ind. awaiting Mr. Culbertsons arrival becoming very impatient—

Wed. 6—Started two Ox carts with some goods to M. Champaigne as we are afraid to delay any longer waiting for Mr. C. who has not turned up today either—Started another saw today but from wind unable to work at *ornamental* work of kitchen. Hauled two loads fire wood

Thurs. 7—All the work of our Fort progressing nicely. Late last evening an Express arrived from Mr. Culbertson for three Mules, as his horses were stolen by some party or another—and today sent him that number with two men also a few goods asked for

Fri. 8—In the evening Mr. Culbertson and party arrived along with some 5 or 6 Indians—Finished roofing and all outer work to Kitchen and began with flooring.—

Sat. 9—Traded with a good many Indians and three started back home Two Carts arrived from M Champaigne with 191 Robes etc Very busy today and having slept but little the past night very glad it has come to a close

Sun. 10—Another busy day trading and giving—got a good many loafers however off our hands. Put up an equipment to sent to Rose and another to Michell in the morning. . . .

Thurs. 14—A Waggon arrived from Rose today and one from Baptiste having together 428 Robes etc. finished flooring our Kitchen Dinning Room.—

Fri. 15—Nothing stirring. Weather very mild in these times, the River runs pure and as free from Ice as in Summer and today after Sun set our Ther. stood at 54°.

Sat. 16 – Mr. Culbertsons B in L started and took with him a few goods for trade – An Indian "Spotted Cow" arrived with some Robes for trade also a large party going to War and another coming from it – Thus it ever is with these dogs.

Sun. 17 – Busy trading. In the afternoon Cadot arrived from F. Union with men who left here with horses 17th ulto. He brings no letters, as Mr. Clark accompanied him so far as Milk River and will be here probably in the morning. – M Champaigne arrived having wound up his trade with Pagans for the present.

Mon. 18 – Waggon and Cart arrived from Michels with balance of his trade 233 Robes. Shortly afterwards Mr. Clark arrived and in the evening B Champaigne arrived stating a Wagn. and Cart will be here tomorrow from Mr. Rose –

Tues. 19 – Wagn. and Cart arrived from Rose with some 240 Robes etc. etc. Put up an equipment to send to him in the morning also one for Baptiste to start with for Blood Ind Camp. Our two Wagns. dispatched 12th inst. for Revais returned today having been wandering about in the prarie ever since without finding their destination. . . .

Sun. 24 – Early a man at long last arrived from our Gros Ventres traders in quest of goods and God knows what. Put up a large equipment to send there on Tuesday, tomorrow being Xmas Late in the evening Mr. Rose arrived from his Camp stating his Wagn. will be here in the morning.

Mon. 25 – Put up a fine equipment to start with Mr. Rose in the morning – His Wagn. has not yet turned up however. In the evening went to a little jolification not only on a/c of the Season but because also Mr. Culbertson intends taking his departure for F. Union in the morning

Tues. 26 – Early Mr. Culbertson and family also Mr. Tevis started for F. Union – Started 1 Ox Wagn. and 1 Ox Cart with Equipment to Gros Ventres Mr. Rose's driver arrived stating his Oxen had given out so sent another man with an additional yoke and towards evening all got back safely. Mr. Rose started with Mr. Culbertson to accompany him so far as the Marias.

Wed. 27 – Early Mr. Rose returned and immediately started him with 3 horse Wagns. containing Equipment put up 25th inst. Hauled two loads fire wood.

Thurs. 28 – Very boisterous and disagreeable day Hauled 2 loads wood. Fort looks very empty in these times. Three Gros Ventres arrived from War but count no coup –

Fri. 29–Wind throughout the past night so very strong as to alarm a good many of us. Even our solid Dobbie walls shook under it, and the whole of the pickets on the S W side were blown down. Put these up again but the wind still continues so strong as to prevent our other out door work.

Sat. 30–Calm but very cold, Ther. in the morning 5 below zero–A party of Pagans with some few Robes and meat arrived to trade. Hauled 2 loads firewood and saws going well.

Sun. 31–Traded with our Pagan friends when a party of 5 Blackfeet arrived with a good many robes for trade, the same number also went to the opposition house. They however put off their trade until morning.–

January 1855.

Mon. 1–Traded with our Blackfeet and two others of their party brought down their Robes from other Fort and traded here. Very cold and considerable snow fell. Gave all hands in the fort a small feast.

Tues. 2–More snow fell throughout the night and Ther. at 10° below zero and on this we have not a stick of firewood in the Fort–Late to recover our Oxen and it was dark before we got any wood home. Our Blackfeet also keep hanging on and begging much to our annoyance.–

■ CAPTAIN JOHN MULLAN

In 1859, Governor Isaac Stevens of Washington Territory appointed Captain John Mullan to build a wagon road connecting Walla Walla, Washington, with Fort Benton, Montana. Mullan completed this important immigrant highway in 1863. His Miners and Travelers' Guide to Oregon, Washington, Idaho, Montana, Wyoming, and Colorado via the Missouri and Columbia Rivers *was published in New York in 1865.*

From Miners and Travelers' Guide

The following pages and accompanying map have been prepared with a view to place in the hands of travelers and emigrants to the North-West and Pacific Coast, such advice and information as they would find useful in their journey, when traveling by the new route.

During the past fourteen years the entire emigration that has sought the Pacific Coast, with the view of there making permanent homes, has taken either the route across the Continent, via the South Pass, involving 2000 miles of land travel, or via the Isthmus of Panama, involving 6000 miles of sea travel; both fraught with heavy expense, danger and discomfort.

The great desire of all has been to secure a route where the sea travel would be avoided in toto; and at the same time have the land transit the shortest minimum. The geography of the section of the Continent west of the Mississippi shows that this can only be attained by ascending the Missouri river to its highest point practicable for steamers, and thence cross to the navigable waters of the Columbia, where we find the land carriage only 624 miles.

Having been occupied for a number of years in the exploration and construction of the wagon road, via this route, I feel warranted in placing in a brief form such advice, facts, and statements as our labors in the field have developed.

Those who desire to make this trip should apply for further information to Charles P. Chouteau, of St. Louis, or to John G. Copelan, of St. Louis, both of whom are interested in forwarding passengers and freight from St. Louis to the Rocky Mountain region, at the headwaters of the Missouri and Columbia Rivers. Their steamers are generally ready to leave St. Louis somewhere between the 4th of March and 1st of May—starting thus early in order to take advantage of the June rise which they meet at or near Sioux City, and which enables them to run over all the bars and shoals found in the difficult stream of the Missouri.

These boats make the trip but once a year, and hence all travelers should make their preparations in time to take the boats by 1st April, either from St. Louis or from Walla-Walla. John G. Copelan will keep constantly a steamer between Fort Benton and the Yellowstone for the accommodation of travelers who wish to return east in early spring, or late in the autumn. Wagons and outfits of all kinds can at present be secured at Fort Benton.

Travelers will probably find fresh vegetables at Sun River, on the Big Prickly Pear, in the Deer Lodge Valley, Hellsgate Valley, at the Coeur d'Aléne Mission, on the Spokane River, on the Touchet River, Dry Creek and Walla-Walla, and fresh beef at each and all of these points.

Fresh animals can be purchased at nearly all these points, and blacksmith shops will be found at the Deer Lodge, Hellsgate and Coeur d'Aléne Mission.

No fear need be apprehended from Indians along the entire route. The trip from St. Louis to Fort Benton will involve from 35 to 40 days, and from Fort Benton to Walla-Walla about the same length of time.

The following more detailed statistics published in an official report, will be found to contain much of interest to those who have never made the trip:

Recommendations for Travelers

For persons who desire to leave St. Louis in the spring on steamer for Fort Benton, where the passage is from $100 to $200, and freight from ten cents to twelve cents per pound, and who desire to make the land transit by wagon, I would advise that they provide themselves with a light spring covered wagon in St. Louis, also two or four sets of strong harness, and transport them to Fort Benton, where they can procure their animals, mules or horses. The former can be had from $100 to $150, the latter from $50 to $75; oxen, from $100 to $125 per yoke. Let them provide themselves with a small kit of good strong tin or plated iron mess furniture; kettles to fit one in the other, tin plates and cups, and strong knives and forks; purchase their own supplies in St. Louis; brown sugar, coffee, or tea, bacon, flour, salt, beans, sardines, and a few jars of pickles and preserved fruits will constitute a perfect outfit in this department. I have found that for ten men for fifty days, the following is none too much on a trip of this kind: 625 pounds of flour, 50 pounds of coffee, 75 pounds of sugar, 2 bushels of beans, 1 bushel of salt, 625 pounds of bacon sides, 2 gallons of vinegar, 20 pounds of dried apples, 3 dozen of yeast powders, and by all means take two strong covered ovens, (Dutch ovens.) These amounts can be increased or diminished in proportion to the number of men and number of days. If your wagon tires become loose on the road, caulk them with old gunny sacks, or in lieu thereof, with any other sacking; also, soak the wheels well in water whenever an opportunity occurs. In loading the wagons, an allowance of four hundred pounds to the animal will be found sufficient for a long journey. For riding saddles, select a California or Mexican tree with machiers and taphederos, hair girth, double grey saddle blanket, and strong snaffle bit.

If the intention is to travel with a pack train, take the cross-tree packsaddle, with crupper and breeching, and broad thick pads. Use lash-rope, with canvas or leather belly bands. Have a double blanket under each saddle. Balance the load equally on the two sides of the animal – the whole not to exceed two hundred pounds. Have a canvas cover for each pack. A mule-blind may be found useful in packing. Each pack animal should have a hackama, and every animal (packing and riding) a picket-rope, from thirty-five to forty feet long and one inch in diameter. For my own purposes, I have always preferred the apparejo for packing, and have always preferred mules to horses. Packages of any shape can be loaded upon the apparejo more conveniently than upon the packsaddle. A bell animal should be always kept with a pack train, and a grey mare is generally preferred. Every article to be used in crossing the plains should be of the best manufacture and strongest material. This will, in the end, prove true economy. Animals should be shod on the fore-feet, at least. Starting at dawn and camping not later than 2 P.M., I have always found the best plan in marching. Animals should not go out of a walk or a slow trot, and after being unloaded in camp they should always be allowed to stand with their saddles on and girths loose, for at least fifteen minutes, as the sudden exposure of their warm backs to the air tends to scald them. They should be regularly watered, morning, noon, and night. Never maltreat them, but govern them as you would a woman, with kindness, affection, and caresses, and you will be repaid by their docility and easy management. If you travel with a wagon, provide yourself with a jackscrew, extra tongue, and coupling pole; also, axle-grease, a hatchet and nails, auger, rope, twine, and one or two chains for wheel locking, and one or two extra whippletrees, as well as such other articles as in your own judgment may be deemed necessary. A light canvas tent, with poles that fold in the middle by a hinge, I have always found most convenient. Tables and chairs can be dispensed with, but if deemed absolutely necessary, the old army camp stool, and a table with lid that removes and legs that fold under, I have found to best subserve all camp requisites. Never take anything not absolutely necessary. This is a rule of all experienced voyageurs.

GARTER SNAKE
as told to Fred P. Gone

This account is of the spiritual voyage of Gros Ventre leader Bull Lodge (1802-1886). Bull Lodge's pilgrimage took place on seven buttes in Montana, ranging from the Judith Mountains to the Bears Paw near the Fort Belknap Indian Reservation and north to the Sweet Grass Hills. Garter Snake (1868-1953), Bull Lodge's daughter, first told the story to tribal historian Fred P. Gone in 1942 as part of the WPA federal writer's project. These excerpts are from The Seven Visions of Bull Lodge *(1980), edited by George P. Horse Capture, a Gros Ventre and curator of the Plains Indian Museum at the Buffalo Bill Historical Center in Cody.*

The Seven Visions on Seven Buttes

The Hudson Bay Company had a trading post on the upper Saskatchewan River, run by a white man whom the Gros Ventres called Crooked Rump. He was called this because he walked with a funny twist in that part of his body. He was the first white man with whom the Gros Ventre tribe had dealings, for they began to frequent the trading post then. This man, who was later called High Crane, married a young Gros Ventre woman named Good Kill and Bull Lodge came from this union. When the tribe moved away from that country, Good Kill left High Crane and lived with her relatives. The people moved south to country lying on both sides of the United States and Canadian border, including Montana, Alberta and the western part of Saskatchewan. I do not know exactly where my father was born. I only know that it was among his people, the Gros Ventres.

Visions of Preparation

When Bull Lodge reached the age of twelve, he knew he was motivated to become a great man of the tribe. Being poor, he had experienced hard times in his childhood. He began to consider how he could fulfill his ambition. Now through the later years of his childhood, he had a deep faith in and affection for the Chief Medicine Pipe which was called the Feathered Pipe. There were other medicine pipes in the tribe, but this one, the Feathered Pipe, was the pipe he chose to call upon as his guide and teacher. So he entrusted his life to it.

One day late in the spring of the year, as the tribe was breaking camp before moving, Bull Lodge wandered away from the others so that he would not be heard. He began to cry. He wandered about the country crying like a lost child. After this, he returned to the deserted camp grounds. Approaching the eastern side, he went from one tipi bed ground to the other, seeking out the tipi marks of the Chief Medicine Pipe which was called the Feathered Pipe. He discovered them by locating the shallow hole directly behind the fire place, where the live coals of buffalo chips are placed and the incense made. Also, he knew that the tipi of the Feathered Pipe must always face south. Starting at the entrance, he circled around the tipi. After making a complete circle he continued on until he reached the back. He knelt by the shallow hole in the ground where the incense was made, then he began to cry, keeping both hands over the hole in homage to the Feathered Pipe.

He remained in that kneeling position for a long time. When he stopped crying, he prayed to the Feathered Pipe to deliver him from his state of poverty. Then he continued to circle the deserted camp ground, crying as he walked. After reaching the point where he had started, he picked up the direction of the tribe's movement, noting the marks of tent poles and travois on the ground. But he did not cease his crying. Finally he said, "I wish there were someone up above who would have pity on me and help me to be a man so that I could live like a man." Each time the tribe moved, he did all these things.

One day after crying around the deserted campground, having followed the tracks of the moving tribe to a place where he was in sight of camp, his eye was attracted to a small coulee full of thick grass. It was so inviting that he lay down on the grass, looking up at the sky. He was tired from crying and walking, and he fell asleep. In his dream an old man approached, wearing a buffalo robe with the hair still on it. The robe was painted red where the old man's shoulders protruded. The waist line too had red paint going around the robe. The old man's long hair was matted, and in his hand he held one of the sweat bath implements, made of buffalo tail. His face was painted with the same dark red paint, exactly as a Chief Medicine Pipe owner paints his face.

The tribe was moving in a northerly direction that spring and early summer, and Bull Lodge continued to wander off when the people were breaking camp. After they moved, he would return to the deserted campground and search for the bed of the Feathered Pipe. Standing at the extreme east of the campground, he would face west, holding his hands up in supplication to the Supreme Being. After praying, he would go from one bed ground to another. He would always begin by circling to the right, never to the left, continuing until he discovered the place of the Feathered Pipe. He would circle round it once completely to the right, to signify the way the Feathered Pipe was handled. Then he would continue to circle the tipi mark until he was directly opposite the entrance mark.

The tipi where the Feathered Pipe was kept must always face south, and the Medicine Pipe owner sits at the back end of the tipi, facing the entrance. After stopping in the place where the Medicine Pipe owner sits, Bull Lodge would kneel down and hold his hands over the hole where the incense is made, making his cries and prayers to the Feathered Pipe. Then he would complete his circle of the entire campground, going to the right in order to go towards the sun. Afterwards he would follow the marks left by the tribe when they moved. When he was in sight of the tipis, he would find some nice secluded spot and lie there until dusk before returning home. Bull Lodge had made it a rule that he could not enter the camp until dusk. And by his own choice he was fasting, for he included this duty in his way of seeking his future.

One day the old man who had appeared to him in his vision spoke to him.

"My child, why do you do these things? Why do you look for me in particular, locating my bed ground in the deserted camp? My child, I have noticed this custom you have adopted for yourself, holding your hands on the place where the incense is made for me. And your cries have moved me with compassion.

"I pity you, my child. You will be powerful on this earth. Everything you have asked for is granted you. Now, my child, look at me. Do you see my hair, my robe, my sweat implement, and how my face is painted?

"I give you all of it. Are you sure that you recognize the robe?"

"Yes," Bull Lodge answered. The robe was the skin of a grizzly bear and the sweat implement was made from the tail of the white buffalo.

"I will give you something very soon, my child."

And Bull Lodge thought, "I am still just a boy, but this old man looks like a medicine man of the Chief Medicine Pipe. Clearly he belongs to the Feathered Pipe which I have chosen as my special guide, and whose incense place I hold my hands upon in the deserted campgrounds."

Then the old man disappeared, and Bull Lodge awoke. He sat up and looked about for the old man. Seeing that he was alone he said, "I wish that this thing which is coming to me might come right away."

And as the day was almost spent, he returned to camp to his tipi.

Bull Lodge followed his customary ceremonies for three months, from late spring into the summer. Then one summer day, after he had finished crying around the deserted camp ground, having followed the tribe's tracks to his stopping place, he lay in the grass on his back with his arms out flat on the ground, elbows bent. He lay in that position for quite a while. As he gazed up at the sky, an object appeared, very small, but he could see that it was moving. It looked like a circling bird. He just lay there, watching that speck in the sky. Then it seemed to him that it was coming down in small circles. It came closer and closer, and the closer it came, the bigger it got, until it came within arm's length. It was a shield, with a string or fine cord attached to it leading up into the sky.

The shield hung suspended before Bull Lodge, as if giving him plenty of time to examine it and to imprint its features on his mind. It was about a foot and a half in diameter. The surface presented to him was painted half red and half dark blue. A painted rainbow went all around the edge. In the center a black bird was painted, and from each side of the bird's head, green streaks of lightning, ending at the rainbow's inside rim. Eagle feathers hung in a double row from the outside rim. In the center of the shield hung a single soft, fluffy feather.

The shield suspended itself a while for Bull Lodge's inspection, then it lowered itself the rest of the way until it rested upon him.

Then Bull Lodge heard a voice. The sound came from behind the shield, which was resting on his face and upper chest. He could not judge whether the voice came from directly behind the shield or from a little way off, but it was quite close to the shield.

"My child, look at this thing. I am giving it to you from above. It is for your living. In times of danger when you need my help, you must always say, 'Help me, Thunder Sing.' I will always hear you when you pronounce my name: Thunder Sing. Now I will instruct you concerning what you must do. There are seven buttes on this earth that you must sleep on. You must do this in imitation of me, for I too have done it.

"From this time on, everything you do will be good. Have you made sure that you have taken a good look at this thing I have presented to you?"

Bull Lodge, still lying on his back, answered "Yes" in his mind.

Then the voice said, "I command you to make one like it for your own use. Your instructions for the shield's use will be given to you later. I will always be watching you and guarding you from above."

Then the voice left, and the shield rose up from Bull Lodge's chest and gradually disappeared into the sky. For a while Bull Lodge just lay on the earth. Then he sat up. "A-ho," he said, "I am glad that my Father has given me a living." He remained there for a long time, pondering the event. Then he rose and went home.

He ate his supper, but he still felt restless. He was too excited to sit quietly, so he took up his robe and went back out away from the camp. He walked to the top of a nearby hill and lay there with his face down. His restlessness gradually disappeared and the quiet and peace of the night overcame him. And as he lay there he heard a voice above him.

"I was sent with a message to you from your Father. You are to go to a particular butte called Black Butte, which stands out away from these mountains to the east.

"On this butte, which stands on the south side of the Big River (the Missouri), you are to stay and fast for seven days and nights. Before you start out to the designated fasting place, it will rain. That will signify your purification."

Bull Lodge lay there for a while without stirring. Then, since nothing else happened, he sat up and looked around. It was dark and peaceful. Since he did not notice anything unusual, he arose and went back to camp.

All the while he was returning, he was thinking of the Chief Medicine Pipe called the Feathered Pipe. He decided to look for the tipi of the man who then owned the Pipe. When he found it, Bull Lodge began to cry at the tipi entrance, and after he had cried for some time, the medicine man spoke to him.

"Child," he said, "come inside." Bull Lodge went in and sat down. The medicine man asked, "What is it you want, and why are you crying at my tipi?" And Bull Lodge said, "I ask you to do me a favor. I ask you not to move the tribe away from this present site until I return. I am going to Black Butte, south of the Big River, to fast."

"I will stay here and wait for you," answered the medicine man. "The tribe will not move from this place until you come back." After leaving the tipi of the Feathered Pipe, Bull Lodge said to himself, "Now I will see if all this that has been revealed to me is to take place as it was told."

The First Vision

Bull Lodge walked out away from the camp, looking for a high hill not too far away. When he found one, he went to the top, took off his clothes and began to cry. He spent a long time crying on this hill, standing facing west. Finally the rain came. It was a brief shower, a heavy downpour which did not last long. It passed as suddenly as it came. He gathered up his clothing and put his robe over himself, carrying his soaked clothes home. Then he went to bed and slept peacefully.

At this time the tribe was camped near White River by a place called Cliffs, on the south side of the Big River (the Missouri) near the Belt Mountains.

Early the next morning, Bull Lodge called his friend Sits Like A Woman and asked him to accompany him to Black Butte, where he was told to fast. They went off together on horseback, and when they reached the butte, the sun was high in the sky. Bull Lodge told Sits Like A Woman to take his own horse back to camp with him. When he was alone at the foot of the butte, he took off his clothes. Then he started his ascent, taking only his robe, his knife and his pipe.

Before he reached the top of Black Butte, Bull Lodge could already feel the pangs of thirst. It was a hot, clear summer day. At the top, he began to cry. He cried for the rest of that day, resting only at short intervals. When evening came he built a small low shelter out of rocks, just big enough to lie in. The rock shelter was about two feet high and as long as he was tall. It was open at one end, in the shape of a "U". He gathered some evergreens and laid them inside as a mat to lie on. He lay down here whenever he rested, but every hour that he was awake, he cried.

Days and nights passed, and Bull Lodge became weaker and weaker. On the sixth day, just before the sun rose, he numbed the little finger of his left hand by hitting it, then he took out his knife and cut the finger off at the first joint below the nail. Taking the severed finger, he laid it on a rock and offered it up as a sacrifice. Shortly after this, he lay down. The loss of blood, coupled with his weakness from fasting, caused him to pass out.

Bull Lodge lay there all day and night, until the next morning after sunrise. During that time he had a vision. An old man appeared to him and said: "This first experience is a test to see if you are truly earnest in your ambition to become a great man of your people. The first test is the most severe, to find out your endurance and your will to become a great man. You have proven yourself worthy. Therefore all the things you desire will be given to you, but you are still obliged to go through the rest of the fasting. From time to time, these things I speak of to you shall be revealed at the designated place of fasting, a little each time. Because of what I now give you, this first of the fasting places shall be known as the place of the gift. At the second place, you will be instructed how to use what I shall give you here. My child, you must go back and live a quiet and respectable life. It will be revealed to you when and where you are to fast again.

"You are destined to complete your fasting on the seven designated buttes. At each one you will be told to go on. The length of time you will spend on each butte will be less and less, until you have finally completed your fasting on all seven. This first time, you were obliged to fast and pray for seven days and nights. The second will be shorter: you will fast and pray on another butte for six days and nights. On the third, you will remain five days and nights. On the fourth butte you will remain four days and nights; on the fifth, three days and nights; on the sixth, two days and nights; on the seventh and last butte you are sent to, you will stay but one day and night. This is all I will tell you for this time, my child. Now look to where the sun comes up."

Bull Lodge looked off, and there on the horizon he saw horses coming. One dark-colored horse ran ahead of the rest. The sun was just topping the horizon, shining on the lead horse's hide so that it looked glossy, like an otter skin. A tanned piece of hide hung around the lead horse's neck, with two buffalo hoofs strung on it like bells. Then Bull Lodge looked to the south of where he was and saw a tipi. It was painted several different colors and faced east to the sun's rising. The horse with the buffalo hoofs strung round its neck led all the horses up to the tipi entrance and stopped there. The whole herd was strung out on the horizon behind him, with the sun behind. And more horses kept appearing on the horizon, to swell the numbers of those at the tipi entrance.

Then the old man spoke again. "My child, I give you horses and a tipi. The first horse you own will be a smoky, buckskin-colored one. Then you will accumulate a herd. I give you that tipi and that herd of horses, my child. You shall do great things in healing and curing. You shall become a great doctor. Now you must go home and wait for the message to go to the next place of fasting. You have endured the most severe experience that was allotted to you, and your wishes are all granted."

When Bull Lodge woke from his sleep, the sun was already quite high. He knew that he had slept out the seventh day and night. He picked up his robe and pipe and started down to the bottom, where he had left his clothes eight days before.

In the meantime, the man who owned the Chief Medicine Pipe called the Feathered Pipe was concerned about Bull Lodge's absence. Bull Lodge said he would be gone a few days, but this was the morning of the eighth day and he still had not returned. The medicine man called Sits Like A Woman and asked him to go back to the place where he had left his friend. He was afraid Bull Lodge had met with some accident, or that a band of warriors from some other tribe had run into him on the butte and killed him. Black Butte was a well-known place for war parties going through. They all wanted to go up and look around.

So Sits Like A Woman set out to find his friend. When he reached the butte where he had left Bull Lodge eight days before, he looked up before climbing it and saw Bull Lodge slowly coming down. He was so weak, he was staggering as he came. When he reached the bottom where his clothes were, he could hardly put them on. Then Sits Like A Woman helped him onto the horse he had brought. They travelled home very slowly because of Bull Lodge's condition.

Thus Bull Lodge made a successful start toward his life's ambition. He set himself to the task of preparation by living a quiet and normal life. He was careful about his behavior. He practiced charity and showed respect for his elders and his tribe. At home, he spent most of his time pondering his experiences. He knew that he was to go through such experiences from time to time, and that they would be spaced at long intervals, but not evenly. Some would come sooner than others. So he bided his time patiently, waiting to be told what to do next.

The Seventh Vision

The tribe in its wanderings camped at that same creek late that summer and Bull Lodge was told in his sleep to go to a butte called Porcupine, on the west side of Three Buttes, the place of his last experience. As usual, Bull Lodge went out the evening before he was to start, to receive cleansing from the rain. The following morning, very early, he woke his brother, whose name was Bear Goes on Side Hill. They went to the butte on horseback, tied their horses at the foot and started up. When they reached the top the sun was just appearing over the eastern horizon. Bear Goes on Side Hill cut his brother's flesh on both thighs. Four small, round pieces of flesh were cut on the right thigh in a vertical line, and three pieces were cut on the left thigh the same way, so that the number of pieces cut would be seven. Then his brother left. Bull Lodge took the pieces of flesh and held them up as a sacrifice to the Supreme Being, praying with them in his hand. Then he laid them on a flat stone and began his crying, which was his usual way of worshipping.

He did this all through that day and into the night. When he was tired he lay down and slept. He began to dream. An old man appeared to him, saying, "My son, I have been expecting you, for I was told of your coming to my place at this butte. I am the last one of the seven who are to help you become famous among your people. You have already got all you asked for and wanted, and have proven yourself worthy of our help. I have just one thing to give you. Come over here, my son."

Bull Lodge followed him, and a short distance from where the old man appeared, they came to a spot that was cleared of grass and smoothed clean. Then the old man said, "Look, my son. There are all the things that have been given to you." Bull Lodge looked over the cleared ground and saw all the things that had been given to him in his experiences. They were painted with red earth. Off to one side lay a whistle. The old man picked it up. "Here is what I am giving you. I will show you how you must use it when the occasion arrives."

Suddenly a man appeared there on the cleared ground. He lay on his back with a bullet hole in his chest. Bull Lodge could tell he was dying, because his breathing came in gasps and far apart.

Standing at the head of the dying man, the old man blew the whistle four times, long and straight. Then he circled to the man's right, stopping at the feet, and blew the whistle four times, exactly as before, four times long and straight. Then he circled again, moving to his left, until he stood again at the head. Once more he blew the whistle, four times long and straight. Again circling to the left, the old man stopped at the dying man's feet. This time the old man blew the whistle four times spasmodically. Bull Lodge noticed that when the old man blew the whistle the third time, there was a change in the wounded man's breathing. It was almost normal. When the old man blew the whistle the fourth and last time, spasmodically, the patient opened his eyes and sat up, looking around.

The old man then turned to Bull Lodge and said, "Now my son, with this whistle I am giving you, you will be able to do just what you saw me do, no matter how near death a person may be. You will be able to restore life and cure him. Any time you do this with this whistle, you shall not fail, because when you blow on the whistle I'll hear it.

"My son, you have now finished with the experiences that were allotted to you. You have made it clear to us that you are sincere in your ambition to become a great man. All of the important things which go to help one become famous have been given to you. Now that your wish is granted and your work done, you are to wait until you are told to begin exercising the powers that are given to you. Go now and prepare yourself, my son. As it was told you, you must get ready for the life you are to live."

Then Bull Lodge woke up. Rising to his feet he prayed long and earnestly to the giver of all things. He thanked him for all that was revealed to him and for the many gifts, but especially for the supernatural powers attached to each one.

Bull Lodge was twenty-three years old when this experience of fasting was completed. He started at the beginning of his seventeenth year, and completed the course at the end of his twenty-third year.

At his leisure he began to gather material to make the articles that were given to him throughout the course of his experiences. First he set out to make the shield, because it was the first article that was revealed and given to him. Then he made the others one by one in sequence, exactly as they were revealed to him.

■ IRON TEETH *as told to* Thomas B. Marquis

Born in about 1834, Iron Teeth led a traditional Cheyenne woman's life on the plains. But in 1877, she and her people were exiled to Indian Territory (present-day Oklahoma) and her life changed dramatically. In 1878, a large group of Cheyennes, including Iron Teeth and her family, escaped from that reservation and made a months'-long trek to Nebraska with Morning Star and Little Wolf's bands. There, in January 1879, she took part in the Fort Robinson Outbreak, when many Northern Cheyennes were killed trying to escape imprisonment by the army. Iron Teeth was ninety-two years old when she told her story to Dr. Thomas B. Marquis in 1926. Marquis, who had been the agency physician, wrote books and articles about the battle of the Little Big Horn and life among the Cheyennes and the Crows. He completed The Cheyennes of Montana *in 1935, shortly before his death.*

Iron Teeth, a Cheyenne Old Woman

Ninety-two years ago I was born in the Black Hills country. The time of my birth was in the moon when the berries are ripe, in the last part of the summer. My father was a Cheyenne Indian, my mother was a Sioux. My parents brought up their family as members of the Cheyenne tribe. Our people traveled over the whole country between the Elk River and Mexico. . . .

My grandmother told me that when she was young our people did not have any horses. When they needed to go anywhere they put their packs upon dogs or on little pole travois drawn by dogs. The people themselves had to walk. In those times they did not travel far nor often. But when they got horses they could move more easily from place to place. Then they could kill more of the buffalo and other animals, and so they got more meat for food and gathered more skins for lodges and clothing.

I remember when parties of our men used to go afoot from the Black Hills far southward to get horses. Each man took along only his lariat rope, his bow and arrows, his sheath-knife, a little package of dried meat, and two or three extra pairs of moccasins tucked into his belt. Their women were sad in heart as they made these moccasins, for sometimes the travelers were gone a whole year, or sometimes they were killed. . . .

We planted corn every year when I was a little girl in the Black Hills. With sharpened sticks we punched holes in the ground, dropped in the grains of corn, then went hunting all summer. When the grass died we returned and gathered the crop. But the Pawnees and the Arikaras got to stealing or destroying our growing food, so we had to quit the plantings. We got into the way then of following all the time after the buffalo and other game herds.

We learned of vegetable foods growing wild. We gathered wild turnips, wild sweet potatoes, and other root foods. We found out the best place for berries. One time, when we were traveling past some white settlements, our people got a few watermelons. These were to us a new kind of food. The women cut them up and put them into pots for boiling. After a while they looked into the pots and found nothing but water and seeds.

Our dolls were made by tying a stuffed buckskin head on the end of a forked stick. Such a doll had hair glued to the head, beads for eyes, and a face painted on the buckskin. The stuffing for the head was buffalo hair. The clothing was of beaded and fringed buckskin. We girls built playhouse tepees for ourselves and our dolls. We would hang little pieces of meat out upon bushes and play like we were drying meat, the same as our mothers did at the home lodges. Sometimes we would play at moving camp. The boys would come with willow baskets. Everything would be put into the baskets and then the boys would drag them to wherever we might want to go. We would ride stick horses. The doll might ride on a stick horse beside the play-mother, or it might be carried on her back.

My mother made me a fine doll that I kept in a rawhide satchel with its extra clothing and moccasins. But I lost it. The Pawnees came and attacked our camp. All of the women and children went running, without stopping to take anything from the lodges. I had to leave my satchel and the doll behind. For a long time afterward, many times I cried over that lost baby. At night I dreamed about the enemy having scalped it and cut up its body.

A great issue of government presents was made to the Cheyennes when I was 15 years old. The place was near the forks of what we called Horse River and Geese River. Soldier houses had just been built there. We were given beef, but we did not care for this kind of meat. Great piles of bacon were stacked upon the prairie and distributed to us, but we used it only to make fires or to grease robes for tanning. We got soda but did not know what to do with it. Green coffee was distributed among us. We supposed the grains were some new kind of berries. We boiled them as they were, green, but they did not taste good. We liked the sugar presented to us. They gave us plenty of it, some of it light brown and some dark brown.

We got brass kettles, coffeepots, curve-bladed butcher knives and sharp-pointed sewing awls, which were better than ours that were made of bone. There were boxfuls of black and white thread for us. The thread was in skeins, not on spools. All of the women got black goods, colored goods and bed-ticking material. We made the cloth into summer clothing for children and draperies for the interiors of the lodges. We were given plenty of colored beads, brass buttons, brass finger rings, and red and blue face paints. Blankets were issued out to everybody. None of them had mixed colors. All were of some one or other solid color–red, blue, yellow, green, white. No shawls were given. It was some time afterward when we first saw shoulder shawls. Also, it was some time afterward when we first saw blankets having mixed colors. I first saw them among the Crows.

Our chief told us: "These presents are given to us because the white people are friendly and they want us to become civilized, as they are." Two certain white men did most of the gift distributing at this time. We called one of them Yellow White Man. He belonged with the Crow Indians. The other was a full white man. He gave us the blankets, so we called him Blanket White Man, or Blanket. The Cheyennes knew him after that time. We learned the white people called him Jim Bridger.

The first time I rode alone on horseback occurred when I was about ten years old. My father gave me a yearling colt. When we were traveling, my mother would put packs upon the colt with me. Usually I had two badger skins filled with dried chokecherries behind me, swinging down the colt's sides. Boys teased me by riding up close and lashing my colt to make it jump. At first I was frightened and they laughed at me. But I soon got used to it, and after a little while I became a good rider.

After I grew older I liked to break horses. When I became a woman I never asked any man to tame my horses for me. Before trying to ride them, my sister and I used to take the wild animals to a sandy place beside the river. Sometimes we would lead one out into deep water before mounting it. A horse cannot buck hard in deep water. One time a bucking horse threw me into a deep and narrow ditch, where I lit upon my back. My sister had to help me out from the ditch, but I was not hurt. I was never badly hurt in this way nor any other way. I never had a broken bone. I have been shot at many times but no bullet or arrow ever hit me.

Lots of wild horses used to be running loose on the plains to the southward. I had a good running horse when I was a young woman, and I always carried with me a lariat rope made of spun and plaited buffalo hair. As a girl I played a romping game we called "wild horses," in which some children would run here and there while others would try to throw lariats about their bodies. In this way I learned to toss the rope. One time, after my marriage, I was riding with my baby strapped to my back when I saw some wild horses. I put the baby in its cradle board down on the prairie and got after the herd. That day I caught two horses.

I was married to Red Ripe when I was 21 years old. But my name was not changed. The Indian women of the old times did not lose their own names on account of marriage. In my girlhood I was called

Mah-i-ti-wo-nee-ni—Iron Teeth. All through my life I have been known to my people by this same name.

My husband was a good hunter and did not need my help for gathering meat, but I often went hunting with him. One time, when we were riding after a small herd of buffalo, he called to me to get in front and turn them uphill. A buffalo cannot run fast uphill, so when I chased them in that direction it was easy to keep close to them. I struck different ones with my hatchet. A bull whirled and knocked down my pony. I fell sprawling, but my husband drove away the angered animal and saved me. Another time, when I was alone and afoot, I roped a buffalo calf. It dragged me, but I held on and finally I led it into our camp.

One time, far up the Powder River, I got after a beaver that was running along the bank. I sprang upon it and grasped the fur on its back. It struggled and tried to bite me. But I held it and threw it upon a high bank and climbed up after it. I knelt upon it and used one hand for beating its head with a stick. Another time I chased a black and white striped little animal. I plunged forward and grabbed it. Right away there was a strong smell. It was a skunk. My eyes were blinded, and I was almost strangled. But I was hungry for meat, so I did not let loose. I pounded it to death with my club. I then caught seven young skunks from a den where the old one belonged. Besides the meat, I got some pretty skins. I tanned all of them and sewed them together for a robe that my little girl wore upon her shoulders. I have caught lots of prairie dogs. They are wary and quick, so they are hard to catch. The best way is to hide beside a hole. If the hunter keeps very quiet and waits long enough, the prairie dog will finally creep out from the hole. Then it can be grabbed and beaten to death. . . .

Any kind of meat tastes good to me if I am very hungry. Young dogs or wolf pups are good enough if I cannot have anything better. Old dogs or full-grown wolves have a strong and unpleasant odor that I do not like. Buffalo, elk, deer, antelope and bighorn sheep used to be the favorite meats of the Cheyennes. The best of all was buffalo. We never grew tired of this food. The worst of all meats I know anything about is the kind the white people have in cans they buy at the trading store. I do not understand how they can eat and enjoy such food. There is no good taste in it. Another thing: I do not like the glistening appearance of that kind of meat when the can is opened.

I never learned how to swim. Many a time I sat on the bank of a stream and watched other girls swim, but I was always afraid of going in where I could not wade.

I never heard of Christmas until I was about 45 years old. The Cheyennes did not know of any such time. All of our religious and other celebrations were in the spring, summer or autumn seasons. We did not have any special festivals in winter. We considered it best to sleep much and eat only a little food during the cold weather, the same as the animals and the trees and grass.

When any woman among us gave birth to a baby, she was kept at rest several days. Her friends took care of her. If the camp was being moved, they stayed behind, or she might be brought along on a travois bed, which does not jolt when being dragged slowly. If enemies were in pursuit, and if the movement was rapid, the sick woman was usually hidden away somewhere. One time, when we were running away from the Pawnees, I and another woman stayed behind to help a friend bring her new baby. We hid in some timber. The Pawnees passed near to us, but they did not see us. We stayed there two days after the baby came. Then we made a bed upon a travois of buffalo skins stretched across two lodgepoles, to be dragged by a horse. Upon this bed we placed the mother and her baby. We knew where our people were going, so we took all of the short cuts and found them after three days of travel. If the Pawnees had found us, they would not have killed us. Indians did not kill each other's women and children. They captured them, to add them to the tribe of the captors.

But the white people did not spare us in this way. I know of one case when a sick young woman and an older helper stayed behind and hid themselves. At that time we were only moving camp, not fleeing from enemies. Two days later, the husband of the young woman went back to see how his wife was getting along, or to help in bringing her to the camp. He found the dead bodies of the mother, the baby and the woman helper. Horse trails showed that a band of white men had killed them. The husband was made crazy by his grief and anger. He vowed after that he would never have pity for any white people.

Very old or disabled people sometimes had to be abandoned to die or to be killed if enemies were in pursuit of us. Friends could not stay with them as all might be killed. Even if no enemies were near, it was so much trouble for old or sick ones to move from place to place that they would often ask to be left alone. . . .

Our children used to ride in woven willow baskets swung between the travois poles, when we were traveling. They would often climb out, play along the way, then climb back in again and go to sleep. One time, when some Pawnees were after us, one of our women lost a little girl from her basket. It was plain that the enemy people had captured and would keep the child. All through that mother's remaining life she mourned on account of the loss of her daughter. . . .

Our men sometimes stole each other's wives. According to our old-time ways, married couples were allowed to break their union at any time either of them might want to do so. Each of them might then take another mate at once. Among us, when any man took another man's wife, the victor got the woman on a horse with him and they rode about the camp. Young people followed them and sang lively songs. In one case of this kind, when I was yet a young girl, the losing husband came with his friends, all bringing their bows and arrows. The old men came and made them go away. The young people went on with their gaiety.

All Indians liked to get women and children from other tribes. Captives were treated kindly, to make them feel contented so they might not try to escape. The women became wives, perhaps second or third wives to some man. The children always found many people anxious to adopt them. . . .

A woman of the Ute tribe was brought to us about the time I was married. She had with her a boy four or five years old. The man who had caught her made her his wife and adopted the boy as his own. They were treated well, but she appeared not to be happy. One day she was down by the Greasy Water River tanning skins. After a while she was missed. Her husband and others searched for her. The boy told them his mother had gone somewhere across the river. Trails showed that she had taken a horse and gone away in a hurry. She left her boy with us, and she never came back. . . .

A white girl four years old came for a time into my keeping. That was about 77 years ago, before I was married. We were in camp on Turkey River. One of our women, out alone digging turnips, was found dead with her pack of turnips on her back. Several bullets had been shot into her body. Some of our boys, hidden in reeds by the water, had seen white men on horseback in that vicinity. Many of our young warriors wanted to go out and fight the white men, but our chiefs decided we should move away from the river into the hills to keep away from any fighting.

As I was packing to go, a woman brought the little white girl to me. She said: "I give you this girl." I asked why she did not want to keep her. She replied: "I am afraid the white people may kill me if they find her with me. If you are not afraid, you may keep her. If the white people get too close, she can be turned loose for them to find her alone, or you can throw her into the river." I thought about the matter a few moments, then I said: "If you promise not to ask her back from me, I will take her." The woman promised. It was raining hard, and the night was beginning to come. I made a blanket sling and put the child into it. I swung her upon my back, between my shoulders. She slept there while I walked and carried her almost all night, until we got to the new place for camping, in the hills.

Two or three days later, when all signs of danger were gone, the woman asked me to give the little girl back to her. "No, I want her for my own," I answered. I was not married though, so I gave her to a cousin of mine who had a husband but no children, who begged for her. All through her girlhood, I made dolls and moccasins and beaded clothing for her. When she became old enough, I taught her how to tan robes. She learned from me that one side of a buffalo must be skinned and the hump cut off before it can be turned over for skinning the other side.

This white girl grew to womanhood as a Cheyenne, not knowing any other language. She married a Cheyenne man, and they had several children. She kept her skin always stained to a brown color, so that white people might not recognize her and try to persuade her to join them. She could not hide, though, her blue eyes and her light brown hair. Several years ago she died, on the Rosebud Valley side of this reservation. Children, grandchildren, and great-grandchildren of hers are living now as full-blood members of our tribe. When I look nowadays upon her little descendants, learning to read and write at the white man school, it seems like I am living in another world. My thoughts go back nearly 80 years to the time when as a big girl I fled through rain and darkness while carrying on my back a sleeping little white girl who afterward became a woman, then an old woman, and then died, and who was their great-grandmother.

When I was about 18 years old a great band of Shoshonis attacked our tribal camp while we were having our annual Willow Dance, the principal Cheyenne religious ceremony of each year. Our camp was on a stream flowing into the upper part of the Powder River. We were surprised, so our young men were not ready to fight. But they got their bows and arrows and guns as soon as they could and put themselves forward so as to give the women and children a chance to escape. Many women fled without packs, and even without horses. They just seized their children and ran away afoot. Many of our young men were killed. For a long time afterward our hearts were sad. That was one of the worst days for the old-time Cheyennes.

I was on a horse and leading another one bearing packs. Two Shoshoni men came running toward me. I heard a Cheyenne voice call out: "They will capture Iron Teeth!" But I had a gun and I fired a shot toward the two Shoshonis. Not many Indians then had guns so I suppose I only frightened them, did not hurt them. Anyhow, they got away from me as fast as they could go. Many of our young women were captured that day. One of these was a cousin of mine. I never heard of her afterward. I suppose she was made the wife of some Shoshoni man and raised a family for that tribe.

White Frog's wife gained a high name for herself when a band of Pawnees attacked the Cheyenne camp. The warriors of that tribe took many of our women, at different times, but in her case they failed. She was running away afoot and alone. A Pawnee man caught her. She made signs that she was willing to go with him. But suddenly she jerked her hatchet from her belt and struck him. His head was split wide open, and he fell dead. After all of us got reassembled in quiet camp, she was heralded as a brave woman. Young warriors led her on horseback about the camp and sang songs in her praise, the same as was done for the regular warriors. Her husband, White Frog, gave away all of his horses and robes and blankets, to show how proud he was of her. . . .

. . . Our tribes were to have a permanent home in our favorite Black Hills country. We were promised that all white people would be kept away from us there. But after we had been there a few years, General Custer and his soldiers came there and found gold. Many white people crowded in, wanting to get the gold. Our young men wanted to fight these whites, but there were too many of them coming. Soldiers came and told us we would have to move to another part of the country and let the white people have this land where the gold was. This action of the soldiers made bad hearts in many of the Cheyennes and Sioux. They said it was no use to settle on any new lands because the white people would come there also and drive us out. The most angered ones went out to the old hunting grounds lying between the Powder and Bighorn Rivers.

My husband and I took our family to the Red Cloud Agency, known to us as the White River Agency, where all Cheyennes had been told to go. He was in bad humor because of our having been driven from our Black Hills home country, but he thought it was best to do whatever the white people ordered us to do. In a year or two we heard that many white soldiers were going out into our old western hunting grounds to fight the Indians there and make them come back to the new reservations in Dakota. Later, in the middle of that summer, we heard that all of the soldiers had been killed in a great battle at the Little Bighorn River.

When we were told of the great victory by the Indians, my husband said we should now go into the Montana lands, to join our people there. With many others, we left Dakota and found the Cheyennes. The tribe traveled together during much of the remainder of that summer, hunting along the Powder, Tongue and Rosebud Rivers. My husband was busy killing buffalo, antelope, deer and other animals, and I was busy tanning skins and storing up meat and berries for use during the winter. We stayed with the main tribal band led by our favorite Old Man Chief, Morning Star, or Dull Knife. When the leaves fell from the trees and the grass died, the tribal camp was made on a small stream flowing into the upper part of Powder River, almost in the Bighorn Mountains. Our men did not want to fight. They wanted to keep entirely away from all white people, wanted to be left alone so they might get food and skins to provide for their families. They said that nobody would trouble us in this place so far away from other people.

But we were not allowed to live in peace. When the snow had fallen deep, a great band of soldiers came. They rode right into our camp and shot women and children as well as men. Crows, Pawnees, Shoshonis, some Arapahoes and other Indians were with them. We who could do so ran away, leaving our warm lodges and the rich stores of food. As our family was going out from camp, my husband and our older son kept behind and fought off the soldiers. My husband had a horse, but he was leading it as he walked, so he might shoot better when afoot. I saw him fall, and his horse went away from him. I wanted to go back to him, but my two sons made me go on away with my three daughters. From the hilltops we Cheyennes looked back and saw all of our lodges and everything in them being burned into nothing but smoke and ashes.

We wallowed through the mountain snow for several days. Most of us were afoot. We had no lodges, only a few blankets, and there was only a little dry meat among us. Some died of wounds, many froze to death. We came down from the mountains to the valley of the Tongue River and followed down this stream. After 11 days of traveling, we found a camp of Oglala Sioux. They fed us and gave us shelter. But the remainder of that winter was a hard one for all of us.

When spring came, all of the Cheyennes surrendered to soldiers or went back to the Dakota agencies. I was afraid of all white men soldiers. It seemed to me they represented the most extreme cruelty. They had just killed my husband and had burned our whole village. There was in my mind a clear recollection of a time, 12 years before this, when they had killed and scalped many of our women and children in a peaceable camp near Mexico. At that time I had seen a friend of mine, a woman, crawling along on the ground, shot, scalped, crazy, but not yet dead. After that, I always thought of her when I saw white men soldiers.

In Dakota, we Northern Cheyennes were told that we must go to Oklahoma, to live there on a reservation with the Southern Cheyennes. None of us wanted to go there. We liked best the northern country. But one of our chiefs, Red Sash, or Standing Elk, made friends with the white men soldier chiefs by lying to them and telling them we were willing to go. My two sons then said it was the only thing our family could do. I suppose all of the other Cheyennes felt the same way. So all of us were taken to lands in the South. . . .

In Oklahoma we all got sick with chills and fever. When we were not sick, we were hungry. We had been promised food until we could plant corn and wait for it to grow, but much of the time we had no food. Our men asked for their guns to be given back to them, so they might kill game, but the guns were kept from them. Sometimes a few of them would take their bows and arrows and slip away to get buffalo or other meat, but soldiers would go after them and make them come back to the agency. The bows and arrows were used at times for killing cattle belonging to white men. Any time this happened, the whole tribe was punished. The punishment would be the giving of less food to us, and we would be kept still closer to the agency. We had many deaths from both the fever sickness and starvation. We talked among ourselves about the good climate and the plentiful game food in our old northern country hunting lands.

After about a year, Little Wolf and Morning Star, our principal Old Man Chiefs, told the agent: "We are going back to the North."

The agent replied: "Soldiers will follow you and kill you."

My two sons joined the band determined to leave there. I and my three daughters followed them. I think that, altogether, there were about 500 Cheyennes in this band. The white soldiers chased us.

They came from every direction. Some of the Indians went back as soon as the bullets began to fly. But my older son kept saying we should go on toward the North unless we were killed, that it was better to be killed than to go back and die slowly.

Only one buffalo, a calf, was killed by our men during the long flight back to the old home country. A few cattle belonging to white people were killed. Our chiefs told the young men not to do this, but our people were very hungry and no other food could be found. I have heard it said they killed some white people not soldiers. If they did, it must have been white people who started the fight. At that time all of us were trying to stay entirely away from all other people, so we could travel without interruption.

Chills and fever kept me sick along the way. We had no lodges. At night, when we could make any kind of camp, my daughter helped me at making willow branch shelters. Day after day, through more than a month, I kept my youngest daughter strapped to my body, in front of me, on my horse. I led another horse carrying the next-youngest daughter. The oldest daughter managed her own mount. The two sons always stayed behind, to help watch for soldiers. For 45 years I kept the Indian saddle I rode during those days. Not long ago I burned it up, with other old things. I never supposed anyone would want that saddle. . . .

We dodged the soldiers during most of our long journey. But always they were near to us, trying to catch us. Our young men fought them off in seven different battles. At each fight, some of our people were killed, women or children the same as men. I do not know how many of our grown-up people were killed. But I know that more than 60 of our children were gone when we got to the Dakota country.

We separated into two bands when we got near the old home regions. The two bands were led by Little Wolf and Morning Star, or Dull Knife. I and my family stayed with Morning Star's band. At Salt Creek, as we got to the old Red Cloud Agency, my younger son and the oldest daughter set off with some other Cheyennes to go forward to the agency. Some of our friends warned them not to do this, that the Pawnees and Arapahoes who belonged to the soldiers would kill them along the way. But they were determined to go. It turned out they did what was best. They got through without any serious trouble. I and my three remaining children and the other people with us had before us many other days of hard trial.

Morning Star said we should be contented, now that we were on or own land. He took us to Fort Robinson, where we surrendered to the soldiers. They took from us all of our horses and whatever guns they could find among us. They said then that we must go back to the South, but our men told them it was better to die by bullets. After a few weeks of arguing, our men were put into a prison house. We women and children were told we might go to the agency. Some of them went there, but most of us went into the prison with the men. In the one room, about 30 feet square, were 43 men, 29 women and 20 or 30 children.

"Now are you willing to go back to the South?" the soldier chiefs asked us.

Nobody answered them. The quantity of food given to us became less and less every day, until they gave us none at all. Then they quit bringing water to us. Eleven days we had no food except the few mouthfuls of dry meat some of the women had kept in their packs. Three days we had no water.

Guns had been kept hidden in the clothing of some of the women. One day, a woman accidentally dropped a six-shooter on the floor. Soldiers came and searched us again, taking whatever weapons they could find. But we kept five six-shooters, with some cartridges for them. I had one in the breast of my dress. We hid all of these under a loose board of the floor. My family blanket was spread over this board.

The men decided to break out of this jail. The women were willing. It was considered that some of us, perhaps many of us, would be killed. But it was hoped that many would escape and get away to join other Indians somewhere. Women cut up robes to make extra moccasins. I made extra pairs for myself and my three children. We piled our small packs by the two windows and the one door, or each woman held her own pack ready at hand. The plan was to break out just after the soldiers had gone to bed for the night. I gave my son the six-shooter I had. He was my oldest child, then 22 years of age.

After the night bugle sounded, my son smashed a window with the gun I had given him. Others broke the other window and tore down the door. We all jumped out. My son took the younger of the two daughters upon his back. The older daughter and I each carried a small pack. It was expected the soldiers would be asleep, except the few guards. But bands of them came hurrying to shoot at us. One of them fired a gun almost at my face, but I was not harmed. It was bright moonlight and several inches of snow covered the ground. For a short distance all of the Indians followed one broken trail toward the river, but soon we had to scatter. My son with the little girl on his back ran off in one direction, while the other daughter and I went in another direction. We had no agreed plan for meeting again.

I and the daughter with me found a cave and crawled into it. We did not know what had become of the son and his little sister. A man named Crooked Nose also came into our cave. We could hear lots of shooting. The next day we still heard shots, but not so many. Each day after that there was some further firing of guns. We stayed in the cave seven nights and almost seven days. More snow kept falling, it was very cold, but we were afraid to build a fire. We nibbled at my small store of dry meat and ate snow for water. Each day we could hear the horses and the voices of soldiers searching for Indians. Finally, a Captain found our tracks where we had gone out of and back into the cave. He called to us. I crept out. He promised to treat us well if we would go with him. He and his soldiers then took us back to Fort Robinson.

My toes and fingers were frozen. Others who had been caught and brought back were in the same condition, some of them in worse condition. A soldier doctor told us to rub snow on the frozen parts. I did this. At first there was great pain and burning, but this soon passed away. The frozen parts continued sore, but finally they got entirely well.

I was afraid to ask anybody about my son and the little daughter, as my asking might inform the soldiers of them. But I kept watching for them among the Indians there. After a while the little girl came to me. I asked her about her brother. It appeared she did not hear me, so I asked again. This time she burst out crying. Then I knew he had been killed. She told me how it had been done. That night, they had hidden in a deep pit. The next morning some soldiers had come near to them. The brother had said to her: "Lie down, and I will cover you with leaves and dirt. Then I will climb out and fight the soldiers. They will kill me, but they will think I am the only one here, and they will go away after I am dead. When they are gone, you can come out and hunt for our mother." The next day she came out, but the soldiers caught her.

Four of my women friends were shot to death the night we broke out. I do not know how many men and children were killed. Some of the people were never seen again after that night. A few of them got away to Sioux camps on the reservation, and afterward they were sent to Pine Ridge Agency. I heard that seven of the soldiers were killed, all of them shot by one man, a son of One Horse, and then the young man received a fatal wound. We who had been recaptured were kept in a group by a high cut bank, where soldiers guarded us. Some coffee and a box of crackers were brought for all of us. This was all we had to eat, although we were as hungry as wolves. The soldiers hurried us, so that many of the people did not have time to eat much. A few put crackers into their blankets and ate them afterward. Some shoes and socks and blankets were given to us. We had no place of shelter. My daughters and I got some cottonwood branches and built for ourselves a kind of lodge. With the blankets given to us, this was the best place for sleeping I had been in for a week.

A day or two later all of us were again put into the prison house. Our number now was only about half what it had been. The soldier chief at the fort came and talked to us through an interpreter. He said he pitied us and did not want to kill any more of our people. He then asked if we were willing now to go back to Oklahoma, so that no more of us would be killed. But we were mourning for our dead and we had no ears for his words. Everybody said: "No, we will not go back there."

We expected then that the soldiers would come at once into the prison and shoot all of us. But they did not. Instead, a few days later we were taken to Pine Ridge Agency. There we were put among the Oglala Sioux. Little Wolf and his small band, who had separated from us in coming from Oklahoma, went to Fort Keogh and then were put upon lands by Tongue River, in Montana. Other Cheyennes were with us in association with the Oglalas on Pine Ridge Reservation. Finally, after 12 years, all of us were brought together on this Tongue River Reservation.

We old Indians never knew of any way of obtaining food except by hunting. The government promised to feed us if we would live on the reservations. But I am given very little food. Each month our Indian policeman brings me one quart of green coffee, one quart of sugar, a few pounds of flour and a small quantity of baking powder. I am told that I might get more if I should go each month and ask the agent for it. I myself must go and get it, as they will not send it by a friend. But my home is more than 20 miles over a mountain from the agency. I have no horse to ride or to drive. My daughter who lives with me is a widow and has no children. She likewise has no horse. When either of us wants to go anywhere we have to walk, unless a friend invites us to ride. This being my case, it should not be expected that a 92-year-old woman get her food by personally going to the agency every month, on a certain day of the month, and during certain hours of the day when the agent or his helper is at the office. It would be hard enough in summer. It is impossible in winter.

To keep myself from starving, I still do some work. I have good eyes yet and good hearing, and I can walk far if given plenty of time. Sometimes I cut wood, but it makes me more tired than it did when I was younger. Last summer, I went by myself and gathered choke-cherries. I pounded them up, dried them, and stored away a sackful of this dried fruit, for winter use. I also gathered seven gallons of serviceberries and dried them. The missionary gave me some squashes and pumpkins, and I cut them into slices and dried them in the sun to keep for winter. He also gave me a dog that barked at people who came to his place. I killed the dog, ate some of the meat, and dried the remainder of it. When a friend gives me any kind of meat, I dry in the sun whatever I do not need for my present hunger. I used to smoke tobacco. But several years ago I quit. I decided it was not good for the health, and also it costs too much money. Prairie woman, who is now interpreting for me in talking to you, sometimes shares her food with me. When winter cold comes, Spotted Hawk lets me stay at his house, to keep warm there. But I do not like to depend in this way upon my friends. I think the government ought to do better in keeping its promise to take care of the old Indians.

This hide-scraper I have is made from the horn of an elk my husband killed, just after we were married. He cut off the smaller prongs and polished this main shaft. The Indian men of the old times commonly made this kind of present to their young wives. Besides using them in tanning the women made marks on them to keep track of the ages of their children. The five rows of notches on this one are the age-records of my five children. Each year I have added a notch to each row, for the living ones. Any time, I can count up the notches and know the age of any of my children. Throughout 72 years it has always been a part of my most precious pack. There were times when I had not much else. I was carrying it in my hands when my husband was killed on upper Powder River. It was tied to my saddle while we were in flight from Oklahoma. It was in my little pack when we broke out from the Fort Robinson prison. It never has been lost. Different white people have offered me money for it. I am very poor, but such money does not tempt me. When I die, this gift from my husband will be buried with me.

This sheath-knife scabbard was also made for me by my husband, soon after we were married. Since then, every day it has dangled from my belt. It is not for sale. Red Ripe was the only husband I ever had. I am the only wife he ever had. Through 50 years I have been his widow, I could not sell anything he made and gave to me.

I used to cry every time anything reminded me of the killing of my husband and my son. But I now have become old enough to talk quietly of them. I used to hate all white people, especially their soldiers. But my heart now has become changed to softer feelings. Some of the white people are good, maybe as good as Indians.

According to our Indian ways, it is considered not right to speak the name of any of our own dead relatives. But mine have been gone many years, and you are well known to us, so I have told you who my husband was. I tell you now the name of my son who was killed: we called him *Mon-see-yo-mon*–Gathering His Medicine. Lots of times, as I sit here alone on the floor with my blanket wrapped about me, I lean forward and close my eyes and think of him standing up out of the pit and fighting the soldiers, knowing that he would be killed, but doing this so that his little sister might get away to safety. Don't you think he was a brave young man?

■ HENRY EDGAR

Henry Edgar was a prospector in Montana's early gold-mining camps. During 1863, he kept a journal detailing his life as a prospector. He also recorded the discovery of gold in Alder Gulch, one of the largest strikes in Montana. Edgar's journal was transcribed by Israel Clem, Meagher County's representative to the Montana Territorial Legislature in 1871-1872 and again in 1881-1882. He served as a state representative from Granite County in 1897-1898. The journal appears in Volume 3 of Contributions to the Historical Society of Montana *(1900).*

Journal, 1863

May 2nd: All went well through the night, but towards morning the horses became restless, and required a good deal of looking after. Just as morning came I took two of them where the boys were sleeping and woke them up. I put the saddles on and was just going out to Bill when the hills were alive with Indians. They were all around Bill and I got on the horse and started for him, but an Indian grabbed him by the head; I pulled my revolver, Simmons was along side of me and told me not to shoot. Well, I got off and gave the rope of the other horse to my Indian. Here they come with other horses and Bill mounted behind another Indian with hat in one hand and rifle in the other, digging his heels in the horse's flanks and yelling like the very devil he is. "How goes it boys?" he asked as he got off. Simmons was talking to the Indians and told us to keep quiet. Quiet, everything we had they had got, but our arms! A young buck took hold of Cover's gun and tried to take it from him. Bill stuck his revolver in the buck's ear, he looked in Bill's face and let go of the gun. We told Simmons to tell them that they had got everything but our guns and that they could not get them without killing us first. We were told to keep them. Everything we had was packed and off to the village. Such a hubbub when we got there. Our traps were put in a pile and a tent put over them. Simmons and the chiefs held a long pow wow. The women brought us some breakfast; good of the kind and plenty. Simmons told us we were prisoners, to keep still and not to be afraid. I went through the village and counted the lodges; there were 180 of them. We talk the matter over and agree to keep together and if it has to come to the worst to fight while life lasts. All the young ones are around us and the women. What fun! We get plenty to eat; Indians are putting up a great big lodge,–medicine lodge at that. Night, what will tomorrow bring forth? I write this,–will any one ever see it? Quite dark and such a noise, dogs and drums!

May 3rd: All is well. What will we get for breakfast, that is the first thing? Barney has got some flour. Bill asks "If we can get some coffee?" I go to the grub pile. Sugar and coffee all gone. An old woman is watching me. I take the coffee pot and show it to her. She knows what I want and hands me some coffee and sugar; buffalo meat in plenty, cut what we want; high living. The Medicine man made medicine all night. Wonder what the outcome will be? The village is on a large, low flat on the left bank of the river, with a large wooded hill back of it. Could we make that? Yes, the boys say when the time comes we will make it. Simmons tells us we are wanted at the medicine lodge; up we go. Bill says, "Ten o'clock, court now opens." We went in, the medicine man sat on the ground at the far end; both sides were lined with the head men Red Bear and Little Crow, the two chiefs of the village, sat beside the medicine man. We were taken in hand by an old buck; in the center of the lodge there was a bush planted,–the medicine bush–and around and around that bush we went. At last their curiosity was satisfied and we were led out to Red Bear's lodge and told to remain there. We had a good laugh over our cake walk. Bill says if they take us in again we will pull up that medicine bush and whack the medicine man with it. We tell him not to, but he says he will sure. An order comes again, and we go in and around the bush. At the third time Bill pulls up the bush and Mr. Medicine Man gets it on the head. What a time! Not a word spoken; what deep silence for a few minutes! Out we go and the Indians after us. We stand back to back, three facing each way; Red Bear and Little Crow driving the crowd back with their whips, and peace is proclaimed. Red Bear mounts his horse and started in on the longest talk I ever heard of; I don't know what he is talking about; Simmons says he is talking for us. He began the talk about noon and he was still talking when I fell asleep at midnight. We are all in Red Bear's lodge and a guard around it.

May 4th: All's well that ends well. We were told this morning what the verdict was. If we go on down the river they will kill us; if we go back they will give us horses to go with. A bunch of horses were driven up and given to us. I got a blind eyed black and another plug for my three; the rest of the boys in the same fix, except Bill, he got his three back. We got our saddles, a hundred pounds of flour, some coffee, sugar, one plug of tobacco and two robes each for our clothes and blankets; glad to get so much. It did not take us long to saddle up. Simmons asked us what was best for him to do, stop with the Indians or go with us. I spoke for the boys and told him he had better stay with the Indians, if he was afraid to risk his scalp with white men. He stayed. We got away at last. Harry Rodgers was riding by my side. I asked him what he thought would be the outcome. His answer was "God is good." The Indians told us to cross at the ford and go up the south side of the river. We met an old Indian woman and she told us not to cross the ford. She made us understand that if we did we would all be killed. When we came to the ford we camped and got something to eat and when it was dark saddled up and traveled all night; took to the hills in the morning; we were about forty or forty-five miles from our friends, the Indians. They told us Stuart was one day ahead. What has become of them? . . .

May 26th: Off again; horse pretty lame and Bill leading him out of the timber; fine grassy hills and lots of quartz; some antelope in sight; down a long ridge to a creek and camp; had dinner, and Rodgers, Sweeney, Barney and Cover go up the creek to prospect. It was Bill's and my turn to guard camp and look after the horses. We washed and doctored the horse's leg. Bill went across to a bar to see or look for a place to stake the horses. When he came back to camp he said "There is a piece of rimrock sticking out of the bar over there. Get the tools and we will go and prospect it." Bill got the pick and shovel and I the pan and went over. Bill dug the dirt and filled the pan. "Now go" he says, "and wash that pan and see if you can get enough to buy some tobacco when we get to town." I had the pan more than half panned down and had seen some gold as I ran the sand around, when Bill sang out "I have found a scad." I returned for answer, "If you have one I have a hundred." He then came down to where I was with his scad. It was a nice piece of gold. Well, I panned the pan of dirt and it was a good prospect; weighed it and had two dollars and forty cents; weighed Bill's scad and it weighed the same. Four dollars and eighty cents! Pretty good for tobacco money. We went and got another pan and Bill panned that and got more than I had; I got the third one and panned that–best of the three; that is good enough to sleep on. We came to camp, dried and weighed our gold, altogether there was twelve dollars and thirty cents. We saw the boys coming to camp and no tools with them. "Have you found anything?" "We have started a hole but didn't get to bedrock." They began to growl about the horses not being taken care of and to give Bill and me fits. When I pulled the pan around Sweeney got hold of it and the next minute sang out "Salted!" I told Sweeney that if he "would pipe Bill and me down and run us through a sluice box he couldn't get a color," and "the horses could go to the devil or the Indians." Well, we talked over the find and roasted venison till late; and sought the brush, and spread our robes; and a more joyous lot of men never went more contentedly to bed than we.

May 27th: Up before the sun; horses all right; soon the frying pan was on the fire. Sweeney was off with the pan and Barney telling him "to take it aisy." He panned his pan and beat both Bill and me. He had five dollars and thirty cents. "Well, you have got it good, by Jove!" were his greeting words. When we got filled up with elk, Hughes and Cover went up the gulch, Sweeney and Rodgers down, Bill and I to the old place. We panned turn about ten pans at a time, all day long, and it was good dirt too. "A grub stake is what we are after" was our watchword all day, and it is one hundred and fifty dollars in good dust. "God is good" as Rodgers said when we left the Indian camp. Sweeney and Rodgers found a good prospect and have eighteen dollars of the gold to show for it. Barney and Tom brought in four dollars and a half. As we quit, Bill says "there's our supper," a large band of antelope on the hillside. We had our guns with us. He took up one draw and I the other; it was getting dark, but light enough to shoot; got to a good place within about seventy-five yards and shot;

the one I shot at never moved; I thought it missed; I rolled over and loaded up my gun, then the antelope was gone. Bill had shot by this time; I went to where the one I shot at was standing, and found some blood, and the antelope dead not ten steps away; Bill got one too; ate our fill; off to bed.

May 28th: Staked the ground this morning; claims one hundred feet. Sweeney wanted a water–a notice written for a water right and asked me to write it for him. I wrote it for him; then "What name shall we give the creek?" The boys said "You name it." So I wrote "Alder." There was a large fringe of Alder growing along the creek, looking nice and green and the name was given. We staked twelve claims for our friends and named the bars Cover, Fairweather and Rodgers where the discoveries were made. We agree to say nothing of the discovery when we get to Bannack and come back and prospect the gulch thoroughly and get the best. It was midday when we left; we came down the creek past the forks and to its mouth, made marks so we could find the same again and on down the valley (Ram's Horn Gulch) to a small creek; the same we camped on as we went out and made camp for the night; a more happy lot of boys would be hard to find, though covered with seedy clothes.

May 29th: All well. Breakfast such as we have, bread and antelope and cold water and good appetites. What better fare could a prince wish! It might be worse and without the good seasoning given by our find. Down and over the Stinking Water along a high level bench twelve miles or more to the Beaverhead River, then up about six miles and camp. We have come about twenty-five miles.

May 30th: All well. Ate up the last of our meat for breakfast; will have supper at Bannack, ham and eggs. Away we go and have no cares. Crossed at the mouth of the Rattlesnake and up to the Bannack trail, the last stage over the hill and down to the town, the raggedest lot that was ever seen, but happy. Friends on every side. Bob Dempsey grabbed our horses and cared for them. Frank Ruff got us to his cabin. Salt Lake eggs, ham, potatoes, everything. Such a supper! One has to be on short commons and then he will know. Too tired and too glad.

May 31st: Such excitement! Everyone with a long story about the "new find." After I got my store clothes on, I was sitting in a saloon talking with some friends; there were lots of men that were strangers to me; they were telling that we brought in a horse load of gold and not one of the party had told that we had found a color. Such is life in the "Far West." Well we have been feasted and cared for like princes.

3

Stories of Early Pioneers and Indians

■ *Better Than Myth*

ANNICK SMITH

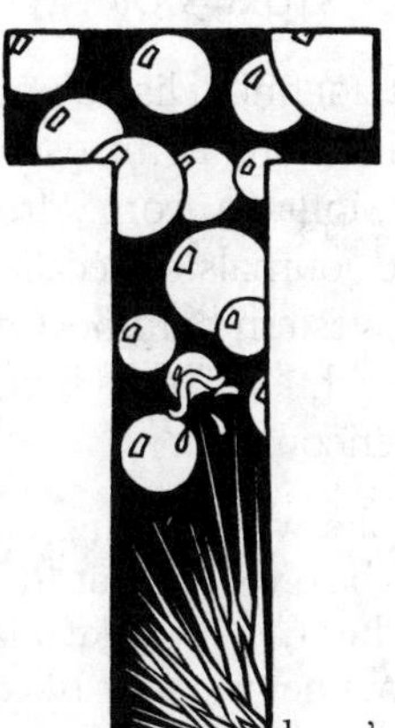

here's a mythological Montana that all Americans know. It is the dwelling place of good cowboys and bad Indians, of sturdy pioneers and ladies of the night—a place of gold and blood and wildness. This Montana is home ground for the Western—the dominant American myth. Names on a map call up magic: Virginia City, Bannack, the Little Big Horn, Yellowstone, Great Falls, Absaroka, the Bitterroots, Deer Lodge. Real names, real places, and legends.

During the nineteenth century, even more than today, plenty of fiction was being written about the Wild West. Stories hit the streets hot on the heels of the events they depicted. We know of 1,700 novels written about Buffalo Bill *during his lifetime*, but not a single one is in print today. The dime novels that popularized the West were invented by eastern writers for the entertainment of large, urban audiences. Imagine Rambo in 1885 but call him Wild Bill Hickok, and you will know how the Western came to be.

No one remembers E. Z. C. Judson, a most prolific pulp writer, but we continue to be enthralled by his more accomplished successors, such as Zane Grey and Louis L'Amour. And the simplistic cowboy code that lies at the heart of the western myth—good guys versus bad guys in a ritual duel—unfortunately still holds great power in American politics and foreign policy. Henry Kissinger once likened himself to the Lone Ranger, Ronald Reagan quotes lines from B-westerns at the drop of a Stetson hat, and Colonel Oliver North has a fan club. John Wayne and Gary Cooper gave face and voice to the mythical cowboys who "won the West." And for millions of people, those movie faces, landscapes, and stories continue to be the only West worth remembering.

We know better. A rich literature of Montana's mining and stockmen's frontiers exists beyond popular novels, comic books, movies, and television. You will not find it listed under "fiction" in your public library, for this is not "literature" in the usual sense. The enduring and true stories of early Montana come from personal experiences recorded in diaries and journals or recalled in reminiscences. Even the self-mythologizing western heroine, Calamity Jane, turns human when an artful writer such as "Teddy Blue" Abbott—a real-life cowboy—recalls an actual encounter:

> It was in 1907, and she was standing on a street corner in Gilt Edge. . . . A few years before . . . some friends of hers had taken up a collection and sent her East to make a lady of her, and now she was back. I joked about her trip and asked her: "How'd you like it when they sent you East to get reformed and civilized?"
>
> Her eyes filled with tears. She said: "Blue, why don't the sons of bitches leave me alone and let me go to hell my own route? All I ask is to be allowed to live out the rest of my life with you boys who speak my language. And I hope they lay me beside Bill Hickok when I die."

This aging Calamity, worn-out and destitute on a street corner in Gilt Edge, is a different creature from the Wild West show caricature of popular fiction. You could run into that old woman in your local bar. No matter where you live, she is someone you might know.

When Granville Stuart does the telling, even a legendary shootout on Main Street—frontier justice in the popular mythology—appears sordid, accidental, and brutal. The demise of two drunken outlaws becomes a black comedy.

> Out in the street "Rattle Snake Jake" mounted his horse and Owen started to mount his, when he spied Joe Doney standing in front of Power's store. Revolver in hand he started to cross the street. When within a few feet of the walk Doney pulled a twenty-two caliber revolver and shot him in the stomach. A second shot struck Owen's hand, causing him to drop his revolver. . . .
>
> "Rattle Snake Jake," revolver in hand started to ride up the street in the opposite direction, when a shot fired by someone in the saloon, struck him in the side. . . . and turning his horse he rode back to his comrade through a perfect shower of lead coming from both sides of the street and together the two men made their last stand in front of the tent [of photographer L. A. Huffman].
>
> . . . When the smoke of battle cleared away examination of the bodies showed that "Rattle Snake Jake" had received nine wounds and Owen eleven, any one of which would have proved fatal.

What was the crime for which these desperadoes paid with their lives? Drinking and "cursing and swearing, declaring that they intended to clean up the town." So much for justice.

Justice. The very word is anathema to the Native American experience. In most popular Westerns, "the Indian" is depicted as a noble savage or a bloodthirsty savage—always savage, in any account, and as incomprehensible as a cigar-store dummy. But the stereotype dissolves in first-hand accounts, such as Andrew Garcia's *Tough Trip Through Paradise*. The old mountain man recalls a time when he got lost in dense mountain forests around Chief Joseph Pass with his Flathead wife, In-who-lise, called "Susie" for short. Their squabbles and strategies of love and revenge as they stumble over deadfalls and crash down rockslides are familiar and heartbreaking and funny. We love this couple, and we understand their domestic situation. In them we find the true literature of Montana.

The mythology is turned on its head again in Frank Linderman's translation of Crow chief Plenty Coups' ugly battle with horse-stealing Blackfeet, "Why I Do Not Like to Fight with White Men." White men are simply too much trouble, Plenty Coups says, even when battling a common enemy. Their ineptness will endanger your whole war party. They wear too many clothes, and they always want to eat. Our stereotypes shatter as Plenty Coups, trying to avoid trouble with white men who have already slaughtered his buffalo and are taking his land, politely yet scornfully denies their equality as men and warriors. This is history in the deepest, most human sense.

Almost every literate adventurer or pioneer knew they were involved in a venture of huge importance, and they wrote a diary or reminiscence to record their participation in it. Out of this hodgepodge of experience and anecdote come a few great stories that shine. With vivid and precise language, these accounts are infused with complex emotions and wit. Characters live, and events compel our interest. You could call them "true stories," but the truth is in the telling.

For instance, Emma Cowan, a ranch wife from Radersburg, wrote a reminiscence about going on a camping trip to Yellowstone National Park in the summer of 1877 with her husband, her brother, and a group of friends. This is a tourist story, but with a twist. Chief Joseph and his people, on the run from the U.S. Army, burst into the picnic. That's how she tells it. A quiet day is invaded by history, and we are given a tale full of horror and bravery. Yet, the same story is filled with surprise and comedy. Emma's matter-of-fact voice carries this historic occurrence completely away from any preconception of the western myth.

A real storyteller creates a world alive with surprise, humor, pathos. He or she speaks in a voice as individual and quirky and full of nuance as your own would be in your best dreams. Here, for instance, is Mary Ronan, remembering her girlhood in the gold-mining camp of Virginia City in 1863:

> There were tall buttercups and blue flags in the valley. Up Alder Gulch snow and timber lilies bloomed, wild roses and syringa grew in sweet profusion and flowering current bushes invited canaries to alight and twitter. . . . Robins, meadowlarks, bluebirds, blackbirds, . . . bluejays, crows and magpies lured us from where men were ravishing the gulch.

And here's what schoolteacher Thomas Dimsdale wrote in his famous *Vigilantes of Montana* about the same town in the same year. He is describing the events that led to the hanging of Captain J. A. Slade:

> J. A. Slade was himself, we have been informed, a Vigilanter; he openly boasted of it, and said he knew all that they knew. . . . He and a couple of his dependents might often be seen on one horse, galloping through the streets, shouting and yelling, firing revolvers, etc. On many occasions he would ride his horse into stores; break up bars, toss the scales out of doors, and use most insulting language to parties present.

Can this be the same place? Which version is truest? What does "true" mean when you are talking about literature? And how has Mary Ronan's experience altered our vision of gold camps and outlaws and vigilantes?

Beyond the voice of the storyteller, serious writing is about character and conflicts and the moral consequences of a person's actions. More often than not such stories deal with the complexities—the changing faces—of love. In her reminiscence, *A Bride Goes West*, Nannie Alderson moves through a series of emotional frontiers as she changes from enthusiastic young ranch wife to isolated and anxious mother and is finally a self-sufficient widow. During the course of her womanhood in Montana, Alderson encounters both friendly and hostile Indians, sees her ranch house burned to the ground, reports on her husband's shooting of the last buffalo in that part of the country, gives birth to a child alone on her kitchen table, and finally moves to Miles City to run a boarding house.

Elizabeth Custer tells a different kind of love story, although here, too, we see the sadness and loneliness and anxiety of frontier women–army wives left behind when their husbands marched off to war. Mrs. Custer remembers a day when the women gathered at the fort to sing and pray at the very moment that their husbands were being killed alongside the Little Big Horn River.

> On Sunday afternoon, June 25, our little group of saddened women, borne down with one common weight of anxiety, sought solace in gathering together in our house. We tried to find some slight surcease from trouble in the old hymns; some of them dated back to our childhood days, when our mothers rocked us to sleep to their soothing strains. . . . All were absorbed in the same thoughts, and their eyes were filled with faraway visions and longings. Indescribable yearning for the absent, and untold terror for their safety, engrossed each heart. The words of the hymn,
>
> *E'en though a cross it be*
> *Nearer, my God, to Thee,*
>
> came forth with almost a sob from every throat.

A most unlikely "love" story is E. C. "Teddy Blue" Abbott's account of his attachment to a handsome and brave young Cheyenne warrior named Pine. Pine was unjustly jailed for a racial incident caused by white cowboys that had begun at Nannie Alderson's place and led to the burning of her cabin.

> While they were all in jail, I went to see Pine every day, and took him presents of tailor-made cigarettes and candy and stuff. . . . The last day he took a silver ring off his finger and gave it to me. The ring had a little shield, and on the shield it said "C Co 7 Cav." That was Tom Custer's company, and Pine took it off the finger of one of Tom Custer's soldiers at the fight, and he was in that fight when he was not yet fourteen years old.

Strange how these stories intertwine and encircle one another. Nannie Alderson, "Teddy Blue" Abbott, Tom Custer, Elizabeth Custer, and a Cheyenne named Pine. Perhaps it is not so strange when you realize how few white people were in Montana before the era of railroads and the hordes of land-hungry settlers. This handful of early pioneers did not live in isolation. Like an extended family, they were connected by necessity and geography and fate.

The literature of Montana's mining and stockmen's frontiers is filled with relationships among whites and Indians, ordinary people trying to come to terms with their consciences. Abbott's prose is sophisticated and moral, a loving and sensitive cowboy writing about the injustice he no longer wants any part of. At about the same time, near the Canadian border in Blackfeet country, another bright young man, adventurer and Indian trader James Willard Schultz, was taking a Blackfeet girl as his bride. In his book of early remembrances, *My Life As an Indian*, Schultz tells about this union with wry tenderness. Life was good and full of promise, but Schultz did not stay in that young man's paradise to witness the succession of broken promises as the buffalo were slaughtered and traditional Indian life began to fall apart. When he returned many years later to visit his Blackfeet friends on the reservation, he found them dying of smallpox and starvation. The U.S. government refused responsibility and did nothing to abet the "Starvation Winter" of 1883-1884. Schultz wrote furious letters and finally got some food to the reservation, although in the long meantime many starved. The voice we hear in his later book, *Blackfeet and Buffalo*, is filled with anger and disillusion. In the few years between adolescence and maturity a way of life older than America's "white" history had been wiped out.

What did Montana's native peoples have to say about their story of dispossession? In Frank Linderman's book-length translations of the memories of Crow chief Plenty Coups and the old medicine woman, Pretty Shield, we see a tragic progression. At first curiosity and trust–the pride of co-equals welcoming a powerful new people to a land full of buffalo and game, plenty for everyone. Their memories are Edenic. But then comes knowledge and, by old age, disillusion–expulsion from the Garden.

Unlike their Indian hosts, the whites were not interested in cohabitation; they had a different, exclusive notion of ownership and land. Pushed onto reservations, with the buffalo gone, the game hunted out, and the tribes decimated by wars and disease, elders and chiefs speak in sad voices in transcribed treaty negotiations. The "Flathead Railroad Treaty Negotiations of 1882" and the "Proceedings of a Council with Sioux Indians of Fort Peck Agency in 1886" read like modern one-act plays, black tragi-comedies in which the Indians try to outsmart the whites at their own game, playing out their hand all the while knowing that the deck is stacked against them. There is wisdom here, irony and candor, and a gift of language that makes you wish you could understand the actual words of Indian orators. And on the other side–from U.S. government agents and mediators–there is oiliness, bluffs and promises, half-truths and outright lies.

The final step in the Native American oral literature of loss goes beyond disillusionment to a fine, bitter anger. We hear it in the famous words that are ascribed to Nez Perce Chief Joseph as he accepted defeat in the Bears Paw Mountains: "I will fight no more forever." And we hear it more vehemently in a speech attributed to the Flatheads' chief, Charlot, pushed out of his tribe's ancestral lands in the Bitterroot and outraged at the notion that his people would have to pay taxes for that privilege. In "The Indian and Taxation," Charlot says:

> Yes, my people, the white man wants us to pay him. He comes in his intent, and says we must pay him–pay him for our own, for the things we have from our God and our forefathers; for things he never owned and never gave us. What law or right is that? What shame or what charity? . . .
>
> And is he not foul? He has filled graves with our bones. His horses, his cattle, his sheep, his men, his women have a rot. Do not his breath, his gums stink? . . . yet he is not ashamed. No, no! His course is destruction; he spoils the Spirit who gave us this country made beautiful and clean. But that is not enough: he wants us to pay him, besides his enslaving our country. Yes, and our people, besides, that degradation of a tribe who never were his enemies.

The battle for property did not end with the conquest of Indian lands. Soon white outlaws were stealing horses and running them over the Canadian border for sale. They were rustling cattle off the open range and hiding out in the rugged canyons of the Missouri Breaks. A new, upper-crust vigilante system was organized to protect such movable property from the riffraff thieves. Its members included a president (Teddy Roosevelt) and a nobleman (Marquis de Mores). As in feudal days, the contest was between life and property, with property ascendant. Granville Stuart, one of the vigilante groups' prime movers, was also Montana's first official historian. He defends the winning side in his essay, "Cattle Rustlers and Vigilantes," from his voluminous reminiscences, *Forty Years on the Frontier*. Readers may wonder if Stuart's stories are history or literature or neither one.

Fortunately, frontier life was not always such a serious matter, and the literature of early Montana is salted and peppered with a great deal of humor. Humor could act as a leavening agent against work and poverty. In *Devil Man with a Gun*, Art H. Watson tells the hilarious tale of a mule skinner called "Stuttering Shorty." Imagine the predicament when his brakes fail, the mules must be spoken to, and the skinner cannot speak! In "Shooting Fish," an ungentlemanly sportsman is blown away along with his game. Other humorous tales act as strategies for survival–fireside warnings, such as John R. Barrows' "Circular Story" from *Ubet*, his book about cowboy life in a small town.

The most famous western humorist of Montana's cowboy frontier days was artist and tall-tale-teller Charles M. Russell. Here is a voice that is self-consciously participating in the western myth, but the participation is altogether self-mocking. In "The Story of a Cowpuncher," Russell's cowpoke persona, Rawhide Rawlins, sizes up the situation:

> "Speakin' of cowpunchers," says Rawhide Rawlins, "I'm glad to see in the last few years that them that know the business have been writin' about 'em. It begin to look like they'd be wiped out without a history. Up to a few years ago there's mighty little known about cows and cow people. It was sure amusin' to read some of them old stories about cowpunchin'. You'd think a puncher growed horns an' was haired over.
>
> "It put me in mind of the eastern girl that asks her mother: 'Ma,' says she, 'Do cowboys eat grass?' 'No dear,' says the old lady, 'they're part human,' an' I don't know but the old gal had 'em sized up right."

Which brings us full circle to the mythological Montana of dime novels and pulp Westerns. Yes, there were cowboys, outlaws, vigilantes, pioneers, six million bison, and fierce Indians in eagle feathers. But the reality we find in the first-hand accounts of Montana's mining and stockmen's frontiers is more complex than the six-gun myth–so much richer in its particularities. Filled with the ambiguities of conquest and colonialism, it is a literature.

Long after comic-book heroes such as the Lone Ranger or Red Ryder have been forgotten, tomorrow's children will be informed, instructed, and entertained by the stories of Plenty Coups, Charlie Russell, Nannie Alderson, and "Teddy Blue" Abbott. When legends fail, we can rely on stories that tell the idiosyncratic human truths.

MARY RONAN

Born in Louisville, Kentucky, in 1852, Mary Ronan came with her family to the Montana mining frontier when she was a very young girl. In this selection from her memoirs–published as Frontier Woman: The Story of Mary Ronan, As Told to Margaret Ronan *(1973)–Ronan presents a lyrical childhood vision of Virginia City, Montana, in 1863, the year of the infamous vigilance committee. In 1873, Mary married Indian agent Peter Ronan and for twenty years lived on the Flathead Indian Reservation. Ronan died in Missoula in 1940.*

Alder Gulch in 1863

Hundreds of tents, brush wickiups, log cabins, even houses of stone quarried from the hills were springing up daily in the windings of Alder Gulch and Daylight Gulch, in the hollows of the hills and along the ramblings of Alder Creek and the Stinking Water. Soon over a stretch of fifteen miles a cluster of towns had assumed the importance of names–Junction, Adobetown, Nevada, Virginia City, Pine Grove, Highland, Summit. In a few weeks the population numbered into the thousands. Every foot of earth in the gulches was being turned upside down. Rough-clad men with long hair and flowing beards swarmed everywhere. Some were digging for bedrock, others were bent over barrow loads of the pay dirt, which they were wheeling to the sluice boxes, and into these boxes yet others were shoveling the dirt. Up and down the narrow streets labored bull trains of sixteen- and twenty-horse teams pulling three and four wagons lashed together, and long strings of packhorses, mules or donkeys. Loafers lolled at the doors or slouched in and out of saloons and hurdygurdy houses too numerous to mention. Frequently the sounds of brawling, insults, oaths echoed through the gulch. When my stepmother sent me down the street on errands she often said, "Now run, Mollie, but don't be afraid." I was never spoken to in any but a kindly way by those men.

Our surroundings I took quite for granted as the way of all places in which little girls lived. Nevada, Central City, Denver and Virginia City were much alike. Here, as in those other towns, was a certain class of women whom I heard called "fancy ladies" because of their gaudy dress, so different from that of the ladies who were our friends.

They were always to be seen either walking up and down or clattering along on horseback or in hacks. Sometimes one was glimpsed through a window lounging in a dressing gown and puffing on a cigarette. They were so in evidence that I felt no curiosity about them. I knew that they were not "good women," but I did not analyze why.

After a while I made the acquaintance of Carrie Crane, Lizzie Keaton and some other little girls; not many though, for few were in Virginia City as long as I lived there. We spent our leisure playing in the back streets or learning the haunts and names of the wild flowers and their times for blossoming.

There were tall buttercups and blue flags in the valley. Up Alder Gulch snow and timber lilies bloomed, wild roses and syringa grew in sweet profusion and flowering currant bushes invited canaries to alight and twitter. There were great patches of moss-flowers with a scent and blossom like sweet-william. And such forget-me-nots—larger and bluer and glossier than any others I have ever seen. On the tumbled hills among and over which the town straggled the primroses made pink splotches in early spring; there the yellowbells nodded and the bitterroots unfolded close to the ground their perplexity of rose petals. In watered draws among the hills blue, yellow and white violets bloomed; in secret places, so we thought, by the creek in Daylight Gulch was a patch of white violets tinted with pink. Wild gooseberries were to be gathered in the Gulch and service berries and choke cherries on its steep sides. Robins, meadowlarks, bluebirds, blackbirds, beautiful as flowers and tantalizingly elusive, and camprobbers, bluejays, crows and magpies lured us from where men were ravishing the gulch.

A walk that was never denied us because it branched away from the diggings, led up Daylight Gulch to a spruce grove called Gum Patch, in a wooded canyon. We learned to distinguish the fir and nut pine and juniper and the dwarf cedar with blue berries. Striped badgers were everywhere among the hills, and so were their holes, which menaced a horse's way. Gophers amused us, whistling, flipping their tails and whisking down their holes. It was fun to startle the cottontails and to watch them dart into the underbrush, or to climb up the mountainside and make the rockchucks scurry away along the sunny walls. Sometimes a deer flashed a white signal of danger as we glimpsed it leaping to cover. On rare occasions we were permitted to go so far out on the benchland that we saw or thought we saw antelope in the distance—sometimes, possibly, a lone buffalo or a wraith of Indian smoke signal. Under the blue, blue sky in the clear air of that high valley, nearly seven thousand feet above sea level, we could see a hundred miles.

My family lived in a big log cabin on Wallace Street, the main thoroughfare running up Daylight Gulch. Because my father was a freighter the Sheehans were well provisioned and always set as good a table as was possible in a remote mining town. My stepmother's and Ellen's dried apple pies and dried peach pies were rare delicacies, much in demand, and so it came about that we began to take boarders. Among them were the "discovery men," as Bill Fairweather, Henry Edgar, Barney Orr and others were called. Among the men who dropped in now and again to a meal was our companion on the journey to Montana, Jack Gallagher. To us he was always courteous and soft-spoken, and yet within the year we came to know that he was one of the most hardened of all the road agents. Another of this gang who came often enough so that I remember him distinctly was George Ives. Childlike, my attention was directed to him because of the long blue soldier's overcoat which he wore. From admiring that I went on to notice that he stood head and shoulders above most of the men who gathered around our table, that unlike the others he was smooth-shaven, and that he was blonde and handsome. Henry Plummer was only a name to me, but after his execution I heard him discussed at home—when he had last come to Virginia City, how picturesque he was in appearance, how gentle in manner. Long before the Vigilantes organized, my father evidently made his own conclusions about the character of some of the patrons of our boardinghouse, for he soon closed the doors of our cabin to the public and moved the family into a little two-room cabin off the main street.

Grasping desperately and by any means for gold, brawling, robbing, shooting and hanging were not all of life in this mining camp. Into our midst came the man of God. He was indeed that, Father Joseph Giordo, S.J., the sweet-faced Italian gentleman whom I came to know so well in later years. He had made the long drive from St. Peter's Mission and had to leave in two days. When he asked where he might say Mass, two young Irishmen, Peter Ronan and John Caplice, placer-mining in partnership, offered a cabin they were having built. Miners from neighboring claims helped to level the floor and to put the cabin in shape for Mass the next morning. My stepmother was asked to dress the improvised altar. She and I covered the roughhewn boards with sheets and arranged the candles. The first Mass in Virginia City was held on the Feast of All Saints, November 1, 1863. It was a simple, reverent congregation that knelt on the dirt floor within the four walls of newhewn logs. By far the majority were bearded miners in worn working clothes. Many received the Holy Eucharist.

I was distracted from contemplating things spiritual to those human by the tinkling sound in large tin cups that were being passed from one man to another. I saw each pour a trickle of gold dust from his buckskin pouch. Then the dust was poured from all the cups into a new yellow buckskin purse and laid upon the altar by Peter Ronan, whom the miners had chosen to make the presentation to the priest.

When Father Giordo went to the stable where he had left his team and asked for his bill, he was told that it was forty dollars for the two days. He turned to Mr. Ronan saying that he had not enough money to pay so excessive a price. Mr. Ronan inquired if he knew how much he had in the yellow purse. Unworldly and unconcerned with money, Father Giordo had not thought of weighing its contents. Together, he and Mr. Ronan did so and found that the purse contained several hundred dollars in gold dust.

Almost every morning the miners cleaned their sluice boxes with a tin contrivance called a scraper, but much fine gold was left in the cracks of the boxes and around the edges. After the miners had gone into their cabins for supper, a little friend and I would take our blowers and hair brushes, which we kept for the purpose, and gather up the fine gold. We took it home, dried it in the oven and blew the black sand from it. Sometimes our gold dust weighed to the amount of a dollar or more. It was the only kind of money I ever saw in Virginia City. I kept my dust in a small guttapercha inkwell, which had traveled with us from Denver, and carried it when I went to the store to buy rock candy. My friend and I thought that this sweet was kept especially for little girl shoppers—the phrase "rock and rye" was familiar to us but not meaningful. Sometimes the storekeeper had stick candy, candy beans, or ginger snaps. Twenty-five cents was the least that was ever accepted across the counter. Once I bought my father a present of a shirt, which cost $2.50 in gold dust.

A man would have entered another's sluice-box at the risk of being shot on sight, but it amused the miners to have us little girls clean up after them. One never-to-be-forgotten evening I busied myself about the property of Peter Ronan. I was wearing my new shaker, a straw poke bonnet, trimmed in pink chambray, which my stepmother had just made. I laid it on a cross-piece of a box while I stooped to brush and blow. Mr. Ronan, not noticing me, lifted a gate above and let muddy water run through his boxes. It splashed on the adored pink chambray "valance." Many times afterward I heard Mr. Ronan tell in his inimitable way how the angry little girl suddenly stood straight, then scrambled from the sluicebox, crying out, "I'll never, never, never again, Mister, take gold from your sluicebox." His dark eyes flashed and he laughed gaily as he apologized and begged me to reconsider. This is my first memory of Peter Ronan.

THOMAS J. DIMSDALE

Thomas J. Dimsdale was the schoolmaster and newspaperman in Virginia City, Montana, during its vigilante period. In 1865, Dimsdale wrote a series of articles for the Montana Post *that he compiled the next year and published as Montana's first book.* The Vigilantes of Montana, or Popular Justice in the Rocky Mountains *became a classic source for countless popular "outlaw" westerns and is available in several editions.*

The Execution of "The Greaser" (Joe Pizanthia) and Dutch John (Wagner)

A marked change in the tone of public sentiment was the consequence of the hanging of the bloodstained criminals, whose deserved fate is recorded in the preceding chapters. Men breathed freely; for Plummer and Stinson especially were dreaded by almost everyone. The latter was of the type of that brutal desperado whose formula of introduction to a Western barroom is so well known in the mountains: "Whoop! I'm from Pike County, Missouri; I'm ten feet high; my abode is where lewd women and licentious men mingle; my parlor is the Rocky mountains. I smell like a wolf; I drink water out of a brook like a horse. Look out, you ——, I'm going to turn loose," etc. A fit mate for such a God-forgotten outlaw was Stinson, and he, with the only and snake-like demon, Plummer, the wily, red-handed, and politely merciless chief, and the murderer and robber, Ray, were no more. The Vigilantes organized rapidly. Public opinion sustained them.

On Monday morning it was determined to arrest "the Greaser," Joe Pizanthia, and to see precisely how his record stood in the Territory. Outside of it, it was known that he was a desperado, a murderer and a robber; but that was not the business of the Vigilantes. A party started for his cabin, which was built on a side-hill. The interior looked darker than usual from the bright glare of the surrounding snow. The summons to come forth being disregarded, Smith Ball and George Copley entered, contrary to the advice of their comrades, and instantly received the fire of their concealed foe. Copley was shot through the breast. Smith Ball received a bullet in the hip. They both staggered out, each ejaculating, "I'm shot." Copley was led off by two friends, and died of his wound. Smith Ball recovered himself, and was able to empty his six-shooter into the body of the assassin, when the latter was dragged forth.

The popular excitement rose nearly to madness. Copley was a much-esteemed citizen, and Smith Ball had many friends. It was the instant resolution of all present that the vengeance on the Greaser should be summary and complete.

A party whose military experience was still fresh in their memory made a rush, at the double-quick, for a mountain howitzer which lay dismounted, where it had been left by the train to which it was attached. Without waiting to place it on the carriage, it was brought by willing hands to within five rods of the windowless side of the cabin, and some old artillerists, placing it on a box, loaded it with shell, and laid it for the building. By one of those omissions so common during times of excitement, the fuse was left uncut, and, being torn out in its passage through the logs, the missile never exploded, but left a clean beach through the wall, making the chips fly. A second shell was put into the gun, and this time the fuse was cut, but the range was so short that the explosion took place after it had traversed the house.

Thinking that Pizanthia might have taken refuge in the chimney, the howitzer was pointed for it and sent a solid shot through it. Meanwhile the military judgment of the leader had been shown by the posting of some riflemen opposite the shot-hole, with instructions to maintain so rapid a fire upon it that the beleagured inmate should not be able to use it as a crenelle through which to fire upon the assailants. No response being given to the cannon and small-arms, the attacking party began to think of storming the dwelling.

The leader called for volunteers to follow him. Nevada cast in her lot first, and men from the crowd joined. The half dozen stormers moved steadily, under cover of the edge of the last building, and then dashed at the house, across the open space. The door had fallen from the effects of the fusillade; but, peeping in, they could not see anything until a sharp eye noticed the Greaser's boots protruding. Two lifted the door, while Smith Ball drew his revolver and stood ready. The remainder seized the boots.

On lifting the door, Pizanthia was found lying flat and badly hurt. His revolver was beside him. He was quickly dragged out, Smith Ball paying him for the wound he had received by emptying his revolver into him.

A clothes-line was taken down and fastened round his neck; the leader climbed a pole, and the rest holding up the body, he wound the rope round the top of the stick of timber, making a jamb hitch. While aloft, fastening all securely, the crowd blazed away upon the murderer swinging beneath his feet. At his request, "Say, boys! stop shooting a minute"–the firing ceased, and he came down "by the run." Over one hundred shots were discharged at the swaying corpse.

A friend–one of the four "Bannack originals"–touched the leader's arm and said, "Come and see my bonfire." Walking down to the cabin, he found that it had been razed to the ground by the maddened people, and was then in a bright glow of flame. A proposition to burn the Mexican was received with a shout of exultation. The body was hauled down and thrown upon the pile, upon which it was burned to ashes so completely that not a trace of bone could be seen when the fire burned out.

In the morning some women of ill-fame actually panned out the ashes to see whether the desperado had any gold in his purse. We are glad to say that they were not rewarded for their labors by striking any auriferous deposit.

The popular vengeance had been only partially satisfied so far as Pizanthia was concerned; and it would be well if those who preach against the old Vigilance Committee would reflect upon the great difference which existed between the prompt and really necessary severity which they exercised and the wild and ungovernable passion which goads the masses of all countries, when roused to deeds of vengeance of a type so fearful that humanity recoils at the recital. Over and over again we have heard a man declaring that it was "a ——— shame," to hang some one that he wished to see punished. "———, he ought to be burnt; I would pack brush three miles up a mountain myself." "He ought to be fried in his own grease," etc., and it must not be supposed that such expressions were mere idle bravado. The men said just what they meant. In cases where criminals convicted of grand larceny have been whipped, it has never yet happened that the punishment has satisfied the crowd. The truth is, that the Vigilance Committee simply punished with death men unfit to live in any community, and that death was, usually, almost instantaneous, and only momentarily painful. With the exceptions recorded (Stinson and Ray) the drop and the death of the victim seemed simultaneous. In a majority of cases, a few almost imperceptible muscular contortions, not continuing over a few seconds, were all that the keenest observer could detect; whereas, had their punishment been left to outsiders, the penalty would have been cruel and disgusting in the highest degree. What would be thought of the burning of Wagner and panning out his ashes "By order of the Vigilantes"? In every case where men have confessed their crimes to the Vigilantes of Montana, they dreaded the vengeance of their comrades far more than their execution at the hands of the Committee, and clung to them as if they considered them friends.

A remarkable instance of this kind was apparent in the conduct of John Wagner. While in custody at the cabin, on Yankee Flat, the sound of footsteps and suppressed voices was heard in the night. Fetherstun jumped up, determined to defend himself and his prisoner to the last. Having prepared his arms, he cast a look over his shoulder to see what Dutch John was doing. The road agent stood with a double-barrelled gun in his hand, evidently watching for a chance to do battle on behalf of his captor. Fetherstun glanced approvingly at him, and said, "That's right, John, give them ——." John smiled grimly and nodded, the muzzle of his piece following the direction of the sound, and his dark eyes glaring like those of a roused lion. Had he wished, he could have shot Fetherstun in the back, without either difficulty or danger. Probably the assailants heard the clicking of the locks of the pieces in the still night, and therefore determined not to risk such an attack, which savages of all kinds especially dislike.

The evening after the death of Pizanthia the newly-organized Committee met, and, after some preliminary discussion, a vote was taken as to the fate of Dutch John. The result was that his execution was unanimously adjudged, as the only penalty meeting the merits of the case. He had been a murderer and a highway robber for years.

The Arrest and Execution of Captain J. A. Slade

J. A. Slade, or, as he was often called, Captain Slade, was raised in Clinton County, Ill., and was a member of a highly respectable family. He bore a good character for several years in that place. The acts which have given so wide a celebrity to his name were performed especially on the Overland Line, of which he was for years an official. Reference to these matters will be made in a subsequent part of this chapter.

Captain J. A. Slade came to Virginia City in the spring of 1863. He was a man gifted with the power of making money, and when free from the influence of alcoholic stimulants, which seemed to reverse his nature, and to change a kind-hearted and intelligent gentleman into a reckless demon, no man in the Territory had a greater faculty of attracting the favorable notice of even strangers, and in spite of the wild lawlessness which characterized his frequent spells of intoxication, he had many, very many friends whom no commission of crime itself could detach from his personal companionship. Another and less desirable class of friends were attracted by his very recklessness. There are probably a thousand individuals in the West possessing a correct knowledge of the leading incidents of a career that terminated at the gallows, who still speak of Slade as a perfect gentleman, and who not only lament his death, but talk in the highest terms of his character, and pronounce his execution a murder. One way of accounting for the diversity of opinion regarding Slade is sufficiently obvious. Those who saw him in his natural state only would pronounce him to be a kind husband, a most hospitable host, and a courteous gentleman. On the contrary, those who met him when maddened with liquor and surrounded by a gang of armed roughs would pronounce him a fiend incarnate.

During the summer of 1863 he went to Milk River as a freighter. For this business he was eminently qualified, and he made a great deal of money. Unfortunately his habit of profuse expenditure was uncontrollable, and at the time of his execution he was deeply in debt almost everywhere.

After the execution of the five men on the 14th of January the Vigilantes considered that their work was nearly ended. They had freed the country from highwaymen and murderers to a great extent, and they determined that in the absence of the regular civil authority they would establish a People's Court, where all offenders should be tried by a judge and jury. This was the nearest approach to social order that the circumstances permitted, and though strict legal authority was wanting, yet the people were firmly determined to maintain its efficiency and to enforce its decrees. It may here be mentioned that the overt act which was the last round on the fatal ladder leading to the scaffold on which Slade perished was the tearing in pieces and stamping upon a writ of this court, followed by the arrest of the judge, Alex. Davis, by authority of a presented derringer and with his own hands.

J. A. Slade was himself, we have been informed, a Vigilanter; he openly boasted of it, and said he knew all that they knew. He was never accused or even suspected of either murder or robbery committed in this Territory (the latter crimes were never laid to his charge any place); but that he had killed several men in other localities was notorious, and his bad reputation in this respect was a most powerful argument in determining his fate, when he was finally arrested for the offense above mentioned. On returning from Milk River he became more and more addicted to drinking; until at last it was a common feat for him and his friends to "take the town." He and a couple of his dependents might often be seen on one horse, galloping through the streets, shouting and yelling, firing revolvers, etc. On many occasions he would ride his horse into stores; break up bars, toss the scales out of doors, and use most insulting language to parties present. Just previous to the day of his arrest he had given a fearful beating to one of his followers; but such was his influence over them that the man wept bitterly at the gallows, and begged for his life with all his power. It had become quite common when Slade was on a spree for the shopkeepers and citizens to close the stores and put out all the lights, being fearful of some outrage at his hands. One store in Nevada he never ventured to enter—that of the Lott brothers—as they had taken care to let him know that any attempt of the kind would be followed by his sudden death, and though he often rode down there, threatening to break in and raise ——, yet he never attempted to carry his threat into execution. For his wanton destruction of goods and furniture he was always ready to pay when sober if he had money; but there were not a few who regarded payment as small satisfaction for the outrage, and these men were his personal enemies.

From time to time Slade received warnings from men that he well knew would not deceive him, of the certain end of his conduct.

There was not a moment, for weeks previous to his arrest, in which the public did not expect to hear of some bloody outrage. The dread of his very name, and the presence of the armed band of hangers-on who followed him, alone prevented a resistance which must certainly have ended in the instant murder or mutilation of the opposing party.

Slade was frequently arrested by order of the court whose organization we have described, and had treated it with respect by paying one or two fines, and promising to pay the rest when he had money; but in the transaction that occurred at this crisis, he forgot even this caution, and goaded by passion and the hatred of restraint, he sprang into the embrace of death.

Slade had been drunk and "cutting up" all night. He and his companions had made the town a perfect hell. In the morning, J. M. Fox, the sheriff, met him, arrested him, took him into court, and commenced reading a warrant that he had for his arrest, by way of arraignment. He became uncontrollably furious, and seizing the writ, he tore it up, threw it on the ground, and stamped upon it. The clicking of the locks of his companions' revolvers was instantly heard and a crisis was expected. The sheriff did not attempt his capture; but being at least as prudent as he was valiant, he succumbed, leaving Slade the master of the situation, and the conqueror and ruler of the courts, law, and law-makers. This was a declaration of war, and was so accepted. The Vigilance Committee now felt that the question of social order and the preponderance of the law-abiding citizens had then and there to be decided. They knew the character of Slade, and they were well aware that they must submit to his rule without murmur, or else that he must be dealt with in such fashion as would prevent his being able to wreak his vengeance on the Committee, who could never have hoped to live in the Territory secure from outrage or death, and who could never leave it without encountering his friends, whom his victory would have emboldened and stimulated to a pitch that would have rendered them reckless of consequences. The day previous, he had ridden into Dorris' store, and on being requested to leave, he drew his revolver and threatened to kill the gentleman who spoke to him. Another saloon he had led his horse into, and buying a bottle of wine, he tried to make the animal drink it. This was not considered an uncommon performance, as he had often entered saloons and commenced firing at the lamps, causing a wild stampede.

A leading member of the Committee met Slade, and informed him in the quiet, earnest manner of one who feels the importance of what he is saying, "Slade, get your horse at once, and go home or there will be —— to pay." Slade started and took a long look with his dark and piercing eyes, at the gentleman—"What do you mean?" said he. "You have no right to ask me what I mean," was the quiet reply, "get your horse at once, and remember what I tell you." After a short pause he promised to do so, and actually got into the saddle; but, being still intoxicated, he began calling aloud to one after another of his friends, and at last seemed to have forgotten the warning he had received and became again uproarious, shouting the name of a well-known prostitute in company with those of two men whom he considered heads of the Committee, as a sort of challenge; perhaps, however, as a single act of bravado. It seems probable that the intimation of personal danger he had received had not been forgotten entirely; though, fatally for him, he took a foolish way of showing his remembrance of it. He sought out Alexander Davis, the Judge of the Court, and drawing a cocked derringer, he presented it at his head, and told him that he should hold him as a hostage for his own safety. As the Judge stood perfectly quiet, and offered no resistance to his captor, no further outrage followed on this score. Previous to this, on account of the critical state of affairs, the Committee had met, and at last resolved to arrest him. His execution had not been agreed upon, and, at that time, would have been negatived, most assuredly. A messenger rode down to Nevada to inform the leading men of what was on hand, as it was desirable to show that there was a feeling of unanimity on the subject, all along the Gulch.

The miners turned out almost en masse, leaving their work and forming in solid column, about six hundred strong, armed to the teeth, they marched up to Virginia. The leader of the body well knew the temper of his men on the subject. He spurred on ahead of them, and hastily calling a meeting of the Executive, he told them plainly that the miners meant "business," and that, if they came up, they would not stand in the street to be shot down by Slade's friends; but that they would take him and hang him. The meeting was small, as the Virginia men were loath to act at all. This momentous announcement of the feeling of the Lower Town was made to a cluster of men, who were deliberating behind a wagon, at the rear of a store on Main Street, where the Ohlinghouse stone building now stands.

The Committee was most unwilling to proceed to extremities. All the duty they had ever performed seemed as nothing to the task before them; but they had to decide, and that quickly. It was finally agreed that if the whole body of the miners were of the opinion that he should be hanged, the Committee left it in their hands to deal with him. Off, at hot speed, rode the leader of the Nevada men to join his command.

Slade had found out what was intended, and the news sobered him instantly. He went into P. S. Pfout's store, where Davis was, and apologized for his conduct, saying that he would take it all back.

The head of the column now wheeled into Wallace street and marched up at quick time. Halting in front of the store, the executive officer of the Committee stepped forward and arrested Slade, who was at once informed of his doom, and inquiry was made as to whether he had any business to settle. Several parties spoke to him on the subject; but to all such inquiries he turned a deaf ear, being entirely absorbed in the terrifying reflections on his own awful position. He never ceased his entreaties for life, and to see his dear wife. The unfortunate lady referred to, between whom and Slade there existed a warm affection, was at this time living at their ranch on the Madison. She was possessed of considerable personal attractions; tall, well-formed, of graceful carriage, pleasing manners, and was, withal, an accomplished horsewoman.

A messenger from Slade rode at full speed to inform her of her husband's arrest. In an instant she was in the saddle, and with all the energy that love and despair could lend to an ardent temperament and a strong physique, she urged her fleet charger over the twelve miles of rough and rocky ground that intervened between her and the object of her passionate devotion.

Meanwhile a party of volunteers had made the necessary preparations for the execution, in the valley traversed by the branch. Beneath the site of Pfout's and Russel's stone building there was a corral, the gate-posts of which were strong and high. Across the top was laid a beam, to which the rope was fastened, and a dry-goods box served for the platform. To this place Slade was marched, surrounded by a guard, composing the best-armed and most numerous force that has ever appeared in Montana Territory.

The doomed man had so exhausted himself by tears, prayers, and lamentations, that he had scarcely strength left to stand under the fatal beam. He repeatedly exclaimed, "My God! my God! must I die? Oh, my dear wife!"

On the return of the fatigue party, they encountered some friends of Slade, staunch and reliable citizens and members of the Committee, but who were personally attached to the condemned. On hearing of his sentence, one of them, a stout-hearted man, pulled out his handkerchief and walked away, weeping like a child. Slade still begged to see his wife most piteously, and it seemed hard to deny his request; but the bloody consequences that were sure to follow the inevitable attempt at a rescue that her presence and entreaties would have certainly incited, forbade the granting of his request. Several gentlemen were sent for to see him in his last moments, one of whom (Judge Davis) made a short address to the people; but in such low tones as to be inaudible, save to a few in his immediate vicinity. One of his friends, after exhausting his powers of entreaty, threw off his coat and declared that the prisoner could not be hanged until he himself was killed. A hundred guns were instantly leveled at him; whereupon he turned and fled; but, being brought back, he was compelled to resume his coat, and to give a promise of future peaceable demeanor.

Scarcely a leading man in Virginia could be found, though numbers of the citizens joined the ranks of the guard when the arrest was made. All lamented the stern necessity which dictated the execution.

Everything being ready, the command was given, "Men, do your duty," and the box being instantly slipped from beneath his feet, he died almost instantaneously.

The body was cut down and carried to the Virginia Hotel, where, in a darkened room, it was scarcely laid out, when the unfortunate and bereaved companion of the deceased arrived, at headlong speed, to find that all was over, and that she was a widow. Her grief and heart-piercing cries were terrible evidences of the depth of her attachment for her lost husband, and a considerable period elapsed before she could regain the command of her excited feelings. . . .

Such was Captain J. A. Slade, the idol of his followers, the terror of his enemies and of all that were not within the charmed circle of his dependents. In him, generosity and destructiveness, brutal lawlessness and courteous kindness, firm friendship and volcanic outbreaks of fury, were so mingled that he seems like one born out of date. He should have lived in feudal times, and have been the comrade of the Front de Boeufs, De Lacys, and Bois Guilberts, of days almost forgotten. In modern times, he stands nearly alone.

The execution of Slade had a most wonderful effect upon society. Henceforth, all knew that no one man could domineer or rule over the community. Reason and civilization then drove brute force from Montana.

One of his principal friends wisely absconded, and so escaped sharing his fate, which would have been a thing almost certain had he remained.

It has often been asked why Slade's friends were permitted to go scot free, seeing that they accompanied him in all his "raids," and both shared and defended his wild and lawless exploits. The answer is very simple. The Vigilantes deplored the sad but imperative necessity for the making of one example. That, they knew, would be sufficient. They were right in their judgment, and immovable in their purpose. Could it but be made known how many lives were at their mercy, society would wonder at the moderation that ruled in their counsels. Necessity was the arbiter of these men's fate. When the stern Goddess spoke not, the doom was unpronounced, and the criminal remained at large. They acted for the public good, and when examples were made, it was because the safety of the community demanded a warning to the lawless and the desperate, that might neither be despised nor soon forgotten.

The execution of the road agents of Plummer's gang was the result of the popular verdict and judgment against robbers and murderers. The death of Slade was the protest of society on behalf of social order and the rights of man.

■ FRANK B. LINDERMAN

Frank Bird Linderman was born in Ohio in 1869 and came west when he was sixteen years old. Although he had a long and colorful career as trapper, guide, newspaperman, and businessman, Linderman's greatest achievements were the writing of two pivotal books about the Native American experience. Linderman transcribed the reminiscences of Chief Plenty Coups (1848-1932) and the old medicine woman, Pretty Shield, from first-hand interviews. John Day in Cleveland first saw these volumes into print as Plenty-coups, Chief of the Crows *(1930) and* Pretty-shield, Medicine Woman of the Crows *(1932). Linderman died at his home on Flathead Lake in 1938.*

From Plenty-coups, Chief of the Crows

Pecunie Coup

Nearly always after telling a story the Chief would spend a little time talking to Coyote-runs and Plain-bull. I had grown to expect it and used these moments to go over my notes. This time his talk was interrupted by the coming of Plain-feather, a friend of mine whom I had not seen for some time. Plain-feather had once told me a story so crammed with horrible detail that I believed I should be obliged to leave it out of a collection I had made among the Crows for publication. However, after much careful work I had included it, and later on was greatly surprised to discover almost the identical tale in a translation from the Sanskrit. Now I wished to tell him, as best I could, of finding his story in the writings of a very ancient people who had inhabited a far-off land across the Big Water. After we had greeted each other, as he could speak no English, I asked the interpreter to relate to him what I wished him to know. He was intensely interested, and, after the interpreter had finished speaking, stood looking for a long time out of the window across the plains. Then he turned to me, his face expressionless. "These things are beyond us," he said simply. When he was gone the chief began again.

"One winter," he said, "when I was quite young, not over twenty, Pretty-eagle carried the pipe for a war-party against the Pecunies [a tribe of the Blackfeet, called Piegans by white men]. He was a brave warrior and picked his party with care. He has now gone to his Father, but Bell-rock, who is older than I and was older than Pretty-eagle, is still alive and will remember what I am going to tell you.

"The weather was cold, but in those days in all kinds of weather men had good times. Cold days were the same to us as warm ones, and we were nearly always happy. We headed for the Beartooth Mountains, with only one horse in the party. He carried our extra moccasins, a few robes, and some pemmican, enough for twenty men. Three times we camped in the mountains, and then turned away for the Judith Basin where we stopped for one night in sight of the Two Buttes. Next morning before the party moved, seven Wolves were sent out to travel ahead, and I was one of the seven. Bear-from-the-waist-down carried the pipe for the Wolf party, who were Fleshings, Bird-on-the-ground, Medicine-rock-goes-out, Little-gun, Gros Ventres-horse, and myself. Besides these warriors there was a pup with us Wolves, a young man on his first war-party. His name was Pounded-meat, a brave man of eighteen years.

"We Wolves were on a high hill looking toward Plum Creek, and saw just below us on the plains a band of buffalo cows. Before we had looked over the country carefully, as we ought to have done to see what besides buffalo was there, somebody–I have forgotten who–said, 'We have been eating bull meat long enough. Let us go down there and kill a fat cow, and fill up.'

"Nobody objected, and all except Gros Ventres-horse and me went down the hill to get some fat meat. I suppose I might have gone too, if I had not been the owner of the only telescope in the party, but I stayed to use my glass and very soon was glad I had not left the hill. I saw a queer thing, a thing I had never seen before. A Pecunie war-party with only one Wolf ahead of it was traveling toward us afoot, through the snow on the plains. And the queer thing, or I mean the thing that made what I saw look queer, was far behind–so far off that without a telescope I might not have seen it at all. It was a Flathead war-party on the trail of the Pecunies! The Flatheads had horses, but were themselves walking in the snow in the Pecunies' trail.

"I was most interested in the Pecunies, of course. They were nearest, and the people we were looking for. Besides, they were heading for the Crow country, but I thought we should soon be able to show them Crows enough, without their having to travel so far. Their Wolf, who was now on a knoll top, stopped, turning back toward his party. This was enough for me, and I howled like a wolf to tell my companions I had seen the enemy.

"I felt certain the Pecunie Wolf had seen only me and not the buffalo hunters down below, who were five against the Pecunie party of exactly that number, but I was mistaken. Before I could reach the trail my companions had made in the deep snow on the hillside when they went down to get a buffalo cow, I saw the Pecunies coming straight for them, and howled again, turning to see how far off our main party was. Seeing our men coming as fast as they could lead the horse along, some of them running ahead, I knew we now had the best of it, and waited for the whole party to come up.

"But the Pecunies, when they discovered us on the hill, turned to run, with the five already down on the plains after them. Most of us dashed down through the snow to join in the chase, but the horse could not walk on that side of the hill, the snow being deeper; so they had to blindfold him and push him over. He slid to the bottom without hurting himself, making a fine trail for those who waited to follow.

"Nobody besides myself knew about the party of Flatheads who were yet far away, but I realized we should have trouble with them after we finished with the Pecunies. We were scattered all the way from the horse to the leaders. The latter were not very far behind the Pecunies, who finally made a stand in a deep wash-out, where they began shooting at the leading Crows.

"We did not have a gun in our party, only bows and arrows. I remember I had twenty good arrows that day, and a bow that would send them where I wished them to go. I had been hoping for an opportunity to count coup, and when I reached the wash-out I found what I wanted. Our party, all that had reached the wash-out, had surrounded the Pecunies, but as yet had done them no harm. There were four of the enemy in a bend of the wash-out not far from me, and one, who had both a gun and a pistol, about two hundred yards further up. This fellow appeared to be the pipe-carrier for the Pecunie party, and I wanted his scalp.

"I tied my medicine beneath the left braid of my hair and sang my war-song. When I had finished, the lone Pecunie in the wash-out stood up. He knew my song! 'Let us not fight,' he called out. 'Let us make peace.'

"Ho! I knew him! His name was The-bull. He had once left his own people, the Pecunies, to live with us. He had taken a Crow woman and then, after a while, left her with children to support. These children yet live on this reservation. I see them quite often. Ho! I knew The-bull. My heart was bad toward him. He had betrayed us and, knowing our country, was even now leading a war-party against us.

" 'I know you well,' I called to him. 'You are The-bull, and this day you shall die!'

"His point of the wash-out bent out toward us, and I saw several large bunches of rye-grass, tall as a man, standing between it and me. Thinking I could use them, I ran zigzag, as the snipe-bird flies, for the nearest.

"The-bull fired, but missed me, and I slid into the first bunch of rye-grass to get my breath. But I was not alone. Somebody's feet touched my shoulders when I landed. Looking back, I saw the Wolf pup, Pounded-meat. He was breathing hard, and his eyes were burning like coals in a lodge fire. I felt proud of him. 'Be careful,' I told him when I stood up to run for another bunch of the rye-grass.

"I slid into it, unhit by The-bull's shot, which spattered snow and little stones around me and Pounded-meat, who was sticking to me like mud. I had again felt the pup's toes against my back when I landed, and now I felt his breath on my neck when I got up on my knees. I was not twenty feet from my enemy, and, if only I could manage to see him, I could finish things quickly from where I was.

"'Get up and fight me! I am here before you!' The-bull's voice surprised me.

"Though I did not believe him, I raised myself up to look over the top of the rye-grass. And there he was! His gun flashed almost in my face. He missed! And my arrow passed through his nose just above his mouth. Its blow whirled him half round, and he staggered backward, falling into the wash-out and looking as though he held my arrow between his lips.

"I realized his hurt was not fatal and was aware that he had a pistol. He would get up to fight again. Springing to the rim of the wash-out I looked over it, into his pistol's smoke that blinded my eyes. Its bullet brushed my hair, but that was all–all he had time to do before my arrow reached his heart.

"I knew there was now another Pecunie under the bank near me and thought I had him located exactly. But he fooled me a little by moving. If his gun had not hung fire he might have finished me, but he had bad luck and missed. I heard my arrow strike bone in his body before I jumped down into the wash-out with the Wolf pup by my side.

"The-bull and the other Pecunie were finished. I realized there might be others under the banks, which were not so high as I had thought; but as I could see none, I raised my bow to tell any Crow who might see it that the fight was over.

"'Look out! Here they come!' cried Pounded-meat.

"I turned, an arrow on my bowstring, and saw a gun flash from the wash-out below me. The-wolf, one of our best men, pitched head-first into the snow, and was still. I jumped upon a rock to climb out and go to him. But Pounded-meat held my arm.

"A lone Pecunie was running toward us down the wash-out with Pretty-eagle and another Crow behind him. We pressed our bodies against the bank until the Pecunie had come abreast of us; then Pounded-meat sprang from my side and slapped his face–counted coup–before Pretty-eagle could get hold of him.

"They fell in the snow and rolled over. Somehow the Pecunie escaped Pretty-eagle, and if Little-gun's arrow had not caught him he might have given us a lot of trouble. He was the last. The fighting was finished, but The-wolf, a good man, was lying on the snow in a circle of blood, and our hearts were beside him.

"We raised him up and got the blood out of his mouth. 'Try to save him,' said Gros Ventres-horse to my uncle, Takes-plenty, one of our Wise Ones, as he untied a fine necklace from his own neck and put it around mine." [It was not customary to offer reward directly to a medicine-man for his services. To show earnestness the necklace was given to Plenty-coups, who was related to the medicine-man.]

"'I will try. We must not leave his body in the Pecunie country,' said Takes-plenty, removing a little buckskin pouch from his shirt.

"The-wolf's mind was yet sound, but he was nearly gone. The bullet hole was in his breast, and blood was coming from his mouth and nose, when Takes-plenty opened his pouch and took out a pinch of The-flower-the-buffalo-will-not-eat [?] and a little of another kind of flower I did not know. He chewed them in his mouth, and, stepping to windward, blew them upon The-wolf's breast. He then walked one-quarter round him and did the same thing, then half round, then three quarters, each time chewing a portion of the two flowers and blowing them upon The-wolf, who lay upon his back with his eyes open. I knew he understood what was going on, and hoped with all my heart he would get well.

"Takes-plenty snorted like a buffalo-bull and jumped over The-wolf's body, and I saw the wounded man turn his eyes and try to move his body a little, as though he wished to sit up. But Takes-plenty did not even look at him. He jumped again and again over his body and legs, each time snorting like a buffalo-bull. 'Bring me a robe with a tail on it,' he said to us, who were watching.

"He shook the buffalo's tail before the seeing eyes of The-wolf, snorting and jumping over his body till The-wolf reached out his hand in a weak effort to take hold of the tail. But Takes-plenty did not even look, or did not seem to. I felt like calling out, 'Wait! wait!' because he did not see and was now even backing away from The-wolf, who reached farther and farther, at last sitting up.

"I stepped out to help him, but Takes-plenty waved me away and kept backing, backing up, his eyes now looking into the dim ones of the wounded man that were growing brighter as he reached out again and again to take hold of the buffalo's tail that fluttered about before them, until he staggered to his feet without help.

"They were walking slowly in a circle, when Takes-plenty, without looking our way or stopping the buffalo's tail that kept fluttering before the eyes of The-wolf, said 'Open his shirt.'

"As I did so, I heard his breath whistling through the bullet hole in his breast. I stepped back, and Takes-plenty, standing a little way from him, told The-wolf to stretch himself. When he did, black blood dropped out of the hole to the snow. When red blood came my uncle stopped it with the flowers from his pouch.

"The-wolf walked alone among us. 'I am all right,' he said, and our hearts began to sing. It was then I thought of The-bull's scalp. My people seldom take an enemy's scalp if a Crow has been killed in the fight. But now that The-wolf was all right I went back and took the scalp of The-bull, the only one I wanted."

Here I interrupted Plenty-coups, to ask about Takes-plenty, the medicine-man who had healed The-wolf. I have heard many such tales, and always from old men. Their replies to my question, "Why are such cures not practiced today?" are the same. Plenty-coups said, "Such things were done long ago by good men who were wise. Nobody now understands what our Wise Ones knew before the white man came to change this world. Our children learn nothing from us, and watching the young whites, have no religion. I hope, if they cannot find and hold firmly to our old beliefs, that they will learn the religion the white man teaches and cling fast to it, because all men must have a religion, if they would live." . . .

"I have not finished with the Pecunies," said Plenty-coups, taking the pipe. "The next morning, when the village moved, snow was falling and the air was sharp as a knife. We who had been on the raid against the Pecunies rode together beside the line of moving travois, singing our war-songs, while young women smiled at us and called our names. It was good to live in those days.

"Suddenly we saw the horses far ahead stop, and men ride out from the head end of the line. One came dashing back along it, calling out some message, but we did not stop to hear it. We lashed our horses into a run to see what was going on, hope for a fight in our hearts. We got our wish. Men were already fighting on the Sweetgrass [creek], and we saw a dead Pecunie, without his scalp, lying on the snow ahead of us.

"Big-nose, who was on a fast horse, and ahead, leaned over as he went by and struck coup on the scalpless one, he being first to fall in the fight. Nobody halted, and just as Big-nose struck his coup I saw a Pecunie sitting on the ground ahead. I think Big-nose discovered him at the same time. Anyway, after striking the dead Pecunie he raced away for the man on the ground, who, although armed, could not stand because of a broken thigh.

"Things told as I am telling them now do not seem to be fast, but they were very fast while they were happening. Big-nose intended to count a double coup and jumped from his running horse beside the Pecunie to take his gun. As he sprang toward him the fellow fired, and Big-nose fell with his own thigh broken.

"They faced each other, each with a broken thigh, neither able to stand, Big-nose wholly unarmed because he had thrown away his gun when he jumped from his horse so that he might count a fair coup. I saw the Pecunie raise his knife and saw Big-nose back away, pushing his body along with his hands.

"I lashed my horse! The Pecunie was edging himself toward Big-nose, who was backing off, each pushing himself along with his hands, the Pecunie's knife always ready. Big-nose was working toward his gun, but it was far away, and he dared not turn his head to keep from circling [going in wrong direction]. And the Pecunie was gaining. I expected to see him throw his knife into the body of the Crow.

"How slow this sounds in spoken words! There were several men behind me, but I did not know it then. I saw only Big-nose, backing in a circle that would never bring him to his gun. He must have heard our horses coming because he gave the Crow war-cry without taking his eyes off his enemy, who was edging along after him with his knife.

"We circled around them, not daring to shoot for fear of hitting Big-nose. The Pecunie knew he was gone now, and gave the Pecunie yell. Several bullets cut it short. I never knew just whose bullets struck him, of course, but that Pecunie was a good man, and brave.

"We did not stop there long. A band of Pecunies had crossed Sweetgrass and had thrown up a breast-work of willows in the brush. Our warriors had twice charged and had been beaten back, losing several men. When we arrived we all charged again and were driven back, with Bobtail-raven shot through the breast, rather low down, and Shot-in-the-hand wounded in the shoulder.

"The best shooting had come from a point in the breast-works where I had seen a Pecunie wearing a white man's hat. I made up my mind to try to get him. Dismounting, I stripped and tied my medicine beneath my braided hair. I knew mine was a desperate game, but I played it, sliding safely to the foot of the breast-works, where I waited to get my breath. To shoot me now the fellow with the hat would have to stand up and lean over the breast-works, and I did not believe he would risk it. I knew he was right behind the breast-work from me because I saw his coup-stick leaning against it. Its feathers waved in the wind over my head, and when I had rested a little I took hold of it and pulled. He hung on, but I got it away from him, and when I saw his face over the brush I struck it with his own coup-stick.

"This started things in our favor, and the Crows charged, only to find nobody behind the breast-works. Burnt-eye shot my man with the hat, as he was following his friends into the willows. However, I had already counted a beautiful coup on him, and with his own coup-stick. The Pecunies had killed three Crows and wounded several. We had four scalps, and of course did not know how many we hurt. We Crows had counted three coups: one by Big-nose, which I have told you about; one by White-bull, who struck the Pecunie breast-works while under fire; and mine. I have finished for today."

I Do Not Like to Fight with White Men

Plenty-coups began his story next morning by pointing out a few of the white man's frailties. "By the time I was forty," he said, "I could see that our country was changing fast, and that these changes were causing us to live very differently. Anybody could now see that soon there would be no buffalo on the plains, and everybody was wondering how we could live after they were gone. There were few war-parties, and almost no raids against our enemies, so that we were beginning to grow careless of our minds and bodies. White men with their spotted-buffalo [cattle] were on the plains about us. Their houses were near the water-holes, and their villages on the rivers. We made up our minds to be friendly with them, in spite of all the changes they were bringing. But we found this difficult, because the white men too often promised to do one thing and then, when they acted at all, did another.

"They spoke very loudly when they said their laws were made for everybody; but we soon learned that although they expected us to keep them, they thought nothing of breaking them themselves. They told us not to drink whisky, yet they made it themselves and traded it to us for furs and robes until both were nearly gone. Their Wise Ones said we might have their religion, but when we tried to understand it we found that there were too many kinds of religion among white men for us to understand, and that scarcely any two white men agreed which was the right one to learn. This bothered us a good deal until we saw that the white man did not take his religion any more seriously than he did his laws, and that he kept both of them just behind him, like Helpers, to use when they might do him good in his dealings with strangers. These were not our ways. We kept the laws we made and lived our religion. We have never been able to understand the white man, who fools nobody but himself. However, even with all our differences, we kept our friendship for him, as I shall show you.

"One winter day when the snow was deep, our Wolves came in and told us the Pecunies had stolen many of our horses. I was camped with about forty lodges on Rock Creek, and our horses were running in the hills where they could paw away the snow and get grass. Because of the slow days that had come to us with the white man, and the lack of long grass to cut with our knives, we had no good horses tied near our lodges ready for trouble, as we always had had when the buffalo were plentiful. We had to go out in the hills and catch horses to ride. That is the way we lived now, like a lot of sleepy people whom anybody might whip.

"Eight of us went out and caught up our best horses, the fastest and strongest. We expected the trail to be a long one, and kept wondering if white men would stop us from getting back our property. Anyway we started, and picked up the Pecunie trail on Elk River. The water was frozen, so we crossed on the ice in the face of a cold wind that kept it wiped clean of snow, which had drifted into piles out on the plains and along the river banks.

"Where Park City now stands we came to a few houses, and the white men who lived in them told us the Pecunies, or somebody, had taken most of their horses too. We talked to them as best we could with signs and a little English (when we knew it was nearly right), and at last four white men who had lost good horses wanted to go along with us to get their stolen property. I believed them able to take care of themselves and agreed, which was one of the most foolish things I ever did.

"They began to show me this soon after we started. Their horses had been eating hay and oats in a house, while ours had been pawing snow for grass in the windy hills. Naturally their horses could travel faster than ours, but because the trail was likely to be a long one I tried to hold the white men back, telling them to save their animals for the trouble ahead. They would not listen but rode on, while we walked, until their animals grew tired. Then the white men camped. When I passed them by their fire they wished me to stay with them, but I told them the Pecunies would not camp and that if we expected to catch them we must keep going. I explained to them, as best I could, that the thieves were driving nearly one hundred horses and would be unable to go so far in a day as we could, if we kept at it. This did no good. They said their horses were tired out, and of course they were, having been ridden all day in the deep snow. So I left them, wishing with all my heart that I had not sent four of my men back to the Crow village when these white men joined me to go after the Pecunies.

"They caught up with us late the next afternoon, and at once began to talk about camping and eating, but this time I pretended not to hear them at all. I kept pushing on with my three men–Plain-bull, who is with us here, Strikes-on-the-head, and Big-sky–thanking luck that no more than four white men were in our party. I saw they were a hindrance instead of a help, and that, if left to themselves, they would never in this life catch a Pecunie horse thief.

"In the middle of the night we came to the headwaters of the Musselshell, and when the Seven-stars [Big Dipper] had turned clear around Ek-kha-ceh-say [North Star] I saw that two of my men were far behind because of the condition of their horses. I knew I should have to give them rest, and stopped to look for a good place. The wind had blown the ground bare of snow where I was standing. I signed all to stop while I looked a little farther, before camping.

"It was well I did so. I had gone but a little way when I became suspicious of a place in the rim-rock where the snow was piled about some boulders, and, stooping low to get the sky between me and the rim-rock, discovered some horses above it. Besides, I smelled a little smoke that was from a fire nearly dead. The Pecunies were near it, I knew.

"Not daring to trust the white men to do the right thing, I hurried back to where they were waiting with Plain-bull. 'Stay here,' I signed to them. 'I will go ahead now and steal their guns before we attack them, if

I can.' But I could not hold my white friends. They were unmanageable, and got on their horses to charge the camp in that dim light.

"I ran ahead, waving them back, but they followed on horseback and began to yell. Yes, I am telling you the truth; they began to yell, and I dodged behind a boulder, leaving them out there sitting on their horses and yelping like coyotes.

"They did not shout long. The Pecunies were not fools. I soon saw rifles poking over the rim-rock, one of which spurted fire. Down went a white man with a bullet over his eye.

" 'Go back!' I called, making the sign. But my words did no good. There they sat on their horses, wearing too many clothes and looking foolish, until another tumbled off his horse with a ball in his forehead. This time the two others moved a little. One jumped from his horse and hid behind a boulder to fight. He was smarter than the others, but just as he poked his rifle over the boulder a bullet struck the rock and glanced into his face. Ho! The lead bullet split and spattered, making a terrible wound that knocked him down in the snow as though finished.

"I looked to see what the other was going to do with himself and saw him running away afoot, as fast as he could go. Next I saw him stagger and fall, get up again and run, and then tumble. I thought he stayed there.

"I would have helped him if I could, even though I thought him worth very little. My two men were coming up now and getting themselves into position to hold the Pecunies from getting away. I had not yet got a shot. Bullets chipped pieces from my boulder every time I stuck my head above it, and I had to be careful. Those Pecunies did good shooting that morning. I kept them wasting their ammunition by making them think my robe was my head, while I watched for a shot at a tall Pecunie who, I knew, had done most damage to the white men. He had seen the two Crows join us among the boulders, and probably thought more were coming and that it was time to move from where he was. I was expecting him to make a run for different cover, but when he did I missed him clean, shooting too low. My bullet made him duck behind another rock that was not so good as the one he had left, and I made ready for him to come out again. When he did, I doubled him up.

"The others saw him fall, which made them wish to move to the rocks higher up on the hill. When they started I made one of the best shots I ever fired, killing one of them halfway up that hill, as easily as though he had been just against my gun barrel. One of the others, who had a Winchester, began a lively spurt of shooting now, but they were in a tight place, and knew it. Their guns were faster than ours, but ours carried bullets farther and could reach their position, even in the higher rocks. However, our own were accomplishing no more than theirs; so, after stationing two of my men to hold the Pecunies where they were, I crept back with Plain-bull to see what we could do for the white man whose face had been smashed.

"We found him breathing like a snorting horse and bleeding badly. We carried him to a safer place, dragged the two dead men together, and then went to look at the trail left in the snow by the white man who ran away and fell down. We followed his tracks only a little way, looking carefully for blood, saw where he had fallen and got up, found where he had tumbled again and then floundered to his feet to run on. He had not been wounded, only scared; so we came back to the job of trying to get the other Pecunies among the rocks.

"On our return we stopped again by the side of the wounded man, and while we were kneeling down to see if there was anything we could do for him, we heard horses coming–a dozen or more of them. We stood up, but not for long. White men began to shoot at us.

"I waved my hand–made the sign for 'friend'–but they did not understand and kept shooting. Their bullets were kicking up the stones around us and we feared they might kill the wounded white man. We dragged him behind a boulder to save him from being finished by his own people, and hid ourselves to think. We were in a bad situation, with white men shooting in front and Pecunies shooting behind us. We thought if we shot up the hill at the Pecunies the white men would understand that we were friends. But when we tried this it did no good. The white men's bullets kept clipping against our boulders. Some other thing had to be done quickly.

"I tied a white piece of buckskin on my wiping-stick and stood up unarmed. Holding my stick high with my right hand, I stretched my left above my head, so that anybody might see that I carried no weapon. In this manner, expecting to be shot down, I began walking toward those men, and more than one bullet was fired at me before they stopped shooting. They at last realized that I was only one man, and unarmed, and that I could not possibly kill them all. When I got near enough to speak my name in English, fortunately one of them knew it. This ended the trouble and we shook hands.

"I led them to the spot where their friends were and, as best I could with signs and a very few English words, explained what had happened. While some of them were examining the wounded man and the dead ones whose bodies were now frozen very hard, two white men went out to find the man who had run away. So Plain-bull and I started again to see what we could do toward killing the other Pecunies. [Pecunies—often spelled Pikunis—means "painted-face," though their enemies declare the word to mean "*scabby*-face."]

"We crept up the hill from rock to rock, while Big-sky and Strikes-on-the-head kept up their fire, until we came to the tall one's body. Here Plain-bull stood up and, walking to the tall one, counted coup on him in the face of the firing up the hill. I took the fellow's scalp, and together we set out once more to get the other whose body was still farther up the hill. But the white men now began calling and beckoning us. They had promised to keep up a fire while we did this, but now when they began calling and beckoning they quit shooting. We turned back, leaving that Pecunie unscalped. I have felt sorry ever since.

"The white men had built a large fire, and also they had gone out and killed a white man's cow, so that they might have meat to eat. All those white men seemed to think about was eating and camping. But we Crows were hungry too, so we ate meat with them, while the Pecunies made good their escape. I wished I had a few more Crows with me instead of those white men.

"While we were eating, the whites who had gone to follow the one that ran away came back with the coward. He was unhit. Two bullets had struck his fur overcoat, and one had knocked him down on the snow. He had got up running and hadn't stopped for a long time.

"I myself had three holes in my capote and one in my shirt, but my skin was not even scratched. We rounded up all the horses and helped the white men pack their dead on gentle animals. Their bodies were so frozen that they broke them across the backs of the horses so that they could carry them away from there. I led the party back to Park City.

"The weather was so cold that the trees popped and snapped, and more than once we were obliged to stop and build fires to warm the white men, who wore too many clothes. The snow in places was drifted very deep, but never did we unload the horses that carried the dead. Many times since then I have remembered how strange the stiff arms and legs looked in the clear moonlight, especially when we were among scattering trees. They did not please me, I remember.

"It was a hard journey for those white men. Two whole days and nights, with little rest, took us to Park City, the white men's village, and it was there I learned that white women mourn as ours do. My heart fell to the ground when I heard them crying and wailing for their men, who need not have died if only they had used their heads a little. I do not like to fight with white men."

Vision in the Crazy Mountains

"I decided to go afoot to the Crazy Mountains, two long days' journey from the village. The traveling without food or drink was good for me, and as soon as I reached the Crazies I took a sweat-bath and climbed the highest peak. There is a lake at its base, and the winds are always stirring about it. But even though I fasted two more days and nights, walking over the mountain top, no Person came to me, nothing was offered. I saw several grizzly bears that were nearly white in the moonlight, and one of them came very near to me, but he did not speak. Even when I slept on that peak in the Crazies, no bird or animal or Person spoke a word to me, and I grew discouraged. I could not dream.

"Back in the village I told my closest friends about the high peaks I had seen, about the white grizzly bears, and the lake. They were interested and said they would go back with me and that we would all try to dream.

"There were three besides myself who set out, with extra moccasins and a robe to cover our sweat-lodge. We camped on good water just below the peak where I had tried to dream, quickly took our sweat-baths, and started up the mountains. It was already dark when we separated, but I found no difficulty in reaching my old bed on the tall peak that looked down on the little lake, or in making a new bed with ground-cedar and sweet-sage. Owls were hooting under the stars while I rubbed my body with the sweet-smelling herbs before starting out to walk myself weak.

"When I could scarcely stand, I made my way back to my bed and slept with my feet toward the east. But no Person came to me, nothing was offered; and when the day came I got up to walk again over the mountain top, calling for Helpers as I had done the night before.

"All day the sun was hot, and my tongue was swollen for want of water; but I saw nothing, heard nothing, even when night came again to cool the mountain. No sound had reached my ears, except my own voice and the howling of wolves down on the plains.

"I knew that our great Crow warriors of other days sacrificed their flesh and blood to dream, and just when the night was leaving to let the morning come I stopped at a fallen tree, and, laying the first finger of my left hand upon the log, I cut part of it off with my knife. [The end of the left index finger on the Chief's hand is missing.] But no blood came. The stump of my finger was white as the finger of a dead man, and to make it bleed I struck it against the log until blood flowed freely. Then I began to walk and call for Helpers, hoping that some Person would smell my blood and come to aid me.

"Near the middle of that day my head grew dizzy, and I sat down. I had eaten nothing, taken no water, for nearly four days and nights, and my mind must have left me while I sat there under the hot sun on the mountain top. It must have traveled far away, because the sun was nearly down when it returned and found me lying on my face. As soon as it came back to me I sat up and looked about, at first not knowing where I was. Four war-eagles were sitting in a row along a trail of my blood just above me. But they did not speak to me, offered nothing at all.

"I thought I would try to reach my bed, and when I stood up I saw my three friends. They had seen the eagles flying over my peak and had become frightened, believing me dead. They carried me to my bed and stayed long enough to smoke with me before going back to their own places. While we smoked, the four war-eagles did not fly away. They sat there by my blood on the rocks, even after the night came on and chilled everything living on the mountain."

Again the Chief whispered aside to the Little-people, asking them if he might go on. When he finally resumed, I felt that somehow he had been reassured. His voice was very low, yet strained, as though he were tiring.

"I dreamed. I heard a voice at midnight and saw a Person standing at my feet, in the east. He said, 'Plenty-coups, the Person down there wants you now.'

"He pointed, and from the peak in the Crazy Mountains I saw a Buffalo-bull standing *where we are sitting now.* I got up and started to go to the Bull, because I knew he was the Person who wanted me. The other Person was gone. Where he had stood when he spoke to me there was nothing at all.

"The way is very long from the Crazies to this place where we are sitting today, but I came here quickly in my dream. On that hill over yonder was where I stopped to look at the Bull. He had changed into a Man-person wearing a buffalo robe with the hair outside. Later I picked up the buffalo skull that you see over there, on the very spot where the Person had stood. I have kept that skull for more than seventy years.

"The Man-person beckoned me from the hill over yonder where I had stopped, and I walked to where he stood. When I reached his side he began to sink slowly into the ground, right over there [pointing]. Just as the Man-person was disappearing he spoke. 'Follow me,' he said.

"But I was afraid. 'Come,' he said from the darkness. And I got down into the hole in the ground to follow him, walking bent-over for ten steps. Then I stood straight and saw a small light far off. It was like a window in a white man's house of today, and I knew the hole was leading us toward the Arrow Creek Mountains [the Pryors].

"In the way of the light, between it and me, I could see countless buffalo, see their sharp horns thick as the grass grows. I could smell their bodies and hear them snorting, ahead and on both sides of me. Their eyes, without number, were like little fires in the darkness of the hole in the ground, and I felt afraid among so many big bulls. The Man-person must have known this, because he said, 'Be not afraid, Plenty-coups. It was these Persons who sent for you. They will not do you harm.'

"My body was naked. I feared walking among them in such a narrow place. The burrs that are always in their hair would scratch my skin, even if their hoofs and horns did not wound me more deeply. I did not like the way the Man-person went among them. 'Fear nothing! Follow me, Plenty-coups,' he said.

"I felt their warm bodies against my own, but went on after the Man-person, edging around them or going between them all that night and all the next day, with my eyes always looking ahead at the hole of light. But none harmed me, none even spoke to me, and at last we came out of the hole in the ground and saw the Square White Butte at the mouth of Arrow Creek Canyon. It was on our right. White men call it Castle Rock, but our name for it is The-fasting-place.

"Now, out in the light of the sun, I saw that the Man-person who had led me had a rattle in his hand. It was large and painted red. [The rattle is used in ceremonials. It is sometimes made of the bladder of an animal, dried, with small pebbles inside, so that when shaken it gives a rattling sound.] When he reached the top of a knoll he turned and said to me, 'Sit here!'

"Then he shook his red rattle and sang a queer song four times. 'Look!' he pointed.

"Out of the hole in the ground came the buffalo, bulls and cows and calves without number. They spread wide and blackened the plains. Everywhere I looked great herds of buffalo were going in every direction, and still others without number were pouring out of the hole in the ground to travel on the wide plains. When at last they ceased coming out of the hole in the ground, all were gone, *all*! There was not one in sight anywhere, even out on the plains. I saw a few antelope on a hillside, but no buffalo–not a bull, not a cow, not one calf, was anywhere on the plains.

"I turned to look at the Man-person beside me. He shook his red rattle again. 'Look!' he pointed.

"Out of the hole in the ground came bulls and cows and calves past counting. These, like the others, scattered and spread on the plains. But they stopped in small bands and began to eat the grass. Many lay down, not as a buffalo does but differently, and many were spotted. Hardly any two were alike in color or size. And the bulls bellowed differently too, not deep and far-sounding like the bulls of the buffalo but sharper and yet weaker in my ears. Their tails were different, longer, and nearly brushed the ground. They were not buffalo. These were strange animals from another world.

"I was frightened and turned to the Man-person, who only shook his red rattle but did not sing. He did not even tell me to look, but I did look and saw all the Spotted-buffalo go back into the hole in the ground, until there was nothing except a few antelope anywhere in sight.

" 'Do you understand this which I have shown you, Plenty-coups?' he asked me.

" 'No!' I answered. How could he expect me to understand such a thing when I was not yet ten years old?

"During all the time the Spotted-buffalo were going back into the hole in the ground the Man-person had not once looked at me. He stood facing the south as though the Spotted-buffalo belonged there. 'Come, Plenty-coups,' he said finally, when the last had disappeared.

"I followed him back through the hole in the ground without seeing anything until we came out *right over there* [pointing] where we had first entered the hole in the ground. Then I saw the spring down by those trees, this very house just as it is, these trees which comfort us today, and a very old man sitting in the shade, alone. I felt pity for him because he was so old and feeble.

" 'Look well upon this old man,' said the Man-person. 'Do you know him, Plenty-coups?' he asked me.

" 'No,' I said, looking closely at the old man's face in the shade of *this* tree.

" 'This old man is yourself, Plenty-coups,' he told me. And then I could see the Man-person no more. He was gone, and so too was the old man.

"Instead I saw only a dark forest. A fierce storm was coming fast. The sky was black with streaks of mad color through it. I saw the Four Winds gathering to strike the forest, and held my breath. Pity was hot in my heart for the beautiful trees. I felt pity for all things that lived in that forest, but was powerless to stand with them against the Four Winds that together were making war. I shielded my own face with my arm when they charged! I heard the Thunders calling out in the storm, saw beautiful trees twist like blades of grass and fall in tangled piles where the forest had been. Bending low, I heard the Four Winds rush past me as though they were not yet satisfied, and then I looked at the destruction they had left behind them.

"Only one tree, tall and straight, was left standing where the great forest had stood. The Four Winds that always make war alone had this time struck together, riding down every tree in the forest but *one*. Standing there alone among its dead tribesmen, I thought it looked sad. 'What does this mean?' I whispered in my dream.

" 'Listen, Plenty-coups,' said a voice. 'In that tree is the lodge of the Chickadee. He is least in strength but strongest of mind among his kind. He is willing to work for wisdom. The Chickadee-person is a good listener. Nothing escapes his ears, which he has sharpened by constant use. Whenever others are talking together of their successes or failures, there you will find the Chickadee-person listening to their words. But in all his listening he tends to his own business. He never intrudes, never speaks in strange company, and yet never misses a chance to learn from others. He gains success and avoids failure by learning how others succeeded or failed, and without great trouble to himself. There is scarcely a lodge he does not visit, hardly a Person he does not know, and yet everybody likes him, because he minds his own business, or pretends to.

" 'The lodges of countless Bird-people were in that forest when the Four Winds charged it. Only one is left unharmed, the lodge of the Chickadee-person. Develop your body, but do not neglect your mind, Plenty-coups. It is the mind that leads a man to power, not strength of body.' "

From Pretty-shield, Medicine Woman

Chickadees

. . . I would try to get Pretty-shield going again by introducing the chickadee.

But I could not make our interpreter, Goes-together, understand which bird I meant. To her, as to most moderns, red or white, a bird is a bird. To these unfortunates there are "little" birds and "big" birds, and here their ornithology ends. I did not know the sign for chickadee, and during all the talking between Goes-together and myself Pretty-shield's face remained amusedly blank. At last, in desperation, I whistled the spring-call of the chickadee, and the day was saved. Pretty-shield reacted instantly. She stood up and with a hand resting on the table, leaned toward me, her eyes shining.

"Ahhh, Ahh! The chickadee is big medicine, Sign-talker," she said, with one hand. "Do you know him well?" she asked so eagerly that I felt my assurance slipping.

But, "Yes," I answered, yet believing in my knowledge of the bird. I had written many stories about him.

"Good!" she signed, emphatically. "Then you have seen his tongue."

Now what was this? Was she joking? No. I knew that she was serious, and that here, as in so many other instances where old Indians had taught me, I should learn a new lesson. "No. I have not looked at the chickadee's tongue," I admitted, feeling like a trifling school-boy.

"Ahhhh!" Pretty-shield sank back into her chair, her face so fallen that I laughed outright. "Tst, tst, tst," she clucked, seemingly unable to believe that I, who could whistle the chickadee's call, did not know about the bird's tongue.

But I intended now to learn. "Tell me about his tongue, Pretty-shield," I begged, again whistling his spring-call to salve her disgust for my ignorance.

"In the fall, when the leaves first begin to change their color," she began, "the chickadee has but *one* tongue. In the springtime, when he begins to say those words you have just spoken [his spring-call] he has *seven* tongues," she said, moving her chair up to the table to place her hand flat upon its top, palm downward.

"It is by the chickadee's tongue that we tell what moon of the winter we are in," she went on, speaking rapidly. "In the first moon the chickadee shows *two* tongues, then *three*, then *four*, then *five*, then *six*, and finally *seven*," she declared, the index finger of her right hand marking imaginary divisions upon the left, that was yet flying flat upon the table-top. "And then," she smiled, "the chickadee says 'summer's near, summer's near,' and goes back to *one* tongue."

She leaned back now. "We do not harm the chickadee when we look at his tongue to see what moon of the winter we are in," she assured me. "We catch them, look quickly at their tongues, and then let them go again."

I could not help feeling doubt in all this. And yet I was determined to investigate; and I did. For days, even weeks, the chickadees, usually plentiful here at Goose Bay, avoided the place as though their "medicine" had warned them of me. It was in April, a little too late in the season to find seven well-defined tongues, as Pretty-shield had said, when I caught two chickadees. With the aid of a jeweler's glass I discovered that their tongues were not alike, one having four sharp points resembling the spines on the cactus plant, two on the right, and two on the left of the tongue's center; the other, seven thread-like strands resembling a raveled edge of cloth. I thought that both tongues were shorter than the beaks seemed to warrant, there being room in each beak for a longer tongue than was present. Anyhow, the tongue of the chickadee is phenomenal and a careful examination of it late in February or early in March may prove Pretty-shield's contention to be correct.

"One day in the moon when leaves are on the ground [November] I was walking with my grandmother near some bushes that were full of chickadees," Pretty-shield continued. "They had been stealing fat from meat that was on the racks in the village, and because they were full they were all laughing. I thought it would be fun to see them all fly, and tossed a dry buffalo-chip into the bushes. I was a very little girl, too little to know any better, and yet my grandmother told me that I had done wrong. She took me into her arms, and walking to another bush, where the frightened chickadees had stopped, she said: 'This little girl is my granddaughter. She will never again throw anything at you. Forgive her, little ones. She did not know any better.' Then she sat down with me in her lap, and told me that long before this she had lost a close friend because the woman had turned the chickadees against her."

Here Pretty-shield was interrupted. A Crow woman, wearing a green blanket, came to tell her that a young man who had been missing for several days had been found dead, and buried in a shallow grave. His head had been split with an axe, she said.

"Bad!" Pretty-shield signed to me, when the woman had gone. "The young man was a little crazy." Then, as though there was nothing that she could do to help matters, Pretty-shield took up her story telling.

"My grandmother's name was Seven-stars," she said. "She was a wise-one. She would have only black horses; and her medicine was the chickadee. She told me that one day when her first child, a little girl, was just beginning to walk, she was dressing a buffalo robe. She said that the day was beautiful, and the moon the last one of winter.

"She and another woman, whose name was Buffalo-that-walks, had built a fire among some bushes, and both were working on robes that were pegged to the ground, with the fire burning between them. My grandmother's little girl, who became my mother, was walking and falling down, and getting up only to fall down again, all around the fire while the women worked on their robes.

"A chickadee flew into a bush beside Buffalo-that-walks. 'Summer's near, summer's near,' he said, over and over, while he hopped about in the bush.

"Buffalo-that-walks was a cross woman. 'Be quiet,' she said to the little chickadee. 'Don't you believe that I have eyes? I can see that the summer is near as well as you can. Go away. You are bothering me.'

" 'Summer's near, summer's near,' called the bird, paying no attention to what she said. 'Summer's near, summer's near.'

"Buffalo-that-walks threw a stick at the chickadee, and he dodged it. 'Ho!' he laughed, hopping higher. 'Yes, I suppose I do bother you,' he said, looking down at her with his black head turned sidewise. 'I bother nearly everybody. And now I will bother you a little more. You are going to be wrapped up in that very robe that you are making so soft. I came here to tell you this, and you threw a stick at me.'

"Then the chickadee flew to a bush that was near my grandmother. 'Summer's near, summer's near,' he said, as though there was nothing else he could think about. My grandmother picked up her little girl. The chickadee had made her afraid. 'I threw no sticks at you,' she said, starting toward her lodge with her child in her arms.

" 'Wait! Do not leave your work. Pay no attention to what the Chickadee-person has said. He will say anything that comes to his mind. Nobody believes his words,' called Buffalo-that-walks.

"My grandmother turned to look back at the woman, her friend. 'Don't say such things,' she warned. 'And I wish you would leave me out of all this foolishness. I am afraid.' Then she went on to her lodge with her little girl. Later she brought some fine back-fat to the bushes, putting it where she thought the chickadee would find it. And he did find it.

"He came while yet my grandmother was there. 'Don't worry,' he told her, picking at the back-fat. 'You are not in this trouble. You have nothing to worry about. It's the other one.'

"Buffalo-that-walks died that very night, and they wrapped her in that very robe, as the chickadee had said. Grandmother told me that as soon as Buffalo-that-walks was put away the village moved, and that the dead woman's man did not go with the village. He stayed behind to mourn for his woman.

"While he was sitting by the tree that held his woman's body the chickadee came to him. The man smoked deer-tobacco, offering his pipe to the chickadee. 'I am sorry that my woman mistreated you,' he said. 'I wish you would be my friend, chickadee.' The little bird sat on the man's hand, and talked to him. 'I am small,' he said. 'My strength is not great. I only run errands for the big ones, and yet I can help you. In the morning a *Person* will come to you. Listen to what he has to say. I must go about my own business now.'

"At daybreak, that was clear and cold and beautiful, a large bird came to the man; and the chickadee was with him. This large bird was Big-claws-on-both-sides [I could not identify this bird from her description]. He said, 'Nobody who has a good heart ever mistreats my friend, the Chickadee. Because you are sorry for what your woman did I will be your Helper for the rest of your life.' And he was a good Helper, my grandmother said.

"It was the next spring after this," Pretty-shield continued, "that one day, when my grandmother was dressing a robe, a chickadee came to her. At first it did not talk, but picked up bits of the fat in the fleshings lying on the robe. [The meat, and fat, scraped from robes, or other skins, are called "fleshings."]

"Grandmother talked to the little bird, and finally after its belly was full the chickadee said, 'Leave your work for a while, and follow me. I wish to talk to you over yonder by that creek. Get somebody to take care of your little girl, and meet me at the creek.'

"Grandmother ran to her lodge, got a woman friend to care for the little girl, who became my mother, took a sweat-bath, put on her finest clothes, and went to the creek."

These "sweat-baths" were taken in tiny, conical, willow lodges, covered tightly with buffalo robes. Heated stones were rolled inside, and freely sprinkled with water, the resultant vapor thoroughly cleansing the occupant's body. The "sweat-bath" was severe, and when taken before or after a "medicine-dream," was symbolic of mental purification.

"At first grandmother did not see the chickadee. She could hear the bird talking and laughing to itself, but could not see it until it came to sit on a willow right above her head. 'Look,' it said, going up into the air, flying higher and higher. Straight up it went, growing larger and larger and larger, until it was as large as a war-eagle [mountain, or golden eagle]. 'See,' it called down to my grandmother, 'there is great power in little things.' And then my grandmother saw that the bird held a buffalo calf in each of its taloned feet. 'I am a woman, as you are. Like you I have to work, and make the best of this life,' said the bird. 'I am your friend, and yet to help you I must first hurt you. You will have three sons, but will lose two of them. One will live to be a good man. You must never eat eggs, never. Have you listened?' asked the bird, settling down again, and growing small.

"'Yes, I have listened,' my grandmother told that chickadee, and from that day she never ate an egg. But her children did, and her man, my grandfather, did. They would not listen. Two of her boys, and her man, my grandfather, were killed by Lacota. It is bad to harm the chickadee, and foolish not to listen to him," she finished, emphatically.

Women Against War

"Of course the Lacota, Striped-feathered-arrows [Cheyenne], Arapahoes, Pecunnies, and other tribes never let us rest, so that there was always war. When our enemies were not bothering *us*, our warriors were bothering *them*, so there was always fighting going on somewhere. We women sometimes tried to keep our men from going to war, but this was like talking to winter-winds; and of course there was always some woman, sometimes many women, mourning for men who had been killed in war. These women had to be taken care of. Somebody had to kill meat for them. Their fathers or uncles or brothers did this until the women married again, which they did not always do, so that war made more work for everybody. There were few lazy ones among us in those days. My people used to be too proud to be lazy. Besides this, in the old days a lazy person didn't get along very well, man or woman."

"Were there always men left in your camps?" I asked, hoping that the answer might remind her of another story.

"Yes," she said, "but sometimes when war-parties were out looking for the enemy, and besides these, many hunters were on the plains after buffalo, only old men were left in camp, old ones, and a few lazy young ones. Once, a long time ago, the Lacota nearly wiped the Crows out, because all the men were gone to steal horses. Nearly all the women were killed, and all the old men that had been left in the village, besides. But this was long before my time. Even in my days young men were always going to war, or to steal horses, leaving the village short of warriors, because they could not marry until they had counted coup, or had reached the age of twenty-five years. Young men do not like to wait so long," she smiled.

"My man, Goes-ahead, was a Fox [member of that secret society] and although we women had no secret societies we sided with our men, so that my heart was always strong for the Foxes. The Foxes were warlike. We women did not like war, and yet we could not help it, because our men loved war. Always there was some man missing, and always some woman was having to go and live with her relatives, because women are not hunters. And then there were the orphans that war made. They had to be cared for by somebody. You see that when we women lost our men we lost our own, and our children's living. I am glad that war has gone forever. It was no good—*no good*!"

The End

I wondered if I could get Pretty-shield to talk of the days when her people were readjusting themselves to present conditions. Plenty-coups, the aged Chief, had refused to speak of the days that immediately followed the passing of the buffalo, saying: "When the buffalo went away the hearts of my people fell to the ground, and they could not lift them up again. After this nothing happened. There was little singing anywhere. Besides, you know that part of my life as well as I do. You saw what happened to us when the buffalo went away."

Now I asked Pretty-shield, "How old were you when the buffalo disappeared?"

She hesitated. "Tst, tst, tst! I haven't seen a buffalo in more than forty years," she said slowly, as though she believed herself to be dreaming.

"The happiest days of my life were spent following the buffalo herds over our beautiful country. My mother and father and Goes-ahead, my man, were all kind, and we were so happy. Then, when my children came I believed I had everything that was good on this world. There were always so many, many buffalo, plenty of good fat meat for everybody.

"Since my man, Goes-ahead, went away twelve snows ago my heart has been falling down. I am old now, and alone, with so many grandchildren to watch," she interposed, and fell silent.

"I do not hate *anybody*, not even the white man," she said, as though she had been accused by her conscience. "I have never let myself hate the white man, because I knew that this would only make things worse for me. But he changed everything for us, did many bad deeds before we got used to him.

"Sign-talker," she said, leaning toward me, "white cowboys met a deaf and dumb Crow boy on the plains, and because he could not answer their questions, could not even hear what they said, they roped him and dragged him to death."

"Tell me what happened when the buffalo went away," I urged.

"Sickness came, strange sickness that nobody knew about, when there was no meat," she said, covering her face with both hands as though to shut out the sight of suffering. "My daughter stepped into a horse's track that was deep in the dried clay, and hurt her ankle. I could not heal her; nobody could. The white doctor told me that the same sickness that makes people cough themselves to death was in my daughter's ankle. I did not believe it, and yet she died, leaving six little children. Then my other daughter died, and left hers. These things would not have happened if we Crows had been living as we were intended to live. But how could we live in the old way when everything was gone?

"Ahh, my heart fell down when I began to see dead buffalo scattered all over our beautiful country, killed and skinned, and left to rot by white men, many, many hundreds of buffalo. The first I saw of this was in the Judith basin. The whole country there smelled of rotting meat. Even the flowers could not put down the bad smell. Our hearts were like stones. And yet nobody believed, even then, that the white man could kill *all* the buffalo. Since the beginning of things there had always been so many! Even the Lacota, bad as their hearts were for us, would not do such a thing as this; nor the Cheyenne, nor the Arapahoe, nor the Pecunnie; and yet the white man did this, even when he did not want the meat.

"We believed for a long time that the buffalo would again come to us; but they did not. We grew hungry and sick and afraid, all in one. Not believing their own eyes our hunters rode very far looking for buffalo, so far away that even if they had found a herd we could not have reached it in half a moon. 'Nothing; we found nothing,' they told us; and then, hungry, they stared at the empty plains, as though dreaming. After this their hearts were no good any more. If the Great White Chief in Washington had not given us food we should have been wiped out without even a chance to fight for ourselves.

"And then white men began to fence the plains so that we could not travel; and anyhow there was now little good in traveling, nothing to travel for. We began to stay in one place, and to grow lazy and sicker all the time. Our men had fought hard against our enemies, holding them back from our beautiful country by their bravery; but now, with everything else going wrong, we began to be whipped by weak foolishness. Our men, our leaders, began to drink the white man's whisky, letting it do their thinking. Because we were used to listening to our chiefs in the buffalo days, the days of war and excitement, we listened to them now; and we got whipped. Our wise-ones became fools, and drank the white man's whisky. But what else was there for us to do? We knew no other way than to listen to our chiefs and head men. Our old men used to be different; even our children were different when the buffalo were here.

"Tst, tst, tst! We were given a reservation, a fine one, long ago. We had many, many horses, and even cattle that the Government had given us. We might have managed to get along if the White Chief in Washington had not leased our lands to white stockmen. These men, some of them, shot down our horses on our own lands, because they wanted all the grass for themselves.

"Yes," she went on, her eyes snapping, "these white men shot down our horses so that their cows and sheep might have the grass. They even paid three dollars for each pair of horse's ears, to get our horses killed. It was as though our horses, on our own lands, were wolves that killed the white men's sheep."

She quickly curbed the anger that these thoughts had aroused. "I have not long to stay here," she said, solemnly. "I shall soon be going away from this world; but my grandchildren will have to stay here for a long time yet. I wonder how they will make out. I wonder if the lease-money that is paid to the Government in Washington by the white stockmen will be given to my grandchildren when it is paid in, or if they will have to wear out their moccasins going to the Agency office to ask for it, as I do.

"But then," she added quickly, the light of fun leaping to her eyes, "I suppose they will be wearing the white man's shoes, because shoes last longer than moccasins."

I felt that my work was finished now. Outside, our backs turned to the cutting March wind that was whipping the cottonwood, I said good-bye to Goes-together; and then Pretty-shield and I walked across the Agency square to the store.

"Fire is good today," she signed, spreading her hands to the warmth of the Trader's big stove. Then, a little regretfully I thought, she asked. "When are you traveling?"

"Tonight," I signed, adding, "You and I are friends, Pretty-shield."

"Bard-ners," she said earnestly, in pidgin English.

May her moccasins make tracks in many snows that are yet to come.

■ ELIZABETH B. CUSTER

Elizabeth Custer, wife of Lt. Colonel George Armstrong Custer, did much to create the myth that made her husband into a national hero—deservedly or not. "Boots and Saddles" or, Life in Dakota with General Custer *(1885) is her account of their life together just before the battle of the Little Big Horn on June 25, 1876. This selection from Elizabeth Custer's book offers a poignant expression of the army wives' situation when their men marched off to battle.*

Our Life's Last Chapter

Our women's hearts fell when the fiat went forth that there was to be a summer campaign, with probably actual fighting with Indians.

Sitting Bull refused to make a treaty with the government and would not come in to live on a reservation. Besides his constant attacks on the white settlers, driving back even the most adventurous, he was incessantly invading and stealing from the land assigned to the peaceable Crows. They appealed for help to the government that had promised to shield them.

The preparations for the expedition were completed before my husband returned from the East, whither he had been ordered. The troops had been sent out of barracks into a camp that was established a short distance down the valley. As soon as the general returned we left home and went into camp.

The morning for the start came only too soon. My husband was to take Sister Margaret and me out for the first day's march, so I rode beside him out of camp. The column that followed seemed unending. The grass was not then suitable for grazing, and as the route of travel was through a barren country, immense quantities of forage had to be transported. The wagons themselves seemed to stretch out interminably. There were pack mules, the ponies already laden, and cavalry, artillery, and infantry followed, the cavalry being in advance of all. The number of men, citizens, employees, Indian scouts, and soldiers was about twelve hundred. There were nearly seventeen hundred animals in all.

As we rode at the head of the column, we were the first to enter the confines of the garrison. About the Indian quarters, which we were obliged to pass, stood the squaws, the old men, and the children, singing, or rather moaning, a minor tune that has been uttered on the going out of Indian warriors since time immemorial. Some of the squaws crouched on the ground, too burdened with their trouble to hold up their heads; others restrained the restless children who, discerning their fathers, sought to follow them.

The Indian scouts themselves beat their drums and kept up their peculiar monotonous tune, which is weird and melancholy beyond description. Their warsong is misnamed when called music. It is more of a lament or a dirge than an inspiration to activity. This intoning they kept up for miles along the road. After we had passed the Indian quarters we came near Laundress Row, and there my heart entirely failed me. The wives and children of the soldiers lined the road. Mothers, with streaming eyes, held their little ones out at arm's length for one last look at the departing father. The toddlers among the children, unnoticed by their elders, had made a mimic column of their own. With their handkerchiefs tied to sticks in lieu of flags, and beating old tin pans for drums, they strode lustily back and forth in imitation of the advancing soldiers. They were fortunately too young to realize why the mothers wailed out their farewells.

Unfettered by conventional restrictions, and indifferent to the opinion of others, the grief of these women was audible and was accompanied by desponding gestures, dictated by their bursting hearts and expressions of their abandoned grief.

It was a relief to escape from them and enter the garrison, and yet, when our band struck up "The Girl I Left Behind Me," the most despairing hour seemed to have come. All the sad-faced wives of the officers who had forced themselves to their doors to try to wave a courageous farewell and smile bravely to keep the ones they loved from knowing the anguish of their breaking hearts gave up the struggle at the sound of the music. The first notes made them disappear to fight out alone their trouble and seek to place their hands in that of their Heavenly Father, who, at such supreme hours, was their never failing solace.

From the hour of breaking camp, before the sun was up, a mist had enveloped everything. Soon the bright sun began to penetrate this veil and dispel the haze, and a scene of wonder and beauty appeared. The cavalry and infantry in the order named, the scouts, pack mules, and artillery, all behind the long line of white-covered wagons, made a column altogether some two miles in length. As the sun broke through the mist a mirage appeared, which took up about half of the line of cavalry, and thenceforth for a little distance it marched, equally plain to the sight on the earth and in the sky.

The future of the heroic band, whose days were even then numbered, seemed to be revealed, and already there seemed a premonition in the supernatural translation as their forms were reflected from the opaque mist of the early dawn.

The sun, mounting higher and higher as we advanced, took every little bit of burnished steel on the arms and equipments along the line of horsemen, and turned them into glittering flashes of radiating light. The yellow, indicative of cavalry, outlined the accouterments, the trappings of the saddle, and sometimes a narrow thread of that effective tint followed the outlines even up to the headstall of the bridle. At every bend of the road, as the column wound its way round and round the low hills, my husband glanced back to admire his men and could not refrain from constantly calling my attention to their grand appearance.

The soldiers, inured to many years of hardship, were the perfection of physical manhood. Their brawny limbs and lithe, well-poised bodies gave proof of the training their outdoor life had given. Their resolute faces, brave and confident, inspired one with a feeling that they were going out aware of the momentous hours awaiting them, but inwardly assured of their capability to meet them.

The general could scarcely restrain his recurring joy at being detained on other duty. His buoyant spirits at the prospect of the activity and field life that he so loved made him like a boy. He had made every plan to have me join him later on, when they should have reached the Yellowstone.

The steamers with supplies would be obliged to leave our post and follow the Missouri up to the mouth of the Yellowstone, and from thence on to the point on that river where the regiment was to make its first halt to renew the rations and forage. He was sanguine that but a few weeks would elapse before we would be reunited, and used this argument to animate me with courage to meet our separation.

As usual we rode a little in advance and selected camp, and watched the approach of the regiment with real pride. They were so accustomed to the march the line hardly diverged from the trail. There was a unity of movement about them that made the column at a distance seem like a broad dark ribbon stretched smoothly over the plains.

We made our camp the first night on a small river a few miles beyond the post. There the paymaster made his disbursements, in order that the debts of the soldiers might be liquidated with the sutler.

In the morning the farewell was said, and the paymaster took sister and me back to the post.

With my husband's departure my last happy days in garrison were ended, as a premonition of disaster that I had never known before weighed me down. I could not shake off the baleful influence of depressing thoughts. This presentiment and suspense, such as I had never known, made me selfish, and I shut into my heart the most uncontrollable anxiety and could lighten no one else's burden. The occupations of other summers could not even give temporary interest.

We heard constantly at the Fort of the disaffection of the young Indians of the reservation, and of their joining the hostiles. We knew, for we had seen for ourselves, how admirably they were equipped. We even saw on a steamer touching at our landing its freight of Springfield rifles piled up on the decks en route for the Indians up the river. There was unquestionable proof that they came into the trading posts far above us and bought them, while our own brave 7th Cavalry troopers were sent out with only the short-range carbines that grew foul after the second firing.

While we waited in untold suspense for some hopeful news, the garrison was suddenly thrown into a state of excitement by important dispatches that were sent from division headquarters in the East. We women knew that eventful news had come and could hardly restrain our curiosity, for it was of vital import to us. Indian scouts were fitted out at the Fort with the greatest dispatch and given instructions to make the utmost speed they could in reaching the expedition on the Yellowstone. After their departure, when there was no longer any need for secrecy, we were told that the expedition which had started from the Department of the Platte, and encountered the hostile Indians on the headwaters of the Rosebud, had been compelled to retreat.

All those victorious Indians had gone to join Sitting Bull, and it was to warn our regiment that this news was sent to our post, which was the extreme telegraphic communication in the Northwest, and the orders given to transmit the information, that precautions might be taken against encountering so large a number of the enemy. The news of the failure of the campaign in the other department was a death knell to our hopes. We felt that we had nothing to expect but that our troops would be overwhelmed with numbers, for it seemed to us an impossibility, as it really proved to be, that our Indian scouts should cross that vast extent of country in time to make the warning of use.

The first steamer that returned from the Yellowstone brought letters from my husband, with the permission, for which I had longed unutterably, to join him by the next boat. The Indians had fired into the steamer when it had passed under the high bluffs in the gorges of the river. I counted the hours until the second steamer was ready. They were obliged, after loading, to cover the pilot house and other vulnerable portions of the upper deck with sheet iron to repel attacks. Then sandbags were placed around the guards as protection, and other precautions were taken for the safety of those on board. All these delays and preparations made me inexpressibly impatient, and it seemed as if the time would never come for the steamer to depart.

Meanwhile our own post was constantly surrounded by hostiles, and the outer pickets were continually subjected to attacks. It was no unusual sound to hear the long roll calling out the infantry before dawn to defend the garrison. We saw the faces of the officers blanch, brave as they were, when the savages grew so bold as to make a daytime sortie upon our outer guards.

A picture of one day of our life in those disconsolate times is fixed indelibly in my memory.

On Sunday afternoon, June 25, our little group of saddened women, borne down with one common weight of anxiety, sought solace in gathering together in our house. We tried to find some slight surcease from trouble in the old hymns; some of them dated back to our childhood's days, when our mothers rocked us to sleep to their soothing strains. I remember the grief with which one fair young wife threw herself on the carpet and pillowed her head in the lap of a tender friend. Another sat dejected at the piano and struck soft chords that melted into the notes of the voices. All were absorbed in the same thoughts, and their eyes were filled with faraway visions and longings. Indescribable yearning for the absent, and untold terror for their safety, engrossed each heart. The words of the hymn,

E'en though a cross it be
Nearer, my God, to Thee,

came forth with almost a sob from every throat.

At that very hour the fears that our tortured minds had portrayed in imagination were realities, and the souls of those we thought upon were ascending to meet their Maker.

On July 5 – for it took that time for the news to come – the sun rose on a beautiful world, but with its earliest beams came the first knell of disaster. A steamer came down the river bearing the wounded from the battle of the Little Big Horn, of Sunday, June 25. This battle wrecked the lives of twenty-six women at Fort Lincoln, and orphaned children of officers and soldiers joined the cry to that of their bereaved mothers.

From that time the life went out of the hearts of the "women who weep," and God asked them to walk on alone and in the shadow.

■ TWO MOON *as told to* Hamlin Garland

Two Moon, a Northern Cheyenne chief, participated in the battle of the Little Big Horn on June 25, 1876. His account of the battle offers an almost Grecian version of the conflict – a battle played out for the amusement of the Great Spirits. Through an interpreter, Two Moon told his story to writer Hamlin Garland, who published the account in the September 1898 issue of McClure's Magazine.

General Custer's Last Fight As Seen by Two Moon: The Battle Described by a Chief Who Took Part in It

"That spring [1876] I was camped on Powder River with fifty lodges of my people – Cheyennes. The place is near what is now Fort McKenney. One morning soldiers charged my camp. They were in command of Three Fingers [Colonel McKenzie]. We were surprised and scattered, leaving our ponies. The soldiers ran all our horses off.

That night the soldiers slept, leaving the horses one side; so we crept up and stole them back again, and then we went away.

"We traveled far, and one day we met a big camp of Sioux at Charcoal Butte. We camped with the Sioux, and had a good time, plenty grass, plenty game, good water. Crazy Horse was head chief of the camp. Sitting Bull was camped a little ways below, on the Little Missouri River.

"Crazy Horse said to me, 'I'm glad you are come. We are going to fight the white man again.'

"The camp was already full of wounded men, women, and children.

"I said to Crazy Horse, 'All right. I am ready to fight. I have fought already. My people have been killed, my horses stolen; I am satisfied to fight.'"

Here the old man paused a moment, and his face took on a lofty and somber expression.

"I believed at that time the Great Spirits had made Sioux, put them there,"—he drew a circle to the right—"and white men and Cheyennes here"—indicating two places to the left,—"expecting them to fight. The Great Spirits I thought liked to see the fight; it was to them all the same like playing. So I thought then about fighting." As he said this, he made me feel for one moment the power of a sardonic god whose drama was the wars of men.

"About May, when the grass was tall and the horses strong, we broke camp and started across the country to the mouth of the Tongue River. Then Sitting Bull and Crazy Horse and all went up the Rosebud. There we had a big fight with General Crook, and whipped him. Many soldiers were killed—few Indians. It was a great fight, much smoke and dust.

"From there we all went over the divide, and camped in the valley of Little Horn. Everybody thought, 'Now we are out of the white man's country. He can live there, we will live here.' After a few days, one morning when I was in camp north of Sitting Bull, a Sioux messenger rode up and said, 'Let everybody paint up, cook, and get ready for a big dance.'

"Cheyennes then went to work to cook, cut up tobacco, and get ready. We all thought to dance all day. We were very glad to think we were far away from the white man.

"I went to water my horses at the creek, and washed them off with cool water, then took a swim myself. I came back to the camp afoot.

When I got near my lodge, I looked up the Little Horn towards Sitting Bull's camp. I saw a great dust rising. It looked like a whirlwind. Soon Sioux horseman came rushing into camp shouting: 'Soldiers come! Plenty white soldiers.'

"I ran into my lodge, and said to my brother-in-law, 'Get your horses; the white man is coming. Everybody run for horses.'

"Outside, far up the valley, I heard a battle cry, *Hay-ay, hay-ay*! I heard shooting, too, this way [clapping his hands very fast]. I couldn't see any Indians. Everybody was getting horses and saddles. After I had caught my horse, a Sioux warrior came again and said, 'Many soldiers are coming.'

"Then he said to the women, 'Get out of the way, we are going to have hard fight.'

"I said, 'All right, I am ready.'

"I got on my horse, and rode out into my camp. I called out to the people all running about: 'I am Two Moon, your chief. Don't run away. Stay here and fight. You must stay and fight the white soldiers. I shall stay even if I am to be killed.'

"I rode swiftly toward Sitting Bull's camp. There I saw the white soldiers fighting in a line [Reno's men]. Indians covered the flat. They began to drive the soldiers all mixed up–Sioux, then soldiers, then more Sioux, and all shooting. The air was full of smoke and dust. I saw the soldiers fall back and drop into the river-bed like buffalo fleeing. They had no time to look for a crossing. The Sioux chased them up the hill, where they met more soldiers in wagons, and then messengers came saying more soldiers were going to kill the women, and the Sioux turned back. Chief Gall was there fighting, Crazy Horse also.

"I then rode toward my camp, and stopped squaws from carrying off lodges. While I was sitting on my horse I saw flags come up over the hill to the east like that [he raised his finger-tips]. Then the soldiers rose all at once, all on horses, like this [he put his fingers behind each other to indicate that Custer appeared marching in columns of fours]. They formed into three bunches [squadrons] with a little ways between. Then a bugle sounded, and they all got off horses, and some soldiers led the horses back over the hill.

"Then the Sioux rode up the ridge on all sides, riding very fast. The Cheyennes went up the left way. Then the shooting was quick, quick. Pop–pop–pop very fast. Some of the soldiers were down on their knees, some standing. Officers all in front. The smoke was like a great cloud, and everywhere the Sioux went the dust rose like smoke. We circled all round him—swirling like water round a stone. We shoot, we ride fast, we shoot again. Soldiers drop, and horses fall on them. Soldiers in line drop, but one man rides up and down the line—all the time shouting. He rode a sorrel horse with white face and white fore-legs. I don't know who he was. He was a brave man.

"Indians keep swirling round and round, and the soldiers killed only a few. Many soldiers fell. At last all horses killed but five. Once in a while some man would break out and run toward the river, but he would fall. At last about a hundred men and five horsemen stood on the hill all bunched together. All along the bugler kept blowing his commands. He was very brave too. Then a chief was killed. I hear it was Long Hair [Custer], I don't know; and then the five horsemen and the bunch of men, may be so forty, started toward the river. The man on the sorrel horse led them, shouting all the time. He wore a buckskin shirt, and had long black hair and mustache. He fought hard with a big knife. His men were all covered with white dust. I couldn't tell whether they were officers or not. One man all alone ran far down toward the river, then round up over the hill. I thought he was going to escape, but a Sioux fired and hit him in the head. He was the last man. He wore braid on his arms [sergeant].

"All the soldiers were now killed, and the bodies were stripped. After that no one could tell which were officers. The bodies were left where they fell. We had no dance that night. We were sorrowful.

"Next day four Sioux chiefs and two Cheyennes and I, Two Moon, went upon the battlefield to count the dead. One man carried a little bundle of sticks. When we came to dead men, we took a little stick and gave it to another man, so we counted the dead. There were 388. There were thirty-nine Sioux and seven Cheyennes killed, and about a hundred wounded.

"Some white soldiers were cut with knives, to make sure they were dead; and the war women had mangled some. Most of them were left just where they fell. We came to the man with the big mustache; he lay down the hills towards the river. The Indians did not take his buckskin shirt. The Sioux said, 'That is a big chief. That is Long Hair.' I don't know. I had never seen him. The man on the white-faced horse was the bravest man.

"That day as the sun was getting low our young men came up the Little Horn riding hard. Many white soldiers were coming in a big boat, and when we looked we could see the smoke rising. I called my people together, and we hurried up the Little Horn, into Rotten Grass Valley.

We camped there three days, and then rode swiftly back over our old trail to the east. Sitting Bull went back into the Rosebud and down the Yellowstone, and away to the north. I did not see him again."

■ EMMA CARPENTER COWAN

In the summer of 1877, Emma Carpenter Cowan from Radersburg, Montana, went on a camping trip to the newly established Yellowstone National Park with her husband, George, and some relatives and friends. As the tourists prepared to leave the park to return home, they encountered Chief Joseph's band of Nez Perce Indians, who were on the run from the U.S. army. Emma's account of their adventures appears in Volume 4 of the Contributions to the Historical Society of Montana *(1903) and is excerpted in Joseph Kinsey Howard's* Montana Margins *(1946). Emma Cowan died in Spokane in 1938.*

A Trip to the National Park in 1877

The summer of 1877 was exceedingly hot and dry. This, together with a grasshopper raid, which was not the least of the trials of the pioneer, made the necessity of closing up the house to keep out the pests almost unbearable. My brother Frank, visiting us from Helena, told us of his intention to visit the Park, and asked us to be of the party. It required but little effort on his part to enthuse us, and we soon began preparations for the trip. Several people from our town, Radersburg, talked also of going, but by the time we were ready, one acquaintance only, Mr. Charles Mann, joined our party from that town. I induced my mother to allow my young sister, a child of a little more than a dozen years, to accompany me, as I was to be the only woman of the party and she would be so much company for me. . . .

Thursday, the 23d of August, found us all at the home camp, as we termed it, ready to retrace our steps towards civilization. We had had a delightful time, but were ready for home. This day we encountered the first and only party of tourists we had seen, General Sherman and party. They had come into the Park by way of the Mammoth Hot Springs. Of them we learned of the Nez Perce raid and the Big Hole fight. We also received the very unpleasant impression that we might meet the Indians before we reached home. No one seemed to know just where they were going. The scout who was with the General's party assured us we would be perfectly safe if we would remain in the Basin, as the Indians would never come into the Park. I observed, however, that his party preferred being elsewhere, as they left the Basin that same night.

That afternoon another visitor called at camp, an old man by the name of Shively, who was traveling from the Black Hills and was camped half a mile down the valley. Home seemed a very desirable place just at this particular time, and we decided with one accord to break camp in the morning, with a view of reaching it as soon as possible. Naturally we felt somewhat depressed and worried over the news received. My brother Frank and Al Oldham, in order to enliven us somewhat, sang songs, told jokes, and finally dressed up as brigands, with pistols, knives and guns strapped on them. Al Oldham, with his swart complexion, wearing a broad sombrero, looked a typical one, showing off to good advantage before the glaring camp fire. They made the woods ring with their nonsense and merriment for some time.

We probably would not have been so serene, had we known that the larger part of the audience consisted of the Indians, who were lurking out in the darkness, watching and probably enjoying the fun. Such was really the fact, as they informed us later, designating Oldham as Big Chief. The advance party of Indians had come into the Basin early in the evening. Before morning the entire Indian encampment was within a mile of us, and we had not heard an unusual sound, though I for one slept lightly.

I was already awake when the men began building the camp fire, and I heard the first guttural tones of the two or three Indians who suddenly stood by the fire. I peeped out through the flap of the tent, although I was sure they were Indians before I looked. I immediately aroused my husband, who was soon out. They pretended to be friendly, but talked little. After some consultation the men decided to break camp at once and attempt to move out as though nothing unusual was at hand. No one cared for breakfast save the Indians, who quickly devoured everything that was prepared. By this time twenty or thirty Indians were about the camp, and more coming. The woods seemed full of them. A line of timber was between us and the main camp. Some little time was required to pull down tents, load the wagons, harness and saddle the horses, and make ready for travel. While Mr. Cowan was engaged elsewhere one of the men—Mr. Arnold, I think—began dealing out sugar and flour to the Indians on their demand. My husband soon observed this and peremptorily ordered the Indians away, not very mildly either. Naturally they resented it, and I think this materially lessened his chances of escape.

So much ammunition had been used on the trip, especially at Henry lake, that the supply was practically exhausted. Mr. Cowan had five cartridges only, about ten all told in the party. It was a fortunate thing probably that we had no more, for had the men been well armed, they would have attempted a defense, which could only have ended disastrously to us. Six men arrayed against several hundred Indians splendidly armed would not have survived long.

We drove out finally on the home trail, escorted by forty or fifty Indians. In fact, they all seemed to be going our way except the squaw camp, which we met and passed as they were traveling up the Firehole towards Mary's lake. A mile or more was traveled in this way, when the Indians for some reason called a halt. We were then a few hundred yards from where the road enters the timber and ascends the hillside. One of the Indians seated on a horse near Mr. Cowan, who was also on horseback, raised his hand and voice, apparently giving some commands, for immediately forty or fifty Indians came out of the line of timber, where they had evidently been in ambush for our benefit. Another Indian, addressing Mr. Cowan and pointing to the Indian who had given the command, said in good English, "Him Joseph." And this was our introduction to that chief. Every Indian carried splendid guns, with belts full of cartridges. As the morning sunshine glinted on the polished surface of the gun barrels a regiment of soldiers could not have looked more formidable. We were told to backtrack, which we did, not without some protest, realizing however the utter futility. The Indians pretended all this while to be our very good friends, saying that if they should let us go, bad Indians, as they termed them, would kill us.

Passing and leaving our morning camp to the right, we traversed the trail towards Mary's lake for two miles. We could go no farther with the wagons on account of fallen timber. Here we unhitched, mounted the horses, taking from the wagon the few things in the way of wraps that we could carry conveniently, and moved on. It gave us no pleasure to see our wagons overhauled, ransacked and destroyed. Spokes were cut from the buggy wheels and used as whip handles. We did not appreciate the fact that the Indians seemed to enjoy the confiscated property. One young chap dashed past us with several yards of pink mosquito bar tied to his horse's tail. A fine strip of swansdown, a trophy from Henry lake, which an ugly old Indian had wrapped around his head turban fashion, did not please me either.

Regardless of the fact that they had been harassed and hard pressed and expected battle any moment–not from Howard's command, whom they termed for some reason "squaw soldiers,"–but from the Bannack Indians, eighty of whom were the advance scouts for General Howard–the majority of the Nez Perces were light-hearted and seemed not to worry over the outcome of their campaign. Perhaps to worry is a prerogative of the white race. The Bannack scouts referred to were following closely at the heels of the Nez Perces and could have attacked them several times had they so desired, but for some reason they did not.

After traveling some ten miles, a noon camp was made, fires lighted and dinner prepared. Poker Joe (we did not learn the Indian name) acted as interpreter. He talked good English, as could all of them when they desired. Through him we were told that if we would give up our horses and saddles for others that would be good enough to take us home, they would release us and we would be allowed to return to the settlement without harm. Many of their horses were worn out from the long, hurried march. Under the circumstances we acquiesced, and an exchange began. I was seated on my pony, watching proceedings, when I observed that two or three Indians were gathering around me, apparently admiring my horse, also gently leading her away from the rest of my party. They evidently wanted the animal and I immediately slipped out of the saddle to the ground, knowing I should never see my pony again, and went over to where Mr. Cowan was being persuaded that an old rackabone gray horse was a fair exchange for his fine mount. He was persuaded.

It occurs to me at this writing that the above mode of trading is a fair reflection of the lesson taught by the whites. For instance, a tribe of Indians are located on a reservation. Gold is discovered thereon by some prospector. A stampede follows. The strong arm of the government alone prevents the avaricious pale face from possessing himself of the land forthwith. Soon negotiations are pending with as little delay as a few yards of red tape will admit. A treaty is signed, the strip ceded to the government and opened to settlers, and "Lo, the poor Indian" finds himself on a tract a few degrees more arid, a little less desirable than his former home. The Indian has few rights the average white settler feels bound to respect.

In a measure I had gotten over my first fright. The Indians seemed friendly and the prospect of release probable. Poker Joe, mounted on my husband's horse, made the circle of the camp, shouting in a sonorous voice some commands relative to the march apparently, as the squaws soon began moving. He came to us finally and told us we could go. We lost no time in obeying the order. Two of our party, Dingee and Arnold, escaped into the timber at this time, though they were not missed by Mr. Cowan or me until later. All went well with us for half a mile or so. Then to our dismay we discovered Indians following us. They soon came up and said the chief wanted to see us again. Back we turned, passed the noon camp, now deserted, and up and on to higher timbered ground. My side saddle had been placed on a poor old horse and given to me, but the others were without saddles. We rode along the trail, my husband and I in advance, followed by my sister and brother and others of our party, Indians on every side, twenty or thirty of them. Their gaiety of the morning was lacking, the silence seemed ominous. The pallor of my husband's face told me he thought our danger great. I hoped we would soon overtake the squaw camp, for I fancied we would be safer. They seemed the same old dirty Indians familiar to all Western people.

Suddenly, without warning, shots rang out. Two Indians came dashing down the trail in front of us. My husband was getting off his horse. I wondered for what reason. I soon knew, for he fell as soon as he reached the ground – fell headlong down the hill. Shots followed and Indian yells, and all was confusion. In less time than it takes me to tell it, I was off my horse and by my husband's side, where he lay against a fallen pine tree. I heard my sister's screams and called to her. She came and crouched by me, as I knelt by his side. I saw he was wounded in the leg above the knee, and by the way the blood spurted out I feared an artery had been severed. He asked for water. I dared not leave him to get it, even had it been near. I think we both glanced up the hill at the same moment, for he said, "Keep quiet. It won't last long." That thought had flashed through my mind also. Every gun of the whole party of Indians was leveled on us three. I shall never forget the picture, which left an impress that years cannot efface. The holes in those gun barrels looked as big as saucers.

I gave it only a glance, for my attention was drawn to something near at hand. A pressure on my shoulder was drawing me away from my husband. Looking back and up over my shoulder, I saw an Indian with an immense navy pistol trying to get a shot at my husband's head. Wrenching my arm from his grasp, I leaned over my husband, only to be roughly drawn aside. Another Indian stepped up, a pistol shot rang out, my husband's head fell back, and a red stream trickled down his face from beneath his hat. The warm sunshine, the smell of blood, the horror of it all, a faint remembrance of seeing rocks thrown at his head, my sister's screams, a sick faint feeling, and all was blank.

Of the others of the party, all had run for the brush, including my brother. An Indian followed him and was about to fire, when Frank for a reason best known to himself, made the sign of the cross. The Indian immediately lowered his gun and told my brother to follow him. No other attempt was made on his life. He saw me ahead of him several times, fastened with a strap behind an Indian. He did not dare to make a point of getting near enough to speak. He was helping to drive the horses. We had overtaken the squaw camp. We afterwards learned that the chiefs, suspecting mischief from a few lawless Indians, had sent back Poker Joe to prevent further trouble.

After coming to my senses my first recollection was of a great variety of noises—hooting, yelling, neighing of horses—all jumbled together. For a while it seemed afar off. I became conscious finally that someone was calling my name, and tried to answer. Presently my brother rode close beside me. He told me later that I looked years older and that I was ghastly white. He tried to comfort me and said the Indians had told him no further harm should befall us. It seemed to me the assurance had come too late. I could see nothing but my husband's dead face with the blood upon it. I remember Frank's telling me my sister was safe, but it seemed not to impress me much at the time.

The Indians soon learned that my brother was familiar with the trail, and he was sent forward. Over this mountain range, almost impassable because of the dense timber, several hundred head of loose horses, pack horses, camp accoutrements, and the five or six hundred Indians were trying to force a passage. A narrow trail had sufficed for tourists. It was a feat few white people could have accomplished without axe or implements of some sort to cut the way. It required constant watching to prevent the loose horses from straying away. As it was, many were lost and recovered by the Bannack Indians later. The pack animals also caused trouble, often getting wedged in between trees. An old squaw would pound them on the head until they backed out. And such yelling! Their lungs seemed in excellent condition.

The wearisome up-hill travel was at length accomplished. Beyond the summit the timber was less dense, with open glades and parks. Finally, at dusk we came to quite a valley, which had already begun to glow with campfires, though many were not lighted until some time later. The Indian who was leading my horse—for I had been allowed to ride alone after recovering consciousness, the Indian retaining a grip on the bridle–threaded his way past numerous campfires and finally stopped near one. As if by a prearranged plan someone came to the horse, enveloped in a blanket. Until he spoke I thought it to be an Indian, and I was clasped in the arms of my brother. Tears then, the first in all these dreary hours, came to my relief. He led me to the fire and spoke to an Indian seated there, who, I was told, was Chief Joseph. He did not speak, but motioned me to sit down. Frank spread a blanket on the ground, and I sank down on it, thoroughly exhausted. A number of squaws about the fire were getting supper. My first question had been for my sister. I was told she was at Poker Joe's camp, some little distance away, together with the old man Shively, who was captured the evening before we were. I was told I could see her in the morning, and with this assurance I had to be satisfied. Food was offered me, but I could not eat.

My brother tried to converse with Chief Joseph, but without avail. The chief sat by the fire, sombre and silent, forseeing in his gloomy meditations possibly the unhappy ending of his campaign. The "noble red man" we read of was more nearly impersonated in this Indian than in any I have ever met. Grave and dignified, he looked a chief.

A squaw sat down near me with a babe in her arms. My brother wishing to conciliate them, I suppose, lifted it up and placed it on my lap. I glanced at the chief and saw the glimmer of a smile on his face, showing that he had heart beneath the stony exterior. The squaw was all smiles, showing her white teeth. Seeing that I was crying, the squaw seemed troubled and said to my brother, "Why cry?" He told her my husband had been killed that day. She replied, "She heartsick." I was indeed. . . .

Only a short distance away, which I would have walked gladly the night before, I found my sister. Such a forlorn looking child I trust I may never again see. She threw herself into my arms in a very paroxysm of joy. She seemed not to be quite certain that I was alive, even though she had been told. Mr. Shively, the old man before referred to, was at this camp, and I was as glad to see him as though I had known him always. He gave us much encouragement. The Indians had talked more freely with him and he had tried to impress upon them the wisdom of releasing us, telling them we had lived many years in the West and had many friends and that it would be to their advantage to let us go.

Poker Joe again made the circle of the camp, giving orders for the day's march. We were furnished with horses and my brother came up leading them. The four of us rode together that morning. We reached the crossing of the Yellowstone near the mud geysers at noon. The Indians plunged into the stream without paying much regard to the regular ford, and camped on the opposite shore. At this point a few days later, the Bannack Indians, scouting for Howard, came to this camp and found a poor old wounded Nez Perce squaw, who, too sick to travel, had been left here with bread and water within reach. They proceeded to kill and scalp her without delay, celebrating this great achievement with a war dance when the General's command arrived. . . .

At the squaw camp, dinner was being prepared. I had begun to feel faint from lack of food. I forced down a little bread, but nothing more. Fish was offered me, but I declined with thanks. I had watched the squaw prepare them something after this wise: From a great string of fish the largest were selected, cut in two, dumped into an immense camp-kettle filled with water, and boiled to a pulp. The formality of cleaning had not entered into the formula. While I admit that tastes differ, I prefer having them dressed.

A council was being held. We were seated in the shade of some trees watching proceedings. Six or seven Indians–the only ones who seemed to be in camp at the time–sat in a circle and passed a long pipe one to another. Each took a few whiffs of smoke, and then one by one they arose and spoke. Poker Joe interpreted for us. Presently he said the Indians had decided to let my sister and me go, together with the soldier who had been captured that morning, but would hold my brother and Shively for guides. I had not been favorably impressed with the soldier. Intuition told me he was not trustworthy, and I refused to go unless my brother was also released. This caused another discussion, but they agreed to it, and preparations were made for our departure. A search was made for my side saddle, but without avail. It was found later by some of Howard's soldiers near where Mr. Cowan was shot.

Some of our own bedding, a waterproof wrap, a jacket for my sister, bread and matches, and two old wornout horses were brought, and we were ready. We clasped hands sadly with our good friend Shively, promising to deliver some messages to friends in Philipsburg should we escape. His eyes were dim with tears. In reality, I considered his chances of escape better than our own, and so told him. The Indians needed him for a guide. "We may be intercepted by the warriors out of camp," I said. "No," he replied, "something tells me you will get out safely."

We crossed the river again, my brother riding behind Poker Joe, who went with us a half mile or more, showing us presently a well defined trail down the river. He told us we must ride "*All Night, All Day, No Sleep*—we would reach Bozeman on second day." He reiterated again and again that we must ride all night. We shook hands and set out, not very rapidly. My brother walked and the horses we rode were worn out. It seemed folly to think we could escape. Furthermore, we placed no confidence in the Indian. I regret to say that as soon as he was out of sight we left the river trail and skirted along in the timber. . . .

About noon the signs of some one ahead of us were apparent. In crossing streams, pony tracks in the wet sand were plainly seen, and the marks of a rope or lasso that had been dragged in the dust of the trail indicated Indians. They often drag the rope thus, I am told. We passed Lower creek and stopped a very short time to rest the horses. A few hours later, in rounding a point of timber, we saw in a little meadow not far beyond, a number of horses and men. At the first glance we thought them Indians. Frank drew our horses back into the timber and went forward to investigate. He returned in a very few minutes and declared them soldiers. Oh, such a feeling of relief!

Imagine their surprise when we rode into the camp and my brother told them we were fleeing from the Indians, the only survivors of our party, as he believed then. The soldier we had left in the Nez Perce camp the day before was a deserter from this company. Retribution closely followed transgression in this case. Mr. Shively escaped after being with the Indians ten days, but the fate of the soldier we did not learn.

This company of soldiers was a detachment from Fort Ellis, with Lieutenant Schofield in command. They were sent out to ascertain the whereabouts of the Nez Perces, and were returning in the belief that the Indians were not in that vicinity. Of them we learned that General Howard was closely following the Indians. Many of their actions were thus accounted for. The soldiers kindly prepared supper for us. I remember being nearly famished. Camp had been made for the night, but was quickly abandoned, and arrangements made for quick travel. We were mounted on good horses, and the poor old ones, that had done us good service notwithstanding their condition, were turned out to graze to their hearts' content.

As we were about to move off, a man came hurrying down the trail. He proved to be one of the Helena party and believed himself the only one alive of that party. He said they were attacked at noon.

Frank and I concluded that Poker Joe knew what he was talking about when he told us to travel all night. A horse was provided for this man, hurry orders given, and we set out for the Springs, some seventeen miles distant. This night, unlike the previous one, was dark and cloudy. We passed over some of the roughest mountain trails near Gardiner that I ever remember traveling. Many of the soldiers walked and led their horses. Near midnight we reached the Mammoth Hot Springs, tired out and stiff from long riding, but truly thankful for our escape. . . .

On Monday, Mr. Calfee, a photographer, invited us to go to Bozeman with him. He said he had a pair of wild mules and a big wagon, but if we wished, he would take us. We were anxious to get home and very glad of so good an opportunity. The Englishmen and their guide also decided to return to Bozeman. Wonderland had lost its attractions for the nonce. . . .

We drove to Bozeman next day. A few miles from the town we met seventy or eighty Crows, escorted by Lieutenant Doane on their way to intercept the Nez Perces. They looked rather more dangerous than any we had yet met. After reaching Bozeman, my brother eventually went with this party nearly to the Mammoth Hot Springs in his endeavor to reach the point where Mr. Cowan was shot, but was compelled to return again to Bozeman without accomplishing that result.

In the meantime I had reached my father's home. Kind friends and neighbors had kept the news of our capture from my people until the day we reached home, then prepared them for our coming, thus sparing them much of the suspense. I reached there worn out with excitement and sorrow. Years seemed to have passed over my head since I had left my home a month previous.

From the time I learned of the close proximity of General Howard's command to the Nez Perces at the time Mr. Cowan was shot, I could not but entertain a faint hope that the soldiers might have found my husband alive. Yet, in reviewing all of the circumstances, I could find little to base such a hope upon. Still, as one after another of the party were accounted for, all living, the thought would come. I believed I should know to a certainty when my brother returned from his quest.

I had been at home a week, when one afternoon two acquaintances drove to the house. My father not being in, I went to the door. They would not come in, but talked a few minutes on ordinary subjects. Then one of them handed me a paper and said news had been received of Mr. Cowan, that he was alive. In the "Independent" extra I found this account:

> COWAN ALIVE. He is with General Howard's Command.
> Whereabouts of Howard.
> (Special to the Independent), Bozeman, September 5.
>
> Two scouts just in from Howard's command say that Cowan is with Howard and is doing well and will recover.
>
> He is shot through the thigh and in the side and wounded in the head.
>
> Howard was fourteen miles this side of Yellowstone lake. This news is reliable. LANGHORNE.

Some way the doorstep seemed conveniently near as a resting place just at that particular time. Presently they told me the particulars. He was badly wounded, but would live; was with Howard's command, and would either be sent back to Virginia City or brought the other way to Bozeman. For the time being, this news was all sufficient. A day or two passed. I learned nothing more. My brother Frank came, but had the same news only that had been given me. The hours began to drag. I decided to go to Helena with my brother, as from that point telegraphic news could reach me much sooner. After arriving at Helena, however, a whole week passed before a telegram came to me, stating that my husband would be in Bozeman the following day.

I lost no time in going. At Bozeman, however, I found he had given out at the Bottler ranch on the Yellowstone. A double-seated carriage was procured for the trip, and once again I found myself traversing the familiar and oft traveled road. But this day the sun shone. My husband had notice of my coming and was expecting me. I found him much better than I dared anticipate, and insistent on setting out for home without delay.

We arranged robes and blankets in the bed of the carriage. With his back propped up against the back seat, he was made quite comfortable. I occupied the back seat, Mr. Arnold and the driver the front. Mr. Arnold, whose escape is elsewhere noted, reached the Howard command and was among the first to aid Mr. Cowan when that command found him, and he had remained with and cared for him like a brother ever since.

We stopped for a hand shake and congratulations at the Ferril home on Trail creek. We had rather a spirited team and made fair progress. Late in the afternoon we were at a point seven miles from

Bozeman in Rocky canyon. The road bed was graded around a steep hillside for some distance. We could look down and see the tops of trees that grew on the stream far below. Presently we experienced the novel and very peculiar sensation of seeing our carriage resting on those self same trees, wheels uppermost, ourselves a huddled mass on the roadside. Merely a broken pole strap, a lunge forward of the horses as the carriage ran up against them. The buggy tongue caught, snapped and threw the carriage completely over. Fortunately the seats were not fastened and we were left, a bundle of seats, robes, blankets and people on the hillside, shaken but not much hurt. The carriage, from which the horses had freed themselves, made one more revolution as it went over and landed as described. We were thankful to have left it at the first tip.

Mr. Cowan was lifted to a more comfortable position by the roadside. Not long after, a horseman leading a pack animal came along. Our driver borrowed the horse, making the trip to Fort Ellis and back in the shortest possible time and returning with an ambulance. The seven miles seemed long ones, and before we reached Bozeman Mr. Cowan was almost exhausted, his wounds bleeding and needing attention. He was carried by careful hands to a room in the hotel as soon as the crowd had thinned somewhat. Mr. Arnold arranged to dress the wounds, and in order to do so seated himself on the side of the bed, when lo, the additional weight caused the whole inside of the bed to drop out and down on the floor. This sudden and unexpected fall, in his enfeebled state, nearly finished him. A collapse followed, from which he did not rally for some time.

A week passed before we were able to travel further. I think the anxiety for my husband alone sustained me during this trying time. As it was, my nerves were all awry. Had I been morbidly inclined, I might have conceived the idea that some avenging nemesis was following in his foot-steps, which nothing but the forfeit of his life would satisfy.

By the time we reached home Mr. Cowan was able to hobble about on crutches. The winter passed however before he was entirely well. A severe gunshot wound through the hip, a bullet hole in the thigh, a ball flattened on the forehead, and the head badly cut with rocks—few, indeed, are the men who could have survived so severe an ordeal. Our month of out-door life and a fine constitution, coupled with a strong will power, worked a miracle almost.

After receiving the pistol shot in the head, some time must have passed before he regained consciousness, as the sun was just tipping the tree tops, proving that the afternoon was far advanced. At the time of receiving the shot in the thigh he supposed the bone broken, as he was unable to stand. By this time, however, the numbness was gone, the blood had begun to circulate, and he could move his foot.

The intolerable thirst that follows gunshot wounds impelled him to try to reach water. Absolute quiet reigned. Yet, as he raised himself by the branch of a fallen tree, an Indian who had evidently been waiting for other Indians observed the movement and immediately fired at him. The ball passed through the point of the left hip, and he fell, fully expecting the Indian to come up and complete the work. Presently several Indians passed along the trail, and again all was silence.

Some time passed before he again began the quest for water, crawling on hands and knees, as he could not now stand. He would go until exhausted and then rest in the branches of some fallen pine tree. Not before noon of the next day did he finally reach a stream of water, though he had crawled parallel with it some miles without being aware of the fact on account of the timber and dense undergrowth. He fairly lay in the water, quenching his thirst. Then with hands and teeth he tore his underwear into bandages and dressed his wounds as best he could.

Even though the month was August the nights were cold in this altitude, so that this was added to his other discomforts. He continued crawling, getting up on the hillside that he might better watch the trail. Several times he heard and saw Indians passing, and one night nearly came upon two who were sleeping.

His idea was to reach the home camp in the Lower Basin, believing he might be found more readily in that vicinity, also that he would possibly find food and matches there. He was four days and nights crawling the ten miles. Tuesday he reached the camp and found a few matches, but nothing to eat. A double handful of coffee was picked up, which he contrived to pound up in a cloth, and an empty syrup can answered very well to boil it in. Nearly half was lost by the can's falling into the fire. Still, enough remained to strengthen him considerably.

In the afternoon of the next day two of Howard's scouts found him and gave him food and blankets, placing him where Howard's command would find him. The scouts were taking rations to the Bannack Indians, who, with Fisher, were scouting for Howard. They had passed

Mr. Cowan the day before and been seen by him, but of course he supposed them Nez Perces. The scouts left him after building a fire which came near being his undoing. A heavy wind in the night caused it to get beyond his control, and a timber fire resulted from which he had great difficulty in escaping. As it was, hands and knees were burned in trying to crawl away.

Thursday brought to him Howard's command, also Arnold and Oldham, of our party, the latter slightly wounded in the face, and he was assured of the safety of his wife, her brother and sister. His wounds were dressed, the bullet that had flattened on his skull removed, and he was made as comfortable as circumstances would permit.

And then began the hard, wearisome travel. Over rough new made roads he was carried by the command where oftentimes the wagon was let down the mountain side with ropes. Over stumps and rocks and fallen timber they made their way. From fever and the sloughing of the wounds, he had become so emaciated that Arnold, though himself a small man, could easily lift him out of the wagon. The trip was indeed a hard one. It would seem that the determination to live, come what would, alone brought him out alive, where others with less will power would have succumbed.

Many years have passed since the events herein narrated occurred, yet retrospection is all that is needed to bring them to mind clear and distinct as events of yesterday – many years, since which life has glided on and on, with scarce a ripple beyond the every day sunshine and shadow that falls to the lot of each and all of God's people.

■ CHIEF JOSEPH

For five months in 1877, Chief Joseph and eight hundred "nontreaty" Nez Perce Indians successfully fought off and escaped the forces of the U.S. Army, who were charged with moving Joseph's people to a reservation in Idaho. Believing they had escaped and were close to safety in Canada, the Nez Perces were surprised in the Bears Paw Mountains by General Nelson Miles and his soldiers. After three days of heavy fighting, the Nez Perces surrendered on October 5, 1877; but instead of being returned to Idaho, they were sent to Indian Territory (present-day Oklahoma), where almost half died of sickness. Seven years later, 280 survivors of the ordeal returned to reservations in Idaho and Washington. In his 1893 report to the U.S. Bureau of Ethnology, James Mooney included the army report of Chief Joseph's famous speech to his chiefs before the surrender of the Nez Perces. Joseph died in 1904 at Nespelem on the Colville Indian Reservation in Washington.

I Will Fight No More

I am tired of fighting. Our chiefs are killed. Looking Glass is dead. Toohulhulsote is dead. The old men are all dead. It is the young men who say yes or no. He who led the young men is dead. It is cold and we have no blankets. The little children are freezing to death. My people, some of them, have run away to the hills and have no blankets, no food. No one knows where they are—perhaps freezing to death. I want to have time to look for my children and see how many of them I can find. Maybe I shall find them among the dead. Hear me, my chiefs. I am tired. My heart is sick and sad. From where the sun now stands I will fight no more forever.

■ ANDREW GARCIA

Andrew Garcia, nicknamed the "Squaw Kid," lived among the Nez Perce and Flathead Indians during their last "free" years on the Northern Plains. Garcia's memoirs were found after his death in 1943, packed into an old dynamite box in his cabin near Alberton in western Montana. Bennett H. Stein edited Garcia's writings and published them under the title, Tough Trip Through Paradise *(1967). "The Only Way Out Is to Fly" is a chapter from those memoirs that begins with Garcia's visit with his wife to the battlefield on the Big Hole River, two years after the Nez Perce fought the army there.*

The Only Way Out Is to Fly

The second day after we returned to the battlefield after burying Susie's father and Red Heart, we were prowling through the willows and found a lance that some Indian must have used in the fight. The long handle was broken off, about a foot of the handle remaining with the lance head. I did not care for it then—maybe I was superstitious. Anyway, my wife was, and she said, "No, you shall not take away that what is of some dead warrior of my people. He may want it yet, he may come back from the land of the dead for it, and

then, if it is gone, he will do evil things to us." "All right," I told her, "we will hide it in this clump of willows for him, or some white man surely will find it," and we hid it there. Many times since I have thought of my good, little squaw and wondered if anyone ever found that lance head. When I started to write this book about her, I knew that I ought to go to the Big Hole, but kept putting it off, as I thought, "What is the use in going there—it will only make me more sorry for her." But, in the fall of 1930, I finally found I would have to go there to refresh my memory.

I went down to the Indian camp place and knew right away where I was. At the monument I asked if I could look over the field. I was told, "You are right in it." I said, "This is only a part of the battlefield, where the white men dug in after the Nez Perces licked the hell out of them. I want to go down in the creek bottom where Gibbon's bunch shot up the bucks and murdered the squaws and papooses. I used to have a squaw that was in this battle. I came here with her in 1879, and I know this place and where I want to go."

"I will go along with you," he said, and he did. He came along to try to learn something about those places. I went back there on the sly in a few days and did my work in peace, though I felt like crying when doing it. I hunted for the lance head, and without much trouble located it in that clump of willows. The lance was rusted badly and I had a hard time getting it out of the willows, as the blade was two feet long and as the old willows had died, the young shoots had grown up and wedged it in. The men at the monument did not try to take the lance away from me. I brought it home.

In-who-lise and I left the Big Hole battlefield in June, 1879, on our way to the Bitterroot Valley, and I was glad to leave this charnel house of sorrow. When we came to a fork in the trail, I started to take the left, or white men's trail. In-who-lise, driving the pack horse behind, said, "No, not that way. Turn right and take the Injun trail, the way my people came over here."

I told her the two white men at the battlefield had told me not to take the Injun trail, that it was full of fallen trees. Susie flies in a rage at this, and starts crying, "Yes, it is now always white men with you, when you know I hate them–them evil white men who helped to kill my people. E-ah, they would have killed you this morning if it were not for your woman's sharp eyes and the gun in her hands. After all of their evil, you are still listening to them, and no more heed the voice of your woman."

Without saying a word, I swung my horse around and headed up the old Injun trail. At first the trail was not bad, as this part of the country was fairly open and flat. Making good time, it was not long till we came to the camp in the pines where the Nez Perce women cut tepee poles to bring with them to the buffalo country nearly two years before this.

In-who-lise, penitent for the tongue-lashing she had given me, wants to make up. Failing at this, she starts in at her old trade, wailing for her people, and said that we must camp here. But I was still mad at her for making me take the Injun trail. Knowing that if we camp here, it will only be for me to attend another Injun funeral, I said, "I am the man, and no woman tells the man where to camp. It is a long day yet; we keep on going."

The trail still was not bad, but I was soon to find out that a good beginning means a bad end. The closer to the summit we came, the thicker the lodge poles grew, until they were as thick as the hair on a dog's back. Tall and majestic, they stood so thick that the sun never shone on the ground. It was a continual jumping of fallen trees across the trail.

Our horses were prairie horses, and not used to dodging through the thick timber with bulky packs. They would rub the lash rope off the corners of the *aparejos*, and get hung up between the trees. I had been on trails in timber, but had never been in anything like this. We came to logs across the trail that my saddle horse refused to jump. I gave Susie the dickens for getting us into a jackpot like this.

In-who-lise said scornfully that this was a good Injun trail and that I did not know much if I could not get my horse through a good trail like this. I told her that it was up to her to get us through. She could lead, and I would drive behind, till we came out in God's country again.

Before this I had heard the story of the American who rode his horse till he was exhausted and fell down on the trail, and, do as he would, the American could not get him up to go any further. Leaving him there, he went on his way. It was only a few minutes later when along comes an Injun. The Injun, in some brutal way known only to Injuns, gets the weary and played-out horse up on his feet, mounts and rides ten miles further, when again the horse fell down exhausted. Do as the Injun would, he could not get the horse up again. Failing in this, in disgust he went on his way. Before the Injun got out of sight, along the trail comes a Mexican, who on seeing the almost dead horse lying by the trail, said to himself, "*Gracias a Dios*, but this is good. Never yet did a Mexican walk when there was a good horse like this lying by the trail for him to ride." The Mexican now like the Injun, and by other brutal means known only to Mexicans, gets this nearly dead horse up on his feet, mounts and goes on his way with him, making ten miles and was congratulating himself on what a good horse he had when the horse, much to the disgust of the Mexican, fell dead on the trail.

Just why this slur was put on the Mexican is hard to say. While the Mexican is a hard rider, there are few people except the Arabs who have a greater love and affection for Allah's pride the horse than the Mexican. I was to find out today, and many times after that the Injun has no affection, gratitude or pity for the horse. Many times after this, I was thankful that, of all things on this earth, I was not born an Injun's horse.

In-who-lise, being now in the lead, needs no second bidding to make her words good. Cutting herself a pine sapling the size of a fish pole, she came up behind my saddle horse who had refused to leap over this fallen tree up to his breast across the trail. One crack from the sapling by In-who-lise was enough. With a snort of terror as the blow landed on his rump, he rears up and like a steeplechaser cleared the fallen tree. As each one of the pack horses came up to the fallen tree she could come down on him with her pole, and over the high log he went.

As we went along, sometimes the fallen trees across the trail would be higher, and the pack horses could not make it the first time, an extra crack or two from In-who-lise, then the poor brutes who could not turn around to get away would rear up, getting their front feet over and scramble over on their bellies. It was not long till all of our horses were bruised and skinned up, besides having long welts on them, where In-who-lise hit them with her pole.

The trail kept getting worse. I told her that I had had enough of this brutality. Telling her to get behind where women rightly belonged, I said that I could do better than her, without having to bruise and smash our horses up.

With Susie sulking behind, we came to a place where I could see that, by cutting a couple of the fallen trees out of the way, we could get out of this eternal windfall into what looked like open timber. I thought we could make it this way and thought I was doing fine.

Soon Susie said, "You are going the wrong way already, and soon we will be turned around and lost among all those trees that look alike."

I told her that I was doing this, and that she should drive them cayuses along faster, so that we could get back on the trail.

I kept on going making good time. Whenever the trees got too thick and blocked me, I could swing off and find another opening that led another way, still thinking that I would find another opening in the thick trees where I could swing back in the right direction.

Susie is still nagging me to turn back to the Injun trail before it is too late. The third time she rode ahead to me, she said that I was lost even if I thought that I was not.

Finally she said, "If An-ta-lee my man will not heed my voice, when I know I am right in this, he can go on his own trail, and I go on mine. Your woman goes no further with you this way. I am going back to the Injun trail and leave you here."

Instead of this threat making peace between us it got worse, and in the end it wound up with me telling her to get back to the Injun trail if she wanted so bad to leave me here, that I would be well rid of her and glad to see her go.

At first In-who-lise did not believe I meant this. But when I offered to whack up everything we had, she refused, saying, "Then if An-ta-lee my man wants me no more, I want nothing from him." With her head bowed down to hide the tears, turning her horse around, she silently rode off, leaving me in this dark timber, to get out the best way I could, with eleven horses packed and six loose besides my saddle horse. Though I would not admit this to her, I knew now that I was lost.

Putting all the blame on her for this, I thought I was well rid of her, as I bitterly thought, "Just let me get out of here. Then it's back to the

Injun buffalo camps, in the Musselshell and Milk River country, no more of this tall timber country for me."

I had been told by the wise ones that there was nothing to it when lost in the woods. "Don't get excited," they said, "sit down and compose yourself." In this way I sat down talking to myself, anathematizing the squaws in general, telling my audience, our seven Injun dogs who are wagging their tails around me, that they are the only friends I now had left, and for them to take a warning from this–to beware of the she stuff.

But as the time went by and the shadows of the approaching night deepened, I missed something, and kept looking back the way In-who-lise had gone, as though expecting to see her coming back like she always did in the end. But no In-who-lise showed up when I needed her bad. Still darker deepened this silent forest of lodge pole pines. It was then that grave doubts began to assail me from all sides; they are whispering what struck terror in my heart, saying with an evil leer, "She is never coming back to you. This is the time you drove her off once too often."

Then I realized the trouble I was in with all this stock to drive, in this forest of trees that all look alike, and, worse still, seems to have no end. The more I thought of this, the worse my terror got. I would go now before it got too late to overtake her and beg her to come back.

Leaving our dogs there, with some of the horses tied, taking my carbine along, I start off afoot, and had only gone a little way when I noticed for the first time, that even with all the horses we had along with us, they left no sign of a trail on the pine needles under the trees.

I ran back to the horses and, discarding my rifle for an ax, I was quickly on my way again, putting a blaze on the trees here and there to keep from getting lost from the horses. I just had to find In-who-lise to pull me out of this. If I could just get my eyes on her once more, never would I be mean to her again. I would be her humble slave all my life.

Climbing over and crawling under the fallen trees, I surely was lost, but suddenly, much to my joy, I heard a horse snuffle. Crawling to where the sound came from, coming out of the windfall, I nearly ran into In-who-lise. She was squatting beside her horse near a fallen tree, a picture of woe with her head bowed down on her knees. Sometimes she would raise her head, and I could see that she was silently crying. Crawling back out of her sight, I lay there watching her. At first I wanted to go and give her a grizzly-bear hug, and my conscience is telling me, "Squaw Kid, you are a damned brute when you do this to the only true friend you have."

But the spirit of evil said, "Don't listen to them foolish thoughts. That fool woman is going to come back to you like she always did. No use in spoiling her. If you coax her, then she will do this she thing every chance she gets, just to make you run after her."

I listened to the voice of evil as usual, saying, "Me humble myself to her? Not on your life. I will see all the squaws in hell first. I will teach her to pull off any more stunts like this."

Hand in hand with the devil, I had no trouble following the blazes, going quickly to arrive at the horses before Susie got back, and found them and the dogs all right. As I expected, In-who-lise soon rode up, and is all sheepish smiles.

She got off her horse and, coming up to me, I could see the sorrow in her eyes. She said, "No, I did not come back to stay. I came back to see if you are sorry like I am. Do you still like me, or do you want me to go away?"

Then I knew my deviltry had gone far enough. In-who-lise had come back to make up. Standing there watching me with sad despair, I could tell that she had made up her mind that this was the end, one way or the other. Her face is now expressionless, her dark eyes now stern and inscrutable.

Once more the spirit of good won out. I swore to God, like I had done many times before, only this time I meant it, that there was no other woman like her to me. The black clouds have cleared away. Hope and love are again beaming in her midnight eyes, as she said never again will she forget her words to Colon Suten and the E-qui-lix, that she would follow her man on his way till the end of the trail.

We camped there, since it was now too dark to travel. The horses were tied to the trees with nothing to eat, and, worse still, without a drink since we left the last Nez Perce camp. Taking the packs off, unrolling our robes and blankets, we ate some dried buffalo meat, and went to sleep without a fire. Susie said it was too dangerous for fires with the thick pine needles under the trees and no water. The horses, hungry and dry as they were, were restless and pawed the ground all night.

At the break of day we were packing up, and soon on our way. I said to In-who-lise that it was up to her to lead the way and pull us out of this. She declined that honor, saying that she was turned around and lost herself, that any way was as good as another now.

On we went through this seeming endless forest of lodge pole pines. Sometimes they were tall, large and majestic, and for a way looked as though they had been planted in rows a certain distance apart by the hand of man. Again we came to thickets of them where they grew tall and slim and so thick and close together, it would have bothered a man afoot to work his way through them. On we went only to run into windfalls, making us swing in another direction. On we went over ridges, and across gulches in this eternal shade. Not a sign of wild life had we seen, no grass or water had we found and only pine needles that in some places carpeted the ground nearly a foot deep. On we went, to tell you the truth, I don't know where. This way and that with only one wish, that will show us an opening between the trees, how to get out of this lodge pole forest that seems to have no end, to where we can find water and grass for the horses and a drink for ourselves.

It must have been near the middle of the day. Yes, God is good, when through a kind of an opening we could see some distance above us bare rocky hills with scattering trees here and there. If we could make it and get up there on the hill, we might be able to tell where we were. We came out of it at last. Taking what looked to be the easiest way, we started sidling to make it to the top, so that we could see over the timber. On our way we found a small rivulet made by snow water, where the horses and us got a drink, the first since before noon yesterday. We came to small patches of buck brush and bear grass, and would let the horses stop to eat. The buck brush was not so bad, but bear grass is too tough and wiry and sour for stock to eat if they can get anything else. Still our hungry horses went at it; it was so tough they sometimes pulled a mouthful out by the roots, and thought it good.

Up we went sidling along this long range of hills, and soon we began to see over a part of the tops of the trees of this forest we had been lost in. It took us some time the way we went, with the horses eating here and there before we reached the top.

Coming to the top nothing entered my mind, except a bitter curse. Where to find a place to get down and back out of here, without having to go through that lodge pole forest again! Every way we could see on both sides of this ridge below us for miles stood out this belt of green trees, between the Big Hole and Ross's Hole on the Bitterroot side. From here not an opening could we see.

Squaw men have been accused of about all the crimes there are, except of being poetical and dreamers, but I must tell you that it was some sight to see and was probably never duplicated before or after this, superb in its gigantic splendor, the mighty mountain peaks in all directions as far as the eye can see, and the bullheaded An-ta-lee and the ornery In-who-lise away up there sometimes almost in the clouds. The scenery was grand even if you can't eat it, as they went on their way, riding along the Continental Divide, the backbone of the Rocky Mountains, driving a pack train and their several loose horses, all their worldly wealth, including seven Injun dogs.

In this way sometimes the going was good, other times bad, as on we went, sometimes up, more times down, again it would be across and over rock slides to wind up on a rocky sideling where a false step of your horse would send you and him rolling and crashing to land down on some rocky canyon a quarter of a mile below, getting by this only to go skirting over loose rock slides around the base of some rocky peak that towered above us, its crests gleaming white with snow, winding our way around this only to run into something far worse and hair-raising.

Time and again we crossed over the ridge from the Big Hole side to the Ross's Hole side, looking down for a way to get down from here and find an opening through the timber below. There was none that we could see, and the only way to get down from here now without going back the way we got up here is to fly. And I should have known that no woman would keep her word of honor, when it comes to keeping her mouth shut, for In-who-lise has broken her word to me, and now again bewails our sad lot. She wants to know where I am headed for, saying it will be better for us to turn back the way we came and try to make it back to the Big Hole Valley through the lodge pole forest, then take the white men's trail this time. Sometimes as she drives the pack and loose horses along, In-who-lise to relieve her feelings is crooning an Injun funeral dirge, but was soon smiling and happy again, when we came on a long stretch of country that was good going. Then our luck changed for the worse again. We came to a divide where this ridge was broken in two, while maybe more than three hundred feet below us lay quite a flat that connected the ridge we were on with the ridge on the other side. Down in this dismal hole were several scrubby pines, bear grass and buck brush.

We had a hell-roaring time, getting down into this hole. It was swift going as long as it lasted. We found ourselves standing on a large slide of gravel, shell rock and sand, at the base of a bluff that rose up and frowned down on us more than a hundred feet high. It stood there almost straight up and down, with its thousands of tons of gravel, shell rock and sand honeycombed into many fantastic shapes. All of them standing there and looking as though a person had only to blow his breath on some of those towering structures of wash to make them topple over and come tumbling down.

Below was the accumulation of many years' cave-ins of them bluffs. We came upon the head of the slide, and, seeing this was the only way to get down, we did not stay long.

I told In-who-lise to say quickly all the prayers she knows in Injun, and for her to watch her saddle horse's step, and not let him get sideways with her, if the slide started to run.

Starting down the slide on the lead, with the horses following down in a long string, we were going at a good fast clip, the horses with their rumps high above their heads, with their front feet braced ahead of them, with the wash up to their bellies, each horse pushing waves of loose gravel, shell rock and sand ahead of it. Down the plunging horses went toward the bottom, accompanied by waves of rattling gravel and shell rock, the sand in it making clouds of dust, that hid what was before or behind. The horses on the lead finally struggled out of the wash onto the flat.

But on looking up the slide, through the rifts in the floating dust, it is with horror I can see that In-who-lise is still not halfway down the slide and that there are several horses still strung out ahead of her. And not far behind her came a large wave of wash that came swishing down from them tottering bluffs and now caught up with her terrified saddle horse. In-who-lise was bravely holding him from getting sideways when the terror-stricken brute rears up and plunges down the slide with her, landing sideways in the fast-moving slide with her still in the saddle, and was quickly swept off his feet and covered over with running wash. In-who-lise leaps out of the saddle on the up hillside, as her horse rolled over. Coming down this way to the bottom, her horse quickly struggled to his feet, and lost no time in rejoining the rest of the horses that were already rambling over the flat, looking for grass or brush to fill up on.

In-who-lise did not have as good luck coming down as her horse did. Springing wildly into the running wash at the bottom, I tried my best to make it up a ways, to try to meet and help her, but for every step I tried to make in the cursed stuff I lost two, and was pushed back out on the flat. Finally, the oncoming wash spreading out more as it reached the bottom, I was lucky enough to be able to grab In-who-lise by the arm as she was coming by. I got her up on her feet, but it was only for an instant, it seemed, when another wave of wash came swishing down into us, and taking us along with it, as we struggled and clung to each other to keep from falling down. We were shoved and pushed along with the wash, a good fifty feet further out on the flat, among some of the scrubby pine trees, and, lucky for us, to where we were able to scramble to safety. All covered with dust, her hair, eyes and ears full of sand, In-who-lise was some sight to see, but, lucky for us, had only a few scratches here and there.

She wished now that she had let me take the white men's trail, from the Big Hole battlefield to the Bitterroot Valley.

I told her not to be down in the mouth for a little thing like this. If we lived through a few more days in this awe-inspiring country, it was going to make a mountain man out of me yet. Besides it was root-hog-or-die with us now, for no horse was ever made that could climb up that slide and back up on the ridge.

Finding a good spring of water and plenty of wood, with some buck brush and a tough sour grass for the tired horses, we went into camp for the night. The packs and *aparejos* were off for the first time in two days. In-who-lise crooned a plaintive ditty, squatting cooking by a roaring fire, with a motherly look on her scratched face. Our campfire sent its beams in a friendly way far out in the night, adding a homelike appearance to this weird scene.

Nearly all night long, as though misery likes company, gusts of wind came passing over us, from someplace on their way across this divide, sighing and moaning, as though a delegation of lost souls were passing by on their way to hell. In the intervals we could hear a large hoot owl using profane language. The moon and stars gleaming on the white snow on the surrounding peaks lit up the night almost like day.

At the break of day the ground was gray with frost. In-who-lise was cooking breakfast, as I moved shivering with the biting cold, putting the *aparejos* on the huddled and shivering pack horses. After investigating both sides of this divide, the only way that was left to us was the main ridge east out of this hole. We soon found ourselves back up, as it looked, a stone throw from the clouds, and looking back we could tell that ever since we started yesterday we had been going higher up in altitude. The mountain peaks we had dodged yesterday were only the babies of the peaks that loomed in front of us. Sidling along steep rocky hillsides, with slopes that looked a good quarter of a mile to the bottom of them, the horses loosened good-sized boulders that rolled down the steep slope. As the boulders increased their speed, they would leave the slope and go flying through the air, to land crashing far away below us.

Again it would be over and across steep and deep rocky gulches, and, though it is the latter part of June, above us they are still full of snow. Suddenly this ridge we had been trying to follow swung abruptly to the north, with high bluffs staring us in the face, hiding all views before us. Plainly we had come to the end of our rope. We could go no further this way up here. In-who-lise wildly protesting that a mountain goat could not get down from here, that ourselves and all the horses were going to be killed, I told her that anything is better than the way we were now.

The outfit in a long string, the horses with their rumps high above their heads, in a half slide and half crawl as they carefully brace one forefoot ahead of the other, down-down and sidling from one rocky ledge to another on we went, trying to follow the base at the side of those bluffs. Climbing along and over ledges of rock that overhang deep rocky canyons far below, we went sidling on our way.

After many ups and down, we came out on another ridge or spur. Losing no time, we started following down this spur, which, though it is far below the ridge we had been on, was no little foothill. On down we went and, while the going was not any too good, still it was a paradise compared to what we had already gone through. It did not take very long to reach the bottom of the divide among a scattering of pine trees. There before our eyes lay what was either an elk or a seldom used Injun trail.

Tired and weary and covered with dust, we had now been on the go through the long June day since a little after sunrise. It was now about an hour to sundown and this was no place to camp, as there was no feed of any kind for the horses.

We went into camp for the night just as the sun went down behind the hills. The dusky shade of the approaching night was now filling up this narrow gulchlike valley, with its towering hills on both sides of us. Turning the horses loose and driving them further down the trail, so they won't come back too soon, I went back to camp through the half-dark, to eat supper.

JAMES WILLARD SCHULTZ

Born in New York in 1859, James Willard Schultz came to Montana in 1877 to hunt buffalo. During his many years in Montana he became a trader, married a Blackfeet woman named Fine Shield Woman, and was adopted into the tribe. Schultz wrote many books about Indian life, including these selections from Blackfeet and Buffalo *(1962) and* My Life As an Indian *(1963).*

Starvation Winter (1883-84)

Detouring around the Indian Agency on our return home, we again camped with our Pikuni friends, and still more pitiful were the tales they told us of their suffering from want of food; of the decimation of their horse herds from a contagious skin disease. Gaunt, weak, and listless, they were themselves proof of their dire need. I at once gave them all the meat that we had in our wagon–that but a mouthful each for the members of the camp. I advised them to go up to the Lakes Inside country where game was still to be found. Sadly they replied that they had no cartridges and no horses to ride. Crying women came and held their skinny children up before us and asked that, as we loved our own children, in some way to help their own hungry ones. I answered that I would do all that I possibly could for them.

I had long been a contributor to *Forest and Stream*, best of all outdoor magazines, published in New York, and so had had much correspondence with its owner and editor, George Bird Grinnell. So now, upon arriving home at Fort Conrad, I wrote him about the destitution of the Pikunis and asked what could be done to help them. In due time I received a wire from him, forwarded by mail from Fort Benton, advising that I go up to the reservation at once, make a thorough investigation of the conditions, and send him a full report on it. Twenty-four hours after getting the message, I rode into a camp of the Pikunis a couple of miles above the agency, on Badger Creek, and was welcomed in the lodge of my brother-in-law Boy Chief. In a lodge near it women were wailing for the dead; in answer to my query, Boy Chief said: "They mourn for old Black Antelope. Dead because of his defiance of the gods. Hunger gnawing him, he caught some spotted fish (trout), they, as you know, the property, the food of the terrible Underwater People–food forbidden to our kind. We all begged him not to do it. He would not heed our warnings. Ordered his women to cook them for him. They would not even touch the spotted ones. He cooked them himself, ate them all, four big spotted fish. That was last night. Just before you arrived, he died."

"Too bad. Poor old man. Forever gone from us," I said. Useless for me to say that trout were healthful, nourishing and that in the many streams of the reservation there were enough of them to keep all the tribe from starving. Nor could I advise them to kill and eat their horses, which to them were sacred animals of almost human attributes–animals that they loved almost as much as they did their children. And, different from other tribes, they believed that dogs were sacred animals and therefore forbidden food.

In turn I visited White Calf's and Three Sun's large camps on Two Medicine Lodges River, then Red Paint's camp of about one hundred lodges on Birch Creek. All alike, they were increasingly suffering from want of food–the weaker, tubercular ones already dying. Of big game none remained, either on the plain or in the near-by mountains, and small game such as rabbits, grouse, porcupines, and beavers were becoming very scarce. It was plainly evident that unless food, and great quantities of it, would be brought out to them, the whole tribe would die from starvation before the coming of another summer.

While I was in Red Paint's camp, the Rev. Prando, S.J., arrived for a talk with its leading men and asked me to be his interpreter. Soon we were thirty or forty gathered in Red Paint's large lodge, as one after another they told of their sufferings and asked the priest in some way to try to get food for them. He replied that he fully realized their needs and would do all that he possibly could for them. In the meantime, he said, they should follow his teachings; having led pure lives, when they came to die, their souls or, as I had to interpret it, "shadows" could go away up in the sky, there join World Maker (God) and ever afterward live happily. And then, concluding, he said impressively: "But mind this: if you fail to live good lives, then, when you die, your shadows will go deep down beneath the ground, down to that bad one, Fire Maker, where he will keep you forever burning."

Followed a long silence, broken at last by Red Paint. Said he, impressively: "Black Robe, the whites can do many wonderful things. I doubt not their ability, when they die, to go to their World Maker, far up in the sky. But look at us: have we wings to enable our shadows to fly up into the blue? No. Impossible for us to go up there. Have we claws like the badger to enable us to dig down to Fire Maker, for him to roast us perpetually? No. Black Robe, it is that, when we die, our shadows walk or ride out to the Sand Hills, north of here, there forever to remain. There to hunt shadow buffalo; roast shadow meat over shadow, heatless fires; live in shadow lodges. That, Black Robe, is what awaits us all. And so, I finish." With that, they all arose and one by one, in silence, left the lodge. And sad and worried was the expression on Father Prando's face.

Well, during the more than fifty years since that time, the priests and other missionaries have failed to change in any way the beliefs of the sun-worshiping Blackfeet tribes. Within the past two months I have attended the impressive ceremonies of the Tobacco Planters society of the Alberta Blackfeet and the medicine-lodge rites of the Alberta Bloods and the Montana Pikunis. I, for one, am glad that they persist in their ancient faith. Their absolute and enthusiastic belief in it—oh, how different from the apathy of white Christian congregations.

Leaving Birch Creek, I returned to Little Dog's camp on Badger Creek and sent Boy Chief to the agency to tell Rutherford and Phemmister that I wanted to have a talk with them. They came long after dark, and I told them why I was there; asked them if the agent, Major Young, was doing anything toward obtaining food for his starving charges; if he had any on hand to give them.

Said Rutherford: "The old devil, he has plenty of shelled corn, brought upriver from Fort Benton, freighted out from there, but what does he do with it? Every mornin' feeds it to his chickens, the Indians standin' by, awful hungry, and lookin' on."

Said Phemmister: "He knows they're starving, but I don't believe he has written to Washington to get grub for them. What you want to do, to get a line on him, is to talk with his clerks, Ed. Garrett and Charlie Warner."

"I don't know them. Perhaps they won't give me the information I want," I said.

"We'll fix it for you to meet 'em anyhow. Come on," Rutherford offered.

We walked down to the agency. Rutherford unlocked the small gate in the stockade and relocked it after we had passed in. The log buildings formed three sides of the square. The clerks had been in bed. They lit a lamp. I was introduced to them, and when I had told them of my mission there they were plainly wary and frightened. But when I had assured them that I would keep to myself the source of what they could tell me, they talked; freely, bitterly they told of Young's cold-blooded supervision of his charges—he a prominent member of an eastern Methodist church. It was that, for some years, in his annual reports to the Secretary of the Interior, he had stated that he was civilizing the Pikunis; making self-supporting farmers of them. Ha! Civilizing them!

Why, they had rarely come to the agency; they had been roaming the plains, living well upon the buffalo, selling buffalo robes for what they needed of white men's goods. Then, suddenly, the buffalo had been exterminated, and Young had had no supplies for the tribe; having reported that they were self-supporting, he dared not ask for help for them and so admit that he was a liar. Yes, and equally as bad as he were his two daughters, also church members. They had confiscated the few blankets remaining to be issued to the Indians and had dyed them, so obliterating the U.S.I.D. (United States Indian Department) with which they had been stamped.

On the following evening I was at home in Fort Conrad writing Grinnell a full report of my investigations on the reservation, urging him to do his utmost in behalf of the starving Pikunis. Mails were slow in those days; it was all of a month before I heard from him; he wrote that he had been in Washington interviewing the powers-that-be, showing them my report, urging that they take quick action on it. President Arthur himself had promised that good supplies of food would be sent to the tribe as soon as possible. So, anxiously, we waited to hear of their arrival. Weeks passed; months; we were learning how slowly the affairs of our government move because of its red tape. More and more families of the starving people came down to camp near us and hunt. Deer and antelope were becoming so few that they could not kill enough of them to supply their needs. We helped them as best we could with staple groceries, at considerable expense. Kipp's frugal, thrifty mother, Earth Woman, and her companion, Crow Woman, had nearly one hundred buffalo robes that they had in one way or another acquired during the last years of the herd. They had Kipp dispose of them in Fort Benton, and the nine hundred dollars worth of groceries that they received from the sale they generously doled out to their hungry Pikuni friends.

Came February, and we learned that, up around the agency, some of the Pikunis were daily dying from starvation. And then it was, when we believed that all were soon to die, that we got most wonderful news from there: Fort Shaw soldiers had arrived with many wagonloads of flour, bacon, beans, and other food for the hungry ones. Beef cattle had been driven in and were being slaughtered for them. One of Our Grandfather's chiefs had come, caused Young Person (Major Young) and his daughters to leave at once, and had put a new agent in his place.

We later made a count of those who had died from starvation that winter: nearly five hundred of the eighteen hundred members of the tribe had passed. So ended the fourth great wrong that the Pikunis had suffered under our government. The others had been: two successive acts of confiscation of their country between the Musselshell and Marias rivers, by orders of Presidents U. S. Grant and Rutherford B. Hayes—both instances in direct violation of the duly ratified treaty which the United States had made with the tribe in 1855; and, earliest of the four, the massacre of 173 men, women, and children of the tribe by Colonel E. M. Baker and his troops on the Marias River on January 23, 1870.

A Winter on the Marias

There was a little town in northern Montana, where upon certain days things would run along as smoothly and monotonously as in a village of this effete East. But at certain other times you would enter the place to find everyone on a high old tear. It seemed to be epidemic; if one man started to get gloriously full every one promptly joined in—doctor, lawyer, merchant, cattleman, sheepman and all. Well do I remember the last affair of that kind I witnessed there. By about 2 p.m. they got to the champagne stage—'twas really sparkling cider or something of that kind—five dollars a bottle, and about fifty men were going from saloon to store and from store to hotel treating in turn—sixty dollars a round. I mention this as a prelude to what I have to say about drinking among the Indians in the old days. They were no worse than the whites in that way, and with them it seemed to be also epidemic.

Quietly and orderly a camp would be for days and days, and then suddenly all the men would start in on a drinking bout. Really, I believe that the Indians at such times, free as they were from any restraint, to whom law was an unknown term, were better behaved than would be a like number of our working-men in the same condition. True, they frequently quarrelled with each other when in liquor, and a quarrel was something to be settled only by blood. But let a thousand white men get drunk together, would there not ensue some fearful scenes? . . . One night that winter on the Marias I was wending my way homeward from a visit at Sorrel Horse's place, when a man and woman came out of the trade room and staggered along the trail toward me. I slipped behind a cottonwood tree. The man was very unsteady on his feet and the woman, trying to help him along, at the same time was giving him a thorough scolding. I heard her say:

"———, and you didn't look out for me a bit; there you were in that crowd, just drinking with one and then another, and never looking to see how I was getting along. You don't protect me at all; you don't care for me, or you would not have let me stay in there to be insulted."

The man stopped short and, swaying this way and that, gave a roar like a wounded grizzly: "Don't care for you; don't protect you; let you get insulted," he spluttered and foamed. "Who insulted you? Who? I say. Let me at him! Let me at him! I'll fix him with this."

Right there by the trail was lying a large, green, cottonwood log which would have weighed at least a ton. He bent over it and tried again and again to lift it, shouting: "Protect you! Insulted! Who did it? Where is he? Wait until I pick up this club and let me at him."

But the club couldn't be picked up, and he became perfectly frantic in his efforts to lift it up and place it on his shoulder. He danced from one end to the other of it with increasing ardour and anger, until he finally fell over it exhausted, and then the patient woman picked him up—he was a little, light fellow—and carried him home.

I knew a young man who always became very mischievous when he drank. He had three wives and at such times he would steal their little stores of fine pemmican, fancy bead-work, their needles and awls, and give them to other women. He was up to his pranks one morning as I happened along, and the women determined to catch and bind him until he became sober. But he would not be caught; they chased him through the camp, out toward the hills, by the river, back to camp, when, by means of a travois leaning against it, he climbed to the top of his lodge, seated himself in the V-shaped crotch of the lodge poles, and jibed the women for their poor running qualities, enumerated the articles he had stolen from them, and so on. He was exceedingly hilarious. The wives held a whispered consultation, and one of them went inside. Their tormentor ceased jibing and began a drinking song:

"Bear Chief, he gave me a drink,
Bear Chief, he gave me a ———"

That was as far as he got. The wife had thrown a huge armful of rye grass from her couch upon the smouldering fire, it blazed up with a sudden roar and burst of flame which reached the tenderest part of his anatomy; he gave a loud yell of surprise and pain and leaped from his perch. When he struck the ground the women were upon him and I know not how many lariats they coiled about him before they bore him inside, amid the jeers and jests of a throng of laughing spectators, and laid him upon his couch.

But there was another side, and by no means a pleasant one to this drinking business. . . .

Out on a hunt one day down on the Missouri, I killed a buffalo which had what the traders called a "beaver robe," because the hair was so exceedingly fine, thick, and of a glossy, silky nature. Beaver robes were rare, and I had skinned this with horns and hoofs intact. I wished to have it especially well tanned, as I intended it for a present to an Eastern friend. The Crow Woman, good old soul, declared that she would do the work herself, and promptly stretched the hide on a frame. The next morning it was frozen stiff as a board, and she was standing on it busily chipping it, when a half-drunk Cree came along. I happened in sight just as he was about to pull her off of the hide, and hurrying over there I struck him with all my power square in the forehead with my fist. The blow did not stagger him. It has often been said that it is nearly impossible to knock an Indian down, and I believe it. Well, the Cree picked up a broken lodge pole the longest and heaviest end of it, and came for me, and as I was unarmed I had to turn and ignominiously run; I was not so swift as my pursuer, either. It is hard to say what would have happened–probably I would have been killed had Berry not seen the performance and hurried to my assistance. The Cree was just on the point of giving me a blow on the head when Berry fired, and the Indian fell with a bullet through his shoulder. Some of his people came along and packed him home. Then the Cree chief and his council came over and we had a fine pow-wow about the matter. It ended by our paying damages. We did our best always to get along with as little friction as possible, but I did hate to pay that Cree for a wound he richly deserved.

We traded several seasons with the Crees and North Blackfeet down on the Missouri, they having followed the last of the Saskatchewan buffalo herds south into Montana. There was a certain young Blackfoot with whom I was especially friendly, but one day he came in very drunk and I refused to give him any liquor. He became very angry and walked out making dire threats. I had forgotten all about the incident when several hours later his wife came running and said that Took-a-gun-under-the-water (It-su'-yi-na-mak-an) was coming to kill me. The woman was terribly frightened and begged me to pity her and not kill her husband, whom she dearly loved and who, when sober, would be terribly ashamed of himself for attempting to hurt me. I went to the door and saw my quondam friend coming. He had on no wearing apparel whatever except his moccasins, and had painted his face, body, and limbs with fantastic stripes of green, yellow, and red; he was brandishing a .44 Winchester and calling upon the Sun to witness how he would kill me, his worst enemy. Of course I didn't want to kill him any more than his wife wished to see him killed. Terror-stricken, she ran and hid in a pile of robes, and I took my stand behind the open door with a Winchester. On came he of the long name, singing, shouting the war song, and saying repeatedly, "Where is that bad white man? Show him to me that I may give him one bullet, just this one little bullet."

With carbine full cocked he strode in, looking eagerly ahead for a sight of me, and just as he passed I gave him a smart blow on top of the head with the barrel of my rifle; down he dropped senseless to the floor, his carbine going off and sending the missile intended for me through a case of tinned tomatoes on a shelf. The woman ran out from her hiding place at the sound of the shot, thinking that I had surely killed him; but her joy was great when she learned her mistake. Together we bound him tightly and got him home to his lodge.

Now, one often reads that an Indian never forgives a blow nor an injury of any kind, no matter how much at fault he may have been. That is all wrong. The next morning Took-a-gun-under-the-water sent me a fine buffalo robe. At dusk he came in and begged me to forgive him. Ever after we were the best of friends. Whenever I had time for a short hunt back in the breaks, or out on the plains, I chose him for my companion, and a more faithful and considerate one I never had.

I cannot say that all traders got along so well with the Indians as did Berry and I. There were some bad men among them, men who delighted in inflicting pain, in seeing blood flow. I have known such to kill Indians just for fun, but never in a fair, open fight. They were great cowards, and utterly unprincipled. These men sold "whisky" which contained tobacco juice, cayenne pepper, and various other vile things. Berry and I sold weak liquor, it is true, but the weakness consisted of nothing but pure water—which was all the better for the consumer. I make no excuse for the whisky trade. It was wrong, all wrong, and none realised it better than we when we were dispensing the stuff. It caused untold suffering, many deaths, great demoralisation among those people of the plains. There was but one redeeming feature about it: the trade was at a time when it did not deprive them of the necessities of life; there was always more meat, more fur to be had for the killing of it. In comparison with various Government officials and rings, who robbed and starved the Indians to death on their reservations after the buffalo disappeared, we were saints.

All in all, that was a pleasant winter we passed on the Marias. Hunting with the Indians, lounging around a lodge fire, or before our own or Sorrel Horse's fireplace of an evening, the days fairly flew. Sometimes I would go with Sorrel Horse to visit his "baits," and it was a great sight to see the huge wolves lying stiff and stark about them, and even on them. To make a good bait a buffalo was killed and cut open at the back, and into the meat, blood, and entrails three vials of strychnine – three-eighths of an ounce – were stirred. It seemed as if the merest bite of this deadly mixture was enough to kill, a victim seldom getting more than 200 yards away before the terrible convulsions seized him. Of course, great numbers of coyotes and kit foxes were also poisoned, but they didn't count. The large, heavy-furred wolf skins were in great demand in the East for sleigh and carriage robes, and sold right at Fort Benton for from three dollars to five dollars each. I had a fancy to take some of these stiffly-frozen animals home, and stand them up around Sorrel Horse's house. They were an odd and interesting sight, standing there, heads and tails up, as if guarding the place; but one day there came a chinook wind and they soon toppled over and were skinned.

So the days went, and then came spring. The river cleared itself of ice in one grand, grinding rush of massive cakes; green grass darkened the valley slopes; geese and ducks honked and quacked in every slough. We all, Indians and whites, wished to do nothing but lie out on the ground in the warm sunshine and smoke and dream in quiet contentment.

I Have a Lodge of My Own

"Why don't you get a woman?" Weasel Tail abruptly asked one evening as Talks-with-the-buffalo and I sat smoking with him in his lodge.

"Yes," my other friend put in. "Why not? You have the right to do so, for you can count a coup; yes, two of them. You killed a Cree, and you took a Cree horse in the fight at the Hairy Gap."

"I took a horse," I replied, "and a good one he is; but you are mistaken about the Cree; you will remember that he escaped by running into the pines on Hairy Gap."

"Oh!" said Talks-with-the-buffalo, "I don't mean that one; we all know he got away; I mean one of those who first fell when we all fired into them. That tall one, the man who wore a badger-skin cap; you killed him. I saw the bullet wound in his body; no ball from any of our rifles could have made such a small hole."

This was news to me; I remembered well having shot several times at that particular warrior, but I never had thought that 'twas my bullet that ended his career. I did not know whether to feel glad or sorry about it, but finally concluded that it was best to feel glad, for he would have killed me if he could have done so. I was turning the matter over in my mind, recalling every little incident of that memorable day, when my host aroused me from my reverie: "I said, why don't you take a woman? Answer."

"Oh!" I replied. "No one would have me. Isn't that a good reason?"

"Kyai-yo′!" exclaimed Madame Weasel Tail, clapping her hand to her mouth, the Blackfoot way of expressing surprise or wonder. "Kyai-yo′! What a reason! I well know that there isn't a girl in this camp but would like to be his woman. Why, if it wasn't for this lazy one here,"—giving Weasel Tail's hand an affectionate squeeze—"if he would only go away somewhere and never come back, I'd make you take me. I'd follow you around until you would have to do so."

"Mah′-kah-kan-is-tsi!" I exclaimed, which is a flippant and slangy term, expressing doubt of the speaker's truthfulness.

"Mah′-kah-kan-is-tsi yourself," she rejoined. "Why do you think you are asked to all these Assiniboin dances, where all the young women wear their best clothes, and try to catch you with their robes? Why do you think they put on their best things and go to the trading post with their mothers or other relatives every chance they get? What, you don't know? Well, I'll tell you: they go, each one, hoping that you will notice her, and send a friend to her parents to make a proposal."

"It is the truth," said Weasel Tail.

"Yes, the truth," Talks-with-the-buffalo and his woman joined in.

Well, I laughed, a little affectedly, perhaps, and turned the conversation by asking about the destination of a war party which was to start out in the morning. Nevertheless, I thought over the matter a good deal. All the long winter I had rather envied my good friends Berry and Sorrel Horse, who seemed to be so happy with their women. Never a cross word, always the best of good fellowship and open affection for each other. Seeing all this, I had several times said to myself: "It is not good that the man should be alone." That quotation is from the Bible, is it not, or is it from Shakespeare? Anyhow, it is true. The Blackfeet have much the same expression: "Mat′-ah-kwi täm-äp-i-ni-po-ke-mi-o-sin—not found (is) happiness without woman."

After that evening I looked more closely at the various young women I met in the camp or at the trading post, saying to myself: "Now, I wonder what kind of a woman that would make? Is she neat, good-tempered, moral?" All the time, however, I knew that I had no right to take one of them. I did not intend to remain long in the West; my people would never forgive me for making an alliance with one. They were of old, proud Puritan stock, and I could imagine them holding up their hands in horror at the mere hint of such a thing.

You will notice that thus far in this part of my story I have substituted the word woman for wife. A plainsman always said "my woman" when speaking of his Indian better half; the Blackfoot said the same: "Nit-o-ke'-man," my woman. None of the plainsmen were legally married, unless the Indian manner in which they took a woman, by giving so many horses, or so much merchandise for one, could be considered legal. In the first place there was no one in the country to perform the marriage service except occasionally a wandering Jesuit priest, and again, these men, almost without exception, didn't care a snap about what the law said in regard to the matter. There was no law. Neither did they believe in religion; the commands of the church were nothing to them. They took unto themselves Indian women; if the woman proved good and true, well and good; if otherwise, there was a separation. In it all there was never a thought of future complications and responsibilities; their creed was: "Eat, drink, and be merry, for to-day we live and to-morrow we die."

"No," I said to myself time and again; "no, it will not do; hunt, go to war, do anything but take a woman, and in the fall go home to your people." This is the line of conduct I laid out for myself and meant to follow. But–

One morning the Crow Woman and I were sitting out under a shade she had constructed of a couple of travois and a robe or two. She was busy as usual, embroidering a moccasin with coloured quills, and I was thoroughly cleaning my rifle, preparatory to an antelope hunt. A couple of women came by on their way to the trade room with three or four robes. One of them was a girl of perhaps sixteen or seventeen years; not what one might call beautiful, still she was good-looking, fairly tall, and well-formed, and she had fine large, candid, expressive eyes, perfect white, even teeth and heavy braided hair which hung almost to the ground. All in all, there was something very attractive about her. "Who is that?" I asked the Crow Woman. "That girl, I mean."

"Don't you know? She comes here often; she is a cousin of Berry's woman."

I went away on my hunt, but it didn't prove to be very interesting. I was thinking all the time about the cousin. That evening I spoke to Berry about her, learned that her father was dead; that her mother was a medicine lodge woman, and noted for her unswerving uprightness and goodness of character. "I'd like to have the girl," I said. "What do you think about it?"

"We'll see," Berry replied. "I'll talk with my old woman."

A couple of days went by and nothing was said by either of us about the matter, and then one afternoon Mrs. Berry told me that I was to have the girl, providing I would promise to be always good and kind to her. I readily agreed to that.

"Very well, then," said Mrs. Berry; "go into the trade room and select a shawl, some dress goods, some bleached muslin – no, I'll select the outfit and make her some white women's dresses like mine."

"But hold on!" I exclaimed. "What am I to pay? How many horses, or whatever is wanted?"

"Her mother says there is to be no pay, only that you are to keep your promise to be good to her daughter."

This was quite unusual, to request that nothing be given over for a daughter. Usually a lot of horses were sent to the parents, sometimes fifty or more. Sometimes the father demanded so many head, but if no number was specified, the suitor gave as many as he could. Again, it was not unusual for a father to request some promising youth, good hunter and bold raider, to become his son-in-law. In that case he was the one to give horses, and even a lodge and household goods, with the girl.

Well, I got the girl. It was an embarrassing time for us both when she came in one evening, shawl over her face, while we were eating supper. Sorrel Horse and his woman were there, and with Berry and his madame they made things interesting for us with their jokes, until Berry's mother put a stop to it. We were a pretty shy couple for a long time, she especially. "Yes" and "no" were about all that I could get her to say. But my room underwent a wonderful transformation; everything was kept so neat and clean, my clothes were so nicely washed, and my "medicine" was carefully taken out every day and hung on a tripod. I had purchased a war bonnet, shield, and various other things which the Blackfeet regard as sacred, and I did not say to any one that I thought they were not so. I had them handled with due pomp and ceremony.

As time passed this young woman became more and more of a mystery to me. I wondered what she thought of me, and if she speculated upon what I might think of her. I had no fault to find, she was always neat, always industrious about our little household affairs, quick to supply my wants. But that wasn't enough. I wanted to know her, her thoughts and beliefs. I wanted her to talk and laugh with me, and tell stories, as I could often hear her doing in Madame Berry's domicile. Instead of that, when I came around, the laugh died on her lips, and she seemed to freeze, to shrink within herself. The change came when I least expected it. I was down in the Piegan camp one afternoon and learned that a war party was being made up to raid the Crows. Talks-with-the-buffalo and Weasel Tail were going, and asked me to go with them. I readily agreed, and returned to the post to prepare for the trip. "Nät-ah'-ki," I said, bursting into our room, "give me all the moccasins I have, some clean socks, some pemmican. Where is my little brown canvas bag? Where have you put my gun case? Where–"

"What are you going to do?"

It was the first question she had ever asked me.

"Do? I'm going to war; my friends are going, they asked me to join them–"

I stopped, for she suddenly arose and faced me, and her eyes were very bright. "You are going to war!" she exclaimed. "You, a white man, are going with a lot of Indians sneaking over the plains at night to steal horses, and perhaps kill some poor prairie people. You have no shame!"

"Why," I said, rather faintly, I presume, "I thought you would be glad. Are not the Crows your enemies? I have promised, I must go."

"It is well for the Indians to do this," she went on, "but not for a white man. You, you are rich; you have everything you want; those papers, that yellow hard rock (gold) you carry will buy anything you want; you should be ashamed to go sneaking over the plains like a coyote. None of your people ever did that."

"I must go," I reiterated. "I have given my promise to go."

Then Nät-ah'-ki began to cry, and she came nearer and grasped my sleeve. "Don't go," she pleaded, "for if you do, I know you will be killed, and I love you so much."

I was never so surprised, so taken aback as it were. All these weeks of silence, then, had been nothing but her natural shyness, a veil to cover her feelings. I was pleased and proud to know that she did care for me, but underlying that thought was another one: I had done wrong in taking this girl, in getting her to care for me, when in a short time I must return her to her mother and leave for my own country.

I readily promised not to accompany the war party, and then, her point gained, Nät-ah'-ki suddenly felt that she had been over-bold and tried to assume her reserve again. But I would not have it that way. I grasped her hand and made her sit down by my side, and pointed out to her that she was wrong; that to laugh, to joke, to be good friends and companions was better than to pass our days in silence, repressing all natural feeling. After that, the sun always shone.

■ FLATHEAD RAILROAD TREATY, 1882

The Flathead Railroad Treaty of 1882 was negotiated by Joseph Kay McCammon, representing the U.S. government and the railroad interests, and Flathead leaders Arlee, Eneas, Adolphe, Michele, and others. The treaty transcript shows the wit and sophistication of the Indian negotiators and also their powerlessness in the face of overwhelming government pressure. These selections are from the "Report in Relation to an Agreement Made Between Joseph Kay McCammon, Assistant Attorney General, on Behalf of the United States, and the Confederated Tribes of the Flathead, Kootenay, and Upper Pend D'Oreilles Indians for the Sale of a Portion of Their Reservation in Montana for the Use of the Northern Pacific Railroad," printed in 1883 by the Government Printing Office.

From Transcript of the Council Meeting

Council held by Hon. Joseph K. McCammon, Assistant Attorney-General, appointed by the Secretary of the Interior to negotiate an agreement with the Indians on the Flathead Reservation for right of way for the Northern Pacific Railroad through the reservation.

AUGUST 31, 1882–3 p.m.

Present: Arlee, Adolphe, Eneas, and Michelle, with headmen and Indians of the Flathead, Pend d'Oreilles, and Kootenais tribes.

Agent RONAN said: Mr. McCammon is here from Washington, representing the United States Government, to meet the Indians in council; and it is desired to have them listen attentively. He is here with the voice of the Great Father, and brings his words to the Indians. I have no further words of introduction.

Commissioner McCAMMON. My friends of the Flathead, Pend d'Oreilles, Kootenais, and other tribes living on the Jocko Reservation: I have been sent by the Great Father at Washington a great many miles to see you and talk with you. He knows how well you have treated the white people these many years; that you have been peaceful and happy, and have taken care of yourselves; that you have always been his friends and the friends of his people. Knowing these things he does not wish to take from you your lands. He knows, however, that a railroad is to be built on the borders of your reservation. Twenty-seven years ago you and your fathers made a treaty with the whites. That treaty which you and the others made provided for a country here in which you and your fathers should live. In that treaty you and your fathers agreed "if necessary for the public convenience roads may be run through the said reservation." . . . The Great Father and the Great council in 1864 gave the Northern Pacific Railroad Company the right to build a railroad through this country. The railroad company now say to the Great Father, "We want to build a railroad through the Jocko Reservation a few miles." The Great Father says, "The Indians on the Jocko Reservation gave me consent, years ago, to have roads of every description built through their land." . . . But the Great Father says that he thinks the Indians should be paid for the little land that will be used by the railroad. He says he thinks the railroad will be good for the Indians as well as for the whites. The building of the road may bring white men on the reservation in order to grade the road, lay ties, &c., but when the road is built, no white men will remain except at stations, and there only so many as are necessary. I will now show you a map of your reservation (shows map). The railroad is to come up here from the Missoula, entering the reservation by the Jocko River, and then going along the Jocko and Pend d'Oreille Rivers to the west line of the reservation. Now, as all the lands on the reservation belong to the Indians the United States wants to pay, and thinks it right to pay, for 100 feet of road on each side of the track, for a distance of 53.26 miles on this narrow line; and also for five squares of ground alongside, to be used as stations, being about 130 acres in addition, fully described on the map. . . . Now the Great Father asks me to inquire of these Indians what will be a fair price for this small tract. He says you ought to be paid a fair, reasonable price, just as much as he would pay a white man, no more and no less. Where the railroad runs through the farms of Indians, those Indians will be paid for their fences, farms, houses, and crops, if interfered with, the money to be paid to each Indian, or to the agent to be used for them. I am appointed to find out how much this will damage each Indian farm. This refers only to houses, fences, crops, &c., that belong to individual Indians.

MICHELLE. You don't know how much individual Indians will get, do you?

COMMISSIONER. No; that we will determine hereafter. . . . I want you to consider this matter and ask questions. I don't want any one to misunderstand. I want to be just to the Indians. I want to protect their rights. I want them to talk. I am ready to hear from Arlee, Michelle, Adolphe, Eneas, or the headmen who know what they want to say.

ENEAS. I presume you will not ask us to answer now. There are some men here who have wild ideas, and we want to adjourn and talk the matter over.

MICHELLE. We don't want to detain you for a lot of humbug. Of course you and the Great Father claim that we ought to be paid for the land taken; we are not to be cheated; we are to be treated just the same as whites.

COMMISSIONER. The Crows last year sold land to this company just the same as you are asked to do. Whatever time you wish will be granted.

ARLEE. I am going to talk not about what you are talking about. The Great Chief don't pity me. I am crowded on both sides. White men go up and down the reservation with cattle. I lose cattle in plenty. I want you to get the whites off the land at the head of Flathead Lake. I am old. I will soon die. There are a lot of young ones. I would like to have them live happy. But they will always be in trouble with white men if they remain so near us. It may be true that the railroad would help the Indians, but I would like to get the whites off the Flathead Lake.

COMMISSIONER. . . . . Fewer cattle will go through the reservation after the building of the railroad, for then many cattle will go through on cars. I will report your wishes to the Great Father. The Great Father did not know them.

ARLEE. The country we gave to the government is very valuable. Lots of white men have made independent fortunes in my country. Since twenty-seven years ago, when my forefathers made the treaty and gave you the country east and south of this, you have been digging gold there; that country is very valuable. You must not think there are so few here. Lots of others think of coming over here and living on this reservation. Be sure to tell the Great Father my wishes. . . .

SEPTEMBER 1, 1882–1.40 p.m.

Commissioner McCAMMON. My friends, I am glad to see you today, and hope your hearts are good towards the Great Father . . . .

ENEAS. I am the chief and you see me now. I have not doubt you are sent to see us by the Great Father. I am the chief and this is my country. I am not joking in telling you I would like to get the Flathead

Lake country back. There are things that the government promised me in that treaty that I have never seen. The government promised me everything we needed. The government told me it would send a blacksmith, and build school-houses, and furnish teachers at the agencies to instruct Indians, and a head farmer, and build houses for us. The government wished us to be like white men, and these were to instruct us. It promised me a tinner, a wagon-maker, a plow-maker, a hospital, and a doctor to look after the sick; and that is the reason we signed the treaty. I was glad to think we were to have these things. We had a big country, and under those conditions we signed the treaty. Seven years after that we learned that the line of the reservation ran across the middle of Flathead Lake. We didn't know that when we signed the treaty. That is the reason we want that country back. Besides, we did not get one-half of the annuities that belonged to us. It was divided among yourselves. You told us that after a while we would be intelligent and rich and like white men. We are poor now. We try to have whites to assist us, and they won't because we are Indians. That is the reason we want to have the whites kept out of that Flathead Lake country. . . .

ARLEE. What is the reason you are not able to treat with the Indians about that country? You have full power.

COMMISSIONER. Arlee is mistaken; I have not power to treat about everything. As I said yesterday, the Great Father did not know what your wishes were about that strip of land. He only knew about the railroad, and he told me to agree to pay for the land to be used by the railroad. . . . Do you understand?

ARLEE. I understand. . . . We will now quit talking about the head of Flathead Lake.

COMMISSIONER. Now, I will be glad to hear about the money to be paid for the use of the land for the railroad.

ENEAS. You know what I said, that the government did not give half it agreed about annuities; and I think I don't wish the road to pass through this reservation. The Great Father is a good man, and when the Great Father tells me a thing I do it. I wish the Great Father to do me a favor and consult my wishes, and not let the road go through this reservation. There is a good way down the Missouri to Horse Prairie. You are a great people, and when you want to do a thing you can do it. What makes you think the railroad can't go down there? This reservation is a small country, and yet you want five depots upon it. These are the best spots on the reservation. What is the reason I should be encouraged when you take the best part of my country? My country was like a flower and I gave you its best part. What I gave I don't look for back, and I never have asked for it back. The Great Father gave it to us for three tribes, Flathead, Upper Pend d'Oreilles, and Kootenais. What are we going to do when you build the road? We have no place to go. That is why it is my wish that you should go down the Missoula River. I am not telling you that you are mean, but this is a small country, and we are hanging on to it like a child on to a piece of candy.

COMMISSIONER. The line selected by the railroad company was selected ten years ago, because it was the best route, and because down the Missoula River would not be a good route. . . . The Great Father has respect for the wishes of the Indians, but he thinks he knows what is best for them, and feeling that way he wants to know what money they want for the land. The Great Father will take care that bad white men do not sell whisky to Indians. He thinks he can do that better with a railroad through your reservation than with one down the Missoula. He wants it here. He says, "You have told me I can build roads through your reservation"; but he also says you shall be paid, he having pity on you. . . .

ENEAS. Who established the lines of this reservation? It was the Great Father that got these lines established. Why does he want to break the lines? If we had no lines I would say no word. Lines are just like a fence. He told us so. No white man is allowed to live and work on the reservation. You know it is so in the treaty. That is the reason I say you had better go the other way. Why do you wish us to go away? It is a small country; it is valuable to us; we support ourselves by it; there is no end to these lands supporting us; they will do it for generations. If you say you will give us money for our lands, I doubt if we get it, because we didn't before.

COMMISSIONER. Eneas and the rest do not understand what I said yesterday. . . . I come here as an honest man to talk to honest men, and I want you to consider well the words of the Great Father.

(An Indian in the audience says, "Railroads are not mentioned.")

The commissioner read from the treaties of July and October, 1855, about roads, and continued: . . . The Great Father will be sorry when he hears that the Indians do not believe in his good faith. Shall I go back and say to the Great Father that these Indians do not believe he is treating them right? He has but one object, and that is your good; and if I go back without your having named a price for the lands, he will say they are not the good Indians and faithful friends I thought.

MICHELLE. I am going to speak to Indians and no word to white men. I told the agent it was useless for us to oppose giving the white men this strip of land. We don't know the plans of the white man; there is no use of us thinking. Just now he has something to compel. You spoke yesterday of the land at the head of Flathead Lake. I agree with you. That is my wish. You were here yesterday. No word he mentioned was bad. I think it was all good. When you get a gentle horse if you beat him he is bound to get mean; and you are to blame when you beat a dumb brute. He spoke to us gentlemanly; he used no hard words; and we ought to be glad. We are all Americans. The British line is north, and beyond that are the British Indians. If the President thinks it best for a railroad to run through this land, I am quite willing. It is true this country has been reserved for us. When Garfield came here he told us this was our country; our agent and another big chief from Washington told us the same. Our agent is acting friendly with us. I do not think this gentleman has said a wrong word to us yesterday or to-day. He only wants a little strip of land; he might take it without asking, but he is going to ask us first, and then leave it to the chiefs. It is a thing that is bound to go through anyhow; and so you must not blame your chiefs.

COMMISSIONER. The whole country is not taken from you; just a little narrow strip is used for railroads; you can use it, except the narrow strip for a track and depot grounds. . . . I want to ask Arlee and Michelle if the wagon road has taken the country from them? If not, then a railroad will not. It is only a road with rail ties and locomotives to go through.

ARLEE. We don't think anything bad, but we don't want the railroad to go through the reservation here, because these white men are bad people. At Camas Prairie they sell whisky; they go there and get whiskey, and our boys bother us about whisky. This is why we don't want the railroad to go through our reservation, because when the white men come in to work there will be trouble; that is all.

COMMISSIONER. About the man who sold liquor, we had him arrested and taken to jail. . . . It won't be as bad as Arlee thinks; I hope not bad at all for the Indians. No liquor will be sold on the reservation at the depots.

ARLEE. It was our old people that were good; we had good chiefs; I don't know how many years it is since the white people came, and we have never had fights between us and the whites; nor have we ever killed you at all; and that is why I want to remain in my country quiet and undisturbed. I hear every few days that other tribes of

Indians are fighting with the whites; then you win their country. You did not win my country from me at all; the big chief made our lines and told us to stay here all the time, and a few years ago Garfield sent me here to stay. But you don't mind what he said at all. Garfield said "Take it easy, don't be uneasy." It was nine years ago that Garfield said "Don't think we will thrust you from that country; that land belongs to you." Last winter I was at home lying down, when they told me men were surveying the place. Some said it did not amount to anything, but I said it would cut our reservation in two; and now to-day I see you here trying to get our land from us for the railroad. But I do not want any railroad here, for this is my country.

COMMISSIONER. This is your country; there is no doubt about that. . . . I will again ask you if you can name what money you want for this right of way. If you cannot, I will name a sum for you. When the railroad is built, the Great Father will probably come out himself to see his country and you. It is too far from the railroad now.

ADOLPHE. It is true that you only want a small strip of my country; it is true that there will be no white men in our country. All will be glad if you only take a small strip of our country. Look at my hand (uplifted); this is what they do in Washington. I lift my hand; the President does the same thing. It is true that what you say is in the treaty in regard to roads. In the treaty at Hell Gate in 1855 the Indians said the white men could have railroads through here. Governor Stevens said to Victor, "You are the head chief of three tribes here, and of the whites here too"; and they said we will talk about this land here by and by; and we are having that talk now. Some time ago I did not know about talking, nor what it was to sign my name; now I know. If the whites are good I am good. When there is blood on my hands, they are not wet with white people's blood. If what you have told me to-day is true, I will be glad. In this country you see no blood; other countries are stained with blood. The line of my country extends from earth up to heaven.

COMMISSIONER. I want to talk again about this road going through your reservation. I want to explain to you that the Great Father sells land near and adjoining your reservation for $2.50 per acre. The railroad sells its land for $2.50 per acre near your reservation. It has land down towards the Missoula. I wish to be liberal. The Great Father told me to propose a fair price, and I think that $10 per acre is a fair price for the 1,500 acres. That is four times as much as the Great Father gets for his land. This would make altogether for the land $15,000. The Crows got only about five thousand, and the Shoshones seven thousand, or nearly eight. In addition, each Indian will be paid for his fences and barns where this railroad interferes with him. The $15,000 will be for the benefit of the whole tribe.

ARLEE. I object to depots.

COMMISSIONER. Arlee never having seen railroads, don't know the amount of land required. Here is a glass with a few drops of water in it (illustrating). The whole tumbler represents the reservation, the water the amount of land wanted for the railroad. The railroad wanted six stations; the Great Father said five would be enough. They wanted these for water for the engines. The railroad wanted a strip 400 feet wide; the Great Father said, "No, 200"; the railroad wanted larger and more stations; the Great Father said, "No, five stations, and these must be small ones." The Great Father was thinking of the wishes and the interest of the Indians. . . .

ARLEE. I want to know about the depots; what are they?

COMMISSIONER. Every railroad in this country has stations once in 10 miles for water, at the side of the track. If the railroad at Spokane has not stations every 10 miles it is because it is not yet finished. I have here the law of the great council, and it says the right of way through the lands of the United States is given for 100 feet each side, and stations for depots, &c., every 10 miles of its road. Let any young Indian read it if you want to hear it.

ARLEE. It is so.

COMMISSIONER. These stations are to accommodate you. We are not trifling with you. Arlee ought to be satisfied.

ARLEE. I want $1,000,000 for it.

COMMISSIONER. The whole reservation would not be worth that.

ARLEE. I thought you were here to help us.

COMMISSIONER. I am. I represent the Great Father, as well as the Indians. . . . Michelle, Eneas, and Arlee, are you ready to come to an agreement with the government. . . .

MICHELLE. When I heard you the first time I was glad; but now when I hear what you offer, I do not feel so well, because now you say that all the reservation is not worth $1,000,000. Now I do not agree with you.

COMMISSIONER. I am sorry if Michelle misunderstands me. I do not mean that the land is not worth $1,000,000 to the Indians, but that the same kind of land would bring no more among the whites. I only referred to that, as they all refused four times what was the selling price of such land among the whites.

MICHELLE. When a railroad runs through the railroad company will get the money back in one day. They will run through my ranch and take my timber to build it with. I would not take $15,000. I do not mean we will make trouble; I only say we will not take $15,000. If you want to go through, go; but we won't take $15,000. I don't speak now, any more, because you offer only $15,000. . . .

ARLEE. We have said.

COMMISSIONER. We will not talk any more about the million dollars; the Great Father will not allow us to talk of that.

ARLEE. All right; then go by the Missoula. If the railroad don't want to give the money, let it go by Frenchtown. . . .

MICHELLE. How would it be if you had a good horse and I offered you a price that you did not think was right; if I took the horse wouldn't you complain? When we made the treaty we did not say railroads could pass through our country, only common roads.

COMMISSIONER. They said roads of every description. Suppose I were to give Michelle a loaf of bread every day, and then were to ask him to return me a very small slice, would he not be a very bad Indian if he did not give me the slice when I needed it? Especially if I had paid him the money for it? So the Great Father says, "You can have this country, but I want a small slice or strip for a road," and afterwards offers to pay for it.

MICHELLE. If you wanted a small piece of bread, I would say, "Here is a piece." If you say it is too small, I would say, "Take what you want."

COMMISSIONER. Michelle does not understand; he never saw a million dollars; he don't know what it is. It is nearly seventy times $15,000. The Great Father could not afford to pay $10 an acre for the Indian lands in the United States. He could not afford to pay the price now offered you, and would not have offered this if these Indians had not always been friends and good. We are not trying to make a hard bargain; we want to be liberal to the Indians. That is all. Do you want me to go home and tell the Great Father, or do you want me to stay till to-morrow?

MICHELLE. Do as you wish.

COMMISSIONER. What do you wish?

MICHELLE. I do not understand. You know it is not done; the agreement is not made.

COMMISSIONER. Then I will stay. Ask them to meet me earlier to-morrow.

SEPTEMBER 2–1.30 p.m.

Commissioner McCAMMON. My friends, I am glad to see you; I hope you did not think I had unkind thoughts yesterday. I had none but kind thoughts in my mind. I desire to hear from you or to answer any questions you wish to ask. . . .

ARLEE. I don't wish to change our calculations. When we heard that you were coming we made up our minds what to say to you. Yes, we are all good Indians, and we have a nice country, and I don't wish the Great Father should bother us by a big railroad through the reservation. When we heard of your coming we made up our minds what to say to you, and I said it to you yesterday. You seem to like your money, and we like our country; it is like our parents. I have the same feeling I had yesterday, and I am not the only one. I told you about the money, what we ask; and you said it was an exorbitant price. We do not wish to change our ideas; we told you yesterday about our wishes.

COMMISSIONER. In the treaty of 1855, made by Governor Stevens, the Indian tribes now represented here sold to the Great Father the country which was then claimed by them. That country was great; it extended from the British line to Big Hole River, and was very broad east and west. The Indians were then satisfied with the treaty, and have never been dissatisfied since. The money paid to your tribes was the sum of $120,000. That was only about one-ninth of what you now claim for a little strip of country through your reservation. You ask about nine times more for this little strip than what you received for all that vast amount of land. So you see you are mistaken as to the value of this little strip of country. I want you to think of this; that the $15,000 I offered yesterday is very much more per acre than the money you received under the treaty of 1855. As I have been fair and reasonable, I have a right to ask that you should be, and that you should trust me. I am afraid some bad white men have been misleading you about the price. No man is your friend who tells you that you should receive $1,000,000 from the government.

ARLEE. We are not any way dissatisfied or hostile towards you or the government. We only want a fair bargain; fair play on both sides. My forefathers, our chiefs, the head chiefs of the tribe, were like men with veils over their heads; they could not see at all; they were like blind men; and when Governor Stevens arrived and he began talking about this part of the country, they had no idea of their country; they were stupid. They signed the treaty. This reservation was offered by the man who made the treaty, and we are holding on to it. Our forefathers are all dead, and we are the chiefs nowadays, and are hanging on it.

COMMISSIONER. You are quite right in holding on to your reservation. As your friend, I say hold on to it; it is your land. I would be willing to give you the land you want up north; but the little line that the railroad wants won't interfere with your land; it will give the Great Father a better chance to protect you. . . .

ARLEE. Now won't you try to raise it a little more?

COMMISSIONER. I will consider for a moment. (After a pause.) . . . I will tell him that you are good Indians, as he knows, and I thought you were entitled to $16,000.

ADOLPHE. How many years will this $16,000 last? (They consult.)

ARLEE. We want the money. The reason we did not get the money before was because we took it in annuities. We prefer the cash.

COMMISSIONER. The Great Father knows more about you than they did years ago; and whatever wrong was done you then, will not be repeated now. This very railroad will bring the Great Father nearer to you. The money will be expended for the benefit of the Indians in the manner the Great Father thinks best. If he thinks, after hearing from you, that it is better to let you have the money, he will pay the money. You must depend upon his judgment as to how the money will be paid. The Great Father will never forget you.

■ NANNIE T. ALDERSON

Nannie T. Alderson was born in 1860 into the southern aristocracy on a slave-holding plantation in Virginia. In 1882, she and her husband Walt moved to southeastern Montana to establish their first ranch. Her memoirs, A Bride Goes West *(1942), were transcribed and co-authored by Helena Huntington Smith when Nannie Alderson was eighty-two years old. It remains one of the finest records of a woman's life on the Montana frontier.*

From A Bride Goes West

The Last Buffalo

. . . That year the buffalo were still so thick that Mrs. Lays had only to say: "Mr. Alderson, we're out of meat"; and he would go out and find a herd and kill a calf, all just as easily as a man would butcher a yearling steer in his own pasture. Yet when I came out, one year later, there was nothing left of those great bison herds, which had covered the continent, but carcasses. I saw them on my first drive out to the ranch, and they were lying thick all over the flat above our house, in all stages of decay. So wasteful were the hunters, they had not even removed the tongues, though the latter were choice meat.

The summer after I came out Mr. Alderson killed the last buffalo ever seen in our part of Montana. A man staying with us was out fishing when he saw this lonesome old bull wandering over the hills and

gullies above our house—the first live buffalo seen in many months. He came home and reported it, saying: "Walt, why don't you go get him?" And next morning Mr. Alderson did go get him.

That afternoon he suggested that we take the spring wagon and go up to where the old bull had fallen. There he lay in the green brush at the bottom of a draw—the last of many millions—with the bushes propping him up so that he looked quite lifelike. I had brought my scissors, and I snipped a sackfull of the coarse, curly hair from his mane to stuff a pillow with.

I am afraid that the conservation of buffalo, or of any other wild game, simply never occurred to the westerner of those days.

First Spring and High Hopes

The men of course knew the truth about our visitors, and I was never left alone at the ranch. No matter how much work there was to be done one man always had to stay with me. During the spring this was simple enough, for the two men building our house were always there, and then there was our partner Mr. Zook. But we knew that Mr. Zook was planning a trip to Chicago in the summer, when the roundup would be keeping both Brown and Mr. Alderson busy. And so, just when or how I don't remember, we acquired a new member of the family, Brown's brother, Hal Taliaferro, whose principal duty was to stay at the ranch and guard me.

Sometimes I wonder if too much hasn't been said about the grim aspects of frontier life. Later on in my marriage I came down to hard, bare facts; to loneliness and poverty. But that first spring and summer I was anything but lonely in spite of the lack of women. I had much to learn and hard work to do. But I had no children to look after, I lived in surroundings of great beauty, I was happy in my marriage, and pioneering still seemed rather romantic.

We had plenty of visitors. Although the ranches were far apart–our near neighbors being five to ten miles distant–the men were always riding around looking for lost horses or moving stock, and as summer time approached, reps from miles away–even hundreds of miles–would come riding by on their way to join the roundup, and they would stop with us. A rep was a cowboy sent out by his outfit to represent them on some other part of the range, and gather up stray cattle bearing their brand. There were no fences, the cattle drifted for many miles, and these riders came to us from long distances–from the Belle Fourche in South Dakota, from Sun Dance on the edge of the Black Hills. Each would be traveling with a string of horses, his bed packed across the back of one. He would ride in, turn his horses in with ours, and stay for a meal or a night. If for the night, he would just throw his bed down out of doors. Later I heard that quite a joke was made on the roundup about the number of reps who found it necessary to pass by the Zook and Alderson ranch.

Once a week the mail came by horseback courier from Birney postoffice, twenty-five miles across the divide. Often it brought belated and unexpected wedding presents. The carrier was a young redheaded cowboy named Fred Banker, who spent the weekend with us, making the return trip to Birney on Monday. As he was a pleasant young fellow with a good singing voice, he was quite an addition to our musical evenings, and he and Johnny, Brown, and my husband, soon learned all the songs I knew on the guitar.

One week he brought a motherless colt he had picked up on the road over. Apparently the Sioux Indians, who were visiting the Cheyennes, had left it by accident, or because it was too weak to travel. When Freddie rode over the hill the appearance of extra bulk in the saddle occasioned some wonder at first. As he rode up he said: "There was no wedding present for you this mail, so I brought you this colt."

About the same time one of the bachelor neighbors brought me a motherless calf, also carried across his saddle, so I sent to Helena, the state capital, to have a brand recorded and thereupon entered the stock business. Our firm's brand was the sugar bowl and spoon; my individual brand was the first three letters of my maiden name with a bar underneath, TIF. The orphan stock that wore my brand was pretty pathetic, especially the calf. He was known as a "poddy," for feeding skimmed milk gave him a big stomach, and there was a sad look in his eyes, due to undernourishment. We called him Jack after the neighbor who brought him, and we kept him till he was a big five-year-old steer. He was what they called a "rough steer"–but he brought enough to buy a much-needed carpet to cover the splintery boards of my room. Those were later and harder times.

In 1883 we were all very young. Mr. Alderson was twenty-eight, and he was the oldest. I was twenty-three at the end of the summer; Johnny Zook and Hal were my age, Brown was a year younger. Our friends were in their twenties or early thirties. If we were empire builders we didn't feel like it or act the part. We made a game of everything, even the garden.

In April Mr. Alderson and Johnny and Brown took the plough and started breaking ground for a garden plot on a level space near the house. I shall never forget how tough the sod was; it didn't want to be ploughed. For longer than human memory the grass had grown and died and its roots had interlaced to form one of the strongest sods ever seen. Our little saddle horses weren't raised for such work, and besides they were only on grass, as we had no grain to give them, so they tired easily. The men could do just a few furrows at a time, and it took several days to make our small garden. But we planted it eventually with peas and lettuce and potatoes, and we turned the sod back over them, which was all we could do. We had fresh vegetables that summer, but the potatoes were quite flat.

While they were ploughing I would finish my housework–or just leave it unfinished, I'm afraid–and would go down there and watch them. When the horses had to rest the boys would come over and sit by me. Mr. Alderson was wearing a gold ring which became too tight as he worked, and he took it off and put it on my finger. A few days later it was gone.

We were working on the garden again when I noticed it was missing. I rushed back to the house and searched. I looked where the wash water had been thrown out, but the ring was nowhere. Brown had followed me up to the house to see what the matter was, and he now said soothingly:

"I'll bet Walt or some of them have hid that ring on you."

I said: "Go back down there and tell them I'm crying my eyes out"– but even that didn't produce the ring.

Next day I discovered a bruise on my forehead, and the moment I saw it I knew where the ring was. A few days before this the boys had taken the wagon and gone up into the hills to load pine poles for a fence. Of course I'd had to take my crocheting along and ride with them, perched on the running gears, and I'd sat under the pine trees and crocheted while they cut the poles. The gnats were thick on those warm spring days and in batting at them, as I now recalled, I had hit myself a crack over the eye with the ring.

I said to Brown: "I know where the ring is. It's up where you all were cutting poles."

He said: "You'll never find it. A magpie has got it by now."

But we saddled and rode up there, and I could see it gleaming in the pine needles before I got off my horse.

No, we were not very serious then. We didn't mind the hard things because we didn't expect them to last. Montana in the early Eighties was booming just like the stock market in 1929, and the same feverish optimism possessed all of us. I believe the same thing was true of many other frontier communities. Our little dirt-roofed shack didn't matter because our other house was building. And even the new house was to be only a stepping stone to something better. We didn't expect to live on a ranch all our lives–oh, my no! We used to talk and plan about where we would live when we were rich–we thought of St. Paul. It all looked so easy; the cows would have calves; and two years from now their calves would have calves, and we could figure it all out with a pencil and paper, how in no time at all we'd be cattle kings.

Well, it wasn't so. But there was a glamour to it while it lasted. Raising cattle never was like working on a farm. It was always uncertain and exciting–you had plenty of money or you were broke–and then, too, work on horseback, while dangerous and often very hard, wasn't drudgery. There was more freedom to it. Even we women felt that, though the freedom wasn't ours.

To me at first ranch life had endless novelty and fascination. There were horses to be broken and cattle to be branded, because new ones that we bought had to have our mark of ownership put on them before they were turned out on the range. Something was always going on in the corral, and I would leave the dishes standing in the kitchen and run down and watch, sometimes for hours. This having a Wild West show in one's own back yard was absorbing but it was terrifying; I never could get used to the sight, but would marvel how anyone could stay on such a wild, twisting, plunging mass of horseflesh. The boys took it all quite calmly, and would call to the rider to "Stay with him!" as though it were just a show. My husband always rode the ones that bucked the hardest. It was awful to see his head snap as if his neck would break, yet I never could stay away. However, Brown learned fast to be a good rider, and before long offered to take the worst ones, as he wasn't married.

Sometimes the boys would run races on their favorite horses, and I would hold the stakes. I often went riding when I ought to have been at work. I had a dark blue broadcloth riding habit, with a trailing skirt, and a tightly fitted coat made à la militaire, with three rows of brass buttons down the front. The buttons were a gift from a cousin who went to Annapolis, but was expelled along with two or three other Southern boys for hazing a negro midshipman. My riding habit was even more inappropriate to the surroundings than the rest of my clothes. But the men liked it, and there were no women around to criticize.

My mounts were a chapter in themselves. Gentle horses, as the term is understood in more civilized parts, were almost as rare in Montana as kangaroos. Therefore it was a routine operation, when I was going riding, for one of the boys to get on the horse first with my side saddle and skirt and "take the buck out of him," after which I would get on and ride off, trusting to Providence that he was through for the day. All cowboys, wherever they worked, had each his "string" of eight or ten horses, which actually belonged to the company but which were regarded as the sacred private property of the man who rode them. What was referred to as my "string" consisted of one elderly bay cow pony known as Old Pete. Old Pete was neither good-looking nor a lady's saddle horse, but he was considered gentle because he didn't buck except on starting out, and he would tolerate a side saddle. One day, however, Brown remarked with a thoughtful expression: "I'm afraid Old Pete's going to blow up with you some day when you're riding him. He did it with me."

If he did "blow up" I knew what would happen, but at the time it was Old Pete or nothing. When the roundup came, however, I acquired a new and safer mount.

Many young people have told me how they envied the freedom of the unfenced range as we knew it. But I fear that to the girls of today we should have seemed very quaint. Being married, I felt like a mother to the bachelors, even when they were older than I was, and none of them ever called me by my first name. As for Mr. Alderson, I never could bring myself to call him "Walt," the way the boys did. We didn't do that, in the South. Back home you would hear women say: "Why, I couldn't call my husband George"–or William or Henry. "You'd call a *servant* by his first name!" Of course I couldn't address my husband as I would a servant–not even in Montana where there were no servants! I believe we stuck all the more firmly to our principles of etiquette, because we were so far from civilization. We could still stand on ceremony, even though our floors were dirt.

I should add that in time Mr. Alderson took to calling me "Pardner," which became shortened to "Pardsy," and that after awhile I called him "Pardsy" too. So perhaps we were not so stiff after all.

The boys were always scrupulous about swearing where I could hear them. But when they were working in the corral, they would forget that the wind could carry the sound up to the house. I caught nearly all of them that way at one time or another. Once I even caught Mr. Alderson. It was one day in the summer while they were finishing the new house. I had taken my darning and gone over there to sit, as I often did–because it was cooler there, and one of our new chairs, still done up in burlap, made a comfortable seat. A half-finished partition hid me from Mr. Alderson and Hal, who were working on the tongued-and-grooved ceiling. This was a difficult piece of work, and when Hal, in his irresponsible way, dropped his end of a board and tore out the whole groove, Mr. Alderson swore at him just terribly. I hated so to hear him, I dropped my work and ran to the shack–greatly to the delight of that scamp Hal.

Tongue River

We stayed only a few more months on Tongue River, as my husband and Mr. Zook had decided to break their partnership. Five years had been the term of the original agreement, and the five years were up. It was a good time to dissolve, because the cattle had to be tallied that spring to see what was left after the hard winter. But Mr. Alderson and I had never expected to give up our home.

It happened this way. In dividing the assets, the two partners would take turn about at setting a value on this or that item; when one had priced it, the other must take it or leave it at that figure. The ranch, the house and the furniture were all lumped together; Mr. Zook had the pricing of them, and he named a figure which Mr.

Alderson felt was too high. Thus it came about that Mr. Zook kept the house and everything in it. Mr. Alderson took his interest in cattle. He located a new ranch near the head of Muddy Creek on the Rosebud, ten miles from our first home. And we moved for the third time in four years.

Mr. Alderson had just time enough to make a trip to Miles City before the roundup started, and come back with one wagon load of bare necessities. He brought a cook stove, some provisions, and a few chairs. He also brought two mirrors. That was absolutely all we had to start with.

Some little time before this the government had started an agency for the Cheyennes, on the site of our old ranch on Lame Deer. The first agent's wife, Mrs. Upshaw, had stayed with us in the spring of 1885, while their house was being built. She now repaid us in kind, by inviting me and children to stay with her. One day in May she sent an Indian over with a wagon to get us. I loaded the children in, with our clothes and some personal pictures, and that was our moving day. We stayed with Mrs. Upshaw for perhaps two weeks, but as soon as the new house had a roof and a floor we moved into it, even before the clay daubing between the logs was finished. And that was when I began to pioneer in earnest.

In many ways this was going back to the beginning–or worse than the beginning, since we were no longer borne up by the belief that our trials were temporary. Once more we were living in two rooms, with a tent outside for the boys to live in during the summer. (When winter came we built two bunks in the kitchen.) We had board floors, but they were put down rough and unplaned. Fay was crawling, and there was the problem of splinters–so I cut a sugar sack in two and hung it over her shoulders with suspenders, thus keeping her clean, besides saving her knees. One of our neighbor stockmen came to see us one day, and was quite taken by Fay's costume.

"Wait till she gets to be sixteen," he said. "Then I'll tell her I knew her when she wore gunny sack dresses."

That fall when Jack, the motherless calf, was sold as a five-year-old steer, I bought a carpet for the bedroom. And as soon as I could I diamond-dyed the kitchen floor brown and oiled it so it wouldn't show grease spots. For furniture, I improvised a couch out of two Arbuckle coffee cases and some boards, padding the top with what the boys called a "sougan," and I called a comfort–the latter taken out of an old roundup bed. Our new hand, Mr. Logan, was very handy with tools, and he made us bedsteads and a bureau. The latter had no drawers, but it had shelves which I covered with cretonne. We made out very well, for make out we must. But I can truthfully say that the six years spent on Muddy were the hardest of my life.

Years later when I was a widow living on another ranch, I had a near neighbor and friend who had moved to the West for reasons of health. She told me that when she was packing to come she debated a long time whether to take her few pieces of silver, her books, her pictures—they seemed so inappropriate to the hard, simple life she was planning to lead. She decided finally in their favor, and she never ceased to be thankful, for those few little luxuries which she had hesitated to bring were all that saved her.

"At times they were all that helped me to keep my head up," she said. "I'd have died without them."

I know just what she meant—for after the fire I had nothing of that sort to cling to.

On Muddy I was more alone than I had ever been. Mr. Alderson was away as much as ever, and we had less help because we had cut down the number of our cattle. So I had less of the boys' cheery companionship, and we were so remote that visitors were few. Tongue River was a thoroughfare, but no white people except ourselves had business up this narrow, lonely valley. Above us our horses ran on the high, windswept divide; below us the valley wound downhill for ten miles before getting anywhere—and "anywhere," when reached, was nothing but a tiny log postoffice, a few houses, and Mr. Young's store.

But the worst of hardships was the consciousness of getting run down at the heel. You *had* to keep up or go under—and keeping up made much hard work. I'm a vain old woman now and I was vain then, and I struggled for daintiness. Yet I never liked to ask for anything because Mr. Alderson was so hard up for cash. Not that we didn't have credit—we had too much credit!

My own clothes gave me no trouble. The good ones that I brought with me or bought in Miles City lasted for years, and when they gave out I made myself gingham dresses of pretty colors. Once or twice I even had a nice Alsatian girl to help with the sewing.

I made all the children's clothes, of course. For several years I dressed Fay and Mabel in a sort of a uniform, a blue and white gingham apron with a sash and a turned-down collar. Children's play overalls had not yet been invented, and it took eight apiece of these pinafores to keep them clean, one for each day of the week and the eighth to carry them over. Even though we did live out in the wilds where no one could see us, I couldn't bear to have them looking like little ragamuffins. So beside all the other washing for the family there were fourteen gingham pinafores to wash every week—and fourteen pairs of white cambric drawers, which were white only once, and that was before the first wearing.

Those much-punished undergarments spent hours and hours astride the top rail of the corral–always a box seat for whatever was going on. By dint of much rubbing on the weathered poles the white drawers acquired a greenish grime which wouldn't come off, or in contact with a new pine pole they would pick up a lump of pitch. They took the brunt of it when the children rode bareback, the effects of a hot little body, a galloping horse, and a warm day being just what you would expect. I take off my hat to whoever was bright enough to think of making bloomers for a little girl out of the same material as her dress. I wasn't bright enough, and by the time someone was, my children were grown.

A mother's life was harder then than now, for the lack of such simple things. There were no zippers, and no snaps which children could fasten themselves. When Fay and Mabel went out to play in the winter, I would have to button up two pairs of jersey leggins, button by button, to the waist. Then when I'd done all that they would be back in no time at all, it seemed, with cheeks like apples and with eyes like stars, announcing that they'd had enough snow and wanted to play *indoors* now.

They were lovely little girls. Mabel kept her curls, and they both had blue eyes set wide apart, and long eyelashes. My mother loved beauty so, it was a pity that we did not live where she could have seen more of her little granddaughters. But I was so busy getting three meals a day, I don't think I ever realized they were pretty, until we moved to town where I saw them with other children.

I don't think there is anyone so unfitted to raise children as a tired mother, and I was always tired. And then too there were the effects of isolation and of living inside four walls. In the early days when I had only Mabel I could, even if rarely, pack her in the spring wagon and go on a day's trip with Mr. Alderson, or visit the roundup when it was working near. My sidesaddle was lost when the Indians burned our house, but once or twice on Tongue River I rode short distances on a man's saddle, knee crooked around the horn, while Mr. Alderson took the baby on a pillow in front of him. Two children, however, made all that a thing of the past, and later there were three, and then four! I've said there were weeks when I didn't leave the ranch. There were weeks, in our long winters, when I scarcely left the house except to hang clothes on the line.

No mother gives her best to her children under these conditions, and I know I wasn't patient with mine. But I religiously sang them to sleep every night, or read to them–though sometimes I was so tired I'd fall asleep myself in the middle of the story. I agree heartily with the modern parents and teachers who say that to do this is nonsense, and bad for the child, but at the time I thought I had to do it. They looked like such angels when they were tucked in bed, in their little white nightgowns, that sometimes I couldn't help saying: "Oh, why can't you be good children in the daytime, and not try me so?"

I remember Mabel's serious reply: "But Mother, we can't be good *all* the time!"

Yet with all my mistakes my children today, I am glad to say, look back to a happy childhood. They had more freedom than many modern children whose mothers know more of psychology than I did. And children thrive on freedom. Most of the time they were outdoors and away from me, living and learning for themselves. For hours they roamed at will, out of the range of "don'ts." When they did come indoors, though, I overworked "don't" until sometimes I myself wished that the word had never been invented. People have asked me since if, living in isolation, I didn't have an unusually close companionship with my children. I suppose I did–but I never noticed it! When you live so close to the bare bones of reality, there is very little room for sentiment.

■ E. C. "TEDDY BLUE" ABBOTT

Cowboy E. C. "Teddy Blue" Abbott rode the cattle-drive trails from Texas to Montana during the 1870s and 1880s. His famous book of recollections, We Pointed Them North, *was published in 1939 with the collaboration of Helena Huntington Smith.*

From We Pointed Them North

A Pious New Englander–Calamity Jane Gets Us a Drink–I Repay a Debt

Although Mr. Fuller didn't know one end of a cow from the other, that didn't stop him from trying to revolutionize the cowboys. He told us down on the Platte that those was his intentions, and when we got up to the Yellowstone he went to work to carry them out. He issued orders forbidding us to bring the *Police Gazette* to the ranch. And when we went to town we were not to take a drink, and he went along to see that the order was obeyed. We couldn't do nothing but give in to him, more or less. We were strangers up north, and winter was coming on. We were getting big wages. We had to take a tumble.

Along toward the end of that fall the outfit was all in Miles City. One day the old man was sitting in the hotel lobby, where he could keep his eye on the bar and see that none of his boys was in there, when in walked Calamity Jane. The first time I ever saw her was five years before this, in the Black Hills in '78, when I went up there from the Platte River with that beef herd. I didn't meet her then, but I got a good look at her, when she was at the height of her fame and looks. I remember she was dressed in purple velvet, with diamonds on her and everything. As I recall it, she was some sort of a madam at that time, running a great big gambling hall in Deadwood.

In Miles City in the fall of '83, I had met her and bought her a few drinks. We knew a lot of the same people. So when she came into the hotel lobby where old man Fuller was, I went over and told her about him, and I said: "I'll give you two dollars and a half if you'll go and sit on his lap and kiss him."

And she was game. She walked up to him with everybody watching her, and sat down on his lap, and throwed both her arms around him so his arms were pinned to his sides and he couldn't help himself–she was strong as a bear. And then she began kissing him and saying: "Why don't you ever come to see me any more, honey? You know I love you." And so forth.

I told him: "Go ahead. Have a good time. It's customary here. I won't write home and tell your folks about it."

The old man spluttered and spit and wiped his mouth on his handkerchief. And he left the hotel and that was the last we saw of him that night.

Latter that winter I met Calamity Jane again at Belly-Ups stage station, which was the first station out of Miles City on the Miles-Deadwood stage line. They named it that in honor of the buffalo hunters, who all went belly-ups in the winter of '83 because the buffalo was all gone. Anyway, I met her there, and I borrowed fifty cents from her to buy a meal. I wasn't broke, because I had plenty of money at the ranch, but I had blowed all I had with me, so it come to the same thing.

I thanked her for the fifty cents and said: "Some day I'll pay you." And she said: "I don't give a damn if you never pay me." She meant it, because she was always the kind that would share her last cent.

And I never saw her again until twenty-four years later. It was in 1907, and she was standing on a street corner in Gilt Edge; which was more of a town then than it is now, since they took half the buildings away. I walked up to her and said: "Don't you know me?" and gave her the fifty cents. She recognized me then and said: "I told you, Blue, that I didn't give a damn if you never paid me," and we went and drank it up. She had been famous a long time then, traveling with Buffalo Bill's show and so on, and she was getting old. A few years before I met her in Gilt Edge some friends of hers had taken up a collection and sent her East to make a lady of her, and now she was back. I joked her about her trip and asked her: "How'd you like it when they sent you East to get reformed and civilized?"

Her eyes filled with tears. She said: "Blue, why don't the sons of bitches leave me alone and let me go to hell my own route? All I ask is to be allowed to live out the rest of my life with you boys who speak my language. And I hope they lay me beside Bill Hickock when I die."

Cheyenne Outbreak of '84—"We Are Even"—In Front of a Tepee—Pine Is My Indian—"C Co 7 Cav"—Nobody Will Ever See It Again

It was just about the time of the big chinook that came in March of '84, and a few snowdrifts still showed up, when a Cheyenne named Black Wolf and his immediate family of seven lodges came over from Tongue River to the Rosebud on a visit to the other Indians. They camped at the mouth of Lame Deer Creek, near where two partners named Zook and Alderson had a ranch. One day the chief, Black Wolf, went up to this ranch by himself, and the boys gave him dinner. There was just two of them there at the time, a fellow named Sawney Tolliver, from Kentucky originally, and another one whose name I don't remember.

After Black Wolf had filled up, like an Indian would, he walked out and sat down in the sun on some poles, and he went to sleep. He had an old black stovepipe hat on, and this Tolliver stood at the door of the ranch house and said to the other fellow: "I'll bet you a dollar I can shoot a hole through his hat without hitting his head."

The fellow took him up, and Tolliver throwed down on the Indian, and he just creased him along his scalp. You could lay your finger in the mark. It knocked him out and they thought they had killed him. So they got on their horses and rode to the next ranch to get help, because they expected to have hell with the Indians, and they expected right. When they got back to the ranch with their reinforcements, Black Wolf was gone. But they knew the Indians would be coming just the same, and pretty soon they come and commenced shooting. When the other cowboys saw how many Indians there was, they just stampeded off, because they had no stomach for the business anyhow. It was a damn fool trick that caused the trouble. Tolliver left, too, quit the country. If he'd been caught, he'd have gone to jail, you bet, and he knew it. The soldiers would have seen to that.

The Indians went to work and burnt the house down, and shot the dog, and then they quit right there. Hank Thompson told me that in talking about it afterwards they put their two forefingers together, which is the sign meaning "We are even." Some people claim that they stole some provisions out of the house, coffee and so on, and that the stuff was found in their tepees after they surrendered. I don't know, I didn't go in the tepees. My sympathies was with the Indians.

The cowboys who ran away got word to the soldiers and to the sheriff in Miles City that the Cheyennes had broke out. The first we knew of it over at the F U F was when my friend Billy Smith, the stock inspector, who was in charge of the sheriff's posse, turned up at the ranch calling for help to arrest the Indians and protect a couple of white families that were in danger at the mouth of Lame Deer. By this time it was two days after the shooting, because it was one long day's ride of ninety or a hundred miles to Miles City, and another one to the F U F. We ate dinner and got on our horses, and along about 2:00 A.M., we got to one of these white families at the mouth of Lame Deer, where the posse was supposed to rendezvous. We found them all up and scared to death—though the Indians hadn't done a damn thing yet, only burn down the house where their man had been shot. It was lucky he didn't die, or there would have been hell.

Next day the posse divided, and fourteen of us, keeping this side of the Rosebud, rode away around and tied our horses in some brush, left two men with them, and after dark crawled up to where we were in between the Rosebud and the Indian camp. It makes me shiver yet when I think of the chance we took. There was no shelter whatever. We were right up against a high cut bank, with the river running fast and churning ice below us, so there was no way out in that direction. The tepees were about seventy-five yards in front of us and a bright moon was shining. Some of the others said the Indians were asleep. My God, I could look into the tepee right opposite me and see the moonlight shining off the barrel of his gun—because they always polish off that black stuff—and I imagined I could see the hole at the end of the barrel, and it followed me everywhere.

At daylight Hank Thompson and the deputy from Miles City rode into the Indian camp, and believe me that was a brave thing to do.

But the Indians liked Hank and trusted him completely. He called to Black Wolf in Cheyenne who they were, and Black Wolf invited them into his tepee and called all the other warriors into council. That's when they told Hank they were even. They hadn't done nothing wrong in their estimation.

The old fellow, Black Wolf, was very tall and dignified, and he had a great big piece of buffalo manure tied on his head over the wound. Hank told them they were surrounded and asked them to surrender, and they all talked and argued. One Indian, Howling Wolf, was determined to fight, not surrender, and he kept tongue-lashing the others; he was all hate, and the white men knew he was dangerous and they was watching him.

Out on the bank we could hear the talking going on, but we couldn't hear what they said or which way it was going until all of a sudden Hank Thompson's voice rang out clear, in English, speaking to Louis King. He said: "If anything starts, get that Indian that's doing the talking."

And Louis said: "I'll get him right between the eyes."

We expected any second to hear the shooting start, after that, and if it had started, God help us. I figure they would have got at least six of us outside, beside the two in the tepee. And we laid there cramped and shivering in the early morning cold–we had been there three hours already–and we waited. And we waited some more. During the World War I read about men going over the top, and I know what it is like. It's the waiting that gets you. You feel your whole self go down in your boots, and you feel the gun in your hand–and then you wait another half hour.

And all the time Hank Thompson was talking, talking in Cheyenne, explaining things to the Indians and promising that they would get a square deal if they surrendered. And after awhile Black Wolf, who was the subchief at the head of this little bunch, agreed. And the Indians all walked out, thirteen of them, and gave up their guns. They built a big fire then, and we came in and surrounded them and searched them for knives. All but one young brave named Pine had given them up, and he put up a big fight for his knife, which he had in his breech clout, and they couldn't get it away from him. But Black Wolf made him give it up. They're obedient in all things to the chief.

We had an awful narrow squeak in that camp, even after the surrender. When we came in and surrounded them, we didn't bother the women, naturally. It was breakfast time and they were busy around the camp, going back and forth to the river for water. And four or five would go down to the river, and three or four would come back. And three would go down, and two would come back. . . . And they kept that up until there was only one old woman left in that camp. There was a trail that led around through some brush, on the top of the cut bank, and they was crawling along that trail on their hands and knees, going to get word to the whole tribe, which was camped only six miles away.

One of our posse happened to see the head and shoulders of one squaw, as she crawled along where the trail went out of the brush a little way, and that woke him up. He took one look around the camp and yelled: "Where the hell's all them women?" After that they rounded them up and brought them back. There was two or three hundred Indians in that bunch six miles away, and if those women had gotten through to them, it would have been the end of us.

After we had disarmed the Indians, we marched them down to Gaffney's house, that was one of the white families I mentioned at the mouth of Lame Deer. And there I was sworn in as a special deputy, on account of Billy Smith knowing me before. Billy Smith was in charge of the posse. We got our breakfast down there, and Mrs. Gaffney done the cooking for all of us and the Indians, too. After breakfast we loaded the Indians in a wagon and started off for Miles City, where they were to be tried.

There was a lot of things happened in that Indian camp after I left that I only know about through hearsay. Frank Abbott, who came over with the rest of us from the F U F, says there was a young squaw, Pine's squaw, that had only been married two weeks, and she tried to follow her husband, and he says he has always been sorry for the way they had to treat her to make her go back. But he was disgusted to beat everything with the whole affair, and we was all disgusted when we found out what it was all about, and what danger we had been in for a damn fool trick. Frank says this squaw tried to go to Miles City, while the Indians were in prison before the trail, and was drowned crossing Tongue River. But I couldn't say as to that, because I never heard anything more about it.

We got down to Carpenter and Robinson's ranch just before dark, and there we heard that the Tollivers hadn't made enough trouble yet, because Sawney Tolliver's brother, Brownie, had said he was going to follow us with a bunch of men and going to shoot the Indians in the wagon. Unarmed Indians. Sawney was in Wyoming by this time. Billy Smith left word at the ranch that if anybody followed us and tried to meddle with the Indians, we would shoot them down like dogs. Those Indians had surrendered without firing a shot.

And that wasn't the only reason that we felt as we did. There was only six of us in the posse that took them to Miles City, and if those thirteen Indians had all give a yell and jumped for it out of the wagon, in the night, we'd never have hit a one of them. But they'd given their word. Or Black Wolf had, and what he said went for the rest of them. They always looked to the chief.

In the meanwhile there was still this main bunch of two or three hundred Indians only six miles up from the mouth of Lame Deer, and they'd have jumped the whole United States Army if their chief had given the word. But he didn't give the word. And there again we owed everything to the honor of an Indian.

For on our way to Carpenter and Robinson's that afternoon we saw this one tepee, out from the side of the road. It was the tepee of Little Wolf, the war chief of all the Cheyennes, who was camped out there by himself. And Hank Thompson rode over to him and begged and pleaded with him to give his word that he would stay where he was for another twenty-four hours instead of going in to join his tribe. This would give us a chance to get to Miles City. For Little Wolf was the Cheyennes' great chief, who had led them up here in '78, and they would not move without him.

He finally promised to stay where he was, and he kept his promise, and that saved all our lives. He was a wise leader as well as a great fighter, Little Wolf was, and I believe he was wise enough not to want any more trouble with the white man. He had had a plenty of it, and I believe he knew that the white man was bound to win in the end.

We traveled all that night, the six of us and the Indians. I kept going to sleep in the saddle, because it was the second night for me, and I remember Billy Smith jerking my horse's head up when he went to grazing on me. About daybreak we got to Rosebud station on the Northern Pacific, and we waited there for the train to take us to Miles City. And there I claimed this young Indian, Pine, that wouldn't give up his knife, for my Indian, my friend, and I looked after him as best I could. He was one of the best-looking Indians I ever saw, six feet, one or two inches tall and as straight as a string. And he was brave–he fought for his knife–and I was sure stuck on him.

We all ate there, while we was waiting for the train, and I handed Pine the grub and water first, but he always handed them up to the chief–everything for the chief. And after they had eaten they all wrapped up in their blankets and laid down on their stomachs and went to sleep. And so did I–right beside Pine.

By and by the train came, and we all got on it and went to Miles City. The whole town was out to see us come in with the Indians. At the station we loaded them all in a bus, to take them to the jail at the fort, and I was on top of the bus, so everybody thought I was the cowboy that done the shooting. There was a very popular demimondaine by the name of Willie Johnson, who was running Kit Hardiman's honky-tonk, as I have mentioned before, and I remember she came to the door of the house and hollered: "Stay with it, Blue! Don't you weaken!"

When we turned the Indians over to the authorities at Fort Keogh, Major Logan, the commanding officer, was as sore as a boil. He said, here was the Indians, but where was the fellow that started the trouble? And when they told him he was out of the country by that time, Major Logan said the posse was a hell of an outfit and gave us the devil, until, as Billy Smith said afterwards, if he'd had one more word out of him, he'd have hit him over the head with his six-shooter.

I'll tell you something about soldiers. At the first news of the outbreak they started a company of them from Fort Keogh, with a cannon. And when we got up to Miles City with the Indians, these soldiers had gone just forty miles, which was less than half the distance to the scene of the trouble, in the same time it took the sheriff's posse to go clear down to the mouth of Lame Deer and get the Indians and get back. But that's the way they always was in the army–had to go by West Point regulations; had to build their campfire in a certain position from the tent regardless of the way the wind was blowing. They was no earthly good on the frontier.

Well, the thirteen Indians was shut up under guard, and the next morning the whole Cheyenne tribe rode into Miles City. The people were scared to death. They didn't know what was going to happen. But the Indian prisoners had been guaranteed a fair trial, and Hank Thompson was among the Cheyennes all the time, talking to them like a Dutch uncle. So nothing happened. They finally fixed it all up. Four of the Indians pled guilty to burning the ranch house and got a year apiece in the pen, and they turned the rest loose. One of them died up there of grief.

While they were all in jail, I went to see Pine every day, and took him presents of tailor-made cigarettes and candy and stuff. And I told him I'd get him out of it, and luckily he did get out of it, and he was my friend for life. The last day he took a silver ring off his finger and gave it to me. The ring had a little shield, and on the shield it said "C

Co 7 Cav." That was Tom Custer's company, and Pine took it off the finger of one of Tom Custer's soldiers at the fight, and he was in that fight when he was not yet fourteen years old. The ring was too small for me, and I wore it around my neck for years, but in the end somebody got away with it.

That business at the mouth of Lame Deer opened my eyes to a lot of things about the Indians. I had it in for them before that, but it was due to ignorance. I had seen a lot of them, but I never associated with them the way I did after I got up to Montana. From that time I was on their side, because I saw that when trouble started, more often than not it was the white man's fault.

Not three months after the so-called outbreak I have been telling about, there was another mix-up with the Cheyennes, and it started in the very same outfit–Zook and Alderson. After the Indians burned their ranch on Lame Deer, they moved the outfit, and instead of staying away from these Indians they moved right up into the thick of them, on Hanging Woman, which is another creek in the Tongue River country. It almost seemed like they were looking for trouble; yet that couldn't have been true, because Alderson and his partner were both nice fellows and I believe they were away, both times, when the trouble occurred.

It was during the spring roundup, and they were all out with the roundup except a cowboy named Packsaddle Jack and a couple of others, who were breaking horses at the ranch. Packsaddle Jack was bringing in his horses, early one morning, and there was a Cheyenne named Iron Shirt who had a little garden near there–corn and pumpkins and stuff. And Packsaddle drove his horses right over the Indian's garden, and when the Indian come out and objected, Packsaddle shot him in the arm.

Well, there was a lot of riding around and excitement, the same story all over again. Except that some of the cowpunchers had got their bellyful by this time. And when a couple of fellows from Zook and Alderson's rode over to the roundup and asked for men to help defend the ranch, Jesse Garland, the roundup captain, told them to go to hell. He said: "You got us into one jackpot this spring, and I won't allow a man to leave this roundup."

It all blew over. The Cheyennes knew they were beaten, and they were trying to keep the peace. Packsaddle Jack was tried in Miles City that fall and acquitted. And the rest of us weren't going against those fighting Indians on account of any more damned foolishness like that.

But it led to more and still more trouble. Several white men were found dead. Then another white man got killed by two young

Indians in a fuss over a cow, which he said they had butchered, and I don't doubt they had. The chief sent word for them to come in, as the tribe would get into trouble for it, and he was going to punish them. They sent word back that they would come, but in their own way.

And they went up on top of a hill, and they sang their death songs, and painted themselves, and braided their horses' manes. And then they rode down from the hill, just the two of them, and charged two companies of soldiers that were sent out to arrest them. Which shows you the desperate courage of those Cheyennes.

I forgot to tell you about one thing that happened that morning on the Rosebud. While were lying out there in the grass, half froze and waiting for all hell to break loose out of that tepee, I saw an old Indian go up a hill and pray to the sun. It was just coming up, and the top of the hill was red with it, and we were down there shivering in the shadow. And he was away off on the hill, and he held up his arms, and oh, God, but did he talk to the Great Spirit about the wrongs the white man had done to his people. I never have heard such a voice. It must have carried a couple of miles.

I have noticed that what you see when you are cold and scared is what you remember, and that is a sight I will never forget. I am glad that I saw it. Because nobody will ever see it again.

■ GRANVILLE STUART

Granville Stuart was born in Virginia in 1834, went to California in 1852, and came to Montana to prospect gold with his brother James in 1857. In 1880, Stuart and some partners established the DHS ranch in Montana's Judith Basin; he was later elected to the Territorial Council. After his herd was decimated by the hard winter of 1886-1887, Stuart worked as state land agent, U.S. minister to Uruguay and Paraguay, Butte public librarian, and finally state historian in Helena. Stuart's autobiographical writings were published in 1925 as Forty Years on the Frontier, *edited by Paul C. Phillips, professor of history at the University of Montana. Stuart died in Helena in 1918.*

From Forty Years on the Frontier

Indian Wars of the Northwest

That section of the country lying west of the Rocky mountains and east of the Bitter Root range was the home of the Salish, a once numerous and powerful tribe who had always been friendly to the whites, but were wholly neglected by the government.

Although living west of the mountains they claimed the head-waters of the Missouri river as their hunting grounds and the entire tribe annually crossed the range to hunt buffalo; only the very old people and young children remained at home. Their old trails across the mountains were worn deeper and had been traveled more and longer than any other Indian trails in Montana.

These hunting grounds were disputed, being claimed by the Blackfeet and from time immemorial bitter war raged between the tribes. In the earlier period of their history the Salish with their ally, the Nez Percé a small but superior tribe that lived on the upper Columbia were more than a match for the Blackfeet and hunted wherever they chose. The advent of the Hudson's Bay Company among the Blackfeet enabled that tribe to procure firearms at a much earlier period than the Salish could. This gave them such superior advantages that they not only drove the Salish from the hunting grounds but followed them across the range carrying the war into their own country and threatened to annihilate that tribe.

The Salish were not a warlike people but they wanted firearms that they might stand an equal chance in their encounters with their enemies. Firearms could only be procured from the white men, so from the first they welcomed the few trappers and traders that found their way into the Salish country.

In 1853 Isaac I. Stevens on his way from St. Paul to the coast with a surveying party looking out a route for the Northern Pacific railroad came into their country and was welcomed by the chiefs and head men of the tribe. Stevens did not promise them firearms but held out the prospects of making a treaty with the Blackfeet so that both the whites and Indians could dwell in peace. This was a welcome piece of intelligence to the Salish for they were heartily tired of the never-ending wars in which they were continually worsted.

In 1855 Governor Stevens returned to the country to make a treaty with them and was accorded a hearty welcome. More than one thousand warriors arrayed in all their savage splendor rode forth to meet him. The council was opened by Governor Stevens setting forth the terms offered by the government. The Indians were asked to cede extensive tracts of land, practically all that they had, and to retire to a reservation. In return they were to receive certain annuities, cattle, farming implements, seed grain; and schools were to be provided for their children. Teachers, farmers, carpenters, and blacksmiths would be sent to teach them to till the soil and to build houses.

The Indians were willing to cede the land and they did not object to the reservation plan but the location of the reservation was the stumbling block. They were in reality one tribe, the Salish but there were three branches, each inhabiting a particular section of country to which they were strongly attached. Chief Michael lived with the Kootenais on the headwaters of the Columbia and north of Flathead lake, Alexander with the Pend d'Oreilles were south of the lake and in the Jocko valley while Victor, chief of the Flatheads and hereditary chief over all, claimed for his home the beautiful valley of the Bitter Root and neither chief was willing to leave his home. The council dragged along for days without reaching an agreement and then the treaty was finally signed without settling the question of the location of the reservation.

A few presents of red paint, beads, bright calico, knives, and blankets were distributed and Governor Stevens departed. Years passed and nothing more was heard of the treaty. No cattle, farming implements, or seed grain arrived, nor farmers to teach the Indians how to till the soil.

The Salish crossed the range and hunted buffalo for their living and carried on the same old wars with the Blackfeet, and their children had no school other than those furnished by the Jesuit Fathers and Sisters of Charity that were among them when Stevens came. White people came and were welcomed and given land by the Indians until the Bitter Root valley was quite well settled and there were two good-sized towns, Stevensville and Corvallis. The old chiefs were dead and their sons reigned instead.

The white settlers begun to clamor for government titles to their lands and they wanted roads and bridges and schools. In 1871 like a bolt of thunder from a clear sky, came an order from the President to remove the Flathead Indians from the Bitter Root valley to the valley of the Jocko.

Without a shadow of right or justice and without warning or provocation these kindly peaceable Indians were to be driven from the home that had been theirs since the beginning of time. Charlot, their head chief, refused to go. In 1872 General Garfield was sent out to make a treaty with them and to try to induce them to go to the Jocko. Charlot, head chief, and Arlee and Adolph, sub chiefs met at the council. Charlot spoke for the Indians. He remembered the treaty and he also remembered that the white men had not kept their word and the Indians could not keep theirs. He pointed out that the white people's farms were all over the Indian's hunting grounds and that the Salish still crossed the mountains and fought with the Blackfeet in order to get food and shelter and clothing. The white men or their fields had never been hurt by the Flathead Indians.

Victor, his father, said they would remain in the land of their fathers and Charlot would not go. He left the council. Later Adolph and Arlee signed the treaty. Gov. B. F. Potts, Congressman William H. Claggett, Wilbur F. Sanders, J. S. Vial, and D. J. Swain signed as witnesses. General Garfield returned to Washington and the treaty was published as having been signed by all the Indians and at the same time Arlee was recognized by the government as head chief of the Flatheads. In reality Arlee was only a half-blood Flathead his father being a Nez Percé. Preparations were hurried forward for the removal of the Indians to the Jocko.

Chief Charlot was a Christian, having embraced the Catholic faith and was honest, just, and truthful in all of his dealings with the whites and had many staunch friends among the settlers in the valley. When he learned of these outrages his indignation knew no bounds, every vestige of confidence that he had had in the white race vanished, his sense of honor and justice was outraged. He declared that he would never leave the Bitter Root valley alive.

Arlee and his following moved but Charlot and his people remained. Those that went to the Jocko received something in the way of annuities but they had, to say the least, inefficient agents and but little was done to better their condition and they fared but little better than those that remained in the Bitter Root and received nothing from the government. They all continued to go to the buffalo country to hunt in order to live.

In 1877 Major Peter Ronan a man who was conversant with Indian customs and habits and of fine executive ability as well as of unimpeachable integrity was appointed agent for the Flatheads, and immediately set to work to straighten out the tangled affairs. Honest and just in all of his dealings with them he soon won their confidence and remained until his death their trusted friend and adviser. Major Ronan was familiar with the Stevens treaty and with the subsequent proceedings. His sympathies were with Charlot but he could see the futility of further resistance and used all of his powers of persuasion to induce the old chief to reconsider his decision. Charlot would not listen, his confidence in government officials was gone.

Settlers continued to pour into the valley and settled on the land. The buffalo were fast disappearing on the ranges and there was but little game in the Bitter Root and the condition of the Indians became desperate; the matter was finally taken to Congress and Senator George Vest of Missouri and Major Maginnis, our delegate in Congress, were appointed to investigate the matter. The investigation brought to light a long story of injustice, ingratitude, duplicity, and an utter disregard of treaty pledges on the part of the government agents in dealing with these Indians and their report to Washington was to that effect. General Garfield was forced to acknowledge that Charlot had not signed the treaty.

In January, 1884, Major Ronan received instructions to bring Charlot and his head men to Washington for a conference; the object being to try to secure Charlot's consent to remove with his band to the Jocko reservation.

Nearly a month was spent in Washington and several interviews held with the Secretary of the Interior but no offer of pecuniary reward or persuasion of the secretary could shake Charlot's resolution to remain in the Bitter Root valley. He treated with disdain and distrust any person connected with the United States government and refused all offers of assistance from the government. He asked only the poor privilege of remaining in the valley where he was born. In March, 1884, Major Ronan held another council at Stevensville with the Indians at which he promised: first—a choice of one hundred and sixty acres, unoccupied land on the Jocko reservation; second—assistance in erecting a substantial house; third—assistance in fencing and ploughing a field of ten acres; fourth—the following gifts; two cows to each family, a wagon and harness and necessary agricultural implements, seed for the first year and provisions until the first year's harvest. Twenty-one families accepted this offer and went to the Jocko.

The department kept its part of the contract and also authorized the construction of an irrigation ditch to cover the land settled upon. So well did this plan work that in a year, other Indians, witnessing the prosperous condition of their friends and relatives also determined to go to the Jocko and eleven more families moved down. But alas! The red tape was in full operation again. Although Major Ronan wrote and urged and explained and finally went to Washington at his own expense to try to get the necessary funds to supply these eleven families with the things given the first twenty it was all to no purpose. The excuse given was no appropriation at that time. Later orders came to issue supplies to Charlot and those at Stevensville and again the eleven families were left out as they were not at Stevensville. Major Ronan issued them supplies assuming the responsibility himself.

Food, seed grain, and a limited amount of farming implements were issued to Charlot's little band at Stevensville; but the Indians were not farmers and they were too far away to receive instructions and supervision necessary to make their efforts a success. The young men were fast becoming addicted to the use of whiskey and the women and children were starving.

In 1891 General Carrington was sent out to see if he could make some sort of treaty whereby the Indians would remove to the Jocko. Charlot was ready to go. He said, "I do not want your land, You are liars. I do not believe you. My young men have no place to hunt, they get whiskey, they are bad. My women and children are hungry: I will go." Into exile went this truly noble Indian.

During all these years of the treating and wrangling with the Flathead Indians, the settlers in the Bitter Root valley were kept in suspense as to the titles to their lands. There was no incentive to make improvements as they did not know whether they might remain and get title or be ordered off to seek homes in some other locality.

Such was the peace policy of the government which was in operation for so many years, during which time the Indians were almost exterminated, the lives of hundreds of white people sacrificed, expensive Indian campaigns carried on, and much valuable property destroyed. A number of Indian agents and traders made fortunes, hied themselves to their eastern homes and spread stories about the murderous capacity of the white settlers who encroached upon the Indians.

Cattle Rustlers and Vigilantes

At the close of the fall roundup (1883) our tallies showed that we had suffered at least a three per cent loss from "rustling." These thieves were splendidly organized and had established headquarters and had enough friends among the ranchers to enable them to carry on their work with perfect safety.

Near our home ranch we discovered one rancher whose cows invariably had twin calves and frequently triplets, while the range cows in that vicinity were nearly all barren and would persist in hanging around this man's corral, envying his cows their numerous children and bawling and lamenting their own childless fate. This state of affairs continued until we were obliged to call around that way and threaten to hang the man if his cows had any more twins.

The "rustlers" were particularly active along the Missouri and Yellowstone rivers and our neighbors in the Dakota bad lands were great sufferers. A meeting of stockmen was called at Helena on October 16 to consider what best to do. The first thing necessary was to discover the leaders and to locate their rendezvous. It was then decided to bring the matter before the Stock Growers' Association at the regular spring meeting.

The second annual meeting of The Montana Stock Growers' Association convened at Miles City on April 20, 1884. There were four hundred and twenty-nine stockmen present. The citizens' welcome was as cordial as it had been the previous year and the same splendid entertainment offered, but the meeting itself was not the harmonious gathering that the previous meeting had been. Everybody seemed to have a grievance. The members of the association that had been members of the legislature the previous year came in for their full share of censure. We were blamed for everything that had happened but the good weather.

The matters for consideration were overstocking the ranges, the dread pleuro-pneumonia, or Texas fever, that was claiming such a heavy toll in Kansas and Nebraska and how to put a stop to "rustling."

The civil laws and courts had been tried and found wanting. The Montana cattlemen were as peaceable and law-abiding a body of men as could be found anywhere but they had $35,000,000 worth of property scattered over seventy-five thousand square miles of practically uninhabited country and it must be protected from thieves. The only way to do it was to make the penalty for stealing so severe that it would lose its attractions. When the subject was brought up some of the members were for raising a small army of cowboys and raiding the country: but the older and more conservative men knew that that would never do.

I openly opposed any such move and pointed out to them that the "rustlers" were strongly fortified, each of their cabins being a miniature fortress. They were all armed with the most modern weapons and had an abundance of ammunition, and every man of them was a desperado and a dead shot. If we had a scrap with them the law was on the side of the "rustlers." A fight with them would result in the loss of many lives and those that were not killed would have to stand trial for murder in case they killed any of the "rustlers." My talk did not have the conciliatory effect that I expected and seemed only to add fuel to the fire. The younger men felt that they had suffered enough at the hand of thieves and were for "cleaning them out" no matter what the cost.

The Marquis DeMores, who was a warm personal friend of mine and with whom I had had some previous talks on the subject, was strongly in favor of a "rustlers' war" and openly accused me of "backing water." The Marquis was strongly supported by Theodore Roosevelt, who was also a member of the Montana Stock Growers' Association from Dakota. In the end the conservative members of the association carried the day and it was voted that the association would take no action against the "rustlers." In some way the "rustlers" got information about what was done at the meeting and were jubilant. They returned to their favorite haunts and settled down to what promised to be an era of undisturbed and successful operations.

While we were absent on the roundup, a party came to the ranch, stole a valuable stallion and a number of other good horses. Another party collected twenty-four head of beef steers from the Moccasin range and attempted to drive them north of the line into Canada; but when they found they could not evade the range riders, drove the cattle into a coulee and killed them, leaving the carcasses to spoil.

At the close of the roundup there was a meeting of a few stockmen at the "D-S" ranch. They and some men employed by the Stock Growers' Association had been watching the operations of the rustlers. The captain of this band of outlaws was John Stringer who answered to the sobriquet of "Stringer Jack." He was a tall handsome young fellow, well educated, and of a pleasing personality. His distinguishing features were his piercing gray eyes, white even teeth, and pleasant smile. He came to Montana in 1876 and hunted buffalo along the Missouri and Yellowstone rivers and was a conspicuous figure around the wood yards, trading posts, and military cantonments. He did not drink to excess but was an inveterate gambler. When the buffalo were gone he turned his attention to rustling cattle and stealing horses and established his headquarters on the Missouri river at the mouth of the Pouchette.

There were rustlers' rendezvous at the mouth of the Musselshell, at Rocky Point and at Wolf Point. J. A. Wells had a herd of cattle on the Judith river in charge of a herder who had eight saddle horses. On the twenty-fifth of June, Narciss Lavardure and Joe Vardner came up the river and camped opposite the Wells' camp. Next day the herder crossed the river to look for some stray stock and as soon as he was out of sight Vardner and Lavardure crossed the river and drove off the seven saddle horses. They were going up Eagle creek on the run when they accidentally met William Thompson, who knew the horses and ordered them to stop. Lavardure answered by turning and firing at Thompson but his horse plunged and he missed his mark. Thompson, who was well armed and riding a good horse, gave chase. He shot and fatally wounded Vardner and after a race of six miles, captured Lavardure and brought him and the horses back to the Wells' camp. Thompson and his prisoner were taken across the river in a skiff and the latter placed in a stable under guard. At 2 A.M.

on the morning of the twenty-seventh the guard was overpowered by an armed posse and Lavardure was taken out and hanged.

Sam McKenzie, a Scotch half-breed, had spent two years around old Fort Hawley on the Missouri river under pretense of being a wolfer but in reality was one of the most active horse thieves. He stole horses in Montana, drove them across the line into Canada, sold them, then stole horses up there and brought them back and sold them around Benton. He had been very successful in dodging the authorities on both sides of the line because of his many friends among the Cree half-breeds in Canada and in the Judith basin. On July 3, McKenzie was caught in a cañon a few miles above Fort Maginnis with two stolen horses in his possession and that night he was hanged from the limb of a cottonwood tree, two miles below the fort.

Early in June two suspicious characters came into the Judith basin with a small band of horses with a variety of brands on them and among them two fairly good "scrub" race horses. Word of their suspicious appearance and actions came to us and we telegraphed to several places to try to find out who the men were and whence they came.

I first met them on July 3, while out range riding, when I accidentally came on their camp at a spring just above Nelson's ranch (The old overland post office). The men were as tough looking characters as I have ever met, especially Owen who had long unkept black hair, small, shifty, greenish gray eyes and a cruel mouth. "Rattle Snake Jake," despite his bad sounding sobriquet, was not quite so evil looking at his pal, although he was far from having a prepossessing appearance. Both men were armed, each wearing two forty-four Colt revolvers and a hunting knife. When I rode into their camp, Fallon was sitting on a roll of blankets cleaning a Winchester rifle. Owen was reclining against a stump smoking and another Winchester lay on a coat within easy reach. Owen was self-possessed, almost insolent, "Rattle Snake Jake" was civil but nervously tinkered with the gun and kept his eyes on me all the time I was in their camp. I knew that they were a bad lot but had nothing to cause their arrest at that time, but decided to keep an eye on them while they were on the range.

On the morning of July 4 Ben Cline came along the road with a race horse on his way to Lewistown. "Rattle Snake Jake" saw the horse and challenged Cline for a race. Cline did not want to race, giving as his reason that he had his horse matched against a gray mare to run at the races at Lewistown and wanted to get his horse over there in good condition. After a little bantering on the part of Fallon a race was arranged between one of his horses and Cline's for fifty dollars a side, and a level stretch of road almost in front of Nelson's house selected for the race course. Owen bet ten dollars on the Fallon horse with one of Cline's companions. The Cline horse won the race and Cline and his companions resumed their interrupted journey to Lewistown.

Shortly after Cline and his friends left, Owen and Fallon packed up their belongings and set out for Lewistown. At this time Lewistown was just a small village, but they were having a Fourth of July celebration and people from a hundred miles in every direction had flocked to the town, to take part in the festivities.

Owen and "Rattle Snake Jake" arrived in town about one P.M., rode up to Crowley's saloon, dismounted, went in and had several drinks and then rode on to the race track. Here they joined the throng around the track but took no part in the betting until almost the last race when they bet quite heavily and lost their money. This, together with a few drinks of bad whiskey, put them in an ugly mood.

A young man by the name of Bob Jackson, dressed in costume, representing Uncle Sam, rode in the parade and afterwards was at the race track, still wearing the grotesque costume. For some unaccountable reason his presence near Owen gave that gentleman offense and he struck Jackson over the head with the butt of his revolver, felling him to the ground; then placing a cocked revolver to Jackson's head, compelled him to crawl in the dust like a snake. Owen then turned to "Rattle Snake Jake" and said, "Well I guess we will clean out this town" and at that shot at random into the crowd, but fortunately did not hit anybody.

The desperadoes mounted their horses and rode back to the saloon where they each had more drinks: then flourishing their revolvers in a threatening way and cursing and swearing declared that they intended to clean up the town, swaggered out into the street.

Quite a number of men who had been at the race track, sensing trouble hurried back to town, went to Power's store and armed themselves with Winchesters and took up positions in the buildings on either side of the street. Out in the street "Rattle Snake Jake" mounted his horse and Owen started to mount his, when he spied Joe Doney standing in front of Power's store. Revolver in hand he started to cross the street. When within a few feet of the walk Doney pulled a twenty-two caliber revolver and shot him in the stomach. A second shot struck Owen's hand, causing him to drop his revolver.

Doney ran into the store. Owen quickly recovered his revolver and fired at Doney just as he disappeared inside the door. The men in the store answered the shot with their Winchesters and Owen retreated up the street toward a tent occupied by a photographer.

"Rattle Snake Jake," revolver in hand started to ride up the street in the opposite direction, when a shot fired by someone in the saloon, struck him in the side. He kept on for a short distance when his cartridge belt fell to the ground and he drew up to recover it. Looking back he saw that Owen was not following him but was wounded and could not get away, and turning his horse he rode back to his comrade through a perfect shower of lead coming from both sides of the street and together the two men made their last stand in front of the tent.

The citizens in the store and saloons and from behind buildings kept up their firing, while the two desperadoes standing exposed to their merciless fire, coolly and deliberately answered shot for shot, emptied and re-loaded their guns and emptied them again until they could no longer pull a trigger.

Two young men, Benjamin Smith and Joseph Jackson, were crossing an open space a short distance from the tent when "Rattle Snake Jake" caught sight of them, and dropping down on one knee took careful aim and fired on them. The first shot grazed Jackson's cheek and the second one pierced his hat and took a lock of his hair. The third one lodged in Smith's brain, killing him instantly.

A few minutes later Owen reached for his rifle, pitched forward and fell to the ground and almost at the same moment a bullet struck "Rattle Snake Jake" in the breast and he dropped. As soon as both men were down the citizens ceased firing but the bandits continued with their revolvers so long as consciousness remained. When the smoke of battle cleared away examination of the bodies showed that "Rattle Snake Jake" had received nine wounds and Owen eleven, anyone of which would have proved fatal.

In the evening Judge Toombs held an inquest over the bodies, the photographer, in front of whose tent they were killed, took their pictures and then they were given burial on a little knoll on the Pichette ranch.

On the afternoon of July 4, a telegram came to me from Buffalo, Wyoming, stating that Charles Fallon, alias "Rattle Snake Jake," and Edward Owen, were desperate characters and were wanted at several places. The two men had spent the winter on Powder river at the mouth of Crazy Woman, gambling, horse racing, and carousing. On their way north they had stolen some good horses from John R. Smith's ranch near Trabing, Wyoming, and traded them to the Crow Indians. Later on we learned that Owen was from Shreveport, Louisiana, and was wanted there for killing a negro. Charles Fallon hailed from Laredo on the Texas border and was wanted in New Mexico for shooting up a ranch and burning buildings and hay stacks.

Billy Downs was located at one of the wood yards on the Missouri at the mouth of the Musselshell, ostensibly to trap wolves, but in reality to sell whiskey to the Indians. His place soon came to be headquarters for tough characters, and it was but a short time until Downs himself was stealing horses and killing cattle. Downs was a married man and his wife was at the wood yard with him. Because of sympathy for the woman, he was warned that he was being watched and that if he did not change his tactics he was sure to get into trouble. He paid not the least attention to the warning, but continued to surround himself with the worst characters on the river and kept on stealing horses and killing cattle.

On the night of July 4, a committee of vigilantes arrived at the Downs' place and called on him to come out. This at first he refused to do but after a short parley he did come out, accompanied by a notorious character known as California Ed. Both men plead guilty to stealing ponies from the Indians but denied that they had stolen from white men, but they failed to account for the twenty-six horses in the corral, all bearing well-known brands. They claimed that the quantity of dried meat found in the house was dried buffalo meat, notwithstanding the fact that there had not been a buffalo on the range for more than two years. In the stable was a stack of fresh hides folded and salted ready to be shipped down the river, all bearing the brand of the Fergus Stock Co. The two men were taken out to a little grove of trees and hanged.

At the time the vigilante committee started for the mouth of Musselshell, another party left for the vicinity of Rocky Point where two notorious horse thieves, known as Red Mike and Brocky Gallagher, were making their headquarters. They had stolen about thirty head of horses from Smith river, changed the brands and were holding them in the bad lands. They had also been operating over on the Moccasin range and stolen horses from J. H. Ming's ranch and from J. L. Stuart.

When the vigilantes arrived at Rocky Point the men were not there but had crossed over on the north side of the river. The party followed after, and captured them and recovered some of the horses. Both men plead guilty to horse stealing and told their captors that there were six head of the stolen horses at Dutch Louie's ranch on Crooked creek.

Fifteen miles below the mouth of the Musselshell, at an old abandoned wood yard, lived old man James, his two sons, and a nephew. Here also was the favorite haunt of Jack Stringer. There was a log cabin and a stable with a large corral built of logs, connecting the two buildings. One hundred yards from the cabin in a wooded bottom was a tent constructed of poles and covered with three wagon sheets. At the cabin were old man James, his two sons, Frank Hanson and Bill Williams. Occupying the tent were Jack Stringer, Paddy Rose, Swift Bill, Dixie Burr, Orvil Edwards, and Silas Nickerson.

On the morning of July 8, the vigilantes arrived at Bates Point. The men were divided into three parties. Three guarded the tent, five surrounded the cabin and one was left behind with the saddle horses. They then waited for daylight. Old man James was the first to appear. He was ordered to open the corral and drive out the horses. This he did but refused to surrender, backed into the cabin and fired a shot from his rifle through a small port hole at the side of the door. This was followed by a volley from port holes all around the cabin and in an instant the whole party was in action.

Two of the vigilantes crawled up and set fire to the hay stack and the cabin. The men inside stationed themselves at port holes and kept up the fight until they were all killed or burned up. The cabin burned to the ground. The tent was near the river bank and almost surrounded by thick brush and it was easier to escape from it than to get out of the cabin. Stringer Jack crawled under the tent and reached a dense clump of willows from which he made his last stand. Dixie Burr had his arm shattered with a rifle ball but jumped into an old dry well and remained until dark. Paddy Rose ran out of the tent, passed back of the men engaged at the cabin and concealed himself in a small washout and after dark made his escape. Nickerson, Edwards, and Swift Bill reached the river bank and crawling along through the brush and under the bank, succeeded in passing above the men at the cabin and hid in some brush and drift wood. Orvil Edwards and Silas Nickerson were the only ones that escaped without wounds. After the fight at the cabin the men went down the river and spent the day looking for the men who had escaped but failed to find them.

On the afternoon of the ninth, the fugitives rolled some dry logs into the river, constructed a raft and started down stream. At Poplar creek agency they were discovered by some soldiers stationed there, ordered to come on shore and were arrested.

Notice of their arrest was sent to Fort Maginnis and Samuel Fischel, deputy U.S. marshall, started at once to get the prisoners and take them to White Sulphur Springs. At the mouth of the Musselshell a posse met Fischel and took the prisoners from him. Nearby stood two log cabins close together. A log was placed between the cabins, the ends resting on the roofs, and the four men were hanged from the log. The cabins caught fire and were burned down and the bodies were cremated.

Paddy Rose lay all day concealed in a little washout in the bad lands and at night struck for Fort Benton, where he had wealthy and influential relatives. With their influence and assistance he succeeded in reaching the Canadian border.

There were one hundred and sixty-five stolen horses recovered at Bates Point and one hundred and nineteen at other places. After the fight at Bates Point the vigilantes disbanded and returned to their respective homes. This clean-up of horse thieves put a stop to horse and cattle stealing in Montana for many years.

Several of the men that met their fate on the Missouri in July, 1884, belonged to wealthy and influential families and there arose a great hue and cry in certain localities over what was termed "the arrogance of the cattle kings." The cattlemen were accused of hiring "gunmen" to raid the country and drive the small ranchers and sheepmen off the range. There was not a grain of truth in this talk.

There were but fourteen members of the vigilance committee and they were all men who had stock on the range and who had suffered at the hands of the thieves. There was not one man taken on suspicion and not one was hanged for a first offense. The men that were taken were members of an organized band of thieves that for more than two years had evaded the law and robbed the range at will. The fact that the stock men loaned milch cows, horses, and farm machinery to settlers on small ranches, branded their calves for them at roundup prices, established schools for them, bought their butter and vegetables at high prices and in every way helped them to get a start is proof that any law-abiding person was welcome in this country.

■ CHIEF CHARLOT

Chief Charlot and the Flathead (Salish) tribe lived in western Montana's Bitterroot Valley under the terms of the 1855 Council Grove Treaty. In 1872, when General James Garfield (who would become president) came to Montana to move the Flatheads from the Bitterroot to the Jocko Indian Reservation north of Missoula, Charlot and his band would not go. The government then demanded that the Bitterroot Flatheads pay taxes, and Charlot refused. This translated speech, made at a conference on taxation in 1876, appeared in the April 26, 1876, Weekly Missoulian *and was attributed to "A Flathead Chief," but it is generally accepted that Charlot was the author. By 1891, conditions had grown so bad for the Bitterroot Flatheads that Charlot marched his two hundred followers to the Jocko Reservation. He died there in 1911.*

The Indian and Taxation

Yes, my people, the white man wants us to pay him. He comes in his intent, and says we must pay him—pay him for our own, for the things we have from our God and our forefathers; for things he never owned and never gave us. What law or right is that? What shame or what charity? The Indian says that a woman is more shameless than a man; but the white man has less shame than our women. Since our forefathers first beheld him, more than seven times ten winters have snowed and melted. Most of them like those snows have dissolved away. Their spirits went whither they came; his, they say, go there too. Do they meet and see us here? Can he blush before his maker, or is he forever dead? Is his prayer his promise—a trust of the wind? Is it a sound without sense? Is it a thing whose life is a foul thing?

And is he not foul? He has filled graves with our bones. His horses, his cattle, his sheep, his men, his women have a rot. Do not his breath, his gums stink? His jaws lose their teeth and he stamps them with false ones, yet he is not ashamed. No, no! His course is destruction; he spoils what the Spirit who gave us this country made beautiful and clean. But that is not enough: he wants us to pay him, besides his enslaving our country. Yes, and our people, besides, that degradation of a tribe who never were his enemies. . . .

But he lives to persist; yes, the rascal is also an unsatisfied beggar, and his hangman and swine follow his walk. Pay him money? Did he inquire, how? No, no; his meanness ropes his charity, his avarice wives his envy, his race breeds to extort. Did he speak at all like a friend? He saw a few horses and some cows, and so many tons of rails. . . . His envy thereon baited to the quick. Why thus? Because he himself says he is in a big debt, and wants us to help pay it. His avarice put him in debt, and he wants us to pay him for it and be his fools. Did he ask how many a helpless widow, how many a fatherless child, how many a blind and naked thing fare a little from that little we have? Did he—in a destroying night when the mountains and the firmament put their faces together to freeze us—did he inquire if we had a spare rag of a blanket to save our lost and perishing steps to our fires? No, no; cold he is, you know, and merciless. Four times in one shivering night I last winter knew the old one-eyed Indian, Kenneth, the gray man of full seven tens of winters, was refused shelter in four of the white man's houses on his way on that bad night; yet the aged, blinded man was turned out to his fate. No, no; he is cold and merciless, haughty and overbearing. Look at him, and he looks at you—how? His fishy eyes scan you as the why-oops do the shelled blue cock. He is cold, and stealth and envy are with him, and fit him as do his hands and feet.

We owe him nothing! He owes us more than he will pay us—yet he says there is a God!

I know another aged Indian, with his only daughter and wife alone in their lodge. He had a few beaver skins and four or five poor horses—all he had. The night was bad and held every stream in thick ice; the earth was white; the stars burned nearer us as if to pity us, but the more they burned the more stood the hair of the deer on end with cold, nor heeded they the frost bursting the willows. Two of the white man's people came to the lodge, lost and freezing pitifully. They fared well inside that lodge. The old wife and only daughter unbound and cut off their frozen shoes, gave them new ones and crushed sage-bark rind to keep their feet smooth and warm. They gave them warm soup, boiled deer meat and boiled beaver. They were saved; their safety returned to make them live. After a while they would not stop; they would go. They went away. Mind you: remember well! At midnight they returned, murdered the old father and his daughter and her mother asleep, took the beaver skins and horses, and left. Next day the first and only Indian they met, a fine young man, they killed, put his body under the ice and rode away on his horse.

Yet they say *we* are not good! Will he tell his own crimes? No, no; his crimes to us are left untold. But the desolater bawls and cries the dangers to the country from us, the few left of us. Other tribes kill and ravish his women, stake his children and eat his steers; and he gives them blankets and sugar for it. We, the poor Flatheads who never troubled him, he wants now to distress and make poorer!

I have no more to say, my people. But this much I have said, and I close, to hear your minds about this payment.

He never begot laws nor rights to ask it. His laws never gave us a blade of grass nor a tree, nor a duck, nor a grouse, nor a trout. No; like the wolverine that steals your cache, how often does he come? You know he comes as long as he lives, and takes more and more–and dirties what he leaves.

A COUNCIL WITH THE SIOUX INDIANS

This document first appeared in the 57th Annual Report of the Commissioner of Indian Affairs in 1888. In 1983, it was transcribed from the original by R. V. Dumont, Jr., and is available in the NAES collection in the Fort Peck Tribal Archives.

Proceedings of a Council with the Sioux Indians of the Fort Peck Agency, Montana–1886

In accordance with notification given by Agent Cowen the Indians assembled on Monday the 27 day of December 1886 in one of the Agency School buildings. There were present in the council 150 or more, including the chiefs and other principal men of the tribe. It was a full representation of the Yankton and other Sioux, living at Poplar Creek and in the country immediately contiguous thereto and several intelligent half breeds and Indians were also present, who reside at a distance from the agency.

At the appointed hour Interpreter John Brugier introduced the Commission to the Council.

Judge Wright arose and said: . . . The Great Father knows that you are now poor–he knows that you have a great deal of land–more than you can work–more than you need–that you live in a cold country and frequently that you cannot raise crops for the want of rain–he also knows that in former times when the buffalo roamed the plains and covered the hills that you were rich and powerful–game was plenty and you could live by killing buffalo, which supplied all your wants–now that game has almost disappeared and the buffalo has ceased to roam over your prairies. He knows that you cannot live as in good times of old–therefore he wants to assist you so that you and your children may be able to settle down and make a living—he desires to help you so that you may live better than you are now doing and to collect about your homes many of the comforts of life. . . . Should you refuse and hold on to all your land you would be no better off at the end of fifty years than you are now, but the Great Father wishes you to sell him a part of this land. He will give you the money to supply all your wants. That land which you reserve will be your own. Each man can have his own little farm, his sheep and his cattle, own his own home as the whiteman and be prosperous and happy.

If you refuse to do this the Great Father can do nothing for you, because he is now offering to you what he thinks is for your own good and for the good of your children. . . .

D. DANIELS said: My Friends. Dakota. I have known you for 30 years. Probably some here have seen me before. I am the Indian's friend. . . .

Remember that the money for your lands will be paid to you each year for a time of ten years and that it will be sufficient to buy all you need.

To encourage and stimulate labor the Great Father promises to give more to those who work, who make for themselves good homes, cultivate their farms, raise crops, tend their cattle—he says to them who help themselves, I will help you—I want to see you comfortable. I want to see you live well. I want to see you enjoy life, and if you will only try, if you will work, if you will do as I say, I will help you. Do you want to be rich, you must do as the whiteman. He works and works hard. I know you want to be rich and if you do, why don't you take hold and work? We do not expect the old men to work, but the young men must go to work. What I say to you, I also say to the Assiniboine. I won't keep your ears open any longer. I am done. If you want to talk, we will listen.

After D. Daniels had taken his seat AGENT COWEN arose and said that he wishes to say a few words to the Council.

AGENT COWEN then said: My Friends, you know that I have been here but a short time but I have been studying your interest. I have an eye single to your welfare, and as you come to my office and talk, I listen and I am thinking of your wants, and have to provide for you and make you as comfortable as I can with the means at my command. I am your agent and your friend.

You know that the whiteman is coming here and that many say that you have no right here—that you do not own the land, but these men sent here by the Great Father say that you have right and they propose to fix and guarantee your rights to the land, and is it not better to let them settle it now and forever. And you know that you cannot use all the land. You do not need it. They offer you more than 500 acres to every man, woman and child in your band. Therefore with this liberal offer is it not better for you to accept it, to take the land offered to you and the title fixed in perpetuity to you and your children. . . .

MAJOR LARABEE said: I am very glad to see you and shake hands with all. . . .

The time has come when Indians cannot hold vast bodies of land as heretofore. White people are coming to America from all parts of the world. Emigrants are flocking over the plains and the prairies. The demand for land increases from day to day. The cry is more land! more land! The government must take care of and provide land for her white children, as well as the Indians but when the Government gets land from the Indians she wants to pay them for it. Now we in the name of the Great Father ask you to sell your surplus land. We will give you its value. We will not rob you, would not take an acre from you that you or your children need, but knowing that you have vast tracts of land that you can neither work nor graze, we ask that you sell this part and for it the Great Father will pay you a certain sum of money. . . . Our proposition is to leave to you and the Assiniboines at Wolf Point a Reservation here–to the Indians at Belknap a Reservation, that they may select and to the Indians at Blackfoot a Reservation that they may select. In addition to this we also propose to give to you and the Assiniboines at Wolf Point and to each of the other bands or tribes a certain sum of money each year for a term of years, so that you will have the means to provide yourselves comfortable homes, gather around you stock, cattle and sheep and to give you a good start in life. . . .

MEDICINE BEAR then arose and addressed the Commission. He said, My Friends, you have told me something. I want to go home and talk over it. I will meet you tomorrow morning.

A general hand shaking was then gone through with, when the Council adjourned and the Indians dispersed to their homes.

PURSUANT TO ADJOURNMENT THE COUNCIL MET AT 11 O'CLOCK TUESDAY MORNING, DECEMBER 28, 1886.

Judge Wright announced to the Indians that the Commission was ready to hear what they had to say.

MEDICINE BEAR arose and said: My Friends, I want to tell you something but first I want to ask you something. Have you had any land given you since you have been out in this business?

It was answered yes. (JUDGE WRIGHT). Other Indians with whom we have treated have sold us some of their land.

MEDICINE BEAR: My people made my father their Chief. He died and his bones rest here. After his death I was made Chief. I want to raise my children here and I want to die here and rest with my father.

What you said yesterday about our rights in this country was right. Now I want to ask you to help us with the Agent. We want more rations and we want more Indian men employed around the Agency.

The Yankton and the Assiniboine can live together. Let the other tribes have their land about us. We will watch our land. Let them watch theirs. The Whites can have the land above the Little Rockies.

There is something else that I do not like. I want to have it fixed right. I want a good store here. The man that has the traders store here is a bad man.

YELLOW EAGLE: I am glad to see you good men come among us. What you told us yesterday was good. Some years ago when I went to Washington, I shook hands with many good men. They told me to watch my land. I have done so. People used to kill each other. I am a soldier and speak right out. I used to kill many, but now when white man comes as friend, I shake hands with him.

We are friendly with all the tribes. I shake hands with all–all good. Every Spring they come down and talk together. Last Spring they came down here and had a talk. They want their lands to join our lands.

I am willing to do what the Great Father says. I want to have the right to use the beef hides. I want the Agent to fix the price at $5.00 per hide.

The Agent now cuts up the beef but I want him to give it to the Indians whole and let them divide among themselves.

BLACK HAWK: I feel bad. My heart is weak. I told the young men if they had anything to say to speak out. I am willing to do what they want.

I am now 58 years old. I never stole anything from the whiteman. I never wronged the white man. A whiteman gave me this paper to help me along to get something for my family. One of my men went away up north and died and I want something for his family. . . . My people were then starving and dying.

Much bacon and many sacks of bran are sent here and stored in the warehouse but I can get nothing. I want the agent to give us bacon, sugar and coffee this winter.

Our young men were working all summer but have never been paid. I want to know when they will be paid.

When I was in Washington the whiteman talked sweet, but when I got back home I got nothing. The Great Father gave us a big piece of land, but now he wants to cut it down. Yet our Head men are willing to take what you offered yesterday.

RED DOOR: Since we have been here there are many things that I don't like. I am glad to see you good men come to see us and am pleased with what you said, but there are somethings that I do not like.

There are some half breeds here that can read and write, but they are not employed about the agency. Half Breeds should be employed about the agency and get the pay. The Whiteman do the work and get all the money.

There are some white men here married to Indian women. I want those men moved outside the reservation.

Some of our young men can learn to work. They do work sometimes but never get any pay.

When at Washington I was but a boy. I was a soldier for six years and I watched our land.

Our Agent has made me Captain of the Police and I will do my duty. I will watch the land. The Agent that was here before was a bad man–never said a good word to me–treated me as a dog. You told me yesterday many good words and I think my people can now live. When you go to Wolf Point, the people there may tell you many things–I don't know much, myself, but they are worse than me. . . .

IRON NECKLACE: Before they never told us any good words. I am glad for what you have said and I can see how we can now live. What you said yesterday was good and all are satisfied. Our agent has made me Lt. of the police to take care of the land and I will do it. On your way from Buford you should have seen a land mark between that Post and the Big Muddy and I want our reservation to extend to that mark. The White people can let their cattle graze on it and use the wood. We will not object nor ask any charge but I want our land to extend to that place.

How are we to take care of our stock in the winter. We want moving machines to cut the grass and save the hay. Our Agent is a good man, but some of the men he has employed are not good men. I want him to make a change. The man does not treat me well.

DEER TAIL: My friends what will become of my people when the ten years have passed?

JUDGE WRIGHT answered and said that the land would be theirs forever and he hoped that during the ten years that people would accumulate some stock and would be in a condition to make a living for themselves.

BIG EAGLE: The Great Father has sent you here. You have two pockets. You must have tobacco in one and money in the other. All the game is now gone. I live down at Box Alder last summer and had a hard time. Liked to have died. I suppose our Great Father appointed our agent and gave him the annuities. I am glad of it. I like to get the annuities. I want sugar and coffee every day.

BIG FOOT handed paper to Judge Wright which the Judge read. It commended him to the kindness of the white man.

BIG FOOT: My friends look at me. The Frenchman treated me better many years ago. I have lived here 23 years. Some of the Cut Heads and of other tribes are here. I am satisfied with what you have told us yesterday, but I want you to help us as much as you can. I want mowing machines to help raise the cattle. We can make a living by raising cattle. The Half breeds can show us how to use the mowing machine, can show us how to work and help us to work.

I have heard ever since I was a boy that the Great Father wanted to help us. It is an old, old story. If we have mowing machines, we can cut the grass, save the hay to feed our cattle in the winter and sell some hay too and get some money.

WHITE MAGGOT: My friends. I am young, but I want to be like the white man. I want to work as they do. I do not understand, tell me how much money you are willing to pay us for our lands.

The amount was explained to him by the interpreter so that he appeared to understand.

WHITE MAGGOT: I want money and am willing to work for it. I have worked but I have got no money for it.

The Government used to send rations here, but then they got none. If you were living away off the Great Father would not send rations and never give you any. They never get any bacon, sugar and coffee. I want to live here. Many of my dead are here and I want to live and die here. I have never spoken out before, because I did not think it would do any good, but I will speak now. The Agent has worked many of our young men, has worked them hard, has killed some and has never paid us a dollar. I am satisfied with what you have said. I want to butcher cattle ourselves as the Indians do at Standing Rock.

AFRAID OF THE BEAR: I am a poor man. You told us yesterday how we are to live hereafter. I am satisfied. I thank you for what you said. When we get what you promised us we will have plenty of beef and will get plenty to eat.

RED LODGE shook hands with all the Commission and said I am satisfied.

RED THUNDER: I was in Washington and talked with the Great Father and shook many good men by the hand. I am now old and am the only man living that was there that time of our people—all are dead. I am satisfied with any arrangement that you make with our young men. I am glad of what you told yesterday.

RUSHING BEAR: We have said what we had to say, we are now done. . . .

MAJOR LARABEE said, My Friends. . . . Some of you Headmen talked of the Eastern Boundary of your Reservation. We have thought much over this matter and we think the Big Muddy is the best line. It is a natural boundary, everybody will know it.

Your reservation is large enough. We think you should be satisfied and if you are satisfied with it we want you to come up and sign this paper. . . .

BLACK HAWK: The Indian always do what the Whiteman ask him to do, but before the time runs out something more is asked, the bargain is changed.

I thought that we owned lands across the river.

MAJOR LARABEE: It never belonged to you, but was simply attached to your Reservation by the Great Father to keep the whiskey men away. This paper gives you the right to get all the timber you need across the river.

BLACK HAWK: I do not understand how the money is to be divided.

MAJOR LARABEE then read that article of the agreement showing how the money was to be expended. All the details were carefully explained. He also told them that the Commission had given the Indians at Berthold but one half this amount and that they counted (beans?) all night and the (beans?) ran out, that the Indians said it was a plenty. And he said that they could not spend it all. That each year the government would put the surplus away for them in the U.S. Treasury and keep it for them after the ten years had passed, and will do the same for you.

YELLOW EAGLE asked permission to address the Indians which was granted. When he ended the signing commenced.

■ CHARLES M. RUSSELL

Charles M. Russell, Montana's famous cowboy artist, was also a skilled storyteller. Born in St. Louis in 1864, Russell came to Montana when he was sixteen years old to work for a sheepman. He was soon cowboying in the Judith Basin and on the plains around Great Falls, recording his observations and experiences in numerous drawings and sketches. After Russell married Nancy Cooper in 1896, he became a full-time, and very successful, professional artist. He died at his home in Great Falls in 1926. Russell published these yarns in Trails Plowed Under *(1937), using cowboy Rawhide Rawlins as his storyteller.*

The Story of the Cowpuncher

"Speakin' of cowpunchers," says Rawhide Rawlins, "I'm glad to see in the last few years that them that know the business have been writin' about 'em. It begin to look like they'd be wiped out without a history. Up to a few years ago there's mighty little known about cows and cow people. It was sure amusin' to read some of them old stories about cowpunchin'. You'd think a puncher growed horns an' was haired over.

"It put me in mind of the eastern girl that asks her mother: 'Ma,' says she, 'do cowboys eat grass?' 'No, dear,' says the old lady, 'they're part human,' an' I don't know but the old gal had 'em sized up right. If they are human, they're a separate species. I'm talkin' about the old-time ones, before the country's strung with wire an' nesters had grabbed all the water, an' a cowpuncher's home was big. It wasn't where he took his hat off, but where he spread his blankets. He ranged from Mexico to the Big Bow River of the north, an' from where the trees get scarce in the east to the old Pacific. He don't need no iron hoss, but covers his country on one that eats grass an' wears hair. All the tools he needed was saddle, bridle, quirt, hackamore, an' rawhide riatta or seagrass rope; that covered his hoss.

"The puncher himself was rigged, startin' at the top, with a good hat—not one of the floppy kind you see in pictures, with the rim turned up in front. The top-cover he wears holds its shape an' was made to protect his face from the weather; maybe to hold it on, he wore a buckskin string under the chin or back of the head. Round his neck a big silk handkerchief, tied loose, an' in the drag of a trail herd it was drawn over the face to the eyes, hold-up fashion, to protect the nose an' throat from dust. In old times, a leather blab or mask was used the same. Coat, vest, an' shirt suits his own taste. Maybe he'd wear California pants, light buckskin in color, with large brown plaid, sometimes foxed, or what you'd call reinforced with buck or antelope skin. Over these came his chaparejos or leggin's. His feet were covered with good high-heeled boots, finished off with steel spurs of Spanish pattern. His weapon's usually a forty-five Colt's six-gun, which is packed in a belt, swingin' a little below his right hip. Sometimes a Winchester in a scabbard, slung to his saddle under his stirrup-leather, either right or left side, but generally left, stock forward, lock down, as his rope hangs at his saddle-fork on the right.

"By all I can find out from old, gray-headed punchers, the cow business started in California, an' the Spaniards were the first to burn marks on their cattle an' hosses, an' use the rope. Then men from the States drifted west to Texas, pickin' up the brandin' iron an' lass-rope, an' the business spread north, east, an' west, till the spotted long-horns walked in every trail marked out by their brown cousins, the buffalo.

"Texas an' California, bein' the startin' places, made two species of cowpunchers; those west of the Rockies rangin' north, usin' centerfire or single-cinch saddles, with high fork an' cantle; packed a sixty or sixty-five foot rawhide rope, an' swung a big loop. These cow people were generally strong on pretty, usin' plenty of hoss jewelry, silver-mounted spurs, bits, an' conchas; instead of a quirt, used a romal, or quirt braided to the end of the reins. Their saddles were full stamped, with from twenty-four to twenty-eight-inch eagle-bill tapaderos. Their chaparejos were made of fur or hair, either bear, angora goat, or hair sealskin. These fellows were sure fancy, an' called themselves buccaroos, coming from the Spanish word, *vaquero*.

"The cowpuncher east of the Rockies originated in Texas and ranged north to the Big Bow. He wasn't so much for pretty; his saddle was low horn, rimfire, or double-cinch; sometimes 'macheer.' Their rope was seldom over forty feet, for being a good deal in a brush country, they were forced to swing a small loop. These men generally tied, instead of taking their dallie-welts, or wrapping their rope around the saddle horn. Their chaparejos were made of heavy bullhide, to protect the leg from brush an' thorns, with hog-snout tapaderos.

"Cowpunchers were mighty particular about their rig, an' in all the camps you'd find a fashion leader. From a cowpuncher's idea, these fellers was sure good to look at, an' I tell you right now, there ain't no prettier sight for my eyes than one of those good-lookin', long-backed cowpunchers, sittin' up on a high-forked, full-stamped California saddle with a live hoss between his legs.

"Of course a good many of these fancy men were more ornamental than useful, but one of the best cow-hands I ever knew belonged to this class. Down on the Gray Bull, he went under the name of Mason, but most punchers called him Pretty Shadow. This sounds like an Injun name, but it ain't. It comes from a habit some punchers has of ridin' along, lookin' at their shadows. Lookin' glasses are scarce in cow outfits, so the only chance for these pretty boys to admire themselves is on bright, sunshiny days. Mason's one of these kind that doesn't get much pleasure out of life in cloudy weather. His hat was the best; his boots was made to order, with extra long heels. He rode a center-fire, full-stamped saddle, with twenty-eight-inch tapaderos; bearskin ancaroes, or saddle pockets; his chaparejos were of the same skin. He packed a sixty-five-foot rawhide. His spurs an' bit were silver inlaid, the last bein' a Spanish spade. But the gaudiest part of his regalia was his gun. It's a forty-five Colt's, silverplated an' chased with gold. Her handle is pearl, with a bull's head carved on.

"When the sun hits Mason with all this silver on, he blazes up like some big piece of jewelry. You could see him for miles when he's ridin' high country. Barrin' Mexicans, he's the fanciest cow dog I ever see, an' don't think he don't savvy the cow. He knows what she says to her calf. Of course there wasn't many of his stripe. All punchers liked good rigs, but plainer; an' as most punchers 're fond of gamblin' an' spend their spare time at stud poker or monte, they can't tell what kind of a rig they'll be ridin' the next day. I've seen many a good rig lost over a blanket. It depends how lucky the cards fall what kind of a rig a man's ridin'.

"I'm talkin' about old times, when cowmen were in their glory. They lived different, talked different, an' had different ways. No matter where you met him, or how he's rigged, if you'd watch him close he'd do something that would tip his hand. I had a little experience back in '83 that'll show what I'm gettin' at.

"I was winterin' in Cheyenne. One night a stranger stakes me to buck the bank. I got off lucky an' cash in fifteen hundred dollars. Of course I cut the money in two with my friend, but it leaves me with the biggest roll I ever packed. All this wealth makes Cheyenne look small, an' I begin longin' for bigger camps, so I drift for Chicago. The minute I hit the burg, I shed my cow garments an' get into white man's harness. A hard hat, boiled shirt, laced shoes—all the gearin' known to civilized man. When I put on all this rig, I sure look human; that is, I think so. But them shorthorns know me, an' by the way they trim that roll, it looks like somebody's pinned a card on my back with the word 'EASY' in big letters. I ain't been there a week till my roll don't need no string around it, an' I start thinkin' about home. One evenin' I throw in with the friendliest feller I ever met. It was at the bar of the hotel where I'm camped. I don't just remember how we got acquainted, but after about fifteen drinks we start holdin' hands an' seein' who could buy the most and fastest. I remember him tellin' the barslave not to take my money, 'cause I'm his friend. Afterwards, I find out the reason for this goodheartedness; he wants it all an' hates to see me waste it. Finally, he starts to show me the town an' says it won't cost me a cent. Maybe he did, but I was unconscious, an' wasn't in shape to remember. Next day, when I come to, my hair's sore an' I didn't know the days of the week, month, or what year it was.

"The first thing I do when I open my eyes is to look at the winders. There's no bars on 'em, an' I feel easier. I'm in a small room with two bunks. The one opposite me holds a feller that's smokin' a cigarette an' sizin' me up between whiffs while I'm dressin'. I go through myself but I'm too late. Somebody beat me to it. I'm lacin' my shoes an' thinkin' hard, when the stranger speaks:

"'Neighbor, you're a long way from your range.'

"'You call the turn,' says I, 'but how did you read my iron?'

"'I didn't see a burn on you,' says he, 'an' from looks, you'll go as a slick-ear. It's your ways, while I'm layin' here, watchin' you get into your garments. Now, humans dress up an' punchers dress down.

When you raised, the first thing you put on is your hat. Another thing that shows you up is you don't shed your shirt when you bed down. So next comes your vest an' coat, keepin' your hindquarters covered till you slide into your pants, an' now you're lacin' your shoes. I notice you done all of it without quittin' the blankets, like the ground's cold. I don't know what state or territory you hail from, but you've smelt sagebrush an' drank alkali. I heap savvy you. You've slept a whole lot with nothin' but sky over your head, an' there's times when that old roof leaks, but judgin' from appearances, you wouldn't mind a little open air right now.'

"This feller's my kind, an' he stakes me with enough to get back to the cow country."

Lepley's Bear

"Old Man Lepley tells me one time about a bear he was near enough to shake hands with but they don't get acquainted. He's been living on hog side till he's near starved. So, one day he saddled up and starts prowling for something fresh. There's lots of black-tail in the country but they have been hunted till they are shy, so after riding a while without seeing nothing he thinks he'll have better luck afoot. So, the first park he hits, he stakes his hoss. It's an old beaver meadow with bluejoint to his cayuse's knees, and about the center (like it's put there for him) is a dead cottonwood snag handy to stake his hoss to.

"After leaving the park he ain't gone a quarter of a mile till he notices the taller branches of a chokecherry bush movin'. There's no wind, and Lepley knows that bush don't move without something pushing it, so naturally he's curious. 'Tain't long till he heap savvys. It's a big silvertip and he's sure busy berrying. There's lots of meat here, and bear grease is better than any boughten lard. So, Lepley pulls down on him, aimin' for his heart. Mr. Bear bites where the ball hits. It makes Old Silver damn disagreeable–he starts bawlin' and comin'.

"As I said before, there ain't no wind. It's the smoke from his gun hovering over Lepley that tips it off where he's hiding. He's packing a Sharp's carbine an' he ain't got time to reload, so he turns this bear hunt into a foot race. It's a good one, but it looks like the man'll take second money. When he reaches the park his hoss has grazed to the near end. Lepley don't stop to bridle, but leaps for the saddle.

"About this time the hoss sees what's hurrying the rider. One look's enough. In two jumps, he's giving the best he's got. Suddenly something happens. Lepley can't tell whether it's an earthquake or a cyclone, but everything went from under him, and he's sailin' off; but he's flying low, and uses his face for a rough lock, and stops agin some bushes. When he wakes up he don't hear harps nor smell smoke. It ain't till then he remembers he don't untie his rope. The snag snapped off, and his hoss is tryin' to drag it out of the country, and Mr. Bear, by the sound of breaking brush, is hunting a new range and it won't be anywhere near where they met. When his hoss stops on the end of the rope, that old snag snaps and all her branches scatter over the park. I guess Mr. Bear thinks the hoss has turned on him. Maybe some of them big limbs bounced on him and he thinks the hoss has friends and they're throwing clubs at him. Anyhow, Mr. Bear gives the fight to Lepley and the hoss.

"Lepley says that for months he has to walk that old hoss a hundred yards before he can spur him into a lope, and that you could stake him on a hairpin and he'd stay."

Some Liars of the Old West

Speakin' of liars, the Old West could put in its claim for more of 'em than any other land under the sun. The mountains and plains seemed to stimulate man's imagination. A man in the States might have been a liar in a small way, but when he comes west he soon takes lessons from the prairies, where ranges a hundred miles away seem within touchin' distance, streams run uphill and Nature appears to lie some herself.

These men weren't vicious liars. It was love of romance, lack of reading matter, and the wish to be entertainin' that makes 'em stretch facts and invent yarns. Jack McGowan, a well-known old-timer now livin' in Great Falls, tells of a man known as Lyin' Jack, who was famous from Mexico to the Arctic.

McGowan says one of Jack's favorite tales is of an elk he once killed that measured 15-feet spread between the antlers. He used to tell that he kept these horns in the loft of his cabin.

"One time I hadn't seen Jack for years," said McGowan, "when he shows up in Benton. The crowd's all glad to see Jack, an' after a round or two of drinks, asks him to tell them a yarn.

"'No boys,' says Jack, 'I'm through. For years I've been tellin' these lies – told 'em so often I got to believin' 'em myself. That story of mine about the elk with the 15-foot horns is what cured me. I told about that elk so often that I knowed the place I killed it. One night I lit a candle and crawled up in the loft to view the horns—an' I'm damned if they was there.'"

Once up in Yogo, Bill Cameron pointed out Old Man Babcock an' another old-timer, Patrick, sayin', "there's three of the biggest liars in the world."

"Who's the third?" inquired a bystander.

"Patrick's one, an' old Bab's the other two," says Cameron.

This Babcock one night is telling about getting jumped by 50 hostile Sioux, a war party, that's giving him a close run. The bullets an' arrows are tearin' the dirt all around, when he hits the mouth of a deep canyon. He thinks he's safe, but after ridin' up it a way, discovers it's a box gulch, with walls straight up from 600 to 1,000 feet. His only get-away's where he come in, an' the Indians are already whippin' their ponies into it.

Right here old Bab rares back in his chair, closes his eyes, an' starts fondlin' his whiskers. This seems to be the end of the story, when one of the listeners asks:

"What happened then?"

Old Bab, with his eyes still closed, takin' a fresh chew, whispered: "They killed me, b' God!"

The upper Missouri River steamboats, they used to say, would run on a light dew, an' certainly they used to get by where there was mighty little water. X. Beidler an' his friend, Major Reed, are traveling by boat to Fort Benton. One night they drink more than they should. X. is awakened in the morning by the cries of Reed. On entering his stateroom, X. finds Reed begging for water, as he's dying of thirst.

X. steps to the bedside, and takin' his friend's hand, says: "I'm sorry, Major, I can't do anything for you. That damned pilot got drunk, too, last night, and we're eight miles up a dry coulee!"

"Some say rattlers ain't pizen," said Buckskin Williams, an old freighter, "but I know different. I'm pullin' out of Milk River one day with 14, when I notice my line hoss swing out an' every hoss on the near side crowds the chain. My near wheel hoss, that I'm ridin', rares up an' straddles the tongue. It's then I see what the trouble is—a big rattler has struck, misses my hoss an' hits the tongue. The tongue starts to swell up. I have to chop it off to save the wagon, an' I'm damn quick doin' it, too!"

"Cap" Nelse, a well-known old-timer around Benton in the early days, tells of coming south from Edmonton with a string of half-breed carts. They were traveling through big herds of buffalo. It was spring and there were many calves. They had no trouble with the full-grown buffalo, Cap said, but were forced to stop often to take the calves from between the spokes of the cart-wheels!

A traveling man in White Sulphur Springs makes a bet of drinks for the town with Coates, a saloon keeper, that Coates can't find a man that will hold up his hand and take his oath that he has seen 100,000 buffalo at one sight. When the bet's decided, it's agreed to ring the triangle at the hotel, which will call the town to their drinks.

Many old-timers said they had seen that many buffalo, but refused to swear to it, and it looked like Coates would lose his bet until Milt Crowthers showed up. Then a smile of confidence spread over Coates' face as he introduces Crowthers to the drummer.

"Mr. Crowthers," said the traveling man, "how many antelope have you seen at one time?"

Crowthers straightens up and looks wise, like he's turning back over the pages of the past. "Two hundred thousand," says he.

"How many elk?" asks the traveling man.

"Somethin' over a million," replies Crowthers.

"Mr. Crowthers, how many buffalo will you hold up your hand and swear you have seen at one sight?"

Crowthers holds up his hand. "As near as I can figure," says he, "about three million billion."

This is where Coates starts for the triangle, but the traveling man halts him, saying, "Where were you when you saw these buffalo, Mr. Crowthers?"

"I was a boy travelin' with a wagon train," replies Crowthers. "We was south of the Platte when we was forced to corral our wagons to keep our stock from bein' stampeded by buffalo. For five days an' nights 50 men kep' their guns hot killin' buffalo to keep 'em off the wagons. The sixth day the herd spread, givin' us time to yoke up an' cross the Platte, an' it's a damn good thing we did."

"Why?" asks the traveling man.

"Well," says Crowthers, "we no more than hit the high country north of the Platte, than lookin' back, here comes the main herd!"

Jake Hoover's Pig

as told to Frank B. Linderman

Charlie Russell's story about "Jake Hoover's Pig" has been retold countless times over the years. In this rendition, Montana author Frank Bird Linderman remembered this story by his old friend for his Recollections of Charley Russell *(1963).*

"They was funny old boys, them fellers," Charley said, thoughtfully, referring to the old-time trappers. "They had a lot of sentiment an' didn't know it. Of course, a man don't look for much sentiment in a trapper–I mean when it comes to killin' an animal." He rolled a cigaret, lighted it, and inhaled a puff of smoke. "But sometimes it's there just the same."

I knew when Charley had a story coming and waited.

"When I was a kid I threw in with old Jake Hoover. Jake was a trapper an' a skin hunter an' killed deer an' antelope an' elk for the market for fresh meat. He did a lot of things that was ornery. His cabin was in Pig-Eye Basin over in Judith country. You could see deer from the door of his shack 'most any day. But do you think he would kill a deer that stuck about his shack? No, sir, he'd as soon take a shot at men as kill one of them deer. An' I've seen the time when there wasn't enough grub in that shack to bait a mousetrap, too. Every livin' thing around there liked old Jake. Pine squirrels would climb into his lap an' sit on his shoulder. Chickadees were dead stuck on him; they'd pick crumbs from his lips an' he always fed 'em plenty.

"One spring a ranchman in the Judith traded old Jake a little suckin' pig for some elk meat. He was tiny, black as ink, an' cute as a kit fox. Jake chucked him into a gunny sack, tied it behind his saddle, an' fetched the pig to the cabin in Pig-Eye Basin, turnin' him loose there. Inside of two days that little pig was follerin' old Jake wherever he went, up hill and down again, just like a dog. He got to be an awful nuisance. We couldn't keep him out of the cabin, an' he was into everythin' that smelled like grub. He even wanted to sleep with us–got sore as a wolf when we wouldn't let him. So we built a pen for him an' shut him up.

"Wheat was scarce in those days. We had to rustle hard to feed that pig. We always had to find ranchmen who'd rather have elk meat than wheat, because we didn't have any money. But shuttin' that pig up was good for him; he seemed to swell up overnight.

"Jake was dead stuck on that pig. He made a reg'lar ceremony of feedin' him, too. Soon's he'd step into the pen with grub in a camp kettle the pig would rub Jake's shins with his snout, an' the old man would lean over an' scratch the pig's back, talkin' all the time. 'Ain't he a dandy, kid?' he'd say when I was around. 'Won't he make fine eatin' this fall, hey? By God, I'm glad I got him. A man's a damn fool that don't have a pig in these here hills. I ain't never goin' to be without one any more, you bet.' Then he'd empty the kettle into the wooden trough an' say, 'There, eat, you damned glutton. Git good an' fat, 'cause when fall comes we'll smash ya a good lick atween yer eyes with the ax. Then we'll have grease till grass starts in the spring. Lucky we got ya.'

"One mornin' we went huntin' an' was gone three days. When we come back an' was comin' down a steep pitch that was near the cabin we heard a tin pan go 'bang' inside it. 'Hold on, kid,' Jake says, cockin' his rifle. 'There's bear in the shack an' he might be a grizzly. Take keer of yaself.'

"I was lookin' over his shoulder when he poked the muzzle of his Winchester through the open door. But it wasn't a bear; the pig had got out of his pen an' got into the cabin. The place was always tidy, but now it was the damndest wreck in Montana Territory. The pig had found Jake's flour an' molasses an' dried apples an' rolled 'em up plenty in a mess. Molasses an' flour was plastered over everythin'. Worse'n all, he'd dragged old Jake's four-point Hudson's Bay blanket off'n the bunk an' had walloped it round in the mess. You remember them old-fashioned dried apples that used to come in round slices with round holes in the middle? Well, one of them slices had stuck fast to the pig's forehead, an' I bet every fly in the Territory had moved in an' camped on the sticky spots on Jake's blanket.

"He was a pig, remember; but snortin' an' blowin' an' rollin' in the flour an' molasses had made rings round his eyes like he had goggles on, an' the slice of apple stuck on his forehead was the funniest thing I ever saw.

"He was tickled to death to see us an' showed it plain; but old Jake was mad clean to his toes. 'This settles it with you, ya damned dirty rooter,' he said, kickin' the pig in the ribs as he went through the door. 'Ya won't see no leaves turn yellow; you'll be bacon. Good God, just look at my blanket, kid,' he says, draggin' it outdoors.

"I wanted to laugh but I was afraid to. I helped clean up the mess without sayin' anythin', but Old Jake was swearin' like a stuck bull-whacker all the time.

"Soon's we had supper old Jake started to sharpen butcher knives. I didn't know he had so many knives. I went to sleep hearin' 'em grit on his whetstone. I felt sorry for the pig.

"At daylight I turned out an' put on my boots. 'Hold on, kid,' Jake says, sittin' up in his bunk. 'It's too warm to kill that pig in this weather, it's too warm; the meat would spoil an' we don't wanta lose it after all the hell we've had with him. Besides, there's some wheat left an' we wouldn't have nothin' to feed it to. We'll wait a spell.'

"I was glad. I liked that fool pig.

"The wheat didn't last long; we had to make another rustle. 'It's the last time, kid,' Jake said. 'I'm plumb sick of the contract. Soon's this sack's gone, zowie! We'll bat him a good one with the ax.' He looked both fierce an' a bit sad. 'It's comin' to him, ain't it?'

" 'Sure is,' I agreed, though I was mighty glad we had another big sack of wheat, just the same.

"The weather was growin' sharp when the last of our wheat was dished out. 'In the mornin' we'll kill him,' Jake said. 'I'll feed him tonight an' bust his damned dirty head in the mornin',' he growled, sharpening butcher knives again.

"At daylight he called, 'Come on, roll out, kid. We'll get rid of that low-down skunk afore we eat. I jest can't put it off any longer. I been layin' there in my bunk thinkin' of that blanket he ruined. An' besides, the wheat's all gone an' I ain't goin' ridin' like a madman to find feed for a damned hawg no more. Come on, roll out.' He picked up a handful of butcher knives an' the camp kettle he'd always used to feed the pig. 'Fetch the ax,' he says like he was mad at me.

"We started for the pigpen. A pine squirrel came down a fir tree an' up the trail to meet us, but old Jake kicked him. An' when a chickadee lit on his shoulder the old feller dropped his camp kettle, snatched off his hat, an' struck at the little bird with it. 'Kid,' he says, 'this gulch is plumb overrun with damn nuisances. It's got so a man can't live here no more. I know what I'll do; by God, I'll move out an' let 'em have it.'

"The pig was tickled to see Jake. He rubbed his snout against Jake's shins as soon's he stepped into the pen. 'Git away from here, damn ya. Ya think this is a friendly visit? Well, it ain't. Here, kid,' he says, handing me the ax, 'smash him a good one while I git the water heatin'.'

" 'Not by a damn sight; he ain't my pig,' I said to Jake, backing away.

" 'Oh, come on, kid; he's knowed me ever since he was a little feller. The wheat's all gone and we need the meat.'

" 'Can't help it,' I said, 'I didn't bring him here an' I won't kill him.'

" 'No, but you'll eat his meat fast enough, I bet,' Jake growled. He leaned the ax against the pen.

" 'Well, I won't kill him, that's a cinch,' I said an' climbed out of the pen.

"Old Jake quit me cold an' went back to the cabin mutterin' to himself, mad as a hornet. I saw him come out with his rifle an' start up the hill. He climbed until the timber hid him. The pig all the time was watching me, waitin' for somethin' to eat.

"I fed him an' he nosed round in the empty kettle an' then looked around for Jake.

"Bang! I jumped a foot high an' the pig tumbled over an' began to kick beside the kettle.

"Old Jake came down off the hill, leaned his rifle against the pen, pulled out a butcher knife, an' stuck the pig. I can see him yet, ashakin' the blood off the knife.

" 'I don't reckon he saw me or knowed who done it, do you, kid?' he asks, looking sorry as a woman."

■ ANDY ADAMS

Born in 1859, Andy Adams ran away from his Indiana home and drifted west through Arkansas and Texas. Adams worked trail drives north to Montana before going to Colorado to prospect for gold. He settled in Colorado Springs, where he wrote novels and stories about the Old West. This selection first appeared in Log of a Cowboy *in 1903. Adams died in Colorado in 1935.*

End of the Trail Drive

There was a fair road up the Teton, which we followed for several days without incident, to the forks of that river, where we turned up Muddy Creek, the north fork of the Teton. That noon, while catching saddle horses, dinner not being quite ready, we noticed a flurry amongst the cattle, then almost a mile in our rear. Two men were on herd with them as usual, grazing them forward up the creek and watering as they came, when suddenly the cattle in the lead came tearing out of the creek, and on reaching open ground turned at bay. After several bunches had seemingly taken fright at the same object, we noticed Bull Durham, who was on herd, ride through the cattle to the scene of disturbance. We saw him on nearing the spot, lie down on the neck of his horse, watch intently for several minutes, then quietly drop back to the rear, circle the herd, and ride for the wagon. We had been observing the proceedings closely, though from a distance, for some time. Daylight was evidently all that saved us from a stampede, and as Bull Durham galloped up he was almost breathless. He informed us that an old cinnamon bear and two cubs were berrying along the creek, and had taken the right of way. Then there was a hustling and borrowing of cartridges, while saddles were cinched on to horses as though human life depended on alacrity. We were all feeling quite gala anyhow, and this looked like a chance for some sport. It was hard to hold the impulsive ones in check until the others were ready. The cattle pointed us to the location of the quarry as we rode forward. When within a quarter of a mile, we separated into two squads, in order to gain the rear of the bears, cut them off from the creek, and force them into the open. The cattle held the attention of the bears until we had gained their rear, and as we came up between them and the creek, the old one reared up on her haunches and took a most astonished and innocent look at us.

A single "woof" brought one of the cubs to her side, and she dropped on all fours and lumbered off, a half dozen shots hastening her pace in an effort to circle the horsemen who were gradually closing in. In making this circle to gain the protection of some thickets which skirted the creek, she was compelled to cross quite an open space, and before she had covered the distance of fifty yards, a rain of ropes came down on her, and she was thrown backward with no less than four lariats fastened over her neck and fore parts. Then ensued a lively scene, for the horses snorted and in spite of rowels refused to face the bear. But ropes securely snubbed to pommels held them to the quarry. Two minor circuses were meantime in progress with the two cubs, but pressure of duty held those of us who had fastened on to the old cinnamon. The ropes were taut and several of them were about her throat; the horses were pulling in as many different directions, yet the strain of all the lariats failed to choke her as we expected. At this juncture, four of the loose men came to our rescue, and proposed shooting the brute. We were willing enough, for though we had better than a tail hold, we were very ready to let go. But while there were plenty of good shots among us, our horses had now become wary, and could not, when free from ropes, be induced to approach within twenty yards of the bear, and they were so fidgety that accurate aim was impossible. We who had ropes on the old bear begged the boys to get down and take it afoot, but they were not disposed to listen to our reasons, and blazed away from rearing horses, not one shot in ten taking effect. There was no telling how long this random shooting would have lasted; but one shot cut my rope two feet from the noose, and with one rope less on her the old bear made some ugly surges, and had not Joe Stallings had a wheeler of a horse on the rope, she would have done somebody damage.

The Rebel was on the opposite side from Stallings and myself, and as soon as I was freed, he called me around to him, and shifting his rope to me, borrowed my six-shooter and joined those who were shooting. Dismounting, he gave the reins of his horse to Flood, walked up to within fifteen steps of mother bruin, and kneeling, emptied both six-shooters with telling accuracy. The old bear winced at nearly every shot, and once she made an ugly surge on the ropes, but the three guy lines held her up to Priest's deliberate aim. The vitality of that cinnamon almost staggers belief, for after both six-shooters had been emptied into her body, she floundered on the ropes with all her former strength, although the blood was dripping and gushing from her numerous wounds. Borrowing a third gun, Priest returned to the fight, and as we slacked the ropes slightly, the old bear reared, facing her antagonist. The Rebel emptied his third gun into her before she sank, choked, bleeding, and exhausted, to the ground; and even then no one dared to approach her, for she struck out wildly with all fours as she slowly succumbed to the inevitable.

One of the cubs had been roped and afterwards shot at close quarters, while the other had reached the creek and climbed a sapling which grew on the bank, when a few shots brought him to the ground. The two cubs were about the size of a small black bear, though the mother was a large specimen of her species. The cubs had nice coats of soft fur, and their hides were taken as trophies of the fight, but the robe of the mother was a summer one and worthless. While we were skinning the cubs, the foreman called our attention to the fact that the herd had drifted up the creek nearly opposite the wagon. During the encounter with the bears he was the most excited one in the outfit, and was the man who cut my rope with his random shooting from horseback. But now the herd recovered his attention, and he dispatched some of us to ride around the cattle. When we met at the wagon for dinner, the excitement was still on us, and the hunt was unanimously voted the most exciting bit of sport and powder burning we had experienced on our trip.

■ JOHN R. BARROWS

In 1880, John R. Barrows came from Wisconsin by railroad to the Judith Gap to live on his father's homestead. The family settled in a rough cowtown called Ubet (now Garneil), located at the foot of the Snowy Mountains. "Yarns" and "Circular Story" are from Barrows' reminiscences, Ubet *(1934), a classic collection of memories and stories from Montana's stockraising frontier.*

Yarns

Fort Maginnis, less than three miles from the DHS ranch was the local metropolis, and the post-trader's store was our base of supplies. But the thriving mining camp of Maiden, seven miles away over the crest of the Judith Mountains was more popular. There was less restraint, a freedom from military red tape, and always a possibility that something might happen. Thither we trooped in the lazy weeks between round-ups, thence we returned and it often happened upon our return that I, being sober and the others not so much so, carried the artillery equipment of the entire detachment hung over my saddle horn. I had no desire to be eccentric and I had read no tract about the "demon rum," but I had seen his work, and my experiences in the "deadfall" at the forks of the Musselshell had convinced me that whiskey was good stuff to leave alone.

The fall and beef round-ups were devoid of special interest although such work can hardly be described as humdrum. I did not accompany the outfit on the beef drive as it was no part of my plan to make another trip east. Upon my return to Ubet I took up the duties of the winter, multifarious, but not exacting. I had a few colts to break, I performed most of the duties of the postmaster, and our post office was rather important, being at the junction of the lines from White Sulphur Springs to Fort Maginnis and from Billings to Fort Benton. The Billings-Benton line handled considerable traffic and was equipped with four-horse Concord coaches and very decent stock. Many of the drivers were old timers who had seen better days before the railroad era and voiced their humiliation at driving four horses instead of six, unaware that in a few years some of them would be driving a team to a spring wagon, for the stagecoach days were passing.

At this time I had a local reputation as an idler, due to the fact that I spent much time in reading, but I had the general management of our little herd of cattle, forty or fifty head, and upon occasions had to look after our small band of horses. In addition I was the handy man of the local blacksmith, and did my share of extra work in the store and saloon.

Ubet is situated in a stormy section. The Judith Gap is a draughty place, and quite often after a blizzard coming in from the north had blown itself out, we would experience what was known locally as a Gap wind blowing back from the south, and quite as disagreeable as the blizzard. But Montana winter is made tolerable by periods of calm weather with moderate or warm temperatures and bright skies. At such times we saw to it that everything was prepared for the coming of the next storm. In the coldest weather our outside activities were reduced to a minimum, and we limited our operations to the necessary chores. At such times we had long hours around a glowing stove and told and retold our adventures and misadventures.

One evening our chatter seemed to run to humiliations, and almost every member of our group had some incident to relate in which he had played an inglorious part. It was a time for confessions. Bill Newton, who happened to be storm-bound with us, told a story which I believe he had never told before.

"While we are exchanging confessions," he began, "I'll tell you about the hardest fall I ever got. Three years ago I was coming down from Fort Benton and I stayed over night at old Colonel Viall's place on Wolf Creek. Next morning I saddled up and started out for Ubet.

"The weather was just what the doctor ordered, the sun was just warm enough, the old grass had been burnt off the year before and the new growth made the country so green that Ireland would look plumb yellow beside it. Everything was just exactly right. I had a good breakfast inside of me, I had a good horse, and I couldn't find fault with my outfit. There was no wind, just a little breeze, not a cloud in the sky and the mountains all around were perfectly satisfactory; the Snowies, the Judiths, and the Moccasins looked like scenery that had been painted to order. Actually I began to feel silly, like those fellows who write poetry.

"When I rode out of the Sage Creek valley onto the bench, I saw that there was something ahead of me and I let my horse have his head to catch up. Pretty soon I was alongside of the darndest looking outfit that I ever saw. It was a sheep herder on a little whittle-dy-dig of a long-tail pony. Now you know my opinion of sheep herders. When a man gets so worthless that he can't fish floaters out of a swill barrel, he goes to herding sheep. Well, this fellow was a sheep herder, I could tell by the smell. The whole outfit was like a bad dream. He was kind of undersized, with a harmless face; his hair was long, and he wore a Buffalo Bill mustache and goatee. He had on one of those English hunting caps with a peak in front and behind (they are all right if a man doesn't know whether he is coming or going), and it had kind of gores in the sides, so that it could be laced up or let out, so that it would fit your head next morning.

"He had a decent old saddle, but his stirrups weren't mates and he wore shoes, the kind that have elastic on the sides, and his pants had worked up and his socks down. The whole outfit was a crime, but the queerest thing, according to my notion, was the way the man was built. He was kind of spindling, but he had a bay window that filled the saddle from cantle to horn. Do you know, I kind of enjoyed riding alongside of this freak? I would take one look at him and then I would kind of stand off at one side and look at myself.

"Of course we were talking as we rode along together, and my curiosity kept growing; no matter what I was talking about, I kept thinking of his circumference and trying to calculate his diameter at the equator. Now I despise sheep herders, but I didn't want to be too rough with this fellow, so I said, 'What tree is that saddle you're riding?' He said, 'It's a long Frieseke.' I knew that but I asked him how long it was. He says, 'It's an eighteen-inch seat.' 'You fill it pretty well,' says I. He agreed with me and I went on, 'You must have punished lots of good grub in your time.' He put one hand on his Tropic of Capricorn and looked at me kind of sad and said, 'This is the result of accident.' 'Accident?' said I, 'blowed up, maybe?' This seemed so darned good to me that I said it again, 'I guess you was blowed up?' 'No,' said he, 'it wasn't an explosion; it was accidental substitution.' Well, of course I kept on worming around until he told me about it.

"He said that when he was a kid he had taken a job in a sawmill where they worked him almost to death and he didn't get any decent grub. Finally he quit and went home to his folks, and the first meal he ate there tasted so good and he was so hungry that he stuffed himself with good things and then went to bed. After a while he waked up with a horrible bellyache; and while he was telling me how he suffered, the old reprobate took out a red cotton handkerchief and wiped his eyes and went on. 'The pain was perfectly intolerable, and finally I got up and went to the medicine closet. I knew just exactly where we kept that bottle of "Perry Davis's Pain Killer," and I found it in the dark and I rubbed myself for about an hour.' 'Didn't it blister you?' said I. 'No,' he said, 'I wish it had. It wasn't "Pain Killer" at all. We had a skinny hired girl working for us that summer and I had got hold of her bottle of "Bustline Guaranteed Permanent." '

"I just took one look at him and then I touched my old horse with the spur, just ahead of the cinch, and said, 'Well, I guess I must be going,' and I rode through to the Gap without stopping."

The Circular Story

One winter night a chinook was blowing and the soft snow was filling the air to the height of twenty feet. The building was trembling and creaking under the varying stresses, and the entire male population was gathered in the saloon. A quiet game of draw poker was in progress but was not so exciting that the players could not listen to the story which a visiting sheepherder had to tell. We had been discussing the old stories about creasing wild horses. Then we had various stories of the pursuit of wild horses by men afoot. The question was academic, for at that time, horses were cheap and wild horses almost nonexistent.

Our sheep herder obtained the floor: "Well, gentlemen, four years ago I was working for Ralph Berry on the Musselshell, and there was a 'shave-tail' come along buying wethers. Berry had about six hundred that this feller wanted, but he didn't want 'em if he couldn't throw 'em in with another bunch he had bought over by Black Butte, so they wanted me to take a letter down to Flat Willow and meet the Black Butte outfit, so that the two bunches could be throwed together at the Musselshell crossing, but they didn't tell me all of this, but just gave me a horse and told me to deliver the letter.

"Well, gentlemen, I started out early in the morning and was getting along all right until I was about ten miles behind the Lavina road. And then wha' d' you know? The letter was gone! Well, gentlemen, it was a still day so the letter wouldn't blow around, so I took the back trail. I had to go slow, of course, but finally I found it, but I lost a lot of time, so I had to sleep out that night. Just after sundown I stopped at a little creek where there was some big cottonwoods, so I unsaddled and watered my horse and picketed him to a sagebrush and then sat down to eat the lunch Mrs. Berry had give me. While I was a setting and eating my sandwiches, I looked up in the tree and I saw a dead Injun. He was up there on a big limb, all wrapped up in his buffalo robes and tied on good and plenty, and about the time I got through eating I began to wonder if I couldn't get him down somehow. Some people think that's just like robbing a grave, but it doesn't seem so to me; he couldn't stay up there forever. Some day he'd fall off his perch, and I can't see what difference it makes whether it's sooner or later. The scientific ducks are digging 'em up all the time in Egypt, and nobody makes a fuss, so I got hold of a branch that hung down and took a run at it and then let go and sure enough the old boy flopped off and turned over two or three times and hit the ground.

"Well, gentlemen, I was kind of sorry I'd done it. There he was, the old robes busted open clear up to his neck. They was thin and brittle like paper, and of course nobody could ever get him back again. There wasn't much left of him except bones. He had about ten feet of heavy brass wire wrapped around each wrist for bracelets, and there was a dipper made from the horn of a mountain sheep, and a spoon of buffalo horn, and a thing-um-a-jig that they carry live coals in, and some red and yellow paint, just what they generally put in so a feller can start housekeeping.

"Then I found a little bundle, and when I opened it up wha' d' you know? It was a Bible! That floored me. I couldn't see what in hell a Bible was doing in a place like that. When I tried to open it up it kinda stuck together and then crumbled so there wasn't a chance of saving it, but when the cover come off I saw some writing and wha' d' you know? It was, 'To Willy, with Mother's love.' That made me feel kind of funny, for my name is Bill and mother always called me Willy.

"Well, gentlemen, I took a stick and opened up his upper end and I never got such a start in my life. His hair was yellow and curly and he had whiskers! He was a squaw man, sure enough, and that explained the Bible. And gentlemen, wha' d' you know, as soon as I found he was a white man I wanted to bury him, but of course there was no chance. And when I lay down on my saddle blanket I couldn't go to sleep. I just lay there thinking about that feller and how he had turned Injun and had held onto his Bible. And I tried to imagine his funeral when he cashed in and his squaw had packed the Bible in with him for his 'medicine.'

"Along about midnight my horse whinnied and I started straight up. You know how a horse whinnies when you come back from a trip and turn him out in his home pasture, and we were out and all alone, twenty miles from anybody, and then he took a run, broke loose, and away he went.

"I had plenty of time between then and daybreak to make up my mind what to do, and I just said to myself, 'I'm no quitter, I'll walk that horse down if I put in the rest of my life. I'm going to camp on his trail.' And as soon as it was daylight I took my rifle and started out. The trail followed the east side of the creek; we were going north up towards the Snowies. After about three miles the trail turned sharp to the right over some high hills where the grass was dry, but I had no trouble in following it, because he was dragging his rope.

"Every time I would raise a ridge, I expected to see him, for the signs were fresh, but there was nothing in sight, not even game. Everything I saw was out of range and I was getting hungry. We must have covered fifteen miles or so on an easterly course, and I was about ready to leave the trail to do some hunting when I shot a jack rabbit. He was tough and stringy, but them was the qualities I had to have in my business. And when I got through with him, there wasn't enough to bait a trap.

"Come dusk, I lay down under some willows in a little draw and went bang to sleep as soon as I hit the ground. I was dead tired. But some time in the middle of the night, I heard that horse whinny again, and right close to, and it worried me. But I got to sleep again and the sun was shining when I waked up. The trail was leading south now, towards the Musselshell, and followed down a little creek. I thought I ought to get a shot at a whitetail, for I was nearly starved, but no such luck. Then we left the creek when we was within three miles of the river and started west over some awfully rough country. After about ten or twelve miles of that kind of work I was about played out, but I gritted my teeth and said, 'I'm no quitter.' I didn't see how that horse was going to last forever, and after a while I killed an old sage-hen. And when I had cooked and eaten her, all except the feet, I felt she had the same qualities as the jack rabbit.

"Late in the afternoon the trail turned northerly along the creek, and I followed it until dark, stopping to rest once in a while, for I was getting leg weary. And I just fell down and went to sleep. I was sure camping on the trail. About midnight I waked up to hear that horse whinny again, and as soon as it was daylight I took my rifle and started out."

At this point a growing suspicion had taken definite form in my mind. Could it be possible that the guileless shepherd was trying to put over a circular story? I glanced at Billy Coates. He responded by lifting a significant eyebrow. The narrator was continuing—

"Every time I would raise a ridge, I expected to see him, for the signs were fresh, but there was nothing in sight, not even game. Everything I saw was out of range and I was getting hungry. We must have covered fifteen miles or so on an easterly course and I was about ready to leave the trail to do some hunting when I shot a jack rabbit. He was tough and stringy, but them was the qualities I had to have in my business. And when I got through with him there wasn't enough left to bait a trap.

"Come dusk, I lay down under some willows in a little draw and went bang to sleep as soon as I hit the ground. I was dead tired. But some time in the middle of the night, I heard a horse whinny again, and right close to, and it worried me. But I got to sleep again and the sun was shining when I waked up. The trail was leading south now, towards the Musselshell."

My suspicions were entirely confirmed. I looked around to see an interchange of knowing glances and winks. We were all wise except a silent man who was sitting near the cue rack; he had come in after supper on the belated Benton coach. He manifested a growing interest in the story, for the sheepherder's attention was concentrated upon him as the only possible victim of his hoax.

"Then we left the creek when we was within three miles of the river and started west over some awfully rough country. After about ten or twelve miles of that kind of work, I was about played out, but I gritted my teeth and said, 'I'm no quitter.' I didn't see how that horse was going to last forever, and after a while I killed an old sage-hen. And when I had cooked and eaten her, all except the feet, I felt she had the same qualities as the jack rabbit.

"Late in the afternoon the trail turned northerly . . ." And on and on around and around the circle the story continued. At last the silent man brought out from an inside pocket a paper tablet and lead pencil and interrupted the story by saying in a harsh monotone, "I am deaf, will you please write it?"

The storyteller turned a despairing eye towards those of us who had escaped his snare and said, with a gesture of frustration, "Oh, what's the use!"

■ ART H. WATSON

Art H. Watson lived on his family's homestead ranch in Montana's Big Belt Mountain country just after the turn of the century. He worked as a cattle rancher and was elected to the Montana legislature as a representative from Meagher County. "Stuttering Shorty 'Freighter'" and "Shooting Fish" are from Watson's reminiscences, Devil Man with a Gun *(1967).*

Stuttering Shorty "Freighter"

After the gold discoveries of Virginia City, Bannack, Last Chance, Diamond City and others, many who had not made their stake in gold were turning their thoughts to cattle, sheep and ranching. Thus they had to spread over the valleys of the vast domain known as Montana Territory. One of the main passes over the mountains to the east was through Diamond City, Benton Gulch–later Watson post office–and on to the Smith River Valley, Judith Basin, site of Charley Russell's original painting "The Last of Five Thousand," and so on to the Dakotas. Ox teams and freight outfits lined the trails and the wheel prints still are very plain across my ranch.

One freighter, only known to anyone, as far as I ever heard, as "Stuttering Shorty," had a terrific handicap of stuttering, but was a master freighter. He drove an eight horse or mule "jerkline" outfit. Where the trail crossed the Big Belt Mountains two miles above Watson post office the road was very narrow and in winter when snow drifted in, very few negotiated that hill without mishap, especially if they weren't familiar with the methods employed in order to keep the wagons from rolling down the mountain.

Shorty always had eight to ten horses or mules and a trail wagon. Being the master of handling his outfit that he was, it was seldom, indeed, that he needed any assistance. One day, however, he came walking down to Watson and some how told Dad that he had piled up his outfit. Dad took a four-horse team, that he kept for just that purpose, and went up to help Shorty out. When they got up to the bottom of the canyon, they found his outfit, both wagons, horses, mules, all piled up. The first thing Dad noticed was that Shorty did not have a roughlock on either wagon.

A roughlock is a log chain fastened securely around the front axle of the wagon and stretched back to the hind wheel on the lower side of the road. The chain is then wrapped around the wheel and fastened so that as the wagon goes forward, the chain comes tight directly under the wheel. The wheel thus does not turn, but slides along riding on the chain. This automatically shoves the wagon up the hill counteracting its natural tendency to slide down. This was the only way a heavily loaded wagon could stay right side up in coming down the mountain and Shorty knew this as well as any man, but there wasn't a roughlock on either wagon. Dad said, "Shorty, you damn fool, why didn't you roughlock?"

Shorty said, "I-I-I-I s-s-s-s-st-t-t-t-started t-t-t-t-to s-s-s-say w-w-w-hoaw-w-w-when I-I-I-I g-g-g-got t-t-t-to t-t-t-the t-t-t-top o-o-o-of t-t-t-the h-h-h-hill b-b-b-b-but I-I-I-I c-c-c-ouldn't g-g-g-get m-m-my d-d-d-d-damn m-m-m-mouth off."

Thus, Shorty was unable to say "whoa" to his team, and had he done so, they would have stopped suddenly so he could have put his roughlock on, but instead he stuttered clear over the hill and piled the outfit, after rolling many times over, clear into the bottom of the canyon. A jerkline outfit was handled almost exclusively by command of the driver, but when excited, Shorty had no audible command at his disposal and the team went on to a mess that took several days to straighten out, and some of which could not be salvaged.

Shooting Fish

The little mountain streams were teeming with native trout, little speckled beauties, that have no equal in sport of catching, or in taste, once caught and fried over a campfire. My brothers and I used to prey upon these unsuspecting creatures of nature at every opportunity and we made the opportunities numerous. Many times they weren't in the mood to bite on our selection of bait or hooks, but that didn't stop our operation.

We all carried heavy black powder shooting rifles and as most of the streams were shallow, we would shoot just under the fish as they reposed in the bottom of the holes. The concussion from the explosion would break their bladder and they would turn over belly-up and float to the surface, whence we picked them up and put them in our pockets or sack, if we had one, or strung them on a willow.

We couldn't reach them if the hole was deep and as we shot, they merely scampered around until the commotion subsided and then went on living their normal life. We never stopped shooting even if we knew the holes were too deep. Each time we came back, we tried again, hoping against hope that we could reach them. We re-loaded our own ammunition and while we were generally somewhat limited, the community sounded like a front line battle most of the time.

Dad bought lead by the ten-pound bar, powder by the keg and caps a gross-box at a time. We had equipment that punched the old cap out of the cartridge, measures that told us how much powder to put in and we melted the bar lead and poured it into bullet molds. We had a crimping device that pressed in a new cap, pushed the bullet in place and crimped the shell, thus we were ready for another prey, whether it might be grouse, predatory animal or fish.

One day as we were trying our luck at shooting fish, a German sheepherder was herding one of our bands of sheep nearby, heard the bombardment and came to investigate. We showed him some of the holes that were too deep for us and he said, "Ach, dot isn't de vay to choot vish. I show you." He, too, was carrying an old black powder rifle. He walked up to the hole, pulled the hammer back, poked the muzzle of the gun down in the water and pulled the trigger. We had been warned never to try any such monkey business, but to our dismay, every fish in the hole turned belly-up and came to the surface.

"Come down here, Dutch," we all chirped, "we know of a better hole." We took him to a hole that was so deep that we never had been able to stir up the mud in the bottom. There were lots of fish that we could see in there. Dutch was so elated over his accomplishment and his display of a superior knowledge that he poked the gun down in the water almost to the breech.

By this time we were starting to give him room for any expansion that he might need. We were convinced that this would be a sight worth seeing, but we preferred to view it from a distance–whatever distance time would permit from the time Dutch started poking the gun in the water until he pulled the trigger. "Boom" went the gun. All of the fish in the water, as well as the water, seemed to leap skyward. But whatever height they went, Dutch and the willows around the hole, went much higher. Dutch had a full beard and peering out through it, with mud and water all mixed up in his whiskers, were his frightened eyes that shone like the lights of a Cadillac on a dark night.

We rushed back to where he was to pick up the pieces, if need be, and see what had happened to the fish. To us Dutch was expendable, but the speckled beauties, that was something else. We wanted to see what had happened to them. Sure enough, when the muddy water cleared enough to see, most of the fish were bottom side up and coming to the surface.

Dutch had blown about ten inches off the gun barrel and was shaking like a leaf, but no bodily injury. Fortunately, the breech of the gun had held tight, forcing all the might of the explosion down to the muzzle of the gun and out into the creek. Dutch took what was left of his rifle and headed for his band of sheep. We picked up the fish and headed for home.

■ CON PRICE

Con Price was born in Iowa in 1869. As a boy of ten, he moved to the Black Hills with his parents, and by 1886 he had become a Montana cowboy. He married Claudia Toole of Shelby and ranched in the Sweet Grass Hills until 1910. Price moved to western Montana and then even farther west to Pasadena, California, where he recorded his Montana experiences in Memories of Old Montana *(1945). "My Marriage" is from that reminiscence.*

My Marriage

In the days that I write of there were very few women folks in the country and a less number of girls, but there was one family who had one girl of about seventeen years and I thought she was very attractive. I worked about twenty miles from where she lived and used to go to see her quite often, but she had two brothers about eight and ten years old and they were wild as Indians and their main sport and pastime was riding wild calves and yearlings. The girl was about as wild as them and usually joined in those bucking contests, so when I went courting her she wanted me to join in on the fun. As my everyday work was riding and handling cattle, this kind of sport didn't interest me. I was serious and wanted to make love, so those boys were a great worry to me, as when I wanted to court the girl the boys wanted to ride calves. One time when I was particularly interested in talking to the girl they wanted me to go out to the corral and ride calves, and of course I wouldn't go, so one of them suggested I act as a horse and he would ride me. To get rid of him I consented. He was to get up on my shoulders, put his legs around my neck and hold on to my shirt collar with his hands. Then I was to start bucking, which I did. When I got to bucking my best I bent over forward and threw him off pretty hard and hurt him some. He got up crying and the girl was laughing at him for being bucked off. He said, "Well, I would have rode the S.B. if he hadn't throwed his head down." Anyway, I got rid of him for that day and had a chance to court the girl.

As most any story is not complete without some love and courtship in it, I am going to write my experience in that matter.

I was married to Claudia Toole in the year 1899. She was a daughter of Bruce Toole, who was a brother to Joseph K. Toole, Governor of Montana at that time. Now Bruce Toole was a very fine aristocratic Southern gentleman and knowing that a cowboy didn't usually climb very high on the ladder of culture he didn't think I was very desirable company for his daughter. So, we had to carry on our courtship secretly from the old gent, and as about the only amusement of those days was country dancing and as we all went to them on horseback (which usually was 15 or 20 miles) we would ride to a dance. As I could not go to my girl's home to get her, we would designate a certain rock or creek out on the range to meet at and would go from there to the dance. That is where I would leave her the next morning after the dance. Her father thought she went to those parties with her brother, who was in on our secret, so in all our courtship it was unknown to him and it was the shock of his life when we slipped away and got married. . . .

When we got married we had to steal away like we did when we were courting. I borrowed a team and spring wagon and we had to drive forty miles and the snow was about belly deep on the horses. Then we had to wait over in Shelby until the next day to go to Great Falls. The job of getting her away from the ranch was the hard part of it. My wife's room was upstairs in her home and we agreed that she would throw her stuff out the window about eight o'clock at night and I would pick it up and carry it to the wagon I had parked about 100 yards from the house. I didn't have any idea how much stuff she had until she began throwing it out—clothes, suitcases, shoes and everything else that a woman ever wore, and besides, she used to play the piano and she had great bales of sheet music and every time one of those bales of music hit that frozen ground it sounded like someone had shot a high powered rifle and the stuff fell right in front of a window down stairs and the window curtains were up. Her father sat reading about ten feet from where I was picking it up. I would take all I could carry on my back to the wagon and come back for another load, and as she was still throwing stuff out while I was gone there would be a bigger pile than ever when I got back. I believe she would have thrown the piano out too if the window had been big enough, and the worst part of it was her father had two bloodhounds and they bellowed and howled every time she threw out a fresh cargo. It was a very cold night and I wore a big fur overcoat and every time I bent over to pick up a package they would howl louder than ever. They thought I was some kind of animal. I tried whispering to them to get out and keep still and that would bring a bigger howl than ever. I was watching her father pretty close through the window and every once in a while he would cock his head sideways to listen and acted like he was going to get up and come out, then would settle down and go to reading again. During those intervals, my heart was sure pounding and I was all sweaty with fear. I have often heard of people being very nervous when they placed the bride's ring on her finger, but I know that is nothing compared to the ordeal I went through. I forgot, and left a lot of things around where I loaded the wagon and it snowed a lot after that. Every time my wife missed something of hers, we would go to that spot and shovel snow.

Neither one of us had any idea of what it took to set up housekeeping and it is amazing what we bought. One thing we both agreed on was a carpet, as we intended to move into an old cabin that had big cracks in the floor. When we got home and checked our outfit, it seemed to be mostly carpet. Then I think every friend we ever had gave us a lamp for a wedding present, so we had a whole wagonload of carpets and lamps. We had hanging lamps, floor lamps and lamps to throw away, but hardly anything else in the way of housekeeping. When we arrived back in Shelby there were about 25 cowboys in town that had come to celebrate Christmas (it being Christmas week we were married) and they were all at the train to meet us. Most of them had a good sized Xmas jag on and the different congratulations I got from that bunch would sure sound funny today if I could remember them all. They were all old time cowboys that I had worked with for years. We all went to a saloon to celebrate the event. Each one would take me aside to pour out his feelings and congratulations, and give me hell for stealing away to get married without telling them. Some of the names they called me wouldn't look good in print but that was their way of showing their true friendship. One old bowlegged fellow that I had known from the time I was a kid had a little more joy juice aboard than the others. He didn't have much to say, but stood at the end of the bar and drank regularly while the celebration was going on. He had one cock eye and kept watching me all the time until he got an opportunity to attract my attention. He nodded to me to come over to where he was. I went over to him and he looked at me silently for a moment and said, "Well, you're married, are you?" I said yes, and he asked, "Did you marry a white woman?" I answered yes, and he said "You done damn well, but I feel sorry for the girl." In the meantime, while we were away getting married, my wife's father wrote her a letter to Shelby where we had our team and wagon and told her all was forgiven and to come home, which we did.

I went to work for him and as he owned plenty of cattle and horses I seemed to be just the kind of a son-in-law he needed, but we sure had a supply of carpet and lamps that we didn't know what to do with.

L. A. HUFFMAN

Laton Alton Huffman, one of Montana's pioneer photographers, was born in Iowa in 1854, the son of a farmer and photographer. Huffman apprenticed with Northern Pacific Railroad photographer F. Jay Haynes in Moorhead, Minnesota, before coming west in 1878 to be post photographer at Fort Keogh near Miles City. He was elected county commissioner and state representative from Custer County, owned photographic studios in Miles City and Billings, and ranched on the Rosebud. Huffman died in Billings in 1931. "Last Busting at Bow-Gun," which appeared in Scribner's Magazine *in 1907, describes the end of the stockman's frontier.*

Last Busting at Bow-Gun

A hundred and six in the shade of the cook's tent-fly at the Hat X Camp on the Big Dry. It was a mid-August afternoon near the end of the general roundup. The sand flats and dunes of the Lower Dry were radiating heat like griddles. Not a breath of air, not a suggestion of a breeze. Yet in some mysterious way little dust- and sand-laden whirlwinds were born, sprang up and chased each other sportively, and sometimes savagely, noisily, across the bars and up the dunes to die in the sage or fringe of cottonwoods.

The cook was flinging out a kettle of stewed raisins, which, he explained—to no one in particular—"would assay eighty per cent grit, since once of them damn whirligigs got tangled up with his pie preparations."

The great herd had watered and lain down by thousands upon the narrow strip of cool, moist sand that bordered the half-mile-long pool—a tempting pool, with smooth sand and silt floor. Yes, but the first splash of a swimmer might start that entire herd rolling their tails for the hills, the pine ridges of Woody, twenty miles back, from whence the Circle, at much pains and expense of good horseflesh, that morning had brought them. No one there needed cautioning, but a veteran puncher remarked: "Big difference in cattle. They are sure always wolfy that range the pine ridges. Nev'r could savvy why they should be so much wilder than prairie rangers, but they never do stand for no herdin' afoot, or swimming parties."

So we did not swim. We did the next best thing—lay in the shade swapping hunks of cow and horse wisdom; rode broncs, headed stampedes, "fit" prairie fires, killed whole dens of rattlesnakes, burned incense, watched, from the thickly bedded herd, the overthirsty ones rise stretchingly and plod in straggling lines to the water, drink deep, plod back again, *always* to *their* particular family group to lie down again; changing sides, too, of course, same as you or I going back to bed.

To the west on the wide bench, columns of dust and smoke told of the cut of cows and calves and the branding fire where Webb, Charley and Smoky would soon be in a *real* roping contest, bringing quite a hundred and fifty calves for the boys at that fire to wrestle within the space of an hour and a half. Across the flat to the north, which was the roundup ground this morning, the Cross Anchor boys were pushing the biggest throw-back of the year. From the bedwagon I took a shot at the drag end of it as it passed; and you would not believe me, nor would the assessor, if I let you in on my estimate of how many horned creatures there were in that more than a milelong line of drift, bound Redwater way.

Also from my perch on the bedwagon, 'twixt yarns and snapshots and burnings of incense, I saw far down the flat a string with a bed-horse in the lead, making our way through the dust-laden, shimmering heat.

The "Rep" that belonged to that string proved to be Sandy B of the Bow-Gun, who presently bunched the string ropes and unloaded the bed-horse and unsaddled his sweating, blowing mount.

"Me?" said Sandy, after he had drunk his fill from the keg beside the wagon and squatted among us, munching from a hunk of bread in one hand and a hunk of cold beef in the other, "ME? Why, I've been moonshinin' the breaks below Hell and Crooked Creek, with a bunch of breeds from Poplar River way for ten days. Mess-wagon looks good to me. Hot? Say cattle boys, these sand-flats is cool to them . . . Me?"—to no one in particular—"if I had time and a string of my own, I sure would go moonshinin' the breaks for horses. There's a wild maverick bunch in there that would give two honest, capable punchers a start in life. This cowpunchin' is gettin' to be a *sorry trade*. These breeds I reps with tells me it's no josh that them Neidrings that owned the N–N and have driven in more Oregon broncs and trailed more cattle than anybody are *sure* starting a hog ranch. Yessir, a *hog* ranch, wooshers, rooters, thousands of 'em. They are building her right now somewheres on the Missouri not far from Prairie Elk. Hain't goin' to be no room on this earth for 'ery *real* cow-hand a few years more. He goes to the tremblin' room *final* for his check–with 'er *hog* in the corner. This throwback settles it with old Bow-Gun, I guess. I am on my way to the ranch now to help gather the horses. We are short of saddle stock–going to break a bunch before the beef-gather begins. Better come out and see a touch of high life"–this with a nod in my direction–"and bring along your snappin' machine."

The fiery orb touched the tops of the cottonwoods. They began to push our herd from its bed-ground on the bar. The squad from the branding fire galloped campward. The horses were bunched behind the ropes.

The roundup was to split the long drive to Hungry Creek, where they would make the roundup next day, by an evening move to a dry camp high in the divide back of Sand Arroya. Next morning when I awoke Sandy was just cutting his string from the Hat X bunch, and with his bobbing bed-horse in the lead was soon a speck against the first slanting beams of the sunrise.

But I did not forget Sandy's tip to be in on the "busting"; so it fell out that one raw windy September evening I pulled up at the Bow-Gun, one of the old-time cow camps of the north country, built nearly twenty-five years back, and now sadly fallen to dilapidation and decay.

I had come twenty miles to see "broncs busted" by new methods; and I thought, as I unhitched, of the Bow-Gun boys of a far time, and harked back to the days when the environs of Milestown–aye, its main thoroughfare withal–was the daily chosen arena for the busters of those times, when a hand rode out his string whenever or wherever it was dealt to him, and was of the sort that resented the appellation, "Horse Fighter" or "Buster." He was born to the saddle and lariat, as farmer lads are born to the milking pens and the furrows.

Foreman Bob bade me welcome. He and his crew were enjoying a rest between the general and the beef roundup, and lending a hand with the broncs. The old place seemed deserted until the cook, a tall, bony, four-eyed rooster, let out a yell that searched the crannies of the old place and echoed back from the buttes, "It's a-l-l right with m-e-e!" The cry brought foregathering from the one-time "buckaroo" house and sundry tepees pitched beside the dry washout, the hungry crew of the Bow-Gun, fifteen strong, to file by the lay-out box, where each man supplied himself with an outfit–plate, cup, knife and fork–and straightaway to load the same with ribs of young beef, pot-roasted, hot biscuits, stewed corn, and the ever-present "Blue Hen" tomatoes, and to top it, a portion from the Dutch oven, of pudding with raisins galore, and sauce too à la vanilla magoo, and strong black coffee, of course.

While we supped I looked about me to see if I could pick out the bronco rider, whose fame had been long familiar to the countryside. "Weak head and strong back for a horse fighter" is an old and common saying; and likewise it had not infrequently chanced in old days that gentleman could, with certainty, almost unerringly at any time or place, be spotted by his swagger, his display of artillery, his unfailing weakness for wearing heavy bearskin or llama leggings, even in the hottest weather, and his spurs.

But times have changed. There's little doing in bearskin chaps. Fewer men are drawing fifty a month, making up in hat rim what they lack in skill and brains. And here was the old Bow-Gun almost at the end of it, soon to become a third-rate sheep camp.

As Foreman Bob and I supped elbow to elbow in the firelight, listening to the chaff of the crew, I asked him which was Lee Warren, who was to begin on the following morning to ride the wild Bow-Gun horses at the rate of six or eight a day. Pointed out, he proved to be about the least conspicuous, least loquacious man of the bunch. Short to stubbiness and dressed like a farm hand, declining the proffered weed with thanks, saying he'd never learned to smoke. . . .

He'd have six, not more, raw onion-eyed four- and five-year-olds, for his morning's work–when Lem was ready–and six horses, mind you, that had never smelled oats or felt weight of rawhide since they had had that Bow-Gun brand burned on their shoulders, some terrible day of their colthood.

While we waited for the horses, Warren took stock of his outfit. Just a plain, ordinary, single-rigged cow saddle, bridle and lariat, spurs, quirt and some short pieces of grass rope for the cross-hobbling. Presently the voice, its owner elbow-deep in his bread-pan, announced, "Hy-ar they come a f-o-g-g-i-n'."

Swiftly across the wide flat, flanked by half a dozen well-mounted riders, the little band swings in a wide circle, leaving adrift behind it a long ribbon of dust. The big gate is flung open, and the day's work is corralled. An inner gate swings, another swift rush and the six beautiful beasts are bunched, snorting and trembling, in the round corral, the one with the snubbing-post in the center, where legions of wild, carefree, young horses before them have bitten the dust, bidding sudden and painful farewell to the glad, work-free life of the prairie.

Warren, as he looks them over with critical eye, uncoils the rawhide, adjusts hondo and loop. At his first step of approach they break away. Round and round they circle, in vain effort to dodge that flying noose, which, at the second cast, falls true, and the bright bay leader of the bunch, Oscar Wilde (a name that Warren flung to him with the first throw that he so neatly dodged, and Oscar he will be to the end of his days in the Bow-Gun saddle bunch) is in the toils, leaping, bucking, striking savagely at the thing that grips him by the throat, now held taut by Lee and his two helpers, who, when his first desperate lunges are past, take a turn of the rope around the snubbing-post set deep in the earth.

"Easy, easy now! Snub him too sudden and he kinks her or breaks her [his neck]. Steady now!" He is facing the post, feet braced and wide apart, straining at the rope until in his final, blind struggle for breath, he throws himself. Quick as a flash, Warren has his knee on Oscar's neck, grips him by the underjaw, tilts his head so that his nose points skyward. Instantly the turn is thrown from the post. The noose slackens, is slipped off, passed bridle-wise over his ears and, by a dextrous and simple turn, made fast curbwise to his underjaw.

For a full half-minute Oscar has found that dust-laden air so good that he has relaxed, forgotten to fight. Deftly and quickly Warren hobbles his feet together and slips on the bridle. Oscar bounds to his feet, but quickly finds that his struggles to free himself only result in a succession of falls that cause him to hesitate, until, in some mysterious way, he finds his near hind foot, too, caught in a noose and made fast to his near front one. He's cross-hobbled now and ready for the saddle.

Here the skill and patience of the bronc rider are put to a severe test. He must hold his horse by the reins and rope, lay the saddle blanket, then with a one-hand swing place the forty-pound saddle where it belongs. Dazed, cross-hobbled as he is, the horse resents the blanket to the twentieth time, often, and may frustrate as many attempts to reach with the latigo strap that swinging cinch ring, and often he will slip from under the saddle a good many times before it is caught and the first hard pull cinches the saddle firmly in place.

Oscar has been in the toils for fifteen minutes – no doubt it's seemed longer to him. His hobbles are now being removed – often quite as exciting a task as putting them on. They are off, those hobbles, but Oscar does not know it. His attention is distracted by a pain in his ear. Lee has it twisted firmly, gripped in his strong left hand. Strange, but true, nine times out of ten, the wildest outlaw will stand motionless for a minute or more if you get just the right twist on his ear.

Cautiously, tensely, without the shadow of hesitation, Warren lightly swings to his seat. The critical moment has come. For five breathless seconds after that ear is released Oscar stands frozen, wide-eyed, nostrils distended, muscles strained until under the rear of that saddle-skirt there's room for your hat 'twixt it and his back.

In response to the first pull at the rein, by one or two quick, short, nervous steps he discovers that his legs are once more unshackled. Up he goes in a long, curving leap like a buck. Down goes his head, and he blats that indescribable bawl that only thoroughly maddened, terrified broncos can fetch, something uncanny, something between a scream and a groan, that rasps the nerves and starts the chill, hunted feeling working your spine.

The Voice, drawing water at the well, sends a hail: "N-o-w he t-a-k-e-s her. S-t-a-y with him, Lee. S-t-a-y with him," as round and round he leaps, reined hard, now right, now left, by his rider. Again and again he goes high, with hind feet drawn under, as if reaching for the stirrups. Forelegs thrust forward, stiff as crowbars, driving hoof prints in the packed earth, like mauls, as he lands; yet light and tight, seeming never to catch the brunt of the jolt, sits his rider.

Now the little horse begins to sulk, backs suddenly, and rears high, as if to throw himself backward. If he should succeed, should rid himself in that way, of his rider, he would surely try it again. His first lesson might end in failure, and he'd have a good start toward becoming Oscar, the outlaw.

But Lee has also another card looped to his wrist, one that he is loath to use, that stinging rawhide quirt, which now descends, fore and aft, round his ears, and raising welts on his quivering flanks at each stroke. Oscar is quickly distracted from rearing and backing. Again he sulks, refuses to respond to word, rein or quirt.

Now, for the first time it's the steel – the spurs – and the horse chooses doing the circle, the thing of the least punishment. Oscar has been in the corral forty minutes. Sweat runs from belly and nose, and in little rivulets down his legs. Warren swings off gently, then quickly up again, mounting and dismounting rapidly half a dozen times, each time, with his gloved hand, patting the blowing horse on flank, rump, and neck.

Almost in one motion, saddle and bridle are off—flung together at the post. Oscar's first lesson is finished. The gate swings, he dashes through to the outer corral, while Foreman Bob, where we're perched on the fence, says to me: "Old Lee knows when to quit. He's careful; never baked a horse for us yet. Keeps his temper. *That's* where most of us lose out in that game. Feller we had here last summer—good rider, stout as a mule—loses his, and his job. Bakes the first one he tackles. Fights him an hour saddlin', then sifts him outside; throws him the gut-hooks and quirt until the hoss is plumb baked, overhet. Falls dead there a hundred yards from the ranch. Third time's plenty soon to ride 'em outside." . . .

It is eleven o'clock now. Warren, bareheaded, shapeless, sooty as a smith with dust and sweat, is upon "Stripes," his sixth and last horse, when the Voice sings, "B-o-n-e-h-e-a-d-s, take it away," which announces the best meal of the day—roast beef, boiled spuds, fresh bread, cinnamon rolls, and, to trim it, quarters of thick, juicy, blackberry pie.

Always when I sample blackberry pie or snuff the dust of a horse-fight, memory takes me far back on my trail to a distant September day before a yard of wire fence or a horse corral had obtruded between Old Smoky Butte and the Sand-hills, or betwixt the Cannon Ball and Wind River, when horses were dirt cheap and for the most part broken on the trail. Just roped, saddled and rode in the open.

Old Twodot Satchel was our trail boss then, bringing in two big herds of Swinging A cattle. Our camp was among those wonderful red scoria hills on the Big Powder, hills that were full soon to witness the final and big things of the range cattle business.

Old Satchel was scouting the country for shelter and grass and a site for the new ranch, and all hands were "layin' off to turn loose the herds," when this other day of horse-fighting, pie and almost a homicide rolled around.

Old Twodot was a good man to trail with. Never took the best of it, being boss, to shirk night guards on his boys. Come his guard any time between cocktail and breakfast, he would "like to see some blank blank" stand his guard, as he'd lope for the herd prompt as any hand in the outfit. Woe, too, by the same token, to the man he caught overworking the gentle horses in his string, giving the bad ones the go-by cold mornings, hanging back when there was swimming in sight. He was never huntin' shaller crossin's, was old Twodot, but had a well-earned reputation for "chousin" into any river that got in his way.

We all have our failings. Old Twodot had his. Strike him at any time and he had two or three outlaws in his string that he seemed never to ride or to have other use for than to steer unsuspecting strangers against.

"Looks like Old Satchel k'aint have no fun," Andy Williams used to say, "less'n he's sickin' somebody to ride Old Mokey or Zebra, and get k-i-l-l-e-d u-p. It ain't any of my fambly that's takin' risks that way. I shore have knowed fellers, though, to get a gun bent over their nut for less than loanin' such outlaws to parties with a yearn for this glad life."

On the September day referred to, there drifted into that camp of ours a strange, wild specimen of humanity, not only wild-looking, but with that something indescribable in the look of his eye that told of his hunger for this kind.

No puncher need look twice as he approached to learn that the black mare he is ridin' is "Injun" and wild, a stranger to cow camps, unbitted, ridden with something between a one-eared bridle and a hackamore made of untanned skin, that his stirrups are pick-ups that don't mate, that the skirtless seat itself is more like some old castaway, back-number tree that's been hanging on a fence for a year, than a saddle.

That arrival resulted in old Twodot taking a long lay-off and making a trail boss of Andy. It was, to the last day of that worthy's life, worthwhile to hear him regale a bunch of cowhands with the story in somewhat this wise:

"I never did meet up with but one sure-enough hoss-tamer since I works my way, packin' water, into old Rarey's show when I'm a kid, where he's tamin' balky plugs for farmers back in old Misoo' at ten buck a hoss; and that was Stutterin' Bob, that strikes us when we are locatin' the first 'A's' old Satchel brings in on Powder that time. It's this Bob, you see, shoots up old Daniel's dive in Cheyenne that time, and wings one of the Blocker outfit when he's makin' his getaway, headin' north, thinkin' he's a hunted outlaw.

"Keeps goin' from May to July, dodging stage roads and cow camps and every place where he might have got a meal, livin' like a kyot-e, and packin' a hunk of the Blocker boys' lead in his shoulder. When he is about all in he stumbles onto the camp of this old French doctor that's livin' with the Crees and breeds, around Sheep Mountain. Old

Frenchy mines the lead out of him, and fixes him up some, but when he gets so he can crawl out of the wickyup, he ain't got no more horse, saddle or gun than a prairie-d-a-w-g. Them Crees the old sport is a-harboring has set him afoot proper, exceptin' the clothes he's got on and one pop. When he just k'aint choke down another round of the marrowgut and pemmican dawgfeed this outfit feasts on, he borrows a hoss one dark night, and lights out on the back trail. It's a cinch that lone gents ridin' mares ain't so permiscous that away but what this Stutterin' Bob makes a hit with the A outfit, we bein' three hundred miles from a neighboring cow camp or a stage ranch when he shows up on us in that rig of his'n. Starvin', hidin' and hard ridin' fixes it that he gets the red ticket easy over anything that hits Powder River up to then. We all had our prejudices. Old Twodot has his. No squawmen, breeds or Injuns for his'n. He catches a whiff of that tepee smell that's waftin' all the way from the old Doc's Cree wickyup in them remnants of what's onct Bob's clothes; while Bob, all onbeknown'st to them preejidices, is throwin' the feast of his life into hisself; after which he loses no time bracin' old Satchel fer a job, ridin'. 'Well, stranger,' says old Twodot, smooth-like, disguisin' his feelin's, 'We ain't short-handed for riders, just *at present*, but if you-all hain't drawin' the line at *mares*, I might stake you for an old gentle hoss or two, out of my string, so you can help with the cattle for a spell, ontil you can strike something better.'

"That's all right with him. Next thing we see is this wild man leadin' old Zebra out of the bunch with this hackamore of his. Now, Zebra, he's one of these splay-footed old hellyans that'll stand kinder spraddled, thoughtful and meek-like for saddlin' never making a flounce until his man starts swingin' up; then of a sudden he breaks out er-rocketin', hoggin', sunfishin' and plowin' up the yarth for about seven jumps, when he changes ends, caterpillers, goin' over back quicker'n lightnin'. The way the outfit begins to line up watchin' him cinch that old centerfire tree on old Zebra confirms his suspicions. He gives Twodot a savage look like a trapped wolf, tucks the loose coil of that hackamore rope into his belt, and just *walks* onto that hoss; never tries to find the off-stirrup, but stands high in the nigh one, a-rakin' old Zeeb up and down and reachin' for the root of his tail and jabbin' him with his heel every jump until he goes to the earth, feet upwards like a bear fightin' bees. Old Bob ain't under there to get pinched none, though, not on your type; he's jest calmly puttin' a pair of rawhide hobbles on them front feet and a'wroppin' old Zeeb's head and ears in that rag of a coat of his'n, that seems like he shucks before he hits the ground. I'll never tell a man what that long-legged, stutterin' maverick does to a bronc. Zebra ain't the last horse, though, that I sees him mesmerize ontil they'd seem to fergit their past life when he'd let 'em up to foller him around crow-hoppin' in the hobbles like a trick mewl in a circus. Less time than I'm tellin' you, he has them hobbles off again, and is ridin' old Zebra round as quiet as a night hoss.

"The laugh is on old Twodot; and he's that ringy he breaks out intimatin' Bob of some dirty breed work, like slippin' a handful of gravel or a string of buckshot into old Zeeb's ear, and a chow-ow-in' that he never *did* see no Squawherdin' that ride fair. At that Bob climbs down, sayin' quiet like, 'Eat that Injun part and that name or I'll *ride* you.' Old Satchel goes after his gun, but Bob is too quick. He has him plugged through the wrist, and sends another barkin' his scalp that downs him like a beef before he ever gets action. That's however I got *my* start in life, running the old A outfit."

It was a far, far cry between those two September days, between those samples of blackberry pie. Stutterin' Bob, Twodot, Old Andy and Gentleman Bill had passed away. In the shade of this old Bow-Gun blacksmith shop, vaqueros born since their time were listening to tales of their prowess, while tentatively mending gear, from saddles to soogans, through the long afternoon.

It was the third and last day of my stay at the old ranch. Warren, rising from breakfast asked—of no one in particular—"Who all is going to haze me?" Which was to say that Oscar, Flaxey, Stripes and their fellows of that day's work are today to get their first gallop outside—with a hazer, a rider mounted on something wise to the game and swift enough of foot to stay alongside, heading them from washouts, dog towns, and miles on miles of breaks and cut-banks, any direction from the Bow-Gun, where there's such footing as one takes with caution on well-broken mounts.

Now he dispensed with hobbles and helpers, roped, bridled and saddled the horses unaided, mounted them, circled the corral a turn or two, gave the gateman the word, and they went like a shot, buster and hazer neck and neck, off up the flat like a whipping finish in a quarter race. Four rides with a slicker lesson or two, and these daredevil riders call them "plumb gentle," and each man gets his share of the new ones for immediate use in his string.

"Of course," mused Lee, as we lounged by the cook's fire that last evening; "of course, if a buster was getting fifteen bones a head instead of five, all the time he needed, say thirty instead of five days for a bunch like this, horse fighting would be safer, less exciting, less picturesque, as you'd say. We would do our work, too, in a heap safer way for horses and men; but will it pay? is the question. Whether it's bustin' a bronc or a bank, bosses won't stand for a fifteen-dollar finish on a thirty-five-dollar horse."

"Where do you go to ride your next bunch?" I asked.

Warren fell silent, twirling thoughtfully the rowel of a spur, before replying.

"Just between ourselves, I am quitting the game right here–riding my last bronc. She wants that in our 'contrack.' I am to be promoted to run the Flying Eight over on the river. We'll be at home to our friends along about turkey time, and you'll be welcome, if you happen that way, to the best we've got, and the spin of your life behind a pair of flyin' hole colts."

4

Writings About Butte

■ *Butte, America*

RICHARD B. ROEDER

After two decades as a territory, Montana during the 1880s and 1890s was still dotted with isolated gold and silver camps and scattered cattle and railroad towns. It was a boom-and-bust economy. Gold placers were inherently ephemeral, and the Panic of 1893 dealt Montana's silver industry blows from which it never recovered. But by then a promising copper industry had emerged. It all happened in Butte, which had grown from an insignificant placer camp and booming silver town to become the keystone of a copper industry that seemed to guarantee Montana's industrial future. Mines in Butte, smelters in Anaconda, and refineries in Great Falls poured out enormous quantities of the red metal that had become essential to a new age of electricity. The new metals industry created economic opportunities that beckoned to people of all classes. But there were dangers. Although copper gave Montana new economic muscle, it also made the state, and its industrial center in Butte, vulnerable to corporate monopoly and control of basic industries.

This vulnerability attracted that late nineteenth century popular hero, the wealthy and politically powerful business leader who sought to dominate his area of enterprise. Two very different Montanans emerged as classic self-made men during this period: William A. Clark and Marcus Daly.

William A. Clark, a Pennsylvania native of old stock, was a pioneer who had arrived in Montana's placer camps in 1863. By a series of shrewd investments in mining properties and banking, Clark piled up his resources until he became one of America's richest men. Until his death in 1925, Clark's holdings included a good portion of the properties on Butte Hill.

Marcus Daly was an immigrant Irish miner of practical experience who had learned the metals industry from the underground to corporate board rooms. The confidence that Daly inspired enabled him to bring in outside capital to develop Butte's mineral resources, first in silver and then on a massive scale in copper. Daly's creation, the Anaconda Copper Mining Company, dominated Butte mining and Montana's copper industry until the decline of metal mining during the 1970s and 1980s.

Self-made men like Clark and Daly were folk heroes in their day. This was especially true of Daly among Butte's Irish. After his death, Daly's fellow townsmen erected a statue of him by August Saint-Gaudens, which still stands at the foot of the Montana Tech campus peering out over the once bustling city he did so much to create. Daly's appeal was not diminished by the fact that his efforts laid the foundation of a great copper combine that eventually gained complete control of Butte and dominated the lives of its citizens.

Into this situation walked the third figure of Montana's copper wars, the educated and cultured, flamboyant and brazen F. Augustus Heinze. For a brief but dazzling period, Heinze used his technical knowledge, family wealth, and an astute corps of lawyers to fight Butte's copper trust to a standstill. His main tactic was to mire his corporate enemies in a morass of litigation over the ownership of ore veins. But in 1903, the copper trust used a state-wide shutdown of its multifaceted businesses to coerce Governor J. K. Toole and the state legislature into passing legislation that would dismantle Heinze's influence in the district courts of Silver Bow County. By 1906, the fight was over. After making solemn promises to Butte's workers that he would never sell out, Heinze did so, taking a reputed ten to twelve million dollars from the Anaconda Company for his properties. The way was now open for final corporate control of Butte Hill.

Strike-it-rich heros such as Clark, Daly, and Heinze were the most visible figures in Butte, but they represented only the tip of the city's business structure. Butte's wealth also attracted a large and energetic mercantile and professional class. Thousands of workers had to be fed, clothed, and entertained—all of which kept an uptown group of merchants and purveyors hustling around the clock seven days a week. And countless legal cases were guided through the courts by lawyers who received fees and wielded much more power than the ordinary small-town lawyer. Journalists also discovered tantalizing opportunities in Butte. Early in their battles, the copper kings discovered that newspapers were necessary weapons in their arsenals. Every faction—corporate, ideological, and ethnic—had its sheets. Journalism was often scurrilous in Butte, but it was never dull.

Ultimately, Butte's prosperity rested on the backs of the miners who dug the ore from the hill, and on the mill and smelter workers who turned the rock into metals. Butte was always a working-man's town. It came of age with unions whose strength gave it the nickname, the "Gibraltar of Unionism." For a time, the unions secured for their members some of the highest wages in the United States. But the prosperity was uncertain. Union negotiations that found success with earlier business leaders who were personally familiar with the lives of their workers did not always produce favorable results with corporate managers who were determined to convert labor into a commodity. And as immigrants from central and southern Europe joined the original Irish and Cornish work force, labor solidarity suffered from ethnic antipathies and ideological differences over how workers might best share in the wealth their labor created. Aroused by radical ideas (and occasional incidents of violence), company managers adopted a repressive labor policy designed to destroy the miners' unions and imposed a baronial control over Butte's labor supply.

By the beginning of the twentieth century, Butte's past had been brief but colorful and its future promising. It was a cosmopolitan, colorful, vibrant, and sometimes boisterous city that hummed with activity, night and day, both on the surface and a mile underground. To the rest of Montana, Butte was an exotic island. Outsiders were fascinated by but never sure of Butte. It was, as Joseph Kinsey Howard put it, the "black heart" of Montana.

Butte's history, cultural mix, and labor activism, offered exciting material for aspiring writers. Many of the first writers to exploit Butte were newspaper men who described the excitement of mining and the lucky strikes that brought wealth to Horatio Alger-type figures such as Clark, Daly, and Heinze. Although early fictional efforts had little literary merit and have long been forgotten, some journalistic writings proved to be more than ephemeral. Montana's first generation of journalists included imports of excellent talent and education. One such was C. H. Eggleston of Daly's *Anaconda Standard.* Eggleston's obituary writer called him the "West's most brilliant and versatile editorial writer." When presidential candidate William Jennings Bryan visited Butte in 1896 with promises to revive Montana's silver industry, Eggleston responded with "When Bryan Came to Butte," which Joseph Kinsey Howard called "Montana's most famous and remembered poem." More than a generation after it appeared, the *Standard* was still receiving requests for reprints.

Commentary on contemporary affairs in verse was a common journalistic genre of the early 1900s. Berton Braley, one of the country's most successful practitioners of this form, got his start in the *Inter Mountain* and the *Butte Evening News*. Shortly after his arrival in Butte as a fresh 1905 graduate of the University of Wisconsin, Braley attracted national attention with his verses of social criticism of workers as well as public figures. After a few years, he moved on to the East Coast and larger fame and wealth.

Butte's world was masculine, harsh, and violent. But in many ways life in Butte was completely conventional. This was certainly true of prevailing ideas about womanhood. Few doubted that a woman's lot was marriage, motherhood, and a prayerful church life. In 1902, Butte received the greatest literary shock in its history with the appearance of a slim volume, *The Story of Mary MacLane*, written by a recent graduate of Butte High School. Mary MacLane wrote a journal that covers about six months of her life. In it, this nineteen-year-old girl announced that she would have nothing to do with conventional ideas and values and spoke frankly of sexual experiences and urges. The book's impact was felt far beyond Butte and gave MacLane instant national fame and enormous royalties.

Butte's most prolific and best novelist has been largely forgotten. Myron Brinig grew up amidst the Jewish mercantile world of East Park Street. Among his several dozen novels are six that have all or part of their settings in Butte. His first novel, *Singermann*, is a study of Butte's Jewish merchants and of the adjustments they and their families had to make, adjustments that severed vital cultural roots. Most of Brinig's Butte books examine the lives of the bourgeoisie, but his second novel, *Wide Open Town*, recounts Butte's Irish and ethnic world of wage earners—people whose aspirations collided with the realities of defeat, industrial accident, and disease. It describes a working-class world rent by pretensions and ethnic differences.

Brinig's novels invited imitation. Many aspiring local writers thought they had at least one great Butte novel in them. Most of those published exploited well-known episodes from the wars of the copper kings. Some, however, reveal insights into the daily lives of workers. The best of the group is *Glittering Hill* by Clyde Murphy, a lawyer who grew up in Anaconda. Although the plot is weak, many of this novel's scenes graphically describe the lives of Butte's Irish.

By the middle of the second decade of the twentieth century, Butte's labor movement was in confusion. During and after World War I, corporate management exploited the situation through a system of private police and industrial espionage. This repressive system was designed to eliminate "foreign" ideas and to command labor on management's terms. Dashiell Hammett had worked as a Pinkerton detective in Butte during this time. The Butte that his "private op" narrator describes in *Red Harvest* is nicknamed "Poisonville," and the city's most salient characteristic is its capacity to produce violence.

Butte's early literature reached its height at about the same time the city reached its economic zenith, on the eve of World War I. By then a vision of a new Montana community, a rural and a moral one, was emerging, and writers' imaginations shifted to Montana's newest immigrants, homesteaders who were rushing to the vast open plains where an experiment in building a new rural community was about to be carried out.

■ CHARLES H. EGGLESTON

Newspaperman Charles H. Eggleston came to Anaconda from Syracuse, New York, in 1889. Twice elected to the state senate and an editor for The Anaconda Standard, *Eggleston is best remembered for his newspaper verse and his satirical journalistic style. "When Bryan Came to Butte" appeared in the* Standard *on August 13, 1897, the day after William Jennings Bryan had visited Butte. People in Montana's mining regions loved the golden-tongued Bryan for his position on free silver, and Eggleston took the opportunity of Bryan's visit to poke some fun at that adoration.*

When Bryan Came to Butte

I have read of Roman triumphs in the days when Rome played
ball,
When she met all other nations, taking out of each a fall;
When victorious Roman generals marched their legions home in
state,
With the plunder of the conquered–and the conquered paid the
freight.
Gorgeous were those vast processions rolling through the streets of
Rome;
Mad with joy went all the Romans welcoming the veterans home.
Gold there was for fifty Klondikes, silver trinkets big as logs,
Marble statues by the cartload, gems enough to stone the dogs.
Following chariot cars were captives, dainty damsels by the score,
Ballet dancers from far harems, savage men and beasts galore.
Millions cheered and yelled and thundered; shook the earth as by
a storm;
All Rome howled–and yet Rome's howling after all was not so
warm,
For these monster Roman triumphs, at which not a stone was
mute,
Couldn't hold a Roman candle–
When Bryan came to Butte.

I have read of the convulsions of the fiery men of France
When Napoleon came from Elba, eager for another chance.

Marble hearts and frozen shoulders turned the generals to their
chief,
But the people hailed their master with a rapture past belief.
What though France lay stunned and bleeding, she arose and got
too gay;
What though he had cost her fortunes, still the devil was to pay.
Though he'd slain a million soldiers and returned to slay some
more,
The survivors stood there ready to pour forth their inmost gore;
And they wept and sang and shouted, whooped and roared in
sheer delight,
On their knees they begged, implored him to pull off another
fight–
Sure the champion was in training, and in training couldn't lose;
Thus they laughed and cried and acted as if jagged with wildest
booze.
But the passion that they cherished for this brilliant French galoot
Was as zero to that witnessed
When Bryan came to Butte.

I have read of Queen Victoria and her diamond jubilee.
London rose and did the handsome–it was something up in G.
Long and glittering the procession–beat old Barnum's best to
death;
When the queen is on exhibit, even cyclones hold their breath.
Troops of white and black and yellow–regiments from East and
West–
All the glory of Great Britain–pomp until you couldn't rest.
Russia also cut a figure when she crowned the reigning czar.
In the line of fancy blowouts Russian stock is up to par.
There were balls and fetes and fireworks, bands played on and
cannon roared;
Monarchy was at the bat, and all their royal nibses scored.
Add the Moscow show to London's, take the paralyzing pair,
Put the queen and czar together, yoke the lion and the bear–
Swell these pageantries of Europe till you get a dream to suit–
And it's pretty small potatoes–
When Bryan came to Butte.

Bryan has had many triumphs, some ovations off and on
Just a little bit the biggest that the sun e'er shone upon.
You remember the convention in Chicago, do you not,
When the party went to Bryan and the goldbugs went to pot?
You remember the excitement when he rose and caught the
crowd,
When for fully twenty minutes everybody screamed aloud.
Oh, the mighty roar of thousands as he smote the cross of gold,
As he gripped the British lion in a giant's strangle hold!
Oh, the fury of the frenzy as he crushed the crown of thorns,
As he grabbed the situation, as he held it by the horns!
Some there were who leaped the benches, some who maniac
dances led,
Some who tried to kick the ceiling, more who tried to wake the
dead.
'Twas a record-breaking rouser, down to fame it shoots the chute,
But it wasn't quite a fly-speck–
When Bryan came to Butte.

Ah, when Bryan came to Butte! greatest mining camp on earth;
Where the people dig and delve, and demand their money's
worth.
Though the Wall Street kings and princes spurn and kick them as
a clod,
Bryan is their friend and savior and they love him as a god.
Did they meet him when he came there? Did they make a little
noise?
Were they really glad to see him? Do you think it pleased the
boys?
'Twas the screaming of the eagle as he never screamed before,
'Twas the crashing of the thunder, mingling with Niagara's roar,
All the whistles were a-screeching, with the bands they set the
pace–
But the yelling of the people never let them get a place.
Dancing up and down and sideways, splitting lungs and throats
and ears,
All were yelling, and at yelling seemed wound up a thousand
years.
Of the earth's great celebrations 'twas the champion heavyweight,
'Tis the champion forever and a day, I calculate,

For it knocked out all its rivals, and, undaunted, resolute,
Punched creation's solar plexus–
When Bryan came to Butte.

BERTON BRALEY

Born in Madison, Wisconsin, in 1882, Berton Braley came to Butte in 1905 soon after he finished college. He wrote for the Intermountain *for a year before moving to the offices of the* Evening News. *In 1909, Braley went to New York to work for the* Evening Mail. *His long and prolific career included a stint as associate editor of* Punch *and a job as foreign correspondent during World War I. Braley published hundreds of short stories and co-authored* Stand Fast for Freedom *with Lowell Thomas. He was also a prolific writer of newspaper verse, composing over eleven thousand poems, according to one estimate. Braley wrote "When Bryan Came to Butte–Yesterday" for the October 7, 1909,* Intermountain *after his chance sighting of William Jennings Bryan at the Butte railroad station. "Jim" appeared in the* Intermountain *on October 7, 1905, and "The Idealist" is part of an unpublished collection of Braley's poems located in the Montana Historical Society Library.*

When Bryan Came to Butte–Yesterday

(With Apologies to Senator Eggleston of Anaconda.)

Darkness hung about the city when the Peerless Leader came
P. C. Gillis smoked and jollied at a little solo game,
Robert Haydn read his Shakespeare 'mid the comforts of his home,
John O'Rourke was dozing, dozing, in the glimmer of the gloam.
Yet while democrats by hundreds flitted all around the town
Not a one was there to greet him when the train was slowing
down–
Not a bell clanged out a welcome, there was not a whistle's toot,
But a News reporter saw him, when Bill Bryan came to Butte.

Charlie Nevin never knew it, Wally Walsworth hadn't heard,
Tommy Walker, John MacGinniss didn't know it had occurred.
So the silver-tongued and matchless, whom the city used to cheer,
Looked in vain for greeting from them–no one knew that he was
here–

No one, save a News reporter, who was loafing at the train,
And who recognized the features of the Leader once again.
Democrats were dead or sleeping, whistles, bells were silent, mute,
When, upon this sad occasion, Mr. Bryan came to Butte.

Night had spread her sable mantle, something night is wont to do,
And the three-times party leader thus was hidden from the view;
No one tossed his hat or hollered, no one waved a banner high,
There was nary sight of rockets painting fiery red the sky;
But the train rolled inward slowly, slowly rolled upon its way,
Bearing Mr. Bryan onward, there was not a word to say.
It was different, I reckon, from that time of old repute,
From that day of sound and splendor, when Bill Bryan came to
Butte.

Jim

Jim was a dissolute, whiskified man
Who ambled through life on the do nothing plan.
He swore like a trooper, he lied and he stole,
He lacked any morals, he hadn't a soul.
Or if possessed of one–he didn't, I'm sure,
It must have been crooked and mean and impure.

One day, in the middle of Winter, a fire
Began in the courthouse and burned it entire;
And the judge, who so often had sent Jim to jail,
Was caught by the flames as they roared in the gale,
And Jim–here the story commences to turn–
Didn't "rush in and save him," he let the judge burn.

For he said, "I'll be hanged if I 'rush in and die,'
For a man who has acted as mean as that guy.
He put me in jail; let the old lobster roast,
He'll get it still worse when he's changed to a ghost."
Then Jim walked away to the nearest saloon,
Whistling a bar from a popular tune.

The moral's as plain as the hole in the zero;
Though heroes get drunk, every drunk's not a hero,

And a man who is drunken and low and a brute
Doesn't usually rise to a hero's repute.

The Idealist

She's ugly, you say, old Butte is,
And grimy and black and drear?
Why, partner, I never could see it,
And I've lived here many a year.
There's nothing pretty about her,
But somehow she's strong and free,
And big and rugged and—well, comrade,
She looks pretty good to me.

She's beautiful, too, in her fashion,
In her wonderful, strange old way;
With her chimneys and throbbing engines,
Her hillsides marred and gray.
She's the goddess of wealth and power—
It's a thing my words won't reach,
It takes a man to express it
Who's born with a gift of speech.

But some clear autumn morning,
When the air is like a sip
From a spring of sparkling water
That touches the pilgrim's lip,
Go out and look around you
At the mountains against the sky;
Those quiet, immutable mountains
That carry their heads so high.

And then as the day grows brighter,
And the sky is limpid blue,
They come in their grandeur closer
And sort of reach down to you.
And you feel, with a thrill of wonder
That has no stain of pride,
That you are one of the mountains—
That heart of the great divide.

Then at sunset how they fill you
  With a sense of perfect awe,
As the colors bathe and light them
  In faith with God's good law;
Purple and gold and crimson,
  Painted by Nature's hand,
I can't begin to express it,
  But I think I can understand.

And the city, itself, at night time
  When seen from a distant place,
With its many lights a-glistening,
  Like flames on a snow-bank's face.
They sweep in a grand crescendo,
  In glittering rows and lines,
Till they flicker into the starlight
  That shimmers above the mines.

Ugly and bleak? Well, maybe,
  But my eyes have learned to find
The beauty of truth, not substance,
  The beauty that lies behind.
Her faults and her sins are many
  To injure her fair repute,
But her heart and her soul are cleanly,
  And she's beautiful, dear old Butte.

MYRON BRINIG

Born in Minneapolis in 1897, Myron Brinig came to Butte with his immigrant Jewish family in 1900. He left in 1918 to join the army and never came back. Taking his talents to New York City, Brinig worked as a scriptwriter in the early film industry before moving to Hollywood. In 1933, Brinig moved to Mabel Dodge Luhan's artists' colony in Taos, New Mexico, where he remained for forty years before moving back to New York. "Silver Bow" is from Brinig's autobiographical novel, Singermann, *which was published in 1919;* Wide Open Town *was published two years later.*

Silver Bow

You are riding along in the very heart of the mountains. The train is climbing into the sky, and all about are giant boulders and trees whose roots are precarious in pitiless, sheer landslides. Then without any preparation you see, hundreds of feet below, the first houses of a town. It is as if a giant had been sitting on the top of the Rockies playing with many colored dice that he had rattled in his palm and then thrown into the valley below. Certainly, if you look again, the town will not be there. A great rock will have fallen and smashed it into the hard, diamondine earth! But there is Silver Bow, much closer now, less vagrant and poetic, a town of ugly houses and streets. The roofs of Silver Bow look crushed and sullen as if unable to bear the incredible weight of the mountains all about. A few miles away, the atmosphere is as light and intoxicating as champagne; but in the town, each infrequent blade of grass is fighting the smoke and sulphur of the copper mines and smelters. The streets are steep and narrow, rising and falling. You stand on a street-corner and see how the town is fleeing, pursued by the swift, inevitable mountains.

There, on the hill looking down upon Silver Bow, were the copper mines, tall and stately and contemptuous. The copper mines ruled Silver Bow, and the state of Montana as well. Nowhere else in the world was there such a rich treasure of copper as that which ran in ruddy veins under the turbulent, unexpected streets. Thousands of miners were employed, and very few were American born. Mostly, there were blue-eyed lads from Ireland with rich brogues and hard-drinking gullets, tall flat Finns and Norwegians with bony, yellow faces. The Scandinavians worked in the lower drifts and went about, even in their leisure hours, wearing yellow slickers and hip-boots. There was also a conglomeration of Southern Europeans, Montenegrins, Serbs, Bulgarians, Slovaks, Greeks. All these miners had their own societies and clubs and meeting places. And the Finns were always fighting the Irish and the Bohunks, from Southern Europe. Or they were fighting amongst themselves. The Bohunks went about in crowds, ten, fifteen, twenty to a group, and they were all brave together like that, but singly they were furtive and afraid. When a man by the name of James Canestalk came to town and said he was an I.W.W., all the warring factions united for one evening. Canestalk gabbled about higher wages and the leeches of Capitalists. He wore a red necktie and wanted a strike, and he got one for six weeks. But the Big Company that ran the works brought in the State Militia from Helena, and the strikers were bound and gagged. And they had no money to buy clothes or food. So somebody cried, "To hell with Canestalk! To hell with the lousy I.W.W.!" And Canestalk was run out of town on a splintered rail, and the strike came to an end.

The clothing stores of the Jewish merchants were on East Park Street. They caught customers with traps of words, and they were constantly dragging miners inside to sell them shoes, socks, suits of ribbed underwear, and maybe a suitcase to go away with. East Park Street was a beehive with its Jewish stores, its Greek restaurants, and its Irish saloons with swinging doors. You passed by a saloon, a door swung outward and you caught a glimpse of heavy work shoes resting on a brass rail. There was sawdust on the floor, and spittoons; but no one spat in the spittoons. You could see that when the saloon doors swung outward for an instant.

On East Galena Street, not far removed from the busiest part of town, one block was the Red Light District, and the next block was Chinatown. The shacks of Chinatown drooped as though the boards had been infected with the juice of poppies. You went Down The Line and had a hell of a time with the girls; and then somebody would say, "Let's go and see if we can't get a shot of hop off the Chinks." Chinatown was that. Chinatown was chop suey and Chinks carrying huge baskets suspended from either end of a bamboo pole. How mysteriously they moved along in the murky dimness, weird, evanescent figures, silhouettes cut out of black silk! Chinatown was an evil place, some said. But not all the Chinks were in Chinatown. There were Chinks who owned vegetable gardens down on the Flats—the arid, wide plains south of the town. And these Chinamen who lived on the Flats were fresh with the wind and the sky, and their faces were like burned leather.

Silver Bow was a gaudy scramble of races and creeds; but above them all, snapping the whip, was the Copper Hill and the mines. Down below, on the Flats, were the smelters with their fiery smokestacks. They were ugly in the daylight; but at night, their fires burned holes through the dark blue tent of the sky. At night, you could see the red flares of the furnaces and men tending the importunate ovens. At night a smelter is glamorous if you happen to be looking on; but the poor devils who tend the fires miss the glamour. Sometimes an ambulance goes ringing down to the smelter and a workman who has been scalded by the molten copper is borne screaming to the St. James Hospital. He fights the stretcher and the interns and scars the night with bastard words.

On Saturday night, that was the time in Silver Bow when life moved, men hated and loved, and the Jewish merchants on East Park Street did a good business. The Jewish merchants ran up and down the aisles of their stores, made sales and bawled out their clerks. They discovered that shoes and socks and overalls had been stolen from the "show" in front of the windows. Suits disappeared from racks as if by magic; suitcases were casually lifted off benches and carried away on Saturday night.

Drunks swayed from side to side, crashing into plate-glass windows, and then the patrol wagon backed up against the sidewalk and a cop stepped out and lifted the drunk out of the broken glass. The patrol wagon was busy on Saturday night, the horses galloping through the streets, striking fire from the cobblestones. First, the wagon would emerge from the alley where the police station was situated, and it was empty except for the cop standing on the rear step. But a few minutes later, the horses galloped back up the alley. Sometimes there were half a dozen men imprisoned within the wagon. And when you saw a woman screaming and tearing her hair inside the wagon, you ran up the alley to watch her being dragged into the station. That was a terrible thing, a woman like that in a patrol wagon.

On Saturday night, spielers paraded up and down the streets, shouting out, Big sale at the Gent's Furnishing Store. Baseball tomorrow at Columbia Gardens, Northwestern League baseball. On Saturday night, dope fiends shivered and jerked their way along the sidewalks of Silver Bow. Cripples who had been maimed in the mines, sold pencils and shoelaces and damned you for a dirty dog if you didn't help them out. How would you like to be a cripple, you stingy louse? Saturday night was a hell of a night in Silver Bow, for then you saw the race-track touts and the pimps and the ladies from Down the Line. And always the patrol wagons ringing through the streets. But sometimes it was only an ambulance.

On Saturday night, Down the Line, the girls were busy bitches. Roulette wheels and card games were burning holes in the pockets of workers from the Anaconda, Never Sweat, Speculator, Leonard mines. Mechanical pianos were playing, *In the Good Old Summer Time, Rings on my Fingers, Bells on my Toes*; and many a young man was seduced away from godliness on Saturday night.

In his shop on South Montana Street, Rabbi Lachter sold kosher beef and butchered chickens on Saturday night. The room back of the shop was where he took the chicken and slit its throat with a sharp-edged blade. Some said it was the same blade he used for circumcision–but they may have been talking for drama. The chicken flapped its wings and gurgled, and the lids of its eyes fluttered, but the rabbi held on firmly until the bird had given up its impure blood. Now it was a good chicken, fit to eat; but it had been *trafe*, and it had not been Jehovah's chicken before. After he had killed a chicken in the orthodox manner, the rabbi plucked its feathers, and before long the room was fluttering and soft and wheezy with feathers. The rabbi wore a long rusty-black *kaftan* that bore the stains of numberless chickens and cattle. His collar was spotted with blood, and his necktie was frayed and leaked cotton. His shoes were badly in need of a shine and chicken feathers stuck to the soles. But the rabbi's face was perfectly impassive; his eyes were cool and calculating; his mouth was firm. Sometimes, a fluttering chicken feather would stick in his red beard, but he was too busy to notice.

Over on the West Side where lived the respectable merchant families of the town, the mine officials, the wealthy children of pioneers, there was calm. A Mexican vendor of hot tamales moved sinuously from corner to corner, wheeling his barrow before him. He was one of the inevitable and picturesque figures of the town. His voice was clear and ringing as an angelus bell; and as the hour grew later and later, his voice became more and more melancholy, as if pining away for a moonlit night in Mexico, a monastery garden in Mexico, so still except for the tinkling of an invisible fountain. Ta-ma-les! Hot ta-ma-les! Hot! Hot! Hot! He was a figure of romance in the town, and his barrow, illuminated by the flares of kerosene torches, made a spot of gaiety and warmth wherever he chanced to be.

The frenzy of Saturday night in Silver Bow merges gradually into the pallid calm of Sunday morning. The priest at St. Patrick's church on Mercury Street is up before the dawn to celebrate a mass that will be attended by pious Irish girls. Sunday morning is a quiet time, and peaceful. Silence runs along the streets, and for blocks not a man is to be seen; not a sound to be heard. Even the copper mines on the hill have a look of quietude and steel beauty. They are etched against the sky with a fine, purposeful loveliness. The church bells begin to sound, the long, lazy, sonorous bells of the Baptist, Methodist, Catholic churches. It is very pleasant to lie abed on Sunday mornings and hear the iron bells striking through a gauze dream. When the newsboys begin to shout *Butte Miner, Anaconda Standard!* it is quite late then and there are smells of breakfast in the kitchen.

Moses rented a store on East Park Street and partitioned off three rooms in the rear for himself and his family. One room was used as a kitchen, one as a bedroom, and one as a combined bedroom and parlor. Moses had only to step across the threshold of his bedroom and he was in his place of business. But Rebecca despised her new home, it was so cheap and tawdry looking, so hard to keep clean. She wanted a house with proper rooms and a yard. A home is not a home without a yard where you sit and sun your hair on warm days. A yard for the children to play in, that is something to be thankful for. You can stretch a clothesline across a yard, and the wash will smell sweet of the outdoors and not of a close room. Rebecca wept for the comforts and conveniences she had left behind her in Minneapolis. In the evening, after she had cleared the supper table, she wept for the pathetic distance of her girlhood. This was the America every one had praised, the wonderful, golden country they had admired from afar! What a disappointment! For what was the use of all the money in the world if only ugliness and vulgarity were to surround them to the grave? How her father, the creator of sweet melodies on his violin, would have loathed this country! He would have pined away to a quick death, of that Rebecca was certain. Were there dreamers and poets in this country? Poor fellows! Rebecca wept for them, also.

But Moses was too busy to form any estimate of what lay about him, what stretched before him. The moment he stepped across the threshold that separated him from his business, he quivered with the excitement of bargaining and selling. At seven in the morning, he unlocked the front door and started to carry out his "show," a display of samples of his merchandise. Two long benches were placed in front of the show windows, two at the sides. These benches were loaded down with shoes for work and dress, stacks of socks, lunch buckets, candlesticks, caps, hats, piles of shirts and pants and overalls. Slicker coats and rubber boots were hung from hooks screwed into the window framework. There was even a trunk out on the sidewalk with a sign on it, *Sacrificed At A Bargain*.

After he had labored over his show, stopping at intervals to entice customers within, Moses filled a sprinkling can with water and proceeded to "lay" the dust on the floor. The water raining through the holes punched in the neck of the can made pleasing black patterns on the floor and created a damp, musty smell. Sometimes the store smelled of oilskins; sometimes of green overalls; sometimes of dry leather; but the early morning smell of the sprinkling can meant a new day, perhaps prosperous, perhaps slow.

After he had sprinkled and swept the floor in the morning, Moses would rush back to the rear and awaken his children with mighty, ferocious cries. "Joe! Louis! David!" he would call and reproach them where they lay in bed snatching at a few blissful hours of morning slumber. "Already it is eight o'clock and you are like sons of the dead! Ain't it a shame you should snore when all the stores are stealing away our business?" Moses, of course, was exaggerating. His store was the first to open in the morning and the last to close up shop at night. But he was not going to leave anything to chance. It alarmed him that his children should not be up at the same hour as himself. There was much work to be done before they departed for school: windows to be washed, shoe boxes to be marked and put away, bales of overalls to be opened. When words failed, Moses would often snatch the covers off the beds and yank the children up by their legs and ears. His loud cries assaulted the trembling, thin walls, and naked boys ran here and there, dodging impetuous blows. "See, the sun is in the sky! Awake, you healthy but useless drags on my life! This is America, the land of opportunity, of quick sales and small profits!"

Leaving the children to grumble and whimper, Moses would hurry back into the store, eager to create business. If, after a reasonable time, no customer had appeared, Moses would plant himself on the sidewalk in front of the store and importune, cajole, threaten passers-by. There were so many mouths to be fed, so many bills to pay. It was suicide to sit meekly and wait for business to come. And when in his life had prosperity come to him unsolicited? Always he had pursued, given chase to a livelihood, caught opportunity by the coat-tails and strangled it into submission.

"Say, mister, I see by the cracks that you got in your shoes you need a new pair. I got something extra for only three-forty-nine."

"Aw, g'wan. I don't need no shoes. I just bought these I got on a couple weeks ago."

"You was robbed. You don't have to buy any shoes from me, mister, but I tell you, you was robbed. Ain't you ashamed?"

"Say, what right you got to talk to me that way?"

"Because I feel sorry for you, mister. I feel sorry for a man who's a sucker. And that's what you are, just a sucker."

"Is that so?"

"Come inside, and I will show you a pair of shoes for half the price you paid for them what you got on and twice so good."

"Leggo my arm, for Chris' sake. Who d'ya think you're pullin'?"

"Look at that hat you got on, mister. Ain't you ashamed to go home to your wife with that hat?" Moses removed the hat so that the man could study it from a detached point of view. "You call this a hat? Come in, friend. Take a look. It don't cost you nothing to look. I see you're a miner. I know lots of boys from your mine and I treat them like brothers. And also—don't run away, friend—this is what the boys say to me. 'Mr. Singermann,' they say, 'I want I should thank you for that hat what you sold me. It's so good like a Stetson what they charge ten dollars for.' Always I get compliments from my customers. Come in, friend, I show you. Maybe you need a shirt or underwear or socks or a valise for a little money, or maybe I can interest you in a pair of shoes."

"Well, I might come in. Only I don't say I'll buy anything. But I might take a look around."

Moses was constantly bully-ragging his customers and mocking them in Yiddish, but few were offended by his methods, and many came to admire his rough humor and sarcastic temper. He was not a good business man so much as a lover of merchandise; his methods were those of impetuosity and recklessness rather than systematic salesmanship. To the end he remained a tavernkeeper. But he quickly became a character in Silver Bow.

So after two years, he rented a larger place on the same street, installed new fixtures and entered the second phase of his storekeeping career. He also rented a house in South Dakota Street for the family and presented two hundred dollars to the synagogue as a mark of gratitude and respect.

From Wide Open Town

Let us sing in praise of Silver Bow, in the state of Montana, in the United States of America. Crowds that move and surge about the Northern Pacific Railway Station. Oh, swift silver rails that bring the President of the United States to the greatest copper camp in the world. Oh, day of days! . . .

O, the excitement of campaign days in small American towns near the cornfields, by the Mississippi, the Missouri, the Platte. Banners flung across streets, night parades with flaming torches. Vote for McKinley! Vote for Bryan! O, ranting, canting, ringing speeches!

O American saloons, bawdy houses, gambling dens, Winchesters and 44's, pretty ladies and sedate ladies!! Sunflowers growing in court-house yards!

They elected William McKinley to be President of the United States and Theodore Roosevelt to be Vice-President.

Roosevelt was born in New York City of an old-time, respectable family. As a child, he was weak and his life was despaired of, but they pulled him through and he grew a fine set of white teeth.

So he could smile and show his white teeth and say, "Dee-lighted!" So he could go to Harvard and storm San Juan Hill at the head of his Rough Riders and become Police Commissioner of New York City and Governor of New York State. . . .

Theodore Roosevelt was an American. Americans all, I sing your praises! From ditch diggers to college presidents, I sing to you! I love your rocks and rills, your speakeasies and stills, and I love to get over to Canada once in a while!

A dirty anarchist tried to wreck our glorious Government. He took a shot at William McKinley and murdered our beloved William McKinley!

The nerve of him, the dirty dog!

Oh, it was a dark day for America, my friends! May I call you my friends? For you are all, all my friends, from bootleggers to Congressmen! William McKinley lingered for a few days and then died in his wife's arms.

His poor wife, Mrs. McKinley.

And so Theodore Roosevelt became President of the United States and became a friend to the Kaiser of Germany. Oh, the poor Kaiser! Look, what's happened to Wilhelm! He put his head up, Fritzy Boy, and the Tommies took a shot at 'im and so did the Frogs of France! March on! March on! *Vive la France*! Over there! Over there!

O Theodore Roosevelt, you used a Big Stick on the trusts. Three thousand trusts, see how they run, with the Big Stick after them!

And you went hunting in Africa and had your picture taken, one foot planted on poor dead lions, zebras, tigers, hippopotamuses.

And you went to South America and discovered a river.

Oh, you caught a fever in South America, on the River of Doubt.

And you came back to the United States and started a third party called the Bull Moose, and you ran against Taft and Wilson. . . .

Americans all, I raise my glass of bootleg whiskey to you and sing your praises! I sing the great men and the small, the poor immigrants who gaze longingly upon the Statue of Liberty, the Jews, the Swedes, the Irish, the Germans, the I.W.W.'s, the communists, the New York Herald Tribune, and above all, I sing to artists, to writers, painters and musicians!

Hooray! God damn it, there's life in you, America, boiling, moiling, sizzling life! Oh, say, can you see? You're a grand old flag!

George M. Cohan is an American. Isidore Cohen is an American.

America! From the cold, rocky shores of Maine to the sun-drenched boosters of Los Angeles; from the turbulence of Niagara to the darkies dancing on Galveston levees, I sing to you! I would create poems out of all Americans, prostitutes and miners, spielers, grafters, booze-fighters, Presidents, Jew composers of jazz, movie studios in Hollywood, football players of Stanford, Yale, the Army, the Navy! America, you are alive! And Theodore Roosevelt was you, America, all your faults and all your virtues. He was alive!

So when Mr. Roosevelt got off the train, he was met by the Mayor and the Board of Aldermen, and he shook hands with all of them. He caught sight of Roddy Cornett and beckoned to him, saying, "Hello, Roddy! How's that big voice of yours?"

"It's pretty good, Mr. President."

"Do you remember the day we had a wrestling match at Brown's Gulch? You threw me then. I'd like to take you on again. I'm feeling bully."

"Any time, Mr. President."

"Will you come and see me at the hotel before I leave, Roddy? It would be fine to talk over old times, old Western times."

"Yes, Mr. President. Y'know, I'm introducing you tonight at the ball park."

"Are you now? I'm dee-lighted!"

A conversation between two great men in Silver Bow. A flash of white teeth, a strong grip of hands, and Mr. Roosevelt steps into his resplendent carriage. He is driven up Arizona Street where men, women and children of Silver Bow stand cheering him. Teddy raises his hat and smiles and his remarkable teeth seem to become detached in numberless smiles of approbation. In the Mayor's carriage, directly behind that of the President, rides Roddy Cornett, the town-crier of Silver Bow. Two men of America, of the early twentieth century, are meeting for the last time. They knew one another in the old days when Roosevelt was a young rancher in South Dakota and Roddy was a young prospector in Silver Bow. The gorgeous procession passes swiftly up the steep street while flags fly in the breeze and bands glorify the passing moments into mighty rhythms.

Roddy drew upon himself fresh proportions of strength and grandeur from the scene and the experience. He loved the small children who lined the streets and waved American flags. The way they sang *My Country, 'Tis of Thee* was a way of being free of reading and arithmetic lessons in school, a way of looking upon the impossible. Roddy looked down upon the broad, swaying backs, the tingling flanks of the powerful horses that pulled the carriage; their proud pace and progress was a way of America being administrated by Theodore Roosevelt. The harness was of polished black leather fitted together with silver and copper; the metal sparkled in the bright sunlight and the reins gave off tones of swiftness, yet was never loose or inept from the horses. Men and women leaned out of opened windows above the street and sent themselves flying on the wings of their cheers. A group of cowboys on horseback, who had ridden in from Miles City, waved their huge sombreros and some of them stood up on their saddles and gave forth screeching yells of the plains and the bunkhouses . . . Mr. Roosevelt's tall silk hat took on the gloss of Silver Bow's atmosphere, a different sheen from other towns, a different radiance streaking the sides of the hat into proportioned, distinctive measurements.

When the procession reached East Broadway and stopped before the hotel, the President stepped nimbly from his carriage and the hotel manager came rushing out to greet him. The waving tails of the manager's frock coat made him look like a devil with the face of a catering angel. He was restless and agile with many words that rattled in his mouth like ball bearings. "We aim to make you comfortable here, Mr. President. The hotel is yours. And in behalf of the hotel management and its courteous employees, I am tendering you this little present from a grateful heart." The manager thereupon brought forth, from one of the tails of his coat, a miniature mine frame made out of copper. Mr. Roosevelt exclaimed over the gift and held it aloft so that everybody could see it. His trunks were crammed with gifts from cities all over the world, but never before had he received a copper mine that he could hold so easily in the palm of his hand. The bands became more ferocious, eating up the silence with many martial notes, flags made an ecstasy out of the breeze and Mr. Roosevelt bent over to kiss a little girl who was being held up proudly by her father. From that moment onward, Loretta Mooney became famous in Silver Bow as the little girl Mr. Roosevelt had kissed. She grew up to be a haughty, flirtatious woman, and in later years divorced three husbands in succession.

That evening the whole town turned out at the ball-park to hear Mr. Roosevelt speak on "Conditions." Miners and their wives and children, all dressed in their finest; farmers in their broadcloths and farmers' wives in their ginghams and sateens, drove into town in wagons and buggies. They looked like finicky families of birds high on their seats behind the swishing tails of horses. In all the faces of the crowd was an inexpressible awe and wonder. The plains roundabout and the sky above held something of this same magic quality. Because it was summer, darkness had not yet descended; there were broad belts of color in the western sky, long gently green pennants, and, here and there, a robustness of red. The colors of the sky were familiar to the miners of Silver Bow and the farmers from the plains, yet because of Mr. Roosevelt, they now took on an exceptional vividness and strangeness. In the field outside the ball-park, a thousand horses stood flank to flank their bodies quivering with enjoyment as they lowered their heads into feed-bags of oats and hay. Their jaws moved with an incessant, toothsome regularity, and their eyes were gentle and apologetic with the satisfaction of appetites appeased. Inside the park, a fresh, wooden platform had been erected in the middle of the field; benches had been placed in lengthy curving arcs fronting the platform. The Montana State Band of thirty musicians arranged themselves in a compact square in the bleachers; they tested and tuned their instruments so that detached and tentative notes and chords floated out into the liquid air, like restless swimmers striking into dark, unknown seas. With these expectations of music reaching their ears, men and women in the park became familiar with one another and exchanged greetings and sallies. They were beginning to speak more familiarly with their own awe; they could separate the different degrees of their awe from the state of their well-being.

"They're tunin' up the band. Teddy'll soon be here."

"An' I seen him once in South Dakota. He was a young man then, ridin' a horse in the Bad Lands o' Dakota."

"Maybe he'll see to it that the miners get a raise in pay."

"That ain't none of his doin'. He ain't got no truck with the minin' company."

On one of the benches sat a farm woman with her screaming infant. At first she tried to calm the child by dangling a rattle in front of its eyes. Then she turned the baby over on its stomach, and for a moment its cries ceased. When it began to cry again, vociferously, the woman turned to her husband, seated next to her, and entered into a low colloquy with him. He nodded his head several times, and she unbuttoned the front of her dress and slipped out a creamy breast. She held the child's head close to her and looked about fearfully, but no one seemed to notice. The infant made quick sucking sounds of relief, and, after a few minutes, the woman held the child off and buttoned her dress. The child began to coo and kick its legs. The father dangled his watch before its astonished eyes.

A cheer started up outside the ball-park. "He's comin' now," someone said, and strangers on the benches began to talk excitedly with one another. "That must be him, now. Well, it's about time. I'm gettin' a mite restless." Men rose off the benches and looked about, and soon everyone had risen, standing in tense expectation. The band took a sudden, frightful dive into the National Anthem. The President appeared on the platform with the Governor and the Mayor. The men on the platform stood perfectly still, holding their high silk hats against their hearts. When the music stopped, the crowd burst into cheers and applause and Mr. Roosevelt waved his hat, forgetting its formality. The platform became an oasis of light when the electricity was turned on, and no one noticed the colors in the sky any more. The Mayor got up and made a speech, gesticulating freely, but the crowd ate popcorn and drank beer during his speech. When he concluded there was great applause, but it was the applause of relief rather than of enthusiasm. The Governor then rose, but his words scarcely reached the edge of the platform; they could not penetrate the restlessness and impatience of the crowd. He spoke, but as if to himself, for no one cared what he said. He was only the Governor, a Company man. He lived in Helena in a mansion, but no one cared about him except the Company who had placed him in office. The crowd whispered and stirred, and babies began crying all over the ball-park. When the Governor finished, it was dark; the moon and stars seemed to shine with a brilliant eagerness in the sky.

Roddy came up to the front of the platform, his massive bulk making the platform look very small. He stilled the babbling voices with his outflung arms. Men leaned forward to hear what he had to say, some of them cupping their ears in their hands. Roddy's voice came out firm and full-bodied, thundering away to the Rockies, the aftertones creating echoes over the plains. "Fellow citizens, ladies and gentlemen of Silver Bow and of Montana, which is the greatest state in the Union . . ." (applause and cheers). . . . "it is my great privilege an' honor to introduce to you tonight, the President of the United States." The crowd liked that. Roddy's voice had cut through the innumerable words spoken before with a sharp, pointed brevity. He had neither said too much nor too little, but what he had spoken was just right. As he turned back to the rear of the platform, the President came forward, stopped him and shook his hand. That was good and honest of Mr. Roosevelt to do a thing like that, shaking hands with Roddy Cornett like that.

Mr. Roosevelt spoke of many things in a large way. He pronounced curves and angles, cubes and circles of words to his listeners. He made patterns of fine words and lusty words, and some of them he piled one on another and then juggled them on the rims of his glistening spectacles. Sometimes, he would remove his spectacles and wipe the lenses with his handkerchief, rubbing off a mist of words. Sometimes he would joke, and then all his hearers would lean forward in their seats, catching at the drift of his lusty humor. They would drink in his jokes and feel his jokes warming up their insides, resting easy against their ribs. How fine it is to be a speaker like Mr. Roosevelt and travel around the country in a private car and speak to thousands of people from a platform decorated in red, white and blue. Oh, say, can you see Mr. Roosevelt rising on his toes in a fine frenzy and tearing the Democrats to pieces, biting into the Democrats with his powerful teeth, chewing the Democrats and spitting them out? Whose bright eyes and broad smiles through the perilous years guided our beautiful, noble nation through to prosperity and happiness? Why, it was Theodore Roosevelt, of course. The man was Wagnerian, and the way he pounded the table with his fists and slammed away at invisible Democrats, that was a way of life, of living in the full turbulence of the stream. In the same way, he must have galloped up San Juan Hill at the head of his Rough Riders, cutting bloody brooks and rivers through the retreating ranks of Spaniards.

"An' one time I come to Washin'ton, D.C., an' waited in line an' shook his hand," said a farmer from Deer Lodge County.

"The way he spits his words out, now, he's a holy terror," murmured a smelter man from Anaconda. "The way he shapes his words with his tongue an' his teeth is like a fine carpenter."

"All day, I stood in line to shake his hand, an' there was rain fallin', but I had no mind of it."

"With his teeth an' his tongue an' his jaws, the way he shapes his words is a treat to listen to."

"He's a big bluffer," broke in another man, a member of the Industrial Workers of the World. "If you ask me, I'd say he was a tool of Mr. Rockefeller's and the Wall Street interests. An' he's here tryin' to fool us with his big, windy words."

"He's a card one way or another," said the smelter man. "Honest or not, he's a whole show to hisself. An' I'm for him."

"He's nothin' but a big wind-bag," said the Wobbly. "What did he do for the miners when they went on strike last year? What did he do for the harvesters in the wheatfields when they wanted more pay an' decent livin' conditions? Where was he when the street railway men walked out in Sea-attle?"

"He's a friend o' the poor people," maintained the smelter man. "Look at the way he's bustin' up the trusts with his Big Stick."

The two men continued to argue, the Wobbly saying that Roosevelt was nothing but a rich man's tool, a representative of the privileged interests, and the smelter man insisting that it was not so at all. Mr. Roosevelt was a good friend to the poor people, a trust-buster and a gentleman. And after Mr. Roosevelt had concluded his speech and nearly all the people had departed from the ball-park, the Wobbly and the smelter man still sat there arguing, flinging words at one another, working themselves into vivid, spasmodic spurts of argument.

■ BEATRICE MURPHY

During the early years of the century, nurse Beatrice Murphy worked the night shift at the Murray Hospital in Butte, Montana. She kept a candid record of her experiences there in the form of a daily diary, which has been preserved in the Butte-Silver Bow Public Archives. Beginning with the reminder that "Blessed is he who expects nothing for he gets it," these excerpts from Murphy's previously unpublished diary are a microcosm of what everyday (and night) life was like at an important time in Butte's history. This selection is from a manuscript edited by Sister Kathleen O'Sullivan and transcribed by Teresa Jordan.

Diary of a Night Nurse

Butte, Mont. Nov 1st to 30th
In the year of our Lord 1909

"Blessed is he who expects nothing for he gets it."

Monday Night Nov 1st 09
Reported on duty @ 7 P.M. Got orders by the wholesale. Favored everybody with a dazzling smile Rushed madly around trying to get things done till midnight when there was a change for the better. Helped Miss Donegan get supper. Ate supper with feverish haste.

Fixed up miner with scalp wound Ditto with crushed finger Took temperatures, gave medicines, &c. Wrote two letters. Started to write a book on hospital life Answered telephone calls. Started to do my morning work. Finished some of it. Called the day nurses Handed in my nightly report to Miss McGregor She seemed pleased. Tripped down stairs with a light heart. Worked some more Everything done nicely Tired feet, but nothing more. Walked 200 miles all told since 7 P.M. No scraps, no biffs Very uneventful night

P.S. Spoke to Dr. Campbell once. Nothing else of any importance

Tuesday Night Nov 2-09
Reported on duty at 7 as usual. Went around to all my patient's rooms Noted changes in their conditions. Some favorable and some worse. Administered doses of Castor Oil to a privileged few. Fixed oil with lemon juice and "fizz" Thought of a day perhaps in the dim future when I, too, would have to take some. Answered door bell Admitted miner with bruised head, saved his life by performing surgical operation on head. broke one needle (didnt swear) Assisted at operation by Dr. McCrackin first assistant Miss Donegan second assistant Floated up to the 5th floor Ate supper of fried chicken accompanied by Miss Mitchell (no comment necessary) Answered telephone calls Fixed up my records. Answered bells till the Lord called on me to stop. Sympathized with Miss Ylintello on the corn and bunion question. Did my morning work, called the day nurses. Sailed in Miss McGregor's room. Gave my report of night work with confident air. Finished up. Ate breakfast. Very good night

Saturday Night Nov 6-'09
Appeared on the scene at the usual time. Found all the day nurses in good spirits (something unusual going to happen) Walked gracefully down the hall Visited my dear patients One man offered me a bottle of beer. Which I refused with becoming dignity. Elevated my nose among the clouds & tried to look horrified One of my lady patients started to have fits, which lasted one half hour. Nothing slow about the way she screamed. Had to shut all the windows for fear of attracting the attention of some passing policeman. Four miners decided to get hurt for a change. Fixed them all up & sent them on their way rejoicing. Answered telephone bells & door bells as fast as I could go Almost had a fight with Miss Donegan. But didn't think it worth while Took a telephone message for Miss Spelman from one of her many admirers Started to take temps and do my morning work. Called

the day Nurses Reported to Miss McGregor A very mild report. Finished work ate breakfast.
Good Night

Monday Night Nov 8. '09
Came on duty a few minutes late on account of visiting with some of the day nurses. Was afraid to miss something Admitted Dutchman the first thing on the program Forced him to take a bath under penalty of death. Was very kind to the dear sick. Mine accident in the shape of a man with hurt back. Armed myself with a large hammer & proceeded to wake up Dr. McCrackin After pounding on the door for some time was rewarded by a feeble cry of welcome. Dr. appeared before me clad in a London smoke bath robe which took my eye & was certainly very classy Fixed up man's back and sent him home to the bosom of his family Door bell rang again. The offending party was just Dr. Murray who condescended to smile at me. Gave him a look as much to say "Slave bend down and tie my shoestring" Came upstairs & worked awful hard. Almost forgot to eat supper Had a debate with my two partners on the "Man Question" Got disgusted & went to work some more. Called day nurses Reported to Miss McGregor. Finished & ate breakfast. Very good night

Tuesday Night Nov 16–'09
Made a noise like a hoop and rolled down stairs @ 7. Found two new patients awfully sick. Rescued them from the jaws of death and the mouth of hell. Was given a carnation which I will treasure to my dying day in remembrance of my Celtic affinity. Found Miss Tribey in 405 bathroom having a fist fight with two enema cans. Smiled a sad sweet smile at her and departed, leaving her to her fate One of my lady patients got smitten on me to such an extent as to try to hug me. Which proceedings I resented with a ferocious glare of my otherwise mild orbits Called Dr. Rodes to the telephone. Was surprised by a hasty call from Dr. Karsted. Door bell rang wildly. Went down stairs and came face to face with a so called broken arm. Made a bee line for Dr. McCrackin's apartments and roused him from his nightmare. Came upstairs took temperatures &c. Called day watch. Handed in my usual "speel" to Mis McGregor. Felt very important Finished
Charming night

Friday Night Nov 19–'09
Stalked on duty with glad and gallant step Was met on the 4th floor by Dr. Rodes who hurt my feelings to such an extent as to almost make me

weep Walked over by the desk sat down & poured forth my soul in song till the call of duty roused me from my reverie. Went down to answer door bell. Was confronted by a miner with crushed foot. Took him in the dressing room and hypnotized him with my magic power. Fixed his foot with skillful touch and sent him forth to face life's battles afresh. Gave pills to all my patients and tried to be faithful unto death about answering bells. Fixed my charts was called a "ministering angel" by a certain individual. Fussed over a sick baby till things began to swim before my vision Couldn't eat supper. Rested awhile to regain my equilibrium Did my morning work Called day nurses. Reported to Miss MacGregor in the cool gray dawn Went to breakfast. Had a social chat with the kids Retired to my "budvoir" very XXX night

Saturday Night Nov 20–'09
Came on duty a few minutes late on account of holding a meeting in my apartments Went down to the 3rd floor and found every one of Miss Walters patients "spooning" Decided they were following the example of their nurse who gets quite spoony at times. . . .

Sunday Night Nov 21–'09
Reported on deck promptly at 7. Found two new patients awaiting my gentle care. Flipped around from room to room and got thru real early. Pushed a drunken man off the elevator & showed him the door. No bells ringing for some unknown reason Wrote two letters and read the society news. Started to study my "physiology & Anatomy." Felt a wave of sympathy arise in my snowy bosom for Miss Donegan. Went up to the 5th floor and volunteered to get supper, had a very delightful repast, retraced my steps down stairs and sat by the desk. Got to thinking seriously on the vanities of this world Decided that man is but a shadow and life a dream Built some beautiful castles in the sunny land of Spain. Came back to earth after a while & found myself in the unromantic atmosphere of Murray Hospital Pinched myself and went around to see if my charges were all right Started to work taking temps &c. Called day nurses Said my little say to Miss McGregor. Had breakfast. retired. Lonesome night

Monday Night Nov 22–'09
Hove in sight @ 7 P. X Started to feel badly right away it being Miss Donegan's last night on Tried to dispel the awful gloomy feeling which took possession of my inmost soul. Went around to see my

beloved patients. Found them all beaming with happiness at the prospect of seeing my gentle eye Took telephone calls and fixed charts. Answered bells studied the function of the liver Saw the manly form of Dr. Campbell approaching up the hall Felt a strange thrill of delight at seeing him Was sorry for Dr. Kistler because he had such a bad cold. Went upstairs. Ate supper. Doorbell buzzed went down & beheld sorry looking object which on closer inspection proved to be a miner with a red bandana tied gracefully around his Fissure of Rolando. Extended the glad hand and invited him into the dressing room. Sewed up his head with a vim of determination Dismissed him into the mysterious air of night Worked awful hard for 3 hours. Called day nurses Reported to Miss McG. partook of light breakfast retired to dreamland
nifty night

Tuesday Night Nov 23–'09
Reported on duty @ 7. P.M. Visited patients, found everything in fine shape. Was given some rose leaves to make a pillow for my future home. Was asked to read an article on old maids which I refused to do. Answered the usual number of telephone calls & bells gave medicines Fixed charts &C. Read "Tales of the Cloister" didn't like it very well. Saw somebody trying to "spoon" on the 4th floor by the desk. Won't tell who it was for various reasons Was jealous of Miss Greenough because she got new patient in the shape of a Scotch piper who wore kilts. Went up stairs & cooked supper to suit myself. Made a solemn resolution that I would never marry a man unless he could afford a cook. Manicured my finger nails to kill time. Wished that something exciting would happen Got very sleepy and tried to study. Morning came at last. Started my work early. Called day nurses @ 6:30. Reported to Miss McGregor. had breakfast. retired to the arms of Morpheus
very quiet Night

Thursday Night Nov 25–'09
Came on duty after being out to Thanksgiving dinner Examined the patients with critical eye Was glad to find Miss Greenough in the best of humor. Told myself she could be real charming if she wanted to. Saw a man make a fuss over his wife. Was very much surprised. Didn't know that men were "Spoony" after being married (I mean with their wives of course) I dont know very much about such things. Never having been there myself One patient told me she

thought I was the head nurse. Made an immediate dash for the linen room and pinned elastic bandage tightly around my chest to keep from getting swelled up. Didn't dare to think how Miss McGregor would feel if she heard such a remark Dr. McCrackin never came up stairs tonight. somebody felt awful bad. It wasn't "Willie" I am too professional and dignified to harbor such foolish thoughts Didn't eat supper. Did my work extra early. Called day nurses Speeled it off to Miss McG. Had slight nourishment. retired
Dandy night

Friday night Nov 26–'09
Reported at head quarters at 7 P.M. Visited my patients promptly and was very businesslike. Clinic held on Miss Lockey's elbow by Drs. McCrackin & Rodes No bones broken which caused the victim to be sadly disappointed Called up a minister of the gospel to prepare a man for death. Man died before priest arrived Miss Greenough very kindly stayed with him while he was breathing his last Sent for coroner and undertaker to dispose of the remains Got supper unaided partook of some which didn't taste very good Made a raid hunting for furniture for the night nurses room stole a table and three chairs assisted by Miss Greenough. Started morning work. Called day nurses. Told Miss McGregor my "tale of night" Had breakfast Floated down to the dressing room. sharpened razor to cut my corns Tried to steal some pictures for our room but was prevented by Mr. Patterson Cut part of my toe off with razor. Wept & went to bed
strenuous night

Sunday Night Nov 28 '09
Reported on duty at 7 P.M. Visited patients Gave medicines. Answered bells & telephones, manicured finger nails while things were quiet Miss Greenough carried things too far by painting her face & lips Made her look like a fright. She probably thought she would make a hit but got left The excitement of the evening happened when one of Miss Lockey's patients did the acrobatic stunt of the season by falling out of bed and hitting his upper extremity against the radiator I rushed madly down to the field of action and with the Assistance of Divine Providence got him safely back to bed again. The reporters called up wanting to know if there were any accidents I didn't tell them what I knew. Had supper cooked by the expert hand of Miss Greenough. Made plans for organizing a foot ball team among the nurses Appointed Miss Olson as center rush Did the morning work

Reported to Miss McGregor in awe struck tones. Retired to sleep. Swell night

Monday Night Nov 29–'09
Came on deck at 7 P.M. sharp. Found five new patients awaiting my gentle touch. Tried to make an impression on them with my virtuous personality. . . . Had to answer all kinds of bells and telephones Worked till I was perspiring freely. Felt weak all over Almost made up my mind to go out to the fire station and apply for a job attaching the hose Changed my course. Went up stairs ate supper with deliberate haste. Nick named Miss Lockey "Scarey William" owing to her extreme cowardice at night. Worked on worked ever . . . till it came time to call day nurses. Told Miss McG. a very brilliant report. went to my apartments.
Unspeakable night

Tuesday Night Nov 30–'09
Reported at headquarters @ 7 P.M. Work much harder than usual. Every room occupied. Rushed around with the speed of a locomotive. In the midst of my hurry miner arrived suffering from a broken clavical. The attending physician aimlessly remarked that it was caused from trying to walk on his shoulder (very brilliant indeed) Tried to do what I could to relieve suffering humanity. Extended sympathy to Miss Greenough because she got "sat on" Read "The Straw" by Rina Ramsey very racey book Went on an exploring trip down to the first floor accompanied by Miss Lockey Looted the Drs. dining room "bagged" some salad and a dish of nuts. Thought we heard Lena on our trail. Made a wild dash for liberty and escaped by way of the elevator to the 5th floor & the protecting arms of Miss Greenough Had supper. started morning work taking temps &c Felt sorry because it was my last night Called day nurses approached Miss McGregor & told her "the old, old story." retired
Impossible Night

■ MARY MacLANE

"I want Fame," nineteen-year-old Mary MacLane wrote in the first pages of The Story of Mary MacLane, *published in 1902; and her outspoken style and unconventional attitudes gave it to her. MacLane had come with her family to Butte in 1891 when she was ten years old. The publication of her first book,* The Story of Mary MacLane, *made her an instant national sensation and brought her the notoriety that she so obviously desired. In 1917, she presented her unorthodox views again in* I, Mary MacLane *(from which "A Working Diaphragm" and "God Compensates Me" are taken), and her reputation as an independent and eccentric free spirit was confirmed. MacLane died in Chicago on August 7, 1929.*

From The Story of Mary MacLane

JANUARY 17

As I have said, I want Fame. I want to write—to write such things as compel the admiring acclamations of the world at large; such things as are written but once in years, things subtly but distinctly different from the books written every day.

I can do this.

Let me but make a beginning, let me but strike the world in a vulnerable spot, and I can take it by storm. Let me but win my spurs, and then you will see me—of womankind and young—valiantly astride a charger riding down the world, with Fame following at the charger's heels, and the multitudes agape.

But oh, more than all this I want to be happy!

Fame is indeed benign and gentle and satisfying. But Happiness is something at once tender and brilliant beyond all things.

I want Fame more than I can tell.

But more than I want Fame I want Happiness. I have never been happy in my weary young life.

Think, oh, *think*, of being happy for a year—for a day! How brilliantly blue the sky would be; how swiftly and joyously would the green rivers run; how madly, merrily triumphant the four winds of heaven would sweep round the corners of the fair earth!

What would I not give for one day, one hour, of that charmed thing Happiness! What would I not give up? . . .

I am fortunate that I am not one of those who are burdened with an innate sense of virtue and honor which must come always before

Happiness. They are but few who find their Happiness in their Virtue. The rest of them must be content to see it walk away. . . .

JANUARY 18

And meanwhile—as I wait—my mind occupies itself with its own good odd philosophy, so that even the Nothingness becomes almost endurable.

The Devil has given me some good things—for I find that the Devil owns and rules the earth and all that therein is. He has given me, among other things—my admirable young woman's-body, which I enjoy thoroughly and of which I am passionately fond.

A spasm of pleasure seizes me when I think in some acute moment of the buoyant health and vitality of this fine young body that is feminine in every fiber.

You may gaze at and admire the picture in the front of this book. It is the picture of a genius—a genius with a good strong young woman's-body,—and inside the pictured body is a liver, a Mac Lane liver, of admirable perfectness.

Other young women and older women and men of all ages have good bodies also, I doubt not—though the masculine body is merely flesh, it seems, flesh and bones and nothing else. But few recognize the value of their bodies; few have grasped the possibilities, the artistic graceful perfection, the poetry of human flesh in its health. Few have even sense enough indeed to keep their flesh in health, or to know what health is until they have ruined some vital organ, and so banish it forever.

I have not ruined any of my vital organs, and I appreciate what health is. I have grasped the art, the poetry of my fine feminine body.

This at the age of nineteen is a triumph for me.

Sometime in the midst of the brightness of an October I have walked for miles in the still high air under the blue of the sky. The brightness of the day and the blue of the sky and the incomparable high air have entered into my veins and flowed with my red blood. They have penetrated into every remote nerve-center and into the marrow of my bones.

At such a time this young body glows with life.

My red blood flows swiftly and joyously—in the midst of the brightness of October.

My sound, sensitive liver rests gently with its thin yellow bile in sweet content.

My calm, beautiful stomach silently sings, as I walk, a song of peace.

My lungs, saturated with mountain ozone and the perfume of the pines, expand in continuous ecstasy.

My heart beats like the music of Schumann, in easy, graceful rhythm with an undertone of power.

My strong and sensitive nerves are reeking and swimming in sensuality like drunken little Bacchantes, gay and garlanded in mad revelling.

The entire wonderful, graceful mechanism of my woman's-body has fallen at the time—like the wonderful, graceful mechanism of my woman's-mind—under the enchanting spell of a day in October.

"It is good," I think to myself, "oh, it is good to be alive! It is wondrously good to be a woman young in the fullness of nineteen springs. It is unutterably lovely to be a healthy young animal living on this charmed earth." . . .

JANUARY 26

I sit at my window and look out upon the housetops and chimneys of Butte. As I look I have a weary, disgusted feeling.

People are abominable creatures.

Under each of the roofs live a man and a woman joined together by that very slender thread, the marriage ceremony—and their children, the result of the marriage ceremony.

How many of them love each other? Not two in a hundred, I warrant. The marriage ceremony is their one miserable, petty, paltry excuse for living together.

This marriage rite, it appears, is often used as a cloak to cover a world of rather shameful things.

How virtuous these people are, to be sure, under their different roof-trees. So virtuous are they indeed that they are able to draw themselves up in the pride of their own purity, when they happen upon some corner where the marriage ceremony is lacking. So virtuous are they that the men can afford to find amusement and diversion in the woes of the corner that is without the marriage rite; and the women may draw away their skirts in shocked horror and wonder that such things can be, in view of their own spotless virtue.

And so they live on under the roofs, and they eat and work and sleep and die; and the children grow up and seek other roofs, and call upon the marriage ceremony even as their parents before them—and then they likewise eat and work and sleep and die; and so on world without end.

This also is life—the life of the good, virtuous Christians.

I think, therefore, that I should prefer some life that is not virtuous.

I shall never make use of the marriage ceremony. I hereby register a vow, Devil, to that effect.

When a man and a woman love one another that is enough. That is marriage. A religious rite is superfluous. And if the man and woman live together without the love, no ceremony in the world can make it marriage. The woman who does this need not feel the tiniest bit better than her lowest sister in the streets. Is she not indeed a step lower since she pretends to be what she is not—plays the virtuous woman? While the other unfortunate pretends nothing. She wears her name on her sleeve.

If I were obliged to be one of these I would rather be she who wears her name on her sleeve. I certainly would. The lesser of two evils, always.

I can think of nothing in the world like the utter littleness, the paltriness, the contemptibleness, the degradation, of the woman who is tied down under a roof with a man who is really nothing to her; who wears the man's name, who bears the man's children—who plays the virtuous woman. There are too many such in the world now.

May I never, I say, become that abnormal, merciless animal, that deformed monstrosity—a virtuous woman.

Anything, Devil, but that.

And so, as I look out over the roofs and chimneys, I have a weary, disgusted feeling.

JANUARY 28

I am an artist of the most artistic, the highest type. I have uncovered for myself the art that lies in obscure shadows. I have discovered the art of the day of small things.

And that surely is art with a capital "A."

I have acquired the art of Good Eating. Usually it is in the gray and elderly forties and fifties that people cultivate this art—if they ever do; it is indeed a rare art.

But I know it in all its rare exquisiteness at the young slim age of nineteen—which is one more mark of my genius, do you see?

The art of Good Eating has two essential points: one must eat only when one is hungry, and one must take small bites.

There are persons who eat for the sake of eating. They are gourmands, and partake of the natures of the pig and the buzzard. There are persons who take bites that are not small. These also are gourmands and partake of the natures of the pig and the buzzard. There are persons who can enjoy nothing in the way of eating except a luxurious, well-appointed meal. These, it is safe to say, have not acquired the art of anything.

But I—I have acquired the art of eating an olive.

Now listen, and I will tell you the art of eating an olive:

I take the olive in my fingers, and I contemplate its green oval richness. It makes me think at once of the land where the green citron grows—where the cypress and myrtle are emblems; of the land of the Sun where human beings are delightfully, enchantingly wicked,—where the men are eager and passionate, and the women gracefully developed in mind and in body—and their two breasts show round and full and delicately veined beneath thin drapery.

The mere sight of the olive conjures up this charming picture in my mind.

I set my teeth and my tongue upon the olive, and bite it. It is bitter, salt, delicious. The saliva rushes to meet it, and my tongue is a happy tongue. As the morsel of olive rests in my mouth and is crunched and squeezed lusciously among my teeth, a quick, temporary change takes place in my character. I think of some adorable lines of the Persian poet: "Give thyself up to Joy, for thy Grief will be infinite. The stars shall again meet together at the same point in the firmament, but of thy body shall bricks be made for a palace wall."

"Oh, dear, sweet, bitter olive!" I say to myself.

The bit of olive slips down my red gullet, and so into my stomach. There it meets with a joyous welcome. Gastric juices leap out from the walls and swathe it in loving embrace. My stomach is fond of something bitter and salt. It lavishes flattery and endearment galore upon the olive. It laughs in silent delight. It feels that the day it has long waited for has come. The philosophy of my stomach is wholly epicurean. Let it receive but a tiny bit of olive and it will reck not of the morrow, nor of the past. It lives, voluptuously, in the present. It is content. It is in paradise.

I bite the olive again. Again the bitter salt crisp ravishes my tongue. "If this be vanity,—vanity let it be." The golden moments flit by and I heed them not. For am I not comfortably seated and eating an olive? Go hang yourself, you who have never been comfortably seated and eating an olive! My character evolves farther in its change. I am now bent on reckless sensuality, let happen what will. The fair earth seems to resolve itself into a thing oval and crisp and good and green and deliciously salt. I experience a feeling of fervent gladness that I am a female thing living, and that I have a tongue and some teeth, and salivary glands.

Also this bit slips down my red gullet, and again the festive Stomach lifts up a silent voice in psalms and rejoicing. It is now an absolute monarchy with the green olive at its head. The kisses of the gastric juice become hot and sensual and convulsive and ecstatic. "Avaunt, pale, shadowy ghosts of dyspepsia!" says my Stomach. "I know you not. I am of a brilliant, shining world. I dwell in Elysian fields."

Once more I bite the olive. Once more is my tongue electrified. And the third stage in my temporary transformation takes place. I am now a gross but supremely contented sensualist. An exquisite symphony of sensualism and pleasure seems to play somewhere within me. My heart purrs. My brain folds its arms and lounges. I put my feet up on the seat of another chair. The entire world is now surely one delicious green olive. My mind is capable of conceiving but one idea—that of a green olive. Therefore the green olive is a perfect thing—absolutely a perfect thing.

Disgust and disapproval are excited only by imperfections. When a thing is perfect, no matter how hard one may look at it, one can see only itself—itself, and nothing beyond.

And so I have made my olive and my art perfect. . . .

MARCH 8

There are several things in the world for which I, of womankind and nineteen years, have conceived a forcible repugnance—or rather, the feeling was born in me; I did not have to conceive it.

Often my mind chants a fervent litany of its own that runs somewhat like this:

From women and men who dispense odors of musk; from little boys with long curls; from the kind of people who call a woman's figure her "shape": Kind Devil, deliver me.

From all sweet girls; from "gentlemen"; from feminine men: Kind Devil, deliver me.

From black under-clothing—and any color but white; from hips that wobble as one walks; from persons with fishy eyes; from the books of Archibald C. Gunter and Albert Ross: Kind Devil, deliver me.

From the soft persistent, maddening glances of water-cart drivers: Kind Devil, deliver me.

From lisle-thread stockings; from round, tight garters; from brilliant brass belts: Kind Devil, deliver me.

From insipid sweet wine; from men who wear moustaches; from the sort of people that call legs "limbs"; from bedraggled white petticoats: Kind Devil, deliver me.

From unripe bananas; from bathless people; from a waist-line that slopes up in the front: Kind Devil, deliver me.

From an ordinary man; from a bad stomach, bad eyes, and bad feet: Kind Devil, deliver me.

From red note-paper; from a rhinestone-studded comb in my hair; from weddings: Kind Devil, deliver me.

From cod-fish balls, from fried egg plant, fried beef-steak, fried pork-chops, and fried French toast: Kind Devil, deliver me.

From wax flowers off a wedding-cake, under glass; from thin-soled shoes; from tape-worms; from photographs perched up all over my house: Kind Devil, deliver me.

From soft old bachelors and soft old widowers; from any masculine thing that wears a pale blue necktie; from agonizing elocutionists who recite "Curfew Shall Not Ring To-Night," and "The Lips That Touch Liquor Shall Never Touch Mine"; from a Salvation Army singing hymns in slang: Kind Devil, deliver me. . . .

APRIL 2

How can any one bring a child into the world and not wrap it round with a certain wondrous tenderness that will stay with it always!

There are persons whose souls have never entered into them.

My mother has some fondness for me—for my body because it came of hers. That is nothing—nothing.

A hen loves its egg.

A hen!

A Working Diaphragm

To-morrow

I am not Respectable nor Refined nor in Good Taste.

I take a delicate M.-Mac-Lane pleasure in those facts.

I doubt if they are anyway peculiar to me, but they feel like a someway delicious clandestine circumstance: something to enjoy all to myself.

It is difficult to imagine any woman really Respectable on her inner side, the side that is turned toward herself alone. And it's certain no woman is Refined: it feels not possible. (There are yet inland places where the word is used in its smug sense and believed in.) And no woman but a dead woman in her coffin is in complete Good Taste. Every live woman has for instance a working diaphragm: and in a diaphragm there is, in the final analysis, simply no taste at all. . . .

God Compensates Me

To-morrow

It's a Sunday midnight and I've just eaten a Cold Boiled Potato.

I shall never be able to write one-tenth of my fondness for a Cold Boiled Potato.

A Cold Boiled Potato is always an unpremeditated episode which is its chief charm.

It's nice to happen on a book of poetry on a windowsill. It's nice to surprise a square of chocolate in a glove box. It's nice to come upon a little yellow apple in ambush. It's nice to get an unexpected letter from Jane Gillmore. It's nice to unearth a reserve fund of silk stockings under a sofa pillow. And especially it's nice to find a Cold Boiled Potato on a pantry shelf at midnight.

I like caviare at luncheon. And I like venison at dinner, dark and bloody and rich. And I like champagne bubbling passionately in a hollow-stemmed glass on New Year's day. And I like terrapin turtle. And I like French-Canadian game-pie. And artichokes and grapes and baby onions. And none of them has the odd gnome-ish charm of a Cold Boiled Potato at midnight.

I can imagine no circumstance in which a Cold Boiled Potato would not take precedent with me at midnight. If I had a broken arm: if I had a husband lying dead in the next room: if I were facing abrupt worldly disaster: if there were a burglar in the house: if I'd had a dayful of depression: if God and opportunity were knocking and clamoring at my door: I should disregard each and all some minutes at midnight if I had also a Cold Boiled Potato. I love to read Keats's Nightingale in my hushed life. I love to remember Caruso at the Metropolitan singing Celeste Aida. I love to watch the bewitching blonde Blanche Sweet in a moving picture. I love to feel the summer moonlight on my eyelids. And it's disarmingly contented I am with a Cold Boiled Potato at midnight.

Content is my rarest emotion and I get it at midnight out of a Cold Boiled Potato.

Some things in life thrill me. Some drive me garbledly mad. Some uplift me. Some debauch me. Some strengthen and enlighten me. Some hurt, hurt, hurt. But I'm not thrilled nor maddened nor uplifted nor debauched nor strengthened nor enlightened nor hurt, but only fed-up and fattened in spirit by a Cold Boiled Potato at midnight.

I stand in the pantry door leaning against the jamb, with a tiny glass salt-shaker in one hand and the sweet dark pink Cold Boiled Potato in the other. And I sprinkle it with salt and I nibble, nibble, nibble. And I say aloud, 'Gee, it's good!'

I liked Cold Boiled Potato at four and twenty. I liked it at seventeen. I liked it at twelve. At three I climbed on cake-boxes in search of one. And now in the deep bloom of being myself I am made roundly replete at midnight with a Cold Boiled Potato.

■ CLYDE MURPHY

Born in Great Falls in 1899, Clyde F. Murphy left Montana to serve in World War I, but he returned to live in Butte and to attend law school at Montana State University in Missoula. Murphy became a successful attorney in Los Angeles, but he gave up that career to write full time. This selection is from Murphy's novel about Butte, Glittering Hill *(1944), which won E. P. Dutton's first Lewis and Clark prize for the best manuscript submitted by a Northwest writer. Murphy died in 1946.*

From Glittering Hill

Tom Gary and Denny O'Shea were walking to the O'Hara home. The coolness of evening had settled on the Gulch.

"We may be too early," Tom said, uneasily.

"Oh, no," responded Denny.

"What if the family is alone?"

"What of it?" Denny was losing patience.

"What'll we say? That we've been invited? Or what?"

"Aw, Tom, my boy, who's gonna ask questions? Put yourself in the place of the family. A knock comes on the door. One of them goes to answer it. Does he say 'Who are you?' or 'Who asked you here?' "

"Well, maybe not," said Tom doubtfully, "but I'll feel like hell sitting in a strange house not knowing anybody, not even the dead man."

"You're too squeamish, Tom," said Denny, eager to dismiss the subject.

Tom was unequal to further argument. Sullen and quiet, he walked with Denny along the narrow plank sidewalk. The kids in the street—boys wearing overalls and girls in shabby dresses—were playing "Run Sheep Run"; their excited cries rang through the Gulch and their shoes made clapping sounds on the hard-packed clay. Their faces red and shiny and their eyes dancing, they ran themselves short of breath, now in pursuit, and again in wild flight.

A freckled-faced boy of ten impudently rolled a hoop at them, deflecting it with a deft turn of his wrist an instant before it reached them. His grin revealed two rows of gleaming white teeth, with a dark spot left by the loss of a tooth in the middle. Tom and Denny passed a group of larger boys and girls playing "Shinny" with heavy sticks and a battered tin can in the center of the dusty street. Tom reflected gloomily that all about him was noise and laughter, spirit and life, yet here he was being taken, against his will, and his better judgment, to the grim and sorrowful silence, the ghastly whispers and warm heavy air of a house of death. He was a goddamned crazy fool to be going to this wake! A hypocrite too! Why should he perform the mockery of praying for a man, now dead, whom he had never known in life? That wasn't all. Why should he use the poor man's wake as a means of drinking and hobnobbing with people who "counted" in Butte? The whole goddamned thing was insane! For his part in it he should be given a good swift kick in the butt.

Tom really had been afraid of wakes all his life. His mother and father, his brothers and sisters, had been terrified by them. And Tom had always thought that most Irish people to go, loud and jaunty, to a wake must first conquer a deep sense of dread. The Irish went to the houses of the dead because, at them, they were certain to get some kind of a shock to their spirit. They heard the wailing and it did something strange and mystical to them. They murmured their high-blown praises of the dead, gave their word-comforts to the bereaved, joined fervently with their friends and neighbors in the rosary and their hearts were washed free of smallness, enmity and shame. But still they were afraid. When the "keen" was raised over the corpse, that ancient, weird Irish cry, their pulses throbbed, their spirits were swept upward with the rising of the cry, reaching the peak of their terror and ecstasy at the "keening's" highest sustained note. When the cry ended in an abrupt and stricken silence, they were left weak and trembling in that odd zone of the human spirit which borders death itself. . . .

Sounds of whispering came from the dining room, little hissing noises like those from a leaking faucet. Tom looked into the dining room and saw the widow, a thin little soul, sitting with a dark shawl over her shoulders, staring ahead and nodding, ceaselessly, as a well-fed woman, very broad in the middle, told her how to get hold of herself. Touched by the picture of the frail woman, filled with grief and confusion, Tom thought of how Denny and he had butted in, and the reason for their coming, and he burned with anger and shame. He really ought to get up and drag Denny into the street and beg the first man who came along to kick both of them hard enough to jar their teeth loose. That's just what the both of them deserved.

Tom looked at Denny once more and saw that he had not altered his sorrowful expression; he still was somber and priestly though he had begun to slouch in his chair enough to cause the fleshy part of his underchin to sag over his collar.

Just then heavy footfalls sounded on the porch and Weeshy O'Toole rushed to the door.

"Well, well, well, boys," he said.

The words Weeshy used, in themselves, were quite above reproach but the tone of his greeting was a little too festive. In the next few minutes Denny and Tom shook hands with Hogan, who was a paunchy imposing man past fifty, with a rangier specimen named Cassidy about Hogan's age, with Stubby Cavanaugh who was thirty and sandy and wrinkled and had blue eyes that watered when he laughed, with Derg Finley, a tall, dark scowling giant bordering forty, with Phelim Keane, a thin dyspeptic-looking man wearing nose glasses and lastly, with Donner Gribbin, heavy, bug-eyed and a little too loud in the mouth.

These newcomers said their prayers at the kneeling bench with less piety than haste and then they filed gravely into the dining room, shook hands with the widow and whispered hoarse, manly condolences. When they came back to the parlor, Tom and Denny stood and motioned to their chairs but the group, as a group, waved their broad hands and smiled and said they wouldn't think of taking those chairs.

By now the front door was hardly closed at any time. Men and women came in groups, some white and startled and quiet, others eager and alert for cronies. The women took their turns at the kneeling bench, went into the dining room and whispered to the widow briefly and then took chairs and stared straight ahead. Their expressions were seraphic but Tom knew enough about Irish women at Irish wakes to know that their minds teemed with questions of how much their husbands would take aboard, whether anyone would get punched tonight in this house of the dead, and how they would manage to get their husbands home under their own power.

When the parlor became congested, Denny and Tom relinquished their seats to the ladies and then they, too, stood in a corner with Hogan and Cassidy and Stubby and Derg and Phelim and Donner. Singularly enough, all these men seemed to decide, at the same instant, that the parlor had become too crowded and that it was more fitting that the women folks keep the seats in the best part of the house and that they themselves should go to the kitchen.

They left the parlor in a group and, gathering out in the kitchen, began to talk in low assured tones about Toss O'Hara, the dead man, and what a hell of a decent fellow he had been. Some one of them reminded the others that Toss was a damn good miner too, and, not only that, he was a close friend of Magnus Dunn.

Tom Gary pricked up his ears at the mention of Magnus Dunn, and he heard the men about him say that Dunn had discovered that Butte Hill was solid copper and had gotten rich and famous but it hadn't changed him a bit. He still liked to mooch a chew of tobacco from one of the boys and sit on the curb and talk politics by the hour. A great horseman too. His were the finest race horses in the Northwest. He had some Irish horses and some French horses and some Arabian horses, and he was breeding them so as to get their blood all mixed up into a wonder horse he could take back to the Atlantic seaboard and beat the be-Jesus out of those snobbish eastern bastards. That same man Magnus Dunn was going to come to this very house this very night. He never missed the wake of an old friend and Toss O'Hara, God bless him and may God have mercy on his soul, was a friend of Dunn's if ever a man was. . . .

"Yes, sir," Hogan was saying for the fiftieth time, "it's a damn shame that a man like Toss O'Hara had to go. A damn shame, no less. Why is the best the first to go, will you tell me that now?"

Weeshy put a glass in his hand.

"What's this?" said Hogan, astounded. "Well yes, I will," he said to Weeshy. "Not much now, just a little. Whoop, whoop there–wait a minute, wait a minute, that's too much fur me. Well, I'll take it, now that you've poured it, but it's damned heavy and I just had my supper.

"Now wasn't you askin' about Magnus Dunn, Mr. O'Shea?" Hogan coughed daintily. "Well sir, that's a man fur you. He come to Butte twelve years ago, quiet-like, and prowled around the hill laughin' up his sleeve at all the monkeys who was diggin' fur gold and silver. Foxy, he was, as foxy as hell. He writes to his bosses–the Walker Brothers–and, says he, 'these crazy bastards is diggin' fur gold up here in a hill that's solid copper. Send me some money so's I can do a little diggin' o' me own.' That's just what he said only maybe he didn't use that swear word. Well sir, he got the money, that he did, and he used it up and. . . ."

Weeshy tapped Hogan on the elbow. The jug was handy.

"What is it?" Hogan frowned impatiently, then caught sight of the jug. "Oh, thanks, I will." Hogan dispatched the drink he held and thrust his empty toward Weeshy, who poured it full. "Now as I was sayin' about Dunn," Hogan resumed. . . .

Weeshy was reaching at Hogan.

"What is it, man?" Hogan's disposition was getting brittle. "Oh, you want the glass. Well, here's the best, gentlemen."

Hogan put away the second drink with deftness. "Um-um. Tastes like Grogan's best," he said, smacking his lips. "Now Mr. O'Shea, as I was sayin' about Dunn: he got the first batch o' money and spent it trying to find copper. Then he sent fur some more money and his backers was yellow bellies and they got squeamish and they turned him down and he cried like a baby. But he pulls himself together and goes down to California and gets a real wad o' money outa Senator Hearst and a Turk named Haggin and back he comes to Butte and does some more diggin' and, would you believe it, he hit it. Yes, sir, he. . . ."

Weeshy appeared with another glass and began to tilt the jug.

"Well that's right good of you, Weeshy," said Hogan. "Yes, it's right good. Ah–ah, not too much now. Well, gentlemen–here's to the one that ain't here, Toss O'Hara, the finest miner in all of Butte, God rest his soul." . . .

Gribbin began to paw Hogan's coat-front, tears on his cheeks.

"Gribbin," screamed Hogan, backing away, "will you, fur the love o' God, remember that this is Toss O'Hara's last night on earth? Sure I'll drink with you. To Toss, may God rest his soul. Now goddamn you Gribbin, pull yourself together and quit blubberin'. Your eyes is red as a turkey's wattles. There's too goddamned much sadness in this world. Laugh a little is what I say and that's what good old Toss O'Hara would say if he was right here. Are you gonna disgrace this whole affair by cryin' around here instead of takin' care of these gentlemen's wishes? All right, now go along and leave me be."

Hogan leaned into the circle of men about O'Shea.

"Pardon my absence, boys," he murmured graciously, "I had to nip that dummy in the heels. Donner's always getting so drunk he makes a goddamned fool of himself." Hogan stole a peek over his shoulder. "Oh ho," said Hogan in disgust, "what'd I tell you all. See him will you. He's got the jug balanced on his face now. Tsk-tsk-tsk-tsk. There's one that can't drink like a gentleman."

Hogan turned scornfully from the sight of Donner Gribbin.

"Now, Mr. O'Shea, suppose you tell us about your friend. Now what am I sayin'? MISTER O'Shea! Why it's Denny O'Shea." Hogan's voice went into a shout. "Now let's get this boys: no more Misterin' around here tonight. This here's Denny and his partner over in the corner there is Tom." Hogan's voice lowered again. "Say now, Denny, would you be leanin' over just a little closer. This one's on the quiet. Is your friend Gary sore at us or what? Is he the kind that looks down his nose or what?"

"No sir. He's the best ever. A real man."

"Yes? Well he does look tough and he's got a fine cut o' the jaw. A real man I'd say. Now Denny, my old friend, you was goin' to tell us about that lady."

"Well, boys," said Denny, "I'll tell you. Is everything clear there? Well now Mrs. Grundy had a new set of tea dishes with pictures of men in red hunting coats and dogs nosing around in the brush and she asked her neighbor Mrs. Corcoran over to have some tea, outa the brand-new cups. When the two ladies finished their first cup, Mrs. Grundy says: 'And will you be havin' another cup o' tea, Mrs. Corcoran?' Mrs. Corcoran hands over her cup and says: 'Yes, Mrs. Grundy, I will, but this time fill it no higher than that black dog's ass.'"

The roar of laughter shook the house.

"Shh-shh–wait a minute, wait a minute," warned Hogan nervously, "not so loud. After all it's Toss's last night here and let's not–you know."

Weeshy came again with the jug.

"What? Yes, I will thanks, Weeshy, but not too much." Hogan looked into a far corner. "Say Stubby," he said, "would you just step over to the corner there and slip a chair under Donner's butt. He'll close up like a jackknife in a minute." Hogan faced O'Shea again. "Now, Denny, I must say that Mrs. Corcoran was a case and no less. And while we're on the subject let me tell you boys that we laugh at the old country Irish, all right. They're comical characters and all that but there's some pretty wise birds among 'em and don't forget it. They're simple but there's somethin' about 'em that warms my very heart. I hope I never get too high toned fur the ones from the old sod."

Harrigan told Hogan to shut up.

"What? What d'ya mean 'Shut up?' Now lookee here you ring-tailed bastard don't you. . . ."

"Denny's gonna tell us another," protested Harrigan.

"Oh, that's different! Go ahead Denny–say Denny you got the heart of the Irish. . . ."

"For Chrissake, Hogan," yelled Luther.

"All right, all right," said Hogan, "I was just tellin' the man."

Denny cleared his throat. "Well boys, ahem, is everything all right there? Now gather in just a little closer. This same Mrs. Corcoran hated her neighbor Mrs. Lafferty who lived just across the road. Every time Mrs. Corcoran went out, Mrs. Lafferty was sitting in the big bay window of her house lookin' out as proud as you please. One day Mrs. Corcoran was on her way to the center of town and she looked over and she sees Mrs. Lafferty in her window and so she yells: 'Mrs. Lafferty, in God's name, why don't you pull yer face away from that window and stick your big ass out? 'Twould make a better picture than that face, you may believe me.'"

His hearers bellowed their laughter.

"Shh-shh–wait a minute, wait a minute," yelled Hogan, "fur the love of God gentlemen, not so loud. This is the house of the dead. You're all laughin' here like you was back at Grogan's bar."

"Well now I ain't finished yet, boys," said Denny.

"Hogan will you keep that goddamned trumpet mouth o' yours sewed up fur a few minutes 'til Denny gets through with his story?" begged Luther.

Denny went on, after the kitchen quieted. "Well boys, when Mrs. Corcoran told Mrs. Lafferty to take her face outa the window and shove her ass out, Mrs. Lafferty says, quick as a flash: 'Stick my ass out, eh Mrs. Corcoran? Why I did that very thing just yesterday and while my ass was out the window the mail-man comes along and he says to my ass, "How d'ya do there Mrs. Corcoran and when did you move across the road." ' "

This time the laughter was a thundering salvo. . . .

"Now, boys, if we just get in close here, Denny is goin' to give us a little song," said Hogan.

"What in the name of Jesus!" begged Phelim Keane, "here in this house? What can you be thinkin' of, Hogan? Well–be mighty quiet now. Wait a minute, wait a minute don't start it yet. I'll see if everything's clear. All right, but mighty soft now. Say fur cripes' sake, fill Denny's glass, Stubby, what in hell's the matter?"

Tom, still in the corner, took a cigar from his pocket.

Stubby bobbed and weaved toward him and said,

"Where's your glass?"

Tom said, "I had enough, thanks."

Stubby went away with his feelings hurt, muttering,

"The big bastard ought to have his nose punched, comin' to a gatherin' like this and turnin' down the drinks that're bein' passed around to keep everybody's mind from bein' too depressed, what with Toss O'Hara gone and all that."

Tom heard Denny singing softly.

> Oh, Evalina and I went a-fishing one day,
> 'Twas down on the banks of old Chesapeake Bay,
> She caught a sucker and I caught a bass,
> And she fell in the water clear up to her–
> ASK me no question for I'll never tell,
> How far in the water poor Evaline fell.

Now she had a brother down old Brighton Way,
Whose hobby was swimming around Brighton Bay,
He dove and he swam clear out to a rock,
And amused all the ladies by shaking his—
FIST at the p'liceman who pinched him before.
Now. . . .

"Shh-shh wait a minute, wait a minute boys," said Phelim Keane, "the priest is here. We gotta go out. And say Stubby—get a good stiff one fur the Father. He's a great one, Denny. Real old country Irish he is. The real stuff. Wait 'til you hear him sound off. It'll open your eyes and ears my boy. You'll like him. He's real. He's the salt of the earth. Come on, Mr. Gary—you, too."

Tom followed the group out of the kitchen and stood in the dining room. He was startled to see the size of the crowd that was now in the house. The dining room and parlor were packed to the walls. The rooms were hot and the odor of perspiration had mixed with the sweetish odor of flowers to make a ghastly combination that caused Tom's stomach to quiver a little. Of the men and women and children crowded in these small rooms, most were very sad. Some women were sniffling and dabbing their eyes with handkerchiefs. The priest, in the center of all of them, was a short fat man with a very red face and a thick black head of hair. His eyes seemed to shine like shoe buttons. He stood glowering, as if challenging someone to a fight. But soon he got the quiet that he wanted and began to speak in a rich low voice. He gave a short blessing, then went to the coffin and led all in a rosary.

After the ceremony the priest went into the kitchen and promptly took a drink. When he met Denny O'Shea, he looked closely at him and grinned and Denny told him a mild story about a hired man and a calf. The priest laughed a little but not too much. As he looked at Denny he had a foxy expression on his face. Tom could see that soon this priest would be eating out of Denny's hand just as Father Mulcahy had done back home. The priest took another drink with Denny and said he'd have to be going. Several men pressed him to stay but he said he had to get up for early mass in the morning and he would expect to see every one of them at the church and out at the graveyard too. As he went around and shook hands with everyone, he looked straight into their faces as if he were trying to glare a little religion into them. The man next to Tom said it was Father Reardon's way. He looked tough and acted tough but there never was a better man to go to confession to—he never threw the book at you or called a cop when he heard what you had to say. When the priest left, Stubby took up the jug and went the rounds saying in a soft voice that the old pumps needed priming and they might as well have a drop now that the good Father had gone home like the good fellow that he was.

"Now Denny, old boy, you was well into a little song when His Reverence came in," said Hogan. "Wait a minute now, boys, let's give Denny a drink. His glass is empty and that whistle o' his has to be oiled a little, otherwise how would we get a song from him?"

"Wait, wait, wait for God's sake man." It was Weeshy, greatly agitated. "Don't start that stuff now—Magnus Dunn's here."

Tom got excited himself and left the corner of the kitchen where he had been standing. Hogan swung into action, took full authority and began barking orders right and left.

"Stubby, you take that goddamned drunken bum of a Donner Gribbin outside and hide him in the woodshed. Put that jug away Weeshy and be mighty damned quick about it, too. And now fur God's sake men straighten up your ties and fix your hair a little. The place looks like Grogan's back room and Magnus Dunn himself's out there tsk-tsk-tsk-tsk."

A quietness dropped upon the whole house. The kitchen crowd, all trying to get through the door at one time, bumped each other and made so much noise the women in the dining room glowered over their shoulders and pressed their lips tight and thin. Tom was tall enough to see over the heads of the others. A broad man with white hair and a long silvery mustache knelt at the coffin bench and said his prayers slowly, his head bowed. All other persons in the house were quiet and reverent, hardly breathing as they wondered just what would happen when that man completed his prayers. Who would shake hands with him and what should be said? When Magnus Dunn finished praying, he stood up and gravely looked around. Hogan the Wise saved the occasion by coming quickly out of the crowd, grasping Mr. Dunn's hand and saying loudly that it was a blessing Mr. Dunn could attend. And was the missus here? Mr. Dunn motioned toward a quiet slender woman, seated in a corner and Hogan bowed low. Magnus Dunn nodded kindly here and there, shook himself free of Hogan and went to the widow. As he held her hand she commenced weeping and she tried to say something about how grateful she was and the lady next to her said, "shh." Everyone knew that Magnus Dunn had given her a thousand dollars to help bury poor Toss and to keep the wolf away until her children were big enough to earn wages, but it might embarrass Mr. Dunn if he knew that information had been passed around.

When Dunn went into the kitchen, Hogan was at his heels, paying the most respectful attention and ordering everyone else around as if they were his flunkies. But no one minded Hogan's arrogance. They were all grateful that Hogan could see what was to be done. Hogan, himself, launched upon a search for the jug, muttering crossly to himself,

"Now where did that brainless bastard of a Weeshy stow that crock. Must be suspicious of the rest of us, the way he keeps things outa sight."

Hogan, of course, had not let Dunn hear his grumbling. He soon found the jug and he washed out a glass and put it in Dunn's hand and then started pouring the drink.

"Whoop, whoop, there," said Dunn, "very little now. I just had my supper."

Dunn looked around to see if others might be indulging a little. But they were all smart enough not to take a drink in the presence of the best goddam man that ever came to Butte. Yes sir, Dunn was the man who discovered that Butte Hill was solid copper. He'd bought himself a lot of Irish jumping horses and furthermore, he had built a big hotel in Anaconda that was the pride of the Northwest, and no less.

Tom met Dunn through the good offices of Denny O'Shea who had breezed right up to Dunn the instant he got in the kitchen and told him that he had heard a lot about Magnus Dunn and a small part of what he had heard was good. As Dunn chuckled, his body shook and he sipped a little of his whiskey and told Denny that if anyone ever heard anything about Magnus Dunn that was good it would be a wonder indeed. With that, every man in the kitchen stiffened for an instant, then waved their hands and said "pshaw" to ridicule any talk that would reflect on the good name of Magnus Dunn.

Stubby Cavanaugh, who, for a man as full as he was, had been quiet a long time, got in front of Dunn with his face red and his mouth ends twitching. His eyes became watery and he began to whimper like a child. Then suddenly, in a lion-like rage, he stamped his feet on the floor, threw up his two fists, and yelled he could lick any two or a dozen sonsabitches that had the guts to breathe an unkind word against Magnus Dunn, the best goddamned man that ever set foot in Butte. Magnus Dunn nodded gravely and coughed and took a sip of his drink and cleared his throat.

Cassidy and Derg Finley promptly took hold of Stubby, who had disgraced himself and all his friends. As they whisked him out the back door he was whimpering and bellyaching. There was only a short scuffle outside and the thudding of some limp object and Derg and Cassidy came in brushing their clothes. Dunn looked up and frowned and took another little sip of his drink and ran his tongue over the center of his silver mustache to catch the little brown drops that had stuck there.

Tom, standing near Dunn, suspected that Dunn did not like the whiskey but hadn't refused it for fear of offending. He was making it last as long as possible so that the men would not thrust another upon him. Denny kept talking and Dunn let him talk, watching Denny closely and listening to him with amusement in his eyes. Denny did not forget to mention that he and Tom Gary had just come to Butte and were working at the Python mine. Then Denny said:

"That reminds me of a story."

Hogan stood behind Dunn and glared fiercely at Denny and he shook his head vigorously. His pantomime was skillfully executed and it warned Denny that there should be none of his goddamned smut in front of Magnus Dunn. Denny kept nodding and winking and assuring Hogan, by equally expressive pantomime, that he was going to try out only a few of the mild ones on Dunn. Hogan let Denny go ahead and as Denny told his stories, Dunn kept eyeing him keenly, chuckling a little now and then, until finally he said that he must go because the next day he was to take a party of guests through the Python mine.

"You're not goin' to be at the funeral, Mr. Dunn?" asked Hogan, in amazement.

"No, I guess not," replied Dunn. "I came tonight because I wanted to pay my respects but I have some friends here from Chicago and they've made all their plans to see the mine tomorrow. So I'll do that, I guess."

When Dunn left, the whole kitchen gang tagged him to the front door and on their way back to the kitchen, they sighed and told each other there never was another man able to measure up to Magnus Dunn. . . .

By this time Denny's face was red, his eyes bleary and bloodshot and his mouth was hanging open, with patches of dried mucus in the corners. He rocked back and forth, seeming unable to focus his eyes. Tom said very sternly,

"Get your hat, Denny."

Hogan, laying a hand on Tom's arm, asked politely if Tom didn't think it was a bit early for O'Shea to be goin' home when everyone was countin' on the good fellows to keep the family's mind off their troubles. Tom said with equal politeness that he knew Denny O'Shea of old and he knew that Denny was filled to the gills right now and if he wasn't taken out he'd drink 'til he embalmed himself. Hogan at first tried to reason with Tom but when Hogan saw Denny coming through the crowd staggering and pigeon-eyed, he left off arguing. Tom took Denny by the arm and led him into the dining room. There were only a few people left and everything had quieted. Denny tried to put on his hat but Tom took it away from him and bowed to the widow and the few women sitting near her, sore as boiled owls as they waited for their husbands in the kitchen. When Tom got Denny into the street at last, he breathed a deep sigh of relief.

The Gulch was dark and quiet as Tom hauled Denny up the narrow plank sidewalk. He thought of the kids that had played "Run Sheep Run" and "Shinny" on this same street a few hours ago. They were all in bed now, tired from their day of play. A good thing they were for he was carting Denny home as he would a sack of potatoes. Denny's feet went in all directions, his body drooped forward so that to keep from falling on his face he took quick stumbling steps. On the Clancy porch Tom took a good grip around Denny's middle and practically carried him up the stairs and into the room and put him on the bed. Denny kept falling backward and to the side as Tom pulled off his clothes. It was quite a struggle to get Denny's coat and shirt off. When Tom had stripped him to his underwear he took him by the shoulders and shook him.

"Denny what was that talk about laying off tomorrow?"

Denny nodded wearily.

"Yeah, we're goin' to the funeral, Tom."

Tom shook him roughly.

"Are you crazy Denny? We only worked one day and now we're laying off to go to a funeral of a man we don't know. What's eating you anyway?"

Denny stared red-eyed at Tom for a moment.

He moistened his lips and shook his head from side to side.

"Tom, my boy," he mumbled, "have a little charity in your heart. Toss O'Hara was a great fellow and the least we can do fur his family is to see them through this ordeal of grief. . . ."

Denny slumped back on the bed, gurgled a few times and began to snore. Arranging the covers about him, Tom made up his mind that when things ironed out for Denny he was going to sit right down and have a heart-to-heart talk with him and put him right. . . .

DENNIS "DINNY" MURPHY

For many years Dennis "Dinny" Murphy worked in Butte mines owned by the Anaconda Copper Mining Company. Most of the time he worked as a motorman and was for a short time a contract miner. Murphy also worked as a nipper, carrying tools and supplies to other miners underground. His recollections of his experiences, his fellow miners, the working conditions, and Company policies have been preserved in an oral interview transcribed and edited by Teresa Jordan.

"I found my likings in the mines"

as told to Teresa Jordan

I always remember when I went to St. Mary's school, one day I was sitting in a desk looking out the window into the mine yard. I had an Irish nun for a teacher, Sister Laurentia, and she cracked me on the knuckles with her ruler and told me to sit up. Years later, I was on Park Street one day and I saw her. I told her that now I was in the mine yard looking up at St. Mary's. She grabbed my hand, she said, "Dennis, we all have to be something. Some of us had to be doctors and some of us had to be priests and you were put here–what you do is vitally important." She tried to make me feel good anyhow.

People use to always think that you had to be really dumb to be a miner, that you couldn't have an education, that it was nothing to go down and drill a round. But I saw some of these "old country men" who probably couldn't read very much, or maybe they didn't speak English too well, but on measuring day, they could figure in their way faster than the graduate of the School of Mines. Everybody down in the mine wasn't just an ignoramus.

I tell some of these kids, you ought to be pretty proud of your heritage. Your dad, he wasn't a slob, he worked in the mines. You should be as proud as your friend over there who says his dad is a doctor or his dad is a engineer. They wouldn't be doctors or engineers if it wasn't for miners, either. I looked for other things, but I found my likings in the mines.

They had pretty places down in the mine where copper water would drip and it would form crystal icycles. When you touched them, they'd disintegrate. They'd be the prettiest colors—amber green, emerald, even flecks of deep red would flicker. There were places at the St. Lawrence that went back to the days of the Copper Kings. There had been fires in there that were just left to burn until they went out. You'd get a piece of wood, and the knot of the wood would be filled with pure copper. A fire had probably burned in there for years and years until it went out and had melted the copper right out of the rock. They were interesting mines, the St. Lawrence and the Anaconda and the Neversweat, they had a history. They weren't just holes in the ground.

Every mine probably smells different, but when you left surface and fresh air to go down, it had a real different smell. Nothing on surface ever reminds you of that smell. Whether it's the humidity in some of the hot places, the smell from copper water or from decaying timber in certain places, it just has a different aroma. It's hard to describe.

You could never understand how hot, how really hot and humid, it would be in some of these places. You work in your yard and the sweat might roll down your face. Well, down in the mine, it was nothing to take off your mine undershirt and ring it out. And when you take your mine hat off sometimes, the water would just fall right down from the band. Or you took your mine boots off and dumped the water out. People would probably think that you couldn't really sweat that much to pour water out of your boots, but you could. In some places it was so hot that the men would get cramps from the loss of salt in their systems. The Emma and the Travonia were cool mines. The Belmont was noted for being a hot box and then the Con, when it got down 5000 feet, had some pretty hot spots. Some of the places had names, like the Chinese Laundry at the Stewart mine, if you worked in there, you could work any place because that was one of the hottest spots.

Some days I would just hate to go to work because I knew where I was going to be working and I knew it was going to be hot and would probably be gassy. When I was servicing a drift, or even pulling out of a raise, the minute I started letting that rock into the mine car that gas would come out of the rock and my headache would start at the base of my neck and go up. I'd get a pounding, pounding headache. But then you get on surface and go up to Big Butte Tavern and have a beer and a hamburger sandwich and talk it over, and you were back the next day to hate the same thing all over again.

But there were good people you worked with underground. They used to really tease you [when you were green]. You know, getting on the cage, you just shook with fright because you never knew what to expect and the older men would tease you and tell you stories about big wrecks they had going down. Just anything to frighten you more. But once you were down there, they were very, very concerned for your safety. All that harassing and teasing but they made sure that nothing was going to happen to you.

I'm five feet five, and I weighed then probably a hundred pounds. We used to have to dump these one-ton cars. The man I was put to work with was a big husky kid and he was very good to me and showed me how it's easy if you do it right. And if I'd be on the station and maybe be a little bit behind, these station tenders would stop and help me dump rock. Other men, like pipemen that took care of the water pipes and the air pipes, if I had a chute that was hung up or something, they'd come and give me a hand. They didn't ridicule you, say something like, "Look, Shorty, get out of the way," or "Here, weakling, let me do it." They used to just say, "Here, Murph, I'll give you a hand."

These older men are gone, that I think about. You know, they called them Bohunks, Harps, Cousin Jacks. Some people probably didn't like to be called a Bohunk or whatever, but underground, these men were loving guys. There were two guys, Gabe and Keiser, they were brothers. One was as round as a refrigerator. And that poor guy worked in the stope and you could hear him huffing and puffing, he used to have to take his mine lamp off to get through the landing. He'd struggle for 20 minutes to get his hind end down. And then he waddled. He was such a loving guy. If he knew you liked Povititza, he'd bring a piece in his bucket for you.

There was another guy there, Dago John, he took these quarter inch steel sheets they have in the mine and walled his house with them because of the bomb – the "bome," he'd say – the bomb was going to come, the end of the world. He used to take a can of beer wrapped in newspaper. One day, he put his bucket down, and I stole the can of beer and rolled a piece of wood up in the paper. He was going to kill me – not me, he didn't know I did it. I just did it to tease him. But he used to tell me about his inventions. Great big man that was more powerful than he himself actually knew. He could do things.

I used to work with a guy, he was a Montenegran, from Yugoslavia, and he used to grab me by the cheeks and say, "Murphy, good kid, son of a bitch. Too bad you Irish." I was always invited down to his home for their Serbian Christmas. Same way when I worked down at the Leonard and all those people down there would always want you to come home to eat, or they'd bring you whatever was good in their bucket.

The rope men were nearly all Norwegians and Swedes. Like Judge Arnold Olsen, his dad was a ropeman. And they were the ones that lowered all that stuff down the mine. You may have seen pictures where they moved a whole gallus frame without dismantling it. These are all guys that never got out of grade school, but with winches and different rope pulleys, they did marvelous things.

I worked with the Finnlanders at the St. Lawrence and they were the nicest, cleanest people. They would give you the shirt off their back, want to feed you. And boy, they would come to work soused. But I never saw any of them knocked down and dragged out like the Irish. Seemed like they always kept on working, where an Irishman would fall by the wayside.

When I think of people like Gabe and Keiser, and like this John–I get a lump in my throat. "Too bad you Irish, you son of a gun." That camaraderie–that's probably what made working in the mines so interesting. I could just never explain why I liked the mines.

Men were different in the pit. There were really nice, nice guys at the pit, but their work was so different. You know, down at the mine, at lunch time, there was a lot of tomfoolery, a lot of playing. They'd nail your bucket to a post or, if you were sleeping, they'd tie your boots together or build a fire under you.

Underground, you got together at lunchtime. You'd pick a spot that was well timbered and had good ventilation. All the motormen would eat at the motor barn because when you get your motor [ore train engine], you put your coat and your bucket there. A raise miner would probably just come down to the bottom of the raise, find a good cool spot, eat in there. In farther, maybe by the tool shed where it was always cool, the pipemen and the fan bag man and some of the miners would come out and eat there. Everybody had a laggin, that's a three inch board, probably six feet long, and you'd stretch your laggin out and you'd sit on it to eat your lunch. That's when the fantastic stories would come out. You'd hear all about their wives' fights, all about their broken hearts, how tough they were, what good miners they were. Just some good stories. And then everybody would sleep for half an hour. But down at the pit, they had a lunchroom. It was just a lot different.

When I worked at the St. Lawrence, we used to eat in a place that was the old horse barn. And there was five or six guys that worked there when they had the horses. And they'd tell you stories about the horses that would just make you wonder.

The Company treated the horses ten times better than they did the miners. They used to bring the horses up out of the mine and put them out here to pasture. A skinner could stay down in the mine until he died of silicosis.

I always remember some of my uncles, we were going to Gregson past the pasture where the horses were, they would say, "Yeah, look at them over there. They were only down five or six years. We've been down thirty and we're still down there. No one puts us to pasture."

But some skinners were as proud of their horses as they were of their kids at home. Well, I guess they just did some fantastic things. Renegade horses would break out of their stalls and sneak off into a corner some place because they didn't want to go to work. If they weren't tied in their stalls, they'd back out and walk around the level. And they'd tip the tops off of lunch buckets and eat what was in them. The horses would pull a six car train and the skinner might go back in the drift and find another car that he wanted to bring up, so he'd sneak the car up and put the chain on real slow, but every time that horse or mule started to pull, he'd almost count as the cars would click, click, click–he'd get to the seventh one, he'd stop. He'd pull six and that was all.

Some of those skinners, a horse would do something fantastic, and they couldn't wait to get home to tell their family about it. I guess the horses all had names, and when the skinner'd go down in the mines, he'd have a chew of Peerless, he'd give his horse a chew of Peerless also. That's the stories that they told me.

The poor oldtimer, he was the one who paved the way for all of us. Where I lived was what they called Corktown and it was mostly all Irish Catholics. And it was nothing to see the woman walk her husband to the door in the morning. She would always kiss him, always tell him "God bless you." Some women would flick holy water on their husbands. And when the men came home, they were entitled to their shot and their homemade beer. These are places I'm thinking about; this didn't happen to everybody, because some poor guys went home to nothing, you know.

My uncle was the most loving guy. I don't say this just because he was my uncle. He was stern and tough, but he was so loving. He was a station tender here in the mines.

He used to come home and he'd had a few drinks and one of his daughters would say, "Oh Papa,"–they always called him Papa–"you've been drinking." And my aunt would say, "The poor critter, he's tired and he had a few shots and that's all he needs." Now–(laughs)–now people are married six months and they want to try going another way.

My wife really didn't like the mines. I seldom worked overtime, but one night right at the outbreak of the war they came down and wanted us to work overtime. There was no way to call home. I worked four hours overtime and when I came up out of the mine, I heard somebody holler, "Anybody seen Murphy?" I couldn't imagine what they wanted, so I went over to the time keeper and he said, "Murph, your wife has been up here a hundred times." After I showered I went out, and my wife was standing out by the guard shack. It was snowing. She wouldn't go in. When we were walking down Excelsior Street from the Anselmo, she looked back at the mine and said, "I hate those things."

Sometimes I think that the women had it tougher than the men. The men just did the work and that was it. But the women, they had to take care of the kids, do the wash and the cooking, see their husbands off for work. If their husband was late coming home from work, if they were drinking someplace–the wife didn't know. She couldn't call the mine to see if he was all right. She'd get killed if she did that. There were a lot of widows that you don't hear much about anymore. Some of the young kids that got killed left young women that never married again. I don't know how they did it. It was a sad thing.

I guess another thing I liked about working in the mines, you'd come off work and everybody would be at a saloon, you know, a fifth of whiskey, a shot and a beer. Like Finntown, one bar right after the other. I was 24, come off nightshift, and you could get a shot and a beer for a dime. And then the bars always kicked back [bought you a drink for every two or three you bought]. So you'd have 50 cents, and you wouldn't even get out of Finntown. Hell, by the time you got down to Park Street, you were smashed. Then you'd go home and eat, take two hours sleep and go out and get smashed again (laughs).

I worked when I wanted to work. And I never worked really steady until I got married the second time and had children. If I wanted to go to California and I had the money, I took off. You could always get hired again. You liked to drink so you'd just drink. I never ever thought I would turn out to be an alcoholic because I saw so much of it in the neighborhood where I lived. But I got to where I couldn't go to work without having a drink, couldn't come off of work without having a shot. Then I got so that I didn't work.

I got a lot of "quits" because I drank an awful lot. I'd work two days and I'd be gone for a week. I went to work so drunk, the shift boss would do me a favor and send me home. He wouldn't tell me to go down in the mine and sweat it out. I had my job held for three weeks one time. [Personal note: Dinny has been a member of Alcoholics Anonymous for twenty-seven years.]

At one time, my belief is, life didn't mean a lot compared to the profits of the company. Not only in the Butte mines, but any mines, any steel factories or anything else. Life was pretty cheap for the money that some of these companies were making. It was nothing to go into one of these miners' wards and see all the beds full. A lot of broken legs and broken backs. Before they had hard hats, it was nothing to see guys going up the hill with white cones on their head. If they got cut on the head, the doctor used to just shave around the wound and put the stitches in and then put this cone on the wound–I don't know how they made it, but it would foam and then turn hard. And then the miner'd go to work the next day. Towards the end, after all these safety regulations came in, it wasn't that bad. There was guys that got hurt, but it really and truly wasn't that bad.

There was no competition for labor. At one time, you couldn't work for anyplace but the Anaconda Company. Nothing else could ever come in here. The Company had a labor monopoly they wouldn't let loose of. They would probably tell you that they welcomed other business, but they never. Because when a guy got in the mines, he stayed in the mines. He couldn't say, well, I'll quit and go to the sawmill or I'll quit and go to the glassworks, and he stayed. He stayed because he had his home here and he had his family started, he had kids in school. Not all the miners liked the mines. Some of them stayed here because they had everything here and couldn't leave. My uncle used to always say he'd rather have his kids any place but in the mines, but he didn't want them to leave Butte, so they had no choice.

I never ever thought I'd live to see the day that one wheel wouldn't be turning. When I was in my 50's, I never ever thought I'd retire. I thought, you know, I've been around a long time and I know some of the guys in the mine, some of the foremen, I can get a watchman's job. But then when they just pulled out and closed everything, I thought that was really a crying shame. I thought there'd always be one mine.

All these Irish people bought plots–did you ever go to the cemetery and see these plots that they bought? You could raise a couple of sheep on some of them. And now there's not going to be anybody buried in them.

We never knew how good Anaconda was until they left us.

■ DASHIELL HAMMETT

In 1915, when Dashiell Hammett was twenty-one years old, he went to work for Pinkerton's National Detective Agency. Over the next six years, his job with Pinkerton's took him from the East Coast to the Northwest and finally to California, exposing him to situations he later described in what many critics consider to be the best detective fiction of the century. Hammett spent some of those years in Butte, where Wobblies and Socialists were pressuring the Anaconda Copper Mining Company to pay higher wages and improve working conditions. He was also there to control the "radicals" during the 1920-1921 miners' strike. Hammett liked to tell stories about being a detective in Montana, and he used those memories to create his first novel, Red Harvest, *in 1929. The story is set in "Poisonville," a western mining town that is easily recognized as Butte. This excerpt from the first chapter of* Red Harvest *has been reprinted in* The Novels of Dashiell Hammett *(1965). Hammett died in 1961.*

A Woman in Green and a Man in Grey

I first heard Personville called Poisonville by a red-haired mucker named Hickey Dewey in the Big Ship in Butte. He also called his shirt a shoit. I didn't think anything of what he had done to the city's name. Later I heard men who could manage their r's give it the same pronunciation. I still didn't see anything in it but the meaningless sort of humor that used to make richardsnary the thieves' word for dictionary. A few years later I went to Personville and learned better.

Using one of the phones in the station, I called the *Herald*, asked for Donald Willsson, and told him I had arrived.

"Will you come out to my house at ten this evening?" He had a pleasantly crisp voice. "It's 2101 Mountain Boulevard. Take a Broadway car, get off at Laurel Avenue, and walk two blocks west."

I promised to do that. Then I rode up to the Great Western Hotel, dumped my bags, and went out to look at the city.

The city wasn't pretty. Most of its builders had gone in for gaudiness. Maybe they had been successful at first. Since then the smelters whose brick stacks stuck up tall against a gloomy mountain to the south had yellow-smoked everything into uniform dinginess. The result was an ugly city of forty thousand people, set in an ugly notch between two ugly mountains that had been all dirtied up by mining. Spread over this was a grimy sky that looked as if it had come out of the smelters' stacks.

The first policeman I saw needed a shave. The second had a couple of buttons off his shabby uniform. The third stood in the center of the city's main intersection–Broadway and Union Street–directing traffic, with a cigar in one corner of his mouth. After that I stopped checking them up.

At nine-thirty I caught a Broadway car and followed the directions Donald Willsson had given me. They brought me to a house set in a hedged grassplot on a corner.

The maid who opened the door told me Mr. Willsson was not home. While I was explaining that I had an appointment with him a slender blonde woman of something less than thirty in green crêpe came to the door. When she smiled her blue eyes didn't lose their stoniness. I repeated my explanation to her.

"My husband isn't in now." A barely noticeable accent slurred her s's. "But if he's expecting you he'll probably be home shortly."

She took me upstairs to a room on the Laurel Avenue side of the house, a brown and red room with a lot of books in it. We sat in leather chairs, half facing each other, half facing a burning coal grate, and she set about learning my business with her husband.

"Do you live in Personville?" she asked first.

"No. San Francisco."

"But this isn't your first visit?"

"Yes."

"Really? How do you like our city?"

"I haven't seen enough of it to know." That was a lie. I had. "I got in only this afternoon."

Her shiny eyes stopped prying while she said:

"You'll find it a dreary place." She returned to her digging with: "I suppose all mining towns are like this. Are you engaged in mining?"

"Not just now."

She looked at the clock on the mantel and said:

"It's inconsiderate of Donald to bring you out here and then keep you waiting, at this time of night, long after business hours."

I said that was all right.

"Though perhaps it isn't a business matter," she suggested.

I didn't say anything.

She laughed–a short laugh with something sharp in it.

"I'm really not ordinarily so much of a busybody as you probably think," she said gaily. "But you're so excessively secretive that I can't help being curious. You aren't a bootlegger, are you? Donald changes them so often."

I let her get whatever she could out of a grin.

A telephone bell rang downstairs. Mrs. Willsson stretched her green-slippered feet out toward the burning coal and pretended she hadn't heard the bell. I didn't know why she thought that necessary.

She began: "I'm afraid I'll ha–" and stopped to look at the maid in the doorway.

The maid said Mrs. Willsson was wanted at the phone. She excused herself and followed the maid out. She didn't go downstairs, but spoke over an extension within earshot.

I heard: "Mrs. Willsson speaking. . . . Yes. . . . I beg your pardon? . . . Who? . . . Can't you speak a little louder? . . . *What*? . . . Yes. . . . Yes. . . . Who is this? . . . Hello! Hello!"

The telephone hook rattled. Her steps sounded down the hallway–rapid steps.

I set fire to a cigarette and stared at it until I heard her going down the steps. Then I went to a window, lifted an edge of the blind, and looked out at Laurel Avenue, and at the square white garage that stood in the rear of the house on that side.

Presently a slender woman in dark coat and hat came into sight hurrying from house to garage. It was Mrs. Willsson. She drove away in a Buick coupé. I went back to my chair and waited.

Three-quarters of an hour went by. At five minutes after eleven, automobile brakes screeched outside. Two minutes later Mrs. Willsson came into the room. She had taken off hat and coat. Her face was white, her eyes almost black.

"I'm awfully sorry," she said, her tight-lipped mouth moving jerkily, "but you've had all this waiting for nothing. My husband won't be home tonight."

I said I would get in touch with him at the *Herald* in the morning.

I went away wondering why the green toe of her left slipper was dark and damp with something that could have been blood.

I walked over to Broadway and caught a street car. Three blocks north of my hotel I got off to see what the crowd was doing around a side entrance of the City Hall.

Thirty or forty men and a sprinkling of women stood on the sidewalk looking at a door marked *Police Department.* There were men from mines and smelters still in their working clothes, gaudy boys from pool rooms and dance halls, sleek men with slick pale faces, men with the dull look of respectable husbands, a few just as respectable and dull women, and some ladies of the night.

On the edge of this congregation I stopped beside a square-set man in rumpled gray clothes. His face was grayish too, even the thick lips, though he wasn't much older than thirty. His face was broad, thick-featured and intelligent. For color he depended on a red windsor tie that blossomed over his gray flannel shirt.

"What's the rumpus?" I asked him.

He looked at me carefully before he replied, as if he wanted to be sure that the information was going into safe hands. His eyes were gray as his clothes, but not so soft.

"Don Willsson's gone to sit on the right hand of God, if God don't mind looking at bullet holes."

"Who shot him?" I asked.

The gray man scratched the back of his neck and said:

"Somebody with a gun."

I wanted information, not wit. I would have tried my luck with some other member of the crowd if the red tie hadn't interested me. I said:

"I'm a stranger in town. Hang the Punch and Judy on me. That's what strangers are for."

"Donald Willsson, Esquire, publisher of the *Morning* and *Evening Heralds,* was found in Hurricane Street a little while ago, shot very dead by parties unknown," he recited in a rapid singsong. "Does that keep your feelings from being hurt?"

"Thanks." I put out a finger and touched a loose end of his tie. "Mean anything? Or just wearing it?"

"I'm Bill Quint."

"The hell you are!" I exclaimed, trying to place the name. "By God, I'm glad to meet you!"

I dug out my card case and ran through the collection of credentials I had picked up here and there by one means or another. The red card was the one I wanted. It identified me as Henry F. Neill, A. B. seaman, member in good standing of the Industrial Workers of the World. There wasn't a word of truth in it.

I passed this card to Bill Quint. He read it carefully, front and back, returned it to my hand, and looked me over from hat to shoes, not trustfully.

"He's not going to die any more," he said. "Which way you going?"

"Any."

We walked down the street together, turned a corner, aimlessly as far as I knew.

"What brought you in here, if you're a sailor?" he asked casually.

"Where'd you get that idea?"

"There's the card."

"I got another that proves I'm a timber beast," I said. "If you want me to be a miner I'll get one for that tomorrow."

"You won't. I run 'em here."

"Suppose you got a wire from Chi?" I asked.

"Hell with Chi! I run 'em here." He nodded at a restaurant door and asked: "Drink?"

"Only when I can get it."

We went through the restaurant, up a flight of steps, and into a narrow second-story room with a long bar and a row of tables. Bill Quint nodded and said, "Hullo!" to some of the boys and girls at tables and bar, and steered me into one of the green-curtained booths that lined the wall opposite the bar.

We spent the next two hours drinking whiskey and talking.

The gray man didn't think I had any right to the card I had showed him, nor to the other one I had mentioned. He didn't think I was a good wobbly. As chief muckademuck of the I.W.W. in Personville, he considered it his duty to get the low-down on me, and to not let himself be pumped about radical affairs while he was doing it.

That was all right with me. I was interested in Personville affairs. He didn't mind discussing them between casual pokings into my business with the red cards.

What I got out of him amounted to this:

For forty years old Elihu Willsson—father of the man who had been killed this night—had owned Personville, heart, soul, skin and guts. He was president and majority stockholder of the Personville Mining Corporation, ditto of the First National Bank, owner of the

Morning Herald and *Evening Herald*, the city's only newspapers, and at least part owner of nearly every other enterprise of any importance. Along with these pieces of property he owned a United States senator, a couple of representatives, the governor, the mayor, and most of the state legislature. Elihu Willsson was Personville, and he was almost the whole state.

Back in the war days the I.W.W.—in full bloom then throughout the West—had lined up the Personville Mining Corporation's help. The help hadn't been exactly pampered. They used their new strength to demand the things they wanted. Old Elihu gave them what he had to give them, and bided his time.

In 1921 it came. Business was rotten. Old Elihu didn't care whether he shut down for a while or not. He tore up the agreements he had made with his men and began kicking them back into their pre-war circumstances.

Of course the help yelled for help. Bill Quint was sent out from I.W.W. headquarters in Chicago to give them some action. He was against a strike, an open walk-out. He advised the old sabotage racket, staying on the job and gumming things up from the inside. But that wasn't active enough for the Personville crew. They wanted to put themselves on the map, make labor history.

They struck.

The strike lasted eight months. Both sides bled plenty. The wobblies had to do their own bleeding. Old Elihu hired gunmen, strike-breakers, national guardsmen and even parts of the regular army, to do his. When the last skull had been cracked, the last rib kicked in, organized labor in Personville was a used firecracker.

But, said Bill Quint, old Elihu didn't know his Italian history. He won the strike, but he lost his hold on the city and the state. To beat the miners he had to let his hired thugs run wild. When the fight was over he couldn't get rid of them. He had given his city to them and he wasn't strong enough to take it away from them. Personville looked good to them and they took it over. They had won his strike for him and they took the city for their spoils. He couldn't openly break with them. They had too much on him. He was responsible for all they had done during the strike.

Bill Quint and I were both fairly mellow by the time we had got this far. He emptied his glass again, pushed his hair out of his eyes and brought his history up to date:

"The strongest of 'em now is probably Pete the Finn. This stuff we're drinking's his. Then there's Lew Yard. He's got a loan shop down on Parker Street, does a lot of bail bond business, handles most of the burg's hot stuff, so they tell me, and is pretty thick with Noonan, the chief of police. This kid Max Thaler–Whisper–has got a lot of friends too. A little slick dark guy with something wrong with his throat. Can't talk. Gambler. Those three, with Noonan, just about help Elihu run his city–help him more than he wants. But he's got to play with 'em or else–"

"This fellow who was knocked off tonight–Elihu's son–where did he stand?" I asked.

"Where papa put him, and he's where papa put him now."

"You mean the old man had him–?"

"Maybe, but that's not my guess. This Don just came home and began running the papers for the old man. It wasn't like the old devil, even if he was getting close to the grave, to let anybody cop anything from him without hitting back. But he had to be cagey with these guys. He brought the boy and his French wife home from Paris and used him for his monkey–a damned nice fatherly trick. Don starts a reform campaign in the papers. Clear the burg of vice and corruption–which means clear it of Pete and Lew and Whisper, if it goes far enough. Get it? The old man's using the boy to shake 'em loose. I guess they got tired of being shook."

"There seems to be a few things wrong with that guess," I said.

"There's more than a few things wrong with everything in this lousy burg. Had enough of this paint?"

I said I had. We went down to the street. Bill Quint told me he was living in the Miners' Hotel in Forest Street. His way home ran past my hotel, so we walked down together. In front of my hotel a beefy fellow with the look of a plain-clothes man stood on the curb and talked to the occupant of a Stutz touring car.

"That's Whisper in the car," Bill Quint told me.

I looked past the beefy man and saw Thaler's profile. It was young, dark and small, with pretty features as regular as if they had been cut by a die.

"He's cute," I said.

"Uh-huh," the gray man agreed, "and so's dynamite."

5

Remembering the Agricultural Frontier

Country, Town, and Reservation

RICHARD B. ROEDER

In the early twentieth century, the new state of Montana began to define itself as an agricultural outpost in the West. Although Montana's metals industry had generated enormous wealth, mining provided an uncertain economic base for a permanent community. Prices for copper, silver, and gold depended upon an unreliable, volatile world-wide market, and Montanans were nagged by the realization that no matter how rich the ore, the veins would one day be dug out. People referred to Butte as a mining "camp" or as "the Big Butte Camp."

The livestock industry was not an adequate alternative. Hard winters and fluctuating prices made cattle and sheep raising as uncertain as mining. Moreover, livestock production rested on a sparse, isolated population that could not support the schools, churches, and libraries that were the essentials of American civilization.

When Montanans imagined an alternative economy, they imagined agriculture. The development of a vast agricultural community would supply a stable economy and at the same time tame the wilderness. People yearned for fulfillment of the Jeffersonian dream, where rural community was the keystone of the good society. Unfortunately the dream ran up against an immovable reality.

Montana is subject to large variations in precipitation, but the vast bulk of its arable lands receive only fifteen inches of rain or less a year, which is barely enough to raise crops. Developers knew the land was fertile. All that it needed was water. During the 1890s and the first years of the twentieth century, those who hoped for a bright agricultural future looked to irrigation. Enthusiasm for the ditch system was wild at first, as boosters vastly overestimated the amount of land that could be watered. As new projects got underway after 1903, more realistic estimates of irrigable acreage deflated the enthusiasm.

Just as this was happening, another craze brought hopeful farmers to the state. Using dry-land farming methods, crops could be raised, especially grains, without irrigation. The introduction of hardy Turkey Red Wheat from Crimea, new moisture-conserving techniques of working the soil, and machinery to work large acreages seemed to hold great prospects. The new technology and changes in the homestead laws, which doubled the acreage homesteaders could claim and reduced the prove-up time, brought thousands of new homesteaders to the state. To boosters, the rural community of their dreams seemed about to materialize.

A few were skeptical about the promises of dry-land farming. Typical of these was Will Sutherlin, editor of Montana's leading farm journal, the *Rocky Mountain Husbandman.* Sutherlin argued that dry-land farming was a will-o'-the-wisp; year in and year out it would not yield enough crops to support a family. But Sutherlin was opposed by the most eloquent and respected advocate of dry-land farming, Paris Gibson, a pioneer of Minneapolis who had founded the city of Great Falls. Gibson saw Montana's pastoral economy as a wasteful, anti-social use of land; and on his own farm south of Great Falls, Gibson proved in his own mind that farming without irrigation was practicable.

During the decade before America's entry into World War I, favorable grain prices, wet years, and the lure of dry-farming methods combined to produce a Montana homestead boom unequalled in any other state. There is no accurate estimate of the number of people who came to Montana during those years, but surely there were several hundreds of thousands. The homesteaders came from all over the country and from abroad, but a majority probably came from the Midwest where land prices made it difficult for young people to break into farming. The most common denominator of these homesteaders was their diversity, but most of them were young, sometimes single, and, despite pockets of foreign-born, literate. Most came as family groups just starting out.

Some homesteaders would have come to Montana under any circumstances, but many more came in response to an extensive promotional campaign. Railroads, especially the Milwaukee and James J. Hill's Great Northern Railway, advertised widely in the United States and abroad. Most of these homesteaders arrived by railroad (although some would come in new Ford automobiles). For a few dollars an immigrant family could rent a freight car and haul its belongings, even livestock, to a town within reasonable distance of its homestead site.

Promotion of homesteading was not confined to railroads. Boosterism was pervasive, supported by local businessmen's clubs and above all by local newspapers; the taking up of land also created a booming frontier of small towns. Farmers were not self-sufficient. They relied on a mail-order house for many of their needs, but they also depended on merchants, tradesmen, and bankers in the nearest town. Towns mushroomed as enterprising small businessmen responded to the new opportunities. Before paved roads and modern automobiles and trucks, a town could serve a hinterland population within a ten- to fifteen-mile radius. Railroad agents and independent speculators laid out town sites, hoping their town would at least become a county seat and with luck maybe a new Chicago. Many towns prospered for a time, and then died. They have become Montana landmarks. Homestead ghost-towns far out-number the mining ghost-towns that preceded them.

Overproduction of wheat, an unexpected removal of federal price supports, a precipitous decline in grain prices, and a drought that affected the entire state by 1919 combined to produce a sudden, sharp deflation. The ensuing suffering, animal as well as human, caused political analysts such as Joseph Kinsey Howard to seek out villains. Howard blamed the boosters, and especially James J. Hill who had enticed land-seekers with vain hopes that could only be blasted by the realities of a harsh land.

Those who participated in the homestead frontier, especially those who took up land, have left behind a large body of reminiscence literature. Much of it is hard to come by. The books and articles were printed by private subscription in small numbers, often by vanity presses and sometimes even with mimeograph machines. Some of this literature—for example, Pearl Price Robertson's memoir—reflects the hardships of isolation, the death-dealing winter storms, the backbreaking toil, the penury, and what it was like living close to the economic margin of survival. But for the most part this literature of reminiscence leaves an impression somewhat different from the tale that Howard tells. Homesteaders took pride in their accomplishments and their survival over adversity. They did not feel victimized nor did they need to place blame for failures. Their reminiscences are suffused with positive memories of family unity and recreation, such as performing their own music or reading aloud to each other at night. This literature reflects a sense of community and recalls with fondness group activities such as building a church or school, neighborhood dances, cooperative harvests, picnics, and rooting for the home baseball team.

Nevertheless, critics like Howard make an important point. The collapse of Montana's homestead frontier left lasting scars, perhaps most importantly on the psychology of its survivors. The end of the boom erased a pervasive innocence and optimism about taking up the land and controlling one's future and that of one's community. Those who lasted made economic and technological adjustments that turned Montana into one of the world's great grain baskets. But the old feeling of brotherhood and sense of community has been replaced by a lasting sense of insecurity and a nagging fear of a recurrence of hard times.

For some of the pioneer homesteaders who hung on, the 1920s brought occasional years of fair times and happy memories, such as those of Orland Esval who came of age as a teenage member of a threshing crew. For others, such as Charles Vindex, bad times continued uninterrupted from the initial collapse through the Great Depression of the 1930s. Still others, like Peggy Czyzeski, found hardship and calamity in social and familial problems rather than natural causes such as weather or grasshopper plagues.

The expansion of agriculture added to the diversity of Montana's economic life, but it did not obliterate older life styles. Seldom does the sheep industry receive its due in memories of Montana. The beginnings of sheep raising in Montana are coterminous with the raising of cattle, and the sheep industry assumed great significance for the state and nation, especially after the hard winter of 1886-1887. During the late nineteenth and early twentieth centuries Montana was among the nation's leading wool producers, and towns like Big Timber were important wool-shipping centers. The recollections of Matthias Martinz call attention to some aspects of the unsung sheepherder's life and the fact that herders were often recent immigrants.

The cattle industry remains one of the fixtures of Montana life, and no legacy is more important to American popular culture than the cowboy. The Big Dry country that Paul E. Young tells about was one of the last holdouts of the open-range days. This huge, remote area, part of what Miles City photographer L. A. Huffman called the "Big Open," was only minimally affected by homesteading. The rodeo, now a fixture of popular western entertainment, had its origins in challenges of old cowboy skills. Goyins' anecdotes record a time of transition from local, neighborhood contests to standardized shows with professional performers who travel a large circuit.

While critics like Howard decry the drabness of the homestead town as opposed to the earlier cowtown, Dan Cushman's recollections of a boyhood in Box Elder suggest that life in them may have been more colorful than Howard let on. And Dan Whetstone's account of a meeting of country editors indicates that small-town newspapermen, although boosters, were sharp-witted and idiosyncratic. Taylor Gordon's tales about White Sulphur Springs give a unique vision of an older town–in this case a center for sheep and cattle raising and mining–which had its own sources of vitality. Finally, John Hutchens' memoir of his journalistic apprenticeship in Missoula reveals aspects of the lives of urban newspapermen and the towns they covered. Although the Anaconda Company controlled Montana newspapers, blighting some aspects of Montana's journalism, it could not completely eradicate the vigor of the state's early press.

The homestead years had an enormous impact on the lives of Montana Indians, especially those who lived on reservations. One of the federal government's goals was to surround Indians with white neighbors who would provide "models" of a civilized way of life which, presumably, Indians would imitate. Another goal was to open Indian lands to white settlement, reducing the power and wealth of the tribes. Homesteading achieved both goals. The allotment system opened reservations to non-Indian settlement. White neighbors came, especially on the Flathead and Fort Peck reservations. New roads and motorized transportation broke down some of the isolation of other reservations.

White invasion and the reservation system presented years of difficult adjustments for reservation Indians, but these devices did not completely achieve the goal of swamping Indians into forgetting the old ways and disappearing into the mainstream of white society. As John Stands In Timber recalls, his generation of Northern Cheyenne made a conscious effort not to lose the stories that formed the basis of their old culture. And Walter McClintock describes how in spite of efforts by white Indian agents the Blackfeet perpetuated sacred customs such as the Sun Dance. Montana Indians learned to deal with white technology and confusing language barriers, often with humor and sometimes with deep pathos. Schools presented a real dilemma. Some leaders, such as Plenty Coups, the last of the great Crow warrior chiefs, realized that education was essential if Indians were to come to terms with modern life. Yet schools were whites' most effective tool for deculturalization. McClintock documents the painful generation gaps that occurred as older people lost authority and their young were left without cultural rudders.

The literature of Montana at the turn of the century marks a period of transition into the complexities of a modern world. There would be no simple solution for economic well-being or social or cultural identity. Agriculture, small-town boosterism, and the assimilation of Indians had failed in one way or another. It was time to begin looking inward.

■ JOSEPH KINSEY HOWARD

Born in Iowa in 1906, Joseph Kinsey Howard lived in Canada before moving with his family to Great Falls in 1919. At age seventeen, Howard began his career with the Great Falls Leader *as a reporter and later served as news editor for several years. As a founding member of the Montana Institute of the Arts and a leader of the Montana Writers' Conferences, Howard had a hand in shaping the cultural development of the state. In 1944, Howard joined The Montana Study, a project designed to find ways of improving rural life, and collected selections for* Montana Margins *(1946), an anthology of Montana authors. "They Bought Satin Pajamas" is a selection from Howard's incisive collection of essays entitled* Montana: High, Wide, and Handsome, *which was published in 1943. Howard died in Great Falls in 1951.*

They Bought Satin Pajamas

But it was a great frontier while it lasted.

There had been bonanzas before in America, and there had been more picturesque land rushes than this—to Iowa, to Kansas, to Oklahoma. The Model T and the Studebaker wagon had replaced the prairie schooner. There were no Indians to fight. Yet there never had been anything like the homestead rush in Montana in the second decade of this century, and there never had been anything like the collapse which ensued.

Overnight, homestead shacks sprang up on lonely prairies over which a few vicious gray wolves still prowled. The shacks usually were of one room, about twelve by fourteen feet, with a gable roof, a window in each end, and a door in the middle of the long side. They were set flat on the ground without foundation, but often had a tiny "cellar" under a trap door in the floor, to serve as a refrigerating compartment. The better houses were clapboarded, but thousands of them merely had tar-paper tacked over the exterior siding; the first strong wind ripped much of it off.

Old newspapers, especially rotogravure sections, were pasted up for wall covering. A sagging bed, stools, a table made of boxes, and curtained shelves for cupboards made up the furniture. There was a cast-iron cookstove. Outside the door a washpan sat on an up-ended box; a dispirited cake of soap rested on two nails driven into the wall, and a ragged, grimy crash towel or strip of grain sack hung above.

Usually the doors and windows did not "hang." Few of the honyockers were experienced builders. Their materials were the cheapest available, and the extremes of Montana's climate quickly warped the window frames and lintels. Rags had to be stuffed into widening cracks. Even then the prairie wind in winter, whipping the shack in fury, sliced through the thin walls: tiny drifts of snow blew in under the door and twisted and ran about the splintered, untreated floor. The honyocker and his family then huddled about the cookstove or the heater, which was sometimes a cheap commercially produced "airtight," sometimes just an old oil barrel resting on a cradle of strap iron.

Starvation threatened thousands of the newcomers in their first winter. Then the honyocker would trudge off through the snow to find a job and feed his family, leaving behind a frightened but courageous wife.

"When he went away," said one of these wives, "I was left once more on the homestead without a man, and this time with nine children, the youngest a baby three weeks old. He sent every dollar of his wages home as fast as it was earned, yet with me the winter was one long struggle to keep my family warmed and fed, and to save our horses from starvation. Upon the horses depended our ability to put in one more crop."

Three of their horses froze to death that winter. When feed for the pigs was exhausted, the woman butchered the eight of them with the help of her son and two neighbor boys. Hung in a shed, the carcasses froze, and the job had to be finished in the living room, the only place they could be kept warm. It was then 30 below zero.

Her husband wrote her: "If your fuel gives out, burn the fence posts, tear boards from the barn and burn them, burn anything about the place—don't take any chance of freezing!"

That was the ever-present danger, the nightly horror for the honyocker's wife after her family was asleep. Coal had to be brought from town, and recurring blizzards closed the road and isolated the family. Even water had to be hauled a considerable distance. The crusted snow gashed through the flesh on the horses' legs, and the horses were weak from hunger. Water had to be rationed, finally; and so did food and fuel. The children's faces whitened and the flesh was drawn tautly over cheekbones and jaws. Each day the relentless cold which walled them in pressed a little farther into the room. The chilled wood which had been gathered to augment the dwindling stock of coal would char but would not burn. . . .

This woman and her family came through that winter; ultimately they prospered. Many others did not come through. Those who did put in "one more crop." And in the spring it rained.

"The mushroom towns bustled with activity," said a veteran of those few good years. "It was no uncommon sight to see long strings of wagons full of sacked wheat . . . all drawn by a tractor, moving along the country road bound for the shipping point. The little stores were packed and clerks worked overtime putting up huge orders which included everything from harness to satin pajamas. Optimism ran high. Real estate dealers talked largely of future values and began laying out new additions; but a series of dry years followed."

A little Montana town, Scobey, with a population of less than fifteen hundred, once was the largest single primary wheat loading center in North America. In the "good year" of 1924 which followed the long period of drouth, more than 2,750,000 bushels of wheat were shipped from that village.

Some of the grain had been hauled by horse-drawn wagons for forty-five miles over rutted and muddy trails. Hundreds of wagons stood for days in Scobey waiting to be unloaded. Jim Hill's railroad ran out of cars. Elevator men handling the grain passed out tickets to the waiting outfits to record the order in which they had arrived. Loading the cars was a twenty-four-hour job, and farmers went off to the hotels to snatch a little sleep as they awaited a call that a trainload of empties had come in.

Strikes of railroad workers in two successive years complicated the Great Northern's problem of supplying cars. Angry farmers and elevator men, watching an uncertain market, cursed Jim Hill, his railroad, and the unions.

The usual "grain box" wagon held 125 bushels. Most of the honyockers could load four to seven of these; but sometimes by the time they had reached the elevator the market had fallen and the value of their grain was less than the cost of the haul. Sometimes double-decked sheep wagons were used. There were a few mechanical rigs, tractors usually of 30 horsepower hauling seven 125-bushel wagons, but the cost of this form of transport was high and horses still were favored.

Although the rush came immediately after harvest—from September through November—the hauling continued until snow had made the roads impassable, and sometimes in bumper crop periods it was resumed in the spring.

Frequently the haul was too long for one day. "Halfway houses" appeared and flourished on the trade of temporarily prosperous homesteaders. A few of these grew and became towns as the railroads built spur lines and they acquired elevators of their own.

The log cabin, tent, and tepee town of the open range, with its Indians, dogs, horses, and saloons, was displaced by the hideous "shack town" of the honyocker: a one-street, one-side-of-the-street "business section," stores with dirty showcases and third-rate goods with unfamiliar brands, soda fountain without charged water, firetrap movie theater. By day the angry sun blazed upon the treeless, dusty street; by night the town lay dead and cold and insignificant under the great sky while howling coyotes circled it and sometimes slunk into its alleys to fight the dogs nosing its garbage. Perhaps no one has ever pictured better the loneliness of such towns, their cheap and alien tawdriness in the grandeur of the prairie scene, than did Burchfield in a great painting he called "November Evening."

The sterility of their community life was the most serious shortcoming of these homestead towns, the one which was most damaging in the long run to the whole social structure of the state. In the rural east and middle west and in the better-settled Pacific coast states, there exist hundreds of "cultural communities"–groups of neighborhoods about a central medium-sized city. These fulfill the cultural needs of the residents of that section, and through education, entertainment, and the building up through generations of an intangible but stalwart community loyalty, they tend to hold people within their borders.

Such communities have no counterparts in Montana. The few cities are scores of miles apart, and none of them has a surrounding group of rural communities. The rural towns, with some exceptions, have a deadly sameness and frequently consist of nothing but a grain elevator or two, a general store, a saloon, a church, and a handful of nondescript houses.

The worst of these starved towns (and many others have vanished in the last twenty years) were the creation of the honyocker. They were grimly utilitarian, uncompromisingly ugly; and when the economic excuse for them passed, those which did not perish at once lingered on year after year to become grayer, dirtier, more shrunken, as if they were becoming dehydrated.

Most of these towns grew out of a largely speculative movement. Their founders and some of their customers were in the state primarily to "clean up" and get out. Thousands of the newcomers (though not all, by any means) had no intention of permanently occupying their homesteads–but it was not from such as these that the railroads obtained testimonial letters! They took up their lands as a miner would stake out a placer claim. Others, sincere homeseekers, were either too young to have felt the need for a community culture, or too old and too burdened to bother about it. When the time came for that need to be realized, the towns were dying and the people had been broken by economic disaster.

In the absence of a cultural community there was nothing to hold even successful homesteaders in the state except continued profit. When the cash returns began to dwindle, they sold out and moved on.

Many Montana towns missed the opportunity to become such cultural communities. Out of the rowdy pioneer tradition grew the belief that "bigness" and "toughness" were synonymous. Several of the larger towns, when they set out to attract visitors or even settlers, did so frankly on the promise that within their borders "anything (within reason) goes." Butte still advertises its attractions thus, but

Butte is a special case and outside this particular phase of our study; it has never been the center of a rural region. The scheme works for the metropolitan mining city, Montana's biggest; it failed for others.

There were attempts, during the homestead days, to make the shack towns more livable and to give them character. Many of the honyockers were well educated and reasonably cultured: hundreds had been teachers. But homestead life was harder than they had expected, and for the first few years they had neither time nor strength for much community activity. They started a few feeble clubs, financed a few Chautauquas; then, suddenly broke and disheartened, they gave up.

A few of the newcomers brought their culture with them, refused to modify it to fit the land, and died or fled with it. Among these were the tragic Mennonites, many of them foreign-born; some of their communities were established by children of Mennonites whose colonies had prospered in Minnesota or Canada. The young people pushed out for themselves, to the new promised land; they knew nothing of dryland farming, and such was the stubborn isolation forced upon them by their faith that they could not learn. In addition, many of them feared and distrusted government in any form, even that of relief. They were splendid farmers—somewhere else. They loved the soil, they worked with single-minded intensity; they lived cleanly and thriftily—and they failed. They failed, and starved; they built rude coffins for their dead and came to town to buy from the undertaker a few gewgaws for the pine boxes, some handles or crape. One bereaved family put the corpse under the house and surrounded it with ice because there was no time for burial until after the harvest. They took their farming that seriously, and still they failed. . . . And in the end they could only look at their parched fields, at the gray, flaked soil underfoot, and pray humbly for the strength to go back whence they had come.

The honyocker destroyed the roistering cattleman's town. Its character may not have been of the best, but it had character of a sort, nevertheless: there was more friendship and less commercialism, and the town was loved and remembered. Its resources were slight, for the cattle industry only needed its towns occasionally; besides, towns cluttered up the range, and the fewer of them the better.

Principal establishments of the homestead town, in order of importance, were the grain elevator, the bank, the general store, restaurant, and hotel. None resembled cowtown Glasgow, which a year after it was founded consisted of eight saloons, three restaurants, and one store–all but two of the enterprises housed in tents.

There was some boisterousness in the honyockers' towns, but there was none of the cavalier spirit of the cowtowns, none of their jaunty rowdiness which survives to this day, though sadly watered down, in a few remote Montana villages which subsist precariously upon the periodic visits of the free-spending puncher.

The latter part of the homestead era coincided with prohibition, during which, according to the Federal Writers' Project Montana almanac, "baffled federal blotters ranged this huge state in a vain effort to dry up millions of gallons of 'mountain dew' made for 537,606 prospective drinkers who had 94,078,080 acres to hide it in." Significantly, prohibition made little difference to the honyockers, and in fact was supported by many of them, while it was bitterly opposed by most of the stockmen, and numerous cowpunchers found in border rum-running a new and profitable adventure.

The honyocker drank sparingly, usually beer. He gambled hardly at all. He could not afford either indulgence, and usually he was thinking of the folks at home. The puncher's home was wherever he dropped his war bag and his bedroll, and he seldom had any "folks" dependent upon him. Without liquor, cards, and women occasionally, his life would hardly have been worth living.

Sometimes the antagonistic cultures of cowman and honyocker fought for supremacy in the same town. Such a struggle was waged over dying Ubet, once the most famous stage station of Montana Territory. Ubet, born in 1880, had a two-story log-cabin hotel, a barn for the stage teams, a livery stable, blacksmith shop, ice house, saloon, and post office. It survived until 1903 when a railroad passed it by to put its station three miles away. The railroad named the station Ubet, however, and the old town was moved over there. But that happened to be the site of a new trading post named Garneill in honor of Garnet Neill, wife of a prominent cattleman, and Garneill determinedly maintained its identity, much to the bewilderment of train passengers.

Homesteaders arrived, and the sadly divided community of Ubet-Garneill was still further rent. The newcomers frowned upon the free-and-easy ways of traders' and drummers' Ubet, clustered about the depot, and of cattlemen's Garneill, which by this time boasted a pretentious hotel, a saloon, blacksmith shop, and several stores. So the honyockers built their own Garneill, just north of the other two communities. Thereafter, for a few years, there existed in uneasy neighborhood, North Garneill (of high moral tone), South Garneill (not so particular), and Ubet (fast becoming only a memory). The railroad, despairing, finally dropped Ubet, changing the depot's name to Garneill. Perhaps it was the wages of sin, but probably it was the collapse of the livestock industry and a fire, which killed South Garneill. North Garneill, the honyockers' town, survives; but it is a flag stop filled with abandoned buildings.

In 1878 Powell envisioned communities in his "colony" system which would have grown, not out of speculative hopes, but out of the common needs and aims of the settlers in a well-balanced agricultural economy. These communities would have been small and their institutional and cultural services limited, but they would have been integrated with the economic lives of their people far better than were the dryland towns, including those which have survived to this day. In a few instances this integration is now being sought in Montana planned communities. Until such planning is extended and its ends achieved, however, much of rural Montana must be served by the shack towns, shabby residue of the homestead jamboree.

The dreams of great men often live a long time, as dreams. That of Jim Hill, which he sought to bring to life in fact, became a witless nightmare. His trains rattled empty through dying towns. His neat little green fields were transformed as if an evil spirit had sped overhead, laying a curse upon them: suddenly they were fenced deserts in which the trapped tumbleweed spun and raced nowhere all day. The little houses stood slack-jawed and mute, obscenely violated by coyotes, rats, and bats, and finally faded into the lifeless fields.

■ PEARL PRICE ROBERTSON

Pearl Price Robertson came from New York to Montana's Judith Basin in 1910 with her husband and three children. In 1911 they homesteaded land west of Big Sandy, Montana, where Mrs. Robertson bore six more children. She also farmed and taught in a one-room schoolhouse until drought and an infestation of grasshoppers forced the family out in 1922. While living at a considerably more prosperous farm near Ronan, Montana, in 1933, Robertson finished her memoirs and sent them to H. G. Merriam's Frontier *magazine, where they were published.*

Homestead Days in Montana

Yes, we lived on a homestead once, not so many years ago. Back in 1910 it was—twenty-three years ago in March—that we made our grand adventure by coming west to live on one. We were young then, Alec and I, and life was full of promise. We had been married four years, but somehow had never been able to reconcile ourselves to the bread-and-butter sort of existence led by the people in our native state—so smug and safe and comfortable, the same yesterday, today, and tomorrow—you know, just being born, growing up, living and dying, all in the same cramped space. There must have been an adventurous streak in the make-up of both Alec and me. Anyway, a restlessness of spirit made us both long to get away, though neither of us ever quite admitted that longing.

At the time of our marriage, four years before, there was nothing we wanted so much as a home and a baby. We had no capital other than our love for each other—very much of that—youth, inexperience, unshaken faith in the future, a willingness to work. The home always came first in our plans and was as beautiful as any dream home could be, with wide lawns, gardens, and orchards, great barns and fertile fields—a farm built up out of the raw land by the work of our own hands, a place to create beauty, to build projects, to change visions to reality; a haven and a refuge never to be completed throughout the years—we did not wish ever to come to the place where we could sit down with folded hands, saying, "It is finished; there is nothing more we can add."

But somehow things did not work out the way we had dreamed them; in three and a half years we had three pink-and-white, golden-haired babies; and our only home was a rented one—a little farm which we tended faithfully, partly from sheer joy at digging in the soil and watching green things grow, and partly for means to provide baby shirts and little shoes and other things so necessary to the proper bringing up of the cherubs.

When we learned, somewhat by accident, of Uncle Sam's free homestead land in Montana, it seemed such a happy solution to our problem of acquiring a home of our very own that we decided to avail ourselves of the opportunity at once. But well-meaning friends and relatives had heard many lurid tales of Indian depredations, of outlawry, and of a rigorous Montana climate, and tried to dissuade us from so rash an undertaking. My own ideas of Montana had been gleaned from much that had been written of "the wild and woolly West," and, I must confess, I myself had thought of it as only a barren waste covered with cactus and sagebrush, inhabited by rattlesnakes and blood-thirsty savages. But the more we investigated Montana's home-making possibilities, the more enthusiastic we became, so that in the end nothing could deter us from our purpose. Hand in hand with Alec, I would have gone to the ends of the earth seeking a home! . . .

Facing westward from Big Sandy we drove twenty miles to the quarter-section which was to be our home on the wide windswept prairie; and just before sundown we stopped on the spot where our shack was to be. Westward lay the Goosebill, long and low; northward the Sweetgrass Hills on the Canadian border, crowned with snow; behind us the Bear Paws made a jagged line against the sky; far to the south in the blue distance loomed the Highwoods. The sun shone on the grass sparkling with raindrops; the wild sweet peas nodded their yellow heads in friendly greeting. As I looked across the rolling expanse of prairie, fired with the beauty of a Montana sunset, I sent up a little prayer of thanksgiving from my heart for this, our very first home. Only a rectangle of prairie sod, raw and untouched by the hand of man, but to us it was a kingdom.

I loved the prairie, even while I feared it. God's country, the old-timers called it. There is something about it which gets a man—or a woman. I feared its relentlessness, its silence, and its sameness, even as I loved the tawny spread of its sun-drenched ridges, its shimmering waves of desert air, the terrific sweep of the untrammeled wind, burning starts in a midnight sky. Still in my dreams I can feel the force of that wind, and hear its mournful wail around my shack in the lonely hours of the night. . . .

The rollicking wind promptly bowled our tent over, that first night at our new home, so again we slept in our wagon. The only water we had for any purpose was contained in a gallon jug, and we did not know how soon nor where we could get more. Consequently, we drank sparingly and in little sips, and bathed our hands and faces in the dewy grass of the morning. We never could keep the tent up—but what matter? Our neighbor lent us the use of a little shack across the way until our own shack was built. There we camped the first few weeks. We had no stove or firewood that first day—no, I had not learned to burn cow chips yet—that was an innovation which came later.

Alec went back to town to bring out our first load of lumber, and the children and I put on our wraps and, to keep out the chill, huddled beneath our blankets in the shack. It took most of the day and well into the night to make the trip into town and return with a load, so in the evening I hung up a lighted lantern to guide Alec on his return to the shack.

At first we set the kitchen range out of doors, but rain and disagreeable weather made this impractical; then we moved it within and, since there was no hole in the roof, stuck the pipe out through the little hole in the side which served for a window. The stove and the folding bed filled almost the entire space. There was no room for table or chairs, so mostly when mealtime came we stood and ate from the plates which we held in our hands. The walls were of unmatched lumber which let in the wind and rain, but at least over us there was a roof. We were real westerners now, and could not shrink from anything which was to be our portion.

The greatest hardship of all was the scarcity of water. The first settlers had dug wells, which eighty to ninety feet down were still dry as dust. At first we were filled with dismay to find no water anywhere. Sometimes we had none even to drink until Alec bought a barrel which he filled with water each day when in town and brought home on top of his load of lumber. We had to stint ourselves extremely for water for bathing, and as for our clothing I washed it a few pieces at a time in the washbasin, because there was no water to fill the tub! We located some water holes and coulees where occasionally we could get water for our horses, but often we had to go many miles for it. My throat constricted with pain when I thought of the well we had planned with which I meant to irrigate my lovely dream garden. It now seemed very remote indeed! Later a shallow well was dug in the coulee a mile away which yielded us a small amount of water each day.

Once that spring when we went to the coulee for water the cattlemen were holding their last big roundup on that prairie since the homesteaders had taken their range; they had established camp by the water hole and had just butchered a young steer. Here was a bit of the old West about which I had read–the branding iron on the smoldering fire, the rope corral, the chuck wagon, the riders with wide sombreros, hairy "chaps," and jingling spurs! While we were filling our water barrel one of the cowboys came over and with a grand sweep of his broad hat smilingly proffered us a piece of the freshly butchered beef. Could he have known how much we appreciated his gift, or by any chance have guessed how lean was the larder in the little shack at home?

We worked happily at our building during every minute of our spare time. I held the boards while Alec sawed and nailed them, and in a few weeks the new shack, fourteen by twenty feet, with two windows and a door, was ready to move into. Joyfully I worked with rugs, curtains, and other things dear to a woman's heart, making it pretty and livable.

Alec plowed a small plot for a garden and I attempted the disheartening task of planting it–disheartening because amid the hard dry chunks of sod I could find no loose soil for covering the seeds. Patiently I took up the sods one by one, and with my hands pounded and shook soil from the matted grass roots and carefully patted it over my seeds. But disillusionment sat heavy upon me. As I worked the tears fell, and truly I "watered my furrows with tears." No more rains came, the grass shriveled and dried up, and shimmering heat waves danced across the landscape. The only seeds in my garden which found moisture enough to grow were the beans, and then as soon as the seed leaves appeared above the ground the chickens promptly snapped them off. My first garden on the homestead became only a sad memory.

How much I feared the rattlesnakes, not on my own account alone, but for the sake of my little children! I warned them repeatedly as they played about the dooryard to look out for "ugly creeping things" and to beware of buzzing noises. But we never saw any–*not one*. One day, as Alec and I walked about our so-called garden, we noticed a great black beetle shambling along among the clods and pointed it out to our little son. Imagine how I felt when the little fellow shrank back, his face pale and eyes round with fear as he gasped out, "A rattlesnake!"

Life on the homestead was becoming a serious problem to us now, for our money was all gone and food supplies almost exhausted. There was still a little flour and a bit of lard, I remember. There was no yeast or other leavening; for bread I mixed the flour with water and a little lard and baked it in small cakes. There was rice, but no sugar, so I put in a few raisins for sweetening. There was absolutely nothing else, so far as I can now recall.

Alec was faced with the necessity of leaving his family on the homestead while he went in search of work. I tried to be very brave, but my heart sank at the thought of facing life in that lonely place without Alec. Many of our neighbors, too, went away looking for work, so that I was left very much alone except when some distant settler passed by, sometimes bringing my mail and supplies. At times for days I saw no one; and then the terrifying loneliness and silence of the great prairie appalled me, and I sobbed aloud to shut out the eerie sound of the coyote's wail, or the dreary soughing of the wind beneath the eaves of my shack.

I went to the coulee a mile away each day for water, and occasionally the children and I made the trip afoot to the store and post office; but as these trips always left us all very much exhausted, we did not attempt them often. Alec wrote every week, sometimes oftener, and his letters were always a delight—long, and filled with details of his work and associations. After one of his letters came I could forget my loneliness and sing at my work for hours.

I busied my mind and my hands with homely little tasks, making over garments for the children's wear and preparing a layette for the new baby soon to come. I sighed over the layette, for mostly it was composed of clothes which my other babies had worn, and I found myself longing intensely for at least *one* new little garment for the precious darling. I had a large-sized sugar sack which had been carelessly tossed into Alec's wagon one day at the store; this I carefully ripped open, washed, bleached in the sun, and pressed. I drew threads painstakingly and made a drawn work yoke of exquisite pattern, hemstitched ruffles for the neck and sleeves, and with a deep hem at the bottom it became a dainty little dress which with a sense of deepest satisfaction I laid away in readiness for my baby's coming.

Summer waned, and the frosty mornings and the calm sunshiny days of autumn came on. Alec was to come for us soon, as he was making plans to take us to the Judith Basin where he worked, so that I might have the care of a doctor and a nurse in my hour of need. I wrote to Alec setting the date for his coming in early October, since I expected my baby in November, giving myself, or so I thought, ample time to make the trip and get rested afterward. Twenty-four hours after mailing that letter I was startled by premonitory pains of an alarming nature, and as they constantly recurred at decreasing intervals I became more and more uneasy. Could I have been mistaken in the time? Could this be approaching childbirth? Maybe if I rested quietly for a while . . . maybe, oh, maybe–no, there was no longer any doubt–my baby would arrive before the letter could reach Alec, before competent help could ever reach me! Pains oftener now, and more severe! Heaven help me now, I must think what to do!

Calmly I went about preparations; trying hard to keep a firm grip upon myself, trying hard not to become panicky. I *must* be brave; I *must* keep my head. Babies had been born before like this. Everything was all right. Oh, if I were only sure what to do! If I only had someone–anyone, to look to for help! I watched for a little boy who occasionally rode past my shack in search of his cows which roamed the prairie, and luckily tonight he came within calling distance. "Johnnie, take this note to your mother!" "What is it, a party?" the boy asked eagerly, as he took the note. "I want your mother, I need her help. Oh, please hurry!" I gasped. The gray pony bounded forward and disappeared into the gathering dusk. As darkness came on I put the children to bed and waited tensely for the help which *must* not fail me! Prayerfully I waited, and walked the floor listening, listening–almost in despair as my need grew greater. Such a wave of relief surged over me as I heard scurrying footsteps in the darkness! My sister-in-law arrived, frightened and tearful, and Mrs. Warren, capable, motherly, master of the situation at once. An hour later my wee new daughter was born!

Call it premonition or otherwise, Alec decided to surprise me by coming home much sooner than I was expecting him, and at the same hour that I was waiting for help to come in my desperate need, he was speeding toward home as fast as a train could take him. The train pulled into Big Sandy a few minutes after midnight and Alec stepped out into the darkness without a moment's pause and set out afoot to walk the twenty miles to the shack on the great brown prairie, which held his loved ones. He arrived home soon after daybreak, to find me in bed, flushed with happiness, a newborn daughter by my side.

The children, wakened from their sleep by Alec's arrival, climbed upon him as he sat on the edge of my bed and began opening the parcels he had brought to them. Suddenly they discovered a tiny sister nestled in mother's arms, whereupon they fell upon Alec with fervent hugs and kisses, calling him "the dearest daddy in the world" for bringing them, besides new shoes and stockings, a brand-new baby sister!

The settlers of our prairie were of many kinds and classes and had hailed from many different states, both east and west, but we were all one great brotherhood. If a man had a homestead alongside the others, he was accepted by all the others without question. We helped one another; what one had, he shared with the next. If one man owned a team, his neighbor some harness, and a third one a plow, they managed a plowed strip for each of the three. Many were the makeshifts and privations which made us all kindred souls. One old man bought a boy's farm wagon in which he used to take his supplies home; another brought his things from town in a wheelbarrow; while I, truth to tell, took my baby carriage and trundled it across the prairie to bring home my sack of flour and other groceries.

Always we were handicapped by the scarcity of water. Alec spent many long hours hauling water for our livestock and for our domestic uses. We lived on the homestead during the spring and summer months; there was never money enough for us to spend a whole year there. The winters we spent in the Judith Basin in various ways and places at whatever work came to hand, but spring always found us returning like homing pigeons to the little shack on the prairie, each year putting in more crops and adding to the improvements on the farm. Many times we made the trip across country in our wagon, but later it had a canvas cover in regulation prairie schooner style, and for bad weather a stove. Once we started out, after a week of balmy weather in March, only to be overtaken by a howling blizzard. For two days we drifted with the wind and flying snow, so that the stove and fuel we had in the wagon saved us from probable freezing.

Two more boys were born to us, and then in rapid succession two more daughters. The family prospered, so that at last we could spend all our time on the homestead. We owned a car and the fourteen-by-twenty shack became a five-room cottage—but never was it the home of our youthful dreams. My lovely garden, so soul-satisfying and enchanting, was never aught but a beautiful dream—the trees we planted pined away and died for lack of water, while my flowers bent their frail heads and the brazen sun turned them into nothingness.

The war had come, bringing with it high prices for the farmer's grain, and copious rainfall had blessed the settlers' efforts with bounteous harvests. The four elevators of the prairie town were kept filled to overflowing with golden grain, and every day the golden flood poured in, hundreds of wagons waiting for freight cars, so that the farmers might take turns unloading their precious cargoes. With wheat at $1.87 a bushel and granaries and bins filled to bursting, the settlers bought more land and high-priced machinery to grow more and bigger crops "to help win the war."

But the bad years came when we staked our *all* on the caprice of the weather and a wheat crop which might never be harvested. As drouth, weeds, cutworms, and hailstorms took their toll from the grain fields, the eager illuminating light of hope died out of the settlers' faces and gave place to a look of morbid apathy and despair. We looked across the broad acres of stunted, shriveled crops, dotted with Russian thistles, and the mortgages mounted higher and the bankers clamored for their interest.

Then came a year when no rains fell and no crops grew, and the bewildered settlers faced a winter with no money, no food, no clothing for their families, no feed of any kind for their livestock, no work. Dumb with despair, the men set about finding some means of providing for their families. Most of them went away to work while the women and little children stayed on in the homes, carrying on as best they might. Alec found a job on a ranch near Billings. When he went away I was left on the homestead once more without him, but this time with nine children instead of three, the youngest a baby three weeks old.

Alec sent every dollar of his wages home as fast as it was earned, yet with me the winter was one long struggle with circumstances to keep my family warmed and fed and to save our horses from starvation. Upon the horses depended our ability to put in one more crop. With the help of my twelve-year-old boy I braved the storms, waded snowdrifts to keep the horses fed, and stood upon an icy platform in below-zero weather drawing water while the horses crowded and pushed about the watering trough. Topsy, the black mare, had a young colt running with her and we decided it was best to wean the colt, so we shut him in the barn, leaving the mare outside. But the faithful mother refused to desert her offspring and took up her post just outside the barn door, calling to him in anxious whinnies or soft nickers of love. All night long she kept the vigil. Refusing to seek shelter for herself, she stood where the keen blasts of an icy wind struck with fullest force. When morning came Willie and I found her crumpled form in the snow by the barn door, frozen dead! Mother and son, we wept together over the loss of a faithful friend, while the wind ruffled the icy mane and sent little eddies of drifting snow across the frozen body. Two other horses we lost that winter and each time I felt the loss keenly, as that of a valued friend; but when spring came we still had nine left of our twelve–gaunt, shaggy creatures, covered with vermin.

The feed for my pigs gave out. When a week had gone by I thought desperately of trying to butcher the sorry little creatures. I wept over their plight, and my woman's nature quailed at the thought of undertaking the butchering alone with no help but Willie's. At last my brother-in-law and two neighbor lads came to help, but the day we set for the butchering was bitter cold with freezing blasts of snow-laden wind sweeping out of the north. Scalding and scraping the pigs was a painful task as the water cooled and changed to ice rapidly; but at last the eight of them were cleaned and scraped after a fashion and left hanging in the shed while we ate our dinner. We ate hurriedly, so as to return to our task before freezing interfered with cutting the meat into pieces for curing. But when one of the lads hurried out ahead to examine the pigs he called back, "They're frozer'n hell right now!" Stiffly swinging from the rafters, they hung like graven images carved of stone; no knife could penetrate the frozen forms. To save fuel we moved the kitchen range into the large living room—here, too, had been placed our beds—and here we carried the frozen pigs and placed them in formidable array across the dining table. They stood at various rakish angles, each firmly upon his feet, ears outspread and tails extending stiffly straight out behind, to be left until they thawed out.

I sat up late that night keeping a brisk fire burning and writing a letter to Alec. It was so cold the timbers of the house popped and the frost crept higher and ever higher up the door. The hands of the clock pointed almost to midnight. Suddenly I was startled by footsteps in the frozen snow and my name called in a familiar voice, "Open the door quick! We've got a girl out here who's nearly frozen!" Hastily I opened the door and recognized Dan, a friend of the family, and another man supporting between them a slender young girl. We carried her inside, where I removed her thin shoes and rubbed her aching hands and feet. When she was warmed and resting comfortably Dan turned about, glanced at my sleeping children in the cots, and then at the frozen pigs upon the table. "My God!" he said.

The girl—a homesick child—had been attending school in Big Sandy, and longing to spend the Thanksgiving vacation with home folks, had attempted a twenty-five-mile ride atop a load of coal, when the thermometer stood at thirty degrees below zero. I took her into bed with me for the rest of the night and the men went to a neighbor's.

Thanksgiving morning dawned clear and cold; the morning sun shone across a white and frozen world lying crisp and still in the crinkling frosty air. The Russian thistles had caught the drifts and each was a hummock of glittering snow—no sign of life in the white expanse except for the smoke which curled lazily upward from the housetops dotting the prairie. My little guest of the night before continued her journey that day and reached home in time to partake of Thanksgiving dinner with home folks.

One of my greatest problems was bringing supplies from town, especially hay and fuel. Never having money enough at a time to buy any great quantity, I lived in abject terror of exhausting my supply before I could get more. Alec wrote: "If your fuel gives out, burn the fence posts, tear boards from the barn and burn them, burn *anything* about the place–don't take any chances of freezing!" Sometimes when food supplies ran low I was driven to parceling out our meals in bits, and at times the pinched, ill-nourished look on the faces of my children made me sick with apprehension.

Once in the coldest weather it was imperative that we get supplies from town. I hesitated to send my boy, small and frail as he was, but there seemed no other way. Pridefully, manfully, he set out with the team and sled, in company with his uncle, to bring hay, coal, potatoes, flour, and sugar–there was little else we could afford to buy. The roads were piled with frozen drifts so that bringing out a loaded sled was a slow and tedious matter, and the boy, inadequately clothed and with ragged overshoes many sizes too large, walked stumblingly through the snowdrifts all the long way from town behind the slow-moving sled. It was hours after dark before I heard the jingling of the harness and the creaking runners of the returning sleds. The boy reached home shaking with cold and reeling with exhaustion.

As I worked over the worn-out child, rubbing with snow his numbed hands and frostbitten feet, my mother's heart swelled with fierce, hot rebellion over the fate which imposed such hardship upon so young a child. I made a swift, determined resolve not to let my children be crushed by the sordidness of circumstances, to secure for them their just measure of the beauty and brightness of life, and to make up to them by every means at my command for the privations they now endured.

December brought a chinook and the snow disappeared with the warm southwest wind like ice beneath a July sun. Water filled the puddles, overflowed the ponds, and rushed in torrents down the coulees. No longer need I worry about hauling water, for the rest of that season at least!

Christmas Day the neighbors gathered at my home for a community Christmas dinner. None had much, but all brought something, and assembled, it seemed an abundance. Jollity, friendship, and goodwill radiated from the fun-loving crowd, the day being shadowed for me only by the lack of Alec's presence. It was but one of many good times the community shared together.

Alec returned with the coming of spring and together we planned the planting of one more crop. During the long winter months another plan had been slowly forming in my mind, a plan to which I gained Alec's reluctant consent. Leaving my nine-months-old baby in the care of a neighbor, I washed and pressed my one dress, mended the only shoes I possessed, and in a shabby black coat and khaki hat I went to town to write the examinations for a Montana teacher's certificate. Timidly at first, then glowingly as I warmed to my subjects, I wrote and wrote, and then feverishly awaited the returns from Helena. When I was once more the happy possessor of a teacher's certificate I went to my local board of trustees and asked for a position, and they were too surprised to say "No." Three years I taught my own and my neighbors' children and some of the happiest hours of my life were spent in that tiny prairie schoolhouse where zealously I tried, out of my own knowledge and experience, to bring beauty and joy into the lives of the thirty-three children whose only experiences had been those of the drab life on the bleak prairie. All the love I put into my work there has been returned to me a thousandfold. The money I earned helped to feed and clothe my family and started my boy to high school.

Courageously but hopelessly the settlers struggled on, trying vainly with borrowed money to battle the elements, to tame the desert, and to carve home and fortune out of the raw land. Then came the grasshoppers, newly hatched, swarming out of the unplowed fields and covering the growing crops with a gray, slimy, creeping cloud which hour by hour steadily advanced, wiping out the greenness of the land, leaving only dry, bare clods in the fields. Despair over the ravaged crops filled the farmer's hearts.

On the billowing, russet prairie stands an empty farmhouse, its windows gone and doors sagging; beneath its eaves the wind soughs mournfully, the desert sand drifts around its doorstep, and the Russian thistle tumbles past. Desolate, silent it stands, grim witness to the frustration of a man's hopes and a woman's dreams.

We have no regrets; life is fuller and sweeter through lessons learned in privation, and around our homestead days some of life's fondest memories still cling. We are of Montana, now and always, boosters still—and in a fair valley of western Montana where the melting snows of the Mission Range trickle out in clear streams across the thirsty land, our dreams of the long ago are slowly taking on life.

The grass grows green about my doorstep, the vines clamber about my porch, the flowers bloom, the birds sing, and Alec's much-loved Brown Swiss cattle graze in lush fields. . . .

Tonight, as I write, the mellow glow of our electric lights shines over our happy home circle, the rooms vibrant from the tinkle of a piano, the melodious wail of a violin, and the lilt of happy youthful voices. I feel that creating a home and rearing a family in Montana has been a grand success, and my cup seems filled to overflowing with the sweetness and joy of living.

■ MATTHIAS "MIKE" MARTINZ

In May 1904, when he was sixteen years old, Austrian immigrant Matthias "Mike" Martinz arrived in Maine by ship. Within hours he was on a train to meet his relatives in Montana, where he entered the lonely life of a sheepherder near Sweetgrass on the Canadian border. He stayed in the sheep business in Malta, Montana, until his retirement. This selection is from Martinz' reminiscences, which he donated to the Montana Historical Society in 1983.

Sheepherding on the Sweetgrass

. . . Portland in Main where we landed on the first of May 1904. Then we were sorted out going thrue a chute just like the way they sort out the Sheep on the western Ranches some had red tickets some have green some have Blue or pink or yellow then we were locked in a room where nobody could get out until train time then a guide would come and take us to the train oure next change of trains was in Chicago and I dont remember now but I dont think we had to change again anyway we landed in Garrison Mont. on May 5th where Mr Gorz awaited us and we stayed in the Garrison Hotel over night. On the following day it was parting Day for oure traveling Party so it was decided that we all go to the Knapp Ranch where oure Onkel Simon Petschar was herding Sheep and Franz Petschar was to take his Place. Onkel Simon wanted a lay off and was ready for his spree as Sheepherders usually do after a long siege with a Band of Sheep and the Elements and lonley life. After Dinner one of the Knapp boys hitsched up a team to a lumber wagon and we piled in and drove to Onkel Simons Sheep Camp up over rough and steep Mountain

Roads. We finaly reached the Camp which was located on a small creek with some scattering trees and Brush almost hiding the Cabin. Onkel Simon was still at the Camp but the Sheep had gone early in the morning out to graze. That was the way and style of herding in the Mountains at that time. You just get up and look in wich direction they started and then you follow them later. Well after some greetings and hand Shakes Onkel started to instruct Mr Franz Petschar in his new duties as a Sheepherder. It went something like this. Now we go to the Cabin here is where you will live and sleep cook your Food and here is your gun you must allways have it handy. There are Wolfs Caiotes Wild Cats Mountain Lions and Bears against which you must protect yourself and your Sheep. Well you can imagine how the poor man felt who was never called opon in his young life, he was about 25 years old to wash a shirt cook a meal or do any chores like that. And my Onkel not being a very tidy man everything was in a mess, Potato peelings all over the dirt floor Bones that the Dogs had been chewing on a roll of Bedding on the dirt Floore and from the looks of things it hadnt been swept for ages. There was no Stove just a fire place in the middle of the cabin Built of Rocks and a couple of Iron Bars across for the Pots and Pans the most disgusting scene a man ever looked at. Then the instruction about the dogs how to handle them and feed them and the dogs are to with him allways sleep with him seat (?) with him since he would have nobody else with him the dogs would be his only companions to talk to. Well Mr. Knapp was trying to console Franz by telling him that things are not as bad as Simon was making out and that he would get used to things and in time would like it. And as for the Wild Animals Simon was talking about he would be lucky if he ever got to see one. So he told him I will take the sheep for one day and you can go back to the Ranch with your Companions and take over the next day. So we went back to the Ranch and there we parted by Sister and myself and Florian Guldenbrein with Mr. Gorz left for Deer Lodge to Mr. and Mrs. Gorges Homes and wondering what oure lot would be. We didn't know where Dad was and asked Mrs. Gorz about it since Mr. Gorz was a man of few words and and no information. Mrs. Gorz explained to us that Mr. Gorz had bought a Ranch and Sheep near the Canadien line West of the Town of Sweetgrass Mont. and Dad was up there and me and Florien Guldenbrein would leave accompagnied by Mr. Gorz for Sweetgrass and Mary was to be Mrs. Gorzes personal Maid. . . .

The Ranch was located on the Red River 1½ miles from the Canadian Border. There I met Dad and a fellow Old Country Man by the name of Andrew (?) Barthaloth. Dad was herding about 4000 head of Sheep and they had allready started lambing so we pitshed right in the following morning started to work. There were eight of us all told Otto was the Cook Andrew was the Shed man Florian and Dad were Day men with the Band 2 American Boys and myself were Bunch herders. Well it didnt take long for me to catsh on to the game and as the Bunches were increasing and getting bigger it was decided that they would have to get the oldest Lambs away from the Ranch to a Camp that was one and one half miles from the ranch allmost on the Canadian Border. And I was the Goat that was selected for that job. It really is the easiest job if you know how to cook. Dad was the one who insisted that I take that job. If he only knew to what misery he put me to I doubt that he would have done so. I had never cooked a meal in my life although there was plenty of Grub there so that a person could have lived good if he only knew how to prepare things. There were all kinds of can goods such as Tomatoes corn, peas several kinds of Dried Ham, Oatmeal, corn Meal, Cheese, Coffe, Can Milk, Sugar, Rice, Beans. and a Pound of Tobacco Seal of North Carolina several Corn Cob Pipes floure for hot cakes and Buissquits Lard and everything. But what can a Boy of 14 do with all that stuff when he doesnt know how to cook it, of course when you get hungry you will try anyway but nothing tasted good no matter how Id try. So I ate things Raw without cooking it. But that wasnt the wort [*sic*] yet a good health Person can go a long ways as long as he has something to chew on, if it wasnt for the lonliness of such a life. I had never been alone before in my life I used to run several times a day up on on the hihest Hill about a quarter of mile away to see if there was a human being anywhere in sight But no luck noting but empty Prarie could I see. So I would go back to Camp and try a pipefull of Tabacco but that didnt taste good so out I would go to look at the Sheep but they resented to have me around they could eat grass and drink water without my help. Nothing to doo So I started exploring the Country to see if I could discover something that would take my mind of this damnable lonliness. I went up in to Canada but when I reached the Highest, there was nothing there only another piece of prairie and another high Hill, in the distance, when I got on that Hill it was exactly the same as the Hill before so back again to Camp look at the Sheep and they were doing fine without me. At long last night would come and sleep. In the first few days I could at least sleep good but as the time went on it was getting worse instead of better my sleep was fitt-full I would wake up at the slightest noise a sheep Bell ringing or the wind blowing around The cabin would wake me up. Smoking my corn cob pipe wasnt helping either it was going on my nerves. I knew it but I had to pass the time somehow. About once a week someone would bring me another Bunch of Ewes and Lambs but it happend to be one of the American Boys allthough we couldnt talk or understand each other at least it was a human being. After a few minutes he would return to the Ranch and I was left alone again. Five weeks of that Hell went by before I was relieved of my job of lonliness. Its no wonder that Sheepherders go crazy.

■ PEGGY CZYZESKI

Peggy Czyzeski was a young bride and mother on eastern Montana's agricultural frontier during the 1920s. This excerpt from an oral history by Laurie K. Mercier tells of Czyzeski's futile attempts to prevent her husband and his domineering parents from taking away her children. The interview is part of "Montanans at Work, 1910-1945," an oral history project conducted in 1986 by the Montana Historical Society.

"And I was alone, all alone"

as told to Laurie K. Mercier

MERCIER: How did your life differ? You were sixteen, that was quite young although at the time it might not have been considered young to get married–how did your life as a wife differ from your work on the ranch when you had been a kid?

CZYZESKI: Well, I was sayin' my husband, he didn't have my father anymore to direct him and he done a lot of foolish things and he was operating on *his* father's money. And he would do foolish things. He bought a brand new mowin' machine, we had our team, one of them was a runaway and he drove up in the yard with that brand new mowin' machine and was gonna' mow the hay and he come in the house to have a cigarette and I said, "Kenneth, did you tie your team up," I said, "Molly might run away with that mowin' machine." And I no more 'n got it outta' my mouth and Molly went with the mowin' machine. And she just riddled it, and it was an expensive mowin' machine, it was a team mower but at that time we paid a lot for it. And so there we didn't have no mowin' machine.

And he went to a sale one time and bought six head of the prettiest bay mares all matched. For work. And four of them was broke, gentle, but two of them wasn't. And he hooked all six of 'em on a disk and he was very careless, he hooked all six of 'em up on this disk and it crippled all of them. We had one horse left. It killed one right out and we had one mare left outta' that and he paid—at that time horses were high priced—he paid 600 dollars apiece for those mares. And so we only had one left and one crippled one. And the others died, they were just, oh they were just cut up and beat up awful. That was one accident. Then the mowin' machine, and it was one thing after the other. He went then one time and he bought some milk cows, milk heifers—they were three-year-old heifers—Holsteins, went to this sale at Winnett and he bought them and brought 'em home. We had an old truck at that time, and they were hungry, they'd been in the sale ring and on the truck all day and they were hungry and the alfalfa field was right there and he dumped 'em out into the alfalfa field. And I told him, I said, "Kenneth." I had been raised on a ranch, I knew what bloat was. I said, "Those cows will bloat, those heifers they're hungry and they'll fill up on that alfalfa and go to the river and drink and die. And he said, "Oh no they won't." He said, "They'll just eat what they want," and I said, "That's, that's," I said, "they'll bloat on that." Well, he couldn't, he didn't listen, he left them there and I had by that time my little girl, too, my two little children and I couldn't run after him all the time, run after the cattle and stuff. Sure enough, pretty soon I noticed that they was gone and I ran down to the river and there laid three of 'em dead in the river. They had bloated. So that was an awful expense, I forget how much he paid for them. It was quite a price, stock was high then. It was after everybody in this country had kinda' lost their stock, from that 1919 winter that we had, such a winter and stock was high-priced. There went those cows, and it was just one thing like that after the other. He was not a manager. He couldn't manage a ranch, by himself. He done pretty good when my father was there to tell him everything to do, but not by himself.

Well, he had a bunch of hogs, a hard winter come, and he had a bunch of hogs and he didn't keep grain there for them to eat. And I had to get on the horse, leave him baby-sit the children and I got on the horse and I rode seven miles to the neighbor and got a sack of grain to try to save the hogs. Nearly all the hay, if we'd a had an alfalfa stack they coulda' survived, but we didn't; we had a blue joint stack of hay and he thought those hogs could eat that blue joint and survive, and they, I told him they couldn't, that they would die. Well, they started dying on us, they got so poor, starvin' to death. And we had no grain. And I went to the neighbors and got a sack, big sack of grain, carried it home on the horse, but that only lasted for a few days. And our hogs gradually all died. Just from starvation. And the poor guy, he just couldn't manage.

Well, then we had to move from there to the oilfield, and we had, he had worked in the oilfields some for my brother, and my little daughter was born in the Cat Creek oilfield. My mother delivered her, she weighed eleven pounds. And I had ta', I had ta' walk. It was the 16th day of December but it was good weather, it happened to be a beautiful day, beautiful weather, no snow yet, and I had ta' walk from where I was to the pumphouse where he was working to get help.

I took sick. It was about three o'clock in the morning, and I went in my bathrobe, so you know it wasn't cold, down to where he was working, about a quarter of a mile. And I was in hard labor, and I come back, had walked back, and then he had to go get my mother. And that walk caused me ta', caused my labor to come on fast and hard, and I could see that I possibly would be all alone. But he got my mother there just in time to deliver that baby, and she weighed eleven pounds. Little fat and cute little thing (laughs), and I thought she was the homeliest baby I ever saw in my life cause she had a great big nose when she was born and I just, oh I thought, and my mother teased me, she said, "Well I think, Peggy, you probably marked your baby after Shorty Thorsen," and that was my stepfather and he had a huge nose, and then I cried and my mother laughed, and she said, "Oh, I'm just kiddin' ya'," she said, "When she grows up she'll be a beautiful girl" and (laughing) she said, "I'm just teasin' ya'."

But anyway, my husband did go and get the doctor because mother couldn't get the afterbirth, and so he went, rode to Grassrange and got the doctor. And we had an old car, old Model T Ford and he drove that, got the doctor down and mother, she knew she hadn't got it all because the way the doctor acted. So mother worried about it, and on about the third day I got awfully sick, high fever and I was awfully sick and my mother knew what was the matter. I had infection from that, and I nearly died. But my mother took care of me and I come out of it. She really doctored, my mother knew what to do, anyway, for that. So she took care of me and we lived there then until my daughter was about . . . well, we still had this ranch and we went back to the ranch after that, but before Dolly was born we plowed up a big sagebrush flat. I could show you a picture of that ranch, where I picked sage. Two weeks before Dolly was born I picked sagebrush offa' that flat, and piled it. We just plowed the field and plowed up the sagebrush. And I could work, it never hurt me, nothing ever hurt me, I was so healthy and strong.

Then we were living on the ranch . . . and Arnett woulda' been four in September and Dolly woulda' been three in December. We were livin' on the ranch and doin' fine, and his [my husband's] father and mother wrote and said they were coming out to visit us. They were just there three days and before they come I had went out—my husband was careless, he left the harnesses and the saddles down in the barnyard and everything—and I went out and hung up everything and took care of everything. I had a big garden and a lot of chickens and I'd raised some hogs and everything, and we were gettin' along good.

We had bought a bungalow. Our old house that was my dad's and mother's, we had used that for a barn, the bottom part of it, the log part of it, we tore it down and used it for a barn. And we moved a four-roomed house down from the oilfield with four head of horses and a wagon into our ranch, and we'd moved in that. And you know what I did in that house? I could do carpenter work. We had dug a basement and put that house over it, and I went down into the basement, it was a sand basement, and I dug a well down as far as I could. Then I took a sandpoint, I don't know whether you know what a sandpoint is or not, but it's a thing that's sharp on the end, a pipe about this big, and it's, oh that long, and it's sharp on the end and then it has a screen in it to let the water come into it, you know. And you drive them sandpoints down into the water and the water seeps in there, and then you got a well, like, see and I drove a sandpoint down into that, myself, and put the pipe on it. And I built my own cabinets in that house outta' beaded ceiling lumber. You know, beaded ceiling is a narrow lumber like that and it's grooved along and each board matches; they seal together like, you know, and they called it beaded ceiling. Well, I built me my cabinets in that kitchen myself out of this beaded ceiling lumber and I had this well in my basement and it come up through the floor and I put a pitcher pump on it. You probably never seen one of those. It was a little red pump and you primed it and you could pump water up into my sink, and I did that. I was eighteen years old. And I, I don't know, I was just talented that way, I guess I took after my father and mother both, they were very talented people. And so I had my nice cupboard, and water in the house; and we were just getting along fine.

I had everything cleaned up and my garden, I had a nice garden out the end of the house and that ranch was really a nice little ranch, it was sandy soil and real good gardens grew there and everything. And I got pictures of that I could show you. We had this nice house and we was just doin' great and his folks come and they stayed three days and while they were there they leased the ranch–without us even knowin' it–went up the river and leased the ranch to John O'Day, one of the neighbors about six or seven miles up the river. And then, after they come back, they didn't say anything. After they come back we had the ranch across the river yet that they had bought for Kenneth to begin with and we just lived on my dad's and mother's place. We didn't own it or anything and, my oldest brother owned it at that time, but he didn't charge us nothing, we just lived there and operated it. And we had run my brother's horses for him. He had a lot of wild horses on the range and we run those horses and our horses came from that herd of horses that we'd lived, worked on the ranch. And I had one beautiful black saddle horse that had run a wild stallion and I got him in and broke him myself. I broke him for my children, gentle for my children to ride. He was a precious horse and I broke him myself. Well, I had him that I claimed for my very own because my brother told me I could have him from his herd, and he had good horses. So the stuff in my house was what my mother left me when she moved away, all my furniture, my cookstove and all my furniture and everything. I was real proud of that. And we were just doin' what we thought was really good, but still operating on his folks' money. I didn't have anything in the line of clothes or anything like that but we had plenty and with mother's furniture and everything, we had it pretty nice.

So the next day, after they come, and she wouldn't let the children touch her, she didn't want my children to touch her and they thought they was gonna' see a grandmother like my mother, you know. They was old enough to realize what my mother was, and I had told them their grandmother was comin'. But she was a very sophisticated, high-toned lady and she come into the house and she sat down and 'course Dolly and Arnett was little and they went up to her and she would take her hand and push them away. And it just made me sick, and I *was* sick to begin with.

I had this awful sore throat and I was cooking dinner and my husband and his dad went across the river to see about that ranch across the river and while they were gone Mr. Green rode in, a man that was an old man and him and his wife had moved onto the ranch about three miles from our ranch. They was people from Oklahoma, southern people, and they were awfully good to us. When we couldn't get across the river to our ranch they would always take us in and take care of us. And we stayed at their house a lot, in the summertime and spring when the river was flooding, and so we thought of them. In our country it was nothing for a rider to ride in and you'd always ask 'em to have dinner or invite them in regardless of who they were because people lived far apart in them days and they'd be horseback or wagon. So his mother and I was at the house, and Kenneth and his father was at the other ranch, and Mr. Green rode up horseback. It was about noon and I was getting dinner and I, we called him Paul Green, and I said, "Paul Green, won't you get off and come in?" And he said, "No, not this time, Peggy. I want to ride over, I haven't seen Bob Bailey for a long time. I want to ride over and see him." And he said, "But I would like a glass of water." Well I took him out a glass of water, he was on his horse, and I took the glass of water out to him.

I went back in the house and she started in on me. She said, "You know," she said, "you asked that man to come in and have dinner when your husband wasn't home." And she said, "You know, you're not much of a lady." And she said, "I want you to understand this food up here in this cupboard and everything is mine and dad's, it's not yours to give away." And she said, "That's why we have spent so much money on you and Kenneth, you have give it to neighbors . . . your friends and everybody, and I don't think you're very much of a lady for my son." Oh, I was just squelched. And she said, "We have done more for you than your own father and mother ever done for you and all you want to do is have a bunch of kids for my Kenneth to have to raise like your mother did." I, oh, I was just squelched, I didn't know what to do. I went out behind the house and set down and took my kids and cried.

And pretty soon they come home and he come around, my husband come around the house where I sat and he said, "Why are you setting out here cryin'?" And I said, "Your mother talked awful to me." And I told him what she had said. And he said, "Oh, don't pay any attention to Mother, she's getting old." But she wasn't so old, she was a woman in her late fifties, I guess. And she run the roost. Kenneth went into the house, he went back around inta' the house and she was finishing dinner and he said, "You come in and bring the children in and have dinner, Peggy." And I said, "No. I won't eat her food." I said, "I won't, I'm goin' to walk over to Paul Green's, Paul and Ma Green."

It was about three miles over the hill and it was a hot day, it was in August. And he said, "No, you stay here and come in and have dinner." And he kept coaxin' me, so finally I got up and I took the children and I went to the door to go in and have dinner and she had three plates on the table, one for Kenneth and her husband and her, and I looked at the table and I turned around and walked out, took my children out. And I set out behind the house and I cried, and I cried, and I cried and I didn't know what to do.

The next day they went up to this John O'Day's and this John O'Day was a good friend of my father and mother's and they sold him my saddle horses, my two that I had drove. They sold everything in the house. They leased the ranch out and the third day they left, with my children. They told me when they was packin' their things. I had a little trunk that my brother brought to me when he come home from the world war, first world war. And she told me, she said, "We're takin' Kenneth back to Oregon, but we don't want you because you're just a eatmate, you're not a helpmate, we don't want you." And I said, "Well, you might take him but you're not takin' my children." I said, "If he wants to go with you, that's fine, but you're not takin' my children." She said, "Well, we don't want them, they're too much like you." Oh, I was, it was just terrible. I didn't fight back because I didn't know how. I never had fought back and I didn't know how, so I tried to talk to Kenneth and he said, well he said, "I'll have ta' go with 'em and work until I can pay 'em off and I'll send for you—you and the children." And I said, "O.k."

I had five cents in my pocket and we got up to the oilfield where my friends were, and he left me there at my friends' or was gonna' leave me there at my friends', and me and my children; and I had this little trunk packed with all our clothes in it, it was just a trunk about that long and about that wide, little round top on it. I was so proud of it, 'cause my brother gave it to me. And that held all of my children's clothes and my clothes and I had 'em in that and we had an old Model T with no top on it, and they had a Model T, it was a big, it was 'sposed to be a touring car. It had that old-fashioned top and everything. And we got up to the oilfield and there he left me with Bessie Barden, she was the lady that cooked there at that time. And I was gonna' take my children's clothes and my stuff in there and Kenneth said, "Oh," he said, he told 'em, "I'm not gonna leave my wife and children, I'm not gonna' go." He said, "I'm not going to go," and he was gonna stay with me, and get a job or something around the oilfield. And she said, "If you don't go with us, we'll cut you off of everything

. . . our will and everything. You'll not get a dime." And she said, "We don't want her because," she said, "she's not good enough for you." But, she said, "If you want the children, we will take 'em. We don't want them, but we will take 'em." And she kept naggin' at him, and finally he decided to go, and the last minute they took my children. And I was alone, all alone. Mrs. Barden wasn't home, there was nobody around much. I had to walk about a mile before I could get to somebody, and there they left me standin', five cents in my pocket. I was just, well I was just a real sick girl.

■ ORLAND E. ESVAL

Orland Esval was born into a Norwegian family in North Dakota in 1904. He grew up in eastern Montana, where he became an electrical engineer before retiring to North Carolina. Esval's memoir about working on a threshing crew near Scobey was published in 1977 in Montana the Magazine of Western History. *A later version is included in Esval's reminiscences,* Prairie Tales: Adventures of Growing Up on a Frontier *(1979).*

Member of the Crew

After reaching my teens, an annual obsession was to join the neighborhood threshing crew on its fall circuit. While I had wistfully aspired, ever since childhood, to be an engine operator, there was no chance for that. My only possible place on the crew was as a bundle hauler. It was very hard work, and any youth who could hold his own on that job through an entire threshing season was accepted as a man. No longer did he have to take second place boy status. Each year, it seemed, Papa would not let me join the crews, feeling that I just did not have the necessary stamina. It hurt, because I knew younger fellows who could do it. To be sure, they had short, stocky builds, and were physically well developed for their age. Papa, I knew, was a little disappointed in me, for I had not inherited his solid frame and was tall but very slender. Papa encouraged me to wrestle, and even bought me some boxing gloves. But nearly always I came out second best. I had helped only as an alternate for a few hours at a time on crews of previous seasons, until the summer of 1921, when I was sixteen years old. That year I finally wore Papa down. He had misgivings, but he agreed to equip me with a good team of horses and a wagon bundle rack and let me hire out as a regular on the threshing run.

Our neighbor, Loren Fladager, operated the local threshing rig. He was at our place one Sunday before the start of the run, and agreed, with some misgivings of his own, to take me on. The pay: $5.00 plus $2.00 for the team and bundle wagon–a grand total of $7.00 per working day. I was jubilant. For the first time in my life, a man's pay! I quickly calculated that if the season lasted thirty days I would have earned $210.00. It was an opulent, but really not an impossible, dream.

Loren, however, soon brought me back to earth: "We are starting at my place tomorrow morning. The wheels are rolling at six o'clock and you had better be there."

The alarm woke me up at 4:30 on Monday morning. After a quick breakfast, I harnessed Mable and Queen, hitched them to the wagon, and drove off in the brisk pre-dawn air. Papa had let me have two of his best work horses. I was also equipped with a bedroll, the essential three-tined pitchfork, and what proved to be my lifesaver–a canvas bag for drinking water. Mama and Papa wished me well on a venture they knew was going to be very rough on me. But I was on top of the world and could see no reason for their concern. As it turned out, it was a bumper crop year for Montana, and a vintage (although painful) year of growing up for me.

The sun, a huge golden orb, was just rising through the morning mists of this portentous day in late August. The horses trotted and the wagon rattled as we passed field after field of grain standing in shocks, waiting for threshing. This was a bountiful year, the growing crops having eluded a gamut of hazards throughout the season. The precious grain kernels would soon be stored in granaries, provided the threshers were allowed a few weeks of dry, clear weather.

Never had the farmers' outlook, or mine, been rosier. Proudly, I was taking Papa's place on the team. Moreover, for practical reasons, it was good that Papa had a replacement. The new County of Daniels had just been formed from portions of Valley and Sheridan Counties, and he had been elected to the first Board of Commissioners. Occupied in setting up the new county government, and establishing a new courthouse in Scobey, he had to do so much traveling that he bought his first automobile–a second-hand Model T Ford. Thus aside from the excitement of harvest, my ego was bolstered because I was *needed*.

True enough, as I approached the base of operations the "wheels were rolling," the endless belt on its perpetual journey from engine to separator and back. The separator was moaning, groaning and throwing out plumes of yellow straw. Loren Fladager, standing in the cab of his giant, rumbling, four-cylinder Avery traction engine, had a watchful eye on everything. The romantic steam threshing engines were already outdated; simpler to operate, more efficient, powerful gasoline tractors had taken their place.

Waving from the cab, Loren indicated to me the field from which I was to start loading. Following a row of shocks, I was soon pitching bundles into the rack as fast as I could. The reins were tied to the side of the rack so I could easily reach them in guiding the horses to follow the row. After a few days of training, they followed the row at proper distance with very little reining. Starting and stopping them by "gid-dup" and "whoa" was all that was necessary.

Soon I had the bundles piled high on my rack and the load was getting heavy for the horses to pull over the soft ground. But I wanted to be sure my load was a big one as I pulled up to the machine, because I knew all eyes would be on the "greenhorn" to see if he might try to get by with lighter loads than the other haulers. I knew their code and I was determined to abide by it.

Driving in on top of the swaying load, I had hopes of arriving soon enough to have a bit of rest before unloading. The line, however, was nearly empty. There was no time to sit on the ground or even to say hello to anybody. Immediately I had the precarious job of guiding the horses to the feeder box of the growling, shaking separator.

The first time of the season, this was a frightening experience, even for the gentlest of horses. It was necessary to approach as close as possible to the feeder without colliding with belts, pulleys, conveyers and shakers. Luckily I had Mable and Queen–fine, placid draft horses of the Belgian breed–but even for them, coming so close to the noisy monster and the blinding dust was asking too much. At the first pass, I was too far away. The next time I managed to get closer. After calming the mares the best I could and tying the reins back, hopefully to make them stand still until my load was emptied into the machine, I started pitching into the feeder.

I had been joined by a "spike pitcher" to speed up the unloading and to keep the separator working to capacity. Since my rack was still not close enough to the feeder conveyer and we had to pitch the extra distance, the helper gave me a disgusted Bronx cheer.

The grain bundles had to be tossed "heads first" into the feeder for efficient separation of kernels from straw and chaff. A canvas conveyer transported them head-on into revolving knives which cut the twine with which they were tied, then they disappeared into the machine. Presently the mass became a rubbing, tearing, shaking, screaming and blowing holocaust that eventually diverted the kernels into bags or wagon boxes. It was the farmers' "pay dirt."

Quickly my load was gone, and I was on my way for another. It was not yet 7:00 A.M., but the sun was climbing rapidly in a cloudless sky. The day was going to be hot, with little breeze, but there was no time to think about that. I rushed out to load as fast as I could. This time I pulled in before all those ahead were unloaded, so I gained some precious minutes of rest. And my mares allowed me to maneuver my rack closer to the feeder.

Things were going well. At each load I was earning two or three minutes of rest; Mable and Queen were behaving beautifully as we established ourselves in a slot behind Ole Lien and ahead of Nels Sundby. We were, however, on the belt side of the machine, where, because of the heavy drive belt from the engine, there was a greater distance for pitching the bundles. As it turned out, this was to be my working position for the whole threshing run.

I knew that Ole and Nels were very nice men and that gave me courage. Since Ole unloaded just ahead of me, it was my aim to arrive at the rig before he started to unload, affording a moment to chat with him. Most important, there would be rest during his unloading. But as the morning went on, it became harder and harder to get any rest between loads.

Already I was getting weary, plagued with incessant thirst. I gulped water time after time from my blessed canvas bag. Even so, after about seven rounds, I began to wonder if I could make it until noontime dinner. The bundles were feeling awfully heavy, and actually, because the crop was good, they were. The straw was short and every bundle compact, the heads heavy with ripe grain.

At midmorning there was coffee and donuts at the rig if you had time to get off your load and take some. But I was getting behind so I passed it up. At 10 o'clock the sun was blistering, my head aching. No longer could I toss the bundles up into the rack; they had to be lifted all the way. Sweat was in my eyes and dust was crusting on my face. I could hardly see.

Just as I was pulling in with my tenth load, the threshing stopped for dinner. Staggering, I unhitched the mares and took them to the long watering trough where they drank great quantities before they would leave it. With bridles off, I tied them to the feed box at the back of the rack and poured oats out for them. After washing my face in cool water, I was somewhat revived. The dinner was very good, a typical harvest time meal; but however tasty it was, I could scarcely touch it. I crawled under my rack, in the shade next to the horses, and rested.

In no time, it seemed, Loren started the engine, a signal to hitch up and start unloading into the machine. The afternoon was worse, the sun white hot in an ashen sky. The bundles were pitched, loaded, hauled and unloaded in endless repetition in a semi-conscious kind of daze. In my mind, the threshing machine became a hungry demon, demanding more and more bundles for its awful appetite. Unreasoning and unrelenting, it devoured everything in its gaping maw. To deny the monster its tribute was too horrible to contemplate.

So the day went on–aching muscles, pounding heart, ominous thoughts, continuous thirst. Coffee and cake–but it was ignored again. Finally, came the saturated state of fatigue. It could get no worse.

The sun was no longer so blistering, but the routine just as perpetual. Like a cog in a chain between Ole and Nels, I never got out of place or missed my turn. This was the code, especially for greenhorns.

Unbelievably, the moan and groan of the separator finally stopped, leaving a hollow, silent void. As everyone began unhitching, there was low talk and a little tired joking. The animals had to be attended to first–find them a sheltered place for the night, after watering them. Unharness and rub down the sweat-caked bodies, find hay and bedding, then give them their ration of oats.

At about 7 o'clock, with hands and face washed, I joined the rest of the crew for supper in the Fladager house. Mrs. Fladager gave me a concerned look and motioned me to come with her. Speaking as a former nurse, she said, "You look terrible. How do you feel?"

Without much conviction, I said I was all right. Giving me two white pills, she said, "Take these and go to bed right after supper."

What these pills were I never knew, but now it occurs to me that they might have been salt tablets. It is likely that I had a salt deficiency from perspiring and drinking so much water.

Again, I could hardly touch the good meal. Ignoring the banter around me, I left the table to find a place to unroll my bed. But first I had to lead the mares to the watering trough. That done, I laid down, but it was a restless sleep. I pitched heavy bundles all night, and tossed as if in high fever.

A loud clamor aroused me. The crew was getting up for the day's work, but even to move in my bedroll was painful. Pulling on socks, overalls, shirt and boots was agony. At 5:00 A.M. it was chilly, so I put on a warm jacket. Rolling up the bedroll was more misery. When I limped over to the horses, they were in surprisingly good shape and hungry for their oats. It took excruciating effort to lift the heavy harnesses over their backs, but after a face wash in cold water, I was rejuvenated enough to eat a fried egg and a pancake.

Sad to relate, however, the second working day was truly worse than the first. Loading the first rounds with stiffened muscles took painful effort. Then there was some limbering relief. But the day was even hotter. Somehow I survived, not thinking, not questioning. I continued as a cog, never slipping my place in the chain. This is not fantasy; it is fact, because Ole Lien was always about finished unloading as I drove up to the machine. Sometimes Nels Sundby was there ahead of me to enjoy a long breather while I unloaded.

At dinner the second day I still had no appetite. Lying in the shade until work started again, there were lurking thoughts of quitting, going home, being sensible; it would be so easy to end the agony. Mama would be relieved. But the idea had to be rejected. It would mean a permanent loss of status, and I simply could not disappoint Papa.

In my numbing weariness that second afternoon, I was, in fact, a menace to myself and others. In unloading at the machine I was unsure of my footing on the spongy load of bundles. A fall into the feeder was sure tragedy. Al Lawson was the spike pitcher on the belt side. Blinded by sweat and dust, I accidentally scratched him twice with my pitchfork. He was a great mountain of a man and my unfortunate jabs did not even cause him to break the rhythm of his pitching. But he edged over to me for a moment, and over the noise shouted, "Boy, you better not do that again!"

It was fortunate that Mama did not know about my travail. There was a story that circulated at harvest time about a hapless bundle hauler who, after accidentally jabbing a spike pitcher with his fork several times, was thrown to his destruction in the feeder. Such a thing could happen to Mama's one and only son.

At coffee time that afternoon, I climbed down and tried to swallow some of it. Others of the crew were standing around, Selmer Fladager one of them. He was one who enjoyed needling me, and he said as I was holding my cup, "Is that you or is it your shadow? You are so skinny I believe I can see right through you." The others laughed. The dried sweat on my face cracked as I smiled wanly and retreated up on my load, heart pounding.

Two days of heavy exertion in extremely hot weather, profuse sweating and little nourishment had indeed taken their toll. My shirt and overalls hung on me loosely. I had been thin, but now I looked like a cadaver.

While I avoided jabbing Al with my pitchfork again, there were other problems. In my fatigue, some of the bundles I pitched to the feeder landed on top of others or even lay crossways as they entered the machine. This caused the separator to snort and slow down. This was bad for the threshing process, causing loss of grain in the straw pile.

Witnessing all this, Loren ran from the engine, climbed up on my rack, came close to me and yelled, "You feed this machine right or get out of here! Understand?"

I did understand. Perhaps it was anger, causing the adrenalin to flow, sharpening my wits, that gave me strength to deliver the bundles in better position after that. And even this awful day came to an end, as the groaning rumble of the rig suddenly stopped. In my stupor, it gave me a start. But this time I was not quite so indifferent. There came a small restoration of my wits, and in my thoughts, even food took on a slight appeal. Caring for my two faithful mares took super effort, but at supper, I did more than just toy with my food. Almost oblivious to the table chatter, I hurried through the meal and quite literally hit the hay (straw).

Sleep this time was not quite so nightmarish, but waking up in the morning was just as miserable, my muscles sorer than ever. The harnesses were heavier, too, and the mares nuzzled me as if in sympathy.

But this day—it was Wednesday—was the turning point. The hot weather continued and the threshing was as steady as ever, but I was less an insensible robot. There was more appetite, and more consciousness of the whole operation. That morning there was one nagging worry: a substitute spike pitcher was on the job to replace Al Lawson, and he didn't have Al's skill. This bothered me, especially since I had heard the reason Al was absent. He had a weakness for liquor, and the night before had gone to the town of Tande and treated himself to a bottle of bootleg whiskey (this was during Prohibition). It took him half a day to sober up, but he was on the job in the afternoon as if nothing had happened.

The next day, although the work was steadily getting easier for me and I finally was really hungry before mealtime, the jabbing episode with Al and his brief absence from the job was still to haunt me. This mental misery was in some ways worse than the physical torture I had known. At supper that night, one of my tormentors turned to Al Lawson and said, "I hear you took off and went to Scobey to see a doctor yesterday morning."

Al looked up in surprise, since the statement was obviously not true. But he caught the drift, grinned, and growled into his plate, "Who me? Oh ya, ya."

Following up his chance, the wise one went on: "Yeah, and I hear you got stuck with a pitchfork and got blood poisoned." This brought down the house and, of course, it was at my expense. New-found hunger gone, I stared down at my plate and blushed to my ears.

Saturday night, after pitching the last bundle for the day, I headed straight for home without waiting for supper with the crew. Never had home been so appealing. Mable and Queen knew our destination at once and maintained a trot all the way. The rig was now at Willy Fladager's, a couple of miles further away.

I had a gala reception. Papa's oldest sister, my cultured Aunt Aagot, was there as well as my parents, my sisters and Uncle Torstein. A conquering hero could not have been better received. Papa even took care of my horses for me. I surprised Mama by requesting, first of all, a washtub full of water in the back shed. For the first time in my life I loathed being filthy dirty. It was a glorious feeling to be cleansed of six days of sweat and grime and to put on fresh clothes.

Mama peeked at me in the lantern light before I got dressed and gasped, "Orland, you have lost so much weight. I think this is bad for you. Please do not go back to it."

I brushed her off, but surprised her at the number of helpings I had of her delicious supper. She had all my favorites, including strawberry shortcake and heavy cream. After supper there was music and singing, a real party atmosphere, but I could not stay awake and went right to bed. I did not wake up until 4:00 the next afternoon, when it was nearly time to go back to the threshing location.

Mama pleaded with me to give it up, but although I had misgivings, I hitched my horses to the bundle wagon and drove off. At this point, I knew I could take the physical part of being on the crew. What I still could not handle was the mental part, the needling. This feeling could not be shared with anyone, not even my parents. The complete rest at home had, however, done wonders. Rolling out of bed so early in the morning was still painful, but endurance had been developed to cope with the hard labor and hot weather. Most important, while I knew I might still be needled, I would no longer be singled out for it.

In the third week of the run there was an early September snowstorm. Fair weather quickly followed it, but the operations were halted for several days, allowing a welcome vacation for me at home.

With it came the opportunity to hear from Papa about his interesting work with the County Commissioners in setting up the new government of Daniels County.

After this hiatus, I was really glad when the harvested wheat, standing in shocks, was again dry enough so threshing could resume. What a great feeling it was to take my place on the crew again, this time as a regular. I was especially proud of this when, in due course, the operation got to our farm.

My chief problem now was a ravenous hunger that plagued me the last couple of hours before dinner and supper. The mares, too, were thriving in spite of the long hours of hard work. By now they were so accustomed to the routine that I scarcely had to speak to them as they pulled the wagon along the shock rows while I tossed the bundles into the rack. I loved the gentle brutes. I loved it all. Too soon it would end.

With a final groan the machine swallowed the last bundle and stopped for good. The crew dissolved in all directions, hurrying home to attend to many things that had been neglected during the run.

Until that instant I could not comprehend that the finish would be so complete and final. A sudden tight feeling in the throat betrayed the attachment I had formed for these men, machines and animals. There had been a challenge, a mountain to be climbed. With painful effort and teamwork, it had been conquered. But now at the pinnacle it had collapsed into a valley of emptiness for me. The crew had disbanded abruptly, indifferently, leaving a void of silent desolation. I felt let down, deflated.

Loren and Carl Lien stayed with the rig, coupling up everything, including the cook car, for towing back to the Fladager place. I lingered for my pay. All the rest of the crew were farmers who applied their wages on their threshing bill. Loren took out his worn timekeeper book and tallied up my working days. I had not missed an hour of threshing time and it totaled 25 and 3/4 days. I had earned $180.25. As he handed me the check, Loren paid me his best compliment: "You're gonna be a good worker."

Mable and Queen sensed the run had ended. They would have galloped all the way home if I had not held them in. For me, it was high time I entered school. I would be deprived, even, of the companionship of my beautiful horses. Did they know they would be enjoying a well earned vacation? It seemed so. Within an hour they were in the big pasture, reveling, whinnying, snorting, free of leather collars and straps. They rolled on the ground, squealing in ecstacy. In their freedom it would take days before the heavy harness marks would no longer mar their furry coats.

I did not know it then, but not only had I parted company with Mable and Queen, a fine crew and a great team spirit, but with the only lifestyle I had ever known. Never again would I harness and drive fine horses, or ride windswept prairies looking for stray cattle, or plow fields, or harvest tall standing grain. Never again would I see limitless winter whiteness, or sense the pungent barn smells where cows are milked while dogs and cats wait hungrily for their dish of foaming milk.

Most of all, I didn't realize, and it is well that I didn't, that those noble people, bonded together by an austere environment, would become for me only a misty memory.

■ CHARLES VINDEX

Born in Minnesota, Charles Vindex taught school and worked at many other jobs in the West before retiring to his home state to write about local history and life in the American West. His memories about rural Montana during the Great Depression are from "Survival on the High Plains," which originally appeared in Montana the Magazine of Western History *(1978).*

Survival on the High Plains, 1929-1934

At the end of October 1929 a plains blizzard drove southwest from Hudson Bay. To my family and me, then residents of northeastern Montana, it was far more swift in terms of disaster than the financial storm already sweeping America. I had just brought my wife and our week-old daughter home from the hospital in Plentywood when the warm blue afternoon haze dissolved into gentle rain—the first rain since early July. We welcomed its beginning as only plainsmen welcome rain. But about nightfall it turned to sleet, and the wind rose. Within moments the grim Montana winter burst about us. When that first fury abated, after seventy hours of wild opaque whiteness, the machines with which our road crew had gouged all summer at the brown prairie sod and gravel stood ice-encased and buried under snow. The work on which we had been living was not resumed until 1934.

My wife and I had been married seven days short of a year and had put much of that year's earnings into repairing and furnishing the house in which we lived. To supplement my very seasonal income we had bought a large incubator and 1,200 hatching eggs the previous spring. But white diarrhea had scattered half our downy flock in hideous bedragglement. Now, confused by cold, the brooder-accustomed survivors ignored their roosts, huddled together on the floor for warmth and smothered one another, ten to fifty at a time.

Early in April our landlord required his house. After a week of vain search we moved into a tall gabled four-room structure eleven miles northwest of town, which had stood gathering dust for years. All windows not boarded up were broken. With the hostile haunted air that grows in company with the smells of vacancy, mold, and vermin, it faced south near the northwest corner of a 160-acre wheatfield. A crude trail ran south toward the Plentywood road. . . .

This region, short of manpower since its very beginning, had always imported help, had in consequence been devoted to the work ethic. Now with blinding suddenness came an ethical revolution: the simple and forthright obligation to work was ousted overnight by something describable only as the doctrine of the prior claim. Every man who sought a job, unless he could prove some special right to it, emerged willy-nilly as a threat to some other man's survival. . . .

1929-30

West of the house three stony acres sloped toward the road. I turned what I could of this ground with a battered walking plow, and planted most of our first garden about May 1. Earlier attempts were self-defeating; there seemed to be always another cold spell waiting to come back. The wind, which seldom died down for more than a few hours, whipped up incredibly penetrating dust. The best houses were not free of it; in ours it gathered daily on every level surface. It even came up through the floor.

A whole folklore of methods for shutting out dust grew up among our neighbors. For us the most effective immediate way was to enlarge and deepen the cellar, then bank the removed material around the house to close small wind-admitting gaps between its sills and the foundation. Meanwhile, cleaning remained a task without end.

Our surviving chickens were laying several dozen eggs daily. Local markets paid around 15 cents a dozen for them, in trade. There was no longer any market at all for the chickens themselves. As feed grew scarcer and values inexorably fell, while our new chicks grew to usable size, we ate so many chickens and eggs that both became tiresome.

The distance from suppliers made milk for the baby a problem from the start. There was a good dairy just outside Plentywood; but our wheat-farming neighbors kept few cattle. At length, one, only a mile distant over the fields, informed us that he had a young cow he disliked to milk because "her teats are so small you can't get hold of 'em." He offered us her morning milk if I would walk over and extract it myself. She gave two to four quarts that summer, depending on the changing quality of pasturage.

East of the house a 40-foot windmill tower surmounted a well 300 feet deep. The pump was out of order; without hoisting equipment I could not repair it. I carried drinking and cooking water from a neighbor's well; for other purposes I hauled water from a coulee dam which did not go dry until late summer. We caught every drop of the run-off from the roofs when, rarely, it rained. When winter came we continuously melted snow in a wash boiler on the kitchen stove and in a barrel beside the stove. We kept adding snow as the level sank; when we had a boilerful of water finally heated we poured it into the barrel to accelerate melting there. There were many steel barrels, once containers for oil or gasoline, blown into nearby coulees, where boys had used them for targets. I soldered metal patches on the smaller holes and bolted pieces of discarded tires over the large ones. . . .

After midsummer most of our hens stopped laying; only the growing grasshopper infestation saved the flock. It was pathetic but comic to see twenty cockerels advance like a skirmishing party in the shimmer of heat–wings drooping, beaks panting–alert to pounce upon hoppers too drowsy with sunglare to escape. . . .

Only a few people used poison against hoppers that first year, but during the following half-dozen years the method was adopted throughout the region. The active ingredient, arsenic, was mixed with a wet bran mash baited with amyl acetate. The hoppers went for the banana-scented chemical, voraciously took the arsenic with it, and died in such numbers that their corpses piled up in windrows, like drifted soil or snow. It developed later, however, that human skins could be badly injured by the mixture; I knew one man whose hands still suffered a disabling eczema three years after handling the mash.

1930-31

I stripped the ears from the desolated corn and the heads from the sunflowers, and spread them to dry for chicken feed. At the same time I had to shut the chickens up in their shed to prevent them from eating the freshly poisoned hoppers; then I cultivated the rows deeply to turn the bodies safely under. Our roots (apart from the onions) yielded fairly well. We traded $11 worth of the best potatoes and carrots to a Plentywood grocer, and stored the rest. I helped a neighbor dig his potatoes and received in payment a sack of speltz, a valuable addition to our supply of chicken feed.

Cold weather multiplied our problems. Our cash income for 1930 had been about $65, a fact so truly ghastly that it did not at all amuse us to be told that we were safe from the internal revenue people. We could not buy winter clothing. The things that might have improved the house–stucco, plaster, paint–were as inaccessible to us as to the first settlers. . . .

Wood is not plentiful in the Plentywood region. Except along stream courses, there aren't even bushes. Under the prairie lie veins of lignite coal from an inch to fifteen feet thick, but good ones are seldom available to the man who digs his own. The one I found, halfway up a coulee wall two miles east of us, was only one foot thick.

I tried to mine it by removing one foot of earth beneath the coal, but ended by removing two. Swinging a pick in a space three feet high and three feet wide, I still had to work in a difficult kneeling-crouching attitude. When my head touched the untrustworthy ceiling, cold grit showered down my neck. Taking out a ton of this fuel was a bitter twelve hours' toil. It meant knuckles flayed so often that they never really healed–hardly a day without its minor quota of blood lost. I did no blasting, but broke the coal down with a bar after removing the dirt beneath it as far back as I could reach with pick and shovel. Loading out was almost as bad as digging; I had to leave the wagon at the foot of the hill and trudge up and down, slipping, sliding, and being wrenched about. I was able to haul only when some neighbor could spare me a wagon and team.

In February, 1931, the temperature power-dived from summery readings to forty below zero in a single night; the wind mourned around our shell of a house. On the second day I made two trips to the mine on foot. Each time I brought home a large block of coal in a sack on my back, smaller chunks in a bucket. The path up from the coulee was coated with ice; the wind met me at the top with the spiteful authority of a whip. Every few hundred feet I had to swing my arms violently to restore circulation; almost before I could get the sack back on my shoulder my hands were chilled.

That night my wife wore overshoes and overcoat while washing dishes at the red-hot kitchen stove. . . .

1931-32

My wife's tasks included such drudgeries as hair cutting, which she dreaded more than the severities of scrubbing floors. After midwinter she taught me such things as doing the laundry, but she continued her hardest job, the preparation of three meals a day from materials that grew more dismayingly scanty as the months wore on. The only variety possible lay in the choice of forms and combinations in which to serve the same carrots, potatoes, parsnips, beets. She made a mixture of finely chopped vegetables into a hauntingly delicious sandwich spread. Green tomatoes she transformed by some miracle into mince pie. . . .

Our chickens, again on short rations, laid few eggs. By April only forty hens remained. We ate bread without butter, vegetables flavored only with salt, and an occasional jackrabbit. Rabbits were so plentiful that young people organized rabbit drives to get rid of them. Long lines of beaters trudged the dun prairies herding the animals into chicken-fence enclosures where they were clubbed to death by the hundreds. Fried rabbit was delicious, but many people rejected this "wild" food for fear of rabbit plague. We ourselves examined the meat very thoroughly and discarded more than we used.

The winter's light snow seemed not to thaw but to evaporate, moistening nothing. Throughout spring and most of summer it rained not a drop. But how the wind blew! The soil of neighboring fields swept over us in dense black clouds and pattered like sleet against the windows. Large but weightless thistles wheeled across the fields or bounded into the air like a new, insane bird life. They lodged high in the windmill and formed solid gray walls in fences. A screaming gale tore out miles of such fence and dragged posts, wire, and thistles far over the fields. It was like living in a permanent hurricane with grinding, sand-blasting dirt to face at each moment instead of salt spray. . . .

At 3:00 A.M. on the first of May, I took my wife to the hospital in a neighbor's car. By the time I had hiked back to town after returning the car, our son was two hours old.

Any mother of two small children can arrive at my wife's problems thereafter by squaring the sum of her own. We had no new clothing for the boy; everything he wore was either taken from the older child's layette or adapted from things never meant for such service. Luckily he was a quiet fellow who, like his sister, set about life's beginning calmly. . . .

A friend gave us five turkey eggs, of which four hatched. Our chicks and poults got through the early summer chiefly on milk and bread scraps. In June we used the last of our flour. For weeks we ate coarse cakes made of corn ground and reground in our own hand mill. Our young birds subsisted on insects.

Wells went dry all over the prairie that year. Knowing that ours was deep and had staying power, two neighbors helped me repair it in return for water for their stock. That saved us. I fitted up a conduit of bits of pipe, garden hose, old inner tubes, and wooden troughs, and pumped tons of the blessed fluid into the garden by the well. To the larger patch I carried it in buckets, a severely limited method of irrigation.

Suddenly in late summer it rained–rained briefly but so hard that the coulees ran like rivers. For minutes after the sky cleared the rush of water echoed among the hills. Almost overnight the scorched grass turned a rich green, and rectangles of countryside miles away had the brief heart-stopping beauty, the look of absolute freshness, that is never seen elsewhere to such advantage as on the Great Plains. Unhappily, it came six weeks too late.

One disaster remained to round out that wrenching summer. For two days we noticed army worms on roadside thistles; then as if these scouts had reported favorably, they attacked in force. They crawled so thickly over the fields, yards, buildings–always over; never, apparently, around–that it was impossible to avoid them, impossible not to touch the brown, greasy abomination. Wriggling food offered itself to our chickens in such abundance that they watched it with every sign of boredom. When the instinct to move on relieved us of the creatures, they left the same desolation that the hoppers had left the year before, except that where the hoppers had wiped out onions and other strong-flavored plants, the worms preferred the mild members of the cabbage family. They took every trace of our cauliflowers, for example, which I had babied along with hand watering all summer. . . .

At this point, despite our terrible second summer, we fully intended eventually to raise everything we needed for food–salt excepted, of course. We hoped to make shoes and mittens of farm-tanned skins and to limit clothing purchases to textile fabrics. I did make sound bootees and slippers of the lining of an old sheepskin coat. My wife made attractive dresses from low-priced mill-ends; her old ones she made over for the children. My clothes became marvels of reconstruction. Small patches patched large patches, and larger patches covered all; these in turn were spotted with smaller patches until Joseph's coat of many colors wasn't a patch on my shirt. When all strata of a garment wore out, my wife tore them into strips and knitted them into thick warm rugs with a pair of needles I made of a springy wire barrel hoop.

In utilizing odds and ends I believe we went our pioneering forebears one better. Waste of many things was common on the frontier; for us any waste at all was felony. We made odd bits of metal, leather, wood, and what not into children's cribs, various garden and household tools, and innumerable repairs. Once I went too far: I experimented by half-soling a shoe with a piece of tin cut from an old oilcan. Every time I stepped with this shiny sole on snow or ice I became an irresistible force sitting down on an undentable surface.

The third winter was our nadir—the winter I cut ice for 75 cents a day. The house seemed colder; during storms we had to keep hot ashes and a lighted lantern in the cellar to protect our precious vegetables. Our chickens had starved too often, lost all resistance, and now died one by one. Somehow we saved the turkeys. . . .

1932-33

By no standard was 1932 a good year. Cutworms menaced growing crops; some farmers had to plant their cornfields twice. Brassy-looking wireworms dug tunnels through the best potatoes until another shiny insect—the savage, venomous black larva of the click beetle—came along and killed them by the millions. But things grew despite worms, despite the continuing plague of hoppers. Knowing now what was too difficult or costly to produce, we traded off our 600-egg incubator and raised few chicks, but as many turkeys as possible. In the garden our mainstays were corn, potatoes, and carrots. Of other seeds we planted as much as space permitted. The vine crop was the surprise of the season. Pumpkins grew so large that our scales would not weigh them. We stored them upstairs, in the cellar, in the living room; we piled them outdoors. We ate pumpkin pies and pumpkin butter; baked pumpkins for the chickens, the turkeys; gave pumpkins to anyone who would take them. We traded vegetables in general for things we would ordinarily have had to buy; even the newspapers of Plentywood accepted vegetables for subscriptions that fall. We heard of others who traded produce to their doctor for medical attention. (Try that in 1978!)

Brief jobs became available several times that summer. The pay was a dollar for a ten-hour day until harvest, when it rose to a dollar fifty. One neighbor without money paid me in wheat valued at 25 cents a bushel and delivered it to the Plentywood flour mill, which ground it for us on shares. This solved the problem of bread for a full year. Another man paid me partly in cash, partly with a half-grown pig, partly by lending me a wagon and team for hauling.

We were by no means overprosperous during our penultimate winter on the land. Through the coldest months we had, for example, no eggs or milk. But we had plenty of bread, almost every vegetable of our latitude, a pig to slaughter, a few turkeys to sell. And at last we had hope: we and our neighbors had begun to take the measure of the Depression. We had proved that if the breadth of a man's shoulders and the nimbleness of a woman's hands are not salable for cash, they are not therefore valueless. Having something others needed, we did not really have to jingle coins to live. . . .

In the spring of 1933 we found a better house on the edge of an irrigable coulee. This would have been an earth-shaking change for us except that the land belonged to others; our tenure there, as in our first house in 1930, would end at their need. Far more important in practical terms were the changes taking place in the whole community's approach to common problems. In 1933 something like two dozen of our neighbors pooled their resources of labor and equipment and opened a cooperative coal mine in a good vein. Some contributed horses, tractors, or trucks; others, like myself, only their own labor. My share was informally computed to be one week's work; then neighbors with trucks hauled the coal we needed and dumped it in our fuel shed. After the endless struggle of digging and carrying all winter for three years, it was like a personal emancipation proclamation. . . .

■ PAUL E. YOUNG

Paul E. Young was ninety-one years old when his life story was published in 1983. In 1979, while working on a project for the American Folklife Center of the Library of Congress, folklorist Paula Johnson discovered both Young and his memories of cowboying in eastern Montana. Nellie Snyder edited Young's reminiscence and published it as Back Trail of an Old Cowboy *(1983).*

From Back Trail of an Old Cowboy

After the foreign governments quit buying horses, early that summer I went out to the Big Dry to break horses on Dad Brunson's X Bar ranch. I broke out a bunch of X Bar horses, and some for Ledson McLain, Jeff Nicks, Dunc McDonald and some others, all at the X Bar. That summer the district built a log schoolhouse on Bob Roebuck's homestead, across the Big Dry from the X Bar.

Bob was old Dad Brunson's son-in-law, who lived, or slept, in the log cabin on his homestead but ate at the X Bar, unless Big Dry was rolling high. I remember one time he got caught at Brunson's for three days and nights when the Dry came up after a summer cloudburst. It was August and Dad had decided to give a dance in a new log wing they were building. The wing, about sixteen by thirty feet in size, was roofed and floored, and after the dance they were going to partition it into two rooms. Dad was proud of that roof, made of cottonwood poles between the ridge logs and chinked with gumbo and covered with about eighteen inches of dirt for insulation, and red scoria rock on top of that.

Bob was a pretty good hoe-down fiddler and they had a piano that one of the Roebuck girls had won as a prize for getting subscriptions to the Miles City paper. Monte Roebuck and her sister, Pearl, could both chord on the piano to Bob's fiddling, but they expected other musicians to show up for the dance, as there were many homesteaders, from all walks and trades, in the country.

Sure enough, on the day of the dance a man walked in with a violin under his arm in a black case. He told Mr. Brunson that he wanted to buy a horse and a cheap saddle. Dad took him to the pen and showed him two or three gentle horses in a bunch I had just corralled. I had just finished tying up a blue roan in another pen and had turned back to get another horse when I heard Bob say, "Take a look at that!" I turned, and what I saw was that dude trying to walk up to the bronc, his hand out to pet his rump, and saying, "Nice horsey, nice horsey."

He had the horse cornered and I don't know what kept it from kicking him right out of the corral. Brunson said the Lord must have his arms around people like that to protect them. Anyway, that blue roan was the only one he liked and he said he'd buy him at a reasonable price. Brunson asked if I thought I could get him gentle enough in four days. I told him I could try, and the dude said he'd wait that long if I concentrated on the roan.

The night of the dance the fellow turned out to be an expert piano player—and loved to play. About ten that evening, with a big crowd taking turns on the dance floor, the rain started and gradually increased. Dad, with his Texas drawl, said, "By shotts! That thar roof won't leak, so y'all jest fergit th' rain." But after a while a drop or two came through, then more and more. We put pans and pails under the leaks and danced around them.

Not long after refreshments were served at midnight we could hear the Big Dry in flood. That meant that all except those that came horseback were stranded at the X Bar till the Dry was crossable again. The only road out from the ranch was either up or down the creek, for the home buildings were built in a bend that had to be crossed to get out.

Naturally, the dance lasted for three days and nights—until the Dry went down enough for wagons and buckboards to cross it. Brunsons had a good supply of food, as they had just been to Terry for supplies and the guests had brought plenty of cake and sandwiches along. But no ranch had beds enough to bed down that many extra people. Since there were plenty of musicians to keep the dance going, the folks took turns sleeping in what beds there were while the rest danced all night, every night, and often in the daytime.

I had to take time off from dancing to ride the blue roan every day. On the sandy bends of the Big Dry there was always good footing, even when it rained, so I worked on that three-year-old early and late. We kept him in and fed him hay and I used him to wrangle on. The fourth day I told Dad I thought the pilgrim could get along with the horse if he'd leave his violin case at the ranch, to be shipped by express later when he got where he was going.

I explained to the pilgrim that it'd be hard to tie that wooden case on the saddle so it wouldn't shake and spook a green horse, unless it was all wrapped up in a slicker or a blanket, and he didn't have either one. He mumbled something, but paid for the bronc and ten dollars for an old A fork saddle Bob had brought up the trail from Texas and discarded.

To make the bronc foolproof, I had put the old double-rigged saddle on him and then had mounted him several times from the wrong side and dismounted the same way. I had even ridden him behind the saddle, but all of this didn't prepare the colt for the crazy stunt that pilgrim pulled on him the first few minutes he was on his back.

He had ridden the horse a little, but the day he left he ate early, before noon, so the rest of us were at the table when someone said, "For Pete's sake, take a look out that window." We did, and there was that pilgrim, mounted on the roan and ready to leave–all but his fiddle, in the black case and on the ground about twenty feet in front of the horse. The pilgrim had a twine string in his hands, the far end tied to the fiddle, and was slowly pulling in the string.

Every inch he pulled moved the case a little closer, and the nearer it came the more nervous it made the bronc. "How in the world does he think he can pull that big black case up onto that spooky horse?" one of the fellows said. But he did just that. The horse stood with his ears pointing toward the case, snorting and stomping every time it moved, while the pilgrim pulled it slowly and kept talking to him.

The horse was trembling when he pulled the case up–and everyone knew he was ready to break in two, bucking or running for sure, but he didn't. I don't know why. Maybe for the same reason that he didn't kick the fellow out of the corral when he walked up and put his hand on its rump the first time he'd ever been tied up. Anyway, the last we saw of that pilgrim he was riding down the Big Dry heading for the Missouri River. We got reports on him from time to time, always closer to the big river, so I guess he got there. Dad said he would, because the Lord had his arms around tenderfeet and pilgrims.

BLAINE ALLEN GOYINS

Blaine Allen Goyins was born in Great Falls in 1924 and grew up in Stanford, Montana. After serving as a bombardier in the U.S. Air Force, he spent his summers as a rodeo cowboy and his winters as a skilled leather craftsman. His way of life and his many injuries contributed to his early death in 1966. Snake Tracks, *Goyins' illustrated memoirs of the old rodeo days, was published in 1970 by his widow.*

From Snake Tracks

Down south, one winter, I ran into a real smart con man. He always had a stack of loot to flash around. I had been following this one string pretty steady and was winning some of the bull ridin' at every pitchin'. This guy was a rodeo nut and was around every show. He just liked to be around the performers. He would stake you to entry fees for a fourth of your winnings. Being always broke, he and I had quite a bit of business. I could ride any bull in this string. How much I won depended on how tough an ox I drawed. He was a gambler and was always bettin' with some well-heeled gent on whether next rider would buck off or not. Sometimes the bets were bigger than the total purse at the show. He asked me if I would like to make some real dough without robbin' a bank. Naturally I'm all ears. My champagne taste on beer income is always welcoming a boost. We made an attractive deal with the stock contractor and go from there. I didn't even enter up anymore, but bought a light suit, and a pair of oxfords. When he got a good mark on the string I'd mix in with them some and play a little drunker along about bull riding time. I'd make a lot of derogatory remarks about any bull rider who bucked off, and when a good bull bucked someone off I would flash a good roll and offer to bet the bundle even I could ride that one. My pardner would con the mark into calling me as I am drunk and don't need the money anyhow. That is, if they can get the promoter to run this bull in again.

We all go get a hold of the promoter and make a deal with him to run the ox back in. He finally agrees, after I sign a release showing he ain't responsible. He was a fair con man too and is so sympathetic to me and what lays ahead for a greenhorn, that the mark nearly breaks his wrist givin' the stake money to the promoter to hold.

While they are waitin' for the bull to be brought back, I head for the car to get dressed into my wearing apparel and my rope and bell.

When I get back to the chutes, the mark can see he has probably been took and can only hope I get throwed. Fortunately this never happened this season on our deal. There were a couple times though it would have been easier to have got dumped for some of these greedy bastards could scrap a bit too. I never felt sorry for one though. He just got took on what he figured was a sure thing. We wintered real good on this racket. Then spring came along and the urge to see the local snakes come out of hibernation finds me back in Lewistown.

Miller and I went top city in Miles City one time and before we had to resort to the doorknob in a heavy sock we ran into a couple old friends. They were both good but had given up the steady poundin' and jarrin' of the ponies for a little more comfortable method of survival. They had a set of dies made up to make quarter, half, and dollar slugs. Slot machines were illegal in Montana but every joint and club had a string of them anyway. There wasn't anything the owner of these could do to you, but bodily harm, when he caught you gyppin' one. These two boys and Miller are very tough men and if they are cornered it takes lots of help to chastise these three. They had a Coleman gas stove with a booster on it. We would buy a few pounds of high speed babbitt, rent a motel and sit up all night pouring and trimming a couple gallon cans of slugs. Then off to work we'd go. While two are sittin' at the bar keeping the bartenders busy and talking up a storm, the other two are pulling the one-armed bandit's arm off. If the man smells a rat, the two at the bar can generally detain him long enough for the others to take the face off the machine. (Puttin' five good coins in rapid order, so when he looks in the glass of the machine, he sees nothing but good U.S. coins.)

The very first time I run slugs was a disaster. We stopped at a little bar and the bartender knew our two friends, so Miller and I beat it to the machines in back. These machines were really ripe and payin' off ten to eighteen real regular. Too regular, in fact, 'cause here comes the man. We had plenty time to take the face off, but being nervous, I was frantically puttin' coins in the bandit, but was puttin' in slugs instead of good dollars. I was excited and took a hand full out of the wrong pocket. When I looked at the glass I saw what I had done, but time had run out so I beat a hasty retreat out the back door. The man came immediately to the machine I'd just vacated. He let out a shriek and grabbed Miller by the arm. He says, "Just look what that guy was doing!" Bill looked at his machine and damned if he hadn't done the same thing. He makes a dive for the back door too. By the time the man gathers his wits, we were in the back end of the panel truck under a tarp. The two boys at the bar soothes his temper some and tell him we were a couple hitchhikers they had just picked up, but would sure sack us out for him if they ever see us again. Needless to say, that doesn't happen again. The worst thing that can happen is to hit a jackpot. This brings everyone in the country on the run to share in your good fortune. So catch all you can in your hat and depart like you're going to break the three-minute mile. We toured the state in short order. For you are not very welcome anywhere long. At four to five hundred a town though we made stake enough to rodeo like playboys for a time.

One boy stayed with us on the circuit and bought a new car to travel in while the other picked a couple more tough boys and a girl up in the snake den, and made the loop again. I heard later, she got real good at the game and made more loot than all of us combined. Who would suspect a pretty, excited gal of beatin' a nice honest illegal machine?

We three hit a lot of shows and developed a way to turn the odds a little in our favor at some of the shows where the pets won all the loot. This one boy held a card and was pretty well known in the rodeo game. When we would get to a show he would put on a real authentic-lookin' arm sling. Then we would start the propaganda machine to work, telling everyone that we could get to listen to us, how tough he is havin' it with his broken arm. He can't ride with it and needs the pay from the judgin' job at this show to get home on, so let's all spread the word to vote for him as judge. The kindhearted generally voted him in, too. This gives us one judge that is damn sure going to mark us high enough to corner part of the loot, regardless of the pets.

About half the time I was riding with a broken bone or so. If it was a knee, ankle or wrist, anything a ways from your face, get a can of ether from a drug store. They aren't supposed to sell it without a prescription, but I have used gallons of it and never been turned down anywhere. Just a while before you ride, keep pouring a little ether on the break, and it will freeze up a leg to where you can run on a broken bone with no pain till the freeze wears off, then you better be taking on some hundred proof to deaden it.

I found out, quite by accident one day, that it was also real handy in another way. I was standing on the back side of the chute over my bull, puttin' the final freeze on a busted wrist. This old brammer has a bad habit of eating cowboys if they come down and has a spin that's hard to weather. He was tryin' to tear the chute down and I accidentally spilled some ether on his tender nose. When we came out he bucks good, but is slower than usual and don't have the snap to him he did. I won the bull ridin' that day and gained some valuable knowledge along with it. After that whenever I would draw a double rank I'd manage to give him a face full of ether. It sure took the tiger out of his tank. I couldn't keep a good thing to myself though, so got to helping a few friends out with this gimmick. It wasn't long till the knowledge was a community project. An arena smelled like an operating room along about bull time. Consequently, the stock contractors got the word, and put a bounty on anyone around the chutes with as much as too strong a shavin' lotion on.

I was helpin' a kid out one time with the ether on a bull. The kid was scared to death of him and had no business in that event, anyhow. More to bolster his morale than anything else, I put a couple drops on the bull's face. I didn't put on enough to do anything though cause I knew the old ox, and the kid can't ride him even if he just runs. The old bull is gentle and won't hurt a fly on the ground. I figured to just let him get bucked off and forget the bulls, or the brand of fear he has of them will get him killed. The damn fool don't think I got enough sleep medicine on him so he got the can out of my sack and dumped half of the can on the old bull. By the time he is supposed to come out the old ox is sound asleep. The chute boss gives him another bull that is in the chutes but not drawed. This one is a real wampus cat and everyone is waiting so he doesn't have time to do anything to this one. The bull damn near broke his neck. This drowsy bull nearly got me. I was just kinda keepin' an eye on him for his old pappy who was a good friend of mine. Unlike his old daddy, though, he just didn't have it.

My old runnin' mate, Con Pernot, and I were in front of the chutes at Greybull, Wyoming. I had a boot full of ether to keep a busted ankle froze to ride my bull. Con's saddle bronc is in the chutes and we got him all saddled and ready to go. He's got a busted shoulder, and says it is really actin' up. We were both pretty full of a different kind of pain killer too, but he wants me to freeze his shoulder. I says it's too close to his head to use this, but he says to try it. There is a little breeze blowing so he points his nose upwind, and I start drippin' ether on his shoulder. The wind musta changed about then for as soon as he says it don't hurt anymore he collapses in my arms. When he comes to, he is in a big rush to get out of the car and to the chutes to ride his horse. The only thing wrong with this is the show has been over for about three hours, and we're uptown.

■ DAN CUSHMAN

Dan Cushman was a small boy when he arrived in Box Elder, Montana, in 1914. When he was fifteen, he went to work as a linotype operator and reporter for Big Sandy's weekly newspaper. After graduating from Montana State College in Missoula, he moved to Great Falls and became a correspondent for the Great Falls Tribune. *Cushman also worked as a miner, prospector, and geologist, but he is best known for his novel about reservation life,* Stay Away Joe *(1953). This selection is from Cushman's reminiscences,* Plenty of Room and Air *(1975).*

A Toad in Hell

Pa liked atlasses. He liked to sit down at night by the kerosene lamp and study maps, picking out places with names like *Kamloops*, and wondering what it was like there? Some new country was always opening up, full of opportunities, so he'd leave the family while he went and looked at it. At first, hailing from Michigan, he limited himself to the Lake Superior country, the Vermilion Range and the Mesabi, both great iron regions, the Keweenaw copper district, and the many sawmill towns. Then he got to ranging farther. He went down to North Carolina when he read how you could get an entire terrapin supper for 15¢ standing at a counter, or 25¢ sitting at a table with a white cloth, but in a couple of months he was back saying yes, the terrapin was fine, though the oysters were better, all you wanted on the halfshell for a dime, but he didn't care for the country or the people. The people were bone-lazy. No better way of describing them. In fact he never saw such stupefying people in his life, white and black; you'd ask a question and they'd just stand with their jaws sagging open. He was sure glad to be back where prices might be high but people had some ambition. You never did see gold money down there, or even a silver dollar. So the family no longer heard about the Sunny South. Now it was the Golden West.

I don't know why he bought a ticket to such an unlikely place as Box Elder, but as soon as he stepped off the train he knew it was what he'd been looking for. He had the sense of being set free. Of not being hemmed in. He could see and breathe. And nobody was standing at his elbow telling him to do this and that.

"I'd finally got out of the woods," he said.

He certainly had. In Box Elder you could look and look, no trees except a thin line of brush along the creek, all else prairie and sky. There were mountains on the horizon, but offering no limits, you knew there was plenty of open country beyond.

"They sure let the daylight in this swamp," Pa liked to remark. "They pulled the stumps." . . .

Pa had arrived alone. The rest of the family was still in the East. We were in Minnesota, in some sawmill town, or up on the Iron Range. It was always the same order of things. Pa would set out to look things over. To "get located." We'd hear from him by color postcard always depicting some *nonpareil* feature of the new land. On the other side would be a note in Pa's hand, all abbreviations—he was a terrible speller, and knew it, so he would just indicate and put a period, the result an exciting, telegraphic style. Sometimes by postcard we could follow him about three days late all around some part of the nation as he went from town to town trying to get located. What Pa wanted was a place where he could "put down roots and grow with the country." Wherever we went we intended to stay permanently. When he found where it was to be he'd send a telegram. Almost invariably Mama had to have the ticket agent look it up in the railroad directory, and often as not he couldn't find it because it was some boom town unknown a year ago. He'd claim there wasn't any such place. Then she'd show him the telegram to prove there was.

He'd want to sell her tickets to some city that was close but Mama wouldn't stand for it because it might cost extra. "You get right on that wire and find out how much it is!" Mama would say. All those small depot agents were telegraph operators and paid extra by Western Union, so he'd do it–Mama wouldn't budge until he did do it–and sure enough, there *was* such a place, and he'd get ready to write the ticket, a strip of paper about one foot long. Then Mama would say, "I want to go tourist rate." At that time the transcontinental lines like the Great Northern were trying to get people to go West and settle, so they had all manner of homeseekers' specials, generally referred to as the *tourist sleeper*, throwing in the berths free. Mama asked on general principles, and the agent didn't know; it would be on some line such as the Grand Trunk or the Copper Range & Duluth; he was like as not to go leafing through his rate and route schedules for about three years back and find something that answered, or almost. "Yes, this must be what you're talking about. There are so many of these it's a full-time job keeping up."

He was certainly glad to write those tickets and get her away from his window, where she'd never be heard of again. Then she got on the train primed for the conductor in case he tried to cause trouble. "You're on the wrong train," he was likely to say, pretending we were lucky not to be put off at the next flag stop, let alone get berths. "This is a Pullman Palace train, not a tourist sleeper."

No, Mama would say, this is *not* the wrong train, because this was how she'd been routed, and as far as the sleeper was concerned it was up to the railroad to either provide what had been bought and paid for or something equally good. He might try walking off, but she didn't let him get away with that! He'd go to his little office and Mama would find him and *demand* an answer. She would tell him to telegraph the General Passenger Agent in Chicago at the next stop, and if he didn't, she would. That did the trick! Pa said such a threat always worked because conductors made a good thing of it knocking down on the line, and hence would be leery of telegrams which might make it seem they were sleeper-full without the corresponding fares. So, he'd say all right, he had every intention, only he was busy for a few minutes. *etc., etc.* And Mama would park right there until he finished and allotted the berths, family style, which meant an upper and lower together, and not two uppers which was one of their tricks you had to watch out for. "They see you're a woman and they think they can get the start of you," Mama remarked each time afterward, when we'd been moved to our proper seats. "These are Pullman seats. They give us the right to go sit in the observation car whenever we want to." But not hers if it meant leaving the seats unoccupied. Like staking a claim in a new camp, it was risky to be absent from the ground.

Anyhow, when Mama got the telegram we set out. She'd had plenty of practice. She sold everything that couldn't be packed into trunks. We'd ride and ride and the country would change. All would be forest when you went to sleep but you'd wake up and be traveling along a broad river; or you'd be in red dirt hills and wake up on the prairie and not a living thing as far as the eye could see. Finally after what seemed like days of travel we'd get off in an utterly strange place with Pa the only familiar sight, standing there on the depot platform.

He'd sure be glad to see us. Oh, it was a wonderful country. Exceeded all expectations! Yes, he'd found a place for us to live. He'd take us to it and it would be pretty bad.

Mama: "Oh dear!–I *swore* I'd never move into another Injun shack."

It was a shame because Pa would have been so proud of what he'd been able to find. You see there'd be a boom on, the town had doubled in size, and was expected to treble by year's end. People were living in wickiups and dugouts, but Pa had rustled around and found a *house*.

"You don't realize how things are here, Rose. I was lucky. Anyhow, it's just camping out for a while until we can get squared around."

I don't actually recall our first place in Box Elder. It was summer, one could watch the tan-brown prairie from the train window, and sparse trees along a white-rimmed river, which must have been the Milk River in that desolate alkali country between Wolf Point and Chinook. Then it was winter and we were living in some rooms, up a flight of outside stairs, over a saloon where Pa had a barber chair.

Years later, after Pa's death, Mama refused to admit we'd ever lived over a saloon, right over it, anyway. "*No, we did not*! Why do you keep telling over and over *what is not true*?"

It must have been very close because I can remember lying with the side of my head pressed against the floor and hearing voices downstairs. A person would get used to the quiet mutter of voices and never notice them, but every once in a while there'd be an eruption of merriment. You could never actually hear the things being said, but you'd know Pa's voice, it would come through louder than anyone's.

"Happier than a toad in hell," Mama would say.

She would catch me lying with my ear to the floor and God! she'd jerk me away.

"Stop that! I won't have you listening to that foul language."

When she had callers she would talk to drown out any sound that might come from downstairs. She thought if she talked loudly enough they wouldn't realize we were living over a saloon.

I liked it down in the saloon and went down there every chance I got.

"Oh, it has a *devilish* attraction for him," she would say to Pa. "Now, the instant you see him there he's to be *grabbed*. And he's to be *let know in no uncertain terms* he's never to go in there again."

Pa would agree, but he'd be sitting in his barber chair, probably, with nothing to do, the place perfectly quiet and harmless, no sin or corruption, just ordinary fellows standing around, so he'd let me stay for a little while. In fact, he'd give me quite a friendly greeting.

"I can jig." This was my opening.

"Go ahead and jig," somebody would say.

I'd jig and then the fellow would be a piker if he didn't give me a nickel.

"That calls for a drink," the bartender would say.

When Luke Murphy was tending bar he would pour about a tablespoonful of raspberry cordial in a glass and fill it up from the fizz bottle. It tasted just like pop, but it was better than pop. It tasted as good as pop going down, but then it would spread out and, *whoo*! I'd light out jigging, and I'd jig and jig.

"Look at him go!" they'd yell; and cheer and clap; and *laugh*; and I'd jig until I was so tired I could hardly stand up, but I'd keep jigging until finally they'd make me stop.

"Enough, enough. Enough of the jigging."

"Save some for tomorrow," Pa would say.

Or it might just be warm, quiet and friendly. There'd be a poker game with several empty chairs, just a quiet sort of a game with only a few dollars worth of chips on the table, and I'd sit with my chin on the green cloth and watch. Montana had about three men to every woman, there were very few children, and men who were lonesome for a family would want to get their hands on me, and lug me around. What I really liked was to sit on some fellow's lap while he played poker. He'd let me peek at his hole card and whisper in his ear what it was, and he'd let me put chips in the pot.

Whenever he won he'd say I was a good poker player and that I brought him luck.

"How about sitting on my lap and see if you bring me some of that luck?" another player would ask.

I thought it was true. I thought I won for them.

It was a wonderful place, the Bear Paw saloon, and I couldn't understand why Mama made such a fuss about it.

Mama would miss me, or maybe she'd be working around, thinking I was right in the next room when she'd get to hearing the commotion downstairs, my voice raised in a big rollick. She'd wait for me as long as she could stand it, hoping Pa would send me home, but he never would, and I'd never come by myself, so she'd put a shawl around her and come down.

She wouldn't go inside the saloon. She wouldn't even come and stand in the door. In those days not even fallen women entered saloons. Ten or twelve year old girls, perhaps, trying to get their fathers to come home with them, but never a grown woman until prohibition erased the taboo.

Mama would walk back and forth outside, and stand in front of the window, in the little place where it wasn't covered over by curtains, potted palms and signs, in the hopes Pa would see her, but it never happened: the best she could do was wait until somebody came along that she could send inside.

"Mr. Fisher, I wonder if you'd go in and see if my son is there, and if he is, send him right out?"

God, she'd jerk me up the stairs when she finally got her hands on me.

"I'll teach you to go in there! I'll teach you not to hang around a saloon!"

She was down on saloons and liquor. Worse than anyone on earth she despised saloon owners.

"He's all right down there, Rose," Pa would say when he came home. "He doesn't bother anybody. If he got to be a pest I'd be the first one to chase him out."

How that would annoy Mama. "You don't think I care about *them*, do you? I'm worried about that child. What if he gets a taste for liquor? Or for gambling, which is just as bad?"

Then she'd aim one right at Pa:

"God knows I've put up with enough drinking without having the kids start in!"

He wouldn't say anything. Perhaps something like, "Well, yes, but every man has to take a drink now and then to be friendly."

This was a real sore point with her, because Pa was such a friendly drinker. He had no overpowering thirst for alcohol. There could be a bottle around the house for months and he'd hardly ever take a nip out of it. But he was always saying "Here's happy days," with his friends.

"Charlie Phelps came in," Pa might say when he got home to a warmed-over supper, two hours with Mama sighing and glancing from the window, and sighing, and listening at every sound. "I hadn't seen him in six months, and you know how Charlie is. We had a couple and time just slipped away."

"Why does it have to be liquor? Why can't you be friendly over a cup of coffee?"

It was Mama's dream to have Pa stay out of saloons and come home at six o'clock "like other people." She wanted him to have a steady job, to stay in one place, to live in a decent house in a good neighborhood so we could "hold our heads up in public." She wanted to *save and have*. "Save your pennies and dollars will come," Mama would say, quoting John D. Rockefeller.

In every one of the little towns we lived in, boom or no boom, there'd be an upper-crust society of a few people, typically Methodists, and women who belonged to Eastern Star. These were the people Mama secretly envied. Pa, however, liked the hail-fellow rough-and-tumble types. "Water finds its own level," Mama would say when Pa immediately took up with the roisterers, bartenders, gamblers, jockeys, pistoleers, Irish tenors, town marshals, and the more flambuoyant foreign born. Why couldn't he choose friends from the better class?—church goers, men whose idea of a good time was cranking an ice cream freezer on the lawn Sunday afternoon. Pa would say yes, she'd change her tune in a hurry if she was ever married to one. He figured all people were equally prone to evil, only some kept it hidden. There were hypocrites and those who did it in the open.

Pa wanted to have a nice house and all that. He really did. He had grandiose dreams of large yards, trees, gardens, places for cows and chickens, special compost areas, *etc*., but finding the right town in the right country, that was the problem. As for saving one's pennies Pa said, "It's not what you spend but what you make. You can be a pinch-penny all your life and never have a God damned thing." As for the steady job part, he wouldn't even give it a civil tip of the hat. "Let me give you a piece of advice," Pa said to me one time, years later, when I was leaving for college. "Learn something so you can be your own boss. Don't ever get tied down where you'll have to spend your life taking orders from some son of a bitch. I'd rather have a liverwurst stand on the corner than the best God damn job in the United States."

What Pa liked was to have living quarters attached to his place of business. We'd be eating and a customer would come in, and he'd get up and wait on them. Or he'd say, "Just sit down, George, I'll be right with you." They'd come hammering on the door at midnight and he'd get up and wait on them.

"If we could just get away from this place and have some peace and quiet," Mama would say.

But we'd move across town to a house and they'd come there, even at midnight.

"Don't get up!" Mama would whisper. She had a whisper you could hear through walls. "You can't tell *who* it is."

"Oh hell, who could it be? Nobody's going to harm me."

It would be somebody from away out in the mountains who had left a parcel in the joint; or who wanted to buy a pound of Spearhead chewing tobacco.

So Pa would get up and dress and go away with him.

Mama wouldn't go back to sleep. There might be a couple or three fellows, they'd be strangers to her, and she'd worry.

"They could knock him over the head just as *easy*."

Pa would be gone for half an hour and someone would fire a shot. It was always happening along in the night, somebody would get up and shoot to scare off a cat, or a cowboy would take a shot in the air as he left town, celebrating, and then go home and tell the boys how he'd shot up the town.

"Oh, dear God!" Mama would whisper, up in the dark, looking out the window. "What *can* he be doing?"

Hours might pass, there wouldn't be a place open, and he couldn't come, and he wouldn't come. But finally he came, I'd hear his step and wake up, and Mama whispering furiously "what in the world?" *etc.*

Pa couldn't understand that anyone would be worried. He'd run into Charlie Boland, or someone, who was waiting for it to get a little bit lighter to start driving out to his ranch with a wagonload of supplies, and they'd stood around talking.

"It's just beautiful outside, Rose. You ought to come outside and see."

"Humph!" Mama would say. "Well, let's get some sleep. There's a *little* of the night left."

Pa always slept till around ten o'clock; everyone in town would long have been at work when Pa sallied forth.

Mama was a good deal more resigned to our quarters above the Bear Paw Saloon once cold weather set in. It was very cold. C. D. Herzog, the U.S. weather observer, posted lows of 62 and 65 below zero. Actually the winters in northern Minnesota, up in the Vermilion country and the Iron Range, were worse because the cold was more continuous, but the houses there were built for it. Box Elder was just claptrapped together. Dave Cowan, our leading citizen, had a well-built house with siding, storm sash, *etc.*, but most of the places were rough, unpainted, or covered with tarpaper. Every fall you'd see people with shovels out banking up their houses with dirt so the draft wouldn't get beneath, and some of them would bank all the way to the windowsills. Lacking storm windows they would pack rags, strips of fleece-lined underwear preferred, in the cracks around the windows and other places where, by holding a candle and watching the flame, drafts could be detected. In the coldest weather they'd close off part of the house, nail quilts over doors to the livingroom and bedrooms and just live in the kitchen and one other room on the south side. Perhaps they only had one stove, which was the kitchen range. They might have a small heating stove in the parlor, but it would just sit there, polished and cold.

There was a *big* heater in the saloon. It stood higher than a man's head. Luke Murphy would walk over from behind the bar, tucking his white apron up so it wouldn't catch fire, open the door, and pitch in an entire scuttle of coal with one heave. He would open the door with his toe and close it the same way, because it was too hot to touch. He would adjust the draft just right, and the heavy fluted firebox would hold a translucent red, hue of iron taken from a blacksmith's forge. If you hit it with a poker it would emit a dull thud, no ringing sound, and in the summer, when it was cold, you could go around one of those big, coal heating stoves and see the dents where things had been bumped against it when hot and malleable.

The heating stove sat about two thirds of the way back, and in the middle of the room. The pipe rising from it was guyed and slung by wires from the ceiling, traversing about twenty feet to the brick chimney. The pipe would become dull red from heat for about three feet above the stove, and beyond that, when it turned at an elbow and traveled horizontally, all the dust and bat turds would burn off; but next to the chimney there'd remain some unsinged cobwebs fluttering in the heat. They needed real long stovepipes to get all the heat out of the flames, but there had to be a certain balance of cold outside and fire in the stove to get a draft. The colder it got the better it worked.

Everything centered around that big heating stove during cold weather. Customers would gather at the deep end of the bar to be close to it, Pa would move his barber chair around to occupy the territory from behind, and the card tables would gather in along the wall.

In the beginning Pa had a little laundry stove where he kept a boiler of water hot for his barbering. When it got cold and he moved closer to the big heater he took the boiler along, and set it where it would keep hot, steaming but not boiling. It would be just right to dip his steam towels in and wring them out. On a bracket stand high on the stove sat a tea kettle which he used for the shaving mug; shared with the bartender who tapped it for hot rums, whisky slings, and the like. During cold weather when men came in for a shave he would lay them back in the chair so the soles of their shoes were flat toward the stove. They'd lie there and their feet would toast, it was one of those little extra services that people appreciated, and a help to his business.

"Ouch!" you'd hear them say when they got out of the chair and put their weight down. They'd do a little dance, and fellows would wait for it and laugh, but still those hot shoe soles felt good after the chilblain cold of the sidewalks outside.

When the front door opened a cold wave rolled along the floor; it struck people from the waist down, and if the door was open too long they'd all yell in chorus, "Close the door! Where were you raised, in a barn?"

Then the fellow who came in would say, "Good God, it stinks in here. It smells like a cave." Or, "Where you keeping the bear? I can smell him but I can't see him."

In hot weather people favored the front of the saloon where the screen door kept opening and closing, and there was breeze, and they could see what was going on in the street. Not in winter. Up front it would be so cold along the floor that the spittoons would freeze; the sponge in the cigar case would turn hard as a piece of pumice and the cigars would turn solid from cold so a man would have to warm them by rolling them between the palms of his hands, breathing on them, before they would draw. Even by the stove the floor would be cold so you'd see the poker players sitting with their legs folded under them. The heat rose dense under the ceiling and sometimes Luke would have to stand on the bar to fix one of the hanging lamps and he'd get down as fast as he could saying, "Whew! You can hardly breathe up there."

The heat warmed the ceiling and our floor at the same time. It was real comfy upstairs. We got a lion's share of the heat together with the smell of cigars and those raucous sounds.

Box Elder settled in for winter, very quiet. Weeks went by with always the same crowd, same loafers, same drinkers; the same fellows in for a shave, same poker players, the same money going from hand to hand, and some of it, torn bills and blemished coins, would be recognizable, be given names, "Old Broken Nose" for a half dollar cut half through by a chisel, *etc.* But it wasn't true that counterfeit coins circulated fast; they'd be tossed to one side, left to collect in a box under the cash drawer, and maybe once every six months somebody would take it all to Havre and see if he could pass it off. No charge, they'd just give it to him through their goodness of heart. "Get this God damn stuff out of town."

Then, right in the dead of winter, with no reason anyone could detect, business would pick up. People would start coming in from the ranches. They'd ride in on woolly-haired horses, in mackinaws, scarfs tied over their ears and hats set on top, in blanket-lined overalls or hair chaps, with gunny sacks full of hay tied to the stirrups to put their feet in. They'd been wintering at some ranch, caring for the stock, and finally they couldn't stand it any longer–dark old bunkhouse, greasy deck of cards, beef, beans and rice pudding with canned milk day after day–so they'd set out for town, cold or no cold.

Often the boss would come in with them, and who was taking care of the stock was a question. All of them would have a little money, and they'd start throwing it around. The poker games which had just yawned along would stiffen up. All the seats would be filled. I'd go in looking for an invitation to sit in somebody's lap, but they wouldn't look at me. Then strangers would start showing up. News of the big game would go out. Gamblers came from Big Sandy and Havre. One of those big games might go on for upwards of a week. The players wouldn't know whether it was night or day under the gasoline mantle lamp, behind the curtained, leaded and smoked-over windows.

A big poker game meant good business for Pa. During the frozen month just past he'd been lucky to take in $1.50 per day. A fellow would get in the chair for a shave and Pa would work on him for half an hour, giving him steam towels, a massage, a neck shave that was itself half a haircut, and a bay-rum hair rub, all for 25¢; but when things got to booming that same customer would find himself in and out of that chair before he knew what happened.

"Next!" Pa'd say, whipping the hair cloth off him, and the fellow would look so *surprised*! He'd stand rubbing his chin hardly able to believe it had happened to him.

Pa had no cash register. In those silver dollar days he did all his business from his pants pocket, and you could tell what kind of a day he was having by the way his pants swung and jingled. On a good day he'd look as if he were carrying two flatirons around. He might take in as much as $10.00–very big money in those times when clerks got $60.00 per month, and round steak, the Box Elder staff of life, was two pounds for a quarter at Meat Axe John's butcher shop.

The out-of-town gamblers were particularly good for Pa. They all wanted to be known as high rollers and big spenders. They'd get in the chair and ask for shampoos, tonics and massages. Pa had a special deal which he called "Around the World for a Dollar"–haircut, shave, massage, shampoo and tonic, but it was only a trade stimulator for quiet times. He'd never mention it when the gamblers hit town, because they'd fork over $2.00 for the same thing and not blink an eye.

Even on busy days Pa never worked more than half the time. He finished the last customer and then pumped up the chair with the foot pedal–it had a rachet elevator which worked like an old-fashioned car jack that raised it high for barbering children–allowing him to sit away up like a lookout at a faro spread and watch the game from the best vantage point in the house. Snap-snap went the cards, followed by a moment of utter silence as everyone looked at his hole card. They looked at it over and over as if they had forgotten what it was. Only movement from the house man, taking care of the pot, keeping it nice and neat. The house man took chips out of every pot, except the very smallest, and that was his rake-off, the house percentage. He did it openly, very openly, but he did it just as the cards were being dealt and the result was some people might play all night and never realize he'd taken a chip.

The out-of-town gamblers would know he'd taken a chip. They might give him a hard look, or say "Arm getting tired there, Bob?" But joking, they wouldn't get into any quarrels. If there was one thing those hustlers found out it was never to start trouble in another man's town. But poker games were not violent. I've read many times about shoot-outs in Western poker games, and how true gamblers always carried their guns in a shoulder sling rather than on their hip because they couldn't get at it sitting at a table, but if a gambler ever carried a gun in Box Elder I never saw it; and I never, there or anywhere, saw real trouble at a poker game. In fact, men playing poker are as near to being happy as men can be, too happy to laugh, except quietly, a few words after a hand was played out, or to drink, or leave the table except reluctantly to go to the can.

Poker players would get so tied in with the game they'd send out and have their meals brought to them and eat without missing a turn of the cards. I've read that the Earl of Sandwich did the same thing, and his piece of meat between two pieces of bread became naturally the sandwich. But the Box Elder hustlers were partial to the sirloin steak, and they'd sit there with a napkin tied around their necks and the platter on a chair beside them, the table being too crowded for the platter. They'd chew, and wipe their fingers so as not to get the cards greasy, and bet, only maybe pass the deal when it came their turn. They'd need sleep and, that being unthinkable–an entire four or five hours away from the table–they'd get rid of their boozy headedness, buzzing ears, and falling eyelids by having a shave, a bay rum rub, and hot and cold towels applied over the head and the back of the neck. Pa was really good at it, he knew just what they needed. He never gambled himself, but he knew gamblers. He'd do it right at the table; they'd sit with their heads tilted away back while he shaved them, and forward when he massaged their necks, but they'd still be able to see every card that fell, and signal to show what they wanted to do, call, pass or whatever, and when he was through they'd probably give him a blue chip, worth one dollar. The regular price would be 50¢, but nobody ever made change for a chip, that was understood.

Pa was really working his way out of hard times. He'd come up at night and empty his pockets out for Mama to see–silver dollars, halves, quarters, gold pieces, which in that day were still common, and blue chips. The gold was particularly beautiful, it always had such a shine in the light of a kerosene lamp–and the blue porcelain chips! He wouldn't cash the chips in right away because he wanted to show Mama. I'll tell you, that gold against blue chips really looked like something.

"Well, what do you think of the hard winter now?"

And Mama would have to admit, grudgingly, that it was turning out pretty good.

"Real nice and comfy up here," Pa would say. "You have the warmest place in town."

Yes, we were wintering real good. He had the last laugh on Mama.

■ TAYLOR GORDON

Born in 1893, Taylor Gordon was raised in White Sulphur Springs, Montana, with six older brothers and sisters. His father was a chef, and his mother had been a slave on a Kentucky plantation. In addition to the job described in this excerpt from his memoirs, Born to Be *(1929), Gordon worked as a personal porter for circus impresario John Ringling. He left Montana for New York, where he became a well-known singer of Afro-American spirituals during the "Harlem Renaissance" of the 1920s. During the 1930s and 1940s, Gordon was out of work and suffering from mental illness. He returned to White Sulphur Springs, where he died in 1971.* Born to Be *includes introductions by Muriel Draper and Robert Hemenway, a foreword by Carl Van Vechten, and illustrations by Covearrubias.*

Mother's Foresight

Big Maude, a new landlady who came to town with four new girls, made me page and cash boy in her new house on the sporting line. Maude claimed to be of big English stock, some kind of Lords or Dukes, but because her people wanted her to marry some Knight, whom she didn't love, she ran away from home and decided to be a worldly woman to spite them. With her was a pretty little black-haired Irish girl who had a real brogue, and three American girls who claimed their families were rich too. But love drove them to prostitution. Maude had a real idea and mind for the business. She was the first to build an extra room especially for dancing on the old log house, put in a piano and redecorate the rooms. You could tell that Maude knew what a man wanted, although she claimed to be a green-horn at the business.

With her big-city air, dressed every night in swell gowns, making all the girls dress too, her house was the Palace on the line. In all the other cribs, the girls worked in gingham gowns, kimonas, Spanish shawls, semi-nudes, or a large ribbon tied around the bust with a hip sash hanging down on one side.

Before Maude came, a round of drinks cost a dollar anywhere on the line, no matter if you were alone or ten, a dollar right on. She raised it to five dollars.

Maude dressed me up in a blue suit with brass buttons. I was surely proud of that suit and my job, the only page in town. I was on duty from eight-thirty until one every night except Saturdays and Sundays. Later on, those nights. All the miners, farmers and city folks were out hitting it up on week-ends and the crowds lasted longer.

You'da died laughing if you'da been there one night. Old Billy Leapopa, a rich Scotch farmer and stock-man, always came in town on Saturday nights. He drove two fast trotting black horses hitched to a spring buggy. The big red barn was his put-up, a building with over two hundred stalls. Old Billy. Everyone called him by his first name, in fact the whole of Meagher County lived as one big family.

Well, Billy fell into Maude's half lit up, and ordered a drink for himself and the girls. This was around nine o'clock. Maude was the only one dressed for the evening. She told me to serve the drink while the girls were getting ready. I did. But when I asked for the five spot, Billy like to hada fit. He told Maude he had been buying drinks in whore-houses for twenty years and he knew what the price was. But Maude was his master. She sprung her high English on him, telling him she was ashamed of him as one from her land across the water. Old Billy became embarrassed and coughed up the five. He kinda laughed and told Maude that he had heard of her beautiful lasses and her wonderful self and he wanted to meet all.

Maude called for the girls to hurry dressing, like a dowager would shout to her guests when she called them to gather in the parlor to explain the rules of the game they were going to play. The words had hardly fallen from her lips when the door bell rang.

I opened the door. A lot of fellows fell in, most of them town boys who had been away to college from White Sulphur Springs. I won't call their names. They were a fast lot with plenty of noise. The piano player came in and began playing the *Midnight Fire Alarm*, his opening number. He called that his fast classic and masterpiece, although I think *A Hot Time in the Old Town* his best. He played that out of this world. The young fellows were too fast for Billy. He was kinda lame, having been shot in the leg for something—I never did learn for just what. So as fast as the girls would come in from their rooms, one of these collegiates would grab her and start dancing. After the dance he'd hold her for a chat. It looked like a bad night for Billy in Big Maude's Palace of Joy.

The stage coach was unusually late that night. The train was late at Dorsey. (That old Jawbone Road was never on time in the summer, so you can imagine what time it made in the winter.) I heard Butch Norse, the stage driver, whistle and crack his six horse whip. I'd know that whistle if I heard it in Purgatory. The custom was that as long as the mail came in before midnight it would be distributed, and the general delivery window would be opened. I told Maude the mail was in and asked permission to go for it. We had to be in the Postoffice when the window was opened, because after eight o'clock at night they never kept it open longer than when the last person had left the waiting room at that time.

Maude gave me permission to go. To get a letter at night, from the right person to the right girl, usually meant an extra two or four bits for me: from the wrong one to a girl not feeling too good meant a cussing out for me. They always laid the jinks on me as well as saying I was good luck. (Voluptuous moods.)

The next half hour I spent with the milling mob, jammed in the lobby of the Postoffice, talking, half whispering because the clerks couldn't work fast if the people made too much noise. At ten o'clock I got my bundle of mail. I knew every girl on the line by her real name and nickname. At times I ran for nearly fifty, steady, and more on off days, such as fast Saturdays and slow Monday evenings.

It was five blocks from the Postoffice to the first crib on the line, the Brown House. There were twelve girls in there at that time. I dropped their mail and hit on up the line—Blue House, the Cabins, then Bennett's place, the last and biggest house on the east end of the string, a big gray frame house with seven large rooms on the ground floor. I always saved Maude's mail until the last because I worked there steady.

There was a new girl at Bennett's, sent to her by some friend in Butte, without letting Bennett know that she was coming. The girl had just gotten off the stage coach. She still had her coat on. Her suitcase was setting in the parlor. Bennett's was all filled up. (Agnes Bennett was her name. Seldom anyone ever called her Agnes.) She asked me if I knew any house that needed a girl. I told her that Maude had an extra room, if she would take her. (Maude was so funny.) Bennett asked me to find out if Maude wanted the girl. I ran down the hill to Maude's and told her of the girl. Maude asked me what she looked like. Her house was full of men. I told her–five foot six, thirty-eight bust, blue eyes, chestnut hair, and young. Maude said, "My God! Yes! Get her quick!"

I went back to Bennett's, got the girl, her bag, and we hurried down to Maude's. I took her in the back door and called Maude to the kitchen. She gave the girl a surveying look from head to feet. Then they had a little chat. Drinks were selling too fast for Maude to have time to put over her fine points regarding her method on the business.

Jewell, that was her name, Jewell Hooks, was assigned to the Daisy Room. All the rooms in Maude's were named after flowers–Daisy, China Aster, Lily of the Valley, Tuberose, Rose Geranium, and over the maid's door she had Heliotrope. On Maude's door were large Orange Blossoms, painted by her own hands. Maude said she knew the language of the flowers and their interpretations expressed so much. Jewell was soon dressed and in the parlor, entertaining the guests *ad lib.* Old Billy fell for her, hook, line and sinker, and asked to be served in a private room with her. I took them one drink and had the time of my life again getting my five spot. I had to threaten him by saying that I'd tell Maude.

You know, a girl working for a name in Maude's was supposed to drink a drink every five minutes, or at least order them while on duty. Such a thing as bringing a bottle of whiskey of your own into any of the houses was a crime, but in Maude's it was murder in the first degree. Jewell, for whom Maude had chosen the right room, knew nothing about these rules. She was a novice of the first water. In the hands of old Billy Leapopa, a man nearly fifty with twenty years' experience in buncoing lewd women, Jewell was too soft for him.

At two o'clock, Maude called me to send me home, being an hour late. We checked up on my collections for the evening. Maude had a mind like an electric adding machine, started and stopped by a time clock: there was no way to fool her on her business. I counted out a hundred and eighteen dollars in her lap as she sat on the big low sofa, legs cocked and spread so that her dress pulled tight like a fireman's life-saving canvass.

When I said "a hundred and eighteen–that's all," there came a funny sort of grin over her face and a grunt through her nose. *Humph*! Her lips tightened as her head turned kinda sidewise. Her eyebrows formed a high arch. Before a knowing smile came to her red face, she spoke. "You're holding out on me putty heavy tonight, aren't you?"

"Holding out?" I said. (Really I didn't know much about holding out at that time.) "No, that's all I collected."

"Who's laying down on the job tonight, then?" she asked.

You know, I hadn't learned to lie good yet, especially to Maude. She was hypnotic, so I told the truth. "No one," I answered.

"Did that new girl do any business tonight?" she inquired.

"Yes," I said.

"How much?" she questioned.

"One drink."

"One drink! My God! One drink in three hours! What kind of house does that d—— b—— think I'm running?"

I was shocked pink. I had heard plenty of cussing before, but that was the first time I had heard Maude Healdyne cuss or even lose her city manners.

In a second she was on her feet. By the way, I have never seen such shapely feet on a woman of her height since. Nimble too. They carried a hundred and eighty pounds of violent woman down to the end of the hall into the Daisy Room without knocking in two jiffies. Old Billy Leapopa had smuggled a quart of Kentucky Bourbon into the house. How? You'll never know, with Maude's eagle eyes on the watch. He and Jewell had drank most of it up. I heard Maude say, "And so, Miss Hooks, a bottle of Bourbon? That's why you have only called for one drink tonight, eh? Selling it yourself, what?" The girl was frightened stiff and didn't answer. Maude continued to talk in her high English tones. "Don't you know the rules of my house–that I don't allow any one to bring liquor in here? What do you think I'm running the business for?"

Jewell answered in a quivering voice, "I didn't bring the liquor in here. It's my first night to be employed as a useful companion for a gentleman and I don't quite understand it all. I heard it was not very thrilling work, although there was lots of money to be had for it, but so far both statements are wrong!"

Maude told her to put on her kimona and step out of the room as she wanted to talk to the gentleman. Her voice was so calm. Jewell had hardly gotten out of the door before Maude began playing the dozens with Billy. He tried to defend himself. The more she talked, the madder she got. She picked up Billy's clothes and threw 'em out the back door. The Daisy Room wasn't over six steps to the back door. Then she grabbed old Bill and yanked him out of the house, into the back lot. He was almost nude. Such cussing. My! oh my! You know, cussing coming unexpectedly and well rendered from some seemingly refined woman, is so effective. . . . She slammed the door after him and bolted it.

Jewell had gone into the parlor. She was lying on the sofa, crying like a whipped child. Maude came in and read the riot act to her. She told her all the fine points of the business in order to be successful. I thought she might turn on me with a slap for not telling her before that they were not drinking in the Daisy Room, so I slipped out the front door.

In order to get home quickly I started around the west corner of the house and turned south through the back lot. Old Billy Leapopa was trying to find his clothes in the dark on a half muddy ground. He heard someone coming and hollered, "Hey there, friend," rolling the r's laboriously, "help me find me clothes."

In those days I had eyes like an owl. In a few minutes he was dressed, but dirty for fair. He had stepped on some of his clothes and he put on his shoes without socks, after stumbling around in the muck ever since he had been outside. He handed me a bill. When I got home I found it was a twenty.

The next morning I had almost thirty dollars. I gave mother the twenty and she questioned me as to how I came by it. It was hard to make her believe the tale about Maude's acting. At any rate, she kept the twenty but told me I was getting too big to work around the girls, and that I should stop. I swelled up and began to pout. Ma threatened to whip me within an inch of my life if I didn't dry up. I knew she really carried out her words, so I sulked out of the house. At the end of the week, I quit Maude's. She gave me a new suit of clothes, a pair of shoes, a hat and a hand-painted picture of flowers–white pinks, canary grass laurel for good service.

I must look that combination up in Webster's dictionary some time, and see just what she had in mind.

■ ELLIOT PAUL

Elliot Paul came to Montana as a young man in 1907 to work on a U.S. Bureau of Reclamation irrigation project on the Yellowstone River. During his varied career, he was a jazz pianist, the author of the Homer Evans Murder Mysteries, a gourmet cook and cookbook writer, and a member of Boston's Beacon Hill Old Bohemian Colony. This selection is from A Ghost Town on the Yellowstone *(1948), which Paul based on his experiences in Montana.*

Preceding the Baptism of Frost

One week, early in September, the east bank of the Yellowstone, near the Glendive bridge, was lined with people about nine o'clock each morning, to watch two elephants from a traveling circus stand in the shallows and spray each other joyously from their trunks. The school hours were shifted, so the children could see the frolic, and everyone, including the elephants, had a marvelous time. Bert Lacey met the proprietor of the show in the bar at the Jordan and offered him special inducements if he would move the circus through the lower valley and give Saturday and Sunday performances on the baseball field at Trembles. As usual, when he set his heart on anything, Bert closed the deal.

Just about that time, the first motor vehicle to be owned and operated by a resident of the valley was shipped in by Frank Banks, a civil engineer who now is in charge of construction work on the All-American Canal in southern California. Banks was an enthusiastic pioneer motorist, but after he had had a few embarrassing experiences on account of the fact that the Montana livestock stampeded and ran for their lives whenever he passed near them, he took his practice runs early in the morning, before rigs were likely to be on the road near the dangerous barbed wire fences.

Banks started southward from Trembles. Because the leading circus wagon was in a slight declivity when he approached, at twenty miles an hour, Frank did not see it in time. That wagon contained the two circus lions, one male and one female. It was drawn by four horses which bolted for their lives when the chugging motor bike, raising a formidable cloud of dust, rushed toward them. The wagon driver, who had been dozing and was caught unawares, did his best to get his team under control. Frank, always considerate, swerved off the road, and bumped over the sagebrush until his machine tipped over on him. The terrified horses missed the wire fence, but in doing so tilted the wagon and the lions' cage at a perilous angle, and smashed the side into a solid corner fence post. The smashed wagon righted itself and kept going, but the lions leaped out and instantly were lost to sight in a cloud of dust.

Worthington T. Stackpole was spending that night in the Clark Hotel at Trembles. He had taken a strong liking to the town and its people, and enjoyed especially his long talks with Charley Swift and Howard Wise, the hotel clerk. Also his expansive nature had responded to the warm admiration Annie Rongfto, the chambermaid and waitress, developed for him. Since both of them were by nature discreet, and the hotel was usually quite busy and active in the late evenings, Mr. Stackpole made a practice of leaving his door unbolted, in order that he and Annie might chat in whispers in the early mornings.

The two lions streaked northward along the road and when the dust thinned and they found themselves among buildings, they both loped into the first dim opening they saw. That chanced to be the front door of the Clark Hotel. Wise, who had a room off the hallway near the door, was a sound sleeper. He said afterward that he heard a faint sound of paws running over the floor outside, but he assumed that a couple of stray dogs had got in and would go out again when it pleased them.

The male lion, in the lead, dashed up the wooden stairs and along a narrow corridor, facing which, at the end, was Mr. Stackpole's door. The lion stood up on his hind legs and let his front paws rest against the panels. Inside the bedroom, Stackpole, in his elegant silk pajamas, was wide-awake. Hearing the slight scratch on his door, he smiled happily and tiptoed across the floor to open it. He saw, teetering before him, not Annie Rongfto, his impulsive Montana sweetheart, but the underside of a full-grown king of the beasts that smelled stronger than U.S. Indian Affairs. Too startled to be frightened on the instant, the big engineer bellowed, "Down, sir, dammit," and slammed the door.

Annie, in a near-by room, heard Mr. Stackpole's hearty voice and what seemed to be a commotion in the corridor. She decided it would be more discreet to postpone the twosome they had planned, so she went back to bed for a twenty-minute snooze. Meanwhile the he-lion slunk downstairs and out the front door again, just in time to avoid astonishing Lela Weckerling, who, wrapped in a toweled bathrobe, with her hair in braids, was on her way to the washroom for a morning bath. Bert had not been able to install modern plumbing, but provided on the second floor of the Clark Hotel a small room with zinc-lined floor, a large rubber bath mat, kerosene stove and washboiler filled with water, and an enameled bathtub set on griffin's legs.

Having modestly pulled down the window shade, and locked the door behind her, Mrs. Weckerling slipped off her robe and hung it on a hook. She looked at her limbs and well-rounded curves, smoothed with satisfaction her clear olive skin, glanced in the wall mirror to detect gray hairs and, finding none, she smiled, then took a dipper of warm water from the boiler and was about to pour it in the tub. At that moment she saw Queenie, the lioness, who was cowering in the tub. Queenie snarled and recoiled, coming up on her haunches.

Mrs. Weckerling sank noiselessly down to the floor in a dead faint.

The lioness was one of the tamest wild animals in the circus. She calmed herself, got out of the tub cautiously, sniffed the inanimate form of the naked woman, then went over to a corner and sat down to think things over. How many times Lela revived, saw the beast staring at her and swooned again, she was unable, afterward, to remember.

Lam McGlynn, coming down the corridor for his morning wash, tried the bathroom door and found it locked. He paced up and down the hallway a few times, then tried the door again. Little Helen, who always was somewhere near by when her mother was out of her sight, appeared at the head of the stairway and told Lam who was bathing.

"I didn't hear any water splashing," Lam said.

The little girl went over to the bathroom door, listened, then peeped through the keyhole. She saw and heard nothing but a sound like a lot of cats purring. Puzzled, she tapped on the door. There was no answer. Alarmed, she knocked, louder and louder. No response.

Lam, intending only to gain admittance for the child, pushed hard on the door. The lock gave way, and the lioness darted out, dodged little Helen who was screaming, and dashed down the stairs, just in time to knock Bert Lacey, who was on his way up to see what was wrong, bum over bandbox.

Inside the bathroom, Lela regained consciousness just in time to realize that Lam McGlynn, in his shirtsleeves, was sprawled over her, with a mad grimace on his face. She fainted again, and Lam, completely rattled, picked her up, bare as an egg, and rushed up and down the hallway with her draped across his shoulder, trying to find a room in which to deposit her.

Finally, Annie opened her door, gasped, and said:

"Mr. McGlynn! This is a respectable house!"

Lam, weak from shock, shoved his way in, unceremoniously, dumped Lela on the bed, and took flight.

"What's going on here?" Bert asked.

Little Helen dashed across the hall with her mother's bathrobe.

About that time, the circus wagons drove up the street, and the lion tamer rounded up his two fugitives.

Engineer Stackpole descended to the café for his breakfast, beaming. When Bert showed up, having cleared up the incidents in his mind, as best he could, Mr. Stackpole remarked:

"Mr. Lacey! You have here a unique establishment. Never banal. By no means dull. I envy you, sir."

■ JOHN K. HUTCHENS

Born in Chicago in 1905, John K. Hutchens moved to Missoula when he was twelve years old. Hutchens attended public schools in Missoula and later worked as a cub reporter for his father's newspapers, the daily Missoulian *and its evening edition,* The Sentinel. *In 1927, he moved to New York, where he wrote for the* New York Evening Post, Theatre Arts Magazine, *and the* New York Times. *Hutchens ended his career as a member of the editorial board of the Book-of-the-Month Club. This selection is from* One Man's Montana *(1964), Hutchens' collections of autobiographical and historical essays.*

City Room

The office of the *Missoulian*, as I have said, was as much my home as any other, for me an unceasingly fascinating place from the day I first entered it. Into it came the great outside world, on The Associated Press wire chattering in an alcove where George M. Reeves, lightning-fast telegrapher, transformed dots and dashes into typed bulletins. Piled on a table in the corner were the newspapers from the big cities—the "exchanges"—telling of life as lived elsewhere by foreign correspondents, columnists, drama critics, sports writers, their names by-words as well as by-lines. Who knows where one's education begins? But I believe that mine began here.

"Read those papers and see what you can learn," said French T. Ferguson, the *Missoulian*'s managing editor. "But don't start trying to imitate anybody in particular, or you'll get mixed up."

Mr. Ferguson, who as a young man had emigrated to Montana from Illinois, was slight and of medium height. He endlessly rolled straw-colored cigarettes, wore gold-rimmed eyeglasses and a green eyeshade, wrote editorials for the *Sentinel*, conducted a lively column entitled "The Oracle" for the *Missoulian* (a sort of local counterpart of Franklin P. Adams' "Conning Tower" in the New York *World*), supervised the news gathering and make-up for both papers, worked from 8 A.M. until well into the evening, and described himself as lazy. If my father was my major mentor, he was also a figure of some awe, at least in the office. Mr. Ferguson, sometimes severe, frequently aphoristic, was instructive on a different level.

I stood before his desk on the first morning of a high school vacation during which my aptitude, if any, for the newspaper life was to be tested. Mr. Ferguson counted out twelve pennies and handed them to me. "You will weigh yourself on twelve different weighing machines around town, note the discrepancies in the machines, and see what kind of story it makes," he said, and cautioned me to eat and drink nothing while on this assignment.

The story it made was a somewhat heavily jocular one, which to my great satisfaction was printed almost as written.

"Do you think the story proved anything?" Mr. Ferguson asked me at the end of the day.

I said I supposed it proved that people should be careful about taking things for granted.

"That was the idea," said Mr. Ferguson. "It applies especially to would-be newspaper reporters."

I was not yet equipped to handle anything remotely important in the way of straight news, and I might have grown restless if Mr. Ferguson's supply of feature story ideas had not been inexhaustible. When they were unsuccessfully executed, it was my fault usually, although not always.

"A Mrs. Deschamps, down in Grass Valley, has just given birth to her twentieth child," he said one morning. "You might go and see her about it."

I did, and finally got around to asking her the obvious question.

"Difficult?" said Mrs. Deschamps, who was constructed along the lines of a French-Canadian earth mother. It was no more difficult, she said, but more tersely, than having a bowel movement. I reported back to Mr. Ferguson.

He sighed.

"It is one of the misfortunes of our profession," he said, "that a good deal that is interesting cannot be reported in newspapers exactly as it is said and done. You may live to see the day when it is, but in the meantime you may as well cultivate the art of euphemism. Perhaps you can have Mrs. Deschamps say that giving birth to her twentieth child was no more arduous than drinking a glass of that terrible dandelion wine they make down there."

He was not always so calm. A few moments after I turned in what I regarded as a witty account of a weird cult's revival meeting, he summoned me. A blue pencil line ran through the story. His gaze was cold.

"I should not have thought it necessary to tell you," he said, "that a reporter does not make fun of *anybody's* religion, no matter how funny it seems to him. Who are you to pass judgments?" He relented somewhat. "That also goes for certain things that people get foolishly sentimental about, like the schools they went to, and dogs, and the virtue of womanhood, or anyhow American womanhood of a certain class."

That summer and the next, while I was still occupied with little feature stories, I could observe my highly professional elders. It was as important a part of my education as any. It would be years before I fully realized how lucky I was—that in this little city room were men who would have served well on any newspaper in the country.

Presiding over the telegraph desk was the low-voiced, efficient Ralph Swartz, who expertly read the copy and wrote the heads for about half of the *Sentinel*. The *Sentinel*'s city editor, Eddie Rosendorf, ran the city desk with dispatch and a certain waggish touch that brightened a paper on a day when there happened not to be much news. Reporter Jim Faulds covered hotels, conventions and other local matters with a deceptively easygoing countryman's air that commanded the confidence of people who regarded him on first meeting as an old friend and thereafter submitted their news to him without being asked. Mrs. Bessie K. Monroe, the *Missoulian-Sentinel*'s Bitter Root Valley correspondent in Hamilton, sixty miles away, phoned and wrote in stories, tips and features with a tireless, round-the-clock accuracy. "The Montana Nellie Bly," my father used to call her, with affectionate admiration. And there was Ray T. Rocene.

He was the wonder of our paper, this lean, intense, fast-working man who drummed at his typewriter like a frenzied pianist and on any given day wrote half a dozen stories besides assembling the sports section and turning out his "Sports Jabs," a column read throughout the Northwest. Forestry service and railroad news comprised most of his reportorial circuit outside sports. He covered it—train wrecks, forest fires, conservation projects—with unfailing skill and speed. But sports were his passion as a newspaperman, and had been so since he, a child of Swedish immigrant parents, joined the *Missoulian* staff in 1916. He remains one of the half-dozen finest sports writers I have ever read, his integrity shining through every line, his authority and style enlivening the literally countless baseball, football and boxing pieces which kept local sports fans better informed than newspaper readers in many a place much larger. He frequently angered University of Montana athletic coaches with his candid appraisals of their performance. Inevitably they came to value his advice. He described a "fixed" fight exactly as he saw it and was threatened with extinction by the manager of one of the participants.

"Go over to the hardware store across the street, get a gun, and shoot him in the belly," said the *Missoulian*'s editor, Martin Hutchens, reaching for a voucher on the *Missoulian*'s till. Ray didn't need anything like that, then or ever. Meeting the murderous manager on the street, he stared him into speechlessness.

We were a happy office and, I think, a good one. (Even the neophyte feature writer, on vacation from high school, early included himself in that "we.") To be sure, the *Missoulian-Sentinel* was a "Company paper," which is to say, the Anaconda Copper Mining Company then held a controlling interest in it, as it did in most Montana dailies. But the *Missoulian*, at least in my father's time, enjoyed a high degree of autonomy. It frequently opposed political candidates supported by other Company papers. When, in 1919, the Chancellor of the University of Montana suspended an economics professor about to publish a book criticizing The Company's virtually tax-free status, the *Missoulian* defended the professor. I recall no story suppressed or distorted on orders from The Company, although former United States Senator Burton K. Wheeler—whom the *Missoulian* despised, and vice versa—might have had a different view of this.

"I don't have to read the *Missoulian*! I can smell it!" the Senator used to bellow when out on the hustings.

"Some day Mr. Wheeler will come to a crossroads in his career, and when he arrives there you will see him taking the opportunist's path," my father would say when I offered a word in praise of the then liberal Mr. Wheeler, a courageous United States District Attorney in Butte, a progressive Senator in the 1920's.

Mr. Wheeler, when his political career abruptly ended in 1946, was contentedly accepting the support of The Company.

Editor Martin Hutchens was one of the last of the old-school "personal" western editors, and on occasion he could be very personal indeed. Directly across West Main Street, in a second-story office facing his own, was the local headquarters of the Industrial Workers of the World. They, including their officers, were regularly denounced on the *Missoulian*'s editorial page as murderers and thieves–as, indeed, they were, despite a romanticizing tendency now to portray the I.W.W. as a Robin-Hood-like band. The local I.W.W. sent word to Editor Hutchens that it would be an easy gun shot from their office to his. The Editor put a Smith & Wesson revolver in his desk drawer and left his window shade up. The I.W.W. sent word again, this time to the effect that they respected his courage. The armed truce remained unbroken.

The Editor could be rough on his own staff, too, when he thought it advisable. That the *Missoulian-Sentinel* had no local daily paper competition was no excuse, he held, for slipshod practice. When an eight-column, Page 1 headline in the *Missoulian* appeared later in the day, by accident, in the first press run of the *Sentinel*, the building shook with his wrath; even Miss Margaret Marshall, the Editor's secretary, as calmly efficient as she was beautiful, appeared for once to be alarmed. Advertisers who ventured to suggest news treatment or ask favors never did so again. In moments of crisis–for instance, a politician charging victimization at the hands of a reporter–the Editor stood behind his man against the outsider, however he might later deal with the reporter. Not for nothing had the Editor been trained in the Pulitzer tradition.

So we all worked hard, and the days and nights went joyfully. In due time I was allowed to work later shifts, much to my pleasure. There was something special about the office then, the green-shaded lamps concentrating the light on the paper-strewn desks, the cigarette smoke curling away into the shadows. Now and then I tried rolling a cigarette myself, in the manner of Mr. Ferguson, if I had reason to think my father was not coming into the city room. When he did, in that relaxed time after the paper had gone to bed, it might be to tell a story about traveling with William Jennings Bryan in the presidential campaign of 1896. Or George Reeves would spin a tale of his days with The Associated Press in South Carolina. Or Ray Rocene would dip back into the years and his astounding memory to reconstruct a prize fight, round by round.

In that city room, night lent an extra glamor, an excitement, to encounters that would have been more nearly routine in daytime. Late in an evening when I happened to be alone in the office, a tall, well-built, well-dressed man came in and asked to see the *Missoulian* for October 5, 1892. I found it for him, and he said, "See this?" as he pointed to a paragraph announcing that Emmett Dalton, youngest of the Dalton brothers who had memorably set out to raid a bank at Coffeyville, Kansas, was about to die.

"He didn't, though," the man said. "That's me."

The city room was suddenly a street in that Kansas town where nine people, including Emmett's brothers, Bob and Grattan, died in a roar of gunfire and Emmett himself, wounded, was saved from lynching only by a quick-thinking coroner who told the townsfolk that Emmett, too, had died. Facing the sometime bandit, I trembled a bit but tried not to show it. This, it occurred to me, was like meeting one of Henry Plummer's gang in person. Wouldn't a genuine Dalton as soon shoot you as look at you?

However, Mr. Ferguson's admonitions about credulity came to the fore.

"How do I know you're Emmett Dalton?" I asked. "He went to the penitentiary for a long time."

"Fourteen years," the man said, and produced evidence: letters, clippings, pictures. I wished that someone would come back to the office, Ray Rocene or Mr. Ferguson, but no one did, and so I went to the morgue, or library, and looked into the Dalton file. Some fairly recent pictures of Emmett Dalton were certainly pictures of this man. And then he offered the final proof. He was in Missoula to lecture in advance of a crime-doesn't-pay movie, "Beyond the Law," in which he had the leading role.

Hearing this, I sensed a distinct let-down. None of Harry Plummer's boys would have gone straight as Emmett Dalton had done. I kept asking questions, as Mr. Ferguson had told me a reporter should do, and at last he came up with an answer suggesting that neither he nor the world had suddenly become perfect. Was he really sorry about all of his past? Would he relive any part of it if he could?

"Only if I had to," said Emmett Dalton. "If anybody depending on me needed food or clothes, I'd sure as hell steal it, I certainly would."

I felt a lot better as I sat down to write a story about him.

DANIEL W. WHETSTONE

Montana journalist Daniel Whetstone had a sharp tongue, a hard-boiled sense of humor, and an acerbic style. The founder of the Pioneer Press *in Cut Bank, Montana, Whetstone was a staunch Republican and a critic of the Anaconda Copper Mining Company's inclination to control the editorial policies of the daily newspapers it owned in Montana. Whetstone's memories of a meeting of a group of Montana newspapermen is reprinted from* Frontier Editor *(1956).*

Meeting with Montana Journalists

During this period of enforced leisure on my part, Phil "Punk" Holden, editor of the *Sweet Grass Banner*, announced a meeting of the newspaper publishers of northern Montana, at Shelby, July 2nd, to consider and act upon matters of mutual benefit. I was glad to attend, and during this to me memorable powwow, got quite an insight into the techniques used by editors of small-town newspapers in Montana in those days.

The place of the meeting was the business office of Slim Martindale, owner of the *Gold Butte Bar*, on West Main Street, in Shelby, a place set aside for serious public forums and gatherings of horse raisers and cattlemen.

The meeting was well attended. I was one of the first to put in an appearance and Holden was on hand to greet me and the other journalists.

Mose Pettijohn had written notes to all, to say that there would be dinner and refreshments at the adjoining Gold Butte Cafe and that he would be host.

A little knot of early arrivals, having sociable drinks, wondered if Jack Fergus of the *Conrad Observer* would show up at the meeting and if he did, might there not be an embarrassing situation, because of the bitter feuding between him and Pettijohn. "Punk" Holden giggled a little about this concern of one or two of the brethren. He said he had heard from Fergus, who promised to be present.

Pettijohn had joined the group, gulping down beer and the harder stimulants. The only one who didn't sit in with the drinking crew was Lars Gilbertson, editor of the *Galata Herald*. Lars was a rather sanctimonious-looking Scandinavian who had come out west from the Norwegian holy land near Northfield, Minnesota. He had studied for the ministry at Gustavus Adolphus college in Northfield but later came down with the journalism fever. He homesteaded near Galata, edited his paper and preached in the Lutheran church on Sundays.

He had followed with fear and regret, he said, the editorial warfare between Fergus and Pettijohn and expressed the hope that the matter would be taken up at this meeting, to try and heal the ever-widening breach between the two, which he feared might result in violence.

While he was expressing this misgiving to me, there was a knock and a kick on the door of the conference room and in bounded Jack Fergus, who tossed a dirty gray Fedora into the center of the table and shouted greetings to one and all. Mose Pettijohn jumped up from his chair, tipping over his glass of beer.

"This," I said to myself, " 'is it'!"

Mose rushed at Pettijohn. Lars Gilbertson braced himself where he sat in a far corner, as if prepared for the ultimate in violence. He was pale and looked pretty scared.

But then, to our utter amazement, Fergus grabbed Mose around the neck and began shouting: "Why you old, mangy catamount," to which Mose replied with: "You darned old worm-eaten timber wolf!" And they were pounding each other on the back like long-lost brothers. Then Fergus ordered a round of drinks to celebrate, and after that was consumed, Mose ordered another round or two.

But the pious Lars Gilbertson couldn't be induced to hoist even one. He was still too scared.

It was brought out that Fergus and Pettijohn had served in the same regiment in the Spanish-American war and while toasting and "tossing 'er down the old hatch" they sang snatches of regimental songs, some not appropriate for mixed company, and told of their experiences in the Philippines, paying tribute to some of the torrid and bosomy maidens on Mindanao.

Joe Johnstone, later editor of the *Brady Booster*, was *en rapport* with the fun that was being staged by the Fergus-Pettijohn duo and urged postponing the serious side of the session until later in the evening, but "Punk" Holden who felt a little eclipsed while Fergus and Pettijohn were putting on their act, insisted that the meeting go into executive session and take up the order of business.

Holden led off by saying that it was about time the saps in the newspaper game got hep to themselves and quit sucking around the deadhead merchants for a few dimes in advertising. "The goddam whelps'll only give you a four-inch double-column ad and all they'll say is 'John Jones, Dealer in General Merchandise, your patronage solicited,' and then expect you to boost their game and help 'em keep out competition, the lazy-livered no-goods.

"I gave the bastards, and that includes the hometown bootleggers and the rumrunners from Canada, who somehow get past the customs with their fancy stuff, a runout pill about a year ago and business picked up with a bang. I got myself elected constable of Sweet Grass and then started to turn 'er on, hot and cold. One week I'd come out for a moral cleanup of the town and the little handful of bluenoses 'ud whoop it up at the churches and praise my courage for standing for the right.

"Purty soon a delegation of the sporty crowd 'ud call at my office in the back room and leave a bundle of nice green lettuce and the paper 'ud say nuthin' or a little article on fairness and moderation and live and let live. When these sporty boys and girls started to forget the *Banner* and the constable, I'd give 'em another prod and along 'ud come another package of the folding mazuma. Sweet Grass is just a wide open place on the rumrunners' road from Alberta, but, fellows, I've the best plant in this part of the state and not doing badly. No going hat in hand to the little prune peddlers for me no more."

Some received the speech in silent amazement. Joe Johnstone seemed a bit bored. Out of narrow slits of eyes he appraised Holden, with a cynical sneer. His mental reactions seemed to reveal that he considered the member of the Fourth Estate from Sweet Grass a rather crude braggart.

The subject turned to final proofs to be filed on by the homesteaders, and Joe, who had made the tarpaper circuit in North Dakota, was asked to give of his ripened experiences. His recital was listened to with interest and appreciation.

He related that after being hired and fired and quitting a dozen or more shops in the kerosene-lamp towns, mostly because printing interfered with his poker, he launched a paper at Grano, the metropolis of the Mouse River country north of Minot.

"The banker, the town's best stud player, loaned me the money after a gainful night with a couple of wealthy flax farmers. Aware of my talents with the pasteboards, he advised that I devote as little time as possible to printing a paper. He suggested that I lay in a good supply of boiler plate, set the final proofs and not neglect to change the dateline. I followed his advice with meticulous detail and did pretty well."

Then he lapsed into a more serious vein and relieved himself of a little righteous indignation on a subject not directly pertinent to the printing business. "Young as I was and reckless and unthinking as I was, I became sickened of the coarse grafting in Dakota in those settlement years. The businessmen, bankers, real estate men and grain dealers were a woman-chasing, poker-playing, racketeering lot; they exploited and robbed the honest grangers in grain grading and confiscating interest rates. They sold 'em rotten lumber at two prices, shoddy clothing and groceries at double the value, then foreclosed at the wink of an eye in years when it didn't rain. The first farmers were conservatives politically. Later they and their sons staged a rebellion and went to a far extreme. Sometime later they embraced Townleyism, financed state-owned elevators and mills. Rampant radicalism swept the state. The servile, blackmailing, big and little newspapers in that day in Dakota must share the blame." Fixing a stare at Holden: "If this is a moral sermon, make the most of it."

Pettijohn wanted Johnstone to tell the assembly more about how final proofs were handled in the homesteading days in North Dakota since the subject was timely; soon there would be a final proof harvest in this part of Montana.

Joe obliged. "In the first days of homesteading back there the proof publication patronage went to the papers printed nearest the land which was to pass to the homesteader from Uncle Sam. He explained that three years after date of filing on a homestead final proof could be made before a United States Commissioner when it could be shown that residence and cultivation requirements were lived up to. To make commutation proof, similar requirements, but only a residence of fourteen months and a payment of $1.25 an acre.

"Then it became political patronage and only the papers that supported the national administration in power were given proof publications. The registrar of the land office was the political appointee of the senators and if they were not of the same faith as the prevailing powers in Washington, the national committeeman was the federal boss.

"The registrars first posed as men of fairness, honor and rectitude. They would scorn the thought of a split for mailing a few proofs to a newspaper man who wasn't politically accredited. But as time went on this stern code started to slip.

"A fellow who had served for a spell as receiver of the United States land office at Bowman (the receiver is the money taker and accountant for the government) bought himself a "parent" plant and some "packhorse" plants. A "packhorse" plant, in the Dakota argot, is one that can be moved from place to place on a horse's back; an exaggeration of course.

"Well, he put in the 'parent' plant at Thunder Butte and twelve 'packhorse' plants at crossroads postoffices and back-country blacksmith shops. He must have known the attitude of the registrar of the Bowman land office. The proofs for all the packhorses were set in the parent office. The one-sheet papers supposedly printed in the satellite places were also printed at Thunder Butte. All the legal publications in southeastern North Dakota were the gravy of this one editor. It was probably the biggest rural newspaper chain in existence at that time. It might happen here; I leave the details to your imagination."

He explained further that contest notices (contesting the claims of homesteaders) were exclusively the patronage of the local United States Commissioner and suggested that these worthy officials be regarded as leading citizens of their towns, that when their wives gave an afternoon tea or their daughters were "rushed" into a sorority at Missoula, the story be given page one, alongside straight reading matter. As a final suggestion he advised that a quart of the best bourbon be placed behind the commissioner's desk regularly, when he wasn't looking.

Ben B. Weldy, telegrapher, U.S. Commissioner, justice of the peace, owner of the *Chester Sentinel*, mine host of the Prairie Inn and pastor of the Gospel Reformed church at Chester, danced in just before dinner. He announced that he had used his credit to buy a web press, a monotype, six typesetting machines and other modern equipment, and would soon launch the Weldy chain of weeklies that would cover northern Montana like the dew. His boasts got no response from brother publishers, by this time so far removed from sobriety that they could not bother to be impressed or resentful.

Two overpainted and under-dressed ladies, slightly intoxicated, peeped through the open door of the Gold Butte Cafe and tried to start a flirtation with the gentlemen of the press. Fergus arose weavingly and bade them begone. "Get going, you dowdy chippies; this meeting is for serious business matters. I ain't got no time for women in public places, they belongs in the home. Scat out of here, you strumpets."

The more brazen of the two shot back: "You talk like one of them saintish pulpit pounders; no one is trying to vamp you, you homely old coot. Go home to your mother, sourpuss."

Pettijohn and Fergus were the top entertainers at the lively dinner and at about three the next morning Mose got to his feet with a mighty effort and thanked those who had taken time to attend such an important and profitable meeting, a meeting not only profitable to the printers but the entire communities they served.

Holden, who had called the meeting, was sleeping soundly under the table.

■ JOHN STANDS IN TIMBER MARGOT LIBERTY

John Stands In Timber and Margot Liberty first met in 1956 when Liberty was teaching Cheyenne children in a government school in eastern Montana. Stands In Timber, a Northern Cheyenne elder, had clear memories of growing up in Montana during the reservation period, which Liberty recorded and edited in Cheyenne Memories. *Stands In Timber died in 1967, just as the book went to press.*

From Cheyenne Memories

An old storyteller would smooth the ground in front of him with his hand and make two marks in it with his right thumb, two with his left, and a double mark with both thumbs together. Then he would rub his hands, and pass his right hand up his right leg to his waist, and touch his left hand and pass it on up his right arm to his breast. He did the same thing with his left and right hands going up the other side. Then he touched the marks on the ground with both hands and rubbed them together and passed them over his head and all over his body.

That meant the Creator had made human beings' bodies and their limbs as he had made the earth, and that the Creator was witness to what was to be told. They did not tell any of the old or holy stories without that. And it was a good thing. I always trusted them, and I believe they told the truth.

Now I am one of the last people who knows some of these things. I am telling them as they were told to me during more than eighty years among the Cheyenne people. I can tell only what I know; but I have not added anything or left anything out.

The old Cheyennes could not write things down. They had to

keep everything in their heads and tell it to their children so the history of the tribe would not be forgotten. There were tales of the Creation, and the early days before the Cheyennes lived in the Plains country. Many of these have been forgotten, but some have lasted to this day. And there were tales of the hero Sweet Medicine, the savior of the Cheyenne tribe, who gave us our laws and way of living. And there were history stories, of travels and fights, and stories of a funny person, Wihio, told for the children.

Trouble with the Language

Another trouble in those early years was with the language. Most Cheyennes still do not talk English at home, even today. The languages do not exactly compare. I know from interpreting. Some things in one language cannot be said very well in the other.

One story they still tell is about the fellow who translated a certain kind of tobacco as "powder." You can scrape this black stuff out of a pipe when you have smoked store tobacco, and mix it with kinnikinick. It tastes pretty good. This one Cheyenne went to his friend's house and smoked some for the first time. He asked what it was and his friend said "powder."

So he went home and got his kinnikinick sack and some gunpowder, and mixed it up. "You must be crazy," his wife said. "That stuff explodes." "Don't tell me," he said to her. "I just smoked some and it sure tasted good." He loaded his pipe up tight. "Well, I don't want to see you exploded," said his wife. She went out, and there was a big bang. He had touched a charcoal from the fire to light up. When he came out of it a piece of the stem was blown way back inside his mouth. And his wife was mad. "Go ahead," she said. "Smoke some more of that powder."

Another time they got mixed up translating was when they started to play baseball. They were still telling the story in Oklahoma five years ago.

Some boys had learned baseball at school and they had a game going in the middle of the village. They were teaching each other, all talking Cheyenne. One boy who was in his first game had come around and was on third, and this other fellow was coaching him. "Lie down on your hands," he told him, "and get ready to jump out and run like a foot race. When the pitcher raises his arm, run home and slide in."

So this boy got down and watched. When the pitcher raised his arm he took off. But he did not go to the plate. He ran straight to his tent in the village and when they yelled at him he ran faster. He slid in and knocked the pole down and spilled some pots of food his wife was giving to visitors. He crawled out in a hurry and ran back to the game. "Well, I did it," he said. "How many points did we get?" They had told him to "run home and slide in," in Cheyenne.

■ WALTER McCLINTOCK

Walter McClintock came to Blackfeet country as a young forester at the turn of the century. He made friends with a Blackfeet guide and was adopted into the tribe by Mad Wolf, a renowned orator. In 1908, McClintock presented the results of his studies of the Blackfeet to anthropological societies in Germany, England, and Ireland. He returned to visit the tribe a few years later and found the old life nearly gone, the people plagued by sickness and poverty. These poignant excerpts are from McClintock's The Tragedy of the Blackfoot, *published in 1930.*

From The Tragedy of the Blackfoot

We arrived at the Indian camp on Cutbank River, and found the people still in doubt whether their agent would allow them to give the sun dance. By this time they were losing interest, because of the uncertainty of having the circle-camp.

The women straightaway pitched my traveling lodge close to the tipi of the Mad Wolf family. I did not ask them to do this, and it was not the custom for Indians to serve anyone. But it was their idea of hospitality. They wanted to do the right thing by me before the tribe.

They brought a fresh pail of water and piled firewood beside my door. Takes In The Night, a daughter of Little Creek, brought me a present of a miniature squaw saddle, with a little shield and medicine cases attached. Her mother, Strikes On Both Sides, came with a bunch of strawberry plants covered with ripe fruit which she gathered in a meadow. They were all hospitable and on the lookout to do something kind.

Little Creek had some relics from the ancient Beaver Bundle of Mad Wolf. They had been replaced in the Bundle and were no longer used in the ceremony. He asked me to look them over, and, surrounded by the Mad Wolf family we examined them. I found the hoofs of a young antelope, skins of a prairie dog, squirrel, mallard duck, eagle feathers, buffalo sinew, bird wings, and pieces of bone whistles.

Then Little Creek spoke for the family and asked me to take charge of these relics. He said I should place them in the medicine case of my Iniskim, which they had given me. I could hang them all together on a tripod behind my tipi in the conventional way. They agreed this was the best thing to do. It would bring me greater power and give protection from illness and misfortune.

Then the head men of the camp held another council and decided to give the sun dance. Their agent was still away and it was too late to withdraw from the ceremony. Women had made vows to the Sun; it might bring death and misfortune if their vows were not carried out. Better to risk the disapproval of a new agent than stop the ceremony now; there was nothing harmful in the ceremony; it was for the benefit of the tribe, to help them lead better lives and to restore to health those who were ill.

So it was agreed among the leaders to go ahead. The ceremony of the tongues was finished in haste, and a messenger sent to the southern division of the tribe which was camped on Two Medicine, to move on the following day. They would all gather on the broad plain south of the agency. There the sun dance would take place.

Early next morning I was wakened by sounds of confusion—herds of horses driven into camp, shouting of herders, barking of dogs, and neighing of horses. I dressed and went out from the lodge. The sun had not risen. Along the horizon was a supernatural light—a glow of pale yellow, mingled with touches of red and gold. It spread upwards towards the zenith; the glow grew stronger and the sun rose. Its bright rays of yellow light streamed across the plain, and touched the snow-capped summits of the Rocky Mountains.

Soon a change came over the camp. Places where tipis had stood the night before were vacant now. In other places were stacks of bare poles, women were pulling away lodge covers which were flapping in the wind.

Now the camp was full of horses, some tied to wagons, others wandering loose and busily feeding. All about were piles of robes and blankets, bundles, saddles, and cooking utensils; women gathering their property together, tying up and packing on horses. Noise and confusion. Colts screaming shrilly, mares neighing, camp dogs excited and barking, howling, yelping. Boys shouting and whooping, running races, wrestling. Anxious mothers, worried by the labor of packing and looking after children and horses, calling to people in shrill voices; the crying of frightened and angry babies.

A line of wagons began to form, headed south, towards the river valley and the direction they would move to the circle-camp. Soon there was a long line of Indians in wagons piled with household goods. The old and middle aged and children were in the lead in wagons, and behind them came a throng of young men riding their best horses.

The strong voice of the herald was still heard as he rode about the camp urging the people on, saying: "Listen! Everybody hurry and get ready. Now we are going to start. So the chiefs have ordered." He repeated this over and over.

Now the last families were nearly ready. They were packing furiously, ashamed to be the last. The women had a sort of pride in being ready with the others–a superstitious fear of being left.

White Grass, the aged medicine man, was in the lead. He carried a Sacred Lance wrapped in an elk-skin and attached to a pole. With him were the chiefs Middle Calf and Bear Child. They followed no road, but took a short route through the hills, towards the big flat near the agency, the meeting place agreed upon for the circle-camp.

I joined this strange procession and rode with the Mad Wolf family where I belonged. But I kept moving along the line stopping now and then to chat with friends. They liked to hear me speak in the Blackfoot tongue. A joke was always greeted with smiles and laughter. They had an unfailing sense of humor and liked any kind of repartee; it was the spirit that counted. No matter how depressed an Indian might feel, bantering always brought a laugh, and they rattled off something foolish in reply.

This journey to the circle-camp was an impressive occasion and to me deeply moving; traveling with that long line of Indians, slowly over the prairies on their way to the sun dance, their greatest ceremony–and I believed it would be the last. A strange scene for this modern age–those primitive children of nature, stone men, a last remnant of our aborigines, soon to disappear forever and be forgotten, submerged by the onrush of a materialistic civilization.

I watched their eager, rapt faces. Forgetful for the moment of their agent and white men; oblivious to anything but the circle-camp which brought associations dear to the Indian heart–old friends, feasting and social dances, singing and religious ceremonies.

We passed through a grassy valley and climbed to the summit of a ridge. Here we had our first view of the big camp distant on the prairie–

already many tipis were there and the great circle was being formed.

As soon as the Indians caught sight of the camp, they began traveling faster down the long slope. Along the line they shouted to each other with excitement–nothing escaped them, the Painted Tipis of head men, where different bands were camped, what families had arrived, and where each family belonged in the circle.

In the line was a dilapidated vehicle drawn by an aged horse, blind, and lame, hobbling painfully on three legs, with head down and eyes closed. Three aged women rode in the wagon, laughing and chattering, as excited as young girls, eager to keep up with the procession and to get quickly to the big camp. They hated being left, but the line moved too fast for them.

During the first day of the big camp there was confusion. The Indians from the north and the south did not come in two divisions as in former years when their strong leaders were alive. This time they kept straggling in, and many families were late.

Vacant places were in the camp-circle which were depressing to see. They were mostly on the north side, where prominent men had died. The families of White Calf, Mad Wolf, Bear Paw, Double Runner, Siksikaikoan, the scout, and many others were in mourning. They did not join the circle, but camped outside in the hills. They held themselves aloof and took no part in the ceremonies; it was not proper for them to be with the crowd. The bands of Small Robes and Worm People were not represented by any families; all of them were dead.

On my arrival, there was a council of the head men of the camp, as to a suitable place for my lodge,–Curly Bear of the band of Buffalo Chips, Bear Chief of the Don't Laughs, Big Moon of the All Chiefs, Bull Calf of the Bloods, White Man of the Lone Eaters, and Wades In Water of the Grease Melters. They said my tipi should be on the inside-circle among the chiefs.

In former years when Mad Wolf, my Indian father, was alive, there was no question where I belonged. I always went with his band. Now he was gone; his family were in mourning and not included in the circle. The head men of the south realized this and wanted me to camp with them. I had many friends in the south and decided to accept; I wanted to get to know them better. This was the cause of trouble; I was too popular in the camp.

They pitched my tipi on the south side, in a prominent place on the inside-circle next to the Black Buffalo Tipi–where the best families were. Now I was more prominent than ever.

Near-by were White Man in the Striped Tipi, Big Moon in the Bald Eagle Tipi, Mountain Chief, Calf Robe, and Onesta–all old friends;

and they were outspoken in their expressions of good will and pleasure at my joining them.

An interesting feature of this camp-circle was a band of visiting Blood Indians from the north, who came to fulfill vows made to the Sun for people who were ill. They too were on the inner-circle and had a group of Snake Painted Tipis, which had black tops to represent a cloudy sky at night, with discs for constellations on both ears and serpents in color round the center.

My lodge was so close to Cold Body and Wolverine I could hear everything. Cold Body was dying of tuberculosis and had a cough. It was so bad he could not sleep. But his son snored contentedly through the night.

I was so interested in the camp life, I did not want to sleep, but lay awake listening to all that was going on. It was so different from life in civilization I wanted to record everything. The striking extremes of wealth and poverty so evident in large cities were absent, but the lights and shadows of domestic joy and sorrow, of health and sickness, of pathos and humor, were all present in this Indian camp, with even sharper contrasts, because of the close association of the people.

In the lodge of Wolverine, his children were restless and a young baby cried fretfully. The mother rocked it in a little hammock cradle fastened to the lodge poles, singing an old cradle song: "Come wolf eat this baby if he don't sleep."

Beyond Wolverine, was the lodge of Okyio, a poor young man. He had one wife and their only child was dying. It grew worse in the night and a doctor came. I heard the monotonous beating of his medicine drum, not loud but very soft and regular. It had a solemn sound in the night, and continued until I saw the first sign of light in the sky.

When day was beginning to dawn, the drum of the medicine man stopped; and I knew the child had died. For a while there was stillness, not a dog barked. Then I heard the sobbing of the young mother, and soon it became a mournful wail.

With the day came a light breeze from the mountains, making a humming sound against the ropes of my lodge and the ears at the top flapped gently in the changing wind. Through the smoke-hole I saw two morning stars in the sky—bright and beautiful in the clear air of that high altitude. On the ground sounded the quick thud of horse-hoofs. It was the day herder crossing the meadow towards the hills to watch the horse herds.

Then I heard the strong voice of Elk Horn, the herald, as he rode through camp and made announcements for the day. People began talking in near-by lodges and women were preparing the morning meal.

Soon after sunrise the women of neighboring lodges went to the tipi of Okio to help with the body. A small box was secured, the dead child was washed and dressed, wild flowers of the prairie placed in its hands and on its breast. Many Indians came to the funeral. That afternoon the solemn procession passed my tipi, going to the summit of a lonely ridge where the body was placed. The young father and mother walked close to the little box, weeping and with heads bowed.

In the meantime, the warriors of the camp were assembling, dressed in fine costumes, with feathers and war paint. They gave horseback dances and sham battles. They galloped through the camp with shrill cries, in imitation of war parties of former days. Then the society of Brave Dogs came forth from their lodges and marched and danced and assembled to feast at the tipis of prominent chiefs.

Again I heard the continuous drumming of a doctor at work on a boy who was dying. He was the grandson of Little Plume, the famous war chief. In his behalf a woman relative had made a vow to give the sun dance. But the agent had interfered and now the boy was dying; it caused a superstitious fear.

Big Plume, the medicine man, also was dying. I heard a strange tale as to the cause of his illness; it shows the fear Indians have of disobeying the rules of their medicine bundles.

Big Plume found an old flageolet or reed pipe in a field and took it home, not knowing anything was wrong. He suddenly became ill. They could not tell what was the matter, until some one examined the place where the flageolet was found and discovered an old grave. Now Big Plume as the owner of a Medicine Pipe should not use anything that belonged to the dead. The flageolet he had found was therefore taboo. It was said to be the cause of his illness—the penalty for his disobedience.

There were signs in the sky that bad weather was coming—heavy clouds enveloped the mountains and spread over the plains. I made ready my tipi for a blow from the north, roping it to the ground on the north side, with lariat noosed round the tops of the lodge poles and fastened to strongly driven stakes. I adjusted the ears at the top and drove the pegs into the ground, so my lodge would not be overturned by the wind.

That night a heavy gale with rain and sleet came straight from the north and beat violently against the tipi. But it held fast. I built a wood fire to last through the night and went to bed.

It was not a night for sleep. I heard the wailing and crying of women, mourning for their dead. It came from all sides, distinctly through the storm. They kept it up through the night. Many families were in mourning and illness widespread. It added to the gloom of the Indians, already depressed by the ban placed upon their religious ceremonies by the agent.

In the middle of the night, Mountain Chief whose tipi was near mine, began a sort of chant in a strong voice to drive away the storm. Then his women joined in, with a chorus in a minor key. This was to add power to their prayers. They kept up this chanting and singing until day began to dawn.

Their prayers were answered later in the morning, when the cloud banks rose over the Rocky Mountain chain and the sun was soon shining in a clear sky.

Some of the women who were in mourning, were accustomed to go daily at sunset and sunrise to lonely hills outside the camp, to weep and gash themselves with knives. They did this to excite the pity of the Great Spirit; to show their indifference to pain and their high regard for the dead. As a sign of deep mourning, they might cut off a finger, generally the first joint of the small finger. People in mourning wore old clothes and gave up painting themselves and ornaments. They kept away from public gatherings, dances, and religious ceremonies. When a prominent chief died, as in the cases of White Calf and Mad Wolf, the family lodge was placed outside the circle-camp, among the hills and at a distance from the others.

With their strong leaders dead and no one to restrain, there was confusion in the big camp. Young men of the new generation, eager for excitement rode wildly at night. For a practical joke, they lassoed the small tipi of an old woman; she lived alone and had no one to defend her. They threw a rope round the top of her lodge, the other end fastened to the horn of a saddle. The rider rode at a gallop and jerked the lodge from its foundations, leaving the old woman bewildered in bed, exposed to public view, surrounded by all of her possessions.

They played a joke on an unpopular chief, by taking a colt and pushed it into his lodge at night. Inside it made havoc in the dark, kicking and squealing and racing about.

Bad whiskey was freely distributed by white peddlers. It was against the law to sell whiskey to Indians, but there was no sign of enforcement.

The young generation were beyond control. They were returning to their families and primitive conditions, coming from distant schools and colleges. Now they had short hair, modern clothes, and manners strange. At first they made a fight and failed, as anyone would fail, without employment and exposed to the ridicule of families and friends. Quickly disillusioned, their education became a bitterness. They deteriorated morally and physically. White men took away their old culture and gave nothing to take its place.

■ HENRY TALL BULL TOM WEIST

In this selection, Henry Tall Bull and Tom Weist put a humorous twist on a story about how one Cheyenne Indian adapted to the white man's technology. The setting for this tale is the Cheyenne Indian Reservation during the early years of the century, and the machine requiring domination is the Model T Ford. The story was first published in 1970 by Montana Reading and Publications in Billings as part of its Indian Culture Series.

Grandfather and the Popping Machine

My grandfather, old man Raven, was one of the first Cheyennes to buy a car (taomeamoeoxzistoz – that which runs by itself). He called it a popping machine because of the pop-pop-pop noise the engine made. Grandfather had always been good at handling horses, but learning to drive a car was something different. That was an adventure!

Grandfather bought his popping machine in Forsyth. The salesman at the garage cranked the engine for us. Bang! Boom! Bang! Pop-pop-pop! The car shook and the noise was awful. Grandfather held tightly to the steering wheel.

"You have to watch out when you crank it to get it started," shouted the salesman. "Sometimes it kicks."

Grandfather nodded. "Like horse, only kick at other end," he said in his broken English.

The salesman looked worried. "Have you ever driven a car before?"

Grandfather shook his head. "My grandson, Johnny, help me break it on the way home," he said.

"This will tell you how to drive a car," said the salesman, and he handed a small book to Grandfather. *Driving Lessons*, it said on the cover. "I'll show you how to make it go." Then the salesman explained to us about the foot pedals and how to shift gears and where the horn button was located. "Now," he said, "If you'll wait a minute, I'll get my tools and fix the brakes. Why don't you practice shifting gears so you'll get used to it." Then he went into the garage.

Grandfather did what the salesman told him to do. Maybe his foot slipped off the clutch pedal, or maybe he was just anxious to go. The engine roared, and the car jerked and bucked, and suddenly we were moving!

I heard a shout and looked back. The salesman was running after us, waving his tools and yelling something, but I couldn't hear what he was trying to tell us because of all the noise. We were going faster and faster! Grandfather had found out that the car jerked and bucked only when it was going slowly. So, like a horse, he gave it its head and ran it fast. Now I couldn't see the salesman at all because of the smoke and dust blowing up behind us.

The first thing Grandfather had to learn was how to steer. We raced down the main street of Forsyth, weaving back and forth. Ahead of us, a woman was crossing the street. She didn't see us until Grandfather blew the horn. Ooga! Ooga! went the horn. The woman screamed and ran. After that, Grandfather decided to keep blowing the horn to warn people that we were coming.

Just about that time, this cowboy rode out of a side street. Both he and his horse looked like they were half asleep. Well, when we drove by, that horse really showed his spirit! The horn seemed to wake him up. He surprised me, the way he suddenly began bucking and jumping like he was the wildest thing on four legs. Of course, I wasn't half as surprised as the cowboy who was riding him! He put on quite a show, hanging on as that horse bucked, kicked, and fishtailed his way down Main Street. The last thing I saw of the cowboy, he was still on the horse, headed in the general direction of Miles City. Then the smoke and dust hid everything. I began to hope that it was covering our trail, too.

By now, Grandfather was getting better at steering his popping machine. We made a left turn and came to the railroad tracks. Just ahead, a big steam locomotive was coming down the track. Grandfather blew the horn and the engineer blew his whistle. The locomotive was picking up speed and getting closer. Grandfather decided that he had better stop, so he hit the brake pedal. Nothing happened! I couldn't bear to look, so I shut my eyes good and tight. I kept waiting for the terrible crash of the train hitting us, but it never came. Very slowly, I opened my eyes and saw that, somehow, we had made it across the tracks. Behind us, the locomotive thundered past.

Now we knew why the salesman had run after us. The brakes didn't work!

"Where is the book the salesman gave you?" I asked Grandfather.

"Drop book when popping machine start moving," said Grandfather.

I bent down and searched the floorboards hoping he had dropped it inside the car, but it wasn't there. "Oh, Grandfather!" I exclaimed. "Now we are in trouble. The brakes don't work and we've lost the driving lessons book!"

Grandfather took it calmly. "Not have book when I learn to ride war pony."

That was true, but a car wasn't a war pony. And we had a long drive ahead of us before we reached home. Then I looked over at Grandfather, sitting tall and straight behind the wheel, his braids moving in the wind. He was steering straight down the road. His eyes twinkled with pleasure. He was getting used to driving his popping machine. Somehow I wasn't so afraid anymore.

The road was dusty but fairly smooth. We began to enjoy our trip, though each hill we came to frightened us. The road was narrow in places and it would be hard to pass, should we meet a wagon. When the road flattened out, Grandfather sang his wolf song. This was the same song he had sung as a young warrior when he returned to camp with horses taken from the enemy.

We went a long way, then crossed Armell's Creek and neared the place where the Cheyennes camped on their way to and from Forsyth. It was getting late in the afternoon and we could see the smoke from the camp fires long before we reached the camp.

Grandfather began blowing the horn. Ooga! Ooga! Everyone laughed and yelled when they saw who it was. As we drove by the camp, we could smell the coffee, meat and greasebread cooking. Grandfather took his foot off the gas pedal and tried to slow down, but the car began to buck and jerk, so he drove faster once more.

Suddenly I felt very tired and hungry. How I wished we could stop and eat! But, without any brakes, all we could do was keep going. Grandfather did try to shift gears, but, when he heard the sharp, grinding noise he was making, it scared him and he gave up. He was afraid he might break his popping machine.

We left the camp behind us. Finally, after a time, I curled up on the front seat beside Grandfather and fell asleep.

Well, if I had known what was going to happen, I never would have fallen asleep. There I was, sleeping soundly, when Grandfather came to this straight stretch of road and decided to take a little nap himself. He was used to dozing on his horse sometimes when he rode home. The horse knew the way. But he soon learned that his popping machine couldn't be trusted.

Bump! Bump! Bump! I suddenly woke up. We were hitting something! I looked over at Grandfather. He was sitting behind the wheel, his chin on his chest, sound asleep! It took four or five bumps to wake him.

He was really surprised when he saw that we were driving right down a new fence line. Luckily, the posts were loose in their holes. By the time Grandfather turned the car back on the road, we must have knocked down ten or fifteen posts.

Then I noticed where we were. Directly ahead lay the reservation. We were almost home!

It was nearing sundown when we drove through Lame Deer. A few people waved to us and several dogs ran off with their tails between their legs. On we went.

Before long we came to a fence. The gate was closed, so I told Grandfather to drive on through after he circled so I could jump off and open the gate. He circled again; I ran after the car and jumped onto the running board.

We drove across the field. We reached the other side, and there stood a big Hereford bull between us and the next gate. He watched us coming closer and began pawing the ground. Grandfather began to circle just as the bull charged. Off we went through the field with the bull right behind us. When I looked back, all I could see of the bull were his head and horns in front of a dust cloud. I yelled at Grandfather to drive along side the fence. Then I waited until just the right moment and jumped off the running board. The bull raced past, still chasing the car. I rolled through the sagebrush, then got to my feet and ran for the fence.

Grandfather saw me open the gate. He was still circling with the bull right behind. He drove towards the gate and started blowing the horn. That startled the bull and he turned just as Grandfather drove on through. I closed the gate, then ran after the car and jumped onto the running board. I was out of breath, very tired, and very sore. Grandfather and I were learning that there was a lot more to driving a car than we had thought.

Before long, we saw the house up ahead. We still couldn't stop the car, so Grandfather decided to begin circling once more. He had planned to surprise Grandmother with his new popping machine. Well, as it turned out, he *really* surprised her.

Grandmother had been having trouble with her hearing; otherwise, she would have heard us coming a long way off. She was just coming out the back door to feed the chickens as we drove around the side of the house. We turned the corner, and suddenly the air was filled with chickens, all of them trying to fly at once! Grandmother screamed and ran into the house and locked the door behind her!

When we came around to the front of the house, I jumped off. It took a while before Grandmother realized who it was and finally unlocked the door.

"Come see Grandfather's popping machine!" I told her.

Grandfather came around again, and this time, he was loudly singing his wolf song. Grandmother just stood in the doorway and shook her head like she didn't believe what she was seeing. She watched him come around several more times. "Old Man is crazy," she said, finally, and went back into the house to fix supper.

I ate a piece of greasebread while I told her about our adventures on the way home. I told her all about the car and the things the salesman had told us. When I got to the part about there being thirty horses under the hood, she looked up at me sharply and I had to look away. I couldn't believe that one, either.

I explained that we weren't sure just how to stop Grandfather's popping machine, so she fixed a plate of meat, beans, and greasebread for Grandfather, which I took outside. Grandfather came around again, and I dashed after him, jumped onto the running board, and handed him his supper. Then I jumped down and went after his coffee. When I brought that out, Grandfather was eating and driving at the same time. After he nearly missed hitting his sweat lodge, he told me to drive and slid over on the seat.

I was really excited about driving the car. I drove around the house three or four times until I started to get dizzy, then I switched to doing figure eights for a while, but that wasn't much better. It was dark, but the moon was out and it wasn't hard to see.

After a time, Grandfather took the wheel once more. I was getting sleepy. I thought about sleeping in the car beside Grandfather to keep him company, but the ride was awfully bumpy, and I was still dizzy. Finally, I told Grandfather that I was going to bed. I told him to make sure he didn't fall asleep at the wheel. Then I jumped down and stood for a moment, watching Grandfather drive his popping machine off through the moonlight.

Grandmother looked up from her beading when I came in. "Don't worry about Grandfather," I told her. "He'll be all right. Tomorrow we'll really learn how to drive the popping machine. Then we'll all go for a ride."

I went to bed and lay for some time, listening to the pop-pop-pop of the machine as Grandfather circled the house. I wondered how long he had yet to drive before he ran out of gas.

I thought of Grandfather, sitting tall and straight behind the wheel of his popping machine. How pleased he was! I thought of all the things that had happened, and how this had been a day that neither of us would ever forget.

Then, just as I was falling asleep, I heard, above the noise of the engine, the high, clear sounds of Grandfather's wolf song rising on the night wind. Good sounds, such good sounds.

■ FRED NAULT

Fred Nault was a Metis—a Northern Cree of mixed French and Indian descent. He was born at Dupuyer, Montana, in 1901 and spent his last years on the Chippewa/Cree Rocky Boy's Indian Reservation. For most of his life Nault worked as a cowboy, but this story delves deep into Metis history. Nault traces the lives of his ancestors who came from Canada in the late 1870s with Catholic leader, teacher, and rebel Louis Riel. "Old Man Boushie," Nault's recollection of his maternal grandfather, is from Fred Nault: Montana Metis, As Told By Himself *(1977).*

Old Man Boushie

Old Man Boushie was one-eighth French and the rest Cree. In his early days he was a great hunter and tracker. When he was a young man William Boushie married Suzanne Collins and for many years was a mountain man.

The Boushies were from away North, somewhere in Canada. They just sort of followed the game around. By the time they got to Montana most of the buffalo were killed off.

He and his wife used to move around on pack horses because there were no roads. They moved around the foothills of the Great Rockies from Augusta to around Chief Mountain near the Canadian Border, a distance of almost 100 miles. He did a lot of trapping of fur-bearing animals. The pelts he sold for money, which he used to buy whatever he needed such as shells for his rifles. He had more than one rifle because he stayed out all Winter. His wife also was a good shot.

Every Fall he bought a supply of salt, sugar, tobacco, matches, a lot of tea and coffee. Enough to last him and his wife all Winter. This was before they had any children so they were free to go anywhere and live. They also would carry flint and steel in case they ran out of matches, plenty of fish hooks and line because in the creeks and beaver dams were a lot of fish.

They would ride their horses and set camp near the Mountains where there were a lot of dry wood and straight poles to build a wooden tipi–because a wooden tipi would stand up no matter how deep the snow got where a tent of canvas would rip.

He would tie the poles at the top over-and-over to make it strong with strips of rawhide. He would make his tipi about 22 feet across and 14 to 16 feet high so they could build a fire inside and hang dry meat and dry pelts during the cold, stormy months.

Then the hunt would begin. As the snow got deeper up higher the big game would come down lower to feed where the snow was not too deep. That's when Old Man Boushie got a lot of game to make dry meat. His wife would tan hides. When he killed a large, fat bear they would get a lot of grease. Sometimes in Winter they would find a bear's den. They would kill the bear in his den. He said whenever they saw steam coming out of the deep snow there was a bear den. When they got the bear out of his den the bear would not put up too big a fight because he was still sleepy and groggy.

The Boushies lived on wild game, big and small. Big game was elk, deer, bighorn sheep. Small game was snow-shoe rabbit, cottontail rabbit, grouse, beaver, fish. In Summer the Boushies also had berries of different kinds.

Toward Spring Old Man Boushie would be running out of shells for one of his guns. This one time he had only five shells for this one gun although he had a lot more for his other guns. But he took five shells which were left for the one gun. And as it was starting to get warm he went out on his last hunt for the season with just five shells. He came over a hill with timber all around. Usually a hunter always sneaks around, and that is how he came upon a mountain lion stalking an elk. Not far from the elk was a large, black bear grubbing for ants.

Boushie sat down behind a large tree, wondering which animal he should shoot first. He finally decided to shoot the mountain lion.

Next would be the elk. Last would be the bear. He decided this way because the mountain lion was quickest. Then the elk hearing the shot would jump once and then look around. That way he would get an easy shot. Last would be the bear being that he was mean. He would stand on his hind legs to look around for a fight. That is what he did.

When Old Man Boushie went home he had to make a return trip with two pack horses to bring back his kill to camp, so his wife could prepare the meat for dry meat and pemmican.

When Spring finally came to stay he would move down the hills to sell his pelts. All Summer he would take jobs around the ranches. This he would do until late in the Fall. Then again he would move to the mountains with his wife. But later on when they started to have children he did not hunt much.

The Boushies had three sons, and six daughters. Nancy, Maggie, Lorraine, Olive, Cecilia were the daughters. One daughter was my mother, Louise. The boys were Ed, Joe and Pete Boushie. Pete still lives here in Rocky Boy with a lot of children. Pete Boushie is now an old man.

All the years the Chippewa and Cree tried to get a reservation there were people who depended on Old Man Boushie to give them advice about what to do next. He was a wise man in very many ways. It is because of him and some others that there is a Rocky Boy's Reservation. Every day I remember him.

My grandfather was respected for his wisdom. He and Pennato had been associated with Little Bear, chief of the Crees. The Little Bear Crees and the Rocky Boy Chippewa were really not a single group until they camped at where Johnny Morsette's place is now in 1914. This was after Little Bear got the land for a campground. There was never peace from the time of the first Riel Rebellion on to the second Riel Rebellion. The Crees and Riel's group of mixed bloods got together and organized. Gabriel Dumont was selected as a vice president, I guess you would call him.

After the United States Government abandoned Fort Assinniboine Military Reservation, Old Man Boushie suggested to Little Bear that they ask for the military reservation. Little Bear then went about it by asking Paris Gibson and C. M. Russell. Those two men got together with the Cascade county commissioners and city officials of Great Falls because those Indians were never accepted very well anywhere. That was after Little Bear had wandered around Montana trying to settle his people and after Little Bear's people were denied the right to settle near Browning with Rocky Boy. Little Bear was trying to get in with Rocky Boy but the Crees were denied this right because they were from Canada. Little Bear and his people were even denied camping rights.

From Browning they went to the Flathead where some of the band stayed. Quite a few of them stayed at the Flathead because they were tired of roaming around.

From the time he came into Montana, Old Man Boushie was making his living as a mountain man up by Dupuyer, as I have said. Every now and then all three of them–Boushie, Pennato and Little Bear–would meet up. They'd talk about a reservation, as to how they could go about getting recognition by the government. Sometimes they met with Gibson and C. M. Russell, also Frank Linderman, and William Bole of *The Great Falls Tribune*. They finally all got together and decided to ask for this Reservation here.

Gibson, Linderman, and Russell got busy to assist Little Bear to get the campground set up. They kept after that for years. The tribal-owned land concept grew out of that campground. Now when Rocky Boy and his people were allotted by Browning, Little Bear finally came down here with his people who did not stay on at Browning or Flathead.

Boushie, those first years, was here practically every year. He would travel back and forth from here to the Dupuyer country. We–his family–were up there at the foot of the Rocky Mountains where my grandfather had planned on proving up his homestead. But as I said before he could not establish a permanent home being he was Indian. He was really a mixed blood. He was a Metis. Now awhile back, I think I mentioned his efforts to establish a home in general. He really tried twice. The first time he went up to the foothills of the Rocky Mountains they would not give him his rights to the land he had settled, so he sold his improvements. That place was 14 or 15 miles south of Dupuyer. He then moved to another site near Dupuyer, this one 17 or 18 miles west of Dupuyer. Both places were in the foothills. He stayed at the second site even if he could not prove up on it. He wanted to settle down. Eventually a fellow from Conrad went to the land office and discovered this place was open for homestead–a fellow by the name of Witherspoon. My grandfather sold his improvements and cattle to this man in 1917. That's when he came down here. He got himself enrolled, along with his wife and me and my sister and his sons. None of my aunts were enrolled here because they were married to people not recognized by

Little Bear and Rocky Boy. One of my aunts–Nancy Boushie–was married to Francis Munroe, who was enrolled on the Blackfeet. Mary was married to Ezare LaFromboise. I really don't know why he was not recognized. Mary and Ezare were one of the families who had stayed at Flathead.

Ed Boushie, Joe Boushie, and Pete Boushie were enrolled by my grandfather also.

Old Man Boushie suggested to Little Bear that each family be given a homesite. This suggestion he made as early as the people were living in what was called the Rocky Boy Campground, before there was the Reservation. And, of course, he repeated this suggestion after the executive order making it a reservation.

Boushie suggested to Little Bear that the people ask for issuance of machinery and wagons to start farming to work their sections. He believed in farming because he knew that was what they had to do to survive because non-Indian people were drifting into Montana and taking up the land. Just about then was the beginning of the Homestead Act.

I did not take any interest in what he told my uncles, his sons. I was too young. But I knew he was a stockman after being a mountain man, although periodically he'd go back into the mountains to hunt elk or deer.

Old Man Boushie stayed here three years before going to Canada in 1921. He returned to the United States in 1925 and stayed with his children on and around the Blackfeet Reservation. He never returned to Rocky Boy. For one thing he was too old, and he was plumb broke, and he did not have any means of traveling other than by horse, and that would be too hard a trip. But, anyway, he did manage to stay alive until 1931 when he died at Heart Butte where his older daughters lived. They were Mary LaFromboise and Maggie Salois.

6

Literature of Modern Montana

■ *Frontier Dreams*

MARY CLEARMAN BLEW

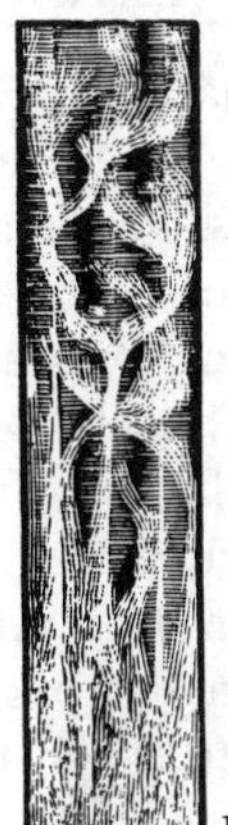n 1947, Montana's most famous novel appeared into a post-war world that barely had begun to comprehend the existence of the nuclear bomb. With the conviction brought by its new realism to the old theme of the irrevocable loss of the past, A. B. Guthrie's *The Big Sky* inevitably became a best-seller. To Montanans it was more: It was a parable of their lives as they understood them to have been shaped by their sense of place and their fear of invasion. So embedded has the novel become in the self-consciousness of Montanans that its title is used as the state's nickname and as a slogan on license plates.

To read *The Big Sky* is to recognize, in the story of seventeen-year-old Boone Caudill running away from the brutality and disease of the Midwestern white frontier into idyllic seclusion with the Blackfeet in the Teton Mountains of Montana in the 1820s, a belief in lost innocence that today seems overlaid by many layers of irony. In reinventing our past out of the wealth of stories and diaries and accounts from the preceding periods, how could we ever have believed in so much innocence to be lost? And yet how, in the violence of life in late twentieth century Montana, can we deny the self-destructiveness personified by Boone or escape sharing the guilt that drives him, drunken and dehumanized, reeling out of paradise?

Innocence and self-destructiveness converge in today's Big Sky country with its awareness of being the end of a tradition, the last best place, a fortress of the mind. *Having lost so much, how can we keep the little that is left?* This is the unspoken fear behind public policy debate in Montana, from concerns about protecting the wilderness, the water, and the air to promoting free enterprise, economic development, trade, and growth.

In this convergence lies the attraction A. B. Guthrie's novel continues to hold for readers, and herein are found the concerns of the majority of writers in Montana during the middle decades of the twentieth century. Here also, in what we imagine ourselves to have been and in our worst fears of what we may become, lies the continuing importance of *The Big Sky* for a succeeding generation of writers.

The assumption of an innocent past is shared by writers as divergent as Dorothy M. Johnson in her classic western fiction and Grace Stone Coates in her dark probings of the soul. Growth for both writers—whether personal, as explored painfully in Coates' prose and poetry, or as social development from the unfettered frontier into a modern state—is achieved only through loss. While both writers treat the loss of innocence with poignance, both tacitly accept its inevitability as well as its price.

To examine Johnson's stylized treatment of the western adventure story is to test the cutting edge between myth and formula. All western adventure stories look back to the innocent days, but the formula in "The Man Who Shot Liberty Valance" is crafted into an elegiac whole that surpasses its origins. Through an irony that is underlined by the name of the gunslinger, Liberty Valance, we are forced to recognize the dualities of innocence and brute strength, liberty, and chaos, which discolor perceptions of our frontier heritage.

It is a heritage as recently vanished as a dream, and as troubling. "Bert Barricune died in 1910," the narrative begins before it dissolves into timelessness. Equally dreamlike is the portrayal of Liberty Valance himself, who exists only as a threatening shadow until he appears in silhouette, "burly and broad-shouldered," for the ritual shoot-out in the town street. Of greater significance than Liberty Valance to the central action of the story is the cowboy, Bert Barricune, whose courage and naive code of honor make possible the ultimate confrontation between Valance and the young man from the East who not only reads Plato but comprehends the applications of the legal and political systems of civilization. For the young easterner to achieve an ordered state and elected office, however, he must earn his manhood, first by surviving the shooting of Liberty Valance and then by outgrowing the cowboy, who dwindles gradually into obsolescence and death. "He was my enemy; he was my conscience; he made me whatever I am," muses the Senator over the cowboy's coffin.

Nowhere can be found a greater contrast to Johnson's dream frontier than in the psychological landscapes of Grace Stone Coates; but Coates, too, is preoccupied with the theme of betrayed innocence. Unlike Guthrie or Johnson, Coates allows an authentic female voice to surface throughout her work. In the poems, the speaker usually is acquiescent or subversive, and she often identifies her body with landscape.

While the female voice in the poems avoids confrontation with the male either through passiveness or through secret strategies of the mind, Coates presents a direct confrontation between male and female in a chapter from her novel, *Black Cherries*. This selection begins and ends with the naive child narrator questioning her identification of her mother with a cherry tree that bears a particularly sweet and exotic dark fruit. The mother, however, is not permitted to retain for long her simplistic identification with nature. Against the counterpoint of her child's questions, she moves through the story in a series of responses to violation: flight through the dark pastures with her own daughters while her ten-year-old stepdaughter begs her not to abandon her; avoidance in her return to the farmhouse and her ministering to the stepdaughter with towel and basin; and finally, when outraged beyond endurance, confrontation:

> She walked to the table where father sat. He did not look up. I could hear the air being still around her before she spoke. A small sharp singing began, that I could always hear when I listened hard, especially when I listened for something that had not happened yet. Mother said, "I will not live in a house where children are abused."

The story closes with our knowledge that not only her marriage but also the perceptions of the eavesdropping child narrator will be altered beyond return. It is a courageous conclusion, not only because it allows the female viewpoint to expand beyond her own identification with a natural world that may be used, abused, or exploited by the questioning male, but also because it implies that life continues and actually may be strengthened after the loss of innocence. The courageousness of Coates' conclusion may be appreciated by comparing her with writers who never bring themselves to challenge the limitations imposed on them by the assumption of an innocent past: Gwendolyn Haste, whose ranch wives wither away or go mad in the solitude of scenic grandeur, or Hughie Call, the eternally self-deprecating woman forever trapped in a world of disapproving men.

In his *Partisan Review* essay of 1948, "The Montana Face," Leslie Fiedler stung Montanans by comparing their preoccupation with their past to the story of dance hall girls panning the ashes of a road agent for the gold it was rumored he had been carrying. So long as white Montanans fail to come to terms with the Indians and the reality of their past, Fiedler argues, they will fail the possibility for tragedy and poetry.

Indians, for whom Montana never was empty, have realized the potential for tragedy. Well before the appearance of "The Montana Face," D'Arcy McNickle confronted the ghosts of a destroyed culture and exposed the dark side of the Big Sky tradition. In *The Surrounded*, which Fiedler might have read in 1948, McNickle writes about the survivors of a past that is anything but innocent and, in his themes of alienation and confrontation, opens the way for a younger generation of writers.

For Archilde of *The Surrounded*, whose father is white and who has been educated as a white, the past is nonexistent, unreal. That his mother and uncle take seriously the lost culture of the past seems to him humorous, and he believes that he himself exists exclusively in the present. When his uncle begins a round of storytelling around the fire, however, Archilde listens at first with condescension and then with growing interest. Although the same stories often have been told in his presence, he realizes that this is the first time he has been able to hear them. One coyote legend kindles his amusement, another his sense of wonder. And finally, after listening to his uncle's narrative, Archilde experiences illumination:

> For the first time he had really seen it happen. First the great numbers and the power, then the falling away, the battles and starvation in the snow, the new hopes and the slow facing of disappointment, and then no hope at all, just this living in the past. He had heard the story many times, but he had not listened. It had tired him. Now he saw it had happened and it left him feeling weak. It destroyed his stiffness toward the old people. He sat and thought about it and the flames shot upward and made light on the circle of black pines.

The medium of storytelling may make it possible for a young man of mixed blood and white values, like Archilde, to retrieve his identity and understand himself as the culmination of the past. But the white man, however well-intentioned, is locked outside the Indian experience. Without the common experience of the past on which to draw, he can neither hear the stories nor comprehend what is left of their power.

Even a man like Adam Pell in McNickle's *Wind from an Enemy Sky*, who sees the Indians' plight and acknowledges his own culpability, cannot convey to his white friends his sense of desperation on the

Indians' behalf. However many times he tells their story, his words are met with incomprehension; and indeed Adam himself fails to understand that the dam under construction, in flooding the valley, will cause damage more profound to the Indians than the economic loss he tries to explain to his friends. Out of the failure of understanding is borne confrontation and disaster.

The failure of language in the face of impenetrable cultural differences is the occasion for Mildred Walker's historical novel, *If a Lion Could Talk.* Confronted by the refusal of an Indian woman to speak English, Walker's young missionaries retreat back to civilization in bewilderment that rapidly turns to shame at the inadequacy of their own faith. The wilderness experience eventually leads the missionaries through suffering and personal sacrifice to a painfully won self-understanding. But for the Indian woman and her white husband, the path is just the opposite. Neither can endure in the other's culture, and eventually she returns to her people, leaving him in despair and their children in limbo. The significance of the novel lies in Walker's refusal to find innocence in the past.

For D'Arcy McNickle, the sacred past is tied directly to specificity of landscape. For Wallace Stegner, however, landscape is almost accidental. "It has no meaning," Stegner has written, "it can hardly be said to exist, except in terms of human perception, use, and response." Stegner, whose celebrated "rootlessness" leads him into territory much further reaching than the boundaries of Montana, never treats the homestead frontier as a wilderness waiting to be transformed, nor does he equate its emptiness with innocence. Stripped of its mythology, Stegner's prairie is revealed as a harsh setting for natural, cyclical life. But lacking a culture or even a rudimentary sense of the past, Stegner's family succeeds only in creating the most fragile of paths on the side of a homestead too barren to provide a living or sustain a dream.

As Stegner demonstrates in *Wolf Willow*, a history of prairie settlement exists, and one who is willing to put aside nostalgia and search for it will learn something about the present. By coming to terms with the historical past, by understanding his place in the natural life cycle, by discovering the significance of human activities like path-making, the boy will become a man in a sense very different from the romantic, despairing mountain man of *The Big Sky*. In the search for the last best place, Stegner has recognized the past and its mythology, what it reveals, and what it hides.

■ GRACE STONE COATES

For many years, Grace Stone Coates conducted her literary career from a ranch in Martinsdale, a small community in central Montana. Coates was a frequent contributor and associate editor of H. G. Merriam's literary journal, The Frontier, *which was published by the University of Montana in Missoula. Coates also completed two volumes of poetry*—Portulacas in the Wheat *(1932) and* Mead and Mangelwurzel *(1933). Her most lasting creative work is* Black Cherries, *a novel published in 1931. Coates died in Bozeman in 1976.*

Black Cherries

The black-cherry tree that stood beyond the kitchen door was mother's. At first, at the very earliest, I thought the tree *was* mother. I thought it was mother-being-a-tree. Later I thought it was a mother-tree. But my sister Teressa explained to me that it was mother's tree because she liked its sweet black cherries. She could not eat the sour pie-cherries we gobbled greedily. It was her tree.

Mother liked all trees, except the two palm-like strangers standing outside the pantry window. She loved trees, and the black-cherry best of all. Only by her permission could we break one splayed white blossom. For her we snapped bare winter twigs, with smooth dark ice-glazed bark. For her, in summer, we dug "gum," well bedded with ants and Kansas dust. There was a curious thing about our gifts of amber sap. Although I often stood at her side, for the vicarious rapture of seeing a bit of shiny "gum" slip between her lips, I could never catch the exact moment when she tasted the treasure. Always the fire needed attention, or a pail must be emptied. Once when I had brought her an unusually ample lump, I turned back at the door to reclaim a morsel for myself. She said it was all gone. I was puzzled. I was so puzzled I asked to look in her mouth. I thought there must be a small piece, somewhere, she didn't know she hadn't swallowed. Mother acted bothered. She said part of the gum had had bark on it, and she hadn't eaten that. After I went outdoors I wondered for a long time how she could swallow a sticky thing so quickly.

It was for mother we guarded the cherry tree's black fruit.

Because of something that happened, once, as I gathered her an offering, the tree stands forever in the disquieting twilight which haunts unhappy dreams—the shadow that prevents any dream from being happy.

It was the edge of evening, in the slow, long summer half-light. I was alone, peering into the branches of the tree, picking a cherry here and there. The season was almost over; little fruit was left. I held the cherries by their stems as I gathered them, making a tight bouquet. As I thought of mother taking them, I could feel her smooth fingers flatten against mine, transferring the cluster deftly to preserve its careful shape. Some of the cherries I touched slipped from their pits and smeared my fingers. These I ate. When I had pulled a branch down within reach, I would catch a twig in my teeth to hold it. The leaves brushed my face. The bark was pungent in my nostrils and on my tongue. I pretended I was part of the tree.

While I was looking into the branches' deepening blackness, mother came from the house with Teressa at her side. She held Teressa's hand, and that was queer; Teressa didn't like to be touched. I went toward them, offering mother my cherries. She pushed my hand away as if I were not there, and said, "Not now." Her face was white in the dusk. I looked at her and she said again, still as if I were not there, "I couldn't taste them. They would sicken me. Come, we are going for a walk."

She took my free hand, and still holding Teressa's, started across the yard. Suddenly she dropped our hands and turned back to the house, saying, "Stay there!" over her shoulder as she went. We waited. I rubbed the cherries up and down against my cheek. I knew this was not nice, but I did it anyway. I liked the way they felt. If doing it stayed in my mind and bothered me, I would rinse the cherries off at the pump before I gave them to mother. They felt like glass. I could smell them and make them smell like blossoms, or I could smell them and make them smell like bark. I told Teressa this, and she said, "I hate you."

It grew darker while mother was in the house. She came out of the kitchen door, walking fast. As she stepped from the low platform to the path, my oldest sister, Augusta, came running after her, crying, "Don't go! Don't go!"

Without turning her head, or stopping, mother said, "Go back," but Augusta ran around in front of her, crouched down, and caught mother around the knees. She kept saying, "Please, please, please don't leave me." I wondered why Augusta didn't go with us.

Mother did not move. She looked straight ahead and said, "Go back." I saw the buttons on the back of Augusta's dress, and her bent head, and the way her braids jerked when her shoulders shook. Augusta was old. She was more than ten. She did not speak or cry on her way back toward the house, but her shoulders went up and down.

Mother came toward us and took our hands. She almost ran. Usually mother did not take short cuts, or climb fences. She went on paths. But this time we went straight through the orchard without going by the road. We went through deep grass, past sunflowers in the corner where sand burrs grew, to the fence. It was a board fence. I hurried to get through first, because I wanted to see how mother went through a fence where there was no gate. I caught myself between two tight boards, and when I could look again mother and Teressa were through. Past the fence we were in a plowed field. We went so fast I had to take little running steps to keep up. My fingers ached from holding the cherry stems. It was strange to be walking fast and not talking. I wondered why Augusta didn't want us to go, and why she had not come with us. I asked. I knew it was naughty to ask. Mother's voice sounded far away. She said Augusta had to study her lessons, and for me not to talk.

We walked a long time. I was tired. All at once mother turned around, and leaving us both, began to run toward the house. It was like the horrible queerness of a dream to see her running over the plowed ground in the darkness. Teressa took my hand and we began to run, too. We caught up with mother on the other side of the fence. I wondered again whether she went between the boards or climbed over them. As we came out of the orchard she looked over her shoulder and said, "Stay back," just as she had before; only this time she said it to Teressa.

Teressa said we must go to the granary to gather eggs she had forgotten. It took her a long time to look for them, and she didn't find them.

When we came to the house there was a light in the kitchen. Father was sitting at the table by my brother, teaching him square root. I knew it was square root, because Carl was crying onto his slate. Mother went through the kitchen with a washbasin in her hand, and a towel. She went to Augusta's room. When she came out I asked her if Augusta had a headache, and she said, "Yes. Keep out of her room."

Father and Carl had a worse and worse time. Father said, "I can make you see it with a strap." He said that whenever he taught Carl. Mother did something that seemed strange, as all the rest of the evening had been. I had never known her to help Carl, before, when father was teaching him. She said in a clear voice that sounded loud, "Carl, put up your books. Wash your face and go to bed." Carl looked at her with his mouth a little open. She said again, "Put away your books." His eyes were round, and he tiptoed when he crossed the room.

After he had gone, mother walked toward the porch door. A strap hung beside it, high on a nail. The strap was long, and had holes in one end. Mother took it down, and rolled it in her hands as she walked toward the stove. She was saying, "You shall never touch a child again, yours or mine, as long as I live in this house." She lifted the stove lid and put the strap on the coals.

I wondered why she said yours *or* mine.

She walked to the table where father sat. He did not look up. I could hear the air being still around her before she spoke. A small sharp singing began, that I could always hear when I listened hard, especially when I listened for something that had not happened yet. Mother said, "I will not live in a house where children are abused."

She turned and saw me. I had been sitting by the window, almost hidden by the curtain, and she had forgotten me. She told me sharply to go to bed, and added that I should have gone without telling, when Teressa did. I laid the cherries on the window sill. They lay there in the morning when I got up, tumbled on their heads. I did not eat them.

The next day I played alone all day. I knew things I had not known the morning before. There were things one learned, and things one knew without learning. Things I learned were like pictures to paste in a scrapbook. Things I knew were like pages to paste pictures on. I had learned that Augusta and Carl were not like Teressa and me. They were different the way things we bought were different from things we raised in the garden. What I knew was this: learning about one thing that puzzled me only made other things to wonder about. Why were Carl and Augusta different? Why did they cry when they studied? Why did father teach them, when mother always taught us? And why had the entire evening been so queer?

The questions came, and burrowed, and lay still, and wriggled again, always with the tickling brush of cherry leaves against my face, the scent and tang of cherry bark, and forbidden red-black smoothness across my cheek; always with the choking mystery of twilight, and the strangeness of plowed ground under hurrying feet.

Ransom

Harried by flesh I gave my body away,
A trifle, a toy its lover loved, not I.
Let nudging neighbors whisper and say what they say,
That I fed my soul to the jaws of lust. They lie.

How shall women holding their flesh so dear
   Their wan lives sicken guarding it, understand
That any ransom setting my spirit clear
   Were less to me than a pebble dropped from my hand.

Topers

On that bad night when I was drunk
With wine, and you were drunk with life,
You made your heady tipple mine;
And life in me was furious brew
You sipped, till you were drunk with wine,
And I was drunk with life and you.

Since separation was a knife,
We cut away restraint, and threw
The blade behind us, past the reach
Of time; while night, the miscreant, slunk
Unnoticed toward the western gate.
We rose unsobered, each with each
Eternally inebriate.

The Answer

What does the twisted sand dune say
   In answer to the wind that drives?
Her acquiescent atoms lay
   Their pattern as the wind contrives.

You are the wind; my body knows
   The answer of the shaken hill;
My undulated spirit shows
   The motion of your will.

Village Satiety

Satire sits on a satin cushion,
   Cups her chin, and looks at the street;

Questions: lethargy—or devotion?—
  Prisons me here on this window seat

To watch the villagers empty ashes,
  A wagon rattle to two white horses,
Purse-gut grocers strut like Pashas,
  And willows stagger the water courses.

Satire broods at the empty window:
  I will be *thus*, and I shall do *so*,
Hug my knees as wise as a Hindu,
  And watch stupidity come and go,

While I live a hidden life more sparkling
  Than lights that scream on a city street,
With secret ways of thought, more darkling
  Than crypt where cavern and river meet.

Ergot is on me. I shall be festive
  While life conceived in me is dying.
When I sit passive I shall soar restive
  Till I look down on great birds, flying.

I am deception to those who see
  Only coifed hair and tints that perish,
A flat bosom and crooked knee.
  In me is what the gods cherish.

Nights of Evil

Lean coyotes on the hill
Mock their own wailing
With ribald laughter.
Their lewd staccato cries excite my ear.

The wind explores my hair
With lecherous fingers,
They thrust at my throat and breast,
My mouth is stopped with his kiss,
I am ravished by the wind.

The moon is a forger
in his high chamber
Issuing checks on spent emotion
And signing them with my youth.

He is a counterfeiter
Whose false dies stamp
The spurious moidores of desire.

The moon, a sly procurer,
Waylays my heart coercing it to lust.

Country Doctor

I want loose women and a bawdy song—
Big white arms to pull me along
In a rowdy dance; and lips that are equal
To a kiss or a curse or a dirty sequel
To a dirty story.
God, I'm tired!
What do I care if their fun is hired—
At least they can laugh.

I want to forget
That I drove all night in the mud and the wet
Skidding tires and tearing my guts
To keep the damned car out of the ruts,
Half way to hell and back, so I
Could watch a girl watch her baby die.
Little fellow hadn't a chance. . . .
I want to forget it. I want to dance
And drink and be noisy. I want to drink
And forget that baby.

Some folks think
A doctor's an oiled machine, to run
Without sleep or meals or rest or fun—
We all need uplift. . . .

Well, I get this—
Rough-house racket and a floozy kiss.

D'ARCY McNICKLE

Born in St. Ignatius, Montana, in 1904, D'Arcy McNickle spent much of his early life on the Flathead Indian Reservation. He was graduated from the University of Montana in 1925 and completed his education at Oxford University and the University of Grenoble before becoming a field representative for the Office of Indian Affairs in Washington, D.C. McNickle worked for the U.S. Indian Bureau for sixteen years and was one of the founders of the Congress of American Indians. He was also a professor of anthropology at the University of Saskatchewan and program director at the Newberry Library in Chicago until his death in 1977. His many publications included books of fiction, ethnohistory, and biography. These selections are from his novels, The Surrounded *(1936) and* Wind from an Enemy Sky *(1978).*

From The Surrounded

On the same day that Max Leon visited Father Grepilloux at the Mission, Archilde's mother invited her relatives and friends to a feast in honor of her returned son. She killed one of her own steers—of which she had more than a few head, as she had horses also—and before sundown the fires were burning. Five tepees had been set up in the low ground by the creek, where they were hidden from the big house. After nightfall the flames would light up the black encircling pines and the reflection would fall upon the windows of the house and cast a soft glow in Max's bedroom. There would be voices rising up to him, too. He would lie in bed, swearing at the noise and wondering what it signified, whether the voices were sad or happy.

Archilde sat near the entrance of the principal tepee, that of old Modeste, the blind chief, who was either the uncle or the brother-in-law of his mother. Indian relationships, in the old style, were always a bit vague to him. Modeste he knew as a gentle old man who had appeared at intervals during his life in some act of generosity, either giving him, as a child, a finely wrought bow and bone-tipped arrows, such as had not been made in many years, and teaching him to shoot it; or sending him, when he was going away to school, a "safe-keeper" which the old man had carried since his own boyhood (Archilde still possessed two such amulets from Modeste's hand, one an eagle-bone whistle and the other the polished claw of a grizzly); and then, when Archilde had quite grown, giving him a horse, saddle and bridle. That was old Modeste. There he sat, smoking and waiting for the women to serve the meat, his sightless eyes blinking to his thought.

Archilde's mother occupied a place of distinction in the tribe. She was the daughter of the chief Running Wolf who had welcomed the Fathers, and since the title was hereditary she was still of the chief's family. More than that, she was a woman whose opinions were valued, and they were given only when sought. Just now she was directing the several women who were preparing the meal and drawing laughter from the women with her sharp comments. "Rose has such big buttocks now she can't bend to stir the fire. Look! Mine? Aih, you see I keep them out of sight. I sit on them."

This was true of his mother, but Archilde had never thought of it as a matter of any importance. It did not count in his scale of values. Old Modeste, more than his mother, made what he was seem important. If he had commanded an action, you would have to do it; while if his mother commanded you might do it, but you would be amused, you would smile and tease her a little by pretending that you weren't going to do it. Actually, in the way he was learning the world, neither Modeste nor his mother was important. They were not real people. Buffaloes were not real to him either, yet he could go and look at buffaloes every day if he wished, behind the wire enclosure of the Biological Survey reserve. He knew that buffaloes had been real things to his mother, and to the old people who had come to eat with her tonight. To him they were just fenced up animals that couldn't be shot, though you could take photographs of them.

Amusing was what it was. After living in Portland, playing the violin, living in a boarding house, reading baseball scores–it was funny to come home and sit at his mother's feast. His eyes saw the old faces, faces he had forgotten about, never thought to see again; and now to be sitting in the circle of firelight and looking at them–but it wasn't really funny, not deeply funny. The deeper feeling was impatience, irritation, an uneasy feeling in the stomach. Why could he not endure them for just these few hours? Why did they make him feel sick? It was not to be reasoned with. It did no good to remind himself that the old faces were not at fault; that his mother, who had never struck him, scarcely even spoken angrily to him, was in no way to blame for what he felt; and neither were the buffalo to blame for being no longer free. Reason wouldn't quite do the trick, but he would try it. He would sit quietly and try not to see or hear or smell too much. He would try not to speak, lest he say more than was necessary. And in a few hours, days–He had come home this time because it would be the last time. When he went away again–this he knew–he would not return.

He tried to eat, the way one had to at a feast. He tried to play the part. But when he had devoured about a pound of roasted meat he began to feel sick. The old people joked him.

"Here is a lump of hot fat the size of your head. That will do you good!"

His stomach turned. He felt the blood drain out of his face.

"That would kill a dog." His voice sounded weak.

"A pleasant death. A dog wouldn't mind dying with a full belly."

"Asilde"—the native Salish had no r's and the old people could not pronounce his name the way it was written—"in the old days your mother would have been ashamed of you." An ancient aunt, Mrs. Beaverfoot, made this observation. She never had got over the fact that Catharine was *Pu-Soiapi*; that is, she had married a white man.

"If I had been born in the old days"—Archilde tried to be unconcerned in his tone, though the remark made him angry—"then I would not be as I am now. You people talk about the old days as if they were here. But they're gone, dead. So don't tell me what I ought to do to be like that."

"Aih! The boy is right." This was Modeste. "You old women forget that what our children are like they cannot help. It began before their time." At that they all shook their heads and looked mournful. All conversations among the old people ended in this way. No matter what they talked about, before they had finished they were shaking their heads and thinking about what was gone.

Now that they were started, they would go on digging up their troubles and telling stories of the old days. Archilde with his impertinent new ways of thinking would be forgotten. He could sink back, glad not to be noticed and let them talk. Time would pass that way.

The first story was told by an old woman. Her scarcity of teeth gave an odd sound to some of her words but the story was an old one and nothing was lost.

"In the long ago the animals had tribes just like men. Coyote had his own tribe and this was one of the mightiest. Now he was hungry and all his people were hungry. They had nothing to eat. He sat in his tepee and pulled his blanket close.

" 'If I just had something to put on my arrow,' he said.

"It was like this. He had nothing to put on his arrow. He had just bark and you can see that would not go through a buffalo. When he shot something with the bark it just bounced off and the buffalo said 'Now I will eat that fly if he doesn't go away.'

"And Coyote had nothing to eat.

"Next day he went to see Fox, and Fox was cooking a piece of meat on a stick. He was holding it to the fire. Coyote sat down and watched the meat getting cooked. And he smelled the hot fat. And he got very hungry. Then when it was all cooked Coyote jumped and grabbed the meat and put it in his mouth all at once. But when he bit there was something hard in it. And it was the Flint.

" 'Now why didn't you tell me you had the Flint?' Coyote asked. 'When did the Flint go along here?'

"Fox said it was three days now since the Flint went by.

"Then Coyote took his blanket and his things and started after the Flint. When he had walked all day he said, 'Here is where the Flint camped.' Then he slept. Another day he traveled and then he said, 'The Flint made his bed here.' And he slept in that place. Then he walked the next day and at night he said, 'The Flint started from here this morning,' and so he slept again. Next morning he got up early and walked fast and there he saw the Flint going along the road. Coyote went out that way and then went faster and got ahead of the Flint and waited. And when the Flint came Coyote said:

" 'So here you are. Come here now and I will fight you.'

And the Flint said, 'All right. We will fight.'

"Then they were fighting and going this way and that way and Coyote took what he had in his hand–it was a war club–and he hit the Flint very hard and the Flint broke all to pieces.

" 'Hoh!' said Coyote. 'It is done.' And he put the pieces in his blanket and put it on his shoulder and started back. And he said to his people 'Just put some flint on the point of your arrows and we will kill buffalo.' Then he went to all the tribes and gave them flint and after that they did not have to starve.

"That is the story of Flint."

When the story was told everybody laughed. It was a very old story, the kind grandmothers told to grandchildren, and it always made people laugh. Archilde had not intended to listen, yet he had heard every word. The story had amused him in spite of himself. It left a spark of gay remembrance in his mind.

The next story was told by Whitey, an old man who had been born, they said, with a streak of white hair running through the black. His story was about "The Thing that was to make life easy." It went like this:

"There was an old man who had a dream and in this dream it said that something was coming that would make life easy. They would not have to hunt or dig for roots or do any kind of work. But they had to watch out and not let this thing that was to make life easy escape their notice.

"When the old man had this dream he was astonished and he went about telling people 'Something is coming that will make life easy.' Then he sat down to watch for it. He would not go on the hunt and he would not dig for roots or do any kind of work. He did not want to miss it. His people laughed at him. They said 'He was always a lazy man. Now he will never work.' So they went off to hunt and get food and left him sitting. And it went that way for many years. He sat in front of his lodge and waited. Sometimes he got very hungry because the hunters brought him nothing. Only his little grandchild kept him from starving. She took a piece of meat from her mother and brought it to Old Man. She did this every day.

"One day Old Man went away. They did not see him go but when they came by his lodge he was not sitting there. 'Where did Old Man go?' they asked. Nobody knew. Even the grandchild did not know. 'He just found a softer seat some place,' they said. And then they went hunting. All the men went out from the village and left only the women and children and the very old ones. They were gone a long time, as they had to cross the mountains in the east and go to the plains where they hunted buffalo. So there were no men in the village when Old Man came back. Yes, he came back finally, that old man. He carried something under his blanket. They looked at him but they were afraid to ask what it was. He sent out a call that all were to come to his lodge, and when they came there he said, 'Make me a meal and then I will show you the thing that is to make life easy.'

"When he had eaten he said, 'Come with me to the woods and I will show you this thing.' He went first carrying a bundle in his arms, and all those women and children and the very old ones followed. Their eyes were big and they said, 'Is it true or is Old Man a fool now?' And the old ones grumbled because everybody was walking so fast.

"He stopped when he came to a young cottonwood by the water. He put his bundle on the ground, then he spoke to the people who had crowded near. 'Oh, you foolish ones!' that was how he spoke to them. 'You did not believe it would come, but it is here. The thing that will make life easy is here now.' So he opened his bundle, and there it was. The people looked at the shiny thing and they were full of wonder.

" 'I will strike that tree five times and it will fall.' That was what he told them. It was not a very large tree but even so in the old days it would take a man maybe half a day to make it fall because in those times their axes were made of stone. And this thing that was to make life easy was an iron axe.

"Now the people could not believe what he said. They laughed. 'Hoh! Old Man! You can hit that tree ten times–twenty times–and it will not fall.' But some were not so sure. They looked at that shiny thing and it seemed to wink at them. And these said, 'Yes, it will fall. It will fall.'

"Old Man was angry at those who would not believe even now, and he went to that tree and struck it a mighty blow. A big chip flew out. Then he hit it a mighty blow on the other side. Again a big chip flew out. Once more on each side, four blows in all, and the tree died. It fell on some old people who had come too close and did not expect it to fall.

"The old man wrapped the axe in his bundle again and did not wait for their cries of astonishment. He went quickly to the trail which led away from the village. That way the hunters would come when they returned from across the mountains. And there he began to chop down the trees. He chopped every tree that stood near the trail and made a pile of the big chips right in the trail. Then he went home.

"When the hunters came from across the mountains they just stopped and cried in astonishment. Then they sat down around that pile of big chips and stared at it. 'It has come!' they said. 'The thing that is to make life easy has come and we were not here to meet it.'

"When the men entered the village Old Man was waiting for them. He began to laugh when he saw them and then everybody began to laugh. It made them happy. Now they had the thing that was going to make life easy.

"That is the story."

Archilde heard that story also. He wondered at it. And the more he reflected on it the more wonderful it grew. A story like that, he realized, was full of meaning.

Others told their stories, then they turned at last to Modeste, the blind chief. He would have to tell a story. They urged him. His sightless eyes blinked rapidly as he gathered his thought before speaking. He was going far back into the past.

"These stories make the heart light," he said in his high voice. "My story will have to be a different one. I will tell it for this boy who has just come home after traveling out to the world. You have just heard him say that those old days are dead and won't come again. And it's true. But let me tell this story so he will see better just what it was like back in those times.

"I will tell you first that in old times, before any white men came, his people were a mighty race and their land went from the plains east of the mountains to the Snpoilshi [Columbia] River. This is no boast about something that never was. When we made a treaty with the Government they saw how it was, and that was the country we owned. We had a strong nation and those who later became our greatest enemies, the Blackfeet and their kinsmen, and the Crows too, they respected us. We went twice a year to hunt on the Missouri and there were few who dared invade our hunting ground. It had been that way for longer than any man can say. And then it happened. How it was I cannot say. Up there at Fort-des-Prairies they began to give guns to the Blackfeet. No other Indians got these guns, only the Blackfeet. That was when our trouble began.

"The years that followed were bad. When we went to hunt on the Missouri the Blackfeet were there ahead of us with their guns. We had bows and arrows and our war clubs. Our people were frightened out of their senses. They had never seen that kind of fighting. A man dropped dead before he came near the enemy. Every year when we came back from the hunt there were lodges of women and children with no men. There were lodges of old people too with no young sons. At our councils there were some who said we should stay away from the buffalo country and that we could live just as well on mountain game. But those weak ones were not listened to. That land belonged to us and we had always hunted the buffalo. If we did not fight they would treat us like dogs and in a little while they would take the mountains away too. No, we would not listen to those weak ones.

"It went on that way a long time, and then the white men came to us in the mountains. There were foolish ones in our councils who said that we ought to just kill every white man that came along because they had given the guns to the Blackfeet. These foolish ones were not listened to either. We made peace with the first ones that came and helped them to find their way through the mountains, and we kept that peace with all of them. Today we can say that we never had the blood of any white man on our hands. It was not that we feared them, but we had to have their guns. And we could not stop being friendly once we had got some guns, as the foolish ones wished, because we had to have more guns. It was a different world from that time. In the old days of our wars a few men would be killed and fighting was a thing you could enjoy, like hunting. But now it became a bitter thing. Old scores of blood revenge could never be settled because too many were killed. Maybe this year it was your son, next year it would be your father, then your brother, then your wife, and each time your heart grew heavier. You cut off your hair so many times that men forgot how they had lived before all this happened. The old ones could say it had not always been thus, but the young ones thought they talked in dreams. For them the world had always been bitter.

"When we got our guns we had a great battle with the Piegans, the kinsmen of the Blackfeet. They did not know we had these guns and they rode foolishly at us. We were lying down on a ridge. They rode quite close and then we fired all at once. Their confusion was so great that some just fell off their horses. Their war chiefs tried to get them to come at us again but instead they ran the other way and left their wounded behind. That was a great battle."

At that point he paused and once more addressed himself to Archilde, for whom this story was intended. "Perhaps this talk of fighting and men dying means little to you. It is a little thing now, but when it was happening it seemed big. You will die easily, but if you had lived then you might have died fighting to live."

Modeste continued his story. "We thought guns would save our hunting grounds and make the old times return. But that was a mistake. This new kind of fighting just meant that more men were killed. It was bitter fighting. And we gained nothing. The Piegans made a peace but it was not to be trusted. Men said: 'We used to sleep all night, but now that we have peace with our enemies we sleep in the day and watch all night.' It was this way, that a man feared to go hunting alone or in a small company, for the Piegans were always waiting. We dared not leave our villages unprotected, for our enemies would shoot our women and children and carry off everything. That was what it had come to.

"Our wise ones said we had to try something else. They began to look about. Many went off alone on praying-fasts. It was clear that something had gone wrong, the people had lost their power. We had so few fighting men left we were afraid to count. It might be a bad thing to count men. So our wise ones began to say that we must find something new. Our voices, they said, no longer reach Amotkan [the Venerable One]. Maybe he has gone too far away or maybe our voices have become weak, but when we speak in the old ways we are not heard.

"Now some Indians came to us from the East. Perhaps you know about them. They were from the Iroquois nation. They came here to trap, but when they had been here a while we made them our brothers and asked them to live with us. They were the ones who told us about the black-robe Fathers. We must send for them. The Fathers would help us to be strong. They had a power, a Somesh, and it was like this: it was two sticks, one stick across the other like this. The black-robe Fathers called it the crucifix. If they brought it to us we would be strong again. That was what they told us and it was what our own wise ones were looking for. This was the new thing.

"So we sent for the black-robe Fathers. Four different times we sent our people all the way to St. Louis. And finally the Fathers came to us here. They built a church. They baptized us. . . ."

Here Modeste paused. No one looked up. No one stirred. In their thoughts they dwelt on that time in the past to which the old man had carried them. Then they heard him sigh.

"We thought they would bring back the power we had lost–but today we have less. This boys tells us the truth." Then his lips mumbled "Ies choopminzin" (I stop talking to you).

Archilde, listening closely, felt something die within him. Some stiffness, some pride, went weak before the old man's bitter simple words.

For the first time he had really seen it happen. First the great numbers and the power, then the falling away, the battles and starvation in the snow, the new hopes and the slow facing of disappointment, and then no hope at all, just this living in the past. He had heard the story many times, but he had not listened. It had tired him. Now he saw that it had happened and it left him feeling weak. It destroyed his stiffness toward the old people. He sat and thought about it and the flames shot upward and made light on the circle of black pines.

In the big house Max tried to sleep but his eyes would open and there would be the glow of light on the walls of his bedroom. Voices would come up to him. He would frown and turn his face away. He tried to be angry at them for the noise they made, but pity was there ahead of his anger. Why was it that after forty years he did not know these people and was not trusted by them? He had never interfered in their affairs, and he had never cheated them. They had lost a way of life, as Father Grepilloux said, but–damn it! why couldn't just one of his sons have the sense and the courage to make himself a new way of life! He rolled away from the glow of light, but still the voices reached him. What were they saying? Why didn't they talk to him?

From Wind from an Enemy Sky

It was a winter of heavy traveling, and every time Adam Pell returned to New York he wanted to know what information had been assembled during his absence. Not that he spent much time with the folders and documents that were accumulating on his desk.

"I'll get to it–just keep the stuff coming," he would tell Miss Mason, his long-time secretary, as another flying trip called him to Canada or Mexico or the West Coast.

Miss Mason knew the pattern. She had worked with it, and around it, and in spite of it, for twenty-odd years. When he had an idea stirring around in his mind, he seemed to put off coming to a decision and was satisfied to have staff members crowd his desk and his office with impedimenta, which once included a number of pickled specimens in tall glass jars that gave off a bad odor. If the idea failed to survive this trial by inertia, Miss Mason knew it when he exclaimed, coming fresh from a trip:

"For God's sake, Miss Mason! What is this junk all over the place? Get rid of it!"

She dressed properly: dark skirt and white shirtwaist closed at the throat with a pink cameo or silver brooch. But in the inner office where she performed prodigious feats with typewriter and filing cabinets, she often swore colorfully and at length and smoked cigarettes in a blue haze. Adam never entered her domain, though he had once come to the threshold and had staggered away at the sight of her pounding the typewriter keys, her skirt pulled above her knees, and a cigarette hanging from her lower lip.

A letter from A. T. Rafferty, Superintendent and S.D.A., managed to go unanswered, in spite of Miss Mason's usual vigilance about such matters. It simply dropped out of sight among accumulating documents.

"I have in mind," the letter ran, "your offer to look for the medicine bundle and the possibility that you might return it in person, when you locate it. Needless to say, the Indians here set great store by the object. It seems to represent a kind of controlling force in their universe–if that is the proper way of expressing it. I trust we may have a report soon. The Indians seem to think I can do something about retrieving this lost treasure."

While the letter did not immediately stimulate the search that had been promised, it did encourage an inquiry of a different, though not unrelated, sort.

Adam's office, one of several through which he moved, occupied a large second-floor corner suite of his museum, The Americana Institute, which sat on a gentle knoll overlooking an uptown park. The building was a great quadrangle of limestone and marble occupying most of a city block, with a glass-sheltered Mexican garden of banana palms and shrieking parrots filling the hollow center. And here, soon after his return from the West, he began at first to browse and presently to dig avidly through the accumulation of reports, Congressional hearings, surveys, and a miscellany of public and private petitions and protests borrowed from various libraries across the country. Miss Mason was content to see him thus occupied. It meant that her labor and the labor of other staff members in assembling the material would not be wasted.

And browsing and digging, he began to discover a history of events that shocked him. He would call out from his desk: "Great jumping Lucifer! How can such things be? Miss Mason! Get me the senator on the phone!" And he meant the senior senator from New York State with whom he had been associated as client and friend for many years.

And later: "This is monstrous! Get me the judge. Ask him to have dinner with me, if he's free." The judge, a member of the appellate court, was another close associate from his first years in the East.

All he obtained from these students of the law, and from others, including finally the solicitor for the Department of the Interior, was a confirmation of what he found in the public record and had rejected as unworthy. The conversations left him feeling exposed and naked, and considerably embarrassed. He had rushed into these discussions with some confidence, expecting his good friends, lawyers all, to click their tongues and nod their heads in agreement. He had not permitted his mind to wander in the mystic realms of legal remedy, realizing that the events, however fresh and strong the stench, were ex post facto—events of fifteen, twenty, even fifty years past. But at least he had been sure of sharing a common sense of outrage. The past might not be remedied, perhaps never could be, he thought, but ways might be found to devise a present equity.

What denuded him was the discovery that his sentiments were *not* shared, that what he expressed, however indignantly he said it, was just a personal sentiment. With kindly hands, they led him through the jungle of the law: to John Marshall: *By common accord, the nations of the world recognized the right of each to chew off what it could, and to keep what it could hold*; to Vattel: *The nation with superior skill could appropriate to its own use the domain of a less accomplished people.* They even led him to the Christian Bible: *Multiply, and make the earth bear fruit.*

These were not sentiments, these were principles of international politics – and how was it that he, a businessman of the world, should be raising such questions?

Indian lands had been taken because they would be put to a higher order of use, because they would contribute to the advancement of a higher order of society – and the law had legitimized such taking. The law was in society and society was in the law. Could he imagine what it would be like otherwise? Whose law, whose society, were irrelevant and immaterial questions.

Adam had not placed his query at such sublime heights, but the judge, Judge Carruthers, liked to elevate simple legal questions to levels of abstraction which discouraged argument over particulars. Moreover, their talks took place in the decorous air of the Harvard Club, usually at a remote dinner table for two, where the speaking voice was instinctively modulated. The judge preferred the Harvard Club over the Yale Club, of which he was also a member, because of a tendency at the latter for gentlemen to shout to one another across the dining room. And he knew that Adam had a tendency to get up and stride around when his mind was exercised – an activity not encouraged at the Harvard, in either the dining room or the lounge.

So Adam sat aghast, but helpless, while the judge exposed him as a romanticist without, of course, resorting to that word.

"A great nation, one of the powers of the modern world, has been built on this continent. Should we have left it in virgin forest where the red man chased his dinner through the undergrowth?"

Adam's fading blond hair looked especially ashen in the lamplight. His very long upper body, clothed in tweed, yielded only slightly to the necessity of bending forward to the table – and be-damned if he would yield in any degree to the judge's chauvinism. That's what it was, but Adam was equally considerate and did not utter the word aloud.

"I'm not talking against progress. That's how I make my living," he said in a voice as mild as the lamplight. "But these people should also share in that progress, which is not going to happen if they are robbed of their resources and chased off into the desert.

"I'm not trying to argue legal principles with you, I know my limitations. I'm against thievery, and that's what happened out there. The law was clear – and I'm not raising the question whether such a law should have been passed. It was on the books, and it said clearly that the President, at his discretion, could divide up an Indian reservation held in common ownership and give each man, woman, and child a piece of that common property. The President didn't have to ask the Indians whether they wanted it that way, and even if they opposed it to a man, he could still do it. The law was clear. He could go further, consulting only his political advantage. He could invite white men to come into that reservation—though it might be protected by treaty against alienation—and take up homesteads on any lands left after each Indian had been given a little piece of his own earth.

"All right. That was in the law and it was very clear. But now I'm talking about what happened at the Little Elk Reservation. After the land was divided among the Indians and white men were invited—exhorted, really, with literature advertising the rare qualities of soil and climate and mountain wealth—a grave miscalculation was discovered. The land was really too arid and parched to make a crop oftener than once every four or five years. It needed to be irrigated. While this conclusion was being verified by expert studies and discussions were going on about what to do, the first homesteaders began to go broke and everybody set up a great outcry. So Congress authorized the construction of an irrigation system.

"The law didn't authorize the President to divide up the water as well as the land, but Congress—our Congress, you and I—decided to do just that. There were several perennial streams that came out of mountain snowpacks and flowed out of the valley to join a river flowing through an adjoining valley. The mountains were still owned by the Indians—no white man wanted to homestead a mountain peak—and the water flowing out of them was certainly their property.

"So Congress said, 'Build dams, collect the water, and put it on the land.' I built one of those dams—or rather, a construction company in which I am involved built it. The last of a series of dams, the largest, and I believe the best. I had no knowledge of this background when I went out there. It was just a job of construction and my company built a good dam.

"Now, two things emerge. One: Very few Indians had taken pieces of land in the open valley when the reservation was divided up. They knew about the hot, dry summers, the treeless, unsheltered flats. They made their selections in the foothills, in the timber country, along forested streams. Consequently, when their main perennial streams were blocked off and diverted out to the dry valley, only the white homesteaders benefited. No compensation went to the Indians for this appropriation of their property.

"Two: The Indians had received money for the land which had been taken over by the homesteaders—at a dollar and a quarter an acre, I believe. This was not a negotiated price. The government, our government, you and I, just said, 'That's what we'll pay, in order to encourage strangers to come and take your land.' This revenue was deposited in the United States Treasury as it was paid to the government. And would you believe it, these funds which, like the land itself, were held in common ownership for the Little Elk Indians—this money was used by the government to pay for surveys, soil studies, engineering estimates and all manner of preliminary work that went into the development of the irrigation project, to benefit the government-invited homesteaders. I haven't yet found out whether any of this diverted money has been replaced.

"The latest thing I've discovered, and I haven't reached the bottom of the pile yet, is that the reservoir sites—these are areas containing thousands of acres in which the mountain water is impounded, the ownership of which is still in the tribe—these sites were taken without agreement or compensation of any kind, as far as I can determine, and again, without benefit to the Indians.

"Now, Judge," and Adam's voice finally began to climb to a level just noticeably above the modulated tone of the room, "will you tell me that such conduct is what makes a nation great? The Indians say we killed the water, and damned if they aren't right!"

"But Adam," the judge said, advancing his white head as if to convey a very private thought, "you know as well as I that political action is often hasty and not well considered."

Adam pulled away from the confidential tête-à-tête. "The actions I've been describing occurred over a twenty-year period. One could hardly say they were taken in haste. I would say they were well and ingeniously considered as devices to exploit the Indians."

He broke off, then veered the direction of his thought. "I'm too old to be making these discoveries. A younger man would feel he could do something about it—like Carlos, when he set out to remake the world at Cuno."

The judge looked puzzled. "Cuno? Never heard of it."

"Well, it's too long a story for now. Carlos had this advantage at the beginning—he had something to give, he could show good faith—"

At that point he smacked the table with the flat of his hand. The clapping sound went through the murmuring shadows like a pistol shot. Dishes jumped and faces turned toward the judge's table.

Adam excused himself as gracefully as he could. "Maybe I do have something to give! Maybe I do!" He left the club, trailing the topcoat he retrieved from the cloakroom.

His first act when he reached his desk the next morning was to call for Rafferty's letter, and for the first time he gave it a careful reading.

What followed after that, or what failed to follow, involved Adam in the final disaster at Little Elk.

"Ah, my kinsmen! My journey has been long since I left camp two days ago. A long journey. Almost to the end. But, you see, I came back!"

Two Sleeps would say no more. Not then. He needed to sit by himself, smoking his long-stemmed pipe. He huddled close to Veronica's morning fire, his stubby old feet pushed toward the warm ashes. He knew the camp waited to hear what he would say, but he would not talk about it. He let his pipe go cold and drop from his hands, and he seemed to sleep.

It had been, as he said, a long journey. Behind his closed eyes, shutting the others out, he traveled again out of the camp, as he had traveled two days before. If he could follow it out, just as it happened, if he could see everything again, he might escape the fear. It might then be that he could talk about it.

It had been afternoon when he left camp. Snow lay deep and quiet under the pine trees, and a fresh storm was moving darkly against the mountains. Weather made no difference for what he had to do. He wrapped his old legs in strips of woolen blanket; a robe made from a winter-killed buffalo calf weighed upon his body, and his white head was swathed in otter fur. He toiled up the trail like a slow-footed bear after eating heavily.

The winter night came quickly, the storm bringing it on, but he moved even so. Old men who have lived a long time with their own thoughts know how to be at ease with the night. And storms are filled with the voices they wish to hear.

So he moved up a trail that was not there, and when the wind paused and seemed to listen, his own voice sang steadily on, as if to encourage the wind.

"My friend, the storm, I am still with you," he chanted. His voice was like laughter.

He moved in what he saw as a shower of light, a mantle that spread from him and moved with him in the night—but only darkness encompassed him. The ice crystals which formed on his lashes refracted the bright-lying snow and tricked his faltering eyes.

He remembered another such night of cold-blowing wind and snow, at a time so distant now that it was scarcely more than a feeling of fear, the pictures were so dim and ragged. He was with his own people then, a people who lived east of the mountains, far out in the prairie along a big river. He had been with a hunting party following a buffalo herd which moved upstream toward the mountains. Another hunting party was also there—waiting. A heavy snowstorm came during the night, and in the morning while the snow still fell and muffled all sound, the waiting mountain people charged the camp, and red blood streaked the white snow. He was then a young man, and a young wife waited for him on the bank of the big river. For two days he lay as dead from a skull blow. The small hunter's tepee had been knocked over during the attack and the raiders missed him when they gathered up their prizes and rode away.

When he came from the dead and crawled into daylight, he didn't know where he was or where he came from, and he didn't know which way to go. And he was alone, without a horse or a weapon. He walked into the mountains, following a snow-buried stream. He saw game, but could not reach it. He chewed twigs and ate snow. One day, from a ridge, he watched a great herd of buffalo in a sheltering valley—but by then he was too weak to go down to it.

That night, when he knew he had reached the end, he saw a small fire throwing a pale glow against pine trees. He stood up tall, singing his death song—and that was when he joined the people, of which Enemy Horse, Bull's father, was then headman.

Now it was another night of cold-blowing wind and whipping snow. It might be the night to finish off what did not end the first time. But a man learned much in a lifetime, including one special thing. Above all else, a man learned to be strong in support of his kinsmen. A man by himself was nothing, a shout in the wind. But men together, each acting for each other and as one—even a strong wind from an enemy sky had to respect their power.

This night he was acting for those who took him in as a kinsman—nothing else would prevail, not even death.

He emerged from the heavy timber and skirted an open face of the mountain, where a sharp-edged wind swept fiercely up from the black depths of the valley and lashed the snow into a fury of whirling ice clouds. He slowed, wavered. He crawled on all fours for a while, a dark creature pushing its way into a nameless and forbidding world.

When he could get to his feet again and his breath returned, he still sang: "My friend, the storm, I am here with you! My brother, the storm wind, stay here with me!"

The wind came roaring again, turned shrill, and exploded against a barrier of thrusting rock.

The frost reached his blood and his face turned to stone, but he crawled ahead. The fire within his body would keep him going awhile longer. And then he would dream. The dreams that come just this side of death were the strongest of all, but only a strong man dared go that far. Only the very strong came back.

It was becoming difficult to hold his thoughts together. They flew up and away from him and it was necessary to hold on to them. He had to work out what it was like to be in the world, to have an understanding. If death was to come, he wanted to be full of understanding. Even to be smiling at what he understood.

To be born was not enough. To live in the world was not enough. How was it, then? He stood there, swaying slightly, trying to hold it in his mind. When he moved again, he was following his thought once more, but it was getting dim. One had to reach. That was what a man had to do. It pulled him along. He had to reach with his mind into all things, the things that grew from small beginnings and the things that stayed firmly placed and enduring. He had to know more and more, until he himself dissolved and became part of everything else – and then he would know certainly. Reaching with his mind was part of that, a kind of dissolving into the mist that was at once the small seed from which the pine tree would grow and the mountain that endured forever. And a man was there, in the middle, reaching to become part of it. That was something of what it was like to be in the world.

And yet, there was more – if he could hold fast to it.

By the time he had crossed the mountain's face and was again in a sheltering grove, his strength was leaving his quaking body. Breath came in fast and shallow gasps. Numbness began to seal off all feeling. While he still knew what he was about, he crawled under the spreading arms of a spruce tree, where he dug a hole in the quiet snow. There he rolled himself into a ball within his buffalo robe.

And there he dreamed.

■ NORMAN MACLEOD

Born in Oregon in 1906, Norman Macleod lived in Missoula during the 1920s, when his mother taught in the University of Montana's Speech Department. He received a master's degree from Columbia University in 1936 and was the founder of the New York Poetry Center, which he directed from 1939 to 1942. Macleod taught at many colleges throughout the country before his death in 1986. "The Trouble with Girls" is from The Bitter Roots *(1941), and "We Played the Flatheads at Arlee" is from Macleod's* Selected Poems *(1975).*

The Trouble with Girls

I.W.W. no worse than La Follette. Dean Larsson discusses freedom of speech at Public Forum. Another point of view was expressed by an unknown questioner who asked: "How far do you think you would get in an argument with Max Eastman or Emma Goldman? . . . Charles M. Schwab, president of the Bethlehem Steel Corporation, declared in an address at a dinner here tonight that the time was near at hand "when the men of the workingclass—the men without property—would have control of the destinies of the world."

The New Year had come and gone.

Betty Darling had the shakes for many months after her cruel experience with Harold. It took time to rebuild the confidence she'd had in herself. If Betty were to rope any Romeos, first of all she would have to get the incense of evil out of her mind. The letter she had received from Lonely comforted her. Her brother was learning all there was to know about France. He'd be going up to the front line trenches soon. And if the Boche hadn't heard about Montana so far. . . . Powder River, Let 'Er Buck!

Betty went to the high-school drags that were thrown in the local gymnasium, where the balconies were draped with purple and gold brocade. The baskets were swung up against the roof. By such simple magic, a basketball court was turned into a seventeenth-century salon. Most of the time, Betty refused to dance. She wanted to make up her mind about life and you couldn't do that very well in the arms of some boy!

School every morning. At night, there was the stiff figure of her father, the lines of worry creasing his forehead. The bank was not well these days, for people were land-poor.

When Betty went upstairs to go to bed in a lonely house, she worried; and at night she dreamed about Harold. The man who had described and questioned her body, and left it unanswered. The boy who had made a jest of her. While blizzards swept over the mountains, Betty slept in a house that was not her home. She lived in the house of her father, where smoke of expensive Havana tobacco lay heavy on the air at suppertime. The maid came and went along the dark hallways. There were too many rooms in the Darling house, now that the mother was dead, and Lonely had gone to fight the war on another continent.

Who was there now to warm the heart of a young girl in a world that was too big for her?

Betty had thought herself a tomboy. She had admired Lonely when he wasn't too drunk, but Harold had changed that! Now, Betty didn't know what to think.

When it came to the dance held at the gymnasium in January, the snow had frozen and the ground was hard. Betty appeared in a white dress that revealed her growing loveliness, with her hair curled and a white ribbon tied neatly over her left ear. There was no use in being a tomboy, now that she was fast on the way to being grown-up. Her breasts grew larger as the winter advanced. She'd forget Harold if it was the last thing she ever did, Betty thought.

Betty was all right!

Augie was sure of that, as he came barging down the basketball floor. He'd give her a swing, Augie would, for Betty was tender. She was young as the sprout. The greener the flower, the whiter the root! Augie was definitely impressed with Betty, and the Pastor couldn't possibly object to her father. Not that Augie was the marrying kind, and him so young, but if it ever came out! Should Sullivan say, for instance, "I hear you're goin' fancy!"

The banker's bank would shut that out.

For Betty was tender!

"May I have this dance?" Augie said in his best Sunday-school English.

Betty floated into his arms like a dream, her flesh was so soft and her dress was so white, and she moved like a cloud. You'd never have guessed, from the overalls she used to wear and her raucous speech, that Betty could be so lovely. But Lonely was long gone in France and Betty had changed. She should be interesting out on a date, from what Stiff Sullivan said. Augie was sure that Harold had missed a few points. Harold would! How in hell a lady like Betty had gone for that fag was more than the Pastor's son could understand.

But he'd soon find out!

Between dances, Augie sneaked out to the lockers to get a snort. Drinking was a new angle he'd learned from his last trip to Butte, when he'd tangled with Serafimovitch and that crowd. Pocketful of Sen-Sen, and you munched it hard, and didn't come home until late. Pastor never guessed what went on. Sen-Sen worked.

Betty knew that Augie was drinking. She didn't mind it if he didn't get goofed up too much. Like when she remembered Lonely's fraternity brothers and the way they had pushed her around in the billiard room in the cellar of her father's house to the fox trots they'd played on the victrola. So she knew what whiskey felt like from the breath of it on her cheek. It was better than the five-and-dime incense of Harold and his chicken coop! Augie was a boy that Lonely would've liked. It took boys like that for Betty to grow fond of! But for several months she had wondered if there was something wrong with her that Harold should have acted so bad.

She'd find out tonight!

Augie had stoked the furnace of the Pastor's house well. He could stay out as long as he pleased. He'd borrowed the Pastor's car. He'd take Betty for a ride, after the dance was over. If he got goofed up enough.

Augie would sow his wild oats while he was young, while Norval was strewing his grain on the fertile fields of France.

When Sullivan had suggested going to see Penny, Augie was scared half out of his pants. They'd gone down to the rooms of Madam Nellie's Hotel. They'd walked up the stairs to the second floor lobby. The Madam with skirts flowing like *Thais* floated up the hall.

"Yes, what will you boys have?" she asks real polite.

Augie, no kidding, is weak at the knees!

No good to let Sullivan know, so Augie swaggers up to the Madam and says, "The best in the house!"

Madam smiles faintly, but is too much of a lady to let out she catches on. She ushers Sullivan and Augie into the sitting room, and they both sit down on the edges of their chairs, formally, only Augie a little more so. He keeps his lips buttoned!

"What comes now?" says Augie.

"Keep your pants on!" Sullivan sneers. "All in good time."

So Augie droops back into his chair, but tries to get a cynical look in his face.

Well, of course, Penny comes in and she is a sight for sore eyes. Long and slinky, black hair and dark eyes. She has a kimona over her body. She's not too careful about covering up the breasts, either. Penny looks at Augie, who is new to the place.

"A friend of yours?" she asks, turning to Stiff.

"We knock around some," Sullivan admits.

The other nest takes Sullivan, and Penny goes off with Augie into her bedroom. And that was where the trouble began!

Augie fumbled with fear. His bones went soft as gumbo mud in the rain. His whole body wilted, and he thought of the sturdy rocks of mountain crags, steadfast and clean, the smell of pine cones, and the prickle of kinnikinnick, whittled by the wind. The wild parsnips of summer white on the plain. Augie was new at the game, and remembered everything that his mother never told him. The Pastor, his father, believed in God, but had never gotten around to giving his son any practical advice. The only coaching Augie had ever received had been from his older brother.

But Norval was far away.

Augie did the best he could! He fought a losing fight facing the stiff current. He came up, like Honey Pie, clutching for straws. Drowned. In the soft red lushness and the simpering sneers of Penny that would make him a man! Augie had carried it off in seeing the Madam and on the trip upstairs. For the rest, it was a quick passage through strange waters, and then a battery of instruments that frightened him half out of his wits. "What d'yuh think I mean?" Penny had said. "Think I want to shake hands?" and she had laughed pleasantly in a professional sort of way. Damn! But there was a helluva lot of white fat on her behind!

Going back down the hallway, Augie recovered enough to become curious. "You ever go out?" he asked. "Do you go out to eat, you go out to get the air, you go out to smoke or buy a newspaper, or go to a movie or have a sundae?"

"No," Penny replied. "I stay here!"

She laughed to the other garden: "He ain't planted much around here!" Penny snickered and Stiff Sullivan looked wise. OK, the Pastor's son was all right. You'd never see a better guy with a cue or a collection plate come Christian Sundays when the Pastor was talking about the war!

"Augie'll learn," Stiff Sullivan said to the girls.

But the Madam didn't show and Augie felt like on some of those mountains at night. You're up twelve thousand feet in the snows in a barrack of rocks to hide you from the storm. You light the fire and it casts some rainbows in the sky. Eyes glow in the underbrush around you. And you measure the space between the eyes and you match coins to see whether it's a coyote, a cougar, a lynx, or a plain damn figment of the imagination. And you always win! No referee. And it's fine fun! Then, you start gassing, or remembering, about all the girls you took out that you've never seen since. You open a can of beans, fry some bacon, burn some spuds, and the fire begins to die out.

It's cold.

The dawn comes up grey over the mountains.

And you're lonely. Afraid! And you go out of the whorehouse feeling like that, and wishing the Madam was around so you could crack wise.

"Come back again when you're more at attention," Penny laughed, as she turned around her fat behind and walked down the hallway.

Augie hoped to Christ he didn't get himself in a sling. He wished Norval were around to give him some good advice!

Augie finished the bottle of whiskey in the locker room. He felt fine! Wiping his mouth with his handkerchief, he turned and walked back to the dance floor where Betty was waiting for him. They danced around the place a few times as the orchestra was playing *Home, Sweet Home*. After the dance was over, Betty wrapped herself warmly in the coat her father had given her for Christmas. Outside the gymnasium, Augie opened the door of the car for Betty to climb in. It was a sedan. Rare in these parts. And fairly warm in winter! Augie lit a cigarette and stepped on the starter.

He wondered if Betty was warm? She looked bright enough in the fair beauty of her skin. She was sweet and human in a way that Penny never had been. Augie saw that the banker's daughter was tucked in securely with the robe around her feet and thighs. Only her soft face showed clearly in the light coming from the dashboard.

Augie shifted gears.

Skidding crazily around the corner down Higgins Avenue, he gunned the car on the straightaway, pressing the throttle hard. The wind rode past like buffalo in stampede. The mountains shining in the stiff, white light of the moon, were remote as remembered desire. His car, a black beetle, shot forward in the steel-encased jacket that kept the world outside. Augie's silent exhilaration was running the clock!

With the alcohol deep in his veins and Betty beside him.

Not that Augie was interested in girls to the extent of marriage! But all of his life he'd known and admired Lonely. He'd never have dared to talk to his sister if he had wanted to in those early days. Now, Lonely was gone and Betty was no longer the stripling kid in overalls.

She was full-blown and soft like a question. One he would know the answer to:

And why was Harold?

The car was parked in the blind alley of a coulee beyond Fort Missoula, where the mountains began. In the back seat of the sedan, Betty was serving as a cushion. She felt the strong masculine odor of whiskey and cigarette breath on her cheek. The lisp of liquor on Augie's lips tasted good. At least, the Pastor's son had kissed her the way she should be kissed! She went soft under the hard muscle of Augie's body. It was clean because it was like Lonely. It was like Missoula, and Lonely's fraternity brothers, and like all of the life she had been through, and yet it was strange and undiscovered. Betty was on guard, for all her softness!

She marveled at Augie's movement and boyhood strength. His rosy cheeks were hot under the thin white threads of her fingers. But when his hands drew up along her naked thighs and felt like fever on her belly–

Betty Darling cried. She jacknifed like the snap of long and steel-sharp scissors. Nothing like Harold would come again in her life! Not until words meant something real to her heart, not until lips could speak and eyes could sense the loneliness of her thought. Silence shut in the valley of her body.

On the road back to Missoula, Augie sulked.
Returning to the outhouse of God, Augie was sore.
He hoped to Christ Sullivan had himself in a sling!
For teaching him about love.

We Played the Flatheads At Arlee

From miles around the Indians came to see us
Play basketball against the Flatheads at Arlee.
The stakes were high and the floor narrow–
The Indians wore their black hair parted,
Drawn back sharp as the split edge of a tomahawk
From both sides of the copper forehead.
        The game was angry–
Never until the dead end were we

Sure of winning.
    But if they lost,
We knew it had not always been their habit
To be losing.
    Never had basketball on a Jesuit court
Been a game of their own choosing.

■ HUGHIE CALL

Born in Trent, Texas, in 1890, Hughie Florence Call attended Trinity University in San Antonio. She and her husband raised sheep near Ennis in the Madison and Yellowstone river valleys of Montana. Call wrote several books for young people, but her most popular work is Golden Fleece *(1942). This selection from* Golden Fleece *offers an inside view of community and connection in an isolated country that was just beginning to experience the technology of the twentieth century. Call died in 1969.*

The Rural Telephone

The country telephone is something more than mere wires strung on tall poles, than receivers and mouthpieces. It is a living, vibrant thing which welds the interests and problems of isolated communities in a way that is past understanding.

The telephones are even equipped with a convenience for the eavesdropper–a little gadget on the left side of the instrument which can be released if you want to talk or left in place if you'd rather listen. Thus is quiet ensured. A mother can balance a fretting baby on her hip and get the news without having to worry lest the noise disturb her neighbors.

Many ranch wives do their own work and have only snatches of time between dishwashing and potato-peeling and the cooking and serving of three huge meals a day. They may have a spare moment to listen, but no time to become involved in talk. The country telephone has all the advantages of the radio or the talking machine. It can be turned on or off at will. No danger of your pies burning while you learn the latest local news, for you can leave your post without seeming rude, take a peek at the pies and come back again. You may have missed a little, but you can always catch up if the conversation interests you enough.

I shall never forget my first contact with "listening in." I walked into the dining-room one morning to find Jennie leaning indolently against the wall, the receiver glued to her ear. This surprised me. Until that day I had never seen Jennie idle. Ordinarily she whizzed around with a purpose and energy that put me to shame. I was pleased to see her take time off for–I suppose–a chat with a friend.

I had come downstairs to ask some question and I went on into the kitchen to wait until she was through. She didn't get through. Moments elapsed before it dawned on me that Jennie was eavesdropping.

Grim with disapproval, I came back to the dining-room, pulled a chair out from the table and sat down. Jennie might have me bested and on the defensive where ranch work was concerned, but I felt I could teach her a thing or two about ethics and I meant to do it.

I waited and Jennie listened.

The moments ticked on and finally I said, "Jennie, I'd like to speak to you." I was not handling this matter well and the knowledge put an edge of sharpness to my voice.

I expected her to drop the receiver sheepishly, but not Jennie. She gestured for silence and listened ten minutes longer. When at last she put the receiver back on its hook and turned about, I was too angry to care what I said and I voiced my distaste in no uncertain terms. Her calm eyes widened with surprise.

"Why, Missus," she told me, as though conveying a fact I'd be delighted to hear, "that's all right. Everybody listens. You're supposed to. It's a good thing I did. Ellison's ditch broke and flooded the road for a quarter of a mile. Old man Thayer's stuck down there with a truck full of hogs and Jim Anderson's taking a team to pull him out. He . . ."

I cut her short and explained with all the patience I could muster that I was not interested in other people's business. I should have said more, but she interrupted excitedly: "But Missus, it *is* our business. The Boss's trucks was coming that way with cottonseed cake. If they get stuck, it'll take a block and tackle to get them out. I'm going to ring down the line and ask the Thextons to send them up through the field."

That took a little of the wind out of my sails, but I was still unconvinced and indignant. When she had delivered her message, I warned her that I never wanted to see her "listening in" again.

She took me literally. I never *saw* her do it, but oh, how she listened! That woman knew everything that happened within a radius of fifty miles and she naïvely regaled the ranch hands at meal time with the gossip. She knew that the Ellisons had sowed their oats before the "shiftless Burtons" had more than broken their ground. She knew when the Lawtons sold their hogs and what they got for them. She was righteously indignant when the doctor in a near-by town refused to bring the Burton baby into the world, because he hadn't yet been paid for the last five Burton heirs. This story shattered my heroic reserve and I urged Jennie to go right down and see what she could do; I even offered to take her down.

"Grandma Bassett'll go. She's the closest."

"But she may not know about it. It would be criminal to leave that poor woman alone at a time like this!"

She looked me squarely in the eye before she turned back to her work. "Don't worry," she said. "She *knows*."

She did know. I later learned that Grandma Bassett had taken immediate charge of the Burton affairs, had browbeaten the doctor into making another entry on the debit side of his ledger, and furthermore had stayed with the mother until she was up and about again.

Several months later a lamb buyer telephoned Tom and offered him nine dollars per hundredweight for his lambs. Tom would not commit himself, but promised to think it over. No sooner had he put down the phone than our ring came through. I answered, and a woman's excited voice called over the wire: "Tell Tom not to take nine dollars for his lambs. I heard that lamb buyer make Jim Anderson the same offer last night and Jim upped him to nine dollars and a quarter."

I did a sum in mental arithmetic before I replaced the receiver. That message would make Tom some money. Jennie eyed me expectantly as I turned away from the phone, but I took a mean advantage. I refused to relay the message until Tom and I were alone.

These two incidents gave me food for thought, but it took something that struck even closer to bring me into line. Leigh was not quite a year old at the time. Jennie had married a "dry farmer" and we had a man cook. I wouldn't admit that it was dull without Jennie, for if it was, I knew why. I missed her chatter—and her "listening in."

One afternoon during the first lamb drive of the season, the ranch was deserted save for Cy, the cook, my young son and I. Cy adored the baby and spent all his spare time amusing him. I had letters to write, so I left them together on the back porch and went upstairs to my desk. Cy had been peeling green apples, and upon my return I found the baby alone, gurgling gleefully, with his small mouth full of apple peelings. I was frightened, of course, and worried throughout the balance of the afternoon because I couldn't be sure just how many peelings he had swallowed.

By ten o'clock that night I knew he had swallowed too many. He grew restless, cried out repeatedly in his sleep and began to run a temperature. I did everything I knew to do, but my efforts were futile. Around midnight his body began to twitch and draw. I considered calling Cy, but to do so I should have to go to the bunkhouse, some eight hundred yards away, and I dared not leave my son.

Terrified, I sped down the stairs and tried to call the doctor. His wife answered the telephone. She told me he was out in the country, on a maternity case; she doubted if she could get word to him.

"You've got to get word to him!" I gasped. "I'm all alone, and I'm afraid my baby is having convulsions!"

She assured me she would try, but she didn't sound encouraging. I was frantic with fear, and for a moment I clung shakily to the receiver, wondering if there was anything else I could do. Even now Leigh could die before the doctor got back to town and then drove all those miles to our ranch . . . Just as I was on the point of returning the receiver to the hook, a woman's voice called out:

"See here, child, have you any hot water?"

"Yes . . . *Yes.*"

"Put your baby into a warm bath right away, and get some cold compresses on his head. Jeff's backing out the car this minute and I'll be with you as soon as I can make it."

If you've ever been alone, ignorant and helpless, with someone you love slipping away before your eyes, you'll know what that message meant to me. I carried out her instructions, eased the small, rigid body of my son into a warm bath and placed cold compresses on his head. After what seemed hours to me, my neighbor arrived.

She took charge with the efficiency that comes of long practice, while I carried out her orders. We fought shoulder to shoulder—I, white and shaken and no doubt clumsy and ineffectual; she, grimly, but very, very surely. Ah, that woman, that blessed woman. I can hear her now . . . "There, he's comin' out of it . . . Look, his eyes is back natural . . . Now his breathing's easier . . . You ain't sick, you onery rascal. You're just tryin' to scare your poor ma to death."

When the doctor's car drove up to our door, Leigh was sleeping quietly and naturally. The doctor assured me that everything had been done as he himself would have done it.

There are some things you can't thank people for, things that are too big for words, but I clung to my neighbor's work-worn hand and did my feeble best. She patted my shoulder in her friendly fashion and laughed.

"Lord, child, you needn't thank me, just give thanks for the party line. I knew nobody would be ringing town that time of night unless they were in trouble. I just naturally had to get up and listen."

She didn't think she'd done anything unusual. She'd have done the same thing for anybody. But I had learned a lesson. From that time on I "listened in" brazenly and I was never dull any more.

One afternoon I overheard a rancher's wife call him in town and tell him to bring home some bread. They expected the threshers the next day, and she couldn't bake because something had gone wrong with her yeast. Her husband was so absent-minded that he was a community joke, and I worried about that bread until I heard his car rattling down the hill. It was a mere skeleton—that car. A box, nailed to a few boards, formed the seat. Nothing was hidden; even the engine had no hood. If the bread was there I couldn't help but see it, and I rushed out to the yard to have a look. Sure enough, he'd forgotten the bread. Before I had time to think, I found myself running down the road in his wake.

"You've forgotten Bertha's bread!" I shrieked. "We baked today. You'd better take some of ours."

The car stopped with a sudden grinding of brakes. He got out and thanked me sheepishly. As I packed the still warm loaves in a box it never occurred to him to ask, "How did you know that Bertha needed bread?" and it never occurred to me to enlighten him.

Another time, in the busiest part of haying season I overheard a hardware merchant in town telling a rancher that it would take three days to get new teeth for a broken rake. "Hay-diggers" work against time in this country. The season is so short that every hour counts. I knew that the laying up of a rake for three days was nothing short of a tragedy. We had the same kind of rakes and some extra teeth. I got into my car and took them down to him. He was grateful, but not a whit surprised.

I don't think I ever knew the real meaning of neighborliness until I came to Montana. Ours was a large, closeknit family. We were sufficient unto ourselves, and had few contacts with our neighbors. In my home city I sometimes sent flowers when I happened to learn that a neighbor was ill. In this country, with the doctor miles away, illness can assume alarming proportions. You always know about it, via the rural telephone line. You don't send flowers, you *take* an extra hot-water bottle, a bag of ice or a change of bed linen. Sometimes the only help you can give is releasing a worried mother from the kitchen, for ranch work must go on, illness or no. But whatever there is to do, you do it gladly, knowing full well that when trouble strikes, the same will be done for you.

I never complain now when I'm trying desperately to hear over long distance, although every receiver that goes down weakens the telephone circuit more and more. I just yell a little louder.

I'll have to confess that there are times when I wish I had the courage of a Forest Ranger in our district. There was a rumor abroad that the Government intended lowering grazing fees on the Forest, and this was a matter of vital importance to every sheepman on the line. All the receivers were down and it became increasingly harder for the Ranger to hear. Presently he could no longer hear. Patience exhausted, he slammed the receiver down on the hook and gave the general ring.

"Listen, folks," he begged, "I can't make head nor tail of what the supervisor says unless you hang up. Do it as a favor to me and when I'm through talking, I'll ring back and tell you what he says!"

He didn't keep his word, though, and I've always had a grudge against him. I had to learn the Government's decision from a neighbor who was "on to him" and wasn't taking a chance on missing a single thing.

■ JASON BOLLES

Henry Jason Bolles was born in Denison, Iowa, in 1900. As a young boy, he came to Montana with his widowed mother to homestead near Lewistown. Bolles was graduated from Montana State College in Bozeman in 1924. He worked as a surveyor for the Federal Bureau of Fisheries and was an ore sampler in Butte before returning to Bozeman in 1934 to teach in Montana State University's English Department. Bolles' collected poems, Magpie's Nest *(1943), were published by his widow soon after his unexpected death in 1942.*

Agency Town

Last evening I drove past the Agency.
A full-blood man in middle life came out,
Cat-footed down the sidewalk. He was well dressed;
That is, the nondescript assortment of clothes
He wore was fairly new, of average quality.
His broad gray Stetson was a better hat

Than most Indians can buy. "There goes a man
Of some importance in the tribe," I thought.
I was rolling along very gently, almost stopped
To give him plenty of room to cross in front of me.
I saw his lips move as he jerked anxious
Glances over his shoulder, made awkward haste
Across the road, looked back again suspiciously,
Then went in dignity on his soundless way.
I drove to the store to get a few supplies.
A little girl was standing in the doorway,
About ten years old, very dark and thin,
Her shapeless little dress faded and stained.
I touched her neat black hair, said, "Look out, Sis."
With a startled turn she got out of my way;
Not looking at me again, she stood behind
Her mother, who sat in a blanket on the floor.
The girl feigned great absorption in a showcase.
After a little while I saw her reach
Behind her quickly and feel the back of her head.
I went in the post office, stood at the writing stand
Addressing some letters. A young man came in,
Exchanged a few slurred syllables with the clerk,
And brought a post card over where I stood.
I did not notice that there was only one
Bottle of ink. He took a pen, looked about.
Then, instead of reaching in front of me,
He walked around behind me and dipped his pen
And said, "Excuse me, please." Nothing odd at all,
Except that his voice was just a shade too loud,
His accent more careful than it need have been.

Cows

My cows come up from pasture, walking slow,
The biggest leading by a little space.
Their feet are lifted, moved, set down just so,
With stinginess of effort that is grace.
My cows come up from pasture before night,
Reluctantly, their bellies taut and round,

Their long heads swinging at their shoulders' height.
Stiffly they inch across the trampled ground,
And snuff the barnyard gate that blocks their way.
They feign torpidity, and seem to drowse;
But soon they bellow, malcontent that they
Have come, that they must halt, that they are cows.
In the faint shining of the early stars,
I bring the buckets and let down the bars.

■ WALLACE STEGNER

Born in Iowa in 1909, Wallace Stegner spent his early childhood in North Dakota and Washington, his boyhood in Saskatchewan and Montana, and his adolescence in Utah. Stegner received his Ph.D. from the University of Iowa in 1935 and taught English at the universities of Utah and Wisconsin and at Harvard before taking a position at Stanford University. He became one of Stanford's distinguished professors and was director of the university's writing program until his retirement in 1969. Stegner's novel, Angle of Repose, *won the Pulitzer Prize in 1971, and his* The Spectator Bird *was awarded the 1977 National Book Award for fiction. His new, highly praised novel,* Crossing to Safety, *was published in 1987. These selections are from Stegner's autobiographical novel,* Big Rock Candy Mountain *(1943).*

From Big Rock Candy Mountain

In this summer of 1918, because Chet was staying in town to be delivery boy for Mr. Babcock in the confectionery store, the homestead was isolation and loneliness, though he never felt it or knew it for what it was. Only when his mother looked at his father and said they should never have let Chet take that job, it left Brucie too much alone. Then he felt vaguely disturbed and faintly abused, but he never did really believe he was lonely, because he loved the homestead, and the Sunday school hymns he sang to himself down in the flowered coulee meant to him very definite and secret and precious things, meant primroses and space and the wet slap of a rare east wind, and those tunes would mean those things to him all his life.

Still he was almost always alone, and that summer he somehow lost his identity as a name. There was no other boy to confuse him with; he wasn't Bruce, but "the boy," and because he was the only thing of his kind in all that summer world he needed no name, but only his own sense of triumphant identity. He knew the homestead in intimate and secret detail because there was so little variety in it that the small things took the senses. He knew the way the grass grew curling over the lip of a burnout, and how the prairie owls nested under those grassy lips. He knew how the robins tucked their nests back under the fringes of the prairie wool, and their skyblue eggs were always a wonder. He could tell, by the way the horses clustered in a corner of the pasture, when something was wrong, as when Dick got wound up in the lower strand of the fence and almost cut his leg off trying to break loose. He could tell instantly when a weasel was after the hens by the kind of clamor they made. Nothing else, for some reason, ever caused that fighting squawk from the mother hens. He could tell a badger's permanent burrow from the one he made in digging out a gopher. The yapping of coyotes on a moonlit night was lonely and beautiful to him, and the yard and chicken house and fireguard and coulee were as much a part of him as his own skin.

He lived in his own world in summer, and only when hail or wind or gophers or Russian thistle threatened the wheat on which he knew his father yearly gambled everything, was there much communication with the adult world whose interests were tied down to the bonanza farming and the crop. Wheat, he knew, was very high. The war did that. And he knew too that they were not well off, that every spring his father scraped together everything he had for seed and supplies and hoped for a good year so that he could clean up. He knew that they had less than most of the homesteaders around: they didn't have a barn, a cow (they had two in town, but it was a hard trip to bring them out), a seeder, a binder, a disc, a harrow. They didn't have much of anything, actually, except a team, a plow, and a stoneboat. Anything he didn't have tools for his father either borrowed tools to do, or hired done. But that frantic period of plowing and seeding came early, before his senses had adjusted themselves completely to the homestead, and later, in the period when they did practically nothing but sit and wait and hope that the weather would give them a crop, he moved in a tranced air of summer and loneliness and delight.

At the end of the first week in this summer he caught a weasel in one of his gopher traps, and brought it, still twisting and fighting in the trap, to the house. His father and mother came to the door; his mother made a face and shivered.

"Ugh!" she said. "Ugly, snaky thing!"

But his father showed more interest. "Got something special, uh?" he said. He came down and took the ringed chain from the boy's hand, held the weasel up. The weasel hissed in his face, trying to jump at him, and he straightened his arm to hold the swinging trap away.

"You've got to hand it to them," he said. "There isn't anything alive with more fight in it."

"Take it and kill it," Elsa said. "Don't just keep it in the trap torturing it."

Bruce was looking at his father. He ignored his mother's words because this was men's business. She didn't understand about weasels. "Maybe I could keep him till he turns into an ermine," he said.

"Why not?" his father said. "You could get three bucks for his pelt, these days. We ought to be able to make a cage that'd hold him."

"Oh, Bo," Elsa said. "Keep a weasel?"

"Give Boopus here something to do," Bo said. "You've been telling me we ought to get him a pet."

Bruce looked from one to the other, wondering when they had talked over getting him a pet. "We've got old Tom now," he said.

"Old Tom," his father said, "is so full of mice his mind is all furry."

"We ought to get a dog," Elsa said. "Not a vicious thing like a weasel."

"Well, we've got the weasel, and we don't know any place to get a dog." Bo looked down at the boy and grinned. He swung the weasel gently back and forth, and it arched its long yellow body against the trap and lunged. "Let's go make a cage for this tough guy," Bo said.

"Can I have a dog too?"

"Maybe. If I can find one."

"Holy catartin," Bruce said. "A cat, a dog, and a weasel. Maybe I can catch some more and start a weasel farm."

"I'd move out," his mother said. She waved them away. "Hurry up, if you're going to keep that bloodthirsty thing. Don't leave it in the trap with its broken leg."

They made a cage out of a beer-case, screened under the hinged top and with a board removed at the bottom, leaving an opening over which they tacked a strip of screen. They had trouble getting the weasel out of the trap, and finally Bo had to smother him in a piece of horse blanket and spring the jaws loose and throw blanket and all in the cage. For three days the weasel sulked in the corner and would eat nothing, but when the boy said he didn't think it was going to live his father laughed at him. "You can't kill a weasel just by breaking his leg. Put a mouse in there and see what happens."

Next day the boy rescued a half-dead mouse that Tom was satedly toying with under the bed, and dropped it in the cage. Nothing happened, but when he came back later the mouse was dead, with a hole back of his ear and his body limp and apparently boneless. The boy fished the carcass out with a bent wire, and from then on there was no question of the weasel's dying. The problem was to find enough mice, but after a few days he tried a gopher, and then it was all right.

There had been a wind during the night, and all the loneliness of the world had swept up out of the southwest. The boy had heard it wailing through the screens of the sleeping porch where he lay, and he had heard the wash tub bang loose from the outside wall and roll on down the coulee, and the slam of the screen door, and his mother's padding feet as she rose to fasten things down. Through one half-open eye he had peered up from his pillow to see the moon skimming windily in a luminous sky. In his mind's eye he had seen the prairie outside with its woolly grass and cactus white under the moon, and the wind, whining across that endless oceanic land, sang in the screens, and sang him back to sleep.

Now, after breakfast, when he set out through the pasture on the round of his traps, there was no more wind, but the air smelled somehow recently swept and dusted, as the house in town smelled after his mother's cleaning. The sun was gently warm on the bony shoulder blades of the boy, and he whistled, and whistling turned to see if the Bearpaws were in sight to the south. There they were, a tenuous outline of white just breaking over the bulge of the world; the Mountains of the Moon, the place of running streams and timber and cool heights that he had never seen—only dreamed of on days when the baked gumbo of the yard cracked in the heat and the sun brought cedar smells from fenceposts long since split and dry and odorless, when he lay dreaming on the bed with a Sears Roebuck or a T. Eaton catalogue before him, picking out the presents he would buy for his mother and his father and Chet and his friends next Christmas, or the Christmas after that. On those days he looked often and long at the snowy mountains to the south, while dreams rose in him like heat waves, blurring the reality of the unfinished shack and the bald prairie of his home.

The Bearpaws were there now, and he watched them a moment, walking, his feet automatically dodging cactus clumps, before he turned his attention to the scattered stakes that marked his traps. He ran the line at a half-trot, whistling.

At the first stake the chain was stretched tightly down the hole. The pull on its lower end had dug a little channel in the soft earth of the mound. Gently, so as not to break the gopher's leg off, the boy eased the trap out of the burrow, held the chain in his left hand, and loosened the stake with his right. The gopher tugged against the trap, but it made no noise. There were only two places where they made a noise: at a distance, when they whistled a warning, and in the weasel's cage. Otherwise they kept still.

For a moment he debated whether to keep this one alive for the weasel or to wait so he wouldn't have to carry a live one all the way around. Deciding to wait, he held the chain out, measured the rodent, and swung. The knobbed end of the stake crushed the skull, and the eyes popped out of the head, round and blue. A trickle of blood started from nose and ears. The feet kicked.

Releasing the gopher, the boy lifted it by the tail and snapped its tail fur off with a smart flip. Then he stowed the trophy carefully in the breast pocket of his overalls. For the last two years he had won the grand prize offered by the province to the school child who destroyed the most gophers. On the mantel in town were two silver loving cups, and in the cigar box under his bed in the farmhouse were already seven hundred forty tails, the catch of three weeks. In one way, he resented his father's distributing poison along the wheat field, because poisoned gophers generally got down their holes to die, and he didn't get the tails. So he spent most of his time trapping and snaring in the pasture, where poison could not be spread because of the horses.

Picking up trap and stake, Bruce kicked the dead gopher down its burrow and scooped dirt over it with his toe. They stunk up the pasture if they weren't buried, and the bugs got into them. Frequently he had stood to windward of a dead and swollen gopher, watching the body shift and move with the movements of the beetles and crawling things in it. If such an infested corpse were turned over, the carrion beetles would roar out, great, hard-shelled, orange-colored, scavenging things that made his blood curdle at the thought of their touching him, and after they were gone and he looked again he would see the little black ones, undisturbed, seething through the rotten flesh. So he always buried his dead, now.

Through the gardens of red and yellow cactus blooms he went whistling, half-trotting, setting his traps afresh whenever a gopher shot upright, whistled, and ducked down its hole. All but two of the first seventeen traps held gophers, and he came to the eighteenth confidently, expecting to take this one alive. But this gopher had gone in head first, and the boy put back in his pocket the salt sack he had brought along for a game bag. He would have to trap or snare one down by the dam.

On the way back he stopped with bent head while he counted the morning's catch of tails, mentally adding this lot to the seven hundred forty he already had, trying to remember how many he and Chet had had this time last year. As he finished his mathematics his whistle broke out again, and he galloped down through the pasture, running for very abundance of life, until he came to the chicken house just within the fireguard.

Under the eaves of the chicken house, so close that the hens were constantly pecking up to its door and then almost losing their wits with fright, was the weasel's cage. The boy lifted the hinged top and looked down through the screen.

"Hello," he said. "Hungry?"

The weasel crouched, its snaky body humped, its head thrust forward and its malevolent eyes steady and glittering.

"Tough, ain't you?" the boy said. "Just you wait, you bloodsucking old stinker, you. Won't I skin you quick, hah?"

There was no dislike or emotion in his tone. He took the weasel's malignant ferocity with the same indifference he displayed in his gopher killing. Weasels, if you kept them long enough, were valuable. He would catch some more and have an ermine farm. He was the best gopher trapper in Saskatchewan. Why not weasels? Once he and Chet had even caught a badger, though they hadn't been able to take him alive because he was caught by only three hind toes, and lunged so savagely that they had to stand off and stone him to death in the trap. But weasels you could catch alive, and Pa said you couldn't hurt a weasel short of killing him outright. This one, though virtually three-legged, was as lively and vicious as ever.

Every morning now he had a live gopher for breakfast, in spite of Elsa's protests that it was cruel. She had argued and protested, but he had talked her down. When she said that the gopher didn't have a chance in the weasel's cage, he retorted that it didn't have a chance when the weasel came down the hole after it, either. When she said that the real job he should devote himself to was destroying all the weasels, he replied that then the gophers would get so thick they would eat the wheat down to stubble. Finally she had given up, and the weasel continued to have his warm meals.

For some time the boy stood watching his captive. Then he turned and went into the house, where he opened the oatbox in the kitchen and took out a chunk of dried beef. From this he cut a thick slice with the butcher knife, and went munching into the sleeping porch where his mother was making the beds.

"Where's that little double-naught?" he said.

"That what?"

"That little wee trap I use for catching live ones for Lucifer."

"Hanging out by the laundry bench, I think. Are you going trapping again now?"

"Lucifer hasn't been fed yet."

"How about your reading?"

"I'ne take the book along and read while I wait. I'm just going down by the dam."

"I *can*, not I'ne, son."

"I can," the boy said. "I am most delighted to comply with your request of the twenty-third inst." He grinned at his mother. He could always floor her with a quotation out of a letter or the Sears Roebuck catalogue.

With the trap swinging in his hand, and under his arm the book–*Narrative and Lyric Poems*, edited by Somebody-or-Other–which his mother kept him reading all summer so that "next year he could be at the head of his class again," the boy walked out into the growing heat.

From the northwest the coulee angled down through the pasture, a shallow swale dammed just above the house to catch the spring run-off of snow water. Below the dam, watered by the slow seepage from above, the coulee bottom was a parterre of flowers, buttercups in broad sheets, wild sweet pea, and stinkweed. On the slopes were evening primroses pale pink and white and delicately fragrant, and on the flats above the yellow and red burgeoning of the cactus.

Just under the slope of the coulee a female gopher and three half-grown pups basked on their warm mound. The boy chased them squeaking down the hole and set the trap carefully, embedding it partially in the earth. Then he retired back up on the level, where he lay full length on his stomach, opened the book, shifted so that the glare of the sun across the pages was blocked by the shadow of his head and shoulders, and began to read.

From time to time he looked up from the book to roll on his side and stare out across the coulee, across the barren plains pimpled with gopher mounds and bitten with fire and haired with dusty, woolly grass. Apparently as flat as a table, the land sloped imperceptibly to the south, so that nothing interfered with his view of the ghostly mountains, looking higher now as the heat increased. Between his eyes and that smoky outline sixty miles away the heat waves rose writhing like fine wavy hair. He knew that in an hour

Pankhurst's farm would lift above the swelling knoll to the west. Many times he had seen that phenomenon, had seen Jason Pankhurst watering the horses or working in the yard when he knew that the whole farm was out of sight. It was heat waves that did it, his father said.

The gophers below had been thoroughly scared, and for a long time nothing happened. Idly the boy read through his poetry lesson, dreamfully conscious of the hard ground under him, feeling the gouge of a rock under his stomach without making any effort to remove it. The sun was a hot caress between his shoulder blades, and on the bare flesh where his overalls pulled above his sneakers it bit like a burning glass. Still he was comfortable, supremely relaxed and peaceful, lulled into a half trance by the heat and the steamy flower smells and the mist of yellow from the buttercup coulee below him.

And beyond the coulee was the dim profile of the Bearpaws, the Mountains of the Moon.

The boy's eyes, pulled out of focus by his tranced state, fixed on the page before him. Here was a poem he knew . . . but it wasn't a poem, it was a song. His mother sang it often, working at the sewing machine in winter.

It struck him as odd that a poem should also be a song, and because he found it hard to read without bringing in the tune, he lay quietly in the full glare of the sun, singing the page softly to himself. As he sang the trance grew on him again, he lost himself entirely. The bright hard dividing lines between senses blurred, and buttercups, smell of primrose, feel of hard gravel under body and elbows, sight of the ghosts of mountains haunting the southern horizon, were one intensely-felt experience focussed by the song the book had evoked.

And the song was the loveliest thing he had ever heard. He felt the words, tasted them, breathed upon them with all the ardor of his captivated senses.

The splendor falls on castle walls
And snowy summits old in story . . .

The current of his imagination flowed southward over the shoulder of the world to the ghostly outline of the Mountains of the Moon, haunting the heat-distorted horizon.

Oh hark, oh hear, how thin and clear,
And thinner, clearer, farther going,
Oh sweet and far, from cliff and scar . . .

In the enchanted forests of his mind the horns of elfland blew, and his breath was held in the cadence of their dying. The weight of the sun had been lifted from his back. The empty prairie of his home was castled and pillared with the magnificence of his imagining, and the sound of horns died thinly in the direction of the Mountains of the Moon.

From the coulee below came the sudden metallic clash of the trap, and an explosion of frantic squeals smothered almost instantly in the burrow. The boy leaped up, thrusting the book into the wide pocket of his overalls, and ran to the mound. The chain, stretched down the hole, jerked convulsively, and when he took hold of it he felt the life on the other end trying to escape. Tugging gently, he forced loose the digging claws and hauled the squirming gopher from the hole.

On the way up to the chicken house the dangling gopher with a tremendous muscular effort convulsed itself upward from the broken and imprisoned leg, and bit with a rasp of teeth on the iron. Its eyes, the boy noticed impersonally, were shiny black, like the head of a hatpin. He thought it odd that when they popped out of the head after a blow they were blue.

At the cage he lifted the cover and peered down through the screen. The weasel, scenting blood, backed against the far wall of the box, yellow body tense as a spring, teeth showing in a tiny soundless snarl.

Undoing the wire door with his left hand, the boy held the trap over the hole. Then he bore down with all his strength on the spring, releasing the gopher, which dropped on the straw and scurried into the corner opposite its enemy.

The weasel's three good feet gathered under it and it circled, very slowly, along the wall, its lips still lifted to expose the soundless snarl. The abject gopher crowded against the boards, turned once and tried to scramble up the side, fell back on its broken leg, and whirled like lightning to face its executioner again. The weasel moved carefully, circling, its cold eyes hypnotically steady.

Then the gopher screamed, a wild, agonized, despairing squeal that made the boy swallow and wet his lips. Another scream, wilder than the first, and before the sound had ended the weasel struck. There was a fierce flurry in the straw before the killer got its hold just back of the gopher's right ear, and then there was only the weasel looking at him over the dead and quivering body. In a few minutes, the boy knew, the gopher's carcass would be as limp as an empty skin, with all its blood sucked out and a hole as big as the ends of his two thumbs where the weasel had dined.

Still he remained staring through the screen top of the cage, face rapt and body completely lost. After a few minutes he went into the sleeping porch, stretched out on the bed, opened the Sears Roebuck catalogue, and dived so deeply into its fascinating pictures and legends that his mother had to shake him to make him hear her call to lunch.

■ ELLIOTT C. LINCOLN

In 1908, the young Elliott Lincoln boarded a train for Montana. He homesteaded near Lewistown, married a local girl, and taught school to the town's children. He then moved to California to teach in a private school. Lincoln published two books of poetry about Montana, Rhymes of a Homesteader *(1920) and* The Ranch *(1924). This selection is from* Rhymes of a Homesteader.

A Song of the Wire Fence

Millions of miles of shining metal threads
   Cutting the plain in geometric lines,
   Climbing aloft among the mountain pines,
I show the way wherever Progress treads.

I bound the cultivated fields of man,
   Divide his cattle from the masterless,
   I form a barrier to the wilderness;
I end that which has been since time began.

My barbed and twisted strands have marked the change
   That comes when Nature pays the debt she owes.
   I whisper to each heedless wind that blows
The last low dirges of the open range.

■ A. B. GUTHRIE, JR.

Born in Bedford, Indiana, in 1901, A. B. Guthrie, Jr., grew up in Choteau, Montana, where his father was principal of the high school. After being graduated from the University of Montana in 1923, Guthrie went to Kentucky to work as a

journalist, short-story writer, and creative writing instructor. Twenty years later, he returned to Choteau, where he finished writing The Big Sky. *In 1950, Guthrie received the Pulitzer Prize for* The Way West, *the second novel in his historical series about the West. He also wrote the screenplay for* Shane, *a classic film about the Old West. Guthrie lives near Choteau, where he continues to write and to advocate the protection of the wilderness he memorialized in his works. These selections are from* The Big Sky *(1947).*

From The Big Sky

The long western sun lay flat on the river and plain. Down the hills to the northeast a string of pack animals filed, looking black against the summer tan of the bluffs.

"Could be that's Zeb," Summers said, squinting. "McKenzie said likely he'd get in afore dark." He and Jim Deakins and Boone stood behind the fort. The *Mandan* was moored two miles up river, where Jourdonnais was watching cargo and crew. Summers had suggested that the three of them come back to the fort to talk to Calloway. "That hoss knows a heap," he had said to Jourdonnais, "besides bein' kin to Caudill. I figger I better see him."

A little piece from where they stood a dozen lodges of the Assiniboines, set in a half-circle, pointed at the sky. Once in a while smoke came from one of them, rising from the smoke hole at the top in a thin wisp, as if a man with a pipe was blowing through it. The voices of the Indians, of the men talking and the squaws laughing and squabbling and a baby squalling came clear in the evening air. Dogs nosed around the lodges and sometimes faced around in the direction of the three white men and barked as if they had suddenly remembered to do something forgotten.

"Let's set," said Summers, letting himself down to the ground.

The pack string snaked down from the hills and headed toward them across the plain. A mounted man was at the head of it, and another one at its tail.

Summers smoked and watched and said presently, "I do believe it's your Uncle Zeb, Caudill."

It was Uncle Zeb, all right, looking older, and gray as a coon. A man couldn't go wrong on that long nose and the eyes that peered out from under brows as bushy as a bird's nest.

Boone wanted to get up and shout hello and go out and give his hand, but something held him in.

Summers got to his feet easy, so's not to affright the mules that were packed high and wide with meat. "H'ar ye, Zeb?"

Uncle Zeb stared out of his tangle of brow like a man sighting a rifle. "How," he answered, his voice stiff and cracked as a man's is after a long silence. Then, "This child'll be a Digger if it ain't Dick Summers."

Summers motioned. "This here's someone you seen afore."

Uncle Zeb fixed his gaze on Boone. He spit a brown stream over the shoulder of his horse. "So?"

Summers waited, and Uncle Zeb looked at Boone again and said, "Ain't my pup, I'm thinkin'."

"Close," answered Summers. "Don't you know your own nephy, old hoss?"

Boone asked, "How you, Uncle Zeb?"

"For Christ sake!"

"I reckon you don't know me, I've changed that much."

Uncle Zeb spit again and put his mind to remembering. "One of Serenee's young'ns, ain't ye?"

"Boone Caudill."

"For Christ sake!"

Uncle Zeb didn't smile. He sat on his horse, his shoulders slumped and his mouth over at one side, making his face look crooked. A calf was bawling inside the fort as if he had lost his ma. "Stay thar," Uncle Zeb said at last. "I'll get shet of these here mules. Ho, Deschamps." The string got into slow motion, the heads of the mules jerking as the slack went out of the tie ropes. The rider at the tail was an Indian, or a half-breed anyway. For a bridle he had a long hair rope tied about the lower jaw of his horse. The stirrups of his saddle were made of skin and shaped like shoes. He stared as he went by, lounging on his horse, with his rifle carried crosswise before him.

Jim and Summers glanced at Boone. He picked up a blade of grass and tied a knot in it. "It's a spell since he seed me."

The Assiniboine squaws were playing a game, laughing and squealing as they played. Three bucks passed by, making toward the fort. They stopped on the way to ask for some tobacco. A little sand rat that Summers called a gopher came out of a hole and sat up, straight as a peg. He whistled a thin pipe of a whistle that struck the ears like the point of an awl. Boone tossed a pebble at him, and he dived into his hole and then nosed back up, just his head showing, and the black unwinking eye. The sun had got behind a bank of clouds and painted them blood red. It was like an Indian had spit into a hand of vermilion and rubbed the western sky with it. Boone got out the pipe he had traded for down river.

In a little while Uncle Zeb came back, walking stiff and uneven from the saddle. His leggings were black and worn, with no more than a half-dozen pieces of fringe left. He wore an old Indian shirt smeared with blood, which had a colored circle on the chest made of porcupine quills. Instead of a hat he had a red handkerchief tied around his head. He took a bottle out of his shirt and sat down and got the cork out, not saying anything. Summers brought out another bottle. Uncle Zeb passed the first one round, watching it go from hand to hand as if he could hardly wait. The first thing he said was, "Can't buy a drink on'y at night, goddam McKenzie!"

It was getting cold, with the sun low and hid, too cold even for the gnats that like to ate a man alive. A little breeze ran along the ground, making Boone draw into himself. Off a piece he could see some whitened bones, and beyond them some more, and beyond them still more where buffalo had been butchered. Three Indian dogs that looked like wolves except for one that was blotched black and white were smelling around them. The dogs were just bones themselves, with spines that humped up and ran crooked so that the feet didn't set square underneath them. The calf inside the fort was still bawling.

As if it didn't make much difference Uncle Zeb asked, "How's Serenee makin' out?"

"All right, last I seen her."

Uncle Zeb grunted and lifted the bottle and took a powerful drink. He slumped back, in a mood, as if waiting for the whisky to put life into him. He said, "Christ sake!" and took another drink.

Summers said, "This here's Jim Deakins, crew of the *Mandan*."

"Pleased to meetcha," Jim said.

Uncle Zeb got out tobacco and stuffed it in his cheek and let it soak. "Why're you here?"

"I fit with Pap."

"Measly son of a bitch. By God! If'n you're any part like him–?" He spit and sucked in his lower lip afterward to get the drop off.

"He's some now," Summers said. "He's true beaver. Catched the clap and fit Indians and killed a white b'ar a'ready."

Uncle Zeb looked at Summers. "Never could figger why my sister teamed up with that skunk, less'n she had to." He turned. "How old be ye?"

"Comin' eighteen."

Uncle Zeb thought for a while, then said, "You got no cause to be set up, account of your pap."

"Be goddammed to you! You take after Pap your own self."

"Sic'im, Boone!" It was Jim, looking across at him with a gleam in his blue eye.

Uncle Zeb only grunted. He started the bottle around again, taking a swig of it first himself and ending the round with another. "This nigger's got a turrible dry."

Summers was smiling at the ground as if he was pleased. "Caudill and Deakins, here, aim to be mountain men."

"Huh! They better be borned ag'in."

"How so?"

"Ten year too late anyhow." Uncle Zeb's jaw worked on the tobacco. "She's gone, goddam it! Gone!"

"What's gone?" asked Summers.

Boone could see the whisky in Uncle Zeb's face. It was a face that had known a sight of whisky, likely, red as it was and swollen-looking.

"The whole shitaree. Gone, by God, and naught to care savin' some of us who seen 'er new." He took the knife from his belt and started jabbing at the ground with it, as if it eased his feelings. He was silent for a while.

"This was man's country onc't. Every water full of beaver and a galore of buffler any ways a man looked, and no crampin' and crowdin'. Christ sake!"

To the east, where the hill and sky met, Boone saw a surge of movement and guessed that it was buffalo until it streamed down the slope, making for them, and came to be a horse herd.

Summers' gray eye slipped from Boone to Uncle Zeb. "She ain't sp'iled, Zeb," he said quietly. "Depends on who's lookin'."

"Not sp'iled! Forts all up and down the river, and folk everywhere a man might think to lay a trap. And greenhorns comin' up, a heap of 'em—greenhorns on every boat, hornin' in and sp'ilin' the fun. Christ sake! Why'n't they stay to home? Why'n't they leave it to us as found it? By God, she's ours by rights." His mouth lifted for the bottle. "God, she was purty onc't. Purty and new, and not a man track, savin' Injuns', on the whole scoop of her."

The horses were coming in fast, running and kicking like colts with the coolness that had come on the land. The gopher was out of his hole again, moving in little flirts and looking up and piping. It was beginning to get dark. The fire in the west was about out; low in the east one star burned. Boone wished someone would quiet that calf.

Summers said, " 'Pears you swallered a prickly pear, hoss."

"Huh!" Uncle Zeb reached in and fingered the cud from his mouth and put a fresh one in.

"Beaver's a fair price, a mighty fair price. It is, now."

"Price don't figger without a man's got the beaver," Uncle Zeb said while his mouth moved to set the chew right.

The horses trotted by, kicking up a dust, shying and snorting as they passed the seated men. Behind them came four riders, dressed in the white blanket coats that the workmen at the fort wore.

"I mind the time beaver was everywhere," Uncle Zeb said. His voice had turned milder and had a faraway tone in it, as if the whisky had started to work deep and easy in him. Or was it that he was just old and couldn't hold to a feeling? "I do now. Everywhere. It was poor doin's, them days, not to trap a good pack every hunt. And now?" He fell silent as if there was nothing fitting a man could lay tongue to.

"Look," he said, straightening a little, "another five year and there'll be naught but coarse fur, and it goin' fast. You, Boone, and you, Deakins, stay here and you'll be out on the prairie, hide huntin', chasin' buffler and skinnen' 'em, and seein' the end come to that, too."

"Not five year," said Summers. "More like fifty."

"Ahh! The beaver's nigh gone now. Buffler's next. Won't be even a goddam poor bull fifty years ahead. You'll see plows comin' across the plains, and people settin' out to farm." He leaned forward, bringin his hands up. "They laugh at this nigger, but it's truth all the same. Can't be t'otherwise. The Company alone's sendin' twenty-five thousand beaver skins out in a year, and forty thousand or more hides. Besides, a heap of buffler's killed by hunters and never skinned, and a heap of skins is used by the Injuns, and a passel of 'em drownds every spring. Ahh!"

"There's beaver aplenty yit," replied Summers. "A man's got to go after them. He don't catch 'em inside a fort, or while makin' meat."

"Amen and go to hell, Dick! On'y, whisky's hard to come by off on a hunt. Gimme a pull on your bottle. I got a turrible dry."

Boone heard his own voice, sounding tight and toneless. "She still looks new to me, new and purty." In the growing darkness he could feel Uncle Zeb's eyes on him, looking at him from under their thickets–tired old eyes that whisky had run red rivers in.

"We're pushin' on," said Summers, "beyant the Milk, to Blackfoot country."

"This child heerd tell."

"Well, now?"

"This nigger don't know, Dick. It's risky–powerful risky, like you know. Like as not you'll go under."

"We got a heap of whisky, and powder and ball and guns, and beads and vermilion and such."

"You seen Blackfeet drunk, Dick?"

"A few."

"They're mean. Oh, by God, they're mean! An' tricky and onreliable. But you know that as good as me. Got a interpreter?"

"Just this hoss. I know it a little, and sign talk, of course. We ain't got beaver for a passel of interpreters."

"You dodged Blackfeet enough to learn a little, I'm thinkin'."

"Plenty plews there."

"They don't do a dead nigger no good. Pass the bottle."

"How are you and McKenzie?"

"The bourgeway bastard, with his fancy getup and his tablecloth and his nose in the air like a man stinks! Y'know the clerks can't set to his table without a coat on? And the chinchin' company, squeezin' hell out of a man and chargin' him Christ knows what for belly rot!

McKenzie pays this child, and this child kills his meat, but that's as fur as she goes. I'm just tradin' meat for whisky."

"Zeb," Summers said, "this here's secret as the grave. Wouldn't do for it to get out. It wouldn't now."

"My mouth don't run to them cayutes, drunk or sober."

"We got a little squaw, daughter of a Blackfoot chief, she says, that was stole by the Crows and made a getaway. A boat picked her up, nigh dead, and took her on to St. Louis last fall. We're takin' her back."

"Umm. Injuns don't set much store by squaws."

"Blackfeet like their young'ns more'n most."

"A squaw?"

"I know, but still?"

"Might be." Uncle Zeb was silent for what seemed a long time. "This nigger heerd something from the Rocks about that Crow party. Heavy Otter—ain't that the chief?"

"That's the name she gave. We're countin' on her a heap, Zeb."

"Umm."

"We make talk purty slick, what with her l'arnin' a little white man's talk and me knowin' some Blackfoot. Me and her together, we don't need no interpreter."

"This nigger don't like it."

"Your stick wouldn't float that way? We'll cut you in, and handsome. Better'n bein' a fort hunter."

In the darkness Boone could see Uncle Zeb's head shake. "It ain't a go, Dick. It ain't now."

"I recollect when it would be."

It seemed to Boone that all of time was in Uncle Zeb's voice. "Not now, hoss. Not any more. This child ain't scared, like you know, but it ain't worth it. It's tolerable here, and whisky's plenty even if it costs a heap."

"What you hear about the Blackfeet?"

"The Rocks say they're away from the river, gone north and east to buffler. Me, now, I'd say go to Maria's River, or along there, and fort up, quicker'n scat."

"Too fur. Take a month, even with Jourdonnais blisterin' the crew. Buffler an' Blackfeet would be back afore we could set ourselves."

"Uh-huh. There's mostly some Injuns around Maria's River all the time. Anyways, get your fort up fast."

"That's how this child figgered. A little fort, quick, ready for 'em when they come back to the river."

"It's risky doin's, anyways you lay your sights."

"You figger the Company's like to take a hand in this game?"

"McKenzie's got plans for the Blackfeet. He's makin' medicine. He is, now. Come fall or winter, he'll p'int that way, or try to. But he'll let ye be, likely, thinkin' the Blackfeet and the British'll handle things. He's slick. He ain't wantin' a finger p'inted at him, now you're so fur up."

"He said he might send a boat up, to buck us."

"No sech. He ain't got the hands right now. If this nigger smells a stink afore you pass the Milk, he'll get word to you one way or t'other."

"Heap obliged, hoss."

Uncle Zeb got up unsteadily, his knees cracking as he straightened them out. "If it gits to talk, ask for Big Leg of the Piegans, and give a present, sayin' it's from me. We're brothers, he said onc't."

"That's some, now. Obliged again."

Uncle Zeb walked away, swaying some and not saying good-bye. The three others made off in the direction of the *Mandan*, waking the Indian dogs, which started barking all at once. They could hear loud voices and laughs and sometimes a whoop from inside the fort. "Liquorin' up," said Summers. The calf had stopped bawling.

Boone's head swam with the whisky. It was the first he had let himself drink much of in a long time. "I reckon old age just come on Uncle Zeb," he said. After a silence he added, "It's fair country yit." Summers was keeping them in the open, away from the river.

"It's fair, sure enough," Deakins agreed.

Summers said, "Watch out for them pesky prickly pear. They go right through a moccasin." . . .

When Boone had a mood on, there was nothing to do but let it wear off. He would be silent and grumpy no matter what, not answering to talk or laughing at jokes but going along with his lips tight and his eyes dark until the trouble in him eased. If a man understood, he just let him alone, knowing time would take care of him. Time would make him himself again; he would get used to his baby's being blind and so not have to take his hurt out on others as if it was their fault the young one couldn't see. Leave him be and he would get friendly sooner or later and take pleasure in things in his corked-up way. Boone never was one to let out what was in him, being a silent man, mostly, and too proud to show himself. Only it must be hard on Teal Eye, living with him now and him not speaking except to grunt and his eyes clouded and far away.

Jim flicked his horse with the tail end of his reins. He was on his way to Fort McKenzie, where he would drink himself some whisky and maybe lie around for a few days and earn a dollar or so by killing meat for the fort or interpreting for Chardon, the bourgeois. By the time he got back to Red Horn's band Boone might feel like speaking a word to him once in a while.

From the plain he could look down on the wooded valley of the lower Teton. Magpies cried from down there, and a crow called, sounding like a hoarse whisper against the wind that flowed out of the northeast. Up on the plain, ground larks flitted from under his horse's feet and jackass rabbits leaped out of hiding and went bounding away, stopping to look after a while, their front feet held up dainty and their coats already turned from snow-white to dirty gray. Spring was coming even if the weather didn't know it. A week of good weather and the cottonwoods would bust their buttons and the diamond willow run out leaves as narrow as snakes' tongues, and at sundown a man would hear the killdeer crying.

Spring made a man feel good and sad, too, and wild sometimes, wanting to howl with the wolves or strike north with the ducks or fork a horse and ride alone over the far rim of the world into new country, into a fresh life. Spring was a good hurting inside the body. It made laughter come easy, and tears if a man didn't shut them off. Come a soft night, and he could sit under the sky and watch the stars or moon and listen to running water, and he would feel a pushing inside of him, a reaching for things he couldn't single out—for a woman, maybe, who was all he ever could think up and more, for the quietness a man never seemed to have until he looked back and saw he had passed it by, never knowing. Old times came back to him then, so's he felt like crying over them, and old friends he had traveled with and parted from, never thinking that those times and those friends would come to be an aching in him. Jourdonnais and Dick Summers and Poordevil, and long days on the *Mandan* and nights on the Powder and that evening in Colter's Hell with the first people and the fine, high singing overhead and the air itself breathless, and all of them gone from him now except as pictures in the heart.

Spring made a man a little crazy. It gave him ideas he wouldn't want to own to—ideas like baying the moon or flying with ducks, sharp beginnings of ideas, like finding a certain woman willing, that he pushed quick from his mind. Anyhow, spring made some men crazy. Maybe not Boone. Maybe not a man that had a Teal Eye for his squaw and wanted nothing but to go on as he was. Maybe there was just one big hunger that other hungers grew from.

Jim rode down into the valley of the Teton where the stream turned north. He climbed the far slope and halted his horse on the high nose that separated the Teton from the Missouri. He saw Fort McKenzie below him, with only three tepees pitched about. Beyond it the Missouri flowed wide, shining silver in the sun. The valley would be green with leaf soon, and a man stopping on the nose would feel shriveled with the wind and sun and would kick his horse downhill to meet the cool breath of the valley. The breeze was still raw now, and the trees stood naked below. Cold had followed that first taste of spring along the Medicine, as Jim had said it would.

The feel of the country settled into Jim, the great emptiness and age of it, the feel of westward mountains old as time and plains wide as forever and the blue sky flung across. The country didn't give a damn about a man or any animal. It let the buffalo and the antelope feed on it and the gophers dig and the birds fly and men crawl around, but what did it care, being one with time itself? What did it care about a man or his hankerings or what happened to him? There would be other men after him and others after them, all wondering and all wishful and after a while all dead.

Jim tried to shake the miseries from his head. It was Boone being so sully that made his thoughts sorry, or the wound he had got and the long hunger. He clucked to his horse and rolled in the saddle to its downhill jolt. Where the ridge leveled off, he spurred the horse to a gallop and pulled up short before the outer gate. A Frenchman peeked through the pickets and swung the gate open to let him through and closed it tight afterwards. There wasn't an Indian in the store except for a couple of squaws that showed by fancy fixings of ribbon and red cloth that they belonged to the men in the fort.

"Where's the customers?" Jim asked.

The Frenchman gestured with his hands, saying only God knew. A clerk eyed Jim, his hands palms down on the counter. "Only customers we get these days are ugly customers," he said.

"They'll be liftin' your hair if you ain't careful, from what I hear."

The guard at the inside gate carried a good Hawken in the crook of his arm. He studied Jim as if to make sure he didn't need killing.

There wasn't much doing inside the grounds. Over by a shop three pork eaters were sorting and mending gear. They and the guard were the only men in sight except for Alexander Harvey, next man in line to Chardon, who sat in a doorway out of the wind sunning himself. The flag overhead snapped in the breeze, and the sun ran along the cannon that was kept aimed at the gate.

Jim said "How" to Harvey and slid off his horse. He rested his rifle by the door and sat down in the dust. The horse nosed off, hunting for a spear of grass on ground that the company horses had picked bare while being kept up for fear of Indians.

GWENDOLEN HASTE

Gwendolen Haste was born in Streator, Illinois, in 1889. An accomplished poet of national reputation during the 1930s and 1940s, Haste spent several years in Montana during her girlhood and college years. After being graduated from the University of Chicago, Haste won The Nation's *poetry prize in 1922. She also worked with her father to edit* The Scientific American *in Lincoln, Nebraska, and in Billings, Montana, and later moved to New York City, where she joined the staff of* The Survey. *These selections from her "Montana Wives" poetic sequence are from* Young Land, *published in 1930.*

The Ranch in the Coulee

He built the ranch house down a little draw,
So that he should have wood and water near.
The bluffs rose all around. She never saw
The arching sky, the mountains lifting clear;
But to the west the close hills fell away
And she could glimpse a few feet of the road.
The stage to Roundup went by every day,
Sometimes a rancher town-bound with his load,
An auto swirling dusty through the heat,
Or children trudging home on tired feet.

At first she watched it as she did her work,
A horseman pounding by gave her a thrill,
But then within her brain began to lurk
The fear that if she lingered from the sill
Someone might pass unseen. So she began
To keep the highroad always within sight,
And when she found it empty long she ran
And beat upon the pane and cried with fright.

The winter was the worst. When snow would fall
He found it hard to quiet her at all.

The Wind

The cabin sits alone far up a hill
Where all the year the mournful wind blows shrill.

She used to tell him sometimes: "No one knows
How hard it is to listen while it blows."

He never touched a plow again, they say,
After he found her there, but went away.

And tenants wouldn't live upon the place
Because, the neighbors said, they saw her face

Pressed close against the little window-pane
Watching the twisting storm clouds in the rain,

And in the night time they could hear her cry
And moan and whimper if the gale was high.

So now through barren fields the great winds blow
Where fan weed and the purple wild pea grow.

They said she had no cause to die, but still
The wind was always blowing on that hill.

Vengence

The sun came up with a nice display
    Of amber and rose;
    And at end of day
There was orange or crimson or amethyst
    Whichever you chose.
    But she never saw.
The storms hurried up from behind the mountains
    And spread great clouds
    Like boiling fountains
And covered the fresh blue sky with shrouds.
    She only said "Pshaw!"
And went out to gather the clothes from the line.

Then the cottonwood tree in the yard
Danced like a virgin before a shrine.
She looked at it hard
And said "Cottonwood trees are so messy."
At last she died
And was buried in black, very dressy.
Her relations cried;
But the sunset poured out scarlet and blue
Purple and gold;
While the cottonwood danced the whole day through
When they put her away to mould.

Deliverance

The screaming kingbirds in the poplars woke her,
And since lately there had been no joy in waking,
She thought it well to end such things, together
With floors to scrub and baking.

So instead of lifting up the pails, she turned
Down to the river rushing brown in flood
And watched a moment the June sunlight sifting
Through a lone cottonwood.

An easy way it was to end all wakings,
To hear no more the flooded river's strife,
Nor noisy birds at dawn, nor cows at milk-time,
Nor any voice of life.

The Stoic

She guessed there wasn't any time for tears
Because her heart had held them all unshed
While one by one her little hopes had fled
Down through those racking, windy, drouth-filled years.
The frozen winter when the cattle died,
The year the hail bent flat the tender wheat,
The thirsty summers with their blazing heat–
She met them all with wordless, rigid pride.

But when, sometimes, the children in the spring
Searching through barren hill or ragged butte,
Would heap her lap with loco blooms, and bring
Clouds of blue larkspur and bright bitter-root,
Then would she run away to hide her pain
For memory of old gardens drenched with rain.

Horizons

I had to laugh,
For when she said it we were sitting by the door,
And straight down was the Fork,
Twisting and turning and gleaming in the sun.
And then your eyes carried across to the purple bench beyond the river
With the Beartooth Mountains fairly screaming with light and blue and snow,
And fold and turn of rimrock and prairie as far as your eye could go.

And she says: "Dear Laura, sometimes I feel so sorry for you,
Shut away from everything—eating out your heart with loneliness.
When I think of my own full life I wish that you could share it.
Just pray for happier days to come and bear it."

She goes back to Billings to her white stucco house,
And looks through net curtains at another white stucco house,
And a brick house,
And a yellow frame house,
And six trimmed poplar trees,
And little squares of shaved grass.

Oh dear, she stared at me like I was daft!
I couldn't help it. I just laughed and laughed!

NAOMI LANE BABSON

Naomi Lane Babson was born on Cape Ann, Massachusetts, in 1895. After attending Radcliff College, in 1922 she traveled to Canton, China, where she taught the children of staff members at Lingham University. She and her husband, Paul Greider, returned to the United States in 1935 and settled in Bozeman, Montana, where she lived for many years. Babson published her first novel, The Yankee Bodleys, *in 1936. This excerpt is from the opening of her novel,* I Am Lidian, *published in 1951.*

From I Am Lidian

Grandview Montana Daily Herald, June 29, 1928

It was your correspondent's privilege this afternoon to spend an hour with that dainty and aristocratic little lady known to us all as the first white woman to make her home in our fair valley, so fitly titled by the Red Man, Vale of Flowers, and this at a time some sixty years in the past when instead of the prosperous busy city, upwards of ten thousand population estimated, with paved streets and electric lights, fine residences, flourishing business concerns, daily newspaper, three banks, not to mention educational and religious advantages equal to the best, there was only the virgin wilderness undefiled, the waving bunch grass often so lush and high that feeding antelope were hidden from sight until they raised their heads to stare with gentle amazement at the rude intruders into their erstwhile Paradise. . . .

The June sun never seemed to shine more brightly. A vagrant breeze stirred the window draperies and gently caressed the petals of a stunning bouquet of roses sent by who but the Governor of our fair state himself on the auspicious occasion of this anniversary. But hush, hush! Speak softly, not a sound. The frail small figure in the rocking-chair has dropped asleep.

A single petal drifted from the Governor's bouquet to lie on the table like a blood-red tear. Roses smaller than these but just as red used to blossom long ago on the thorny bushes in the Annsville garden. They had been brought from England on sailing ships. And there were English violets darkly purple under the apple trees. She wet her feet in the dew-spangled grass and got her best tier draggled picking a bunch of violets before breakfast on Dear Ma's birthday.

That was the same morning Minnie had found a blown-down robin's nest with the speckled eggs in it, unbroken but quite cold. Aunt Pet showed them how to prick the shells with a needle and blow them clean. One had cracked but they kept the others for a long time. Yes, she remembered, though it was better than eighty years since two little girls in identical sprigged frocks stood tiptoe at the china closet choosing a gilt-edged sass dish for their blue eggs. Calico dresses glossy with laundering, two or three petticoats each, and pantalettes and aprons. What a sight of work somebody had to do. There were five children in the family, all girls. But in those days she hadn't spared a thought to soap and starch and sadirons. It was only later on . . . later on. . . .

Behind her closed eyelids the pictures wavered and dissolved, then formed again. Two little girls, but these were not Sister Minnie and herself. She was seeing Rose and Amy in the limp dark frocks and sunbonnets and clumsy shoes they wore across the Plains. Hideous clothes, but, oh, how flaxen fair their hair shone by contrast. She had made them each a collar of bright beads that could be worn a long time without showing dirt. She had the bead collars still in the keepsake trunk upstairs, wrapped away in flannel long ago, but Rose and Amy . . . darling Rose . . . dear little Amy.

That girl from the newspaper thought she was asleep. Let her think it, then. When you are ninety it's your privilege to go to sleep in company if you choose. She was tired of answering questions anyhow. Wagon-train, redskins, road-agents, fiddle-de-dum. Folks were mighty funny about the past, picking it over like rats on a rubbish heap; the greatest trash was what they fancied most, and Plummer cast a longer shadow nowadays than a dozen better men who had helped hang him. Nobody ever asked her about the first shingled house in town or the first piped water, nor cared who had brought rose slips and p'inies all the way from the States, whose hands built the grain elevator, whose the church, who had put up the first bridge across West Fork.

Ninety years old, and so the Governor sent her a bunch of posies, and there would be a piece written up in the newspaper, just as if a woman ever was pleased with being old. As if it were by her own choice that she had lived so long. *The days of our years are threescore years and ten, and if by reason of strength*—Nobody used to count her very strong. A puny young one, not near as peart as the rest of them, never make old bones.

A bee had got in from somewhere and was buzzing around the flowers. Roses and bumblebees hadn't changed a mite in ninety years. *Annsville, Massachusetts, A.D. 1838, 29th Day of June. Born to us this day of God's great grace a daughter*—Just as her father wrote the final word a bee had stung him on the nose, and the blot he made in consequence still stood against her name in the big Bible, and still would stand when she was dead and gone. Things lasted. People passed away. Her hands tightened in her lap. She seemed to crush the hours and days and minutes of all the years like the thin blown shells of the robin's eggs so long remembered, so long gone to dust. *The days wherein Thou hast afflicted us, and the years wherein we have seen evil.*

Evil and good together, joy and sorrow, love and hate. The longer she lived the harder it was to tell tother from which. The checkered pattern of the past flickered in memory like shadow pictures against a sheet, sharp enough, plain enough, but erratic and unrelated, making no sense in all the world except to her. Cradle to rocking-chair in ninety years: life came full circle at the last; the end and the beginning were all one. She had wanted her supper the day she was born, no doubt, and she wanted it now.

Her eyes came open, and the rockers squeaked. Tell that writing woman something and let her go. Didn't matter an iota what she said, because the paper would print the same old story. Wagon-train, redskins, road-agents, fiddle-faddle. Words formed in her mind and sentences shaped up, and her lips moved, but not a sound came out. She was talking only for herself, just as she used to long, long ago. She had retreated so far into the past that a forgotten terror bound her tongue. She was a little, little girl again, and she was dumb.

Turn the mind back and search for the beginning. The dark lifts slowly. Forms and faces are already there, familiar, recognized, needing no explanations. They exist and are eternal. Dear Ma and Papa and Minerva. Then she came, and she was Lidian.

■ HOBART McKEAN

Hobart McKean, from Circle, Montana, has been an outspoken socialist journalist, writer, and poet in the farming and mining regions of the Great Plains. This versified rendition of the McCarthy era in Montana was written in about 1952 to the Farmers Anti-Communist Club of Circle. It offers a taste of recent history that many might wish to forget.

A Poem on McCarthyism

Up the rugged mountain top of controversial thought,
And through the vastly complicated social glen,
We dare not go a-hunting truth
For fear of little men.

Let me join the Farmers Anti-Communist Club,
And fight this wicked Socialism
I'm as good a repeater and apologist as any dub,
And as full of patriotism.

When I join up and pay my dues (if any)
One rascal less the boys will have to fight,
For I shall then be one among the many
Helping to prove that might makes right.

I promise to forget my aspirations,
My conscience too, I'll hold in check,
And trade my unseen intellectual integrity
For the safety of my much seen neck.

What's in a name? Not much indeed,
For what may be the home for owner to abide in,
Can prove to be an empty shell, supplying need
For some rank imposter just to hide in.

Forgive me boys if I am slow to see, After twenty years of treason,
The Russian menace in desire for parity Or brain-washing as the threat in reason
I shall abjure to Sir Gallahad, Who only claimed the strength of ten,
And swear allegiance to Don Quixote Dulles with his strength of all "free" men.

Man has been called the son of God,
And as such, a born creator,
But now, to save his wretched neck
He must become an imitator.

Okay boys, I'll tread the paving stones, Your good intentions pave the path so well; Too big a coward to seek the unblazed trail, I'll go along with you to Hell!
Sez Who?

■ MILDRED WALKER

Born in Pennsylvania in 1905, Mildred Walker received a Masters degree in English from the University of Michigan. She came to Great Falls, Montana, in 1933 with her cardiologist husband, Dr. Ferdinand Ripley Schemm. Walker's first novel, Fireweed *(1934), received the Avery Hopwood Award, and her* The Body of A Young Man *(1960) was nominated for the National Book Award. Probably her best-known book is* Winter Wheat, *published in 1941. Walker has recently moved to Missoula from her home in Vermont to be near her daughter, poet Ripley Schemm Hugo. This excerpt from* If a Lion Could Talk *(1970) is based on the lives of fur-trader Alexander Culbertson and his Blackfeet wife, Natawista.*

From If a Lion Could Talk

They came up the walk to their own house in the dark, like fugitives. Behind them, the cab they had been lucky to get at such an hour retreated over the cobblestone street, the hoofbeats of the horse and the creak of the wheels lightly muffled in a thin layer of snow. When Mark turned the big brass key in the lock, the door still held, bolted on the inside.

"I never thought of the bolt!" Harriet murmured.

"Isn't Hannah here?" Mark started to lift the knocker.

"There was no reason for her to stay when we expected to be gone so long."

He put the knocker down without letting it sound, as though he didn't want to disturb the silence of the street. "You wait here, Harriet. I think I can get in through the study window, or if I can't, I'll find some way to break in."

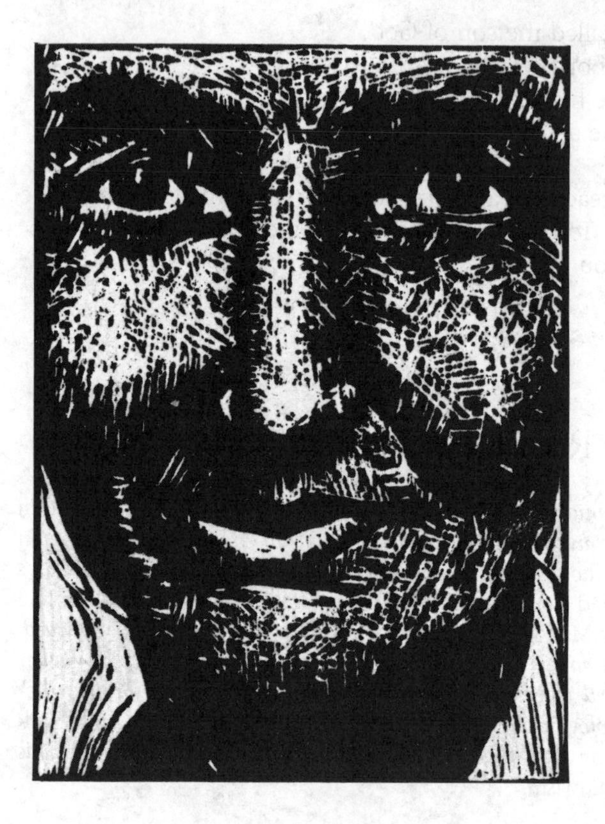

But to stand outside their own door in the chilling dark, with a bag at her feet, to have Mark climb in through a window like a thief in the night made her feel stealthy. This was her home; she had been born here, had lived all her life in this house. Now she looked over her shoulder down a street that had become suddenly unfamiliar, almost hostile in the dark. The houses reared up tall, with sharp pointed roofs, and the trees crowded close. She shivered and drew her fur cape more tightly around her; yet she had been far colder on the way. On either side, the houses were dark. What would Miss Dinwiddie or the Allens think when they saw that she and Mark were back? What would the Church think, for that matter?

She remembered how eagerly she had gone out of this door, leaving Hannah to close it and wave a tearful good-bye. Never before in her life, except of course when she married Mark, had she felt so sure of what she was doing; for how could she not follow her husband into the Wilderness? But now he was back. And she was with him.

It seemed a long wait before she saw, through the glass panes on either side of the door, a small flame moving through the house. Mark set the kerosine lamp down on the little table beside the card tray, not stopping to light the gas jet, and shot the bolt back with a grating sound. The door stuck as he pulled it open and reached out to draw her in. A powder of snow came, too, on the hem of her skirt. Then he brought in the bag. Of all they had taken—the melodeon, the four trunks, the boxes of books and beads, the rolls of cotton flannel and calico and the patterns for underwear for the Indian children that she had never unfolded, the religious tracts and the colored Bible pictures—a single carpetbag was little to bring back.

Major Phillips had said he would send their trunks on the first boat down river in the spring, but she knew very well that his wife would dress up in her clothes and promenade in front of the giggling squaws. Harriet stepped into the parlor, away from the remembered sound of squaw laughter, feeling rather than seeing the heavy furniture and the great square piano assembled there in the dark.

She watched Mark hanging his fur cap and heavy skin coat on the hatrack, which creaked under its strange burden. He looked foreign to this hall in his elkskin shirt and trousers, with his ruddy face and his beard.

An odd silence had fallen on them both for an instant, as though they couldn't quite realize where they were; then Mark came to her. "We're home, Harriet," he said solemnly. "The Lord has brought us through all the dangers of the Wilderness." He put his arm around her, but his voice had a formal sound in the stillness of the cold, dimly lit room. She was afraid he was going to kneel in prayer.

Her own "yes" came out small and inadequate to the occasion, she felt. That time when the river was blocked by ice, and in the blizzard, she hadn't been sure they would ever reach home. It wasn't that she was not grateful to the Lord, but she was suddenly too tired to kneel or try to pray. The clock in the church tower struck one, startling her. She had forgotten how town clocks sounded.

"Mark, the clock!"

"What, dear?"

"The clock," she managed to repeat.

"Oh, yes." Mark seemed to bring his thought from a long way off. "We're back in civilization. Come, Harriet, you need to get to bed."

She watched their shadows climb with them up the staircase, her hand on the mahogany rail that had been polished until it was smoother than her own palm. The white wallpaper was patterned in red and blue flowers, like the beaded pattern on Mrs. Phillips' white elkskin dress, the one that had become all spotted with blood when she ate the raw buffalo brains. Against the wall Mark's shadow, with his long hair and beard, seemed to belong to some trapper; but her own shadow, in bonnet and cape, looked strange to her, too.

Their bedroom was enormous, and cold. The head of the bed lost itself in the shadows of the high ceiling, and the marble top of the dresser gleamed like gray ice and grated beneath the lamp Mark set on it while he lighted the gas light. It seemed to take him a long time, and the first match didn't catch. Then the yellow light flared out with a low hissing sound.

Harriet stood in front of the dresser, taking off her bonnet. That thin woman in the mirror, with the wind-reddened face between lank loops of light hair, was herself. Behind her she saw Mark, just standing there, looking around the room. No, his hair and beard gave him the look of a prophet, not a mountain man. Getting here seemed to have taken all their strength; they seemed unable to go about the motions of undressing or the effort of talking. Then she felt Mark's hands taking off her cape.

"Are you all right, Harriet? The terrible trip hasn't hurt you?"

"No. I'm all right, only so tired." Her words came out with an unexpected quaver. Mark lifted her up and laid her on the bed. She closed her eyes, hardly aware that he was unhooking her jacket, covering her with a quilt, murmuring comforting things to her about building a fire . . . warm in a minute. His voice drew farther and farther away. She fell asleep before she could get any words out to protest.

The buffalo skin was warm beneath them, rough-haired and yet not rough. The hide had a sharp, raw smell, so different from the lavender-scented sheets at home. Animal feet ran on the roof–were they squirrels or rats? Outside, in the black dark, was the Wilderness, where savages roamed, and animals, wild animals, lurked. But she didn't care. She had made the long trip by herself to be with Mark, and now she lay in his arms, naked on the fur skin. At home they had never lain naked together. Mark lifted his mouth from hers to whisper, "You should never have come, my darling, but you don't know how I wanted you."

The walls were thin between the rooms. Curses in a hard voice burst through the cracks, words she did not understand, had never even heard. Mark drew the blanket up over their heads. "This is no place for you, Harriet, but I'm thankful the Major's wife is a lady."

The Major's wife's eyes were shining and black. Now her face was bending over Harriet instead of Mark's. The gold cross she wore on her red silk bodice swung on its leather thong, just above Harriet's eyes. But she didn't speak.

"Why won't you speak for Mark, Mrs. Phillips? He wants you to interpret for him." The Major's wife's black bright eyes only smiled.

Mark sat on the bed with his face in his hands. "She wouldn't speak to me, Harriet."

"Don't mind, Mark. Maybe she listened."

But Mark just shook his head. His face was drawn; there were smudges of black and white paint on it, like the paint on Mrs. Phillips' face. He didn't look like Mark; he looked terrible. "Harriet, can't you see? I failed."

She put her hands up to his face to draw him to her, but it wasn't Mark's face. A mutilated, masklike, horrible face leered down at her. The face was Aapaaki's. The black eyes on either side of the holes of her nose stared at Harriet. Harriet tried to scream, but no one came. Where was Mark? Why did Aapaaki follow Mark around all the time? Harriet tried to drive her away. She had a big stick in her hand, but Aapaaki ran off after Mark.

Mark was holding a service at the end of the big room in the Fort. He was reading from the Bible: "He that is without sin among you, let him first cut off her nose." But the young braves who cut off Aapaaki's nose weren't there; only some squaws, and the Major's wife.

Now it was time for the hymn, and she was playing the melodeon, but only she and Mark were singing. The Indian children kept up a crazy yah-yah-yah. "Stop it!" She swung around from the melodeon, waving her big stick, but Mrs. Phillips was laughing at her.

"But why won't she listen to me, Harriet? Why?" Mark kept asking.

"What do you want to say to her, Mark?"

"I want to say 'loved.' 'God so loved. . . .'"

"But she knows all that; she's a Christian already. The Catholic priest converted her; don't you know that? She wears a gold cross around her neck."

Mark was walking away, down by the bank of the river. She saw him lifted up into the air by a great bird, and Mrs. Phillips was with him, holding his hand. They were going up and up into that enormous sky, beyond the cliff of rock, where she could never find them. And she was standing on the ground, calling. Aapaaki was beside her, holding her there, so she couldn't run after them. Harriet couldn't bear to watch, and hid her face in the big pillow of goose down, plump in its cold linen case, and soft. . . .

She dropped down into a sleep too deep for dreaming.

Mark stared into the dark of the furniture-filled bedroom. They were home and safe in their own bed. Harriet had kept turning and tossing, moaning in her sleep out of sheer exhaustion, but now she was sleeping quietly. Why couldn't he sleep instead of lying as rigid as though he were squeezed into that Mackinaw boat, close to the icy water, feeling the current under them? That was the closest thing to being in the belly of a whale he could think of. Might as well have been; he felt like Jonah. He hadn't refused to go to Nineveh, but he had refused to stay there long enough to accomplish the Lord's work. . . . But would he have accomplished it if he had stayed?

He got out of bed and went down through the cold house to his study, feeling his way. He had paced the study floor often enough to cross to his desk in the dark, and he managed to light the green-shaded lamps. He picked up the afghan that lay as it always had on the couch, pulled it around him like an Indian blanket, and sat down in his high-backed leather armchair.

Almost reluctantly, his eyes reached up to the high shelves where the books marched rank on rank in stern array. The gold word "Exegesis" leaped from the backs of one row, broken by a gap where he had taken two volumes out when he left. No one at the Fort would ever try to read them; they would be tossed into the fire some bitter cold night, along with those tracts and the colored Bible pictures for the children.

His eyes came back to his desk. Twin circles of yellow light spread over the blotter pad that he had left bare when he went away; blotted into its surface was his own confident handwriting, perhaps from one of his many letters to the Mission Board, perhaps from his last sermon here at Calvary Church. He spread his cold hands in the light to warm them, and saw the scrap of paper folded under the inkwell—some quotation or idea he had scribbled down. He pulled it out, curious because it belonged to that other time, before he went away. "What I must do is all that concerns me, not what the people think." Emerson, of course. Emerson had said so many things he had taken unto himself.

But it hadn't been Emerson that had sent him to the Wilderness; it had been that single sentence in Isaiah: "The voice of him that crieth in the wilderness, Prepare ye the way of the Lord, make straight in the desert a highway for our God." He remembered his excitement, sitting here at this desk. He had read it plenty of times before and never thought of it as directed at him. He had even looked with a slight curiosity at classmates in the seminary who were going to the mission field. But that day he had thought of John the Baptist preaching in the wilderness. And then he had thought of himself there.

The next Sunday, when he stood in his pulpit and looked down at the placid faces framed in their bonnets, and the faces above the beards and high white collars and cravats–almost anonymous in their similarity–he had felt a powerful urge to go to the Wilderness, to preach to ignorant heathen who had never heard the Word. He had felt called of God. Or had he put it that way to himself? He was sick of questioning.

He had been convinced of his call, even though he had been at Calvary Church so short a time and it would mean leaving Harriet until the next year, perhaps longer. He had told himself that a man called of God must make sacrifices and endure hardships, that surely the experience in the Wilderness would be a period of growth in power for himself, power he would use in the work of the Lord.

How little he had known, or the Mission Board either, of what such a mission would be! The ignorant savages had not been eager to hear him, and he knew now what a fool he had been to think he could make them listen to him, let alone understand him, unless he spoke their tongue. He had sat here at this desk and imagined himself with redskins thronging around him!

There had never been any throngs, except for the one time seventy lodges had come to the Fort to see the Major. The Major, Ephraim Phillips, had introduced him to them as their white brother who had come to bring them "good medicine," and he had stepped forth into that great circle of dark faces, feeling stirred as never before, full of a sense of his power to bring them to God.

But after that there had not even been crowds. He had preached to a handful of children, half a dozen braves at best–usually old ones–a dozen or more squaws, and the Major's wife. The Major was always too busy to come.

How stupid he had been not to know it would be difficult to preach through an interpreter. Pierre, that conceited little French Canuck clerk, translated his evangel into some kind of Indian dialect that sometimes set them laughing. He had accused Pierre of adding comments of his own, but Pierre swore he only repeated what Mark preached. "But what you tell them sometimes is crazy to them, *mon père*. One time you tell 'em God is fisher of men. They laugh to think of Indian jerked up out of river! And they don't know what the hell is shepherd. Better when you say God is burning bush."

"I said God appeared to Moses *in* a burning bush," he had pleaded with him hopelessly.

That next Sunday he had begun so simply: "God is a mighty hunter, the mightiest and bravest of all hunters. His arrow is more swift and sure than the arrow of the greatest Indian brave." Then he had to wait for Pierre to turn the words into an unintelligible chain of t's, k's, and s's. He was always relieved when Pierre came to a stop, but startled.

"It is the arrow of truth," he would begin again. . . . If Mrs. Phillips had only translated for him, it could have been so different. He still believed he might have reached them through her, but she would never even try.

Mark jerked his body up straight in the chair to pull his mind out of its memory. He lifted the silver top of the cut-glass inkwell and saw that the ink had dried and the nibs of the pens on the tray were crusted with dry ink. He pulled open the left drawer and saw the sermons he had written, each one folded three times. He raised one and looked at the inscription on the back as though someone else had written it.

CALVARY BAPTIST CHURCH
WOOLLETT, MASS.
The Foundations of Faith

He dropped it back in its place without unfolding it; without, in fact, having any sense of recognition that he had ever conceived and composed it.

Yet, though Mrs. Phillips had never tried to speak to him, and had never translated for him, he had always to remember that it was through her that his vision had come. If it was a vision.

He had been over it a hundred times, resorting to the Scriptures to prove the importance of visions. "Your young men shall see visions." And the inverse statement: "Night shall be unto you that ye shall not have a vision; it shall be dark unto you." Now he would look at the incident coldly, under the light of his own study lamps, and determine whether or not he had had a vision.

That day, the very first week at the Fort, he had ridden from sunup until late afternoon with the Major, hunting a site for the church that never got built. He had been so lame and hot when he came back that he had thrown himself down on the bank above the river and fallen asleep, even as Jacob had been asleep when his vision came. Mark covered his face with his hands, giving himself up to the memory, almost fearfully.

A drop of water fell cold on his face, waking him instantly, but he lay still, not moving the arm that covered his eyes. His skin crawled with fear, and he had trouble keeping his breathing even. There was no sound. Another drop hit his face, then another. Someone was close to him . . . above him. Human breathing.

A cold drop struck lower down, on his neck, and he had an impulse to jump up and confront that breathing presence hovering over him, but he held himself rigid. Pretending that he was stirring restlessly in his sleep, he moved his arm ever so slightly, trying to see beneath it.

Something was coming down; he felt it just above his face. It blocked the light that seeped under his sleeve. Still trying to imitate the unconscious movements of sleep, he threw back his arm and found himself gazing up into a widespread of feathers.

The wings came closer. The soft, downy feathers of a great bird's breast brushed against his face with coolness. He could have thrust out at it with his arm, but he lay still, staring up, blinking as a cold drop of water fell from the wings into his eye.

The wings were lifting! He felt himself rising with them. Now he could see the interlacing feathers, edged with color, white-shafted, and the strong bony joinings of the wide-spread wings. Eagle wings . . . infinitely strong, infinitely soft. He felt light of body, weightless, translated out of his own lame flesh, up, up . . . infinitely free.

"I bare you on eagles' wings, and brought you unto myself."

The wings lowered again, touching lightly, coolly against his face, then lifted, drawing him with them.

Mark let out his tight-held breath in a sigh, and opened his eyes. He hadn't lost it. Even back here in his own study that incredible sense of weightlessness, of holiness, returned. He lifted his hand and let it fall on the desk in triumph. The vision was all he had brought back from the Wilderness, really. But wasn't it enough? Just once in a lifetime to feel caught up far beyond ordinary human experience!

He tried to stop his mind there, but that laugh, high and sharp as a bird's cry, still sounded in his brain. His head had bumped against the wings as he sat up, and the bird fell heavily onto his knees. Mrs.

Phillips was standing in front of him, bending double with laughter, her heavy black hair, which had come unbraided, falling over her face. Her elkskin dress was dark with water, and water ran from it onto the ground, even onto his Testament, which had slipped out of his pocket. She had pointed at him, speaking some Indian word that sent her off again into swoops of laughter.

When he picked up the bird, the head wobbled forward; its eyes staring blindly. It was a duck, black with green feathers.

He remembered asking where it had come from; and without a word she had slid down the steep bank. Just as he got to his feet, still holding the dripping duck, she disappeared under water.

Where the current slackened into smooth water, ducks moved back and forth, flashing the sun from their wings in nets of sudden light. Even now he could see that whole stretch of river. Some bird shrilled ceaselessly on the sand bar, but there was no sign of Mrs. Phillips. While his eyes searched for her one of the ducks bobbed out of sight, then rose again, feet first, in a human hand, and Mrs. Phillips' laughing face appeared for a moment before she swam back, this time half out of water, the bird cutting the ripple ahead of her as she held it in her hand. He had left the duck on the ground, picked up his Testament, and gone back into his room at the Fort. It had been dark after the light outside, he remembered, as dark as his own angry disillusionment.

He had told himself then that there had been no vision. He was only confused by being wakened so suddenly with that cold drop of water and the sense of fright. It had been some kind of Indian trick to scare him to death. Maybe just a prank, as Harriet had said.

Yet how could he not have had a vision when he had felt himself drawn up by those wings? The duck's wingspread could not have been more than twelve to fifteen inches. How could he possibly have thought the interlacing feathers stretched far out beyond the reach of his eyes unless the illusion *was* a vision? Those drops of cool water had touched his hot eyelids like some heavenly ichor, and he had had an incredible sense of nearness to God. Not incredible; he had known it.

Nor did it matter that at dinner that night Mrs. Phillips was again the Major's lady, in a black silk dress, with gold earrings and the gold cross around her neck. Her hair was brushed smooth and polished with grease, a braid down over each shoulder. He had met her eyes once as she dropped them to the table for the grace he asked, but they gave no sign. The kettle of stew that sometimes reeked nauseatingly of wild meat gave off a savory aroma, and he spoke of the good smell. Mrs. Phillips, who seldom spoke to the Major during the meal, said something to him in her own tongue, and the Major told him she wanted him to know that the stew was made from a couple of ducks she had caught that day. "Then I should thank you," he had said, not sure she would detect the sarcasm in his tone. He remembered the way she inclined her head so that half her face was shadowed and only the smooth brow shone between those tight-drawn bands of hair; she lifted her face and her eyes met his. They were alive with laughter.

But there was her other face, painted black and white with green lines across the forehead, a hideous mask of horror; the eyes dull and staring as blindly as the dead duck's. And her hair standing up in ragged clumps, chopped off all over her head.

He sat a long time, lifting the top of the inkwell with one of the dry pens and letting it fall closed. Then he flung the pen down on the desk. He could never tell anyone about that time on the butte; neither could he ever get it out of his mind. That monotonous, inhuman cry of despair–like a voice out of hell, or some woman wailing for her demon lover in the mad kingdom of Kubla Khan. She had seemed beyond human power to reach, and no divine power was given him. Even his faith had failed him.

He hadn't been able to tell Harriet how it had been, except that he had failed. But it was the night after he came back, as though she might not have spoken of it so soon otherwise, that Harriet told him about the child. And that, too, his tired mind must go back over. He had seemed to get nothing settled on the long trip back; he had been too much on edge. Here in his study, where he had once been so confident, he could think about what they had done. He had to look squarely tonight at all that had happened to him, for tomorrow he would have to announce himself and explain why they had returned so soon.

They had wanted a child, and had prayed for one; yet when Harriet told him, he had turned around from his table and sat dumb and half incredulous–the way Joseph must have felt, he thought now, with a sense of not irreverent amusement. He had looked at Harriet speaking so calmly over there on the bed. He couldn't remember what he had said, if anything. Their eyes held in the wonder of it, and they were drawn so close together that he had no need to go to her. Then his mind had leaped at the thought of the coming child as a reason for leaving the Wilderness. And, almost at the same instant, Harriet had said perhaps they should try to go back home, as though their eyes, looking into each other's, had propagated the same thought.

It would be terrible to be there in winter, she had said. She could only stay huddled up inside most of the time. Pierre had told them there weren't many Indians at the Fort then, only coming and going; mostly the *engagés* who worked at the Fort, and Mark knew how little they came to the services. He could only say a prayer over them if one got stabbed in a drunken fight.

Of course that was true enough, but it startled him to have Harriet speak so cynically. He had listened, half wondering if she was saying these things or if they were his own thoughts.

Could he accomplish very much during the winter, really? Ever since she had heard that the Phillipses were making the trip all the way to St. Louis, she had been thinking . . . Maybe he should talk to the Major.

He remembered how he had gone over to sit beside her. "You want terribly to go, don't you, Harriet?" he had asked. She was slow in answering, not looking at him. It all depended on him; he would have to decide, she said finally. She would have the baby there if he thought they should stay.

And he had said that of course it would be better for her to be at home; he would be relieved to have her under Dr. Fothergill's care. But the trip would be dangerous. It might be too rugged in her condition, and if she should lose the baby . . . She had said she was sure she could stand the trip. Hadn't she come up all alone? She knew what it would be like. That was quite another thing, he had said, although it had taken plenty of courage, and she should never have tried it. But this time it would be in October and November.

If she hadn't come, she had started to say, but he had said quickly that he could come back up with the first boat in the spring, because there was no use going into that. He could spend the winter working with the Mission Board–studying the language, he had said vaguely; or it might be that Calvary hadn't settled on a permanent pastor, though he doubted that. It did seem, with the baby coming and the Phillipses leaving just then, so they could go with them, as though Providence. . . . Another name for God, but at one remove, he always thought. He had used the term when he wrote the Mission Board.

Then the thought had struck him, as it should have in the very beginning. He had asked her point-blank whether she was suggesting their going just to give him an excuse for leaving, because of his–

and it had been hard, suddenly, to say it, but they were speaking so clearly and honestly together—because of his *failure*.

For answer she had put her arms around his neck and brought his face down to hers. "Oh, Mark, I love you," she had said. "If you hadn't asked that, I would have minded. I don't care if you tell the Major that I want to go home to have the baby; you can even say that I'm afraid to have it without a doctor, and you can tell the deacons and the Mission Board that, too. It's a good enough reason that anybody could understand, and it's better to have them blame me. But, Mark," she had said, "I would hate it if you didn't know really that I'm not afraid to have the baby here, if you're with me."

Put that way . . . so their going *was* mostly for his sake; and the word "blame" . . . If that was her chief reason for going, then they had better stay, he had said. He winced now, hearing himself. And he remembered how he had gone on, insisting that just because he wasn't satisfied with his progress so far didn't mean that in time, when he had learned the tongue and was adept at sign language . . . He hadn't looked at Harriet when he said it; he had kept his eyes on his worktable, imagining himself sitting there working. He had even reminded her that he had been able to communicate with Two Knives, and often smoked a pipe with him. Two Knives had given him that eagle feather. "Until this experience with Mrs. Phillips . . ." he had said. His whole ordeal in the Wilderness seemed caught between those two experiences with that woman, both the confirmation of his mission and the negation of it. What did that mean?

But he hadn't finished his sentence about Mrs. Phillips, and Harriet had said, "What, Mark?"

"I believed I could persuade her to talk for me in the services. She could make all the difference."

"But now?" Harriet persisted.

It had been hard to say it; he had never quite admitted it to himself. "Now I don't think I can. I don't know why, but I can't seem to get to her." It was a relief to tell Harriet he had been dreading the winter. "It would be just as you said, I'm afraid." As he thought of leaving, his desire to go became so strong he had crowded it down by talking of the danger of the trip for Harriet. For if something should go wrong, if the trip should be too hard—and she knew anything could happen—she might blame him. That word again. She might not say it, but she might think that if he hadn't been so discouraged—

given up is what it amounted to – she would have stayed and had her baby safely, whatever the discomforts, he had said.

Her eyes had held his in a long look again. "Do you really think I am like that, Mark? Don't let's ever think one thing and say something else to each other," she had said. He remembered, too, how they had clung together that night in such oneness of understanding and love that he was absolved, for a little time, of his sense of failure.

Mark was stiff from sitting in the cold, and he got up to hunt for paper he could burn in the study grate. On impulse he opened a drawer of sermons, running his finger over them to read their titles, remembering certain ones quite distinctly. He came on "The Hidden Life" and flipped up the page to read the text. From Corinthians: "For what man knoweth the things of a man, save the spirit of man which is in him?"

No one, not even Harriet, knew the things he had felt, and thought, and tried to do in the Wilderness. It wasn't a bad sermon, but he had hardly understood the full meaning of the word "hidden" when he wrote it. He crumpled the neatly written pages, stuffed them under the single stick that had been left in the grate, and lit them. They flamed up and thrust grabbing fingers at the wood, but fell back again. Still, there was a momentary flash of heat. He went back to his drawer and pulled out another: "April 2nd." The Sunday before he left. He looked curiously to see what the man he then was had preached on.

"Untrodden Paths." Joshua 3:4. "For ye have not passed this way heretofore." That was an understatement! And he had certainly been thinking entirely of himself rather than the congregation. How wrapped up in himself he had been! He tore the pages across, adding them to the fire, and went back to his desk.

It was easier to amuse himself with his old sermons than to force his mind back over leaving the Wilderness: how he had put off going to the Major all that next day, but known he would go. The Major's lack of surprise had given him a flat feeling. Harriet's condition struck him as a quite logical reason – just as she had said it would. He was even a little grateful to give it to the Major.

"A white woman, naturally," the Major had said. The Indian women often dropped back and had their children on the trail; quite amazing. But their grief when they lost a child was more frightful than any white woman's, he believed; Mrs. Phillips was still living in a tipi by herself. Mark began to tell him how he had tried . . . but the

Major interrupted him in that brusque way of his saying she had to take it in her own way. A woman like Eenisskim didn't lean on anyone else.

It would always hurt him to remember how little the Major seemed to mind his giving up the mission. Clearly, he felt Mark had been a failure in the Wilderness. Many men were, Mark supposed, not just missionaries. But the Major had been a success; he was as good as any mountain man, could outride, bareback, most of the young braves, and outshoot them, of course. The chiefs listened when he called a council. All of that somehow lined the Major's tone of voice, and the way he made it easy for them to leave. They'd be going that week, the Major had said, while the weather was still good. October first was late; danger of the river freezing before they got down, and snow and blizzards. Mustn't expect an easy trip; part of the way in an open Mackinaw boat. But they'd make it, one way or another. They were taking the two children with them to his sister in Illinois; going to put them in proper schools. Since the younger boy's death, Mrs. Phillips was willing; and he felt it was time for them to be educated like white children. He had been silent for a long minute before he said, quietly, that he was retiring from the fur trade in the spring. Several years ago he had bought quite a piece of country in Illinois, and had a house built. He'd had men working on it, laying out the grounds. It was waiting for them to furnish.

The Major had seemed to forget Mark's presence, and as he stood waiting for him to go on, Mark had wondered how Mrs. Phillips would manage in civilization. Perhaps she would talk English then; she would have to.

Mark went back over to stand in front of the fire. One end of the stick had caught, but the fire was only smouldering. If he had been there at the Fort alone, as he had planned, that first winter, at least, it wouldn't have occurred to him to leave. That thought gave him some small satisfaction. But then, of course, he would have had no legitimate excuse for leaving.

He thought of their departure. He had been as glad to leave the Fort as he had been eager to arrive there. The salute from the cannon as they left belched in his ears with wry derision. He could never forget Aapaaki running along the shore as they pushed off, or the handful of Indians who laughed and pointed at her. Even Mrs. Phillips laughed. Harriet kept her face turned away toward the other shore, he remembered.

When the Black Robe left, Pierre had told him, the Indians, a hundred or more, followed him for three miles to get a last glimpse, and he had to stop and give them his blessing again. "He loved 'em like they were his children," Pierre had told him. When Marcus Ryegate left, he was followed by a single woman, an adulterous outcast with a cut nose. He had been relieved when she stood still; then he saw she was crying, and he had to wave to her.

He and Harriet hadn't talked much about their going, once the Major agreed to it if they thought they could stand the trip. That day when they snagged for the third time in the river, capsizing one boat, so most of their stuff was soaked, Mark had whispered to Harriet that it might be better if they cast Jonah out of the boat. She had known what he meant, but she only smiled and put her hand on his under the buffalo robe.

Mark leaned his head against the mantel. God, he called in his mind. God in Heaven, here am I, back in the place from which I started. Thou knowest that I have failed miserably, that I wanted to leave. But Thou hast brought us safely home after all that long journey, so Thou must want me for something.

He was so tired he stumbled on his way back upstairs, although the morning light was sifting through the stiff lace curtains.

Beneath the layers of sleep Harriet was aware of the sound of swishing water she had wakened to so many mornings, water turning the sidewheel of the Missouri River boat; but there was no movement under her, no sound of timbers straining or of engine chugging, no loud voices. The swishing stopped abruptly, then began again in fast chopping sounds. She sat up in bed and looked around the room, at Mark sleeping soundly beside her.

Crossing to the window, she saw a maid sweeping the white steps of Miss Dinwiddie's house, a woman whose name was Maggie, whom she had known as a child. With a rush of gladness, she realized she was home.

DOROTHY M. JOHNSON

Dorothy M. Johnson was born in McGregor, Iowa, in 1905 and grew up in Whitefish, Montana. She was graduated from the University of Montana in 1928 and worked as a book and magazine editor in New York from 1935 to 1950. She also wrote short stories for popular magazines such as The Saturday Evening Post. *Johnson returned to Montana in 1950 to become news editor for the* Whitefish Pilot *and taught journalism at the University of Montana in Missoula until 1967. Several of Johnson's short stories were adapted for the movies, including "A Man Called Horse," "The Hanging Tree," and "The Man Who Shot Liberty Valance." In 1982, Johnson published* When You and I Were Young, Whitefish, *a humorous recollection of her girlhood in Whitefish. Johnson died at her home in Missoula in 1984.*

The Man Who Shot Liberty Valance

Bert Barricune died in 1910. Not more than a dozen persons showed up for his funeral. Among them was an earnest young reporter who hoped for a human-interest story; there were legends that the old man had been something of a gunfighter in the early days. A few aging men tiptoed in, singly or in pairs, scowling and edgy, clutching their battered hats—men who had been Bert's companions at drinking or penny ante while the world passed them by. One woman came, wearing a heavy veil that concealed her face. White and yellow streaks showed in her black-dyed hair. The reporter made a mental note: Old friend from the old District. But no story there—can't mention that.

One by one they filed past the casket, looking into the still face of old Bert Barricune, who had been nobody. His stubbly hair was white, and his lined face was as empty in death as his life had been. But death had added dignity.

One great spray of flowers spread behind the casket. The card read, "Senator and Mrs. Ransome Foster." There were no other flowers except, almost unnoticed, a few pale, leafless, pink and yellow blossoms scattered on the carpeted step. The reporter, squinting, finally identified them: son of a gun! Blossoms of the prickly pear. Cactus flowers. Seems suitable for the old man—flowers that grow on prairie wasteland. Well, they're free if you want to pick 'em, and Barricune's friends don't look prosperous. But how come the Senator sends a bouquet?

There was a delay, and the funeral director fidgeted a little, waiting. The reporter sat up straighter when he saw the last two mourners enter.

Senator Foster—sure, there's the crippled arm—and that must be his wife. Congress is still in session; he came all the way from Washington. Why would he bother, for an old wreck like Bert Barricune?

After the funeral was decently over, the reporter asked him. The Senator almost told the truth, but he caught himself in time. He said, "Bert Barricune was my friend for more than thirty years."

He could not give the true answer: He was my enemy; he was my conscience; he made me whatever I am.

Ransome Foster had been in the Territory for seven months when he ran into Liberty Valance. He had been afoot on the prairie for two days when he met Bert Barricune. Up to that time, Ranse Foster had been nobody in particular–a dude from the East, quietly inquisitive, moving from one shack town to another; just another tenderfoot with his own reasons for being there and no aim in life at all.

When Barricune found him on the prairie, Foster was indeed a tenderfoot. In his boots there was a warm, damp squidging where his feet had blistered, and the blisters had broken to bleed. He was bruised, sunburned, and filthy. He had been crawling, but when he saw Barricune riding toward him, he sat up. He had no horse, no saddle and, by that time, no pride.

Barricune looked down at him, not saying anything. Finally Ranse Foster asked, "Water?"

Barricune shook his head. "I don't carry none, but we can go where it is."

He stepped down from the saddle, a casual Samaritan, and with one heave pulled Foster upright.

"Git you in the saddle, can you stay there?" he inquired.

"If I can't," Foster answered through swollen lips, "shoot me."

Bert said amiably, "All right," and pulled the horse around. By twisting its ear, he held the animal quiet long enough to help the anguished stranger to the saddle. Then, on foot–and like any cowboy Bert Barricune hated walking–he led the horse five miles to the river. He let Foster lie where he fell in the cottonwood grove and brought him a hat full of water.

After that, Foster made three attempts to stand up. After the third failure, Barricune asked, grinning, "Want me to shoot you after all?"

"No," Foster answered. "There's something I want to do first."

Barricune looked at the bruises and commented, "Well, I should think so." He got on his horse and rode away. After an hour he returned with bedding and grub and asked, "Ain't you dead yet?"

The bruised and battered man opened his uninjured eye and said, "Not yet, but soon." Bert was amused. He brought a bucket of water and set up camp–a bedroll on a tarp, an armload of wood for a fire. He crouched on his heels while the tenderfoot, with cautious movements that told of pain, got his clothes off and splashed water on his body. No gunshot wounds, Barricune observed, but marks of kicks, and a couple that must have been made with a quirt.

After a while he asked, not inquisitively, but as one who has a right to know how matters stood, "Anybody looking for you?"

Foster rubbed dust from his clothes, being too full of pain to shake them.

"No," he said. "But I'm looking for somebody."

"I ain't going to help you look," Bert informed him. "Town's over that way, two miles, when you get ready to come. Cache the stuff when you leave. I'll pick it up."

Three days later they met in the town marshal's office. They glanced at each other but did not speak. This time it was Bert Barricune who was bruised, though not much. The marshal was just letting him out of the one-cell jail when Foster limped into the office. Nobody said anything until Barricune, blinking and walking not quite steadily, had left. Foster saw him stop in front of the next building to speak to a girl. They walked away together, and it looked as if the young man were being scolded.

The marshal cleared his throat. "You wanted something, Mister?"

Foster answered, "Three men set me afoot on the prairie. Is that an offense against the law around here?"

The marshal eased himself and his stomach into a chair and frowned judiciously. "It ain't customary," he admitted. "Who was they?"

"The boss was a big man with black hair, dark eyes, and two gold teeth in front. The other two–"

"I know. Liberty Valance and a couple of his boys. Just what's your complaint, now?" Foster began to understand that no help was going to come from the marshal.

"They rob you?" the marshal asked.

"They didn't search me."

"Take your gun?"

"I didn't have one."

"Steal your horse?"

"Gave him a crack with a quirt, and he left."

"Saddle on him?"

"No. I left it out there."

The marshal shook his head. "Can't see you got any legal complaint," he said with relief. "Where was this?"

"On a road in the woods, by a creek. Two days' walk from here."

The marshal got to his feet. "You don't even know what jurisdiction it was in. They knocked you around; well, that could happen. Man gets in a fight–could happen to anybody."

Foster said dryly, "Thanks a lot."

The marshal stopped him as he reached the door. "There's a reward for Liberty Valance."

"I still haven't got a gun," Foster said. "Does he come here often?"

"Nope. Nothing he'd want in Twotrees. Hard man to find." The marshal looked Foster up and down. "He won't come after you here." It was as if he had added, *Sonny*! "Beat you up once, he won't come again for that."

And I, Foster realized, am not man enough to go after him.

"Fact is," the marshal added, "I can't think of any bait that would bring him in. Pretty quiet here. Yes sir." He put his thumbs in his galluses and looked out the window, taking credit for the quietness.

Bait, Foster thought. He went out thinking about it. For the first time in a couple of years he had an ambition – not a laudable one, but something to aim at. He was going to be the bait for Liberty Valance and, as far as he could be, the trap as well.

At the Elite Cafe he stood meekly in the doorway, hat in hand, like a man who expects and deserves to be refused anything he might ask for. Clearing his throat, he asked, "Could I work for a meal?"

The girl who was filling sugar bowls looked up and pitied him. "Why, I should think so. Mr. Anderson!" She was the girl who had walked away with Barricune, scolding him.

The proprietor came from the kitchen, and Ranse Foster repeated his question, cringing, but with a suggestion of a sneer.

"Go around back and split some wood," Anderson answered, turning back to the kitchen.

"He could just as well eat first," the waitress suggested. "I'll dish up some stew to begin with."

Ranse ate fast, as if he expected the plate to be snatched away. He knew the girl glanced at him several times, and he hated her for it. He had not counted on anyone's pitying him in his new role of sneering humility, but he knew he might as well get used to it.

When she brought his pie, she said, "If you was looking for a job . . ."

He forced himself to look at her suspiciously. "Yes?"

"You could try the Prairie Belle. I heard they needed a swamper."

Bert Barricune, riding out to the river camp for his bedroll, hardly knew the man he met there. Ranse Foster was haughty, condescending, and cringing all at once. He spoke with a faint sneer, and stood as if he expected to be kicked.

"I assumed you'd be back for your belongings," he said. "I realized that you would change your mind."

Barricune, strapping up his bedroll, looked blank. "Never changed it," he disagreed. "Doing just what I planned. I never give you my bedroll."

"Of course not, of course not," the new Ranse Foster agreed with sneering humility. "It's yours. You have every right to reclaim it."

Barricune looked at him narrowly and hoisted the bedroll to sling it up behind his saddle. "I should have left you for the buzzards," he remarked.

Foster agreed, with a smile that should have got him a fist in the teeth. "Thank you, my friend," he said with no gratitude. "Thank you for all your kindness, which I have done nothing to deserve and shall do nothing to repay."

Barricune rode off, scowling, with the memory of his good deed irritating him like lice. The new Foster followed, far behind, on foot.

Sometimes in later life Ranse Foster thought of the several men he had been through the years. He did not admire any of them very much. He was by no means ashamed of the man he finally became, except that he owed too much to other people. One man he had been when he was young, a serious student, gullible and quick-tempered. Another man had been reckless and without an aim; he went West, with two thousand dollars of his own, after a quarrel with the executor of his father's estate. That man did not last long. Liberty Valance had whipped him with a quirt and kicked him into unconsciousness, for no reason except that Liberty, meeting him and knowing him for a tenderfoot, was able to do so. That man died on the prairie. After that, there was the man who set out to be the bait that would bring Liberty Valance into Twotrees.

Ranse Foster had never hated anyone before he met Liberty Valance, but Liberty was not the last man he learned to hate. He hated the man he himself had been while he waited to meet Liberty again.

The swamper's job at the Prairie Belle was not disgraceful until Ranse Foster made it so. When he swept floors, he was so obviously contemptuous of the work and of himself for doing it that other men saw him as contemptible. He watched the customers with a curled lip as if they were beneath him. But when a poker player threw a white chip on the floor, the swamper looked at him with half-veiled hatred–and picked up the chip. They talked about him at the Prairie Belle, because he could not be ignored.

At the end of the first month, he bought a Colt .45 from a drunken cowboy who needed money worse than he needed two guns. After that, Ranse went without part of his sleep in order to walk out, seven mornings a week, to where his first camp had been and practice target shooting. And the second time he overslept from exhaustion, Joe Mosten of the Prairie Belle fired him.

"Here's your pay," Joe growled, and dropped the money on the floor.

A week passed before he got another job. He ate his meals frugally in the Elite Cafe and let himself be seen stealing scraps off plates that other diners had left. Lillian, the older of the two waitresses, yelled her disgust, but Hallie, who was young, pitied him.

"Come to the back door when it's dark," she murmured, "and I'll give you a bite. There's plenty to spare."

The second evening he went to the back door, Bert Barricune was there ahead of him. He said gently, "Hallie is my girl."

"No offense intended," Foster answered. "The young lady offered me food, and I have come to get it."

"A dog eats where it can," young Barricune drawled.

Ranse's muscles tensed and rage mounted in his throat, but he caught himself in time and shrugged. Bert said something then that scared him: "If you wanted to get talked about, it's working fine. They're talking clean over in Dunbar."

"What they do or say in Dunbar," Foster answered, "is nothing to me."

"It's where Liberty Valance hangs out," the other man said casually. "In case you care."

Ranse almost confided then, but instead said stiffly, "I do not quite appreciate your strange interest in my affairs."

Barricune pushed back his hat and scratched his head. "I don't understand it myself. But leave my girl alone."

"As charming as Miss Hallie may be," Ranse told him, "I am interested only in keeping my stomach filled."

"Then why don't you work for a living? The clerk at Dowitts' quit this afternoon."

Jake Dowitt hired him as a clerk because nobody else wanted the job.

"Read and write, do you?" Dowitt asked. "Work with figures?"

Foster drew himself up. "Sir, whatever may be said against me, I believe I may lay claim to being a scholar. That much I claim, if nothing more. I have read law."

"Maybe the job ain't good enough for you," Dowitt suggested.

Foster became humble again. "Any job is good enough for me. I will also sweep the floor."

"You will also keep up the fire in the stove," Dowitt told him. "Seven in the morning till nine at night. Got a place to live?"

"I sleep in the livery stable in return for keeping it shoveled out."

Dowitt had intended to house his clerk in a small room over the store, but he changed his mind. "Got a shed out back you can bunk in," he offered. "You'll have to clean it out first. Used to keep chickens there."

"There is one thing," Foster said. "I want two half-days off a week."

Dowitt looked over the top of his spectacles. "Now what would you do with time off? Never mind. You can have it—for less pay. I give you a discount on what you buy in the store."

The only purchase Foster made consisted of four boxes of cartridges a week.

In the store, he weighed salt pork as if it were low stuff but himself still lower, humbly measured lengths of dress goods for the women customers. He added vanity to his other unpleasantnesses and let customers discover him combing his hair admiringly before a small mirror. He let himself be seen reading a small black book, which aroused curiosity.

It was while he worked at the store that he started Twotrees' first school. Hallie was responsible for that. Handing him a plate heaped higher than other customers got at the café, she said gently, "You're a learned man, they say, Mr. Foster."

With Hallie he could no longer sneer or pretend humility, for Hallie was herself humble, as well as gentle and kind. He protected himself from her by not speaking unless he had to.

He answered, "I have had advantages, Miss Hallie, before fate brought me here."

"That book you read," she asked wistfully, "what's it about?"

"It was written by a man named Plato," Ranse told her stiffly. "It was written in Greek."

She brought him a cup of coffee, hesitated for a moment, and then asked, "You can read and write American, too, can't you?"

"English, Miss Hallie," he corrected. "English is our mother tongue. I am quite familiar with English."

She put her red hands on the café counter. "Mr. Foster," she whispered, "will you teach me to read?"

He was too startled to think of an answer she could not defeat.

"Bert wouldn't like it," he said. "You're a grown woman besides. It wouldn't look right for you to be learning to read now."

She shook her head. "I can't learn any younger." She sighed. "I always wanted to know how to read and write." She walked away toward the kitchen, and Ranse Foster was struck with an emotion he knew he could not afford. He was swept with pity. He called her back.

"Miss Hallie. Not you alone–people would talk about you. But if you brought Bert–"

"Bert can already read some. He don't care about it. But there's some kids in town." Her face was so lighted that Ranse looked away.

He still tried to escape. "Won't you be ashamed, learning with children?"

"Why, I'll be proud to learn any way at all," she said.

He had three little girls, two restless little boys, and Hallie in Twotrees' first school sessions–one hour each afternoon, in Dowitt's storeroom. Dowitt did not dock his pay for the time spent, but he puzzled a great deal. So did the children's parents. The children themselves were puzzled at some of the things he read aloud, but they were patient. After all, lessons lasted only an hour.

"When you are older, you will understand this," he promised, not looking at Hallie, and then he read Shakespeare's sonnet that begins:

No longer mourn for me when I am dead
Than you shall hear the surly sullen bell

and ends:

Do not so much as my poor name rehearse,
But let your love even with my life decay,
Lest the wise world should look into your moan
And mock you with me after I am gone.

Hallie understood the warning, he knew. He read another sonnet, too:

When in disgrace with Fortune and men's eyes,
I all alone beweep my outcast state,

and carefully did not look up at her as he finished it:

For thy sweet love rememb'red such wealth brings
That then I scorn to change my state with kings.

Her earnestness in learning was distasteful to him–the anxious way she grasped a pencil and formed letters, the little gasp with which she always began to read aloud. Twice he made her cry, but she never missed a lesson.

He wished he had a teacher for his own learning, but he could not trust anyone, and so he did his lessons alone. Bert Barricune caught him at it on one of those free afternoons when Foster, on a horse from the livery stable, had ridden miles out of town to a secluded spot.

Ranse Foster had an empty gun in his hand when Barricune stepped out from behind a sandstone column and remarked, "I've seen better."

Foster whirled, and Barricune added, "I could have been somebody else–and your gun's empty."

"When I see somebody else, it won't be," Foster promised.

"If you'd asked me," Barricune mused, "I could've helped you. But you didn't want no helping. A man shouldn't be ashamed to ask somebody that knows better than him." His gun was suddenly in his hand, and five shots cracked their echoes around the skull-white sandstone pillars. Half an inch above each of five cards that Ranse had tacked to a dead tree, at the level of a man's waist, a splintered hole appeared in the wood. "Didn't want to spoil your targets," Barricune explained.

"I'm not ashamed to ask you," Foster told him angrily, "since you know so much. I shoot straight but slow. I'm asking you now."

Barricune, reloading his gun, shook his head. "It's kind of late for that. I come out to tell you that Liberty Valance is in town. He's interested in the dude that anybody can kick around – this here tenderfoot that boasts how he can read Greek."

"Well," said Foster softly. "Well, so the time has come."

"Don't figure you're riding into town with me," Bert warned. "You're coming in all by yourself."

Ranse rode into town with his gun belt buckled on. Always before, he had carried it wrapped in a slicker. In town, he allowed himself the luxury of one last vanity. He went to the barbershop, neither sneering nor cringing, and said sharply, "Cut my hair. Short."

The barber was nervous, but he worked understandably fast.

"Thought you was partial to that long wavy hair of yourn," he remarked.

"I don't know why you thought so," Foster said coldly.

Out in the street again, he realized that he did not know how to go about the job. He did not know where Liberty Valance was, and he was determined not to be caught like a rat. He intended to look for Liberty.

Joe Mosten's right-hand man was lounging at the door of the Prairie Belle. He moved over to bar the way.

"Not in there, Foster," he said gently. It was the first time in months that Ranse Foster had heard another man address him respectfully. His presence was recognized – as a menace to the fixtures of the Prairie Belle.

When I die, sometime today, he thought, they won't say I was a coward. They may say I was a damn fool, but I won't care by that time.

"Where is he?" Ranse asked.

"I couldn't tell you that," the man said apologetically. "I'm young and healthy, and where he is is none of my business. Joe'd be obliged if you stay out of the bar, that's all."

Ranse looked across toward Dowitt's store. The padlock was on the door. He glanced north, toward the marshal's office.

"That's closed, too," the saloon man told him courteously. "Marshal was called out of town an hour ago."

Ranse threw back his head and laughed. The sound echoed back from the false-fronted buildings across the street. There was nobody walking in the street; there were not even any horses tied to the hitching racks.

"Send Liberty word," he ordered in the tone of one who has a right to command. "Tell him the tenderfoot wants to see him again."

The saloon man cleared his throat. "Guess it won't be necessary. That's him coming down at the end of the street, wouldn't you say?"

Ranse looked, knowing the saloon man was watching him curiously.

"I'd say it is," he agreed. "Yes, I'd say that was Liberty Valance."

"I'll be going inside now," the other man remarked apologetically. "Well, take care of yourself." He was gone without a sound.

This is the classic situation, Ranse realized. Two enemies walking to meet each other along the dusty, waiting street of a western town. What reasons other men have had, I will never know. There are so many things I have never learned! And now there is no time left.

He was an actor who knew the end of the scene but had forgotten the lines and never knew the cue for them. One of us ought to say something, he realized. I should have planned this all out in advance. But all I ever saw was the end of it.

Liberty Valance, burly and broad-shouldered, walked stiff-legged, with his elbows bent.

When he is close enough for me to see whether he is smiling, Ranse Foster thought, somebody's got to speak.

He looked into his own mind and realized, This man is afraid, this Ransome Foster. But nobody else knows it. He walks and is afraid, but he is no coward. Let them remember that. Let Hallie remember that.

Liberty Valance gave the cue. "Looking for me?" he called between his teeth. He was grinning.

Ranse was almost grateful to him; it was as if Liberty had said, The time is now!

"I owe you something," Ranse answered. "I want to pay my debt."

Liberty's hand flashed with his own. The gun in Foster's hand exploded, and so did the whole world.

Two shots to my one, he thought—his last thought for a while.

He looked up at a strange, unsteady ceiling and a face that wavered like a reflection in water. The bed beneath him swung even after he closed his eyes. Far away someone said, "Shove some more cloth in the wound. It slows the bleeding."

He knew with certain agony where the wound was—in his right shoulder. When they touched it, he heard himself cry out.

The face that wavered above him was a new one, Bert Barricune's.

"He's dead," Barricune said.

Foster answered from far away, "I am not."

Barricune said, "I didn't mean you."

Ranse turned his head away from the pain, and the face that had shivered above him before was Hallie's, white and big-eyed. She put a hesitant hand on his, and he was annoyed to see that hers was trembling.

"Are you shaking?" he asked, "because there's blood on my hands?"

"No," she answered. "It's because they might have been getting cold."

He was aware then that other people were in the room; they stirred and moved aside as the doctor entered.

"Maybe you're gonna keep that arm," the doctor told him at last. "But it's never gonna be much use to you."

The trial was held three weeks after the shooting, in the hotel room where Ranse lay in bed. The charge was disturbing the peace; he pleaded guilty and was fined ten dollars.

When the others had gone, he told Bert Barricune, "There was a reward, I heard. That would pay the doctor and the hotel."

"You ain't going to collect it," Bert informed him. "It'd make you too big for your britches." Barricune sat looking at him for a moment and then remarked, "You didn't kill Liberty."

Foster frowned. "They buried him."

"Liberty fired once. You fired once and missed. I fired once, and I don't generally miss. I ain't going to collect the reward, neither. Hallie don't hold with violence."

Foster said thoughtfully, "That was all I had to be proud of."

"You faced him," Barricune said. "You went to meet him. If you got to be proud of something, you can remember that. It's a fact you ain't got much else."

Ranse looked at him with narrowed eyes. "Bert, are you a friend of mine?"

Bert smiled without humor. "You know I ain't. I picked you up off the prairie, but I'd do that for the lowest scum that crawls. I wisht I hadn't."

"Then why—"

Bert looked at the toe of his boot. "Hallie likes you. I'm a friend of Hallie's. That's all I ever will be, long as you're around."

Ranse said, "Then I shot Liberty Valance." That was the nearest he ever dared come to saying "Thank you." And that was when Bert Barricune started being his conscience, his Nemesis, his lifelong enemy and the man who made him great.

"Would she be happy living back East?" Foster asked. "There's money waiting for me there if I go back."

Bert answered, "What do you think?" He stood up and stretched. "You got quite a problem, ain't you? You could solve it easy by just going back alone. There ain't much a man can do here with a crippled arm."

He went out and shut the door behind him.

There is always a way out, Foster thought, if a man wants to take it. Bert had been his way out when he met Liberty on the street of Twotrees. To go home was the way out of this.

I learned to live without pride, he told himself. I could learn to forget about Hallie.

When she came, between the dinner dishes and setting the tables for supper at the café, he told her.

She did not cry. Sitting in the chair beside his bed, she winced and jerked one hand in protest when he said, "As soon as I can travel, I'll be going back where I came from."

She did not argue. She said only, "I wish you good luck, Ransome. Bert and me, we'll look after you long as you stay. And remember you after you're gone."

"How will you remember me?" he demanded harshly.

As his student she had been humble, but as a woman she had her pride. "Don't ask that," she said, and got up from the chair.

"Hallie, Hallie," he pleaded, "how can I stay? How can I earn a living?"

She said indignantly, as if someone else had insulted him, "Ranse Foster, I just guess you could do anything you wanted to."

"Hallie," he said gently, "sit down."

He never really wanted to be outstanding. He had two aims in life: to make Hallie happy and to keep Bert Barricune out of trouble. He defended Bert on charges ranging from drunkenness to stealing cattle, and Bert served time twice.

Ranse Foster did not want to run for judge, but Bert remarked, "I think Hallie would kind of like it if you was His Honor." Hallie was pleased but not surprised when he was elected. Ranse was surprised but not pleased.

He was not eager to run for the legislature—that was after the territory became a state—but there was Bert Barricune in the background, never urging, never advising, but watching with half-closed, bloodshot eyes. Bert Barricune, who never amounted to anything, but never intruded, was a living, silent reminder of three debts: a hat full of water under the cottonwoods, gunfire in a dusty street, and Hallie, quietly sewing beside a lamp in the parlor. And the Fosters had four sons.

All the things the opposition said about Ranse Foster when he ran for the state legislature were true, except one. He had been a lowly swamper in a frontier saloon; he had been a dead beat, accepting handouts at the alley entrance of a café; he had been despicable and despised. But the accusation that lost him the election was false. He had not killed Liberty Valance. He never served in the state legislature.

When there was talk of his running for governor, he refused. Handy Strong, who knew politics, tried to persuade him.

"That shooting, we'll get around that. 'The Honorable Ransome Foster walked down a street in broad daylight to meet an enemy of society. He shot him down in a fair fight, of necessity, the way you'd shoot a mad dog–but Liberty Valance could shoot back, and he did. Ranse Foster carries the mark of that encounter today in a crippled right arm. He is still paying the price for protecting law-abiding citizens. And he was the first teacher west of Rosy Buttes. He served without pay.' You've come a long way, Ranse, and you're going further."

"A long way," Foster agreed, "for a man who never wanted to go anywhere. I don't want to be governor."

When Handy had gone, Bert Barricune sagged in, unwashed, unshaven. He sat down stiffly. At the age of fifty, he was an old man, an unwanted relic of the frontier that was gone, a legacy to more civilized times that had no place for him. He filled his pipe deliberately. After a while he remarked, "The other side is gonna say you ain't fitten to be governor. Because your wife ain't fancy enough. They're gonna say Hallie didn't even learn to read till she was growed up."

Ranse was on his feet, white with fury. "Then I'm going to win this election if it kills me."

"I don't reckon it'll kill you," Bert drawled. "Liberty Valance couldn't."

"I could have got rid of the weight of that affair long ago," Ranse reminded him, "by telling the truth."

"You could yet," Bert answered. "Why don't you?"

Ranse said bitterly, "Because I owe you too much. . . . I don't think Hallie wants to be the governor's lady. She's shy."

"Hallie don't never want nothing for herself. She wants things for you. The way I feel, I wouldn't mourn at your funeral. But what Hallie wants, I'm gonna try to see she gets."

"So am I," Ranse promised grimly.

"Then I don't mind telling you," Bert admitted, "that it was me reminded the opposition to dig up that matter of how she couldn't read."

As the Senator and his wife rode home after old Bert Barricune's barren funeral, Hallie sighed. "Bert never had much of anything. I guess he never wanted much."

He wanted you to be happy, Ranse Foster thought, and he did the best he knew how.

"I wonder where those prickly-pear blossoms came from," he mused.

Hallie glanced up at him, smiling. "From me," she said.

Confessions of a Telephone Girl

I used to be a switchboard operator in Whitefish. Not everybody had a telephone—at $1.75 a month on a four-party line, it was a luxury that lots of people could do without. . . .

A girl on steady, working 56 hours one week and 48 the next, got $50 a month. The relief girl was paid $1.65 for eight hours. If she worked part of a shift for one of the steady girls, that girl paid her 20 cents an hour. When I was relieving, I maintained that $1.65 divided by eight hours ought to be 21 cents, but the steady girls stood shoulder to shoulder against inflation.

These jobs were much in demand. There were usually two or three girls hopefully waiting for a chance to learn. The relief operator (unless she was me, not intending to make a career of it) hoped that one of the steady girls would get married, move away, or drop dead.

We all taught the learners willingly; it gave us status to have someone to admonish, because nobody hesitated to admonish us. And any of us could tell, after a couple of hours, whether she was ever going to be any good. If she was phlegmatic and didn't get upset when she made a mistake, there wasn't much hope. Slow and steady did not win that race. The plowhorse type would never learn to be nimble, to keep track of the time on a long distance call while handling a lot of local calls and trying to hunt down a doctor and the Great Northern call boy. The fire-horse type worked out best—nervous, dedicated, quick. To this day, when the timer on my electric range buzzes, I jump a foot.

There were no flashing lights on our switchboard. It had rows of black eyes, each with a number under it. When a subscriber wanted to make a call, he ground a crank. The little black eye above his number flipped over and showed red. Our board was modern enough, though, so that the operator didn't grind a crank to ring. She pulled a little peg called a key–and it had better be the right key or she'd ring somebody a blast in the ear, which was a dreadful thing to do because it hurt.

The board was a vast expanse of eyes, with, at the base, a dozen or so pairs of plugs on cords for connecting and an equal number of keys for talking, listening, and ringing. On a busy day these cords were woven across the board in a constantly changing, confusing pattern; half the people using telephones were convinced that Central was incompetent or hated them, and Central–flipping plugs into holes, ringing numbers, trying to remember whether 44 wanted 170K or 170L, because if she went back and asked him, he'd be sure she was stupid–was close to hysterics.

It was every operator's dream that when her ship came in she would open all the keys on a busy board, yell "To hell with you," pull all the plugs and march out in triumph, leaving everything in total chaos. Nobody ever did. We felt an awful responsibility toward our little corner of the world. We really helped keep it running, one girl at a time all by herself at the board.

We were expected to remember quite a lot of things. There were two rural lines with lots of people on them and multiple rings, like three shorts and one long for a store out in the woods somewhere. Mostly these subscribers tended to their own affairs and did their own handle grinding, calling between isolated lumber camps, timber claims, and ranger stations. We were supposed to ignore them unless they buzzed one long ring. That meant they wanted the switchboard to connect them with someone on another line. The theory was fine. It just didn't work very well.

Consider: A girl is trained to stab a plug into every hole that buzzes, but she is also trained to ignore two of them. That's hard enough. But she is supposed to NOT ignore them if one long buzz sounds. When there are buzzes all over the board, she probably does the wrong thing. Either she forgets to ignore those two lines, says "Number, please?" and is told by an impatient caller twenty miles away to get off the line, or she remembers to ignore them and doesn't notice when one of them gives a long buzz that she's supposed to answer.

So way out there on a mountain somewhere a frustrated smoke chaser grinds the crank harder and harder and gets madder and madder because he has a forest fire to report and why the hell doesn't Whitefish answer? When she finally remembers not to ignore that long buzz, the smoke chaser naturally gives her a piece of his mind, hot off the griddle, and her feelings are hurt and maybe she cries. It's a wonder ALL the forests didn't burn up, with the flames fanned by gusts of high emotion.

We were also supposed to keep in mind that two other lines were pay stations, and when anyone phoned from there, it cost money. We were suspicious of anyone who was willing to pay a nickel for a local call. He was obviously up to no good. Why didn't he call from the pool hall? So he wanted privacy, did he? He didn't get it. A charming fellow I had met while swimming over at Whitefish Lake once called from a pay phone. Recognizing his voice, of course I kept the key open. He made an appointment with a fallen woman over at the Red Flats, so after that I didn't need any more swimming instruction from him.

On a pay-station call, when the operator got the called number to answer, she said, "Hold the line, please," closed the key, opened the key to the pay phone, said, "I have your number. Deposit five cents, please," and waited until the nickel clanked. Then she connected both lines and advised benignly, "go ahead."

For long distance it was harder, counting clanks of varying tones for various coins and doing mental arithmetic. Mr. Tills collected the money from the pay stations once a month. There was always too much money, and this he couldn't forgive. We always thought he ought to be pleased. But we were supposed to make out a ticket for every dratted five-cent call, and when we were busy, we couldn't. When the monthly day of accounting came, we quivered under the lash of his tongue—"Two dollars and sixty-five cents too much in zero—what do you girls think you're *doing*?" We would gladly have divided the surplus among ourselves to keep him happy, but he had the key to the money boxes.

On one ghastly occasion the total was almost nine dollars short, and of course collecting too little money was worse than collecting too much. It was my fault, too. A man had phoned all the way to New York from the pay station at the Cadillac Hotel. New York, mind you! Who ever heard of such a thing?

The combined efforts of operators in cities all across the United States, their voices getting fainter with distance as they bandied around a lot of bewildering code abbreviations, put the call through in a hurry. It didn't take more than a couple of hours. And I was so flushed with triumph when the connection was completed that I forgot to tell him to drop in his money. By the time the shortage was discovered, he had left town–the rat–and the hotel had no forwarding address for him. Mr. Tills came close to apoplexy.

There were two other lines about which we had to remember something special: "Don't say 'Number, please.' Say 'Whitefish.'" Those lines were long distance connecting Kalispell, and we stood, in relation to any Kalispell operator, as an erring child to a stern stepmother who is a practicing witch. All our long-distance calls went or came through Kalispell. Why, over there they had an operator who handled nothing but long distance!

We couldn't really imagine so idyllic a situation. A girl at our switchboard was everything–local, long distance, and information. We also turned on the fire alarm and the police signal. We used to tell inquirers what time it was until somebody missed a train because our clock was slow. After that, Mr. Tills made us refer such inquiries to the Great Northern depot, and the agent on duty there didn't like it a bit. Some subscribers even expected us to know whether No. 2 was going to be on time, but the railroad didn't think we ought to be responsible for information like that.

For Mr. Tills, life was a constant battle, him against us. We seldom came up to his standard. He had spent some years in Chicago, and he mentioned it often. Telephone users in Whitefish didn't come up to his standard, either. Everybody tended to be too informal.

If Mrs. Smith asked for 73X, which was her sister, and we knew 73X wouldn't answer because she wasn't home, we were likely to say, "She's at 190-L–I'll ring there." This was fine with Mrs. Smith and her sister, but Mr. Tills couldn't stand it. They didn't do things that way in Chicago. We were supposed to keep trying 73-X until Mrs. Smith got tired and hung up or we got tired and announced, "That number does not answer."

Since our switchboard had no lights to flash on or off, the only way a girl could find out when people had finished a conversation was to open the key, listen, and inquire, "Are you waiting? Are you through?" If nobody said anything, she pulled the plugs. If somebody did say something, it was usually, "No, we're not through. Get off the line!"

The telephoning public had a dark suspicion that we spent our spare time listening in, and very often the public was right. Mr. Tills felt that listening in was a crime just short of manslaughter. They didn't do it in Chicago. Of course not. Nobody in Chicago knew anybody.

Another thing they didn't do in Chicago was to ring a number that the calling party couldn't look up because she had mislaid her glasses or the baby had torn that page out of the phone book. In cases like this, Mr. Tills expected us to assume another aspect of our triple personality. The local operator became Information. When requested to ring Charlie Turner's house, she mustn't admit that she knew the number. She was supposed to refer the calling party to Information. Then she said, "This is Information. May I help you?" and after letting enough time elapse to look up "Turner, Charles," which she didn't need to do, she announced his number.

Naturally the calling party then said, "All right, ring it, will you?" But Information was too superior to ring numbers; all *she* did was reveal them. So Information said with a tinge of reproach, "I will connect you with the operator." Thereupon she clicked the key a couple of times to indicate that big doings were afoot and came back on the line to say, "Number, please?"

This nonsense puzzled the customers, who knew very well that there was only one girl on the board, so what was all the fuss about? But Mr. Tills liked the formality: it was as close as possible to the way they did it in Chicago.

Sometimes in the evening when he had nothing better to do, he strolled around downtown and checked up on us from various phones. He was seldom successful in catching an operator doing something wrong. We recognized his voice. We recognized a lot of voices. Voices were our business. If he tried to make a girl mad by being grumpy or downright rude, she became sweeter and sweeter; she dripped the honey of courtesy until he was up to his ankles in it.

If he tried to catch her knowing a number without referring to her all-wise other self, Information, she gave him more key clicks than anyone else got; also she kept him waiting a while and came back on the line to apologize abjectly for the delay and explain that the board was terribly busy. This was part of our continuing war with Mr. Tills. We insisted that only a genius with four hands could handle the job. He was convinced that we had nothing to do and really should mop the floor once in a while.

Once he tried to prove we weren't overworked and couldn't possibly need two girls during the busiest part of the day. (Occasionally a day operator, pushed past the endurance point, simply burst into hysterical tears.) He would have us keep an accurate count of local calls.

So he gave us a little gadget that we were supposed to tap every time we plugged in. If there was anything an overworked operator didn't need, it was one more gadget to keep track of. Naturally, what we did was ignore it until a lull came; then we caught up with our tapping, plus a good big bonus on account of resentment.

One of the perquisites of Mr. Tills' job as manager was a rent-free apartment just down the hall from the room the switchboard was in, and one of his duties (he said) was to supervise; i.e., to snoop and try to catch the night operator taking a nap. He removed the lock from our door, leaving a big round hole suitable for peering through. We always knew when he was there, because the floor squeaked. Mr. Tills had an affliction that made one of his eyes roll around sometimes. It was enough to stand your hair on end to glance over at the peep hole and see that whirling eye.

One night a newly trained girl on her first all-alone shift saw it and was terrified–but not paralyzed. With great presence of mind, she switched on the downtown light that signaled the police, rang the police station and left the key open so the night cop could hear her death struggle if it came to that, and then ran to the open window and screamed for help. It was all terribly embarrassing for Mr. Tills. After that there was a big cork in the peep hole.

I came home from the University one June to find that a new girl had been hired, and she was trying to reform our methods, also Mr. Tills'. She worked in Minneapolis, which was almost as awesome as Chicago, both being big cities way back east. She was determine to introduce big-city usages in little old Whitefish. For her, the Great Northern depot was nigh-un nigh-un and Hori's Cafe was thu-rrree thu-rrree. She said "Oppiteh" when she meant operator, and her "Number please" came out like "No place." These elegancies confused the customers quite a lot, they being used to our home-grown pronunciation. Unless, I suppose, they had lived in Minneapolis.

We resented her, partly because she was married and didn't need the job, but we grudgingly admired her, too, because she bullied Mr. Tills and sometimes seemed to have him on the ropes. After all, his gospel about how they did things in Chicago was only hearsay; he had never been an oppiteh there. But Florence, or whatever her name was, had the True Word about Minneapolis from personal experience.

She yearned to be our Chief Oppiteh and sometimes claimed she was, but Mr. Tills said she wasn't. Our real Chief Oppiteh was in Kalispell. We never laid eyes on her. We thought of her as a goblin that would get us if we didn't watch out, but we loved her as compared with Florence. So we went along as before, without any resident Chief Oppiteh. In Whitefish we were all first among equals.

When Florence departed, she left us a legacy. She used very fancy penmanship on long distance tickets, and for a while we all put little circles over our *i*'s instead of dots.

I was a pretty good operator but not the best one Whitefish ever had. We had two girls in the years I worked there who were wonders. Carrie and Faye were the fastest draws in the West. Either of them could ring a number (front key plus a button for L, K, Y or X) with the left hand while flipping a back plug into a hole with the right hand and caroling "That party doesn't answer" with no hands to somebody else. Meanwhile she could remember that 90 had blinked before 144 and therefore deserved to be answered first and, when she had a second to spare, open two or three keys to inquire "Are you waiting? Are you through?" and pull out the plugs without disconnecting anybody. Those girls' hands darted around like a pair of hummingbirds.

Along with all this, Faye or Carrie could remember that when Kalispell called back to report, "On your 15 to Spokane, W.H." the man who had placed the call on Ticket 15 at the Cadillac Hotel pay station wasn't in the booth any more but she should ring the desk clerk, who would trot down the hall to his room to get him.

W.H. meant "We have the party you want, anyway within shouting distance, so now try to find yours." W.H.L. meant "We have the party on the line with the key open, so let's be formal." H.L. meant "Hold the line, I'll be right back." D.A. stood for "Doesn't answer; might as well give up." N.A. was less final—"No answer, but remind me later and I'll try some more." A.Y. meant "The calling party will talk to anyone who answers at that number." A.B. meant he would settle for anybody who could talk business. B.Y. meant "The line is busy."

We never knew why long distance operators had to communicate in that esoteric way. We simply accepted the idea that ordinary people trying to connect with someone far away were not supposed to know what was going on until one or another operator emerged from the sacred mystery and translated into plain language. I loved those code letters. They made me feel like part of an international spy ring instead of a relief operator whose eight-hour shift was worth $1.65. . . .

We took care of a lot of little things that a dial system won't do for you. If a brakeman's wife, expecting the doctor to phone because the baby was sick, asked us to ring lightly because Henry had to catch some sleep before going out on his run, we rang lightly.

Sometimes we were trapped. When the roundhouse whistle wailed over and over, we braced for a flood of calls because that signal called out the wrecker. Somewhere east or west a train was in bad trouble. Men might be hurt, might be dying. Frantic wives phoned, demanding the dispatcher's office, wanting to know at least in which direction that wrecked train was. But everybody who might know was busy getting a crew together, making arrangements for the emergency, and couldn't answer such calls. All we could do was help the women worry. A dial system can't even do that. . . .

One of our sins that I'm not sure Mr. Tills ever caught onto was what we called "talkin' to a fellah." Late evenings and at night there was nothing much to do at the switchboard. When a girl had read all the dog-eared confession magazines, frowning because some other girl had already clipped the coupons that would bring a free sample of face powder, life was pretty dull. There wasn't room to lay out a game of solitaire. So when some man about town called in and crooned, "Hey, kid, you wanna talk?" she usually did. . . .

A really bold romeo might ask for the privilege of walking Central home after her shift was over (the evening shift, that is; nobody cared to walk home the night girl who got off at seven in the morning), and she might lead him on a little. But she probably refused him in the end and sneaked out the back way, just in case he might be the type who wouldn't take No for an answer. She didn't really want to meet him. He might be an absolute monster. She just liked the sound of his voice, and he helped pass the time.

I carried on an affair intermittently all one summer with a smokechaser far away in the woods. Both of us had to stay awake. He could make a conversation about nothing last until 3:00 A.M. and sound like Don Juan arranging a seduction without ever saying a thing I couldn't have repeated to my mother. I remember his voice fondly and with gratitude. Murmuring and cooing, we kept each other awake while he guarded the forest and I took care of Whitefish.

JOHN J. TATSEY

John Tatsey, a Blackfeet policeman and reporter, was born in 1894 on the Blackfeet Indian Reservation, where he attended an Indian mission school. Tatsey ranched and worked in the cattle business before moving to Heart Butte in the 1950s, where he was a tribal peace officer for eighteen years. From his vantage point at the Heart Butte police headquarters and jail, Tatsey wrote a weekly column for the Browning Glacier Reporter, *and his "Heart Butte News" columns have become an important part of Montana lore. These selections are from* The Black Moccasin, *edited by Paul De Vore and published in 1971.*

From The Black Moccasin

Heart Butte News

The best ever happened at Heart Butte was last Sunday when there were between 75 and 100 cars in front of the church. The church was jammed so there were a lot of people stood outside. Hope their prayers were heard.

Mr. Richard Little Dog has been coming to Heart Butte on Sundays. Tatsey had to put him in jail for the night. He came again last Sunday and someone reported so the police went to investigate, found him out in a car. Police asked his wife what was wrong. She said he was sick and his heart was stopping on him coming from Browning and stopped altogether when they got to Heart Butte. Police told them to leave and Richard's heart got back in motion. Too much gallo.

Francis Bull Shoe and partner Stoles Head Carrier are two fine men, staying home behaving.

Last week the Heart Butte twins were seen having trouble on the road with their legs. They were holding one another up to keep from falling. They got home sometime during the night.

Heart Butte people are expecting a lot of people for Easter Sunday if the weather permits. All will enjoy going to church and picnics and games in the afternoon.

The reporter from Heart Butte missed last week's news on account of the bad weather and blizzards, but will report what happened then this week.

On Tuesday the Council sent a load of Buffalo meat to Heart Butte and it was given out to the people and everyone had meat during the cold spell.

James Spotted Eagle was at police headquarters and reported dogs killing his sheep right in his shed at night. Police went to the party who owned the dogs and they were taken off the living list.

Leo Bull Shoe had a dream last week. He dreamed that he could take live coals from the fire and not burn himself so he tried it by putting live coals under his arm pits. Next day he had blisters under each arm so he is no medicine man.

Leslie Grant went on a party with some young men last week. He did not want to go home, he was afraid of his wife so he went to Jerry Comes at Night's house and asked if he could sleep there till he felt better. They showed him a place to sleep where there was a person sleeping and it was his wife and it was all over.

Frank Comes at Night came to Heart Butte Sunday in a team and wagon and someone said the team and wagon blowed away with Mrs. Comes at Night in it.

Louie Red Head and son Lewis went out to look for their team of horses late one evening. Horses came home so Mary Red Head went out to look for her man. Louie landed in Dupuyer and found a team of Gallos. They ran away with him and Tribal police were called and finally caught him red hot, and kept him in the Heart Butte cooler and then over to J. W. Walter's quarters.

There is a new place at Heart Butte just south of the government square, where there are several people living. It has been raided a few times by Tatsey Tribal Police and now the name is Dizzy Land. There is competition between George Night and Maggie Jiggs for mayor in Dizzy Land.

Mr. & Mrs. Running Crane were not at Heart Butte Sunday and were soon missed by the people. They were stuck in a mud hole on Big Badger.

Sunday the Heart Butte children made their first communion. Fifteen boys and eight girls.

Heart Butte News

The reporter last Friday morning drove out to check on the sheep he supposed to herd. While looking around saw a white tail buck. Wanted liver so bad for breakfast, couldn't shoot to hit. No guts there.

There were George Horn from Durham at Heart Butte with a Canadian and his wife. They were at the stick game all feeling really light. The Canadian asked someone where the rest room was, and he was told there was none, but to do the best he could to find one.

The wedding dance at Little Badger turned out pretty rough. Towards morning a free for all, but the bride and groom got home without a mark.

John Tatsey has an invitation from Governor to attend inaugural for 16th of January. First Republican ever invited a Democrat, but the tribe has no traveling money.

As I say, I write the news that really takes place and happens. I won't make up any lies, just the truth. I'll back up anything I write.

Our long time stockman Gordon DuBray passed away last week. All felt sorry for him.

The reporter has been doing cowboy work for the last three days rounding up cattle. Painful to walk now.

The reporter from Heart Butte lost all his blankets out at the self service laundry last week. Some one came and asked if the blankets were ready and he got them. When the reporter went after them, the other John had already taken them. The manager said someone just looked like me. Hope for return.

Reporter took his pickup to Valier for an overhall job. He has been driving a sorrel horse instead of a buckskin Ford.

The reporter and Louie Red Head will see their names on the bill board next week. Let's have another full blood Indian name for the council. Louie Red Head is a full blood and very smart, with a lot of experience in life and the condition of the full blood tribe. Very kind and good hearted to both old and young.

Thanksgiving day was rather poor for a dinner at some Indian homes, but were thankful for what they had. The full blood Indian shared what he had with Mother Earth by taking some of the food and putting it in the ground. That's how thankful they were.

Joe Running Crane took his oldest son to Shelby last week to shop. He told Joe he want a long sheepskin overcoat. He found one cost him $65.00 and no money left for groceries. He'll keep warm till the next check comes in.

Felix Running Crane has been busy plowing road in Mad Plume community from one house to another and the short piece to the main road. He is the only one that has a team of horses.

Sam New Breast received an invitation to the President's inaugural which will be Jan. 20 in Washington. Have to get along without Sam. No money.

John Tatsey, the reporter, Carson Boyd, Peter Red Horn, Earl Old Person were at the Montana Mansfield dinner which was at Helena last Saturday. There were a lot of people there around 7 or 800. There were ten tables and all full. There was not any fancy stuff on the tables but the roast meat was real good because it was black angus beef. That's what Mike Mansfield enjoyed. All Montana officials were there. There were a lot of good words for Mike. The reporter from Heart Butte talked to him, and he said to the Reporter, it's been a long time since we ate together. The reporter said yes, and Mike said yes and it's been a long time since we got any news from Heart Butte.

■ LESLIE FIEDLER

Literary critic and novelist Leslie Fiedler came to Missoula in 1941 to teach English at the University of Montana; he remained there until 1964. Throughout his career, Fiedler taught at Princeton, Columbia, and Indiana universities and at the universities of New York, Wisconsin, Vermont, Rome, Bologna, and Athens. He published widely and is probably best known for his Love and Death in the American Novel *(1960),* Waiting for the End *(1964),* An End to Innocence *(1972), and* Freaks: Images of the Secret Self *(1984). Outspoken and controversial, Fieldler created a furor in the state when he published "The Montana Face" in the* Partisan Review *in 1949. He later amended his impressions of Montanans in "Montana P.S." (1956) and "Montana: P.P.S." (1984), which are reprinted in* The Collected Essays of Leslie Fiedler *(1971). Fiedler now lives in Buffalo, New York, where he is Professor of English at SUNY-Buffalo.*

The Montana Face

There is a sense, disturbing to good Montanans, in which Montana is a by-product of European letters, an invention of the Romantic movement in literature. In 1743 a white man penetrated Montana for the first time, but there was then simply nothing to *do* with it: nothing yet to do economically in the first place, but also no way of assimilating the land to the imagination. Before the secure establishment of the categories of the *interessant* and the "picturesque," how could one have come to terms with the inhumanly virginal landscape: the atrocious magnificence of the mountains, the illimitable brute fact of the prairies? A new setting for hell, perhaps, but no background for any human feeling discovered up to that point; even *Sturm und Drang* was yet to come.

And what of the Indians? The redskin had been part of daily life in America and a display piece in Europe for a couple of hundred years, but he had not yet made the leap from a fact of existence to one of culture. *The Spirit of Christianity* of Chateaubriand and the expedition of Lewis and Clark that decisively opened Montana to the East were almost exactly contemporary, and both had to await the turn of the nineteenth century. Sacajawea, the Indian girl guide of Captain Clark (the legendary Sacajawea of course, shorn of such dissonant realistic details as a husband, etc.) is as much a product of a new sensibility as Atala–and neither would have been possible without Rousseau and the beautiful lie of the Noble Savage. By the time the trapper had followed the explorer, and had been in turn followed by the priest and the prospector, George Catlin in paint and James Fenimore Cooper in the novel had fixed for the American imagination the fictive Indian and the legend of the ennobling wilderness: the primitive as Utopia. Montana was psychologically possible.

One knows generally that, behind the thin neo-Classical facade of Virginia and Philadelphia and Boston, the mythical meanings of America have traditionally been sustained by the Romantic sensibility (the hero of the first American novel died a suicide, a copy of *Werther* lying on the table beside him); that America had been unremittingly dreamed from East to West as a testament to the original goodness of man: from England and the Continent to the Atlantic seaboard; from the Atlantic seaboard to the Midwest; from the Midwest to the Rocky Mountains and the Pacific. And the margin where the Dream has encountered the resistance of fact, where the Noble Savage has confronted Original Sin (the edge of hysteria: of the twitching revivals, ritual drunkenness, "shooting up the town," of the rape of nature and the almost compulsive slaughter of beasts) we call simply: the Frontier.

Guilt and the Frontier are coupled from the first; but the inhabitants of a Primary Frontier, struggling for existence under marginal conditions, have neither the time nor energy to feel *consciously* the contradiction between their actuality and their dream. Survival is for them a sufficient victory. The contradiction remains largely unrealized geographically sundered; for those who continue to dream the Dream are in their safe East (Cooper in Westchester or New York City), and those who live the fact have become total Westerners, deliberately cut off from history and myth, immune even to the implications of their own landscape. On into the second stage of the Frontier, it is dangerous for anyone who wants to *live* in a Western community to admire the scenery openly (it evokes the Dream);

such sentiments are legitimate only for "dudes," that is to say, visitors and barnstorming politicians.

But the schoolmarm, pushing out before her the whore, symbol of the denial of romance, moves in from the East to marry the rancher or the mining engineer (a critical cultural event intuitively preserved as a convention of the Western movie); and the Dream and the fact confront each other openly. The schoolteacher brings with her the sentimentalized Frontier novel, and on all levels a demand begins to grow for some kind of art to nurture the myth, to turn a way of life into a culture. The legend is ready-made and waiting, and speedily finds forms in the pulps, the movies, the Western story, the fake cowboy song–manufactured at first by absentee dudes, but later ground out on the spot by cultural "compradors." The Secondary Frontier moves from naivete to an elementary consciousness of history and discrepancy; on the one hand, it falsifies history, idealizing even the recent past into the image of the myth, while, on the other hand, it is driven to lay bare the failures of its founders to live up to the Rousseauistic ideal. The West is reinvented!

At the present moment, Montana is in some respects such a Secondary Frontier, torn between an idolatrous regard for its refurbished past (the naive culture it holds up defiantly against the sophistication of the East, not realizing that the East *requires* of it precisely such a contemporary role), and a vague feeling of guilt at the confrontation of the legend of its past with the real history that keeps breaking through. But in other respects, Montana has gone on to the next stage: the Tertiary or pseudo-Frontier, a past artificially contrived for commercial purposes, the Frontier as bread and butter.

In the last few years, Montana has seen an efflorescence of "Sheriff's Posses"; dude ranches; chamber of commerce rodeos, hiring professional riders; and large-scale "Pioneer Days," during which the bank clerk and the auto salesman grow beards and "go Western" to keep the tourist-crammed coaches of the Northern Pacific and the Great Northern rolling. The East has come to see its ancient dream in action–and they demand it on the line, available for the two-week vacationer. What the Easterner expects, the Montanan is prepared to give him, a sham mounted half in cynicism, half with the sense that this is, after all, what the West really means, merely made visible, vivid. There is, too, a good deal of "play" involved, a not wholly unsympathetic boyish pleasure in dressing up and pulling the leg of the outlander, which overlays and to some degree mitigates the cruder motives of "going Western." But in Montana's larger cities and towns, a new kind of entrepreneur has appeared: the Rodeo and Pioneer days Manager, to whom the West is strictly business. There is scarcely a Montanan who does not at one remove or another share in the hoax and in the take; who has not, like the nightclub Negro or the stage Irishman, become the pimp of his particularity, of the landscape and legend of his state.

Astonishingly ignorant of all this, I came from the East in 1941 to live in Montana, possessing only what might be called the standard Eastern equipment: the name of the state capital (mispronounced); dim memories of a rather absurd poem that had appeared, I believe, in *The Nation*, and that began: "Hot afternoons have been in Montana"; some information about Burton K. Wheeler; and the impression that Montana (or was it Idaho) served Ernest Hemingway as a sort of alternative Green Hills of Africa. I had, in short, inherited a shabby remnant of the Romantic myth; and, trembling on an even more remote periphery of remembering, I was aware of visions of the Indian (out of Cooper and "The Vanishing American") and the Cowboy, looking very much like Tom Mix. I was prepared not to call cattle "cows," and resolutely to face down any student who came to argue about his grades armed with a six-shooter.

I was met unexpectedly by the Montana Face. What I had been expecting I do not clearly know; zest, I suppose; naivete, a ruddy and straightforward kind of vigor–perhaps even honest brutality. What I found seemed, at first glance, reticent, sullen, weary–full of self-sufficient stupidity; a little later it appeared simply inarticulate, with all the dumb pathos of what cannot declare itself: a face developed not for sociability or feeling, but for facing into the weather. It said friendly things, to be sure, and meant them; but it had no adequate physical expressions even for friendliness, and the muscles around the mouth and eyes were obviously unprepared to cope with the demands of any more complicated emotion. I felt a kind of innocence behind it, but an innocence difficult to distinguish from simple ignorance. In a way, there was something heartening in dealing with people who had never seen, for instance, a Negro or a Jew or a Servant, and were immune to all their bitter meanings; but the same people, I knew, had never seen an art museum or a ballet or even a movie in any language but their own, and the poverty of experience had left the possibilities of the human face in them incompletely realized.

"Healthy!" I was tempted to think contemptuously, missing the conventional stigmata of neurosis I had grown up thinking the inevitable concomitants of intelligence. It was true, certainly, that neither the uses nor the abuses of conversation, the intellectual play to which I was accustomed, flourished here; in that sense the faces didn't lie. They were conditioned by a mean, a parsimonious culture; but they were by no means mentally incurious – certainly not "healthy," rather pricked invisibly by insecurity and guilt. To believe anything else was to submit to a kind of parody of the Noble Savage, the Healthy Savage – stupidity as mental health. Indeed there was, in their very inadequacy at expressing their inwardness, the possibility of pathos at least – perhaps even tragedy. Such a face to stand at the focus of reality and myth, and in the midst of all the grandiloquence of the mountains! One reads behind it a challenge that demands a great, liberating art, a ritual of expression – and there is, of course, the movies.

The seediest moving-picture theater in town, I soon discovered, showed every Saturday the same kind of Western picture at which I had yelled and squirmed as a kid, clutching my box of jujubes; but in this context it was different. The children still eagerly attended, to be sure – but also the cowhands. In their run-over-at-the-heels boots and dirty jeans, they were apparently willing to invest a good part of their day off watching Gene and Roy, in carefully tailored togs, get the rustlers, save the ranch, and secure the Right; meanwhile making their own jobs, their everyday work into a symbol of the Natural Gentleman at home.

They *believed it all* – not only that the Good triumphs in the end, but that the authentic hero is the man who herds cattle. Unlike, for instance, the soldier at the war picture, they never snickered, but cheered at all the right places; and yet, going out from contemplating their idealized selves to get drunk or laid, they must somehow have felt the discrepancy, as failure or irony or God knows what. Certainly for the bystander watching the cowboy, a comic book under his arm, lounging beneath the bright poster of the latest Roy Rogers film, there is the sense of a joke on someone – and no one to laugh. It is nothing less than the total myth of the goodness of man in a state of nature that is at stake every Saturday after the show at the Rialto; and, though there is scarcely anyone who sees the issue clearly or as a whole, most Montanans are driven instinctively to try to close the gap.

The real cowpuncher begins to emulate his Hollywood version; and the run-of-the-mill professional rodeo rider, who has turned a community work-festival into paying entertainment, is an intermediary between life and the screen, the poor man's Gene Autry. A strange set of circumstances has preserved in the cowboy of the horse opera the Child of Nature, Natty Bumppo become Roy Rogers (the simple soul ennobled by intimacy with beasts and a virginal landscape), and has transformed his saga into the national myth. The boyhood of most living Americans does not go back beyond the first movie cowpuncher, and these days the kid without a cowboy outfit is a second-class citizen anywhere in America. Uncle Sam still survives as our public symbol; but actually America has come to picture itself in chaps rather than striped pants. Since we are comparatively historyless and culturally dependent, our claim to moral supremacy rests upon a belief that a high civilization is at a maximum distance from goodness; the cowboy is more noble than the earl.

But, on the last frontiers of Montana, the noble lie of Rousseau is simply a lie; the face on the screen is debunked by the watcher. The tourist, of course, can always go to the better theaters, drink at the more elegant bars beside the local property owner, dressed up for Pioneer Days. The cowhands go to the shabby movie house off the main drag and do their drinking in their own dismal places. And when the resident Easterner or the visitor attempts to pursue the cowpuncher to his authentic dive, the owner gets rich, chases out the older whores, puts in neon lights and linoleum–which, I suppose, serves everybody right.

But the better-educated Montanan does not go to the Westerns. He discounts in advance the vulgar myth of the Cowboy, where the audience gives the fable the lie, and moves the Dream, the locus of innocence, back into a remoter past; the surviving Cowboy is surrendered for the irrecoverable Pioneer. It is the Frontiersman, the Guide who are proposed as symbols of original nobility; Jim Bridger or John Colter, who outran half a tribe of Indians, barefoot over brambles. But this means giving up to begin with the possibilities that the discovery of a New World had seemed to promise: a present past, a primitive *now*, America as a contemporary Golden Age.

When the point of irreconcilable conflict between fact and fiction had been reached earlier, the Dream had been projected westward toward a new Frontier–but Montana is a *last Frontier*; there is no more ultimate West. Here the myth of the Noble Woodsman can no longer be maintained in space (the dream of Rousseau reaches a cul-de-sac at the Lions Club luncheon in Two Dot, Montana); it retreats from geography into time, from a discoverable West into the realm of an irrecoverable past. But even the past is not really safe.

Under the compulsion to examine his past (and there have been recently several investigations, culminating in the Rockefeller Foundation-sponsored Montana Study), the contemporary Montanan, pledged to history though nostalgic for myth, becomes willy-nilly an iconoclast. Beside a John Colter he discovers a Henry Plummer, the sheriff who was for years secretly a bandit; and the lynch "justice" to which Plummer was brought seems to the modern point of view as ambiguous as his career. The figure of the Pioneer becomes ever more narrow, crude, brutal; his law is revealed as arbitrary force, his motive power as—greed. The Montanan poring over his past comes to seem like those dance-hall girls, of whom a local story tells, panning the ashes of a road agent who had been lynched and burned, for the gold it had been rumored he was carrying. Perhaps there had never been any gold in the first place . . .

It is in his relations with the Indian that the Pioneer shows to worst advantage. The record of those relations is one of aggression and deceit and, more remotely, the smug assumption that anything goes with "Savages." There are honorable exceptions among the early missionaries, but it is hard for a Protestant culture to make a Jesuit its hero. For many years the famous painting of Custer's Last Stand hung in the state university, where the students of history were being taught facts that kept them from taking Custer for the innocent Victim, the symbolic figure of the white man betrayed by crafty redskins that he is elsewhere. In Montana it is difficult to see the slaughter at Little Big Horn as anything but the result of a tactical error in a long warfare with whose motives one can no longer sympathize.

Driving across Montana, the conscientious sightseer who slows up for the signs saying "Historic Point 1000 Feet" can read the roadside marker beside US 2 at Chinook, which memorializes "The usual fork-tongued methods of the white which had deprived these Indians of their hereditary lands," "One of the blackest records of our dealings with the Indians. . . ." Or at Poplar he can learn how the Assiniboines "are now waiting passively for the fulfillment of treaties made with 'The Great White Father'."

It is at first thoroughly disconcerting to discover such confessions of shame blessed by the state legislature and blazoned on the main roads where travelers are enjoined to stop and notice. What motives can underlie such declarations: The feeling that simple confession is enough for absolution? A compulsion to blurt out one's utmost indignity? A shallow show of regret that protects a basic indifference? It is not only the road markers that keep alive the memory of the repeated betrayals and acts of immoral appropriation that brought Montana into existence; there are books to document the story, and community pageants to present it in dramatic form. The recollection of a common guilt comes to be almost a patriotic duty.

What is primarily involved is, I think, an attempt to *identify* with the Indian. Notice in the sentences quoted from highway signs the use of Indian terminology, "fork-tongued," "Great White Father"–the attempt to get *inside* the Indian's predicament. If the Pioneer seems an ignoble figure beside the Indian, it is perhaps because he was, as a Noble Savage, not quite savage enough; as close as he was to nature, the White Pioneer, already corrupted by Europe and civilization, could not achieve the saving closeness. "Civilization," a road sign between Hysham and Forsyth ironically comments, "is a wonderful thing, according to some people." The corpse of Rousseau is still twitching.

At the beginnings of American literature, Cooper had suggested two avatars of primeval goodness: Pioneer and Indian, the alternative nobility of Natty Bumppo and Chingachgook; and the Montanan, struggling to hang on to the Romantic denial of Original Sin, turns to the latter, makes the injured Chief Joseph or Sitting Bull the Natural Gentleman in place of the deposed Frontiersman.

But the sentimentalized Indian will not stand up under scrutiny either. "The only good Indian is a dead Indian," the old folk saying asserts; and indeed the Montanan who is busy keeping the living Indian in the ghetto of the reservation cannot afford to believe too sincerely in his nobility. The cruelest aspect of social life in Montana is the exclusion of the Indian; deprived of his best land, forbidden access to the upper levels of white society, kept out of any job involving prestige, even in some churches confined to the back rows, but of course protected from whisky and comforted with hot lunches and free hospitals–the actual Indian is a constant reproach to the Montanan, who feels himself Nature's own democrat, and scorns the South for its treatment of the Negro, the East for its attitude toward the Jews. To justify the continuing exclusion of the Indian, the local white has evolved the theory that the redskin is *naturally* dirty, lazy, dishonest, incapable of assuming responsibility–a troublesome child; and this theory confronts dumbly any attempt at reasserting the myth of the Noble Savage.

The trick is, of course, to *keep* the Indian what he is, so that he may be pointed out, his present state held up as a justification for what has been done to him. And the trick works; the Indian acts as he is expected to; confirmed in indolence and filth, sustained by an occasional smuggled bout of drunkenness, he does not seem even to have clung to his original resentment, lapsing rather into apathy and a certain self-contempt. The only thing white civilization had brought to the Indian that might be judged as good was a new religion; but one hears tales now of the rise of dope-cults, of "Indian Christianity," in which Jesus and Mary and the drug *peyote* are equally adored. Once I traveled for two days with an Indian boy on his way to be inducted into the Army; and, when he opened the one paper satchel he carried, it contained: a single extra suit of long underwear and forty comic books—all the goods, material and spiritual, with which our culture had endowed him.

On the side of the whites, there is, I think, a constantly nagging though unconfessed sense of guilt, perhaps the chief terror that struggles to be registered on the baffled Montana Face. It is a struggle much more difficult for the Montana "liberal" to deal with than those other conflicts between the desired and the actual to which he turns almost with relief; the fight with the Power Company or the Anaconda Copper Mining Company for the instruments of communication and the possibilities of freedom. The latter struggles tend to pre-empt the liberal's imagination, because on them he can take an unequivocal stand; but in respect to the Indian he is torn with inner feelings of guilt, the knowledge of his own complicity in perpetuating the stereotypes of prejudice and discrimination. In that relationship he cannot wholly disassociate himself from the oppressors; by his color, he is born into the camp of the Enemy.

There is, of course, no easy solution to the Indian problem; but so long as the Montanan fails to come to terms with the Indian, despised and outcast in his open-air ghettos, just so long will he be incapable of coming to terms with his own real past, of making the adjustment between myth and reality upon which a successful culture depends. When he admits that the Noble Savage is a lie; when he has learned that his state is where the myth comes to die (it is here, one is reminded, that the original of Huck Finn ended his days, a respected citizen), the Montanan may find the possibilities of tragedy and poetry for which so far he has searched his life in vain.

ANNORA BROWN

Annora Brown was born and raised in Ft. MacLeod, Alberta. Her father was a North West Mounted Policeman who came to Canada from London in 1885. Brown attended the Ontario College of Art and later taught at the Extension Department of the University of Alberta and the Banff School of Fine Arts. She retired to Vancouver Island, B. C., where she painted and wrote until her death. Over 200 of her paintings of flowers are in the permanent collection of the Glenbow Foundation in Calgary. These selections are from Old Man's Garden *(1954).*

From Old Man's Garden

Bear Grass
Xerophyllum tenax

Visitors to Waterton Lakes or Glacier Park cannot fail to notice the bear grass which rises like tall lighted candles against the dark evergreens.

Clusters of sharp wiry grass-like leaves grow from a thick root. A woody flower stalk covered with smaller awl-shaped leaves, thin, dry and whitish, rises above this basal cluster and bears a dense raceme of creamy white flowers. The individual flowers are tiny white stars.

The leaves of the bear grass were used by the Indians for making baskets. The blade, which is about two feet long and three-eighths of an inch wide, is smooth and strong and pliant. The young blades particularly, because not exposed to the sun and air, have a smooth, bright appearance and were generally preferred.

As Lewis and Clark returned from their long journey to the Pacific coast, they met the Indians of the mountain regions, laden with neatly packed bundles of bear grass which they were taking to the coast to trade with the coastal Indians for wappatoo roots and for blue beads obtained from the small trading ships that were beginning to find their way up the coast. This bear grass was used by the Indians of the coast in combination with cedar bark for baskets so closely woven that they were watertight, without the aid of gum or resin. The form was generally conic, or rather the segment of a cone, of which the smaller end was the bottom of the basket. They were of all sizes from that of the smallest cup to a capacity of five or six gallons and answered the double purpose of either a covering for the head or a container for water. Some of them were highly ornamented with strands of bear grass, woven into figures of various colours. For the construction of these baskets the bear grass formed an article of considerable traffic.

On the strength of the information collected by Lewis and Clark, who first called it bear grass, it was given the scientific name of *Xerophyllum tenax*—the dry leaf that holds fast.

David Douglas, the botanist whose name is familiar to all who have heard of the Douglas fir, sent specimens to England for garden use and one species is named in his honour, *Xerophyllum douglassii.*

Blackfoot visitors to the mountains usually harvested a store of leaves and roots for their own use, and to carry as gifts to their medicinally inclined friends of the prairies who, for one reason or another, were unable to travel so far to replenish their own supplies. They did not need its leaves for baskets, as the buffalo supplied all their requirements along that line, but they boiled the roots and used the resulting infusion for a hair tonic as well as for the easing of sprains. Farther south the infusion was evaporated and the residue used for soap.

Even the ground squirrels find a use for this versatile plant. They cut down the flower stalks and use them for food.

Such a conspicuous plant must naturally have collected many names. A few of the most common are moose grass, pine lily, squaw grass, turkey beard and basket grass.

Kinnikinik
Arctostaphylos uva-ursi

When the heavily laden canoes of the fur traders crossed the threshold of the unknown west, the men took with them, as part of their pay, ten or fourteen pounds of strong tobacco done up in long rolls like the ship's perique that sailors carried with them to sea. Since all their supplies had to be carried with them, either by canoe or on their shoulders, they were fortunate to find growing in the country a plant whose leathery leaves could be added to the tobacco to make it milder and to eke out their slender supplies.

Even before the beginning of the nineteenth century, David Thompson and his fellow traders of the North West and Hudson's Bay Fur Companies had learned from the Indians to call this plant 'kinnikinik'. "The natives collect the leaves," he says. "It is mixed with tobacco for smoking, giving it a mild and agreeable flavour." Fifty years later Captains Lewis and Clark recorded that their *engagés* were calling it '*sacacommis*' because the *commis* or clerks of the fur companies carried it in their *sacs* or pouches.

Sir George Simpson found the Indians calling it 'atcheskapesekwa' or smoking weed and Sir James Hector recognized in this plant the smoking weed of the Scotch hills. We often read in journals of the time that the evening was spent in the making of tobacco.

The botanists ignored all this in choosing their name for the plant. This little prostrate red-berried shrub, so common on all our hillsides, boasts the generic name of *Arctostaphylos* which means bearberry. Its specific name, *uva-ursi*, also means bearberry. So there it is: family name, *Arctostaphylos*; specific name, *uva-ursi*; common name, bearberry. Three times repeated it begins to sound quite convincing.

It is not only the bears that find this flat-tasting berry irresistible. It is the favourite food of the grouse also and its fruit is borne close to the ground within easy reach of them.

The small white or pink urn-shaped flowers, growing clustered amongst the dark leathery leaves, is one of the loveliest of the springtime flowers, while in autumn the shrub produces not only bright red berries, but leaves brilliantly tinted and tipped with scarlet. The plant spreads in mats one or two yards across, from a single root.

It is often used for winter decorations. Being evergreen, it is little affected by the cold winds of winter. On the hills it may be gathered in January with the berries still fresh and red and the tips crowned with flower buds all ready to open at a moment's notice when the sun gets warm. In early spring, flowers, berries and leaves appear on a branch together.

Blueberry and Cranberry

"The common huckleberry, oftener seen in pies and muffins by the average observer than in its native thickets, unfortunately ripens at fly time, when the squeamish boarder in the summer hotel does well to carefully scrutinize each mouthful." So Neltje Blanchan begins the huckleberry, blueberry and cranberry section in her book on eastern wild flowers.

Such are the joys and trials of civilization. To James Hector, who broke five days of enforced fasting in the Kicking Horse Pass when he came across a patch of blueberries, to Daniel Harmon, David Thompson, Alexander Mackenzie and many others who staved off starvation with them, they were connected with neither flies nor pies, but were in themselves deliciously nourishing meals.

Huckleberry, whortleberry, bilberry, blueberry are names applied to members of the huckleberry family that are so closely related as to be almost indistinguishable. Usually the blacker berries are referred to as huckleberries while the bluish one with the pale bloom are called blueberries. By whatever name we know them, and whatever the specific name, we know that in pies or muffins, or raw with a garnish of cream, they are hard to beat.

There are two berries popularly known as cranberries. The true cranberry is a denizen of swamps and marshy places. It is a delicate little trailing vine with small leaves that are dark green above and white beneath. The four or five tiny, narrow pink divisions of the corolla are pendant from slender, swaying stems and are as pretty as the round red fruit.

Cranberries are members of the huckleberry family and justly popular in the kitchen. Frederick V. Coville, however, draws a fine distinction between them and their near relatives. The blueberry, he says, has the cranberry beaten "because you can't use cranberries without buying a turkey." This distinction would not trouble a pioneer who would just go out and shoot whatever wild game he fancied.

The other type is known as the high bush, mountain or Swedish cranberry and is especially plentiful through the northern sections. This berry grows on low shrubs. Its leaves are thick, dark green and shiny above, pale and black dotted beneath, with curled margins. Growing as it does in rocky places and open woods, and about two feet off the ground, it is more easily gathered and in more common use as a wild fruit than the true cranberry.

7

Contemporary Fiction

■ *Montana Renaissance*

WILLIAM KITTREDGE

t is almost impossible to sort recent storytelling in Montana into schools or even traditions. And that's good, as I see it, a sure sign of maturity. Our writers are no longer paying much attention to the old hide-bound mythology of the Western; they are writing from their own experiences, discovering and defining their own demons and battles, engaged in the constant business of the artist—renaming the sacred.

In 1974, the Native American writer James Welch published *Winter in the Blood*, which a *New York Times Book Review* critic called an "almost perfect first novel." Among other things, *Winter in the Blood* is a quite unflinching look at the possibilities of reservation life on the Montana Hi-Line, a story concerned with finding a meaningful life in connection with a place distant from the so-called Great World, which is nevertheless made sacred by the history of a people.

Winter in the Blood gave considerable heart to an emerging group of writers who had elected to stay and work in Montana, writing about Montana subjects. It was a work that said a thing they wanted to hear, about staying home. It was also an artistic success.

Then Norman Maclean published *A River Runs Through It* in 1976. Maclean had retired from a long and distinguished career at the University of Chicago in 1973, determined to try his hand at some stories about growing up as a Presbyterian minister's son in western Montana. In the title novella, with the constraint of an impeccable resonating style, Maclean details for us the story of his father and himself and his mother and the death, in 1937, of his brother Paul, the transcendent fly fisherman.

"A River Runs Through It" is a story about delineating the ways in which we can and cannot help one another, in the unlikely event we might know what help would be. Its glory lies in Maclean's willing reverence, always implied in the precision of his language as he goes at his business of naming the sacred aspects of his own life. And there's more. Perhaps the story's most profound glory lies in Maclean's ability to convince us that all of our lives contain elements that are sacred on any scale of things. Quirky and idiosyncratic as it is, "A River Runs Through It" is to me as valuable as any other single piece of American writing.

James Crumley left the University of Montana in 1969, but like so many he kept coming back and writing about Montana. In 1975, he published *The Wrong Case*, which takes place in the bars and along the highways between various wildernesses in Montana, both real and metaphoric. Crumley had moved the hard-boiled detective novel out of Los Angeles to the rural West; it was a brilliant notion. Detectives guide us down the mean, bewildering streets of our times; and Milo is our Virgil, leading us through the circles of corruption in a very real Montana we hadn't seen in books before. *The Wrong Case* was followed by *The Last Good Kiss* (which starred a fat poet much on the model of Dick Hugo) and *Dancing Bear*. These books are honest and smart and contain some of the most insightful writing we have about contemporary life in the American West.

About this time Tom McGuane began to write about his chosen home ground in Montana. He had included some Montana episodes in *The Bushwhacked Piano* (1971), but when I read "The Heart of the Game" in the first issue of *Outside Magazine*, I realized that McGuane had moved in to stay. He wrote: "He [the buck] wasn't in the browse at all, but angling into invisibility at the rock wall, racing straight into the elevation, bounding toward zero gravity, taking his longest arc into the bullet and the finality and terror you have made of the world, the finality you know you share even with your babies with their inherited and ambiguous dentition, the finality that any minute now you will meet as well." The language was always gorgeous, and now it was directed toward us.

Rick DeMarinis came to Montana in the Air Force and was stationed in Havre. He studied with Dick Hugo during the 1960s, went away to various teaching jobs, and came back to Montana in the 1970s. Working from the most relentlessly modernist vision of any writer in this anthology, DeMarinis' fiction has been deeply admired by other writers for almost two decades. He never leaves us comfortable in our preconceptions as he tells us news we often don't want to hear, performing the true work of an artist, helping us reexamine ourselves. All of this is evidenced by *The Burning Women of Far Cry* (1986), a story of a modern Montana where romances of any dimension do not thrive. He recently won the Drue Heinz Award for his book of stories, *Under the Wheat* (1986). The wide popularity that his work deserves must be only around the corner.

Mary Clearman Blew, another writer less well-known than she ought to be, studied in Missoula and Missouri and then returned to the high plains of central Montana to teach at Northern Montana College in Havre and to write about that piece of the world where she had grown up. Her stories have twice been included in the annual Best American Story Collections, and in 1977 the University of Missouri Press published her book of stories, *Lambing Out*. It is our misfortune that she interrupted her writing to spend a number of years as Dean of Arts and Sciences at Havre, a job that left her little time to write; it is our good luck that her situation has changed. Mary Blew illuminates the things she knows about living amid the ranchland people of central Montana with candor and insight, and we don't get many like her in any generation. We should cherish them.

Ivan Doig went from Valier High School to Northwestern University and then spent some years as a magazine journalist and editor. Like Norman Maclean, Doig had a tough time finding a publisher for his autobiographical book about growing up in Montana, *This House of Sky* (1978). But when the book was finally in print, it almost at once attracted a considerable local and national audience and a nomination for the National Book Award. Doig is currently in the midst of publishing a trilogy of novels set in his home country along the Rocky Mountain Front. The first, *English Creek*, came out to considerable notice in 1984; the second, *Dancing at the Rascal Fair*, to even better word of mouth in 1987. The trilogy is drawing a justifiably large national readership to its examination of Montana life along the Rocky Mountain Front over a long sweep of years, a precise evocation of life as it was and how it got to be the way it is.

But Doig's reputation is still irrevocably anchored to his accomplishment in *This House of Sky*, a book that so vividly rewarded readers who were "longing for an explicable past." And more. Readers keep coming back to *This House of Sky* to renew connections with Doig's people. It is his success in connecting the affections of his readers to his major characters, his father Charlie and his grandmother Bessie Ringer, that established *This House of Sky* so centrally in the canon of major Montana literature. Bessie Ringer and Charlie Doig were real people, of the kind we understand and care about in Montana, and so we care deeply about their story, because it is in so many ways our own.

By the late 1970s, a renaissance of wonderful narrative writing was clearly on the bloom in Montana. Jim Harrison came to visit Tom McGuane and wrote *Legends of the Fall* (1979), a novella that is regarded by a large public as one of the most vivid and compelling stories ever written about Montana. It should be read whole, and it is our regret that the whole is too long to reprint in this anthology.

A year later, in 1980, Steven Krauzer and I were editing an edition of the literary magazine, *TriQuarterly*, which was to be devoted to stories about the American West. We got some work from a man named David Quammen, who had come to Montana with a novel published in his senior year at Yale and a Rhodes Scholarship behind him. He had worked as a bartender in Missoula and a fishing guide in Ennis. We published a story called "Walking Out," which details a father/son hunting trip into the Crazy Mountains. The story has since been anthologized nationally maybe a half-dozen times; again, we don't include it because of its length. Rather, because Quammen has gone on to become one of the finest natural history essayists in America, a career capped in 1987 by the National Magazine Award for Essays and Criticism, we include one of his essays.

Richard Ford is a man at a delicate place; at this writing he is emerging as one those fortunate few American writers who have been identified in the popular mind as likely to have a major career. Ford seems to have lived everywhere at one time or another. He grew up in Little Rock and Jackson, went to school in Ann Arbor and Los Angeles, lived in Mexico and New York City, taught at Princeton and Williams, moved to the Mississippi delta, and then to Montana. His writing reflects the width of sympathy and unrest and speculation that led him to try so many homes, that restlessness that seems to find its proper residence in the American West. This is true not only of Ford, but also of other writers who have come to settle in Montana, such as David Long and Patricia Henley.

I remember reading a story of Ford's called "Rock Springs" when it first appeared in *Esquire* in 1982 and wondering how these outlanders should be able to write so accurately about the West, often more insightfully than many of us who have lived here all our lives. Much of the answer lies of course in the amount of time they have spent learning their craft, learning to see and pay attention to the life around them. But there are other answers that may be of more interest, at least to other writers in the American West who presumably have spent their own time honing their craft.

I am talking about the perceptions of people who have moved around extensively, looking for places and people they can identify as uniquely valuable and who then can live with them in emotional comfort. In America, these days, that's a tall order.

From Ford and Long and Henley we get stories about escape from that threatening world, in which the only hope seems to lie in finding a calm place where we can go at some decent tasks, engage in straight talk with a few friends, and find a lover with whom to share life as truly as we can manage. Behind this escape we sense a certain rattled despair. We also sense a profound relationship with the truths of our own lives here in Montana, where so many of us have lived an elaborate history of getaway.

This seeking after a good place in which to conduct a good life is the most evident pattern in Montana narratives. In this we are together, both natives such as Maclean and Welch and Doig and those who came from somewhere else such as Hugo and DeMarinis and Crumley and McGuane and Ford. All of these stories seem to be focused mainly on naming, one way or another, what they value in the Montana they were born to or found. What we find in these stories, over and over again, is talk of home, lost or sought after, or in some conditional way discovered or rediscovered – the possibility of a coherent life in a last best place.

■ NORMAN MACLEAN

Born in Iowa in 1902, Norman Maclean grew up in Missoula, Montana, where his father was a Presbyterian minister. From the age of fourteen through his college years at Dartmouth, Maclean worked for the Forest Service in the Bitterroots. With a doctorate from the University of Chicago, Maclean joined the English Department there, where he remained until he retired in 1973 as William Rainey Harper Professor of English. While living at his family's log cabin on Seeley Lake, Montana, Maclean has spent most of his summers fly-fishing the Blackfoot River. These selections are from his American classic, A River Runs Through It and Other Stories, *which was published in 1976 and was nominated for a Pulitzer Prize. Maclean is currently working on a new book about the disastrous Mann Gulch forest fire of 1949.*

A River Runs Through It

Paul and I fished a good many big rivers, but when one of us referred to "the big river" the other knew it was the Big Blackfoot. It isn't the biggest river we fished, but it is the most powerful, and per pound, so are its fish. It runs straight and hard – on a map or from an airplane it is almost a straight line running due west from its headwaters at Rogers Pass on the Continental Divide to Bonner, Montana, where it empties into the South Fork of the Clark Fork of the Columbia. It runs hard all the way.

Near its headwaters on the Continental Divide there is a mine with a thermometer that stopped at 69.7 degrees below zero, the lowest temperature ever officially recorded in the United States (Alaska omitted). From its headwaters to its mouth it was manufactured by glaciers. The first sixty-five miles of it are smashed against the southern wall of its valley by glaciers that moved in from the north, scarifying the earth; its lower twenty-five miles were made overnight when the great glacial lake covering northwestern Montana and northern Idaho broke its ice dam and spread the remains of Montana and Idaho mountains over hundreds of miles of the plains of eastern Washington. It was the biggest flood in the world for which there is geological evidence; it was so vast a geological event that the mind of man could only conceive of it but could not prove it until photographs could be taken from earth satellites.

The straight line on the map also suggests its glacial origins; it has no meandering valley, and its few farms are mostly on its southern tributaries which were not ripped up by glaciers; instead of opening into a wide flood plain near its mouth, the valley, which was cut overnight by a disappearing lake when the great ice dam melted, gets narrower and narrower until the only way a river, an old logging railroad, and an automobile road can fit into it is for two of them to take to the mountainsides.

It is a tough place for a trout to live—the river roars and the water is too fast to let algae grow on the rocks for feed, so there is no fat on the fish, which must hold most trout records for high jumping.

Besides, it is the river we knew best. My brother and I had fished the Big Blackfoot since nearly the beginning of the century—my father before then. We regarded it as a family river, as a part of us, and I surrender it now only with great reluctance to dude ranches, the unselected inhabitants of Great Falls, and the Moorish invaders from California.

Early next morning Paul picked me up in Wolf Creek, and we drove across Rogers Pass where the thermometer is that stuck at three-tenths of a degree short of seventy below. As usual, especially if it were early in the morning, we sat silently respectful until we passed the big Divide, but started talking the moment we thought we were draining into another ocean. Paul nearly always had a story to tell in which he was the leading character but not the hero.

He told his Continental Divide stories in a seemingly light-hearted, slightly poetical mood such as reporters often use in writing "human-interest" stories, but, if the mood were removed, his stories would appear as something about him that would not meet the approval of his family and that I would probably find out about in time anyway. He also must have felt honor-bound to tell me that he lived other lives, even if he presented them to me as puzzles in the form of funny stories. Often I did not know what I had been told about him as we crossed the divide between our two worlds.

"You know," he began, "it's been a couple of weeks since I fished the Blackfoot." At the beginning, his stories sounded like factual reporting. He had fished alone and the fishing had not been much good, so he had to fish until evening to get his limit. Since he was returning directly to Helena he was driving up Nevada Creek along an old dirt road that followed section lines and turned at right angles at section corners. It was moonlight, he was tired and feeling in need of a friend to keep him awake, when suddenly a jackrabbit jumped on to the road and started running with the headlights. "I didn't push him too hard," he said, "because I didn't want to lose a friend." He drove, he said, with his head outside the window so he could feel close to the rabbit. With his head in the moonlight, his account took on poetic touches. The vague world of moonlight was pierced by the intense white triangle from the headlights. In the center of the penetrating isosceles was the jackrabbit, which, except for the length of his jumps, had become a snowshoe rabbit. The phosphorescent jackrabbit was doing his best to keep in the center of the isosceles but was afraid he was losing ground and, when he looked back to check, his eyes shone with whites and blues gathered up from the universe. My brother said, "I don't know how to explain what happened next, but there was a right-angle turn in this section-line road, and the rabbit saw it, and I didn't.

Later, he happened to mention that it cost him $175.00 to have his car fixed, and in 1937 you could almost get a car rebuilt for $175.00. Of course, he never mentioned that, although he did not drink when he fished, he always started drinking when he finished.

I rode part of the way down the Blackfoot wondering whether I had been told a little human-interest story with hard luck turned into humor or whether I had been told he had taken too many drinks and smashed hell out of the front end of his car.

Since it was no great thing either way, I finally decided to forget it, and, as you see, I didn't. I did, though, start thinking about the canyon where we were going to fish.

The canyon above the old Clearwater bridge is where the Blackfoot roars loudest. The backbone of a mountain would not break, so the mountain compresses the already powerful river into sound and spray before letting it pass. Here, of course, the road leaves the river; there was no place in the canyon for an Indian trail; even in 1806 when Lewis left Clark to come up the Blackfoot, he skirted the canyon by a safe margin. It is no place for small fish or small fishermen. Even the roar adds power to the fish or at least intimidates the fisherman.

When we fished the canyon we fished on the same side of it for the simple reason that there is no place in the canyon to wade across. I could hear Paul start to pass me to get to the hole above, and, when I realized I didn't hear him anymore, I knew he had stopped to watch me. Although I have never pretended to be a great fisherman, it was always important to me that I was a fisherman and looked like one, especially when fishing with my brother. Even before the silence continued, I knew that I wasn't looking like much of anything.

Although I have a warm personal feeling for the canyon, it is not an ideal place for me to fish. It puts a premium upon being able to cast for distance, and yet most of the time there are cliffs or trees right behind the fisherman so he has to keep all his line in front of him. It's like a baseball pitcher being deprived of his windup, and it forces the fly fisherman into what is called a "roll cast," a hard cast that I have never mastered. The fisherman has to work enough line into his cast to get distance without throwing any line behind him, and then he has to develop enough power from a short arc to shoot it out across the water.

He starts accumulating the extra amount of line for the long cast by retrieving his last cast so slowly that an unusual amount of line stays in the water and what is out of it forms a slack semiloop. The loop is enlarged by raising the casting arm straight up and cocking the wrist until it points to 1:30. There, then, is a lot of line in front of the fisherman, but it takes about everything he has to get it high in the air and out over the water so that the fly and leader settle ahead of the line—the arm is a piston, the wrist is a revolver that uncocks, and even the body gets behind the punch. Important, too, is the fact that the extra amount of line remaining in the water until the last moment gives a semisolid bottom to the cast. It is a little like a rattlesnake striking, with a good piece of his tail on the ground as something to strike from. All this is easy for a rattlesnake, but has always been hard for me.

Paul knew how I felt about my fishing and was careful not to seem superior by offering advice, but he had watched so long that he couldn't leave now without saying something. Finally he said, "The fish are out farther." Probably fearing he had put a strain on family relations, he quickly added, "Just a little farther."

I reeled in my line slowly, not looking behind so as not to see him. Maybe he was sorry he had spoken, but, having said what he said, he had to say something more. "Instead of retrieving the line straight toward you, bring it in on a diagonal from the downstream side. The diagonal will give you a more resistant base to your loop so you can put more power into your forward cast and get a little more distance."

Then he acted as if he hadn't said anything and I acted as if I hadn't heard it, but as soon as he left, which was immediately, I started retrieving my line on a diagonal, and it helped. The moment I felt I was getting a little more distance I ran for a fresh hole to make a fresh start in life.

It was a beautiful stretch of water, either to a fisherman or a photographer, although each would have focused his equipment on a different point. It was a barely submerged waterfall. The reef of rock was about two feet under the water, so the whole river rose into one wave, shook itself into spray, then fell back on itself and turned blue. After it recovered from the shock, it came back to see how it had fallen.

No fish could live out there where the river exploded into the colors and curves that would attract photographers. The fish were in that slow backwash, right in the dirty foam, with the dirt being one of the chief attractions. Part of the speckles would be pollen from pine trees, but most of the dirt was edible insect life that had not survived the waterfall.

I studied the situation. Although maybe I had just added three feet to my roll cast, I still had to do a lot of thinking before casting to compensate for some of my other shortcomings. But I felt I had already made the right beginning—I had already figured out where the big fish would be and why.

Then an odd thing happened. I saw him. A black back rose and sank in the foam. In fact, I imagined I saw spines on his dorsal fin until I said to myself, "God, he couldn't be so big you could see his fins." I even added, "You wouldn't even have seen the fish in all that foam if you hadn't first thought he would be there." But I couldn't shake the conviction that I had seen the black back of a big fish, because, as someone often forced to think, I know that often I would not see a thing unless I thought of it first.

Seeing the fish that I first thought would be there led me to wondering which way he would be pointing in the river. "Remember, when you make the first cast," I thought, "that you saw him in the backwash where the water is circling upstream, so he will be looking downstream, not upstream, as he would be if he were in the main current."

I was led by association to the question of what fly I would cast, and to the conclusion that it had better be a large fly, a number four or six, if I was going after the big hump in the foam.

From the fly, I went to the other end of the cast, and asked myself where the hell I was going to cast from. There were only gigantic rocks at this waterfall, so I picked one of the biggest, saw how I could crawl up it, and knew from that added height I would get added distance, but then I had to ask myself, "How the hell am I going to land the fish if I hook him while I'm standing up there?" So I had to pick a smaller rock, which would shorten my distance but would let me slide down it with a rod in my hand and a big fish on.

I was gradually approaching the question all river fishermen should ask before they make the first cast, "If I hook a big one, where the hell can I land him?"

One great thing about fly fishing is that after a while nothing exists of the world but thoughts about fly fishing. It is also interesting that thoughts about fishing are often carried on in dialogue form where Hope and Fear—or, many times, two Fears—try to outweigh each other.

One Fear looked down the shoreline and said to me (a third person distinct from the two fears), "There is nothing but rocks for thirty yards, but don't get scared and try to land him before you get all the way down to the first sandbar."

The Second Fear said, "It's forty, not thirty, yards to the first sandbar and the weather has been warm and the fish's mouth will be soft and he will work off the hook if you try to fight him forty yards downriver. It's not good but it will be best to try to land him on a rock that is closer."

The First Fear said, "There is a big rock in the river that you will have to take him past before you land him, but, if you hold the line tight enough on him to keep him this side of the rock, you will probably lose him."

The Second Fear said, "But if you let him get on the far side of the rock, the line will get caught under it, and you will be sure to lose him."

That's how you know when you have thought too much—when you become a dialogue between *You'll probably lose* and *You're sure to lose*. But I didn't entirely quit thinking, although I did switch subjects. It is not in the book, yet it is human enough to spend a moment before casting in trying to imagine what the fish is thinking, even if one of its eggs is as big as its brain and even if, when you swim underwater, it is hard to imagine that a fish has anything to think about. Still, I could never be talked into believing that all a fish knows is hunger and fear. I have tried to feel nothing but hunger and fear and don't see how a fish could ever grow to six inches if that were all he ever felt. In fact, I go so far sometimes as to imagine that a fish thinks pretty thoughts. Before I made the cast, I imagined the fish with the black back lying cool in the carbonated water full of bubbles from the waterfalls. He was looking downriver and watching the foam with food in it backing upstream like a floating cafeteria coming to wait on its customers. And he probably was imagining that the speckled foam was eggnog with nutmeg sprinkled on it, and, when the whites of eggs separated and he saw what was on shore, he probably said to himself, "What a lucky son of a bitch I am that this guy and not his brother is about to fish this hole."

I thought all these thoughts and some besides that proved of no value, and then I cast and I caught him.

I kept cool until I tried to take the hook out of his mouth. He was lying covered with sand on the little bar where I had landed him. His gills opened with his penultimate sighs. Then suddenly he stood up on his head in the sand and hit me with his tail and the sand flew. Slowly at first my hands began to shake, and, although I thought they made a miserable sight, I couldn't stop them. Finally, I managed to open the large blade to my knife which several times slid off his skull before it went through his brain.

Even when I bent him he was way too long for my basket, so his tail stuck out.

There were black spots on him that looked like crustaceans. He seemed oceanic, including barnacles. When I passed my brother at the next hole, I saw him study the tail and slowly remove his hat, and not out of respect to my prowess as a fisherman.

I had a fish, so I sat down to watch a fisherman.

He took his cigarettes and matches from his shirt pocket and put them in his hat and pulled his hat down tight so it wouldn't leak. Then he unstrapped his fish basket and hung it on the edge of his shoulder where he could get rid of it quick should the water get too big for him. If he studied the situation he didn't take any separate time to do it. He jumped off a rock into the swirl and swam for a chunk of cliff that had dropped into the river and parted it. He swam in his clothes with only his left arm–in his right hand, he held his rod high and sometimes all I could see was the basket and rod, and when the basket filled with water sometimes all I could see was the rod.

The current smashed him into the chunk of cliff and it must have hurt, but he had enough strength remaining in his left fingers to hang to a crevice or he would have been swept into the blue below. Then he still had to climb to the top of the rock with his left fingers and his right elbow which he used like a prospector's pick. When he finally stood on top, his clothes looked hydraulic, as if they were running off him.

Once he quit wobbling, he shook himself duck-dog fashion, with his feet spread apart, his body lowered and his head flopping. Then he steadied himself and began to cast and the whole world turned to water.

Below him was the multitudinous river, and, where the rock had parted it around him, big-grained vapor rose. The mini-molecules of water left in the wake of his line made momentary loops of gossamer, disappearing so rapidly in the rising big-grained vapor that they had to be retained in memory to be visualized as loops. The spray emanating from him was finer-grained still and enclosed him in a halo of himself. The halo of himself was always there and always disappearing, as if he were candlelight flickering about three inches from himself. The images of himself and his line kept disappearing into the rising vapors of the river, which continually circled to the tops of the cliffs where, after becoming a wreath in the wind, they became rays of the sun.

The river above and below his rock was all big Rainbow water, and he would cast hard and low upstream, skimming the water with his fly but never letting it touch. Then he would pivot, reverse his line in a great oval above his head, and drive his line low and hard downstream, again skimming the water with his fly. He would complete this grand circle four or five times, creating an immensity of motion which culminated in nothing if you did not know, even if you could not see, that now somewhere out there a small fly was washing itself on a wave. Shockingly, immensity would return as the Big Blackfoot and the air above it became iridescent with the arched sides of a great Rainbow.

He called this "shadow casting," and frankly I don't know whether to believe the theory behind it–that the fish are alerted by the shadows of flies passing over the water by the first casts, so hit the fly the moment it touches the water. It is more or less the "working up an appetite" theory, almost too fancy to be true, but then every fine fisherman has a few fancy stunts that work for him and for almost no one else. Shadow casting never worked for me, but maybe I never had the strength of arm and wrist to keep line circling over the water until fish imagined a hatch of flies was out.

My brother's wet clothes made it easy to see his strength. Most great casters I have known were big men over six feet, the added height certainly making it easier to get more line in the air in a bigger arc. My brother was only five feet ten, but he had fished so many years his body had become partly shaped by his casting. He was thirty-two now, at the height of his power, and he could put all his body and soul into a four-and-a-half-ounce magic totem pole. Long ago, he had gone far beyond my father's wrist casting, although his right wrist was always so important that it had become larger than his left. His right arm, which our father had kept tied to the side to emphasize the wrist, shot out of his shirt as if it were engineered, and it, too, was larger than his left arm. His wet shirt bulged and came unbuttoned with his pivoting shoulders and hips. It was also not hard to see why he was a street fighter, especially since he was committed to getting in the first punch with his right hand.

Rhythm was just as important as color and just as complicated. It was one rhythm superimposed upon another, our father's four-count rhythm of the line and wrist being still the base rhythm. But superimposed upon it was the piston two count of his arm and the long overriding four count of the completed figure eight of his reversed loop.

The canyon was glorified by rhythms and colors.

I heard voices behind me, and a man and his wife came down the trail, each carrying a rod, but probably they weren't going to do much fishing. Probably they intended nothing much more than to enjoy being out of doors with each other and, on the side, to pick enough huckleberries for a pie. In those days there was little in the way of rugged sports clothes for women, and she was a big, rugged woman and wore regular men's bib overalls, and her motherly breasts bulged out of the bib. She was the first to see my brother pivoting on the top of his cliff. To her, he must have looked something like a trick rope artist at a rodeo, doing everything except jumping in and out of his loops.

She kept watching while groping behind her to smooth out some pine needles to sit on. "My, my!" she said.

Her husband stopped and stood and said, "Jesus." Every now and then he said, "Jesus." Each time his wife nodded. She was one of America's mothers who never dream of using profanity themselves but enjoy their husbands', and later, come to need it, like cigar smoke.

I started to make for the next hole. "Oh, no," she said, "you're going to wait, aren't you, until he comes to shore so you can see his big fish?"

"No," I answered, "I'd rather remember the molecules."

She obviously thought I was crazy, so I added, "I'll see his fish later." And to make any sense for her I had to add, "He's my brother."

As I kept going, the middle of my back told me that I was being viewed from the rear both as quite a guy, because I was his brother, and also as a little bit nutty, because I was molecular.

Not only was I on the wrong side of the river to fish with drowned stone flies, but Paul was a good enough roll caster to have already fished most of my side from his own. But I caught two more. They also started as little circles that looked like little fish feeding on the surface but were broken arches of big rainbows under water. After I caught these two, I quit. They made ten, and the last three were the finest fish I ever caught. They weren't the biggest or most spectacular fish I ever caught, but they were three fish I caught because my brother waded across the river to give me the fly that would catch them and because they were the last fish I ever caught fishing with him.

After cleaning my fish, I set these three apart with a layer of grass and wild mint.

Then I lifted the heavy basket, shook myself into the shoulder strap until it didn't cut any more, and thought, "I'm through for the day. I'll go down and sit on the bank by my father and talk." Then I added, "If he doesn't feel like talking, I'll just sit."

I could see the sun ahead. The coming burst of light made it look from the shadows that I and a river inside the earth were about to appear on earth. Although I could as yet see only the sunlight and not anything in it, I knew my father was sitting somewhere on the bank. I knew partly because he and I shared many of the same impulses, even to quitting at about the same time. I was sure without as yet being able to see into what was in front of me that he was sitting somewhere in the sunshine reading the New Testament in Greek. I knew this both from instinct and experience.

Old age had brought him moments of complete peace. Even when we went duck hunting and the roar of the early morning shooting was over, he would sit in the blind wrapped in an old army blanket with his Greek New Testament in one hand and his shotgun in the other. When a stray duck happened by, he would drop the book and raise the gun, and, after the shooting was over, he would raise the book again, occasionally interrupting his reading to thank his dog for retrieving the duck.

The voices of the subterranean river in the shadows were different from the voices of the sunlit river ahead. In the shadows against the cliff the river was deep and engaged in profundities, circling back on itself now and then to say things over to be sure it had understood itself. But the river ahead came out into the sunny world like a chatterbox, doing its best to be friendly. It bowed to one shore and then to the other so nothing would feel neglected.

By now I could see inside the sunshine and had located my father. He was sitting high on the bank. He wore no hat. Inside the sunlight, his faded red hair was once again ablaze and again in glory. He was reading, although evidently only by sentences because he often looked away from the book. He did not close the book until some time after he saw me.

I scrambled up the bank and asked him, "How many did you get?" He said, "I got all I want." I said, "But how many did you get?" He said, "I got four or five." I asked, "Are they any good?" He said, "They are beautiful."

He was about the only man I ever knew who used the word "beautiful" as a natural form of speech, and I guess I picked up the habit from hanging around him when I was little.

"How many did you catch?" he asked. "I also caught all I want," I told him. He omitted asking me just how many that was, but he did ask me, "Are they any good?" "They are beautiful," I told him, and sat down beside him.

"What have you been reading?" I asked. "A book," he said. It was on the ground on the other side of him. So I would not have to bother to look over his knees to see it, he said, "A good book."

Then he told me, "In the part I was reading it says the Word was in the beginning, and that's right. I used to think water was first, but if you listen carefully you will hear that the words are underneath the water."

"That's because you are a preacher first and then a fisherman," I told him. "If you ask Paul, he will tell you that the words are formed out of water."

"No," my father said, "you are not listening carefully. The water runs over the words. Paul will tell you the same thing. Where is Paul anyway?"

I told him he had gone back to fish the first hole over again. "But he promised to be here soon," I assured him. "He'll be here when he catches his limit," he said. "He'll be here soon," I reassured him, partly because I could already see him in the subterranean shadows.

My father went back to reading and I tried to check what we had said by listening. Paul was fishing fast, picking up one here and there and wasting no time in walking them to shore. When he got directly across from us, he held up a finger on each hand and my father said, "He needs two more for his limit."

I looked to see where the book was left open and knew just enough Greek to recognize *Aóγos* as the Word. I guessed from it and the argument that I was looking at the first verse of John. While I was looking, Father said, "He has one on."

It was hard to believe, because he was fishing in front of us on the other side of the hole that Father had just fished. Father slowly rose, found a good-sized rock and held it behind his back. Paul landed the fish, and waded out again for number twenty and his limit. Just as he was making the first cast, Father threw the rock. He was old enough so that he threw awkwardly and afterward had to rub his shoulder, but the rock landed in the river about where Paul's fly landed and at about the same time, so you can see where my brother learned to throw rocks into his partner's fishing water when he couldn't bear to see his partner catch any more fish.

Paul was startled for only a moment. Then he spotted Father on the bank rubbing his shoulder, and Paul laughed, shook his fist at him, backed to shore and went downstream until he was out of rock range. From there he waded into the water and began to cast again, but now he was far enough away so we couldn't see his line or loops. He was a man with a wand in a river, and whatever happened we had to guess from what the man and the wand and the river did.

As he waded out, his big right arm swung back and forth. Each circle of his arm inflated his chest. Each circle was faster and higher and longer until his arm became defiant and his chest breasted the sky. On shore we were sure, although we could see no line, that the air above him was singing with loops of line that never touched the water but got bigger and bigger each time they passed and sang. And we knew what was in his mind from the lengthening defiance of his arm. He was not going to let his fly touch any water close to shore where the small and middle-sized fish were. We knew from his arm and chest that all parts of him were saying, "No small one for the last one." Everything was going into one big cast for one last big fish.

From our angle high on the bank, my father and I could see where in the distance the wand was going to let the fly first touch water. In the middle of the river was a rock iceberg, just its tip exposed above water and underneath it a rock house. It met all the residential requirements for big fish—powerful water carrying food to the front and back doors, and rest and shade behind them.

My father said, "There has to be a big one out there."

I said, "A little one couldn't live out there."

My father said, "The big one wouldn't let it."

My father could tell by the width of Paul's chest that he was going to let the next loop sail. It couldn't get any wider. "I wanted to fish out there," he said, "but I couldn't cast that far."

Paul's body pivoted as if he were going to drive a golf ball three hundred yards, and his arm went high into the great arc and the tip of his wand bent like a spring, and then everything sprang and sang.

Suddenly, there was an end of action. The man was immobile. There was no bend, no power in the wand. It pointed at ten o'clock and ten o'clock pointed at the rock. For a moment the man looked like a teacher with a pointer illustrating something about a rock to a rock. Only water moved. Somewhere above the top of the rock house a fly was swept in water so powerful only a big fish could be there to see it.

Then the universe stepped on its third rail. The wand jumped convulsively as it made contact with the magic current of the world. The wand tried to jump out of the man's right hand. His left hand seemed to be frantically waving good-bye to a fish, but actually was trying to throw enough line into the rod to reduce the voltage and ease the shock of what had struck.

Everything seemed electrically charged but electrically unconnected. Electrical sparks appeared here and there on the river. A fish jumped so far downstream that it seemed outside the man's electrical field, but, when the fish had jumped, the man had leaned back on the rod and it was then that the fish had toppled back into the water not guided in its reentry by itself. The connections between the convulsions and the sparks became clearer by repetition. When the man leaned back on the wand and the fish reentered the water not altogether under its own power, the wand recharged with convulsions, the man's hand waved frantically at another departure, and much farther below a fish jumped again. Because of the connections, it became the same fish.

The fish made three such long runs before another act in the performance began. Although the act involved a big man and a big fish, it looked more like children playing. The man's left hand sneakily began recapturing line, and then, as if caught in the act, threw it all back into the rod as the fish got wise and made still another run.

"He'll get him," I assured my father.

"Beyond doubt," my father said. The line going out became shorter than what the left hand took in.

When Paul peered into the water behind him, we knew he was going to start working the fish to shore and didn't want to back into a hole or rock. We could tell he had worked the fish into shallow water because he held the rod higher and higher to keep the fish from bumping into anything on the bottom. Just when we thought the performance was over, the wand convulsed and the man thrashed through the water after some unseen power departing for the deep.

"The son of a bitch still has fight in him," I thought I said to myself, but unmistakably I said it out loud, and was embarrassed for having said it out loud in front of my father. He said nothing.

Two or three more times Paul worked him close to shore, only to have him swirl and return to the deep, but even at that distance my father and I could feel the ebbing of the underwater power. The rod went high in the air, and the man moved backwards swiftly but evenly, motions which when translated into events meant the fish had tried to rest for a moment on top of the water and the man had quickly raised the rod high and skidded him to shore before the fish thought of getting under water again. He skidded him across the rocks clear back to a sandbar before the shocked fish gasped and discovered he could not live in oxygen. In belated despair, he rose in the sand and consumed the rest of momentary life dancing the Dance of Death on his tail.

The man put the wand down, got on his hands and knees in the sand, and, like an animal, circled another animal and waited. Then the shoulder shot straight out, and my brother stood up, faced us, and, with uplifted arm proclaimed himself the victor. Something giant dangled from his fist. Had Romans been watching they would have thought that what was dangling had a helmet on it.

"That's his limit," I said to my father.

"He is beautiful," my father said, although my brother had just finished catching his limit in the hole my father had already fished.

This was the last fish we were ever to see Paul catch. My father and I talked about this moment several times later, and whatever our other feelings, we always felt it fitting that, when we saw him catch his last fish, we never saw the fish but only the artistry of the fisherman.

While my father was watching my brother, he reached over to pat me, but he missed, so he had to turn his eyes and look for my knee and try again. He must have thought that I felt neglected and that he should tell me he was proud of me also but for other reasons.

It was a little too deep and fast where Paul was trying to wade the river, and he knew it. He was crouched over the water and his arms were spread wide for balance. If you were a wader of big rivers you could have felt with him even at a distance the power of the water making his legs weak and wavy and ready to swim out from under him. He looked downstream to estimate how far it was to an easier place to wade.

My father said, "He won't take the trouble to walk downstream. He'll swim it." At the same time Paul thought the same thing, and put his cigarettes and matches in his hat.

My father and I sat on the bank and laughed at each other. It never occurred to either of us to hurry to the shore in case he needed help with a rod in his right hand and a basket loaded with fish on his left shoulder. In our family it was no great thing for a fisherman to swim a river with matches in his hair. We laughed at each other because we knew he was getting damn good and wet, and we lived in him, and were swept over the rocks with him and held his rod high in one of our hands.

As he moved to shore he caught himself on his feet and then was washed off them, and, when he stood again, more of him showed and he staggered to shore. He never stopped to shake himself. He came charging up the bank showering molecules of water and images of himself to show what was sticking out of his basket, and he dripped all over us, like a young duck dog that in its joy forgets to shake itself before getting close.

"Let's put them all out on the grass and take a picture of them," he said. So we emptied our baskets and arranged them by size and took turns photographing each other admiring them and ourselves. The photographs turned out to be like most amateur snapshots of fishing catches—the fish were white from overexposure and didn't look as big as they actually were and the fishermen looked self-conscious as if some guide had to catch the fish for them.

However, one closeup picture of him at the end of this day remains in my mind, as if fixed by some chemical bath. Usually, just after he finished fishing he had little to say unless he saw he could have fished better. Otherwise, he merely smiled. Now flies danced around his hatband. Large drops of water ran from under his hat on to his face and then into his lips when he smiled.

At the end of this day, then, I remember him both as a distant abstraction in artistry and as a closeup in water and laughter.

My father always felt shy when compelled to praise one of his family, and his family always felt shy when he praised them. My father said, "You are a fine fisherman."

My brother said, "I'm pretty good with a rod, but I need three more years before I can think like a fish."

Remembering that he had caught his limit by switching to George's No. 2 Yellow Hackle with a feather wing, I said without knowing how much I said, "You already know how to think like a dead stone fly."

We sat on the bank and the river went by. As always, it was making sounds to itself, and now it made sounds to us. It would be hard to find three men sitting side by side who knew better what a river was saying.

On the Big Blackfoot River above the mouth of Belmont Creek the banks are fringed by large Ponderosa pines. In the slanting sun of late afternoon the shadows of great branches reached from across the river, and the trees took the river in their arms. The shadows continued up the bank, until they included us.

A river, though, has so many things to say that it is hard to know what it says to each of us. As we were packing our tackle and fish in the car, Paul repeated, "Just give me three more years." At the time, I was surprised at the repetition, but later I realized that the river somewhere, sometime, must have told me, too, that he would receive no such gift. For, when the police sergeant early next May wakened me before daybreak, I rose and asked no questions. Together we drove across the Continental Divide and down the length of the Big Blackfoot River over forest floors yellow and sometimes white with glacier lilies to tell my father and mother that my brother had been beaten to death by the butt of a revolver and his body dumped in an alley.

My mother turned and went to her bedroom where, in a house full of men and rods and rifles, she had faced most of her great problems alone. She was never to ask me a question about the man she loved most and understood least. Perhaps she knew enough to know that for her it was enough to have loved him. He was probably the only man in the world who had held her in his arms and leaned back and laughed.

When I finished talking to my father, he asked, "Is there anything else you can tell me?"

Finally, I said, "Nearly all the bones in his hand were broken."

He almost reached the door and then turned back for reassurance. "Are you sure that the bones in his hand were broken?" he asked. I repeated, "Nearly all the bones in his hand were broken." "In which hand?" he asked. "In his right hand," I answered.

After my brother's death, my father never walked very well again. He had to struggle to lift his feet, and, when he did get them up, they came down slightly out of control. From time to time Paul's right hand had to be reaffirmed; then my father would shuffle away again. He could not shuffle in a straight line from trying to lift his feet. Like many Scottish ministers before him, he had to derive what comfort he could from the faith that his son had died fighting.

For some time, though, he struggled for more to hold on to. "Are you sure you have told me everything you know about his death?" he asked. I said, "Everything." "It's not much, is it?" "No," I replied, "but you can love completely without complete understanding." "That I have known and preached," my father said.

Once my father came back with another question. "Do you think I could have helped him?" he asked. Even if I might have thought longer, I would have made the same answer. "Do you think I could have helped him?" I answered. We stood waiting in deference to each other. How can a question be answered that asks a lifetime of questions?

After a long time he came with something he must have wanted to ask from the first. "Do you think it was just a stick-up and foolishly he tried to fight his way out? You know what I mean—that it wasn't connected with anything in his past."

"The police don't know," I said.

"But do you?" he asked, and I felt the implication.

"I've said I've told you all I know. If you push me far enough, all I really know is that he was a fine fisherman."

"You know more than that," my father said. "He was beautiful."

"Yes," I said, "he was beautiful. He should have been—you taught him."

My father looked at me for a long time—he just looked at me. So this was the last he and I ever said to each other about Paul's death.

Indirectly, though, he was present in many of our conversations. Once, for instance, my father asked me a series of questions that suddenly made me wonder whether I understood even my father whom I felt closer to than any man I have ever known. "You like to tell true stories, don't you?" he asked, and I answered, "Yes, I like to tell stories that are true."

Then he asked, "After you have finished your true stories sometime, why don't you make up a story and the people to go with it?

"Only then will you understand what happened and why.

"It is those we live with and love and should know who elude us."

Now nearly all those I loved and did not understand when I was young are dead, but I still reach out to them.

Of course, now I am too old to be much of a fisherman, and now of course I usually fish the big waters alone, although some friends think I shouldn't. Like many fly fishermen in western Montana where the summer days are almost Arctic in length, I often do not start fishing until the cool of the evening. Then in the Arctic half-light of the canyon, all existence fades to a being with my soul and memories and the sounds of the Big Blackfoot River and a four-count rhythm and the hope that a fish will rise.

Eventually, all things merge into one, and a river runs through it. The river was cut by the world's great flood and runs over rocks from the basement of time. On some of the rocks are timeless raindrops. Under the rocks are the words, and some of the words are theirs.

I am haunted by waters.

■ JAMES WELCH

James Welch was born in 1940 in Browning, Montana. Blackfeet on his father's side and Gros Ventre on his mother's, Welch attended grade schools on the Blackfeet and Fort Belknap Indian reservations before leaving to study literature and writing with Richard Hugo at the University of Montana. Welch has been on the faculties of the University of Washington and Cornell University and serves on the Montana Board of Pardons. The selections reprinted here are from some of Welch's best-known work: Winter in the Blood *(1974),* The Death of Jim Loney *(1979),* Fools Crow *(1986), and* Riding the Earthboy 40 *(1971). Welch currently lives and works in Missoula, Montana.*

From The Death of Jim Loney

Thanksgiving and the streets were empty. Loney walked slowly, eating a piece of bread and trying to think what it had been like with his aunt. In the two years he had lived with her, they must have celebrated Thanksgiving, but the only holidays he could remember were Christmas and Easter. He remembered them because of church—midnight mass at Christmas, sunrise service at Easter. He wondered about her men friends because they never seemed to be around on holidays, at least on Christmas and Easter. But maybe they were around on the other holidays; maybe that's why he couldn't remember the other holidays; maybe they took her away with them on Thanksgiving.

Then Loney saw himself and his aunt sitting on the floor, quietly watching the lights on a small tree. It was Christmas Eve and they were drinking cocoa—no, he was drinking cocoa; she was drinking water because she was going to take communion that night—and she lowered her head and started to cry. He was twelve and he put his hand on her hair. He couldn't look at her, but he held his hand there until she stopped. She was good and he moved his fingers through her hair until she stopped. He had felt like a man, and after mass they opened presents and he felt as happy as anyone in the world. She never told him why she had cried and he never asked. It had been enough to feel her hair and smell the Christmas tree. She gave him a pen that wrote in three colors and he gave her a magazine that had beauty secrets, and they ate the pudding that tasted like butterscotch but wasn't.

As he nibbled at the bread, he felt a small regret that she had gone to him. It was no longer a question of a life with her, of a kind of family, which used to fill him with pain; rather, it was a simple regret that he did not get to know her. He wanted to believe that she was beautiful and he wanted to believe that he knew the color of her hair, but he could not, for he didn't know either of these things. The only thing he was sure of was that of all the women in his life, she was the one he had tried hardest to love.

Her name started with an S and she had left and he had been sent away to a mission school in southern Montana. Kate had already left. She had never lived with the aunt. Instead, she had gone away to another mission school, in Flandreau, South Dakota, right after their father had left them. Loney often wondered why she never lived with him and the aunt. It would have been better than any mission school. He had hated his school; he worked hard at his studies, but he hated the dormitory and early morning mass and the pasty cereal. He didn't like the fathers and the brothers—except for Brother Gerard, who taught science and taught him how to play basketball. Loney always believed that it was Brother Gerard who got him sprung too.

It had been in the spring of his second year there. Brother Gerard's class had gone on a field trip to a slough to collect water bugs, and Loney had left the group and followed a cattle trail to the far end of the slough. There, he sat on a beaver-chewed log and stared at the remains of a muskrat that had been trapped but never retrieved. It had crawled up on the bank from the entrance to its hole and its fur was almost gone and its tail had been chewed off. It was leather and bone and past stinking, but it made Loney cry and he thought that he would die, too, if he did not leave that school.

That evening he and Brother Gerard were taking a break after a one-on-one game and Loney told him he had to leave. The brother had sat there on the floor, his back against the folded-up bleachers, in his T-shirt and khaki pants and white sneakers, and he didn't say anything and Loney stood up and walked out on the court and took a last shot—he believed it would be the last shot of his life—and left the gym. But he didn't go back to the dormitory.

They picked him up the next morning on the highway to Billings. He got into a lot of trouble over that, but a couple of weeks later the priest who ran the school told him he had found Loney a place to stay in Harlem. Loney continued in Brother Gerard's science class until the end of the spring term, but they were never close again. Loney never went to the gym and he did not say goodbye when he left.

He lived during his high school years in a boardinghouse run by a minister and his wife. He didn't know much about ministers and he thought it strange that there was no church connected to the boardinghouse. He didn't believe that the man was a real minister. He had no church, and as far as Loney knew, no God. No midnight mass, no sunrise service. Loney did remember saying prayers before meals, but the minister never ate with them. He ate in the kitchen with his wife, after she had served the food to the five or six boys at the table in the dining room. Although the number of boys stayed about the same, the faces changed frequently. Loney outlasted all of them, living at the boardinghouse until the day he graduated. Then he packed his suitcase with his clothes, the small gold basketball pins that he'd won in the three years he played, and the Bible that the minister's wife had given him as a graduation present. He caught the bus up to Havre to enlist in the army and he never saw the minister and his wife again.

As Loney ate his bread and thought about these things, he became aware that he had been watching a small boy squatting beside a rough shape at the edge of an alley. He crossed the street.

The boy stood and stepped back.

"What have you got there?" said Loney.

"Nothing," said the boy.

Swipesy lay on his side, his mouth open and his blind blue eye staring up at nothing. There was something odd in the way he lay, as though he had been split lengthwise. Then Loney saw that he was frozen into the mud.

"What's your name?" he said to the boy.

"Amos," said the boy.

"Can you hold these, Amos?" And Loney handed him the sack of groceries.

Loney tried to lift Swipesy out of the frozen mud, but he had no luck. As he moved his hands down the dog's body, he heard Amos rustling in the sack for a piece of bread. He grabbed two handfuls of Swipesy's fur and tried to lift him. Then he tried the two free legs.

"Can't do it," he said. He stood and looked down at Swipesy, then at Amos. "Damn."

Amos set the groceries on the ground and dug into his coat pocket. Then he handed Loney a knife. It was a fat old pocket-knife with one blade completely gone and the other broken off about half its length.

Loney worked with the broken knife, chipping away flakes of the frozen mud. Once he stopped to rest his hand and said, "How old are you, Amos?"

"My name is Amos After Buffalo."

"This old dog of mine was ready to die, Amos. He was ninety years old."

"I'm seven."

Loney went back to work. He worked carefully, chipping away the mud from around Swipesy's head, then his back, his belly, his legs.

"What are you going to do with him once you get him out?"

"That's a good question."

"Are you going to throw him away?"

"No—I guess I'll bury him."

"That's what I'd do." And Amos After Buffalo squatted to watch. He liked to watch the man work. And he liked being the man's helper. "I'd bury him out there," he said, pointing in the general direction of the Little Rockies.

"Maybe that's just what I'll do."

"That's where I live. I live way out there." He thought for a moment. "Do you know where I live?"

Amos After Buffalo stood with the sack of groceries in his arms and watched the man walk away from him. The man cradled the dog the way Amos carried firewood. But today was Thanksgiving and he didn't have to carry logs or anything if he didn't want. He was visiting his aunt and uncle in town and his aunt was cooking a big venison roast. Amos didn't understand Thanksgiving. It was a holiday, but it wasn't like Christmas or Easter or the Fourth of July. It was a time to eat. He wished they had a turkey. A turkey seemed more like a holiday. He had never eaten turkey, but he thought it might be sweet.

Amos After Buffalo watched the man turn the corner at the end of the street. Then he set the groceries down and started to run home. He ran and he thought it was funny that the man didn't seem to be sad about his dog. He had wanted to watch the man bury the dog. But he remembered that his aunt had made a roast and he had been gone for a long time. He would have to break his old record to get home in time.

Loney stood behind the old woman and the girl. They were looking out the large windows at the airplane about to land. It came in so slowly and quietly that it seemed to be gliding. Loney could read the letters on the fusilage above the windows—FRONTIER—and he felt a kind of panicky excitement.

The right wheel touched the ground first, sending up a spray of blue smoke; then the left wheel touched, and finally the nose wheel settled on the runway. Suddenly the roar of the engines shook the windows of the little terminal and the old woman took a step back, almost bumping into Loney. She wore an old cloth coat and a black silk scarf and moccasins and leggings. Loney guessed that she was from Rocky Boy, because the old women still dressed that way out there. The girl was wearing a blue parka and checkered slacks and white sneakers. She looked to be about fifteen or sixteen. She stared with awe at the airplane, which was taxiing toward the gate. She hadn't noticed that her grandmother was now standing directly behind her, between her and Loney. The grandmother was frightened at the sight of the large plane bearing down on the terminal, but she didn't show it. She seemed impassive, and as Loney looked down at her shoulders and her silver, yellowing hair, he thought, That's the way old Indian women get; they've seen so much in their years, so many of these winters. . . .

The left engine came to a stop and a door behind the cockpit opened. Metal stairs slowly unfolded and lowered to the pavement.

Loney patted his hair down. He had got it cut that morning in Harlem and it felt slick and neat. He had also shaved and put on his best white shirt. He was excited because he knew that Kate would be perfect. He always loved to look at her and her beauty always affected him and he knew it was because he hadn't seen much of her since he was ten and she was fifteen. Now she was like a beautiful stranger to him until they got reacquainted. He had seen her only four or five times, all in the last ten years, since they parted as children. He had last seen her three years ago and he remembered how she looked–tall, willowy, maybe a little skinny, but no skinnier than some of the magazine models Loney had looked at. And he remembered the high wide cheekbones, which gave her face a soft diamond shape that he found lovely and strong.

Again he wondered why she had never married. He wondered that a lot, at odd moments. Sometimes he thought it was because of her job: she was just too busy flying around the country, telling people what to do and how to do it. At other times he thought it was because she was too strong. He couldn't imagine any man being equal to her. He smiled because he had been dreading this moment all morning for just that reason. But now he was excited. He knew that they would get reacquainted and everything would be fine. She would be his sister again.

A man carrying a briefcase emerged first, hurrying down the stairs without looking up, as though he expected to be taken for a celebrity. An elderly couple followed him, waving toward the terminal, but as far as Loney could tell, only he and the old woman and the girl were waiting. Then a young Indian in a green army uniform got off. His hat was back on his head and his tie was loose. He looked as if he had been traveling for days. The girl said something in Cree to the old woman and they moved toward the boarding area. Loney continued to stare at the door behind the cockpit. Nobody appeared for a few moments. Then a stewardess emerged from the darkness and descended the stairs. She was carrying a clipboard, holding it up to shield her hair from the slight wind. Loney could see a gold bracelet on her slender wrist.

He waited a while longer. Then he walked over to the Frontier counter, but there was no one around. He read the schedule board: FLIGHT 72, 11:43 A.M. The clock at the far end of the building said 11:48. It had to be the right plane.

The stewardess had walked up to the counter and was writing something on the clipboard.

"Excuse me," said Loney. "Did everybody who was supposed to get off that plane get off?"

The stewardess glanced out the window at the plane. Then she looked at her clipboard. "Four passengers . . . Um hum, yes."

"But my sister . . ."

"Was she by any chance coming from the south?"

"Arizona."

"Okay, um hum, I understand. It's been happening all day. Sir, the Denver airport has been closed because of blizzard conditions. I assume she would have had to change planes in Denver. But she was probably rerouted to Salt Lake, in which case"–she squinted at the schedule board–"she'll probably catch a later flight to Billings and connect up with our flight forty-three, which comes in here at five-thirty."

"You mean she'll be here later today?"

"Unless her plane landed in Denver. Some planes landed there earlier this morning. But all traffic is grounded now and likely will be for the rest of the day. I wouldn't worry. She probably went on to Salt Lake. You just be here at five-thirty." She smiled and walked briskly toward the boarding gate.

Loney watched her until she passed the soldier and the girl and the old woman. Then he watched them. They had their arms around each other; rather, the soldier had his arms around them and the girl had her arms around him. They both had their heads bowed as though they were saying a prayer. The old woman had her arms at her sides, accepting the soldier's hug. She was thinking that it was a bad world when her grandson comes home to her on a machine that flies. Later, when he told her stories of where he had been and what he had seen, she would realize that she had lost him. She sensed this now and it filled her with sadness, for she knew that what he had gained would never make up for what he had lost. She had seen the other boys come home. And she stared past her soldier at Loney's wolfish face and she thought, That's one of them.

From Winter in the Blood

First old Bird tried to bite me; then he tried a kick as I reached under his belly for the cinch. His leg came up like a shot turkey's, throwing him off-balance, and he lurched away from me. He tried a second kick, this time more gingerly, and when his hoof struck the ground, I snaked the cinch up under his belly and tightened down. As soon as he felt the strap taut against his ribs, he puffed his belly up and stood like a bloated cow. He looked satisfied, chewing on the bit. He was very old. I rammed my elbow into his rib cage and the air came out with a whoosh, sending him skittering sideways in surprise. The calf stood tense and interested by the loading chute. Lame Bull cradled his chin on his arms on the top rail of the corral and smiled.

It was a hot morning and I was sweating as I grabbed the saddle horn, turned the stirrup forward and placed my foot in it to swing aboard. As soon as Bird felt my weight settle on his back, he backed up, stumbled and almost went down. Then we took off, crow-hopping around the corral, old Bird hunkering beneath me, jumping straight up and down, suddenly sunfishing, kicking his back legs straight out, and twisting, grunting. We circled the corral four times, each jolt jarring my teeth as I came down hard in the saddle. He started to run, racing stiff-legged at the corral posts, changing directions at the last instant to make another run. Each time we passed Lame Bull, I could see him out of the corner of my eye, head thrown back, roaring at the big white horse and the intent, terrified rider, both hands on the saddle horn, swaying in the wrong direction each time the horse swerved. The calf had started to run, staying just ahead of Bird, bucking and kicking and crapping and bawling for its mother, who was circling on the other side of the corral.

Finally Lame Bull opened the gate, ducking out of the way as calf, horse and rider shot by him out onto the sagebrush flat between the toolshed and slough. I gave Bird his head as we pounded clouds of dust from the Milk River valley. The escaped calf had peeled off and pulled up short, swinging its head from side to side, not sure whether to follow us or return to its mother. We were beyond the big irrigation ditch by the time Bird slowed down and settled into a nervous trot. He panted and rumbled inside, as though a thunderstorm were growing in his belly. We reached the first gate and he was walking, trying to graze the weeds on the side of the road. I got down and opened the gate, leading him through and shutting it. A garter snake slithered off through the long grass, but he didn't see it.

We followed the fence line to the west between a field of alfalfa and another of bluejoint. Through the willows that lined the banks of the irrigation ditch I could see our small white house and the shack in front where Mose and I used to stretch muskrat pelts. The old root cellar where Teresa had seen a puff adder was now a tiny mound off to the side of the granary. A crane flapped above the slough, a gray arrow bound for some distant target.

Bird snorted. He had caught his breath and now walked cautiously with his head high and his dark eyes trained on the horizon in front of us. I slapped a horsefly from his neck but he didn't shy, didn't seem to notice.

"Tired already?" I said. "But you're an old war pony, you're supposed to go all day—at least that's what you'd have us believe."

He flicked his ears as if in irritation but lumbered ahead.

My bad leg had begun to ache from the tenseness with which I had to ride out Bird's storm. I got down and loosened the cinch. He took a walking crap as I led him down the fence line toward the main irrigation ditch. The wooden bridge was rotten. There were holes in the planks and one could see the slow cloudy water filled with bugs and snaky weeds. Bird balked at crossing. I coaxed him with soft words and threats, at last talking him across and down the bank on the other side.

Before us stood a log-and-mud shack set into the ground. The logs were cracked and bleached but the mud was dark, as though it had been freshly applied. There were no windows, only a door dug out of the earth which banked its walls. The weeds and brush stopped a hundred feet away on all sides, leaving only a caked white earth floor that did not give under one's feet. The river flowed through jagged banks some distance away. The old man stood at the edge. As we approached, he lifted his head with the dignity of an old dog sniffing the wind.

"Howdy," I said. The sun flared off the skin of earth between us. "Hello there, Yellow Calf."

He wore no shoes. His suit pants bagged at the knees and were stained on the thighs and crotch by dirt and meals, but his shirt, tan with pearl snaps, seemed clean, even ironed.

"How goes it?" I said.

He seemed confused.

"I'm First Raise's son–I came with him once."

"Ah, of course! You were just a squirt," he said.

"It was during a winter," I said.

"You were just a squirt."

I tied Bird to the pump and pumped a little water into the enamel basin under the spout. "My father called you Yellow Calf . . ." The water was brown. I loosened the bridle and took the bit out of Bird's mouth. It must have tasted strange after so many years. "And now Teresa says you are dead. I guess you died and didn't know it."

"How's that–dead?" He dug his hands into his pockets. "Sometimes I wish . . . but not likely."

"Then you're still called Yellow Calf."

"I'm called many things but that one will do. Some call me Bat Man because they think I drink the blood of their cattle during the night."

I laughed. "But you should be flattered. That means they are afraid of you."

"I have no need to be flattered. I am old and I live alone. One needs friends to appreciate flattery."

"Then you must be a wise man. You reject friends and flattery."

He made fists in his pants pockets and gestured with his head toward the shack. "I have some coffee."

It was only after he started walking, his feet seeming to move sideways as well as forward, that I realized he was completely blind. It was odd that I hadn't remembered, but maybe he hadn't been blind in those days.

He gripped the doorframe, then stood aside so that I could pass through first. He followed and closed the door, then reopened it. "You'll want some light."

The inside of the shack was clean and spare. It contained a cot, a kitchen table and two chairs. A small wood stove stood against the far wall. Beside the pipe a yellowed calendar hung from the wall. It said December 1936. A white cupboard made up the rest of the furniture in the room. Yellow Calf moved easily, at home with his furnishings. He took two cups, one porcelain, the other tin, from the cupboard and poured from a blackened pot that had been resting on the back of the stove. I coughed to let him know where I was, but he was already handing me a cup.

"Just the thing," I said.

"It's too strong. You're welcome." He eased himself down on the cot and leaned back against the wall.

It was cool, almost damp in the banked shack, and I thought of poor old Bird tied to the pump outside. He might get heatstroke.

"You're a good housekeeper, old man."

"I have many years' practice. It's easier to keep it sparse than to feel the sorrows of possessions."

"Possessions can be sorrowful," I agreed, thinking of my gun and electric razor.

"Only when they are not needed."

"Or when they are needed—when they are needed and a man doesn't have them."

"Take me—I don't have a car," he said.

"But you don't seem to need one. You get along."

"It would be easier with a car. Surely you have one."

"No."

"If you had a car you could take me to town."

I nodded.

"It would make life easier," he went on. "One wouldn't have to depend on others."

I wondered how the old man would drive a car. Perhaps he had radar and would drive only at night.

"You need a good pair of shoes to drive a car," I said.

"I have thought of that too." He tucked his feet under the cot as though they were embarrassed.

"There are probably laws against driving barefoot, anyway."

He sighed. "Yes, I suppose there are."

"You don't have to worry—not out here."

"I wouldn't say that."

"How so?"

"Irrigation man comes every so often to regulate the head gate—he keep his eye on me. I can hear him every so often down by that head gate."

I laughed. "You're too nervous, grandfather—besides, what have you got to hide, what have you done to be ashamed of?"

"Wouldn't you like to know . . ." His mouth dropped and his shoulders bobbed up and down.

"Come on, tell me. What have you got in those pants?"

"Wouldn't you like to know . . ." With that, his mouth dropped open another inch but no sound came out.

"I'll bet you have a woman around here. I know how you old buzzards operate."

His shoulders continued to shake, then he started coughing. He coughed and shook, holding his cup away from the cot, until the spasm of mirth or whatever it was had passed.

He stood and walked to the stove. When he reached for my cup, his hand struck my wrist. His fingers were slick, papery, like the belly of a rattlesnake. He poured to within half an inch of the cup's lip, to the tip of the finger he had placed inside.

"How is it you say you are only half dead, Yellow Calf, yet you move like a ghost. How can I be sure you aren't all the way dead and are only playing games?"

"Could I be a ghost and suck the blood of cattle at the same time?" He settled back on the cot, his lips thinned into what could have been a smile.

"No, I suppose not. But I can't help but feel there's something wrong with you. No man should live alone."

"Who's alone? The deer come–in the evenings–they come to feed on the other side of the ditch. I can hear them. When they whistle, I whistle back."

"And do they understand you?" I said this mockingly.

His eyes were hidden in the darkness.

"Mostly–I can understand most of them."

"What do they talk about?"

"It's difficult . . . About ordinary things, but some of them are hard to understand."

"But do they talk about the weather?"

"No, no, not that. They leave that to men." He sucked on his lips. "No, they seem to talk mostly about . . ."–he searched the room with a peculiar alertness–"well, about the days gone by. They talk a lot about that. They are not happy."

"Not happy? But surely to a deer one year is as good as the next. How do you mean?"

"Things change–things have changed. They are not happy."

"Ah, a matter of seasons! When their bellies are full, they remember when the feed was not so good–and when they are cold, they remember . . ."

"No!" The sharpness of his own voice startled him. "I mean, it goes deeper than that. They are not happy with the way things are. They know what a bad time it is. They can tell by the moon when the world is cockeyed."

"But that's impossible."

"They understand the signs. This earth is cockeyed."

A breeze came up, rustling the leaves of the tall cottonwoods by the ditch. It was getting on in the afternoon.

I felt that I should let the subject die, but I was curious about Yellow Calf's mind.

"Other animals—do you understand them?"

"Some, some more than others."

"Hmmm," I said.

"This earth is cockeyed."

"Hmmm . . ."

"Of course men are the last to know."

"And you?"

"Even with their machines."

"Hmmm . . ."

"I have my inclinations."

"The moon?"

"Among other things—sometimes it seems that one has to lean into the wind to stand straight."

"You're doing plenty of leaning right now, I would say," I said.

"You don't believe the deer." He was neither challenging nor hurt. It was a statement.

"I wouldn't say that."

"You do not believe me."

"It's not a question of belief. Don't you see? If I believe you, then the world is cockeyed."

"But you have no choice."

"You could be wrong—you could believe and still be wrong. The deer could be wrong."

"You do not want to believe them."

"I can't."

"It's no matter."

"I'm sorry."

"No need—we can't change anything. Even the deer can't change anything. They only see the signs."

A pheasant sounded to the east but the old man either did not pay attention or thought it a usual message. He leaned forward into the shadows of the shack, holding his cup with both hands, looking directly at me and through me. I shifted from one buttock to the other, then set my cup on the table.

"It's not very good," he said.

"No—that's not true. It's just that I have to leave; we're weaning a calf . . ."

"I'm old."

"Yes."

"You must say hello to Teresa for me. Tell her that I am living to the best of my ability."

"I'll tell her to come see for herself," I said.

"Say hello to First Raise."

"Yes, yes . . . he will be pleased." Didn't he know that First Raise had been dead for ten years?

We walked out into the glare of the afternoon sun.

Bird tried to kick me as I swung my leg over his back. "Next time I'll bring some wine," I said.

"It is not necessary," he said.

"For a treat."

I started to wave from the top of the bridge. Yellow Calf was facing off toward the river, listening to two magpies argue.

From Fools Crow

The infant had died during the early night, but still, in the gray light of dawn, the young woman hugged the body to her. Earlier she had bared a breast and put the small mouth to it, as though life would begin again with the simple act of suckling. But the mouth did not move and the body did not move, so the woman put away her breast and rocked back and forth, whispering soothing words into the tiny ear.

Her husband and his two other wives had tried to take the infant from her, but now they sat and watched and listened to the gentle murmur of the mother. They knew it would be for the best to get the infant away from camp, to bury it someplace far away. One of the other wives had prepared a winding cloth, a small dress and moccasins and some food to accompany the infant on the journey to the Sand Hills.

There was an air in the lodge of both expectation and resignation. This was the first death caused by the white-scabs in the winter camp of the Lone Eaters. It had not been a drawn-out death, full of agony and grief. Less than two sleeps ago, the mother had first noticed the red sores on the infant's scalp and chest. They were small and the women thought they were a rash, and like a rash they began to spread, first to the upper arms and then down to the belly. The women put salve on the red areas that they had obtained from Mik-api. If they had been more observant, they would have noticed his silence as he made the paste. But these wives were young, the oldest not yet twenty winters, and so they chattered among themselves and did not remark on the old man's faraway face.

The end was very quick. No sooner had the women applied the salve than the infant, whose name was Long Tail because it had cried like a long-tail when it appeared in the world, convulsed and passed into the Shadowland.

Now the mother hugged the small body to herself, then handed it gently to one of the other young women, who placed the infant on the winding sheet. She and the other wife then dressed the infant and rolled it and a small sack of pemmican in the sheet.

The husband, who had already saddled and bridled his horse, took the bundle and left the lodge. The women inside heard the squeak of leather as the man put his weight in the stirrup. Then the horse danced a bit before it took off at a fast trot. The women listened to the muffled hoofbeats on the frozen earth. The mother began to sing to herself, a sleeping song that her mother had sung to her. The other two looked at each other. In spite of their youth and inexperience, they knew, had known for some time, that the infant had died of the white-scabs. One stood, as though in that silent communication she had been chosen, and hurried out of the lodge.

The sickness spread rapidly. There was no longer any talk of moving the camp to the land of the Siksikas. Three families who appeared to be still healthy did leave the winter camp but they traveled in the direction of the Four Horns agency. Some who watched them leave felt both envy and betrayal. Most of the others were too busy caring for the ill ones to notice the three circles of bare earth on the edge of the camp.

During the first three or four days, Mik-api and Boss Ribs went from lodge to lodge, performing their curing ceremonies. Fools Crow, who had returned to camp the night the infant died, stayed busy too, conducting purifying sessions in the sweat lodge, taking whole families who had not yet been touched by the sickness into the small skin-draped lodge. In between sessions he mixed medicines and took them to the two many-faces men. He built up the fires, heated stones, sweated, prayed and even tried his own healing on two members of Sits-in-the-middle's family. Soon after the long ceremony the two were dead. It was then that Fools Crow knew the ceremonies were futile—the healing and purifying were as meaningless as a raindrop in a spring river. Even if the healing worked, by the time the ceremony was over, twenty others would come down with the sickness.

Boss Ribs seemed to share this feeling of hopelessness. On the fifth day Fools Crow went to his lodge to deliver some fresh-ground medicine. Upon entering, he noticed that the many-faces man sat alone, hunched over a small fire. Beside him, the Beaver Medicine bundle lay open, its many skins and paraphernalia strewn about. At first, Fools Crow thought that Boss Ribs had been conducting the beaver ceremony and he felt his heart quicken with faint hope, but when he looked into the deep, sad eyes, he knew that whatever magic the keeper of the bundle had been searching for was not there.

"Are we lost then?" said Fools Crow as he squatted before the heap of objects. He was tired and his own words did not alarm him. The dying had begun and would continue. He had seen it on the yellow skin.

"The Above Ones will stop the suffering when they see fit. Our medicines are as powerless as grass before Wind Maker." Boss Ribs indicated the contents of the bundle. "I have been through the bundle three times since daybreak, searching for a ceremony, a song that might have some effect. . . ."

Fools Crow looked at the packet of herbs in his hand. "This white-scabs—it takes the strong as well as the weak, the young, the healthy ones, just as easily as the old and the sick. Whole families have perished!"

"How is it with your family, Fools Crow?"

"Nothing in my father's lodge, or in Yellow Kidney's. And Red Paint, she is healthy too. I have asked her to stay in the lodge, to open up to no one, but I saw her this morning going into her mother's lodge. I'm afraid for our soon-to-be son."

"You should take her away. Leave this camp. Go into the Backbone until this is over. There is plenty of meat there and no sickness. Sun Chief will watch over you."

Fools Crow thought of Feather Woman in the green bowl of the Backbone of the World. In the small pause that filled the lodge, the two men could hear the wailing of women in the next tipi. It was difficult to tell how many there were or who they mourned. Wailing no longer carried the urgency of grief; instead, it seemed more a ritual to be enacted because the Pikunis had always mourned their dead. Even the young had become inured to the deaths that surrounded them. Fools Crow placed the packet of herbs before Boss Ribs, then stood.

"And what of your family?" he said.

"A daughter died during the night–Bird Rattler. She was six winters." Boss Ribs pointed with puckered lips.

Fools Crow saw the small winding sheet. He touched the many-faces man on the shoulder and left, his thoughts far away and centered on the woman who mourned each new dawn with the wailing of a thousand geese.

He saw it in her eyes even as he entered his lodge. It was a look he had seen much of recently.

"One Spot and Good Young Man have the sickness!" The words came out in a breathless rush, but it took a space of time for them to register.

"Where?" he said dully.

"In my mother's lodge. She won't let me in!" And now Red Paint began to weep. Her small shoulders shook beneath the blackhorn robe and her sobs drove the yellow dog slinking out the entrance. Fools Crow crossed to her, his mind alert, and held her to his chest.

"She won't let me in," wailed Red Paint. "She won't let me help, she says I am not needed–and yet my two brothers are sick and dying of the dreadful spirit. I pray and pray to the Above Ones, but it is not enough. They know Red Paint is not significant and they laugh at her puny voice. Oh, she is a nothing-one and her own mother doesn't want her around!" She put her face into the folds of Fools Crow's shirt, but the muffled sobbing only increased.

As he held her, he felt her round belly jump each time her breath caught and he imagined the life within and he wanted to take her away, to the Backbone, to the land of the Siksikas, anywhere. But it was too late now. She would never leave her family. He caught her hands in his and pressed them flat against his chest. Her fingers were cold.

"Your mother is right to send you away. You must protect our child. He must be born strong, full of life. I am afraid for the Pikunis now, but we must think of the moons and winters to come. Our son must survive."

Fools Crow was gone all that day and far into the night. Three times Red Paint left the lodge, each time intent on going to her mother's. The second and third times she walked across camp and stood outside the lodge where her brothers lay sick. She heard the drumming and Fools Crow's husky chant. When darkness fell, she looked up at the stars and saw the Seven Persons and the Dusty Trail and the Star-that-stands-still. They were far away and bright and she noticed that Moon was not among them. She has chosen to hide her face from our troubles, thought Red Paint. She had always thought of Night Red Light as a protector, one who watched over the people while Sun Chief slept in his lodge. She was strong and her light betrayed many an enemy that sought to steal Lone Eater horses to take revenge on the sleeping village. Once, as a girl, Red Paint had become lost with two companions and had wandered across the monotonous prairies until Moon rose and showed them the way home. Now, not even Moon would help her people against this powerful sickness.

Red Paint returned to her lodge and lay down in her sleeping robes. There was a dull ache in her stomach and she knew she should eat something; instead, she closed her eyes and saw her father and brothers in happier times. She saw herself as a girl in that lodge with all of life before her. She shuddered as she thought of the day the men brought Yellow Kidney's body in on the makeshift travois. She had thought she would have to be strong for her mother's sake, to help her through the mourning period. But her mother surprised her by displaying very little emotion. The next day they had taken the body up into a grove of quaking-leaf trees in the upper Two Medicine River. There, they built a platform of branches and hoisted her father's body in place. When they rode back to the village, Red Paint noticed the look of peace on her mother's face.

A wave of guilt passed through her body and her cheeks burned. The thought confused her but the feeling was real enough. She would have remained that girl forever—she would have forsaken her life with Fools Crow—if it would have brought her father back healthy from the Crow raid and restored her mother's spirit, and if it would make her brothers well and happy again. If it had not been for her exhaustion, if she had not slipped away into a deep sleep, she might have made a vow that would have taken away what little comfort and happiness she knew, a vow as irretrievable as the leaves which fell each autumn.

As it was, when Fools Crow returned and lay down beside her, his arm flung over her shoulder, she became aware, for the first time since their marriage, that he was a person apart from her. She smelled his odor and she felt the weight of his arm, and she tried to remember his face, his smile of reassurance, but she couldn't. She lay there and thought of her family and of the new life within her, and she trembled beneath the dead weight of his arm.

Harlem, Montana: Just Off the Reservation

We need no runners here. Booze is law
and all the Indians drink in the best tavern.
Money is free if you're poor enough.
Disgusted, busted whites are running
for office in this town. The constable,
a local farmer, plants the jail with wild
raven-haired stiffs who beg just one more drink.
One drunk, a former Methodist, becomes a saint
in the Indian church, bugs the plaster man
on the cross with snakes. If his knuckles broke,
he'd see those women wail the graves goodbye.

Goodbye, goodbye, Harlem on the rocks,
so bigoted, you forget the latest joke,
so lonely, you'd welcome a battalion of Turks
to rule your women. What you don't know,
what you will never know or want to learn–
Turks aren't white. Turks are olive, unwelcome
alive in any town. Turks would use
your one dingy park to declare a need for loot.
Turks say bring it, step quickly, lay down and dead.

Here we are when men were nice. This photo, hung
in the New England Hotel lobby, shows them nicer
than pie, agreeable to the warring bands of redskins
who demanded protection money for the price of food.
Now, only Hutterites out north are nice. We hate
them. They are tough and their crops are always good.
We accuse them of idiocy and believe their belief all wrong.

Harlem, your hotel is overnamed, your children
are raggedy-assed but you go on, survive
the bad food from the two cafes and peddle
your hate for the wild who bring you money.
When you die, if you die, will you remember
the three young bucks who shot the grocery up,
locked themselves in and cried for days, we're rich,
help us, oh God, we're rich.

The Man from Washington

The end came easy for most of us.
Packed away in our crude beginnings
in some far corner of a flat world,
we didn't expect much more
than firewood and buffalo robes
to keep us warm. The man came down,
a slouching dwarf with rainwater eyes,
and spoke to us. He promised
that life would go on as usual,
that treaties would be signed, and everyone—
man, woman and child—would be inoculated
against a world in which we had no part,
a world of money, promise and disease.

In My First Hard Springtime

Those red men you offended were my brothers.
Town drinkers, Buckles Pipe, Star Boy,
Billy Fox, were blood to bison. Albert Heavy Runner
was never civic. You are white and common.

Record trout in Willow Creek chose me
to deify. My horse, Centaur, part cayuse,
was fast and mad and black. Dandy in flat hat
and buckskin, I rode the town and called it mine.

A slow hot wind tumbled dust against my door.
Fed and fair, you mocked my philosophic nose,
my badger hair. I rolled your deference
in the hay and named it love and lasting.

Starved to visions, famous cronies top Mount Chief
for names to give respect to Blackfeet streets.
I could deny them in my first hard springtime,
but choose amazed to ride you down with hunger.

THOMAS McGUANE

Born in Michigan in 1939, novelist Tom McGuane was graduated from Michigan State University and received an M.F.A. from Yale in 1965. McGuane's The Bushwhacked Piano *(1971) won the Richard and Hinda Rosenthal Award of the American Academy of Arts and Letters, and his* Ninety-Two in the Shade *(1973) was nominated for a National Book Award. His screenwriting credits include* Rancho Deluxe, Tom Horn, *and* Missouri Breaks. *"Visitors" is from McGuane's novel,* Something to Be Desired, *published in 1985. "Heart of the Game" originally appeared in* Outside Magazine *in 1977 and is reprinted in* An Outside Chance *(1980). McGuane and his family live on a ranch near McCleod, Montana, where he raises cutting horses.*

The Heart of the Game

Hunting in your own back yard becomes with time, if you love hunting, less and less expeditionary. This year, when Montana's eager frost knocked my garden on its butt, the hoe seemed more like the rifle than it ever had before, the vegetables more like game.

My son and I went scouting before the season and saw some antelope in the high plains foothills of the Absaroka Range, wary, hanging on the skyline; a few bands and no great heads. We crept around, looking into basins, and at dusk met a tired cowboy on a tired horse followed by a tired blue-heeler dog. The plains seemed bigger than anything, bigger than the mountains that seemed to sit in the middle of them, bigger than the ocean. The clouds made huge shadows that traveled on the grass slowly through the day.

Hunting season trickles on forever; if you don't go in on a cow with anybody, there is the dark argument of the empty deep-freeze against headhunting ("You can't eat horns!"). But nevertheless, in my mind, I've laid out the months like playing cards, knowing some decent whitetails could be down in the river bottom and, fairly reliably, the long windy shots at antelope. The big buck mule deer–the ridge-runners–stay up in the scree and rock walls until the snow drives them out; but they stay high long after the elk have quit and broken down the hay corrals on the ranches and farmsteads, which, when you're hunting the rocks from a saddle horse, look pathetic and housebroken with their yellow lights against the coming of winter.

Where I live, the Yellowstone River runs straight north, then takes an eastward turn at Livingston, Montana. This flowing north is supposed to be remarkable; and the river doesn't do it long. It runs mostly over sand and stones once it comes out of the rock slots near the Wyoming line. But all along, there are deviations of one sort or another: canals, backwaters, sloughs; the red willows grow in the sometime-flooded bottom, and at the first elevation, the cottonwoods. I hunt here for the white-tail deer which, in recent years, have moved up these rivers in numbers never seen before.

The first morning, the sun came up hitting around me in arbitrary panels as the light moved through the jagged openings in the Absaroka Range. I was walking very slowly in the edge of the trees, the river invisible a few hundred yards to my right but sending a huge sigh through the willows. It was cold and the sloughs had crowns of ice thick enough to support me. As I crossed one great clear pane, trout raced around under my feet and a ten-foot bubble advanced slowly before my cautious steps. Then passing back into the trees, I found an active game trail, cut cross-lots to pick a better stand, sat in a good vantage place under a cottonwood with the ought-six across my knees. I thought, running my hands up into my sleeves, this is lovely but I'd rather be up in the hills; and I fell asleep.

I woke up a couple of hours later, the coffee and early-morning drill having done not one thing for my alertness. I had drooled on my rifle and it was time for my chores back at the ranch. My chores of late had consisted primarily of working on screenplays so that the bank didn't take the ranch. These days the primary ranch skill is making the payment; it comes before irrigation, feeding out, and calving. Some rancher friends find this so discouraging they get up and roll a number or have a slash of tanglefoot before they even think of the glories of the West. This is the New Rugged.

The next day, I reflected upon my lackadaisical hunting and left really too early in the morning. I drove around to Mission Creek in the dark and ended up sitting in the truck up some wash listening to a New Mexico radio station until my patience gave out and I started out cross-country in the dark, just able to make out the nose of the Absaroka Range as it faced across the river to the Crazy Mountains. It seemed maddeningly up and down slick banks, and a couple of times I had game clatter out in front of me in the dark. Then I turned up a long coulee that climbed endlessly south, and started in that direction, knowing the plateau on top should hold some antelope. After half an hour or so, I heard the mad laughing of coyotes, throwing their voices all around the inside of the coulee, trying to panic rabbits and making my hair stand on end despite my affection for them. The stars tracked overhead into the first pale light and it was nearly dawn before I came up on the bench. I could hear cattle below me and I moved along an edge of thorn trees to break my outline, then sat down at the point to wait for shooting light.

I could see antelope on the skyline before I had that light; and by the time I did, there was a good big buck angling across from me, looking at everything. I thought I could see well enough, and I got up into a sitting position and into the sling. I had made my moves quietly, but when I looked through the scope the antelope was 200 yards out, using up the country in bounds. I tracked with him, let him bounce up into the reticle, and touched off a shot. He was down and still, but I sat watching until I was sure.

Nobody who loves to hunt feels absolutely hunky-dory when the quarry goes down. The remorse spins out almost before anything and the balancing act ends on one declination or another. I decided that unless I become a vegetarian, I'll get my meat by hunting for it. I feel absolutely unabashed by the arguments of other carnivores who get their meat in plastic with blue numbers on it. I've seen slaughterhouses, and anyway, as Sitting Bull said, when the buffalo are gone, we will hunt mice, for we are hunters and we want our freedom.

The antelope had piled up in the sage, dead before he hit the ground. He was an old enough buck that the tips of his pronged horns were angled in toward each other. I turned him downhill to bleed him out. The bullet had mushroomed in the front of the lungs, so the job was already halfway done. With antelope, proper field dressing is critical because they can end up sour if they've been run or haphazardly hog-dressed. And they sour from their own body heat more than from external heat.

The sun was up and the big buteo hawks were lifting on the thermals. There was enough breeze that the grass began to have directional grain like the prairie and the rim of the coulee wound up away from me toward the Absaroka. I felt peculiarly solitary, sitting on my heels next to the carcass in the sagebrush and greasewood, my rifle racked open on the ground. I made an incision around the metatarsal glands inside the back legs and carefully removed them and set them well aside; then I cleaned the blade of my hunting knife with handfuls of grass to keep from tainting the meat with those powerful glands. Next I detached the anus and testes from the outer walls and made a shallow puncture below the sternum, spread it with the thumb and forefinger of my left hand, and ran the knife upside down to the bone bridge between the hind legs. Inside, the diaphragm was like the taut lid of a drum and cut away cleanly, so that I could reach clear up to the back of the mouth and detach the windpipe. Once that was done I could draw the whole visceral package out onto the grass and separate out the heart, liver, and tongue before propping the carcass open with two whittled-up sage scantlings.

You could tell how cold the morning was, despite the exertion, just by watching the steam roar from the abdominal cavity. I stuck the knife in the ground and sat back against the slope, looking clear across to Convict Grade and the Crazy Mountains. I was blood from the elbows down and the antelope's eyes had skinned over. I thought, This is goddamned serious and you had better always remember that.

There was a big red enamel pot on the stove; and I ladled antelope chili into two bowls for my son and me. He said, "It better not be too hot."

"It isn't."

"What's your news?" he asked.

"Grandpa's dead."

"Which grandpa?" he asked. I told him it was Big Grandpa, my father. He kept on eating. "He died last night."

He said, "I know what I want for Christmas."

"What's that?"

"I want Big Grandpa back."

It was 1950-something and I was small, under twelve say, and there were four of us: my father, two of his friends, and me. There was a good belton setter belonging to the one friend, a hearty bird hunter who taught dancing and fist-fought at any provocation. The other man was old and sick and had a green fatal look in his face. My father took me aside and said, "Jack and I are going to the head of this field"–and he pointed up a mile and a half of stalks to where it ended in the flat woods–"and we're going to take the dog and get what he can point. These are running birds. So you and Bill just block the field and you'll have some shooting."

"I'd like to hunt with the dog." I had a 20-gauge Winchester my grandfather had given me, which got hocked and lost years later when another of my family got into the bottle; and I could hit with it and wanted to hunt over the setter. With respect to blocking the field, I could smell a rat.

"You stay with Bill," said my father, "and try to cheer him up."

"What's the matter with Bill?"

"He's had one heart attack after another and he's going to die."

"When?"

"Pretty damn soon."

I blocked the field with Bill. My first thought was, I hope he doesn't die before they drive those birds onto us; but if he does, I'll have all the shooting.

There was a crazy cold autumn light on everything, magnified by the yellow silage all over the field. The dog found birds right away and they were shooting. Bill said he was sorry but he didn't feel so good. He had his hunting license safety-pinned to the back of his coat and fiddled with a handful of 12-gauge shells. "I've shot a shitpile of game," said Bill, "but I don't feel so good anymore." He took a knife out of his coat pocket. "I got this in the Marines," he said, "and I carried it for four years in the Pacific. The handle's drilled out and weighted so you can throw it. I want you to have it." I took it and thanked him, looking into his green face, and wondered why he had given it to me. "That's for blocking this field with me," he said. "Your dad and that dance teacher are going to shoot them all. When you're not feeling so good, they put you at the end of the field to block when there isn't shit-all going to fly by you. They'll get them all. They and the dog will."

We had an indestructible tree in the yard we had chopped on, nailed steps to, and initialed; and when I pitched that throwing knife at it, the knife broke in two. I picked it up and thought, *This thing is jinxed.* So I took it out into the crab-apple woods and put it in the can I had buried, along with a Roosevelt dime and an atomic-bomb ring I had sent away for. This was a small collection of things I buried over a period of years. I was sending them to God. All He had to do was open the can, but they were never collected. In any case, I have long known that if I could understand why I wanted to send a broken knife I believed to be jinxed to God, then I would be a long way toward what they call a personal philosophy as opposed to these hand-to-mouth metaphysics of who said what to who in some cornfield twenty-five years ago.

We were in the bar at Chico Hot Springs near my home in Montana: me, a lout poet who had spent the day floating under the diving board while adolescent girls leapt overhead; and my brother John, who had glued himself to the pipe which poured warm water into the pool and announced over and over in a loud voice that every drop of water had been filtered through his bathing suit.

Now, covered with wrinkles, we were in the bar, talking to Alvin Close, an old government hunter. After half a century of predator control he called it "useless and half-assed."

Alvin Close killed the last major stock-killing wolf in Montana. He hunted the wolf so long he raised a litter of dogs to do it with. He hunted the wolf futilely with a pack that had fought the wolf a dozen times, until one day he gave up and let the dogs run the wolf out the back of a shallow canyon. He heard them yip their way into silence while he leaned up against a tree; and presently the wolf came tiptoeing down the front of the canyon into Alvin's lap. The wolf simply stopped because the game was up. Alvin raised the Winchester and shot it.

"How did you feel about that?" I asked.

"How do you think I felt?"

"I don't know."

"I felt like hell."

Alvin's evening was ruined and he went home. He was seventy-six years old and carried himself like an old-time army officer, setting his glass on the bar behind him without looking.

You stare through the plastic at the red smear of meat in the supermarket. What's this it says here? *Mighty Good? Tastee? Quality, Premium, and Government Inspected?* Soon enough, the blood is on your hands. It's inescapable.

Aldo Leopold was a hunter who I am sure abjured freeze-dried vegetables and extrusion burgers. His conscience was clean because his hunting was part of a larger husbandry in which the life of the country was enhanced by his own work. He knew that game populations are not bothered by hunting until they are already too precarious and that precarious game populations should not be hunted. Grizzlies should not be hunted, for instance. The enemy of game is clean farming and sinful chemicals; as well as the useless alteration of watersheds by promoter cretins and the insidious dizzards of land development, whose lobbyists teach us the venality of all governments.

A world in which a sacramental portion of food can be taken in an old way–hunting, fishing, farming, and gathering–has as much to do with societal sanity as a day's work for a day's pay.

For a long time, there was no tracking snow. I hunted on horseback for a couple of days in a complicated earthquake fault in the Gallatins. The fault made a maze of narrow canyons with flat floors. The sagebrush grew on woody trunks higher than my head and left sandy paths and game trails where the horse and I could travel.

There were Hungarian partridge that roared out in front of my horse, putting his head suddenly in my lap. And hawks tobogganed on the low air currents, astonished to find me there. One finger canyon ended in a vertical rock wall from which issued a spring of the kind elsewhere associated with the Virgin Mary, hung with ex-votos and the orthopedic supplications of satisfied miracle customers. Here, instead, were nine identical piles of bear shit, neatly adorned with undigested berries.

One canyon planed up and topped out on an endless grassy rise. There were deer there, does and a young buck. A thousand yards away and staring at me with semaphore ears.

They assembled at a stiff trot from the haphazard array of feeding and strung out in a precise line against the far hill in a dog trot. When I removed my hat, they went into their pogo-stick gait and that was that.

"What did a deer ever do to you?"

"Nothing."

"I'm serious. What do you have to go and kill them for?"

"I can't explain it talking like this."

"Why should they die for you? Would you die for deer?"

"If it came to that."

My boy and I went up the North Fork to look for grouse. We had my old pointer Molly, and Thomas's .22 pump. We flushed a number of birds climbing through the wild roses; but they roared away at knee level, leaving me little opportunity for my over-and-under, much less an opening for Thomas to ground-sluice one with his .22. We started out at the meteor hole above the last ranch and went all the way to the national forest. Thomas had his cap on the bridge of his nose and wobbled through the trees until we hit cross fences. We went out into the last open pasture before he got winded. So we sat down and looked across the valley at the Gallatin Range, furiously white and serrated, a bleak edge of the world. We sat in the sun and watched the chickadees make their way through the russet brush.

"Are you having a good time?"

"Sure," he said and curled a small hand around the octagonal barrel of the Winchester. I was not sure what I had meant by my question.

The rear quarters of the antelope came from the smoker so dense and finely grained it should have been sliced as prosciutto. We had edgy, crumbling cheddar from British Columbia and everybody kept an eye on the food and tried to pace themselves. The snow whirled in the window light and puffed the smoke down the chimney around the cedar flames. I had a stretch of enumerating things: my family, hayfields, saddle horses, friends, thirty-ought-six, French and Russian novels. I had a baby girl, colts coming, and a new roof on the barn. I finished a big corral made of railroad ties and 2×6s. I was within eighteen months of my father's death, my sister's death, and the collapse of my marriage. Still, the washouts were repairing; and when a few things had been set aside, not excluding paranoia, some features were left standing, not excluding lovers, children, friends, and saddle horses. In time, it would be clear as a bell. I did want venison again that winter and couldn't help but feel some old ridge-runner had my number on him.

I didn't want to read and I didn't want to write or acknowledge the phone with its tendrils into the zombie enclaves. I didn't want the New Rugged; I wanted the Old Rugged and a pot to piss in. Otherwise, it's deteriorata, with mice undermining the wiring in my frame house, sparks jumping in the insulation, the dog turning queer, and a horned owl staring at the baby through the nursery window.

It was pitch black in the bedroom and the windows radiated cold across the blankets. The top of my head felt this side of frost and the stars hung like ice crystals over the chimney. I scrambled out of bed and slipped into my long johns, put on a heavy shirt and my wool logger pants with the police suspenders. I carried the boots down to the kitchen so as not to wake the house and turned the percolator on. I put some cheese and chocolate in my coat, and when the coffee was done I filled a chili bowl and quaffed it against the winter.

When I hit the front steps I heard the hard squeaking of new snow under my boots and the wind moved against my face like a machine for refinishing hardwood floors. I backed the truck up to the horse trailer, the lights wheeling against the ghostly trunks of the bare cottonwoods. I connected the trailer and pulled it forward to a flat spot for loading the horse.

I had figured that when I got to the corral I could tell one horse from another by starlight; but the horses were in the shadow of the barn and I went in feeling my way among their shapes trying to find my hunting horse Rocky, and trying to get the front end of the big sorrel who kicks when surprised. Suddenly Rocky was looking in my face and I reached around his neck with the halter. A 1,200-pound bay quarter horse, his withers angled up like a fighting bull, he wondered where we were going but ambled after me on a slack lead rope as we headed out of the darkened corral.

I have an old trailer made by a Texas horse vet years ago. It has none of the amenities of newer trailers. I wish it had a dome light for loading in the dark; but it doesn't. You ought to check and see if the cat's sleeping in it before you load; and I didn't do that either. Instead, I climbed inside the trailer and the horse followed me. I tied the horse down to a D-ring and started back out, when he blew up. The two of us were confined in the small space and he was ripping and bucking between the walls with such noise and violence that I had a brief disassociated moment of suspension from fear. I jumped up on the manger with my arms around my head while the horse shattered the inside of the trailer and rocked it furiously on its axles. Then he blew the steel rings out of the halter and fell over backward in the snow. The cat darted out and was gone. I slipped down off the manger and looked for the horse; he had gotten up and was sidling down past the granary in the star shadows.

I put two blankets on him, saddled him, played with his feet, and calmed him. I loaded him without incident and headed out.

I went through the aspen line at daybreak, still climbing. The horse ascended steadily toward a high basin, creaking the saddle metronomically. It was getting colder as the sun came up, and the rifle scabbard held my left leg far enough from the horse that I was chilling on that side.

We touched the bottom of the basin and I could see the rock wall defined by a black stripe of evergreens on one side and the remains of an avalanche on the other. I thought how utterly desolate this country can look in winter and how one could hardly think of human travel in it at all, not white horsemen nor Indians dragging travois, just aerial raptors with their rending talons and heads like cameras slicing across the geometry of winter.

Then we stepped into a deep hole and the horse went to his chest in the powder, splashing the snow out before him as he floundered toward the other side. I got my feet out of the stirrups in case we went over. Then we were on wind-scoured rock and I hunted some lee for the two of us. I thought of my son's words after our last cold ride: "Dad, you know in 4-H? Well, I want to switch from Horsemanship to Aviation."

The spot was like this: a crest of snow crowned in a sculpted edge high enough to protect us. There was a tough little juniper to picket the horse to, and a good place to sit out of the cold and noise. Over my head, a long, curling plume of snow poured out, unchanging in shape against the pale blue sky. I ate some of the cheese and rewrapped it. I got the rifle down from the scabbard, loosened the cinch, and undid the flank cinch. I put the stirrup over the horn to remind me my saddle was loose, loaded two cartridges into the blind magazine, and slipped one in the chamber. Then I started toward the rock wall, staring at the patterned discolorations: old seeps, lichen, cracks, and the madhouse calligraphy of immemorial weather.

There were a lot of tracks where the snow had crusted out of the wind; all deer except for one well-used bobcat trail winding along the edges of a long rocky slot. I moved as carefully as I could, stretching my eyes as far out in front of my detectable movement as I could. I tried to work into the wind, but it turned erratically in the basin as the temperature of the new day changed.

The buck was studying me as soon as I came out on the open slope: he was a long way away and I stopped motionless to wait for him to feed again. He stared straight at me from 500 yards. I waited until I could no longer feel my feet nor finally my legs. It was nearly an hour before he suddenly ducked his head and began to feed. Every time he fed I moved a few feet, but he was working away from me and I wasn't getting anywhere. Over the next half hour he made his way to a little rim and, in the half hour after that, moved the 20 feet that dropped him over the rim.

I went as fast as I could move quietly. I now had the rim to cover me and the buck should be less than 100 yards from me when I looked over. It was all browse for a half mile, wild roses, buck brush, and young quakies where there was any runoff.

When I reached the rim, I took off my hat and set it in the snow with my gloves inside. I wanted to be looking in the right direction when I cleared the rim, rise a half step and be looking straight at the buck, not scanning for the buck with him running 60, a degree or two out of my periphery. And I didn't want to gum it up with thinking or trajectory guessing. People are always trajectory guessing their way into gut shots and clean misses. So, before I took the last step, all there was to do was lower the rim with my feet, lower the buck into my vision, and isolate the path of the bullet.

As I took that step, I knew he was running. He wasn't in the browse at all, but angling into invisibility at the rock wall, racing straight into the elevation, bounding toward zero gravity, taking his longest arc into the bullet and the finality and terror of all you have made of the world, the finality you know that you share even with your babies with their inherited and ambiguous dentition, the finality that any minute now you will meet as well.

He slid 100 yards in a rush of snow. I dressed him and skidded him by one antler to the horse. I made a slit behind the last ribs, pulled him over the saddle and put the horn through the slit, lashed the feet to the cinch dees, and led the horse downhill. The horse had bells of clear ice around his hoofs, and when he slipped, I chipped them out from under his feet with the point of a bullet.

I hung the buck in the open woodshed with a lariat over a rafter. He turned slowly against the cooling air. I could see the intermittent blue light of the television against the bedroom ceiling from where I stood. I stopped the twirling of the buck, my hands deep in the sage-scented fur, and thought: This is either the beginning or the end of everything.

Visitors

Lucien got up at daybreak. When he went outside, the moisture was still in the ground and the ground itself seemed to be beginning a day-long respiration as the smell of grass and open dirt and evergreens hung on the unmoving air. He walked down to the corral and opened the gate to the upper pasture. The horses crowded each other in the passage, then ran and bucked onto the new ground.

There were flatiron clouds over the far ranges, and they were the color of wet slate. Lucien put his cup of coffee on top of a post and threw some hay up into the metal feeder. He reached through with his jackknife and cut the binder twine, pulled the strings out, looped them and hung them on a plank. The salt was all cupped out from the working of tongues, but more than half the block was left. He could hear the whine of a cold-starting tractor down at the neighbor's ranch. He'll do that until the battery is dead, thought Lucien, then go in and watch the soaps. An old-timer.

He went back up to the house and got a few things. He had a notion. He got a camouflage net and some welder's gloves. He got the little box of bird bands and some pliers, and the long-handled net. He got his wire pigeon cage out of the basement and two pairs of goggles that were hanging on a nail next to the airyway window. He ignored the phone and turned off the low flame under the coffeepot. On the wall was a picture of his father being presented with a spit of roasted meat in a restaurant in Arequipa, Peru. The phone rang again and Lucien did not pick it up. He had come to know when the calls were not urgent, just as he could count heads at the hot spring right through the wall.

He got everything loaded into the car and went over to the White Cottage. He knew it was early. He knew Suzanne would be wandering around in her robe trying to wake up, keeping sleepy responsible eyes on the waking day. As he reached the door in the gate, a cloud of warblers lifted out of the yellow-flowered caragana. He could hear James singing, and when he knocked on the door the singing stopped. "It's Pop!" Lucien called into the quiet. The gate opened and there was Suzanne. Lucien was happy to see her. She smiled with faint embarrassment and murmured something about not coming through at dinner. "Not to worry," said Lucien. "There'll be another time." There was a plate of pastries on the outdoor table, and a pitcher of juice. Lucien recognized every pattern and whorl of the pastry: Suzanne had learned to get what she needed from the kitchen. He took a couple of sweet rolls.

James came out of the cottage, quickly waved, then turned to look at his mother. "Can't you say good morning to Pop?" she said.

"Good morning."

Lucien ate a sweet roll and watched him for a moment. That made James nervous. "James, I'm going to band some hawks today. I want you to help me. We're trying to figure what all we've got on this place. It's pretty exciting."

"Weren't we going into town today?" James asked his mother.

"We can go anytime," she said, trying to messenger some reassurance James's way with a bright smile.

"But I need gym socks," James said in a panicky voice. "Remember?"

"I can pick those up."

"Last time they didn't fit," he said in a desperate whisper.

"You go band hawks with Pop," she said firmly. "I've got to get dressed." She went back up to the house, hiking the terrycloth robe around her angular hips. Lucien and James were alone. Lucien quickly made to open the door.

"Do I need a coat?"

"You're fine. Let's go."

They went out through the gate to the car with the net-handle sticking out of the back window. "We didn't bring enough socks," James explained. "And I only got these one pair of glasses. Me and Mom didn't plan so good, I don't think."

"Anything you need, you tell me," said Lucien. James was embarrassed.

By the time they had wound out past the buildings and started across the ranch, James had his small face angled unmovingly at the side window of the car. Lucien didn't know what to do. "James, have I said something wrong?" The land here was flat and brushy and there was an absolutely horizontal butte a few miles ahead.

"No."

"Are you sure?"

"Yes."

Lucien thought for a long, hard moment. "Then why are you treating me like this?"

"Because you're never going to let me go," James said bitterly. "You're going to keep me and never let me go." He began to cry, silently heaving in the huge space of his seat. Lucien shook his head as if to say that weren't true, but he didn't actually say anything. He just kept on driving until James finally sighed.

By that time they reached the old homestead, and Lucien stopped and got out. "Reach me the net, James. We've got to get us a pigeon for bait."

The two of them carried the net into the old barn and were momentarily blinded by the sudden near darkness. Immediately a number of pigeons went out the old haymow; the remainder cycled back and forth overhead, making a hollow, woody racket in the closed space. Lucien gave James the net and the little boy walked around swiping and missing pigeons. Soon he was running after them, and in a minute he brought his net down with the thrashing lump of a pigeon tangled in its mesh. As they put the pigeon into the wire carrying cage, the others assembled cooing on the whitened log joists. Lucien praised him and they took everything back out to the car.

Lucien drove on the zigzag dirt road toward the butte. James carried the cage in his lap and stared in at the now apparently tame pigeon that walked red-eyed back and forth on the wooden floor cooing in an inquiring and flutey voice. "I wonder what that bird is thinking about!" said James.

The road came up under the butte, so close that the rock wall was just outside the window of the car. They drove around to where the end of the butte melted back into the surrounding hills and drove partway out onto the butte itself and stopped. Here the wind had a warm westerly sweep from the valley floor, and they could see the small dust devils from a great distance. The cars on the river road didn't seem to be moving at all.

"I can see some hawks now," said Lucien. "They're in the thermals."

"What's thermals?"

"Warm rising air. Easy for the hawks to fly in. You get the pigeon. I'll get the camouflage net and the rest of it."

Lucien watched James trying to carry the pigeon's cage and look into its side at the same time and thought, as the little boy stumbled along, I can see a beginning.

They carried the gear a half mile out onto the warm top of the butte. Lucien watched James until the boy began to see the hawks. Sometimes the heated gusts would come through the deep grass in cat's paws and they would have to lean into the wind as they walked. Suddenly James looked straight at Lucien and grinned, put down the cage and said, "Gotta rest up."

"I shot a big pronghorn out here when I was a kid," said Lucien.

"With your dad?"

"Nope. By myself. Then I couldn't haul it home. An old cowboy came along with a dog and a pair of binoculars looking for his cattle and we packed it on his horse and we walked out together even though he had real bad knees, real bad. I always thought that was something special. I told the kids at school it was my dad that packed it out, but actually it was this old cowboy and I didn't really even get his name. We gave his dog some antelope. When I was bigger I had some horses of my own, just crow bait–"

"What's 'crow bait'?"

"Used up. I lived with my mother and we didn't have money, not much of it anyway. But even with those old horses, I could go. I could go clear over the top. I could go anywhere." Why am I rambling on like this, Lucien wondered.

James looked all over the top of the butte. "How did we end up in the State Department?"

"I don't know. College. I used to make pictures of all this stuff. I got sick of pictures of this butte. But I never got sick of the butte. I came up here a while ago when there'd been a chinook and there were these wild old patches of snow and I came that close to making one more picture of the place. But I felt like I'd covered that. I just wonder if you have a clue about what I'm saying." James was smiling nervously, one lens of his glasses glinting shut, trying so to please.

They kept on until they came to an oval of rocks on the flattened ground. "I'm ninety-nine percent certain that this is where the Indians caught their birds." Lucien like so many had always felt the great echoes from the terminated history of the Indians–foot, dog and horse Indians. How could a country produce orators for thousands of years, then a hundred years of yep and nope? It didn't make sense. It didn't make sense that the glory days of the Old South were forever mourned while this went unmentioned. Maybe the yeps and nopes represented shell-shock, a land forever strange, strange as it was today to a man and a boy with a caged bird and makeshift camouflage. Well, thought Lucien, it's not a bad spot for coyotes, schemers and venture capitalists.

Lucien laid out the trap carefully. He put on the heavy gauntlets, and they each put on their goggles. He removed the pigeon from the carrying cage and seized its feet in his fingers. The wings beat hard and scared James. The two of them got under the camouflage and Lucien held the bird outside the netting atop their reclined bodies.

The camouflage consisted of numerous yellow and olive strips sewn to a piece of netting. From underneath it, the wind seemed diminished and the sky behind the mesh harsh and clear, vast as a cathedral. The longer they stayed under the net, the more it seemed to curve high over them, as though its sides were somehow not far away and its center absolutely vertical overhead.

"What's going to happen?"

"We hope a hawk will come to us."

"Then what?"

"Then we'll see what he is and we'll put one of those bands on his leg and turn him loose."

"Why's a hawk going to come to us?"

"He's going to try to get our pigeon." The pigeon was murmuring faintly. It had shortened its neck and flared its feathers in peace. Lucien could feel that the clenching of its feet in his hands had stopped. He could sense the heat of the pigeon's body on his own chest and thought he could let go of it without losing the bird.

"I think he's sleepy," said James.

"Don't you get sleepy."

"I won't."

"Time passed slowly. Lucien's arm was cramping and James was quietly knocking the sides of his tennis shoes together. Then James fell asleep. So Lucien, not concerned about their talk, was able to drift off in a fashion himself. Oddly, he thought about Dee; she'd been with him when he thought he was going to crack, or maybe had cracked. He wondered if she could really be as brutal a floozy as she seemed, always clambering onto all fours to receive her sacrament stern-on. Wonderful how that kind of cartooning took the heat off, made time fly. When he was young he used to shadowbox for the same reason, dancing around, throwing punches, going fifteen rounds in his own world. Then came drinking. Then came Emily and the Lost Sweetheart and the spring, the Lost Sweetheart Spring. Why couldn't he stand success? Suzanne was success. Suzanne was whole. Why was he just beginning to see that?

The pigeon moved. Lucien remained still but noted his head was erect once more, his limpid eyes unmoving. Lucien looked on up to the sky. There was the hawk. The falconers called it waiting-on: the hawk made no motion in the circle of sky but hovered with a blurred wing-beat straight overhead, taking the pigeon's position. The pigeon felt this happening to him. Lucien knew that if he nudged James it would spook the hawk and they'd lose him. Instead he regulated his own breathing and watched until the distant wing-beat stopped, the hawk tightened its size and fell.

When the impact came, James jumped up screaming and began to crawl off. Lucien sat up, holding the hawk by the feet in one gauntleted hand. There were feathers everywhere, and the hawk beat in a blur of cold fury, striking at Lucien with his downcurving knife of a beak and superimposing his own screech over the noise of James. "We've got him, James!" James, quiet now, looked ready to run. The hawk had stopped all motion but kept his beak marginally parted so that the small, hard black tongue could be seen advancing and retreating slightly within his mouth. "It's a prairie falcon. It's the most beautiful bird in the world. I want to come back as a prairie falcon."

"Where are you going?"

"Nowhere very soon. Reach me a band and the pliers." James handed these things to him gingerly. It fascinated Lucien that he was such a timid boy. Lucien hadn't been particularly timid and he rather liked having a boy who was. But James was shaking.

Each time the bird's wings beat, Lucien could actually feel the lift in his forearm, could feel the actual pull of the falcon's world in the sky. He had seen hawks on the ground, graceless as extremely aged people, and he knew their world was sky. He'd seen old cowboys limp to their horses, then fly over the land, and he knew what their world was too. He wanted his own life to be as plain.

By concentration and by ignoring the prospects of a bite, Lucien managed to get the band on. "We're married at last," he said to the hawk. James raised his eyebrows. Lucien held the terrifying bird out before him and released his grip. The falcon pulled vertically from his glove and with hard wing-beats made straight into deep sky, swept straight off and was gone.

When Lucien looked over at James, he was holding the pigeon in his hands. Its eyes were closed. Its head was angled harshly onto its back. Blood ran from the nostrils down the domestic blue feathers of its narrow shoulders. Lucien said nothing.

"We both fell asleep at the same time," said James in an unsteady voice.

As Lucien thought about it, he really didn't know what the effect of trapping the hawk had been on James, what kind of day it had made. When Lucien had dropped him off, the White Cottage was full of Suzanne's relatives, mostly cousins and including a good number of no-accounts who had nothing better to do than give Lucien a dirty look as one who'd done a good girl wrong. There was a cousin from Great Falls who used to run a greasy spoon up that way that was open twenty-four hours a day and therefore had no doorknobs. On days he wanted to fish and could find no one to spell him, he wrapped a hundred feet of logging chain around the building and padlocked it. He alone smiled at Lucien standing awkwardly in the doorway, the unwelcome host. But early Tuesday morning Suzanne called and said that James had enjoyed his day.

"Did he say anything about the pigeon?"

"Yes."

"Did that upset him?"

"He seems to appreciate that you and he had some kind of adventure. When I said it was sad about the pigeon, he said that's how hawks have to live. He was kind of taking up for you in that, I thought."

"That's nice."

"So things aren't as bleak as you may believe."

"It serves my purposes to feel that I am singled out. I get mad. Which serves me to get out of bed in the morning."

"Do you remember my cousin Danny?"

"Not really."

"Well, he wants to know if you can use an irrigator."

"I want to hold you and kiss you."

"You stop this right now."

"We don't need an irrigator. We put in a wheel-line sprinkler and we don't use it. We just write it off. Lying there, it underscores the nothing-is-real atmosphere that people on holiday demand. Your cousin Danny would ruin that."

"You're not kidding about the atmosphere. I've seen some lulus around that spring."

"I know."

"But I also noticed a lot of the old local yokels."

"They get to have it both ways. Their thing is to come just out of curiosity, night after night. I humor them. We elbow each other in the ribs. We point. They keep coming back. I specialize in catering to the big-spending local dipso. If I didn't have the out-of-towners, I'd have to hire topless dancers."

A long and awkward silence followed, maybe not awkward but full of something that brought pain without impatience. So it was a question of where it would end. Finally Lucien broke the quiet. "Why can't we just see each other in a normal kind of way?"

"Because we had that. And you left it. It has not returned just because we occupy the same real estate at the moment. I'm surprised you asked that question."

"You're surprised that I asked that question?"

"Yes, because it implies that I am either stupid or have no memory."

"I'm very much alone, Suzanne," Lucien said and was immediately sorry for even having tested this lame idea out loud. He received an actual Bronx cheer. "I'm coming over," he said and hung up.

When he got to the White Cottage, Suzanne let him in and said, "Will someone tell me why I'm even opening this door?" Lucien swept her into his arms and held her tight. His hands slid down over the roundness of her buttocks and felt them grow solid. He sensed himself getting suddenly hard. At least it will have something other to do than soak my foot through the top of my shoe, he thought confidently.

"I'm not going to fuck you," she said.

"Oh, yes you are."

"Oh, no I'm not." Her pelvis was firm and unmoving against him. He had never wanted to make love with anybody so much in his life. He couldn't remember how it had been with her because he had never really cared.

She planted the tips of her ten fingernails against his chest lightly and pushed him away. He glanced down. His nicely fitted slacks had a grim off-center bulge in them, and there was a spot too. Love.

Suzanne's eyes flickered away. Lucien remembered when she was a virgin. Virgins are bores, he thought, like people with overpriced houses. I suppose we could show you the living room; but we're not even sure we want to sell and we're very particular about the buyer. Lucien remembered Suzanne's virginity as something that one approached like a root canal. Against the precociously carnal Emily it seemed a little sappy.

So instead they had tea. Suzanne seemed so beautiful that Lucien stared too much and made gestures that were either not appropriate or off in their timing. The wind blew the door open and a strange dog came in while they watched. He drank from the spring and turned a gaunt brindle muzzle toward them coolly. When Lucien tried to shoo him, he merely watched, then left at his own speed, jogging angularly out through the door again.

■ JAMES CRUMLEY

Novelist and screenwriter James Crumley was born in Texas in 1939 and grew up near San Antonio. With an M.F.A from the University of Iowa Writers' Workshop, Crumley came to the University of Montana in 1966 as an instructor of creative writing. Although he has lived and taught in many places, Crumley always returns home to Missoula, where he is co-owner and captain of the Montana Review of Books softball team. Crumley is the author of One to Count Cadence *(1987), a war story set in the Phillipines, and three western detective novels, including* The Last Good Kiss *(1978) and* Dancing Bear *(1983). This selection is from* The Wrong Case, *published in 1975.*

From The Wrong Case

After I filled my wallet with my two thousand, I added a thousand of Nickie's and hoped I could cover it somehow. Then I sat down at the desk to have a drink and take a quick look at the folder Mrs. Crider had given me. But I thought about her instead. She was a hell of a woman. She had asked me to kill without even flinching. I liked that, but it also scared me. We weren't even on first-name terms yet, but she assumed because I had lied to her that I owed her a murder. Just as Jamison assumed that I owed Simon one too. Unfortunately, I didn't know who was owed what. And I began to wonder about their judgment of my character. So I opened the folder. It was the beginning of his thesis on Dalton Kimbrough and Western justice. As I had told Helen Duffy, my great-grandfather [Milodragovitch] made his way into law enforcement and capital gains by killing Dalton Kimbrough, so I had always been interested.

But the thesis wasn't a simple history of Dalton Kimbrough or an estimation of Western justice. It was an examination of the difference between myth and reality in the Western hero and villain. The Duffy kid began with the distance between the Wyatt Earp created by Ned Buntline and the often too human lawman, then passed on through the careers of Billy the Kid, Joaquin Murieta, Jack Slade, et al.—the easy research—and on to the life and hard times of that infamous outlaw, highwayman and killer, Dalton Kimbrough. As it turned out, Dalton was a man ahead of his times: he handled his own public relations. The first thing he did was change his name from Ernest Ledbetter to the more heroic Dalton Kimbrough, then out of a spotty criminal career that included one arrest and one gunfight he made a name for himself throughout the gold fields of the post-Civil War West.

His solitary arrest record was for shoplifting in St. Joe, Missouri, where he had been raised. The shopkeeper had collared Dalton with a pocketful of .44 rounds and an old Navy Colt under his coat. The revolver was a paperweight with no firing pin. Dalton did his thirty days, then headed west for a life of crime and excitement in the gold camps. Dalton drank, tried mining, and probably hung around the bars more than he should have, looking for trouble. One winter, over in Montana, in a log-cabin bar just large enough for a four-foot plank bar, one table and two bunks on the opposite wall, Dalton finally found a gunfight in the midst of a poker game.

When the gunfire ended, everybody's revolver empty, there was a great deal of smoke and powder burns, but nobody had been hit. Except the bartender's dog, which had been killed by a single round through the lungs. The game resumed peacefully amid smoke and the good feelings that come with survival, only to be disturbed again. This time by odd groans from a miner sleeping off a drunk in the lower bunk. When they turned him over to tell him to shut up, they found a large puddle of blood beneath his body from a round that had passed through his thigh. He groaned once more, then died from the loss of blood. Dalton, ever ready for fame, claimed both killings as his very own, and nobody bothered to dispute his claim.

Dalton also boasted of numerous stage holdups and bank robberies, all of which either never took place in recorded history or were committed by other men, who had never heard of Dalton Kimbrough. As far as anybody knows, Dalton took part in only one stage holdup, his last one. Perhaps the gunfight in the bar went to his head. Later the same winter, he and two men stopped the Salt Lake stage as it topped the south pass into the Meriwether Valley, the stage carrying my great-grandfather to his new home, an Army wife with her young son, and a strongbox.

As the horses were blowing at the top of the pass, three armed men appeared on horseback, demanding the strongbox, which was bolted to the coach floor. Dalton fired five rounds at the lock, but it didn't open. So he went after the passengers. My great-grandfather couldn't speak English but he could count, and he was often courageously surly. When Dalton tried to open his coat to see if he carried a money belt, he met an unhappy Russian, who grabbed him in a clumsy hug. As they struggled, one of the mounted outlaws pulled off a round. Right through Dalton Kimbrough's kidneys. He fired once more from his wildly bucking horse, hitting the frightened stagecoach driver in the chin, then his horse pitched him off. When he hit the frozen ground, he went out cold. The third outlaw, who finally decided to take control, also began to fire, but for reasons unrecorded—probably either wet or forgotten percussion caps—his revolver wouldn't fire. He cocked the hammer and pulled the trigger several times, then rode away in disgust, never to be heard of again.

After being shot through the kidneys, Dalton lost his taste for holdups and fights. He fell to the ground in my great-grandfather's embrace, where his skull was crushed by a large stone in a Russian peasant's burly hand. When the snow had settled, my great-grandfather trussed the unconscious outlaw like a pig and tossed him into the boot with Dalton's body, bound the driver's face, helped the lady back into the stage, then drove into history. As soon as his English was passable, he was hired as Meriwether's constable, then elected sheriff, and nearly appointed territorial governor. In death, Dalton Kimbrough's public relations paid off. For my great-grandfather.

And in a less obvious way, for the stagecoach driver too. He stayed around town for years, wearing a scarf over his missing chin, becoming a local curiosity and drunk. The Army wife found her husband shacked up with a Willomot squaw, which she might have forgiven if he hadn't been cashiered too, so she went back East, where people were civilized. Dalton Kimbrough's body was hung next to his partner's, the good folk of Meriwether deciding that stringing him up dead was nearly as good an example to potential outlaws as hanging him if he had been alive.

As the years passed in the usual manner, the story bloomed into heroics with the aid of imaginative newspaper editors and my great-grandfather's whiskey. According to Duffy's thesis, my great-grandfather encouraged the Kimbrough myth to further his own political ambitions, which was probably true. At the end of the typed pages, he scrawled a sour note: *A fucking klutz.* I got the impression that although he believed his thesis, he didn't especially like it, preferring myth to reality even as he cast the terrible light of a debunking truth across the years of Dalton Kimbrough's petty life.

All this was twice as sad because the truth about Kimbrough and my great-grandfather had been known for years before Raymond Duffy found Willy Jones and his papers. Even the B Western filmed in the early fifties had to invent a hero: the chinless stage driver. In the movie, he knows the truth of the Milodragovitch pose and the puniness of Kimbrough's villainy, but is unable to tell anybody. Until he is taught to write by a gentle schoolmarm from Philadelphia. Then he is able to expose the character of my great-grandfather as a cowardly and overbearing sham. In the last scene, the actor playing Milodragovitch lies sprawled in the middle of a dusty, back-lot street, the victim of unfounded pride and drunkenness. As the camera draws back, the sober, upright storekeeper, who has shotgunned the mad Russian and his knouted hand, is seen advancing like a cartoon hunter clutching a hammerless double-barreled shotgun. Then the frame widens to include the chinless hero, his eyes above the scarf suggesting a triumphant but sad smile, his hand on the schoolmarm's delicate arm. She is smiling too, but in a rather pinched way, as if the chinless wonder needs a bath. They do not embrace. Music rises. Dissolve to list of cast.

Just to set the record straight: my great-grandfather died quite bitterly sober in an old folks' home.

There is a quaintly modern notion that information will eventually equal knowledge, which is neatly balanced by the cliché that the more one learns, the less one knows. Both ideas are probably more or less accurate, but neither is particularly useful in dealing with the human animal.

As I thought of Raymond Duffy, nothing came to mind. An image remembered from a bar, his eyes as black as gun barrels glistening with pleasure above his pale cheeks. They were murderous, not suicidal. And even though Reese had said that the kid was very depressed over the death of Willy Jones, I couldn't see him killing himself. *Maybe it was an accident, pure and simple, dumb-ass, a mistake.* But I still needed a reason, if not for his death, then at least for his depression beforehand. If I knew what caused the depression, then I would be able to justify accidental death. Mistakes do happen. Like my father's death, which I had always thought of as an accident caused by the mistake of leaving the bolt open on his deer rifle, of not looking at the shotgun as he lifted it out of the closet, of not checking the safety when he put it away . . .

But as I thought of these things, an odd feeling came over me. I was missing something. And suddenly I knew and was damned sorry that I did. I remembered his first lecture about guns: Always keep them loaded, a full magazine and a round in the chamber, and you'll never be killed by an empty gun; keep the safety on, check that always, but keep them loaded. Drunk or sober, he had never made a mistake with a gun; he put them away loaded, the safety on. But I remembered as clearly as I remembered the bloody stain on the hallway ceiling that the bolt of the deer rifle was open, the chamber empty. I wondered how long he had planned it, that accident planted in the hall closet like a bomb.

I had a sip of whiskey, which seemed proper, but I was too tired and sore to feel any real grief. If that was the way he had wanted it, then I wasn't about to disagree with him. I wondered if my mother knew, and decided that she did. Some knowledge rises out of information, disorganized but nonetheless true. If he couldn't kill himself with a whiskey bottle, my father had to make do with guns, which made me wonder why the Duffy kid had chosen drugs instead of his pistols . . .

"Bingo," I said to myself and sat up straight in my chair.

Even though it seemed that my father's death wasn't caused by a mistake after all, I'd bet good, or bad, money that Willy Jones's had been. If you play with guns long enough, my father had told me, eventually you'll kill somebody. And I saw the Duffy kid, drug-crazed, playing with guns, drawing and snapping the trigger in the old drunk's face, saw the round left in the cylinder by mistake, saw the old man's face explode, the back of his head hit the far wall, skull fragments and blood and brain matter all over the room. That would do it to a kid raised on bloodless violence, Hollywood and quick-draw contests; that would drive him over the edge. When he saw what firearms are meant to do, when he saw the effect of an unjacketed lead round fired into a human face, that would make him throw his pistols away, cut his hair and discard his gunfighter clothes. I knew. At that range, when a bullet enters the human head, the hydrostatic pressure blows the face up like a cheap balloon; the eardrums burst, the eyes pop out, and the head seems to dissolve in a shower of blood. Oh God, did I know, and not want to at all.

Assuming that I had had a hard day that morning, I had a long drink, then another before I called Amos Swift. He agreed that he might have missed powder burns and a gunshot wound in Willy Jones's head because the body had been so badly burnt. But he bet money that he wouldn't miss it a second time. If I could come up with something solid enough to convince a judge to sign an exhumation order. I told him I hoped it wouldn't be necessary, then hung up.

What a mess, I thought, what a hard day. I called Helen just to hear her voice, to remind myself why I was doing all this. She came to the telephone on the ninth ring, answered it breathlessly, timidly.

"Hello?"

"It's nice to know you're still there," I said.

"Oh. I'm still here. I just–didn't know if I should answer your telephone–I was in the backyard–and I tripped coming in the back door."

"Are you all right?"

"Oh yes–I'm fine. How are you?"

"I'm not in jail, anyway. I'm in pain," I said lightly, "but free."

"Oh–I'm glad."

"Are you going to be there when I get back?"

"Are you–coming home–right now? I didn't know . . . when you were coming back."

"Well," I said, thinking about the trip up the north fork with Muffin's money, "I've got a few things to do yet. It'll take three or four hours, but I'll be home to take you out to dinner. If you don't mind being seen in public with me."

"Of course not," she answered, sounding happy instead of confused. "It's a date."

"Okay," I said. "Hey, you know it's nice to call my house and have you answer the phone."

"Oh–oh–I'm sorry about–this morning."

"So am I, but let's forget about it."

"Okay–if you want . . . I'll–see you tonight."

"Take care," I said.

"You too," she answered hesitantly, then we both hung up.

Whatever I'd expected out of the call to make me feel better hadn't been there, but telephones had always had some sort of curse on me anyway, so I didn't worry about it. I started to take the office bottle with me but decided to put it back in the drawer. By the time I reached the top of Willomot Hill the weight of the morning made me regret my decision. I turned into the empty parking lot of the Willomot Bar, thinking to get a couple of drinks in go cups and maybe have an unfriendly chat with the owner, Jonas. I could depend on him not to change character, not to confuse me. He had hated my guts for years, and there was something reassuring about that.

Jonas was sitting at the first table inside the door, leaning back in a chair, his tiny boots crossed on the battered tabletop, his narrow eyes watching the tourist traffic avoid his place like the plague, watching the rectangle of sunlight retreat across his dirty floor toward the doorway. Standing in the bright doorway, I assumed I must have been an anonymous shade because Jonas smiled as I stepped in. I guess the smile was too much. I lifted my foot and shoved his table. He went over backwards, thumping his head solidly against the cement floor.

Jonas was small, but stout as a stump and meaner than a sow bear, with quick hands and agile feet. He wasn't a big man but he was damn sure a handful of trouble. I had taken him before, three or four times, but that had been in the line of duty, sort of, and I had used the sap or a billy. I had a frozen moment to remember my face and all the aches and pains, especially my nose, and to regret most of my life. Two middle-aged bucks sat over shot glasses at the end of the bar, working on their hangovers, and the thick-faced barmaid stood across from them. The three heads swiveled toward the crashing sound of Jonas and furniture. One buck banked toward the back door past the dark shadow of the bear, but the other raised his glass, either toasting me or trying to hustle a drink. The barmaid simply looked away in boredom.

But Jonas wasn't bored. He rolled once, came up ready, his feet spread, his short thick arms cocked, his head bobbing and weaving like that of a punch-drunk fighter, then he saw me and broke out in a mean grin.

"What the hell's happening, Milo?" he asked happily. "You drunk 'fore noon, you old son of a bitch? What the hell happened to your face? Hey, man, I heard 'bout poor ol' Simon. What a fuckin' shame. He usta be a hell of a man. Did I ever tell you 'bout the time he got my old man off a manslaughter bust? The old man found two goddamned tourists cleanin' a cow elk up in that timber on the other side a the ridge and he cut down on the dumb-asses, and . . ."

As he rattled on with his favorite Simon story, he came around the table, kicking chairs out of the way with an absent-minded violence that amazed me all over again. He grabbed my arm and led me to the bar, shouting for shots and beers, shaking my hand over and over, pausing only long enough to gun his shot and half the beer chaser. By the time he finished his story, he had forgotten why he was telling it to me.

"Oh yeah. Simon. Goddamned old drunk. Goddammit, I'm sorry 'bout him. That's a nasty way to go, man, ugly. I seen a bum one time when I was a kid been hit by a train, and that was bad as I ever wanna see, but when I heard 'bout how Simon got it, man, I nearly got sick," he prattled. "And goddammit, Milo, you know nothing makes me sick." Then he laughed happily.

"Wish I could say the same," I said, but he didn't hear me through the laughter. Then an odd thing happened: I almost liked the little bastard, even after all the trouble. Of course, it had been at least ten years since we had tangled, but those times didn't count the nights when he had been drunk enough to argue with me about who to arrest but sober enough to remember that I had fifty pounds and a badge on him. When he stopped laughing, I said, "You know it's a goddamned sorry day when I can't even pick a fight with you, Jonas."

That made him laugh so hard that he blew beer foam all over the bar and his dark face. As he wiped his face, he said fondly, "Goddamn, we usta have some dandy times, didn't we. Seems like ever other night you'd come in here and put knots on my head a goddamned goat couldn't climb. Hey, you still got that little flat sap?"

"Yeah, I think so," I said, trying to remember where it had gone to. "No, I think the police have it. Hell, I don't know."

"I tell you, Milo, that thing was mean," he said, as if that was the nicest compliment he knew. "Goddamn, those were some times. Shit, somma the boys up on the reservation are still 'bout half afraid of you. You see that ol' boy take off when you come in?"

"Yeah."

"Well, that was his older brother knocked you cold that time and drove you down to the jailhouse. Half-brother, I think it was. Anyway, he ain't near as mean. That's why he took off when you come in."

"That was a long time ago, Jonas."

"You tellin' me–shit, we're too old for rough and tumble, Milo, and hell, you already sewed up and taped together like a busted watermelon. Hell, you look so bad a fella'd be afraid to give you a good shot. Might kill you," he said, and as if to prove his point, he thumped me in the ribs with a short, affectionate punch that nearly knocked me down.

"Not in the ribs, Jonas," I grunted, trying to breathe.

"Sorry 'bout that. Heard you took a hell of a beatin'. Got that one son of a bitch, huh? Blew his fuckin' head right off, huh. That'll teach them goddamned hippies not to mess around with home folks, huh."

"He was a construction worker, Jonas," I explained, knowing it wouldn't make any difference.

"Yeah, whatever, he ain't gonna mess with nobody no more, right?" he said, lifting a new shot.

"Right."

He waited for me to lift my shot, but I didn't know if it would stay down behind the memories, the new and bitter knowledge of the morning. It did but it didn't want to.

"So how's business?" Jonas asked, thumping me again.

"Not so good," I said. "Say, were you in here the night the kid OD'd in your john? About a month ago?"

"Don't remind me of it, Milo. The goddamn Liquor Control Board tried to take my license, but hell, that's nothing new," he said, then laughed again. "Why?"

"That's what I'm working on now."

"Who for?" he asked, his eyes squinting with suspicion.

"The family. They weren't too happy with the sheriff's investigation."

"What investigation? That old bastard can't find his ass with either hand. Hell, there wasn't anything to investigate anyway."

"They just wanted to know what happened."

"Nothing happened, Milo. The kid comes in, orders a drink, then goes into the john. A couple hours later somebody complains that they can't take a crap because the stall door is locked, so I climb over and find him dead, sittin' there like he's passed out, but when I seen that needle in his arm I figured he was dead. That's funny, he didn't look the type."

"Had he ever been in before that night?"

"Hell, Milo, they come and go. I don't know. But probably not. He was such a clean-cut-lookin' kid, not like that bunch a mangy god-damned hippies in town, that I'd probably remember. He didn't look the type to be on that dope."

"That's what I hear," I said. "Did he come in with anybody?"

"Well, Milo, I was busier than a one-legged man at an ass-kicking contest and I was a hair drunk, so I don't know."

"What was he drinking?"

"A draw," Jonas answered quickly. He had a bartender's memory for faces and drinks. "And there wasn't nobody with him, 'cause that's all I got was the one beer."

"Where did he sit?"

"All the way down at the end of the bar."

"Anybody sitting next to him?"

"Shit, Milo, I don't know," he answered, sorry that he couldn't help.

"That's okay," I said, "it's not really important." Then I thought about the guy with long black hair and a beard. "Hey, there didn't happen to be a hippie in here that night, a guy with black hair and a beard?"

"I'll be damned. There sure was. Sittin' right next to the kid. I remember 'cause they ain't welcome here and they figure that out real quick, so we don't get many. Yeah, and 'cause he was a little old to be runnin' around like a goddamned hairy ape. He had on sunglasses too, but hell, I could tell he wasn't no kid."

"You remember what he was wearing?"

"Milo, I could shut my eyes right now," Jonas said, "and I wouldn't be able to tell you what you was wearing."

"What was he drinking?" I asked, sipping at my beer.

"Brandy and soda, no ice," he answered quick as a shot, then motioned for another round.

Bingo. Goddammit, how could I be so dumb? Goddamned Nickie. Jesus.

"Help?" he asked.

"I don't know," I said, forcing the thoughts and feelings out of me, retreating to hide the fear. "Lots of people drink brandy and soda."

"Yeah," he said as he raised his glass. "Sorry I don't remember more."

"Thanks anyway, Jonas. Next time you're in town, stop by. The drinks are on me," I said, then had a sip of beer and started to leave, but Jonas grabbed my arm.

"Wanna do me a favor, Milo?" he asked in a conspiratorial whisper so I would know it was an illegal favor. I shrugged, and Jonas took that as an affirmative answer. "You seen Muffin lately? I got this friend on the other side of the mountains, and he's buildin' this motel. One big son of a bitch, two hundred units. But he's kinda strapped for capital right now, goddamned inflation, and he ain't got the bread for the color TV's and he can't come up with no credit he can afford. You know what I mean?"

"I'll act like I don't, Jonas. Muffin's out of business anyway."

"That's too bad. There's a pretty penny in this deal, Milo. How 'bout puttin' me in touch with somebody else?"

"I don't know anybody, sorry."

"Don't shit me, Milo," he said, grinning like a small animal.

I wanted to grin back, but couldn't. Just like I wanted to rub my tired, hot face. Jonas was mean and crooked and slightly dumb, but the face he turned toward me was warm with affection. That has to count for something.

"Okay," I said.

"How big a piece you want?"

"Nothing. I owe you, Jonas."

"What?"

"Hell, I don't know. Maybe all those lumps on your head. I don't know."

He grinned again, his tiny yellowed teeth nearly as dark as his Indian face, and started to poke me in the ribs. But he remembered not to.

"That don't matter none, Milo, not at all. Those were good times. Hell, you never tried to shake me down or run me in for some petty shit. You were fair, Milo, and I could count on you," he said. "Hey, by God, next time I'm in town, let's you an' me just get drunker than pigs in shit, then go down to them hippie bars and just kick the shit outa somebody. Anybody messes with us, we'll blow their fuckin' heads off. How 'bout it? Be like the old days, 'cept we'll be on the same side."

"We've probably been on the same side all along and just didn't know it, Jonas, but I damn sure don't want to kill anybody . . ."

"Hey, you all right?" he asked as I headed for the john to heave it all up.

All drunks have theories, endlessly tedious arguments, both vocal and silent, with which to justify their drinking. They drink to forget or remember, to see more clearly or discover blindness, they drink out of fear of success or failure, drink to find a home and love or drink to get away. Their lives revolve around drink. Some of the theories may well be true, but because drunks lie so much, it's difficult to divide the sharp perceptions from the sorry rationalizations. Once, my father talked to me about drinking and drunks, and in my memory it sounds not at all sorry. Just sad.

I was a boy, but old enough to have already realized that even the simplest life was too complex, that my parents lived together without very much love, that I was both curse and prize in their battles; old enough to love my father without thinking that I had anything for which to forgive him. It was then, when I was old enough to be sad, that one afternoon my father and I had gone fishing. As it usually happened, we lodged in a country bar to wet our whistles before we wet our lines, and as usual, we stayed in the bar, letting the trout, as my father said, grow one more day. "Tomorrow, son," he'd say, "they'll be just the right size." Tomorrow. And every time we caught a trout, he'd hold it up and tell me, "See, son, just right."

But this afternoon we stayed in the bar, and sometime during the long hours of drinking, he disappeared into the john and stayed much longer than usual. I was a child among strangers, a youth to be regaled with the hopes they no longer possessed because I had a future and they had only pasts. Slightly frightened by all this weight, I went to look for my father.

He was kneeling at the toilet, his eyes fearfully shot with blood from the efforts of his retching. A long string of glutinous spittle looped heavily from his trembling lips to the stained toilet bowl.

He spit and asked how I was doing; knowing I was frightened, he was calm. "Don't worry about me, son," he said, "I'm all right. I been bellied up to this trough a time or two before. You go on out and wait for me, okay? I'll be out in a minute." As I went out the door, I tried not to hear the convulsive, heaving rasp, tried not to be disgusted by the only person in the world I loved.

But I heard and was disgusted. I went all the way outside the bar to the porch, where I watched the afternoon steal across green hayfields and pastures, the shadows of the mountain ridges reaping light, sowing darkness. After the dank, torpid air inside the bar, air more like smoke, the air outside seemed as fresh and clean as spring water, and I filled my lungs with gasp after gasp, sucking down the sobs, vowing as seriously as only a frightened child can that I would grow up and never drink, ignoring the fact that I already sipped from my father's glass whenever I pleased. I vowed, promised in innocence already lost.

He came out behind me, a huge dark man smiling tiredly, a glass of neat whiskey in his large hand. With the first swallow, he rinsed out his mouth, then spit off the porch into the dust that rimmed the parking lot. The second, he drank, emptying the glass. Then he patted me on the head, perhaps sensing what I felt. Even at his drunkest, he was kind and perceptive, at least around me. As he held my head in his great hand, I was warm in the lingering sunset chill.

"Son," he said without preamble, "never trust a man who doesn't drink because he's probably a self-righteous sort, a man who thinks he knows right from wrong all the time. Some of them are good men, but in the name of goodness, they cause most of the suffering in the world. They're the judges, the meddlers. And, son, never trust a man who drinks but refuses to get drunk. They're usually afraid of something down deep inside, either that they're a coward or a fool or mean and violent. You can't trust a man who's afraid of himself. But sometimes, son, you can trust a man who occasionally kneels before a toilet. The chances are that he is learning something about humility and his natural human foolishness, about how to survive himself. It's damned hard for a man to take himself too seriously when he's heaving his guts into a dirty toilet bowl."

Then he paused for a long minute and added, "And, son, never trust a drunk except when he's on his knees."

When I glanced up, he was smiling an oddly distant smile, like a man who can see his own future and accepts it without complaint.

If he had left it at that, I might not have understood, but he raised his empty glass and pointed at the vista. The fields, a lush, verdant green, grew dark with shadows, nearly as dark as the pine-thick ridges, but the sky above still glowed a bright, daylight blue. A single streak of clouds, like a long trail of smoke, angled away from the horizon, flaming a violent crimson at the far end as if it had been dipped in blood. But the middle was light pink, and the end nearest us was an ashen gray.

"A lovely view, isn't it, son?"

"Yes, sir."

"But it's not enough," he said, smiling, then he walked back into the bar, laughing and shouting for whiskey, love and laughter, leaving me suspended in the pellucid air.

Vomiting into the toilet of the Willomot Bar, not from the drink but from the knowledge and the dying, I felt my father's hand holding my head. He had left me this legacy of humility, and I accepted it. Where her little brother lost his life, I found mine, and understood that I wasn't going to kill anybody, except myself, and not myself for a long time yet. I remembered Simon telling me to slow down, not to drink myself to death before I had time to enjoy it. When I finished puking, I went back into the bar to wash out my mouth with whiskey.

■ RICK DeMARINIS

Born in New York in 1934, Rick DeMarinis grew up in California and came to Montana in 1955 as a radar operator for the Air Force. After working for Boeing and Lockheed, he entered the University of Montana and in 1967 was graduated with an M.A. in English. DeMarinis has taught at San Diego, Arizona, and Wichita state universities. He is currently directing the Creative Writing Program at the University of Texas at El Paso. His most recent works include Under the Wheat, *a collection of short stories that received the 1986 Drue Heinz Prize for Short Fiction, and* The Coming Triumph of the Free World *(1988). This selection is from his novel* The Burning Women of Far Cry *(1986).*

Gent

A year after my father shot himself my mother married a two-faced hardware salesman named Roger Trewly. In public, Roger Trewly smiled as if someone holding a gun on him had said, "Look natural, Roger." At home, though, he was usually cross and sullen and would rarely answer civilly if spoken to. He was a crack salesman and was once awarded a plaque engraved with the words *Ace of Hand-Held Tools*. There is a photograph that records the event. He is standing with the owner of the store, Mr. Fenwick, in front of a display of braces and bits, hammers, ripsaws, and planes. Both men are smiling, but the difference in their smiles has stuck in my mind through the years. Mr. Fenwick is smiling like a man who has just been found naked in the girls' gym and isn't at all humiliated by it. There's a ferocious gleam in his eyes challenging anyone to file a complaint. He looks like a well-to-do madman, capable of anything, absolutely sure of everything. Roger Trewly is smiling as though he's just spilled boiling coffee in his lap at the church social. His face shines with desperate sweat and his begging eyes are fixed on Mr. Fenwick. If you cover the lower half of Roger Trewly's face with your thumb, you will see that his small, pale eyes have no smile in them at all. They have a puzzled, frightened cast, wide with adrenalin. They are the eyes of a man who has understood nothing of the world in his thirty-five years. That anxious, kowtowing smile tries to hide this terrifying vertigo, but I don't think Roger Trewly fooled very many people. Mr. Fenwick, steely-eyed and successful, looks as though nothing had ever fooled him. When my father, who was a war hero, shot himself through the heart with his deer rifle, everyone was shocked. But when Roger Trewly jumped off the Mill Avenue bridge into the heavy rapids of the Far Cry River, no one in town was surprised, least of all my mother. "I saw it," she said. "I saw it coming."

Mother was only thirty-two years old the spring that Roger Trewly drowned himself, but four years of living with a terror-struck two-faced man had taken the bloom off her spirit. She didn't have gray hair yet, she didn't have wrinkled skin, she had not become bent or shaky or forgetful, but she acted like an older woman with not a whole lot left to live for. If you weren't a child, and could see things for what they were, you would have called her beautiful in spite of the lines and hollows of weariness that masked her true face. She was a petite, almost tiny woman with high, youthful breasts and her hair was the color of polished mahogany. She kept it long and she brushed it until it crackled with a suggestion of dark fire. She had large, widely spaced eyes, the gray-specked green of imperfect emeralds, and a smile that made you want to jump up and do chores. My father, who was a large, powerful man, called her "doll" or "midge." He loved to pick her up in his strong arms and whirl her through the house whistling or singing, like a happy giant whose dreams had come true at last.

"Ma, you're so pretty!" my sister, LaDonna, said one bright summer afternoon in 1952. This was a little over a year after Roger Trewly killed himself. Mother was dressed up for the first time since the funeral. "Look, Jack!" LaDonna said, pulling me into Mother's bedroom. "She looks like a princess!"

It was true. She was beautiful in her dark blue dress and white high-heeled shoes and little pillbox hat. Her face had recovered its sharp-edged prettiness. She looked young and exotic. Her perfume struck me like a shocking announcement. We both put our arms around her and hugged her tight. "Princess! Princess!" we yelled, imprisoning her in our linked arms. I'd turned twelve years old that spring and shouldn't have been carrying on like that, but I was as overwhelmed by her as LaDonna was. She had come out of herself at last, like a butterfly out of its winter cocoon, and we clung to her as if we knew there was a real danger of her flying away from us. But she pried off our greedy arms and said, "Don't! You'll wrinkle me! I'm only going out on a date!"

She went out into the living room where the man was waiting. I hadn't realized that a stranger had entered the house. His name was Gent Mundy, the owner of Mundy's Old Times Creamery. LaDonna and I stood in front of Mother like a double shield between her and this man, but we were only a nuisance and she sent us outside to play. And when Gent Mundy asked her to marry him several weeks later, we accepted the news like the condemned victims of a rigged jury.

Gent lived in a large, slate-gray house next to his creamery on the main east-west street of Far Cry. We were all invited there to have dinner with him. After cookies and coffee in the living room, he gave us a tour.

"This would be your room, Jackie," he said to me. "My" room was on the second floor. It had a large dormer window that looked out on the parking lot of the creamery where all the milk trucks were kept when they were not making deliveries. The room was about twice as big as the one I had at home, and the walls had been freshly painted light blue. There was a "new" smell in the room, and I realized then that all the furniture still had price tags on it.

Next he showed us the room he and Mother would have. It was half again as big as my room, and the bed in it had a bright pink canopy. Mother sat on the bed and bounced lightly up and down twice. "This *is* something," she said, the thin light of greed sharpening her eyes. Gent sat next to her and the bed wheezed. The depression he made in the bed forced her to sag against him. She looked like a child next to his bulk.

"I think she's warming up to the idea, kids," he said, winking nervously. He was bald, and the top of his head was turning pink in mottled patches. It looked like a map of Mars, the rosy, unknown continents floating in a white, fleshy sea. Gent Mundy was a tall man. He had a heavy torso, but his legs were painfully thin, almost spindly. His chest sloped out into a full, belt-straining stomach. His large head made his shoulders seem abnormally narrow. He had alert, pale blue eyes and a wide, friendly mouth that was fixed in a permanent half-smile, a smile warned off suddenly, as though by a cautionary second thought. He was an odd-looking man, but he was friendly and alive and open to everything that was going on around him. He wasn't powerful and wild like my father, but he wasn't two-faced and careful like Roger Trewly, either.

He was especially attentive to Mother. If she sighed, he would put his arm around her small waist as if to boost her morale. If she touched her nose before sneezing, he would quickly have his handkerchief ready. If she looked bored or disinterested, he would smoothly change to a livelier subject of conversation. If she began to rant at length about some ordinary injustice, he'd listen carefully to every word, and then, to prove he shared her concern, he'd repeat verbatim certain things she had said.

Some deep and fragile longing made him fall colossally in love with her. I almost winced to see it, even though I didn't understand what I was seeing or why it moved me to wince.

He made something of her name, Jade, and of her size. "Tiny perfect jewel," he once called her. "Jade, Jade, how I'd like to set you in gold and wear you on my finger!" When he said things like this, his eyes would get vague with tears.

LaDonna's prospective room was next to mine. Instead of fresh paint on the walls, it had new wallpaper—fields of miniature daisies against a light green background. "I had this done especially for you, honey," he told her, his voice low and secretive, as if it were a private matter between just the two of them.

Gent was forty-eight years old and had never been married. "I think I have a lot to offer you," he said, after the tour. We returned to the living room and sat down uneasily in the large, overstuffed chairs. Gent made some fresh coffee and poured each of us a cup. I picked up a *National Geographic* and thumbed through it. LaDonna picked up the silver cream pitcher. She brought it close to her face to study it. Mother held her steaming cup of coffee several inches from her lips, blowing thoughtfully. Careful lines appeared on her forehead. A tall clock ticked patiently in the polished hallway. A black woman with low-slung breasts and dusty feet was talking to a white man in a sun helmet. I turned the page to an article about funeral customs in Sumatra. Gent was sweating now, and he mopped his head with his napkin. "Well, no," he said, as if agreeing to some unspoken criticism. "I'm no Casanova, I grant you that. I'm no Tyrone Power, that's for sure! But I am moderately well off. I can provide handsomely for all three of you. The milk business . . ." and here he seemed to be stumped for the precise words. A dreamy look came over his face and he smiled at the perplexity of the thing in his mind. ". . . is, is a *good* business." His face reddened, and his forehead was lacquered again with sweat.

Mother put the cup to her lips and drew a little hissing sound from it that made all three of us lean toward her. We were poor. Mother had a little pension, but it barely put food on the table and paid the rent. My father was out of work when he shot himself, and Roger Trewly, even though he was the Ace of Hand-Held Tools, never made enough to keep up with the bills.

Mother set the cup down and said something. Her back was straight and some untameable pride made the small muscles around her mouth rigid.

"What was that, Jade?" Gent said, leaning closer to her. "What was that your wonderful mother said, kids?"

LaDonna stood up. "It was yes," she said sternly. "Our wonderful mother said yes, she will be happy to marry you, Mr. Mundy."

LaDonna was like that. She saw things for what they were and she spoke her mind easily, and often with a sharp tongue. Though she was only eleven years old at the time, she had her future planned. She was going to be a scientist. She had no doubts about this. Her hero was Albert Einstein. A picture of the long-hair genius hung on her bedroom wall. She claimed to understand the general drift of his writings, if not all the math involved. She said that Einstein knew everything he would ever know when he was sixteen, he just hadn't found the words to put it in. She had an aggressive curiosity about nearly everything, and an ice-cold, relentless intelligence to back it up. I always thought she was something special, one of the world's truly unique people, but her detached brilliance sometimes worried me.

When she was seven she made a jigsaw puzzle out of a frog, a salamander, and a cat-killed flicker. She spread out their innards on the back-yard picnic table, trying to match them, organ for organ. The big and small differences fascinated her. Mother threw a fit when she saw the slimy, sun-pungent mess and called her Little Miss Frankenstein. But LaDonna was also affectionate and full of ordinary eleven-year-old ideas.

So when LaDonna said yes for Mother, it was with such crisp authority that Gent clapped his hands together and said, "Oh, Jade, you don't know how happy you've made me! You'll never regret this, I promise!"

LaDonna and I liked Gent, though he was overly neat and too concerned with cleanliness. One day, while visiting our house, he began to fidget. We were all sitting at the kitchen table waiting for Mother to take a box cake out of the oven. Finally Gent pushed away from the table and found himself an apron. "I'll clean up a little while we're waiting," he said. He began to sponge-clean the sink and the counter next to it. Then he went after the greasy stovetop with Ajax and a hard-bristle brush. When he finished that, he knelt down and searched the floor for dust balls. There were no dust balls. Dust that found its way into the kitchen got mixed almost instantly with the haze of grease that covered everything. Mother wasn't a very good cook and preferred to fry most of our food. When she cooked for us, grease hung in the air like fog. Gent ran a finger along the base of the counter. He stood up then, a gummy gray wad stuck to his uplifted finger, his half-smile bravely in place.

"Christ on a crutch, Gent," Mother said. "You don't have to do that." She stood up and tried to yank loose his apron ties. But Gent danced nimbly out of reach.

"No, no, Jade," he said. "Honestly, I don't mind at all. In fact, I like to tidy up. I've been a bachelor for nearly half a century!" He scraped and scrubbed until the whole kitchen gleamed. Mother watched him from her place at the table. She lit a cigarette and blew smoke noisily through her teeth. After Gent finished mopping the kitchen floor, he found the vacuum cleaner and went to work on the living-room carpet.

"No, no!" he yelled over the sucking roar, as if someone were trying to change his mind. "Let me do it! I don't mind a bit!"

He was wearing a suit. The apron had pink and white checks, with a ruffled trim. He had thrown his green, hand-painted tie over his left shoulder as if to keep it out of the way of the machine.

Mother got up and went outside. I watched her through the kitchen window. She crossed the back yard slowly and sat down at the picnic table. She lit another cigarette and stared into the hedge at the end of our property. A neighborhood cat jumped up on the table next to her, its vertical tail quivering, but Mother swept it away with a quick flash of her arm.

The night before Gent and Mother were to be married, Gent gave me a present. It was a dark blue suit with powerful gray stripes running through it. He also gave me a stiff, blue-white shirt and a shiny red tie with a picture of a trout painted on it. The trout had a red-and-white lure in its mouth. Big drops of water flew off its head like sweat.

"Christ God!" Mother said when she saw me in my new outfit. "Look at you, Jackie! It's the president of the First National Bank himself!" She was honestly taken by my appearance. She pressed both hands flat against her stomach and laughed nervously. I went into her bedroom and looked at myself in the full-length mirror. I raised an eyebrow and frowned and curled my lips, one side of my mouth up, the other side down. I didn't look bad. I felt I looked handsome in that ugly gangster way. "Say your prayers, sucker," I snarled, imitating Edward G. Robinson.

Gent fixed us dinner that day. Mother had allowed the kitchen to get grimy again, but Gent cleaned it before he started cooking. He was a good cook. He made a standing rib roast, scalloped potatoes, and three kinds of vegetables blanketed in a rich yellow sauce. I wore my blue suit to the table. LaDonna had received a new dress for the occasion. Gent was very generous to us. I had found a ten-dollar bill in the inside coat pocket of the suit, and LaDonna had found a five pinned to her skirts. I ate dinner like a steel robot, but still managed to get salad dressing on my tie and yellow sauce on my coat sleeve.

The wedding took place in a minister's back office. It was stuffy and hot in there, and my blue suit made me feel sick, so I slipped out the door just as the minister was getting up a head of steam on the subject of the good marriage and how easily it can jump the tracks and wreck itself in the rocky ravine of neglect. Good grooming, for instance, said the minister. Married folks tend to let themselves go as they gradually become familiar with one another. I saw Gent wink at Mother when the minister said this, for Gent was nothing if not neat.

And then, said the minister, there are the cat-footed evils of spite, inattention, and the always misguided sense of independence. Amen, Doc, said Gent, under his breath.

I felt better out in the street. It was a cool day in early autumn. I walked to the closest drugstore and bought a pack of cigarettes. The clerk didn't blink an eye. I guess I looked smoking-age in my blue suit, shirt and tie. I also bought a cigarette lighter that had the shape of a leaping fish. It looked pretty much like the trout that was jumping on my tie. The idea of my tie and cigarette lighter matching each other appealed to me.

I walked back to the church learning how to inhale. The smoke made me dizzy in an agreeable way. I knocked the ash off my cigarette several times so that I could use my fish-shaped lighter to light up again. Lighting up needed a style, and I studied myself in store windows trying to perfect one. When I reached the church, I sat down on the front steps and lit up again. Some kids ran by pointing at me and yelling, "I'm gonna te-ell, I'm gonna te-ell," but I blew some smoke at them and laughed suavely at their childishness.

After the wedding we went for a drive in the country in Gent's Buick Roadmaster, a black four-door sedan the size of a hearse. Gent parked next to an abandoned railroad depot. Mother and Gent walked down the old weedy railbed, and LaDonna and I explored the decaying brick depot. I actually found a set of ancient water-stained tickets that would have taken someone all the way to Chicago.

The windows of the depot were broken out and the floor was littered with a dank mulch of shattered glass and slimy leaves. I lit up a cigarette. LaDonna watched me with slowly widening eyes. I acted as though smoking were a trifle boring, as though smoking for us veterans were something to be endured fatalistically, like old wounds that would never quite heal.

I gave LaDonna a drag. Her brave curiosity wouldn't let her refuse. She drew a lungful of smoke. I could see that she wanted to choke it out, but she wouldn't let herself. "Give me one," she said, the words grating on her parched vocal cords. I gave her one and lit it for her. She inhaled again and blew the smoke furiously out her nose, her teeth grinding together in a tough smile.

"L.S.M.F.T.," I said, imitating the radio commercial.

"What?"

"Lucky Strike means fine tobacco," I said.

She looked at the white cylinder in her hand. "Tastes like burning rubber," she said.

We walked out onto the crumbling platform where people from another generation caught trains for Chicago. We could see Mother and Gent hugging down the railbed in the shade of an old rusted-out water tower. They kissed. Gent in his dark brown suit looked like a top-heavy bear. He was so much taller than Mother that he had to lean down and hunch his back as he gathered her in his arms. The kiss was long and awkward and Mother dropped her purse into the weeds. She tried to lean away from him to retrieve it, but Gent held her fast in his desperate arms, his legs spread for power. It looked like a bear had caught up with a Sunday picnicker. I took out my fish lighter and watched them through the orange flame.

My suit and tie made me look older, and smoking made me feel older. Feeling older widened my interests. I took a bunch of Gent's magazines up to my room once. I got them out of his office, which was a large paneled room next to the kitchen. Some of the magazines had full-color pictures of women wearing skimpy bathing suits. Others were of a more general interest. I read an article about the home life of Stone Age people. There were some drawings to go along with the article. The drawings showed short stubby women with furry tits tending a fire. They had faces only a zookeeper could love. In the hazy distance, a group of short men without foreheads were carrying a huge woolly carcass of some kind. The caption under this drawing said: "The Backbone of Domestic Harmony is the Successful Hunt."

I set the magazine aside and looked at the pictures of the women in bathing suits. These were modern women—long-legged, smooth, with faces that were angelic and yet available. They seemed to radiate heat. The Stone Age men in the other magazine would have murdered entire forests full of woolly animals for a smile from one of those faces.

I'd been lying on top of my bed in my pajamas, but now I felt too restless and warm to go to sleep. I got up and put on my suit. I watched myself smoke cigarettes for a while in the mirror above my dresser. I looked good, I was developing style. I wished my neck weren't so skinny. I cinched my red tie, drawing the loose shirt collar tighter around my throat.

It was late, but I went into their room anyway. I guess I wanted some adult company. I snapped on the overhead light. There was a great rolling commotion in the canopied bed. I sat down in the chair next to Mother's vanity and lit a cigarette.

"Say, listen to this," I said, flipping open the magazine I had brought with me. "This story is about a day in the life of a linoleum cutter. It tells about this Stanley Wallach. He cuts linoleum twelve hours a day in Perth, Australia, and hopes to save enough money in twenty years to buy his own island. He's going to call it New Perth and crown himself king. King Stanley the First."

"Jackie," Mother said, sitting up in bed. "You shouldn't come barging into a bedroom like that. You're old enough to know better."

I felt suave in my suit. I put out my cigarette just so I could light another one. I wanted them to see my style. Gent was sitting on the edge of the bed, his back to me, his large pale head in his hands. He was in his shorts. I blew a recently perfected smoke ring toward them, winking.

"When did you start smoking?" Mother asked.

But I only crossed my legs and laughed in a sophisticated way, sort of tossing my head back and winking again, this time at the ceiling. I felt clever. I felt that I more or less had an adult's grasp of things.

"And there's this family," I continued, "who talk backasswards to each other, if you can swallow it. No one but themselves can get what they're saying. It's like a foreign country right in the middle of the neighborhood."

"Jack, old boy," said Gent, getting heavily to his feet. The lump in his long shorts swung as he stepped around the big bed. His bulky stomach rolled above his thin white legs. "Jack, you really ought to tap on a door before storming in like that."

I thought for a few seconds, then said, "Sklof, taht tuoba yrros."

"What?" Gent said.

"That's how they must do it," I said. "Talking backasswards."

Mother took a deep breath. It looked like she was about to smile. "Jackie . . ." she said.

I blew a fat doughnut straight up into the ceiling. "Okay, okay." I chuckled. "I can take a hint." I winked at them. Smoking had also given me a stylish chuckle, a husky little bark that trailed off into a world-weary wheeze. I stood up and yawned. I stubbed out my cigarette in their ashtray. "Guess I'll hit the old sackeroo," I said. "See you people in the morning."

I strolled slowly out of their room, as if the reluctance were theirs, not mine.

Money and a nice big house made all the difference to Mother. She now looked young and happy again. She had a lively bounce to her walk and she wore makeup every day. She bought herself a new dress on the first of every month and her collection of shoes outgrew her closet. She looked beautiful in the morning in her red silk duster and blue mules and she looked beautiful in the afternoon in her expensive dresses.

Gent was proud to have such a good-looking young woman for his wife and he made no secret of it. Her small size thrilled him, just as it had my father. But where my father would pick her up and dance her through the house, Gent seemed almost afraid to touch her, as if she were made of rare porcelain.

He would take us for Sunday rides in the Roadmaster just to show her off to the town. Mother would sit in the front seat next to Gent with her skirts hiked up for comfort, and LaDonna and I would sit in the back, reading the comic section. The Roadmaster had a radio, and Mother would search the dial for music as we idled in second gear through the streets of Far Cry.

The town on the north side of the river was usually smoky because of the teepee-shaped chip burners the lumber mills used to get rid of waste. On the south side, the air had a sulfurous sting to it because of the paper mill. On Sundays, though, the air on both sides of the river was not so bad. We'd drive down the tree-lined streets of the north side, and then, if we felt like it, we'd cross the Mill Avenue bridge and cruise the wider, treeless streets of the south side. Sometimes Gent would pull over and park and we'd listen to the radio for a while. People on the sidewalks, looking into the car, would smile and nod as if to approve our way of killing Sunday.

Mother had a baby by Gent Mundy. It was a big baby and the delivery was an ordeal. It gave her milk leg and she had to stay in bed for nearly a month after she got home from the hospital. The head of the baby was so large that for a time the doctor thought it would not be able to pass through the birth canal. And when it did pass, it tore her badly. Gent felt terrible about this. I saw him once kneeling at her bedside, crying loudly, his face in his hands. But Mother healed quickly and soon the big, happy-dispositioned baby became the central attraction at our house.

They named him Spencer Ted. Spencer Ted looked like Gent, and Gent couldn't get over it. "The Mundy heir," he'd say, amazed. If I was in earshot, he'd get flustered and add, "No offense to you, Jack." But it didn't matter to me since no boy of thirteen cares much about inheriting a creamery. "My precious strapping fellow," Gent would coo to the big, round-headed baby, and if either LaDonna or I was nearby, he'd insist, "But, say, I love you kids too, just as if you were my own!"

All this didn't matter to LaDonna or me. We liked Gent because he was easygoing and generous. He gave us practically anything we wanted. LaDonna hinted for a microscope of her own, and Gent went right down to the Sears outlet and ordered an expensive binocular microscope complete with lab kit. I barely complained one day about having to ride my old, rusty Iver-Johnson bike, and the next afternoon after school I found a beautiful new Schwinn on the front porch, complete with basket, headlight, foxtails, and horn.

It didn't matter to me or LaDonna that Gent loved Spencer Ted best because we loved the new baby too. He was happy as a cabbage and cute in an odd sort of way. All babies are more or less cute, but Spencer Ted's cuteness wasn't baby-cuteness. It was the cuteness of joke postcards, where unlikely combinations are relied on to produce a humorous effect. Like a fish wearing a saddle and a cowboy in the saddle twirling a rope, or a poodle smoking a pipe and reading the newspaper. With Spencer Ted, it was a fringe of red hair around his ears, which made him look like an old scholar, and a round, tomato-red nose, which made him look like a seasoned drinker. He had deep-set, coal-black eyes that missed nothing, and radiantly pink ears that bloomed under his fringe of hair like roses.

Spencer Ted seemed as pleased with the brand-new world as Gent was with his brand-new heir. Often LaDonna and I would take Spencer Ted out for a walk in his stroller, and when we did this, LaDonna liked to pretend that we were his parents. It was a game that tickled her, and she would say things such as "We must find a suitable nurse for our darling little man, dear." She would speak in a stagey voice and people near us would wink and chuckle, for we were only children ourselves.

Sometimes we would sit down on a park bench and LaDonna would hold Spencer Ted in her lap. Being held in a lap was a signal for him and he would begin turning his big round head impatiently, looking for a full breast. This made LaDonna nervous and she would give him his pacifier which only gentled him for a few seconds. He would spit the pacifier out, arch his back angrily, and then grind his soft, drunkard's face into LaDonna's milkless ribs.

"Mamma spank!" La Donna once said, embarrassed by Spencer Ted's aggressive search for satisfaction, and Spencer Ted, arrested by her sharp, scolding voice, studied her like an old scholar studying an obscure text, his black eyes wide with alarm. LaDonna immediately regretted her tone. "Oh no, Spencey," she said. "Mamma would never spank *you*."

We always went to Grassy Lake on the Fourth of July. Grassy Lake was a recreational area for the people of Far Cry. There was a beach and several boat-launching ramps. In the late fall, old men would fish off the ramps with cane poles, but in the summer there were only bathers and boats at the lake.

Spencer Ted was almost one year old by the Fourth of July, and we took him up to the lake thinking that he'd be thrilled with the fast boats, the long expanse of deep blue water, and the evening fireworks. But he was cranky and balked at everything we tried to interest him in. He sat under the beach umbrella with Gent, fussy and critical, while LaDonna and I made sand castles and Mother swam.

I didn't know Mother could swim, but she swam like a young girl out to the diving platform which was about fifty yards from shore. LaDonna and I watched her, amazed. When she reached the platform, she pulled herself easily out of the water and stood on the planks, shimmering with wet light. She took off her bathing cap, releasing her long shining hair. Then she found a sunny spot and lay down on her back.

The arch of her ribs, her nicely muscled legs, the graceful reach of her relaxed arms, and the mass of dark glossy hair pillowing her head and shoulders made all of us gaze out across the water like the stranded victims of a shipwreck afflicted with thirst-caused visions. It was like a spell. Finally Gent said, in dreamy baby talk, "Thaz you booly-full mamma, Spencey," and Spencer Ted, recognizing at last the impassable gulf between him and Mother, released a ragged forlorn sob.

LaDonna and I turned our attention back to our sand castles. They weren't very elaborate and we didn't mind wrecking them as soon as we got them built. We erected a city full of sloppy skyscrapers. "Let's A-bomb it," LaDonna said.

I was the B-29, arms out, rumbling through the hot sky, radio chatter of the crewmen alive in my head, sighting in on the muddy skyline of our city. Then, as I approached it, I picked up speed, bomb-bay doors open, crew tense, and I released the bomb, Fat Boy. I had to be Fat Boy then, and I fell on the city, back first, squashing it flat, and LaDonna made the A-bomb noise, the rolling boom and bleak sigh of the high sweeping wind.

We did this several times, and then I dove into the lake to wash off the mud. I swam out toward the diving platform, thinking to join Mother, but when I looked up I saw that there was a man standing behind her. He was big and heavily muscled. He had black hair, bright as freshly laid tar. He lifted his arms and flexed. The biceps jumped impossibly tall with cords of angry veins, violet under the oiled skin. Then he put his hands on his hips and drew in his stomach until his ribcage arched over the unnatural hollow like an amphitheater. His thighs from his kneecaps to hips were thick with bands of visible muscle. He moved from one pose to another, finally relaxing, hands on hips at a cocky angle, a swashbuckler's smile on his tanned face. Mother glittered like booty at his feet. But she acted as though she didn't see him, or even know he was there.

I swam back to shore and joined Gent and Spencer Ted under the umbrella. LaDonna was building another city. This one was futuristic, with tall spires and cylinders and oddly concave walls. I got a half-dollar from Gent and bought a package of firecrackers—"ladyfingers"—and a package of "whistlers." I thought we could blow this city up with ordinary explosives, one building at a time. Gent and Spencer Ted took a nap. Gent was lying flat on his back with a towel over his face and Spencer Ted was tucked in the crook of his arm. I was afraid the "whistlers" might wake them, but they didn't.

After the city was wrecked, I watched Mother swim. She stroked the water like a professional channel swimmer, but she wasn't swimming back to us. She was swimming parallel to shore, away from the platform. The muscleman with the black hair was in the water too. He didn't swim as gracefully as Mother. The water churned around him and his black hair whipped from side to side. Even so, he swam much faster than Mother and was soon even with her. They treaded water for a while, about one yard apart. I thought I could hear them talking. Then they swam back to the platform, side by side. He tried to match his stroke to hers, but it wasn't easy for him. While she looked smooth and natural, he looked drugged.

He climbed out of the water first, then helped Mother. He pretended that she was too heavy for him and that she was pulling him off balance. He somersaulted over her into the water with a gigantic splash. Mother climbed up onto the platform, laughing. He joined her and then did a handstand. He began to walk around the perimeter of the platform on his hands while Mother shook out her hair. Mother leaned sharply to one side and then to the other, combing her hair with her fingers, while the muscleman walked on his hands. It looked like some kind of crazy dance.

Gent and Spencer Ted were awake now and looking out across the water at Mother. Spencer Ted's bald head looked like a smaller version of Gent's. Spencer Ted lifted his fat white arm and pointed toward the diving platform. He moaned crankily and blew a fat spit bubble.

It was nearly evening. Soon the fireworks would begin.

■ WAYNE UDE

Wayne Ude was born in Minneapolis in 1946, and he grew up in Harlem, on Montana's Hi-Line. He was graduated from the University of Montana in 1969 and received an M.F.A. degree from the University of Massachusetts in 1974. During the early 1970s, Ude worked in Community Action Programs and was on the Planning Board of the Fort Belknap Indian Reservation. He has taught at Colorado State University, Mankato State University, and Old Dominion University in Virginia. This selection is from Buffalo and Other Stories, *published in 1975.*

Enter Ramona, Laughing

As usual in the evening, Ramona Laughing sits on a stool at the bar's end farthest from the door and stares at her hands, spread out before her on the polished bar-top. They are small hands, like her grandmother's, but useless: good only to excite a man. Ramona's glass is neglected, half-filled with warming beer. The bar as yet is quiet; it will fill up later, and Ramona may or may not notice: she also is quiet tonight. Some nights she may be feverish in her conviviality, and others sullen, almost murderous in her silence. She once stabbed a man, though not seriously, and it is widely agreed that he should have known better.

Ramona's dark features are passive tonight, almost the look for which these Indians are famous. She lets her mind wander, south to the little ranch in the mountains which is still, from time to time, home. Her father is, no doubt, irrigating his alfalfa; a good rancher, he grows his own feed, repairs his own machines, teaches his sons to work the land, and leaves his daughters for his wife to raise. That wife, Ramona's mother, presides over the house, competent in the midst of her appliances and canned goods. The ranch and house are no different from those off the Reservation.

The glass makes a damp circle on the bar-top; Ramona makes absent designs with a negligent finger—circles, lines, no apparent pattern. The bartender watches carefully from the bar's other end. He may propose a few rolls of dice for the jukebox; some music would break the monotony until a crowd shows. He decides against it; if Ramona will be peaceful, he is wiser to leave her alone.

Grandmother lived in a small log cabin a few miles from the ranch. Each spring she erected a tipi in the yard and closed the cabin door until fall. Grandfather, of course, went with her, but it was Grandmother who decided, Grandmother who moved, Grandmother in whose wake he followed. Ramona's memory of him is vague; he seems a mere appendage.

Ramona's hands cease their dampened bar-top design. The fingers spread slowly, flat on the bar, the hands turn over and back. The palms and fingers are not calloused, the wrists are slim, the forearms promise little strength. On one wrist is a scar, white, straight, smooth across the dark skin. Hair on these arms is fine and black. Grandmother's hair was white and coarse, thick on her head if not her arms. Her hands were strong, capable: Ramona, if she had the words, would call them alchemist's hands.

Ramona has seen things at her grandmother's, and remembers them: an uncle brought a deer once, and Grandmother deftly removed the entrails, the hide, cut up the meat. Ordinary things enough, but then came the alchemy: Grandmother made sinew into string, hooves into glue, bones into tools, hide into clothing, entrails into pouches, meat into pemmican, teeth into necklaces, and on, and on. It took several days, while Ramona watched with a kind of awe. She had never imagined anything like this: to create, out of a single deer, what seemed to be all the material of living; to create one's own life. Ramona had forgotten that it was, after all, an uncle who brought the deer, and she gave her Grandmother credit for that, too.

Grandmother, pleased by the child's attention, said nothing until the work was nearly done. Then one morning she astounded Ramona by asking: "Would you like to learn?" For a moment Ramona was unable to answer. It had not occurred to her that such skills could be learned; they seemed rather the result of an inborn magic. And Ramona's mother, Grandmother's own daughter, had no such skills.

The lessons began immediately, and Ramona spent a happy week working alongside her Grandmother. Then the visit ended and Ramona returned home.

She began to watch her mother closely, with a newly awakened eye. Mother had always seemed to her the most competent being she had known, but now her mother's competence appeared as a series of make-shift, artificial half-measures designed to hide a creative failure. The sink, gas stove, sewing machine, refrigerator, cupboards of canned foods, closets full of ready-made clothes, all seemed merely inferior ways to prop up what seemed her mother's fading vitality. Grandmother had magic, which was life, in her hands; Grandmother could create, she could make things, she could reshape them into other things; Mother obviously could not.

Ramona drinks off her flat beer, waves to the bartender for another. He approaches warily. She is too quiet for his taste. Ramona, knowing what is in his mind, laughs as he nears; she is a little proud of her reputation, and a little intimidated by it, as though it belongs properly to someone else who will someday come and claim it from her. People come into the room, scatter along the bar's scarred front, lean on the railing or crouch on stools, talking, as yet, quietly.

There were more lessons with Grandmother, but not nearly enough. Ramona was only ten when the old woman died. At first she thought that mother had learned of the lessons and sent Grandmother away, but when she saw the frail, shrunken body she realized what had really happened: Grandmother had transformed herself and become something else. What lay in the coffin was no more than a deer after all its parts have been turned into other things: nothing resembled what it had been. For a long time Ramona watched for her Grandmother's return, and she has never given up watching; only now she seldom remembers what it is she watches for.

Ramona drinks the second beer more rapidly than the first, though with no more notice and perhaps less pleasure. She doesn't like this bar, but the others have thrown her out so often she no longer enters them until later in the evening. This is the worst of the lot: bare dusty floor, no tables, jukebox with the last decade's songs listed under "Hit Parade."

The bar fills up and people begin to jostle one another, though no one jostles Ramona. Near the door, a commotion: Charley Many Rivers has come in, already drunk, talking louder than anyone else. Tonight he curses the men who carve statues for the Foundry where he sweeps. They are, Charley says, hack artists: he can do as well. His friends shout agreement, urge him to buy another drink. He throws money at the bar, roaring his disdain for second-rate art.

Ramona glances his way, shakes her head. At least she is sometimes quiet, while this man never is. Someday someone will cut him up in little pieces and feed him to the fish. Perhaps it will be her. Just now he is shouting again: "Aren't these the hands of an artist?" When Charley thrusts out his hands, Ramona stops smiling.

These are large hands, strong, covered with scars and callouses, the nails bitten off short; but no one looks at them. Even Charley doesn't seem to take his call quite seriously, and his friends laugh and look to their drinks, now that he has paid. Ramona slips from her barstool and makes her way toward him.

Charley Many Rivers admires the backs of his hands. He raises and clenches them into fists, which he opens again; he spreads his fingers, turns both hands over and admires his palms, then turns them again so the palms are raised away from him, and slowly lowers his arms. Along the bar, people draw back as Ramona passes, watch her warily. The friends closest to Charley try to warn him, but he will not allow his concentration to be broken.

Ramona reaches with one small hand, touches Charley's, timidly, running her fingers over his scars and blisters, searching his palms. She takes his hands with both hers, draws them to her.

Charley has stopped admiring. His mouth is open, he stares at Ramona Laughing as though she's never been seen before. She is intent on his hands, ignores his eyes; he hears her murmur, cannot catch the words. The bar is very quiet. Ramona pushes him toward the door, and he goes, uncomprehending.

Ramona is watching herself in the mirror behind the bar. Her face is wasted more than her years should merit; the man she leans against is apparently a little drunk, probably stupid. She knows, with a certainty a little surprising in its suddenness, what all this will come to: what everything has come to. And yet, she tells herself, perhaps . . . perhaps Charley Many Rivers is a man; perhaps she can find a way to be a woman, no longer a little girl. Perhaps. Her grandmother is most certainly dead. She pushes Charley Many Rivers toward the door, and he goes. Ramona watches herself in the mirror until the door closing behind her cuts off the sight.

■ MICHAEL E. MOON

Born in Missoula in 1948, Michael Moon attended both Montana State University and the University of Montana, where he received his degree in 1974. Moon worked as a logger, a firefighter, and information specialist for the Forest Service. This selection is from his novel, John Medicinewolf, *published in 1979. Moon's promising literary career was cut short in 1986, when he died of cancer.*

Raising Goats

We have three goats, which provide us with nine to twelve quarts of milk a day. About half of the milk I use, and the other half I sell. We drink the milk as well as cook with it. Our goats are half Nubian and half French Alpine. Their names are Rachel, Esther, and Ruth.

It is not necessary to own purebreds. A grade doe can still be a good milker. Just make sure you buy her from someone you know, or from a reputable dealer. Make sure the herd has never had brucellosis or tuberculosis.

You can tell a good milker by looking at her. First, milk her and taste the milk. Then examine her teeth to see how old she is. Examine the coat and skin and feel her udder. It should be soft and not have warts or scars. If she walks with a limp, don't buy her; and if she is fat, she will probably be a poor milker.

We let our goats browse in the woods. Goats are natural browsers, and any place that is good for deer will be good for goats. I supplement their diet with beets and carrots. Like any stock, you have to feed them hay and grain during the winter. If they get six months of good pasture, each goat will need about 500 pounds of hay during the rest of the year, and about 450 pounds of grain.

I have kept accurate records, and paying for hay and grain still comes out far cheaper than buying the milk. This is because the dairy industry and the government conspire to set the price of milk unreasonably high.

I usually tether the goats, although they are not likely to leave unless they are dry. Wet nannies need to be milked, and they know it. Avoid letting goats get near anything they can climb upon, because they will. Milking twice a day is usually enough, unless the nanny has just kidded. The best method for milking is to build a platform with a stanchion. I built one that works pretty well. It's about eighteen inches high, built of number three rough lumber. Once the goats get used to it, they hop right up there without any coaxing.

Wash the udder each time you milk her, and don't drink the first few squirts. Cool the milk as soon as possible. I usually put the milk in jars and set them in the creek—this cools them faster than the refrigerator.

A nanny will come into heat every twenty-one days, but only between September and January. If you don't get her bred during this time she will not take again until the following August. When she is in heat she will be restless and shake her tail.

Breed her to the best billy you can find for the price. This is not solely for her enjoyment, but partly. Try to find a billy who has thrown good milkers in the past. Don't keep a billy yourself; it's not worth the money. Besides, they stink; and if you don't keep them away from the nannies, the smell will get in the milk.

The nanny will kid in 149 days. A few days before she's due, put her in a warm, dry place where she can be alone and keep her watered. It's best not to feed her too much just prior to kidding.

They almost never have trouble kidding, so I will not go into all that. They usually have two, although occasionally three. In a normal delivery, number one will come out front feet and head first, and number two will come out hind feet and tail first. The kids are up and around within an hour, and they are the cutest animals you've ever seen.

If the kids don't nurse right away, milk some of the colostrum and give it to them, either in a bucket or with a bottle. Colostrum is her first milk, and it contains vitamins and antibodies important to the kids.

The best way to wean them is to just keep them away from momma. If you need the milk yourself, you can wean them as early as a week or so. If you're not going to keep them for milkers, sell them. That includes all the billies. Of course, you can eat them if you want to. It is the custom in some Mediterranean countries to eat the billy kids for Easter. But I never could bring myself to do this.

You can use goat's milk in any way you use regular milk. We drink it, cook with it, make cheese with it, and sell it. Another extremely good way to use goat's milk is to make it into yogurt. You take the milk and warm it to 180° F. (use a candy thermometer), then cool it slightly and mix each quart with three tablespoons of yogurt. Then run hot water through a thermos bottle until it is very hot, pour out the water, pour in the yogurt/hot-milk mixture, and put on the lid. In eight hours it will have set into yogurt and can be refrigerated for further setting.

Yogurt is both delicious and quite nutritious. It is especially good with fruit or berries. Cooked apples and cinnamon is another good combination.

There are two important things to remember about making yogurt: first, the thermos bottle must be absolutely undisturbed for the first eight hours. Second, always remember to keep enough of the yogurt to "start" the next batch.

All in all, goats are a very satisfactory livestock.

Protecting goats from winter chill is the biggest problem we have. Pneumonia is common if young goats get a chill. In fact it is probably the chief cause of death among goats. We don't have a barn for our goats, and I know that one of these winters we'll lose them all to pneumonia.

It's fairly easy to raise goats. Certainly easier than keeping a cow.

Goats are somewhat more hardy and will eat a wider variety of things. You get much more milk per pound. They're not as expensive, and it wouldn't take as much of a barn to keep them in. A goat barn could be much smaller than a regular barn.

My husband claims to be a carpenter, yet he refuses to even consider building a barn for the goats.

If you ask me, he's the goat.

■ RICHARD BRAUTIGAN

Novelist and essayist Richard Brautigan wrote with an imaginative, critical, and innovative style that earned him a large and loyal audience. His early experimental novel, Trout Fishing in America *(1967), found an international reputation and became a "cult" classic through the early 1970s. Brautigan also published such imaginative works as* The Pill Versus the Springhill Mine Disaster *(1973),* The Hawkline Monster *(1981), and* So the Wind Won't Blow It All Away *(1983). Although Brautigan always headquartered in San Francisco, he found refuge for many years at his home in the Paradise Valley near Livingston, Montana. In 1986, at the age of fifty-three, Brautigan committed suicide near San Francisco. "The Good Work of Chickens" is reprinted here from* The Tokyo-Montana Express, *published in 1980.*

The Good Work of Chickens

The sweet turbines of revenge purred gently in his mind like the voice of a beautiful woman and relaxed him to the point that it didn't feel strange or even out of the ordinary for him to be driving a dump truck full of chicken shit down a quiet street with his lights out in a prosperous middle-class residential neighborhood.

He had bought the truckload of chicken shit earlier that day at a huge chicken ranch in White Sulphur Springs, Montana, and had driven it to the town of View, Montana, a distance of over two hundred miles.

He had never done anything like this before and he enjoyed the whole procedure of borrowing a friend's dump truck and driving it to White Sulphur Springs to buy the chicken shit and watching it being loaded onto the truck.

"This sure is a lot of chicken shit," one of the men said who was helping load the truck.

"Yes," said the proud new owner of the chicken shit. "It is a lot, isn't it?"

"What are you going to do with all this shit?" the man asked who liked to talk with people because he spent so much time with chickens.

"I'm going to make sure that it gets to the right place."

"Well," the chicken shit loader said, for lack of anything better to say. "I hope this chicken shit works out for the best."

"It will," the man said, who we'll call Mike, though his name was C. Edwin Jackson because his right name is not important. It's what he did with that chicken shit that's important.

Mike drove slowly almost anonymously past house after house in the early evening of a cold February night, looking for the right house. He had muddied up the license plates of the truck, so that it would be hard to trace.

That's how he had gotten the address of his destination, a house on Butte Street, by tracing the owner's license plate number when their car drove away leaving a bewildered little dog in its wake.

The people in the car had abandoned the dog in the country near his place. When he saw what the people were doing, he ran out of the house but it was too late to stop them. He yelled at them but they drove away ignoring him and leaving the little dog standing there frightened in the road as its masters drove off, abandoning it to the cruel fates of the Montana countryside.

Mike thought about getting his shotgun and pursuing them, but then he memorized their license plate number and went into the house and wrote it down right away because he had decided to put into operation a revenge fantasy that he had courted in his mind like a beautiful woman for years now.

He had a small ranch out in the country about ten miles from the small town of View and people were always driving out and dumping their unwanted animals on his property. Poor dogs and cats doomed to the shock of abandonment, *farewell, nice home*, and to the agonies of starvation and survival in a world where they could not survive.

One minute they were happy domestic pets and as soon as they were put outside the car or truck, they were just another wretched creature doomed to a slow and agonizing death.

Domestic animals cannot survive by themselves in this country. They suffer minute to minute, hour to hour, day to day until kind Death touches their lives with the shadow of his life.

Country people don't want these animals. They already have their own animals. Why do people think that strangers will take care of their animals after they no longer want to take care of them themselves?

There simply is not room for a hundred cats and fifty dogs at every house in the country. People at the most have a few dogs or cats and that's about it.

There truly is no room at the inn.

It's full.

Anyway, Mike or C. Edwin Jackson had had it up to his ears with the cruelty of people abandoning their pets in the country to die a slow and painful death.

He had seen puppies starved down so much that they looked like the shadows of string with no other response to life than hunger like bowling going on in their stomachs.

He once saw a kitten eating an ear of corn in the garden and he had seen a cat standing in a creek, the water was a very cold six-inches deep, trying to catch a fish.

Hunger had driven a house cat to become a fisherman.

Yes, he had no love in his heart for people who would do things like that to animals and he had slowly evolved this fantasy of revenge upon those who abandoned the helpless without even the mercy to take their unwanted animals to the veterinarian and let him painlessly take care of the business, so that no suffering would occur. Sometimes he thought that people abandoned their animals just to save the few dollars that the vet would cost.

Mike tried to think of what those people thought about when they took their animals away from their homes and drove them out to the horror of trying to stay alive in the country.

But now there was going to be an element of fairness introduced into it and he was only a few blocks away from 14 Butte Street and the beauty of his revenge.

It was a quiet house, large and spacious and occupied by a middle-aged man and his wife and their conveniently-absent dog.

"Have you found your dog yet?" one of their neighbors asked the day after it had "disappeared."

"No, Little Scott is still missing."

"Well, we hope you find him. He's such a cute dog."

"So do we. We love that dog."

"Don't worry. You'll find him."

The man and woman were watching *The Six Million Dollar Man* on television when Mike backed the truck up over the curb and across their lawn to the front porch and dumped three tons of chicken shit on it.

The man jumped up from the television set. He jumped up so fast that you'd think he was the Six Million Dollar Man.

The woman screamed.

She didn't know it yet but she was going to have to cancel her appointment at the beauty parlor tomorrow. She would be doing something else.

The weight of the chicken shit forced the front door open and it poured into their living room like an avalanche.

Three tons of chicken shit is a lot of dedicated chickens and their work had not been in vain.

SPIKE VAN CLEVE

Spike Van Cleve was born on November 7, 1912, on a ranch near Melville, Montana, which his grandfather had established in 1880. He grew up on the ranch and, after attending Harvard University, he returned to run the operation as a horse and dude ranch until his death in 1982. A member of Western Writers of America, Van Cleve was a prolific storyteller and writer. He published his memories of his life in the the shadow of the Crazy Mountains in Forty Years' Gatherin's *(1977) and* A Day Late and a Dollar Short *(1982). "Cody and Terry," which appeared in* Forty Years' Gatherin's *and is one of Van Cleve's best-known stories, won the Wrangler Award from the National Cowboy Hall of Fame.*

Cody and Terry

I am a horse man. I was raised with them, have lived with them all my life, and I hope I'll die with them. I've known a lot of good ones and a few bad ones. But looking back, while I've ridden—and still do—some popping fine saddle horses, it seems to me that I've known more really great work horses than I have riding horses. Maybe it's because none of the work stock bucked me off when I was breaking them—I never was a bronc rider by any stretch of the imagination—but I can well remember some real juicy go-rounds the first time I hooked up a stout old colt, so I guess the bucking off hasn't anything to do with it! It wasn't that we had more work horses, or that I was around them more, because we didn't and I wasn't. It was, I have finally decided, because while the saddle stock were individuals sufficient unto themselves, the work teams were just that, teams. Two individuals who, in the course of time, became almost one individual; two horses which were one unit. To this day I can't mention a work horse without thinking of the teammate, too! Somehow or other I got closer to them, with a few glaring exceptions, than I did saddle horses, and it is an interesting fact that I have heard the same thing from other ranchers. Funny–and I mean that peculiar, not ha, ha–but true.

Lord, but I've known some fine teams! They were mostly Percheron, and the first I can recall was Tex and Mex. Iron grey geldings and perfectly matched, with Tex a quiet gentleman and Mex a boogery, dangerous son of a gun. I remember them mostly because of the time when I, a little guy, toddled into the stall between them–something a grown man did pretty gingerly–and while Mex stood humped and quivering, old Tex blew his warm breath down the back of my neck and nosed me under his broad belly as he sidled over and braced himself against Mex until Dad could talk me into coming out on his off side. I might add that I got the living hell paddled out of me, too, when I got within Dad's reach. I did the same to Buckshot years later, come to think of it, when she was about five and wandered into the stall where I had a bronc tied up. The bronc was bay, and so was her mare, Mickey!

Another of the old teams was Fitz and Sharkey. Dad loaned Fitz to a rancher over on the Musselshell, and every time they turned him loose he came home to his sidekick. A matter of thirty-odd miles, too. After about the third trip over for him the rancher gave Fitz the fight, and he and Sharkey looked positively smug about it for a month at least.

There were others, and I'm not just naming names, I'm naming friends I knew well: Jack and Dinah; Margaret and Jessie; Toodles and Tacho–Toodles was out of Margaret, and Margaret was out of Dinah; Jack and Kelly; Sigurd and Sharkey–Young Sharkey; Betty and Babe–Babe was Toodles' colt; Modoc and Thunder–the latter another of Toodles'; and what I think was the finest team I ever broke, and one of the best I ever threw a line over, Bullet and Young Babe. She was out of Babe, and Bullet out of a grey Percheron we got from Frank Mackey of Billings. Only colt the grey ever had, worse luck. And, of course, the only team I have left on the place now, Chief, he was out of Bullet by a Belgian stud and so damn big I had to buy a Belgian gelding to match him. I named the newcomer Bill, though I am certain that for the first month he didn't know for sure that it wasn't "You big sonofabitch!" Good team, the big gunsels, but I haven't enough work to keep them toned down, so we have some rapid feeding circles, and I'd sure hate to try and put them up alongside a threshing rig!

There were lots of others, but names don't mean much to anybody who didn't know them, and what I am getting at anyhow is Cody and Terry. I won't forget them.

I couldn't have been very old when they were foaled, for I remember coming in from school one winter evening and hearing Dad remark to my granddad, "Those two colts I drove today are sure going to be a fine pair. Both are geldings, and what'll we name them?" From the vintage of the names I suspect Gramp came up with them. Anyhow, it was Cody and Terry, and a team, from then on for better than twenty years. Still is, really.

Funny how unalike they were, and yet how perfectly matched. Cody was black, pretty chunky, and operated on a hair trigger. Terry was bay, rawboned and levelheaded. Both were gentle and good natured. Terry was absolutely honest and accepted things as they came, while Cody was wise, suspicious and put in a lot of time trying to make things happen the way he figured they should. Neither ever scotched his share of the work, but Cody had a sneaky, grain-thieving bent that would preclude calling him plumb honest. In fact we had to devise such an intricate rigging on the oat box to keep Cody out that a human had trouble getting in, and the best way to run the son of a gun through a gate was to try and head him off from it, and swear as he thundered by. Funny he never wised up, either. I guess because he had a devious mind. We all loved Terry, for his heart and dependability. We loved Cody, for he had a great heart, and his rapscallion ways were something you could depend on, too. Often I've heard a teamster remark, "Ol' Terry," even when he was a green colt, followed by, "That damn Cody," but always with a grin. They were a pair to draw to!

There was a bad alkali bog out north of the buildings about a mile, an innocent white crust covering a soupy blue muck, and before we finally got it well fenced we lost an animal in it from time to time. Anyhow, one morning Cody showed up alone, more fidgety than usual, wouldn't let himself be caught, and he kept heading off north, stopping to see if we were coming, and then thundering back to fuss around and get in our way. Making a general nuisance of himself.

"He's trying to tell us something," Dad said. "Terry's in trouble. Get Jack and Kelly, all the chains we've got, and let's go. I'll bet it's that damn bog hole, and I sure hope we aren't too late."

We weren't, but Terry was sure enough in trouble. He was in so deep that only his head and fore quarters showed above the muck, but he wasn't fighting. Too smart, and he never moved while we shoved a plank out and got a log chain around his chest and the grab hook fastened. Then ever so carefully the team eased him towards the edge, and finally the old fellow lurched to his feet on comparatively solid ground. Naturally by that time he was pretty well covered with blue slime. Cody, who had been messing around, worrying and bothering us and the team, took one look at this great blue monster that had emerged from the bog, let out a snort and headed for the barn as hard as he could go, Terry right behind and calling for him to wait. How the old horse did dig–this horrible thing had his partner's voice, maybe had eaten him even, and was trying to trick him to where it could catch him, too. By the time we got to the barn with our very interested team Cody was backed into a corner of the corral, in a state of near collapse, desperately threatening his mate, and it was only after we had taken Terry down to the trough and washed him off that his partner would have anything to do with him. But then Cody fussed around like a mare with her first colt–sniffing, nuzzling, nickering and reassuring himself that everything was in good shape, and all with a puzzled, disbelieving look. We laughed, but our eyes were misty.

Another time, along in January, Dad and I were feeding down on the Sweet Grass some six miles from home. We drove down in a little sleigh and then hooked the old team to a bobsleigh and rack to feed. We had quite a string of cattle, and it took most of the day to haul the six or seven loads of loose hay we needed, and it was cold! There are no thermometers on a hay rack, but it must have been thirty-five or forty below, with at least four sun dogs glaring balefully through the frost haze. About the time we'd finished the last load a stiff breeze sprang up, right square in our faces, and the snow started moving, whispering wickedly across the crust. By the time we'd changed sleighs it was shoulder high, and after we'd gotten the dog in and on our feet, the lines tied up and the lap robe pulled up over our heads, all we could see were two powerful rumps ahead of us. We spoke to them, and those two fine gentlemen took us home. Twice they stopped and one of us would get out, fumble up to their heads and open the gate they'd stopped for. They'd go through, wait until they felt somebody get into the sleigh and then head doggedly into the ground blizzard again. I wouldn't have believed anything could have faced it alone, and I still don't believe anything could have, except that old team. And after they'd brought us home – I can still see it, smell it and hear it – side by side in their stall in the warm barn, harness marks in the frost on their broad backs, the sweet scent of hay, the regular munching as they contentedly ate their oats and the tinkle of the icicles on their fetlocks as they shifted their weight from time to time. Fine friends in rough going, those two!

Years passed, and the two got pretty grey around the heads, but whatever they were asked to do they still did in a workmanlike fashion. There were younger teams for the hard work, and finally we only used them for getting out a little timber in the winter, mainly really so we'd have an excuse to see to it that they had plenty of grain in the rough weather. Right down Cody's alley, since it was all light, downhill work, but that didn't keep the smart son of a gun from talking Terry into slipping off to the barn with him any time they were left alone in the timber. It got so a man automatically took a hitch around the nearest stump with the log chain before dropping them, and it was worth it to slip back quietly to where you could watch Cody stealthily test out the hitch first one way and then the other to see if it was solid.

By the time the snow melted off the skid trails and the soft haze of a Montana spring crept into the air, they were fat and slick. A good time to end their work, so one bright day in late May I saddled up and led them over to the high benches on Otter Creek and turned them loose. There was plenty of grass; only a few fences broke the miles of rolling foothills, and they had it all to themselves. Come fall, before the weather got rough, I'd come up and take them down home for the winter.

Spring seemed to have gotten into the old devils' blood, for they tore away like two overgrown colts, circling, neighing, bucking ponderously and ripping up the tender grass with their joyous hooves. Then they swung back to me, touched noses with my saddle horse, scowled and nipped at him like they'd never seen him before, and turned to the serious business of feeding. As I rode home I could see them grazing shoulder to shoulder, outlined against the sky on a distant rise, partners.

It was maybe three months later that I happened to be in the vicinity again, and though several times during the summer I had caught distant sight of two black spots close together on some grassy ridge, for some reason I decided to see how they were getting along. I located them without any trouble, but as I rode down the green draw where they were feeding I could feel that something was wrong. Cody met us half way, eyeing us suspiciously, with the distrust and wildness of an old horse long on the range, his ears pricked inquiringly. He was fat and shiny as a two-year-old, but Terry, down the draw a little, barely lifted his head, and as I got closer I could see that he was pitifully thin and that a festering barb-wire cut slashed to the bone on one hind leg from hock to hoof. I hurriedly got down, and while Cody was scorning the friendly advances of my saddle horse I carefully examined the leg. No chance; the foot was almost off, flies and hot weather had done the rest. There was one thing to be done, and I looked up at the old fellow who was watching me so trustfully and hopefully. The partners would have to be split up. I straightened and slapped the old horse reassuringly, "Terry, old friend, I guess I've got to." I stood there rubbing the soft nose that nuzzled me in hopes of some oats, while Cody, his wildness forgotten at the possible prospect of a handout, crowded in on my other side. I stayed quite a while talking to those two, and petting them, and I cried a little, too. Finally I swung into the saddle and headed home, cursing barbed wire, and myself.

The next day when I got back to them, with rifle under my leg and grain in the sack tied behind my cantle, Terry was down. This made things a must, and after making friends with a very worried Cody, who was all ready to fight for his sidekick, I got down and poured them the grain and knelt with my arm over Terry's neck while they ate. At last the oats were nearly finished, so, sneaking the halter I'd brought over Cody's head, I led him to some aspens on the side of the draw and tied him back in them. He knew something was wrong, and he fumed and pawed as I left. Terry was just cleaning up the grain, and for just a minute I fondled the greying head. Then, hating myself, I jacked a shell into the chamber. The grand old fellow was just getting the last oat munched; he was happy, happier than he'd been for quite a while, as fine a gentleman as I'd ever known. I didn't look at his great soft eyes, I couldn't—and the rifle barrel crept up to the base of a silky ear—.

As the last trembling echo died slowly away there came a soft, frightened nicker from the aspens. A silence. Then a call, a lonely, lost call, followed the gunshot out through the evening twilight over the quiet hills. A heartbroken call. Cody knew.

It was a broken old horse that I led home that evening. The sparkle was gone from his eyes; his head, usually so alert, drooped; even his flanks looked gaunt and thin. He looked terribly old and lonesome, paying no attention to anything, plodding along beside my saddle horse and occasionally trying to turn back up country. It was a slow, sad trip. Even my horse was subdued, and the only sound was the slow beat of hooves through the grass and a coyote crying in the distance. When we got to the ranch, however, a change came over the old gelding which brought tears to my eyes. At the sight of the barn he brightened–for twenty years and better Terry had always been around the barn, and Cody plainly thought that there might be a chance that his partner was still there, somehow. He looked eagerly toward the open door when we arrived at the corral gate, and the minute I turned him loose he hurried to the barn whickering anxiously. In a moment he thundered out the door and around to the hay corral behind; perhaps Terry was there. Then down to the watering trough–perhaps–. But no, as I turned my pony loose I saw him come up from the waterway, head low, tail drooping, feet dragging. Hay, grain, cake; he showed not the least interest in any of my offerings, and as I went down to the house I could see him standing there, old and alone.

Time seemed to help a little. The old fellow slicked up again after a month or so, but he wasn't the same. Something was gone, and though once in a while he perked up and acted a little like himself, I believe it was just that, like any old person, he got to remembering and imagined that he and his partner were together again. Such times were few, though, so figuring it might cheer him up, toward spring I put him in with the weaner colts. I don't think he ever really noticed them; not even scowling when one of the little pests would slip in and steal a bite of his grain! So I was sort of glad one lovely May morning, with the red winged blackbirds trilling in the willows and the white collars of the killdeers bobbing as they prospected the banks of the spring, to find him sleeping when I went down at daylight to feed the stock. Or so I thought, at first. Just about a year from the time I'd turned the two of them out in the upper country.

Betty and Babe and I took a slip and opened a spot under the cottonwoods on the creek bank in the colt pasture and put the old horse in it. Then I saddled Smoky Joe, put a pack outfit on Snip, and we brought Terry down and laid him beside Cody. When the spot was covered and smoothed I hunted up a small slab of sandstone, chiseled their names on it and put it there.

The willows and chokecherries have pretty well covered the spot by now, and the stone is hard to find. The birds and the cottontails know where it is, though, and I hope all the colts that have grazed the pasture since then, and those that will do so in the future, know too. For I am horseman enough to believe that it has been, is, and will be, good for the little colts; for where those two great horses lie, there too, certainly, will be gentleness, honesty, courage, loyalty and love. *Cody and Terry.*

■ IVAN DOIG

Born in White Sulphur Springs, Montana, in 1939, Ivan Doig grew up in a family of Scottish ranchers and sheepherders. Doig attended Valier High School and left home as a scholarship student at Northwestern University, where he received an M.A. in journalism in 1962. After working as a journalist in the Midwest, Doig moved to Seattle and earned a Ph.D. in American history from the University of Washington in 1969. In 1978, This House of Sky, *Doig's memoir about growing up in Montana, was nominated for a National Book Award. Doig then went on to use his talents as historian and writer in* Winter Brothers *(1980) and* The Sea Runners *(1982). Doig is currently completing his Montana trilogy, which recounts the generational experiences of the McCaskell family in Montana.* Dancing at the Rascal Fair *(1987) is the second novel published in the trilogy.*

From This House of Sky

For the first time, mortality was crowding Charlie Doig slowly enough that he could think it through, and across that charring summer it brought him to the greatest change of mind he could make. He needed someone in readiness to step into his place in my life. The readiest person on the face of the planet was the one who had loomed in his dark musings all this while.

My father had everything to gulp back, then, when he set out to make truce with this phantom grandmother of mine. I can hear, as if in a single clear echo, the pivoting of our lives right there: Dad beginning his desperate phone call in the lobby of the Sherman Hotel, spelling out her name in an embarrassed half-shout to the operator, staring miserably at the cars nosing off around the prow of the hotel as the long-distance line hummed and howled in his ear. Then: *Ah. Hullo, Bessie, This is Charlie. Charlie, Charlie Doig. No, Ivan's fine, fine, he's right here. Ah. Say, would ye gonna be home on Sunday? We could, ah, come over maybe and see ye. All right. All right, then. G'bye.*

The Magnusson farm, in the county south of us, lay in what we called the Norskie Country—a coverlet of farmed slopes and creek bottoms coming down along the watershed of the Shields River from the icy snaggled peaks of the Crazy Mountains. It was better growing country than our valley—lower, milder—and the Scandinavian immigrants were exactly the thrifty and stubborn people to make it pay. After her years at the sage flats of Moss Agate, my grandmother's job at Magnusson's must have seemed almost silken. As we drove to his farm, the furrowed fields were ruled straight and brown on one side of the road, the green flow of hayfields curving with the creek on the other.

Magnusson's house, brown as the plowed earth, came out like a rampart from the slope which led down into the creek's slim valley. As we went up the outside flight of stairs, a man and a woman stepped onto the lofty porch and looked down at us with curiosity. Magnusson proved to be a steady-eyed, stocky farmer in his seventies, with white eyebrows and a mustache stained considerably less than white. His rumbled accent came like a growl against Dad's burr, but he said we were welcome in his house always, then withdrew to the front room with his newspaper from Norway.

That left us with my grandmother, whom I barely remembered from three or so years before. She gave Dad a thin *Hello*, beamed down at me and said, *Where's a kiss for your gramma?* I pecked her cheek and husked a *Hello* as close as I could to the tone she had given Dad.

The three of us bunched ourselves at the table in the vast kitchen, which was where serious visiting was done in the coffee-habited Norskie Country. As she and I munched our way through a plate of cookies, Dad lit cigarettes nervously and between puffs chewed away at the inside of his cheek. In a fashion, he was courting this wary woman much as he had courted her daughter twenty years earlier, but with grimness instead of love. What was unspoken but being said more plainly than anything in his careful chat was this: *We need you. I may die soon. Ivan must have someone to raise him.*

How much of their old rift between them was mended that Sunday, I do not know. I was too young to read the presence of the past, although I could sense it was somehow there in the kitchen with us. But rilesome as both of these figures could be about whatever might have happened in some yesterday, that first visit surely undid some of the anger just by not becoming a brawl.

I remember that at the late end of the afternoon I went out with her to feed the white geese in the farmyard, and that they hissed and founced around us until her dog, Shep, came barking, delirious to have an excuse to scatter the bullies. *Shoo 'em, Shep*! I remember her encouraging in a kind of angry pleasure: *Shoo 'em good! Sic 'em out of here, the goshdarn old fools!* I remember too that by the time Dad and I left, I was calling her *Grandma.*

For his part, Dad had seemed not to know what to call his own mother-in-law. He avoided calling her anything at all during our kitchen stay. But from the bottom of the stairs, he finally said up to her: *G'bye to ye, Lady. We'll come again next Sunday.*

Almost every weekend after that we would make the long drive to Magnusson's to visit her. The bargain Dad needed was being forged. It would take effect sooner than even he dreamed, because one among us in that odd group was dying, all right, but it was not my father. It was Martin Magnusson.

Just before old Magnusson slumped into the series of hospital stays which saw him decline to death, Dad bluntly asked my grandmother further into his plan. The doctoring in Montana was not helping him; his stomach flamed more and more now, he felt himself growing weaker. He was going to a place in Minnesota called the Mayo Clinic, and he wanted not to go alone, to have me with him—and her. Would she come?

In a week, the three of us stepped up into the eastbound train at Ringling. I remember of the trip only that Dad wearily slept and slept, and that when Grandma drowsed with her head back against the coach seat, she sometimes snorted herself awake with a long *kkkhhh* of a snore, and that I abandoned the pair of them to sit by the hour in the dome car and watch the worldscape of my first train journey.

At the destination in Minnesota, Dad hardly had the strength to carry a suitcase into the hotel where we would stay. He checked into the clinic, and immediately the doctors began days of tests on him. Grandma and I watched the people below from our hotel room far above the street, and spent time with Dad at the clinic whenever he was not in tests.

On the fourth day we were startled by a telegram for Grandma. Tom Ringer had died. His last torment of my grandmother was that she still felt something for him which made her want to return to Montana for his funeral. Dad agreed there was no choice, although it seemed to me there was all the choice in the world. She and I took the train back to Montana, leaving Dad to the doctors' solemn tests.

After the funeral, I went to stay again with Dad's brother Angus and his family, Grandma returned to Magnusson's farm. Several weeks dragged by before Dad followed us home to Montana, and when he came, he was a bony ghost with only a third of his stomach. That severe surgery was all that could keep him alive, the doctors had told him, and he would not be able to do any work for many months.

There the doctors had the matter backwards. Staying away from work, from knowing what ability was left in him, was what Charlie Doig could not do. Within a few weeks, he had hired on at a ranch at the western edge of the valley and there, pale and retching if he ate a spoonful too much at any mealtime, my father began slamming away at the job as he always had.

And he arranged a second matter, as much against the odds as the first. Grandma and I now were to live in Ringling, in the shambled small house where she had managed to put her own children through school and out into the world. From there I would ride the bus to school in White Sulphur Springs. That part of life changed little. But under a new roof with this restored woman called Lady and Grandma, almost all else did.

Ringling lay on the land, twenty miles to the south of White Sulphur Springs, as the imprint of what had been a town, like the yellowed outline on grass after a tent has been taken down. When the roadbed of the Milwaukee and St. Paul Railroad was diked through the site early in the century, a community – it was called Leader then – snappily built up around the depot: three hotels, several saloons, a lumber yard, stores, a two-story bank, a confectionery, even a newspaper office. When John Ringling's little railroad bumped down the valley from White Sulphur to link onto the Milwaukee and St. Paul main line, and the rumor followed that the headquarters of the great circus would be established there – surely the century's record for unlikelihood – the village was optimistically renamed Ringling. But before the end of the 1920's, the grandly adopted name was almost all that was left: many of the businesses had burned in a single wild night of flame. It was said, and more or less believed, that a Ku Klux Klan cross had blazed just before the lumber yard caught fire and spewed the embers that took half the town to the ground.

A few years later, another fire even less explainable than the first mopped up almost all of what was left. By the time Grandma and I moved there, Ringling stood as only a spattered circle of houses around several large weedy foundations. The adult population was about 50 persons, almost all of them undreamably old to me, and the livelihoods were a saloon, a gas station, a post office, Mike Ryan's store, the depot, and exactly through the middle of town, the railroad tracks which glinted and fled instantly in both directions.

Mornings, an eastbound passenger train tornadoed through, then came one tearing westward; afternoons, as people said, it was the same except opposite. My first days there I wondered about the travelers seen as tiny cutouts against the pullman windows – what they were saying when they looked out at us and our patchy, sprawled town-that-was-less-than-a-town. If they looked out.

These orange-and-black passenger trains whipped in and went off like kings and queens, potent and unfussed, on the dot. But freight trains banged around at all hours, and for a few weeks in autumn, Ringling made its own clamoring rail traffic as boxcars of sheep and cattle trundled back and forth from the loading pens at the edge of town. Otherwise, the town did almost nothing but doze, kept sleepily alive by the handful of people who lived there out of habit and the few ranchers who used it as their gas-and-mail point. The single wan tendril to its past was Mike Ryan's store, which I lost not a moment before visiting.

Mike Ryan was a very ancient man by then, near-blind, looming in his goggling spectacles and flat cap amid a dust-grayed avalanche of hardware, harness, stray dry goods, and stale groceries such as the bakery goods his cats liked to sleep on. The second words Mike spoke to you, after a broguey *Hello* and learning what it was you wanted, always were: *Now it's here if I can just find it.*

And it would be, for Mike Ryan's had been a perfect country store in its time, a vast overstocked bin of merchandise behind its high false front and under its roof with the yellow airplane signals painted hugely on. But now, as if the years were caving in on it, the enterprise was becoming more and more muddled, dim, musty. At times Mike himself would dim away into some reverie and would no longer see a person come in the door, and you could stand for moments, watched only by his brindle cats, and hear him breathe an old man's heavy resigned breathing.

Just as Mike Ryan's was the fading memory of a general store and Ringling itself the last scant bones of a town, Grandma's house turned out to be the shell of a place to live in. It counted up, all too rapidly, into a kitchen, living room and bedroom, each as narrow as a pullman car and about a third as long. The rooms had stood empty for more than ten years–empty of people, that is, for the flotsam of Grandma's earlier family leaned and teetered everywhere. Diving into the dusty boxes and dented metal suitcases, I came up with a boomerang sent by the son who had moved to Australia after the war, a lavender-enameled jewelry box which had been my mother's, albums of strange people in stiff clothes.

The place was stacked with dead time, and the first few days Grandma could not move in it without tears brimming her eyes. When at last she could, she called me into the bedroom and wordlessly began to dig down through the stacks and piles atop a low reddish wooden chest just larger than a seaman's trunk. As I watched, she propped the lid, looked down into the tumble of old clothes and ancient bedding inside, and snuffled. Then a quick honk into her handkerchief, and she began talking in a tone angrier than I had yet heard from her: *This here was your mother's hope chest. The kids' dad made it back at Moss Agate, when she first started going with Charlie. With your dad, I mean. He worked on this at nights for the longest time. See, he didn't have anything to make it from but some pieces of flooring, but he wanted her to have a hope chest of some kind. He did a good job with it. He could when he wanted to. It's sat here all these years. I want it to be yours now.* The back of my throat filled and tightened as she talked. I gulped, managed to say *All right*, and walked carefully from the room so as not to plunge from it.

Life with Grandma proved to be full of squalls of emotion of that sort. For one thing, she had a temper fused at least as short as Dad's. But where he would explode into words, she would go silent, lips clamped. If she could be persuaded to say anything, the words were short and snapped, displeasure corking each sentence, and you discovered you were better off to let her be wordless.

I know now that such silences came out of years of having no other defense: of being alone on a remote ranch, nowhere to go, no other person to unbend to, when a stormy husband went into his own black moods. But I did not understand it then, and found myself suddenly in a household which could change as if a cloud had zoomed across the sun.

The quickest annoyance I could cause was to look at her when she had her false teeth out for brushing, and after a time or two of blundering into that, I would veer off or turn my back if I saw it in prospect. There even was a way she could rile herself: as I had guessed on the train trip to Minnesota, Grandma was a thunderous snorer, and in the middle of the night was apt to snort herself awake and mutter irately about it.

But other of the unexpectednesses which kept tumbling out of her were entirely easy-tempered. To be doing something even when there was nothing to be done, Grandma sat at the kitchen table and played game after game of solitaire. When the cards continued to turn up wrong for her, she would cheat just once to try to get the game moving again, which I thought was balanced good sense. And whenever she won, the identical proclamation: *I got that game, boy. What do you think of that?*

Also, she was perpetually ready to go into a full-sail version of my childhood I had never heard before. When she had visited my father and mother so often in the first three or four years of my life, it had been she who spent many of the patient hours to teach me to read, the words fastening in my mind as I sat in her lap and watched her finger move along with her reading. And much else: *Oh, how you used to coax me to sing. 'Ah-AH-ah! SING, gramma!' you'd say. So I'd have to hold you in the rocker and sing by the hour. . . . 'Poor me,' you'd say when you didn't get your way, and you'd pooch out your lower lip so sad. . . . Lands, you used to scare me half to death, the way you ran down that hill at the Stewart Ranch. There was a big tree way up on the slope, and you'd take your dog up there and here the both of you would come, straight down. I used to hold my breath. . . .*

And back beyond all that, she had the news of how I'd arrived into the world: *You were born in Dr. McKay's hospital in White Sulphur, it's that building just up the hill from—oh, what's the name of that joint? Hmpf. The Stockman, just up the hill from the Stockman. When you were born, you had two great big warts right here in front of your ear, and your right foot splayed off like this, and you had the reddest hair. You were something grand to see, all right . . .*

Nor was that nearly all. At times she talked a small private language which must have come from those two islanded times of childhood, her own growing up on the Wisconsin farm and her children's years at Moss Agate. Words jigged and bellied and did strange turns then: *I'll have a sipe more of coffee, but if I eat another bite, I'll busticate. . . . Get the swatter and dead that fly for me, pretty please? . . . Hmpf, I been settin' so long my old behinder is stiff. . . .* Anything which lay lengthwise was *longways* to her; the stanchions of a milking barn were *stanchels,* the cows themselves were a word of my mother's as a child, *merseys.*

Her sayings too took their own route of declaring. That it was time to get a move on: *Well, this isn't buying the baby a shirt nor paying for the one he's got on.* Or to take a doubtful chance: *Here goes nothin' from nowhere.* Or when she did not understand something I read to her from one of my books: *Like the miser man's well, too deep for me, boy.* Or when she did understand: *I see, said the blind man to his deaf wife.* Neighbors were rapidly tagged with whatever they deserved: *She goes around lookin' like she's been drawed through a knothole backwards. . . . That pair is close as three in a bed with one kicked out . . . That tribe must never heard that patch beside patch is neighborly, but patch upon patch is beggarly.*

Each time the prairie wind swirled up her dress, there would be said: *Hmpf! Balloon ascension!* At least one meal of the day, she would pause between forkfuls and pronounce like a happy benediction: *I hear some folks say they get so tired of their own cooking. By gee, I never have.* And whenever something irked her, which was sufficiently often, she had her own style of not-quite cussing: *Gee gosh, god darn, gosh blast it. . . .*

And always the stories, such as the one of an early Moss Agate neighbor, a homesteader, who had a head huge and twisted as an ogre's. After a lifetime of despair over his own ugliness, the man began rethinking it all and soon before he died proudly willed his skull to medical science. As I shivered a bit at the tale, Grandma chuckled and said in her declaring style: *Headless man into heaven, think of that.*

To my surprise, dogs and cats fully counted into her conversations. Dad likely had not glanced in a cat's direction since the last time my mother had scratched Pete Olson's gray ears, and he spoke to dogs only to send them kiting off after strayed livestock. But Grandma communed with them all, especially all dogs. There had been one or another of them, generally named Shep, in her households ever since a huge woolly sheepdog back on her parents' Wisconsin farm, and the last of that name had moved to Ringling with us.

A fine white-and-tan with a hint of collie about him, Shep had gone old and as lazy as my grandmother would allow anything to be. He panted as he walked and spent most of life stretched under the kitchen table, where he filled all the space there was. Several times a day grandma would shift her feet as she sat at the table playing solitaire, and there would be an explosion of pained howling and outraged sympathy: *Well, you shouldn't be there right under my feet, that's what you get! Serves you right, you aren't hurt, big baby. Come here, let me pet it, pretty please, that's all right, there you're all better now . . .*

Grandma's sure sign of good humor was to break into roughhouse play with Shep or any other available dog, setting off wild barking and leaping which invariably ended with fresh bleeding scratches on her arms. By then, all the skin between wrist and elbow carried white nicks of scar, as if she had been lightly scored with a scalpel time after time. But that annoyed her less than the bathroom habits Shep and the others ungratefully put on display in front of her. Their natural post-sniffing and leg-lifting sent her into prompt fury: *Shep! Don't be so sappy! Get away from there, you darned fool!*

Cats, too, aloof wayfarers that they were, did not manage to live up to her standard of expectation. Any that passed by, she fed as if they were famished but naughty orphans, scolding and huffing over them all the while she filled the dish with milk and bread: *What do you mean bumming around here? Why don't you stay to home where you've got good grub? I ought to let you go hungry, sappy old thing! Here, eat!* The only creatures in her world which got no affection with their scoldings were magpies. She hated their scavenging habits, and when she saw one making its black-and-white flash of glide in the air anywhere within range of her voice, she cut loose: *GIT! Git yourself out of here, god darned old thing, there's nothing gonna die here for you to peck on! Git! GIT!*

Grandma and I settled in, if living amid such salvoes could be called settling in, by somehow coaxing the tiny Ringling house to stretch and once more make way for people. When the single closet was full, we stashed boxes and suitcases under the bed and davenport as if ballasting the place. All the time we lived there, Grandma grumbled things in and out from under the bed, vowing someday she'd not have to do so. The ironing board went in with a tangle of fishpoles behind a door, my mound of paperback books covered the hopechest at the foot of the one bed.

My bed, for I learned at once that living with my grandmother always meant that she claimed the worst accommodations for herself, and the dreariest chores. This inside-out chivalry she must have formed in the Moss Agate years, when she found that she minded the drudgeries there less than did her edgy husband or my frail mother or her frisky sons and so took most of them upon herself. Beyond that, there simply was her assumption that if I was to be a special benefit, she would happily pay any price in chores.

Dad had been thoroughly right about one high matter: my grandmother did want me as a child to raise, the way a retired clipper captain might have yearned to make one last voyage down the trade winds under clouds of sail. Despite Dad's wariness of it, there had been little chance that she could have arrived in my life without his arranging it. Now that he had done so, here I was as the bonus child for her penchant about family–by several years the oldest of her grandchildren, and the shadow-son of her lost daughter. Everything in her said to treat me as a gift, and in terms of this new Ringling household it came out as her granting me the bed and the bedroom while she slept on the davenport in the living room, her climbing out first in the chilly mornings to light the kitchen stove with fuel oil and match, her doing every other task the place needed–until blessed common sense edged through and suggested that what might do me more good would be to have duties of my own. *How do you feel about that?* she offered cautiously. *I think it wouldn't hurt you none, do you?*

Unarguably it wouldn't, and I began then to take my turn at keeping the woodbox piled with firewood and the ashes emptied from the bottom of the kitchen range. But the main and everlasting chore was the water bucket, because the house had no well, and a neighborhood pump had gone rusty from years of disuse. The rain barrel at a corner of the house did the job for laundering clothes and a washtub bath apiece for us once a week. But every dipperful of the water for our daily use had to be pumped next door–I paced it at seventy steps in one of my earliest trudges–at the house of Grandma's long-time friends, Kate and Walter Badgett. And by unexpected fortune that perpetual bucketing carried with it something new and rich, for necessity's water was the least of what this ancient pair could add to our Ringling life.

There were enormities about the Badgetts which somehow seemed to bolster us simply by existing so near at hand. These began with size and age, and went on through manner. Side by side, the two weathered figures loomed like barn and silo. Kate was pillowed in fat, so wide that she seemed to wedge apart the arms of the huge easy chair where she spent her days. Atop that crate of a body was an owlish face, and a swift tongue that could operate Walter all day long and still have time to tell what the rest of Ringling was doing. On her desk by the front window which looked across the tracks to the gas station and post office-store, Kate kept her pair of binoculars. Who had come to town, for how long and maybe even what they bought—it all came up the magnifying tunnel of vision to Kate, then went out with new life, as if having added to itself while re-echoing through that bulk of body.

Then in some midsentence of hers, Walter would appear from one or another of his chores, in his pauseful way looming tall as a doorway, and nearly as still—a rangy silent sentinel with great hands hung on poles of arms. His face was more an eagle's than any other I have seen on a man: the spare lines of brow and cheek and the chisel of nose, somehow with the hint of a beak, and beneath it all, the mouth which turned down sharply at its corners not from mood but just the decades of pursing around a cusp of chewing tobacco.

Walter's eyes were a pale, flat, seen-it-all-before shade of blue. Once I heard someone tell of seeing him angry, which I never had. *He was tending bar for the day at the saloon there in Ringling, and one of Rankin's cowboys came in with a load on. He was helling around up and down the bar, and Walter told him, 'Better settle down a bit.' The Rankin man cussed him and said, 'Who the hell're you, old feller?' Walter came leaning across that bar, those blue eyes snapping sparks. 'I said you'd better settle down, or I'll settle you.' The Rankin man never said another word.*

Both coming onto eighty years old, the Badgetts were in the kind of outliving contest which very old couples sometimes seem to have, each aging only against the other instead of against time. Naturally, Kate was going to win, and she did, by nearly a decade. But at this point they both seemed as little changing as glaciers, and Walter in particular had slowed life to the exact amble he wanted. Midmornings, he would stroll to his woodpile halfway between his house and ours, and begin chopping with giant strokes: the axe easily high, then down in a slow arc, a *whunk!* as the wood blasted apart and spun away into the dirt. Walter would straighten, loose a long splatter of tobacco juice, study around town for anything to report to Kate, reach with one hand to set another piece of wood on the chopping block, then *whunk!* again.

Multiplying that woodpile, which would have kept half the county snug for a winter, spent his mornings. After lunch, he could be seen, in his slow angular stroll, headed for the post office to bring Kate the day's letters and any capturable gossip. Even his responses to her could come slow as a measuring now because he had a fitful mild deafness which gave him the excuse to answer an innocent uncomprehending *Hnnh?* while he mulled the latest of her constant orders.

Theirs was a household at once curt and cordial. Knock on the door, and Kate's voice boomed a single word like an empress's: *COME!* I was puzzled that she had the habit of calling other women only by their last names. Grandma always was simply *Ringer* to her. But Kate's brusqueness had a vast gap in it. Over the years she had ironed every thinkable vice out of Walter except for his habit of chewing tobacco; for that, he was permitted a coffee can behind the stove to spit in. Yet when she talked to him for any reason besides an order, the tongue that banged bluntly on every other life in town suddenly went soft and crooned, of all words, *Hubby*.

Walter had drifted north from Texas as a young cowboy, and I would learn from men who had worked with him in the valley that he was a storied man with horse and rope. The stories included the hint that he had departed Texas after a scrape against the law. Even here, Kate matched him: out of her background wafted the whisper that in Prohibition times she had been one of the area's most reliable vendors of bootleg whiskey.

In all their ways, then, these two serene old outlaws put forth a steadiness, a day-upon-day carol out of the valley's past, and for all I knew, out of the past of all the world.

Up the slope from our house, the other regular chimes in our Ringling life spoke weightier accents, graver outlooks. Mr. and Mrs. Brekke both had been born in Norway, and both come young to the new life in America: they met and married, found a small ranch beyond Ringling where they endured through to prosperity, and now, their family long grown, the pair of them lived at the top of the tiny town like gentlefolk quite surprised at their own new position of courtliness.

Each early afternoon, Mr. Brekke's serious singsong—*HEL-lo*—would sound on our porch, and he would hand in the mail he had brought from the post office, already backing away with a gentle smile from our thanks and invitations to come in for a moment. Mrs.

Brekke did come, at least once a day either to our house or to the Badgetts', to hear the doings of the town with a steadily astonished *Ohh, myy!* Leaving, she invariably turned and urged: *Why don't you come up sometimes for ice cream and cake?*

The Brekkes owned the one house in all of Ringling that looked as if it truly had been built to live in rather than just to hold boards up off the ground. A white-fenced yard rulered neatly around it, framing half a dozen small tidy trees–the only ones in town–and a many-windowed sun porch which opened the entire front of the house. The first owners were a husband and wife who had been the local schoolteachers, a couple storied for their learning, and their books and a decade or so of magazines came to the Brekkes with the house. These I mined weekend after weekend, carrying home an armload of old issues of *National Geographic* and *Life* and *Collier's* and *Saturday Evening Post* at a time, reading them lying on my bed with the hot bedlamp at my ear. Mr. and Mrs. Brekke admired education almost as if it were a magic potion. When their own children were growing up and one or another would protest not knowing the answer to something, Mary Brekke had a single iron reply: *Well, you better learn!* Now they encouraged me into each new printed trove as soon as I had finished the last one–*Done with that batch?* Mr. Brekke would cry: *Come in for some more!* And Mrs. Brekke would cry after: *Then sit a minute for some ice cream and cake, can't you?*

The Brekke household's secondhand magazines and books became a second school for me, more imagination lit from it than from the one I rode the bus to in White Sulphur Springs each weekday. I read straight through whatever shone dark on the snowfield pages, a visit to Scintillating Siam lapping on into the swashbuckling of Horatio Hornblower, which likely took place back-to-back with a Clarence Budington Kelland shoot-out in the Arizona Territory. I read, that is to say, as an Eskimo who had never before seen a movie might watch the newsreel and then the cartoon and then the feature film without ever knowing to separate them in his mind, simply letting himself be taken with the habited flow of flashing images.

It all began adding up in my head in deposits which astonished Grandma. Her own information about the world was as spotty as mine was swirlish. She had been born when a man named Grover Cleveland was President. That she had no idea of this merely spoke her own unusual way of having been brought up. She was perplexed that there had been two Presidents named Roosevelt; Franklin Delano had served such a span in her adult life that she could easily believe he had been in the White House back at the turn of the century as well. The labor leader John L. Lewis and the boxing champion Joe Louis consistently mixed their names for her, and I was not at all surprised when she asked me if the Hemenway who intoned the news on the radio was the Hemingway whose books showed up now and then in my rummage from the Brekkes. She seemed entirely pleased with my knack for knowledge, and quickly learned to use it as a kind of utility, asking me to spell out stubborn words when she wrote a letter, to work out the balance in her checkbook, to comparison-shop the Monkey Ward and Sears, Roebuck mail-order catalogues for our items of clothing.

But lore ran both ways between us, and generally hers was more useful than mine, having come straight out of life instead of from printed pages. She recalled for me a pastime that her sons once tried, setting up a lemonade stand and taking turns to shout across town the advertising she taught them: *Lemonade, lemonade! Stirred by an old maid! With a spade!* I thought it over, but at last decided the business wasn't worth reviving; Ringling's population had plummeted so far that the only buying traffic I could foresee was Walter Badgett and Mr. Brekke. But another idea Grandma recalled had the right feel. The same enterprising sons had sent away for any free mailings they came across in magazines and, since Ringling had no street names, conjured for themselves whatever elaborate addresses they could think of. I got out paper and envelopes and set to work on the most current Brekke magazines. Quickly, offers for stamp collecting kits or pleas for me to get rich selling salve were pouring into the post office in care of *I. Clark Doig, 776 Sagebrush Acres* or *14 Jackrabbit Boulevard* or *801 Gopher Gulch* or whatever other elegancy I'd been able to dream up. Grandma much admired my gaudy mail; I much admired her for the lode of boy-raising behind it.

That exact lode, I began to find, came ready more and more as adolescence perked in me. Together, she and I pondered the pale frizz of hair taking over my upper lip. At the precise age when other boys were praying for some hint of whiskers, I badly wanted to be rid of that downy white shadow. Grandma of course had been through this—and apparently everything else—before. She came up with a salve called a depilatory which erased the fuzz, right enough, and felt as if my lip were being scorched away with it.

Impressed with her results, I asked if she knew anything to be done about my hair, which had a stubborn tendency to divide itself floppily on the exact top of my head, as if I had been bashed there with a cleaver. At once she dug out one of her discarded nylon stockings and snipped and sewed it into a snug skullcap. *We'll damp your hair down before you go to bed and you sleep with this over it, and we'll see how that does.* How it did was that within weeks her remedial yarmulka tamed the thatch into the pompadour I had worn out a lifetime of combs trying to achieve.

She was as handy with my other disquiets, such as the passion for baseball which had been brewing in me. The onset of this likely had come from Dad, who in his try-anything youth had played catcher for the Sixteen community team. *Did I tell ye the time we had a big Fourth of July game goin' while Jack Dempsey was fightin' Gibbons up in Shelby? Nineteen twenty-three that would have been. We were havin' a helluva game down there by Sixteen Creek, but somebody'd run down from the telegraph office at the end of every round and tell us what was happenin' with the fight, so it took us half the afternoon to play an inning or two. . . .* Then at World Series time in 1946, Dad had got tired of listening to his saloon chums mutter about the invincibility of the vaunted Boston Red Sox team and uncharacteristically began betting them that it wasn't so. He quickly had bets in every bar in town, and they added up to a couple of hundred dollars, undoubtedly the easiest money of his life, when the St. Louis Cardinals won for him.

Whether it was that windfall or some other encouragement–it may simply have been that Ringling was a perfect place to tinker at imagination, because so little else about the town was in working order any more–I had begun to daydream of myself as a shortstop or a pitcher, or maybe both, strolling across the infield to the mound every fourth day or so to fire fastballs. Now, all of a sudden, I had a teammate. Grandma tirelessly would toss a rubber ball for me to bat back and forth across Ringling's emptinesses. Our audience was Walter Badgett, launching his contemplative splatters of tobacco juice as he glanced over from his woodchopping. Once in a while the ball would bounce toward Walter, and he would pick it up and fling it back in a sweeping stiff-armed motion, like a weathered old catapult which still could crank up. Grandma and I went on with this even if it rained, playing catch inside the house by bouncing the ball between us the scant twenty feet from the kitchen door through the living room to my bedroom.

It comes as a continual surprise to me to realize that even here, where she first came into my life, my grandmother already was nearly sixty years old. Everything I can remember of this time has the tint of her ageless energy. All other entertainment failing, she was even willing to wrestle, and we would tussle stiff-armed against one another until we both giggled to a halt and she panted herself down into a chair saying *Whoof! Nosir, you're just too tough for your old gramma, I can't keep up with a wildcat like you.* And in half a minute, she would be up and in the kitchen, into the making of the next batch of bread or cinnamon rolls or butter cookies.

From Dancing At the Rascal Fair

Adair had barely come across the threshold when Rob and I had to trail his wethers and my lambs to the railhead for shipping. Quick after that, school began again and I was making the daily ride from homestead to the South Fork and then back. In weekends and other spare minutes, winter had to be readied for. It sometimes seemed I saw more of Scorpion than I did of my new wife.

She said nothing of my here-and-gone pace, just as I said nothing of her beginning attempts at running a household. Accustomed to tea, Adair applied the principle of boiling to coffee and produced a decoction nearly as stiff as the cup. Her meals were able enough, but absentminded, so to speak; the same menu might show up at dinner and at supper, then again at the same meals the next day, as if the food had forgotten its way home. Courage, I told my stomach and myself, we'd eventually sort such matters out; but not just yet. There already was a problem far at the head of the line of all others. Adair's lack of liking for the homestead and, when you come all the way down to it, for Montana.

Again, her words were not what said so. I simply could see it, feel it in her whenever she went across the yard to fling out a dishpan of water and strode back, all without ever elevating her eyes from her footsteps. The mountains and their weather she seemed to notice only when they were at their most threatening. I counted ahead the not many weeks to winter and the white cage it would bring for someone such as Adair, and tried to swallow that chilly future away.

Before the winter found its chance to happen, though, there was a Friday end-of-afternoon when a session of convincing Ninian on the need for new arithmetic books—*ay, are you telling me there are new numbers to be learned these days, Angus?*—didn't get me home from the schoolhouse until suppertime. During my ride, I had watched the promise of storm being formed, the mountains showing only as shoals in the clouds by the time I stepped down from Scorpion.

"Sorry, Dair," I said, providing her with a kiss, and headed sharp for the washbasin while she put the waiting food on the table. "It's just lucky I didn't end up arguing with Ninian by moonlight."

"The old dark comes so early these days," she said, and took the glass chimney off to light the lamp wick.

"We get a little spell of this weather every year about now," I mollified her as I craned around to peer out the window at the clouds atop the mountains, hoping they would look lessened, "but then it clears away bright as a new penny for a while. We'll be basking in Indian summer before you know what's hap–" The sound of shatter, the cascade of glass, spun me to Adair.

She was staring dumbstruck at the table strewn with shrapnel of the lamp chimney, shards in our waiting plates and in the potatoes and the gravy and other food dishes as if a shotgun loaded with glass had gone off. In her hand she still held a glinting jagged ring of glass, the very top of the chimney.

I went and grasped her, wildly scanning her hands, arms, up the aproned front of her, up all the fearful way to her eyes. No blood. *Mercy I sought, mercy I got.* Adair gazed back at me intact. She did not look the least afraid, she did not look as if she even knew what the fusillade of glass could have inflicted on her. Tunnels of puzzle, those eyes above the twin freckle marks. She murmured, "It just–flew into pieces. When I went to put it back on the lamp."

"That happens the rare time, the heat cracks it to smithereens. But what matters, none of it cut you? Anywhere? You're sure you're all right, are you, Dare?"

"Yes, of course. It surprised me, is all. And look at poor supper." Adair sounded so affronted about the surprise and the stabbing of supper that it could have been comical. But my heart went on thundering as I stepped to the shelf where I kept a spare lamp chimney.

In the morning I said what had lain in my mind through the night.

"Dair? You need to learn to ride a horse today."

She thought it was one of my odder jokes. "I do, do I. What, do I look like a fox-hunting flopsie to you? Lady Gorse on her horse?"

"No, I mean it. As far back in here as we are, no one else near around, it'd be well for you to know how to handle a horse. Just in case, is all." In case lamp chimneys detonate in innocent moments, in case any of the accidents and ailments of homestead life strike when I am not here with you, I was attempting to say without the scaring words. "I'm living proof that riding a horse isn't all that hard. Come along out, Scorpion and I'll have you galloping in no time." I got up from my breakfast chair and stood waiting.

"Now?"

"Now. Out to the barn." I put my arm in hers, ready escort. "Scorpion awaits."

Her gaze said *all right, I will humor you, show me what a horse is about if you must.*

At the barn I demonstrated to her the routine of saddling, then unsaddled Scorpion and said: "Your turn."

"Angus. This is—"

"No, no, you don't do it with words. Hands and arms are unfortunately required. They're there at the ends of your shoulders if I'm not wrong." No smile from her. Well, I couldn't help that. "Just lift the saddle onto him and reach slowly under for the cinch."

Beside the big gingerbread-colored horse, Adair was a small pillar of reluctance.

"Now then, Dair," I encouraged. "Saddle him and get it over with."

She cast me a glance full of *why?*

"Please," I said.

The saddle seemed as big as she was, but she managed to heave it onto Scorpion. Then in three tries she struggled the cinch tight enough that I granted it would probably hold.

"There," she panted. "Are you satisfied?"

"Starting to begin to be. Now for your riding lesson. *Over Pegasus I'll fling my leg/and never a shoe will I need to beg.*" Verse didn't seem to loft her any more than the rest of my words. "What you do is put your left foot in the stirrup," I demonstrated with myself, "take hold of the saddle horn, and swing yourself up this way." From atop Scorpion I sent my most encouraging look down to Adair, then swung off the horse. "Your turn. Left foot into stirrup."

"No." She sounded decisive about it.

"Ah, but you've got to. This isn't Nethermuir. Montana miles are too many for walking, and there are going to come times when I'm not here to hitch up the team and wagon for you. So unless you're going to sprout wings or fins, Dair, that leaves you horseback."

"No, Angus. Not today. I have this dress on. When I can sew myself a riding skirt—"

"There's nobody around to see you but me. And I've glimpsed the territory before, have I not?" I hugged her and urged her, wishing to myself that I knew how to snipper Barclay stubbornness into five-foot chunks to sell as crowbars. "You can do this. My schoolgirls ride like Comanches."

"I'm not one of your wild Montana schoolgirls. I'm your wife, and I–"

"I realize that makes your case harder, love, but we'll try to work around that handicap." She didn't give me the surrendering smile I'd hoped that would bring, either. By now I realized she wasn't being stubborn, she wasn't being coy, she was simply being Adair. At her own time and choosing, riding skirt newly on, she might announce her readiness. Fine, well, and good, but this couldn't wait. "I'm sorry, Dair, but there's no halfway to this. Come on now," I directed. "Up."

"No."

I suppose this next did come out livelier than I intended.

"Dair, lass, you came across the goddamned Atlantic Ocean! Getting up into a saddle is no distance, compared. Now will you put your foot here in the stirrup–"

"No! Angus, I won't! You're being silly with all your fuss about this." Adair herself wasn't quite stamping that foot yet, but her voice was. She sounded as adamant as if I'd wakened her in the middle of the night and told her to go outside and tie herself upside down in the nearest tree.

The only thing I could think of to do, I did. I stepped to Adair and lifted her so that she was cradled in my arms. Surprised pleasure came over her face, then she giggled and put her arms rewardfully around my neck. The giggling quit as I abruptly took us over beside Scorpion.

"Angus, what–"

"Upsy-daisy, lazy Maisie," I declared. "Whoa now, Scorpion," and with a grunt I lifted Adair, feet high to clear the saddle horn and I hoped aiming her bottom into the saddle.

"Angus! AnGUS! ANGUS, quit! What're you–"

"Dair, let yourself down into the saddle. Whoa, Scorpion, steady there, whoa now. Don't, Dair, you'll scare the horse. Just get on, you're all but there. Whoa now, whoa–"

Her small fists were rapping my back and chest, and not love taps, either. But with no place else but midair to go, at last she was in the saddle, my arms clasped around her hips to keep her there. Scorpion gave us a perturbed glance and flicked his nearest ear. "Dair, listen to me. Sit still, you have to sit still. Scorpion isn't going to stand for much more commotion. Just sit a minute. You have to get used to the horse and let him get used to you."

She was gulping now, but only for breath after our struggle; her tears were quiet ones. "Angus, why are you doing this?"

"Because you have to know how to handle a horse, Dair. You just absolutely do, in this country." I buried my face in her dress while the sentences wrenched themselves out of me. "Dair, I'm afraid for you. I could never stand it if something happened to you on account of marrying me. An accident, you here alone, this place off by itself this way . . ." The ache of my fear known to both of us now. I had lost one woman. If I lost another, lost her because of the homestead–"But this place is all I've got. We've got. So you have to learn how to live here. You just have to."

A silent time, then I raised my head to her. She was wan but the tear tracks were drying. "Hello you, Dair Barclay. Are you all right?"

"Y-yes. Angus, I didn't know–how much it meant to you. I thought you were just being–"

I cleared enough of the anxiety out of my throat to say: "Thinking will lead to trouble time after time, won't it. Now then, all you need do is take these reins. Hold them in your right hand, not too slack but not too tight either, there's the way. Don't worry, I'll be hanging tight onto Scorpion's bridle and first we'll circle the yard. Ready?"

You won't find it in the instructions on the thing, but for the first year of a marriage, time bunches itself in a dense way it never quite does again. Everything happens double-quick and twice as strong to a new pair in life–and not just in the one room of the house you'd expect.

Here, now, in the time so far beyond then, when I see back into that winter after Adair and I were married, it abruptly is always from the day in May. The day that stayed with us as if stained into our skins. Take away that day and so much would be different, the history of Adair and myself and–

Even on the calendar of memory, though, winter must fit ahead of May, and that first winter of Adair and myself outlined us to one another as if we were black stonepiles against the snow. After the first snowfall the weather cleared, the air was crisp without being truly cold yet. Being outside in that glistening weather was a chance to glimpse the glory the earth can be when it puts its winter fur on, and Rob and I tried any number of times to talk Adair into bundling up and riding the haysled with us as we fed the sheep. "Come along out and see the best scenery there is. They'd charge you a young fortune for an outing like it in the Alps." But nothing doing. Adair quietly smiled us away, brother as well as husband. "Adair can see the winter from where she is," she assured us.

For a while my hope was that she was simply content to be on the inside of winter looking out, the way she paused at any window to gaze out into Scotch Heaven's new whiteness. That hope lasted until a choretime dusk soon after the start of the snow season when George Frew, quiet ox in a sheepskin coat and a flap cap, trooped behind me into the house. "Anything you'd like from town besides the mail, Dair?" I asked heartily. "George is riding in tomorrow."

"Yes," she responded, although you couldn't really say it was to George or myself. Times such as this, conversing with her was like speaking to a person the real Adair had sent out to deal with you. Wherever the actual mortal was otherwise occupied at the moment, the one in front of us stated now: "Adair would like a deck of cards."

George positively echoed with significant silence as he took those words in. Flora Duff might want darning thread, Jen Erskine might want dried peaches for a pie, but what did Adair McCaskill want but a—

"You heard the lady, George," I produced with desperate jollity. "We're in for some fierce cribbage in this household, these white nights. Kuuvus's best deck of cards, if you please. I'll ride down and pick it up from you tomorrow night."

Thereafter, Adair would indeed play me games of cribbage when I took the care to put my reading aside and suggest it in an evening. But her true game was what I had known she intended. Solitaire. After the deck of cards arrived, I began to notice the seven marching columns of solitaire laid out on the sideboard during the day. Aces, faces, and on down, the queues of cards awaiting their next in number. Adair amid her housework would stop and deal from the waiting deck to herself, play any eligible card where it belonged, and then go on about whatever she had been doing, only to stop again her next time past and repeat the ritual.

But I soon was repeating my own silent ritual that winter, wasn't I. My own solitary preoccupation. Against every intention in myself, I was soon doing that.

The schoolhouse dances brought it on. At the first dance in my schoolroom, fresh silver of snowfall softening the night, I was in mid-tune with Adair when I caught sight of Anna and Isaac Reese entering. The sensation instantly made itself known within me, unerringly as the first time I ever saw Anna. Toussaint Rennie once told me of a Blackfeet who carried in his ribcage an arrowhead from a fight with the Crow tribe. That was the way the feeling for Anna was lodged in me: just there, its lumped outline under the skin same and strong as ever. *Dair, here in my arms, what am I going to do with myself and this welt inside me? Marrying you was supposed to cure me of Anna. Why hasn't it?* Until that moment of Anna entering from the snow-softened dark, not having laid eyes on her since the day Adair and I were married, I was able to hope it was my body alone, the teasing appetite of the loins, that made me see Anna so often as I waited for sleep. *I am not inviting any of this, Dair, I never invited it.* Her in the midst of this same music, that first night of glorious dancing here in my schoolroom. Her in the Noon Creek school, turning to me under a word in the air, her braid swinging decisively over her shoulder to the top of her breast. *Dair, I wish you could know, could understand, could not be hurt by it.* Anna beneath me, watching so intently as we made the dawn come, arousing each other as the sun kindled the start of morning. Double daybreak such as I had just once shared with a woman, not the woman I had wed. Night upon night I had been opening my eyes to explode those scenes, driving sleep even farther away. Beside me, Adair who slept as if she was part of the night; there in the dark was the one place she seemed to fit the life I had married her into. But this other inhabitant of my nights–I knew now, again, that whether she was Anna Ramsay or Anna Reese or Anna Might-Have-Been-McCaskill, every bit of me was in love with the woman as drastically as ever.

How many times that winter, to how many tunes, was I going to tread the floor of my South Fork schoolroom or her Noon Creek one, glimpsing Anna while Adair flew in my arms? I couldn't not come to the dances, even if Adair would have heard of that, which she definitely would not have. To her, the dances were the one time that Montana winter wasn't Montana winter.

"She's another person, out there in the music." This from Rob. He meant it to extol, but that he said anything at all about an oddness of Adair was a surprise.

"She is that," I couldn't but agree. Dancing with Adair you were partnered with some gliding being she had become, music in a frock, silken motion wearing a ringleted Adair mask. It was what I had seen when she danced with Allan Frew after the shearing, a tranced person who seemed to take the tunes into herself. Where this came from, who knew. At home she didn't even hum. But here from the first note to last she was on the floor with Rob or me or occasional other partners, and it was becoming more than noticeable that she never pitched in with the other wives when they put midnight supper together. To Adair, eating wasn't in the same universe with dancing.

"Angus, you look peaked," Adair remarked at the end of that first schoolhouse dance. "Are you all right?"

"A bit under the weather. It'll pass."

■ MARY CLEARMAN BLEW

Born in Lewistown in 1939, Mary Clearman Blew was raised on a ranch on the Judith River. She received an M.A. in English from the University of Montana in 1963 and continued her studies at the University of Missouri, where she earned a Ph.D. in 1969. From 1969 to 1987, Blew taught at Northern Montana College in Havre, where she was chairman of the English Department and Dean of Arts and Science. In 1977, the University of Missouri Press published Lambing Out, *a collection of Blew's short stories. The story reprinted here, "Forby and the Mayan Maidens," appeared in* The Georgia Review *(1980). Blew teaches English and creative writing at Lewis-Clark State College in Lewiston, Idaho, and has completed a new collection of short stories,* Runaway *(1989).*

Forby and the Mayan Maidens

It is your belief, I take it, that undertaking this narrative will, in shedding light upon my *alleged* role in Richard's death, allow me to sleep nights. I have no faith at all in the efficacy of this project. The events leading up to Richard's choice, insofar as they had to do with me at all, were a part of my adult and conscious life. I have no reason to feel guilty. It is the irrevocability of his turning from me that I simply cannot—allow myself to dwell upon.

But lest I be charged with unwillingness to cooperate in my own cure, I have begun this account, to use your words, of the authoritarian figures of my childhood. What a phrase! Its illogic is manifest, for all children stand in the shadows of giants. My particular giants, my parents, were ordinary farm people. I am the younger of two brothers. My brother, Miles, still farms the old ground. He and I remain on good, if remote, terms. My father is dead, my mother senile.

It is not at all unusual for a man like me to come from such a background. Few of my graduate-school acquaintances, as I recall them, or of my present colleagues enjoyed the advantages of a cultured or even sympathetic background. My personal history is depressingly commonplace: the bookish and sensitive child, rebuffed

and belittled by puzzled or contemptuous parents and playmates, turns more and more to the rewards of scholastic achievement that eventually lead to escape through a scholarship at the state university and thence to the teaching assistantship and the painfully acquired advanced degree which in its turn, if one is fortunate, returns one to the teaching position at the undistinguished four-year college. The infrequent rewards, the Richards whose sensitivity and promise provide one with the opportunity to perform the rescue that was one provided for oneself, must suffice. Hundreds, possibly thousands, can tell my story. Reason enough for my reluctance to reexamine it. In my case I was fortunate to have a brother like Miles who, in fulfilling perfectly the expectations of our little community, lessened the need to press me into the same deadening mold.

As I think upon it now, however, I admit that few among those thousands can boast of overcoming an initial encounter with public education as stultifying as was mine. For even in my boyhood, rural schools were beginning to disappear from farming communities just as remote as ours. Hardly a one of those schools can exist today. In his Christmas letter Miles mentioned that our very school had recently been purchased by a neighbor and hauled away to serve as a grain bin. A far more useful function than it had served in many years!

It was their inability to hire a teacher, wrote Miles, that convinced the local school board to bow to the inevitable. High time, indeed. Even in my boyhood it was difficult to find a teacher who would accept a position isolated by miles of muddy or snowbound roads beyond even the reach of telephone lines, without plumbing and without electricity and with the very drinking water carried from the spring–do I bore you? Those teachers were hardly the authoritarian figures you imagined. Only the halt, the blind, the dregs of the profession would accept positions in the rural schools.

It was my brother Miles's teacher's dropping dead in his shoes before the astonished eyes of the school's ten or eleven pupils that delayed my own enrollment in school for two fatal years. I do not exaggerate. It was during those two years that I grew into myself–or are you curious about poor old Professor Wentworth who dropped dead? Do you want to know the details? I really know very little, having been only six years old and kept in the dark at the time it happened. I do know that Professor Wentworth was ninety years old when they hired him. He had had a respectable teaching career but at his age no town school would have taken a chance on him. He was spry and alert but he, too, bowed to the inevitable shortly before Thanksgiving. Miles had to be driven ten miles to a school in the next district for the rest of the year, and I, who should have started the first grade in the fall, was kept at home by my mother for two more years. She was worried, I suppose, about the effect the sudden death might have upon me. Its effect on Miles? You may well ask. I've never known. Did he, I wonder, lie awake at night as I do and watch the electric streetlight outside my window bleach the unresisting elm leaves and slowly fade as they resume their daylight greens one more time?

Why, why in the name of God must I bother with all this? Can you tell me what point it has? Do you think I can possibly care about elm leaves or Miles or country schools? I was begotten, born, and will–should I be fortunate enough to follow Professor Wentworth's example–drop dead before the momentarily startled eyes of thirty freshmen composition students. Meanwhile I cannot sleep. You have implied that you can grant oblivion in return for these details, and God knows it is an exchange I would make joyously if only I believed in its terms; what else could I ask at three in the morning when, brain aching from the unrelenting roller coaster of associations it can no longer contain, I prowl from window to window in the dark and note how still the leaves hang in the artificial light? If only I could ask him, talk with him, have ten minutes back out of all time to plead my cause–as I say, it is the irrevocability of a suicide that leaves the living without an alternative.

In any event, I was at last enrolled in school, the wife of a neighboring farmer having agreed to open ours. Large for my age, self-taught to read from my brother's schoolbooks, longing for school with a misplacement of expectations that is pathetic in retrospect, I was set up for disillusionment in a way no one recognized.

"I think he'll be all right," I remember my mother saying. I remember that she sounded doubtful, but memory is a notorious liar. Certainly it seems as though I recall perfectly her sharp voice and the line gouged between her eyes as she turned in the long September twilight to carry the supper dishes to the drainboard–but do I? Of course it was September, time for school to start. Of course she frowned; her frown was permanent. But if, by one of the technological feats that have reduced our young to illiterate victims of a box of flickering shadows, I could witness a, so to speak, metaphysical videotape of my mother's kitchen on that September evening, what would I see? Or hear (assuming a sound track)? Was she doubtful? Angry? Relieved to get me off her hands?

I think I remember her turning as my father pushed back from the wooden table and lifted his cup of coffee in a hand horny and permanently grimed from his fields–"Why wouldn't he be all right? Only place for him. Goddamn kid would get himself killed if I let him around the machinery. Even if you could get his nose pried out of his book he'd forget his head if it wasn't for Miles keeping track of him. Miles, now–" Some of this diatribe he may have repeated to my mother on that September evening, some of it at other times. How I feared him, and feared the certainty of his voice and the wallop of his hand! His assessment of me was the assessment which my first schoolmates made immediately and which has been made of me repeatedly since then: in a world split between the real and the unreal, my only province lies in the latter.

Miles, for example, knew what to expect. He drove grain trucks up to the day school started. Then he submitted reluctantly to a bath and clean clothes–"If I could skip the first week, Dad, and help you finish harvest?"–but at last dug out his baseball bat and glove and cheered a little at the sight of them.

But I couldn't wait to get to school. I tried to get out of the car before it came to a full stop in the schoolyard that morning, earning me a shout from my mother, but my feet were on the sod by then and nothing could stop me. I stood in the dry September grass that was still knee-high on the playground, squinting against the glare of the sun on white siding and smelling the fields of stubble and the dust that converged from the horizon from all directions upon one point.

The school was cool in the anteroom. Underfoot the old pine flooring was hollowed from the feet of hundreds of children. Under the row of coat hooks sat the earthenware water cooler with its tap at the bottom and its row of drinking cups on the shelf behind it. In the classroom itself, light flooded through a dozen long north windows and fell in blotches across the waxed floor and the rows of desks in graduating sizes that were connected with the back of each seat supporting the desk of the next. The blackboard was clean. At the front of the school was the teacher's desk and a large flag. At the rear was the oil heater. A door behind the heater led to the teacherage, as everyone but me knew. Perhaps even in that first excitement, something about the teacherage warned me off. I do remember its smell, yeasty and cramped from the generations of women who had lived and cooked for themselves behind the schoolroom.

"And this is Wayne," said my mother, catching me by the neck and pushing me forward with a smile so unlike her that I struggled to escape her fingers. "Oh yes?" smiled the teacher and I got my first good look.

You understand, don't you, what a crime it was? From Miles's social studies and science readers I had not only taught myself to read but had also caught a glimpse, so I thought, of a heaven on earth made concrete in a third- or fourth-grade classroom presided over by a smiling Miss White or Miss Bell who guided twenty or so small companions all united in their desires to examine the sources of weather changes or common modes of transportation or the lives of children around the world. Do you understand what I imagined lay ahead?

Mrs. Skaarda had taught for several years previously at our school, its proximity to her home being, I suppose, its one attraction. She was considered to be a fine teacher with a proper regard for phonics, those tiresome objects whose unpredictable fallings in and out of pedagogical fashion so worry the parents of young children—Mrs. Skaarda, as I have said, was strong on phonics, and her willingness to teach at our little school was considered a stroke of fortune for the neighborhood until her unexpected illness forced her to a long stay in a distant hospital and brought about the hiring, after a frantic school board meeting, of poor old Professor Wentworth. Miles, my senior by four years—and six grades ahead of me because of my late start—had already gone to school under Mrs. Skaarda and liked her. This fall, after nearly three years of an illness I never heard named, Mrs. Skaarda felt well enough to return to the school, and my mother thought it safe at last to enroll me.

I do not remember ever seeing Mrs. Skaarda before that morning. Unlike my mother and the other farm women, who were heavy-handed and heavy-hammed from work and fatigue and over-feeding, Mrs. Skaarda was a small slim woman with bones as insubstantial as a bird's. While considerably older than the Miss Whites and the Miss Bells of Miles's old readers, she radiated something of their storied warmth. Her hair was dark and her eyes, too, were dark and apprehensive in their setting of fine wrinkles. Her smile for me was tremulous: "And this is Miles's little brother? Wayne? Oh-h-h-h-h! We'll be fine!"

After all the parents drove away, Mrs. Skaarda rang a little bell and called the small children off the swings and Miles and the big Snapp girls and Charlie Connard away from the baseball diamond to crowd through the cloakroom into the fresh sun-dappled schoolroom to try out desks for size. Mine, I remember, had hardly room for my legs under it; as the year wore on I was continually being cursed by Shelley Snapp for tripping her on her way to the pencil sharpener, which I could not help, my desk having been assigned me because of my primary status and not my size. Yes, from that first day I was paired with Forby Weston.

But back to Mrs. Skaarda. As I recall her small, anxious face, the way she cupped her chin in her hands while her eyes searched our twelve faces for reassurance, I must ask myself again: how well do I really remember her? And I answer firmly: oh surely I remember her as she was! For on that first day, whether she knew it or not, I recognized a kindred spirit in her, a fellow sensitive in the land of the unfeeling. From the time when, instead of beginning an arithmetic lesson, Mrs. Skaarda leaned across her desk and began to tell us how glad she was to be well again and how she looked forward to learning with us, I knew her for what she was.

For Mrs. Skaarda, too, stood in the shadows of giants. Her sister-in-law, her father-in-law, her professors at college, a man who taught her niece in a city school, the director of a theater group to which she had once belonged—"I begged her to understand the man was dying!"

Mrs. Skaarda's tremulous whisper reduced us to silence as we sat in our rows between the north windows and the blackboard. "But it didn't matter to her! It didn't matter!"

The accounts of her conflicts, begun in lieu of opening exercises, swelled through the mornings and sometimes continued after we had eaten our sandwiches at noon. We were a willing audience, for none of us had heard such tales; and, as though by agreement, we never discussed what we heard with our parents or even among ourselves. More and more those long mornings and lengthening afternoons became a matter of awe among us.

Mrs. Skaarda's brother was dying of cancer. Every morning she brought us reports, not only of the callousness of her sister-in-law, but of each step her brother took as he yielded his body to decay. "Cancer has its own terrible smell," she whispered. "I gag when I sit at my own brother's bedside. Anybody would. And to think that he must lie there, never able to walk away from the putrid smell of his own body! And we'll all come to the same thing in the end. Every body in the room will someday be putrid!"

"I'd shoot myself before I died like that," said daring Shelley Snapp.

"It's all the same in the end," Mrs. Skaarda told her sadly.

A few days later she told us that her brother could eat nothing. For three days he had eaten nothing. Then it was a week.

"He can't eat nothing! He'd die!" said my brother Miles stoutly.

"They give him liquids through a tube," she explained. "But it isn't enough nourishment to live on. He would starve to death if he weren't dying first of cancer." Then she told us the dreadful family secret: it didn't matter to her sister-in-law whether her brother died or not.

One morning she came to school red-eyed. "He's dead," she told us, and burst into tears. The youngest Snapp girl cried, too, and the rest of us tried not to cry. Only Forby Weston showed no emotion, and, not for the first time, I focused my anger on Forby, my companion in the first grade, for his lack of sensitivity. He sat coloring in his workbook and paid no attention. I had always disliked him for his appearance and his inability to read; now I whetted my dislike by staring at him. He was as large-framed as I, with pale skin and fishy eyes and a large mouth like a fish.

"I sat up with him all night," Mrs. Skaarda recovered enough to tell us as we waited, rapt, for more. "I held his hand. No one else would stay with him. It happened about three o'clock this morning."

The schoolroom was so quiet that I could hear the soft rub of Forby's crayon across the paper. "Did you know that dead bodies fart?" Mrs. Skaarda confided. "His did."

After her brother died, Mrs. Skaarda become fearful. For a few days fitfully spent on ordinary lessons, her eyes searched the schoolroom, lingering on the three shelves of old library books I had already read from cover to cover, the wainscoted cabinet that held chalk and paper, the twelve of us in our three rows, and coming to rest more and more often on our old oil heater.

"If it exploded, it would kill us, of course," her voice broke the silence. We looked up hopefully from our science readers, blinking against the sunlight now strained thin through frost-covered windows. "They might be able to identify my body. My desk is on the far side of the room. But most of you would be mutilated beyond recognition."

We all turned to look at the glowing heater, once our ally against the freezing December weather that kept us cooped in the schoolhouse during recess, but now transformed into a squat smug force capable of blotting us all out of existence.

"If it started to explode, I'd jump up and run," said Shelley loudly.

"You wouldn't have time to run," said Mrs. Skaarda.

For the rest of the week before school mercifully was dismissed for Christmas, we all watched the oil heater and breathed as tentatively as we could. For as Richard once took pains to point out to me, it is the threat from the familiar, from the recognized companion, that is the true rack of anxiety. Not, of course, that those were his words–no. You do not need to hear his words. I will never rid myself of them, and that they are drawn from the impoverished vocabulary of his generation does not make them the less poignant. Let it suffice that not only did he hold me responsible for his growing estrangement with his background, but he found insubstantial what I could offer in return. But this you have heard before. I have, as I have said, no reason to feel guilty.

I must say! (For you see, I am determined not to stray long from the assigned subject.) Although I earlier described my first educational experience as stultifying in the extreme, it strikes me now that in some respects, at least, Mrs. Skaarda's brand of education far exceeded the trite doses fed most farm children stuck in a snowbound country school. If I remember anything exactly as it was, it is the way we sat through those winter mornings, hands folded on our desks and mouths slightly ajar as we listened to the unfolding installment of the slow death of one of Mrs. Skaarda's relatives or of the details of Mayan sacrifice. And oh, yes! Her teaching went much further.

I had long thought of myself as one of Mrs. Skaarda's own, a member of a small loyal flock that stood firm against the insensitives of the world. Gradually I became aware that all of us, however, were not of the flock. Mrs. Skaarda's eyes lingered more and more—no, not upon me, but upon Forby Weston.

Because of our common grade assignment, Forby and I were often enforced companions. We took the pail for water together when it was our turn. We were supposed, ridiculously, to be doing lessons together. And oftener than not we were paired in the recess games like Last Couple Out or Prisoner's Base that the older children taught us. Forby, although large for his age, was in fact better coordinated that I; my clumsiness had rapidly won for me the dishonor of always being the last chosen for sides (out of doors, mind you! In schoolroom games I was always first in spite of my age). "You may be the smartest one in school, but you're the dumbest one outside it!" Shelley Snapp once taunted me. Such designations come early, as you see.

Forby was content to sit quietly at his desk and color while Mrs. Skaarda talked to the rest of us, and for a long time he gave no indication of being aware of her increased scrutiny. Perhaps he, too, assumed that as one of the chosen he was safe.

"There is something the matter with Forby," Mrs. Skaarda confided to Shelley over the water cooler. I, eavesdropping as usual, turned with Shelley to look at Forby where he sat coloring peaceably in his spelling workbook. "Why does he always color with the black crayon?" whispered Mrs. Skaarda. "Or the brown?"

"Why don't you use the red crayon?" she asked Forby. I winced, for her voice held the forced good will my mother turned on her neighbors. "Okay," said Forby, picking up another crayon at random and going on with what he was doing. Mrs. Skaarda turned and shrugged significantly at Shelley.

Even in retrospect I can offer little insight into the mystery of Forby. I once tried to explain the incident to Richard—"He probably just didn't know his colors," said Richard. I was disappointed. I had looked forward to sharing the story with him; Richard, I had felt sure, would understand, if not the causal relationship that set Forby crashing out of his small world, at least the effect his crash has had upon me ever since. But it was not to be. I misjudged Richard, as I have misjudged so many others. But to return.

At the time I only knew that Forby had unaccountably taken the place of the Mayan civilization in Mrs. Skaarda's interests. We had considered the Mayans with her for–days? weeks? I don't remember. Sometimes it seems as though we were occupied with the Mayans for most of the winter, and yet surely at one time or another we did ordinary lessons? Wouldn't my mother or some other mother, have become suspicious sooner than she did and visited the school? And yet I recall only the Mayans.

Mrs. Skaarda had lent to Miles, her favorite, a book about the Mayan civilization to read over Christmas vacation. He shared generous portions of it with me. One episode haunted me for nights. It had to do with the sacrifice of Mayan maidens into a pool thought to be bottomless until recently fathomed by curious archaeologists who fetched up skeleton after delicate skeleton of hapless children cast down to appease their ancestor the sun. I daresay neither I nor the now-forgotten author of the book understood the mythology, but no matter. It was important, he said, that the maiden be cast into the pool at the precise moment dawn cracked over the horizon. He himself was so fascinated with the maidens that one night he waited by the pool until sunrise and, with its first rays, cast himself into the pool (but survived the fall and swam out). He said the pool smelled bad.

Mrs. Skaarda was, as I said, fascinated with the Mayans and their sacrifices until Forby claimed her attention. Loyally we shifted our attention with hers.

"There is something the matter with Forby," Mrs. Skaarda whispered to Miles. "I'm so thankful you're here." Such was her intensity that even my unimaginative brother looked at Forby, while I trembled in my impotent rage that it was to Miles her clouded eyes turned for reassurance. Who was Forby to cause us such distress? Fish-eyed Forby!

"If he were ever to–you know–lose control, it would be more than any one of us could do to subdue him. The insane have strength beyond all normal measures," she explained to Miles in her troubled whisper. "That's what I'm afraid of. That he'll slip over the divide and overpower us all."

By this time every pair of eyes in school was glued on Forby. Could we have possibly believed the child was insane? was Richard's question. I don't know. Perhaps more accurate to say that, stimulated by the vicarious threat of death and destruction and awakened to the promise of sacrifice, we suspended our disbelief for the course of the action. For who could say what Forby might do? Was it impossible that his was the pale mien of homicidal mania? And Forby gradually looked up from his crayons and his paste and his other simple pursuits to find a wall around him.

Within doors and out—for by this time winter had yielded to early spring mud—we all watched Forby. No longer chosen on anyone's side in games, he took to hovering at a distance of a few yards and pawing with his overshoes at the greening sod, while I, once the clumsy outcast, shone in a new role. For I, who had been Forby's peer against my will, was now privileged to be his licensed tormentor.

"Get away!" Shelley might bellow across the few yards of unthawing prairie grass at dumb, uncomprehending Forby in his thick winter coat and cap. "Keep away from us! We don't want you hanging around us, so quit being so stupid!"

But Shelley could do no more than shout; anything further would be "picking on the little kids" and outside the pale of country-school convention. But—"You chase him off, Wayne!" Shelley could urge. "Kick him. That's right. See? He's even scared of Wayne." And I, riding on a crescendo of encouraging yelps from the other children, ran at Forby and made him withdraw another ten or fifteen feet. "That's right!" "Kick him, he's got it coming!" they shrilled, and I raised an overshoed foot and planted its mud on Forby's undefended leg. For the first time in my life, I was flooded with joy. How thankful I was for Forby! How I fed my dislike upon his thick pale features! How I doted on his otherness that made me complete! Oh, the pure joy of my new mindlessness! How I capered in the April sun, freed by Forby from my old self as surely as though, snakelike, I had shed a skin!

As for what follows—the particular occasion when two mothers converged—that incident, as you will understand, I never confessed nor wished to confess to Richard. For it is one thing, is it not, to confess to the pleasure I took in another child's torment, but quite another to admit to its reverse? Why, indeed, continue now? Only because it is almost dawn and a few more paragraphs will suffice.

I even had some small part in bringing to an end my time in the sun, for I took to bragging of my exploits to my parents—little enough I had had to brag of in the past—at about the same time that Forby's mother somehow divined through her son's phlegmatic exterior that all was not well with him, bringing the two women separately and coincidentally to school the day Forby was at last driven out of his skin.

Driven out of the circle and pelted with mud balls by the older children and teased and kicked and even bitten by me, Forby had made no attempt to defend himself. His eyes withdrew into the stolid white plane of his face as though no taunt, no pummel, could penetrate. But that day, I bolted my sandwiches and raced out of doors, quite beside myself in the mellow young sunlight—"Get away!" I shrilled at Forby. "Get away!" Screwing my face into ferocious indignation, I hurtled myself at the unmoving figure in the plaid cap and coat and decently buckled overshoes just like mine, only to stop in astonishment when he broke and ran.

After my first surprise, I ran after him, of course. We all ran, ten of us pelting across the mushy, wet grass back of the school (Miles, whose presence might have made a difference, had taken to staying in the schoolhouse and talking to Mrs. Skaarda during recess), down the coulee that sliced the schoolyard and panting up the other side, gulping the sharp spring air that stung our young lungs, ecstatic because we saw we were going to corner Forby against the barbed-wire fence that separated the schoolyard from the neighboring grain fields—but the others had unaccountably fallen back and I was alone at Forby's heels when, instead of turning to accept his punishment from my hands, he crashed into the barbed wire and set it vibrating for yards in both directions.

Forby hung on the wires. Gradually they ceased their humming. Shelley and the others stood in a silent group. They had seen, as I had not, Forby's mother coming across the back lot. As I turned, she broke into a run with her coat flapping around her legs. She ran past me without looking at me and plucked Forby off the fence. Carrying him, she turned back toward the school. In his mother's arms Forby looked astonishingly long and limp.

The others turned and trailed in her wake back toward the school. I tried to catch up. "Did you see how dumb old Forby ran?"

Nobody would look at me. "You're the dumb one," Shelley muttered.

My mother and Mrs. Skaarda were waiting on the steps as we came around the corner. Forby's mother had put him in her car and had just slammed the door on him, but I caught a glimpse of his white face lolling against the seat.

I hardly dared to breathe, for Mrs. Skaarda's chin was trembling and her eyes were wells of fear. Even in that moment so indelibly etched that I can still remember the warm rotten smell of the spring thaw and the whistle of a meadowlark from the gatepost and the force of all eyes fixed on me, it was her fear I pitied.

Her hands were clenched in two small white fists at her waist. "I have been so worried," she said to my mother. Her voice shook. "I didn't know what to do. He's been worse and worse since the weather turned warm—hasn't he?" Her appeal was to my schoolmates. Solemnly they all nodded.

My mother's face was bright red. "You go in the teacherage," she said to me, "and stay there until we're ready for you."

I remember I took two steps toward the cloakroom door and stopped, still too dazed to cry or protest, to squint against the glare of eyes that pinned me there against the peeling white siding of the school. The realization, if not the comprehension, was dawning on me that it was I who was to be offered up to whatever gods she feared.

As I walked through the cloakroom and past the cold and harmless oil heater, I heard the burst of voices eager to tell what I had done. I walked into the teacherage and shut the door on all but an unintelligible buzz.

No one had lived in the teacherage since the days of old Professor Wentworth. The shades were pulled over the windows and a single beam of sunlight glared through a torn place. On the bed was a mattress. Mrs. Skaarda's coat hung on the back of the door.

I sat down on the bed to wait, where, in a sense, I have been waiting ever since. After a while, I got up and stood by the door and put my face against her coat. The moment on the steps, when I knew it was I who had been fixed outside the circle, had been as painful as a rotten tooth under a probe, but it has been the aftermath that has returned in the wake of Richard's choice to overwhelm me with its dim associations of dust and yeast. As you see, I can go no further. No, I am not responsible for Richard's death. It is the awful suspicion that once again the tables have been turned that keeps me here, bleareyed but unable to sleep, as a raucous sunrise breaks into my window.

■ WILLIAM KITTREDGE

Born in 1932, William Kittredge grew up and worked on his family's cattle ranch in southeastern Oregon until it was sold in 1967. He received a degree in general agriculture from Oregon State University and later earned an M.F.A. from the University of Iowa Writers' Workshop. Since 1969 Kittredge has been a professor of English and is the director of the Creative Writing Program at the University of Montana. His stories have been published widely and are collected in The Van Gogh Field *(1979), which won the St. Lawrence Short Fiction Prize, and* We Are Not in This Together *(1984). "Phantom Silver," which appeared in the* Iowa Review *in 1977, was re-edited as a chapbook for Missoula's Kutenai Press in 1987. "Drinking and Driving" is excerpted from* Owning It All, *published in 1987. Kittredge's novel,* Sixty Million Buffalo, *is forthcoming.*

Drinking and Driving

Deep in the far heart of my upbringing, a crew of us sixteen-year-old lads were driven crazy with ill-defined midsummer sadness by the damp, sour-smelling sweetness of night-time alfalfa fields, an infinity of stars and moonglow, and no girlfriends whatsoever. Frogs croaked in the lonesome swamp.

Some miles away over the Warner Range was the little ranch and lumbermill town of Lakeview, with its whorehouse district. And I had use of my father's 1949 Buick. So, another summer drive. The cathouses, out beyond the rodeo grounds, were clustered in an area called Hollywood, which seemed right. Singing cowboys were part of everything gone wrong.

We would sink our lives in cheap whiskey and the ardor of sad, expensive women. In town, we circled past the picture show and out past Hollywood, watching the town boys and their town-boy business, and we chickened out on the whores and drank more beer, then drove on through the moonlight.

Toward morning we found ourselves looping higher and higher on a two-truck gravel road toward the summit of Mount Bidwell, right near the place where California and Nevada come together at the Oregon border. We topped out over a break called Fandango Pass.

The pass was named by wagon-train parties on the old Applegate cutoff to the gold country around Jacksonville. From that height they got their first glimpse of Oregon, and they camped on the summit and danced themselves some fandangos, whatever the step might be.

And we, in our ranch-boy style, did some dancing of our own. Who knows how it started, but with linked arms and hands we stumbled and skipped through the last shards of night and into the sunrise. Still drunk, I fell and bloodied my hands and stood breathing deep of the morning air and sucking at my own salty blood, shivering and pissing and watching the stunted fir and meadow aspen around me come luminous with light, and I knew our night of traveling had brought me to this happiness that would never bear talking about. No more nameless sorrow, not with these comrades, and we all knew it and remained silent.

Seventeen. I was safe forever, and I could see 70 miles out across the beauty of country where I would always live with these friends, all of it glowing with morning.

We learn it early in the West, drinking and driving, chasing away from the ticking stillness of home toward some dim aura glowing over the horizon, call it possibility or excitement. Henry James once said there are two mental states, excitement and lack of excitement, and that unfortunately excitement was more interesting than lack of excitement. Travel the highways in Montana, and you will see little white crosses along the dangerous curves, marking places where travelers have died, many of them drunk, and most of them searching and unable to name what it was they were missing at home. It's like a sport: you learn techniques.

For instance, there are three ways to go: alone, with cronies of either sex, or with someone you cherish beyond all others at that particular moment. We'll call that one love and save it for last.

Although each of these modes can get tricky, alone is the most delicate to manage. Alone can lead to loneliness, and self-pity, and paranoia, and things like that—the trip can break down into dark questing after dubious companionship.

The advantage of going it alone lies, of course, in spontaneity and freedom. You don't have to consult anybody but your inclinations. You touch that warm car, and you climb in for a moment and roll down the window, just to see what it would be like.

And then, it's magic—you're rolling, you're gone and you're riding. Shit fire, you think, they don't need me, not today. I'm sick. This is sick leave. You know it's true. You've been sick, and this day of freedom will cure your great illness. Adios.

Say it is spring, as in *to rise or leap suddenly and swiftly*, the most dangerous and frothy season, sap rising and the wild geese honking as they fly off toward the north. "Ensnared with flowers, I fall on grass." Andrew Marvell.

It might be the first day of everything, in which we rediscover a foreverland of freedom and beauty before the invention of guilt. A day when the beasts will all lie down with one another. Hummingbirds in the purple lilac.

What we are talking about is the first day of high and classical spring here in the temperate zones, one of those pure and artless mornings somewhere toward the latter part of May or early June in the countries where I have lived, when the cottonwood leaves have sprung from the bud and stand young and pale green against the faint, elegant cleanliness of the sky. We are talking about walking outside into such a morning and breathing deeply.

Where I like to head out of Missoula is upstream along the Blackfoot River, the asphalt weaving and dipping and the morning light lime-colored through the new leaves on the aspen, with some fine, thin, fragile music cutting out from the tape deck, perhaps Vivaldi concerti played on the cello. Such music is important in the early day. It leaves a taste as clean as the air across the mountain pastures, and it doesn't encourage you to think. Later, there will be plenty of thinking.

But early on all I need is the music, and the motion of going, and some restraint. It always seems like a good idea, those mornings up along the Blackfoot, to stop at Trixie's Antler Inn just as the doors are being unlocked. One drink for the road and some banter with the hippie girl tending bar.

But wrong.

After the first hesitation, more stopping at other such establishments is inevitable. And quite enjoyable, one after another. The Wheel Inn on the near outskirts of Lincoln, Bowmans Corner over south of Augusta, with the front of the Rockies rearing on the western skyline like purity personified.

Soon that fine blue bowl of heaven and your exquisite freedom are forgotten, and you are talking to strangers and to yourself. No more Vivaldi. It's only noon, and you are playing Hank Williams tapes and singing along, wondering if you could have made it in the country music business. By now you are a long and dangerous way from home and somewhat disoriented. The bartenders are studying you like a serious problem.

You have drifted into another mythology, called lonesome traveling and lost highways, a place where you really don't want to be on such a fine spring day. Once, it seemed like pure release to learn that you could vote with your feet, that you could just walk away like a movie star. Or, better yet, load your gear in some old beater pickup truck and drive. Half an hour, the vainglorious saying went, and I can have everything on rubber. Half an hour, and I'll be rolling. You just watch, little darling.

For some of us, the consequences of such escape tended to involve sitting alone with a pint bottle of whiskey in some ancient motel room where the television doesn't work. The concept was grand and theatrical, but doing it, getting away, was oftentimes an emotional rat's nest of rootlessness. Country music, all that worn-out drifter syncopation, turned out to be another lie, a terrific sport but a real thin way of life.

So, some rules for going alone: Forget destinations; go where you will, always planning to stay overnight. Stop at historical markers, and mull over the ironies of destiny as you drive on. By now you are listening to bluegrass, maybe a tape from a Seldom Seen concert. And you are experiencing no despair.

Think of elk in the draws, buffalo on the plains, and the complex precision of predator-prey relationships. Be interesting, and love your own company. There is no need to get drunk and kill somebody on the road. Quite soon enough it will be twilight, and you can stop in some little town, check in at one of the two motels along the river, amble down to the tavern, and make some new friends. Such a pretty life.

Traveling with cronies is another matter. Some obvious organizational efforts are implicit. There stands your beloved car, warm in the sun. You touch a fender and turn away and backtrack toward your telephone, which magically starts ringing. Others have the same idea. My rig, your ice chest, bring money, we're traveling.

But the real logistical niceties lie in the chemistry of compatibility. Not just every good friend is a fit companion for the heedless expeditions of a summer drive. Each stop and turnoff must seem the result of consultation with mutual inclination. Nothing spoils traveling more quickly than endless debate, or any debate at all. Trust the driver. Everybody knows what we're looking for. Take us there.

Which is where? Looking for what? Call it ineffable—that which cannot be expressed or described and is not to be spoken of. Traveling with cronies can't be heedless without unspoken agreement.

Back when we were young and idiot, we would head up to The Stockman's in Arlee, hit the Buffalo Park in Ravalli, move on to the 44

Bar north of St. Ignatius, and then make the Charlo turn to Tiny's. From there whim led the way until we ended up in the Eastgate Lounge in Missoula around midnight. The circuit was called The Inner Circle.

Say the afternoon sky is streaked white, and spring winds drive storm clouds over the peaks of Montana's Mission Mountains. This is the Flathead Valley, and the town is Charlo, and though it may seem impersonal now, it need not be. If you are in any way sensible, your next move should be simple and clear and rewarding. You and your companions will clump down the stairs and into Tiny's Tavern. The place used to be called Tiny's Blind Pig, *blind pig* being prohibition code for tavern. The old name, for those of us who stopped by when we were passing through, implied a connection with the romance we were seeking–an outlaw dream of prohibition, dusty black automobiles just in from a rum-run to Canada, blond gum-snapping molls. As newcomers we ached to be a part of Montana–and here it was, the real goddamned item.

One night my brother was shooting pool at Tiny's with a wiry old man, an electrician by trade as I recall. During a lull in the bar talk I heard something that stood the hair on the back of my neck. "Son of a bitch," my brother said, "I wouldn't have to cheat to beat you."

Oh, pray for us, Lord. Outlanders in a bar filled with local ranchers and their brawny sons celebrating another victory for the best eight-man football team in the history of Montana. Do not let them beat on us–at least, not on me. Take my brother.

The rancher next to me, about a foot taller than I will ever be, looked sideways and grinned. "Don't know about you," he said, "but I ain't going over there. Them old black eyes take about three weeks to heal." By the time I had bought him and me a drink, my brother and the electrician were finishing their game without any further hint of warfare.

Well, I thought, got myself home again. Home is a notion such backcountry taverns seem to radiate–at least if they're places that longtime patrons and their barkeep hosts have imprinted with the wear and damage of their personalities. Tiny's was shaped as much as anything by the old man who owned it when I first went there–ancient and hurting, hobbling around on crutches, a former police chief from Miami, Florida, with a huge collection of memorabilia in glass case around the bar–over 5000 different kinds of beer bottles, intimate snapshots of Hitler taken in the 1930's, fine obsidian arrowheads, gem-quality Kennedy half-dollars. Tiny is dead now, and they've changed the sign over the doorway. But his collections are still in place.

Homes and love, if they are to exist as more than fond children of the imagination, most often take us by surprise on back roads. On my way to Missoula almost every day I pass the old Milltown Union Bar, where Dick Hugo used to do his main drinking in the days when he was serious about it. Above the doorway white heads of mountain goat and bighorn sheep, sealed in plexiglass bubbles, contemplate those who enter. As Hugo said in a poem about the Milltown, "You were nothing going in, and now you kiss your hand." In another poem, about another barroom, Hugo named the sense of recognition and homecoming I expect upon going into one of the taverns I love. His poem begins, "Home. Home. I knew it entering."

Indeed, what are we looking for? In July of 1969 I came to Montana to stay, bearing a new Master of Fine Arts degree from the flooding heartland of Iowa. I had just finished up as a thirty-five-year-old, in-off-the-ranch graduate student in the Iowa Writer's Workshop, and I had lucked into a teaching job at the University of Montana. I was running to native cover in the west; I was a certified writer, and this was the beginning of my real life at last.

During that summer in Iowa City–drinking too much, in love with theories about heedlessness and possibility–I was trying to figure out how to inhabit my daydream. We lived in an old stone-walled house with a flooded basement out by the Coralville reservoir, listening to cockroaches run on the night-time linoleum and imagining Montana, where we would find a home.

Every morning the corn in the fields across the road looked to have grown six inches, every afternoon the skies turned green with tornado-warning storms, and every night lightning ran magnificent and terrible from the horizons. My wife said they ought to build a dike around the whole damned state of Iowa and turn it into a catfish preserve. The U-Haul trailer was loaded. After a last party we were history in the Midwest, gone to Montana, where we were going to glow in the dark.

The real West started at the long symbolic interstate bridge over that mainline to so many ultimately heart-breaking American versions of heaven, the Missouri River. Out in the middle of South Dakota I felt myself released into significance. It was clear I was aiming my life in the correct direction. We were headed for a town studded with abandoned tipi burners.

But more so—as we drove I imagined Lewis and Clark and Catlin and Bodmer and even Audubon up to Fort Union on the last voyage of his life in 1843, along with every wagon train, ox-cart, cattle drive, and trainload of honyockers, all in pursuit of that absolute good luck which is some breathing time in a commodious place where the best that can be is right now. In the picture book of my imagination I was seeing a Montana composed of major post cards. The great river sliding by under the bridge was rich with water from the Sun River drainage, where elk and grizzly were rumored to be on the increase.

Engrossed in fantasies of traveling upriver into untouched territory, I was trying to see the world fresh, as others had seen it. On April 22, 1805, near what is now the little city of Williston in North Dakota, Meriwether Lewis wrote:

> . . . immense herds of buffalo, elk, deer, and antelopes feeding in one common and boundless pasture. We saw a large number of beaver feeding on the bark of trees along the verge of the river, several of which we shot. Found them large and fat.

By 1832, at the confluence of the Missouri and the Yellowstone, the painter George Catlin was already tasting ashes while trying to envision a future—just as I was trying to imagine what had been seen. Catlin wrote:

> . . . the native Indian in his classic attire, galloping his wild horse, with sinewy bow, and shield and lance, amid the fleeting herds of elks and buffaloes. What a beautiful and thrilling specimen for America to preserve and hold up to the view of her refined citizens and the world, in future ages! A *nation's park*, containing man and beast, in all the wild and freshness of their nature's beauty!

Think of Audubon responding eleven years later, on May 17, 1843, in that same upriver country around Fort Union:

> Ah! Mr. Catlin, I am now sorry to see and to read your accounts of the Indians you saw—how very different they must have been from any that I have seen!

On July 21, Audubon writes:

> What a terrible destruction of life, as it were for nothing, or next to it, as the tongues only were brought in, and the flesh of these fine animals were left to beasts and birds of prey, or to rot on the spots

> where they fell. The prairies were literally covered with the skulls of victims.

On August 5 Audubon finishes the thought:

> But this cannot last; even now there is a perceptible difference in the size of the herds, and before many years the Buffalo, like the Great Auk, will have disappeared; surely this should not be permitted.

In our summer of 1969 we poked along the edge where the Badlands break so suddenly from the sunbaked prairies, imagining the faraway drumming of hooves, Catlin's warriors on their decorated horses coming after us from somewhere out of dream. Not so far south lay Wounded Knee.

We studied the stone faces of our forefathers at Mount Rushmore and didn't see a damned thing because by that time in the afternoon we were blinded by so much irony on a single day. We retired for the night to a motel somewhere south of the Devil's Postpile in Wyoming. I was seeing freshly, but not always what I hoped to see. The distances were terrifying.

By the time we reached Missoula, I had disassociated my sensibilities with whiskey, which gave me the courage to march up the concrete steps to Richard Hugo's house, only a block from the Clark Fork River, where the Village Inn Motel sits these days. I rapped on his door. He studied me a moment after I introduced myself. "You're very drunk," he said.

Well hell, I thought, now you've done it.

"Wait a minute," Hugo said. "I'll join you."

Home, I thought, childlike with relief. This was the new country I had been yearning for, inhabited by this man who smiled and seemed to think I should be whatever I could manage.

I was lucky to know Dick Hugo, and his collected poems, *Making Certain It Goes On*, heads my list of good books written about the part of the world where I live. Dick loved to drive Montana, his trips imaginative explorations into other lives as a way toward focusing on his own complexities. He made the game of seeing into art, and his poetry and life form a story that lies rock bottom in my understanding of what art is for.

Once we drove over to fish the Jefferson River on a summer day when we were both hung-over to the point of insipid visionary craziness. We didn't catch any fish, and I came home numb, simply spooked, but Dick saw some things, and wrote a poem called "Silver

Star." Each time I read "Silver Star" I rediscover a story about homes, and the courage to acknowledge such a need, a story about Dick and his continual refinding of his own life, and an instruction about storytelling as the art of constructing road maps, ways home to that ultimate shelter which is the coherent self. Montana is a landscape reeking with such conjunction and resonance. They fill the silence.

Not long ago, on a bright spring morning, I stood on the cliffs of the Ulm Pishkun where the Blackfeet drove dusty hundreds of bison to fall and die. Gazing east I could dimly see the great Anaconda Company smokestack there on the banks of the Missouri like a finger pointing to heaven above the old saloon-town city of Great Falls where Charlie Russell painted and traded his pictures for whiskey—only a little upstream from the place where Meriwether Lewis wrote, having just finished an attempt at describing his first sight of the falls:

> After writing this imperfect description, I again viewed the falls, and was so much disgusted with the imperfect idea it conveyed of the scene, that I determined to draw my pen across it and begin again; but then reflected that I could not perhaps succeed better. . . .

After so many months of precise notation, all in the service of Thomas Jefferson's notion of the West as useful, in one of the most revealing passages written about the American West, Lewis seems to be saying: *But this, this otherness is beyond the capture of my words, this cannot be useful, this is dream.* The dam-builders, of course, did not see it his way.

Behind me loomed the fortress of the rock-sided butte Charlie Russell painted as backdrop to so much history, with the Rockies off beyond on the western horizon, snowy and gleaming in the morning sun. This listing could go on, but I was alone and almost frightened by so many conjunctions visible at once, and so many others right down the road: the Gates of the Mountains and Last Chance Gulch and even make-believe—Boone Caudill and Teal Eye and Dick Summers over west on the banks of the Teton River, where it cuts through the landscapes of *The Big Sky*—history evident all around and the imaginings of artists and storytellers intertwined. Charlie Russell and Bud Guthrie and Dick Hugo and Meriwether Lewis created metaphoric territory as real as any other Montana in the eye of my imagination.

We all play at transporting ourselves new into new country, seeing freshly, reorienting ourselves and our schemes within the complexities of the world. It is a powerful connection to history, and the grand use we make of storytelling as we incessantly attempt to recognize that which is sacred and the point of things.

Which brings us to our most complex option, traveling with lovers. In Missoula, in the heart of winter, if you are me, you talk in a placating way to the woman you love. It is about three days after you forgot another country custom, *The Valentine Party*. You suggest ways of redeeming yourself. You talk to friends. An expedition forms.

This paragon of a woman owns an aging four-wheel-drive Chevrolet pickup, three-quarter-ton, and she and I and her twin boys set off in that vehicle. Only praying a little bit. Good rubber, but a clanking U-joint. The friends—a southern California surfer hooked on snow skiing of all varieties, and a lady of his acquaintance—set off in that lady's vintage Volvo. We also pray for them. The Volvo wanders in its steering, in a somewhat experimental way. But no need for real fear. These are Montana highways.

Out of Missoula we caravan south through the Bitterroot Valley, where—before the subdivisions—Tom Jefferson could have seen his vision of pastoral American happiness realized. The Volvo wanders, the U-joint clanks, and we are happy. We wind up over Lost Trail Pass, where Lewis and Clark experienced such desperate vertigo in the wilderness on their way west. At the summit we turn east, toward the Big Hole Basin and a town named Wisdom. At 6,000 feet, the altitude in the Big Hole is too much for deciduous trees. The only color is the willow along the creeks, the red of dried blood.

We pass along the Big Hole Battlefield, where Joseph and Looking Glass and the Nez Percés suffered ambush by Federal troops under General Oliver Otis Howard on the morning of August 11, 1877. Casualties: Army, 29 killed, 40 wounded; Nez Percé, by Army body count, 89 dead, most of them women and children. We are traveling through the rich history of America.

Winter has come down on this country like a hammer, but the defroster is working perfectly and there is a bar in Wisdom with dozens of stuffed birds and animals on display around the walls. The place is crowded with weekend snowmobile fans in their bright insulated nylon coveralls. There is a stuffed quail on a stand with its head torn off. All that's left is just a little wire sticking out of the neck. What fun that night must have been.

The bar is fine. No one cares when we bring in our own cheeses and stoneground wheat crackers. We slice on the bar top, scatter crumbs. The bartender cleans up our mess. Smiles. The kids play the pinball machine all they want. We have hot drinks. So we are slightly tipsy, not to say on the verge of drunk, when we line out south toward Jackson. This is the deep countryside of Montana, and no one cares. The Volvo doesn't wander as erratically. The U-joint has made peace with itself. Which is something country people know about mechanical devices. They oftentimes heal. At least for a little while.

The Big Hole is called the "Land of 10,000 Haystacks." Nearby, a country man is feeding his cattle. Pitching hay with ice in his mustache. He has been doing it every day for two months. He has a month to go. Feeding cattle never was any fun. We do not think about such matters.

Beyond Polaris we head up a canyon between five-foot banks of snow, and we are arrived. Elkhorn Hot Springs. Right away, we like it. Snowshoeing and cross-country in all directions, and for our surfer friend, a dandy little downhill area only about three miles away. We have a cabin with a fireplace that works fine after the wood dries out. Up in the lodge they are serving family-style dinners. And cheap. You know–roast beef and meat loaf and real mashed potatoes and creamed corn and pickled beets. And on and on. Maybe this is the moment to break out the bottle of rum.

Eventually we wander down to the hot baths, the indoor sauna pools and the outdoor pool, and the snow falling into our mouths. Snowball fights in the water. Rowdiness. Young boys in swimming suits created from cut-off Levis. And the next day, sweet red wine in the snow and white chilled wine in the evening, and the ache from all the skiing melting out of our knees into the hot water.

But electricity is in fact the way nature behaves. Nothing lasts. That was winters ago. My surfer friend went off hunting the last good wave. He wrote from Australia, extolling the virtues of the unexamined life. The Volvo is dead; the U-joint is fixed. Desire and the pursuit of the whole is called love.

Phantom Silver

The great white horse rears above the rolling horizon, which is golden and simple in the sunset, and those sparkling hooves strike out into the green light under dark midsummer thunderclouds. Far away there is rain, and barn swallows drop like thrown stones through clouds of mosquito near the creek. A single planet and then stars grow luminous against the night, and the great horse is gone.

Moths bat against the screen around the veranda porch, and we are left in that dreamed yesteryear where the masked man rides away. The light is cold in the early morning, and the silver bullet rests on the mantle like a trophy. Only in the morning is it possible to think of that masked man as old and fat and slow and happy.

They were all brave and unmasked in that beginning, that crew of clean-shaven Texas Rangers, before the Cavendish gang did them in, leaving him for dead and alone, all his comrades sprawled around him and killed. They had ridden into a box canyon, and rifle fire crackled from the surrounding rims. They were ambushed; horses reared and screamed; the good men fell, and in only a few beats of a heart it was over. The Cavendish boys walked the stony ground amid the bodies and smiled as if they would live forever.

But he was not dead, only scarred. Revenge became his great obsession, revenge and justice, notions which served him like two sides of a coin as he changed like a stone into gold. He rode that white stallion named Silver, he disguised himself behind that mask, he traveled with his dark companion, the Indian named Tonto, and they began their endless conquest of wrong-doing. There was ranch after ranch saved from eastern bankers and monied second sons from Baltimore. Always another gold shipment to be rescued. Another sod-buster and his family to be protected. Another evil lawman to be confounded. Another wagon train to be saved from the clutches of circling savages—anyone would have grown weary, or even bored. How many rustlers died, how many homesteaders' wives stood in the doorway of plain unpainted cabins with that silver bullet still warm in their hands while they wondered aloud who that masked man could have been, while the great stallion reared?

The real beginning of this end was a mortal family, a strong-handed father and a mother who split their wood, and two children, a brother and a sister, all of them having come west to Texas after the Civil War. They had been living happily in a juniper log cabin alongside the Brazos River before that summer morning when Comanche came down like slaughtering, screaming rain.

They thought they were safe. The Comanche had been corraled for seven years on the Oklahoma Territory, eating mainly on dole meat, and the father was a slow-spoken German other white men did not deal with easily, and so left mostly alone. But there on that bright morning was the truth, Comanche out of season, and killers. But look away from that cabin and the killing for a moment.

Down there in the bullrushes near the water of the Brazos there was another morning sort of time, there was the dumb blankness of eyes rolled back to their extreme station, the hardness of lean hip-bones under the flesh, handholds as this brother mounts his sister from behind, the younger brother, the older sister, her skirt tossed up where they were down there on the matted grass, hidden from the house by tules and nodding downy cattails, the sister on her knees and elbows and the brother plugged in from behind, going weak and dizzy that morning with her and afraid the screaming he heard so distantly might be her or even himself, but that was foolish, they were practiced and wouldn't. He stopped, crouched over her, listening, and she thrust herself back against him.

"Don't you quit now," she said.

But he did. He had. The screaming he heard was not really screaming, not fearfulness, that came later, but high-pitched joyous whooping and ki-yiing, and now he could hear the horses, the hooves beating down the hard-packed wagon road. There was lots of them, and riding hard.

"Don't you stop," she said, but it was too late for that, already he had fallen back away from her, turning, knowing there was no way to see anything from where they were, that was why they were safe there on those hidden mornings down near the river. Already he was frightened, and later he would sense she had always been stronger, had always cared more than he did about what was going on right at the time; later he would understand it was an undivided mind that gave her what proved in time to be the strength of her indifference.

"Dammit," she said. "Then get yourself together."

What she meant was for him to pull up his pants and tuck in his shirttail, and to do it quietly. It was her that kept him quiet and crouching there those next hours as the smoke from the burning cabin and the barns rose thin and white into the clear sky, after the first bellowing from their father and their mother's frantic shrieking, after the horses had gone away, as the smoke dwindled and twilight came and the frogs called to one another in the quiet. It was her that kept him crouching and hidden there, until the next day they were saved, at least saved in the sense that they could walk away, they were not killed and not captured, not bloody and hairless like the bodies of their father and mother.

She was sixteen that summer of 1867, and he was two years younger, and for a few months, after they had walked those miles upstream to the nearest homestead on the Brazos, toward the Palo Pinto, they were pitied and fed. Then October began to settle into fall, and in November the green-headed Mallards and the Canada geese and the Sandhill Crane began coming south, circling and calling as they settled toward the river. The clump of pink-blooming roses on the south wall of the cabin froze, the tamarack hung darker red against the gray hillslopes and the big cottonwood flared yellow one morning in the sun, but the real cold came all in one day the week before Thanksgiving, weather a line of shadow on the morning horizon, the air greasy and hushed all that day, then at twilight a hard northerner wind and driven sleety rain. But they didn't leave until after the Thanksgiving meal, goose and all the fixings. It was her that decided.

"We are going," she said.

By Christmas they had hooked wagon rides south to San Antonio, and she would no longer let him touch her. "If we had been going to stay there we would have stayed forever," she said, and after the beginning of the new year she took to leaving him alone for days while she went around to the taverns on the banks of the San Antonio River, and she came home with money. She had her blankets in the room they shared, but she would not let him come under them with her. "You have done me what damage you could," she said. It was not that she did not love him, she explained, it was simply that the damage was done. He took to breaking horses for a livery stable. He had always been good with horses. He could not remember his parents, they had gone away into those scalped bodies the Comanche left behind, he could not think about them at all, and the thing he hated most was the notion of horses he loved being driven north toward the territories by those savages.

Three summers later, when he was seventeen, she left him behind altogether. "You are man enough," she said. "You take care of yourself like I am going to take care of myself." She was loading just a few things into saddle bags, rich-looking carved-leather bags provided by the tubercular-looking white-haired man she was with, a man who wore one quick gun and claimed to be a medical doctor, although no one had ever known him to cure anything. "We are going to settle in the north," she said, talking about her reasons for traveling, as though the white-haired man meant nothing. "He is going to do some work," she said, talking about the eastern Wyoming Territory around Laramie. "Things are cleaner in the north," she said, before she rode off alongside her man. "But you stay around here. You can be what you want to be around here."

By the next summer he was riding with the Texas Rangers, all of them young and clean-handed and shaven, except for the older ones with brushy mustaches, and he was thinking about the man she had ridden away with, going north to some trouble centering around the long-horned cattle being driven that way out of Texas in the great herds, thinking about how he was going to learn this law business clean, getting set for another one-day meeting with that white-haired medical doctor. He could not stop thinking about her with that man, in his bed, on her knees and her elbows as she had been when the Comanche struck. He knew she was that way with the white-haired man, and he watched them in the darkness and kept his hands off himself, getting ready.

Then in the spring of 1876 the Cavendish gang left him there shot in the face, thinking him dead on the rocky dry riverbed, and there came along a single Indian, the man without a tribe on the paint horse, the good dark man who found him and nursed him, and he recalled that long-ago morning the Comanche struck and knew this was a different life. As he recovered, he knew childishness was left behind, that somewhere in the kindness of this new companion there was a force he would hold always steady against what, until now, he had thought he loved: her white flesh in the sunlight that morning while she crouched with her skirt thrown forward.

For a long while things were so easily clear, there was this new friend and there was the great white horse, and both sides of what was right, like the Indian and buffalo on the United States nickel. The mask and silver bullets were emblems of the need to be austere and distant if you were to be great and right. He understood emblems were only emblems, ways of getting work done, even though the mask covered that dark purple scar, the twisted hole that had been his nostrils before the Cavendish gang shot him down and rode away, thinking he was dead, seeing as he looked drowned in blood.

What luck that he could shoot so perfectly without any sense of aiming, the silver bullets being after all part of him, the way he thought, the shooting more a business of balance and intent than anything he understood, the bullets just going where he thought they would, as though he could see a pistol in the hand of some craven man and shoot it away with only a thought.

Those were the legendary wandering years, when he did not think about his sister. There was plenty of time; time was a trapeze that only swung you back and forth. Those were the years our Union advanced in its skip-step way toward the Pacific and the meeting of fresh water with salt tides in the Golden Gate, the years our passenger pigeons were clubbed out of trees and Indian children were clubbed out of bushes as the nation made ready for the clubbing of Cuba and the Philippines and China. The Pony Express riders mounted their quickly saddled horses at a run while savages burned the way stations behind them; all but the impounded remnants of our sixty-odd million buffalo were slaughtered for their tongues and humps and hides and bones; the long-horned cows wore their way north to the grassy plains of Montana and Wyoming, surviving stampede while the lightning flashed, surviving quicksand on the Platte, only to perish in the snowy blizzard of 1885. The horse-drawn stages scattered dust between towns like Helena and Butte, Goldfield and Tonapah, carrying treasure in their strong-boxes and enticing weak black-hatted men into banditry; the railroads came, building their graded roadbeds inexorably up through the passes, over Donner Summit and through the Marias in the northern Rockies; the nester fought the cattle barons; the cattle men fought the sheep and the rich fought the poor; the barbed wire went up and fought the wind; the sod-grass was plowed under; the streets of Carson City were paved with brick that had served as ballast on sailing ships from China; Joseph and Looking Glass fought off tourists in Yellowstone, which was already a National Park, before losing everything they had suffered for in the Bear Paw Mountains. Somewhere far away the last visionary chiefs were dying. Crazy Horse was dead, and what there was to defend was somehow over as the first popping of the internal combustion engine began to be heard. There was nothing right left to do most of the time, nothing at all to do, and our man who began down on the Brazos was not yet fifty years of age, still quick-handed as he had ever been, and bored.

In 1912 Tonto found a woman and stayed in Grants Pass, Oregon, amid blossoming spring apple and cherry trees and what the masked man called wine-berries. The woman had come west as a child from the plains after her toes were frozen off in the aftermath of the great Ghost Dance massacre on the Pine Ridge Reservation of South Dakota in December of 1891. "We were like animals," the woman said, "so they let us run."

The earth shook San Francisco, where he knew she was, where she had to be, that most sin-filled and elegant city, with water all around. The trench warfare began in Europe, and he was too old. Over there they fought each other from craft in the air, he would have liked that, it seemed right, and he was too old. Then the war was over and he started toward the coast, rode the white horse through the mountains of northern New Mexico, along the old trails that had been graded into roadways, wintered alongside a lake in the Sierras, and in spring drifted down to the valley towns of California, wondering what next, trying to stay furtive now, hiding out, taking his time on this way to San Francisco, perfecting disguises.

He was growing old, alone with the white horse, almost seventy and getting ready for San Francisco, thinking of her hair, the dark marks of age on her hands, which would be like his. The man she left San Antonio with was no doubt dead, but she would have another. There would be something. In some elegant house on one of those hills she would be pouring tea from a silver service, pouring steadily, her hands not shaking at all. He would lift the delicate cup made of fragile English porcelain, and perhaps she would smile.

The summer day was cool that close to the ocean as he came up the old mission road, the El Camino, into the Mission District of San Francisco. Off west the Twin Peaks were green with forest and above them gray fog stood like an arrested wave. The Pacific was over there, and he had never seen the ocean, never seen real waves coming from Asia. The solid ground felt precarious, like it might tip, as though it could slip away without the strength of the continent spread around. He wished he were back on the solid ground of the interior, and smiled at himself, knowing he should have come here when he was not old, when he would have liked this walking on eggs, this vast uneasiness, so much more important to confront than some fool with a model 1873 Colt revolver. So he stabled the white horse in a barn on the swampy ground of the upper Mission, and he rode an electrified trolley car out toward the ocean, to see what it was.

It was like he was invisible, disguised as an old man with a shot-off nose that was impossibly ugly to look at. The black man in the livery stable had treated him like a customer, and the people crowding around him on the trolley car talked and laughed like nothing at all was the matter, like this was what they did all the time.

As though his wound were only a matter of accident. Four seats down there was an old woman with an enormous goiter on the side of her neck, and no one looked at her either. Except for him, he watched her, and once she looked up and caught him and smiled.

They passed beyond the Twin Peaks, beneath the fog and out onto the grassy dune-land that descended toward the sea, and it was necessary to walk. The trolley line ended, and a board walk went on. He strolled, feeling he was coming toward the edge of what he had always been. But it wasn't. It was heavy with dampness, the fog thick around him, the waves gray and white the little way out he could see, but it wasn't like the edge of anything. He took off his boots and left them in the sand, and walked down to the water, which was cold as hell lapping on his blue-white feet. He backed out and rolled himself a cigarette, pulled a few drags of smoke, and flicked the cigarette into the water. It was like being at the center of something, standing barefoot on warm damp ground beside the house where you have always lived in the center of Kansas. He fired one shot out into the very center of that gray circle of oncoming water and fog and smiled at himself because there was nothing there to disarm.

Of course she wasn't up there in those hills, in some rich man's house. He knew that. She would not have gone that way. Down on Market Street, the next day after he slept in the stable beside the white horse, that was where she would be. She would understand that much, and be in the right place, down there with the injured, where arrogance was equal to foolishness. Over the years she would have figured it out. She would have left the white-haired man before he died, she would have gone right and poor.

But she was not there. This day he went without his guns again, without his mask and the gun-belt stocked with silver bullets. The white horse stayed where it was stabled, munching oats calmly as if this were not a new world, and he walked the barrooms, expecting to see her laughing and quarreling, maybe selling flowers on a street-corner. That night he stayed in a room which smelled of urine and ammonia, slept on sheets that smelled of old nervous sweat, not really sleeping, just resting there and dreaming, feeling she was nearby somewhere, knowing she was there, close by, waiting. But she was not. He walked the muddy streets toward the outskirts of the city as a common man, and she was not there.

At least he had not recognized her.

So it was her turn.

He went back to the only things there were: his mask, his silence, those guns, the great white horse. No matter what the comforts of nearby water, he would not be a common man. Trussed out in his black leather gun-belt, so she would see, he would be what he had always been, so totally prepared for whatever happened he had always been able to see the moment of his own death: the lurking coward, the high-power rifle and the shot from behind, the loud after-crack echoing where the Staked Plains fall on the Cap Rock in west Texas, swallows flushing and turning through the afternoon, deer in thickets by the river lifting their heads after the impact, as the darkness closed and the far-away silence began. These last gunless days of searching in this city, where even the sound of the last rifle shot would be lost amid the cobbled streets, as he went aimlessly where she might be, that moment of dying seemed closer.

But he would not die dumb and amiable. So he made inquiries. Who was the most evil and wretched man in this town? She would see, he thought, as the great horse cantered on the bricks. He would not be a common man.

There was no worst man, but there was the man rumored to own the worst men. There from far away we see the city on the hills in the sunlight of that morning, the water gleaming around the ferry boats, the sidewalk crowds along Market Street and the trolley cars clanging, the square black automobiles and the masked man on his white horse riding proudly between the stone buildings, up from the Mission and then down Market toward the building where the ferry boats were docking.

The white horse prances and his mane blows in the sea-breeze. The masked man stops before an Irish tavern, and calms his horse. In through the gleaming clean windows of the tavern he can see faces peering out, old men and old women, and great depths. In his deep, steady voice he calls out the worst man in San Francisco, an old Chinese gentleman with a white thin beard and so the story goes, hundreds of killer functionaries, both white and oriental, some brutal, some cunning. The masked man sits his horse with his hands poised at his guns. At least that old magic will bring down one or two before he goes, even though the deer along the Brazos will never hear of it. But the old Chinese gentleman comes out alone, wearing a long brocade gown decorated with silver and gold thread, and he holds his hands together before him, as though praying.

"You come in," he says in his quavering voice, gesturing at the masked man.

"You come in with us," he says.

"You shake your hands at your sides," he says, "and you feel the sun on your back, and the great knot will untie itself."

"Feel the warmth," he says, "move your fingers."

"Twist your head on your neck, and feel the cracking as things come loose. Feel the movement of each finger, the warmth of the sun and the coolness of the sea." The Chinese gentleman begins moving his hands up and down at his sides in motions like those of newborn birds, the deep sleeves on his embroidered gown flapping as if he might at any moment fly.

As if his body were at last doing what it wanted with him, the masked man found his fingers flexing and unlocking and his head slowly turning from one side to the other, lifting and falling as he twisted and the small old bones of his upper spine began to crack apart from one another. "Feel the movement of each finger," the Chinese gentleman says, "and the aching in your joints as it all comes loose."

Like a child out on that street astride his great white horse, as his arms begin to lift and his fingers feel like feathers, the masked man knows it is important now, in this old age, to risk foolishness. Something new has begun, and the heavy revolvers at his sides will never again be part of what he is; he feels light and only encumbered by these trappings of greatness, the guns and heavy silver bullets in the stiff leather belt. "Step down," the Chinese gentleman says, "and accept this present from an old man." From the folds in his gown the Chinese gentleman produces an orange, which he holds as a gift toward the masked man.

"They are the sweetest and oldest in all the world," the Chinese gentleman says. "The golden apples. In the south of China they are like fire amid the emerald leaves."

Thus the masked man comes to stand in the cool and cavernous darkness of the tavern with his fingers feeling like feathers, and a China Orange before him on the hardwood surface of the bar. "The outside is golden," the Chinese gentleman says. "The inside is sweet."

The people crowding around the masked man are old, and they are talking as old people will, standing in clusters and sometimes gesturing, sometimes talking angrily, but talking. A fat old woman with bright red lipstick and a pink flowered dress, who could never have been his sister, rubs at his neck, digging her thumbs into the knot he feels now between the blades of his shoulders, and there, as the masked man stands twisting his head on his neck, listening to the cracking of small bones loosening themselves from one another, he knows the knot is coming undone, unstringing him from what he has always been, and the guns at his side are a heavy and foolish weight.

"You stay here with us," the Chinese gentleman says.

The masked man lifts his guns from their holsters and places them carefully on the worn mahogany surface of the bar. Alongside them he places a silver bullet, and he orders a drink, a round for the house, for what he calls his friends, and an Irish bartender in a stiff collar sets him up a bottle of whiskey and accepts the silver bullet as payment.

The masked man peels off his mask and stands barefaced beside the aged Chinese gentleman and does not feel mutilated as he sips his drink and listens to this society he has joined, the old Finns and the French and Britishers around him talking, the cackling of old men, old women telling of childbirth after raising the drinks he has bought to toast him silently.

"There was a morning . . ." the masked man says. No one is listening. The masked man begins to peel the soft glowing China Orange, stripping the peel away in a long spool and then separating the sections and aligning them before him on the bar before eating the first one. The juice is cool and rich. For him it is over. He will be ancient when the great fires blossom over Dresden and Japan, after the millions died, and he will not know he should care. Salmon die in turbines and he does not know at all.

But there was a moment when great silence descended and beyond the Staked Plains and the Cap Rock of west Texas, where the swallows flushed and turned through the afternoon, deer in the thickets by the Brazos lifted their heads. In that silence amid bullrushes by the river, a girl crouches on her knees with her skirt thrown forward, her flesh so perfectly white under the fresh morning sun. "Don't you stop," she says, and that great white horse rears above the rolling horizon, which is golden and simple in the sunset. Those sparkling hooves striking out into the green light under dark midsummer thunderclouds, and far away there is rain as the stars grow luminous.

■ DAVID LONG

David Long was born in Massachusetts in 1948. He studied with William Kittredge and Richard Hugo and received an M.F.A from the University of Montana in 1974. From his home in Kalispell, Montana, Long has taught in the Montana Poets in the Schools Program and at Flathead Valley Community College. His stories and poems have been published widely. "Eclipse" is reprinted here from Home Fires, *which was awarded the St. Lawrence Short Fiction Prize for 1982. Long's latest collection of stories is* The Flood of '64, *published in 1987.*

Eclipse

I came home on borrowed rides, east across the sun-blinded distances of Nevada and Utah, north into the forests of Montana, slouched on the cracked seats of pickups, remembering indistinctly what had taken me away and more vividly what I had found. In the back of my mind was the idea that being home would put an end to it. The green-painted man was dead in the bathtub, overdosed beyond bliss. The shower head had dripped all night on his startled face, rivulets of poster paint streaking the porcelain, as if the life inside him had putrified and drained itself. He was nobody I knew. None of them were. So I had stepped into the early morning glare, made my way out of San Pedro's dockyards, squinting at the furious light, fighting off the stink of casualties. The curiosity had burned off me like a dusting of black powder. It was nothing religious after all, only rumors and attractions, an itch in the bloodstream I had taken with full seriousness. The Indian dropped me on the corner by the western-wear store. "Hey, you take care of yourself," he yelled, pulling away, the beer cans rattling in the empty bed of his truck.

The wind blew dust in my eyes. I recognized nobody on the streets. I found that the wave that had carried off so many of us who grew up here had left only the most stubborn, and in my absence they had made families and leaned into their work as if they were born to it. I felt born to no work in particular and had long ago been absolved of kin, having no brothers or sisters, a father who had filled his veins with a substance used to euthanize household pets, and a mother who had found religion in an Arizona retirement community. Though I figured it was as much mine as anyone's, I was not carefully remembered in this town, and I thought I could use this fact to begin a normal, unobtrusive life for myself. Within a year I married Johanna, a big, pleasant girl whose red curls hung thick and guileless around her shoulders, whose skin smelled of salt and flour, who tended to simple jokes and loose clothes of khaki and checked flannel. If she was on a quest it was for nothing ethereal or terribly hard to locate. I must have seemed like a survivor of distant wickedness, a man in need of good intentions. It was true, and I was grateful for the real affection she lavished on me, never understanding it clearly, always fearful she loved the mothering more than its damaged object. I ate her carob cookies, her hardly raised soybean breads, her breakfast rolls suffocating in honey. I never yelled, I never threatened. After suppers on late summer nights, after the thunderstorms had cleared the air, we'd walk the bank of the low-running river, the swifts darting around our heads, the silence between us comfortable enough. I would watch her sit in the debris of washed-up stones, her soft chin lifted to the light as she studied the familiar pattern of mountains that surrounded us, her eyes unable to hide their satisfaction. Saturday nights we drank Lucky Lager at the Amvets and danced around and round to the soothing tunes of Jan Dell and her band, Johanna's favorite. Home again in the insulated darkness of the trailer's bedroom, she would clutch me, so full and earnest I thought I had succumbed–to her, to every bit of it.

Johanna's father, Darrell, was the district Petrolane distributor, and, though he took me with suspicion, he was persuaded to give me a job driving one of his gas trucks. Every day I followed a lazy loop of junctions and wheat towns, contemplating the horizon–stubbled or rich-tasseled, depending on the season. Sometimes the sheer size of the panorama gave me a taste of the planet's curvature, a glimpse of the big picture, but I couldn't hold it. When I stopped, I would stand by the truck and listen to the troubles of the ranchers, nodding as if I truly sympathized. Every night I came home and kicked my boots off and stretched out on the recliner by the TV like a thousand other husbands in town.

Johanna had a son the next year, and when he had grown past earliest infancy he looked so much like her I saw none of myself in him. She named him Eric after her father's father who had died some months before. He was solid and cheerful, everything I was not. Johanna grew less tolerant. When she wanted to lighten my mood, she could come and tell me, "You have a boy you can be proud of." It was not pride but panic I felt. I would often wake and see his round clear-eyed face inches from mine as though he had stood for hours waiting for me. I knew there was something that should flow between us, as unasked for as spring water or moonlight. At night I would lay him in the bottom of the bunkbed he, so far, shared with only the dark room. I would try to make up stories to send him off to a good sleep. Nothing came.

"Tell him what it was like when you were a boy," Johanna said. "He'd like *anything* from you."

"It's a blur," I told her.

"What is it with you?" she said.

"If I knew, I'd fix it," I said.

"Would you?"

I turned away from her and went out and started the pickup and backed it out as far as the mailboxes and couldn't decide which way to turn. I shut off the engine and in a moment lay down on the bench seat and tried to clear my head. I fell asleep hugging myself in the cool November air. When I woke, there was a skim of snow on the hood of the truck. I walked back to the trailer. She had left a message on the refrigerator door, spelled out in Eric's magnetic letters. *Give or Go.* I went to the bedroom. A brittle ballad was coming from the clock radio. "Listen," I said, shaking her shoulder, but she was deep asleep.

One Friday afternoon, after the long, wasting winter had gone, I came home from my route, later than normal since I'd stopped along the way for two Happy Hours, and found Johanna and Eric gone. In fact, it was all gone, the trailer house and everything. I climbed out of the truck, dumb-struck, a fine rain soaking my hair. Deep tracks curled through the shoots of pale grass I'd finally made grow. The muddy plywood skirts were strewn like a busted poker hand. I was wiped clean. The only thing left on the lot was the empty dog house, canted and streaked after a bad season.

In his office the next morning Darrell handed me my last paycheck in a licked-shut envelope and went back to what he was doing, punching digits on his pocket calculator as if they were bugs.

"That's all you're going to tell me?" I asked him.

"That's about got it," Darrell said.

"What'd I do? Tell me that!"

Darrell's eyes disappeared in a squinty smile. He slid the snoose around inside his mouth.

"Near as I can tell," Darrell said, "you didn't do a goddamn thing."

I took a third-story room at the Frontier Hotel and sat on the cold radiator and watched the spavined old horse-breakers limp in and out of the cafe across the street, their straw hats stuck to their heads like barnacles. I quietly considered the loss of my wife and child and felt nothing sharp—except surprise, and when I focused on that I realized that the breakup had been a sure thing all along. Her letter came without a return address. Don't worry, she said, she wouldn't be hounding me for money, Darrell had taken care of her. About Eric she said: *He won't remember you. I believe it's just as well.* About her reasons she said only: *I'm sorry; I won't be your rest cure.*

The sun finally took control of the valley. Lilacs flowered outside the dentist's office, road crews patched chuck holes up and down Main Street, the foothills shone in a green mist above the roof of the abandoned Opera House. Strangers nodded *howdy* on the sidewalks. Everything was repairing itself, and I was out of time with it. Years before, I had felt myself choking in this town and blamed its narrow imagination, and had gone off looking for something Bigger Than Life. Now I didn't have the heart to move nor any trace of destination.

I found work at a small outfit south of town that manufactured camper shells for pickups. There I met Clevinger, a scrawny, tiny-eyed man my age, a twice-wounded survivor of Vietnam patrols. He'd worn the others out with his chatter and fixed on me as soon as I arrived. I listened as long as I could. Clevinger's idea of heaven was twenty acres up the North Fork, heavily timbered and remote, a place to disappear to. Every afternoon after work he drove out and looked at parcels of land that only a few years earlier he might have afforded, and every morning he jabbered about the bastards who owned the money. As he talked, he flexed the muscles in his arms, as white and hard as if they had grown underground. He was a man who'd changed, so certainly I didn't need to know how he'd been before. It showed as visibly as cracks running across his face. Seeing him like that made me know that I was not so different, though I had nothing like jungle warfare to blame it on.

It was a hot, rainless summer. The wilderness areas flared with fire time and again, and one afternoon in early September a burn started in a tinder-dry draw near town and crept over the nearby foothills. Clevinger and I left the shop and stood in the parking lot watching the black smoke billow above the fireline. A World War II bomber rumbled over our heads and banked toward the trees, spraying bright reddish streams of fire retardant, through which the sunlight came streaked and bloody. Clevinger said nothing, his arms hugged tight against his skinny chest, the pale skin around his eyes jerking as the smoke drifted over us. It was the next day Clevinger exploded in the shop. All of a sudden he was down in a fiery-eyed crouch, strafing the room with his pneumatic nailing gun. I was caught in the open, carrying a half-built assemblage with a boy named Buster. Clevinger hit us both. The first cleat took Buster above the wrist; he yipped and let go of his end, the weight of it all falling to me. My back snapped like a pop bead. As I went down a second cleat shot through my mouth, taking with it slivers of jawbone.

I lay flat on the concrete, choking on pain, staring up at the moldering light coming through the Quonset's skylight, hearing shouts and grunts and finally the sound of metal striking Clevinger's skull. For weeks afterward I could see the dark luster of Clevinger's eyes, the look that said it didn't matter who we were. It was nothing personal.

My back was badly torn but would heal if I behaved myself. My jaw had to be wired. When they let me out of the hospital, I returned to my room at the Frontier and ate broth and Instant Breakfasts and anything else I could get to seep through my closed teeth. I called Workman's Comp and discovered I was the victim of a policy called the Coordination of Benefits. My caseworker, Wayne, treated me like I was both childlike and dangerous. It was months before I saw a dollar. In the meantime there wasn't much to do but stay put. My body began to mend, but my imagination had time to dwell on things in earnest.

One night I woke from a late afternoon sleep, got out of bed, took two or three steps across the room, and halted in momentary amnesia. I had no idea who I was. I stood there in my underwear, becalmed, entranced by the blue prayerlike light filling my window, and then a few heartbeats later it all came back: the pain in my back, the peculiar tingle of mortality, shards of waking dreams that added up to nothing but the sense of being orphaned. I turned back to the bed, half-expecting to see a woman's body curled in the sheets, but there was no one at all.

I wandered across the hall to the bathroom, a narrow slot of a room with only a lidless commode. When I hit the light switch, the bulb flared and died. I sat on the can with only the last smudge of light in the dusty glass high over head. When I was done, I discovered that my key was twisted in the lock in such a way that the door would not open. I rattled the handle. Nothing. A strong cry might've summoned one of the other tenants of that dim corridor, but their ears were old and tuned a lot out, and, besides that, the hardware in my mouth let me only growl, like a groggy yard dog.

I sat down.

The darkness was complete. Minutes went by, and I didn't move, didn't holler, didn't lift my head. I felt perfectly severed, as though I had waked into a world I had always known would be there, a silent starless place where the species began and died in utter solitude, one by one by one. I thought of Johanna and Eric, saw their faces floating like reflections, the blackness shining through them. I knew I had not been brave in losing them, only stiff and sullen. I hadn't understood until now the truth of it: that I had not loved her, that I wasn't able to. I had wanted a family for comfort and retreat. All the times I had mumbled love in the dark were counterfeit. And she had known it first, known it pure and simple.

I had gone on and made a son and covered my lack of father feeling with an impatient, tin-faced act. Maybe it was true and good he would not remember me, maybe he would grow toward his own adulthood with only a strange hulking shadow lurking in the backwaters of his memory. Or maybe Johanna would turn up a big-hearted man who could believe a small boy's love was worth the world, and Eric would grow into such a man himself.

The sadness oozed around me like primeval silt. I was stuck in a closet stinking of mold and old men's urine and didn't care to free myself. I could blame myself, or not. I could curse the luck of the draw or the God I never knew. None of it mattered. The world takes it from you, regardless–even the thrill, even the energy to complain. There was nothing holy and nothing magical and no point believing it was a quest of any kind.

Shivering, in my Jockey shorts and faded Grateful Dead T-shirt, I started to cry, so hard it was more like a convulsion, every beat of it wincing up and down my backbone. Some time later I became aware of a pounding on the door and then the clicking of a key. It was then, for the first time, I saw Mr. Tornelli, his great head haloed by the red light of the EXIT sign across the hall.

"What's this?" Mr. Tornelli said.

I could say that Mr. Tornelli saved my life, but it wasn't right then, nor did the man seem a likely redeemer.

"Listen, Jack," he said, squinting into the cubicle, "You move your belly-aching out to the hall a minute, OK? I need the shitter."

In a moment I was in the world again, suddenly quieted. I didn't go back to my room but stood on the strip of balding carpet, waiting. Mr. Tornelli emerged after awhile, his eighty-year-old back a little straighter, his suspenders fastened, his collarless white shirt glowing in the weak light. His head seemed too big for the wickery body it rested on, and his moustaches–there were clearly two of them–were folded down over his mouth like wind-ruffled ptarmigan wings. Composed now, he studied me like a puzzle.

"You got pants?" Mr. Tornelli said.

I didn't answer.

He shook his head gravely. "Listen," he said, "you put your pants on and come down to my room. I'll wait right here."

A moment sometimes arrives when you see the different people you are and have been all at once. It happens without warning, the way a sudden shift of light will show depths in water. Before I'd gone into the bathroom I would have shirked the old man's offer, made a note to shun him in the halls. But I stood nodding at him, found myself pulling on my jeans and accompanying him to his room, the last one on the floor, the one next to the fire escape.

"You know this vertigo?" Mr. Tornelli said.

He walked slowly, both hands a little elevated as if holding imaginary canes.

"Afraid of heights?" I said.

He bent to hear my muffled voice. "No, no," he said. "Not afraid of high places. It's. . . ." He stopped and swiveled his head toward me and twirled his fingers in the air. "Feels like everything whirls."

"Bad," I said.

Mr. Tornelli smiled. "You get used to it."

Rooms at the Frontier were stark, unremitting. Out of superstition I had refrained from making mine any more attractive. Just passing through, the bare walls said. It was immediately clear that Mr. Tornelli didn't see it that way. His was bright and well-appointed: the bed was neatly made, covered with a star-pattern quilt; succulents and African violets and Wandering Jews were crowded on the desk by the southwest window; the walls were obscured by maps and star charts and color blow-ups. A giant photo-illustration of the full moon hung directly over his pillow.

Mr. Tornelli urged me to make myself comfortable. That wasn't possible, of course, but I eased into his straight-backed chair and looked at his little kingdom. He nodded matter-of-factly and sank into his white wicker rocker and folded his hands.

"So," Mr. Tornelli said, widening his great sapphire eyes, "you are a troubled boy and not in a good position to talk about it."

I tried to push the words forward with my tongue, a futile effort. Mr. Tornelli waved me off.

"Don't bother," he said. "You'll just swim around in it." He made an extravagant two-handed pulling motion. "Then you'll want a rope. Forgive me, but I'm not up to it anymore." He laughed with a kind of brittle pleasure. "When you get it down to one sentence, then I'll listen. Would that be all right?"

He rousted himself from the chair and went to the dresser.

"But then you won't need me, will you? No, for tonight's trouble the best thing is brandy," he said. "Perhaps I should shoot it into your mouth with a syringe. Would you like that?"

So Mr. Tornelli and I drank the brandy. It worked on me as it does in the high timber, back to the wind. I stopped shivering. The cipher of ice in my middle began to melt under its heat.

I noticed after awhile that right above his chair was a brilliant photograph of a total eclipse: a golden ring shining around a black disk. Mr. Tornelli admitted having taken it.

"Kenya, 1973. Extraordinarily clear, no?"

I nodded.

"A good turnout that year, but blistering. Some of these young watchers are real zealots. It's good to see. I'll tell you, I spent most of my time under a beach umbrella. There was also, I remember, a type of flying ant that laid eggs in your hair." He threw open his hands. "Ah, but I wouldn't have missed it. Over seven minutes dark. I had planned that it would be my last one, but maybe I was wrong."

He smiled at me curiously. "You know, I might live to see the one here."

"Too many clouds," I managed to say.

"I know," Mr. Tornelli said. "A bad season for the sun. But I think we might be fortunate that day."

He stood, momentarily fighting the spinning in his head, then began giving me the guided tour: Caroline Islands, 1934: Boise, 1945; Manila, 1955; the Aleutians, 1963. A trajectory of blotted suns progressing across his wall.

"I hope you forgive me my fascinations," he said. "Let me tell you a secret. I was born during the eclipse of 1900. My mother was crossing Louisiana on the train and stopped long enough to have me. Do you think I am a marked man?"

He laughed again, and for the first time in a long while I smiled.

"Do you know," he began again, "*eclipse* means *abandonment*? It does. Abandonment. Can you imagine what it would be like if you didn't know about it? Everything's going along just like always, then *poof*, no sun. Imagine. You'd have some fancy explaining to do.

"The Ojibways thought the sun was going out so they shot burning arrows at it so it would catch on again. Another tribe thought all the fire in the world was going to be sucked up by the darkness so they hid their torches inside their huts. People have come up with a number of stories. . . ."

In the coming months the local papers would have a bonanza with the eclipse, playing science off legend. They told about Hsi and Ho, two luckless Chinese astronomers so drunk on rice wine they blew their prediction and were executed. They explained about coronas and shadow boxes and irreparable damage to the eye. In all I read I felt a strange longing for an ignorance that could make it crucial and magical. I thought about Mr. Tornelli's attraction, and it seemed that some of the raw amazement survived in him.

"We had a great friendship in those days," Mr. Tornelli said. "We would meet every few years, take in the spectacle and then go back where we came from. Never saw one another in between. It was all unspoken. Well, many of them are surely dead by now."

"Why are you here?" I asked him finally. It was the only important question I had for him.

"Why this fleabag? That's very good," Mr. Tornelli said, stroking the feathers of his moustache. "Where do you go when you can go anywhere? You think it matters? Well, I guess it does. To tell the truth, I knew a woman in this town once. A married lady, I'm afraid." He drifted a few moments. "Well, I remember how it was to be here and love somebody. Amazing, isn't it? Sometimes I ask myself if this was all the same life."

A few minutes past three, Mr. Tornelli finally stood again and insisted on walking me to my room. A comic, paternal gesture, it seemed. He said good night. Neither drunk nor sober, I lay in bed listening to the silence of the old hotel, the place the old man and I had come to. I imagined what it was made of: dentures soaking in a water glass, an old woman's dotted Swiss hanging in a closet with a lavendar sachet, dreams beginning and ending in some rooms and in others only the silence that follows the departure of one of our number. It was a powerful chord. I realized that Mr. Tornelli had done nothing except come between me and myself. Alone again, the trouble was with me. In the moments before sleep I tried to say its name in the simple sentence he wanted, but I could not.

Autumns here aren't the fiery poignant seasons they have in country with hardwoods and rolling hills. They are as abrupt here as the terrain. Indian summer vanishes overnight, clouds pour in from the northwest and smother the valley like dirty insulation. The rain comes quickly and strips the few maples and elms in a day, leaving the slick leaves puddled around their trunks like fool's gold. I woke late that next morning and a single look at the color of the light in my window told the story. My back had seized up overnight. It took many minutes to get upright, shuffle to the sink, and rinse the scum from my mouth with hydrogen peroxide. Mr. Tornelli seemed like a figment of last night's gloom.

I dressed carefully and went down to the pay phone and called Wayne at Workman's Comp. He sounded edgy. The computer in Helena had spit out my claim again. "Of course," Wayne said, "you know that *personally* I feel you're qualified. You know that, don't you?" I hung up on him and walked two blocks to the bank where the story was no better. Coming out I saw my ex-father-in-law heading toward the cafe. He speeded up to avoid me, then apparently thought better of it. He stopped and took me by the shoulders and gave me a good American once-over.

"You look like shit, you know that?" Darrell said.

"That's good news."

A logging truck rumbled past us, downshifting at the intersection, snorting black smoke in a long vibrant blast.

"How's that now," Darrell said, leaning in a little.

"I'd kick you down to the Feed & Grain," I said.

"No, you wouldn't," Darrell said. "You wouldn't do nothing. Boy, let me tell you, she had the angle on you all right."

He let go of me and shook his big pinkish head and walked off.

For weeks nothing seemed to change but the tiresome thaw and freeze of my back. When I could walk any distance, I scuffed through the town park, the sad remains of the founding family's estate, watching the ducks and Canadian honkers gather in the safety of the brackish pond. Mothers knelt in the cold grass behind their kids as they tossed wads of stale bread at the birds. I never had anything to give. Back at the hotel, I would sit on the edge of the mattress and feel the tightening set in.

I saw almost no one, except Mr. Tornelli. Days he didn't answer his door I went away undernourished, aimless, and vaguely dizzy. But most often he was there and ushered me in with a bright courtesy, as if he'd waited all day for me. He took my silence for granted. He talked freely, sprinkling the air with different voices. Sometimes I truly thought there were more than one of him. He had stared through the giant telescope at Mount Palomar; he had ridden boxcars from San Diego to the Midwest, once delivering the baby of a homeless woman in the light of a mesquite fire near the tracks; he had been an optics engineer at Polaroid. He had once been fired from a teaching position in Wisconsin for being a Communist, which he wasn't, and later asked to guest lecture as a blackballed scientist, which he declined. He had once shaken hands with Neils Bohr, the physicist, outside a hotel in Stockholm. He had taken peyote with Indians in a stone hogan in the mountains of New Mexico. In his vision he had become water, felt himself evaporating from the leaves of the cottonwood and rushing into the upper air and being blown high over the mountains with others like himself, then a great sense of weight and of falling at terrific speed through the darkness.

"*Outstanding*," Mr. Tornelli said. "I wish you could have been there."

I listened patiently. I came to suspect that his talks were something more than reminiscences, that they were aimed at me as if he knew the dimension and velocity of my mood. He always seemed to stop short of conclusions, though. The stories hung there, unresolved.

"Puzzling, isn't it?" he would say with a quick opening of the hands, as if he were releasing a dove, or maybe just giving up his grip on all that his mind had tried to bring together. I was entertained, diverted, moved.

Eight weeks to the day after Clevinger's outburst, the wires were removed from my jaw.

"So," Mr. Tornelli said. "Your tongue is out of its cage. A drink, to celebrate?"

"Thank you."

He handed me a gold-rimmed glass and retired to his chair.

"Now, maybe you can tell me about all this gloomy stuff?" he said.

"I think you know about it," I told him.

Mr. Tornelli leaned forward on his elbows, the light glowing on the waxy skin of his forehead. He looked at me a long time before speaking.

"There was a time," he said finally. "I was at sea aboard a freighter in the North Atlantic." He paused, as if squinting the memory into focus. "I couldn't sleep and there wasn't a soul to talk to. I went out and stood at the railing and stared at the ship's wake. My mind was empty, I could see nothing but the picture of my feet disappearing, then my shirt, my head, no brighter in the moonlight than a trace of the ship's foam. Let me tell you, I was *right there*. . . ."

"What was it?"

"Who knows? A bad time, a bad year. I was sick to death of my failures. I thought the world was a hopeless place. I stayed there all night, and then the horizon lightened a little, the wind came up, and I realized. . . ."

"What?"

He smiled lightly. "I was freezing. Freezing."

Other times he just let me in and returned to his chair and said nothing. As winter descended on us, these occasions seemed more frequent. The silences weren't painful, but it was those times that I could see him without distraction. Surrounded as he was by the battery of eclipses, the piles of spine-cracked books, *Scientific Americans*, fliptop steno pads filled with his faint ciphering, he seemed little and doomed. As he breathed, his ribs creaked like a ship's rigging. Sometimes he closed his eyes, battling the vertigo that spun fiercely in his head, fingering the gold medallion he wore around his neck. I finally understood that I had seen a man in his last brilliance. If my affliction was elusive and hard to name, his was as common as birth.

January was a menace. Days of cold froze the ground many feet deep and left anything exposed to the air brittle. Great clouds of exhaust drifted down the rows of pickups idling on the side streets, so thick they would hide a man. Steam rose to the ventricles of the top-floor radiators and we kept warm, the air in our rooms so humid we might have been in a sanitarium. Mr. Tornelli's plants flourished, but he seemed more and more unwell. His cheeks were smudged with shadows. I remembered how Johanna bent to the bedroom mirror smearing rouge on her face to invoke the same illusion. Mr. Tornelli was coming by it with a swiftness that prickled the darker chambers of my imagination. He had shown himself to be a man who took care of himself–with grace and dignity–but now I realized there were entire days he failed to eat.

I began escorting him around the block to a small restaurant that served steamed vegetables with its dinners. It catered to the nearby old folks home crowd, and there, in the midst of his peers, Mr. Tornelli nursed languid bits of Swiss steak and seemed to me for the first time no eccentric, no quaint loner. Sometimes I would catch him staring at the others and blinking.

"I don't know, Jack," he said softly. "Who are they?"

Midway through February the cold broke, and in the space of ten days the temperature rose fifty degrees. We could scarcely look at things for the sheen of the melting everywhere. As the date of the eclipse came nearer, I expected Mr. Tornelli's enthusiasm to rekindle. Surely he would muster some sort of celebration. He said nothing. I told him I could get a car and drive us up to Glacier Park, just the two of us. I told him I would help him get out his cameras again. He didn't want to talk about it. He was as short with me as I'd ever heard him. I backed off and waited.

The night of the 25th, Sunday, I went to his door convinced some excitement would show in him. There was no answer to my knocks. He had been sleeping irregularly then, so I swallowed my worry and left the hotel. The sky was streaked, but when I entered the darkness of the alley across the street I could see a few stars. Months ago he had known the sun would shine. I leaned on a dumpster behind one of the bars and stared up through a film of tears. A police car flashed its spot down the alley, and I recovered myself and went in and had a few glasses of beer, though the liveliness of the bar seemed desperate and stupid. It was almost midnight when I came out. From the sidewalk I could see the lights blazing in Mr. Tornelli's window.

I ran upstairs and knocked again and this time the silence was terrifying. I shook the doorknob hard against the deadbolt. I thought I was already too late. Finally I heard his voice, high and boyish.

"Are you all right?"

"Good enough," Mr. Tornelli said through the locked door.

"Could I come in?"

There was a long silence.

"Mr. Tornelli?"

"Jack."

"Right here."

"Could you let me be alone tonight? Would that be all right?"

"I want to be sure you're OK."

"Goodnight, Jack," Mr. Tornelli said with a queer force. I turned and went back to my room. I left all the lights on, thinking I'd get up in a few minutes and check on him. When I woke the sun was up, blasting gold off the windows of the abandoned Opera House.

It was after eight. The moon was already nearing the face of the sun. Still in last night's clothes, I ran down the hall and found Mr. Tornelli's door ajar. I walked in, but he wasn't there. The walls and bed and desk were stripped. A black steamer trunk sat in the middle of the floor, heavy and padlocked. Even the plants were gone.

I ran down to the desk and asked what was going on with Mr. Tornelli, but nobody'd seen him. I ran to the restaurant and stood at the end of the counter scanning the old heads bent over their poached eggs, but Mr. Tornelli's wasn't among them. Back at the Frontier I was desperate. I went up and down the corridor knocking on doors. He wasn't in the can. Mrs. Bache hadn't seen him. No one answered in 312. Mr. Karpowicz in 309 offered to break my jaw again. It was just after his door slammed that I saw what I had missed.

The door to the fire escape was propped open with one of Mr. Tornelli's African violets. The other plants huddled together on the metal slats of the landing. I turned and saw Mr. Tornelli's little medallion looped through the bottom rung of the old ladder that led eight steps to the roof. My heart pounded in my ears.

As I poked my head over the edge of the roof, the sunlight was growing gently dimmer on Mr. Tornelli. He was seated on half a hotel blanket laid over the moist tar and pea stones, cross-legged and tiny. This old man who knew the science of light, who had followed the shadow of the sun around the world, was at this moment sitting here staring naked-eyed into the eclipse.

He patted the empty spot next to him.

"Just in time, my boy," Mr. Tornelli said. "Sit please, keep me company."

I joined him on the blanket.

"Keep your eyes down now; don't ruin them," he said.

Darkness came over our part of the world in waves, stronger and faster now. The sparrows fell silent, the sound of tires faded from the streets below. The corona emerged brilliant from the black disk of the moon.

I took Mr. Tornelli's hand and held it in both of mine.

"I didn't know where you were," I said.

"Yes," Mr. Tornelli said. "You had to find me."

"I didn't know."

"So," he said, whispering, though in the stillness his words were bright and clear. "You see how it is with trouble and happiness. There are some good moments, aren't there. Were you asking for more than that?"

All at once the stars were everywhere, pelting their grace down on us.

"This is, ah, what can I say. . . . We come this far and you and I change places. It's good."

He shut his eyes, smiling still. I leaned over and drew his head down to my shoulder and stroked it as the breath labored in and out of him. The darkness began to ease; there was the slightest lightening visible at the edge of things.

■ DAVID QUAMMEN

Born in Cincinnati, Ohio, in 1948, David Quammen was graduated from Yale in 1970 and received a degree in literature from Oxford University in 1973. He worked as a bartender in Missoula and was a fishing guide on the Madison River before turning full-time to his career as a writer. From his home in Bozeman, Montana, Quammen has written three novels, including The Soul of Victor Tronko *(1987), a spy thriller, and* Blood Line *(1988), a collection of three novellas. His "Natural Acts" column, which appears regularly in* Outside *magazine, received the 1987 National Magazine Award for Essays and Criticism. This selection, which first appeared in* Audubon *magazine in 1982, is reprinted from* Natural Acts, *a collection of essays published in 1985. Quammen's latest book is* The Flight of the Iguana *(1988).*

Jeremy Bentham, the *Pietà*, and a Precious Few Grayling

Rumor had it they were gone, or nearly gone, killed off in large numbers by dewatering and high temperatures during the bad drought of 1977. The last sizable population of *Thymallus arcticus*—Arctic grayling—indigenous to a river in the lower forty-eight states: *ppffft.* George Liknes, a graduate student in fisheries at Montana State University, was trying to do his master's degree on these besieged grayling of the upper Big Hole River in western Montana, and word passed that his collecting nets, in late summer of 1978, were coming up empty. The grayling were not where they had been, or if they were, Liknes for some reason wasn't finding them. None at all? "Well," said one worried state wildlife biologist, "precious few."

Grayling are not set up for solitude. Like the late lamented passenger pigeon, grayling are by nature and necessity gregarious, thriving best in rather crowded communities of their own kind. When the size of a population sinks below a certain unpredictable threshold, grayling are liable to disappear altogether, poof, evidently incapable of successful pairing and reproduction without the circumstantial advantage of teeming fellowship. This may have been what happened in Michigan. Native grayling were extinguished there, rather abruptly, during the 1930s.

The Michigan grayling and the Montana strain had been from time beyond memory the unique and isolated representatives of the species in temperate North America. They were glacial relicts, meaning they had gradually fled southward into open water during the last great freeze-up of the Pleistocene epoch; then, when the mile-thick flow of ice stopped just this side of the Canadian border and began melting back northward, they were left behind in Michigan and Montana as two separate pockets of grayling. These were trapped, as it turned out, cut off by hundreds of miles from what became the primary range of the species, across northern Canada and Alaska. They were stuck in warmish southern habitats overlapping the future range of dominance of *Homo sapiens*; their own future, consequently, insecure.

The Michigan grayling went first. They had been abundant in the upper part of Michigan's Lower Peninsula and in the Otter River of the Upper Peninsula. One report tells of four people catching 3,000 grayling in fourteen days from the Manistee River and hauling most of that catch off to Chicago. By 1935, not surprisingly, the Manistee was barren of grayling. Before long, so was the rest of the state. Sawlogs had been floated down rivers at spawning time, stream banks had been stripped of vegetation (causing water temperatures to rise), exotic competing fish had been introduced, and greedy pressure like that on the Manistee had continued. By 1940, the people of Michigan had just the grayling they were asking for: none.

In Montana, where things tend to happen more slowly, some remnant of the original grayling has endured—against similar adversities in less intense form—a bit longer. Even while disappearing during the past eighty years from parts of their Montana range, grayling have expanded into other new habitat. More accurately, they have been introduced to new habitat, in the zoological equivalent of forced school-busing: hatchery rearing and planting. As early as 1903, soon after the founding of the Fish Cultural Development Station in Bozeman, the state of Montana got into the business of manufacturing grayling; and for almost sixty years thereafter the planting of hatchery grayling was in great vogue.

The indigenous range of the Montana grayling was in the headwaters of the Missouri River above the Great Falls; they were well established in the Smith River, in the Sun River, and in the Madison, the Gallatin, and the Jefferson and their tributaries—notably, the Big Hole River. They had evolved as mainly a stream-dwelling species and existed in only a very few Montana lakes. However, they happened to be rather tolerant of low dissolved-oxygen levels, when those levels occurred in cold winter conditions (but not when the oxygen was driven out of solution by summer warming). This made them suitable for stocking in high lakes, where they could get through the winter on what minimal oxygen remained under the ice. In 1909, 50,000 grayling from the Bozeman hatchery were planted in Georgetown Lake. Just a dozen years later, 28 million grayling eggs were collected from Georgetown, to supply hatchery brood for planting elsewhere. And the planting continued: Ennis Lake, Rogers Lake, Mussigbrod Lake, Grebe Lake in Yellowstone National Park. Between 1928 and 1977, millions more grayling were dumped into Georgetown Lake.

Unfortunately, that wasn't all. Back in 1909, hatchery grayling were also planted in the Bitterroot and Flathead rivers, on the west side of the Continental Divide, in stream waters they had never colonized during their ancestral migration. An innocent experiment, and without large consequences, since the grayling introduced there evidently did not take hold. But then, in what may have seemed a logical extension of all this hatchery rearing and planting, the Big Hole River was planted with grayling. The Big Hole already had a healthy reproducing population of wild grayling, but that was not judged to be reason against adding more. From 1937 until 1962, according to the records of the Montana Department of Fish, Wildlife, and Parks (FWP), more than five million grayling from the Anaconda hatchery were poured into the Big Hole, from the town of Divide upstream to the headwaters: hothouse grayling raining down on wild grayling.

This was before FWP biologists had come upon the belated realization that massive planting of hatchery fish in a habitat where the same species exists as a reproducing population is the best of all ways to make life miserable for the wild fish. Things are done differently these days, but the mistake was irreversible. The ambitious sequence of plantings was very likely the most disastrous single thing that ever happened to the indigenous grayling of the Big Hole.

At best, each planting instantaneously created tenement conditions of habitat and famine conditions of food supply. In each place where the hatchery truck stopped, the river became a grayling ghetto. At worst, if any of the planted fish survived long enough to breed with each other and interbreed with the wild fish, the whole planting program served to degrade the gene pool of the Big Hole grayling, making them less capable of surviving the natural adversities—drought, flood, temperature fluctuation, predation—of their natural habitat.

But here's the good news: Very few of those planted grayling would have survived long enough to breed. The mortality rate on hatchery grayling planted in rivers is close to 100 percent during the first year, and most don't last even three months, whether or not they are caught by a fisherman. These planted grayling come, after all, from a small sample of lake-dwelling parents, with little genetic variety or inherited capacity for coping with moving water. Reared in the Orwellian circumstances of the hatchery, cooped in concrete troughs, without a beaver or a merganser to harry them, eating Purina trout chow from the hand of man, what chance have they finally in the most challenging of habitats, a mountain river? The term "fish planting" itself is a gross misnomer, when applied to dropping grayling or trout into rivers; there is no delusion, even among the hatchery people, that these plants will ever take root. More realistically, it's like providing an Easter egg hunt for tourists with fishing rods.

In 1962 the Big Hole planting ceased, and the remaining wild grayling, those that hadn't died during the famine and tenement periods, were left to get on as best they could. Then came the 1977 drought and, the following year, the George Liknes study. One of Liknes's study sections on the Big Hole was a two-mile stretch downstream from the town of Wisdom to just above the Squaw Creek bridge. On a certain remote part of the stretch a rancher had sunk a string of old car bodies to hold his hayfield in place. From that two-mile stretch, using electroshocking collection equipment that is generally reliable, Liknes did not take a single grayling. This came as worrisome news to me because, on a morning in late summer of 1975, standing waist deep within sight of the same string of car bodies and offering no great demonstration of angling skill, I had caught and released thirty-one grayling in four hours. Now they were either gone or in hiding.

Grayling belong to the salmonid family, as cousins of trout and whitefish. In many ways they seem a form intermediate between those two genera; in other ways, they depart uniquely from the salmonid pattern.

The first thing usually noted about them, their distinguishing character, is the large and beautiful dorsal fin. It sweeps backward twice the length of a trout's, fanning out finally into a trailing lobe, and it is, under certain specific conditions, the most exquisitely colorful bit of living matter to be found in the state of Montana; spackled with rows of bright turquoise spots that blend variously to aquamarine and reddish-orange toward the front of the fin, a deep hazy shading of iridescent mauve overall, and along the upper edge, in some individuals, a streak of shocking rose. That's in the wild, or even stuck on a hook several inches underwater. Lift the fish into the air, and it all disappears. The bright spots and iridescence drain away instantaneously, the dorsal folds down to nothing, and you are holding a drab gun-metal creature that looks very much like a whitefish. The grayling magic vanishes, like a dreamed sibyl, when you pull it to you.

Except for this dorsal fin, the grayling does resemble that most maligned and misunderstood of Montana fish, its near relative, the mountain whitefish. Both are upholstered–unlike the trout–with large stiff scales, scales you wouldn't want to eat. Both have dull-colored bodies, grayish-silver in the grayling, brownish-silver in the whitefish–though the grayling is marked along its forward flank with another smattering of spots, these purplish-black, playing dimly off the themes in the dorsal. They are also distinguishable (from each other and from their common salmonid relatives) by the shape of the mouth. A trout has a wide, sweeping, toothy grin; a whitefish's mouth is narrow and toothless–worse, it is set in a snout that is pointed and cartilaginous, like a rat's, probably the main single cause of the whitefish's image problem. The grayling, as you can see if you look closely, has been burdened with a mouth that is an uneasy compromise between the two: The narrow mouth is set with numerous tiny teeth and fendered with large cartilaginous maxillaries, but its shortened nose couldn't fairly be called a snout. The point is this: The grayling is one of America's most beautiful fish, but only a few subtle anatomical strokes distinguish it from one of the most ugly. A lesson in hubris.

But a superfluous lesson, since the grayling by character is anything but overweening. It is dainty and fragile and relatively submissive. With tiny teeth and little moxie, it fails in all territorial competition against trout–and this is another reason for its decline in the Big Hole, where rainbow and brown and brook trout that have been moved into the neighborhood now bully it mercilessly. Like many beautiful creatures that have known fleeting success, it is dumb. It seeks security in gregariousness and these days is liable to find, instead, carnage. When insect food is on the water, and the fish are attuned to that fact, a fisherman can stand in one spot, literally without moving his feet, and catch a dozen grayling. Trout are not so foolish: Drag one from a hole and the word will be out to the others. The grayling cannot take such a hint. In the matter of food it is an unshakable optimist; the distinction between a mayfly on the water's surface and a hook decorated with feathers and floss is lost on it. But this rashness, in the Big Hole for example, might again be partly a consequence (as well as a cause) of its beleaguered circumstances. The exotic trouts, being dominant, seize the choice territorial positions of habitat, and the grayling, pushed off into marginal water where a fish can only with difficulty make a living, may be forced to feed much more recklessly than it otherwise would.

At certain moments the grayling seems even a bit stoic, as though it had seen its own future and made adjustments. This is noticeable from the point of view of the fisherman. A rainbow trout with a hook jerked snug in its mouth will leap as though it were angry, furious—leap maybe five or six times, thrashing the air convulsively each time. If large, it will run upstream, finally to go to the bottom and begin scrabbling its head in the rubble to scrape out the hook. A whitefish, unimaginative and implacable, will usually not jump, will never run, will stay near the bottom and resist with pure loutish muscle. A grayling will jump once if at all and remain limp in the air, leaping the way a Victorian matron would faint into someone's arms—with demure, trusting abdication. Then, possibly after a polite tussle, the grayling will let its head be pulled above the water's surface, turn passively onto its side, and allow itself to be hauled in. Once beaten, a rainbow can be coaxed with certain tricks of handling to give you three seconds of docility while you get the hook out to release it. A whitefish will struggle like a hysterical pig no matter what. A grayling will simply lie in your hand, pliant and fatalistic, beautiful, placing itself at your mercy.

So no one has much use for the grayling, not even fishermen. It grows slowly, never as large as a trout, and gives unsatisfactory battle. It is scaly, bony, and not especially good to eat. Montana's fish and game laws will allow you to kill five of them from the Big Hole River in a day [at the time this essay appeared in *Audubon*; since then, the regulations have been changed in the grayling's favor], and five more every day all summer—but what will you do with them? Last year a Butte man returned from a weekend on the river and offered a friend of mine ten grayling to feed his cat. The man had killed them because he caught them, very simple logic, but then realized he had no use for them. This year my friend's cat is dead, through no fault of the grayling, so even that constituency is gone. A grayling does not cook up well, it does not fight well. It happens to have an extravagant dorsal fin, but no one knows why. If you kill one to hang on your wall, its colors will wilt away heart-breakingly, and the taxidermist will hand you back a whitefish in rouge and eye shadow. The grayling, face it, is useless. Like the auk, like the zebra swallowtail, like Angkor Wat.

In June of 1978, the U.S. Supreme Court ruled that the completion of the Tellico Dam on the Little Tennessee River was prohibited by law, namely the 1973 Endangered Species Act, because the dam would destroy the only known habitat of the snail darter, a small species of perch. One argument in support of this prohibition, perhaps the crucial argument, was that the snail darter's genes might at some time in the future prove useful—even invaluable—to the balance of life on Earth, possibly even directly to humanity. If the *Penicillium* fungus had gone extinct when the dodo bird did, according to this argument, many thousands of additional human beings by now would have died of diphtheria and pneumonia. You could never foresee what you might need, what might prove useful in the line of genetic options, so nothing at all should be squandered, nothing relinquished. Thus it was reasoned on behalf of snail darter preservation (and thus I have reasoned elsewhere myself). The logic is as solid as it is dangerous.

The whole argument by utility may be one of the most dangerous, even ominous, strategic errors that the environmental movement has made. The best reason for saving the snail darter was this: precisely because it is flat useless. That's what makes it special. It wasn't put there, in the Little Tennessee River; it has no ironclad reason for being there; it is simply there. A hydroelectric dam, which can be built in a mere ten years for a mere $119 million, will have utility on its side of the balance against snail darter genes, if not now then at some future time, when the cost of electricity has risen above the cost of recreating the snail darter through genetic engineering. A snail darter arrived at the hard way, the Darwinian way, across millions of years of randomness, reaching its culmination as a small ugly perch roughly resembling an undernourished tadpole, is something far more precious than a net asset in potential utility. What then, exactly? That isn't easy to say, without gibbering in transcendental tones. But something more than a floppy disc storing coded genetic lingo for a rainy day.

Another example: On a Sunday in May, 1972, an addled Hungarian named Laszlo Toth jumped a railing in St. Peter's Basilica and took a hammer to Michelangelo's *Pietà*, knocking the nose off the figure of Mary, and part of her lowered eyelid, and her right arm at the elbow. The world groaned. Italian officials charged Toth with crimes worth a maximum total of nine years' imprisonment. Some people, but no one of liberal disposition, said aloud at the time that capital punishment would be more appropriate. In fact, what probably should have been done was to let Italian police sergeants take Toth out into a Roman alley and smack his nose off, and part of his eyelid, and his arm at the elbow, with a hammer. The *Pietà* was at that time 473 years old, the only signed sculpture by the greatest sculptor in human history. I don't know whether Laszlo Toth served the full nine years, but very likely not. Deoclecio Redig de Campos, from the Vatican art-restoration laboratories, said at the time that restoring the sculpture, with glue and stucco and substitute bits of marble, would be "an awesome task that might take three years," but later he cheered up some and amended that to "a matter of months." You and I know better. The Michelangelo *Pietà* is gone. The Michelangelo/de Campos *Pietà* is the one now back on display. There is a large difference. What, exactly, is the difference? Again hard to say, but it has much to do with the snail darter.

Sage editorialists wrote that Toth's vandalism was viewed by some as an act of leftist political symbolism: "Esthetics must bow to social change, even if in the process the beautiful must be destroyed, as in Paris during *les èvènements*, when students scrawled across paintings 'No More Masterpieces.' So long as human beings do not eat, we must break up ecclesiastical plate and buy bread." The balance of utility had tipped. The only directly useful form of art, after all, is that which we call pornography.

Still another example: In May of 1945 the Target Committee of scientists and ordnance experts from the Manhattan Project met to hash out a list of the best potential Japanese targets for the American atomic bomb. At the top of the list they placed Kyoto, the ancient capital city of Japan, for eleven centuries the source of all that was beautiful in Japanese civilization, the site of many sacred and gorgeous Shinto shrines. When he saw this, Henry L. Stimson, a stubbornly humane old man who had served as Secretary of State under Herbert Hoover and was now Truman's inherited Secretary of War, got his back up: "This is one time I'm going to be the final deciding authority. Nobody's going to tell me what to do on this. On this matter I am the kingpin." And he struck the city of shrines off the list. Truman concurred. Think what you will about the subsequent bombing of Hiroshima–unspeakably barbarous act, most justifiable act in the given circumstances, possibly both–think what you will about that; still the sparing of Kyoto, acknowledged as a superior target in military terms, was very likely the most courageous and imaginative decision anyone ever talked Harry Truman into. In May of 1945, the shrines of Kyoto did not enjoy the balance of utility.

"By utility is meant that property in any object, whereby it tends to produce benefit, advantage, pleasure, good, or happiness (all this in the present case comes to the same thing), or (what comes again to the same thing) to prevent the happening of mischief, pain, evil, or unhappiness to the party whose interest is considered: if that party be the community in general, then the happiness of the community; if a particular individual, then the happiness of that individual." This was written by Jeremy Bentham, the English legal scholar of the eighteenth century who was a founder of that school of philosophy known as utilitarianism. He also wrote, in *Principles of Morals and Legislation*, that "an action then may be said to be conformable to the principle of utility . . . when the tendency it has to augment the happiness of the community is greater than any it has to diminish it." In more familiar words, moral tenets and legislation should always be such as to achieve the greatest good for the greatest number. And *the greatest number* has generally been taken to mean the greatest number of *humans*.

This is a nefariously sensible philosophy. If it had been adhered to strictly throughout the world since Bentham enunciated it, there would now be no ecclesiastical plate or jeweled papal chalices, no Peacock Throne (vacated or otherwise) of Iran, no Apollo moon landings, no Kyoto. Had it been retroactive, there would be no Egyptian pyramids, no Taj Mahal, no texts of Plato; nor would there have been any amassing of wealth by Florentine oligarchs and hence no Italian Renaissance; finally, therefore, no *Pietà*, not even a mangled one. And if Bentham's principle of utility—in its economic formulation, or in thermodynamic terms, or even in biomedical ones—is applied today and tomorrow as the ultimate touchstone for matters of legislation, let alone morals, then there will eventually be, as soon as the balance tips, no snail darter and no. . . .

But we were talking about the Big Hole grayling. George Liknes was finding few, and none at all near the string of car bodies, and this worried me. I had some strong personal feelings toward the grayling of the Big Hole—proprietary is not the right word, too presumptuous; rather, feelings somewhere between cherishing and reliance. I had come to count on the fact, for cheer and solace in a very slight way, that they were there, that they existed—beautiful, dumb, and useless—

in the upper reaches of that particular river. It happened because I had gone up there each year for a number of years–usually in late August, which is the start of autumn in the upper Big Hole Valley, or in early September–with two hulking Irishmen, brothers. Each year, stealing two days for this pilgrimage just as the first cottonwoods were taking on patches of yellow, we three visited the grayling.

At that time of year the Big Hole grayling are feeding, mainly in the mornings, on a plague of tiny dark mayflies known as *Tricorythodes* (or, for convenience, trikes). One of these creatures is roughly the size of a caraway seed, black-bodied with pale milky wings; but they appear on the water by the millions, and the grayling line up in certain areas to sip at them. The trike hatch happens every August and September, beginning each morning when the sun begins warming the water, continuing daily for more than a month, and it is one of the reasons thirty-one grayling can be caught in a few hours. The trike hatch was built into my understanding with the Irishmen, an integral part of the yearly ritual. Trike time, time to visit the Big Hole grayling.

Not stalk, not confront, certainly not kill and eat; visit. No great angling thrills attach to catching grayling. You don't fish at them for the satisfaction of fooling a crafty animal on its own terms, or fighting a wild little teakettle battle handicapped across a fine leader, as you do with trout. The whole context of expectations and rewards is different. You catch grayling to visit them: to hold one carefully in the water, hook freed, dorsal flaring, and gape at the colors, and then watch as it dashes away. This is good for a person, though it could never be the greatest good for the greatest number. I had visited them regularly at trike time with the two Irishmen, including the autumn of the younger brother's divorce, and during the days just before the birth of the older brother's first daughter, and through some weather of my own. So I did not want to hear about a Big Hole River that was empty of grayling.

A fair question to the Montana Department of Fish, Wildlife, and Parks is this: If these fish constitute a unique and historic population, a wonderful zoological rarity within the lower forty-eight states, why let a person kill five in a day for cat food? FWP biologists have offered three standard answers: (1) Until George Liknes finished his master's thesis, they possessed no reliable data on the Big Hole grayling, and they do not like to make changes in management procedures except on the basis of data; (2) grayling are very fecund–a female will sometimes lay more than 10,000 eggs–and so availability of habitat and infant mortality and competition with trout are the limiting factors, not fishing pressure; and (3) these grayling are glacial relicts, meaning they have been naturally doomed to elimination from this habitat, and mankind is only accelerating that inevitability.

Yet, (1) over a period of twenty-five years, evidently without the basic data that would have showed that it was all counterproductive, the department spent a large pile of money to burden the Big Hole grayling with five million hatchery outsiders; and (2) though fishermen are admittedly not the limiting factor on total number of grayling in the river, they can easily affect the number of large, successful, genetically gifted spawning stock in the population, since those are precisely the individual fish that fishermen, unlike high temperatures or low oxygen or competitive trout, kill in disproportionate number. There might be money for more vigorous pursuit of data, there might be support for protecting the grayling from cats, but the critical constituency involved here is fishermen, and the balance of utility is not on the side of the grayling; as for (3), not only are the rivers of Montana growing warmer with the end of the Ice Age, but the Earth generally is warming; it is in fact falling inexorably into the sun, and the sun itself is meanwhile dying. So all wildlife on the planet is doomed to eventual elimination, and mankind is only et cetera.

The year before last, the Irishmen and I missed our visit: The older brother had a second daughter coming, and the younger brother was in Germany, in the Army, soon to have a second wife. I could have gone alone but I didn't. So all I knew of *Thymallus arcticus* on the upper Big Hole was what I heard from George Liknes: not good. Through the winter I asked FWP biologists for news of the Big Hole grayling: not good.

Then one day in late August last year, I sneaked away and drove up the Big Hole toward the town of Wisdom, specifically for a visit. I stopped when I saw a promising arrangement of water, a spot I had never fished or even noticed before, though it wasn't too far from the string of car bodies. I didn't know what I would find, if anything. On the third cast I made contact with a twelve-inch grayling, largish for the Big Hole within my memory. Between sun-on-the-water and noon, using a small fly resembling a *Tricorythodes*, I caught and released as many grayling as ever. As many as I needed.

I could tell you where to look for them, I could suggest how you might fish for them, but that's not the point here. You can find them yourself if you need to. Likewise, it's tempting to suggest where you might send letters, whom you might hector, what pressures you might apply on behalf of these useless fish; also not exactly the point. I merely wanted to let you know: They are there.

Irishmen, the grayling are still there, yes. Please listen, the rest of you: They are there, the Big Hole grayling. At least for now.

■ BILL STOCKTON

Bill Stockton was born in 1921 on his family's homestead in Winnett, Montana. He graduated from Grass Range High School and then left Montana to study at the Minneapolis School of Art. During World War II, Stockton went to France, where he remained to study art at the Ecôle de la Grand Chaumiere. As one of the original abstract expressionists of the 1950s, Stockton has exhibited his art widely. He has also taught at Montana State University, Eastern Montana College, and the College of Great Falls. A working rancher from 1950 to 1983, Stockton is now retired and lives at Grass Range. This selection is from his illustrated book, Today I Baled Some Hay to Feed the Sheep the Coyotes Eat, *published in 1982.*

Pages from My Notebook

Pregnancies take on many shapes, but the only real judgment one can make of the expected event is to have seen the ewe bred, count the days, look up her past history (which is usually impossible) and then hope she'll do as well, or better, this time around.

All ranchers, cattlemen or sheepmen, are guilty of the wrong prognosis when anticipating an animal's time to give birth. This is important since we might have to be prepared to help deliver her young, or to bring her to shelter. We try to read the signs: such as the fullness of the abdomen, size of the udder, the looseness around the vulva, etc. But unless the ewe is within one hour of giving birth, we can be wrong as many times as we are right.

In the sheep business, which is unlike the cattle business in one respect, a rancher is always trying to predict if a ewe is going to have twins.

Personally, after years in the business, I'm still learning, still guessing, and still hoping that someone will come along and fill me in on the vital signs. I even find it difficult to predict if a ewe will bear another lamb after the first one is born. My percentage of good guesses has risen in the last few years, but I can still "goof," and badly.

There are certain broken umbilical cords which dangle outside the vagina after the birth. They vary slightly if the ewe has completed lambing, or if there is another lamb still tucked away in the uterus. They vary, also, if the first lamb born was an identical twin. Of course, there is always the possibility she will have triplets, and then all prognoses will be shot down. . . .

Births . . . births . . . births. . . . I have seen thousands of them, not only in sheep, but in cattle, horses, pigs, dogs, cats, rabbits and mice. Once, I almost caught a skunk at it.

It is so common; yet, I'm drawn to this phenomena with the same wonderment I had when I was a boy. When it is right, it is so simple. When it is wrong, it is nature's cruelest method of paralleling birth with pain and death.

The lamb's little nose, along with his two front feet, is the first part of his anatomy to appear in the outside world. If he doesn't begin his arrival in this order, there is trouble ahead.

A ewe's pelvic cavity is only so large. (I have never understood why nature designed it with such small tolerances.) If it is too small to let both the feet and head pass at the same time, one leg will be forced back into the womb; again, if it is still too small, both legs will be forced back. The mother ewe is now unable to complete the birth—at least in the time frame for life to continue in her offspring—since the lamb's shoulders are too large to be forced past the pelvic opening by the force the ewe can exert.

This syndrome is the most common lambing problem we have. Obviously, in such cases, the lamb will have to be pulled or it will die, as well as the mother. The technique of pulling the lamb is very simple. The ewe has to be caught and turned on her side; next, depending if one or two legs are stuck behind the pelvic opening—because it is often possible to pull the lamb by one leg and his head—it is necessary to push the head back into the uterus. Now, by holding on to the lamb's jaw with two fingers and clasping the feet with the remaining fingers and thumb, one starts pulling, taking advantage of whatever pushes the mother ewe might exert, since, after all, the lamb puller just doesn't have that good a grip. Above all, patience is the order of the moment.

As soon as the feet and nose have been oriented into the birth canal and progressed far enough to the outside so one can get a firm hold on a leg, one pulls the leg out so the shoulder is past the pelvic opening. At this point, by manipulating the legs and forcing the vulva over the lamb's forehead, the puller can pop the lamb right out.

I tried to sneak up on the young ewe and hook her by a hind leg, but I missed on my first pass, and the frightened animal took off at full gallop across the field. The neck and head of the lamb she was trying to birth dangled from her vagina; it bounced and whipped as she ran. Next, I tried to chase her into a fence corner, but again she escaped me. Finally, after a chase of over one half mile, I managed to corner the ewe in a corral.

Even from a distance of one hundred feet, I could see that the lamb's tongue was protruding and that his head was dry and swollen, almost twice its normal size. The ewe, no doubt, had been trying to give birth for several hours.

I could only guess whether the lamb was still alive; God, after all that jostling, it would be a wonder if his neck wasn't broken.

I managed to pull the lamb—as I had managed others in the past—by one leg, and with a force sufficient, one would think, to tear his little body to pieces.

I pumped his left leg, and blew in his mouth for a minute or so, until he was able to breathe on his own; his head was so swollen, he could barely lift it or open his eyes. I managed to squirt some of his mother's milk past his swollen tongue and massage it down his throat. This was by far the best medicine I could give him.

The poor little lamb (or should I say, the great big single) lived. Oh yes, for days I had to help him nurse, but after four days the swelling receded, and he was on his own. For two weeks, he had problems keeping up with his mother and was unable to play "run-across-the-pasture" with the other lambs. But by the third week, though unable to play "flanker," he did "sub" for the "tailback" from time to time.

Recently, a little "dude" girl asked me if I used soap as an antiseptic and lubricant when I pulled a lamb. (She had just acquired a few head of ewes and was very apprehensive about lambing them.) Well, there is very little time for such preparations and no need, really, since the natural lubricants and antibiotics of the mother are sufficient. To tell the truth, since little lambs are so slippery, there are many times I would have given a day's wages for a handful of rosin.

My wife, working her shift during lambing, once pulled a big single who was coming hind end first by his tail. This might be a convenient handle but it is not an advisable way to deliver a lamb if it is at all possible to poke him back into the womb and turn him around. This lamb lived, but he did have a broken tail.

Oh, how many times I've been "up to my elbows" in lambing. I wonder if my old ewes appreciate my small hands and long, slim arms. I have known a lot of "big handed" sheepmen, and I have often been curious as to how they make out at lambing time. Apparently, most of them do make out; but, my God, what stresses they must inflict on those poor old ewes. Anyway, I do know a couple of my neighbors who went into the cattle business because of their handicap.

Once, I pulled for 15 minutes on the head and legs of a little lamb, but I was unable to get his shoulders past the pelvic opening. Finally, to my embarrassment, I discovered I was pulling on the head of one lamb and the legs of another. This happens quite often; a set of twins will start down the birth canal together and get stuck in the opening.

I have worked on many ewes with this problem, as have all sheepmen. To deliver these lambs, I push the lambs far back into the womb, and then feel around with my fingers to sort out, among the eight extremities, the legs that go with the appropriate body. (Need I explain the difficulties involved if there are triplets all mixed up down in that dark, slippery hole.) This isn't easy, since the pressures of the ewe's vagina sap the tone from one's hand and arm muscles to the point where they are partially paralyzed. (In a cow the pressures are four times what they are in a sheep—imagine!) It is sometimes difficult to feel the difference between the front legs and the hind legs. Often I have had to orient myself by the lamb's tail, and even it will sometimes feel much like another leg.

But, in time, after switching arms several times and with the help of a patience I have had to acquire over the years, I have always managed to clamp my hand around the lamb's front feet and neck, and then by merely holding on, I would let the ewe give birth to both her lamb and my hand.

The second lamb is usually much easier to deliver since by this time the birth trail has been well blazed.

RICHARD FORD

Richard Ford was born in Jackson, Mississippi, in 1944. He left Jackson and the South to attend Michigan State University and the University of California at Irvine, where he received an M.F.A. in creative writing. Ford, who has taught at Williams College and Princeton University, has published his essays and stories in Esquire, The New Yorker, *and other magazines. He has written several novels, including* A Piece of My Heart *(1976),* The Ultimate Good Luck *(1981), and the widely acclaimed* The Sportswriter *(1986). In 1983, Ford moved to Montana, where he now lives near the Rattlesnake Wilderness on the outskirts of Missoula. "Communists" first appeared in* Antaeus *in 1985. This version appears in Ford's collection of short fiction,* Rock Springs, *published in 1987.*

Communist

My mother once had a boyfriend named Glen Baxter. This was in 1961. We–my mother and I–were living in the little house my father had left her up the Sun River, near Victory, Montana, west of Great Falls. My mother was thirty-two at the time. I was sixteen. Glen Baxter was somewhere in the middle, between us, though I cannot be exact about it.

We were living then off the proceeds of my father's life insurance policies, with my mother doing some part-time waitressing work up in Great Falls and going to the bars in the evenings, which I know is where she met Glen Baxter. Sometimes he would come back with her and stay in her room at night, or she would call up from town and explain that she was staying with him in his little place on Lewis Street by the GN yards. She gave me his number every time, but I never called it. I think she probably thought that what she was doing was terrible, but simply couldn't help herself. I thought it was all right, though. Regular life it seemed, and still does. She was young, and I knew that even then.

Glen Baxter was a Communist and liked hunting, which he talked about a lot. Pheasants. Ducks. Deer. He killed all of them, he said. He had been to Vietnam as far back as then, and when he was in our house he often talked about shooting the animals over there–monkeys and beautiful parrots–using military guns just for sport. We did not know what Vietnam was then, and Glen, when he talked about that, referred to it only as "the Far East." I think now he must've been in the CIA and been disillusioned by something he saw or found out about and been thrown out, but that kind of thing did not matter to us. He was a tall, dark-eyed man with short black hair, and was usually in a good humor. He had gone halfway through college in Peoria, Illinois, he said, where he grew up. But when he was around our life he worked wheat farms as a ditcher, and stayed out of work winters and in the bars drinking with women like my mother, who had work and some money. It is not an uncommon life to lead in Montana.

What I want to explain happened in November. We had not been seeing Glen Baxter for some time. Two months had gone by. My mother knew other men, but she came home most days from work and stayed inside watching television in her bedroom and drinking beers. I asked about Glen once, and she said only that she didn't know where he was, and I assumed they had had a fight and that he was gone off on a flyer back to Illinois or Massachusetts, where he said he had relatives. I'll admit that I liked him. He had something on his mind always. He was a labor man as well as a Communist, and liked to say that the country was poisoned by the rich, and strong men would need to bring it to life again, and I liked that because my father had been a labor man, which was why we had a house to live in and money coming through. It was also true that I'd had a few boxing bouts by then–just with town boys and one with an Indian from Choteau–and there were some girlfriends I knew from that. I did not like my mother being around the house so much at night, and I wished Glen Baxter would come back, or that another man would come along and entertain her somewhere else.

At two o'clock on a Saturday, Glen drove up into our yard in a car. He had had a big brown Harley-Davidson that he rode most of the year, in his black-and-red irrigators and a baseball cap turned backwards. But this time he had a car, a blue Nash Ambassador. My mother and I went out on the porch when he stopped inside the olive trees my father had planted as a shelter belt, and my mother had a look on her face of not much pleasure. It was starting to be cold in earnest by then. Snow was down already onto the Fairfield Bench, though on this day a chinook was blowing, and it could as easily have been spring, though the sky above the Divide was turning over in silver and blue clouds of winter.

"We haven't seen you in a long time, I guess," my mother said coldly.

"My little retarded sister died," Glen said, standing at the door of his old car. He was wearing his orange VFW jacket and canvas shoes we called wino shoes, something I had never seen him wear before. He seemed to be in a good humor. "We buried her in Florida near the home."

"That's a good place," my mother said in a voice that meant she was a wronged party in something.

"I want to take this boy hunting today, Aileen," Glen said. "There're snow geese down now. But we have to go right away, or they'll be gone to Idaho by tomorrow."

"He doesn't care to go," my mother said.

"Yes I do," I said and looked at her.

My mother frowned at me. "Why do you?"

"Why does he need a reason?" Glen Baxter said and grinned.

"I want him to have one, that's why." She looked at me oddly. "I think Glen's drunk, Les."

"No, I'm not drinking," Glen said, which was hardly ever true. He looked at both of us, and my mother bit down on the side of her lower lip and stared at me in a way to make you think she thought something was being put over on her and she didn't like you for it. She was very pretty, though when she was mad her features were sharpened and less pretty by a long way. "All right, then, I don't care," she said to no one in particular. "Hunt, kill, maim. Your father did that too." She turned to go back inside.

"Why don't you come with us, Aileen?" Glen was smiling still, pleased.

"To do what?" my mother said. She stopped and pulled a package of cigarettes out of her dress pocket and put one in her mouth.

"It's worth seeing."

"See dead animals?" my mother said.

"These geese are from Siberia, Aileen," Glen said. "They're not like a lot of geese. Maybe I'll buy us dinner later. What do you say?"

"But what with?" my mother said. To tell the truth, I didn't know why she was so mad at him. I would've thought she'd be glad to see him. But she just suddenly seemed to hate everything about him.

"I've got some money," Glen said. "Let me spend it on a pretty girl tonight."

"Find one of those and you're lucky," my mother said, turning away toward the front door.

"I already found one," Glen Baxter said. But the door slammed behind her, and he looked at me then with a look I think now was helplessness, though I could not see a way to change anything.

My mother sat in the backseat of Glen's Nash and looked out the window while we drove. My double gun was in the seat between us beside Glen's Belgian pump, which he kept loaded with five shells in case, he said, he saw something beside the road he wanted to shoot. I had hunted rabbits before, and had ground-sluiced pheasants and other birds, but I had never been on an actual hunt before, one where you drove out to some special place and did it formally. And I was excited. I had a feeling that something important was about to happen to me, and that this would be a day I would always remember.

My mother did not say anything for a long time, and neither did I. We drove up through Great Falls and out the other side toward Fort Benton, which was on the benchland where wheat was grown.

"Geese mate for life," my mother said, just out of the blue, as we were driving. "I hope you know that. They're special birds."

"I know that," Glen said in the front seat. "I have every respect for them."

"So where were you for three months?" she said. "I'm only curious."

"I was in the Big Hole for a while," Glen said, "and after that I went over to Douglas, Wyoming."

"What were you planning to do there?" my mother asked.

"I wanted to find a job, but it didn't work out."

"I'm going to college," she said suddenly, and this was something I had never heard about before. I turned to look at her, but she was staring out her window and wouldn't see me.

"I knew French once," Glen said. "*Rosé*'s pink. *Rouge*'s red." He glanced at me and smiled. "I think that's a wise idea, Aileen. When are you going to start?"

"I don't want Les to think he was raised by crazy people all his life," my mother said.

"Les ought to go himself," Glen said.

"After I go, he will."

"What do you say about that, Les?" Glen said, grinning.

"He says it's just fine," my mother said.

"It's just fine," I said.

Where Glen Baxter took us was out onto the high flat prairie that was disked for wheat and had high, high mountains out to the east, with lower heartbreak hills in between. It was, I remember, a day for blues in the sky, and down in the distance we could see the small town of Floweree, and the state highway running past it toward Fort Benton and the Hi-line. We drove out on top of the prairie on a muddy dirt road fenced on both sides, until we had gone about three miles, which is where Glen stopped.

"All right," he said, looking up in the rearview mirror at my mother. "You wouldn't think there was anything here, would you?"

"*We're* here," my mother said. "You brought us here."

"You'll be glad, though," Glen said, and seemed confident to me. I had looked around myself but could not see anything. No water or trees, nothing that seemed like a good place to hunt anything. Just wasted land. "There's a big lake out there, Les," Glen said. "You can't see it now from here because it's low. But the geese are there. You'll see."

"It's like the moon out here, I recognize that," my mother said, "only it's worse." She was staring out at the flat wheatland as if she could actually see something in particular, and wanted to know more about it. "How'd you find this place?"

"I came once on the wheat push," Glen said.

"And I'm sure the owner told you just to come back and hunt anytime you like and bring anybody you wanted. Come one, come all. Is that it?"

"People shouldn't own land anyway," Glen said. "Anybody should be able to use it."

"Les, Glen's going to poach here," my mother said. "I just want you to know that, because that's a crime and the law will get you for it. If you're a man now, you're going to have to face the consequences."

"That's not true," Glen Baxter said, and looked gloomily out over the steering wheel down the muddy road toward the mountains. Though for myself I believed it was true, and didn't care. I didn't care about anything at that moment except seeing geese fly over me and shooting them down.

"Well, I'm certainly not going out there," my mother said. "I like towns better, and I already have enough trouble."

"That's okay," Glen said. "When the geese lift up you'll get to see them. That's all I wanted. Les and me'll go shoot them, won't we, Les?"

"Yes," I said, and I put my hand on my shotgun, which had been my father's and was heavy as rocks.

"Then we should go on," Glen said, "or we'll waste our light."

We got out of the car with our guns. Glen took off his canvas shoes and put on his pair of black irrigators out of the trunk. Then we crossed the barbed wire fence, and walked out into the high, tilled field toward nothing. I looked back at my mother when we were still not so far away, but I could only see the small, dark top of her head, low in the backseat of the Nash, staring out and thinking what I could not then begin to say.

On the walk toward the lake, Glen began talking to me. I had never been alone with him, and knew little about him except what my mother said—that he drank too much, or other times that he was the nicest man she had ever known in the world and that someday a woman would marry him, though she didn't think it would be her. Glen told me as we walked that he wished he had finished college, but that it was too late now, that his mind was too old. He said he had liked the Far East very much, and that people there knew how to treat each other, and that he would go back some day but couldn't go now. He said also that he would like to live in Russia for a while and mentioned the names of people who had gone there, names I didn't know. He said it would be hard at first, because it was so different, but that pretty soon anyone would learn to like it and wouldn't want to live anywhere else, and that Russians treated Americans who came to live there like kings. There were Communists everywhere now, he said. You didn't know them, but they were there. Montana had a large number, and he was in touch with all of them. He said that Communists were always in danger and that he had to protect himself all the time. And when he said that he pulled back his VFW jacket and showed me the butt of a pistol he had stuck under his shirt against his bare skin. "There are people who want to kill me right now," he said, "and I would kill a man myself if I thought I had to." And we kept walking. Though in a while he said, "I don't think I know much about you, Les. But I'd like to. What do you like to do?"

"I like to box," I said. "My father did it. It's a good thing to know."

"I suppose you have to protect yourself too," Glen said.

"I know how to," I said.

"Do you like to watch TV," Glen said, and smiled.

"Not much."

"I love to," Glen said. "I could watch it instead of eating if I had one."

I looked out straight ahead over the green tops of sage that grew at the edge of the disked field, hoping to see the lake Glen said was there. There was an airishness and a sweet smell that I thought might be the place we were going, but I couldn't see it. "How will we hunt these geese?" I said.

"It won't be hard," Glen said. "Most hunting isn't even hunting. It's only shooting. And that's what this will be. In Illinois you would dig holes in the ground and hide and set out your decoys. Then the geese come to you, over and over again. But we don't have time for that here." He glanced at me. "You have to be sure the first time here."

"How do you know they're here now?" I asked. And I looked toward the Highwood Mountains twenty miles away, half in snow and half dark blue at the bottom. I could see the little town of Floweree then, looking shabby and dimly lighted in the distance. A red bar sign shone. A car moved slowly away from the scattered buildings.

"They always come November first," Glen said.

"Are we going to poach them?"

"Does it make any difference to you," Glen asked.

"No, it doesn't."

"Well then, we aren't," he said.

We walked then for a while without talking. I looked back once to see the Nash far and small in the flat distance. I couldn't see my mother, and I thought that she must've turned on the radio and gone to sleep, which she always did, letting it play all night in her bedroom. Behind the car the sun was nearing the rounded mountains southwest of us, and I knew that when the sun was gone it would be cold. I wished my mother had decided to come along with us, and I thought for a moment of how little I really knew her at all.

Glen walked with me another quarter-mile, crossed another barbed-wire fence where sage was growing, then went a hundred yards through wheatgrass and spurge until the ground went up and formed a kind of long hillock bunker built by a farmer against the wind. And I realized the lake was just beyond us. I could hear the sound of a car horn blowing and a dog barking all the way down in the town, then the wind seemed to move and all I could hear then and after then were geese. So many geese, from the sound of them, though I still could not see even one. I stood and listened to the high-pitched shouting sound, a sound I had never heard so close, a sound with size to it—though it was not loud. A sound that meant great numbers and that made your chest rise and your shoulders tighten with expectancy. It was a sound to make you feel separate from it and everything else, as if you were of no importance in the grand scheme of things.

"Do you hear them singing," Glen asked. He held his hand up to make me stand still. And we both listened. "How many do you think, Les, just hearing?"

"A hundred," I said. "More than a hundred."

"Five thousand," Glen said. "More than you can believe when you see them. Go see."

I put down my gun and on my hands and knees crawled up the earthwork through the wheatgrass and thistle, until I could see down to the lake and see the geese. And they were there, like a white bandage laid on the water, wide and long and continuous, a white expanse of snow geese, seventy yards from me, on the bank, but stretching far onto the lake, which was large itself—a half-mile across, with thick tules on the far side and wild plums farther and the blue mountain behind them.

"Do you see the big raft?" Glen said from below me, in a whisper.

"I see it," I said, still looking. It was such a thing to see, a view I had never seen and have not since.

"Are any on the land?" he said.

"Some are in the wheatgrass," I said, "but most are swimming."

"Good," Glen said. "They'll have to fly. But we can't wait for that now."

And I crawled backwards down the heel of land to where Glen was, and my gun. We were losing our light, and the air was purplish and cooling. I looked toward the car but couldn't see it, and I was no longer sure where it was below the lighted sky.

"Where do they fly to?" I said in a whisper, since I did not want anything to be ruined because of what I did or said. It was important to Glen to shoot the geese, and it was important to me.

"To the wheat," he said. "Or else they leave for good. I wish your mother had come, Les. Now she'll be sorry."

I could hear the geese quarreling and shouting on the lake surface. And I wondered if they knew we were here now. "She might be," I said with my heart pounding, but I didn't think she would be much.

It was a simple plan he had. I would stay behind the bunker, and he would crawl on his belly with his gun through the wheatgrass as near to the geese as he could. Then he would simply stand up and shoot all the ones he could close up, both in the air and on the ground. And when all the others flew up, with luck some would turn toward me as they came into the wind, and then I could shoot them and turn them back to him, and he would shoot them again. He could kill ten, he said, if he was lucky, and I might kill four. It didn't seem hard.

"Don't show them your face," Glen said. "Wait till you think you can touch them, then stand up and shoot. To hesitate is lost in this."

"All right," I said. "I'll try it."

"Shoot one in the head, and then shoot another one," Glen said. "It won't be hard." He patted me on the arm and smiled. Then he took off his VFW jacket and put it on the ground, climbed up the side of the bunker, cradling his shotgun in his arms, and slid on his belly into the dry stalks of yellow grass out of my sight.

Then, for the first time in that entire day, I was alone. And I didn't mind it. I sat squat down in the grass, loaded my double gun, and took my other two shells out of my pocket to hold. I pushed the safety off and on to see that it was right. The wind rose a little, scuffed the grass and made me shiver. It was not the warm chinook now, but a wind out of the north, the one geese flew away from if they could.

Then I thought about my mother, in the car alone, and how much longer I would stay with her, and what it might mean to her for me to leave. And I wondered when Glen Baxter would die and if someone would kill him, or whether my mother would marry him and how I would feel about it. And though I didn't know why, it occurred to me that Glen Baxter and I would not be friends when all was said and done, since I didn't care if he ever married my mother or didn't.

Then I thought about boxing and what my father had taught me about it. To tighten your fists hard. To strike out straight from the shoulder and never punch backing up. How to cut a punch by snapping your fist inwards, how to carry your chin low, and to step toward a man when he is falling so you can hit him again. And most important, to keep your eyes open when you are hitting in the face and causing damage, because you need to see what you're doing to encourage yourself, and because it is when you close your eyes that you stop hitting and get hurt badly. "Fly all over your man, Les," my father said. "When you see your chance, fly on him and hit him till he falls." That, I thought, would always be my attitude in things.

And then I heard the geese again, their voices in unison, louder and shouting, as if the wind had changed again and put all new sounds in the cold air. And then a *boom*. And I knew Glen was in among them and had stood up to shoot. The noise of geese rose and grew worse, and my fingers burned where I held my gun too tight to the metal, and I put it down and opened my fist to make the burning stop so I could feel the trigger when the moment came. *Boom*, Glen shot again, and I heard him shuck a shell, and all the sounds out beyond the bunker seemed to be rising–the geese, the shots, the air itself going up. *Boom*, Glen shot another time, and I knew he was taking his careful time to make his shots good. And I held my gun and started to crawl up the bunker so as not to be surprised when the geese came over me and I could shoot.

From the top I saw Glen Baxter alone in the wheatgrass field, shooting at a white goose with black tips of wings that was on the ground not far from him, but trying to run and pull into the air. He shot it once more, and it fell over dead with its wings flapping.

Glen looked back at me and his face was distorted and strange. The air around him was full of white rising geese and he seemed to want them all. "Behind you, Les," he yelled at me and pointed. "They're all behind you now." I looked behind me, and there were geese in the air as far as I could see, more than I knew how many, moving so slowly, their wings wide out and working calmly and filling the air with noise, though their voices were not as loud or as shrill as I had thought they would be. And they were so close! Forty feet, some of them. The air around me vibrated and I could feel the wind from their wings and it seemed to me I could kill as many as the times I could shoot—a hundred or a thousand—and I raised my gun, put the muzzle on the head of a white goose, and fired. It shuddered in the air, its wide feet sank below its belly, its wings cradled out to hold back air, and it fell straight down and landed with an awful sound, a noise a human would make, a thick, soft, *hump* noise. I looked up again and shot another goose, could hear the pellets hit its chest, but it didn't fall or even break its pattern for flying. *Boom*, Glen shot again. And then again. "Hey," I heard him shout. "Hey, hey." And there were geese flying over me, flying in line after line. I broke my gun and reloaded, and thought to myself as I did: I need confidence here, I need to be sure with this. I pointed at another goose and shot it in the head, and it fell the way the first one had, wings out, its belly down, and with the same thick noise of hitting. Then I sat down in the grass on the bunker and let geese fly over me.

By now the whole raft was in the air, all of it moving in a slow swirl above me and the lake and everywhere, finding the wind and heading out south in long wavering lines that caught the last sun and turned to silver as they gained a distance. It was a thing to see, I will tell you now. Five thousand white geese all in the air around you, making a noise like you have never heard before. And I thought to myself then: this is something I will never see again. I will never forget this. And I was right.

Glen Baxter shot twice more. One he missed, but with the other he hit a goose flying away from him, and knocked it half falling and flying into the empty lake not far from shore, where it began to swim as though it was fine and make its noise.

Glen stood in the stubbly grass, looking out at the goose, his gun lowered. "I didn't need to shoot that one, did I, Les?"

"I don't know," I said, sitting on the little knoll of land, looking at the goose swimming in the water.

"I don't know why I shoot 'em. They're so beautiful." He looked at me.

"I don't know either," I said.

"Maybe there's nothing else to do with them." Glen stared at the goose again and shook his head. "Maybe this is exactly what they're put on earth for."

I did not know what to say because I did not know what he could mean by that, though what I felt was embarrassment at the great numbers of geese there were, and a dulled feeling like a hunger because the shooting had stopped and it was over for me now.

Glen began to pick up his geese, and I walked down to my two that had fallen close together and were dead. One had hit with such an impact that its stomach had split and some of its inward parts were knocked out. Though the other looked unhurt, its soft white belly turned up like a pillow, its head and jagged bill-teeth, its tiny black eyes looking as they would if they were alive.

"What's happened to the hunters out here?" I heard a voice speak. It was my mother, standing in her pink dress on the knoll above us, hugging her arms. She was smiling though she was cold. And I realized that I had lost all thought of her in the shooting. "Who did all this shooting? Is this your work, Les?"

"No," I said.

"Les is a hunter, though, Aileen," Glen said. "He takes his time." He was holding two white geese by their necks, one in each hand, and he was smiling. He and my mother seemed pleased.

"I see you didn't miss too many," my mother said and smiled. I could tell she admired Glen for his geese, and that she had done some thinking in the car alone. "It *was* wonderful, Glen," she said. "I've never seen anything like that. They were like snow."

"It's worth seeing once, isn't it?" Glen said. "I should've killed more, but I got excited."

My mother looked at me then. "Where's yours, Les?"

"Here," I said and pointed to my two geese on the ground beside me.

My mother nodded in a nice way, and I think she liked everything then and wanted the day to turn out right and for all of us to be happy. "Six, then. You've got six in all."

"One's still out there," I said and motioned where the one goose was swimming in circles on the water.

"Okay," my mother said and put her hand over her eyes to look. "Where is it?"

Glen Baxter looked at me then with a strange smile, a smile that said he wished I had never mentioned anything about the other goose. And I wished I hadn't either. I looked up in the sky and could see the lines of geese by the thousands shining silver in the light, and I wished we could just leave and go home.

"That one's my mistake there," Glen Baxter said and grinned. "I shouldn't have shot that one, Aileen. I got too excited."

My mother looked out on the lake for a minute, then looked at Glen and back again. "Poor goose." She shook her head. "How will you get it, Glen?"

"I can't get that one now," Glen said.

My mother looked at him. "What do you mean?" she said.

"I'm going to leave that one," Glen said.

"Well, no. You can't leave one," my mother said. "You shot it. You have to get it. Isn't that a rule?"

"No," Glen said.

And my mother looked from Glen to me. "Wade out and get it, Glen," she said, in a sweet way, and my mother looked young then, like a young girl, in her flimsy short-sleeved waitress dress and her skinny, bare legs in the wheatgrass.

"No." Glen Baxter looked down at his gun and shook his head. And I didn't know why he wouldn't go, because it would've been easy. The lake was shallow. And you could tell that anyone could've walked out a long way before it got deep, and Glen had on his boots.

My mother looked at the white goose, which was not more than thirty yards from the shore, its head up, moving in slow circles, its wings settled and relaxed so you could see the black tips. "Wade out and get it, Glenny, won't you please?" she said. "They're special things."

"You don't understand the world, Aileen," Glen said. "This can happen. It doesn't matter."

"But that's so cruel, Glen," she said, and a sweet smile came on her lips.

"Raise up your own arms, 'Leeny," Glen said. "I can't see any angel's wings, can you Les?" He looked at me, but I looked away.

"Then you go on and get it, Les," my mother said. "You weren't raised by crazy people." I started to go, but Glen Baxter suddenly grabbed me by my shoulder and pulled me back hard, so hard his fingers made bruises in my skin that I saw later.

"Nobody's going," he said. "This is over with now."

And my mother gave Glen a cold look then. "You don't have a heart, Glen," she said. "There's nothing to love in you. You're just a son of a bitch, that's all."

And Glen Baxter nodded at my mother, then, as if he understood something that he had not understood before, but something that he was willing to know. "Fine," he said, "that's fine." And he took his big pistol out from against his belly, the big blue revolver I had only seen part of before and that he said protected him, and he pointed it out at the goose on the water, his arm straight away from him, and shot and missed. And then he shot and missed again. The goose made its noise once. And then he hit it dead, because there was no splash. And then he shot it three times more until the gun was empty and the goose's head was down and it was floating toward the middle of the lake where it was empty and dark blue. "Now who has a heart?" Glen said. But my mother was not there when he turned around. She had already started back to the car and was almost lost from sight in the darkness. And Glen smiled at me then and his face had a wild look on it. "Okay, Les?" he said.

"Okay," I said.

"There're limits to everything, right?"

"I guess so," I said.

"Your mother's a beautiful woman, but she's not the only beautiful woman in Montana." And I did not say anything. And Glen Baxter suddenly said, "Here," and he held the pistol out at me. "Don't you want this? Don't you want to shoot me? Nobody thinks they'll die. But I'm ready for it right now." And I did not know what to do then. Though it is true that what I wanted to do was to hit him, hit him as hard in the face as I could, and see him on the ground bleeding and crying and pleading for me to stop. Only at that moment he looked scared to me, and I had never seen a grown man scared before—though I have seen one since—and I felt sorry for him, as though he was already a dead man. And I did not end up hitting him at all.

A light can go out in the heart. All of this happened years ago, but I still can feel now how sad and remote the world was to me. Glen Baxter, I think now, was not a bad man, only a man scared of something he'd never seen before—something soft in himself—his life going a way he didn't like. A woman with a son. Who could blame him there? I don't know what makes people do what they do, or call themselves what they call themselves, only that you have to live someone's life to be the expert.

My mother had tried to see the good side of things, tried to be hopeful in the situation she was handed, tried to look out for us both, and it hadn't worked. It was a strange time in her life then and after that, a time when she had to adjust to being an adult just when she was on the thin edge of things. Too much awareness too early in life was her problem, I think.

And what I felt was only that I had somehow been pushed out into the world, into the real life then, the one I hadn't lived yet. In a year I was gone to hard-rock mining and no-paycheck jobs and not to college. And I have thought more than once about my mother saying that I had not been raised by crazy people, and I don't know what that could mean or what difference it could make, unless it means that love is a reliable commodity, and even that is not always true, as I have found out.

Late on the night that all this took place I was in bed when I heard my mother say, "Come outside, Les. Come and hear this." And I went out onto the front porch barefoot and in my underwear, where it was warm like spring, and there was a spring mist in the air. I could see the lights of the Fairfield Coach in the distance on its way up to Great Falls.

And I could hear geese, white birds in the sky, flying. They made their high-pitched sound like angry yells, and though I couldn't see them high up, it seemed to me they were everywhere. And my mother looked up and said, "Hear them?" I could smell her hair wet from the shower. "They leave with the moon," she said. "It's still half wild out here."

And I said, "I hear them," and I felt a chill come over my bare chest, and the hair stood up on my arms the way it does before a storm. And for a while we listened.

"When I first married your father, you know, we lived on a street called Bluebird Canyon, in California. And I thought that was the prettiest street and the prettiest name. I suppose no one brings you up like your first love. You don't mind if I say that, do you?" She looked at me hopefully.

"No," I said.

"We have to keep civilization alive somehow." And she pulled her little housecoat together because there was a cold vein in the air, a part of the cold that would be on us the next day. "I don't feel part of things tonight, I guess."

"It's all right," I said.

"Do you know where I'd like to go?"

"No," I said. And I suppose I knew she was angry then, angry with life, but did not want to show me that.

"To the Straits of Juan de Fuca. Wouldn't that be something? Would you like that?"

"I'd like it," I said. And my mother looked off for a minute, as if she could see the Straits of Juan de Fuca out against the line of mountains, see the lights of things alive and a whole new world.

"I know you liked him," she said after a moment. "You and I both suffer fools too well."

"I didn't like him too much," I said. "I didn't really care."

"He'll fall on his face. I'm sure of that," she said. And I didn't say anything because I didn't care about Glen Baxter anymore, and was happy not to talk about him. "Would you tell me something if I asked you? Would you tell me the truth?"

"Yes," I said.

And my mother did not look at me. "Just tell the truth," she said.

"All right," I said.

"Do you think I'm still very feminine? I'm thirty-two years old now. You don't know what that means. But do you think I am?"

And I stood at the edge of the porch, with the olive trees before me, looking straight up into the mist where I could not see the geese but could still hear them flying, could almost feel the air move below their white wings. And I felt the way you feel when you are on a trestle all alone and the train is coming, and you know you have to decide. And I said, "Yes, I do." Because that was the truth. And I tried to think of something else then and did not hear what my mother said after that.

And how old was I then? Sixteen. Sixteen is young, but it can also be a grown man. I am forty-one years old now, and I think about that time without regret, though my mother and I never talked in that way again, and I have not heard her voice now in a long, long time.

■ EARL GANZ

Earl Ganz was born in New York in 1932. With an undergraduate degree from Tufts College, Ganz received an M.F.A. from the University of Iowa Writer's Workshop in 1964 and a Ph.D. in English and creative writing from the University of Utah in 1975. A professor of English at the University of Montana since 1966, Ganz was the director of its Creative Writing Program for many years. Ganz has published several stories and is currently working on a novel, The History of Jews in Montana. *This selection is printed here for the first time.*

The Medicine of Albert Heavyrunner

He stopped chewing and wondered if he had pulled the plug on the polygraph? He'd left it on overnight before. There was terrible heat distortion the next day. He remembered shutting off the hissing oxygen tank. Then there'd been the squishing sound the heart made when the injected air reached it. But what about the polygraph? The squishing sound had grown weaker as the heart began to lose its beat. Then there'd been the quiet shimmering over its red surface, each cell firing separately and for the last time. Then? No polygraph hum. And he swallowed his tenseness with the salty gray warmth of the veal in his throat.

"Gimme!" Near the bar a tall man was holding the jukebox plug over his head. Beside him a small man was jumping for it. Albert thought of the dogs and the way they jumped for the ball in the weighing room, their forelegs tucked, their back ones pointing toward the floor. He liked the dogs. He always meant to take one home.

"Harold!" a girl shouted at one of the men. "You're an ass!" They ignored her. But Albert stopped chewing. She had slid the whole length of the leatherette wall bench to be next to him. "I've been watching you," she said mysteriously. He looked at her. She was a Jew or maybe an Italian. He'd never seen her in the Kiwi before. "You're a very big man." He began chewing again. "And you're a beautiful color."

"Thanks." He wasn't offended. She had said it to surprise him. He wouldn't show surprise and went on eating. There was a silence. But he was interested and he wondered what she would say next.

"You've got sauce on your cheek," she said.

"Blood," he corrected. She frowned as if it were a bad joke. But if the light had not been so weak and his skin the color of copper she would have seen the tiny stains around the larger ones. It was the dried spray from the internal mammary artery they had nicked with the autopsy saw. He'd been too tired to wash carefully.

"May I?" She was dipping the end of his unused paper napkin to his half full glass of water. "My name's Tanya . . . Tanya Greenberg," she said as she rubbed at the spots.

"Mine's Albert Heavyrunner," he answered. She stopped rubbing and looked at him. He fed himself the last piece of veal.

"That's a great name." She was smiling. He saw her crooked lower teeth. "You're an Indian?" He nodded. "I didn't know there were any Indians in New York."

". . . sssssssky gathered again." The light in the juke box flashed on. The sound rose from inert silence all the way up to its previous 33⅓ tenor. The bartender had intervened for the small man. "And the sun grew round that very day."

"You like poetry?" Tanya asked.

"Some." He tore at his last piece of bread.

"I like this one," she said. "It's Dylan Thomas. I mean that's really his voice." And Albert listened a moment to the man with the funny accent. Then he felt her looking at him again. He stopped listening, pushed the bread through the red sauce and put the soaking dough in his mouth. She took his hand and matched it palm to palm with hers. "God, you're big!"

"Yes," he agreed and turned his palm, wrapping his fingers around hers and returning her hand to her lap. He felt the softness of her stomach and the top of her pelvis. Small boned, he thought. He was tired. He'd been on his feet over twelve hours and didn't really want a girl tonight.

"Where are you from?" she asked.

"Montana," he answered though he hadn't been back there in twenty years. "Browning."

"Really?" He nodded. "You really are an Indian! I was sure it was ManTan or iodine and baby oil or something like that. That's why I wanted to rub it." He looked at her. She had black hair in braids and gold hoops that hung from pierced ear lobes. "What tribe are you from?" she asked.

"Blackfeet."

"Never heard of 'em," she said and she was laughing. "Do you have black feet?" He almost laughed too, the old joke like a long lost friend. He shook his head no and then he was telling her all he knew about the name. Then she was asking other questions about Indians and why he had left, and as he spoke he decided he liked her, that is liked her company. So after dinner and a few drinks he took Tanya up to his apartment on Macdougal Street where it began at Sixth Avenue. Now he was lying on his side facing the wall. Naked on top of the sheet, he was dreaming of home, a little boy up on horseback behind his grandmother. The sun had just risen. To him it seemed her outstretched arms had called it forth.

"Look!"

"What!" He struggled up.

"Just leaving the Dardanian Gate!" Tanya was pointing at the ceiling. She was naked also but beneath the sheet. "The Trojan Horse!"

"A roach." He sank back onto the sheet and watched the insect near the light fixture as it moved its head from side to side.

"Make it go away!" she ordered. He didn't move. "Go away," she enunciated at the bug. "Shoo! Begone!" She had begun talking like this after they made love. He had ignored it. Now he leaned across her, picked one of his blood-spattered socks off the floor, balled it up and threw it at the ceiling. It missed but the panicked insect ran back under the light. He lay back down.

"Go to sleep." He felt her tenseness. "At least turn out the light."

"It dropped something on me," she whispered after a long pause. The sock had fallen back to the floor. "It dropped something on me." She was pressing the back of her head into the pillow as if she were trying to hide her face behind the mound her breasts made under the sheet. He sat up again.

"It's only an egg sac," he explained. He picked the tiny thing off the part of the sheet that covered her stomach and pushed it around the palm of his hand. It looked just like a grain of fried rice. "They like dark places. Usually they put 'em in my sock drawer."

"Destroy it!" ordered Tanya.

"Know what's in here?"

"Flush it down the toilet!"

"Maybe twenty or thirty little roaches." He nudged it some more. "Each one no bigger than the head of a pin."

"Destroy it," she said and turned on her side, her back to him. "You do it to the dogs." He'd told her about the experiments. She had asked about his socks, had finally believed it was blood on his face. He shouldn't have talked so much. She was only a kid. Like most kids she wasn't really interested in anyone but herself. And she was female. If you told a woman something about yourself she'd use it against you sometime. He thought of his young wife. Over twenty years and he was still angry.

"Roaches are the only insects that have their young like this," he persisted. She didn't say anything. "Know what color they are?"

"Shit brown," she snapped, "like their mommy." Then Tanya turned to him, her face entirely changed. "I'm sorry," she said. Her lower lip relaxed and he could see her crooked teeth. "I didn't mean it the way it sounded." He smiled, more at her thinking he would take offense than in acceptance of her apology. She smiled back and stroked his face. "What color are they?"

"No color at all. Absolutely clear."

"Really?" She was trying to sound interested.

"Yeah." He paused. "Lemme show you." He leaned over and held the egg sac in front of her face, his heavy thumbnail against it.

"Nooooo!" she squealed and pulled the sheet over her head.

"Just wanted to show you." He sounded hurt. Then he was scrambling over the top of her. "Oooooops." He was kneeling by the side of the bed searching the strands of her hair that the sheet didn't cover. Slowly she slipped the white material down her face. "Don't move," he warned. She stopped the sheet, her eyes wide, her mouth still covered. He knew he shouldn't go on with it, that she was really going to get mad. But that's what made it so good. "Might break open any time." He searched her hair a moment longer and then, with the flourish of a magician, revealed the egg sac to her.

"That's not funny," said Tanya. "That's not funny at all." He stood. "How old are you? Too old for those kind of jokes."

"It's very Indian," Albert answered. "A race of practical jokers." He walked back into the bathroom. Wide awake now he decided to do something he had wanted to do for a long time. He lay the egg sac on the edge of the sink, took a scalpel from the medicine chest and, with the aid of surgical tweezers he'd taken home from the lab to pluck his beard, made a delicate incision into it.

"Look!" Tanya cried out after a while. He didn't turn. "How amusing." He was using two pair of tweezers now, the curved points of one spreading the sac walls, the straight points of the other tweezing out the tiny transparencies into a row on the sink's edge. "Troy is burning and I'm not in it." He stopped and peeked over his shoulder. He worried about fires in the old tenement. All he saw was Tanya lying on her stomach looking at the floor.

"That's lucky," he said and turned back to the sink. The sac was empty. He counted the embryos. Twenty-one. He examined them carefully. He could see their roachness. But they were perfectly clear, their colorless outer skeletons like jelly under the tweezer points.

"Dream shadows moving on the floor below," chanted Tanya. "Ghost Cressida from Greek to Greek does go."

"That's good," he said and turned again. "That's very good." And his admiration was genuine. He really liked people to use words well. "You want to see the roaches?" She didn't answer and he turned back to the sink to form them into a double row nursery on its edge.

"At exactly," and he looked at his watch, "3:36 A.M." He was talking to the bathroom mirror. "Mrs. Tanya G. Roach was delivered of twenty-one beautiful babies." He smiled at his image. "Dr. Heavyrunner in attendance." He liked the sound of that. But he would never be an obstetrician. From his old hunting days, from dressing out the game, he had learned animal anatomy. Now he did almost all of the dog preparations, the open-heart surgery.

"You're the first Indian I've ever known," said Tanya in a normal tone.

"Yeah," he agreed. Then he asked her again. "Want to see these roaches?" He poked at them and arranged the lines better. But he couldn't really tell how they were doing. They were just lying there.

He didn't know if they were dead or what. Then he thought of the microscope in the lab. Because they were transparent he could probably see their circulatory system. He could tell that way.

"Did you hear me?" Her voice was petulant. "You're the first Indian I've ever slept with."

"You haven't slept yet." He took a surgical sponge from a package in the cabinet, wet it and tweezed the tiny roaches on to it. Then he folded the sponge and put it in the amber specimen jar he'd taken pills home in. He left the jar on the edge of the sink so he wouldn't forget it. Then he put the surgical tools away, shut the light and came out. He stopped. It was startling to see her like that. She had rolled over on her back and was looking at him backwards, the top of her head flat against the pillow. Upside down her face seemed disembodied. He sensed danger for her, almost couldn't look.

"Is that the mace that crunched a thousand hips," the upside down mouth was reciting. "And spawned the foppish flowers of aluminum?" The lip movements were not synchronized with the words. And her eyes, focused on the center of his body, floated free of her head. He couldn't look anymore. Instead he rushed at her pulled the sheet down and buried his face between her legs.

"Oooooo," she groaned. "Oooooo, Sudden Diomed!" He moved up, kissing her stomach, then her breasts. "Oooooo," she moaned and shook her head from side to side. "Oooooo, chivalrous Greek Knight!" Then he was at her mouth, sliding into her. "Hector's dead," she grunted, her large eyes squinting at the ceiling. Her face had returned to her body. "Priam's laid low on the royal bed."

"Shut up," he murmured and gently, as an animal, he took her jaw flesh between his teeth.

"Please!" She pulled her face away. He felt her bottom contract, grab. "Wait a minute!" He raised his shoulders and looked down. Her eyes were closed and she was shaking her head from side to side. She looked like a small child who would not take her medicine. "Bastard! Stoppit!" Now she was arching her back, trying to throw him off. But he was stubborn too and pressed his great bulk down again. He felt her nails scratching at his back. "Please!" she gasped. But he was moving faster, getting larger.

Then, because he didn't know what it was, he almost did stop. He felt the warmth spreading over his stomach and thought it was blood, that he had hurt her insides. And he felt it on his hands that held her backside and on the sheet beneath. He didn't know what it was, not until it burned a cut on his finger. She was wetting, short bursts with each thrust. He thought of the dogs, how they would sometimes let go in the middle of an experiment, unconscious, supine on the dog board, their bellies shaved and pink, the yellow fluid arching into the air. Grab it, the doctor would yell and Albert, laughing, would try to squeeze the dog shut with one hand while reaching for a beaker with the other.

"Please!" she begged. "Please!"

"Can't," he gasped and felt the bed getting wetter, her closing down harder. But it was funny. She had drunk beer. Why hadn't she peed before?

"Please!"

"Can't!" And finally she let him in all the way. They went off together, he pounding in short bursts, she returning fire, one long final stream. He rolled off, laughing while she scrambled back toward the bathroom. He lay in the warm wetness. Then he was back with his grandmother. She was much older, gray haired and wrinkled. Both of them held their arms outstretched but he watched his grandmother. He knew she would soon die. Then the first rays lit her face and she was young again. So he turned to the sun. But for him it was too strong. Surprised, he lost his balance and felt himself falling.

"Well," he said as he looked up sleepily. "You're dressed." She had on her white turtleneck and short skirt and was standing over him. "Where are you going?"

"Home," she said coldly. He sat up, grabbed a corner of the contour sheet and pulled it off. Then he balled it up and, with the dry part, wiped the plastic mattress cover that he'd brought from the hospital.

"There." He threw it toward the bathroom. "Another sheet and it's good as new."

"I need money for a cab."

"Can't get a cab this time of night."

"I'll take the subway."

"It's not safe."

"I have to go."

"No you don't. Look," and he hesitated. "I'm sorry. I didn't . . ."

"No," she interrupted. "It's not that." Tanya looked down. "My father died yesterday. I have to go to the funeral." And once again he was wide awake. That explains the poetry, he thought, and his feelings when he'd looked at her face, maybe her being there at all.

"I'm sorry," he said.

"Don't be," she snapped. "I hated the bastard." He looked at her and saw she meant it.

"Go home!" he ordered. He didn't know why her remark made him so angry. "Go home!"

"Bastard!" And Tanya fled, not toward the front door because he was in the way, but back into the bathroom. She slammed the door, then locked it with the hook and eye.

There was a moment of silence. Then he heard the breaking of glass and the toilet flush. He thought she was hurting herself and rushed at the door which gave easily. She was standing there with her back to the sink looking at him, a little smile on her lips. He looked around. Amber lights were moving on the white ceiling. He didn't understand. It was only by chance that he looked into the toilet. Like pebbles in a stream the glass of the shattered specimen jar shimmered beneath the water. He turned to look at her face. She was waiting to see what he would do.

He reached out to her and his left hand closed around the back of her neck. Slowly, as in a dream, he was bending her down. There was no resistance except the stiffness of her body and her smile. And her eyes remained on his until she was on her knees. She saw what he was going to do before he did. Her hands gripped the porcelain edge. For a moment it was a stand-off. Then she gave way and he forced her head down into the bowl. Was it her silence that infuriated him, her refusal to struggle even now? Was she saying there was something in her stronger than his strength?

And he might have held Tanya under forever if she hadn't brought her legs up and pushed against the floor. It was her struggling rump that broke his fury. He smacked at it with his open right hand and felt the force traveling through her body into her neck. He left her sitting on the bathroom floor, coughing and sobbing. He went back to the bedroom, got a clean sheet and began making the bed.

"I can't go home like this." She came out sooner than he expected. Her hair was dripping all over her shoulders, her white turtleneck soaked. She had his towel in her hands.

"Sleep here then." He put on his bathrobe, went into the kitchen and took a can of beer and half a salami from the refrigerator. He brought them into the front room and sat on the couch in the darkness looking out the window. The traffic was beginning to pick up on Sixth Avenue. Trucks were coming out of the Holland Tunnel. In an hour it would be light. He sat looking down at the cobblestones. He heard her come out of the bathroom again and get into bed. He nibbled on the salami and sipped the beer from the can. He got up once to check on her. Her breathing was deep and quiet. Then he went back to the couch and waited. After a while the sky turned gray.

But when the sun came up it was behind his building so he couldn't see it. But he did see when its rays struck the painted gray brick of the tenement across Sixth Avenue. It was a much taller building than his and the shadow his cast appeared only a little beyond its midpoint before it began going down. He watched it move from the fifth to the fourth floor. And he saw the street filling with exhaust fumes, the puffy people hurrying toward Spring Street, toward the busses and the subway. And he decided to get a couple of hours of sleep before work. He went back to the bedroom. In the darkness he saw Tanya next to the wall. She was curled beneath the sheet.

He pulled the stopper on the alarm clock on the dresser. But he didn't get in. He was thinking of his grandmother, Jenny Pipewoman. He was very young when he would sneak into her bed at night to hold her warmth. He never knew how she did it but when he awoke, there'd be the old pinto and the dark pines passing slowly until they came out on top of a ridge that he could see was red rock even in the crumbling darkness. What was the name of that ridge? They were living in Babb then and the sun rose behind St. Mary, the little town just to the east.

He looked down at the sleeping girl as if she might know. But he knew she didn't. He shrugged, lifted the sheet and got into bed. Lying there he thought of his grandmother again. "Mmmmmm," he hummed after a while for that was how she called to the sun. "Mmmmmm." He hummed it quietly so as not to disturb Tanya. And he tried to remember what his grandmother said, what her prayer was. He remembered the smell of cottonwood smoke coming out of her sweater and her sounds as they came through her back into his ear. Then he turned to Tanya and put his large arms around her. As if to show welcome, without waking she moved her back into his chest.

"Mmmmmm," he murmured over the top of her head, then let the sound fade. "Listen," he whispered after a moment. "Listen, Sun." And it all came back, the old language. "Listen, Old Man! Let us survive! Look down on our sick children this day. Pity them and give them a complete life. Listen, Old Man . . ." And he would have said it again but Tanya stirred in his arms and he was afraid he would wake her. It had been a long time since he'd watched the sun rise, a long time since the time of his dreams.

But when the dream came it was of the laboratory. The garbage can was full. So he did what he usually did. He took out the top animals, Dr. Kahn's two decerebrate cats and Dr. Wang's five headless guinea pigs, and pushed them into the open chest of his collie. Then he lifted his animal into the can. But the lid would not remain down. Slowly, the sightless eyes of this dog rose over the can's edge, the metal cover resting on its head like a coolie hat.

He knew what he had to do, empty the can into the incinerator. So he wheeled it down the hall to the service elevator. He pressed for the basement. The door closed. But when it reached bottom the door did not open. He pressed the buttons. Nothing happened. He flipped the alarm switch. The alarm bell rang. He flipped it off. The alarm bell stopped ringing. He turned, sat up and found Tanya was gone.

■ RALPH BEER

Ralph Beer was born and raised on a ranch near Clancy, Montana, and, except for a stint of cowboying in British Columbia, has lived in Montana all his life. In 1982, Beer received his master's degree in English from the University of Montana, where he edited Cutbank, *the university's literary magazine. A contributing editor of* Harper's *magazine, Beer has taught creative writing at Carroll College in Helena and continues to operate the family ranch. His first novel,* The Blind Corral, *was published in 1986. This selection appears here in print for the first time.*

The Harder They Come

When he hit the second wind-slabbed drift on Cutler Grade, Gregor MacIvers knew he wouldn't make it home that night without his chains. A spume of fine snow lofted from the hood and misted his windshield, and as the engine stalled, the truck shuddered to a stop. Spindrift sluiced off the plow berm at the west edge of the road, rising in tight vortices beyond the reach of his lights. And for an instant in the swirling space at the edge of darkness, MacIvers saw or imagined a woman standing in a light summer dress, her coiling black hair tracing the currents of wind behind her. He started his engine and rubbed the windshield with the flat of his hand; even with the lights switched to high beam, he saw nothing ahead but a ground-blizzard at night.

MacIvers backed a few yards down his tracks, and watched as grooves cut by his truck's undercarriage began again to fill with snow. He snapped on the dome light and reached for his insulated coveralls. He'd known all day he would have to feed when he got home, yet he had lingered in town over a solitary dinner, celebrating again, as he had for the past four Friday nights, the torment of his divorce. It was an expensive ritual that seemed to do him no good.

As he opened his door and began to step out, MacIvers saw in the confusion of tools and winter clothes crowding the bright cab, that he'd forgotten his felt-lined winter overshoes. He wiggled his toes in the hand-tooled Mexican riding boots he wore and said without heat, "Real pretty."

Stars appeared beyond torn clouds as he zipped the coveralls over his herringbone sports jacket, an extravagance he'd allowed himself a month before on the day he appeared in court. The coat had seemed a good idea at the time, an excusable self-indulgence, a last minute defense against town and what waited there beyond his control. Now it was only a coat, and not very warm at that.

MacIvers ran the coverall zippers down his legs, pulled on a wool Scotch cap, and plowed around to the toolbox in the back. He moved fast, knowing his feet would suffer. In wind that cut through any cloth made, MacIvers wrestled his chains into place on the lugged tires. He crawled under the truck behind each wheel and fastened the first three inside hooks without trouble. As he struggled for slack on the last one, he wondered if he'd set the emergency brake. A premonition of the truck rolling back drove him to squirm out and check. The brake handle was pulled all the way up; that he couldn't remember touching it gave MacIvers a moment's pause. Sometimes in the past few weeks he would set off on an errand to one of his outbuildings and on the way forget what he'd meant to do. That could be dangerous when a man worked alone. It was the little mistakes, MacIvers knew, that got you in trouble.

He forced each V-bar cross-chain around the tire, straining slack toward the inside hook. Snow, packed in the channel iron frame above him, melted under the heat of the idling engine and dripped on his neck. "We're having fun now," he grunted, gripping the length of sidechain with both bare hands and feeling the links bite his calloused fingers as he applied his strength. After he fastened the hook, he lay on his side a moment to rest, his face relaxed in the endearing chill of snow.

Headlights swept the grade below as he finished, the snapping of chains on fenders rising to him on the wind. He slammed the toolbox closed, cursed his numb feet, and stepped back as a new Dodge flatbed, loaded with several tons of cattle cake, eased to a stop beside his truck. Melvin Rathbone rolled down his side window and showed his teeth. He was wearing a Swiss alpine hat with feathers.

Melvin and his younger brother Junior lived on a remnant of their long-dead parent's heartbreak homestead which they hadn't yet subdivided, like the rest of their place, for summer homes. In their eighties, both Rathbones stood less that five feet tall, and their teeth, which hadn't seen a dentist since the Great War, made even MacIvers wince.

"Told you he was stuck," Melvin said, looking MacIvers right in the face.

Brother Junior stared ahead under the loop of steering wheel at snow purling through his lights. "Wouldn't be if we had our new road. Screw him."

Melvin knotted his wrinkled little face like a wizened fist. "Hard guy, yeah. But," he decided, his hooded eyes hot slits in the corrugated ruin of his face, "you're alone now."

"I was 'til you came along," MacIvers said. "You get moving, I'll take my lonesomeness home and warm it up."

"She's not coming back, Gregor," Melvin nickered. He waved as the Dodge churned ahead, gaping back for an instant like an evil dwarf in a child's fevered dream. MacIvers climbed into his truck, held his hands above the defroster and waited until the funnel of receding light ahead disappeared beyond the crest above him. Without spinning a wheel, he eased into the fresh tracks, shifted to second gear, and drove steadily on to his first gate, an elaborate structure he'd built in idle hours from scrap iron. He groped for his keys, watching snow swirl through rusted filigree around what he'd meant to be Pegasus in flight. But in the headlights, the iron figure he'd hammered from boiler plate with a cold chisel looked instead like a winged goat.

MacIvers knew how his neighbors felt about his refusal to let the County cross his place with a better road. And although he still thought he'd been right, he understood how that singular choice of land over community had isolated him for good. Maybe that had advantages, he reflected, with neighbors like his.

He closed the gate behind his truck and held the padlock for a moment in his heavy hand, then pitched it into the dark and replaced it with one of several he'd bought that day after paying off his lawyer.

Not that he disagreed with Melvin and thought she might come back. No, it was only a way of reminding himself that she couldn't.

A stranger in that country would not have made the next mile, but by leaving his summer road below and following sagebrush ridges swept bare by the wind, MacIvers kept his truck moving toward home. He was now upon his own land, land which in the past decade had burdened him with debt, greyed his hair early, worn him out. Four square miles of sidehill grassland, it was still as wild and untouched as the day he bought it, unchanged, probably, since the day Lewis and Clark had passed on their way to the Pacific.

Three months after his father died, MacIvers had gambled on this pasture, and until now, with the added expense of divorce, he'd gained so steadily on the balance that he could almost see an end to it. Land values around him had soared, but years of debt made him cautious; land lasted, and man's mark upon it, long after the man was gone. His father's death had taught him that, and right or wrong, MacIvers knew there would be no roads here until his own death paved their way.

The wind dropped as he entered a pine woods, and he drove on in sudden quiet to his second gate, a massive pole affair topped by a burled yellow pine log, which had marked the former boundary of the ranch. An ox yoke hung on tug chains from the knotted header, and on the yoke, facing what had then been the outside world, MacIver's great-grandfather had seared his name, one flaming letter at a time, with a red-hot length of angle iron.

He changed this lock too, and as he snapped the new one closed MacIvers felt again a wary sense of misgiving—one which he'd lately kept at bay with relentless labor and whiskey. He was alone as he'd never been, completely, and so it seemed, by choice. Voiceless days and nights, welcome at first after the final days his wife had spent in the house, had soon begun to wear on his nerves. And as he looked at the lock and chain, he knew this would be his answer, his reply to her and the life she wanted. What bore his name he intended to keep untouched, no matter what the price in silence or cash.

He made water in the dark beside the gate and noticed that the wind had completely stopped. To the west, the sky was salted with stars, yet in the absence of wind the night seemed even colder. He would change clothes at the house and build a fire in the range before going to the barns. The kitchen would be warm when he returned, and he could re-map his life with bourbon at the lamplit table in peace.

MacIvers fiddled with the radio as he drove on, picking up a rock station in Bozeman, the Country FM in Helena, then classical music from Butte. He made a practice of playing the radio whenever he worked around cattle in the dark, imagining they were calmed by music. He turned up the volume, found the bottle under his seat, and while holding the first hot slash of whiskey tight against his lips, tried to guess Monteverdi or Scarlatti. With the satisfying burn of Walker's came too the vague but familiar pride of having once again made it home on a bad night. Fighting roads was something of a family tradition – dozens of nights, dimmed now by time and run together in memory, young MacIvers had waited at the highway with a team of Belgian horses to pull his parents' car the rest of the way home. That urge toward home on a hard night was something he had wanted to pass on. His eyes watered as MacIvers drank again. "To us," he said in mock-toast to his image in the windshield, "the dead and the stillborn." The music, he realized, was Henry Purcell's, and he put the bottle away.

Yet his eyes still teared as he drove past the house and down the long hill to the barns. When he caught his mistake, he stopped the truck and hardened his mouth. He would have to put his mind on one thing at a time until his work was done. It could wander all it wanted later, in the lamplight. Hereford cattle, their iridescent eyes turned blindly toward him, milled in the truck lights, smoky breath rising over their frosted backs. Beyond them stood the haybarn, massive, cribbed high along the outside with corral rails, and filled to the rafters with sweet alfalfa hay. From the air, the three barns together looked like a giant galvanized T, the haybarn and adjoining log cowbarn intersected midway by a long tin feedshed. MacIvers knew it would be dry in the haybarn and in the plank-floored feed manger next door. He wouldn't have to worry about his feet if he hustled, and then, he thought, he'd be through for the night. The idea of feeding cattle in the herringbone jacket brought a smile; he turned off the lights and engine, letting the radio play in the dark.

MacIvers climbed a ladder to the first level, then another, up to the very top of the stack, some thirty feet above the feedshed door. From there he dragged one bale at a time with a long-handled hook to the edge of the stack, and by the strings, pitched them out into the darkness below. He needed fifty, which he would then pull into the plank-floored feed bunk and break for the cows. The lack of light didn't matter; his eyes gradually adjusted, and besides, he knew the place by heart.

The musty smell of dry alfalfa reminded him, as it often did, of his father, a silent, patient man remembered for his ability with animals. It was said that MacIvers' father could gentle anything with hair; that when you brought him a colt, you'd take home a horse. The haybarn had been their last shared labor, one which brought them together at the time of his father's failing health, when during the dangers of working at such heights, they had wordlessly exchanged the roles of father and son.

After he dropped thirty bales, MacIvers stopped to rest. Though his body seemed warm in the padded coveralls, his feet were wooden again, and his face, which had been badly frostbitten several times, burned with a dull ache. I should have stopped at the house first, he thought and slapped his gloved hands together.

High in the hayshed rafters, where they joined the log barn his grandfather had built, MacIvers noticed his cat coming toward him along a beam. The man made a sound with his lips; the cat paused then came on. A peculiar animal, he didn't meow or purr or mingle with the other cats. Except for MacIvers and mice, he left other living things alone. But when MacIvers worked at the barns, the cat followed him like a shadow.

He began to drag bales again, heaving each one with a grunt toward the feedshed door below. As he walked back and forth across the slick hay, his mind turned to another winter night nearly a dozen years before, when, for thirty dollars and a bottle of Walker's, he'd taken a group of college students for a hayride with his father's last team. Among them was a slender girl who had come alone. Before the end of the first mile she moved up to the seat beside him to watch the heavy horses pull in the moonlight. And as the hayboat cut the brittle night, MacIvers discovered a feeling he would later attach to expanses of undisturbed land.

He stopped, realizing he'd lost count. His face had numbed, and even his legs were chilled. "Close enough?" he asked the cat, who watched from a jackbrace overhead. The cat made no sound. "Right you are, Caliban," MacIvers said and started back along the edge toward the uppermost ladder. He felt his outside boot skid on a loose bale, felt the hemp strings, rotted through by mildew or chewed thin by mice, snap under his weight. MacIvers made an off-balance stab at a cross-brace with his hook, missed, and tipped headlong into the cavity between cribbing and stack. He heard his voice as he fell and what sounded like a rifle fired into his neck when he hit. And as the vertical column of his weight bore down upon his burning face, Gregor MacIvers discovered that he could not move.

He opened his eyes. The left side of his face lay flush against the frozen ground, so flat he knew the shoulder beneath him must be smashed. By rolling his eyes, he could see his legs above him, resting against all logic between an upright post and the wall of hay. He could also see through the rail fence in front of him a small portion of meadow and piece of sky. MacIvers knew he'd fallen almost forty feet but guessed he'd been slowed some by the stack and barrier of poles. Perhaps he'd only lost his wind, broken an arm or collarbone, and jarred loose some teeth; that was nothing new. It was the noise in his neck when he'd landed that frightened him.

The thing to do was relax, right himself as carefully as he could, and get to the house, even if he had to crawl, before he froze his feet. But he couldn't feel his feet. Or his legs. He wasn't really sure where his right arm might be, although his left one seemed to lie somewhere under him. Just catch your wind, he told himself. Take a deep breath and keep thinking. What happened to the hook? But the weight of muscle and bone and gut above him made breathing hard, and he knew he'd have to move soon or suffocate like a bull caught on its back. He strained to bend his legs and nothing moved; a sound in front of his face startled him: the long vowel A. He was shamed by the noise, and he quieted.

Most of the cattle had gone to the far side of the stack, expecting to be fed there as usual. A few, confused by the delay, began to wander back, bawling occasional plumes of smoke. Above the squeal of their hooves on the frozen snow, MacIvers could hear the radio in his truck. A yearling heifer found him, and stretching her neck, peered through the rails at his upturned face. She shook her head and snorted, and he could smell the rich stench of her cud. Above the bulk of the animal, he noticed a few dull stars. It will get colder, he thought, and remembering the cold which he no longer felt, brought MacIvers back to life. Try one thing at a time, man. Find your right hand and wiggle your fingers. At least try. Again he strained in the darkness but found nothing, felt nothing but his own great weight bearing down upon him.

MacIvers worked at breathing. From the angle at which he lay, he studied the roof above him, some rafter ends, the roughcut fir beam they rested on, and a crossbrace rising from post to beam. They had cut the trees during a hard winter, and in the gentle evenings of that wet spring, he and his father had milled the logs into lumber. Working together, they hauled the green, thirty-foot rafters from the mill and ricked them like a charcoal pyre where the barn now stood. That autumn they raised the lodgepole posts and with block and tackle lifted the lintels into place. Every hour of spare time they had, they worked on the barn, through the fall and early winter, sheathing the rafters with pine boards, then nailing down bright sheets of tin. MacIvers remembered the hope which had filled him then, as joining the old barn, their luminous structure rose like a landmark of endurance.

The cattle had begun to bed, as if they'd given up on their feed and forgotten MacIvers, who for some time had been unconscious. He held his breath when he woke, catching the melody of a Handel Sarabande that had been used as the theme for the film, "Barry Lyndon." MacIvers tried to smile at that, although he was no longer sure what he did with his mouth resembled irony. By moving his tongue, he could feel the sharp edges of a broken tooth toward the back of his jaw. He searched for fragments, worrying what might have been a crown toward his lips to spit it out. That's it, he told himself, just hang in there. You've stood frostbite before. Stay calm and try to keep awake. Someone might come.

But MacIvers knew better than that. After the calamity of his wife's second miscarriage, their neighbors and friends gradually stopped dropping by, soured perhaps by MacIver's increasing obsession with work, discouraged by his obvious desire for privacy, his preoccupation with boundaries. And yet, he saw, as he'd isolated himself in work, a distance had grown between him and his work, between him and his land, between him and himself. It hadn't been the County's planned road, MacIvers realized, but a distance he'd created that so finally set him apart.

He felt the sweet dullness creeping over him again and drew as much of the sharp air as he could into his lungs, forcing his mind to range, if not toward escape then at least for a moment of memory he could grasp to pull himself awake. He went back, he thought to the beginning of the trouble, when his father had opposed the marriage—not, MacIvers knew, because the old man hadn't liked Margaret, but because, as he'd said, it would be better to wait. Thinking of that time, MacIvers guessed his father had wanted him to wait on himself, until he had time to season sound enough to stand disappointments like the ones that followed. And he had waited for nearly two years, working longer days, buying and selling cattle with a vengeful cunning that made him respected by older men, and raging continually within himself at the courtship that dragged on, and at the very work which he took more and more upon himself. He lost his sense of humor, and any feeling for fun. During those two years he grew hard; fast to anger, he abused his body as he sometimes abused horses and machines. He became hard on everything and everyone around him, and most of all, he was hard on himself.

Six weeks before the day set for their wedding, MacIvers found his father, sitting as if asleep in the sunny south door of the log barn, facing the vast hayshed which waited for the first time to be filled. He had sat down to rest not fifty feet from where MacIvers now lay and died with no sign of pain upon his face. As if sharing his rest, MacIvers sat down beside him in the dovetailed shadows and thought about harvesting alone.

After that, he began to ease up. In his thirties his hair had turned the color of new iron while his body toughened like green wood. He planned his work carefully, hired good help and treated his help well, pacing himself and the hired men with long but gradual days. He might have been happy then except for a vague and abiding regret over the two fevered years he'd ruined. Children, a son especially, he believed would have eased him, but even that had been beyond his power. When the second child died inside his wife, their life together began to die too. She withdrew into a world of magazines, television, and cigarettes at the house, and MacIvers abandoned her for his woods and fields. In the evenings he engrossed himself in books, music, and a growing lust for more land. He put money they couldn't spare on the Hammerstorm place to the south and spent most of his time there building new fences. It was then that men like the Rathbones, who were old enough to remember, began to compare MacIvers with his great grandfather, and although it was often with anger when they spoke of "that overreaching old son of a bitch," MacIvers was drawn, almost in spite of himself, to emulate a man he'd never known.

"This is one way to get it done," he said, his voice rising from habit. "You just get down here like this, beside each post, and check its alinement with the rest."

Margaret seemed doubtful; she stood just beyond the cribbing in a summer dress, holding her elbows cupped in her hands, cradling her breasts. "I don't see what difference it makes now, Mac," she said.

"I don't guess you would," he answered, watching the wind lace her raven hair into veils across her face.

"I'm sorry about the whole deal," she said.

"Maybe we ought to give it another try," and MacIvers was about to say he was sorry too, when Melvin Rathbone lurched up on stumpy legs and clicked his amber teeth. "No!" Melvin said. "You changed your locks!"

"Maggie?" MacIvers said, coming awake enough to notice his cat walking a rail above him. The animal brushed his leg. Arching its back it turned and seemed to touch him again. MacIvers pursed his lips, then thought better of it. He wished he had stopped to change his clothes like he'd planned, wished he could stay awake, even wished for a drink. Glancing between the rails toward the dark house, MacIvers was startled to see lights coming through the trees beyond the pole gate. Someone, for a reason he couldn't begin to guess, was driving down his lane. He blinked to make certain it wasn't still a dream, then thought, kids–drinking and cruising around. Likely they'd found the maze of development roads at Rathbone's, got lost, and cut his fence. But if they stopped at the gate, they might hear his radio.

Although he couldn't open his mouth, he knew he could make sound. He drew and held a deep breath, straining to hear the approaching vehicle and telling himself to wait a little longer before making his shameful noise. But as he strained his aching eyes, the light left the road, climbing into the dry lower limbs of trees beyond the gate where no road ran. And with absolute clarity MacIvers saw the terrible joke of his life; he released the air he'd held and gasped for more to laugh at the moon, rising as it would for eternity, upon his land.

■ PATRICIA HENLEY

Raised in Indiana and Maryland, Patricia Henley attended St. Mary's College and received a master's degree in creative writing from Johns Hopkins University in 1974. For a time, Henley lived at the Tolstoy Farm, an anarchist commune in Washington. She moved to Bozeman in 1984 and worked as a counselor at Women in Transition. In 1987-1988, Henley was a visiting teacher at Purdue University in Indiana. This selection is from her collection of short stories, Friday Night At Silver Star, *which won the Montana Arts Council's First Book Award in 1985.*

The Birthing

One shot and the killing was over, quickly as trimming a thumbnail. Morgan walked away from the alfalfa field toward the dead goat. It was early evening and the sun had long ago loosened its hold on the canyon.

Angel came running from behind the house. She wore a loose white shirt and was barefooted and soil crept up her ankles like socks. Her braids flew behind her.

"Why the hell did you *do* that?" she said.

Morgan stood near the dead gray nanny goat and with one hand he absently thinned green apples from the dwarf tree. He held the .22 in the other hand, the barrel at an angle to the ground.

"Told her I would if she didn't keep her penned," he said. "Here. You take this back to the house." He handed her the rifle and lifted the goat in his arms and began walking toward the county road, toward the goat woman herself who had heard the shot and was waiting in the middle of the gravel road, but near her house, a quarter mile farther toward the lake. Morgan could see her waiting, arms akimbo, in a long skirt and a big picture hat. The pine woods behind her were blackening and the goat was still warm in his arms.

It was their custom to hold meetings to resolve disputes among their kind. The authorities had never been called in. At the meeting Morgan showed no remorse. He had changed his shirt, wet his head under the garden hose, and slicked back his wavy blond hair. He sat nudging loose tobacco into the careful crease of a rolling paper, his feet propped on an applewood stool next to the cold woodstove.

Angel stood up first thing and defended him. "Morgan was forced to this. He didn't want to do it." She sat down then on the sagging sofa and pulled the nearest young child into her lap, murmuring to his neck and smoothing his forehead.

The schoolhouse was lit by kerosene lamps with soot-black globes and the light was a little skittish, like a feline creature among them.

Georgia, the goatherd, sat in an overstuffed chair surrounded by her four children. She tapped her boots on the linoleum floor and, head bent, stared at Morgan through slitted eyes. Theirs was a longstanding feud. When the little one named Banjo whimpered, she put him to the breast to quiet him.

After Angel spoke no one said anything for a long time. A coyote howled from the rimrock and two dogs wrangled on the schoolhouse porch, their growls low and menacing. At last a tall woman in an old band uniform jacket stood and spoke. "We've got to think about what we're trying to do. We can't be shooting one another's animals." Her hands were grimy with garden soil and she ran them through her frizzy red hair. "What do we believe in?" she asked.

Everyone started talking at once and no one was accorded attention. Morgan said nothing and Angel didn't look at him. She didn't like to think the father of her unborn child would kill a neighbor's goat just for eating apples.

"Hold it. JUST HOLD IT, PEOPLE," Sam hollered, his arms high, gesturing for their attention. The jabbering subsided, like air seeping out of a balloon.

Sam was respected, a leader, a hard worker, a strong wiry man people rarely challenged.

"I can't sit here all night listening to this," he said. "I've got chores. I'll wager most of you do, too." He wiped his face with a blue bandana. There were murmurs of assent.

"Okay," Sam said. "I'm going to ask Morgan to relinquish his .22 for three months. All we can do is let him know we disapprove." No one disputed him.

"What about the goats?" Morgan asked.

"And we will put pressure on Georgia to pen up the goats. I will help you build a pen," Sam said directly to the goatherd before she could say one word in defense of animals running free. She slumped in her chair, defeated. The lines were deep around her mouth and eyes.

"Meeting adjourned," Sam said. The people filed out of the schoolhouse, resuming conversations and laughing, drifting home in the cool night, quick to forget the conflict. Angel and Morgan were last. They stood on the porch and looked at the stars while the others dispersed. The cloying smell of the lilac bush was thick in the night air.

"Want to feel the baby moving, Morgan?" Angel said. She reached for his calloused hand.

"Sure, Sugar," Morgan answered, dutifully placing his hand on her abdomen. He kept it there until the baby kicked. Then he hugged her with the baby like a bundling board between them.

"Are you scared about the baby?" Morgan said.

"Scared?" Angel loved for Morgan to ask her how she was feeling. He didn't ask her often since they had quit courting and settled down to have a baby. She was nineteen. He was twenty-four. They had met a year ago at a healing gathering in British Columbia, linking hands in a circle of two hundred people dancing and not letting go.

"I mean scared of the delivery," he said.

"No," Angel said. "So many ladies have done it before me. It must be almost foolproof."

"Let's go home," Morgan said, and he took her hand to guide her in the shadows to the red house beside the rushing creek.

The holy folks came the first of July when the sun was relentless and the people sometimes gathered in the afternoon to soak in the deepest part of the creek, watching the water striders skim across the water and the nightshade curling around the cottonwood roots. They drove into the canyon in a rattletrap Ford stationwagon, circa 1956, blue and white beneath Arizona and California dust, and overloaded. The tailpipe scraped the first real bump the car came to off the blacktop and the tailpipe was lost, so that the holy folks made quite an entrance, a noisy entrance disturbing the quiet rising of the heat waves.

Morgan watched from the grove of aspens shielding the creek pool. They stopped by the mailbox and all three piled out of the car, two women and one man, dressed in graying, once-white clothing. Morgan stepped from the shade and waved them in his direction.

The three strangers walked abreast down the lane, kicking up small dust clouds. They stepped into the shade where they had seen Morgan. Morgan, Angel, and Sam soaked in the creek.

"Come on in here," Morgan said. He was sitting on a submerged log, thigh deep in the cool water, the lingering branches of a willow trailing around him. Angel's freckled breasts bobbed in the water like some lush riparian fruit.

The three strangers sat down beside the creek, but didn't get in. The women pulled their skirts above their knees and hung their legs over the bank so that their feet splashed in the water. The man sat a little way from them and took off his raggedy straw hat and fanned himself. He was young, younger than the women, perhaps Morgan's age, and slender and white-skinned, as if he ate too many vegetables and not enough meat. His shirt was open to the waist and a brass fish hung on a thin chain around his neck. His chest was hairless and white as wax. The faces of the women were lined and creased. Morgan reckoned they were in their thirties, though one seemed older than the other. They looked alike, slightly plump, with the same dull black hair in braids. There were rings of dirt around their necks and wrists, as though they hadn't been able to bathe in a long time.

"My name's Adam and this here is my family, these women," he said, and he gestured with an open palm toward the women, who lowered their eyes in a modest way. "Greta and Gail." He had a slur of an accent.

"Where'd you come from?" Morgan said. He was curious, but not wary. They were used to strangers passing through.

"We been on the road awhile. Started in east Texas. Tennessee before that," Adam said. "We're lookin' for a place to settle down for a bit."

Morgan and Sam exchanged glances and Sam shrugged and nodded his head. The milk cow mooed long and loud close to the barbed wire fence on the other side of the creek.

"We got a spot not far over there—across the road—where we allow folks to camp for a few days," Morgan offered. "It's right by the creek and off in the woods so you can have a little privacy."

"We'd appreciate it," Adam said.

"I'll take you over there if you like," Sam said.

"That's mighty friendly of you," the older woman said, her voice thick and sweet.

The holy folks set up a tipi before dark, a bright canvas structure like a temple in the juniper woods. That night they had a campfire and the people heard the rhythm of a tambourine and singing, a strange high wail and syllabic chanting in a language they could not decipher.

Angel went to visit them the next morning and took a pint of pickles as a gift. When she came home, Morgan was watering the rhubarb, wearing only cut-offs and sandals.

"How was it?" he said.

"How was what?" Angel said.

"The visitors," Morgan answered. He held his thumb over the end of the hose so the water sprayed and made a fine prism.

"They're okay. They deliver babies, Morgan." She knelt beside the first row of onions and pulled some pigweed.

"Deliver babies?"

"One of 'em's a midwife," Angel said.

"Do they all sleep together?" Morgan said.

"How should I know? They call one another 'brother' and 'sister'."

Morgan absorbed this information in silence.

"Morgan," Angel said, still squatting, "we're going to need a midwife soon."

"Maybe they came here for that reason," Morgan said.

Angel stood up satisfied and went into the house. "Maybe so," she said.

That night Angel baked a rhubarb-strawberry pie and presented it to Morgan. He insisted they whip the last bit of cream. The sun gave way to evening and they ate supper on the narrow deck of the red house. The cool air soothed them. Morgan talked enthusiastically about planting more fruit trees and maybe raising turkeys next year. Angel liked it when he talked about the future.

Nighthawks swooped and rose like rags on the grassy slope before the alfalfa field began. From away high on the canyon wall they heard the coyote cries of children at play. Angel felt the baby flutter inside her. An owl sang from the shadows and Angel held her breath and listened for the holy folks. They were so far away, a quarter mile at least, and she couldn't tell if she heard them or just imagined she heard them.

Morgan went into the house and returned with a sweater for each of them. "Here," he said, "it's chilly already."

Angel just draped the sweater around her shoulders.

"He's a man of the Lord, Morgan," she said.

"Who?"

"Adam. You know," Angel said.

"Oh yeah?"

"He talks about the Lord's will and the Lord's love all the time."

"Talk's cheap, Angel," Morgan said.

Angel seethed inside. "You don't believe in anything, Morgan Riley."

Morgan didn't respond and after a minute Angel went into the house. Morgan followed her and in the loft under the blanket he said, "I do believe in you and me and our land, Angel." He put his arms around her and cradled her head in his hand.

The holy folks stayed into August and became almost a part of the community. Greta and Gail offered to help with the barn repairs. They didn't seek out a winter dwelling, so no one figured they would stay past the first frost, if that long.

One rare rainy day Angel went to make the final arrangements to have Greta, the older of Adam's women, deliver her baby. Her time was near and she needed assurance. She found the holy people inside the tipi with a small fire crackling in the center fire ring. The younger woman, the quiet one, was working yarn around two sticks, weaving a rainbow god's eye. Greta stirred a blackened pot near the edge of the fire while Adam sat, back straight, legs crossed, with fingertips resting on his knees.

"May I come in?" Angel said.

"Come in before you soak to death," Greta said.

Angel settled beside Adam on a rag rug. He placed his white hand on her belly. "You'll be delivering soon," he said. His touch was warm through her thin shirt and Angel was uncomfortable with the touch. He was the only man besides Morgan to touch her like that.

"Yes," Angel said, and he took his hand away. "I need someone to help me."

"I'll help you. I already told you that," Greta said. She had a cocoon-like voice, enveloping Angel, making her feel safe. She was motherly, with soft large breasts free under her dress and a body that looked as though she had given birth herself.

"Morgan says to find out what you want for helping me."

"Not a thing. Just a healthy baby."

"Well, we'll give you something," Angel said.

"Whatever," Greta said, and she began to hum some Bible song, as if to end the discussion.

On the way home Angel looked in the give-away box in the schoolhouse and found a pink dress. She took it home and bleached it in a bucket for three days. Scrubbed and pressed, it was near white with just a wash of color left in the seams like the petals of a rose down close to the stem. She bathed and plaited her hair and wore the dress to the tipi one evening. The holy folks welcomed her as one of their own and together they shared tea and made their plaintive music long into the night. Near ten o'clock, as the moon was setting, they were joined by Georgia, the goatherd. It seemed it was her habit to join them, and Angel felt a tug of loyalty to Morgan, as though she should leave the gathering when Georgia arrived, but she could not bring herself to leave. She felt ecstatic whirling in her cotton dress as the fire danced on her bare legs.

When she went home in the dark, she felt her way along the lane with her bare feet and knew the pleasure of her familiarity with each rock and ridge. The baby was kicking up a storm and Angel suddenly realized Morgan might be lying awake in the loft waiting for her.

She closed the screen door, cushioning its slam with her hand. She pulled the white dress over her head and laid it on the sofa before she climbed the loft ladder to the bed. It was black in the loft, but she knew the way by heart and lifted the blanket on her side and crept under. Morgan rolled over and nested against her back and said, "Let's get to sleep. We got plenty work to do tomorrow, Angel."

Another evening when Angel returned from the tipi she found Morgan under the truck in the day's last light.

"What are you doing under there, Morgan?" she asked. Her voice sounded dreamy, even to herself. She just stood beside the left front wheel, since squatting and rising had become strenuous.

Morgan stuck his head out from under the truck. "Fixin' the brakes, 'case we have to take you to town," he said. His hands and bearded face were streaked with grease.

"Sure is a nice night tonight," Angel said. She sighed and looked toward the creek, keeping her hands folded on her belly. "I saw the heron that lives back there."

Morgan disappeared under the truck again. Angel heard the gravelly sound of him scooting in the dirt on his back. The sky and the horizon seemed to meld in a blue wash and she thought she saw the silhouette of a deer in the alfalfa field.

"Adam plays a silver flute, Morgan," she said.

"Is that right," Morgan said. His voice was faint, disinterested.

"He says he can heal the sky after rain with his flute."

"You got a package today, Angel," Morgan said. "From your mother."

Angel's eyes opened wide. "Where is it?"

"In the house by the radio. Sam brought it from town."

Angel walked to the house and Morgan worked on the brakes until dark.

It was the end of August and the grass was brown as palominos. The people were beginning to journey into the fir woods to gather firewood. Each day Angel and the other women laid out sliced apricots and peaches and pears to dry in the sun. Against the coming barrenness they stored great glass jars full to the brim with the leathery fruit. Batches of wine were begun in clay crocks and the smell attracted insects to the sweet rot. Tomatoes were bending their mother stems and even melons ripened despite the short growing season. There was a sense of accomplishment among the people. They had worked the land and the land had yielded a good harvest. Weather had been with them.

Angel's water broke at high noon while she gathered small green eggs from her chickens. The wetness spilled down her left leg and she remembered wetting her pants as a child and feeling ashamed.

"Morgan, Morgan," she shouted from the fenced-in chicken yard. Morgan looked up from the black plastic pipe emerging from the shower tank he was repairing. The hens chattered around Angel and she waved like someone arriving home.

"My water broke," she said. Then she shooed the chickens and slipped through the gate and locked it.

Morgan met her on the path and put one arm around her shoulders.

"I feel a tightening down there," she said. She held one hand on the underside of her belly.

"Does it hurt?" Morgan said, squinting in the sun.

"No, it doesn't hurt," she said. "I'll take the eggs to the house. You go tell Greta."

"You want me to go to the house with you first?"

"No, I'm okay," Angel said. She lifted the egg basket and then said, "Morgan, I want to have it here. No hospital."

"We will, Angel," Morgan said and he walked down the path toward the county road. He didn't look back. His worn workshirt was the same color as the bachelor buttons bordering the path.

Angel carefully placed the eggs in a cardboard carton and set them in the cooler in the shade of the back porch. The creek curved behind the house, silver from the sun, gurgling incessantly in a comforting way. Rude Steller jays hawked at Angel and she knew a small sadness, an awareness that she would never be the same again, that time was passing, that something irrevocable was about to occur. She went in the house ravenously hungry and ate two banana muffins with butter. Then she sat rocking and rocking next to an open window with the pocket watch on the cedar chest beside her.

"I'm coming, Angel," Greta said, as she slammed the screen door.

"No hurry," Angel said.

Greta unloaded a woven shopping bag on the kitchen counter, then turned to Angel with her hands on her hips. She wore a pale shirtwaist that nearly trailed the floor. Her hair was braided and pinned like a helmet against her head. She was sunburned, the skin at her neck fleshy and wrinkled.

"Are you timing the contractions?" she asked.

"Uh-huh," Angel said. "They're not real regular yet."

"Well, keep timing. They'll most likely get regular as they get closer."

"Where's Morgan?" Angel said. She glanced out the open window.

"Checking something on the truck," Greta said. "Where are the sterile linens?"

"Up there," Angel said, and she nodded toward the high shelf of the pantry, above the canned peaches and cherries and pickles.

Greta reached high and brought down the brown grocery bag which Angel had stapled shut and baked in a slow oven. It contained two white sheets and several towels.

"What about the floss and scissors?" Greta asked.

"Right here on the cedar chest," Angel answered. "We got plenty of time." She smiled at Greta in a shy way, then lowered her eyes and folded and unfolded the hem of her smock. It barely reached her knees and she wore nothing underneath.

"Did you buy the shepherd's purse?" Greta said.

"Yes. It's in that little brown crock."

"I'll make a tea of it just in case we need it. Won't hurt to let it boil and boil. You'll need a strong brew if there's much bleeding." And Greta set to work building a fire in the cookstove.

The two rooms were joined by a step up and a double open doorway and Angel could see Greta as she bustled around the kitchen, crumpling newspaper for firestarter, poking around for kindling. It felt good to have someone there to build a fire, make tea, and keep her company. Angel gathered a bundle of yellow yarn from the floor and began crocheting, the shiny silver hook slipping in and out of the yarn like a cat. She was making a bootie the length of a matchstick.

After a while Morgan came in with an armload of split wood. He stacked the wood, then came and stood between the kitchen and the main room. Angel stopped rocking.

"How are you?" he said. He seemed far away.

"Okay. Twenty minutes apart," she said. "Maybe it's a false alarm."

"Do you think so?"

"No, not really, Morgan. This is it."

"Do you need me yet? I thought since Greta was here I could finish fixing the shower and maybe do some other chores."

"I guess I don't need you yet."

"Okay. Just holler, Greta, if she gets close," Morgan said, and he was gone, out the front door into the sun's glare. Angel watched him until he walked out of sight past the garden's tall corn stalks.

"He'll be back," Greta said from the kitchen. "You got a ways to go yet."

"I know," Angel said, and she commenced rocking again and was comforted by the rocker's squeak.

Greta made a cool hibiscus tea with raw honey and the two women sat suspended in the afternoon, in the shade of the main room, gossiping and sharing a secret now and then, a shard of the past. It might have been any lazy afternoon, two women drinking tea and talking, but for the pocket watch ticking away Angel's innocence. The contractions grew closer and more intense so that when one came Angel's speech was slow and distant and she would still be telling her story but it was as if another person spoke and she, Angel, had gone way inside, concentrating on the force certain as moontide, the force that would wash the child into the world.

When evening came and the nighthawks began their ritual swing across the yard, Angel had reached a plateau and her contractions grew no closer.

"I should fix Morgan's supper," she said.

"Don't you worry 'bout his supper," Greta said. "He'll eat somewhere, no doubt. Or I'll fix him something when he comes home."

"Where is he, I wonder?" Angel said.

"I'm home," Morgan shouted, a grin on his face. "Thought I'd never get through at Sam's. They fed me, then I felt obliged to help with the milking."

Angel met him at the door and hugged him hard.

"I'm glad you're here," she said. In the back of her throat her voice flinched in fear.

"I figured Greta would call if you needed me," he said.

"I would have," Greta said. She dealt herself a hand of solitaire on the kitchen table.

"Why, you haven't even made the bed yet," Morgan said. He had built a plywood platform for a single mattress because he didn't want her climbing the loft ladder.

"We don't do that until it's real close," Angel said. "To keep the sheets sterile." She held his large, stained hand as though it were an anchor in rough sea. The light around them dimmed and Angel danced into her next contraction.

Greta silently picked up the watch and noted the time.

"Does it hurt?" Morgan said.

"Yes. Yes, it hurts," Angel said. "But maybe that means it'll be over soon."

"Let me clean up a bit, Sugar. Then I'll sit with you," he said, and he untangled her hands from his arm.

Morgan went into the kitchen and Angel lit a lamp beside the single bed. She sat on the bed for a moment, but then moved to the rocker. She liked to think of rocking the baby to sleep in her arms. And she would sing.

Greta finished her cards and sat shuffling the deck.

"How long could this go on?" Angel asked.

"First babies generally take their time," Greta said. "We might as well settle in for the night."

The night was a long one. At first Morgan and Angel and Greta tried to play hearts, but Angel could not concentrate and Morgan's presence disturbed the intimacy the two women had earlier established, so the talk was dull and desultory. Morgan grew restless and often went to the porch to watch the stars in the sky. Angel sweated and her hair grew tangled and she was alternately subdued and fretful. Once when Morgan was outside fetching kindling–they had let the fire die out–he heard a sharp cry and he ran to the door, but only looked in and saw Angel was still in the rocker and the bed still unmade, so he returned to his task.

In the dark hour before dawn, Greta made the bed with the sterile sheets and Angel, spent and trying to breathe in the proper way, but often crying out, went into the bed and bathed herself with wheat germ oil to lessen the chance of tearing. Her contractions were two minutes apart. They waited and her screams reverberated around the small house, shaking the salvaged barn-board walls and Morgan's heart.

Roosters fiddled at the skywash and Venus pinned the pink shell above the canyon. It was a cool morning, portending autumn. Morgan had dozed fitfully, unable to stay awake during the last hour. Angel longed for sleep and release from the pain. And still the baby would not be born. Greta had held her hand all night and once said, "You've got the hands of a child." The words stuck in Angel's mind.

When the morning grew light enough to see, Greta stirred from Angel's side and blew out the lamp.

"Greta," Morgan said, "don't you think she needs a doctor?"

"Not yet," Greta answered. "It's just hard work, Morgan."

Angel looked as though she had worked hard, her eyes puffy, her face pale. She lay on the bed with her legs bent and apart, the sheet covering her like a tent. The tent was open at her feet and Greta reached under now and then and measured her dilation.

"Four fingers," Greta announced. "Morgan, she needs you now. You stay by her. I must go out for a moment." And she left the house in a hurry, her skirts switching.

"Morgan, it hurts so bad. I can't believe how much it hurts," Angel said. She spoke quickly, desperately.

Morgan took her hand but didn't answer. When her body clenched, she clenched his hand, but it was limp and his eyes avoided hers.

"I want Greta," Angel said.

"She'll be back."

"Morgan." She screamed his name. "Mor-GAN!" And her body tensed, her back and legs arching in the pain and she could not believe it hurt the way it did. She wished to die.

When Greta returned, she had Adam with her. He walked in as though he belonged there and he was fresh and clean in white pants and a white shirt. He was like a vision to Angel. He went to her side.

"You're having a hard time, Angel?"

"Yes, God, yes, it's awful," Angel said, and she cried.

"When did this labor begin?" Adam asked.

"Yesterday noon," Morgan said.

"We've got to help her have this baby. She's wearing herself down," Adam said.

"Listen, Adam, I want to take her to the hospital," Morgan said. His hands shook like aspen leaves.

"No. NO," Angel screamed.

"We can do it here," Adam said.

Then Morgan saw the other man's eyes lock with Angel's and his heart spoiled within, ripe with bitterness.

"Adam, I'm afraid," Angel said. She groped for his hand.

"There's nothing to be afraid of," Adam said. "Be strong."

"I said I'm taking her to town," Morgan blurted. He spread his feet in a defensive stance.

"She needs a coach, someone to help her through. It won't take long," Adam said. "I can do it."

Morgan felt as though he were invisible.

"Yes. Yes," Angel said, breathless and panting and up on her elbows. "Adam, stay with me."

Then she cried in longing, a cry so raw with want and need that Morgan turned away.

"Son-of-a-bitch," he whispered, beating his fist into his palm.

His face was flushed and contorted in anger. He slammed the door hard and rode the morning like a man in a foreign country, a man with no home, working to obliterate the sound of Angel screaming.

And even as she held the waxy child, so new, with sky and clouds in each pale eye, Angel could hear the dull thud of Morgan splitting sugar pine as he had split her.

■ CYRA McFADDEN

Cyra McFadden's father, Cy Taillon, was a famous Montana rodeo announcer, and her mother was a dancer and trick rider. Born in Great Falls in 1938, McFadden grew up on the rodeo circuit and attended high school in Missoula. She was graduated magna cum laude from San Francisco State University in 1972 and went on to receive an M.A. in English, with honors, in 1974. McFadden wrote a column for a Marin County, California, newspaper, which she later expanded into the best-selling novel and feature film, The Serial *(1977). This selection is from her autobiographical reminiscence,* Rain or Shine: A Family Memoir *(1986).*

From Rain or Shine: A Family Memoir

When they were young, my parents believed they were indestructible, so fast and flashy nothing could touch them. Cy was a lady-killer, a small, natty man whose riverboat-gambler good looks struck women down like lightning bolts. My mother, the former Patricia Montgomery, was a vaudeville dancer, the star of the St. Louis Municipal Opera in the late twenties. When she married Cy, she turned trick rider in the rodeo equivalent of halftime shows. You can take the girl out of show biz, but you cannot take a little girl from Little Rock, or Paragould, which is close enough, and turn her into a house pet.

At least not Pat, with her performer's ego, her longing to shine. Tiny-waisted and white-skinned, her black hair slicked to her cheekbones in sculptured spit curls, she was Cy's equal in recklessness, matching him drink for drink, seduction for seduction, irrational impulse for irrational impulse. Together they shot off sparks and left behind scorched earth, and if they ever thought about how their travels might end, they didn't waste much time on sober reappraisal.

They had more pressing concerns, the main one how to get to the next town with little money, a child and hangovers. My father's schedule took him from Butte, Montana, to Salt Lake City, Utah, from Puyallup, Washington, to Baton Rouge, Louisiana, and sometimes the travel time was a couple of days. We lived in a 1937 blue Packard, spending endless, viciously hot days in it going from Canada to New Mexico and back up to Wyoming, Utah and Idaho—wherever there were rodeos. We slept in that car, ate breakfast, lunch and dinner in it, sang along with the Sons of the Pioneers in it, quarreled in it. My parents must have made love in it, when I was asleep and the Packard parked behind the bleachers in some small-town fairground, waiting for daylight and the rodeo. Between them, there was a strong erotic pull. They walked with their hips touching and had flaming fights over each other's real and imagined flirtations.

Raised on a North Dakota farm, one of nine children of a French Canadian family, Cy had been a law student, a self-taught musician who led dance bands and played in movie-theater pit orchestras, a boxer and a radio personality in Billings and Salt Lake City. In both towns, he was a celebrity, known as "The Singing Announcer" because until a tonsillectomy put an end to this facet of his career, he sang with his bands.

The huge leather scrapbooks he kept all his life document some of these successes; but he claimed triumphs in everything he did, telling a writer for a trade paper called *Hoofs and Horns*, early in his rodeo career, that he'd won a Golden Gloves championship when he was boxing and given a recital at Carnegie Hall as a child prodigy violinist.

How much of that interview is true, I don't know, nor do I think Cy did. For much of his life, he was engaged in the game of inventing himself–adding to what was true what was desirable, stirring counterclockwise and serving up the mix. He must have swallowed much of it himself.

What is fact is that after leaving law school with a theatrical troupe, he ended up, in his early twenties, in Great Falls, where he became a radio announcer and moonlighted as a musician. His hillbilly band, reported in the Great Falls *Tribune*, drew 14,600 letters to the local radio station in six and a half weeks. This was roughly the population of Great Falls at the time. It must have been a letter-writing town.

After two months in St. Paul, Minnesota, as "announcer and entertainer," Cy came back to Great Falls, and in 1929 was leading a trio during the dinner hour at the Hotel Rainbow and picking up other band jobs around town. "The Green Mill gardens, dinner and dancing resort on the paved extension of Second Avenue North, will be formally opened tonight. Eddie Stamy will be director of the orchestra that will play for at least four dances a week. Cy Taillon, Minneapolis, who handles the drums, violin, bells, piano, and most anything else, is charged with providing the sweet numbers."

"Cy Taillon and his orchestra will entertain you again at the Crystal Ballroom . . . Featuring 'The Crystal Ballroom Red Jackets.'"

"Tree Claim Park presents Cy Taillon and his 'Rocky Mountaineers.' Master of Ceremonies, Waddie Ginger, Admission 50 cents."

To the list of instruments he played, another ad for a resort added xylophone, banjo, and "relatively smaller string instruments."

The woman who became Cy's second wife got her first glimpse of him during those days. She was a schoolgirl. He was playing one of the twin pianos in the window of a music store. Their eyes met, she told me, and it was Romeo and Juliet, only more intense. If my mother got in their way for twelve years, that was only because Dorothy was fourteen at the time. My father also had his hands full with other women.

A personal archivist, Cy kept copies of every letter he ever wrote, including one to the city attorney of Great Falls in those years. A woman was harassing him, he complained, accusing him of being the third party in a "spiritual triangle" and fathering her three children by remote control. "Further proof she is hopelessly irrational," he wrote, "is her obsession that I have money."

In my teens, I met a woman who knew Cy in Great Falls. "He was the most beautiful man who ever lived," she said. "You don't look very much like him."

She wasn't rude so much as disappointed. I offered to say hello to him for her.

"He wouldn't remember me. There were too many of us. I'll tell you what, though, say hello for the Willis sisters and let him wonder which one."

The student's pilot license Cy took out in 1933 lists his age as twenty-five, weight 139 pounds, height five feet seven and three-quarters inches, hair black and eyes gray-green. It doesn't describe the movie-star handsomeness of his regular features, his olive skin, his wavy black hair and those eyes–as slate green as the ocean, and when he was angry, as cold.

He looked enough like Robert Taylor to double for him, later, in the riding scenes of the movie *Billy the Kid*.

Rodeo stock producer Leo Cremer tapped him for the crow's nest in the early thirties. Cy left radio for what he said was a three months' leave and never went back. Cremer was famous for his Brahma bulls, whose average weight was three-quarters of a ton: Black Devil, Yellow Jacket, Deer Face, Tornado, Joe Louis, Dynamite. He also had good instincts when he signed my father, despite Cy's reputation as a hard drinker and man-about-town.

Because he'd been attracted to it since his childhood, "Roman riding" the horses on the family farm, Cy was a natural for rodeo. He'd mainly swallowed a lot of dust. After he broke a shoulder, he gave up any ambition to be another Casey Tibbs.

He had cards printed, giving his address as the Mint Cafe, Great Falls, and offering "a New Technique in Rodeo Announcing."

A rodeo announcer keeps up a running commentary on the cowboys and the way they fare in the events, calf roping, Brahma-bull riding, bareback and saddle-bronc riding and, more recently, team roping. Cy was the best, a showman who could play a crowd the way he played stringed instruments, by instinct and with perfect pitch. At the piano, he held to the theory that the more keys you used, the better you played. At the mike, he also used the equivalent of all the pedals. "Ladies and gentlemen, this next waddie broke his wrist and three ribs down in Abilene a few weeks ago, and now he's back in competition. That's called courage in my book. Tiny Rios out of Tulsa, Oklahoma, on a mean hunk of horseflesh called Son of Satan. . . . Let's give him a little encouragement."

From his law school days, when he won prizes in debate, he had a sophisticated vocabulary. He used it, never talking down to his audience of cowboys, stock producers and their wives, ranchers and rodeo-loving kids. Nor did he often forget a cowboy's name, or where he came from, or how he fared in previous rodeos, no matter how chronic a loser the cowboy. So they loved him, even when he borrowed their prize money or their wives. He always paid the money back, and the wives straggled home, moony but unrepentant, on their own.

The reviews began to come in early. Cy never got a bad one, any more than he ever took an unflattering photograph, or if there were any, they never wound up in his scrapbooks, a researcher's nightmare because he clipped articles without the name of the newspaper or magazine and frequently without the date. Sometimes he clipped only the paragraphs that mentioned his name, which he underlined. The articles described him as silver-voiced, golden-voiced, gold-and-silver-voiced, crystal-voiced, honey-voiced. They talk about his clear, bell-like voice. They run out of adjectives and call him the Voice.

In them, he's also spare, handsome and hard as nails; lean, wiry and a natty dresser; suave and dapper; the man who knows rodeo;

the possessor of an encyclopedic memory. Said one writer, consigned to anonymity by my father's clipping methods, "Taillon keeps the show going like a golf ball swatted down a concrete highway."

Rodeo was used to announcers who treated the sport as a Wild West show, part vaudeville, part circus. Cy dignified it, with his ten-dollar words, his impeccably tailored, expensive suits and his insistence that the cowboys were professional athletes. When he intoned "Ladies and gentlemen," women became ladies and men became gentlemen; the silver-tongued devil in the announcer's box, as often as not a rickety structure over the chutes and open to the rain, spoke with unmistakable authority. In a world where pretending to be an insider earns the outsider dismissal faintly underlined with menace, he counted as a working cowboy, though he earned his living with his mouth rather than his muscle.

Like the contestants, he lived from rodeo to rodeo, making just enough money to keep us in gas and hamburgers. He worked in all weather: heat, cold, freak rainstorms that turned arenas into mudholes. If he had extra money, everybody drank, and when we rented a room in a motor court, a luxury, cowboys bunked on the floor with their saddles for pillows. Despite his slight frame, he never hesitated about piling in when there was a fight; you had to get through him to get to somebody bigger, and because he was light on his feet and fast with his fists, few made it. Someone wading into my father also had to take on my mother, not one to sit on the sidelines letting out ladylike cries of dismay. A hundred-pound woman can do substantial damage with teeth, fingernails and a high-heeled shoe, and Pat had an advantage going in. No man would hit her back, though she was swearing ripely and trying to maim him, because no self-respecting Western man hits a lady.

The bars were my parents' living rooms. We spent our nights in them, our mornings in the Packard or a motor court—with Cy and Pat sleeping off their headaches and begging me to stop that goddamn humming—and our afternoons at the Black Hills Roundup or the Snake River Stampede, rodeos that blur into one.

Pat sat in the bleachers, if she wasn't trick riding. I sat in the crow's nest with Cy, sometimes announcing the Grand Entry or the national anthem for him or testing the p.a. system. "One two three four, testing testing testing." I wanted to be a movie star. Cy said you had to start somewhere.

The high point of those afternoons, for me, was when Cy played straight man for the rodeo clowns, who sometimes railed at him because he wouldn't allow off-color material, the crude jokes that were a staple. Not present just to entertain, the clowns also divert the bulls or horses when a rider is down. The cowboys and the crowd love and respect them. So did I, and when my father bantered with them from the stand, he took on added luster.

Pinky Gist and his two mules, Mickey and Freckles, George Mills, John Lindsay, the great Emmett Kelly and a dozen others–sad-faced men in baggy pants, absurdly long shoes and long underwear, out in the arena, and my father aiding and abetting them:

"Eddie, there are ladies present here today. Would you mind pulling up your pants?"

"Sure, Cy." Eddie did a flawless double take, pulled his pants up and doffed his porkpie hat to my father. When he lifted the hat, his pants fell down again, revealing long johns with a trapdoor.

"I'm sorry, Cy. I was asleep in the barrel over there and a train hit me. It tore the buttons off my suspenders."

"That wasn't a train, Eddie," Cy said, kingly at the microphone. "That was a two-thousand-pound Brahma bull, and there's another one coming out of the chute right now."

Eddie screamed hoarsely, stumbled across the arena, clutched at his pants and fell over his shoes. "I wondered why I never heard the whistle."

No matter how many times I heard these routines, they never paled for me. Such is the power of early-childhood conditioning that I still love slapstick; mine is the lone voice laughing at a club act in which the comic gets hit with a pie.

I'm less taken with exhibition roping. The great trick-rope artist on the circuit was Monty Montana, a handsome man who could do anything with a rope, including roping Cy Taillon's daughter. On my father's command, I pretended to be a calf; bolted through a string barrier and into the arena; ran like mad until Monty lassoed me, ran down his rope, threw me and tied me. He never hurt me. The crowd loved it. I hated it.

Not to be upstaged, Pat sometimes followed with her breakneck trick riding–headstands at the gallop, vaulting to the ground from a standing position in the saddle. She was so fearless that the cowboys gathered at the fence to watch her, wondering if this would be the night Cy's crazy wife killed herself.

I still have part of her trick-riding costume, a red Spanish bolero with white scrollwork, silver spurs with tooled-leather straps and canted-heel boots. The full-sleeved white satin shirt disappeared, as did the high-waisted red pants that would fit a twelve-year-old boy. Pat's life in those years is recorded in a few bits of her rodeo wardrobe, her own mutilated scrapbook, in which she also obliterated the supporting cast, and not much else.

Constants from those countless rodeos: the smell of sweat and horses that rose out of the open stalls, just below the booth; the fine dust that floated over the arena, powdering evenly cowboys, animals, the crowd, my father's suit and his pointy-toed boots; the haze of cigarette smoke over the stands; the whinnying of horses, the bawling of calves and howling of dogs, left in pickup trucks out in the parking lot.

Always present too were the high voices of women, wives and girlfriends and rodeo groupies, the "buckle bunnies" who were, and are still, the wives' natural enemies. They set the standards of female dress, with their starched curls and their pinkish pancake makeup, ending in a line at the chin. The buckle bunnies wore tight frontier pants and tooled-leather belts, into which they tucked their nailhead-studded shirts. One who was always around, and whom I admired, had a belt with beads spelling out her name, just above her neat rump: "Bonnee."

As for the wives, they were a tight-knit and wary bunch, sitting in the stands afternoon and night, watching their husbands compete and watching the single women through the smoke from their cigarettes. Those that had children left them sleeping in the trailers, and protected their primary interests. Cowboys then, and cowboys now, bear watching.

If the rodeo was in some two-dog town, we might be there for only one daytime and one evening performance, and then it was back on the road again, with a tour of the local bars in between. These had a certain classic similarity—a jukebox playing cowboy songs about lost love and lost illusions, beer signs with neon waterfalls and on the wall the head of a deer with brown glass eyes.

Such bars did not bother to throw kids out, and so we played the pinball machines, or listened to the bragging and the laughter, or put our heads down on the table, among the shot glasses and beer bottles, and slept. Because slot machines were legal in Montana and Nevada, I liked the bars there best; they weren't legal for children, but who was watching? In Helena, Montana, with money I pried loose from my mother by practiced nagging, I won a jackpot. The quarters poured through my hands and onto the floor, a silver river of money.

No one would have thrown me out of the bars whatever I did, because I was Cy Taillon's daughter, his namesake, a miniature version of Cy in my own hand-made boots and my Stetson.

Bartenders served my ginger ale with a cherry in it. Cowboys asked me to dance to the jukebox, and asked Pat if she knew my father had himself another little gal. Expansive on bourbon, Cy sat me on the bar and had me sing "Mexicali Rose." I have no voice, and hadn't then, but what I lacked in musicality, I made up for in volume. I could also imitate my father at the mike, booming out: "The only pay this cowboy is going to get tonight . . ." and other crowd pleasers.

Not only did rodeo people live like gypsies, traveling in an informal caravan from town to town; my father and I looked like gypsies, both dark-skinned to start with and tanned by the sun pounding down on us, both with dark hair and high cheekbones. Mine softened as I grew older. Cy's became more pronounced, until, just before he died, the flesh receded from the bone. Once, when I was ten, and he and I were having lunch in the Florence Hotel in Missoula, Montana, a woman asked to take a snapshot of us. She was from out of town, she said, and we were the first Indians she'd ever seen. We posed for her in front of the Florence's corny Indian murals, palms raised in the B movie "how" sign.

All of which I took for granted, when our family lived on the road, as the way everyone lived, though a social worker might have taken a dim view of it and I already knew at least one person who did. It was normal to have a dapper, charming father whose public self bore little resemblance to the private Cy, the one who drank too much and flared into an alcohol-fueled temper. It was normal to have a trick-riding, ex-chorus-girl mother who still did dancer's limbering-up exercises every morning, sinking into splits and sitting on the floor spraddle-legged, bending her head first to one knee and then to the other. "You better stay in shape when you grow up," she told me as I watched, "because a woman's looks are all she's got."

It was normal to spend days and nights at the rodeo, listening to Cy's molasses voice and the voices of the cowboys, jawing, swearing and bantering with each other, smelling leather, calves in their pens and horse manure; to sit high above the bleachers in the announcer's stand and all but melt with love and pride when, on cold nights, Cy took his jacket off and put it around me.

It wasn't just normal to live in a Packard, it was classy. A Packard was still a classy car when it was ankle deep in hamburger wrappers.

Some rodeo people pulled trailers and thus had the equivalent of houses, but most drove pickups or the kind of cars which, if they were horses, would have been taken off and shot.

I also believed then that Pat would stay spirited and taut-bodied forever, like a young racehorse, and that my father, whenever he wanted to, could make himself invisible. He told me that he could, but not when anybody was watching, and in the somewhat deflected way he always told the truth, he was telling it then.

■ PETER BOWEN

Born in 1945, Peter Bowen grew up in Bozeman, Montana. During the 1960s, he attended the University of Michigan and is currently working on his B.A. degree at the University of Montana. For the last eight years, Bowen has lived in Boise, Idaho, and Ovando, Montana. He has published a chapbook of poems, Brave to the Point of Madness, *and a novel,* Yellowstone Kelly *(1987). This essay appeared in* Northern Lights *magazine in 1986.*

The Blue Bear

It was fifty degrees below zero. Even the wind was frozen still and blue. Colter felt a tear form and trickle down his cheek; the flesh beneath the wet track froze as it ran. He breathed through his nose, slowly so he wouldn't sear his lungs. The hood of the parka was thrown back. He needed to see.

Dawn would come in a little while. The snow was glowing with the rising light. Far away a tree burst from the cold, making a sharp report, like a gun. The sound rocked back and forth between the hills, like water in a carried basin.

This was the fifth morning he had waited here in the tree. A frozen steer lay chained to a great log forty yards away. Two hours before, Colter had lit a fire in the steer's ripped belly. The heavy smoke, full of the smells of fat and flesh and hair, pooled low against the snow and then flowed away in the currents of air, toward the west and the mountains and the bear.

Two weeks before, the grizzly had clawed his way through the walls of the meathouse as easily as a man breaks a stale crust of bread. Colter and his family were sleeping a little ways away. The rising wind filled with the soft snow muffled the noise. The dogs leaped against the mesh walls of the kennel, barking and yelping. The black labrador house dog scratched at the back door, whimpering, his nose pressed to the stream of cold air which flowed beneath it, the hairs on his spine stood up and his lips curled back from his white teeth.

By the time Colter and his father had dressed and gone out, the bear had gone.

The bear would come again. The bear would sleep and grow hungry and return in a week, at most two.

Colter looked at the huge tracks and the destroyed meathouse and left his young notions of pursuit and fair combat lie. Old Mac pointed at the big spruce and said, "Up there," his voice thin in the gelid air.

In the kitchen Mac poured coffee, rubbing an old hurt in his left hip with his free hand.

"Make sure your shots go flat on in," he said, "otherwise the slugs may turn. He'll likely come back between four and seven in the morning. He knows the schedule of this house as well as you or I. We'll wait up in the tree for him."

Colter built a stand fifteen feet up in the big spruce. He nailed boards to climb on into the hard and icy wood. Some of the heavy nails bent over, unable to pierce the frozen living tree.

Colter hung an old tarpaulin from branch to trunk to branch, behind where he would sit. He poured water over the canvas which then froze stiff. When he threw the plastic jerrycan to the ground, it broke into little pieces.

Colter waited now on the twelfth day since the bear had first come. The winter drowse of a male grizzly is not deep. Often he rises and wanders, restless. The females sleep, their tiny cubs buried in the fur of their bellies.

Colter thought of the gun. Would the primer fire in this deep cold? Would the barrel split? Well, he'd find out. Colter clenched and extended his right hand, stuck inside a plastic envelope filled with petroleum jelly he carried inside his shirt next to his stomach. Without the protection of the grease, his sweating hand would freeze instantly to the works of the rifle, just when you have great need of both hand and gun.

Fifteen feet above the drifted ground, sheltered by the frozen canvas, wrapped in down and fur, Colter waited. He would probably see the bear before he heard it, his head and ears were so cold. Colter smiled, thinking of his father's last words as he dressed to go out to the blind.

"Don't believe any of the crap about grizzlies not climbing trees. They climb 'til they get tired of it and then they bite the goddam tree off," Mac said, furious with himself for being sick, feeling somehow a coward. He had pneumonia, the doctor had said, stay in bed, or at least stay in the house, the cold may kill you if you go outside. Colter knew that Mac had dressed as soon as Colter left the house, and he was now crouched at the window of the back door, rubbing away the frost, ready to run out and start shooting if Colter was in peril, and in doing so maybe killing himself.

I come from a long line of fools, Colter thought, look at us all. Look at me, sitting here like some great goddam horse doover on a one hundred foot toothpick.

Colter blinked to clear his vision. The cold made his eyes tear. He could hear the blood slosh and gurgle in his head, hear his heart thud, hear the high whine of his nervous system. He was used to these sounds, he had heard them many times in the deepest winter, when the silence was absolute.

Colter heard a soft, muffled thudding sound, like heavy plates of steel hung in cloth and gently rocked. He lifted his head and squinted at the blue and shadowed line of trees.

The bear had come.

The bear was blue.

Thirsty, the bear had clawed the cloak of ice and snow away from the dark chill water of the river and thrust its muzzle deep past the quickly freezing slush to drink. Maybe the bear had lost his balance, or perhaps the ice had given way beneath the animal's great weight. He went in.

The bear, soaked, clawed his way onto firm ice, the water streaming from his sable coat. The water shimmered for an instant and then froze. The cold had clad the bear in fine crystal armor. The river became cuirass, greaves and vambraces, frozen to cuisses, gauntlets and sabatons faintly blue, like a potter's glaze, from the trapped air within. The bear, still thirsty, returned to the hole he had made in the ice and drank. Again he fell in, again he scrambled out, biting a few times at the suit of ice before forgetting it was there at all. The ice was now several inches thick, in places enough to turn or stop a bullet. The armor upon the bear's body was broken by the coiled power of the great muscles beneath as the beast walked unconcerned toward the distant cache of fine meat. Along the fractures the plates tapped together, bordering the blue with white, where the glassy ice began to crumble.

Now armored and awesome, steam from his breath making the beast of flesh engine-like and monstrous, the bear came close to the frozen steer and thrust his muzzle to the charred and frozen guts. The clanking stopped. Colter aimed at the spine, just where the great skull had pulled the jagged helmet of ice from the blue gorget. Colter squeezed the trigger and heard a tiny sound of steel tapping through his cheekbone, then the rifle fired.

The bear jerked his head up and looked behind. Colter aimed for the great heart just behind the shoulder. He fired two more shots, saw splashes of frost jump like dust where the bullets punched through skin and bone deep to where the life pulsed.

The rifle empty, Colter grabbed another, a saddle gun made for a heavy pistol cartridge. He fired as fast as he could steady his aim true on the bear's heart.

The bear snapped at the stabbing pain behind his shoulder. The bullets had swollen like mushrooms as they plowed through the great chest. Blood pumped down the beast's side and froze in hanging crimson sheets from the shattered armor. The bear moved slowly off through the deep snow, the dry flakes whispering against the icy coat. He carried seventeen bullets, any one of which should have killed him.

Colter watched the blue bear go, unbelieving of its power. Painfully he stood up and tried to catch his rasping breath. His left eye was frozen shut by the lashes. He had fouled himself. He crawled slowly down the tree, feeling the slippery warm feces and the wetness running down his legs turn cold.

In the outer hall he stripped and cleaned himself as best he could with his soiled clothing. He rolled his jeans inside his shirt and threw the bundle outside. He would bury it later, away from the dogs. He wrapped an old towel around his waist and walked into the kitchen. Mac and Dotty sat at the table waiting for him to speak first.

"Crapped my pants," Colter said, edging by, conquering hero.

"Glad to finally see some signs of sense, son," said Mac. "Best get the shotgun and stay away from the windows. I don't think he'll come in here, but all those slugs didn't slow him much that I could see." If Colter had not seen the blood he'd have thought he had missed.

"Leave him for an hour to stiffen up," said Mac. "You sure you hit him good?"

"I hit him good," Colter said. There couldn't be much of the bear's heart or lungs left but shredded mush.

Colter showered, his shivering body drinking in the heat. His lungs began to feel tight and full. Christ, Colter thought, I wonder how bad I seared my lungs. It can kill you, getting excited. That bear may have scared me to death anyway.

Dressed in clean clothes, Colter walked back into the kitchen, rubbing his head with a towel. He thought of the old joke about the trapper outrunning the grizzly, the trapper having the edge because he was on dry ground and the bear had to contend with the wet slippery trail of the trapper's fear.

"Not yet," said Mac, when Colter moved toward the hall and the boots and the gun and the bear. He handed Colter a mug of coffee with whiskey in it. "Let him stiffen up."

Colter waited until Mac nodded. He carried a double shotgun this time, knowing that any shot he got was likely to be quick, and single, and close, and hurried, and final. With one arm clutching the shotgun and the other inside his parka next to his belly, he bobbed from side to side like a bound prisoner as he lifted his snowshoes and laid them down.

The blue bear had moved through the white and silent drifts leaving a wide trail a yard deep. It was easy to follow. At the other side of a little clearing the trail went abruptly to the right. The load of snow carried by a tall tree dimpled the drifts beneath, knocked loose when the bear had fallen against the trunk.

Colter knelt and stared at the tree's roughened bark, yellow under gray. The blue bear had staggered sideways, his armor scraping down the bark as the beast sank, dying. Six feet ahead, there was a small dish in the snow dusted with drops of bright red blood, where the breath from the ruined lungs had melted the snow. The torn chest was filling to drown the blue bear in his own blood.

Not long, not long now, Colter thought, sliding his hand out and slipping the safety of the shotgun off. Two hundred feet beyond, the Blue Bear had stopped and sagged forward on his driving armored legs. Colter moved closer, ten feet at a time, his heart hammering and his lips curled back in a snarl of fear and rage. He looked for any movement, any sign that the Blue Bear waited to rise suddenly and drag his tormentor down with him.

Colter edged to where he could see one of the bear's eyes, still now and rimed by frost. He dropped the shotgun in the snow.

Colter wept. He was sixteen years old and in the dawn had seen a thing of terrible and perfect beauty come and knew now that he would miss this haunting magic crystal beast and the perfection of its very being if he had not by right and choice been waiting there to kill it.

■ KURT DUECKER

Kurt Duecker was born in 1956 in Greybull, Wyoming, and raised in Billings, Montana. In 1980, he was graduated from the University of Montana, and he received an M.A. in creative writing from Columbia University in 1982. From his home in Berkeley, California, Duecker is currently working on a novel. This story first appeared in Shenandoah *in 1982 and was reprinted in* Editor's Choice *in 1985.*

Saving the Dead

I'm the one in the boat, the one in the red plaid parka gripping the oars. The anchorman will never say, "There, that's Dick Lilly," but I'm there, playing my small red part at 5:00 and 11:00. I'm either bent over the side talking to a diver or passing a cup of coffee to Lance. Or sometimes it's a long, clouded shot of me and Lance out on the empty lake, huddled against the mist. But in the end that's always my red hunting parka turned to the camera.

It's not a lake really. It's a gravel pit, hollowed out years ago by the highway department. It was close enough to the Yellowstone that they struck water and it filled in on them. I imagine it just seeped up from the bottom and through the walls. The green highway sign at the turnoff reads "Two Moons Lake." It gives up palm-sized sunfish and one or two soft bass in the summer, and seals over like a tomb in winter. My dad used to take a bunch of us out on it after most of the snow had blown off. We'd knock a tin can around with tree branches. The old man danced and slid among us, trying to ref. He never needed a whistle. His voice could push a tree over in the high-strung winter air. It was the gravel pit then. It's all we've ever called it.

This time it's a girl, a nine-year-old with straight teeth and ribbons around her ponytail. Her eight-by-ten will grow to fill the whole screen. Her mom last saw her at lunch. She'll say it eight or ten times over the air.

"I've told her, I've told Shell a hundred times, *never* go near that pond. She knows she's never to ride her bike past Shiloh Road." The voice is frightened.

Kids don't listen. On those first nice days of spring they're listening to something else. With me it was snakes, and tadpoles, and turtles waiting out in deep water. A couple of afternoons are sunny, almost hot, and then the clouds are there, not many but enough. By morning it's bone-cold and rainy. The sheriff found her bike against a tree last night, her miniature blue license hanging from the seat—SHELLY. The news will make sure to return to that shot, even though they have to restage it.

It must be a horrid thing to find a kid's new bike late in the evening like that, propped against a tree. The mother waits at her kitchen window, hands lying confused in the cooling dishwater. The tan car pulling into the driveway with its dome breathing blue light is the messenger of God. She quick prays to it before the sheriff steps out and opens the back door or trunk. He lifts the bike out, and bent over because they're never more than a twenty-incher, he starts to wheel it towards the front door. That must kill her.

Lance called me at at 5:17 a.m. The wife and I both worry over what the 5:17 call means. As she lies turned away from me I can feel her listening, eyes open, the sheet clutched under her chin. We've been getting a rash of the early rings lately. When I answer there's dead air or breathing on the end. The new boyfriend must be jealous that we're sleeping together. When I hang up she whispers to me.

"Another one?"

"A nine-year-old girl's been missing all night. They found her bike at the gravel pit. No one we know."

I go to the closet and dig out thermals, the mackinaw, and my Hermin Survivors. While I'm getting dressed Pat always makes coffee. She drops a couple of Pop-Tarts in the toaster, tunes the radio into Country Koyn, and checks for the paper. I can see her from the bedroom, sleepy and stretching on the porch. I feel like taking her back to bed. The big head of yellow hair loosens and lets go of her face. Until summer she sleeps in sweatpants and a T-shirt, then just the T-shirt and panties. Her seat hangs well in the sweats. We're usually friends in the morning. Her eyes welcome the light. They're not after anything yet, just half open and nice to look at.

"It's going to rain on you," as I step into the kitchen.

"Spring isn't easy." We agree to smile.

"Be careful," she always says when I leave. Even when I'm off to work at the regular time it's always, "Be careful."

While I'm knocking around the garage after the boat, she finishes her coffee. She might come to the picture window as I'm tying it on the station wagon, but then it's back to bed.

Even when it's raining I like the morning air, the quiet, the cold trying to climb in with you. Even on these mornings when the

Rangers call I like the air. I think it's because the air's always shitty at the refinery. Refineries, they all stink like eggs.

I don't think about who's in the pit until I pull onto Lance's block. It's almost always a child, eight kids in five years (twice that many searched for) and one old man who went in after his stuck lure. They've become mixed up with the other signals of spring, meadowlarks and lawnmowers. It's gotten so the first thaw and longer days scare me.

Lance is a younger guy, a few years out of high school. He still lives with his folks – his mom's always watching from the kitchen window where she's finished making him breakfast and packing a lunch. I'll have to mooch some or stop at the Quickway for microwave. It isn't long before you notice his hands, goddamn hands. That's how he's always referring to them, "These goddamn hands!" They had to be put back together after a can of lighter fluid blew up in them. The flame climbed right up the stream from the briquets, hit the nozzle and blew. The next thing he knew his arms were candles. The skin on both of them is smooth and shiny. Patches of it seem stretched too tight over the bones. It's mostly from his ass. There's feeling and they still work like hands, but they'll stiffen up and ache after long at the oars. "These goddamn hands," he'll whisper and then cross them under his armpits to hide as much as warm them. We rarely speak up on the lake. Other than his hands Lance is a big, strong, good-looking kid. He's got shoulders like an old Ford, thick, corded forearms, and a smooth anvil-shaped face. He's okay company for this.

I pull against the curb. His mom raps good-bye on the window, and he stretches and starts across the wet grass to the car. The rain hasn't turned into much more than mist.

"Morning, Licks."

"BV." I'm Licks to all the Rangers, Licks Dicks. Lance was given Burn Victim. I don't know why men have to pass nicknames around, but they do.

"Goddamn nine-year-old girl! Hope we find her."

"Hope we don't." It's the answer you learn to give, part of a before-search ritual. It reminds us that we're looking for something we don't want to find. We find them and it's over, the real grief can settle in. And if we don't, the awful hoping goes on. Who knows what's worse?

The car whines on the wet highway. The ceiling is low and gray. On clear mornings you can make out the white veins of the Beartooth ski runs. Today the trees have returned to winter, shadowed and paled. The damp cold seeps in along the windows.

The other Ranger cars are parked in a T near a small fire. I pull my wagon in adding a fourth arm. Across Two Moons a couple of sheriff's cars, an ambulance, and the KGHL van are huddled in another small group. Fifty or sixty steps back from them has to be the parents' car. It's a fairly new Buick. A lot of businessmen types do well in Stark City and then move out into ranch-styles and pretend their riding mower's a tractor. The Rangers like to stay a good distance away from the official grief and media show. There's six of us between the four cars. We all have the shield, "Stark City Search and Rescue Ranger," sewn somewhere on our bodies. The divers, Golly Gean and Yikes, have it laminated to the breast of their wet suits. In both cases it's peeling off. Gean's father Ed is the squad chief. He deals with police and sheriff communications, paces the bank with a walkie-talkie, and nurses a cup of coffee in his Bronco. All this crap has become his life, Ed and the dead or just Dead Ed. Leroy Simms is the other ground man. He pours Ed's coffee and scurries around loose picking up the poop. Sometimes I'd like to drown him.

"What say, what say, Licker?" I don't pay much attention to him while I'm unloading the boat. He isn't worth the fart it would take to chase him away. I pass the rope back and forth through the rack, leaning out trying to keep the car water off my coat. I'll be wet and cold soon enough.

"Eddy's with the posse, telling them our game plan. Laura Soring's over there for KGHL, getting her pretty hair wet. She's got big-league knockers, Licker. I was chatting and couldn't keep my eyes off them."

Lims has deep-hooded eyes that spend most of their time pointed at women's tits and tails. He has to stare up to look me in the face, but every once in a while he'll do it. I don't feel at all like talking to him this morning.

"Eddy wants you and Beevy over off humpbank. The frogs'll work their way over to you from where Cowboy Bob thinks she went in. He's had his deputies shake the brush along the bank. No luck. You two can sit and count rubbers till they get there." A laugh the size of a bat escapes between his large teeth.

"Nice Lims, run around there and help me dump this. Watch yourself, we don't want any shit to fall out of your head. Beevy," I shout, "get the phone."

Pat says Lims is needed out there. The couple of times they've met she's kept her distance. "Any woman can feel his eyes making the rounds. But he's needed out there," she said. "His filthy mouth drones out mood music, keeps reminding all you saints where you're at and why." She called him a wastebasket for hard emotions.

"You get lots of anger, sorrow, and hate with no place to dump it, so you dispose of it in the nearest receptacle–Lims."

"Yeah, maybe," I said. She always catches me with those, the way she turns things into neat little packages. Most things I run into hit and scatter like a magpie off the grill. A clump sticks, but I never have time to pull over and collect the pieces. You can tell it's a magpie by the black and white remains.

She called her first affair, over a year ago, a bad taste in her mouth, that simple. Said I was working too much, drinking too much, and nodding off too early. It was turnaround at the refinery. We were offline and had to do a month of 7-10's to get back on. The arc of the welder sparked in my dreams. It all left a bad taste in her mouth, and she tried to wash it out with a school teacher. I chased that one down, traced his plates from the bar parking lot. It was all right out of "The Young and Restless." He was this extra-large jock that taught biology at the high school. I went over to football practice straight from work, still had my greasy coveralls and welding cap on. My face was black and shiny around the beard. I felt a little like Spencer Tracy giving it to Gable. I think it frightened him. When he saw me marching over the chalk lines he blew his whistle and sent the kids into laps. It didn't stop them from watching. He was a big boy, had six inches on me, and oversized thighs pouring out of his coaching shorts. But I delivered the Tracy, told him if I ever saw him with Pat, or even caught whiff of a rumor, I'd weld his dick to the flagpole. All the young girls could pledge allegiance. He acted dumb, which suited his face, and I told him again, same thing, a little louder. I left him standing there in the middle of the field, his kids running in wide circles around him. It felt great. At home I stepped into the ring with Pat.

"I had to get that taste out of my mouth. He came with the pretzels, stingers and juke box."

What could I say. I told her I'd weld her shut. It didn't go over as well. The marriage had begun to smell.

The next course was a gandy dancer, tie-gang foreman for the Burlington Northern. We spoke the same language, and I rubbed his face in it for little more than a chipped tooth. I wanted bad to use the same approach with her, but once I got my hand up over her I couldn't bring it down. I tucked all the anger away for later. Now it's gone. This new voice in the early morning I don't even feel like answering. I'm afraid it might be someone I know. Maybe I'm tired of being the only one trying to save us.

The fire is pretty sad. It's more for company than warmth, hissing and struggling with the light rain. The signboards and flagsticks, tired of fighting, blacken and throw up their flame. As always, there isn't much to say. We share only Stark City Search and Rescue, and we're not close. You can't go out for beers after something like this, get to know a guy. Either way it ends there's nothing to celebrate.

The divers are sitting on Golly Gean's tailgate. Because of the black suits their swinging, white feet almost glow. The rubber fins hang in a cluster off the bedrail. The Manta tanks clank and scrape as they're hauled from the bed. Talking quietly among themselves each double-checks the other's gauge and regulator, and then fastens his partner's bottles. More and more they become twins of another animal, the soft puffy growth of hood bouncing at their necks. Soon they are transformed for water, waiting nervously to enter. We will hardly talk at all until they become comfortable in the lake. BV is busy weatherizing the walkie-talkie. His hands fumble with the plastic bags. He's talking more to himself than the divers. Coming around different sides of the wagon, Lims and I lean against my back end. Golly Gean and Yikes look up long enough to smile and say hi. BV continues to talk into the fire.

"Thermos, blankets, phone, rope, smokes, anchor . . . Yikes, you bring Cremora for your coffee? Woap, here she is. I should have brought more coat than this. It's going to get worse. A day like this, we'll probably find her. A nine-year-old girl, did you hear?"

"Ten," murmurs Lims. "Cowboy Bob told Ed ten. Too old to listen, too young to know."

"I thought they were going to fill in some of them holes last summer, slope out the floor and sand up a beach for kids along here. Goddamn death trap is what it is. They should level some of that near bottom out."

"Can't," Golly Gean breaks in without looking up. "The bottom's loose gravel. It shifts over winter. We never feel the same floor twice out there. They'd have to drain it and bank it up. It's no swimming hole for kids."

BV doesn't answer, just watches the fire. What's there to say? We all grew up swimming in the gravel pit. Across the water the small stocky figure of Dead Ed breaks from the patrol cars and circles quickly around the bank toward us. He jogs a little and then slows back to the walk. Golly Gean does it for Ed, comes out here in the cold looking for bodies, rubbing his hands in the cluttered bottom. Even drags the hook sometimes, all for the Old Man. Yikes just got caught up in it. He chased a girl here from Florida, pushed his Dodge on six cylinders halfway across the country to find her engaged. He got tight with Gean and taught him frogging. They went under a couple of times for the sheriff and checked bottom on some mountain lakes. Then Ed comes up with the idea to form the Rangers. It saved the state sending divers over from Bozeman. Neither boy could say no and took the patches he'd made up. They talk about going to Hawaii or the Caribbean, but they're still on the bank, hanging their white feet from the tailgate, every time I pull in at the pit.

BV's loaded the boat. He's got the phone, wrapped in a plastic bag, clipped to his belt. The divers' masked faces peer at us from out in Two Moons. They're full-fledged creatures of the black now, and turn their heads back and forth in the mist like aliens. I steady the boat and settle myself onto the middle seat. Kicking the orange life jackets away I clear the oars and adjust my shorts. BV's posed at the tip, ready to scrape us out into deeper water. The real rain isn't coming. It waits patiently in the lead sky stretching around us. I turn to Ed's voice. He makes a quick wave of his hand as he speaks.

"You all know where you're headed? Take her slow, Gean. Let's get it over with," and he starts for the Bronco, swinging his short arms.

"Hope we find her," as BV leans his shoulder into the boat's aluminum tip.

"Hope we don't," Ed returns without turning.

When the bottom releases us I swing the oars out, drop the left and point us toward humpbank on the other side. I begin to row in smooth, deep strokes. It's something I enjoy, the oars pressing and curling the water, its quiet response against the hull. The land begins to fade into its soft line of trees. My dad taught me to row with my breathing, to use the whole lake in a stroke. He helped me pick out the boat, the best Sears had. It doesn't fight too hard ahead or drag too much behind. It leaves a clean wake for fishing, and the bottom's fitted deep for less rock. A boat like this deserves better water. We used to take it up to Yellowtail Dam, and I've had it after browns on the Big Horn River. I even sang to Pat across it once on Mystic Lake. It was evening, the fish were rising to mayflies, and my song echoed off the mountains like a voice from shore. That was only two years ago.

The boat's the reason I got into the Rangers. I knew Ed from the refinery, not well. They needed a guy with a boat. It was after Dad died. I needed to save someone. I guess, in the beginning, I thought that's what we'd be doing, not just looking for the dead.

Lately, at the refinery, I've been spending most of my time off the ground, up among the pipes and pots. We've been welding connections, adding some elbows and blinds, and rewelding some old beads. The casual I've got with me is a good man, Jeff Kirkfleet. He's skipping a semester of school to make some fast money; a loose-fisted kid that runs after work, five miles at a clip. He's one of these new clean-living young, but I like him. The mouth isn't running all the time, and his head goes to his hands well on the job. I don't always have to look back or point. With the plant running full we shout or don't talk at all, and like me he only laughs when it's funny or dangerous. When we do have air to talk he steers it toward Zen, a mind cure that goes back to the Samurai. Most of it V's over my head like ducks, but what's stuck is that he's these two people trying to find a third, the real him. I told him if he ever draws close I'll get the boat and the grap-hook and we'll drag for him. He said he's something he's going down after alone. The stuff keeps him calm though; first casual I ever worked with that didn't seem to mind the heights. When the crane lifts us he saddles up on the bucket and watches the ground pass away. I've never learned to enjoy the high work. They say I have to do it, but I don't have to like it. I still keep the eyes straight or up. Jeff says he loves the feeling of rising, of being lifted by the big arm. He says I think too much about the falling that goes along with it. I should just keep my mind on the lift and free it from its partner.

"From the beginning it's the rise that's been the result of the fall, not bass-ackwards like most people have it. You'll rise in the end," he says.

"Tell that to the guys we've had to scrape off the base pipes," I answered. We laughed.

I've quit worrying about gas with him too. He hunts up and down the pipe for it like a weasel, putting gauge to traps and flanges. When he gives me the okay I'm not afraid to spark the welder and set to. Gas is something you never want to find, unless it's there. Three months and we haven't found a live pipe, and he still runs a good check, and keeps the hose on my sparks like it's his first time.

I've talked to Pat about him, about how fond I am of him. She calls him my Zen Master.

"Don't worry," she said. "His butterfly kite will come down some day," and then called me a trickless old dog that shouldn't always be listening to kids. She calls me an old dog at thirty-seven. I told her she's the one that's too old to be turning new tricks. I almost welcomed the evening of cold cuts and cold shoulder. One minute she tells me to grow up, the next it's old man.

Later she comes out and sits in front of the TV. "Can we talk?" She does, about how she's losing herself. I take her for granted. She's sorry she gets mean and hurts. She thinks she has to leave. "Why?" Maybe she doesn't. I'm glad she decides we'll give it some more time. We hug. I tell her I listen to the kids a lot because I have to work with them a lot. I like them, and want a couple of my own someday. I didn't buy a station wagon for the great mileage and easy handling. I tell her the young are life, their heads busting with their own guts. You just can't turn off your old songs. It doesn't seem like what she wants to hear, but she smiles. "What do we do?" I don't know why I can't talk. I search my head for answers but find nothing. I figure at thirty-two she should love me or dump me. She wants to do both.

BV splashes the anchor a hundred yards or so off humpbank; called teenage wasteland by the kids that use it now. It's a flat gravel parking lot that ends at the water in a small cliff. It's got the usual collection of beer cans and black remains of party fires. There's an old cottonwood with some crippled lawn furniture and a gutted couch under it. With the mist all you can see from the water is the cliff. And in the water you do come across rubbers. The loose flat ones we call prick skins, the knotted ones peter eels. I used to knot mine and then shout to it as I threw it in. "If you get out of that, we'll name you Houdini." My old man, I bet, used the same line. Today the women carry the protection. If I ever have a kid his girl will probably be the one that stops his first bullet with a manhole cover.

As we're grumbling and sipping our coffee, the front of the new Buick rolls into view on the cliff. The shiny grill catches what light there is, and you can hear the wheels on the gravel. After a minute the opening and closing of the door is heard, and a man appears at the front of the car. He stands holding the elbows of his overcoat. He looks in every direction he can and then remains still, pointed at us in the boat. We are both hunched over, hoping that he says nothing, that he'll stop and get back into the car. And he does. No matter what he would have said, I wouldn't have been able to answer him with more than a wave. I'm sure his little girl is in the gravel pit.

BV talks to himself about his latest girlfriend. The morning's dragging. The rain has arrived, sweeping in with darker clouds that push into the pale overcast. The gravel pit is alive with the rain, and as it has gotten later, I've begun to watch the water near the boat for bubbles. The divers must be close. My hands are deep inside my parka, my baseball cap tight over my head. BV's yellow slicker, bright with rain, is almost cheerful. His head is thrown back, catching the drops on his face as he talks to the low sky.

"She loves them now, likes to feel them, and feel them on her body. They're always afraid at first, afraid to touch them, to even look, but once they get past the touching phase and see they won't come apart, they enjoy the shit out of them. You know, sometimes I wish my face was messed up too. Nah. You ever been with a gimp, Licks?"

"I was with a cross-eyed lady once. We passed out on a couch together, me in my underwear, her with her clothes on. She had a Doberman, big friendly thing, but he pissed on my socks. I remember leaving them under the seat of her car when she took me home. I forced myself all evening to look her in the eye until it came natural. I decided she was very pretty. You're not a gimp, Beevy, just a little beat up. A girl will put up with a lot worse than you."

"Yeah, like you." He opens his mouth wide to the rain. "The dog peed on your goddamned socks. That's great."

"Yep, I guess he was just staking his claim, or he liked the smell of them."

"Sure." We must look funny, grinning at each other with the rain churning the water around us. "You know Carol Pottsman?" BV continues. "He picked up an old lady once, with one tit, spent the night and said it wasn't out of pity either. He was crazy for her, that night anyway. I would have jumped ship after coming up empty on one side. Think you could stare at one tit until it became natural?"

"Who knows? I bet I'd feel bad if I backed out. I imagine she'd think it was an act of mercy either way. You can't win some of those."

Air bubbles up to the surface. We both bend over to watch more float up. A diver is just below us. We become more serious, waiting for the frog to cover the floor beneath us. BV's face is tight and troubled. I've decided that's why he's here. With all his girling, and boozing and life wasting, he needs this to feel good about himself, to feel like he's got at least one foot out of hell. The bubbles become a stream and then a cluster, and then we can see the black head rising. It's the terrible moment when you're looking hard to see if the frog is bringing someone up with him. There's a second where you can't decide if you want him empty-handed or trudging up the dead. It's Yikes. He comes out of the water and throws both arms over the sides of the boat, spitting out the mouthpiece and sliding up his mask. He used to cry "Yikes!" after coming out of the cold, dark water. He wasn't comfortable not seeing where he was. The eerie, closed-in feeling got to him. BV pours him a cup of coffee and stirs some Cremora into it with his finger.

"Thanks, Burny. Christ almighty it's cold down there. Settle down, teeth."

"Not much better up here. Nothing, huh?"

"Empty. There's lots of holes down there, cold and dark holes. I think I woke up some carp, but nothing. God damn waste of good equipment in this mud puddle. Gean not up yet? I went wide, thought he'd beat me."

"Hasn't been up."

Yikes sips his coffee. His teeth have quit shaking. The father, and this time the mother, have gotten out again, and stand near the Buick. They have a large umbrella. The mother draws the father's raincoat around her shoulders. None of us will look back at them. Gean's bubbles arrive fast and in a herd, with him close behind. He throws one arm up, while coughing out his mouthpiece. In the other hand is the end of his orange fly line. He reaches it out, and I grab it, tying it to the oar lock. BV is already digging the walkie-talkie out of its plastic. Golly Gean speaks quickly across the boat to his partner.

"Yikes, I need your help. She's caught up in some branches."

I hand Yikes the coil of rope, and both divers disappear, following the orange line to the bottom, and the girl.

BV has raised Ed. "Golly found her, Ed. Yep. She's caught on the bottom. They both went down. Get them all over here."

I'm busy clearing the boat, unfolding the thick wool blanket. The rain begins to darken it with small drops. At this point you feel as if you are saving someone. The feeling is gone in my hands, and I work them to get it back. As we wait for the air bubbles to return everything becomes important. I notice that BV's hiking boots are speckled with blue paint. He sees me staring and draws his feet closer, not knowing why. I am glad that we don't have kids. Pat would be either terrible or incredible during the waiting. I want to imagine she would break down in my arms. I find myself thinking a drowned child would help our marriage.

The divers are busy off below us, trying to untangle the girl. They work slowly, unable to see each other in the dark silence. Passing signals by touch they feel for how the small body is caught and try to free her. They also treat her as if she is still alive, unhooking the clothes and releasing the arms delicately. All the vehicles hurry in a parade line along the bank. I finally hear the father shouting at us from the car. Both parents realized, as soon as I tied off the line, what it meant. It's the girl's name he's shouting, maybe even to her and not to us. He has stepped closer to the edge, leaving his wife. She is stuck to the side of the car. The father has taken his umbrella with him, and the rain now reaches her. She does not feel it. She will not yet let go of the girl and cannot come closer to see. Suddenly the father realizes he has the umbrella. He sees his wife standing in the rain and stretches his hand with the umbrella in it back to cover her. He does not go to her because he has to know what is happening. The sheriff will arrive soon and take care of them in his official way.

As the divers' air comes to us, BV and I move to the back of the boat to take the girl. The black figures become visible first, the girl's body only a white shadow or glow. She begins to take shape in their arms as they rise. We see the white legs and then the purple shoes and shorts. You don't want to see her face and concentrate instead on the red top. You know you will have to look at the face later. She bursts into clarity as they all break the water. Resting in their arms as she comes out of the rain-pocked surface into the light she seems asleep for a second, and it frightens me terribly. But I take her from the divers, and BV has her legs, and I take the small shoulders and rest her on the blanket. She is incredibly white, and we are both staring at her against the dark wool. She is now a dead child. The divers push off, moving across the water as if being reeled in. We don't cover her yet because we have to look. Each time we have to look until it becomes only a body. BV straightens her out with his clumsy hands. His face is shaking with her cold. Soon she is not there anymore, and there is just the small, empty picture that I will see again with the others. We wrap her carefully. The sheriff can uncover her for the parents, themselves and the news. After all she's what we've come out to see. But the cameras will not focus on the girl. They'll point to the parents, so at 5:00 and 11:00 we can feel for them, see how hard they try to hold life in the body. The parents will not believe it has left, and will save both, the living and the dead, as one for a long time. God knows why we all have so much trouble giving them up.

I move to the middle of the boat and point it toward shore. Again I am glad my back is to all that is waiting. BV looks past me to the camera. He is collecting himself. He almost appears to draw calm and strength from the bundle he keeps covered against the bottom.

■ DEBRA C. EARLING

Debra C. Earling grew up in Ronan, Montana, as a member of the Confederated Salish/Kootenai tribe. A student of James Welch's at the University of Washington, she is currently working on her master's degree in creative writing at Cornell University. "Perma Red" was first published in Gathering Ground: New Writing and Art by Northwest Women of Color *(1984).*

Perma Red

She had been walking on the highway for almost an hour. Last night's liquor was now just a cotton-dry whisper on her thick tongue, a faint buzz somewhere behind her head. The bastard had let her off outside of Ravalli on Highway 93, and now nearly an hour later, she was nowhere closer to Perma. The armholes of her blouse were tight and wet. The stiff blouse strained across her breast and had ribbed her nipples raw.

Her stomach rumbled. "No," she groaned. She looked for privacy. A lonely bush, a few scrub trees, sage, weeds, and dry grass. Rattlers? She looked to the pine trees a hundred yards or so further. "Hell with it," she said and ducked behind the nearest bush. When Louise stepped back onto the road the heavy August sun was clearing the Mission Range. Her knees felt a little weak, but she was now ready to walk a serious mile or two. A breeze cooled the sweat on her back and fluttered her thin skirt. She felt the hem wet on her calves and shivered. Although she tried to walk fast, she felt as if she were being pulled down. Each landmark she set her sights on remained distant, unobtainable. She shifted her gaze to the blonde hills.

The stiff grass rustled in the breeze. A gust of wind rattled the dry weeds, whirled a tumbleweed and threw a sheet prickle of dust up her legs. Grit stung her eyes. She stopped on the road's shoulder and watched the small whirlwind gather speed, twirling leaves, small twigs, powder dust. Under its path, thin rows of cheat grass collapsed like brittle sticks. She stood transfixed and watched until the swirling talcum dust disappeared in a steady cross-wind, becoming a faint wisp, a tendril of smoke, thin air.

Her grandmother believed whirlwinds were the souls of the dead, departing, becoming sky. Spirit winds. Louise had never really believed this. Now she swallowed a growing desire to run. She forced herself to walk slowly, but little by little, she began to quicken her pace.

She heard the hollow wind sound of an approaching car. She lifted her thumb, but the car swerved a perfect half moon to avoid her and whipped down the road. A glint of chrome and it disappeared over a hillswell. She raised a slender hand to her brow and blinked at the sun. It wasn't even close to noon and already the road was soft beneath her feet. She wasn't worried though; someone would pick her up, someone whom she knew and she would sit red-faced and silent on the way back home, wishing she had made it to Missoula, or Wallace, anywhere, off this reservation. The thought chewed her pride. This time it'd be different—she'd walk all the bitchin' way home. She stiffened her knees and her heart became her drumbeat homeward.

The shallow drone of an occasional passing car eased the monotony of the fields' humming. She listened to the steady flickering tick of the grasshopper and tried to block the image of her mother's fever-swollen face. She tried to think up an excuse for last night's drunk. But she knew excuses didn't matter now. She had come up with convincing alibis in the past. And Grandma would listen intently, nod politely, and excuse her. She would feel a little guilty at first, but later she would feel smug. But she was never sure she had fooled the old woman, only pride made her hold onto the thought that she had.

"Hey Louise! Red! Want a ride?" Behind her, grinning—cousin Victor hung out the window of his rusty '32 Ford pick-up. A slow cloud of dust billowed past her. He squinted at her, chewing on a tooth pick. His black-gray hair was butch block, bristled like a wire brush. Occasionally, he would get a crew-cut and when it grew out it made his head look square. He was wearing the maroon shirt he always wore, rolled up past his forearms, with a white tee shirt underneath. He looked hot.

Louise said nothing, walked to the passenger side and yanked on the door. Victor tried to roll down the window but it stuck. He yelled at her through the window crack. "Door don't open." He gestured with his fingers. "Gotta come around on my side." Louise noticed again the thin white scar that split his upper lip. It occurred to her that white men didn't have scars. He climbed out of the truck. And Louise crawled in. The dull leather seats were hot and she sat close to the passenger door on a seat rip that was sharp. It snagged her skirt.

The truck pulled out on the road and picked up speed until the window crack whistled and the stick shift vibrated. Victor spit out his toothpick. "Whew," he said, "you smell like a white woman. Where you been?" Louise folded her arms across her sore breasts and looked at the dashboard. A bumper sticker sealed off the jockey box. She read its faded letters: "Pray For Me, I Drive Highway 93."

"Got any booze?" she said. He reached across her and pulled out a half-empty quart of beer. The bent bottle cap had been jammed back on and Louise pulled it off with her fingers. She took a long, easy swig of the flat warm beer and passed it to Victor. He chugged a few swallows. "Taste like dog piss!" he coughed.

"I wouldn't know," Louise said and gulped a quick swallow, then recapped it with her fist. She put the bottle between her legs. The seat poked her thighs.

"What'd you do to your hair, kid? It looks faded somehow."

"Got any gum?" she said.

He reached into his pocket, pulled out a stick of clove gum and tossed it in her lap. Last month she had heard you could lighten your hair with peroxide and water, so she had tried it. She stared out the window. "I like it," she mumbled and wiped her wet palms on her knees. Louise watched the clear shadow of a cloud as it moved over the hills. And it seemed to her that the hills were sleeping. She thought of her mother laying still beneath the clouds in the white heat of the day.

He spoke softly. "I heard Annie's been sick. Aunt Susy was up to your Grandma's house last night." Louise chewed the cuticle on her left thumb and busied herself smoothing her skirt. She looked at her brown shoes but said nothing. Her mother had been sick for only a week, but it was a different sickness. A sickness that pulled the muscles behind her eyes as tight as a blind strap and let go.

Now, every night Grandma listened for the owl and burned the thin strands of Annie's hair in the cook-stove. She also kept a tireless eye on Annie's lonely clothing flapping on the line. If she left her post she would call Louise to stand watch—so neither Annie nor her possessions were ever left alone.

Louise listened to the sound of the tires on the road and re-opened the beer. "Want a chug?" she pointed the bottle toward Victor. He shook his head. The truck hit a bump and beer splattered his lap. She gulped the rest, leaned over and tossed the bottle out his window. She heard a distant tinkle as it hit the ground.

"Aunt Susy says it's bad medicine." He looked at her.

"What?"

She had come from Hot Springs, the old medicine woman. Even in the bright sun, her clothes were black as the crows' wings. Louise remembered that the rattlesnakes buzzed her arrival. Rattlesnakes were blind this time of year. They hid in the grass with milk-white eyes. They struck at anything that moved.

"What?"

"Your mother's sickness."

"I don't know." She felt as if a cold, wet hand had just been placed at the base of her spine. She choked a gag.

Victor changed the subject. "Been a bad spell this summer. Road's too hot, even for snakes. You're lucky you have that spring."

Louise nodded, but said nothing.

The spring's creek was a slow mud trickle thick as blood. Grandma had milked the old cow for Annie and sent Louise down to the spring with a small jar of body-warm milk. The spring pool still bubbled, but it had receded and large mosquitos swarmed the cracked clay banks. Louise had slipped the jar in an old stocking and put it in the creek. For an hour she had sat holding onto the sock, slapping blood fat mosquitos.

They were slowly coming into Dixon. Victor shifted into second and the truck whined down. A few cars were parked at the Dixon Bar. Now it was early afternoon and shadows were short. A dirt gray dog slept in the shade of the Dixon Bar.

The milk was cool and sweet when they put it to her lips, but it dribbled through her hot yellow teeth and scummed the inside of her cheeks like phlegm; a gray paste too thick to swallow. Her ragged fingernails, thin and dry as paper.

"This sure is one hell of a town," Victor said. Louise looked over at the Dixon Bar and could see only darkness behind the ragged screen door. She placed her hand to the back of her neck and thought of sleep. Victor scuffed the palm of his hand over his hair and sighed. As they drove out of Dixon Louise noticed a small boy was playing near the edge of town. Louise turned to look back. A slow cloud of dust was passing over a few gray shingle houses built squat on the ground. The small boy had stopped playing. She saw him raise his hand as if to wave but he cupped his hand above his eyes then lifted his dark face to the sun.

Louise slumped back in the seat and crossed her arms. As she saw her Grandma's house in the distance she sat up suddenly and tugged at her door handle. "Let me out here, Victor." He started to protest but slowed down the truck and let her out. She stood squinting on the roadside and watched until Victor's pickup turned the first highway bend and slipped beyond the hill.

The weathered house stood among the weeds. Near the highway was a marshy stretch, thick with fuzzy cattails and cawing magpies.

The rocky terrain of Grandma's land provided a haven for field snakes and rattlers. Louise walked slowly up to the house. She adjusted her skirt and wiped her mouth on the back of her hand.

For a while she stood, stoneblind and blinking in the doorway. She leaned into the queer hot darkness, straining to see. Her eyes gathered the dark room slowly, one inch at a time. Heavy blankets, smelling like singed hair hid the windows and suffocated the afternoon sun. Here and there pinholes of light poked the walls, illuminating golden particles of dust.

In the dim light, she saw the still shadow of Grandma standing near the cook-stove. Grandma opened the cast iron stove drawer and fanned the flames. Her face was washed with yellow light. She threw something into the flames and shut the drawer. Louise watched a thin flicker of fire lick the round edge of the stove lid and her nostrils were filled with the smell of burning sweet grass. Grandma pulled another grass braid from her deep pocket and touched it to the stove top. An orange flame smoked the withering grass. Grandma carried the smoking medicine to the bedroom where Annie lay. The door closed behind her with a quiet click. Louise clasped her hands to keep her fingers from trembling. And sat down in the sleepy heat and waited.

Annie's wake was held at Aunt Susy's house. The first day of the wake Louise waited outside of the small house. For a while she hid in the root cellar and listened to the sound of her heart. That evening Louise stood behind the pine tree in Aunt Susy's front yard. She cupped her hands to her ribs and watched the people who came to visit her mother for the last time. Even outside she could hear them praying. Sometimes she could hear them laughing and joking. And when they cried, Louise would sit on the porch and listen to the wind moving through the cheat grass.

Aunt Susy came out on the porch to sit beside her once. She had reached over and touched Louise's hand. Louise had looked at her in the darkness and thought the old woman's skin resembled the pickled tavern sausages at the Perma Bar. The old woman seemed small to Louise now. When Louise was a little girl she had been afraid of Aunt Susy. The old woman had a wizened hawk-face and a large dowager's hump. She always wore black garments. And some of her dresses had sleeves short enough to reveal the loose, olive flesh of her inner arms. Once Louise mentioned her Aunt Susy's skin color to Grandma. "Too much green tea," Grandma had said.

For three days and three nights they prayed for Annie. Louise watched Grandma in the kitchen sifting flour for fry bread. Louise could see the mouse turds like hard raisins grate the bottom of the sifter. Grandma would toss them out, scoop up another cup and dump it in the sifter.

Louise looked into the living room where her mother lay propped in a wooden box. She clenched her skirt up tight in her fists and stood still. "Go to her," Grandma said. Louise did not move for a moment. "Go on," her grandmother said. Louise walked slowly toward her mother. The candles flickered up on Annie's delicate waxen face. Annie's slender hands had been folded carefully across her bosom.

And Louise noticed that her mother's hands were still and dark. For a long time Louise gazed upon her, looking for signs of life. Twice, she saw her chest expand, gathering air. But looking again, it seemed to Louise that she had never seen anything so motionless. Even dust moved in the wind. And sometimes rocks seemed to shimmer in the heat. But her mother's stillness was uncomfortable to her. Louise passed her hand over her mother's face but did not touch her.

Louise looked above the casket where, haphazardly tacked on the gray wall, were pictures that Aunt Susy had cut out of magazines and catalogues. Fashion models smiled from the windows of their chauffeured cars. Hawaiian girls waved from a tropical paradise. Happy families sat down to dine in their immaculate kitchens.

Friends and relatives began to pray. Louise looked at their faces. Every face seemed distorted to her; continually changed by the candlelights' flickering. It seemed to Louise that they looked at her mother as though she were far away. Their eyes seemed vague and distant to her. Nervous fingers twisted rosaries. Some sang softly, almost inaudibly. Their chants became a low drone that buzzed like the hot fields. She looked at her grandmother in the kitchen. Louise wondered what caused this dark sadness. It seemed she had felt this way for a long time. Louise slipped out the door without a goodbye.

Louise returned home the next morning before the heat could dry the root-wet fields. She saw Victor's gray Ford parked out back. She held her breath, but she soon realized they had left sometime before.

When she opened the back door she called to her grandmother. She looked at the half empty coffee cups on the table. She sat down in the quiet kitchen; her skull felt thin as an eggshell. A meadowlark sang outside the window and she thought it was a lonely sound. She thought a while and went outside. Maybe Victor had left his keys in the truck. She peered in the window. No keys in the ignition. She opened the door and checked under the mat. She found an old gray key. She wondered if it would work.

The truck picked up speed, faster and faster, until the seats lurched and the rusted coil springs screeched with the rhythmic jar of the road's many potholes. Dust motes billowed behind the truck. Louise pressed the accelerator to the floor and gripped the steering wheel. The road gave way to a series of sharp bends that ended in a roller coaster hill. She sighed as the road gradually sloped to a straight tractor road.

Louise could see the small crowd at the burial ground so she began to slow down. She pulled the truck off on the roadside. Her tight chest felt empty and she was breathing hard. Louise rolled the window down and gulped a breath of air. She pressed her forehead to the steering wheel. Over the field, the wind carried the old songs. A warm breeze touched her damp hair. Louise looked over at the people gathered around the grave; eight or nine people she had known all her life. Grandma's red shawl flapped in the hot wind. She saw that all of them were wearing their best clothes. Victor stood close to Grandma in his stiff white shirt.

Louise twisted the mirror round so she could look at her face. In the sunlight she could see that the red color of her hair did not match her dark skin. She looked for something to cover her head. On the floor was an old bandana that Victor used to stuff the window crack. Carefully she tied the scarf over her hair. Louise looked at herself once more and slowly climbed out of the truck. She left the truck door open and walked a little closer. She waited until the small crowd departed. "Grandma?" she called. Grandma and Victor looked up at Louise.

"I'll meet you both at the truck," he said.

Louise moved slowly toward Grandma. "I know, Honey," Grandma said. "It's going to be fine."

Grandma lifted her palms to the sky and chanted in Salish. Her chant became a slow, meandering song that made Louise very sad. She sang to a part of Louise that was lonesome.

8

Contemporary Poetry

■ *Words and Space*

WILLIAM BEVIS

ne of the best readings I've heard in years was in Missoula, with Paul Zarzyski, modern poet and bronc rider, and Wally McRae, cowboy poet and rancher, sharing the stage. But while both poets were excellent and the shared reading a success, I was also aware of how difficult it is for the ear to move from cowboy poetry to modern poetry. You either expect rhyme and regular rhythm, or you don't; you either expect narrative, or you don't. The reading set me to thinking about Montana and its poetry, and at first I suspected that cowboy poetry probably dominated the scene until the Second World War and that slowly, after Dick Hugo came in 1964, modern poetry took over. Things are not that simple, however; old issues of *Frontier* show a variety of modern styles during the 1920s and 1930s, and cowboy poets are now gaining national fame. Each kind of poetry – modern and cowboy – has different roots and aims.

Bill Kittredge, who was a rancher before he became a writer, recalls that rhymed verses were often written on the oilcloth walls of the buckaroo line camps at their Oregon ranch. At the end of the season, crews would record important events. One poem, written by Burt Parker in 1944, found its way to the English Department in Missoula, and with a wicked delight I make it part of history:

Here's to Billy Kittredge
A lad we all know well.
He used to run a scatter rake
out on the I.X.L.
He was driving Dick and Dandy,
When a line from him did fall,
and they shot out across the flat
just like a cannon ball.
Billy is a gritty kid, he said, "I'll show the witch."
He still had one ribbon, when the rake hit a ditch,
He fell over backwards and landed in the straw
and old Dick and Dandy went drifting down the draw.

The poem goes on to draw the obvious but no less useful moral: "When you go out to scatter rake, Don't never drop a line."

We catch a glimpse here of an ancient tradition of oral history, put into verses that are easily memorized and sung. This poem, in ways, is closer to Homer than Hugo's poetry is. Such narrative verse was not "cowboy" in origin; much of the early Butte poetry, much of Rudyard Kipling, and all of Robert Service were in the same style. Montana's state folklorist Michael Korn tells me that after the turn of the century, cowboy poetry became more ironic and humorous, and he points out that such folk verse always suited democratic American instincts: Here was an "art" that anyone could read and, for that matter, most everyone could write.

Modern poetry, on the other hand, comes from the tradition of the lyric poem, in which compression, imagery, language play, and irrational syntax seem to say more than any person ever could "say" in ordinary speech. In the following lines, Dick Hugo stands at the Bear Paw battlefield where the army fought Chief Joseph's people. Hugo relives the battle of ninety-five years before, when Chief Looking Glass was killed:

Bear Paw

The wind is 95. It still pours from the east
like armies and it drains each day of hope.
From any point on the surrounding rim,
below, the teepees burn. The wind
is infantile and cruel. It cries "give in" "give in"
and Looking Glass is dying on the hill.
Pale grass shudders. Cattails beg and bow.
Down the draw, the dust of anxious horses
hides the horses. When it clears, a car
with Indiana plates is speeding to Chinook.

Wind like armies, "Looking Glass" blending into "grass" and cattails, begging and bowing; the Indians are part of a natural world, going down before the army as grass before the wind. The cinematic effect of hiding the horses with dust, then having the dust clear to reveal a car makes us simultaneously aware of our tourist's empathy with the Indian past and our distance from it. We often feel such sympathy, irony, and discomfort as onlookers at historical sites, especially tragic sites where our people were the villains; but rarely are those subtle feelings, and relations between old and new, red and white, captured in ten lines. "It is a little world made cunningly," wrote John Donne.

I chose an issue of *Frontier* magazine, almost at random, to see what Montana's twentieth century poetic heritage really was. The special issue on Frank Linderman, spring of 1939, contains poems typical of the magazine so ably edited by H. G. Merriam and, in this case, Grace Stone Coates. The poems are surprisingly various. Perhaps the biggest single category is what one would expect: four or five descriptive, sentimental, or preachy poems; versified ideas. The others range from cowboy verse to the very modern. Consider these two openings:

> Danny Kirk was a Western Man,
> A ridin', swearin', gamblin' han';
> He was plum locoed over Hanner Work,
> And he wanted to change her name to Kirk.
> (With a Ki and a Yippi and a Yi Oh!)

The roots of this ballad by Ada Farris are in song and story and in respect for dialect and folklore. The name "Hanner Work" is wonderful, suggesting a world far from glamor, art, and leisure. Just a few pages away, however, is a poem by Tom McGrath, now a well-known poet who at that time was just beginning his writing career as a student at the University of North Dakota. He had probably read Yeats and Eliot, the Imagists (1913-1920), possibly E. E. Cummings, and apparently during the Dakota winter had found time for ennui:

> THIS ROOM, IN THIS STREET, IN THIS TIME
> in alien land. natives unfriendly. last night
> patrol ambushed. 5 men dead. no sign
> of enemy warriors—no enemy troops in sight.
> smoke now over mountain. bridges burning.
> land laid waste before us. roads behind
> washed out by fall rain. leaves now turning
> color of dull gold. frost over lowland.
> springs soon frozen. hope for help from north.
> push on. nowhere. no hope. no friendly hand. . . .

By the second and third stanzas we realize that this is not a war story, and we remember that the title, which leads into the poem, had placed us at home. The war is in our minds; this is a poem of imagery and expression, not a narrative. The poem resembles, in ways, Hugo's "Letter to Stafford from Polson," forty years later:

> Dear Bill: We don't know the new heavy kind of wolf
> killing calves, but we've seen it and it's anything but gray.
> We have formed a new heavy kind of posse
> and we're fanning the Mission range for unique tracks.
> The new wolf is full of tricks. For instance, yesterday
> he sat all afternoon in a bar disguised as a trout. . . .

In both poems, an apparent narrative, straightforward and accessible, is soon turned into a mirror of the mind. And in that little world of wolves and war, things are not going well.

Since at least 1921, when *Frontier* began and modern poetry had taken hold in the English language, Montana has had poetry of all kinds. People's delight in ballads and cowboy verse has not diminished, and many have written and enjoyed the more difficult, compressed, and interior modern poetry. This is hardly surprising. The central publisher of modern poetry in English was Harriet Munroe at *Poetry* magazine in Chicago; Pound and Yeats and Eliot and Stevens were sending her poems from 1913 to 1922. The library at Missoula began taking *Poetry* with the first volume in 1912; and from then on, Missoula writers could be reading the very best of the new poetry being invented in Paris, London, Dublin, and New York.

H. G. Merriam's encouragement of writers in 1919 and Richard Hugo's arrival in Missoula in 1964 were turning points in Montana literature. Hugo had studied under Theodore Roethke at the University of Washington in 1947 and there had learned the "singing style" of William Butler Yeats, perhaps the most passionate poet of our century. The style and sensibility of Yeats and Roethke matched Hugo's own obsessions, which included finding his own place after what he perceived as an orphaned childhood and finding the value of others who were also orphaned, dislocated, dispossessed. His was always a personal poetry, written from the point of view of the underdog and based on an honest voice. Word play was secondary to direct expression; in technique he was "a meat and potatoes man," as poet Dave Smith said.

Hugo's early work created the identity he needed, the voice of an urban orphan at camp: intense, street-wise on the riverbank, never far from a bar. He packed lines with strong stresses and relentless energy:

> I'm a poet of density. That is to say at least in my first two books, my syllables are all strongly accented. I achieve this through elisions, a very thick line, a heavy line. I do this through syntactical shifts. . . . swing music is where I developed the idea of getting something else going before the thing died out.

Such fast and toughened poetry was a distinct advantage for Hugo as a young western writer. It suited the western image of a man, terse and hard, and so the tough style allowed his softy self to come forth in the content of the poem. Indeed, Dick's entire personal stance, as well as his poetry, is part of Montana literary history. For Dick, Roethke was a role model for the vulgar and ungainly:

> He was kind of an outrageous man, and had all kinds of problems, and I was an outrageous young man, and I realized one day that silly as this man sometimes appeared, he was able to create beautiful things, and it occurred to me that maybe there was a chance for me, too . . . maybe I can salvage something out of this absurd creature that I am.

In Missoula after 1964, with two books of poems published, Dick, like Roethke before him, could serve as a model for others. The model included a lot of drinking, a lot of weight, and a lot of absurdity out of which the art must be salvaged. But it worked. Here was a kind of poet that western men, especially, could trust. No slender Parisian aesthete, no Boston Brahmin, no pretentious intellectual, Dick was a working-class poet. And that's what cowboys always were—working-class, with space.

So after 1964 the creative writing program in Missoula, which had been started in 1919 by Merriam and had nurtured, among many others, Bud Guthrie and Dan Cushman and Dorothy Johnson, had Hugo at its head. With his no-nonsense style, his remarkable teaching, his insatiable sociability, and his care and love of language, he changed Montana literature.

He told his student Jim Welch that Indians and the Hi-line—Jim's own background—were worth writing about. He encouraged numerous fiction writers—DeMarinis, Kittredge, Crumley—as well as nurturing, along with Madeline DeFrees, a generation of poets, including Lahey, Scanlon, Todd, Whiteman, Alcosser, and Zarzyski, many of whom appear in this anthology. Much of the poetry here bears his stamp: the dense lines, the landscape like a pressure, the sense of loss.

In his poems, Dick often wrote of sad or even desperate people and towns, but it was never to distance himself, never to be separate or superior. Always, it was an act of love. He sought the down-and-out in order to feel at home. And in his poems, once that bottom is reached, once the worst aspects of Montana's boom-and-bust abandonments are faced, some endurance and pride are salvaged from the wreck. "For Hugo," said Jim Welch, "failure *was* the last best place." Hard times, as much as good, have made Montanans what they are.

A number of the poems in this collection deal with work, or diaries, or fishing or hunting–everyday activities–and to me are especially strong, and Montanan. The application of poetic language to daily lives can be very powerful, as in Ed Lahey's "The Blind Horses" down in Butte's Lexington mine:

> Dozens of tramway horses hauled hard
> against whippletrees–rubbed the timbered tunnels clean–
> pulling down the cribbed-up drifts,
> brass lanterns swinging, work bits in their teeth,
> slick with mine damp and cold to the touch.

Work-toughened language permeates our lives, and the humor of the ordinary, as well as its strain, appears in Dave Thomas' "The Ten Thousand Things":

> Well let's see there's
>   shebolts hebolts and stress rods
> there's make-up bolts inbed bolts and
>   carriage bolts
> there's nuts and washers to fit all sizes
>   of each.

These poems stay quite close to spoken speech, with only the rhythm compressed and intensified. Some poets prefer to shape and compress images and syntax too, even when describing everyday events, as in Bob Wrigley's beautiful "Winter Love," a version of two homesteaders in love (from the journal of D. D. Pye, 1871-1899):

>   Love, she said,
> and he too, wadding rags in the heaved log
> walls, kindling in the swollen,
> buckled stove. The wood into flames
> unravelling was their music,
> and the low reports outside

as trees exploded, frozen to their hearts.
One morning the hens were dead,
a frost-tufted egg in each cloaca.
We know, for all the dead
weight of winter, they never wept
to be back in Pennsylvania. . . .

The soft music overlaying the violence, the giving back of life to language in phrases like "the dead weight of winter" two lines after "dead" hens, creates a tone and scene impossible to translate, floating in the cabin like "breath clouds so long before their faces when they spoke."

In such poetry, layers of possibility are draped over each other. The words do not simply go forward, as in linear and rational language, but advance, retreat, remember, avoid, as life is experienced. Statement, then, is subordinate to something bigger; call it perception. The ambiguities and puns and double meanings superimpose possible statements, as Hugo's Indian battle and Indiana plates are superimposed, or as, in Sandra Alcosser's "A Fish to Feed All Hunger," fly-tying, predation, and sexuality begin to mingle:

The fisherman is dressing,
capes of moose mane around him.
In his vise, he wraps the waist
of a minnow with chenille.

Paul Zarzyski concludes our poetry section with a chilling pun on "range," one of our sacred Montana words suggesting the "bigness, distance, wildness, freedom" that Wallace Stegner called the dream of *The Big Sky*. Yet Zarzyski, writing on the "Silos" of missiles across Montana (silo: a pit for corn in ancient Greek, associated for thousands of years with cereal, Ceres, harvest, agriculture) reminds us of that other "range" in a nuclear world,

. . . where cattle stir,
moon to salt lick to moon,
this veteran wind
once bulletproof, this distance
no longer dark, no longer living
out of sight and range.

So one of our most cherished western dreams, of escape, escape from civilization, is gone. It was never our best dream. And cultures change.

Does Montana poetry differ at all from poetry in the rest of America? Not in technique, perhaps, but inevitably our literature is influenced by this "land of few people and a great deal of space," as Joseph Kinsey Howard put it. Dick Hugo, Madeline DeFrees, and visiting poets have often said that there *is* more landscape, weather, and naming of natural objects in our poetry; the fine poems of Matthew Hansen come to mind. There is also, I believe, a slight cultural difference in our region that affects both poetry and prose. That is a kind of humility, of submission to land and weather, that defines inland West, northern plains literature as a sort of subculture:

> Pray hard to weather, that lone surviving god,
> That in some sudden wisdom we surrender.
>
> (Hugo, "Bear Paw")

In many of these poems, "a quiet resignation to the will of things"—pioneer woman Nannie Alderson's phrase—and Hugo's sense of a chastised self join with simple delight in beauty to create a psychological landscape more complex than any "scene." This tone of humility and endurance appears in our art, in our fiction, in movies such as "Heartland," and in our poetry. Montana artists seem more ready than many Americans to acknowledge forces beyond their control; and thus these poems are not only aware of a natural world, but also humble in ways distinctly regional. This region, however, of limited resources and reduced expectations is rapidly becoming the entire earth. Therefore, the "regional" aspects of Montana's humility—which has seemed rooted in nineteenth century life—joins a new world-wide ecological movement to speak for man's limits, and for the beauty of systems larger than man.

RICHARD HUGO

Born in Seattle in 1923, Richard Hugo grew up in the industrial suburb of White Center, Washington. He joined the Air Force in 1943 and went to Italy as a bombardier, earning a Distinguished Flying Cross. Hugo studied under Theodore Roethke at the University of Washington, where he received an M.A. in creative writing in 1952. While working at Boeing as a technical writer, Hugo completed his first book of poems, A Run of Jacks, *which was published in 1961. In 1964, Hugo began his tenure at the University of Montana, where he directed the Creative Writing Program and taught there until his death in 1982. Hugo had a large and enthusiastic audience for his many books of poetry and for his important book on writing,* The Triggering Town, *published in 1979. These selections are from Hugo's collected poems,* Making Certain It Goes On *(1983), and from his posthumously published autobiographical essays,* The Real West Marginal Way *(1986), edited by Ripley Schemm Hugo, James Welch, and Lois Welch.*

The Milltown Union Bar: You Could Love Here

My life was turning to shit. My marriage was breaking up. I was drinking, unable to control my outbursts of anger and my fears that I had become too difficult to live with. What's worse, I was too blurred to know my wife was about to leave me.

We had come to Montana almost directly from Italy. At the age of forty, I was about to start teaching. I knew nothing about Montana, had only been there once, nearly twenty years before had passed through on a troop train. I remember stopping somewhere, and lovely coeds from a college I could see on a hill across the valley handed each of us a basket containing fruit, candy, and magazines. It seemed idyllic that day, the fresh young girls, the innocent looking school in the distance. It seemed like some America that G.I.s imagined overseas in a World War II movie. I don't know where it was. I've never seen that place again. Or if I have, I didn't recognize it.

I was frightened. I'd never taught and didn't know if I could do it. Dean Robert Coonrod of the College of Arts and Sciences, first person I met at the University, said, "The letter from Sol Katz did it." The implication was clear. I nearly didn't get the job. Good old Sol Katz.

When you are as insecure as I was that fall of 1964, everything, including Coonrod's remark, seems important, takes on some extra

dimension it shouldn't. Good things and bad things. And nearly everything happening was bad. My wife and I had grown apart in Italy. The fault was mine. I couldn't hold myself together that far from friends, that uncertain of ever finding employment again. I drank too much, sullen the last two months, walked the streets of Florence in a hopeless state of depression that bordered on psychotic withdrawal.

Bad things. Warren Carrier, my new boss, the new chairman of the English Department, said, "By the way, you're Leslie Fiedler's replacement." Jesus, God. Leslie Fiedler's replacement! One of the most famous teachers in the nation. I hadn't read a book in years. Except for books of poems. I'd never been much of a reader and didn't feel capable of analyzing anything I'd read. I was certain I'd fail.

I made the mistake of trying to teach the survey lit course as I thought someone should teach it. Hard as I worked, I'd overlooked the dictionary as a source, and one day I got hung up on the phrase, "Fierce tiger fell." A student with pointed sarcasm and obvious disdain read the possible meanings of "fell" from the dictionary aloud in front of the class. He had no idea how very close he came to driving me out of the academic world for good. I was about to apologize to the class, to explain that I wasn't qualified, was sorry I'd wasted their time, and walk out. My teaching career came that close to lasting about three weeks.

The house we intended to rent in Missoula was still occupied and typically we found a funny rundown apartment in a place called Milltown. It was in an old frame apartment building run by Goldie and Chuck Towne. Within a week Chuck Towne died. Goldie pounded on our door at 5 AM, yelling that something was wrong. He was almost gone when we got to him. I called an ambulance and tried mouth-to-mouth. I remember I had the irrelevant thought that this was the only time I'd ever kissed a man and he was dead.

There was a long, dreadful scene in the Missoula railroad station when my wife left for good. We sat and cried for hours. We had been close and it was over. The Missoula railroad station is so cheerless, you'd weep there saying goodbye to Hitler. Then she was gone and I was walking alone down Higgins Avenue, for some reason unusually aware of my shoes each step I took. Then, I was sitting in a bar near the station, tears pouring down my face, and the bartender sophisticated enough to say nothing. He'd seen drunks cry before.

I was naive about English departments and didn't understand the animosity of some of the staff. I didn't know that some professors hate you for being a poet. (Not only do I understand that very well now, I can walk into any English department and in a very short time tell you exactly who those professors are. When it comes to spotting *them*, I'm as sensitive as a candlefish.) Every rude remark, every disdainful look was magnified by my situation and my insecurities. I was on the verge of going under and I didn't know where to turn. I was drinking so heavily that my voice caught and betrayed my shaky emotional state in class. Sometimes I broke into tears.

There were kindnesses, too, and they magnified themselves. Carrier telling me he understood what I was going through and that he had enormous faith in me as a human being. Walter Brown, the Chaucerian, and his wife Mackey, having me over several times for dinner. The late Vedder Gilbert, always the gentleman, offering help in small but generous and important ways. And John Herrmann, then director of creative writing, sensing one day that I was far too upset to meet classes and sending me home, telling me not to worry, that he would cover for me.

I moved into the house in Missoula alone when it vacated. I made it clear that students were welcome, that there would always be a drink or a beer when they came by. Since the house was across the street from the school and since students were favorably disposed to free liquor, I guaranteed myself company during this lonely, empty time.

But of all good saving things from that time, one place and one group of people, one man and one woman. Across a small dirt roadway from Goldie Towne's apartments was a frame bar, the Union Milltown Bar. As I write this, I remember how I felt in those days and I hope you heard the trumpets when I put the name of that bar on the page. Trumpets, too, for Harold Herndon, the first man I met in Montana, the owner of the Union Milltown Bar.

A girl was tending bar the first time I walked in. There was one customer, and a man I took to be another who came to me, put out his hand and said, "I'm Harold Herndon. I run this bar. I'm glad you came in." He could not have picked a better time and I could not have picked a better bar. I fell in love with Harold Herndon and that bar from the very first.

Everything seemed right. The animal heads on the wall–goat and ram under plexiglass domes; the habit of the bartender to buy every fourth or fifth drink; the clientele–workers from the Bonner Mill, the railroad and the woods; the funny old tongue-in-groove lumber walls; the strange, not really good but for that bar perfect, paintings of western scenes and events–buffalo hunts, a lynching, and one man alone waving hello to anyone who might be there across the void of the uninhabited plains–oh, aren't we all, buddy, aren't we just fucking all? And isn't this the right bar, this warm, homely bar where people know that waving to be the human condition, and know it better than anyone any place else knows it?

Harold is a short man, stocky, slightly and humorously sarcastic. His face looks like that of an ex-boxer, his nose broken, his jaw firm. He sees the world as the comedy it is and, when he was about to tell me something funny about one of the customers, he preceded his story with a little laugh, a sort of half-smile, half-laugh that signalled his good-humored vision of the world was at work again. For the most part, he enjoyed the people who came in.

Harold had spent some time in an orphanage. I couldn't miss the hard life behind his eyes, the sadness. But I couldn't miss his strength either. There's something durable about him. He is a survivor, an alder tree, a catfish. Sometimes, usually when he is worried about money, his view of his fellow man gets grim. He becomes distrustful, feels people have taken advantage of him. And they have because he has been generous with them for a long time. Harold might run a tab for several weeks for a truck driver and never ask for money. Then, when feeling the pinch, usually because he'd borrowed money from a bank to "improve" the bar (I begged Harold for years to leave that beautiful place alone), he would demand that the truck driver pay him back. Often there would be a scene since Harold in his bad moments, forgets diplomacy.

Despite the kindness of Carrier, Herrmann, Gilbert and Brown, and the supportive company of Norman Meinke and Dave Smith, I did not feel I belonged in the English Department at the University. I was going back to an existence I'd known years before. I'd come from plain, naive working class (even peasant class) people, the kind of people who came into that bar, and it was in that bar I felt at home. With my wife gone, and seemingly much of my life a meaningless failure, I felt free to drink just as much as I wanted to—and that was a lot.

I suppose I felt the need to be with people who had their feet on the ground. Harold, despite his occasional flights of fancy about the bar, his dreams of turning the bar into a major enterprise, had his feet on the ground. Harold is also an engineer with the railroad and, when I first knew him, a train had derailed miles west of Missoula in the mountains. The engineer had been fired. When I asked Harold about it, he said, "Oh, shit. He was drunk." I needed those simple, factual explanations of things. They seemed very important. A down-to-earth attitude I could anchor on.

In those days a wall of tongue-in-groove lumber chopped the room off right where the bar ended. An old furnace stood against the wall. It heated the bar in the winter and the wall gave the bar a snug, comfortable feeling. To go to the bathroom, one had to go through a hinged door in the wall and make his way across a cold room furnished with booths that were seldom used. One thing I loved about the bar was that often I was the only customer, and for some reason being alone there was a good feeling.

Harold was pleased I was a poet. I think I was the first poet he ever met. One day he said, "Say. You like to write poems about ghost towns. You ought to go to Garnet."

"Where is Garnet?" I asked.

"Just go to Bearmouth and turn left." What a beautiful line. The certainty of place, the certainty that we are not lost, the certainty that the world and our lives have checkpoints with names and definite directions we can follow, the certainty.

And so the Milltown Union Bar became a home. Though I lived in Missoula, I headed east to Milltown every chance I had. I drank there so much that the telephone number was kept on file, along with my home phone number, in the English Department.

The first few months I found myself doing hateful things. For no real reason one night I became angry with a sad, embittered little mill worker named Johnson, and I started to yell at him. No real reason as I say. Just a lot of personal anger spilling over because the man bored me. "What did that guy say to you?" Esther the bartender asked. I told her I was sorry. He hadn't really said anything. In the years ahead I went out of my way to be friendly with that grizzled little man who had so little to show for his life. He was a regular and I saw him often.

But gradually I became a good heavy drinker. I took my favorite stool, drank to closing time, left quite smashed but without making a social mistake and drove home without incident. Over and over. From my favorite stool I could see myself in the mirror behind the bar. That was the man I must accept, the one I must make peace with, that big sad face in the mirror. Forty years old. Then another December 21. Forty-one years old. I'd probably never have another woman.

Though I'd had what I guess were good sexual relations with my wife, once she was gone, I was faced with my lack of experience. I had found my sexual adjustment with her and, in the thirteen years we were together, I had cheated but once, and that had been virtually inadvertent (I wasn't looking for anything at the time) and a dismal failure. In the bar of a small restaurant in Missoula, called The Shack, I tried to pick up the bartender one night. She was from Dillon, an attractive enough woman, but my conversation turned her cold. It came to me that I didn't know how to do this, I was making a fool of myself, and I left half a drink on the bar and went home.

No. The Milltown Union Bar was where I belonged, alone or with Harold, or with Jennie his wife who often tended bar, or with Gene Jarvis from the mill who howled with animal pleasure when he felt his booze, or with Guy Weimer with his loud declamatory way of conversing with you and the whole bar at the same time ("Jesus Christ! The Goddam fishing isn't worth a shit this year."), or with friendless Johnson who mumbled the very little he had to say. But mostly alone. The sky could pour east forever.

Fred Miller is a man people like when they see him. He is very good looking, a bit like Tyrone Power, but he has built into his face the look of a mildly mischievious boy who, like W. S. Merwin, is making it through life without the need or desire to use his intelligence, thank you. When you see Fred Miller, you feel better about things. When you talk to Fred Miller, you feel better about things. That Fred Miller is so instantly likeable probably saved his life.

Fred tended bar now and then for Harold. One cold night during a hard winter a mill worker named Scott came into the Milltown Union Bar. It was late, after 1:00 AM, and the only other person in the bar was Fred's wife. Scott ordered a beer and exchanged a few words with Fred. As Fred turned to the cash register, Scott said, "You're a nice guy, Fred." Those were surely the most important words Fred has ever heard. When he turned back to give Scott the change, Scott was pointing a pistol at him.

Fred gave Scott the money, about 140 dollars, and Scott took off in his car while Fred called the cops. Scott raced to Missoula and headed south on Higgins Avenue. The broadcast had gone out and a Missoula policeman named Doug Chase heard it up Pattee Canyon where he was parked. When Scott's car, which seemed to fit the description, approached, Chase stopped it and radioed back to the station. He was instructed to wait for help which was on the way.

Doug Chase is probably the nicest cop in town, maybe in any town. He spends much time talking to school children because his role on the police force involves public relations work. Like a lot of nice people, he tends to trust humanity. He ignored his instructions and walked towards Scott's car, and Scott shot him in the stomach and took off up Pattee Canyon. The road brought Scott to the Clark Fork River where there was no bridge. In the zero weather, ice and snow, Scott swam the river. He was back in the Milltown area where he had started.

Fred was home by now, and when he heard over the radio that Scott had shot a cop, he realized Scott had been quite capable of pulling the trigger earlier in the bar. Fred imagined that Scott knew where he, Fred, lived, and he sat rigid in his kitchen with a shotgun waiting for Scott to come through the door. Though Fred's fear had obviously excited his imagination, and blurred his logic, in fact, Scott was close. Fred lived near the river where Scott had crossed in the freezing night.

At four that morning, Scott phoned the police from the Bonner Railroad station, a small building a quarter of a mile to the east of the bar on the tracks that pass close to the bar. He was freezing to death, he said, and would they come to get him. That night he slept soundly in the warm jail. The next day he didn't ask how Doug Chase was doing in the hospital.

One of the troubles with Freshmen in the comp class, I found, is that they feel they have little to write about. I got Carrier to authorize 50 dollars for Fred to talk to my class. That should give them all something to think about. Fred never showed. When I asked him why he hadn't—it seemed such an easy 50 dollars for less than an hour—he said he was too shy to talk in front of an audience.

Bill Stafford talks about the bonuses of life, things life gives us that trigger and fit into poems. I was drinking at the Milltown one afternoon when a crusty old man approached. He had been living in a cabin out somewhere in the remote countryside and the cabin had burned down leaving him homeless. Harold gave the man free lodging upstairs over the bar. Like many Montanans, the man, who had never seen me before, immediately started talking about his personal life. In Montana, many people assume that with the scarce population, 735,000 people in a state bigger in area than any except California, Texas, and Alaska, loneliness is the norm and when you meet someone else you have license to speak intimately simply because you are two people in a lonely, nearly uninhabited landscape. This luckless man whom Harold had befriended gave me one of Stafford's bonuses, a great opening line for a poem. The first thing he said was "Harold knew I'd been burned out in the valley." It was too good. I never could do a thing with it. I mentioned this to a class at the University of Washington years later and a young poet named Jim Matsui picked up the line and used it in a poem.

One night I was the only customer, sinking into the soft warm light of my new home, and feeling the soft warmth of the cold stinging bourbon, when two young men walked in, one in his late twenties, the other in his mid thirties. Dale Paulsen was bartending.

The older man was fat and had a long, large nose that ran out of rigidity toward the tip. It wobbled and looked false. He sat one stool away from me and started to talk. He was terribly funny. The younger man played the electric slot machine.

The fat man broke us up, Dale and me. It seemed impossible that he couldn't have made it as a professional comedian. Not only was his patter hilarious, he was inherently funny as the great comics are. Perhaps it was his looks, his girth, and that unusual nose. Neither of us had ever seen the men before. During a lull the fat man asked me the direction to Drummond and how far it was. The young man hit the slot machine for 12 dollars in free games and Dale paid him off out of the register.

Then the younger man sat with us while the older man played the machine, which was down the bar toward the door. The younger man was more conventional looking. He had a round face and dark hair. His conversation was usual too. The fat man lost about five dollars to the electric slot machine.

They traded places again. Now the fat man really turned it on. What a funny man and how odd that anyone this entertaining would come to this out-of-the-way bar. It was as if a traveling show had gotten off course. The young man hit the machine again, this time for 27 dollars, and Dale paid him and they left. The next day Harold found the hole drilled in the machine, where the young man had inserted the thin steel rod that kept free games already won from subtracting while they were being played on the machine.

"They asked the way to Drummond," I told Harold after he muttered things about relative intelligences of bartenders he had employed.

"Sure," Harold said glumly, "and the bastards laughed all the way to Great Falls."

I tried other bars of course and enjoyed them, but never like the Milltown. That was love, love of home, love of the possibility that even if my life would never again change for the better, at least there, in that unpretentious watering hole that trembled when the Vista Dome North Coast Limited roared by, I could live inside myself warm in fantasies, or chat with honest people who were neither afraid nor ashamed of their responses to life. It wasn't the worst way to be.

Often friends went there with me, Dave and Annick Smith, Jim Welch, and later, Lois Welch. Alone or with friends, the charm of the place seldom failed me.

I wish the following had happened in the Milltown because it and that bar deserve each other. But it happened at the Double Front, in Missoula, owned by Harold's brother Gene. That bar is gone now. Gene sold his liquor license and retained only the restaurant where he sells chicken and shrimp.

It was there that one night drinking alone I felt a hand on my face and whirled around, angry. It was an old woman next to me. She said, "Don't be mad, Mister. I just wanted to touch your face." I fell all over myself covering up, told her it was alright, that I understood.

I was in love less than two years after I started going to the Milltown, and I don't mean with just the bar. I was smack in the middle of a love affair and I was happy. But, although I intended to ask the woman to marry me, two children and all, I still couldn't shake the remorse of my divorce. I got that February, 1966. It was a breeze. I charged desertion and my wife in Seattle didn't respond or contest. So on February 10, 1966 at 1:56 PM an old judge signed the decree and said, "You are no longer obligated to this person," and I wanted to say, "How in the hell do you know, you old fart?" But I thanked him, took note of the time because it seemed like a dramatic moment in my life, and went outside and sat on a bench and cried for a while. I was never very good at letting things go.

No offense to my wife, now ex-wife, but that affair in '65-'66 was easily the best sex I'd had or would have for several years after. I couldn't believe how passionate it was nor how very easy it seemed each morning when she would drop by on her way to school–she was a graduate student–and we would spend an hour in the sack. I'd never been that good before. My timidity vanished completely.

But I was hard at the booze. Not that she was a model of sobriety. And I still held much affection for my ex-wife. My sentimentality wouldn't vanish despite the sexual satisfaction. What the hell, nearly fourteen years of a marriage where we had been unusually intimate and close even for man and wife, fourteen years of helping each other like man and wife, brother and sister, over some very rough terrain, those years didn't just go away even if I was very much in love now. It was love but it came at the wrong time and I blew it.

I got too drunk too often. I slobbered about my sad moments I had known in my marriage, leaving my lover to feel that I still loved my wife. I made too many demands when I got drunk, a sort of test I was putting my new love through to see if she really loved me because, after all those hours staring in the mirror at the Milltown, I still hadn't decided if that was the face of a man who could be loved. Finally, she took off when school was out in the spring of '66 and I spent the most depressing summer of my life.

Where had she gone? No word. I sat in the Milltown day after warm day, sullen, certain now that the face in the mirror was that of a man who deserved no love, and who would find none. It would have been easier if school had been in session. I had come to love teaching. It was the only job I'd ever had that I took seriously, and the affection I felt for students, and often could feel coming back in the classroom, was a salvation in those days. But this was summer and I had nothing to do but drink and stare at that loveless man in the glass.

When my ex-lover came back married in September, everyone knew about it but me. Finally, a grad student named Lahey came to my house and told me. My first reaction was to make an Alka Seltzer and drink it–my hand shook when I raised the glass–and to announce bitterly that I would never get entangled with another woman as long as I lived.

The next two weeks were ridiculous, but only in retrospect. I locked myself in the house for eight days because I broke into sobbing so suddenly and so frequently, I feared being in public. I wrote silly letters to friends and even people I didn't know. I declared a desire to die in my sleep. Richard Howard wrote back and said, correctly, that he thought I was fooling myself. David Wagoner did too and added, "What would W. C. Fields say to all this?"

It wasn't the loss of the woman, I realized afterward, that drove me to such absurd behavior. It was the fear that I was losing everything, that given my shrimpy sexual history, my timidity with most women, the ease with which I could return to my fantasies, there was a very good chance I would never have a woman again. That even if I could have, I might very well revert to an old self, the man who invited rejection and then retreated to his "cave of sorrow" to stare out jealously at the world of assumed normalcy.

I was bitter. For a short while I thought I'd kill her. How silly can you get? Then, a long period of resolve. It seemed that I had been treated rotten by women all my life. And it seemed that at my age I had to admit that either I was someone who deserved it or I wasn't, that I was either a shit or a good man. And if I was a good man, why then screw them. If there were to be any tears from now on, they would not be mine. All this infantile reasoning required sustenance with booze, of course. I wrote a poem called "The Lady in Kicking Horse Reservoir." That was as close to direct vengeance as I'd come. Earlier that year, after she had first disappeared for the summer, I wrote a poem called "Degrees of Gray in Philipsburg," anticipating the struggle I might have to go through, anticipating that I might never experience kisses like hers for years to come. "The last good kiss/you had was years ago." If a poet is supposed to suffer for his art, I felt I deserved at least the Nobel Prize.

By now Harold had the back wall torn out, the furnace replaced by a new one buried under the building, and the old booths replaced by new booths and plastic tables with chairs. This was the first big improvement. I fought Harold, though not significantly since it was his bar, on every one of them. "Stop," I pleaded. "Don't improve anything. This is a wonderful bar just as it is." But Harold is a determined man. "I'll get the overflow crowd from East Missoula if I fix this place up," he announced.

She came back to school without her husband who would visit when he could. His work kept him in Wyoming and she wanted to finish her degree. The day she came to see me we were in the middle of a melodramatic conversation when Kenneth Hanson called from Portland to tell me he'd won the Lamont Prize. It was good news and it was good coming in from the outside.

The Milltown Union Bar

for Harold Herndon

(Laundromat & Café)
You could love here, not the lovely goat
in plexiglass nor the elk shot
in the middle of a joke, but honest drunks,
crossed swords above the bar, three men hung
in the bad painting, others riding off
on the phony green horizon. The owner,
fresh from orphan wars, loves too
but bad as you. He keeps improving things
but can't cut the bodies down.

You need never leave. Money or a story
brings you booze. The elk is grinning
and the goat says go so tenderly
you hear him through the glass. If you weep
deer heads weep. Sing and the orphanage
announces plans for your release. A train
goes by and ditches jump. You were nothing
going in and now you kiss your hand.

When mills shut down, when the worst drunk
says finally I'm stone, three men still hang
painted badly from a leafless tree, you
one of them, brains tied behind your back,
swinging for your sin. Or you swing
with goats and elk. Doors of orphanages
finally swing out and here you open in.

West Marginal Way

One tug pounds to haul an afternoon
of logs up river. The shade
of Pigeon Hill across the bulges
in the concrete crawls on reeds
in a short field, cools a pier

and the violence of young men
after cod. The crackpot chapel,
with a sign erased by rain, returned
before to calm and a mossed roof.

A dim wind blows the roses
growing where they please. Lawns
are wild and lots are undefined
as if the payment made in cash
were counted then and there.

These names on boxes will return
with salmon money in the fall,
come drunk down the cinder arrow
of a trail, past the store of Popich,
sawdust piles and the saw mill
bombing air with optimistic sparks,
blinding gravel pits and the brickyard
baking, to wives who taught themselves
the casual thirst of many summers
wet in heat and taken by the sea.

Some places are forever afternoon.
Across the road and a short field
there is the river, split and yellow
and this far down affected by the tide.

The Squatter on Company Land

We had to get him off, the dirty elf—
wild hair and always screaming at his wife
and due to own our land in two more years—
a mud flat point along the river
where we planned our hammer shop.
Him, his thousand rabbits, the lone goat
tied to his bed, his menial wife: all out.

To him, a rainbow trail of oil might mean
a tug upstream, a boom, a chance a log
would break away and float to his lasso.

He'd destroy the owner's mark and bargain
harshly with the mill. He'd weep and yell
when salmon runs went by, rolling
to remind him he would never cheat the sea.

When did life begin? Began with running
from a hatchet some wild woman held,
her hair a gray cry in alfalfa
where he dug and cringed? Began in rain
that cut the light into religious shafts?
Or just began the way all hurt begins–
hit and dropped, the next man always righteous
and the last one climbing with a standard tongue?

In his quick way, swearing at us pressed
against the fence, he gathered rags and wood
and heaped them in the truck and told his wife
"Get in," and rode away, a solid glare
that told us we were dying in his eye.

Galileo's Chair

In gold light here a small guard
warns me not to cross the velvet chain
or climb the stairs that might break down
beneath my modern bulk. Galileo's telescope
was not the first but first toward
the sky. The milky way's not milk
and Venus circles in and out of light.

Take air away and even fire falls–
a voice through this tan air, across
these tiers, seducing men to think.
Star without parallax, he measured time
by weight, like men, and moons of Jupiter
were cause for wine. Sagredo warned
of Roman hate so heavy it can crack
the latest lens. No Pope honors proof
we move about the sun. God is weight
enough to bend an unrecanting knee.

He may be wrong. The sun may circle men.
The stairs might hold me but his chair,
inelegant and worn, is the odd star
fixed beyond my chain. The brown wood
turns this hall a darker brown
each year. We'll give in too and air
will darken in Peking. Outside, pigeons
called by bells of Padova
to fan about a tower, highest point
for miles, the first and last to catch
the sun, won't fly or will fly blind.

I never cross the chain. The small guard
tries to talk but my Italian's stuck.
Was the dungeon black? The one he went to
when he'd lied to God, and where he said
eppur si muove and it did.

Spinazzola: Quella Cantina Là

A field of wind gave license for defeat.
I can't explain. The grass bent. The wind
seemed full of men but without hate or fame.
I was farther than that farm where the road
slants off to nowhere, and the field I'm sure
is in this wine or that man's voice. The man
and this canteen were also here
twenty years ago and just as old.

Hate for me was dirt until I woke up
five miles over Villach in a smoke
that shook my tongue. Here, by accident,
the wrong truck, I came back to the world.
This canteen is home-old. A man can walk
the road outside without a song or gun.
I can't explain the wind. The field is east
toward the Adriatic from my wine.

I'd walked from cruel soil to a trout
for love but never from a bad sky

to a field of wind I can't explain.
The drone of bombers going home
made the weather warm. My uniform
turned foreign where the olive trees
throw silver to each other down the hill.

Olive leaves were silver I could spend.
Say wind I can't explain. That field is vital
and the Adriatic warm. Don't our real friends
tell us when we fail? Don't honest fields
reveal us in their winds? Planes and men
once tumbled but the war went on absurd.
I can't explain the wine. This crude bench
and rough table and that flaking plaster–
most of all the long nights make this home.

Home's always been a long way from a friend.
I mix up things, the town, the wind, the war.
I can't explain the drone. Bombers seemed
to scream toward the target, on the let-down
hum. My memory is weak from bombs.
Say I dropped them bad with shaking sight.
Call me German and my enemy the air.

Clouds are definite types. High ones, cirrus.
Cumulus, big fluffy kind, and if with rain,
also nimbus. Don't fly into them.
I can't explain. Somewhere in a gray ball
wind is killing. I forgot the stratus
high and thin. I forget my field
of wind, out there east between
the Adriatic and my second glass of wine.

I'll find the field. I'll go feeble down
the road strung gray like spoiled wine
in the sky. A sky too clear of cloud
is fatal. Trust the nimbus. Trust dark clouds
to rain. I can't explain the sun. The man
will serve me wine until a bomber fleet
lost twenty years comes droning home.

I can't explain. Outside, on the road
that leaves the town reluctantly,
way out the road's a field of wind.

Silver Star

for Bill Kittredge

This is the final resting place of engines,
farm equipment and that rare, never more
than occasional man. Population:
17. Altitude: unknown. For no
good reason you can guess, the woman
in the local store is kind. Old steam trains
have been rusting here so long, you feel
the urge to oil them, to lay new track, to start
the west again. The Jefferson
drifts by in no great hurry on its way
to wed the Madison, to be a tributary
of the ultimately dirty brown Missouri.
This town supports your need to run alone.

What if you'd lived here young, gone full of fear
to that stark brick school, the cruel teacher
supported by your guardian? Think well
of the day you ran away to Whitehall.
Think evil of the cop who found you starving
and returned you, siren open, to the house
you cannot find today. You question
everyone you see. The answer comes back wrong.
There was no house. They never heard your name.

When you leave here, leave in a flashy car
and wave goodbye. You are a stranger
every day. Let the engines and the farm
equipment die, and know that rivers
end and never end, lose and never lose
their famous names. What if your first girl
ended certain she was animal, barking

at the aides and licking floors? You know
you have no answers. The empty school
burns red in heavy snow.

Missoula Softball Tournament

This summer, most friends out of town
and no wind playing flash and dazzle
in the cottonwoods, music of the Clark Fork stale,
I've gone back to the old ways of defeat,
the softball field, familiar dust and thud,
pitcher winging drops and rises, and wives,
the beautiful wives in the stands, basic, used,
screeching runners home, infants unattended
in the dirt. A long triple sails into right center.
Two men on. Shouts from dugout: go, Ron, go.
Life is better run from. Distance to the fence,
both foul lines and dead center, is displayed.

I try to steal the tricky manager's signs.
Is hit-and-run the pulling of the ear?
The ump gives pitchers too much low inside.
Injustice? Fraud? Ancient problems focus
in the heat. Bad hop on routine grounder.
Close play missed by the team you want to win.
Players from the first game, high on beer,
ride players in the field. Their laughter
falls short of the wall. Under lights, the moths
are momentary stars, and wives, the beautiful wives
in the stands now take the interest they once feigned,
oh, long ago, their marriage just begun, years
of helping husbands feel important just begun,
the scrimping, the anger brought home evenings
from degrading jobs. This poem goes out to them.
Is steal-of-home the touching of the heart?
Last pitch. A soft fly. A can of corn
the players say. Routine, like mornings,
like the week. They shake hands on the mound.
Nice grab on that shot to left. Good game. Good game.
Dust rotates in their headlight beams.
The wives, the beautiful wives are with their men.

What Thou Lovest Well Remains American

You remember the name was Jensen. She seemed old
always alone inside, face pasted gray to the window,
and mail never came. Two blocks down, the Grubskis
went insane. George played rotten trombone
Easter when they flew the flag. Wild roses
remind you the roads were gravel and vacant lots
the rule. Poverty was real, wallet and spirit,
and each day slow as church. You remember threadbare
church groups on the corner, howling their faith
at stars, and the violent Holy Rollers
renting that barn for their annual violent sing
and the barn burned down when you came back from war.
Knowing the people you knew then are dead,
you try to believe these roads paved are improved,
the neighbors, moved in while you were away, good-looking,
their dogs well fed. You still have need
to remember lots empty and fern.
Lawns well trimmed remind you of the train
your wife took one day forever, some far empty town,
the odd name you never recall. The time: 6:23.
The day: October 9. The year remains a blur.
You blame this neighborhood for your failure.
In some vague way, the Grubskis degraded you
beyond repair. And you know you must play again
and again Mrs. Jensen pale at her window, must hear
the foul music over the good slide of traffic.
You loved them well and they remain, still with nothing
to do, no money and no will. Loved them, and the gray
that was their disease you carry for extra food
in case you're stranded in some odd empty town
and need hungry lovers for friends, and need feel
you are welcome in the secret club they have formed.

Letter to Hill from St. Ignatius

Dear Bobbi: God, it's cold. Unpredicted, of course, by forecast,
snow and bitter air drove in from Canada while we, some
students and I, were planning a weekend fishing trip

to Rainbow Lake where, just last week, five of us in four
hours took 44 trout. For all I know that lake is frozen tight,
the trout dormant under the ice for the next five months.
We are shut down. This is a quiet town on the Flathead
Reservation, the staggering Mission Range just beyond,
the mission itself of local historical fame. A priest
some 80 years back designed a ceremony for Good
Friday, Indian-Catholic, complete with Flathead chants
in dialect. It's lovely. This early sudden cold I think
of it, how it reminds me of simple times that no doubt
never were, the unified view of man, all that. I wept
the first time I saw it, the beleaguered Indians wailing
the priest to Stations of the Cross. The pall bearers bearing Christ
outside around fires and crying the weird tongue stark
through the night. Bobbi, I don't mind those real old days broke
down.
We had (still have) too many questions. You've known embittering
winds
in Green Bay and you are not bitter for all the license
they gave. I resent you once told me how I'd never know
what being Indian was like. All poets do. Including the
blacks. It is knowing whatever bond we find we find
in strange tongues. You won't believe this but after my grim years
alone, a woman who loves me has come along. And she
chants when she talks in the strangest of tongues, the human.
I take her in my arms and don't feel strange. She is tall
and she curls in bed like a cat. And so, like Indians,
I chant the old days back to life and she chants me alive.
It's snowing, Bobbi. The flakes seem heavy and they fall hard
as hail. I claim they ring like bells. And sure enough the far
cathedral complements my claim. Chant to me in your poems
of our loss and let the poem itself be our gain. You're gaining
the hurt world worth having. Friend, let me be Indian. Dick.

With Ripley At the Grave of Albert Parenteau

He is twice blessed, the old one buried here
beneath two names and a plastic bouquet from Choteau.
He lived his grief out full. From this hill
where Crees bury their dead to give them a view,

he can study the meadow, the mountains
back of mountains, the Teton canyon winding into stone.
I want to say something wrong,
say, this afternoon they are together again,
he and the wife he killed by mistake in the dark
and she forgives him. I don't want to admit
it's cold alone in the ground and a cold run
from Canada with a dog and two bottles of rye.

Say he counted stones along the bottom of the Teton
and the stones counted him one of them.
He scrubbed and scrubbed and never could
rid his floor of her stain.
He smashed his radio and the outside world
that came from it, and something like a radio hum
went on in him the slow rest of his life.
This is the first time I knew his white name.

We won't bring him real flowers this afternoon
jammed with the glitter of lupin and harebells.
This is the west and depth is horizontal.
We climb for a good view of canyons and we are never
higher than others, never a chief like him.
His grave is modern. His anguish goes back–
the first tone from struck rock. You and I,
we're civilized. We can't weep when it's needed or counts.
If you die first, I'll die slow as Big Bear,
my pale days thin with age,
night after night, the stars callow as children.

White Center

Town or poem, I don't care how it looks. Old woman
take my hand and we'll walk one more time these streets
I believed marked me weak beneath catcalling clouds.
Long ago, the swamp behind the single row of stores
was filled and seeded. Roses today where Toughy Hassin
slapped my face to the grinning delight of his gang.
I didn't cry or run. Had I fought him

I'd have been beaten and come home bloody in tears
and you'd have told me I shouldn't be fighting.

Wasn't it all degrading, mean Mr. Kyte sweeping
the streets for no pay, believing what he'd learned
as a boy in England: 'This is your community'?
I taunted him to rage, then ran. Is this the day
we call bad mothers out of the taverns and point them
sobbing for home, or issue costumes to posturing clowns
in the streets, make fun of drunk barbers, and hope
someone who left and made it returns, vowed
to buy more neon and give these people some class?

The Dugans aren't worth a dime, dirty Irish, nor days
you offered a penny for every fly I killed.
You were blind to my cheating. I saw my future certain–
that drunk who lived across the street and fell
in our garden reaching for the hoe you dropped.
All he got was our laughter. I helped him often home
when you weren't looking. I loved some terrible way
he lived in his mind and tried to be decent to others.
I loved the way we loved him behind our disdain.

Clouds. What glorious floating. They always move on
like I should have early. But your odd love and a war
taught me the world's gone evil past the first check point
and that's First Avenue South. I fell asleep each night
safe in love with my murder. The neighbor girl
plotted to tease every tomorrow and watch me turn
again to the woods and games too young for my age.
We never could account for the python cousin Warren
found half starved in the basement of Safeway.

It all comes back but in bites. I am the man
you beat to perversion. That was the drugstore MacCameron
flipped out in early one morning, waltzing
on his soda fountain. The siren married his shrieking.
His wife said, "We'll try again, in Des Moines."
You drove a better man into himself where he found tunes
he had no need to share. It's all beginning to blur
as it forms. Men cracking up or retreating.
Resolute women deep in hard prayer.

And it isn't the same this time. I hoped forty years
I'd write and would not write this poem. This town would die
and your grave never reopen. Or mine. Because I'm married
and happy, and across the street a foster child
from a cruel past is safe and need no longer crawl
for his meals, I walk this past with you, ghost in any field
of good crops, certain I remember everything wrong.
If not, why is this road lined thick with fern
and why do I feel no shame kicking the loose gravel home?

Glen Uig

Believe in this couple this day who come
to picnic in the Faery Glen. They pay rain
no matter, or wind. They spread their picnic
under a gale-stunted rowan. Believe they grew tired
of giants and heroes and know they believe
in wise tiny creatures who live under the rocks.

Believe these odd mounds, the geologic joke
played by those wise tiny creatures far from
the world's pitiful demands: make money, stay sane.
Believe the couple, by now soaked to the skin,
sing their day as if dry, as if sheltered inside
Castle Ewen. Be glad Castle Ewen's only a rock
that looks like a castle. Be glad for no real king.

These wise tiny creatures, you'd better believe,
have lived through it all: the Viking occupation,
clan torturing clan, the Clearances, the World War
II bomber gone down, a fiery boom
on Beinn Edra. They saw it from here. They heard
the sobs of last century's crofters trail off below
where every day the Conon sets out determined for Uig.
They remember the Viking who wandered off course,
under the hazelnut tree hating aloud all he'd done.

Some days dance in the bracken. Some days go out
wide and warm on bad roads to collect the dispossessed
and offer them homes. Some days celebrate addicts

sweet in their dreams and hope to share with them
a personal spectrum. The loch here's only a pond,
the monster is in it small as a wren.

Believe the couple who have finished their picnic
and make wet love in the grass, the wise tiny creatures
cheering them on. Believe in milestones, the day
you left home forever and the cold open way
a world wouldn't let you come in. Believe you
and I are that couple. Believe you and I sing tiny
and wise and could if we had to eat stone and go on.

The Right Madness on Skye

Now I'm dead, load what's left on the wagon
and have the oxen move on. Tell absentee landlord driver,
Harry of Nothingham, slow. I want my last minutes on earth
filled with this island. For a long time
my days were nothing. My remarkable late surge
I attribute to fanciful chefs: cloud in the salad.
My dramatic reversal of fate insists on this will
read aloud in this poem this day of my death.
Have the oxen move on. Tell Harry of Nothingham, slow.

Take my body to Kilmuir cemetery and adorn
according to instructions. Don't forget the mint.
Carve any lines you want on my stone. If mine
double check spelling. I'm dumb. And triple check
high birds. Bring them down and make them state their names.
If none says 'Rhododendron' you know they're fakes.
Throw them out. Give the piper and drum five minutes
and explain to them, dead, I tire fast.
Have the oxen move on. Tell Harry of Nothingham, slow.

Alive, I often wounded my knee begging response.
My turn to put out. I will one eye to the blind of Dunvegan.
I will one ear to deaf salmon climbing the Conon.
And to the mute ocean I leave this haphazard tongue.
You might note on my stone in small letters:
Here lies one who believed all others his betters.

I didn't really, but what a fun thing to say.
And it's fun to be dead with one eye open in case
that stuck-up twitch in Arizona mourns my loss.

Toot, toot, lovers. Now that I'm moving ahead
you eagerly line the roadside to cheer these remains.
Some say, first, get rid of the body. Not me.
I say let the corpse dance. Make the living lie still.
I told you before, five minutes for piper and drum.
I leave vivid instructions and no one, no one listens.
Let's try it once more. I'm dead. I want to milk that wild
for all it's worth to the crowd already turning away.
Have the oxen move on. Tell Harry of Nothingham, slow.

By now you're no doubt saying, "We've got you to rights.
You can't write a poem from the grave."
Remember, I'm not buried. Only cold on the slab.
There's a hell of a difference between being stiff
from rigor mortis and being held rigid by peat.
Harry of Nothingham knows. Don't you, Harry old chap?
And oxen aren't as dumb as you think. Just because
I've no religion don't say heaven can't welcome me back
under the new majority quota now in effect.

Don't back up for cars. Clear the road for the dead.
Cry 'Fat bag of bones coming through.' I heard that note.
I told you, no trumpets. I told you, five minutes, no more
for piper and drum. Who's mouthing that organ for nothing?
Who's humming along and stamping the right time?
That's the wrong madness for Skye, I say. Wrong
for dispossessed crofters who didn't want me to die
and wrong for comedians waiting for final returns.
Have the oxen move on. Tell Harry of Nothingham, slow.

It's a long road that has no break in the blacktop.
It's a crock to say it. Are they really preparing a speech?
He was this, he was that, lies about me over
the open dirt? If so, have the oxen reverse.
Bring Harry of Nothingham back. I was rotten
in Denmark long before something caught the boat,
and I'm still non grata in Venice. Everytime I level

the piper and drum drown me out.
Have the oxen move on. Tell Harry of Nothingham, slow.

If I'm allowed to digress this way, take me on tour.
What the hell. The hole that's waiting can wait.
I want a last look at Seattle and the way light
subtracts and adds miles to the journey.
And I want to ride again the road on the upper Rha.
If you've got a map you think I'm skipping about.
Listen. All places are near and far selves neighbors.
That wouldn't set well with scholars. Don't tell Harry.
Bury my wounded knee at Flodigarry.

Are we on course again? Good. Isle of Skye, right?
This the day of my death. Only feigned tears, like I ordered.
Make sure the flowers are plastic. Five minutes, remember,
piper and drum. Tell the nearly no mourners remaining
I was easy to mix up with weather. The weather
goes on. Me too, but right now in a deadly stiff line.
Tell the laird who tricked me into being a crofter
I never worked hard in my life except on a poem.
Have the oxen move on. Tell Harry of Nothingham, slow.

Tell Harry of Nothingham stop and have the oxen relax,
I want off at the crossroads. That's far as I go.
I was holding my breath all the time. Didn't I fool you?
Come on, admit it—that blue tone I faked on my skin—
these eyes I kept closed tight in this poem.
Here's the right madness on Skye. Take five days
for piper and drum and tell the oxen, start dancing.
Mail Harry of Nothingham home to his nothing.
Take my word. It's been fun.

Making Certain It Goes On

At last the Big Blackfoot river
has risen high enough to again cover the stones
dry too many months. Trout return
from summer harbor deep in the waters
of the power company dam. High on the bank

where he knows the river won't reach
the drunk fisherman tries to focus on
a possible strike, and tries to ignore
the hymn coming from the white frame church.
The stone he leans against, bleached out dull gray,
underwater looked beautiful and blue.
The young minister had hoped for a better parish,
say one with bells that sound gold
and a congregation that doesn't stop coming
when the mill shuts down.

We love to imagine
a giant bull trout or a lunker rainbow
will grab the drunk fisherman's bait
and shock the drunk fisherman out
of his recurrent afternoon dream and into
the world of real sky and real water.
We love to imagine the drought has ended,
the high water will stay, the excess
irrigate crops, the mill reopen, the workers
go back to work, lovers reassume plans
to be married. One lover, also the son
of the drunk fisherman, by now asleep
on the bank for no trout worth imagining
has come, will not invite his father
to the happy occasion though his father
will show up sober and properly dressed,
and the son will no longer be sure of the source
of the shame he has always rehearsed.

Next summer the river will recede,
the stones bleach out to
their dullest possible shade. The fisherman
will slide bleary down the bank
and trade in any chance he has of getting
a strike for some old durable dream,
a dream that will keep out the hymn
coming again from the church. The workers
will be back full shift. The power company
will lower the water in the dam
to make repairs, make repairs and raise rates.

The drunk fisherman will wait for the day
his son returns, divorced and bitter
and swearing revenge on what the old man
has come to believe is only water
rising and falling on climatic schedule.

That summer came and is gone. And everything
we predicted happened, including the death
of the fisherman. We didn't mention that before,
but we knew and we don't lie to look good.
We didn't forsee the son would never return.

This brings us to us, and our set lines
set deep on the bottom. We're going all out
for the big ones. A new technology
keeps the water level steady year round.
The company dam is self cleaning.
In this dreamy summer air you and I
dreamily plan a statute commemorating
the unknown fisherman. The stone will bear
no inscription and that deliberate anonymity
will start enough rumors to keep
the mill operating, big trout nosing the surface,
the church reforming white frame
into handsome blue stone, and this community
going strong another hundred years.

Degrees of Gray in Philipsburg

You might come here Sunday on a whim.
Say your life broke down. The last good kiss
you had was years ago. You walk these streets
laid out by the insane, past hotels
that didn't last, bars that did, the tortured try
of local drivers to accelerate their lives.
Only churches are kept up. The jail
turned 70 this year. The only prisoner
is always in, not knowing what he's done.

The principal supporting business now
is rage. Hatred of the various grays
the mountain sends, hatred of the mill,
The Silver Bill repeal, the best liked girls
who leave each year for Butte. One good
restaurant and bars can't wipe the boredom out.
The 1907 boom, eight going silver mines,
a dance floor built on springs—
all memory resolves itself in gaze,
in panoramic green you know the cattle eat
or two stacks high above the town,
two dead kilns, the huge mill in collapse
for fifty years that won't fall finally down.

Isn't this your life? That ancient kiss
still burning out your eyes? Isn't this defeat
so accurate, the church bell simply seems
a pure announcement: ring and no one comes?
Don't empty houses ring? Are magnesium
and scorn sufficient to support a town,
not just Philipsburg, but towns
of towering blondes, good jazz and booze
the world will never let you have
until the town you came from dies inside?

Say no to yourself. The old man, twenty
when the jail was built, still laughs
although his lips collapse. Someday soon,
he says, I'll go to sleep and not wake up.
You tell him no. You're talking to yourself.
The car that brought you here still runs.
The money you buy lunch with,
no matter where it's mined, is silver
and the girl who serves your food
is slender and her red hair lights the wall.

■ SANDRA ALCOSSER

Sandra Alcosser grew up in Indiana and attended college at Lake Forest Academy and Purdue. She received the M.F.A. degree from the University of Montana in Missoula, where she studied with Richard Hugo. Alcosser taught in the Montana Poetry in the Schools program in 1977 and is currently the director of the Creative Writing Program at the University of California at San Diego. These poems are from her first book, A Fish to Feed All Hunger, *which won the Associated Writing Program's Poetry Award in 1986.*

The Entomologist's Landscape

I go the circuit of my enclosure over and over again.
HENRI FABRE

He picks through the couch grass, here a black-eared
chat on its nest of blue eggs, and there in the red clay
a natterjack bathes its warty back. Henri crouches,
like a scarab in his yellow jacket, and waits.

His son, Little Paul, keeps a birdcage full of peacock moths,
all male. Downstairs a female slips off her pale cocoon
and stands shivering. Wet fur, maroon and white.
On her wings, enormous chestnut eyes. Henri carries her
in a bell jar from room to room. At night he and Little Paul
turn the suitors loose. They storm through the cypress
to the laboratory where they beat against
the white gauze bell.

When the bait is right, anything can find you.
I look across the river this morning where last I saw a grizzly
batting swollen salmon. A large man stands in a thicket
of raspberries, waving. He wears a tweed jacket
and patent leather boots. Perhaps it is the cottonwood bud
I smashed, dabbed behind my ear like bloody perfume.

Mother's gone off to Maine in search of a secret island.
She will gather lobster, rub their green bellies so they hum
as they enter boiling water. On the leeward side
she will meet a Rockefeller who mows his own

boulder-dense lawn. If I stay in one place too long,
grow my hair like a banner, and for the hummingbirds
hang out a red begonia, whose secret island will I be?

Other than the muscular man, only one person comes.
An old painter with a reducing lens, she grades
the landscape: the mountains are a bookcase
full of shale and lichen, the trapezoidal lightning,
the air that tastes of grape jam. By all standards,
she says, we are sublime.

I myself prefer small scenes. I would have liked Henri.
We could have spent the day together on our hands and knees,
year after year the same weed lot, studying the digger wasp
as she squeezed a wild bee to her breast, then turned
to lick honey from its gasping tongue.

Fox Fire

Once I thought we would know everything,
that's what this was for, this fox fire,
this fragrant energy like nighthawks
screaming at dusk.

All winter I stalked elk that were down
from the mountain and starving.
I walked the low places where they galloped
through slush, the rocks where they wallowed
and pawed for new grasses, the tooth marks
on aspen, the mineral lick, the creek
where the water was roiled and milky.
I sweated through immovable snow
and fell down exhausted, but when I imagined
I'd stand in a thicket, my eyes glazed over,
my sharp breath, and know the cold
communion of elk, I was wrong.

Once I thought we were all gods
blessed and strutting this lovely planet.
The earth was a minor passing, like the path

down to our ditch for water, pretty
with serviceberry, but transient.
As a young girl I swung upside down
with other girls as we hung by our heels
from a jungle gym and contemplated heaven.
It was a silky place. I preferred
purgatory, like a dark café,
retrievers curled about the table legs
and the warm abraded doors.

At thirty-eight I'm still the babe
of my family. Once I thought they would teach me,
that even their last breath would be a key,
but now I see them drifting off from their easy chairs,
like a tribe leaving shore together, the television
blaring, their mouths sagged open, and when they
return for brief moments, they stare at me
as if I were a stranger.

All that I will ever know is right here
in the wash and till of my own ten acres.
Frost tonight and behind it the whole summer
so brief I can still see the bronco-faced calf
born to the bloody pasture and the brown trout
suspended in its first glittering insect hatch.
There will never be more than twilight, a valley
receding to glass. In this tiny paradise
of common flowers, the waist-high marigolds
blaze up like golden dowagers. Venus rises alone
and early to a cold black sky.

A Fish to Feed All Hunger

On the porch like night peelings,
bags of red hackles.
The fisherman is dressing,
capes of moose mane around him.
In his vise, he wraps the waist
of a minnow with chenille.

We wade downstream. I am barefoot.
The fisherman stands, thigh deep,
seining insects. Perhaps today
in this blizzard of cottonwood
it is the caddis that rises,
after a year in mud, from larva
to phoenix in four seconds.

The fisherman ties an imitator
of hare's mask and mallard breast.
He washes his hands in anisette,
then casts back, a false cast,
watching the insect's legs
break the water.

I line the creel with hay and mint
and lay in six pale trout. There is a pink
line that runs the length of a rainbow's
belly more delicate than an inner ear.
It makes the whole basket quiver.

The fisherman does not ask why I come.
I have neither rod nor permit.
But I see him watch me afternoons as I bend
to brush down my rooster-colored hair.
He understands a fish to feed all hunger.
And the lure is the same.

■ MINERVA ALLEN

Minerva Allen is an Assiniboine Indian born on the Fort Belknap Indian Reservation in 1943. Allen attended a private high school in Flandreau, North Dakota, and was graduated from Central Michigan University. She received an M.A. in career guidance from Northern Montana College in Havre and an M.A.T. from Weber State College in Ogden, Utah. Her poems were published in Spirits of the Past Trying to Walk Out to the West *(1974) and* Spirits Rest *(1981). Allen is currently administrator for the Hays-Lodgepole Schools on the Fort Belknap Indian Reservation.*

Look Into the Clouds

Moving forward and back from the lands across the sea.
I am a bird, if you wish to see me?
See me in the clouds.

When sadness falls, I will bring rain.
My feathers will sail with the breeze,
and the clear sky will echo my words
with a pleasing sound.
Across the earth everywhere my voice will be heard.

If you seek me look into the clouds,
and in the silence you will hear me. Listen.
I pity myself, for the wind carries me across the sky.

JON DAVIS

Born in 1952 in New Haven, Connecticut, Jon Davis was raised in the East. He received his M.F.A. from the University of Montana in 1984, studying under Richard Hugo, William Pitt Root, and Patricia Goedicke. The assistant editor of the university's literary journal, Cutbank, *Davis won the 1982 Merriam Frontier Award, which led to the publication of his chapbook,* West of New England. *Davis received the 1987 General Electric Young Poets Award and was a fellow at the Provincetown Fine Arts Workshop. His latest collection,* Dangerous Amusements, *was published in 1987.*

Blue Sky, the Girder Falling

All day long I've been thinking about justice,
that young man from Helena – quarterback, scholar,
wife and young son, the girder falling from the sky. . . .
Last week on campus he said we'd beat 'em good this year
and a case of beer was riding on it. I imagine him
kissing his wife good-bye, holding his boy up,
burying his face in the puffy stomach.
Then the long drive north to the work site,
past farmhouses, their windows blazing with sun.
All day long I've been thinking about justice,
the steel falling, Jim Burford smiling,
tanned and shirtless, the yellow hard-hat
on the perched shell of his skull. I think
of the crane operator: stories told over beers at Rudy's:
the flask tucked beneath his belt, his wife
unbuttoning her beaded blouse behind the trailer.
All day long I've been thinking about justice,
when it was done they grappled the iron off the body
and the toughest men in Montana looked away.
This afternoon I rake leaves, trying to forgive God.
When I look up at Mount Sentinel I remember
bitterroot blooming in a secret valley,
ticks clinging to the tender slips.
All day long I've been thinking about justice.
Last night, a thunderstorm
more violent than birth, lightning
falling in sheets, the muddy river slugging trucks.
I sat with my wife in a car, safe from lightning,

and watched. Pine boughs crashed around us,
a ball of lightning sputtered across a field.
My wife took my hand, kicked open the door.
She walked me into the storm: across
startled suburban lawns, swing sets clanging,
a mutt crashing an aluminum door–whimpering,
the glittering cars, dithering birches,
puddled driveways drenched in light.
All day long I've been thinking about justice,
leaves rushing under the rake, blue sky, the girder falling.

■ MADELINE DeFREES

Madeline DeFrees was born in Oregon in 1919. She studied poetry with Karl Shapiro at Portland State University and with John Berryman and Robert Fitzgerald at Indiana, and received an M.A. from the University of Oregon in 1951. DeFrees entered the order of the Sisters of the Holy Names of Jesus and Mary in 1936, and wrote under the name of Sister Mary Gilbert until she was released from her vows in 1973. She taught at Ft. Wright College and others schools in the Northwest before coming to the University of Montana in 1967. In 1980, DeFrees became the director of the Creative Writing Program at the University of Massachusetts at Amherst. Her books include Springs of Silence *(1953) and* From the Darkroom *(1964). These selections are from* When Sky Lets Go, *published in 1978. DeFrees currently lives in Seattle, Washington.*

The Odd Woman

At parties I want to get even,
my pocket calculator rounds everything off,
taught to remember. I'm not so good
at numbers, feel awkward
as an upper plate without a partner.
Matched pairs float from the drawing board
into the drawing room, ears touched
with the right scent,
teeth and mouth perfect.

The cougar jaw yawns on the sofa back,
his molars an art-object.

The old and strange collect around me,
names I refuse pitched at my head
like haloes. This one is a dead-ringer.
It rings dead. I pat the head of the beagle
nosing in my crotch and try to appear
grateful. A witch
would mount the nearest broom

and leave by the chimney. At ten I plot
my exit: gradual shift to the left,
a lunge toward the bourbon. The expert hunters
are gutting a deer
for the guest of honor. Soft eyes
accuse my headlights. I mention early
morning rituals. A colleague
offers to show me the door I've watched
for the last hour.

We come to my coat laid out
in the master bedroom, warm hands curled
in the pocket. I know
how a woman who leaves her purse behind
wants to be seduced. I hang mine
from the shoulder I cry on.
Say goodnight to the Burmese buddha,
hunters in the snow,
and leave for the long river drive to town.

In the Hellgate Wind

January ice drifts downriver
thirty years below the dizzy bridge. Careening traffic
past my narrow walk
tells me warm news of disaster. Sun lies
low, can't thaw my lips. I know
a hand's breadth farther down could freeze me solid
or dissolve me beyond reassembling.
Experts jostle my elbow.
They call my name.
My sleeves wear out from too much heart.

When I went back to pick up my life
the habit fit strangely. My hair escaped.
The frigidaire worked hard while I slept my night
before the cold trip home.
Roots of that passage go deeper than a razor
can reach. Dead lights
in the station end access by rail.
I could stand still to fail the danger,
freeze a slash at a time, altitude for anaesthetic.
Could follow my feet in the Hellgate wind
wherever the dance invites them.

The pure leap I cannot take stiffens downstream,
a millrace churned to murder.
The siren cries
at my wrist, flicks my throat, routine
as the river I cross over.

Existing Light

for Lee Nye

A picture is worth a thousand words
of waiting. I thought I knew and waited
with the turn. The mirrors we were not
supposed to notice, circle my bedroom walls
to help me learn. In the corner of my closet
where that other black self hangs
praying for a pumpkin coach to cart away
the ashes of a prince, something lost or
spirited below, wakes up and stretches
in the early autumn sun, to let a loose wind
trifle with the veil. Outside, the fevered leaves
repeat my fall in choruses more ancient
than my own, and underneath the stairs,
a guttural parrot calls tired
obscenities to a woman who lives alone.

I studied my unknown face in every opaque
glass, searched for the lie I kept

bottled in. Then you shot
with a focused eye to get inside
the compromising skin. Wherever the light
touched my body it left a bruise.
The bruise deepened to shadow, and shadow
flowed into shape. I felt my bones bend
against the vast concrete. Muscles
tell me what they were for in a dark
beginning of hope. Deftly you planned the angles
to cancel out reflections from my glasses.
Your strategies were natural and sure.
Light from a used sun flooded the street
where I stood, half woman, half nun, exposed.

■ ROGER DUNSMORE

Born in Michigan in 1938, Roger Dunsmore received a B.A. in psychology and an M.A. in English from Pennsylvania State University. He began his teaching career as an English instructor in 1968 at the University of Montana in Missoula. He currently is living and working in Tuba City, Arizona. His book of poems, On the Road to Sleeping Child Hotsprings, *was published in 1978. This selection is from his unpublished manuscript,* Blood House.

The Pink Butterfly

for Billie Anna

Seven a.m. radio says 100% snow
and Krishnamurdi is dead.
Five storms in a week.
The tire shop wants $125 for a set of studs.
I pass.
The roads are slippery,
fat crows black-feed on road-kilt deer
half buried in snow.
An immature eagle, yellow-speckled-breast,
in a cottonwood outside the school.

The talk is upstairs, the Library,
fifty girls and teachers wedged into hard chairs.
They want to know about my buckle
(Assiniboine butterfly for a boy's first dance),
are filled with questions—

When they married the animals
did they actually mate with them?
Do they smoke peyote in their pipes?

Afterward, trembling, you approach,
want me to see your father's gift,
a lavender-pink butterfly in your black hair.
I ask if I can touch
(it's against the rules):
smooth feel of Salish beads on the fingertips,
strands of dark hair clasped in the butterfly wings.

The last thing they tell me,
when one of you runs away
(Billings or Seattle),
you come back gladly.
The pimps use lighted cigarettes
and coat hangers.

Krishnamurdi is dead.
I promised to call your aunt.
The butterfly clasps your black hair
in its pink wings.

Montana School for Girls
February 1986

PATRICIA GOEDICKE

Patricia Goedicke was born in 1931 and was raised in New England. She attended Middlebury College and received her M.A. in English from Ohio University. After living in Mexico for fifteen years with her husband, Leonard Robinson, she moved to Missoula in 1982 to teach in the University of Montana's Creative Writing Program. Goedicke has published eight books of poems, including The Wind of Our Going *(1985) and* Listen, Love *(1986).*

Lost

Miles from here, in the mountains
There is no sound but snowfall.

The wind rubs itself against the trees
Under its breath

If a crow calls it is nothing
If a branch breaks it is nothing.

The birches look at themselves in the water,
The long white poles of their bodies waver

And bend a little,
The yellow leaves of their hair

Like pieces of far off stars come falling,
Hissing onto the lake

That is smooth as pewter, that is clear
And tranquil as an eye

Lost up here in the mountains
As if someone had dropped it, but no

The pebbles beneath the surface
Have no nerves, they are calm

If a fish leaps it is nothing
Surrounded by moss and blueberries

Flowers breathe among the rocks
So quietly you forget everything

Up here on the crusty grass
The bushes sparkle with ice

And no footprints anywhere,
If a twig snaps it is nothing

For nothing matters, once you have lost it
Down here in the valleys among the people

The sidewalks are full of holes,
Faint memories of far off lakes

Up there in the mountains,
In the great evergreen forests

If a woodchuck whirrs it is nothing,
If a bluejay shrieks it is nothing,

Pine needles slip from the trees, silently
They pile up on the ground.

This Life

Why this precise moment, just
sitting here, for no reason
content
as the soft tearing sound of a clarinet
solo after lovemaking
spilling out of a tense movie
at last, on a warm whoosh
of air
or, suddenly, the quiet
after the near miss
of slammed brakes, the rush
and pure happiness of absolute
relief

It seems so American,
after all we've seen, the angry
high passions of Greeks
and flaming Arabs,
our own terrors, cruel
sharp tongues over the breakfast table,
love overturned, found wanting
far to the south of us struggling
Mexicans forcing a living
from dry, brutally cracked
clay

Below the gardening gloves,
beneath the puffed
organdy at the open
2nd floor windows
it's high summer,
in the back yard
9:00 P.M. in the West
the house sits on a concrete
platform surrounded by tough
thin grass, clover
new marigolds straggling
in their pots

This life is something new for us
almost luxurious
not to be answering questions
or asking them,
red pencilling essays
in foreign tongues or at home
struggling to impose a system
we know will never heal
all ills, physical
or metaphysical

Settled here behind neat
small conical evergreens
that poke up like a picket
fence against the huge
smooth melon haunch
of the mountain overlooking us

and our tired bones, shifting
from one pained knee
to the other, isn't it enough
finally just to sit
by sheer luck under a pure
fat white cloud shoulder,
you reading a biography
me with my short stories

Over our heads, in the aisle
of the 9:14 Boeing Constellation
from Seattle
the smokers are fidgeting
over the shoulders of the non-smokers
no terrorists are approaching the cockpit
stewards collect tiny bottles,
used coffee cups
and cigarette papers from all over the world
as the passengers collect their briefcases,
run combs through their hair
thinking of home

In the light, evaporating blue
evening sky
we wonder whether we should go back in,
answer the telephone but no,
slouched in our light
plastic lawnchairs drifting
in the well of twilight like clear
wide-eyed bubbles reflecting
everything we notice
you put your feet up
in blunt, snub-nosed
harmless sneakers
why are we so comfortable here
precisely
your son's almost settled
in his new job,
my sister's handing out warm clothes
in Beirut, where we should be
or someplace else
shouldn't we?

For All the Sad Rain

O my friends why are we so weak
In winter sunlight why do our knees knock,
Why do we walk with small steps, ugly
And spindly as baby birds

Whose world do we think this is?
O my friends take it,
O my friends don't look at each other
Or anyone else before you speak.

I have had enough of scared field mice
With trembling pink ears,
I have had enough of damp
Diffident handshakes,

Do you think I haven't been stepped on by giants?
Do you think my teachers didn't stand me in a corner
For breathing, do you think my own father didn't burn me
With the wrath of a blast furnace for wanting to sit on his knee?

Indeed I have been pressed between steamrollers,
I have had both my feet cut off, and the pancreas
And the liver and the lungs of the one I love
Have been sucked out of my life and the air around me

Has turned to cereal, how will I stand up,
What opinions can I offer but I will not be silent,
There are dogs who keep their skinny tails
Permanently between their legs

But also there are sleek horses, as easily as there are curs
There are squash blossoms that flower around fountains
Like white butterflies, there is courage everywhere,
For every reluctant nail-biter

There are a hundred raised fists, for every broken broomstick
There are millions of bent grasses snapping
Back and forth at the sky, beating the blue carpet
As hard as they can, with the frail tassels of their hair

For every pair of eyes squeezed tight
Under colorless lids there are thousands of others
Wide-open, on the proud columns of their necks turning,
Observing everything like King Radar,

O my friends for all the sad rain in heaven
Filling our dinner plates you have ten fingers of honey
Which are your own, stretch them, stick them up
And then wave to me, put your arms around each other's shoulders

When we meet in a field with no fences
The horizon is yours, and the books and all the opinions
And the water which is wine and the best bed
You can possibly think to lie in.

■ ANDREW GROSSBARDT

Andrew Grossbardt received an M.F.A. in poetry at the University of Montana in Missoula, where he studied under Richard Hugo and Madeline DeFrees. He taught at Northeast Missouri State and was a teaching fellow at the University of Utah and editor of Quarterly West *when he committed suicide in 1978. This selection is from* The Traveler, *published in 1976.*

Wounds

for Paul Zarzyski

Picture one horse
on the highway to Ronan
white from the neck up
the rest stained red
from a sudden slash of wire
the flesh opening like a wink
and try hard
not to remember
the rodeo at Miller Creek
the chestnut bronc bouncing
its rider like a sack
then rushing at the fence

the crack of bone
muscles twitching
green shit pouring out like water
and the sudden hush
clinging to everything
like a fine layer of dust

JOHN HAINES

John Haines was born in 1924 in Norfolk, Virginia, and grew up in Washington, D.C., and Seattle, Washington, the son of a Navy officer. After serving in World War II, Haines lived for a time in Alaska and studied art at American University in Washington, D.C., before homesteading in Alaska in 1954. Haines has taught at universities in Idaho, Washington, Montana, and Michigan. His poetry and prose explore the relationships between people and the landscape of the West. These poems about Montana are reprinted here from News from the Glacier *(1982).*

Missoula in a Dusty Light

Walking home through the tall
Montana twilight,
leaves were moving in the gutters
and a little dust . . .

I saw beyond the roofs and chimneys
a cloud like a hill of smoke,
amber and a dirty grey. And a wind
began from the street corners
and rutted alleys,
out of year-end gardens, weed lots
and trash bins;
               the yellow air
came full of specks and ash,
noiseless, crippled things that crashed
and flew again . . .
grit and the smell of rain.

And then a steady sound,
as if an army or a council,
long-skirted, sweeping the stone,
were gathuring near;
disinherited and vengeful people,
scuffing their bootheels,
rolling tin cans before them.

And quieter still behind them
the voices of birds
and whispering brooms:
"This land
has bitter roots, and seeds
that crack and spill in the wind . . ."

I halted under a blowing light
to listen, to see;
and it was the bleak Montana wind
sweeping the leaves and dust
along the street.

News from the Glacier

East from Glacier Park
an immense herd lies buried.

Thighbones, blunt ends of ribs
break through the soil,
a little grass like hair
straying over them in the wind.

Whatever they were, Mastodon,
Great Horse, Bison
or something no one has named,
they were hunted down
by the cold, starved
in the great earth changes.

We read in this landscape
how they came and went:

Faces to the ground, feeding,
following the gusty ridges,
they had lakes for eyes,
and the future drained away
as they moved and fed.

After the twenty thousand year
seige of rain and ice
the broken gates stand open;
a few rocks piled at the portals,
far plains strewn with bones.

From the long march overland,
scouring the rockwalls,
making camp at the foot of moraines,

we came to this sprawling
settlement of wind and dust,
these streets laid out
among the boulders, metal signs
pocked and flapping.

No great encampment stands in view
at Browning. We are awake
in our own desolate time–

clotheslines whipping the air
with sleeves and pockets,
little fists of plastic bags
beating the stony ground.

■ MATTHEW HANSEN

Born in 1961, Matthew Hansen was the son of Ripley Schemm and the step-son of Richard Hugo. A talented young poet, Hansen's work appeared in The New Yorker *and other journals. Graduating with honors from the University of Montana in 1982, Hansen shared his deep love for the West in his written work. At the time of his death from cancer in 1984, he was collecting oral histories of old-time miners, ranchers, and loggers for the Montana Historical Society. These poems are from* Clearing *(1986).*

Walking Into Silence

1.

Blue Mountain by the Bitterroot
is where the lovers go to feel
their lover's breast and thigh,
to rub their lips against the skin,
the cheek, to grab the coarse
and sliding hair. They hear the deep
heart pound in its cage of bone,
a frantic bird with battering wings.

The dead white horse is up again
in my dream, the freckled eye
and yellowed teeth run wild at me
in the moonlight and the snow, breaking
poles and stamping on my chest
with brittle hooves.

Spring was lovely on the open hill
where horses graze. I measured time
by each new bloom of lupine, rose,
or larkspur in the grass. Bitterroot
exploded pink before you left.
I remember Lake Inez, the long
wet mornings in the old brass bed,
the press of skin and swimming
rhythm ended, rain on the roof.

2.
Lonely whiskey by the Teton, bright
midsummer sun. I drove hard
to reach you on the Yampa
where the coal town booms. We
trembled again in the dry dark air.
Sego lilies flowered, your tongue
in my ear was a brown bat
at night blooming cactus.
I walked up Cedar Mountain
with your brother, found an eagle
feather and a smooth green chert.
The wind ran long and unfettered.
Dark lives groaned underground.

3.
Full moons made of stone
rise hard and white, without care
for creatures of blood and bone
that move on the earth. I went back
to stories I knew, spent my time
in worthless rocks, dreaming red
clay thrown into round bowls.

The potter sang with a voice
like clear water. Memories I kept
like beads in my pocket, told
them over and wore them thin.
The Blackfoot and the Clark Fork
join, flow west through Hellgate Canyon
and the sleepless city made of brick.
I found old days dismembered,
scattered into strange corners
of an arc-lit night. Steel rims
on the track, the loaded freight
rumbled on to Spokane.

4.
When I took the crowded trail
through birch and yew, I was already
alone, walking into silence

on the rhythm of my breath.
Everything that lives in sunlight
throws a shadow–golden larch,
dry blades of tall yellow grass,
and the bull elk bugling away
his antlered strength at rut.

The first snow caught me tired
under the red buttes, worn down
to a log hollow bone from steady
miles and White River Pass.
We each have our own pain, and we
carry it with us–charred heart
abandoned at the last camp, lone
coyote howling on a mudflat
in the noonday sun. I come to sere brown
meadows that I know, and watch
gray jays quiet in the great fir.
I want to escape delusion. I want
to keep my voice strong, my boots
greased, and my knife sharp.

Preparing for Dark

Mourning doves call back the night, pull
the quarter moon down, pull my body
under limb to dream of cottonwood root.
I'll name the ones I love–Jacob's Ladder,
Beebalm, Yarrow, and Owl Clover–
then gather my dead ones into my blood.

I'd like to be known for growing good beets,
have some trick of shovel or dirt. When I go
blind, I want my hands to know a dog's limb
by swollen tendon in the flank. I need
to navigate by feel, find the north star
buried deep in my shadow.

Cripples walk the river bridge, I walk
the bridge and wonder how far stone

has to be to break my neck. What good
are strong legs against steel tons and two
sad eyes broken out of air? I welcome
hard rain that chills my body on pavement.

Walking cool at dawn, the loud bronze orb
clangs up, whips the old moon out
to barren day. We're all good friends
and lovers here. At night we plan deceit,
betrayal of charred blood running
cramped through muscle and vein.

Forget the gold slag heap in my dream,
the dark coal and burnt oil flogging black
across the broad blue cloak of sky.
Today I saw a Salish woman
stop on the bridge, show her child
the river and the deep green trout.

I'll leave the trail the way bones do,
take flood path of mountain water.
What I seek is the warm brotherhood
of fir, spruce, and juniper, the fierce
devotion of a redtail hawk
tearing rabbit for her young.

■ BILL HOAGLAND

Bill Hoagland was born in Rock Falls, Illinois. Hoagland attended Northern Illinois University and received an M.F.A. in poetry from the University of Massachusetts at Amherst. Since 1979, he has taught in the English Department at Northern Montana College in Havre. Hoagland's poems have appeared in the Denver Quarterly, Limberlost Review, *and* The Carolina Quarterly, *and he is currently completing his first book,* The Poem You Write In Sleep. *This poem was first published in* Writers' Forum.

December Spearing

It is not yet light on the reservoir,
though the sky is panicked to the east,
a thin smear of orange over earth.

My friend Steve yells into darkness,
some primitive outrage against cold.
Then we take turns with the iron bar
tall as a man, heavy, bevelled
to an edge for gouging ice
which flies at our legs in chunks
until the spearing-hole is cut—
three feet by four feet—
and we pry the bobbing ice-cake loose,
force it down, away, and the hole is clear.

We lift the ice-house from the truck,
pull it like a sled across the reservoir,
raise its hinged walls,
lock the roof in place,
slide it gently over the spearing-hole
as the sun comes up,
the northern and western hills
in high relief above the ice-plane,
bright mounds and shadowed coulees.

We climb inside, turn up the stove,
and sit in lawn chairs,
the luminescence of water

splayed up to our faces:
we're hunched like ghouls.

So Steve and I take turns jigging
the plastic lures–fish painted
like no fish I've seen before–
though it works, as a broad-backed
northern pike glides close, circling,
I can see her gills pumping steadily,
her fins opaque, undulating,
her toothed jaw dropped.

Steve's black iron spear leaps from his hand.
I kick my aluminum chair.
Steve whoops.
The water inks vermillion between us.
The spear-rope uncoils.

Then we bring her in, hand over hand,
until she gushes at the ice-hole,
I tackle her behind her gills,
Steve shoves, I pull,
we burst through the wooden door
into the light,
fall,
I hit my chin on the ice,
the big green fish is writhing
in front of me, bloody,
slapping the ice with its tail,
"*Jesus!*" Steve wailing, "*Jesus!*"

■ GARY HOLTHAUS

Born in Iowa in 1932, Gary Holthaus received his S.T.M. in theological studies from Boston University in 1958. He came to Red Lodge, Montana, as a clergyman in 1958 and taught at Western Montana College in Dillon until 1964. Holthaus currently lives in Anchorage, Alaska, where he has been executive director of the Alaska Humanities Council since 1972. These poems are from Unexpected Manna *(1978) and* Circling Back *(1984).*

Wild Horses

Once, hunting deer,
I saw wild horses
In the Pryor Mountains
Over on the back side
Beyond Bear Canyon

They were jug-headed
Their tails like brooms
Hanging down in the sage
They seemed afire–
The shekina, maybe–
Red sun going down behind them
Like an embolism closing
The autumn afternoon

They graze that meadow still
A memory growing hard to come by
Of things wild and loose
An image unearthed from our own
Dim jurassic past
Wild horses standing in the sunset
Silent as time to come
Men, and all our kind,
Only an image in the memory
Of the earth's unconscious
Like annual rings wrapped inside
The bark of trees, the trees then
Buried in a vein of coal.

Horse

At dawn Horse came drinking
Dawn Horse came,
Small as first light before Sun is up
Small as Dog
Dawn Horse came,
With toes instead of hooves,
Nose too heavy, legs too short.

But he sure looked like somebody
Familiar. Perhaps it was
Coyote! In disguise!
Coyote could do that—
Become anything he liked!
Could have been Coyote,
Changing, preening himself,
Becoming Middle Horse,
Letting go those toes,
Growing stronger, independent,
Learning to run and to be
Tricky. Equus.

We thought they all died a while.
Maybe old Coyote died too!
At the same time!
We weren't too sure about it . . .
Coyote is cunning!

But he wasn't dead.
Horse wasn't dead either,
Just gone from this place
For a time.

Maybe Horse is still
Coyote in disguise,
Maybe that's why some horses
Don't get tame even now—
Just stay wild and flame-eyed and pecky.
Ride 'em a ways
All smooth and feeling peaceful

Then BANG
The world unfolds
Before you, everything opening
Wide for an instant,
Sky, ground, horse,
All mixed up!

Then you know
That's old Coyote
Still hanging around from a million years ago
Roaming those big savannahs,
Raising hell,
Showing who's trickiest,
The toughest–
Free or dead, the only choice
For Dawn Horse
Old Coyote.

■ NANCY HUNTER

Nancy Hunter was born in Texas and grew up on a ranch near Roundup, Montana. She was graduated from Lewis-Clark State College in Lewiston, Idaho, in 1981 and received an M.F.A. in creative writing from the University of Montana in 1986. Hunter now lives in Seattle. "North of Roundup, 1952" appeared in Frontiers *in 1987.*

North of Roundup, 1952

for my daughters

> *We come out of the earth*
> *and the grass, and aspire*
> *to the light.*
> John Haines

From grass shoulder high she is waving, saying O
these are good times–all this
and a cattle market on the rise–
as the summer sun traces wind
in the curling blades and Mother's dark hair.

In the margin you can't see
a country road, dust that boils
when the bottom falls out,
her husband gone off to town, drunk three days running
and gambling, racing ponies all over again
in a dim back room
as though they could chase away failure.

Others leave for good: Eleanor, round-faced
and yellow-haired,
who rests her elbows on Mom's enameled table and listens
till a new job comes up near Lewistown.
And there's the hired man Burt, who jokes
at sullen mealtimes.
Says her laughter reminds him of clouds,
the way they swirl high and graceful, and he means it.
He moves on. Then

I marry young, so young her only chance
to go through me another way
seems a trail of dust and gone.
I see her wave then shield her eyes, watch her grow
smaller until she seems stunted, bound
to land no picture can ever show.

If, in a white corner, there were a tree
or gentle rise, I would point it out
but this is dry land and flat,
country we all come to, with grass
that grows in cycles: The barn cats full
and sassy then hungry and mean.

We do have this picture:
One woman who knew well
the land's contour. In her place
I take in the smell of timothy and dust motes,
hold it long before I breathe it out.
Listen, you may hear clouds, great white swirls,
she is coming up out of grass, right arm
raised in a sign of triumph
or recognition, mouth
a round burn above the green.

■ GREG KEELER

Greg Keeler was born in Oklahoma in 1946. He received an M.A. in English from Oklahoma State University and completed a doctorate in arts and English from Idaho State University in 1973. Since 1975, Keeler has taught English and creative writing at Montana State University in Bozeman, where he is also well-known for his comic-satiric songs. His work has been widely published, and his most recent collection is American Falls *(1987).*

The Glass Trout

It lies over the rocks.
Or at least its shadow does.
It turns to feed.
Or at least its refraction does.

Here is a bright window
on a world where
everything is clear
until it moves
and everything moves.

A nose breaks the surface
in a circle small as
a bracelet for a slender wrist
but the shadow beneath
cannot even hide behind a boulder
so it moves up and back
under the hatch.

It is a rock
then a weed bed
then a sunstruck wave.

Then it arches out into
this world
where everything stops.

■ ED LAHEY

Ed Lahey was born and raised in Butte. He attended the University of Minnesota and studied poetry under Richard Hugo and Madeline DeFrees at the University of Montana in Missoula. Lahey has taught high school and has worked on mining and pipeline operations and in the trucking business. He also taught English at the University of Montana and at Carroll College in Helena. These poems are from Blind Horses and Other Poems, *which won the Montana Arts Council's First Book Award for 1979.*

The Blind Horses

The old man in the hospital bed
with his horny yellow foot
stuck through the stainless rails,
claimed that July night—the one he picked to die on—
he smelled sulphur on his gown.

When he was my age he worked
the lower levels of the Lex in a great underground corral,
yoked iron tongue to wagons
filled with ruby silver and peacock copper rock,
flaked sweet hay to horses, shot the worn out.

Dozens of tramway horses hauled hard
against whippletrees—rubbed the timbered tunnels clean—
pulling down the cribbed-up drifts,
brass lanterns swinging, work bits in their teeth,
slick with mine damp and cold to the touch.

Dry stulls in the crosscut cave
of that stone corral caught fire in '98.
The horses, tunnel-blind from lack of light, burned up
in the green flame that licked the lagging
black in the Lexington Mine.

I met his eyes cracked white
like a drunk's who hasn't had a drink in months.
He said he could hear hoofbeats ring

and click against the granite footwalls.
He complained of being cold. His nostrils flared:
"I hear them breathing, Ed."

Gimp O'Leary's Iron Works

for Big Ed

You hear a lot of lies about O'Leary
but he could seal a crack in steel
no matter what the size.
His arc welder would strike
white fire and a bead
of blue-black rod would slide
along between cherry streaks,
and acrid smoke would curl away
to leave clean married steel,
not too frail, or buttered up
but straight and strong,
hard as mill forged rail.
Of course you might say,
"Don't use that example
as a metaphor for poetry."
"Welding is a matter of utility."
And you'd be right. Still,
I remember the look on his face
when he'd lift his great helmet
and sneak up on the finished
job with his unprotected eyes.
It was always between him
and the piece of steel–
a struggle of molecules and will.

Often others would say to him,
"Damn good job or some such thing."
If it was, he'd grin, and look again,
as if he thought the natural light
would show a flaw, or bridge
that didn't fuse–convinced, I guess,

that in his struggle with the steel
he could seldom really win.
He knew perfection could
conceal the wound
beneath the arc of his art.
I liked him for that.

DON MANKER

Born in Missouri in 1910, Don Manker moved to eastern Montana when he was five years old. He grew up on his family's homestead and has lived and ranched in that area ever since. Manker's poems have appeared in The Christian Science Monitor, Redbook, *and* Good Housekeeping. *His collection,* The Thin Doll, *won the National Federation of State Poetry Associations Award in 1973. This poem is from* An Inkle of Danger *(1982).*

And She Is There With Laughing

Two or three days out of Eden
we stopped (bushed, of course)
running before the Wrath.
Behind us the sword still flamed
and flickered on the horizon
but (we thought) fitfully,
like a storm dying.
Or it was distance
or being tired.
                No matter . . .
we couldn't have gone on.
There was a spring
and, still so near the Garden,
figs (only a little blasted).
I ate and I gave Eve to eat.
That was a new thing, being hungry.
And when she had eaten she spoke my name
in a new way—
          and that was the first thing.
Afterward I made a bed of leaves
for Eve and made one for myself

the old way. Sleep was slow
and when it came I dreamt–
and woke up running–sweating–
slept again and woke, and slept
and woke–and heard my name
and it was she who called. I rose
then and went and crept into her bed
and she laughed like water over stones
and turned to me and I to her–
and that night we forgot the
thunder that muttered of evil,
and did not remember the foolish lightning–
that was the second thing.
The third? Oh, that is a no-thing,
a nothing at all . . . but to me . . .
and to Eve. So much is gone. I am old
but, even so, sometimes I dream–
and wake up running–from the Wrath,
and she is there
with laughing–and gardens in her hair–
and the taste of apples on her mouth.

■ WALLACE McRAE

Wally McRae is the third generation of his family to work the Rocker 6 Ranch on Rosebud Creek in southeastern Montana. He began writing verse in high school, and by the 1970s his poems were being published widely. McRae's poems have appeared in Mother Jones, Mother Earth News, The Windmill, *and the* Plains Truth, *and his first collection,* Up North Is Down The Creek, *was published by the Museum of the Rockies in 1985. These selections are from* It's Just Grass and Water, *published in 1986.*

Reincarnation

What does reincarnation mean?"
A cowpoke ast his friend.
His pal replied, "It happens when
Yer life has reached its end.

They comb yer hair, and warsh yer neck,
And clean yer fingernails,
And lay you in a padded box
Away from life's travails."

"The box and you goes in a hole,
That's been dug in the ground.
Reincarnation starts in when
Yore planted 'neath a mound.
Them clods melt down, just like yer box,
And you who is inside.
And then yore just beginnin' on
Yer transformation ride."

"In a while the grass'll grow
Upon yer rendered mound.
Till some day on yer moldered grave
A lonely flower is found.
And say a hoss should wander by
And graze upon this flower
That once wuz you, but now's become
Yer vegetative bower."

"The posey that the hoss done ate
Up, with his other feed,
Makes bone, and fat, and muscle
Essential to the steed.
But some is left that he can't use
And so it passes through,
And finally lays upon the ground.
This thing, that once wuz you."

"Then say, by chance, I wanders by
And sees this on the ground,
And I ponders, and I wonders at,
This object that I found.
I thinks of reincarnation,
Of life, and death, and such,
And come away concludin': Slim
You ain't changed, all that much."

The Lease Hound

for Harold and Virginia Sprague

A sharpie in a leisure suit,
With eyelets in his shoes,
Who faintly smelled of talcum
And a little less of booze,
Drove into my neighbor's yard
And gingerly got out,
A little gimpy from the drive,
The altitude, and gout.

He tried to pet their barking dog
While edging to the door,
But once inside his confidence
Sallied to the fore.
"I've come to lease your land for coal,"
Was how he launched his spiel,
He'd been given "authority"
To grant a "generous" deal.

"The nation needs the coal," he said,
"As I am sure you know.
We need more power every year
To make our nation grow.
It's the patriotic duty
Of each American
To help to get the coal mined,
And expedite our plan.

"Now, you may not like stripmining,
And tearing up the earth,
But it's your duty, isn't it,
To the land that gave you birth?
For too long you've reaped the benefits
From places far away.
Your turn has now come up," he said,
"And now, you folks must pay."

"Your power, and the food you eat,
And the lumber in your house,
And all the luxuries you have,
Caused other folks to grouse.
But now your chance has come, at last,
To set the old debt straight.
Just sign the papers I have here,
And you can compensate."

All the time this lecture droned,
My neighbor masked his face.
How could he tell this pompous fool
Their food came from that place;
The lumber came from yonder
North-slope of the hill;

That "make-do" was their motto,
That need meant need, not frill.

The stranger felt he'd seldom
Better delivered his stroke,
He had but to get a signature
From these poor country folk.
His boss would be ecstatic,
His stock would surely rise.
The rutted road, a rainbow,
Had led him to this prize.

He'd do these folks a favor,
Save them from this place.
Though it was dusk, he still had time,
Tonight, a bar to grace.
"If we could have some light," he said,
"You folks could sign the forms.
I could leave here in an hour,
The forecast spoke of storms."

"We won't keep you," said my neighbor
"No need to stay an hour.
We'll light a lamp to show you out.
You see . . . we don't have no power."

■ D. LEWIS MOORE

D. Lewis Moore was born in Berkeley, California, in 1951 and has lived in the Puget Sound area, in New York City, and in New Mexico. He has taught English and humanities in South Dakota and Montana, and was editor of Naturegraph Publishers, a small West Coast nonfiction press. Moore is currently on leave from teaching at Salish/Kootenai Community College in Pablo, Montana.

Fanning the Flame

You drew away my love
like wind over warm coals
even when your raven
tears washed my arms,

when your sinewy mix
perplexed me, the utter
disregard and delight,
the thoughtless revolt
from thinking about it all, at all,
as I thought only of your
green eyes swimming, your long
neck tilted down, that soft hunch
of your shoulders around an angle
of family agonies, your breasts
remembering the young mother
before she wilted over you,
your sweet, ambitious hips
welcoming every possible father
that you never had,
all the twists of your sad story
smoothed under as though your skin
had bled white with lullabyes,
as though the iron that wrung
your wrists and neck and ankles
blew into ribbons
that trailed and spun
where you danced, high-stepping into air.
I saw the chains and smelled
the cankers where they rubbed
you raw. I did not see
the breeze of iron and silk
winding me, softening to make ready.
So this is for you
who was, I thought,
those scars inside that baby skin.
You gripped your losses like a phoenix,
your callouses rising where the links
began to slip, that feathered blush
growing redder for the risks,
the risings from the fire.
I send this out
to you whom
chains cannot cut
for your faith dancing on fear,
for wind-random love surprising us
to be more than our sense of how it is.

■ RICK NEWBY

A native Montanan, Rick Newby currently works for the Montana Historical Society Museum in Helena. He was an editor of Scratchgravel Hills, *a literary journal published in Helena, and has seen several of his poems and short stories published. This selection is from his book,* A Radiant Map of the World, *which was awarded the First Book Award of the Montana Arts Council for 1981.*

Gertrude Stein Almost Comes to Helena, Montana, But Does Not

He was the kind that knew that in Montana there are mountains and that mountains have snow on them. He knew nobody is stout in Montana. It does not take long to leave Montana but it takes a long time to get stout, to put flesh on, get rosy and robust, get vaccinated, get everything.

Gertrude Stein, *Ida*

Alice, she says, Alice, the mountains will do us good, good is a word we both like, & the mountains are clear-headed like we are, so let us go to the mountains near Helena, Montana, where my admirer, young Sam Steward, the novelist, lives, Sam whose book, *Angels on the Bough*, has something in it that makes literature, yes, my dearest Alice, Helena, a name to call forth loving sounds, quickly let us go & we will see a gold mine, a ghost town, & a gallows tree from which they hang the poor Chinese with their opium pipes, from which they dangle the soiled doves with their wardrobes of silk, from which they hang the men who laugh behind their masks & demand your money, *to make you less stout*, they say, *here in Montana where nobody is stout*, Helena, a name to conjure with, where the young novelist, Sam, lives, he who admires me, & whom I admire because he admires me, let us go here & make loving sounds to the mountains, O Alice, in the ghost town, at the bottom of the gold mine, at the foot of the gallows tree, in dear Helena, Alice, we will speak with young Sam who understands that artists need praise & not criticism & that those who need criticism are not yet artists, yes, young Sam will make us happy in that mountain town, we will fly across the landscape that looks like a Mondrian, in a small plane, we will fly to Helena, I so stout & you so thin, we will speak to the farmers & the children &

the priests & the miners & the Indians & the wives, in the opera house, I who am so stout will tell the people of Montana about time & the pleasures of time, about growing stout in the city of Paris where I dream of America, of the geographical history of America & the making of themselves, in their opera house I will tell them "a rose is a rose is a rose" & their ardent ears will translate "eros eros eros," will hear the loving sounds we make, will hear them, will hear . . .

Unfortunately, the plan to visit Helena could not be carried out. With several colleges unable to sponsor a lecture, Alice wrote to Steward that the trip to the Northwest would have to be postponed until a future time.
Linda Simon, *The Biography of Alice B. Toklas*

■ ROBERT SIMS REID

Robert Sims Reid was born in Illinois in 1948. After being graduated from the University of Illinois, he attended the University of Montana and received an M.F.A. in creative writing under Richard Hugo and Madeline DeFrees. Since 1980, Reid has been a detective for the Missoula Police Department. He has published two novels, Max Holly *(1982) and* Hostages *(1988).*

An Elegy for Leila

Because family set the tone for your life,
what else could they have named you but Leila?
When the Pattersons found you slumped over
the phone, number half-dialed, past forgetting,
it was the day after Christmas, nineteen
hundred and seventy-eight, your coat hung
on the hall tree, warming after one last
walk to the barn before lunch, the smell of
detergent and tea fading even then
into unbreathed air. Lord, let us retire
that notion of good people we should have been.
Let us close the door softly on that grief
and go home. Already, Leila, hearing
the news about you is memory. Your house
rushes toward a date with anonymous

fields. Every Sunday I watched you beside
Will during church, middle section, right aisle,
two rows from the back. I remember how
your skin felt warm. After that time, I learned
every day I do something my daughter
will try soon to imagine me doing.
For that record, I got up this morning,
read the thermometer: Zero. I write
these words from Montana. I force myself
to believe you're dead. On my wall, I have
a picture of you young, and in my mind
I keep a picture of the room they found
you in, kitchen behind you, oak sideboard
on the far wall. The phone spills from your hand.
Ice hugs the ground you're part of. Once, I stood
in that cold north window and turned away.
I looked past forty acres of stubble
and saw the dirt road to your house, this house,
the view unobstructed, sharp and complete.

From My Partner and I: An Apology

for Steve Ross

Picture this: it is evening.
People, let's say a dozen,
wander north toward the river.
At the island, a young woman
steps off the path and makes her way
through a clump of willows that crowds
the sun-streaked water. There, she kneels
and mashes sand into a mound.
To her left, the river feeds west,
deeper into town. Hellgate
lies east, source tonight of water
and wind. A flight of swallows
strafes a late hatch. You wash the grit
from your hands and splash cold water
on your face. Now it is evening.

Woman, why do you stay this late
along the river? What message
does sand convey to your skin
when you mold battlement and tower,
then scribe a moat with your finger
and watch it fill? Listen—voice
in the current. Believe: that shadow
on your shoulder means only harm.

Once upon a time, that water
was only water, sand nothing more
than rock made small by motion.
Perhaps you sang in those days
and lay your long legs in a patch
of moonlight. Maybe you stared,
unknowing, at the man on the bridge
and for a moment the river caught
its breath before you tried to scream
but couldn't. Later, my partner
and I kept your story alive
for months. The least we could do,
we said, was share what you had to know
forever. When we finally closed
the file, we whispered. We were sorry.
We failed. We could have thrown flowers
from the bridge, but we didn't.
We didn't get drunk, like TV cops,
and swagger home to bed when the bars
chucked us out. We made coffee.
I shut my eyes and put my feet
on my desk and remembered your voice,
the flat cadence that meant too much
to bear. I knew then a river
will never sound the same.

■ LEONARD WALLACE ROBINSON

Leonard Wallace Robinson is a novelist and writer who has worked as a reporter and editor for The New Yorker, *Managing Editor at* Esquire, *and Executive Editor at Holt, Rinehart, and Winston. Robinson has taught at Columbia University, Syracuse University, and Kalamazoo College. His poem, "print," appeared in* In the Whale *(1984), his first volume of poetry.*

print

i have some time and the will and so
drive aimlessly, wandering through
my country, seeing it for the first
time really. i go south, north but always west.

and now i am inside a japanese
print in my friend's house in
high montana, looking out my
bedroom window through a scrim
of pinetree branchings to the top
of the fat gray-brown mountain
not a hundred yards away
lying like a smooth-flanked water-buffalo
on its side in the cold december sun
its sucking calves
hidden from sight by my high window sill.

these western hills are asian, animal, un-
american, connected to history in some
uncanny manner. great stretches
of the tetons and the little rockies
look like vast head-dresses of eagle feathers
stamped on ridges. and gallery on gallery
of granite figures, mongol faces in profile
sit or lie along the skylines, a patience
caught in stone. the mountains
waited for their people and they came.

the print i'm in is japanese all right.
the close by mountain has formal hillocks
colored like a tiger and it has a single
diagonal path with just one person on it,
in a black coat, high-cheeked, gold-
skinned, mongol-eyed they came across
the icelocked bering sea and down
splitting up at times, some staying
along the coast, some moving inland but
always travelling down; down mexico,
down peru, swift skillful hunters,
fighting their terrors, losing everything and starting each time again,
eyeing, at first white-eyed, the frightening
mountain gods until they knew those gods
had waited just for them. slowly then they wove
sun, mountain, serpent, eagle, moon
into familiar tapestries of awe and learned
the runes of power and control; aztec, toltec, mixtec,
sioux, inca, blackfeet, navajo, pawnee.

i leave my asiatic window-view
and in my subaru i follow southward their wild experiments, their
searching, their trial and
error wanderings and see their
waiting patience printed everywhere against the sky, their eagle-
feathers everywhere along the great divide,
the spinal ridges of my country.
mine? no. i am the stranger here.
this is indian country
to the bone, the very marrow
of its being. these mountains have the time
and will to wait forever. my little car
coughs slightly at a pass's freezing height
but clings surefooted to the slippery curve.

■ WILLIAM PITT ROOT

Born in 1941, William Pitt Root spent his early childhood on the Gulf coast of Florida. He has lived in the Southwest and the Northwest and has participated in the Poetry in the Schools program on the Navajo, Hopi, Crow, Northern Cheyenne, and Wind River Indian reservations. Root taught creative writing at the University of Montana for several years before accepting a position at New York's Hunter College in 1986. Root's work has been widely published, and his books include The Storm and Other Poems *(1969),* Striking the Dark Air for Music *(1973), and* Reasons for Going It on Foot *(1981).*

Circle of Struggle

This morning, when I had to kill
a mouse to free it
from my trap,
I remembered the rat's gnawed foreleg
my father made me see—sheer bone
protruding from a thin
clenched paw. And this was our secret,
father's and mine, kept
from mother, safe in her kitchen,
for years.
        When he died at the verge
of my manhood, she fled north
with me. There I learned the seasons
in a long strange year.
I saw the crippled trees
crumple into colors, shedding
their brilliant disease of leaves
that left the branches dead
and trembling in the snow-white wind,
magical and stark
between streetlamps and starlight.

I learned to set out traps
for muskrats, mink, and rabbits—declaring
I would never marry, never.
And each dawn of the long first winter,

silent in the moonlight, I hiked
through the frostbright
dreamlike sleeping trees
that jutted like black bone
from wounded snow. Alone among
the creatured drifts and banks
piled up in the months between
my father's death and my
own beating flesh,
I was fearful and desirous
of the grey silent wolves
a crushed thing's single shriek
could summon from the dark.

With my strong Confederate bayonet
I'd pry slick frozen steel apart,
freeing stiff legs severed
in my traps. Now and then
a worthless skin.
        One morning
early in the wind and while
the blowing moon still wobbled,
jostling the dark fixed trunks
of night, I heard a chain snap tight.
Then beating wings. Something white
was fumbling at the base of the trees.

Like snow rising from snow,
a silver fox locked
in its talons, the great white owl rose,
then fell–dragged back by the trapped weight.
Dazzled by the brightening
air, its lunar eyes blazed
in their mask of blind snow
as I tripped on ice, reared
to meet its stare. It challenged:
I froze.
        White breast wide
with the heavy wings of a warrior
angel, it dipped the hook of its beak
in slow deliberation

and stole a vivid eye from the skull,
then turned to me. Impatient,
in an outburst of brilliance,
it battered up
out of the snow, clumsy at first,
then – transfigured by the high light of ascent –
    aglide
and glowing
    in the pale soaring sky.

Wet blood, bright
in the decomposing snow,
wound in a desparate
circle of struggle, round
and round the strict radius
of the staked chain.

All around me the horizon tensed
for dawn, encircling my vision
with the limits of a saw-toothed land
sharp against the sky,
and from this trap's dead center,
I looked up at the fatal stars
so innocent in their slow prison
of seasons and hours.

This morning, when I
sent my wife and daughter from the room,
they fled as if to witness death
were death itself. *Am I to die?*
– this accusation in their fear
has followed me until
I feel as if my own is the small
nodding skull I've crushed,
and mine the one bright eye
staring from its ruin.
                    So I
am the child again, facing your candor,
knowing this time you must die,
your face pass into my face,
mine into others. What

shall I tell them father? What can
we tell to these strangers
we have made from our love?

Somewhere,
in the belly of the owl and the earth,
we all stare incessantly from
darkness to darkness soaring.

■ DENNICE SCANLON

Dennice Scanlon was born and raised in the mining districts of Butte and Anaconda. She attended the University of Montana in Missoula, where she studied under Richard Hugo and Madeline DeFrees. Scanlon has taught elementary school in Anaconda and contributes feature articles for Butte's Montana Standard. *This poem appeared in* Poetry Northwest *in 1986.*

The Difference in Effects of Temperature Depending on Geographical Location East or West of the Continental Divide: A Letter

I had a mind to begin by scraping April
from the ridge. When in doubt, the saying
goes, dwell on weather. Haven't we been blessed
with dusk, a thousand ways to grieve the sun
receding? You must find spring a welcome
change where little changes. It's easy
to spot along valley fencelines–the new
calves, Hawn's mended coop, snake-edged
alfalfa oddly whipped against the wind.
Rain doesn't mean as much here. Pigeons
clutter the eaves, softball's late
starting but words wear thin for clouds
in season, the sting of long drives home.

At fifty-two hundred feet, torn buildings
soar. You left before mines with names
dull as Alice closed Butte. The big strike

settled like copper rings on branches.
Cottonwoods wrapped around sewerlines to pop
them at the joints and dusted days took
root. I only mention it because land to us
is personal as choice, whether it swells
in bluffs, plateaus or Indian Corn,
we both know what's enough. Yours gives back
what you put in—grain, slim tops
of asparagus, early beets. Mine demands
something hard to thrive, a red metal core.
When it's gone, dying's less complicated,
slow, as one house at a time boards up,
another promise of work falls through, ground
that's left overlaps its people and keeps
them from the boundary of their dreams.

It weighs my mind to write this way
with sky in doubt, bringing April when gray birds
sulk in the eaves. There was more to say
but news is smaller on the page, neighbors
nice to lunch with, the friends we knew
still close. I wanted to tell you nights
are filmy and alive with bugs, invite you
for Shakespeare in the Park beneath a peeling
signboard, find a part for your eyes to play
out in stages or fold you like a paper star.
But I know what mountains divide, some
common ground unsettled. The best country
is one we can sow and leave with fewer words.
And the best letter brief, seasonal as wheat
or old town affairs. One that closes before
weather wilts ridges between with love.

■ RIPLEY SCHEMM

Ripley Schemm was born in Ishpeming, Michigan, in 1929. When she was four years old, she moved to Great Falls with her family. Schemm was graduated from Swarthmore College and received her M.A. in English and Celtic Literature from the University of Montana. She has taught both English and creative writing at universities and in the public schools. She has been a Montana Poet in the Schools for the last two years. Her poems have been published in such journals as The Ohio Review, *and they have been collected in a chapbook,* Mapping My Father, *published in 1981. Schemm is the daughter of novelist Mildred Walker; she was married to poet Richard Hugo and is the mother of Matthew Hansen, both of whom appear in this anthology.*

Headwaters

for Lorman

Keeper of sacred ground,
born Metis in these aspen,
pushed down the South Fork
to jackpine flats with your people,
your wagon rumbles up this canyon
each morning of my life. Your eyes
bring back white goats to the face
of Wind Mountain. I see you driving
to Green Gulch, to the Headwaters,
hollowed to the reins in your hand.

Now that death has let you get back
from town, town where frailness dragged you,
town that called these aspen Breedtown,
pull up here where buffalo willow
used to hide the crossing.
We were quiet as fish fighting for bait
when you let us water the team.
We were your children.

We've each had our exile in country
where rivers run without water.
Even the youngest who raced the jackpine

til the polio hit. A man now,
he keeps time for the highway crew.
Time off, he carves talc, coaxes
a sensual woman out of native stone.
We've all learned to thirst
from you, Lorman, learned to drink
from our hands.

Rules

1. School Bus

I wait in the frozen rut
by the gate, huddled
in a red scarf wound tight
around my chin. My breath
wets the wool, wind stiffens the wool.
I figure by the shadow I stand in
how sun could reach over the rimrock
before the bus, in time
to warm my nose. I wait
for the thing to happen, the thing
I'm reaching for. I have a lot
to figure with. Whether the cow
will calve before I'm back home,
whether the hollow-cheeked kids
from Hound Creek had breakfast,
and if I can toss
my fresh-made curls
when I pass the seat
where Jim Johnson sits.

2. Speech

To have speech perfect
rising in pitch
leading the way to my mind,
I take the pipe, the iron pipe
that shuts the corral gate
after we've milked. I take

the iron pipe in my mouth.
Thirty below and I am eight.
My brother is so afraid for me
he grabs the pipe, yanks it
out of my mouth,
the lining with it.
Then to have pain and no words
hurts less. My bloody mouth
is a kind of speech
the whole school understands.

3. Scales

Only 10 lbs. of cracked corn
I ask the old man for.
Even wait while he takes my time
to shift the wad and spit.
It's to finish my 4-H calf
for the Fair. Well, he might not
sell off any unless I'm willing
to pay the going rate. I know
I'm a tall girl in tight jeans,
small breasts bearing July sun,
eyes level with the old man's.
I can't stay always a 4-H'er
hand heart head home. He hooks
two fingers over his edge
of the heaped scale. My thumb
pushes up my side.

4. Fire on the North Fork

Eighteen singed men slouched
at the pine table, too tired
to lift their hands when I set down
the full plates, so tired
they shove their forearms out,
breaststroking smoke.
I slide between them,
thin Help in braids, glide back

and forth from the kitchen,
carry how they've been recruited
hopeless from 2nd Street South,
their burnt out lives just right
to save a canyon, a forest,
game they'll never hunt.
When their forks clank
the emptied plates, I'm glad
my belt lies flat on my hips,
glad my mouth knows the rules.

5. Leaving

One spring I leave for town,
I leave for love,
for learning, for all
the lives I want.
Town brings a bigger town,
after that cities too big
to beg. I live all the lives
I pass on the stairs,
in the street, in the park,
I hardly know which of the women
is pushing this child in a swing.
My own life gets along at home
by itself. Stubs its toe
on a willow root,
coils old rope in the shed,
cuts the engine when a quail's
limp feathers fly up with the hay,
races against my heart
to the house to save the nest
of hatchlings. I leave
the morning to mould in the field.

Anastasia's Afternoon

She raises the screen door latch
with the back of her hand, her face
to the steady run of the creek.
Her feet know the step to stir
the dog from, the step to sit on
and where to set the bag of plums,
the paring knife, the scoured pan.
She waits for the house to die down
behind her, cool air to lift
her shirt, ease the slope of her back,
the knot in her head,
into the downstream run.

Time to travel the syllables
of her name–the charge of the ranch woman
who could have murmured Shirley Mae
or Jane but named her newborn
Anastasia, intending perhaps
a wistful hint of Athens
for mule deer browsing the buck brush
along Nevada Creek. Or hope for
resurrection among the onion rows.

The knife blade warms the worn step,
plums stain the brown paper purple
in August heat. Anastasia's fingers
work out the pits, her thoughts work back
across the hay meadow to circle the child
curled between her hipbones. The creek runs
down the mountain alone. After the plums,
new potatoes to dig, after the spade thrown
aside, a bath, fresh clothes
and kitchen words to exchange for news
of hay, of horses, of water level.
Anastasia rises, licks the juice
from her fingers, thinking of yesterday
when her men rode in.

■ BARBARA TAYLOR SMITH

Barbara Taylor Smith was born into a pioneer North Dakota family in 1946. She grew up in Havre, Montana, and was graduated from Northern Montana College. After receiving an M.A. in English from the University of South Dakota, she began her teaching career at Western Wyoming Community College in Rock Springs, Wyoming, where she still lives. Smith's poems have been published in Plainswoman, Writers' Forum, *and several other journals and have been collected in a chapbook about pioneer women,* Wyoming Promises *(1985). This poem appears here for the first time.*

Snakes

The trailer house curtains swell slightly
as gusts hit sideways and rustle
the bales stacked around the bottom,
boom to the ghost town.
Books pile with laundry and dishes,
harlequins tucked with cereal coupons.
She makes her way past ash trays
to the counter. She pours a cup for me.

"They write about those pioneers
living out here in sod huts, dying in labor,
nothing, nowhere to go.
There was this one I read,
they built a dugout into this frozen hill,
moved into it, banked a fire for the night,
and woke up to find the whole place snapping
with rattlesnakes, thawed out.
Died that way they did,
whole hill was a snake's den.
Sorry bunch of homesteaders,
couldn't tell what they were looking at."
The wind whistles in the tires
holding the aluminum down.

"I didn't die in childbirth
like some of these book ladies.

Like to after, though.
Doctor sewed me up too tight
when I had Willie.
His daddy didn't care, neither.
Finally got rid of him, doctor too,
married again and had my girl here.
But he kilt hisself, dumbass,
so now I'm on my third man, raising his kids
and my one. Willie's in Worland."

"That pioneer book was fine,
but I like these better.
You know what's going to happen.
It's never March, froze up and blowing,
some guy rescues the woman, sweeps her
off her feet, the sex is always great,
and they ain't no snakes."

She listens to the roof.

■ WILLIAM STAFFORD

Born in Hutchinson, Kansas, in 1914, William Stafford received the B.A. and M.A. degrees from the University of Kansas and the Ph.D. from the University of Iowa. During World War II, Stafford served as a conscientious objector. The author of more than fourteen books, his second volume of poems, Travelling Through the Dark, *won the National Book Award for 1963. Stafford lives in Lake Oswego, Oregon, and is professor of English at Lewis and Clark College. This poem is reprinted from* Stories That Could Be True, *published in 1966.*

Montana Ecologue

I

After the fall drive, the last
horseman humps down the trail south;
High Valley turns into a remote, still cathedral.
Stone Creek in its low bank turns calmly
through the trampled meadow. The one scouting

thunderhead above Long Top hangs to watch,
ready for its reinforcements due in October.

Logue, the man who always close down the camp,
is left all alone at Clear Lake, where
he is leisurely but busy, pausing to glance across
the water toward Winter Peak. The bunkhouse
will be boarded up, the cookshack barricaded
against bears, the corral gates lashed shut.
Whatever winter needs it will have to find
for itself, all the slow months the wind owns.

From that shore below the mountain, the water
darkens; the whole surface of the lake livens;
and, upward, high miles of pine tops bend where a storm
walks the country. Deeper and deeper, autumn
floods in. Nothing can hold against that current
the aspens feel. And Logue, by being there, suddenly
carries for us everything that we can load on him,
we who have stopped indoors and let our faces
forget how storms come. That lonely man works for us.

II

Far from where we are, air owns those ranches
our trees hardly hear of—open places
braced against cold hills. Mornings, that
news hits the leaves like rain, and we
stop everything time brings, and freeze that one,
open, great, real thing, the world's gift—day.

Up there, air like an axe chops, near timberline,
the clear-cut miles the marmots own. We
try to know, all deep, all sharp, even while
busy here, that other; gripped in a job,
aimed steady at a page, or riffled by distractions,
we break free into that world of the farthest coat—air.

We glimpse that last storm when the wolves
get the mountains back, when our homes will flicker
bright, then dull, then old; and the trees

will advance, knuckling their roots or lying in
windrows to match the years. We glimpse
a crack that begins to run down the wall,
and, like a blanket over the window at night,
that world is with us and those wolves are here.

III

Up there, ready to be part of what comes, the high lakes
lie in their magnificent beds; but men,
great as their heroes are, live by their deeds
only as a pin of shadow in a cavern their thought
gets lost in. We pause, we stand where
we are meant to be, waver as foolish as
we are, tell our lies with all the beautiful grace
an animal has when it runs:

Citizen, step back from the fire and let night
have your head. Suddenly you more than hear
what is true so abruptly that God is cold—
winter is here. What no one saw has
come. Then everything the sun approved could
really fail? Shed from your back, the years
fall one by one, and nothing that comes
will be your fault. You breathe a few breaths
free at the thought—things can come so great
that your part is too small to count,
if winter can come.

Logue brings us all that. Earth took
the old saints, who battered their hearts,
met arrows, or died by the germs God sent;
but Logue, by being alone and occurring to us,
carried us forward a little,
and on his way out for the year will
stand by the shore and see winter in,
the great, repeated lesson every year.
A storm bends by that shore and
one flake at a time teaches
grace, even to stone.

■ DAVID THOMAS

David Thomas grew up in Chinook, Montana. According to Thomas, he "survived the Sixties" to write Fossil Fuel *(1977), his book of poems, and "continues to haunt the streets of Missoula, pen in hand." He has "traveled the old hippie, beatnik axis, following Jack Kerouac's ghost around." He is currently writing and working in Missoula.*

The Ten Thousand Things

Well let's see there's
        shebolts hebolts and stress rods
there's make-up bolts inbed bolts and
            carriage bolts
there's nuts and washers to fit all sizes
              of each.
There's rattle guns 18
          and 24 inch
          crescent wrenches–spud
               wrenches
             and porto-power
              jacks.
There's double jacks and jack hammers
        pinking eyes and inbed plates.
There's Foreman Frank for whom
            I work
          and foreman Al and foreman
            Stan and foreman Rags
          the superintendant and his vice.
There's the dry shacks the print shack
            the fire barrels
the lumber stockpile. There's 2×4's
2×6's 2×12's 4×6's 1×2's
            1×4's 1×6's
            in all different lengths.
            There's the Safety Man and
                        "Access Closed"
            signs there's roped off areas
            and KEEP OUT
              DANGER ABOVE signs.

there's water jugs on the cranes
and there's the nip truck
and its driver bringing in the
goods
nobody can find there's okum
and tie wire big rolls of tape
red plugs
and rock anchors
wing nuts
and cable clamps
not to mention cable and their
shackles
and turn-buckles.
There's the sky turning ever more purple
as the shift
swings toward
its end black by
lunch and stars
from then on mercury
vapor lamps and a
heavier coat.
there's pull ropes to the cans up concrete
columns
there's catwalks
and scaffolds
There's times when I wander
about picking up
and sorting bolts
there's times when a chance glance
at a star
trying to outshine
the lamps
is all the rest I get. It happens every night
from 4:30 pm
to 12:30 am
at Libby Dam.

Oh damn! I forgot nails! 16 common
16 duplex 8's the same
roofing nails and blue
heads
There's just no end to it

Sorting bolts on the edge
  of artificial light
the tune of an engine
  the shadow of the dam.

The Headwaters of the Marias

"I walkd
all the way
to Rock City
from here
and took pictures
met an old boy
from Heart
Butte, said
this is heavy
spiritual
turf, taboo
to Indians . . .
pictures
never turnd
out." blank
frame no frame
at all
these sandstone
bluffs
cut by relentless
wind
and water
older
than any name
we lean
on a brand new
Ford pick-up
as Sweetgrass
speaks
and first
a white splash
in the Two
Medicine River

then a quick
dark leap
snaps a fish
clear
of the late
summer water
low and muddy
the fish
finds its tail
and disappears
in the evening
light.

■ PATRICK TODD

Patrick Todd was born in Seattle in 1942 and grew up in Montana. He received an M.F.A. in creative writing from the University of Montana in Missoula in 1977. Todd was a house painter during the 1960s, and he taught in the Montana Poetry in the Schools Program from 1970 through 1972. From 1977 to 1984, he directed the Missoula Poverello Center, which offered assistance to transients and the poor. Todd's first book, Fire in the Bushes, *was published in 1978. These poems are from Todd's* A Fire by the Tracks *(1983).*

Room At Flathead

Up the creaky stairs a bulb hangs
from a cord in the dark hall
Steam heat rattles marbles through the pipes
And this blue chenille spread wears thin where both
faucets rust the sink   The last roomers
were probably winos trading bed and floor till some farmer's
fence went up   Who could be sadder than women
left in old hotels?   Frayed coat

Pink necklace coiled in a glass
Once a lady and I found a room in San Diego
No windows   Ceiling high as a handball court
and nothing but a cot we hugged on

through the night   Morning
on our way out   juke box
blaring   I glimpsed someone's aunt sleeping
on a barstool   Head on the bar   Red
hair fried to steel wool   Left arm out to anyone
Her face sagged limp
as jelly through the Sunday songs

Neola

Kept a small wild park   thick with pine
and cottonwoods   a hundred sparrows wheeled
into rain woods after a storm
When spring run-off dropped away from
banks of The Clarkfork   Clayton Horne and his
buddies claimed half a mile of the shore line
Those were the years they pulled in browns and whitefish
from the bridge   And waded waste deep through soaking weeds
to see winos lying around a campfire   Or the godawful
sight of Rex Chamley stripping down for a swim
in his greasy longjohns   One night
a huge wild moon swelled over the river
and trees   Only his second summer at the mill
and still no more than a sheepish boy
Clayton stood on the porch of an old clapboard house
above the train yard while two friends waited behind the hedge
in a pickup   A small black woman opened the door
and after brief talk in velvet chairs she led him to
a room   complete with antique tassle
lamp shades   burgundy silk sheets and a mirror
on the ceiling   Clayton Horne has never
been to Paris or finished the book
about a dark lady of Madrid   Still Neola
was plenty for any boy from a country town or the city
This morning   twenty years later   he is simply
a man waiting for her to cross the icy street in front of his car
One hand lugging a big suitcase   The other waving stupid
traffic out of her way   She is catching
the 9:03 this time   The train already rumbling
and steaming behind the station

Dark lady with a side-long glint in her eye
and rough laugh   Once he leaned down to
kiss the yellow butterfly on her lovely round hip
and learned the total price for the full dinner of his pleasures
Who is he to her now? Banker in a little car on business?
Family man? No one she remembers in the lost faces
of a hundred men   When she waves him off
dull in his dapper hat and gloves   there is
a reason   Clayton Horne hasn't even been to New York
But he has been to Neola's at the dead end of 4th Street
And grows more careful each day with
what he gives and takes in the fast world

LINDA WEASEL HEAD

A member of the Confederated Salish/Kootenai Tribes, Linda Weasel Head grew up near Arlee, Montana. Married and the mother of five children, Weasel Head is working toward a B.A. degree in English from the University of Montana. "Stone Woman" originally appeared in Cutbank *(1987).*

Stone Woman

A young woman climbed
Into a green and blue stone
Coyote threw her into the river
        right in the middle
        of Winter
        All she heard
                was clinking ice
        All she saw
                was a brown bottle
        All she felt
                were jagged edges
                that cut her fingers
        All she tasted
                was her own dry lips
                thirsty for water

All she smelled
was thick piss
that clung to her hair
She remembered
she had children
somewhere

Rolled downstream
By fast melting mountain snows, she tumbled
Stumbled out an old woman
Her stone broken

■ ROBERTA HILL WHITEMAN

A student of Richard Hugo's, Roberta Hill Whiteman teaches at the University of Wisconsin at Eau Claire. In the spring of 1988, Whiteman toured China with Barry Lopez, Harrison Salzbury, and Maxine Hong Kingston. Three of her poems appear in the latest edition of the Norton Anthology of Poetry. *These selections are from* Star Quilt, *which was published in 1985.*

Star Quilt

These are notes to lightning in my bedroom.
A star forged from linen thread and patches.
Purple, yellow, red like diamond suckers, children

of the star gleam on sweaty nights. The quilt unfolds
against sheets, moving, warm clouds of Chinook.
It covers my cuts, my fed birch clusters under pine.

Under it your mouth begins a legend,
and wide as the plain, I hope Wisconsin marshes
promise your caress. The candle locks

us in forest smells, your cheek tattered
by shadow. Sweetened by wings, my mothlike heart
flies nightly among geraniums.

We know of land that looks lonely,
but isn't, of beef with hides of velveteen,
of sorrow, an eddy in blood.

Star quilt, sewn from dawn light by fingers
of flint, take away those touches
meant for noisier skins,

anoint us with grass and twilight air,
so we may embrace, two bitter roots
pushing back into the dust.

Lynn Point Trail

That rare day we played for real
and left traces of our walking sticks

in last year's leaves. Lynn Point Trail
hid us in rushing green, in the quick
dark of douglas fir where death conceals
itself in blazing moss.

Leading us in the journey,
our children stomp-danced until the ferns
bristled with the authority
of hooded cobras. When they turned
to us for answers, we began to see
fronds tremble with a delicate weight,

as if infinity had stirred the stem.
The scattered light peopled each ravine.
We longed for woods this deep, for this glen
where you knelt to photograph a gleam
inside a bridge of stone. Was it then
Missy wouldn't go on?

Our youngest girl wanted to believe
home could be this emerald grotto.
Nearby, we heard the breaking sigh of waves,
while, bickering in a bird's staccato,
she kept her gesture firm, though naive:
Here we belonged.

A cuckoo's call echoed in the sun.
I, too, wish we could have lived
near the tilted horizon,
close to the fluttering mat that weaves
dun fly and dune into one.

With songs for granite and bluer skies,
children gathered rain-eroded shells.
Let these rocks be eggs until the tides
scorch them, or until the heart reveals
at last the grace we lost.

■ ROBERT WRIGLEY

A native of Illinois, Robert Wrigley was graduated from Southern Illinois University before coming to the University of Montana to study for his M.F.A. degree under Richard Hugo. Wrigley was the editor of Cutbank, *the university's acclaimed literary magazine. The recipient of an NEA literature grant in 1978-1979, Wrigley is currently on the English faculty at Lewis-Clark State College in Lewiston, Idaho. These poems are from his first collection,* The Sinking of Clay City, *published in 1979.*

Winter Love

From the diary of D.D. Pye (1871-1899)

1

They talked about the cold, the cold
each one felt warm in and believed,
breath clouds so long before their faces
when they spoke–months,
indoors and out–that speech became
unwieldy, frozen, cloud talk
and vapors, a rim of ice
on the lip of the morning blankets.

They made love then, and she rose
and knelt above the chamber pot,
a fog of them rising round her thighs,
and he threw back the hides and covers
that his mist in the cabin rafters
might meld and mix with hers.
Love, when they talked, was what
they said. Love, she said,

and he too, wadding rags in the heaved log
walls, kindling in the swollen,
buckled stove. The wood into flames
unraveling was their music,
and the low reports outside

as trees exploded, frozen to their hearts.
One morning the hens were dead,
a frost-tufted egg in each cloaca.

2

We know, for all the dead
weight of winter, they never wept
to be back in Pennsylvania, but loved, and lived
on the frozen deer he hauled back
from the snow-locked meadow, one flank
here and there worried by wolf,
hacked away and abandoned.
He never felt watched in the crystalline woods.

Over years now we see the blunder,
the misfortune: a gorgeous homestead
worthless in trapped-out mountains,
giddy lovers awash in dreams. And winter,
the steel of it driven through their lives,
how it took hold when they touched it–
a kiss of ice in the frozen world
that held them harder than they held each other.

Until the day the fire took the cabin,
when the stove gave way to a last
over-load of wood and they huddled
on the tramped-down path to the outhouse,
warmed in a way they had not been
in weeks, until that day the diary we read from,
in his crisp, formal hand, revealed
only joy, and the color of her eyes.

3

The lovers, see them now, those first few
miles aswim in a snow so light it is never
entirely fallen, but a kind of frigid fog
swirling under the useless sun.
At camp that night, in the deep bowl
wind-scoured round a fir tree's butt,

there is terror in his words,
a darkness malevolent and haunted.

And his love is numbed to a stillness
after violent shivers, her breath fitful,
obscured to him by the wind-sough above them
and the rumble of his heart.
He vows to change course. Damn
the distant town and houses. He knows
a spring that boils beyond the western ridgeline,
and if its heat is from hell,

if he must move aside Satan to sit there,
to lower his love in its curing waters,
if he must carry her all the snow-clogged miles,
"then so be it," he will. That is all
we can read, but for one brief entry,
one line without date, one
sentence scrawled dumbly, simply,
as though the cold at last had killed his will.

4

"She is gone." Only that, and the rest
of the story pieced together by those
who found them, she floating naked
in the steaming waters, he hung from the spar
of a spring-killed tree, his diary
beneath his clothes, frozen there,
a flimsy shield across his chest.
Nothing more, but what we imagine.

Imagine the last morning how she could not
walk, how piggy-back he carried her,
wading through that sea of snow,
feeling against his neck her cheek
foolingly warmed by the touch of him,
the sweat and grunt and ache of how he walked.
Imagine his blackened fingers fumbling her
out of her clothes, his scream

at those same fingers when he held her
in the heat of that pool.
How he must have swayed with her
there, light in his arms
and caught already in the slow, unceasing turn
of the current–two lovers
dancing in the hot and buoyant waters,
below the cloud of steam that hides their breath.

In the Great Bear

Flathead Range, August 1976

At the excavation for marmots, on the lip
of a saucer bowled out by claws as long as
your outstretched hand, you crouch
low and quiet, the rodent's posture, and sight
two dark lanes through dewy meadow
grass: yours and his, splitting ninety acres
and spinning a dish of dirt
like a pendant on its chain. He left
the way he came, and but for minutes
you walked a collision course.

The digging came to nothing, and now
he is gone where you're headed, over the near rise
or the far mountain, asleep, burping
a fill of lilies. Or filled
with an emptiness like the one he just dug,
paused in the blind of lodgepole,
forelegs shaggy with dew and mud, claws

tipped and shiny. He waits upwind, always
prepared for surprise. But that is
the low view on high places. Stand up
and the air goes clear of his summer musk.
Shake off the marmot's small cautions,
that intricate network of tunnels, and walk on,
with him, behind him, singing loudly
and only to yourself.

Ursa Major

Trapper Peak, September 1975

On your back in juniper, a skeletal bear
grows above, a dipper full of dream
some mauled Indian spotted
centuries ago. Astronomers draw lines,
circle the dots with full-tailed bearish
shells as crude and empty as cookiecutters.

Here, you watch the starry bones grow
a body. In this place of pure dark,
constellations and nebulae too dim
in the city beam a silver-tipped coat,
and now and then some
distant sun flashes like a fang.

■ PAUL ZARZYSKI

Born in 1951, Paul Zarzyski grew up in Hurley, Wisconsin. He was graduated from the University of Wisconsin at Stephens Point with degrees in biology and English and came to Missoula to study poetry with Richard Hugo at the University of Montana. He received his M.F.A. in 1975. When he was twenty-six years old, Zarzyski took up bronc riding and now competes on the rodeo circuit and writes poems about rodeoing. He has held teaching positions in the Forestry School and the English Department at the University of Montana. Zarzyski published his first book, Call Me Lucky, *in 1981. These poems are from* The Make-up of Ice *(1984).*

The Heavyweight Champion Pie-Eatin' Cowboy of the West

for Larry, Curt, Joel, Jim, and Bugs

I just ate 50 pies—started off with coconut
macaroon, wedged my way through bar angel
chocolate, Marlborough, black walnut and sour cream
raisin to confetti-crusted crabapple—

still got room for dessert
and they can stick their J-E-L-L-O
where the cowpie don't shine, cause Sugar Plum
I don't eat nothing made from horses' hooves!

So make it something "pie," something light
and fancy, like huckleberry fluffy chiffon, go
extra heavy on the hucks and fluff–beaten
eggwhites folded in *just* so. Or let's shoot
for something in plaid, red and tan lattice-
topped raspberry, honeyed crust
flaky and blistered to a luster, wild
fruit oozing with a scoop of hard vanilla!

Or maybe I'll strap on a feedbag of something
a smidgen more timid: quivering
custard with its nutmeg-freckled fill
nervous in the shell. Come to think of it now,
blue ribbon mincemeat sounds a lot
more my cut: neck of venison, beef suet,
raisins, apples, citrus peel, currants–
all laced, Grammy-fashion, in blackstrap molasses!

No. Truth is, I'm craving shoofly or spiced rhubarb
or sure hard to match peachy praline,
cinnamon winesap apple à la mode, walnut
crumb or chocolate-frosted pecan. *OR*,
whitecapped high above its fluted deep-dish crust,
a lemon angel meringue–not to mention
mandarin apricot, black bottom, banana cream,
burgundy berry or Bavarian nectarine ambrosia!

And how could you out-gun the Turkeyday
old reliables: sweet potato, its cousin
pumpkin, its sidekicks Dutch apple and cranberry
ice cream nut. Ah, harvest moon, that autumn
gourmet cheese supreme, or Jack Frost squash, or . . .
"my favorite," you ask? That's a tough one.
Just surprise me with something new, Sweetie
Pie–like tangerine boomerang gooseberry!

Escorting Grammy to the Potluck Rocky Mountain Oyster Feed at Bowman's Corner

for Ethel "Grammy" Bean

Lean Ray Krone bellers through a fat cumulus
cloud of Rum-Soaked Wagonmaster Conestoga
Stogie smoke he blows across the room,
"They travel in 2's, so better eat them even
boys, or kiss good luck good-bye for good."

Tonight the calf nuts, beer batter-dipped
by the hundreds, come heaped
and steaming on 2-by-3 foot trays
from the kitchen—deep-fat fryers
crackling like irons searing hide.

And each family, ranching Augusta
Flat Creek country, brings its own brand
of sourdough hardrolls, beans, gelatins,
slaws and sauces, custard and mincemeat
pies to partner-up to the main chuck.

At the bar, a puncher grabs a cow-
poxed handful—7 of the little buggers—
feeding them like pistachios
from palm to pinch fingers to flick-
of-the-wrist toss on target.

Grammy, a spring filly at 86, sips
a whiskey-ditch in one hand, scoops
the crispy nuggets to her platter
with the other, forks a couple
and goes on talking Hereford bulls.

And me, a real greenhorn to this cowboy
caviar—I take to them like a pup
to a hoof paring, a porky
to a lathered saddle, a packrat
to a snoosebox full of silver rivets.

I skip the trimmings, save every cubic inch
of plate and belly for these kernels,
tender nubbins I chew and chew till the last
pair, left for luck, nuzzle on the tray
like a skylined brace of round bales.

A cattleland Saturday grand time with Grammy
is chowing down on prairie pecans, then driving
the dark-as-the-inside-of-a-cow grangehall
trail home to dream heifer-fat, bull-necked
happy dreams all night long in my Sunday boots.

Silos

against Augusta, Montana: prairie dovetailed
with Rockies, raptor with hard wind, hard
grass and grain, with cattle and antelope
with Flat Creek–rainbow,
brown and brook trout–with buckbrush
coulee–jack rabbit and mule deer–
with snowberry, cocklebur and rosehip scrub
–Hungarian partridge and sharptail–
with sun and moon with Tabletop
and Steamboat Mountain, with Haystack
Butte, Gobblers' Knob, Bean Lake, and yardlight
to yardlight, that distant dark we love
between stars. Silos against Augusta:
honeybee with Hutterite with family ranch–
the Minuteman launching pads
against everything from Dearborn River
to jackfence to cowhorse and combine
rolling with the camber and cant, rolling
with the land. Ballistic Missile vaults
square off in a chain all their own
against the horizontal grain
of glacier and age: warheads
from Augusta, from earth still festering
cavalry repeating carbines

to the surface–shrapnel
through old scars–where cattle stir,
moon to salt lick to moon,
this veteran wind
once bulletproof, this distance
no longer dark, no longer living
out of sight and range.

Bibliographic Citations and Permissions

NATIVE AMERICAN STORIES AND MYTHS

"How the Summer Season Came" and "Power of the Peace Pipe," by James L. Long (First Boy), are found in *Land of Nakoda, The Story of the Assiniboine Indians* (Helena: State Publishing Company, 1942), pp. 27-30, 35-40. The stories are reprinted in Michael Kennedy, ed. *The Assiniboines* (Norman: University of Oklahoma Press, 1961), pp. 3-6, 10-14.

"The Gambling Contests" appears in Robert H. Lowie, "The Assiniboine," vol. 4, pt. 1, of the *Anthropological Papers of the American Museum of Natural History* (New York: Museum of Natural History, 1909), pp. 218-223.

"How the Morning and Evening Stars Came to Be in the Sky," by Jerome Fourstar, Fort Peck, Montana, is from an unpublished manuscript. Reprinted by permission of Jerome Fourstar.

"Why the White Man Will Never Reach the Sun," as told by James White Calf, appears in Richard Lancaster, *and horns on the toad*, a publication of the Texas Folklore Society, vol. 29 (Dallas: Southern Methodist University Press, 1959), pp. 192-200. Copyright © 1959, reprinted by permission of the Texas Folklore Society, Austin.

"The Story of Marriage," written and compiled by Darnell Davis Rides At The Door, is in *Napi Stories* (Browning, Montana: Blackfeet Heritage Program, 1979), p. 35. Copyright © 1979, reprinted by permission of the Blackfeet Heritage Program and Darnell Davis Rides At The Door.

"Mia-Wa, the Hard Luck Warrior," by George Comes At Night, is from *Roaming Days*, edited by Jane Bailey (Browning, Montana: Blackfeet Heritage Program, 1978), pp. 8-15. Copyright © 1978, reprinted by permission of the Blackfeet Heritage Program and Mrs. Agnes Comes At Night.

"The Twelve Moons" and "Napi and the Sun's Leggings," by Percy Bullchild, are excerpted from *The Sun Came Down* (New York: Harper & Row, 1985), pp. 120-121, 189-195. Copyright © 1985 by Percy Bullchild. Reprinted with the permission of Harper & Row.

"Ē-hyōph'-sta (Yellowtop-to-Head Woman)," compiled by George Bird Grinnell, is from "Some Early Cheyenne Tales," *Journal of American Folklore* 20 (July-September 1907): 173-178.

"The Bear Butte," as told by Jessie American Horse, "The Ghost Owl," as told by Mary Little Bear Inkanish, and "Why the Turtle's Shell Is Checked," as told by Mary Little Bear Inkanish, are excerpted from Alice Marriott and Carol K. Rachlin, *Plains Indian Mythology* (New York: Thomas Y. Crowell Company, 1975), pp. 43-47, 78-81, 99-100. Copyright © 1975 by Alice Marriott and Carol K. Rachlin. Reprinted with the permission of Harper & Row.

"Lodge-Boy and Thrown-Away" is from Robert H. Lowie, "Myths and Traditions of the Crow Indians," vol. 25, pt. 1, of the *Anthropological Papers of the American Museum of Natural History* (New York: American Museum of Natural History, 1918), pp. 74-85. "Divorced Women" appears in *Crow Texts*, edited and translated by Robert H. Lowie (Berkeley: University of California Press, 1960), pp. 219-223. Copyright © 1960 The Regents of the University of California. Used by permission.

"Origin of the Seasons," by Pete Beaverhead, appears in *Stories from Our Elders*, edited by Clarence Woodcock (Pablo, Montana: Flathead Culture Committee, Confederated Salish and Kootenai Tribes, 1979), pp. 46-61. Copyright © 1979 and reprinted by permission of the Flathead Culture Committee.

"Coyote Kills the Giant" and "Coyote Kills Another Giant" are in Louisa McDermott, "Folk-lore of the Flathead Indians of Idaho: Adventures of Coyote," *Journal of American Folk-lore* 14 (1901): 240-241, 242-244.

"How the Sweathouse Came to Be," by Blind Mose Chouteh, is from a mimeographed copy of an oral transcription taken in 1983. It is held in the archives of the Flathead Culture Committee of the Confederated Salish & Kootenai Tribes, Pablo, Montana, 1983. Copyright © 1983, reprinted by permission of the Flathead Culture Committee.

"The Boy Who Was Raised by Seven Buffalo Bulls" and "Moon Child," by Fred Gone, Sr., are in *War Stories of the White Clay People* (Fort Belknap, Montana: Fort Belknap Education Department, 1982), pp. 57-62, 107-113. Copyright © 1982, reprinted by permission of the Fort Belknap Indian Community.

"The Woman and the Horse," as told by Assiniboine, "The Bad Wife," as told by Watches-All, and "The Man Who Acquired Invulnerability," as told by Watches-All, are in A. L. Kroeber, *Gros Ventre Myths and Tales*, vol. 1, pt. 3, of the *Anthropological Papers of the American Museum of Natural History* (New York: Museum of Natural History, 1907), pp. 114-115, 120-122, 122-125.

"Wolf and the Two-Pointed Buck," as told by Simon Francis, appears in Claude Schaeffer, "Wolf and Two-Pointed Buck: A Lower Kutenai Tale of the Supernatural Period," *Primitive Man* 22 (January-April 1949): 8-22.

"The Flying Head," "The Wolves' Sister Marries," "Frog Takes a Mate," and "Mountain Sheep Boy," as told by Pete Beaverhead and Josephine Beaverhead, are in Leslie B. Davis, "Remnant Forms of Folk Narrative Among the Upper Pend d'Oreille Indians," Anthropology and Sociology Paper no. 31, University of Montana, Missoula, 1965, pp. 5-6, 15-17, 19-20, 28-30. Reprinted by permission of Leslie B. Davis.

JOURNALS OF EXPLORATION

Selections from *Original Journals of the Lewis and Clark Expedition, 1804-1806*, edited by Reuben Gold Thwaites, 7 vols. (New York: Dodd, Mead & Company, 1904-1905), 1:344; 2:33-35, 78-79, 91-93, 100-102, 112-116, 130-132, 147-150, 271, 275-278, 281-283; 3:52-54; 5:219-227.

"How the Ancient Peigans Lived," as told by Blood (Kainaikoan) and interpreted by Joseph Tatsey, appears in C. C. Uhlenbeck, *A New Series of*

Blackfoot Texts from the Southern Peigans Blackfoot Reservation, Teton County, Montana (Amsterdam: Johannes Muller, 1912), pp. 1-12.

Excerpts from W. A. Ferris, *Life in the Rocky Mountains: A Diary of Wanderings on the sources of the Rivers Missouri, Columbia, and Colorado from February, 1830, to November, 1835*, edited by Paul C. Phillips (Denver: The Old West Publishing Company, 1940), pp. 1, 111-116.

"Establishment of Fort Piegan As Told Me by James Kipp," by Lieutenant James Bradley, in Bradley Manuscript–Book "F," copy of a manuscript prepared by A. M. Quivey, in *Contributions to the Historical Society of Montana*, 10 vols. (Boston: J. S. Canner and Company, 1966), 8:246-249. Used by permission of the Montana Historical Society, Helena.

Selections from *Letters and Notes on the Manners, Customs, and Condition of the North American Indians*, by George Catlin, 2 vols. (New York: Wiley and Putnam, 1841), 1:49-50, 260-264.

Selections from *Journal of a Trapper*, by Osborne Russell, edited by Aubrey L. Haines (Lincoln: University of Nebraska Press, 1965), pp. 101-107.

"My Country," by Arapooish, Chief of the Crows, as told to Robert Campbell, was reported by Lieutenant James Bradley in "Arrapooash," in *Contributions to the Historical Society of Montana*, 10 vols. (Boston: J. S. Canner and Company, 1966), 9:306-307. Used by permission of the Montana Historical Society in Helena. The selection is reprinted in Joseph Kinsey Howard, ed., *Montana Margins* (New Haven, Connecticut: Yale University Press, 1946), pp. 109-110.

Selections from "The Missouri River Journals, 1843," by John James Audubon, is from *Audubon and His Journals*, edited by Maria Audubon, 2 vols. (New York: Dover Publishers, 1960), 1:496-497, 508-509; 2:10-14, 26-27, 105-107, 128-129, 130-131.

Selections from *Up the Missouri with Audubon: The Journal of Edward Harris*, by Edward Harris, edited by John Francis McDermott (Norman: University of Oklahoma Press, 1951), pp. 99-101, 108-110, 146-148.

"A Journey on a Barge Down the Missouri from the Fort of the Blackfeet to That of the Assiniboines: Particulars Edifying or Curious," by Nicolas Point, S.J., is reprinted in *Wilderness Kingdom: Indian Life in the Rocky Mountains: 1840-1847–The Journals & Paintings of Nicolas Point, S.J.*, translated by Joseph P. Donnelly (New York: Holt, Rinehart and Winston, 1967), pp. 213-225.

"Pretty Busy" is from "Fort Benton Journal, 1854-1855," an anonymous journal published in *Contributions to the Historical Society of Montana*, 10 vols. (Boston: J. S. Canner and Company, 1966), 10:10-15. Used by permission of the Montana Historical Society, Helena.

Excerpts from *Miners and Travelers' Guide to Oregon, Washington, Idaho, Montana, Wyoming, and Colorado*, by Captain John Mullan (New York: Wm. M. Franklin, 1865), pp. 5-9.

"The Seven Visions on Seven Buttes," as told by Garter Snake to Fred P. Gone, is in *The Seven Visions of Bull Lodge*, edited by George P. Horse Capture

(Ann Arbor, Michigan: Bear Claw Press, 1980), pp. 29-37, 56-58. Reprinted with the permission of George P. Horse Capture.

"Iron Teeth, a Cheyenne Old Woman," by Iron Teeth, as told to Thomas B. Marquis, is from *The Cheyennes of Montana*, edited by Thomas D. Weist (Algonac, Michigan: Reference Publications, 1978), pp. 52-81. Reprinted by permission of Reference Publications.

"Journal, 1863," by Henry Edgar, is transcribed by Israel Clem in *Contributions to the Historical Society of Montana*, 10 vols. (Boston: J. S. Canner and Company, 1966): 3:131-134, 137-140. Reprinted by permission of the Montana Historical Society, Helena.

STORIES OF EARLY PIONEERS AND INDIANS

"Alder Gulch in 1863," by Mary Ronan, is in *Frontier Woman: The Story of Mary Ronan, As Told to Margaret Ronan*, edited by H. G. Merriam (Missoula: University of Montana Publications in History, 1973), pp. 17-22. Used with permission of the University of Montana, Publications in History.

"The Execution of 'The Greaser' (Joe Pizanthia), and Dutch John (Wagner)" and "The Arrest and Execution of Captain J. A. Slade," by Thomas J. Dimsdale, are in *The Vigilantes of Montana, or Popular Justice in the Rocky Mountains* (Virginia City, Montana: Montana Post, 1866). Dimsdale's book has been reprinted by the University of Oklahoma Press in Norman (1985), pp. 151-155, 194-201, 204-205.

"Pecunie Coup," "I Do Not Like to Fight with White Men," and "Vision in the Crazy Mountains," are in Frank Bird Linderman, *Plenty-coups, Chief of the Crows* (Lincoln: University of Nebraska Press, Bison Books, 1962), pp. 58-67, 205-216, 219-222, 227-237. Copyright © 1930 by Frank B. Linderman. Reprinted by permission of Harper & Row, Publishers, Inc.

"Chickadees," "Women Against War," and "The End" are in Frank Bird Linderman, *Pretty-shield, Medicine Woman of the Crows* (Lincoln: University of Nebraska Press, Bison Books, 1974), pp. 152-160, 167-169, 248-253. Copyright © 1960 Harper & Row. Used by permission.

"Our Life's Last Chapter," by Elizabeth B. Custer, in *"Boots and Saddles" or, Life in Dakota with General Custer* (New York: Harper & Brothers, 1885), pp. 216-224. The book was reprinted in 1961 by the University of Oklahoma Press, Norman.

"General Custer's Last Fight As Seen by Two Moon: The Battle Described by a Chief Who Took Part in It," by Hamlin Garland, first appeared in *McClure's Magazine* 11 (September 1898): 444-448. A version of Two Moon's account has been reprinted in *Great Documents in American Indian History*, edited by W. Moquin and C. Van Doren (New York: Praeger Publishers, 1973), pp. 226-229.

"A Trip to the National Park in 1877," by Emma Carpenter Cowan, appears in *Contributions to the Historical Society of Montana*, 10 vols. (Boston: J. S. Canner, 1966), 4:160, 165-187. Reprinted by permission of the Montana Historical Society, Helena. Cowan's account is excerpted in *Montana*

Margins, edited by Joseph Kinsey Howard (New Haven, Connecticut: Yale University Press, 1946), pp. 126-141.

"I Will Fight No More," by Chief Joseph, was reported by James Mooney in "The Ghost Dance Religion and the Sioux Outbreak of 1890," *Fourteenth Annual Report of the Bureau of Ethnology*, 54th Cong., 2d sess., 1892-93, H.R. Doc. 230 (Serial 3531).

"The Only Way Out Is to Fly," by Andrew Garcia, is in *Tough Trip Through Paradise, 1878-1879*, edited by Bennett H. Stein (Boston: Houghton Mifflin, 1967), pp. 364-378. Copyright © by the Rock Foundation. Reprinted by permission of Houghton Mifflin Company.

"A Winter on the Marias" and "I Have a Lodge of My Own," by James Willard Schultz, is in *My Life As an Indian* (Lewiston, Idaho: Confluence Press, 1983), pp. 80-85, 86-91. Copyright © Museum of the Rockies, used by permission of Confluence Press, Lewiston, Idaho, in association with the Museum of the Rockies.

"Starvation Winter (1883-84)," by James Willard Schultz, is in *Blackfeet and Buffalo: Memories of Life Among the Indians* (Norman: University of Oklahoma Press, 1973), pp. 76-81. Copyright © 1962 by the University of Oklahoma Press. Used by permission.

The "Transcript of the Council Meeting" to discuss the Flathead Railroad Treaty of 1882 is from a government document entitled "Report in Relation to an Agreement Made Between Joseph Kay McCammon, Assistant Attorney General, on Behalf of the United States, and the Confederated Tribes of the Flathead, Kootenay, and Upper Pend D'Orielles Indians for the Sale of a Portion of Their Reservation in Montana for the Use of the Northern Pacific Railroad" (Washington, D.C.: Government Printing Office, 1883), pp. 8-15.

Selections from *A Bride Goes West*, by Nannie T. Alderson and Helena Huntington Smith (Lincoln: University of Nebraska Press, 1942), pp. 16-17, 48-58, 163-171, are reprinted by permission of the University of Nebraska Press. Copyright © 1942 by Farrar & Rinehart, Inc.

Excerpts from *We Pointed Them North: Recollections of a Cowpuncher*, by E. C. "Teddy Blue" Abbott and Helena Huntington Smith (Norman: University of Oklahoma Press, 1955), pp. 73-76, 158-170. New edition copyright © 1955 by the University of Oklahoma Press. Used by permission.

Excerpts from *Forty Years on the Frontier as seen in the Journals and Reminiscences of Granville Stuart, Gold-Miner, Trader, Merchant, Rancher and Politician*, edited by Paul C. Phillips, 2 vols. (Glendale, California: Arthur H. Clark Company, 1925), 2:87-95, 195-209.

"The Indian and Taxation," attributed to Chief Charlot, appeared in *The Weekly Missoulian* on April 26, 1976. The speech is reprinted in *Montana Margins*, edited by Joseph Kinsey Howard (New Haven, Connecticut: Yale University Press, 1946), pp. 16-19.

"Proceedings of a Council with the Sioux Indians of the Fort Peck Agency, Montana–1886" appears in *57th Annual Report of the Commissioner of Indian Affairs, 1888* (Washington, D.C.: Government Printing Office, 1888). Transcribed from the original in RG 75, Bureau of Indian Affairs,

Special Case 144-5380-1887, National Archives, Washington, D.C.

"The Story of a Cowpuncher," "Lepley's Bear," and "Some Liars of the Old West," by Charles M. Russell, are in *Trails Plowed Under* (New York: Doubleday, 1937), pp. 1-6, 75-76, 191-194. "Jake Hoover's Pig," by C. M. Russell, is retold by Frank B. Linderman in *Recollections of Charley Russell*, edited by H. G. Merriam (Norman: University of Oklahoma Press, 1963), pp. 18-29. Copyright © 1963 by the University of Oklahoma. Used by permission.

"End of the Trail Drive," by Andy Adams, is from *The Log of a Cowboy* (Boston: Houghton Mifflin, 1903), pp. 327-387.

"Yarns" and "The Circular Story," by John R. Barrows, is in *Ubet* (Caldwell, Idaho: The Caxton Printers, 1934), pp. 177-182, 275-282. Used by permission of The Caxton Printers, Ltd., Caldwell, Idaho.

"Stuttering Shorty 'Freighter' " and "Shooting Fish," by Art H. Watson, are from *Devil Man with a Gun* (White Sulphur Springs, Montana: Meagher County News, 1967), pp. 117-119, 143-145. Used by the permission of Shirley Fogland.

"My Marriage," by Con Price, is in *Memories of Old Montana* (Hollywood, California: Highland Press, 1945), pp. 115-116, 118-121.

"Last Busting at Bow-Gun," by L. A. Huffman, originally appeared in *Scribner's Magazine* (July 1907). It was subsequently reprinted in *Montana, the Magazine of Western History* 6 (1956): 12-24, and in *Cowboys and Cattlemen*, edited by Michael Kennedy (New York: Hastings House, 1964), pp. 317-328.

WRITINGS ABOUT BUTTE

"When Bryan Came to Butte," by Charles H. Eggleston, first appeared in the August 13, 1897, *Anaconda Standard*. The poem was reprinted in *Montana Margins*, edited by Joseph Kinsey Howard (New Haven, Connecticut: Yale University Press, 1946), pp. 346-348.

"When Bryan Came to Butte–Yesterday," by Berton Braley, first appeared in the Butte *Intermountain* on October 7, 1909. "Jim" and "The Idealist" can be found in *Poems, 1882-1906*, a collection of Braley's poems compiled by the WPA for the Montana Historical Society Library, Helena.

"Silver Bow," by Myron Brinig, is from *Singermann* (New York: Farrar & Rinehart, 1919), pp. 33-42; selections from *Wide Open Town* (New York: Farrar & Rinehart, 1931), pp. 121-132. Both selections are reprinted by permission of Myron Brinig.

"Diary of a Night Nurse," by Beatrice Murphy, was edited by Sister Kathleen O'Sullivan and transcribed by Teresa Jordan from a manuscript in the Butte-Silver Bow Public Archives. Used courtesy of the Butte-Silver Bow Public Archives.

Selections from *The Story of Mary MacLane, by herself*, by Mary MacLane (Chicago: Herbert S. Stone, c. 1902), pp. 23-24, 27-30, 71-74, 80-85, 184-186, 288. "A Working Diaphragm" and "God Compensates Me" are from *I, Mary MacLane: A Diary of Human Days* (New York: Frederick A. Stokes, 1917), pp. 121, 158-161.

Selections from *Glittering Hill*, by Clyde F. Murphy (New York: Dutton, 1944), pp. 141-142, 146-148, 150-151, 153-156, 158-163, 166-167.

"I found my likings in the mines," by Dennis "Dinny" Murphy, is from an oral interview with Murphy transcribed and edited by Teresa Jordan in 1986. Used by permission of Teresa Jordan.

"A Woman in Green and a Man in Grey," by Dashiell Hammett, is from *Red Harvest*, which is reprinted here from *The Novels of Dashiell Hammett* (New York: Alfred A. Knopf, 1974), pp. 3-8. Copyright 1929 by Alfred A. Knopf, Inc. and renewed 1957 by Dashiell Hammett. Reprinted from *The Novels of Dashiell Hammett* by permission of Alfred A. Knopf, Inc.

REMEMBERING THE AGRICULTURAL FRONTIER

"They Bought Satin Pajamas," by Joseph Kinsey Howard, is from *Montana: High, Wide and Handsome* (New Haven, Connecticut: Yale University Press, 1943), pp. 189-196. Used by permission of Yale University Press.

"Homestead Days in Montana," by Pearl Price Robertson, first appeared in *The Frontier* (1933). Robertson's reminiscence is reprinted in *Montana Margins*, edited by Joseph Kinsey Howard (New Haven, Connecticut: Yale University Press, 1947), pp. 221-222, 230-242.

"Sheepherding on the Sweetgrass," by Matthias "Mike" Martinz, is from Chapter 8 of his reminiscences, which he donated in 1983 to the Montana Historical Society Archives (Small Collection 1786) in Helena.

"And I was alone, all alone," by Peggy Czyzeski, is part of an interview by Laurie K. Mercier for "Montanans At Work, 1910-1945," an Oral History Project by the Montana Historical Society. A transcript of the interview is in the Montana Historical Society Archives in Helena.

"Member of the Crew: The Fladager Crew Threshing on the Albert Estenson Farm, Scobey, 1924," by Orland E. Esval, first appeared in *Montana, the Magazine of Western History* 27 (Autumn 1977): 64-71. Used by permission of the Montana Historical Society, Helena.

"Survival on the High Plains, 1929-1934," by Charles Vindex, first appeared in *Montana, the Magazine of Western History* 28 (Autumn 1978): 2-10. Used by permission of the Montana Historical Society, Helena.

Selections from *Back Trail of an Old Cowboy*, by Paul E. Young, was edited by Nellie Snyder Yost (Lincoln: University of Nebraska Press, 1983), pp. 167-170. Reprinted by permission of University of Nebraska Press. Copyright © 1983 by the University of Nebraska Press.

Selections from *Snake Tracks*, by Blaine Allen Goyins (New York: Carlton Press, 1970), pp. 63-67. © 1970 by Mildred Stough Goyins.

"A Toad in Hell," by Dan Cushman, is from *Plenty of Room & Air* (Great Falls: Stay Away Joe Publications, 1975), pp. 39-40, 45-63. Reprinted by permission of Dan Cushman.

"Mother's Foresight," by Taylor Gordon, is from *Born to Be* (Seattle: University of Washington Press, 1975), pp. 19-28.

Excerpts from "Preceding the Baptism of Frost," by Elliot Paul, is from *A Ghost Town on the Yellowstone* (New York: Random House, 1948), pp. 210-214.

"City Room," by John K. Hutchens, is from *One Man's Montana* (New York: J. B. Lippincott, 1964), pp. 142-149. Reprinted by permission of John K. Hutchens and J. B. Lippincott.

"Meeting with Montana Journalists," by Daniel W. Whetstone, is from *Frontier Editor* (New York: Hastings House, 1956), pp. 25-32. Used by permission of Frank Whetstone.

Selections from *Cheyenne Memories*, by John Stands In Timber and Margot Liberty, with the assistance of Robert M. Utley (Lincoln: University of Nebraska Press, 1967), pp. 12-13, 280-281. Copyright © Yale University Press. Used by permission of Yale University Press.

Selections from *The Tragedy of the Blackfoot*, by Walter McClintock, Southwest Museum Papers No. 3 (Los Angeles: Southwest Museum, April 1930), pp. 38-44.

"Grandfather and the Popping Machine," by Henry Tall Bull and Tom Weist, was published by the Council for Indian Education, Billings, 1970, pp. 2-15. Used by permission of the Council for Indian Education.

"Old Man Boushie," by Fred Nault, is from *Fred Nault: Montana Metis, as told by himself* (Rocky Boy's Reservation, Montana, Chippewa-Cree Research, Rocky Boy School, 1977), pp. 11-15. Used by permission of the Chippewa-Cree Culture Committee.

LITERATURE OF MODERN MONTANA

"Black Cherries," by Grace Stone Coates, is from *Black Cherries* (New York: Alfred A. Knopf, 1931), pp. 13-21. "Ransom," "Topers," "The Answer," "Village Satiety," and "Nights of Evil" are from *Mead and Mangelwurzel* (Caldwell, Idaho: Caxton Printers, 1933), pp. 24, 25, 44, 70, 106. "Country Doctor" is from *Portulacas in the Wheat* (Caldwell, Idaho: Caxton Printers, 1932), p. 51.

Selections from *Wind from an Enemy Sky*, by D'Arcy McNickle (New York: Harper & Row, 1978), pp. 188-198, and *The Surrounded* (New York: Dodd, Mead & Company, 1936), pp. 60-75. Reprinted by permission of Antoinette Vogel.

"The Trouble with Girls," by Norman Macleod, is from *The Bitter Roots* (New York: Smith & Durrell, 1941), pp. 101-108. "We Played the Flatheads At Arlee" is from *The Selected Poems of Norman Macleod* (Boise: Ahsahta Press, 1975), p. 4. Reprinted by permission of Ahsahta Press.

"The Rural Telephone," by Hughie Call, is from *Golden Fleece* (Boston: Houghton Mifflin, 1942), pp. 40-47.

"Agency Town" and "Cows," by Jason Bolles, is from *Magpies' Nest* (Butte: Standard Publishing Company, 1943), pp. 55, 141.

Selections from *Big Rock Candy Mountain*, by Wallace Stegner (New York: Duell, Sloan & Pearce, 1943), pp. 183-191. Used by permission of Wallace Stegner.

"A Song of the Wire Fence," by Elliott C. Lincoln, is from *Rhymes of a Homesteader* (Boston: Houghton Mifflin, 1920), p. 75.

Selections from *The Big Sky*, by A. B. Guthrie, Jr. (New York: Houghton

Mifflin, 1947), pp. 145-151, 326-329. Reprinted by permission of A. B. Guthrie, Jr.

"The Ranch in the Coulee," "The Wind," "Vengeance," "Deliverance," "The Stoic," and "Horizons," by Gwendolen Haste, are from *Young Land* (New York: Coward-McCann, 1930), pp. 36-42.

Selections from *I Am Lidian*, by Naomi Lane Babson (New York: Harcourt, Brace and Company, 1951), pp. 1-4. Used by permission of Paul Grieder.

"A Poem on McCarthyism," by Hobart McKean, is reprinted from the *Billings Gazette* (1952).

Selections from *If A Lion Could Talk*, by Mildred Walker (New York: Harcourt Brace Jovanovich, 1970), pp. 8-21. Copyright © 1970 by Mildred Walker. Used by permission of Mildred Walker and Harcourt Brace Jovanovich, Inc.

"The Man Who Shot Liberty Valance," by Dorothy Johnson, is from *A Man Called Horse* (New York: Ballantine Books, 1953), pp. 82-98. Copyright © 1949 by Dorothy M. Johnson. Copyright © renewed 1977 by Dorothy M. Johnson. Reprinted by permission of McIntosh and Otis, Inc. Excerpts from "Confessions of a Telephone Girl" are from *When You and I Were Young, Whitefish* (Missoula, Montana: Mountain Press Publishing Company, 1982), pp. 100-112. Copyright © 1982 by Dorothy M. Johnson. Reprinted by permission of McIntosh and Otis, Inc.

Selections from *The Black Moccasin*, by John J. Tatsey, compiled and edited by Paul T. DeVore (Spokane, Washington: The Curtis Art Gallery, 1971), pp. 11-13, 56-57. Grateful acknowledgment is made to June Tatsey and the Tatsey family for permission to reprint these selections.

"The Montana Face," by Leslie Fiedler, was first published in the *Partisan Review* 16 (December 1949): 1239-1248. The essay is reprinted in *Montana Opinion* (June 1956), pp. 15-19. Used by permission of Leslie Fiedler.

Selections from *Old Man's Garden*, by Annora Brown (Sidney, British Columbia: Gray's Publishing Ltd., 1970), pp. 35-37, 223-225, 242-243. The volume was first printed in 1954.

CONTEMPORARY FICTION

Selections from "A River Runs Through It," by Norman Maclean, are from *A River Runs Through It* (Chicago: University of Chicago Press, 1976), pp. 12-22, 94-101. Reprinted with the permission of Norman Maclean and the University of Chicago Press.

Selections from *The Death of Jim Loney*, by James Welch (New York: Harper & Row, 1979), pp. 50-58; selections from *Winter in the Blood* (New York: Harper & Row, 1974), pp. 61-70. Copyright © James Welch. Used by permission. Selections from *Fool's Crow*, by James Welch (New York: Viking Penguin, 1986), pp. 365-370. Copyright © 1986 by James Welch. Illustrations and maps copyright © Viking Penguin Inc., 1986. All rights reserved. Reprinted by permission of Viking Penguin Inc. "Harlem, Montana: Just Off the Reservation," "The Man from Washington," and "In My First Hard Springtime" are from *Riding the Earthboy 40* (New York: Harper & Row, 1971), pp. 25, 30-31, 35. Copyright © James Welch. Reprinted by permission. Available in Penguin paperback.

"The Heart of the Game," by Thomas McGuane, originally appeared in the first issue of *Outside Magazine* in 1977. It is reprinted in *An Outside Chance* (New York: Farrar, Strauss & Giroux, 1980), pp. 227-243. "Visitors" is from *Something to Be Desired* (New York: Farrar, Strauss & Giroux, 1985), pp. 311-319. Reprinted by permission of Thomas McGuane and Farrar, Strauss & Giroux.

Selections from *The Wrong Case*, by James Crumley (New York: Random House, 1975), pp. 223-237. Copyright © 1975 by James Crumley. Reprinted by permission of James Crumley and Random House, Inc.

"Gent," by Rick DeMarinis, originally appeared in *Cutbank* (Fall/Winter 1983); a version appeared *The Burning Women of Far Cry* (New York: Arbor House, 1986), pp. 3-21. It is also reprinted in *Best American Short Stories*, edited by John Updike (1984), pp. 56-71. Reprinted by permission of Rick DeMarinis.

"Enter Ramona, Laughing," by Wayne Ude, is from *Buffalo and Other Stories* (Amherst, Massachusetts: Lynx House Press, 1975), pp. 51-55. Reprinted by permission of Wayne Ude.

"Raising Goats," by Michael E. Moon, is from *John Medicinewolf* (New York: The Dial Press, 1970), pp. 88-91. Used by permission of Tonda Moon.

"The Good Work of Chickens," by Richard Brautigan, is from *The Tokyo-Montana Express* (New York: Dell Publishing Company, 1980), pp. 220-224. © 1980 by Richard Brautigan. Reprinted by permission of the Helen Brann Agency, Inc.

"Cody and Terry," by Spike Van Cleve, is from *40 Years' Gatherin's* (Kansas City: Lowell Press, 1977), pp. 83-91. Reprinted by permission of Barbara K. Van Cleve.

Selections from *This House of Sky* (Orlando, Florida: Harcourt Brace Jovanovich, 1978), pp. 122-141. Copyright © 1978 by Ivan Doig. Reprinted by permission of Harcourt Brace Jovanovich, Inc. Selections from *Dancing At the Rascal Fair* (New York: Atheneum, 1987), pp. 202-210, reprinted with permission of Atheneum Publishers, an imprint of Macmillan Publishing Company. Copyright © 1987 by Ivan Doig.

"Forby and the Mayan Maidens," by Mary Clearman Blew, first appeared in the *Georgia Review* (Spring 1980), pp. 83-95. Reprinted by permission of Mary Clearman Blew.

"Drinking and Driving," by William Kittredge, is from *Owning It All* (St. Paul, Minnesota: Graywolf Press, 1987), pp. 91-107. Reprinted by permission of William Kittredge and Graywolf Press. "Phantom Silver" originally appeared in the *Iowa Review* (1977). This version is from a special edition chapbook (Missoula, Montana: Kutenai Press, 1987). Reprinted by permission of William Kittredge.

"Eclipse," by David Long, is from *Home Fires* (Urbana: University of Illinois Press, 1982), pp. 1-16. Reprinted by permission of David Long and the University of Illinois Press.

"Jeremy Bentham, the *Pietà*, and a Few Precious Grayling," by David Quammen, first appeared in *Outside Magazine* (May 1982). This version is reprinted from *Natural Acts* (New York: Nick Lyons Books and Schocken Books, 1985), pp. 105-118. Reprinted by permission of David Quammen and Nick Lyons Books.

Excerpts from "Pages from My Notebook," by Bill Stockton, are from *Today I Baled Some Hay to Feed the Sheep the Coyotes Eat* (Missoula, Montana: Institute of the Arts Foundation, 1982), pp. 15-16, 31-38. Reprinted by permission of Bill Stockton.

"Communist," by Richard Ford, originally appeared in *Antaeus* (1985). This version is reprinted from *Rock Springs* (New York: Atlantic Monthly Press, 1987), pp. 215-235. Reprinted by permission of Richard Ford and the Atlantic Monthly Press.

"The Medicine of Albert Heavyrunner," by Earl Ganz, is previously unpublished. It is reprinted here by permission of Earl Ganz.

"The Harder They Fall," by Ralph Beer, is previously unpublished. It is reprinted here by permission of Ralph Beer.

"The Birthing," by Patricia Henley, is from *Friday Night At Silver Star* (St. Paul, Minnesota: Graywolf Press, 1986), pp. 11-29. Used by permission of Patricia Henley and Graywolf Press.

Selections from *Rain or Shine: A Family Memoir*, by Cyra McFadden (New York: Alfred A. Knopf, 1986), pp. 11-22. Used by permission of Cyra McFadden and Alfred A. Knopf.

"The Blue Bear," by Peter Bowen, appeared in *Northern Lights* (March-April 1986), pp. 21-22. Reprinted by permission of Peter Bowen.

"Saving the Dead," by Kurt Duecker, first appeared in *Shenandoah* (1982). This version is from *The Editor's Choice: New American Stories*, edited by George E. Murphy (New York: Bantam Books, 1985). Reprinted by permission of Kurt Duecker.

"Perma Red," by Debra C. Earling, is from *Gathering Ground: New Writing and Art by Northwest Women of Color*, edited by Jo Cochran, J. T. Stewart, and Mayumi Tsutakawa (Seattle: The Seal Press, c. 1984), pp. 106-112. Reprinted by permission of Debra C. Earling and The Seal Press.

CONTEMPORARY POETRY

"The Milltown Union Bar: You Could Love Here" and "The Milltown Union Bar," by Richard Hugo, are from *The Real West Marginal Way* (New York: W. W. Norton & Company, 1986), pp. 135-147. Reprinted by permission of W. W. Norton and Ripley Schemm Hugo.

"West Marginal Way," "The Squatter on Company Land," "Galileo's Chair," "*Spinazzola*: Quella Cantina Là," "Silver Star," "Missoula Softball Tournament," "What Thou Lovest Well Remains American," "Letter to Hill from St. Ignatius," "With Ripley at the Grave of Albert Parenteau," "White Center," "Glen Uig," "The Right Madness on Skye," and "Making Certain It Goes On," and "Degrees of Gray in Philipsburg," by Richard Hugo, are from *Making Certain It Goes On* (New York: W. W. Norton & Company, 1983), pp. 5-6, 96-97, 107-108, 124-126, 177-178, 210-211, 216, 235-236,

291-292, 329, 373-375, 389-390, 416-419, 446-448. Reprinted by permission of W. W. Norton and Ripley Schemm Hugo.

"The Entomologist's Landscape," "Fox Fire," and "A Fish to Feed All Hunger," by Sandra Alcosser, are from *A Fish to Feed All Hunger* (Charlottesville: University Press of Virginia, 1986), pp. 3-4, 5-6, 19. Reprinted by permission of Sandra Alcosser.

"Look into the Clouds," by Minerva Allen, is used with the permission of Minerva Allen.

"Blue Sky, the Girder Falling," by Jon Davis, is from *West of New England* (Missoula: University of Montana, 1982), p. 26. Reprinted by permission of Jon Davis.

"The Odd Woman," "In the Hellgate Wind," and "Existing Light," by Madeline DeFrees, are from *When Sky Lets Go* (New York: George Braziller, 1978), pp. 19-20, 49, 61. Copyright © 1977 George Braziller. Used by permission of George Braziller Publishers and Madeline DeFrees.

"The Pink Butterfly," by Roger Dunsmore, is from *Blood House*, an unpublished collection. Used by permission of Roger Dunsmore.

"Lost," by Patricia Goedicke, first appeared in *The Hampden-Sydney Review* (1978), and was subsequently reprinted in *Editor's Choice* (Iowa City: The Spirit That Moves Us Press, 1980) and *The Dog That Was Barking Yesterday* (Amherst, Massachusetts: Lynx House Press, 1985). Used by permission of Patricia Goedicke. "For All the Sad Rain" appeared in *Wind of Our Going* (Port Townsend, Washington: Copper Canyon Press, 1985). Used by permission of Patricia Goedicke and Copper Canyon Press. "This Life" is previously unpublished. Used by permission of Patricia Goedicke.

"Wounds," by Andrew Grossbardt, is from *The Traveler* (Lewiston, Idaho: Confluence Press, 1976). Reprinted with permission of Confluence Press Inc. Copyright 1976 by Andrew Grossbardt. All rights reserved.

"Missoula in a Dusty Light" and "News from the Glacier," by John Haines, are from *News from the Glacier* (Middletown, Connecticut: Wesleyan University Press, 1982), pp. 149, 154-155. Reprinted by permission of John Haines.

"Walking into Silence" and "Preparing for Dark," by Matthew Hansen, are from *Clearing* (Missoula: The Kutenai Press, 1986). Reprinted by permission of Ripley S. Hugo.

"December Spearing," by Bill Hoagland, is from *Writers' Forum* 12 (Fall 1986). Reprinted by permission of Bill Hoagland.

"Wild Horses," by Gary H. Holthaus, is from *Unexpected Manna* (Port Townsend, Washington: Copper Canyon Press, 1978), p. 27. Used by permission of Gary Holthaus and Copper Canyon Press. "Horse" is from *Circling Back* (Layton, Utah: Peregrine Smith, 1984), pp. 29-30. Copyright © 1984 by Gary H. Holthaus. Reprinted with the permission of the author and Gibbs Smith, publisher.

"North of Roundup, 1952," by Nancy Hunter, first appeared in *Frontiers* 9:2 (1987). Reprinted by permission of Nancy Hunter.

"The Glass Trout," by Greg Keeler, is from *American Falls* (Lewiston,

Idaho: Confluence Press, 1987). Reprinted by permission of Greg Keeler and Confluence Press.

"The Blind Horses" and "Gimp O'Leary's Iron Works," by Ed Lahey, are from *Blind Horses and Other Poems* (Butte, Montana: Artcraft, 1979), pp. 12, 29. Reprinted by permission of Ed Lahey.

"And She Is There with Laughing," by Don Manker, first appeared in *An Inkle of Danger* (c. 1982). Reprinted by permission of Don Manker.

"Reincarnation" and "The Lease Hound," by Wallace McRae, are from *It's Just Grass and Water* (Spokane: The Uxalis Group, 1986), pp. 19-21, 28-29. Reprinted by permission of Wallace McRae.

"Fanning the Flame," by D. Lewis Moore, is previously unpublished. Used by permission of D. Lewis Moore.

"Gertrude Stein Almost Comes to Helena, Montana, But Does Not," by Rick Newby, is from *A Radiant Map of the World* (Missoula, Montana: Arrow Graphics, 1981), pp. 15-16. Reprinted by permission of Rick Newby.

"An Elegy for Leila" and "From My Partner and I: An Apology," by Robert Sims Reid, are previously unpublished. Used by permission of Robert Sims Reid.

"print," by Leonard Wallace Robinson, is from *In the Whale* (Daleville, Indiana: The Barnwood Press, 1983), pp. 35-36. Reprinted by permission of Leonard Wallace Robinson.

"Circle of Struggle," by William Pitt Root, is reprinted by permission of William Pitt Root.

"The Difference in Effects of Temperature Depending on Geographical Location East or West of the Continental Divide: A Letter," by Dennice Scanlon, appeared in *Poetry Northwest* 27 (Spring 1986): 34-35. Used by permission of Dennice Scanlon.

"Headwaters," "Rules," and "Anastasia's Afternoon," by Ripley Schemm, are from *Mapping My Father* (Story, Wyoming: Dooryard Press, 1981). Used by permission of Ripley Schemm Hugo.

"Snakes," by Barbara Taylor Smith, is previously unpublished. Used by permission of Barbara Taylor Smith.

"Montana Ecologue," by William Stafford, is from *Stories That Could Be True: New and Collected Poems by William Stafford* (originally appeared in *The New Yorker*). Copyright © 1966 by William Stafford. Reprinted by permission of Harper & Row, Publishers, Inc.

"The Ten Thousand Things" and "Headwaters of the Marias," by David Thomas, are previously unpublished. Used by permission of David Thomas.

"Room At Flathead" and "Neola," by Patrick Todd, are from *A Fire by the Tracks: Poems by Patrick Todd* (Columbus: Ohio State University Press, 1983), pp. 15, 36. Reprinted by permission of Ohio State University Press and Patrick Todd.

"Stone Woman," by Linda Weasel Head, first appeared in *Cutbank* 25 (1986). It was reprinted in *Northern Lights* 3 (May/June 1987): 4. Used by permission of Linda Weasel Head.

"Star Quilt" and "Lynn Point Trail," by Roberta Hill Whiteman, are from *Star Quilt* (Duluth, Minnesota: Holy Cow! Press, 1985), pp. 1, 76-77. Reprinted by permission of Roberta Hill Whiteman and Holy Cow! Press.

"Winter Love," by Robert Wrigley, is reprinted from *Cutbank* 27/28 (1987): 80-82. "In the Great Bear" and "Ursa Major" are from *The Sinking of Clay City* (Port Townsend, Washington: Copper Canyon Press, 1979), pp. 22-23. Reprinted by permission of Robert Wrigley.

"The Heavyweight Champion Pie-Eatin' Cowboy of the West," "Escorting Grammy to the Potluck Rocky Mountain Oyster Feed at Bowman's Corner," and "Silos," by Paul Zarzyski, are from *The Make-Up of Ice* (Athens: The University of Georgia Press, 1984), pp. 10-11, 15, 17. Reprinted from *The Make-Up of Ice* by Paul Zarzyski, © 1984. Reprinted by permission of The University of Georgia Press.

THE EDITORIAL BOARD

WILLIAM BEVIS was born in 1941 in New York City. After receiving his Ph.D. in English at University of California, Berkeley, Bevis taught at Williams College before coming to the University of Montana in 1974. Bevis is a specialist in American poetry and western American literature and is the author of *Mind of Winter: Wallace Stevens—Meditation and Literature* (1989). He has just completed a book-length study of Montana literature, *Ten Tough Trips: Montana Writers and the West*, forthcoming in 1989.

MARY CLEARMAN BLEW was born in 1939 and grew up on a ranch in Montana's Judith Basin. After receiving an M.A. from University of Montana in 1963 and Ph.D. from University of Missouri in 1969, she served on the faculty at Northern Montana College from 1969 to 1987. The author of *Lambing Out* (1977), Blew has published her stories in the nation's leading literary journals. Her latest collection, *Runaway*, will be published in 1989. Blew currently teaches English and Creative Writing at Lewis-Clark College in Lewiston, Idaho.

WILLIAM KITTREDGE was born in 1932 and grew up on his family's cattle ranch in southeastern Oregon. After receiving an M.F.A. from University of Iowa Writers' Workshop in 1969, Kittredge came to University of Montana, where he is Professor of English and Creative Writing. His short stories and essays have appeared in *Harper's*, *Outside*, and other national magazines and journals. His books include *The Van Gogh Field* (1979), which won the St. Lawrence Fiction Prize, *We Are Not in This Together* (1984), and *Owning It All* (1986).

WILLIAM L. LANG was born in Portland, Oregon, in 1942, and studied history at Willamette University, Washington State University, and University of Delaware, where he received a Ph.D. in 1973. Lang has taught American and western history at Whitman College, Carroll College, and Montana State University and has been editor of *Montana the Magazine of Western History* since 1978. He is the co-author of *Montana: Our Land & People* (1979) and has written numerous articles on environmental, ethnic, and cultural history.

RICHARD B. ROEDER was born in Schuylkill Haven, Pennsylvania, in 1930, was graduated from Swarthmore College, and received a Ph.D. in history from University of Pennsylvania in 1971. On the faculty at Montana State University from 1962 to 1985, Roeder is co-author of *The Montana Past* (1969) and *Montana: A History of Two Centuries* (1976). Roeder has published widely in scholarly journals on the political and cultural history of Montana and the West.

ANNICK SMITH was born in Paris in 1936 and raised in Chicago. She attended Cornell University and University of Chicago and graduated from University of Washington with a degree in history and literature. An editor and independent filmmaker, Smith made the internationally acclaimed *Heartland* (1979), which won first prize at the Berlin and U. S. film festivals and the Western Heritage Award of the National Cowboy Hall of Fame. Smith lives on a homestead ranch in Montana's Blackfoot Valley.

JAMES WELCH was born in 1940 in Browning, Montana. Born of Blackfeet and Gros Ventre parents, he lived on the Blackfeet and Fort Belknap Indian reservations and later studied literature under Richard Hugo at University of Montana. Welch first gained fame with his collection of poetry, *Riding the Earthboy 40* (1971), and received national acclaim for *Winter in the Blood* (1974) and *Fools Crow* (1986). Welch has taught at University of Washington and Cornell University and lives in Missoula.

THE ARTISTS

KATHLEEN BOGAN was born in 1953 in Chicago, Illinois. A graduate of Williams College, Bogan has worked in Japan and Australia. She has been design director for *High Country News* and *Northern Lights* and is finishing her M.F.A. degree at University of Montana. Bogan lives in Casper, Wyoming, where she teaches art at Casper College and works as a free-lance graphic designer and artist. Bogan's work appears on pages 21, 83, 100, 234, 365, 481, 685, 704, 720, 887, 1101, 1133.

DIRK LEE was born in 1948 in Denver, Colorado, and spent his childhood in Wyoming, Utah, and Montana. Lee attended the University of Oregon and has been an art consultant for Head Start. He has had his work exhibited in galleries in Montana and Oregon. Lee lives in Missoula, where he is a professional artist and signpainter. Lee's work appears on pages 3, 131, 257, 447, 519, 633, 761.

THOMAS CLARK SAILOR was born in 1947 in Wichita, Kansas. After four years of active duty in the Air Force, he was graduated from Kansas State University with a degree in architecture. Sailor's work has been exhibited in invitational and juried shows in New York, Washington, D.C., West Germany, and Montana. He is currently living in Connecticut, where he works as a full-time architect. Sailor's work appears on pages 1, 129, 255, 445, 517, 631, 759.

JAMES G. TODD, Jr. was born in 1937 in Minneapolis and was raised in Great Falls, Montana. Currently a professor of art and humanities at the University of Montana in Missoula, Todd teaches social history and the theory of art. His artwork has been exhibited in East and West Germany, China, Bulgaria, Spain, South America, and throughout the United States. Todd's work appears on pages 138, 139, 191, 330, 406, 459, 525, 577, 590, 766, 784, 803, 865, 1038.